ISBN 978-0-331-71695-5
PIBN 11061313

1 MONTH OF
FREE
READING

at

www.ForgottenBooks.com

By purchasing this book you are eligible for one month membership to ForgottenBooks.com, giving you unlimited access to our entire collection of over 1,000,000 titles via our web site and mobile apps.

To claim your free month visit:
www.forgottenbooks.com/free1061313

English
Français
Deutsche
Italiano
Español
Português

www.forgottenbooks.com

Mythology Photography **Fiction**
Fishing Christianity **Art** Cooking
Essays Buddhism Freemasonry
Medicine **Biology** Music **Ancient
Egypt** Evolution Carpentry Physics
Dance Geology **Mathematics** Fitness
Shakespeare **Folklore** Yoga Marketing
Confidence Immortality Biographies
Poetry **Psychology** Witchcraft
Electronics Chemistry History **Law**
Accounting **Philosophy** Anthropology
Alchemy Drama Quantum Mechanics
Atheism Sexual Health **Ancient History**
Entrepreneurship Languages Sport
Paleontology Needlework Islam
Metaphysics Investment Archaeology
Parenting Statistics Criminology
Motivational

CATALOGUE

OF

THE PRINTED BOOKS

IN

The Library

OF THE

London, Eng. —

INCORPORATED LAW SOCIETY

BY

FREDERIC BOASE

LIBRARIAN

LONDON

Printed for the Society

BY SPOTTISWOODE & CO., NEW-STREET SQUARE, E.C.

1891

PREFACE

THE establishment of the Incorporated Law Society's Library is of comparatively recent date. In June 1828 Mr. Metcalfe, one of the original members of the Society, presented to the Council as a nucleus for the Library a complete set of the 'Statutes at Large.' At the same time Mr. Bryan Holme, whose portrait hangs in the great hall, contributed many valuable books on topography and similar subjects, and continued making gifts to the Library at various times until his death in 1856. In the year 1869 a most valuable and almost unique collection of books which had belonged to the Rev. Joseph Mendham of Sutton Coldfield, Warwickshire, was, after his death, very generously presented to the Society by a member of his family. Among these books are many rare editions of Liturgies, Missals and Breviaries, and also some books and pamphlets relating to Theological controversies, which perhaps even now may sometimes be of value to solicitors.

The Library was first located in the present building in 1832. The number of books in that year was but little over 1,000, in 1841 it amounted to 6,000, and in 1851 to 10,000. There are now 36,466 volumes, and additional space, both for books and readers, is greatly needed.

In recent years the Library Committee has been occupied chiefly in the acquisition of legal works, and it is hoped that in this department the Library is as perfect and complete as possible, but at the same time a considerable number of books of more general interest, including works on Archæology, County and Local History and Heraldry, has been added to the collection.

The present Catalogue has been arranged on the 'dictionary' principle, the names of authors and subjects being placed together in alphabetical order. In most cases books may be found either under their authors' names or under the subject of which they treat, but exceptions have been made in the case of books which are less generally used : for instance, the Old Law Books in the gallery have been entered according to their authors' names only, and the pamphlets according to subjects only. The Modern Law Books are, in nearly every case, entered both under the names of the authors and under the subject matter of the books ; those referred to under the latter heading are arranged chronologically, the latest published works being placed first. A separate catalogue was made of the Mendham Collection in 1871, which will shortly be reprinted.

July 28, 1891.

CATALOGUE

—·◦·—

ABBEYS.

History of the ancient town and once famous Abbey of Waltham, with the history of Abbies abridged, from the year 977 to their dissolution. By John Farmer. 1735. 8vo.
87 E

Index monasticus, or the abbeys and other monasteries, alien priories, friaries, colleges, and hospitals in the diocese of Norwich and the ancient kingdom of East Anglia. By Richard Taylor. 1821. folio.
92 G

Monasticon Anglicanum. Per Rogerum Dodsworth et Gulielmum Dugdale. New ed. by J. Caley, H. Ellis, and Rev. B. Bandinel. 6 vols. in 8. 1817–30. folio.
85 H I

Notitia Monastica, or an account of all the abbies, priories, and houses of friers formerly in England and Wales. By Right Rev. Thomas Tanner ; with many additions by Rev. James Nasmith. Cambridge, 1787. folio.
85 I

[ABBOT, Charles, 1 Baron Colchester.]

Jurisdiction and practice of the court of great sessions of Wales upon the Chester circuit. 1795. 8vo.
177 C

ABBOT, George, Archbishop of Canterbury.

The life of George Abbot, lord archbishop of Canterbury, to which are added the lives of his two brothers, Robert Abbot, lord bishop of Salisbury, and Sir Morris Abbot, knt., lord mayor of the city of London. [By William Oldys.] Guildford, 1777. 8vo.
79 B

A Short apology for Archbishop Abbot, touching the death of Peter Hawkins. By An unknown hand ; with a large answer to this apology by Sir Henry Spelman. See Sir H. Spelman's English Works, 2nd ed., 1727, part 2, pp. 105-126.
78 H

I

ABBOTT, Benjamin Vaughan.

A Digest of the reports of the United States courts and of the acts of congress, from the organisation of the government to November 1874. 6 vols. New York, 1867–74. 8vo. **32 D**

ABBOTT, Charles, 1 Baron Tenterden.

A Treatise of the law relative to Merchant Ships and Seamen. 1802. 8vo. **175 E**

The same. 4th ed. 1812. 8vo. **175 F**

The same. 8th ed. by William Shee. 1847. 8vo. **175 F**

The same. 12th ed. by Samuel Prentice. 1881. 8vo. **11 F**

ABBOTT, Francis George.

Forms of Writs and other proceedings on the common law side of the Court of Chancery issuing out of the Petty Bag Office. 1849. 12mo. **161 E**

ABBOTT, George.

The question of rating tithes argued and the opinions advanced by Mr. Blake examined. 1839. [Pamphlets, vol. 1.] **144 A**

ABBREVIATIONS.

List of Abbreviations and contractions commonly used in writing and printing. See Ogilvie's Imperial Dictionary, vol. iv., 1883, pp. 791-795. **123 E**

List of classical, mediæval, and modern Abbreviations. See Chambers's Encyclopædia, vol. i., 1888, pp. 7–9; and Encyclopædia Britannica, vol. i., 1875, pp. 26–29. **122 D E**

ABBREVIATIONS IN RECORDS.

Table of Abbreviations, especially of those found in MSS. from the sixth to the fourteenth century. See Sir T. D. Hardy's Registrum Palatinum Dunelmense, vol. iv., 1878, pp. cxxxiii–cclxi. **102 E**

Table of the principal Abbreviations used in records. See T. D. Hardy's Rotuli Normanniæ, 1835, pp. xxxvii–l. **98 A**

ABBREVIATIONS, Legal.

Abbreviations of the old law hands. See A. Wright's Courthand restored, 4th ed., 1815. 4to. **78 G**

An Index of Abbreviations used in legal reports or textbooks. See C. C. Soule's Lawyer's Reference Manual, 1883, pp. 345-497. **82 D**

ABDICATED.

The debate between the Houses of Lords and Commons at the conference held 1688, relating to the word Abdicated and the vacancy of the throne. 1695. 12mo. **48 C**

ABDY, JOHN THOMAS and BRYAN WALKER.

The commentaries of Gaius. Cambridge, 1870. 12mo. **63 E**

The commentaries of Gaius and rules of Ulpian. Cambridge, 1874. 12mo. **63 E**

à BECKETT, ARTHUR WILLIAM.

The Maske of Flowers. Edited and arranged by A. W. à Beckett, Master of the Revels of Gray's Inn, 1887. [Printed on the occasion of the reproduction of the Maske, July 7, 1887, with a list of the dramatis personæ.] 1887. 8vo. **91 D**

à BECKETT, THOMAS TURNER

Law-reforming difficulties exemplified in a letter to Lord Brougham, accompanied by an analysis of a bill for the improvement of the law relating to the administration of deceased persons' estates. 1849. [Pamphlets, vol. 6.] **144 A**

Railway litigation and how to check it, with remarks on proposed railway relief bill. 1846. [Pamphlets, vol. 21.] **144 B**

Remarks on the present state of the law of debtor and creditor with suggestions for its improvement. 1844. [Pamphlets, vol. 3.] **144 A**

ABEL, CHARLES DENTON.

Patents, designs and trade marks, British and foreign. 1886. 8vo. **53 B**

ABERCONWAY ABBEY.

Register and chronicle of the abbey of Aberconway. Edited by Sir Henry Ellis. [Camden Society, vol. 39.] 1847. 8vo. **85 B**

ABERDEEN.

Annals of Aberdeen from the reign of King William the Lion. By William Kennedy. 2 vols. 1818. 4to. **95 D**

ABERGAVENNY PEERAGE.

The claim to the dignity of Baron of Abergavenny. See Berkeley Peerage by tenure, vols. 1 and 3, 1858–62. folio. **124 J**

ABERYSTWYTH, CARDIGANSHIRE.

A Chronological summary of the chief events in the history
of the Castle of Aberystwyth. 4th ed. Aberystwyth, 1858.
12mo. **94 E**

ABINGDON, BERKSHIRE.

A Brief memorial of Abingdon free grammar school. By
Bezer Blundell. Abingdon, 1863. [Pamphlets, vol. 16.]
144 B

Chronicon Monasterii de Abingdon. Edited by Rev. Joseph
Stevenson. 2 vols. 1858. 8vo. **101 A**

Description of Abingdon. See A. Rimmer's Pleasant Spots
around Oxford, 1878, pp. 22–53. **92 F**

ABJURATION.

Thoughts on the oath of abjuration, in a letter to the Earl of
Aberdeen. By A Member of the late parliament. 1853.
[Pamphlets, vol. 9, pt. 1.] **144 A**

ABORIGINES.

Humane policy or justice to the aborigines of new settlements. By Saxe Bannister. 1830. 8vo. **78 B**

ABRAHALL, BENNET HOSKYNS.

Reform of the laws relating to bankruptcy and insolvency.
1861. [Pamphlets, vol. 13.] **144 A**

ABRAHAMS, SAMUEL.

The Palace Court in constitution and practice, with reasons
for its immediate abolition. 1848. 8vo. **78 B**

ABRIDGMENTS OF THE LAW.

Abridgment of the Common and Statute law. By Charles
Petersdorff. 2nd ed. 6 vols. 1861–64, and Supplement,
1870. 7 vols. 1864–70. 8vo. **14 C**

Abridgment of the law. By Matthew Bacon. 7th ed., with
additions by Sir H. Gwillim and C. E. Dodd. 8 vols. 1832.
8vo. **14 A**

A Digest of the laws of England. By Sir John Comyns. 5th
ed., with a digest of the cases at Nisi Prius by Anthony
Hammond. 8 vols. 1822. 8vo. **14 B C**

ABRIDGMENTS OF THE LAW—*continued.*

A General Abridgment of Law and Equity, alphabetically digested under proper titles. By Charles Viner. 24 vols. Aldershot, 1742–58. folio. **38 G H**

An Abridgment of the modern determinations in the courts of Law and Equity, being a Supplement to Viner's Abridgment. 6 vols. 1799–1806. 8vo. **14 A B**

The practical register or a general abridgment of the Law. By John Lilly. 2 vols. 1719. folio. **157 E**

Un Abridgment des plusieurs cases et resolutions del Common Ley. Per Henry Rolle. 2 vols. 1668. folio. **38 G**

Gregorie's Moot-Book, being a survey of the general titles of the common law, with the cases thereof, much enlargsd by William Hughes. 1663. 4to. **63 C**

The Grand Abridgment of the Law continued ; or, A Collection of the principal Cases and points of the Common Law of England, contained in all the reports extant, from the first of Elizabeth, to this present, by way of common-place. By William Hughes. [Vol. 1 only.] 1660. 4to. **63 C**

La Graunde Abridgment, collecte et escrie per Sir Robert Brooke. 2 parts in 1 vol. 1586. 4to. **158 D**

La Graunde Abridgement, collecte par le judge Anthony Fitzherbert. 2 parts in 1 vol. 1577. folio. **158 D**

[An Abridgement of cases from Edward I. to Henry VI., in Norman French. By Nicholas Statham. Rouen, 1495.] 4to. **158 D**

ABSTRACTS OF TITLE.

Instructions for preparing Abstracts of title. By Henry Moore. 4th ed. 1886. 8vo. **13 A**

Dissertation on and precedents of Abstracts. See Bythewood and Jarman's Conveyancing, 4th ed., vol. 1, 1884, pp. 1–207. **13 D**

Comyns' Handy book of exercises on a series of Abstracts of title. 4th ed., by A. J. Parker. 1884. 8vo. **13 A**

The evidence of Abstracts of title to real property. By J. Y. Lee. 1843. 8vo. **13 A**

An Essay in a course of lectures on Abstracts of title. By Richard Preston. 2nd ed. 3 vols. 1823–24. 8vo. **13 A**

ACCIDENT INSURANCE.

The laws of Insurance, fire, life, accident, and guarantee. By J. B. Porter. 2nd ed. 1887. 8vo. **10 D**

The law of Life insurance with a chapter on Accident insurance. By Charles Crawley 1882. 8vo. **10 D**

ACCIDENTS, Liability for.

Decisions of the supreme courts of England and Scotland on the liability of proprietors, masters and servants, for reparation of injuries arising from accidents and negligence. By William Hay. Edinburgh, 1860. 8vo. **172 A**

The evils of the unlimited liability for Accidents of masters and railway companies, especially since Lord Campbell's act. By Joseph Brown, Q.C. 2nd ed. 1870. [Pamphlets, vol. 35.] **144 C**

See also Negligence. **11 A**

ACCOUNT STAMP DUTY.

A Practical guide to account stamp duty. By J. A. Gosset. 1887. 8vo. **11 G**

ACCOUNTANTS AND AUDITORS, Society of.

The Society of Accountants and Auditors. List of members, extracts from the articles and bye-laws. 1888, 1889. 2 vols. 1888–89. 12mo. **142 D**

ACCOUNTANTS, Institute of Chartered.

The Institute of Chartered Accountants in England and Wales. List of members and charter of incorporation, 1881, 1883–1886, 1889. 6 vols. 1881–89. 12mo. **142 D**

Proceedings and Resolutions of the second provincial meeting of the members of the Institute of Chartered Accountants in England and Wales. 1888. 8vo. **142 D**

ACCOUNTS.

A Practical treatise on Accounts, mercantile, partnership, solicitor's, private, steward's, receiver's, executor's, trustee's, &c. By I. P. Cory. 1839. 8vo. **160 A**

ACCOUNTS, Estate.

The preparation and completion of an administrator's or executor's estate account. See F. Wood's Solicitor's Reports to next-of-kin, 1887, pp. 188–232. **9 I**

ACCOUNTS, Merchants'.

Amphithalami, or the Accountants closet, being an abridgment of merchants accounts. By Abraham Liset. 1684. See G. Malynes's Lex Mercatoria. 1686. folio. **118 G**

ACTIONS—*continued.*

Proceedings in an Action in the Queen's Bench, Common Pleas
and Exchequer Divisions of the high court of justice. By
Samuel Prentice. 2nd ed. 1880. 8vo. **64 A**

An Action at law, being an outline of the jurisdiction of the
superior courts of common law. By R. M. Kerr. 3rd ed.
1861. 12mo. **160 A**

Dictionary of the practice in civil actions in the courts of
King's Bench and Common Pleas. By Thomas Lee. 2nd
ed. 2 vols. 1825. 8vo. **162 G**

An Historical treatise of an Action or suit at law and of the
proceedings used in the King's Bench and Common Pleas
from the original process to judgment. By Richard Boote.
6th ed. 1823. 8vo. **163 A**

The Attorney's Vade Mecum and Client's Instructor, treating
of actions. By John Morgan. 2 vols. 1787. 12mo. **163 A**

ACTIONS, LIMITATION OF.

The statute law of the Limitation of Actions. By H. J.
Banning. 1877. 8vo. **10 G**

The Limitations of actions at law and suits in equity and
admiralty. By J. K. Angell. 5th ed. by J. W. May.
Boston, 1869. 8vo. **59 F**

Treatise on the Limitation of actions as affecting mercantile
and other contracts. By J. J. Wilkinson. 1829. 8vo. **172 A**

ACTIONS OF DEBT.

Cases in law and equity, with a treatise on the Action of
Debt. By Lord Chief Baron Gilbert. 1760. 8vo. **74 D**

ACTIONS, PARTIES TO.

The rules for selection of Parties to an action. By A. V.
Dicey. 1870. 8vo. **11 A**

ACTIONS, REAL.

A Treatise on the law of actions relating to Real Property.
By Henry Roscoe. 2 vols. 1825. 8vo. **174 F**

The nature and practice of Real Actions in their writs and
process, both original and judicial. By George Booth. 2nd
ed. 1811. 8vo. **174 F**

ACTIONS UPON THE CASE FOR DEEDS.

Actions upon the case for deeds. By William Sheppard.
2nd ed. 1675. 12mo. **49 B**

ACTON, Thomas Harman.
Reports of cases before the lords commissioners of appeals in prize causes, also on appeals to the King in council, 1809–1811. 2 vols. 1811. 8vo. **1 D**

ACTS OF PARLIAMENT.

American Acts.
An Analytical and compared digest of the constitutions and civil public statutes of all the states and territories relating to persons and property in force January 1, 1886. By F. J. Stimson. Boston, 1886. 8vo. **32 C**

Public statutes at large of the United States of America, 1789–1869, 15 vols. 1861–69, and Synoptical Index from 1789 to 1851, 1 vol. 1856. 16 vols. Boston. 1856–69. 8vo. **32 B C**

Colonial Acts.
Statutes and Ordinances of all the British Colonies. 1690–1889. 420 vols. 1734–1889. folio, 4to and 8vo. **34 A–37 G**

Indian Acts.
Statutes of India and of Bengal, Bombay and Madras. 1834–1889. 75 vols. 1834–89. 4to and 8vo. **33 A–H**

Irish Acts.
Acts passed in the parliaments held in Ireland 1310–1800, 12 vols. 1794–1801 and General index, 2 vols., 1818. 14 vols. Dublin, 1794–1818. 8vo. **32 A**

Statutes at large passed in the parliaments held in Ireland from 1310 to 1800 with Index by W. Ball to the acts passed 1310 to 1798 [forming the eighth volume]. 20 vols. Dublin, 1765–1801. folio. **32 G H**

Local and Personal Acts.
The local and personal acts from 1798 to 1889. 409 vols. 1798–1889. folio. **26 D–31 C**

Private Acts.
The private acts from 1700 to 1889. 208 vols. 1700–1889. folio. **23 C–26 C**

Public Acts.
A Collection of the public general statutes, 1832–1865. 34 vols. 1832–65. 8vo. **71 D–G**

The law reports. The public general statutes, 1866–1889. 24 vols. 1866–89. 8vo. **71 G–I**

ACTS OF PARLIAMENT—*continued*.

    The public general acts passed 1883–1889. 7 vols. 1883–89. 4to.   **62 F**

    The public general acts passed 1887–1889. 3 vols. 1887–89. 8vo.   **71 I**

    The public general statutes, 1870–1889. 20 vols. 1870–89. 8vo.   **70 G H**

    The public general statutes from the time of King Henry III. to the year 1848 [except 18, 19, 20 and 21 Charles II]. 252 vols. folio.   **21 A–23 C**

    The revised edition of the statutes, 1235–1878. 18 vols. 1870–85. 4to.   **71 B C**

    The same. 2nd ed. Vols. 1, 2 and 3, 1235–1814. Edited by G. A. R. Fitzgerald. 3 vols. 1888–89. 8vo.   **71 D**

    Statutes at large from Magna Charta to 41 George III. with preface by Owen Ruffhead, and an appendix [in vol. 9], consisting of obsolete and curious acts. 18 vols. 1769–1800. 4to.   **70 C D**

    Statutes of the realm from Magna Carta to the end of the reign of Queen Anne, printed from original records and authentic manuscripts, 9 vols. in 13, 1810–28. Alphabetical Index, 1 vol. 1824. Chronological Index, 1 vol. 1828. 15 vols. 1810–28. folio.   **99 D**

    Statutes of the United Kingdom of Great Britain and Ireland, 1801–1869, with notes and references by T. E. Tomlins, J. Raithby, N. Simons, C. D. Bevan, and G. K. Rickards. 29 vols. 1804–69. 4to.   **70 D–G**

ROAD ACTS.

    Public acts known as Road acts from 26 Geo. II. to 37 Geo. III. 47 vols. 1753–97. folio.   **21 D–22 G**

SCOTCH ACTS.

    Acts of the Parliament of Scotland from 1124 to 1707, with general index, to which is prefixed a supplement to the acts. 12 vols. in 13. 1814–75. folio.   **31 G**

ACTS OF PARLIAMENT, INDEXES OF.

PRIVATE, AND LOCAL AND PERSONAL ACTS.

    An Analytical table of the private statutes 1727 to 1834. By George Bramwell. 2 vols. 1813–35. 8vo.   **31 E**

    An Index to the local and personal acts and private acts in classes from 1801 to 1865. 1867. folio.   **31 E**

ACTS OF PARLIAMENT, INDEXES OF—*continued*.

Index to the local and personal and private acts, 1798 to 1839. By Thomas Vardon. 1840. 8vo. **31 E**

An Index to the local and private acts passed during the period 1866–1877. 1878. folio. **31 E**

Index to the titles of the 604 private acts of parliament passed in the reign of Queen Anne. Privately printed by William Salt. 1863. See Private Acts, 4 & 5 Anne, 1705. folio. **23 D**

Index to the titles of the 382 private acts of parliament passed in the reign of King George the First. Privately printed by William Salt, September 1863. See Private Acts 1 George I., 1714. folio. **26 A**

Index to the titles of the 1,245 private acts of parliament passed in the reign of King George the Second. Privately printed by William Salt, September 1863. See Private Acts 1 George II., 1727. folio. **26 B**

PUBLIC ACTS.

Chronological table and index of the statutes to the end of the session 50 Vict. 10th ed. 1887. 4to. **71 C**

A Digest and index of all the statutes from Magna Charta to 1846. By George Crabb. 4 vols. 1841–47. 8vo. **31 D**

A Digest of the public general statutes from Magna Carta to 6 Geo. IV., with an analytical index. By R. P. Tyrwhitt and T. W. Tyndale. 3 vols. 1822–26. 4to. **31 E**

An Index to the public general acts passed from 1801 to 1865. 1867. folio. **31 E**

Index to the public general statutes 1801–1828. By Benjamin Spiller. 1829. 4to. **31 E**

An Index to the statute law of England. By George Stamp. 3rd ed. by J. E. Davis. 1862. 8vo. **31 D**

A Table of reference to unrepealed public general acts. By John Biddle. 2nd ed. and supplement. 2 vols. 1869–70. 8vo. **31 D**

ACTS OF PRACTICAL UTILITY.

Chitty's Collection of Statutes of practical utility. 4th ed. containing the statutes and cases down to 1880, by J. M. Lely, 6 vols., 1880. Annual Continuations, 1881–1889, by J. M. Lely, 3 vols. 9 vols. 1880–89. 8vo. **70 I**

ADAM, WILLIAM.

The Gem of the Peak, or Matlock Bath and its vicinity, an account of Derby, and a tour from Derby to Matlock. 3rd ed. 1843. 12mo. **87 A**

ADAMS, FRANK MANTELL.

A Treatise on the law of Trade-Marks. 1876. 8vo. **53 H**

ADAMS, HENRY C.

A Juridical glossary, being an exhaustive compilation of the most celebrated maxims, aphorisms, . . . employed in the Roman, civil, feudal, canon, and common law. . . . and also of adages, axioms, proverbs, mottoes, &c. Vol. 1. A to E. Albany, N.Y. 1886 8vo. **123 G**

ADAMS, JOHN, OF THE INNER TEMPLE.

Index Villaris, or an alphabetical table of all the cities, market-towns, parishes, villages, and private seats in England and Wales. 1680. folio. **85 I**

ADAMS, JOHN, PROVOST OF KING'S COLLEGE, CAMBRIDGE.

An Essay concerning self-murther. 1700. 12mo. **78 A**

ADAMS, JOHN, SERJEANT-AT-LAW.

A Letter to Benjamin Hawes, Esq., M.P., and chairman of the Metropolitan Police Committee. 1838. [Pamphlets, vol. 5.] **144 A**

A Treatise on the principles and practice of the action of Ejectment and the resulting action for mesne profits. 2nd ed. 1818. 8vo. **166 C**

The same. 3rd ed. 1830. 8vo. **166 C**

The same. 4th ed. 1846. 8vo. **166 C**

ADAMS, JOHN, BARRISTER.

The doctrine of Equity, being a commentary on the law as administered by the court of chancery. 1850. 8vo. **167 B**

ADAMS, JOHN ROBINSON.

Dulwich college and the endowed schools commissioners. A tract for the times. 1873. [Pamphlets, vol. 33.] **144 C**

ADAMS, ROGER.

A Catalogue of the lords, knights, and gentlemen that have compounded for their estates. Chester, 1733. 12mo. **49 D**

ADAMSON, TRAVERS.

Acts and ordinances in force in Victoria. 2 vols. Melbourne, 1855–56. 8vo.   **35 B**

Acts of the Parliament of Victoria. 1856–57. Melbourne, 1857. 8vo.   ·**35 B**

ADDAMS, JESSE.

Reports of cases in the Ecclesiastical courts, 1822–1826. 3 vols. 1823–26. 8vo.   **8 G**

ADDERLEY, CHARLES BOWYER.

Letter to the Right Hon. Benjamin Disraeli, M.P., on the present relations of England with the colonies. 1861. [Pamphlets, vol. 18.]   **144 B**

ADDINGTON, WILLIAM.

An Abridgment of penal statutes. 1775. 8vo.   **158 B**

The same. 2nd ed. 1782. 4to.   **158 B**

ADDISON, CHARLES GREENSTREET.

The history of the Knights Templars, the Temple church and the Temple. 1842. 8vo.   **91 D**

A Treatise on the law of Contracts. 2 parts in 1 vol. 1845–47. 8vo.   **163 D**

The same. 6th ed. by L. W. Cave. 1869. 8vo.   **163 D**

The same. 7th ed. by L. W. Cave. 1875. 8vo.   **52 C**

The same. 8th ed. by Horace Smith. 1 vol. bound in 2. 1883. 8vo.   **9 E**

Wrongs and their remedies, being a treatise on the law of Torts. 1860. 8vo.   **178 D**

The same. 2nd ed. 1864. 8vo.   **178 D**

The same. 3rd ed. by F. S. P. Wolferstan. 1870. 8vo.   **178 E**

The same. 4th ed. by F. S. P. Wolferstan. 1873. 8vo.   **178 E**

The same. 5th ed. by L. W. Cave. 1879. 8vo.   **53 H**

The same. 6th ed. by Horace Smith. 1887. 8vo.   **11 H**

[ADDISON, JOSEPH.]

The Old Whig. Numbers 1 and 2. On the state of the peerage with remarks upon The Plebeian, 3rd ed. 1720. [Grimaldi's Tracts, vol. 2.]   **118 B**

ADDISON, JOSEPH.
On the admission of the evidence of persons charged with
criminal offences. 1883. [Pamphlets, vol. 32.]   **144 C**

ADEL, YORKSHIRE.
Archæologia Adelensis, or a history of the parish of Adel.
By Rev. H. T. Simpson. 1879. 8vo.   **94 B**

ADLER, MARCUS NATHAN.
The Temple at Jerusalem, a paper read before the Jews'
College Literary Society. 1887. 8vo.   **84 B**

ADLINGTON, JOHN HENRY.
The Cyclopædia of Law, or the correct British lawyer. 1820.
8vo.   **170 G**

ADMINISTRATION ACTIONS.
Administration of the estates of deceased persons by the
Chancery division of the high court of justice. By W.
G. Walker and E. J. Elgood. 1883. 8vo.   **12 F**

ADMINISTRATION BONDS.
Examples of Administration bonds for the court of Probate.
By Samuel Chadwick. 1876. 8vo.   **12 D**

ADMINISTRATION OF ASSETS.
Principles of the administration of assets in payment of debts.
By A. S. Eddis. 1880. 8vo.   **12 F**

ADMINISTRATION OF JUSTICE, DEFECTS IN.
A Brief account of some of the most important proceedings
in parliament relative to the defects in the administration
of justice in the Court of Chancery, the House of Lords
and the Court of commissioners of bankrupt. By C. P.
Cooper. 1828. 8vo.   **78 C**

ADMINISTRATIONS.
Coote's Common form practice and Tristram's Contentious
practice and practice on motions and summonses of the
high court of justice in granting Probates and Administrations. 10th ed. by T. H. Tristram. 1888. 8vo.   **12 D**

ADMINISTRATIONS—*continued*.

Probate and Administration law and practice.   By W. J. Dixon.   2nd ed.   1885.   8vo.   12 D

Browne's Treatise on the principles and practice of the Court of Probate in contentious and non-contentious business, revised by L. D. Powles.   1881   8vo.   12 D

The practice of Wills and Administrations.   By G. S. Allnutt. 4th ed.   1860.   12mo.   177 D

ADMINISTRATORS.

The law relating to Executors and Administrators.   By W. G. Walker.   2nd ed.   1888.   8vo.   9 I

The law of Executors and Administrators.   By S. C. Macaskie. 1881.   8vo.   52 G

The law of Executors and Administrators.   By Sir E. V. Williams.   8th ed. by R. L. V. Williams and W. V. Williams. 2 vols.   1879.   8vo.   9 I

ADMINISTRATOR'S MANAGEMENT OF ESTATES.

Solicitor's Reports to next-of-kin as to the Administrator's management of their intestate's estates.   By Frederic Wood. 1887.   8vo.   9 I

ADMIRALTY, BLACK BOOK OF THE.

Monumenta Juridica.   The black book of the Admiralty. Edited by Sir Travers Twiss.   4 vols.   1871–76.   8vo.   102 D

ADMIRALTY COURTS, REPORT ON.

· Report from the select committee on Admiralty Courts with the minutes of evidence.   1833.   folio.   153 A

ADMIRALTY FORMS.

Admiralty forms and precedents.   By E. S. Roscoe.   1884. 8vo.   12 D

ADMIRALTY JURISDICTION AND PRACTICE.

Admiralty procedure against merchant ships and cargoes.   By R. G. M. Browne.   1887.   8vo.   12 D

The student's probate, divorce, and admiralty.   By Albert Gibson and Arthur Weldon.   1887.   8vo.   64 E

Admiralty actions and appeals.   By R. G. Williams and G. Bruce.   2nd ed.   1886.   8vo.   12 D

ADMIRALTY JURISDICTION—*continued.*

A Summary of the law and practice in Admiralty. By T. E. Smith. 3rd ed. 1885. 8vo. **64 A**

Admiralty jurisdiction and practice. By E. S. Roscoe. 2nd ed. 1882. 8vo. **12 D**

Admiralty practice, also the practice of the Privy Council in admiralty appeals. By H. C. Coote. 2nd ed. and supplement. 1868–69. 8vo. **52 A**

Two lectures on the jurisdiction and practice of the high court of Admiralty of England, delivered before the Incorporated Law Society 14 and 21 Dec. 1859. By John Morris. 1860. [Pamphlets, vol. 13.] **144 A**

The jurisdiction of the high court of Admiralty of England. By Edwin Edwards. 1847. 8vo. **160 A**

The high court of Admiralty. See Law Journal Tracts, 1825–26, pp. 9–16. **144 G**

A Compendious view of Civil law and of the law of the Admiralty. By Arthur Browne. 2nd ed. 2 vols. 1802. 8vo. **48 F**

The practice of the Court of Admiralty of England. By Francis Clarke or Clerke. 1743. 12mo. **160 A**

Of the Admiral jurisdiction and the officers thereof. See Sir H. Spelman's English Works, 2nd ed., 1727, part 2, pp. 215–232. **78 H**

The jurisdiction of the Admiralty of England asserted. By Richard Zouch. 1686. See G. Malynes's Lex Mercatoria, 1686. folio. **118 G**

A View of the Admiral jurisdiction. By John Godolphin. 1661. 12mo. **49 B**

See also SHIPPING. **11 F**

ADMIRALTY LAW, DIGESTS OF.

Digest of Admiralty law. By W. T. Pritchard. 3rd ed. by J. C. Hannen and W. T. Pritchard. 2 vols. 1887. 8vo. **14 C**

A Digested Index of the cases determined in the high court of Admiralty before Sir William Scott, contained in the several reports of Robinson, Edwards, and Dodson. By Joshua Greene. 1818. 8vo. **63 D**

ADMIRALTY PRACTICE OF COUNTY COURTS.

Admiralty and maritime jurisdiction and practice of the county courts. See J. E. Davis's Practice of the county courts, 6th ed., 1887, pp. 765–828. **12 H**

ADMIRALTY PRACTICE OF COUNTY COURTS—*cont.*
Observations on impracticable character of provisions of act for conferring Admiralty jurisdiction on County Courts. By A. J. Johnes. 1868. [Pamphlets, vol. 32.] **144 C**
See ADMIRALTY and COUNTY COURTS. **12 D & 12 H**

ADMIRALTY REGULATIONS.
Regulations and instructions relating to His Majesty's service at sea. 11th ed. 1772. 4to. **158 C**

ADMIRALTY REPORTS.
The law reports. High court of admiralty and ecclesiastical courts reports. 1865–1875. 4 vols. 1867–75. 8vo. **73 B**
Reports of the leading decisions in the High Court of Admiralty in cases of vessels sailing under British licenses. By Thomas Edwards. 1812. [Pamphlets, vol. 29.] **144 B**
Sir James Marriott's argument in giving judgment in the Court of Admiralty in the case of the ship Columbus, 1789. See Collectanea Juridica, vol. 1, 1791, pp. 82–128. **144 G**

ADMIRALTY STATUTES.
A Collection of the Statutes relating to the Admiralty, navy, ships of war, and incidental matters to the eighth year of King George the Third. 1768. 4to. **158 C**

ADOLPHE, CHAUVEAU et FAUSTIN HÉLIE.
Théorie du code pénal. 4me éd. 7 vols. Paris, 1861–63. 8vo. **58 A**

ADOLPHUS, JOHN LEYCESTER and T. F. ELLIS.
Reports of cases in the Court of King's Bench. 1834–1841. 12 vols. 1835–42. 8vo. **4 A B**
Queen's Bench Reports. New series. 1841–1852. 18 vols. 1843–56. 8vo. **5 F–H**

ADULTERATION.
The law on Adulteration. By Thomas Herbert. 1884. 8vo. **9 A**
The law of Adulterations. By Sidney Woolf. 1874. 12mo. **160 A**

ADULTERINE BASTARDY.
The law of adulterine bastardy, with a report of the Banbury case. By Sir N. H. Nicolas. 1836. 8vo. **52 A**

ADULTERY.

The doctrine and law of Marriage, Adultery, and Divorce. By Rev. H. D. Morgan. 2 vols. Oxford, 1826. 8vo. **172 D**

ADVERTISING.

The Advertiser's A B C of official scales and charges and Advertisement press directory of the United Kingdom, India, and the Colonies. 1889. 8vo. **146 G**

The Advertiser's guardian and advertisement agent's guide. By Louis Collins. 1885. 8vo. **146 G**

ADVOCACY.

Hints on Advocacy. By Richard Harris. 9th ed. 1889. 8vo. **11 G**

Solicitors as advocates, practical suggestions. By D. M. Ford. 1881. 8vo. **11 G**

Hortensius. An Historical essay on the duties of an Advocate. By William Forsyth. 3rd ed. 1879. 8vo. **83 H**

ADVOCATES, COLLEGE OF.

Catalogue of the books in the library of the College of Advocates, Doctors' Commons. 1818. 8vo. **82 C**

. A Catalogue of the very valuable and extensive library of the College of Advocates, Doctors' Commons, London. Sold by auction April 1861. 1861. 8vo. **82 C**

ADVOWSONS, LAW OF.

The law of Advowsons. By John Mirehouse. 1824. 8vo. **52 A**

A Compleat parson, or a description of advowsons or church-livings. By Sir John Doderidge. 1641. [Law Tracts and Arguments, 1641.] **144 F**

See also ECCLESIASTICAL LAW. **9 C**

ADVOWSONS, VALUE OF.

The value of Advowsons. By Rolla Rouse. 1868. 8vo. **52 A**

ÆSCHYLUS.

Æschyli Choephoræ ex recensione Porsoniana, adjecti sunt Choëphoron Chorici Cantus sicut dispositi sunt in tentamine V. R. Caroli Burneii. Glasguæ, 1814. 24mo. **47 E**

AETHELWEARD.

Chronicon Aethelweardi. See Monumenta Historica Britannica.
1848. folio. **99 B**

AFFIDAVITS.

The attorney and solicitor's companion or compleat Affidavit-
man. 1725. 12mo. **160 A**
The same. 2nd ed. 1725. 12mo. **160 A**
The same. 3rd ed. 1739. 12mo. **160 A**

AFFILIATION.

The law and practice of orders of Affiliation and proceedings
in bastardy. By T. W. Saunders. 9th ed. by T. W. Saunders
and W. E. Saunders. 1888. 12mo. **9 A**

AFFIRMATIONS.

Forms of Affirmations. See T. W. Braithwaite's Oaths, 4th
ed., 1881, pp. 73–76. **12 G**
See also EVIDENCE. **9 H I**

AFFREIGHTMENT.

The contract of Affreightment. By T. E. Scrutton. 1886.
8vo. **10 D**

AFRICA, SOUTH.

The general directory and guide-book to the Cape of Good
Hope and its dependencies, as well as Natal, Free State and
the Transvaal. Cape Town, 1882. 12mo. **84 B**
Humane policy or justice to the Aborigines of new settlements.
By Saxe Bannister. 1830. 8vo. **78 B**
A Particular of the Royal African Company's forts and castles
in Africa, 1713, and 14 other pamphlets relating to the
same Company. [Parliamentary Pamphlets, vol. 1.] **144 G**

AGABEG, AVIET and W. F. BARRY.

The bills of exchange act, 1882. 1883. 8vo. **52 G**

AGENCY.

The law of Principal and Agent. By William Evans. 2nd
ed. 1888. 8vo. **11 C**
The law relating to the sale of goods and commercial Agency.
By Robert Campbell. 1881. 8vo. **10 B**
A Treatise on mercantile Agency. By J. A. Russell. 2nd ed.
1873. 8vo. **10 I**

AGENCY—*continued.*

Commentaries on the law of Agency. By Joseph Story. 7th ed. by I. F. Redfield and W. A. Herrick. Boston, 1869. 8vo. **11 C**

A Manual of the law of Principal and Agent. By E. C. Petgrave. 1857. 12mo. **174 C**

The law of Principal and Agent, chiefly with reference to mercantile transactions. By William Paley. 3rd ed. by J. H. Lloyd. 1833. 8vo. **174 C**

AGHABOE, QUEEN'S COUNTY.

A Statistical account of the parish of Aghaboe. By Edward Ledwick. Dublin, 1796. 8vo. **95 E**

AGISTMENT.

A Treatise on Agistment Tithe 1778, with an appendix containing copies of the bill answers and decree in the Court of Exchequer, Easter term 1774, in the cause of Bateman against Aistrup and others, for the tithe of the Agistment of sheep and cattle. By Rev. Thomas Bateman. 1779. 8vo. **176 E**

AGNELLUS, THOMAS.

De morte et sepultura Henrici Regis Angliæ Junioris. See R. de Coggeshall's Chronicon Anglicanum, 1875, pp. 263–273. **102 F**

AGNEW, REV. DAVID CARNEGIE A.

Protestant exiles from France in the reign of Louis XIV. 2nd ed. 3 vols. 1871–74. 8vo. **80 G**

AGNEW, WILLIAM FISCHER.

The law and practice relating to Letters Patent for inventions. 1874. 8vo. **53 B**

A Treatise on the Statute of Frauds. 1876. 8vo. **10 A**

AGREEMENTS.

Practical forms of Agreements. By Henry Moore. 2nd ed. by T. L. Mears. 1887. 8vo. **13 F**

Dissertation on and precedents of Agreements. See Bythewood and Jarman's Conveyancing, 4th ed., vol. 1, 1884, pp. 271–646. **13 D**

AGREEMENTS—*continued.*

A Treatise on the validity of Verbal Agreements as affected by the legislative enactments in England and the United States, commonly called the Statute of Frauds. By M. H. Throop. vol. 1. Albany, 1870. 8vo. **59 B**

AGRICULTURAL CUSTOMS.

The law of the Farm, including the agricultural customs of England and Wales. By H. H. Dixon. 4th ed. by H. Perkins. 1879. 8vo. **10 A**

The present state of the Tenancy of Land in Great Britain, showing the principal customs and practices between incoming and outgoing tenants. By L. Kennedy and T. B. Grainger. 1828. 8vo. **170 E**

AGRICULTURAL HOLDINGS.

Agricultural holdings act, 1883. By J. B. Little. 1884. 8vo. **9 A**

Agricultural holdings act, 1883. By J. M. Lely and E. R. Pearce. 1883. 8vo. **9 A**

Agricultural holdings act, 1883. By J. W. Jeudwine. 2nd ed. 1883. 8vo. **9 A**

Agricultural holdings and the law of distress. By Joseph Beaumont. 1883. 8vo. **160 B**

The agricultural holdings act, 1875. By C. W. R. Cooke. 1876. 8vo. **160 B**

The agricultural holdings act, 1875; with notes. By J. E. Norris. 1875. [Pamphlets, vol. 29.] **144 B**

See also LANDLORD AND TENANT. **10 E**

AGRICULTURAL HOLDINGS, FENCING OF.

An Essay on the law relating to the Fencing of Agricultural Holdings. By A. E. B. Soulby. Malton, 1886. [Pamphlets, vol. 39.] **144 C**

AGRICULTURAL IMPROVEMENTS, COMPENSATION FOR.

The law of compensation for unexhausted Agricultural Improvements. By J. W. W. Bund. 2nd ed. 1883. 12mo. **160 B**

AGRICULTURAL POOR.

The education of the Agricultural Poor. By Captain Maxse, R.N. 1868. [Pamphlets, vol. 33.] **144 C**

AGRICULTURAL POOR—*continued.*

An Essay on the improvement of the condition of the agricultural labourer. By George Nicholls. 1847. [Pamphlets, vol. 13.] **144 A**

AGRICULTURAL TENANCIES.

Law of agricultural tenancies. By G. W. Cooke. New ed. 1882. 8vo. **52 B**

AGRICULTURE.

English land and English landlords. By G. C. Brodrick. 1881. 8vo. **83 J**

Essays on agriculture. By Thomas Gisborne. 2nd ed. 1854. 12mo. **83 J**

The library of agricultural and horticultural knowledge. 3rd ed. 1834. 8vo. **83 J**

AIKIN, John.

A Description of the country from thirty to forty miles round Manchester. 1795. 4to. **88 F**

AILREDUS, Abbot of Rievaulx.

Historia, de bello Standardii tempore Stephani regis, Genealogia regum Anglorum, Vita et miraculis Edwardi Regis et Confessoris &c. See Scriptores Decem Hist. Angl. 1652, pp. 337–422. **114 H**

The 'Relatio de Standardo' of St. Aelred, Abbot of Rievaulx. See Chronicles of the reigns of Stephen, Henry II., and Richard I. edited by R. Howlett, vol. 3, 1886, pp. 179–199. **102 H**

AINSWORTH, Robert.

Ainsworth's Latin dictionary, improved by Thomas Morell, revised by John Carey. 2nd ed. 2 vols. 1823. 4to. **123 E**

AIR AND LIGHT.

Light and air, a text-book for architects and surveyors. By Banister Fletcher. 2nd ed. 1886. 8vo. **10 G**

See also EASEMENTS. **9 G**

AIRD, David Mitchell.

Blackstone economized, being a compendium of the laws of England to the present time. 1873. 12mo. **166 E**

AIRD, David Mitchell—*continued.*

The civil laws of France, supplemented by notes, illustrative of the analogy between the rules of the Code Napoléon and the leading principles of the Roman law. 1875. 12mo.   55 C

AIRLIE PEERAGE.

The case of Walter Ogilvy claiming the title of Earl of Airlie, 1813. See Peerage Cases, third series, vol. 1, pp. 1–32 ; and Peerage Evidence, vol. 8.   124 I J

AIRTH PEERAGE.

The case of Robert Barclay Allardice claiming the title of Earl of Airth, 1839. See Peerage Evidence, vol. 14. 124 J

History of the Earldoms of Strathern, Monteith, and Airth, with a report of the proceedings before the House of Lords on the claim of Robert Barclay Allardice to the Earldom of Airth. By Sir N. H. Nicolas. 1842. 8vo.   124 F

AIRY, Osmund.

The Lauderdale papers, 1639–1679. Edited by O. Airy. [Camden Society, n.s. vols. 34, 36 and 38.]   3 vols. 1884–85. 8vo.   85 D

Letters addressed to the Earl of Lauderdale. Edited by O. Airy. [Camden Society, n.s. vol. 31.] 1883. 8vo. 85 D

AITON, William.

An Inquiry into the pedigree, descent and public transactions of the chiefs of the Hamilton family. Glasgow, 1827. 8vo.   80 C

AKERMAN, John Yonge.

Moneys received and paid for secret services of Charles II. and James II. 1679–1688. Edited by J. Y. Akerman. [Camden Society, vol. 52.] 1851. 8vo.   85 B

ALABAMA CLAIMS.

The case of the United States to be laid before the tribunal of arbitration to be convened at Geneva. 1872. 8vo. 59 A

The indirect claims of the United States under the treaty of Washington of May 8, 1871, as submitted to the tribunal of arbitration at Geneva. By W. B. Lawrence. Providence, 1872. 8vo.   59 A

ALANUS DE INSULIS, Bishop of Auxerre.

The poem called Anticlaudianus and the prose work called Liber de planctu naturæ, of Alanus Anglicus. See Satirical poets of the twelfth century, vol. 2, 1872, pp. 268–522.

102 E

ALAUZET, Isidore.

Commentaire du code de commerce et de la législation commerciale. 4 tomes. Paris, 1856–57. 8vo. **58 A B**

ALBANY AND SUSQUEHANNA RAILROAD.

An Inquiry into the Albany and Susquehanna railroad litigation of 1869. By G. T. Curtis. New York, 1871. [Pamphlets, vol. 29.] **144 B**

ALBEMARLE, Christopher Monk, 2 Duke of.

The case of the Duke of Albemarle with the arguments thereon. See Special Cases in Chancery, 3rd ed., vol. 2, 1736, pp. 191–201. **74 G**

ALBERICUS DE ROSATE BERGOMENSIS.

Alberici De Rosate Bergomensis in Codicem et Infortiatum et Pandectas Commentarii. 8 parts in 4 vols. Venetiis, 1586–85. folio.

ALBERONI, Giulio, Archbishop of Seville

A Modest apology for Parson Alberoni, governor to King Philip a minor, and universal curate of the whole Spanish monarchy. [By Thomas Gordon.] 2nd ed. 1719. [Grimaldi's Tracts, vol. 2.] **118 B**

Testament politique du Cardinal Jules Alberoni, recueilli de divers mémoires, lettres et entretiens de son éminence. Par A. M. Traduit de l'Italien par le C. de R. B. M. [Composed by J. M. Durey de Morsan, edited by J. H. Maubert de Gouvest.] Lausanne, 1754. 12mo. **118 B**

ALBERT LIFE ASSURANCE COMPANY.

Albert Life Assurance Company Arbitration act, 1871. Minutes of proceedings before the arbitrator (Lord Cairns), 1871–1873. 2 vols. 1871–73. folio. **145 D**

First, second and final awards, 1872–1875. 1 vol. 1872–75. folio. **145 D**

Lord Cairns's Decisions, reported by F. S. Reilly, parts 1–3. 1872–75. 8vo. **145 D**

ALBIN, JOHN.

A Companion to the Isle of Wight, comprising the history of the island and the description of its local scenery. 9th ed. 1823. 12mo. **88 A**

A new correct and much improved history of the Isle of Wight. Newport, 1795. 8vo. **88 A**

ALCEDO, ANTONIO DE.

The geographical and historical dictionary of America and the West Indies. Translated from the Spanish by G. A. Thompson. 5 vols. 1812–15. 4to. **84 E**

ALCHESTER, OXFORDSHIRE.

An Inquiry into the history of Alchester, a military station of the Dobuni. See J. Dunkin's History of Bicester, 1816, pp. 185–210. **92 E**

ALCOCK, JOHN BERESFORD.

Personal property in the East Indies, in what cases subject to or exempt from legacy and residue duty, with supplement. 1850–51. 12mo. **38 D**

ALCOCK, JOHN CONGREVE and JOSEPH NAPIER.

Reports of cases in the courts of King's Bench and Exchequer chamber in Ireland, 1831–1833. Dublin, 1834. 8vo. **15 C**

ALDRED, PHILIP FOSTER.

The law of Mortgage of real estate. 1883. 8vo. **172 G**

ALEXANDER THE SEVENTH.

Pope Alexander the Seventh and the College of Cardinals. By John Bargrave, D.D. Edited by J. C. Robertson. [Camden Society, vol. 92.] 1867. 8vo. **85 C**

ALEXANDER, WILLIAM.

Abridgment of the acts of Sederunt of the lords of council and session. Edinburgh, 1838. 8vo. **55 F**

An Abridgment of the acts of the parliaments of Scotland, 1424 to 1707, including verbatim all the acts now in force. Edinburgh, 1841. 8vo. **55 F**

Digest of the Bankrupt act for Scotland 2 & 3 Vict. c. 12. 2nd ed. Edinburgh, 1842. 8vo. **55 F**

The practice of the Commissary courts in Scotland. Edinburgh, 1859. 8vo. **55 F**

ALEXANDRA, The.

International Law considered with reference to the trial of the case of the Alexandra, seized under the provisions of the Foreign Enlistment act. By F. H. Hamel. 1863. 12mo.
55 A

ALEXANDROW, A.

A new and complete English–Russian dictionary. 1884. 8vo. **123 B**

A new and complete Russian–English dictionary. 1884. 8vo. **123 B**

ALEYN, John.

Select cases in B. R. [Banco regis] 22, 23, and 24 Car. I. Regis, reported by John Aleyn. 1681. folio. **74 B**

ALGEBRA.

The elements of Algebra in a new and easy method. By Nathaniel Hammond. 3rd ed. 1764. 8vo. **255 H**

A Treatise of Algebra. By Colin Maclaurin. 4th ed. 1779. 8vo. **255 H**

ALIEN PRIORIES.

Some account of the alien priories and of such lands as they are known to have possessed in England and Wales. [By Richard Gough.] 2 vols. 1779. 12mo. **84 A**

ALIENS.

The law of Naturalisation as amended by the act of 1870. By John Cutler. 1870. 12mo. **11 A**

On Nationality, or the law relating to subjects and aliens. By Sir A. E. Cockburn. 1869. 8vo. **11 A**

A Treatise on the law relating to Aliens and denization and naturalization. By George Hansard, with Supplement. 1844–46. 8vo. **52 A**

Droits, privilèges et obligations des étrangers dans la Grande-Bretagne. Par C. H. Okey. 2me éd., revue par N. M. Thevenin. Paris, 1831. 12mo. **160 B**

ALIENS RESIDENT IN ENGLAND.

Lists of foreign protestants and aliens resident in England 1618–88, from returns in the State paper office. Edited by W. D. Cooper. [Camden Society, vol. 82.] 1862. 8vo. **85 C**

ALIMENA, BERNARDINO.
La Premeditazione in rapporto alla psicologia, al diritto, alla
legislazione comparata. Torino, 1887. 8vo.   55 B

ALISON, SIR ARCHIBALD.
History of Europe from the commencement of the French
revolution in 1789 to the restoration of the Bourbons in
1815. 7th ed. 20 vols. 1847–48. 12mo.   113 B
History of Europe from the fall of Napoleon in 1815 to the
accession of Louis Napoleon in 1852. 8 vols., and Index
1 vol. 9 vols. 1853–59. 8vo.   113 B C
The military life of John Duke of Marlborough. 1848.
8vo.   80 B
Practice of the Criminal law of Scotland. Edinburgh, 1833.
8vo.   55 G

ALL THE TALENTS.
All the Talents! a satirical poem in three dialogues. By
Polypus. [Eaton Stannard Barrett.] 6th ed. 1807. 8vo.
118 B

ALLAN, CHARLES EDWARD.
The law relating to Goodwill. 1889. 8vo.   10 B

ALLAN, GEORGE.
Collections relating to Sherburn Hospital in the county palatine
of Durham. Privately printed. 1771. 4to.   118 F

ALLEN, GEORGE BAUGH and W. B. ALLEN.
Forms of indorsements of proceedings in the Queen's Bench
division prior to trial. 1883. 8vo.   12 E

ALLEN, JOHN.
Inquiry into the rise and growth of the Royal Prerogative in
England. A new ed. by B. Thorpe. 1849. 8vo.   83 I

ALLEN, JOSEPH.
The new navy list 1846–1849, August 1852, and February
1853. 10 vols. 1846–53. 8vo.   133 H

ALLEN, THOMAS.
The history and antiquities of the parish of Lambeth and
the archiepiscopal palace in the county of Surrey. 1827.
4to.   93 D

ALLEN, THOMAS—*continued.*

The history of the county of Lincoln. 2 vols. 1833–34.
4to. **89 C**

A History of the county of Surrey. 2 vols. 1831. 4to. **93 D**

A new and complete history of the county of York. 3 vols.
1829–31. 4to. **94 C**

ALLIBONE, SAMUEL AUSTIN.

A Critical dictionary of English literature and British and
American authors. 3 vols. 1859–71. 4to. **82 F**

ALLNUTT, GEORGE STEVENS.

The practice of Wills and Administrations. 4th ed. 1860.
12mo. **177 D**

ALLNUTT, HENRY.

The auctioneer's, land agent's, and estate agent's directory.
4th ed. 1866. 12mo. **146 D**

The same. 5th ed. 1870. 12mo. **146 D**

ALLOTMENTS.

The law of Allotments for the poor. By J. B. Little. 1887.
8vo. **9 A**

The law of Allotments. By T. H. Hall. 1886. 8vo. **9 A**

ALMACK, RICHARD.

Papers relating to proceedings in the county of Kent, 1642–
1646. Edited by R. Almack. [Camden Society, vol. 61.]
1855. 8vo. **85 B**

ALMANACS.

Almanacs for the years 1700–1841, 1846, 1849, 1851–1853, and
1855. By Vincent Wing. 148 sheet almanacs. 1700–1855.
folio. **19 D**

ΑΤΛΑΣ ΟΤΡΑΝΙΟΣ. The celestial atlas. By Robert White.
For the years 1774, 1792–1797, 1799–1815, 1817–1831, and
1833–50. 57 vols. 1774–1850. 12mo. **107 A–C**

The book of Almanacs, by which the almanac may be found
for every year up to A.D. 2000. By A. De Morgan. 1851.
8vo. **107 E**

British Almanac for the years 1828–1890; with the Companion. 63 vols. 1828–90. 12mo. **107 E–H**

ALMANACS—*continued.*

Complete index to the Companion to the Almanac from 1828 to 1843, inclusive. 1843. 12mo.   **107 E**

The British farmers' almanack for the years 1844 to 1848. 5 vols. 1844–48. 12mo.   **107 C**

Calendarium Catholicum, or an universal almanack. 1662. 12mo.   .   **118 A**

Cardanus Rider's British Merlin. 1744–1747, 1749–1754, 1756, 1759–1761, 1763–1777, 1779–1783, 1785, 1787, 1788, 1790–1799, 1801–1820, 1822–1834. 80 vols. 1744–1834. 12mo.   **217 A–E**

Cardanus Rider's Sheet Almanack for the years 1776 and 1787. 2 vols. 1776, 1787. 12mo.   ··**218 A**

A Companion to the Almanack for the year 1752. [1752.] 12mo.   **107 E**

The Dublin Almanac, and General Register of Ireland, 1835–1837 and 1839–1849. 14 vols. Dublin, 1835–49. 8vo. **141 C D**

The English Apollo. By Richard Saunders. For the year 1774. 1774. 12mo.   **107 A**

The Englishman's Almanack for the years 1829–1831 and 1833–1842. 13 vols. 1829–42. 12mo.   **107 C**

The Englishman's and Family Almanack for the years 1843 to 1869. 27 vols. 1843–69. 12mo.   **107 C D**

The Family and parochial almanack for the years 1835 to 1842. 8 vols. 1835–42. 12mo.   **107 C**

The Farmer's Calendar for the year 1843. 1843. 12mo. **107 C**

The Gardener's almanack. By G. W. Johnson. For the years 1844 to 1867. 24 vols. 1844–67. 12mo.   **107 C D**

The Gentleman's and Citizen's Almanack, 1742, 1768. By John Watson. 1779–1789, 1791, 1792, 1795. By Samuel Watson. 1799, 1803, 1805, 1807–1816, 1825, 1827–1829, 1831, 1833, 1838. By J. W. Stewart. 36 vols. Dublin, 1742–1838. 12mo.   **141 A–E**

The Gentleman's diary for the years 1774, 1792–1797, 1799–1815, 1817–1831, and 1833–1840. 47 vols. 1774–1840. 12mo.   **107 A–C**

Irish Almanac and Official Directory, with the Post Office Dublin City and County Directory. By A. Thom. 41 vols. Dublin, 1850–90. 8vo.   **141 D–H & 142 A**

The Ladies' diary for the years 1774, 1792–1797, 1799–1815, 1817–1831, and 1833–1840. 47 vols. 1774–1840. 12mo.   **107 A–C**

The Lady's and Gentleman's diary for the years 1841 to 1871, 31 vols. 1841–71. 12mo.   **107 C D**

ALMANACS— *continued.*

The London almanac, official register, and county calendar for England and Wales for the year 1841. 1841. 12mo.
218 H

The Mechanic's Almanac for the years 1830, 1831, and 1833–1844. 14 vols. 1830–44. 12mo. **107 C**

The Medical Almanack for the years 1835 to 1843. 9 vols. 1835–43. 12mo. **107 C**

Merlinus Liberatus. By John Partridge. For the years 1774, 1792–1797, 1799–1815, 1817–1831, and 1833–1871. 78 vols. 1774–1871. 12mo. **107 A–D**

A Narrative to be used as a companion to an almanac, with suggestions for improvements in almanacs for land and sea. 1885. [Pamphlets, vol. 39.] **144 C**

'Ολύμπια Δώματα. By Tycho Wing. For the years 1774, 1792–1797, and 1799–1805. 14 vols. 1774–1805. 12mo. **107 A**

Parker's Ephemeris for the year 1774. 1774. 12mo. **107 A**

Poor Robin for the years 1774, 1792–1797, 1799–1815, and 1817–1828. 36 vols. 1774–1828. 12mo. **107 A B**

A Secular diary commencing with the new style 1752, and continued up to the year 1900, for ascertaining any day of the week or month within that period. By D. Barstow. n.d. 12mo. **107 C**

Speculum anni, or Season on the seasons. By Henry Season. For the years 1774, 1792–1797, 1799–1815, and 1817–1828. 36 vols. 1774–1828. 12mo. **107 A B**

Vade Mecum, or the necessary pocket companion, containing Sir Samuel Morland's perpetual almanack; also Interest tables. By Israel Falgate. 1735. 8vo. **107 D**

Vox Stellarum. By Francis Moore. For the years 1774, 1792–1797, 1799–1815, 1817–1831, and 1833–1879. 86 vols. 1774–1879. 12mo. **107 A–D**

The Weather Almanac for the year 1838. By Patrick Murphy. 45th ed., 1838; and for the year 1840, 10th ed., 1840. 1 vol. 12mo. **118 A**

Whitaker's Almanack for the years 1869 to 1890. 22 vols. 1869–90. 12mo. **107 H I**

ALMON, JOHN.

Anecdotes of the life of William Pitt, Earl of Chatham, with his speeches in Parliament from 1736 to 1778. [By John Almon.] 4th ed. 3 vols. 1794. 8vo. **79 B**

ALMON, JOHN—*continued.*

An Extinct peerage of England. 1769. 12mo.   **124 B**
A New baronetage of England. 3 vols. 1769. 12mo. **124 B**
The peerage of Ireland. 2 vols. 1768. 8vo.   **124 F**
The pocket herald, or a complete view of the present peerage
of England, Scotland, and Ireland. 2 vols. 1769. 12mo.
    124 B

ALMON, JOHN, TRIAL OF.

A Letter to Sir Richard Aston, Knt., one of the judges of his
Majesty's Court of King's Bench, containing a reply to his
scandalous abuse, and some thoughts on the modern doctrine of libels. By Robert Morris. 2nd ed. 1770. [Tracts
on law of libel, vol. 3.]   **144 F**
The trial of John Almon, bookseller, for selling Junius's Letter
to the K——. 1770. [Tracts on law of libel, vol. 3.] **144 F**

ALPHONSO IX., KING OF LEON AND CASTILE.

Las Siete Partidas del rey Don Alfonso el Sabio, cotejadas
con varios códices antiguos. Por la Real Academia de la
Historia. 3 vols. Madrid, 1807. 4to.   **39 C**

ALPS, THE.

A Handbook for travellers in Switzerland and the Alps of
Savoy and Piedmont. A new ed. 1842. 8vo.   **84 A**

ALTAVILLA, JOHANNES DE.

The poem called Architrenius of John de Hauteville. See
Satirical poets of the twelfth century, vol. 1, 1872, pp. 240–
392.   **102 E**

ALVARADO, FELIX ANTHONY DE.

La Liturgia Ynglesa ó el libro de Oracion Commun. Hispanizado por D. Felix Anthony de Alvarado. 1707. 8vo. **77 B**

AMAR, MOISE.

Dei Diritti degli Autori di opere dell' ingegno, studi teorico-
pratici sulla legislazione Italiana in rapporto colle leggi
delle altre nazioni. Torino, 1874. 8vo.   **56 E**

AMBLER, CHARLES.

Reports of Cases argued and determined in the High Court of Chancery, with some few in other Courts. [1737-1783.] 1790. folio.

The same. 2nd ed., with corrections and references to subsequent cases by J. E. Blunt. 2 vols. 1828. 8vo.   2 A

AMBROSDEN, OXFORDSHIRE.

Parochial antiquities attempted in the history of Ambrosden, Burcester and other adjacent parts in the counties of Oxford and Bucks. By White Kennett. A new ed. 2 vols. Oxford, 1818. 4to.   92 F

AMEER KHAN and HASHMADAD KHAN.

Report of the proceedings in the cases of Ameer Khan and Hashmadad Khan. By C. C. Macrae. Calcutta, 1870. [Pamphlets, vol. 29.]   144 B

AMENDMENTS OF VARIANCES PENDING TRIALS.

A Concise view of the principles, object, and utility of Pleadings, and The practice as to Amendments pending trials at Nisi Prius and before sheriffs. By Joseph Chitty. 2nd ed. 1835. 8vo.   173 F

AMERICA, CIVIL WAR IN.

Peace the sole chance now left for reunion. By J. L. O'Sullivan. 1863. [Pamphlets, vol. 16.]   144 B

Recognition; a chapter from history of North and South American states. 1863. [Pamphlets, vol. 16.]   144 B

Southern secession. A letter addressed to Captain M. T. Maury, Confederate Navy, on his Letter to Admiral Fitzroy. By J. W. Cowell. 1862. [Pamphlets, vol. 16.] 144 B

The true state of the American question. Reply to Mr. Thurlow Weed. By Fairplay. 1862. [Pamphlets, vol. 22.] 144 B

AMERICA, GEOGRAPHY AND HISTORY OF.

The American Commonwealth. By James Bryce. 3 vols. 1888. 8vo.   116 F

B. Bradshaw's A B C dictionary to the United States, Canada and Mexico. 1886. 12mo.   84 A

AMERICA, GEOGRAPHY AND HISTORY OF—*continued.*

European and American excursions and tours. By Thomas
Cook. 1865. [Pamphlets, vol. 25.] **144 B**

The geographical and historical dictionary of America and
the West Indies. By A. de Alcedo. Translated from the
Spanish by G. A. Thompson. 5 vols. 1812–15. 4to. **84 E**

The history and topography of the United States. Edited
by J. H. Hinton. 2 vols. 1830–32. 4to. **84 E**

The history of America. By Wm. Robertson, D.D. [vols.
6–8 of his Works.] 3 vols. 1824. 8vo. **116 F**

The industrial resources of the southern and western states,
with sketches of the states and cities of the Union. By J.
D. B. De Bow. 4 vols. New Orleans, 1853. 8vo. **84 D**

Memorable days in America, being a journal of a tour to
the United States. By W. Faux. 1823. 8vo. **84 D**

The progress of United States of America from earliest periods.
By R. S. Fisher. New York, 1854. 8vo. **84 E**

A Review of the constitutions of the principal states of Europe
and of the United States of America. By M. De La Croix.
2 vols. 1792. 8vo. **113 C**

AMERICA, SLAVERY IN.

The abolition of slavery, the right of the government under
the war power. Boston, 1861. [Pamphlets, vol. 22.] **144 B**

Annual report of the American Anti-Slavery Society for the
year ending May 1, 1860. New York, 1861. [Pamphlets,
vol. 22.] **144 B**

The fugitive slave law and its victims. New York, 1861.
[Pamphlets, vol. 22.] **144 B**

AMERICAN BAR ASSOCIATION.

Reports of the fifth, sixth, and seventh annual meetings of
the American Bar Association, held 1882, 1883, and 1884.
3 vols. bound in 1. Philadelphia, 1883–84. 8vo. **139 C**

AMERICAN CRIMINAL TRIALS.

American criminal trials. By P. W. Chandler. 2 vols. Boston,
1841–44. 12mo. **59 D**

AMERICAN LAW.

The American Law Review, 1866–1889. 24 vols. Boston,
1867–90. 8vo. **139 A B**

AMERICAN LAW—*continued*.

Martindale's American Law Directory, 1885–86. A complete directory of the practising lawyers of the United States and Canada. Chicago, 1885. 8vo. **Hall**

Table of the foreign mercantile laws and codes in force in the principal states in Europe and America. By Charles Lyon-Caen. Translated by N. Argles. 1876. 8vo. **55 C**

See also UNITED STATES.

AMERICAN MINING COMPANIES.

An Inquiry into the plans, progress, and policy of American mining companies. 1825. [Jacob's Tracts, vol. 2.] **144 E**

AMERICAN SECURITIES.

Practical hints on the test of stability and profit for the guidance and warning of British investors. By An Anglo-American. 1860. [Pamphlets, vol. 13.] **144 A**

AMERICANISMS.

Americanisms old and new : a dictionary of words, phrases, and colloquialisms peculiar to the United States, British America, &c. &c. By J. S. Farmer. 1889. 8vo. **123 C**

AMICABLE SOCIETY.

The charters of the corporation of the Amicable Society for a perpetual assurance office. 1823. 12mo. **78 A**

AMOBYR, CUSTOM OF.

A Concise account of ancient documents relating to Clun, Shropshire; with observations on the custom of Amobyr, formerly existing there. Privately printed. [Shrewsbury,] 1858. 8vo. **93 A**

AMORY, SAMUEL.

Statement as to the comparative merits of the two bills coming before Parliament for regulating the bankrupt law of Scotland. 1814. [Pamphlets, vol. 40.] **144 C**

AMOS, ANDREW.

The English constitution in the reign of King Charles the Second. 1857. 8vo. **116 E**

Fortescue De laudibus legum Angliæ. The translation into English published A.D. MDCCLXXV., and the original Latin text with notes. Cambridge, 1825. 8vo. **170 F**

AMOS, ANDREW—*continued.*

An Introductory lecture upon the study of English law delivered in the University of London, Nov. 2, 1829. [Jacob's Tracts, vol. 7.] **144 E**

Observations on the case of The King and Geddington relative to the law of parochial settlement by equitable estate, 1823. [Jacob's Tracts, vol. 1.] **144 E**

Observations on the statutes of the Reformation parliament in the reign of King Henry the Eighth. 1859. 8vo. **116 E**

AMOS, ANDREW and JOSEPH FERARD.

A Treatise on the law of Fixtures and other property partaking both of a real and personal nature. 1827. 8vo. **168 E**

The same. 2nd ed. by Joseph Ferard. 1847. 8vo. **168 E**

The same. 3rd ed. by C. A. Ferard and W. H. Roberts. 1883. 8vo. **10 A**

AMOS, SHELDON.

A Comparative survey of laws in force for the prohibition, regulation, and licensing of Vice in England and other countries. 1877. 8vo. **177 C**

An English code, its difficulties and the modes of overcoming them; a practical application of the science of Jurisprudence. 1873. 8vo. **63 F**

The history and principles of the Civil law of Rome. 1883. 8vo. **63 F**

The Science of Law. 1874. 8vo. **63 F**

A Systematic view of the science of Jurisprudence. 1872. 8vo. **63 F**

AMSINCK, PAUL.

Tunbridge Wells and its neighbourhood, illustrated by a series of etchings and historical descriptions. 1810. folio. **89 G**

AMUNDESHAM, JOHANNES.

Annales Monasterii S. Albani. (A.D. 1421–1440.) Edited by H. T. Riley. 2 vols. 1870–71. 8vo. **101 H**

ANCIENT DEMESNE.

Some observations upon the law of Ancient Demesne. By Pym Yeatman. 1884. 8vo. **87 B**

3—2

ANCIENT LAW.

Ancient law, its connection with the early history of society and its relation to modern ideas. By H. S. Maine. 4th ed. 1870. 8vo.   **83 I**

ANCREN RIWLE.

The Ancren Riwle, a treatise on the rules and duties of monastic life. Edited and translated by James Morton, B.D. [Camden Society, vol. 57.] 1853. 8vo.   **85 B**

ANDERSON, ADAM.

An Historical and chronological deduction of the origin of commerce, from the earliest accounts to the present time. 2 vols. 1764. folio.   **78 H**

ANDERSON, CHARLES HENRY.

A Digest of the principles and practice of common law, conveyancing, equity, bankruptcy, and criminal law. 2 vols. 1867. 8vo.   **168 A**

ANDERSON, EDMUND.

Les reports des mults principals cases, cibien en le Common-Bank comme devant touts les Juges de cest Roialme. 1534–1604. 2 parts in one vol. 1664–65. folio.   **74 B**

ANDERSON, GEORGE CAMPBELL.

The statute law of the Bahamas. 2 vols. 1862–68. 8vo. **36 B**
The same. 1 vol. 1877. 8vo.   **36 B**

ANDERSON, JOHN EUSTACE.

A History of the Independents or Dissenters at Mortlake, with an account of their chapel. 1888. 8vo.   **93 C**
A History of the parish of Mortlake. Printed for private circulation. 1886. 8vo.   **93 C**

ANDERSON, ROBERT.

The prison acts of 1877 and 1865. 1878. 12mo.   **53 E**

ANDERSON, THOMAS KERR.

A Treatise on the law of Execution in the high court and inferior courts. 1889. 8vo.   **12 E**

ANDRÉ, John.

Proceedings of a board of general officers held by order of General George Washington respecting Major John André, charged with being a spy. 1780. See P. W. Chandler's Criminal trials, vol. 2, pp. 155–181 and 384–387.   **59 D**

ANDREAS, or ANDRÉ, Bernard.

Historia Regis Henrici Septimi necnon alia quædam ad eundem regem spectantia. Edited by James Gairdner. 1858. 8vo.   **101 B**

ANDREWS, George.

Reports of Cases in the Court of King's Bench, in the 11th and 12th years of K. George II. 1754. folio.

The same, 2nd ed., with notes and references to 31 Geo. III. by G. W. Vernon. Dublin, 1791. 8vo.   **4 A**

ANDREWS, John.

Precedents of Leases, with notes. 1871. 12mo.   **172 A**

The same. 2nd ed. 1878. 8vo.   **13 B**

Precedents of Mortgages. 1879. 8vo.   **13 C**

ANDREWS, Robert William and A. B. STONEY.

The supreme court of Judicature acts. 1880. 12mo.   **169 F**

The same. 2nd ed. 1883. 12mo.   **169 F**

The same. 4th ed. 1885. 12mo.   **12 G**

ANDREWS, Thomas.

The Church in Ireland. A second chapter of contemporary history. 1869. [Pamphlets, vol. 34.]   **144 C**

ANECDOTES.

Anecdotes and traditions illustrative of early English history and literature, derived from MS. sources. Edited by W. J. Thoms. [Camden Society, vol. 5.] 1839. 8vo.   **85 A**

Curialia Miscellanea ; or anecdotes of old times, regal, noble, and miscellaneous. By Samuel Pegge. 1818. 8vo.   **83 H**

Paramythia, or mental pastimes ; being original anecdotes. By the author. [James Watson.] 1821. 12mo.   **83 H**

Sporting anecdotes, original and select, including characteristic sketches of eminent persons who have appeared on the turf. By An Amateur Sportsman. 1804. 8vo.   **79 B**

ANECDOTES—*continued.*

Westminster Hall; or professional relics and anecdotes of
the bar, bench, and woolsack. [By Henry and Thomas
Roscoe.] 3 vols. 1825. 12mo. **79 A**

See also CALENDAR, THE. **85 G**

ANGELL, JOSEPH KINNICUT.

The limitations of actions at law and suits in equity and
admiralty. 4th ed. by J. W. May. Boston, 1861. 8vo.
59 F

The same. 5th ed. by J. W. May. Boston, 1869. 8vo. **59 F**

The right of property in tide waters. 2nd ed. Boston, 1847.
8vo. **60 B**

A Treatise on the law of fire and life insurance. 2nd ed.
Boston, 1855. 8vo. **59 E**

ANGELL, JOSEPH KINNICUT and SAMUEL AMES.

Treatise on the law of private corporations aggregate. 7th ed.
by John Lathrop. Boston, 1861. 8vo. **59 C**

The same. 8th ed. by J. Lathrop. Boston, 1866. 8vo. **59 C**

ANGELL, JOSEPH KINNICUT, and THOMAS DURFEE.

A Treatise on the law of Highways. Boston, 1857. 8vo. **59 E**

The same. 2nd ed. by G. F. Choate. Boston, 1868. 8vo.
59 E

ANGLESEY.

Mona antiqua restaurata, an archæological discourse on the
antiquities of Anglesey. By Henry Rowlands. 2nd ed.
1766. 4to. **94 D**

ANGLESEY, ARTHUR ANNESLEY, 1 EARL OF.

The privileges of the House of Lords and Commons, argued
and stated in two conferences between both houses, April
19 and 22, 1671. 1702. 12mo. **48 C**

ANGLESEY PEERAGE.

The claims to the Earldom of Anglesey. See Peerage Cases,
third series, vol. i. pp. 33–53; and Peerage Evidence, vols. 3
and 14. **124 I J**

ANGLO-INDIAN CODES.

The Anglo-Indian Codes. Edited by W. Stokes. 2 vols.
1887–88, and Supplement, 1889. 3 vols. 1887–89. 8vo. **38 D**

ANGLO-LATIN POETS.

The Anglo-Latin satirical poets and epigrammatists of the twelfth century. Edited by Thomas Wright. 2 vols. 1872. 8vo. **102 E**

ANGLO-NORMAN LAWS.

Traités sur les coutumes Anglo-Normandes, publiés en Angleterre, depuis le onzième jusqu'au quatorzième siècle. Par M. Houard. 4 vols. Rouen, 1776. 4to. **40 A**

ANGLO-SAXON HISTORY.

The Anglo-Saxon chronicle according to the several original authorities. Edited by Benjamin Thorpe. 2 vols. 1861. 8vo. **101 E**

Codex diplomaticus Ævi Saxonici, Opera. J. M. Kemble. 6 vols. 1839–48. 8vo. **115 A**

The history of the Anglo-Saxons from the earliest period to the Norman Conquest. By Sharon Turner. 5th ed. 3 vols. 1828. 8vo. **115 E**

The rise and progress of the English Commonwealth. Anglo-Saxon period. By Francis Palgrave. 2 vols. 1832. 4to. **114 E**

ANGLO-SAXON LANGUAGE.

Francisci Junii Etymologicum Anglicanum, præmittuntur vita auctoris et grammatica Anglo-Saxonica. Oxonii, 1743. folio. **123 G**

Hickesii Georgii Linguarum veterum septentrionalium Thesaurus grammatico-criticus et archæologicus. 6 parts in 2 vols. Oxoniæ, 1705. folio. **123 G**

The rudiments of grammar for the English-Saxon tongue, first given in English. By Elizabeth Elstob. 1715. 8vo. **123 B**

Vocabularium Anglo-Saxonicum, Lexico Gul. Somneri magna parte auctius, operâ Thomæ Benson. Oxoniæ, 1701. 8vo. **123 B**

ANGLO-SAXON LAWS.

Leges Anglo-Saxonicæ ecclesiasticæ et civiles. By David Wilkins. 1721. folio. **99 C**

Versuch einer Darstellung der Geschichte des Angelsächsischen Rechts. Von G. Phillips. Göttingen, 1825. 8vo. **55 C**

ANGLO-SAXON LITERATURE.

An Essay on the state of literature and learning under the Anglo-Saxons. By Thomas Wright. 1839. 8vo. **78 R**

ANGUILLA.
The statutes of the islands of Saint Christopher and Anguilla, 1711 to 1857. 1857. 8vo. **36 F**

ANIMALS.
Man's injustice to animals. The Brown Animal Sanatory Institution. 3rd ed. 1888. 8vo. **78 C**

On the power, wisdom, and goodness of God as manifested in the creation of animals and in their history and habits. By Rev. William Kirby. 2nd ed. 2 vols. 1835. 8vo. **77 B**

ANNANDALE PEERAGE.
The claims to the Marquessate of Annandale. See Peerage Cases, second series, vol. 1, pp. 1–152; third series, vol. 1, pp. 54–128; and Peerage Evidence, vols. 3, 8, 14, and 22. **124 I J & 125 I**

ANNE, QUEEN.
History of England, comprising the reign of Queen Anne until the peace of Utrecht, 1701–1713. By Earl Stanhope. 4th ed. 2 vols. 1872. 8vo. **115 D**

The history of Great Britain during the reign of Queen Anne. By F. W. Wyon. 2 vols. 1876. 8vo. **115 G**

ANNE, QUEEN, BOUNTY OF.
An account of the augmentation of small livings, by 'The Governors of the bounty of Queen Anne for the augmentation of maintenance of the poor clergy.' By C. Hodgson 2nd ed. with Supplement. 1845–64. 8vo. **100 G**

ANNUAL PRACTICE.
The Annual Practice, 1889–90. By T. Snow, C. Burney, and F. A. Stringer. 1889. 8vo. **12 F**

ANNUAL REGISTER.
The Annual Register, or a view of the history, politics, and literature for the years 1758–1888. 131 vols. 1759–1889. 8vo. **129 C–130 E**

General index to Dodsley's Annual Register, from its commencement in 1758 to the year 1819. 1826. 8vo. **130 E**

ANNUITIES.
The law of Annuities and Rentcharges. See Watson's Compendium of Equity, 2nd ed., vol. 1, 1886, pp. 10–22. **12 G**

ANNUITIES—*continued.*

Dissertation on and precedents of Annuities. See Bythewood and Jarman's Conveyancing, 4th ed., vol. 1, 1884, pp. 647–730.　　　　　　　　　　　　　　　　　**13 D**

The law of fire and life Insurance and Annuities. By Charles Ellis. 2nd ed. 1846. 8vo.　　　　　　　　　　**52 I**

Instructions for the establishment of parochial societies for granting Government Annuities. 1837. 8vo.　　　**144 F**

A practical treatise on the law of Life Annuities. By J. B. Kelly. 1835. 8vo.　　　　　　　　　　　　　　　**160 B**

The law of Annuities. By W. G. Lumley. 1833. 8vo.　**52 A**

The valuation of annuities and assurances on lives and survivorships. By Joshua Milne. 2 vols. 1815. 8vo.　**160 B**

The doctrine of life-annuities and assurances investigated and explained. By Francis Baily. 1810. 8vo.　　**160 B**

A Practical treatise upon the law of annuities. By Robert Withy. 1800. 8vo.　　　　　　　　　　　　　　**160 B**

A Collection of cases on the Annuity act. By William Hunt. 2nd ed. 1796. 8vo.　　　　　　　　　　　　　**160 B**

Observations on reversionary payments ; on schemes for providing annuities for widows and for persons in old age ; also Essays on life annuities. By Richard Price. 5th ed. 2 vols. 1792. 8vo.　　　　　　　　　　　　**160 B**

Opinions on the grant of a perpetual post obit annuity. See Collectanea Juridica, vol. 2, 1792, pp. 292–295.　**144 G**

ANNUITY TABLES.

Annuity tables. By J. Fleming. 1886. 8vo.　　　　**11 G**

The government annuity tables, embracing the values of annuities on single and two joint lives at 3, 4, 5, and 6 per cent. per annum for every combination of age and sex. By Jardine Henry. 2 vols. 1859. 8vo.　　　　　**160 B**

New formulæ in the valuation of Annuities on lives. By J. B. Benwell. 1830. 8vo.　　　　　　　　　　　　**144 F**

The calculations of Life Annuities and the Public funds, simplified and explained. By W. Tate. 1819. 8vo.　**144 F**

Tables for renewing and purchasing of Leases, Annuities, and Reversions. By Sir Isaac Newton. 6th ed. 1808. 12mo.　　　　　　　　　　　　　　　　　　　**176 D**

National Life annuities ; comprising all the tables, and every necessary information contained in the act for granting the same. By E. F. T. Fortune. 1808. 8vo,　　**144 F**

See also BLEWERT, WM.

ANONYMIANA.

Anonymiana, or ten centuries of observations on various authors and subjects, compiled by a late very learned and reverend divine. [Samuel Pegge.] 2nd ed. 1818. 8vo.

83 H

ANONYMS AND PSEUDONYMS.

A Dictionary of the anonymous and pseudonymous literature of Great Britain. By Samuel Halkett and Rev. John Laing. 4 vols. Edinburgh, 1882–88. 8vo. 82 E

Handbook of fictitious names. By Olphar Hamst, Esq. [Ralph Thomas.] 1868. 8vo. 82 D

ANSELM, Saint.

Eadmeri Historia Novorum in Anglia, et opuscula duo de vita Sancti Anselmi et quibusdam miraculis ejus. Edited by Martin Rule. 1884. 8vo. 102 H

ANSON, Sir William Reynell.

The law and custom of the Constitution. Part 1, Parliament. Oxford, 1886. 8vo. 116 E

Principles of the English law of Contract and of agency in its relation to contract. 2nd ed. 1882. 8vo. 163 E

The same. 3rd ed. 1884. 8vo. 163 E

The same. 4th ed. 1886. 8vo. 64 B

The same. 5th ed. 1888. 8vo. 64 B

ANSTED, David Thomas and R. G. LATHAM.

The Channel Islands. 2nd ed. 1865. 8vo. 94 F

ANSTEY, Rev. Henry.

Munimenta Academica, or documents illustrative of academical life and studies at Oxford. 2 vols. 1868. 8vo.

102 C

[ANSTEY, John.]

The Pleader's guide, a didactic poem in two parts, containing the conduct of a suit at law. By the late John Surrebutter, Esquire, special pleader. [John Anstey.] 5th ed. 1808. 8vo. 118 A

ANSTEY, Thomas Chisholm.

A Guide to the laws of England affecting Roman Catholics. 1842. 8vo. 175 C

ANSTEY, Thomas Chisholm—*continued*.
Notes upon 'The Representation of the People Act, 1867.'
(30 & 31 Vict. c. 102.) 1867. 8vo. **166 C**

ANSTIS, John.
Observations introductory to an historical essay upon the
Knighthood of the Bath. 1725. 8vo. **125 E**

ANSTRUTHER, Alexander.
Reports of cases in the Court of Exchequer, 32 George III.
to 37 George III. 3 vols. 1796–97. 8vo. **7 C**

ANTICOSTI, Canada.
Notes on the resources and capabilities of the Island of Anti-
costi. By A. R. Roche. 1885. 8vo. **84 B**
The settler and sportsman in Anticosti. 1885. 8vo. **84 B**

ANTIGUA.
Acts of Antigua for the years 1857 to 1870 and 1876 to 1888.
6 vols. 1857–88. folio. **36 E**
Acts of Assembly, passed in the Charibbee Leeward Islands
from 1690 to 1730 ; and in the Island of Antigua from
1725 to 1760. 2 vols. 1734–64. folio. **36 F**
Laws of Antigua, consisting of acts of the Leeward islands
in force in Antigua and acts of Antigua from 1668 to 1864.
1865. folio. **36 E**

ANTIQUARIES, Society of.
A Catalogue of the printed books and manuscripts in the
library of the Society of Antiquaries of London. 1816. 4to.
82 I

ANTIQUITIES.
The Antiquarian itinerary, comprising specimens of architecture, with other vestiges of antiquity in Great Britain.
4 vols. 1815–16. 8vo. **85 G**
The Antiquarian repertory, a miscellaneous assemblage of
topography, history . . . By F. Grose and T. Astle. A
new ed. 4 vols. 1807–9. 4to. **85 I**
An Apology for the study of Northern antiquities. See E.
Elstob's Grammar, 1715, pp. i–xxxv. **123 B**
The book of days, a miscellany of popular antiquities in
connection with the calendar. Edited by Robert Chambers.
2 vols. 1869–81. 8vo. **85 G**

ANTIQUITIES—*continued.*

A Collection of curious discourses by eminent antiquaries upon several heads in our English antiquities, with Mr. Thomas Hearne's preface and appendix to the former edition. 2 vols. 1771. 8vo.   **85 G**

The same. another ed. 2 vols. 1773. 8vo.   **85 G**

A Dictionary of Greek and Roman antiquities. By various writers, edited by Wm. Smith. 2nd ed. 1873. 8vo. **84 C**

Itinerarium Curiosum, or an account of the antiquities in Great Britain. By Wm. Stukeley. 2nd ed. 2 vols. in 1. 1776. folio.   **85 I**

Romæ Antiquæ notitia, or the antiquities of Rome. By Basil Kennett. 13th ed. 1763. 8vo.   **113 D**

ANTRIM.

A Guide to the Giant's Causeway and the north-east coast of Antrim. By Rev. G. N. Wright. 1823. 12mo.   **95 E**

Letters concerning the northern coast of the county of Antrim. By Rev. William Hamilton. Dublin, 1790. 8vo. **95 E**

Statistical survey of the county of Antrim. By Rev. John Dubourdieu. 2 vols. Dublin, 1812. 8vo.   **95 E**

ANTROBUS, RICHARD and THOMAS IMPEY.

Brevia selecta, or choice writs. 1663. 12mo.   **48 C**

ANYTE OF TEGEA.

Anytæ Tegeatidis Epigrammata. Hamburgi, 1734. 4to.
                                                         47 F

APOCRYPHA.

A Concordance to the books called Apocrypha. By Alexander Cruden. 10th ed. 1831. 4to.   **77 G**

APOPHTHEGMS.

Apophthegmes new and old. By Francis Bacon. 1625. Bound with Bacon's Essaies, 1598, 12mo.   **118 A**

APOSTOLICAL FATHERS.

The genuine epistles of the Apostolical Fathers S. Barnabas, S. Ignatius, S. Clement, S. Polycarp, the Shepherd of Hermas, and the Martyrdoms of St. Ignatius and St. Polycarp, translated with a large preliminary discourse by W. Wake, D.D. 1693. 12mo.   **77 B**

APOTHECARIES.

Addresses by the Society of Apothecaries to the general
practitioners of England and Wales on Bills 'for the better
regulation of medical practice throughout the United Kingdom' 1844, and 'for regulating the profession of physic and
surgery' 1845. [Pamphlets, vols. 11 and 5.]   **144 A**

A Statement by the Society of Apothecaries on the subject
of their administration of the Apothecaries Act. 1844.
[Pamphlets, vol. 5.]   **144 A**

APPEAL CASE.

The law of Appeals to the superior courts of law by Appeal
Case. By George Tayler. 1865. 12mo.   **160 B**

APPEAL CASES.

Cases heard on Appeal before the judicial committee of the
Privy Council from 1854 to 1888. 423 vols. 1854–88.
folio and 4to.

Cases heard on appeal in the House of Lords, with the judgments from the year 1700 to 1888. 517 vols. 1700–1888.
folio and 4to.

The law reports. Appeal cases before the House of Lords
(English, Irish, and Scotch) and the judicial committee of
the Privy Council, 1875–1889. 14 vols. 1876–90. 8vo.
                                                   72 C D

APPEAL PRACTICE.

Practice of House of Lords in English, Scotch, and Irish appeal cases under Appellate Jurisdiction act, 1876. By C.
M. Denison and C. H. Scott. 1879. 8vo.   **12 A**

Appeal practice of supreme court of Judicature and of House
of Lords. By Locock Webb. 1877. 8vo.   **12 A**

Law and practice in appeals from Scotland to the House of
Lords. By Thomas Paton. Edinburgh, 1858. 8vo.   **55 G**

Appellate jurisdiction of the House of Lords, Privy Council,
and Court of Chancery. By C. P. Cooper. 2nd ed. 1850.
[Pamphlets, vol. 7.]   **144 A**

The House of Lords, a court of appeal. By C. P. Cooper.
1850. [Pamphlets, vol. 7.]   **144 A**

Practical treatise on the appellate jurisdiction of the House of
Lords and Privy Council. By J. F. Macqueen. 1842.
8vo.   **52 H**

Observations on the supreme appellate jurisdiction of Great
Britain as it is now exercised by the courts of the Queen in
council and the House of Lords. By William Burge, Q.C.
1841. 8vo.   **55 D**

APPEAL PRACTICE—*continued.*

A Letter to Viscount Melbourne on the present state of the appellate jurisdiction of the Court of Chancery and House of Lords. By Sir Edward Sugden. 1835. [Chancery Pamphlets, vol. 1.] **144 A**

The practice on Appeals from the colonies to the Privy Council. By John Palmer. 1831, with Supplement 1834. [Jacob's Tracts, vol. 12.] **144 F**

The experienced solicitor in proceedings under the appellant jurisdiction of the House of Lords on appeals and writs of error. By George Urquhart. 1773. folio. **156 D**

APPEALS FROM JUSTICES.

Appeals from the convictions and orders of justices. By J. G. Trotter. 1884. 8vo. **12 B**

APPOINTMENT OF NEW TRUSTEES.

Dissertation on and precedents of Appointments of new Trustees. See Bythewood and Jarman's Conveyancing, 4th ed., vol. 2, 1885, pp. 1–64. **13 D**

Observations on and precedents of Appointments of new Trustees. See Davidson's Conveyancing, 4th ed., vol. 4, 1880, pp. 605–62. **13 E**

APPOINTMENT, POWERS OF.

Dissertation on and precedents of Powers of Appointment. See Bythewood and Jarman's Conveyancing, 4th ed., vol. 1, 1884, pp. 731–823. **13 D**

A Concise treatise on Powers. By George Farwell. 1874. 8vo. **13 C**

A Practical treatise of Powers. By Edward Sugden. 8th ed. 1861. 8vo. **13 C**

A Treatise on Powers. By Henry Chance. 2 vols. 1831. 8vo. **53 C**

An Essay on the learning respecting the creation and execution of Powers. By J. J. Powell. 1787. 8vo. **174 C**

APPORTIONMENT.

The law of Apportionment. See Watson's Compendium of Equity, 2nd ed., vol. 1, 1886, pp. 23–29. **12 G**

The law of Apportionment. By F. A. Lewin. 1869. 12mo. **9 A**

See also LANDLORD AND TENANT. **10 E**

APPRENTICESHIP.

Dissertation on and precedents of Apprenticeship. See Bythewood and Jarman's Conveyancing, 4th ed., vol. 2, 1885, pp. 65–93. **13 D**

See also INFANTS, and MASTER AND SERVANT. **10 C & 10 H**

APPROVEMENT.

Treatise on Commons and waste lands, with special reference to the law of Approvement. By C. I. Elton. 1868. 12mo. **52 B**

APULEIUS LUCIUS.

Apuleii Opera omnia, ex editione Oudendorpiana cum notis et interpretatione in usum Delphini. [Delphin Classics, vols. 69–74.] 6 vols. 1825. 8vo. **46 E**

AQUITAINE.

Some account of the English rule in Aquitaine. See M. Burrows's The family of Brocas, 1886, pp. 11–51. **79 H**

ARABIA, LAW OF.

A Succinct account of the civil regulations comprised in The Koran. See B. Barrett's The Code Napoléon, vol. 1, 1811, pp. ccclviii–ccclxxxi. **55 C**

ARABIC.

The Arabick Alphabet, or an easy introduction to the reading of Arabick. By Thomas Burgess. Newcastle, 1809. 12mo. **255 H**

ARATUS OF SOLI.

The Phenomena and Diosemeia of Aratus. Translated into English verse, with notes, by John Lamb, D.D. 1848. 8vo. **83 C**

ARBITRATION AND AWARD.

Dissertation on and precedents of Arbitration. See Bythewood and Jarman's Conveyancing, 4th ed., vol. 2, 1885, pp. 94–251. **13 D**

The law of Arbitrations and Awards. By J. H. Redman. 2nd ed. 1884. 8vo. **9 A**

The power and duty of an Arbitrator. By Francis Russell. 6th ed. by the author and H. Russell. 1882. 8vo. **9 A**

ARBITRATION AND AWARD—*continued.*

The law of Arbitration between masters and workmen. By
C. W. Lovesy. 1867. 12mo. **160 B**

The law and practice of Arbitration and Award. By J. F.
Archbold. 1861. 12mo. **160 B**

The law of Arbitration. By J. S. Caldwell. 1817. 8vo. **160 B**

ARCHÆOLOGY.

An Archæological dictionary, or classical antiquities of the
Jews, Greeks, and Romans. By Rev. Thomas Wilson. 2nd
ed. 1793. 8vo. **123 B**

A Dictionary of the architecture and archæology of the middle
ages. By John Britton. 1838. 8vo. **123 C**

ARCHAIC AND PROVINCIAL WORDS.

A Dictionary of archaic and provincial words, obsolete phrases,
proverbs, and ancient customs from the fourteenth century.
By J. O. Halliwell. 5th ed. 2 vols. 1865. 8vo. **123 B**

Glossary of archaic and provincial words. By Rev. Jonathan
Boucher. [As far as the word Blade.] 1833. 4to. **123 C**

ARCHBOLD, JOHN FREDERICK.

A Collection of the forms and entries which occur in practice
in the courts of King's Bench and Common Pleas in
personal actions and ejectment. 1825. 12mo. **162 D**

The consolidated Criminal Statutes of England and Ireland
passed in the last session of parliament. 1861. 12mo.
165 D

The Justice of the Peace and parish officer. Vols. 1 and 2,
6th ed. ; vol. 3, 10th ed., and vol. 4, 5th ed. 4 vols. 1859–
55. 12mo. **170 C**

The law and practice in Bankruptcy. 1825. 12mo. **160 E**

The same. 11th ed. by John Flather. 1856. 12mo. **160 E**

The law and practice of Arbitration and Award. 1861.
12mo. **160 B**

The law of Bankruptcy and Insolvency as founded on the
recent statute. 1861. 12mo. **160 E**

The law of Landlord and Tenant. 2nd ed. 1855. 12mo.
170 C

The same. 3rd ed. 1864. 12mo. **170 C**

The law of Nisi Prius. 2nd ed. 2 vols. 1845. 12mo. **173 A**

The law relative to pleading and evidence in criminal cases.
6th ed. by John Jervis. 1835. 12mo. **173 F**

ARCHBOLD, JOHN FREDERICK—*continued.*

The same. 15th ed. by W. N. Welsby. 1862. 8vo.			**173 F**
The same. 17th ed. by W. Bruce. 1871. 8vo.			**173 F**
The same. 19th ed. by W. Bruce. 1878. 8vo.			**173 F**
The same. 20th ed. by W. Bruce. 1886. 8vo.			**12 C**

The new practice pleading and evidence in the Courts of common law at Westminster, with all necessary forms. 1853. 12mo. **162 D**

The Parish officer, comprising also the law as to church rates, vestries, watching and lighting. 4th ed. by James Paterson. 1864. 12mo. **173 B**

The same. 5th ed. by W. C. Glen. 1874. 12mo. **173 B**

The same. 6th ed. by W. C. Glen. 1881. 8vo. **11 A**

The Poor Law. 10th ed. 1860. 12mo. **174 A**

The same. 11th ed. 1863. 12mo. **174 A**

The same. 12th ed. by W. C. Glen. 1873. 12mo. **174 A**

The same. 13th ed. by W. C. Glen. 1878. 12mo. **174 A**

The same. 14th ed. by W. C. Glen. 1885. 8vo. **11 C**

The practice of country attornies and their agents in the courts of law at Westminster, with forms. 1838. 12mo. **163 B**

The same. 2nd ed. 2 vols. 1844. 12mo. **163 B**

The practice of the Court of Common Pleas in personal actions and ejectment. 2 vols. 1829. 12mo. **162 A**

The practice of the court of King's Bench in personal actions and ejectment. 2 vols. 1819. 12mo. **162 A**

The same. 2nd ed. 2 vols. 1826. 12mo. **162 A**

The same. 4th ed. by Thomas Chitty, treating also of the practice of the Courts of Common Pleas and Exchequer. 2 vols. 1835. 12mo. **162 A**

The same. 5th ed. by T. Chitty. 2 vols. 1836. 12mo. **162 A**

The same. 6th ed. by T. Chitty. 2 vols. 1838. 12mo. **162 B**.

The same. 7th ed. by T. Chitty. 2 vols. 1840. 12mo. **162 B**

The same. 8th ed. by T. Chitty. 2 vols. 1845–47. 12mo. **162 B**

The same. 9th ed. by Samuel Prentice. 2 vols. 1855–56. 12mo. **162 C**

The same. 11th ed. by S. Prentice. 2 vols. 1862. 8vo. **162 C**

The same. 12th ed. by S. Prentice. 2 vols. 1866. 12mo. **162 C**

Archbold's Practice of the Queen's Bench, Common Pleas and Exchequer divisions of the High Court of Justice in

ARCHBOLD, JOHN FREDERICK—*continued.*

actions, &c., in which they have a common jurisdiction. 13th ed. by S. Prentice. 2 vols. 1879. 8vo. **12 E**

The same. 14th ed. by T. W. Chitty and J. St. L. Leslie. 2 vols. 1885. 8vo. **12 E**

The practice of the court of Quarter Sessions. 2nd ed. 1857. 12mo. **175 D**

The same. 3rd ed. by C. W. Lovesy. 1869. 12mo. **175 D**

The same. 4th ed. by F. Mead and H. H. S. Croft. 1885. 8vo. **12 C**

The practice of the Crown Office of the court of Queen's Bench. 1844. 12mo. **165 D**

The practice of the new county courts. 2nd ed. 1847. 12mo. **165 B**

The same. 9th ed. by J. V. V. Fitzgerald. 1885. 8vo. **52 E**

The same. 10th ed. by C. A. White. 1889. 8vo. **12 H**

The statutes relating to lunacy. 2nd ed. by W. C. Glen and A. Glen. 1877. 8vo. **10 H**

ARCHER, CHARLES PALMER.

An Analytical digest of the reported cases in the several courts of common law in Ireland from the earliest period to the present time. Dublin, 1842. 8vo. **15 F**

ARCHER, THOMAS GOODWYN.

Index to unrepealed Statutes connected with administration of law in England and Wales, 1837–1850. 1851. 8vo. **176 C**

ARCHER, WILLIAM HENRY.

Abstracts of specifications of patents applied for in Victoria, 1854–1866. Metals, part 1. Melbourne, 1872. 4to. **37 G**

Patents and Patentees in Victoria from 1854 to 1866. 5 vols. in 1. Melbourne, 1868–72. 4to. **37 G**

ARCHIBALD, WILLIAM FREDERICK ALPHONSE.

Archibald's country solicitor's practice, a handbook of the practice in the Queen's Bench division of the high court of justice. 1881. 8vo. **12 E**

Forms of Summonses and Orders, with notes for use at judges' chambers and in the district registries. 1879. 12mo. **53 H**

The same. 2nd ed. by W. F. A. Archibald and P. E. Vizard. 1886. 12mo. **12 G**

ARCHITECTURE.

The Antiquarian itinerary, comprising specimens of architecture, monastic, castellated, and domestic, in Great Britain. 4 vols. 1815–16. 8vo. **85 G**

A Dictionary of the architecture and archæology of the middle ages. By John Britton. 1838. 8vo. **123 C**

ARCOT, Nabob of, Ali Khan Muhummad.

Letter from the Nabob of Arcot to the Court of directors of the East India Company. 1777. 4to. **38 A**

ARCTIC REGIONS.

Journal of a second voyage for the discovery of a north-west passage from the Atlantic to the Pacific, performed in the years 1821–22–23 under the orders of Captain W. E. Parry, with Appendix. 2 vols. 1824–25. 4to. **84 F**

Narrative of an expedition in H.M.S. Terror with a view to geographical discovery on the Arctic shores. By Captain Back, R.N. 1838. 8vo. **84 D**

Narrative of a second voyage in search of a north-west passage, and of a residence in the Arctic regions during the years 1829–1833. By Sir John Ross. 1835. 4to. **84 F**

On the exploration of the North Polar region. By Sherard Osborn. 1865. [Pamphlets, vol. 26.] **144 B**

ARGENTINE REPUBLIC.

Códigos y leyes usuales de la República Argentina. Cuarta edicion. Felix Lajouane, editor. 2 vols. Buenos Ayres, 1888. 8vo. **55 C**

Letters concerning the country of The River Plate (The Argentine Republic) being suitable for emigrants and capitalists to settle in. 1869, and 2nd ed. 1869. [Pamphlets, vol 29.] **144 B**

ARGLES, Napoleon.

A Treatise upon French mercantile law and the practice of the courts, with a new translation of the entire code of commerce and special mercantile laws in force in France. 1882. 8vo. **55 C**

ARGOU; Gabriel.

Institution au droit François. 11me éd. par A. G. Boucher d'Argis. 2 tomes. Paris, 1787. 12mo. **58 F**

ARITHMETIC.

The compendious measurer ; being a brief treatise on Mensuration and practical Geometry, with an introduction to decimal and duodecimal arithmetic. By Charles Hutton. 2nd ed. 1790. 12mo. **255 H**

The intellectual calculator, or manual of practical Arithmetic. By J. T. Crossley and William Martin. 68th ed. n.d. 12mo. **255 H**

ARMADA, Spanish.

Catalogue of the exhibition of Armada and Elizabethan relics, held in grand saloon of theatre royal, Drury Lane, London. By W. H. K. Wright. Plymouth, 1888. 8vo. **78 C**

ARMAGH.

Historical memoirs of the city of Armagh for a period of 1373 years. By James Stuart. Newry, 1819. 8vo. **95 E**

ARMORIAL BEARINGS. See Heraldry.

ARMSTRONG, R., J. MACARTNEY and J. C. OGLE.

Reports of cases at Nisi Prius and the commission in Dublin respectively, 1840–1842. Dublin, 1843. 8vo. **15 C**

ARMY, British.

An Historical account of the British army, and of the law military. By E. Samuel. 1820. 8vo. **83 H**

The military forces of the Crown, their administration and government. By C. M. Clode. 2 vols. 1869. 8vo. **83 H**

Preliminary education for the profession of arms. By F. Eardley-Wilmot. 1856. [Pamphlets, vol. 10.] **144 A**

See also Courts Martial and Military Law.

ARMY LISTS.

Army and Navy Calendar for 1882–83. 1882. 8vo. **146 C**

The Army list, January 1818 to December 1889 (imperfect). 251 vols. 1818–89. 12mo. **208 & 209**

East India Register and Directory for the years 1800, 1801, 1803, 1805–1821, 1828, 1829, 1832, 1837, 1838, 1842–1860. 4 vols. 1800–60. 12mo. **214 A–C**

The Indian army and civil service list, January 1861 to July 1889 (imperfect). 56 vols. 1861–89. 12mo. and 8vo. **214 C–G**

ARMY LISTS—*continued.*

A List of the general and field officers as they rank in the army, of the officers in the several regiments of horse, dragoons, and foot. 1759–1761, 1763, 1767, 1784–1788, 1790–1801, 1803, 1805, 1806, 1808–1824, 1826, 1828–1861. 78 vols. 1759–1861. 8vo. **133 A–D**

A List of the Militia officers, to which is added lists of the officers of independent companies and of fencible regiments now raising in Scotland. 2nd ed. 1793. 12mo. **218 A**

The new annual Army list for the years 1841 to 1889. By H. G. Hart. 49 vols. 1841–89. 8vo. **133 E–G**

The new [quarterly] Army list. By H. G. Hart. Feb. 1839 to Oct. 1889 (imperfect). 85 vols. 1839–89. 8vo. **210 F–211 D**

The official quarterly Army list, July 1880 to October 1889. 38 vols. 1880–89. 8vo. **212 A–E**

ARMY PROMOTION.

An Appeal to the public and a farewell address to the army, including some strictures upon the general conduct of our military force. By Denis Hogan. 10th ed. 1808. 8vo. **118 B**

ARMY REGULATION BILL.

The government bill for the better regulation of the regular and auxiliary land forces of the crown, with amendments to be proposed in committee, by Colonel Sir William Russell, inserted in italics. 1871. [Pamphlets, vol. 29.] **144 B**

A Scheme for the reorganization of the land forces. By Colonel Sir William Russell. 1871. [Pamphlets, vol. 33.] **144 C**

Speech delivered on the second reading of the Army Regulation bill. By G. O. Trevelyan, M.P. 1871. [Pamphlets, vol. 29.] **144 B**

ARNOLD, George Mathews.

Robert Pocock, the Gravesend historian, naturalist, antiquarian, botanist, and printer. 1883. 8vo. **79 B**

ARNOLD, Thomas.

Henrici, archidiaconi Huntendunensis Historia Anglorum : the history of the English, by Henry, archdeacon of Huntingdon, from A.C. 55 to A.D. 1154. Edited by Thomas Arnold. 1879. 8vo. **102 G**

ARNOLD, THOMAS—*continued.*

Symeonis Monachi Opera Omnia. Vol. 1. Historia ecclesiæ
Dunhelmensis. Vol. 2. Historia regum Anglorum et
Dacorum. Edited by Thomas Arnold. 2 vols. 1882–85.
8vo. **102 G**

ARNOLD, Rev. THOMAS, D.D.

The life and correspondence of Thomas Arnold, D.D. By
Arthur Penrhyn Stanley. 4th ed. 2 vols. 1845. 8vo. **80 B**

ARNOLD, THOMAS JAMES.

Reports of cases in the Court of Common Pleas and Exchequer
Chamber, 1838–1839. 1 vol. 1840. 8vo. **6 A**

Summary of the duties of a Justice of the Peace out of
sessions. Summary convictions. 1860. 8vo. **179 A**

A Treatise on the law relating to Municipal Corporations.
1851. 12mo. **164 G**

The same. 2nd ed., with chapters on practice by S. G. Johnson. 1875. 12mo. **164 G**

The same. 3rd ed. by S. G. Johnson. 1883. 8vo. **9 F**

ARNOT, HUGO.

A Collection and abridgement of celebrated criminal trials in
Scotland, 1536 to 1784. Edinburgh, 1785. 4to. **49 H**

ARNOULD, JOSEPH.

A Treatise on the law of Marine Insurance and Average.
2 vols. 1848. 8vo. **169 B**

The same. 2nd ed. 2 vols. 1857. 8vo. **169 B**

The same. 4th ed. by David Maclachlan. 2 vols. 1872.
8vo. **169 B**

The same. 5th ed. by David Maclachlan. 2 vols. 1877.
8vo. **169 B**

The same. 6th ed. by David Maclachlan. 2 vols. 1887.
8vo. **10 D**

AROUET, FRANÇOIS MARIE. See VOLTAIRE.

ARRAGON, KATHARINE OF.

Inventories of the wardrobe stuff at Baynard's Castle of Katharine, Princess Dowager. Edited by J. G. Nichols. [Cam-
den Society, vol. 61.] 1855. 8vo. **85 B**

ARRANGEMENTS, FAMILY.

The law of Compromises and Family Arrangements. See
Watson's Compendium of Equity, 2nd ed., vol. 1, 1886,
pp. 62–66. **12 G**

ARRANGEMENTS WITH CREDITORS.

A treatise on the law of private arrangements with creditors,
also precedents of deeds of arrangement. By G. Y. Robson.
1888. 8vo. **12 I**

Precedents of Deeds of Arrangement between debtors and
their creditors. By G. W. Lawrence. 3rd ed. 1888.
8vo. **12 I**

The Deeds of Arrangement act, 1887 ; with introduction and
notes of cases. By Walter Perks. 1888. 8vo. **12 I**

The law of private Arrangements between debtors and
creditors. By Reginald Winslow. 1885. 8vo. **12 I**

Liquidation by Arrangement under the Bankruptcy act, 1869.
By J. S. Salaman. 1882. 8vo. **12 I**

ARRAY.

A Declaration of the Lords and Commons assembled in
Parliament upon the statute of 5 H. IV., whereby the commission of Array is supposed to be warranted. 1642.
8vo. **49 F**

ARREST.

The act for the abolition of arrest on mesne process in civil
actions. By Edward Ings. 1840. 12mo. **160 C**

Remarks on the abolition of the law of Arrest and imprisonment for debt. By A Barrister. 1830. [Law Tracts, vol. 5.]
144 E

The history of the law of Arrest in personal actions, showing
its severity and inexpediency and the mischiefs incident to
the system of Bail, with practical amendments. By P. W.
Crowther. 1828. [Jacob's Tracts, vol. 12.] **144 F**

Thoughts on the present state of the law of Arrest and imprisonment for debt. 1828. [Law Tracts, vol. 5.] **144 E**

Observations on the law of arrest for debt. By An Attorney.
1827. [Law Tracts, vol. 5.] **144 E**

A Treatise on the abuses of the laws, particularly in actions by
Arrest. By James Pearce. 1814. [Law Tracts, vol. 2.] **144 E**

The law of Arrests in both civil and criminal cases. By An
Attorney at Law. 1742. 12mo. **48 B**

ARROWSMITH, Aaron.

Atlas to Thompson's Alcedo, comprising maps of South America and West Indies, dated 1795–1811.　folio.　**19 D**

A New map of Mexico and adjacent provinces.　1810.　4to.
84 E

ARROWSMITH, John.

The London atlas of universal geography.　1838.　folio.　**19 D**

ARROWSMITH, Robert George.

Occupation, or a glance at the property tax and the income tax, 1854.　[Pamphlets, vol. 21.]　**144 B**

ART UNION OF LONDON.

Twenty-first annual report of the council of the Art Union of London, with list of members.　1857.　8vo.　**146 E**

ART, Works of.

The law relating to works of Literature and Art.　By John Shortt.　2nd ed.　1884.　8vo.　**9 E**

Property in works of art.　H.R.H. Prince Albert *v.* Strange and others.　Attorney general *v.* Strange and others.　Report of the judgment of Sir J. L. Knight Bruce delivered in the Court of Chancery, Lincoln's Inn, January 16, 1849.　By J. H. Cooke.　2nd ed.　1849.　[Pamphlets, vol. 23.]　**144 B**

ARTICLED CLERKS.

The Articled Clerk's handbook.　By J. S. Rubinstein and S. Ward.　2nd ed.　1878.　12mo.　**64 A**

The Articled Clerk's handbook.　By Richard Hallilay.　4th ed. by George Badham.　1873.　8vo.　**64 A**

Law students and young attorneys, their conduct, and some of the conditions of professional success.　By C. T. Saunders.　Birmingham, 1866.　[Pamphlets, vol. 27.]　**144 B**

A Manual for articled clerks.　By J. J. S. Wharton　9th ed. 1864.　12mo.　**160 C**

A Manual for articled clerks and other law students.　1836. 12mo.　**160 C**

ARTICLES, The Thirty-nine.

The Catholic doctrine of the Church of England, an exposition of the thirty-nine articles.　By Thomas Rogers.　Edited by Rev. J. J. S. Perowne　Cambridge, 1854.　8vo.　**77 E**

ARTS AND ARTISTS.

Observations on the state of arts and artists in this Kingdom. See John Gwynn's London and Westminster improved, 1766, pp. 22–75.   **89 F**

Polymetis, or an enquiry concerning agreement between the works of the Roman poets and the remains of the Antient Artists. By Rev. Mr. Spence. 1747. folio.   **78 H**

ARTS AND SCIENCES..

De l'Origine des lois, des arts et des sciences et de leur progrès chez les anciens peuples. 2 tomes. Paris, 1758. 4to.   **78 H**

See also ENCYCLOPÆDIAS.   **122 A-H**

ARUNDEL MANUSCRIPTS.

Catalogue of the Arundel manuscripts in the British Museum, with Index. 2 vols. 1834–41. folio.   **81 H**

Catalogue of the Arundel manuscripts in the library of the College of Arms. Privately printed. 1829. 8vo.   **118 F**

ARUNDEL PEERAGE.

The claim to the dignity of Earl of Arundel. See Berkeley Peerage by tenure, vols. 1 and 3, 1858–62. folio.   **124 J**

ARUNDEL, SUSSEX.

The antiquities of Arundel, with an abstract of the lives of the Earls of Arundel from the Conquest to this time. By the master of the grammar school at Arundel. [Charles Caraccioli.] 1766. 8vo.   **80 A**

The history and antiquities of the castle and town of Arundel, including the biography of its earls. By Rev. M. A. Tierney. 2 vols. in 1. 1834. 8vo.   **93 E**

ARUNDELL, JAMES EVERARD ARUNDELL, 10th BARON, and SIR R. C. HOARE.

The history of modern Wiltshire. Hundred of Dunworth, and Vale of Noddre. 1829. folio.   **94 H**

ARUNDELL, JAMES WHITTON.

A practical treatise on the law relating to Mines and mining companies. 1862. 12mo.   **172 F**

ASGILL, JOHN.

An Essay on a registry for titles of lands. 1698. 8vo.   **49 F**

ASHBOURN, Derbyshire.

The history and topography of Ashbourn, the valley of the
Dove, and adjacent villages. Ashbourn, 1839. 8vo. **87 B**

ASHBY, Matthew.

Free Parliaments. The case of Ashby *v.* White. n.d.
[Pamphlets, vol. 11.] **144 A**

Proceedings at law between M. Ashby and W. White in
relation to an election at Aylesbury. 2nd ed. 1721.
12mo. **48 E**

ASHE, Thomas.

Abridgment des touts les cases reportez a large per Monsieur
Plowden. Composee et digest. per T. A. [n.d.] 12mo.
49 A

Un perfect table a touts les severall livers del reportes de Sir
Edward Coke. 1606. 12mo. **49 A**

Promptuaire ou Repertory generall de les annales et plusors
auters livres del common ley Dengleterre. 2 vols. 1614.
folio. **99 E**

ASHLEY, Henry.

The doctrine and practice of Attachment in the Mayor's
Court, London. 2nd ed. 1819. 8vo. **172 D**

ASHMOLE, Elias.

The history of the most noble order of the Garter, to which is
prefixd, a discourse of knighthood in general and the
several orders extant in Europe. Digested and continued
[by T. Walker]. 1715. 8vo. **125 E**

Life of Elias Ashmole. See J. P. Malcolm's Lives of topographers and antiquaries. 1815. **79 H**

The visitation of Berkshire, 1664–6. By Elias Ashmole.
Edited by W. C. Metcalfe. Exeter, 1882. 4to. **86 B**

ASHRIDGE, Bucks.

History of the college of Bonhommes at Ashridge, in the
county of Buckingham. By H. J. Todd. 1823. folio.
91 H

ASIA.

The Asiatic Annual Register, or a view of the history of
Hindustan and of the politics, commerce, and literature of
Asia for the years 1799–1805. 7 vols. 1800–1807. 8vo.
254 G

ASIA—*continued.*

A Catalogue of maps of the British possessions in Asia.
2 parts. 1870–72. 8vo. **82 D**

Histoire générale des Huns, des Turcs, des Mogols, et des
autres Tartares Occidentaux &c.; précédée d'une introduction contenant des tables chronol. & historiques des
Princes qui ont regné dans l'Asie. Par Joseph de Guignes.
4 vols. in 5. Paris, 1756–68. 4to. **113 E**

ASKEWE, ANNE.

The examinations of Anne Askewe. By John Bale. See
Bale's Select Works, 1849, pp. 135–248. **77 E**

ASPIN, JEHOSHAPHAT.

A Complete system of Chronology or universal history,
abridged. n.d. 8vo. **116 E**

ASPLAND, LINDSEY MIDDLETON.

The law of Blasphemy, being a candid examination of the views
of Mr. Justice Stephen. 1884. [Pamphlets, vol. 30.] **144 B**

The law of Blasphemy. By L. M. Aspland, with an appendix
containing an essay on religious offences indictable at
common law, by E. Taylor, and the speech of Lord Mansfield in the House of Lords in 1767 in the case of the
Sheriffs of London—Chamberlain of London *v.* Evans.
1884. [Pamphlets, vol. 30.] **144 B**

ASSESSED TAXES.

A Handy book of the assessed tax laws. By R. R. Davies.
1864. 8vo. **53 H**

Printed Cases relating to Assessed Taxes decided by the
Judges. Nos. 1–2861. 8 vols. 1823–72. folio. **68 B**

Reports of Tax Cases under the act 37 Vict. cap. 16, and
under the Taxes management act. 1875–1883. Vol. 1.
1884. 8vo. **68 B**

ASSESSMENT SESSIONS.

The practice of the court of general assessment sessions
under Valuation (Metropolis) act, 1869. By E. W. Beal.
1883. 12mo. **11 E**

ASSETS.

The law of Assets. See Watson's Compendium of Equity,
2nd ed., vol. 1, 1886, pp. 30–40. **12 G**

ASSETS—*continued.*

Principles of the administration of Assets in payment of debts. By A. S. Eddis. 1880. 8vo. **12 F**

An Essay on Real Assets ; or, the payment of the debts of a deceased person out of his Real Estate, and the means by which that payment ought to be accomplished. By Joshua Williams. 1861. 8vo. **53 F**

A Practical treatise of Assets, Debts, and Incumbrances. By James Ram. 1832. 8vo. **160 C**

A Treatise of the administration of Assets in equity. By Holker Meggison. 1832. 8vo. **160 C**

ASSIZES.

The Crown circuit companion, containing the practice of the Assizes on the Crown side. By W. Stubbs and G. Talmash. 7th ed. 1799. 12mo. **165 F**

The expenses of the judges of assize riding the Western and Oxford circuits, 1596–1601. Edited by W. D. Cooper. [Camden Society, vol. 73.] 1859. 8vo. **85 B**

The history, objects, and advantages of the Assizes. By W. F. Finlason. 1877. [Pamphlets, vol. 29.] **144 B**

ASSO Y DEL RIO, IGNACIO JORDAN DE y MIGUEL DE MANUEL Y RODRIGUEZ.

Institutes of the civil law of Spain. Translated from the Spanish of the sixth edition, with notes by L. F. C. Johnston. 1825. 8vo. **55 C**

ASSOCIATION FOR THE REFORM AND CODIFICA- TION OF THE LAW OF NATIONS.

Reports of the annual conferences, 1876–1883. Bound in 2 vols. 1880–86. 8vo. **78 C**

ASSUMPSIT.

The law of contracts and promises as settled in the action of Assumpsit. By S. Comyn. 2nd ed. 1824. 8vo. **163 D**

ASSURANCES.

The law of Common Assurances touching deeds in general. By William Sheppard. 1669. folio. **49 G**

ASTLE, THOMAS.

The origin and progress of writing ; also some account of the origin and progress of printing. 2nd ed. 1803. 4to. **78 G**

[ASTLE, Thomas, Rev. J. AYSCOUGH and J. CALEY.]
Taxatio ecclesiastica Angliæ et Walliæ auctoritate P. Nicholai
IV. circa A.D. 1291. 1802. folio. **99 C**

ASTON, James Jones.
Fusion practicable; or, a letter to the lord chancellor on the
further assimilation of the jurisdiction of the superior courts
of law and equity. 1863. [Pamphlets, vol. 17.] **144 B**
The jurisdiction practice and proceedings of Court of Chancery
of county palatine of Lancaster. 1852. 8vo. **170 C**
The stock exchange 'a sham market'? or the recent stock
exchange cases of Grissell v. Bristowe and Coles v. Bristowe, as decided on appeal stated by the Economist to be
unreasonable and inequitable, and making a sham market.
1869. [Pamphlets, vol. 38.] **144 C**

ASTON, John.
Warwickshire; being a concise topographical description of
the county of Warwick from the work of Sir W. Dugdale
and other later authorities. Coventry, 1817. 8vo. **93 E**

ASTON, R.
Placita Latine Rediviva; a Book of Entries, containing perfect
and approved Presidents of counts, declarations, barrs, as
well in actions real, as personal. 3rd ed. 1673. 4to.

ASTRONOMY.
Ædes Hartwelliana, or notices of the manor and mansion of
Hartwell. By W. H. Smyth. Printed for private circula-
tion. 1851. 4to. **86 G**
Astronomy and general physics considered with reference to
natural theology. By Rev. W. Whewell. 5th ed. 1836.
8vo. **77 B**
The cycle of celestial objects continued at the Hartwell ob-
servatory to 1859, with a notice of recent discoveries. By
W. H. Smyth. Privately printed. 1860. 4to. **86 G**
The gallery of nature, a pictorial and descriptive tour through
creation. By Thomas Milner. 1855. 8vo. **84 D**
Impeachment of modern Astronomy. By E. E. Middleton.
1879. 12mo. **78 B**
The nautical almanac and astronomical ephemeris for the year
1890 for the meridian of the royal observatory at Green-
wich. 1886. 8vo. **107 H**
The Phenomena and Diosemeia of Aratus. Translated into
English verse by John Lamb, D.D. 1848. 8vo. **83 C**

ASTRONOMY—*continued.*

Sidereal chromatics ; being a reprint, with additions from the
' Bedford cycle of celestial objects ' and its ' Hartwell con-
tinuation ' on the colours of multiple stars. By Admiral
W. H. Smyth. Privately printed. 1864. 8vo. **78 G**

Twelve planispheres, forming a guide to the stars for every
night in the year 1846. 8vo. **78 B**

ASTRY, SIR JAMES.

A General charge to all grand juries. 1703. 12mo. **49 E**

ASYLUMS.

Notes on asylums for the insane in America. By J. C. Bucknill. 1876. 12mo. **78 A**

[ATCHESON, NATHANIEL.]

The history of Churcher's College, Petersfield, Hants ; with a
report of the case in the high court of Chancery between the
Trustees and several of the inhabitants of Petersfield. 1823.
8vo. **88 A**

ATHANASIAN CREED.

Authorized report of the meetings in defence of the Athanasian Creed held in St. James's hall and in the Hanover Square
rooms January 31, 1873. 1873. [Pamphlets, vol. 30.] **144 B**

ATHENRY PEERAGE.

The claim to the dignity of Baron Athenry. See Peerage
Cases, Second series, vol. i., pp. 153–178, and Peerage Evidence, vol. 3, pp. 119–206. **124 I J**

ATHENS.

A Discourse upon improving the revenue of the state of
Athens ; written originally in Greek by Xenophon, and
made English by W. M. [Walter Moyle.] 1697. See C.
Davenant, On Taxes, 1698. 12mo. **49 D**

The speeches of Isæus in causes concerning the law of succession to property at Athens, with a prefatory discourse,
notes critical and historical, and a commentary. By
William Jones. 1779. 4to. **83 J**

ATHERLEY, EDMOND GIBSON.

A Practical treatise of the law of marriage and other family
settlements. 1813. 8vo. **175 E**

ATHOL, Dukes of. /·.

Copies of proceedings before the Privy Council on a petition
of John, Duke of Atholl, for a further compensation for the
sale of the feudal rights of the Isle of Man in 1765. 1805.
folio. 95 H

Opinion of Mr. Hargrave on the case of the Duke of Athol in
respect to the Isle of Man. 1788. 8vo. 94 F

A Short history of the transactions in the Isle of Man on
which the House of Keys founded their late petition to the
House of Commons against the Duke of Athol. Douglas,
1825. 8vo. 94 F

ATKINSON, George.

Letter to Lord Chelmsford on the Circuit System. 1867.
[Pamphlets, vol. 31.] 144 C

A Practical treatise on Sheriff law. 1839. 8vo. 175 E

The same. 2nd ed. 1847. 8vo. 175 E

The same. 3rd ed. 1854. 8vo. 175 E

The same. 4th ed. 1861. 8vo. 175 E

The same. 5th ed. 1869. 8vo. 175 E

The same. 6th ed. by R. E. Melsheimer. 1878. 8vo. 11 F

[ATKINSON, Rowland.]

Notes and Queries. General index to series the fourth (1868–
1873), 1874 ; to series the fifth (1874–1879), 1880 ; and to
series the sixth (1880–1885), 1886. 3 vols. 1874–86.
8vo. 129 I

ATKINSON, Rowland William.

Observations on the scheme of the solicitor general to simplify
the title to and the transfer of Landed Estates. Walling-
ford, 1859. [Pamphlets, vol. 19.] 144 B

ATKINSON, Solomon.

Acts relating to the law of Real Property passed in the last
session of parliament. 1833. 8vo. 174 E

The theory and practice of Conveyancing. 2nd ed. 2 vols.
1839–41. 8vo. 163 G

ATKYNS, John Tracy.

Reports of Cases in the High Court of Chancery, in the time
of Lord Chancellor Hardwicke. 3 vols. 1765–68. folio.

ATKYNS, John Tracy—*continued.*

The same. 2nd ed. 3 vols. 1781–82. 8vo.

The same. 3rd ed. with notes by F. W. Sanders. 3 vols. 1794. 8vo. **2 A**

ATKYNS, Sir Robert.

Parliamentary and political tracts. 2nd ed. 1741. 8vo. **144 F**

> The power, jurisdiction and privilege of Parliament, and the antiquity of the House of Commons asserted.
>
> Argument in the case concerning election of members to Parliament, between Sir S. Barnardiston, plaintiff, and Sir W. Soame, Sherriff of Suffolk, defendant.
>
> An Enquiry into the power of dispensing with Penal Statutes.
>
> A Discourse concerning the ecclesiastical jurisdiction in the realm of England.
>
> A Defence of the late Lord Russell's innocency, by way of answer and confutation of a libellous pamphlet, intituled, An antidote against Poison.
>
> The Lord Russell's innocency further defended, by way of reply to an answer, intituled, The magistracy and government of England vindicated.
>
> The Lord Chief Baron Atkin's speech to Sir W. Ashurst, Lord Mayor elect of the City of London.

ATKYNS, Sir Robert, the younger.

The ancient and present state of Gloucestershire. 2nd ed. 1768. folio. **88 H**

Life of Sir Robert Atkyns. See J. P. Malcolm's Lives of Topographers and Antiquaries. 1815. 4to. **79 H**

ATLAS.

An Atlas of the World. By James Wyld. 1853. 4to. **84 F**

Atlas to accompany the second report of the Railway Commissioners, Ireland. 1838. folio. **19 D**

Atlas to Thompson's Alcedo, comprising maps of South America and West Indies, dated 1795–1811. By Aaron Arrowsmith. 1795–1811. folio. **19 D**

Bacon's New Ordnance Survey Atlas of London and Suburbs. [1882.] folio. **Hall**

County maps of England. By S. Lewis. 1831. 4to. **84 F**

County maps of Scotland. 1822. folio. **Hall**

The English atlas ; or, a set of maps of all the counties in England and Wales. By E. Bowen. 1777. folio. **19 D**

General atlas. By Frederick de Wit. Amsterdam, 1688. folio. **84 H**

ATLAS—*continued.*

The Harrow Atlas of modern geography. 1874. folio. **84 F**

Joannis Jansonii Novus Atlas, sive theatrum orbis terrarum :
in quo tabulæ et descriptiones omnium regionum totius
universi accuratissime exhibentur. 6 vols. Amstelodami,
1656–58. folio. **84 H**

The London Atlas of Universal geography. By John Arrowsmith. 1838. folio. **19 D**

A New general Atlas. Edinburgh, 1817. folio. **19 D**

A New map of Mexico and adjacent provinces. By Aaron
Arrowsmith. 1810. 4to. **84 E**

A New Parliamentary and County Atlas of Great Britain
and Ireland. By W. Hughes. n.d. folio. **Hall**

Philips' Atlas of the Counties of England. By E. Weller.
[1875.] folio. **Hall**

Philips' Imperial Library Atlas. Edited by William Hughes.
1879. folio. **Hall**

Pigot & Co.'s British Atlas of the counties of England. 1831.
folio. **19 D**

Smith's New English Atlas ; being a complete set of county
maps, divided into hundreds. 1835. folio. **19 D**

The Standard Atlas of Canada, to which are added maps
of the United States of America. 1878. folio. **Hall**

ATTACHMENT.

Attachment of debts and Receivers by way of equitable execution in the high court of justice and in the county courts.
By Michael Cababé. 2nd ed. 1888. 12mo. **12 F**

The customary law of Foreign Attachment. By Woodthorpe
Brandon. 1861. 8vo. **52 H**

The law and practice of Foreign Attachment in the Lord
Mayor's Court. By John Locke. 1853. 12mo. **172 D**

The doctrine and practice of Attachment in the Mayor's
Court, London. By Robert Woolsey. 1816. 8vo. **172 D**

ATTAINDER, BILLS OF.

A Discourse concerning treasons and bills of attainder. 2nd
ed. 1717. [Law Tracts, vol. 1.] **144 E**

ATTESTATION.

Dissertation on and precedents of Attestation. See Bythewood
and Jarman's Conveyancing, 4th ed., vol. ii., 1885, pp. 252–
266. **13 D**

ATTESTATION—*continued.*

Practical observations on certain points of frequent occurrence in Conveyancing, arising from an omission to express the fact of signature in the Attestations of the various instruments executing powers. By W. H. Rowe. 1815. 8vo.

163 G

ATTORNEY, Powers of.

Dissertation on and precedents of Powers of Attorney. See Bythewood and Jarman's Conveyancing, 4th ed., vol. 4, 1887, pp. 855–974. **13 D**

ATTORNEYS AND SOLICITORS.

The law relating to Solicitors of the supreme court of judicature. By Arthur Cordery. 2nd ed. 1888. 8vo. **11 G**

The law and practice relating to Attorneys. By Alexander Pulling. 3rd ed. 1862. 8vo. **11 G**

A Treatise on the Lien of Attornies. By Whitley Stokes. 1860. 8vo. **10 G**

A Remonstrance on behalf of the attorneys of Ireland, with a few suggestions for elevating their position. By One of the body. Dublin, 1859. [Pamphlets, vol. 16.] **144 B**

Observations on the remuneration of attorneys and solicitors. By R. A. Parker. 1853. [Pamphlets, vol. 16.] **144 B**

An Argument on the inutility of the distinction between barrister and attorney, addressed to the Lord Chancellor. By W. L. Harle. 1851. [Pamphlets, vol. 8.] **144 A**

The moral, social, and professional duties of attornies and solicitors. By Samuel Warren. 1848. 12mo. **160 C**

Lectures relative to the profession of Attorney and Solicitor, delivered in the hall of the Dublin Law Institute. By T. J. Beasley. Dublin, 1841. 8vo. **144 G**

The employment and charges of Attorneys. 1839. [Pamphlets, vol. 3.] • **144 A**

An Address to the attorneys at law and solicitors practising in Great Britain, and to the Public, upon the proceedings of a committee of the London Law Club, relative to a bill for the incorporating and better regulation of the Practitioners. By Joseph Day. 1796. 8vo. **160 C**

A Report of the proceedings in the cause of Thomas Harrison, chamberlain of the City of London, plaintiff, against John Alexander, defendant, touching the right of the City of London to oblige attornies at law, who practise conveyancing within the said city, to be free of the Scriveners'

ATTORNEYS—*continued.*

Company. 1768. Bound with Scriveners' Case, London. 1748. 8vo. **89 E**

The practising attorney or lawyer's office, containing the business of an attorney in all its branches. By William Bohun. 4th ed. 2 vols. 1737. 12mo. **162 G**

The compleat solicitor, entring-clerk, and attorney. 1683. 12mo. **48 B**

The practick part of the law shewing the office of an Attorney. 1676. 12mo. **48 B**

ATTORNMENT.

Dissertation on and precedents of Attornment. See Bythewood and Jarman's Conveyancing, 3rd ed., vol. 3, 1842, pp. 35–53. **53 D**

ATWOOD, Thomas.

The history of the island of Dominica. 1791. 8vo. **84 B**

[ATWOOD, William.]

Jani Anglorum facies nova : or several monuments of antiquity touching great councils of the kingdom. 1680. 8vo. **49 D**

AUBREY, John.

Life of John Aubrey. See J. P. Malcolm's Lives of Topographers and Antiquaries. 1815. 4to. **79 H**

Memoir of John Aubrey, F.R.S., embracing his auto-biographical sketches, a brief review of his merits, and an account of his works. By John Britton. 1845. 4to. **79 H**

The natural history of Wiltshire. Edited by John Britton. 1847. 4to. **95 G**

AUCTIONS.

A Practical treatise on the law of Auctions. By J. Bateman. 6th ed. by O. Smith and P. F. Evans. 1882. 8vo. **9 A**

A Practical treatise on the law of Auctions. Excise edition. 1838. 12mo. **160 C**

The law of Auctions. By R. Babington. 1826. 8vo. **160 C**

AUDITORS.

Auditors, their duties and responsibilities. By F. W. Pixley. 1881. 8vo. **9 A**

AUGUSTINE, Saint.

Saint Augustine, a poem in eight books. By the late H. W. Cole, Q.C. Edinburgh, 1877. 8vo. **83 H**

AUNGIER, George James.

Croniques de London, depuis l'an 44 Hen. III. jusqu' à l'an 17 Edw. III. Edited by G. J. Aungier. [Camden Society, vol. 28.] 1844. 8vo. **85 A**

The history and antiquities of Syon monastery, the parish of Isleworth, and the chapelry of Hounslow. 1840. 8vo. **89 D**

AURICULAR CONFESSION.

Auricular confession and priestly absolution. Lord Ebury's Prayer-book amendment bill, with letters containing reasons and authorities in support of it. [By George Biller.] 1880. [Pamphlets, vol. 37.] **144 C**

AUSTIN, John.

An Analysis of Austin's Lectures on Jurisprudence. By Gordon Campbell. 1877. 12mo. **63 F**

Lectures on Jurisprudence with Notes and Fragments. Edited by Sarah Austin. 3 vols. 1861–63. 8vo. **63 F**

The same. 3rd ed. by R. Campbell. 2 vols. 1869. 8vo.
63 F

The Province of Jurisprudence determined. 1832. 8vo. **63 F**

The same. 2nd ed. by Sarah Austin. 1861. 8vo. **63 F**

AUSTRALASIA.

The Australasian Federal Directory of Commerce, Trades, and Professions. 1888–89. 8vo. **Hall**

The Australian Jurist. Edited by J. L. Purves and W. McKinley. vol. 1. Melbourne, 1871. 4to. **37 G**

The Centennial supplement to Sydney Morning Herald, with Reports of events in connection with celebration of centenary of Australian settlement. Sydney, 1888. 8vo. **84 D**

A Colonial Directory ; including Sydney, Melbourne, and New Zealand. 1862. 8vo. **195 D**

The laws of the Australasian Colonies as to the administration and distribution of the estate of deceased persons. By J. D. Wood. 1884. 8vo. **55 D**

A Vacation Tour at the Antipodes. By B. A. Heywood. 1863. 8vo. **84 B**

AUSTRALIA, SOUTH.

Acts and ordinances of South Australia, 1837 to 1888. 15 vols.
Adelaide, 1857–88. 4to. 35 A

South Australia, a sketch of its history and resources. By
J. F. Conigrave. 2nd ed. Adelaide, 1886. 8vo. 84 B

AUSTRALIA, WESTERN.

Acts of Council. 1871 to 1888. 4 vols. Perth, 1871–88.
4to. 35 F

Blue-book for the years 1887, 1888. Perth, 1888–89. folio.
35 F

Index to the ordinances. 1832 to 1862. Perth, 1862. 8vo.
35 F

Ordinances. 1858 to 1870. 3 vols. Perth, 1858–70. 8vo.
35 F

The statutes. 2 vols. Melbourne, 1883. 4to. 35 F.

Votes and proceedings of the legislative council during the
sessions 1873, 1874, 1875, 1887, and 1887-8. 3 vols. Perth,
1873–88. folio. 35 F

AUSTRIA.

General civil code for all the German hereditary provinces of
the Austrian monarchy. Translated by J. M. Chevalier De
Winiwarter. Vienna, 1866. 8vo. 55 C

A Handbook for travellers in Southern Germany. 3rd ed.
1843. 8vo. 84 A

AUTHORS.

Illustrations of the plan of a National Association for the
encouragement and protection of authors and men of talent.
By Wm. Jerdan. 1839. [Pamphlets, vol. 3.] 144 A

AUTOBIOGRAPHY.

Autobiography, a collection of the most instructive and
amusing lives ever published, written by the parties them-
selves. 20 vols. 1827. 12mo. 79 A

AUTOGRAPH LETTERS.

Catalogue of Autograph letters, historical and literary documents and engraved portraits; forming part of the collection of a member of the Incorporated Law Society. [John
Young.] 1862. 8vo. 80 I

AUTOGRAPH LETTERS—*continued*.

A Catalogue of Autograph letters &c. selected from the rare collection of H. B. Ray. 1857. 8vo. **80 I**

Catalogue of 5,000 choice autograph letters &c. collected by the late Dawson Turner. 1859. 8vo. **80 I**

Letters selected from the collection of autographs in the possession of William Tite, M.P. [Camden Society, vol. 87.] 1864. 8vo. **85 C**

AVEBURY, Wiltshire.

Abury, a temple of the British Druids, with some others described. By William Stukeley. 1740. folio. **95 G**

The old serpentine temple of the Druids at Avebury in North Wiltshire, a poem. Marlborough, 1795. 8vo. **93 F**

AVERAGE.

The law of marine insurance and Average. By Joseph Arnould. 6th ed. by David Maclachlan. 2 vols. 1887. 8vo. **10 D**

A Handbook of Average. By Manley Hopkins. 4th ed. 1884. 8vo. **9 A**

The law of General Average. By Richard Lowndes. 4th ed. 1888. 8vo. **10 B**

International general average. By David Murray. [1877.] [Pamphlets, vol. 30.] **144 B**

An Essay on Average. By Robert Stevens. 1816. 8vo. **160 C**

See also INSURANCE and SHIPPING. **10 D, 11 F**

AWARDS.

The law of Awards. By S. Kyd. 2nd ed. 1799. 8vo. **160 B**

See also ARBITRATION. **9 A**

AXHOLME, Isle of, Lincolnshire.

A Topographical account of the Isle of Axholme. By W. Peck. vol. 1. Doncaster, 1815. 4to. **90 H**

AYCKBOURN, Hubert.

Forms of practical proceedings in the high court of Chancery. 1854. 12mo. **161 B**

The same. New ed. 1866. 12mo. **161 B**

The same. New ed. 1873. 12mo. **52 B**

The jurisdiction and practice of the Supreme Court of Judicature and of the divisional courts. 1874. 8vo. **169 F**

AYCKBOURN, Hubert—*continued.*

The same. 2nd ed. 1876. 8vo.	**169 F**
The new Chancery practice. 3rd ed. 1849. 12mo.	**161 A**
The same. 4th ed. 1854. 12mo.	**161 A**
The same. 6th ed. 1858. 12mo.	**161 A**
. The same. 7th ed. 1861. 12mo.	**161 B**
The same. 8th ed. by J. N. Higgins. 1866. 12mo.	**161. B**
The same. 9th ed. 1870. 12mo.	**161 B**

The practice in the Chancery division of the high court of justice and on appeal therefrom. 10th ed. by B. F. Lock and C. A. Cook. 1880. 8vo.   **52 B**

AYERS, Edward Thomas.

. A Guide to the law and practice of Petty Sessions. 1884. 8vo.   **12 B**

AYLIFFE, Anne.

Trial of Anne Ayliffe for heresy. See N. T. Moile's State Trials, 1838, pp. 1–93.   **83 H**

AYLIFFE, John.

A New Pandect of Roman civil law. 1734. folio.   **48 I**

Parergon juris canonici Anglicani, or a commentary by way of supplement to the canons and constitutions of the Church of England. 1726. folio.   **77 H**

The same. 2nd ed. 1734. folio.   **77 H**

[AYLOFFE, Sir Joseph.]

Calendars of the ancient charters &c. and of the Welch and Scotish rolls now remaining in the Tower of London, with some account of the state of the public records from the Conquest to the present time. 1772. 4to.   **100 G**

The same. By Sir Joseph Ayloffe. 1774. 4to.   **100 G**

AYRAULT or ÆRODIUS, Pierre.

Petri Ærodii Quæsitoris Andegavi rerum ab omni antiquitate judicatarum Pandectæ. (De origine et auctoritate judiciorum.) Parisiis, 1589. folio.

The same. Another ed. His accessit liber singularis ejusdem auctoris, de patrio jure ad filium. Parisiis, 1615. folio.

AYRES, William Thomas.
A Comparative view of differences between English and Irish
statute and common law. 2 vols. Dublin, 1780. 8vo. **170 G**

AYRTON, Edward Nugent.
The transfer of land act and the declaration of title act. 1863.
12mo. **53 A**

AYRTON, Scrope.
The practice in the Court of bankruptcy relating to Bonds.
1840. 12mo. **160 G**

AYSCOUGH, Rev. Samuel.
A Catalogue of the manuscripts preserved in the British
Museum hitherto undescribed. 2 vols. 1782. 4to. **82 I**
General index to The Gentleman's Magazine, 1731–1786.
2 vols. 1789. 8vo. **128 G**

BABINGTON, Richard.
The law of Auctions. 1826. 8vo. **160 C**

BACK, George.
Narrative of an expedition in H.M.S. Terror, with a view to
geographical discovery on Arctic shores. 1838. 8vo. **84 D**

BACON, Francis, Viscount St. Albans.
Apophthegmes, new and old. 1625. Bound with Bacon's
Essaies. 1598. 12mo. **118 A**
An argument of Lord Bacon on the writ De rege inconsulto
in the case of the grant of the office of Supersedeas in the
Common Pleas, 13 James I. See Collectanea Juridica,
vol. 1, 1791, pp. 167–213. **144 G**
Cases of Treason. 1641. [Law Tracts and Arguments.] **144 F**
Character of Lord Bacon, his life and works. By Thomas
Martin. 1835. 8vo. **79 B**
The elements of the common lawes of England, branched into
a double tract, the one containing a collection of some
principall rules and maximes of the Common law, the other
the use of the Common law. 1635–36. 8vo. **49 C**

BACON, FRANCIS—*continued.*

Essaies, Religious meditations. Places of perswasion and disswasion seene and allowed. 1598. 12mo. **118 A**

The history of the reigne of Henry vii. 1629. 4to. **114 F**

Law Tracts. 2nd ed. 1741. 8vo. **144 F**

   1. A Proposition for compiling and amendment of our laws.
   2. An Offer of a digest of the laws.
   3. The Elements of the Common Laws of England ; containing a
      collection of some principal rules and maxims of the Common
      Law with their latitude and extent.
   4. The use of the Law for preservation of our persons, goods, and
      good names, according to the practice of the laws and customs of
      this Land.
   5. Cases of treason, felony, præmunire, prerogative of the King, of the
      office of a constable.
   6. Arguments in Law in certain great and difficult cases, viz. Of Im-
      peachment of Waste. Low's case of Tenures. Of Revocation of
      Uses. The Jurisdiction of the Marches.
   7. Ordinances in Chancery for the better and more regular adminis-
      tration of justice in the Chancery, to be daily observed, saving the
      prerogative of the court.
   8. Reading on the statute of Uses.

The life of Lord Bacon. By Rev. Joseph Sortain. [1851.]
8vo. **79 B**

The office of Constables. 1610. See G. Jacob's Complete
parish officer. 1754. 12mo. **173 B**

Of the advancement and proficience of learning, or the partitions of sciences. Interpreted by Gilbert Wats. Oxford,
1640. 4to. **78 G**

The works of Francis Bacon. New edition, by Basil Montagu.
16 vols. 1825–34. 8vo. **78 E**

BACON, JOHN.

Liber Regis vel Thesaurus rerum ecclesiasticarum ; with
proper directions and precedents relating to presentations,
institutions, &c. 1786. 4to. **100 G**

[BACON, MATTHEW.]

A New Abridgment of the Law. By a Gentleman of the
Middle Temple. 5 vols. 1736–56. folio. **156 D**

The same. By Matthew Bacon. 4th ed. 5 vols. 1778.
folio. **156 E**

The same. 7th ed. by Sir H, Gwillim and C. E. Dodd.
8 vols. 1832. 8vo. **14 A**

BACON, Nathaniel.
An Historical and political discourse of the laws and government of England. Collected from some manuscript notes of John Selden, by N. Bacon. 4th ed. 1739. folio.   **78 H**

BACON, Roger.
Fr. Rogeri Bacon opera quædam hactenus inedita. Edited by J. S. Brewer. 1859. 8vo.   **101 C**

BADEN-POWELL, Baden Henry.
A Manual of Jurisprudence for forest officers. Calcutta, 1882. 8vo.   **38 D**

BAGEHOT, Walter.
The history of the unreformed parliament and its lessons. An essay. [1860.] [Pamphlets, vol. 15.]   **144 B**
Lombard Street. A description of the money market. 8th ed. 1882. 8vo.   **78 D**
Parliamentary Reform. An essay. 1859. [Pamphlets, vol. 21.]   **144 B**

BAGLEY, William.
The new practice of the courts of law at Westminster with forms embodied in the text. 1840. 8vo.   **163 B**
The practice at the Chambers of the Judges of the courts of common law in civil actions. 1834. 12mo.   **169 E**

BAGSHAW, Samuel.
History, gazetteer, and directory of the county of Kent. 2 vols. Sheffield, 1847. 8vo.   **88 D**

BAHAMAS.
Laws of the Bahamas from 1869 to 1889. 6 vols. Nassau, 1869–89. 8vo.   **36 B**
The statute law of The Bahamas, comprising all acts of the general assembly of the Bahama Islands in force to 38 Vict. c. 36 inclusive. By Sir G. C. Anderson. 1877. 8vo.   **36 B**

BAIL.
The law of Bail in an action at common law. By Herman Schröder. 1824. 12mo.   **160 C**

BAIL—*continued*.
A Digest of the doctrine of Bail in civil and criminal cases. By Anthony Highmore. 1783. 8vo. **160 C**
A Treatise of Bail and Mainprize. See Sir Edward Coke's Three law tracts, 1764, pp. 279–303. **144 F**

BAIL COURT REPORTS.
Bail Court Reports 1846–1848. By T. W. Saunders and H. T. Cole. 2 vols. 1847–49. 8vo. **4 B**
Bail Court Cases 1852–1854. By J. J. Lowndes and P. B. Maxwell. vol. i., parts 1–5. 8vo. **5 C**

BAILEY, ALFRED.
The succession to the English Crown, a historical sketch. 1879. 8vo. **116 B**

[BAILEY, PETER.]
Sketches from St. George's Fields. By Giorgione di Castel Chiusa. [Peter Bailey.] 1820; and second series 1821. 2 vols. 1820–21. 12mo. **118 A**

BAILIFF.
A Treatise on the offices of Sheriff, Bailiff, &c. By George Atkinson. 6th ed. by A. E. Melsheimer. 1878. 12mo. **11 F**

BAILLIE, NEIL BENJAMIN EDMONSTONE.
The Moohummudan law of sale according to the Huneefeea code. Selected and translated from the original Arabic. 1850. 8vo. **38 B**

BAILLY, LAMBERT.
Coustumes du pais de Normandie, anciens ressors, et enclaves d'iceluy. Paris, 1586. 4to. **118 F**

BAILMENTS.
Commentaries on the law of Bailments. By Joseph Story. 8th ed., by E. H. Bennett. Boston, 1870. 8vo. **9 A**
Remarks upon the law of Bailment. By J. B. Wallace. 1840. [Law Tracts, vol. 7.] **144 E**
An Essay on the law of Bailments. By Sir William Jones. 4th ed. by W. Theobald. 1833. 8vo. **9 A**

BAILY, FRANCIS.
The doctrine of life-annuities and assurances analytically
   investigated and explained. 1810, 8vo.   160 B

BAINBRIDGE, WILLIAM.
The law of Mines and Minerals. 2nd ed. 1856. 8vo.   172 F
The same. 3rd ed. 1867. 8vo.   172 F
The same. 4th ed. by A. Brown. 1878. 8vo.   10 I

BAINES, EDWARD.
History, directory, and gazetteer of the county palatine of
   Lancaster. 2 vols. Liverpool, 1824–25. 8vo.   89 A
The history of the county palatine of Lancaster. 4 vols.
   1831–35. 4to.   89 G

BAINES, THOMAS.
Yorkshire past and present, including an account of the
   woollen trade of Yorkshire, by Edward Baines. 2 vols.
   [1871–77.] 4to.   95 G

BAKER, CHARLES CONYERS MASSY.
The laws relating to young children. 1885. 8vo,   10 C

BAKER, GEORGE.
The history and antiquities of the county of Northampton.
   2 vols. 1822–30. folio.   93 H

BAKER, SIR RICHARD.
A Chronicle of the Kings of England from the time of the
   Romans' government unto the death of King James.
   8th ed. 1684. folio.   114 G

BAKER, THOMAS.
The law of Highways in England and Wales, including
   bridges and locomotives. 1880. 8vo.   52 H
The laws relating to Burials, with notes, forms, and practical
   instructions. 2nd ed. 1859. 12mo.   161 A
The same. 4th ed. 1873. 12mo.   161 A
The same. 5th ed. 1882. 12mo.   9 B
The laws relating to Public Health. 1865. 12mo.   174 G

BAKER, THOMAS—*continued.*
The laws relating to Salmon Fisheries in Great Britain.
1866.   12mo.   168 E
The same.   2nd ed.   1868.   12mo.   168 E

BAKER, REV. THOMAS.
History of the college of St. John the Evangelist, Cambridge.
Edited by J. E. B. Mayor.   2 vols.   Cambridge, 1869.   8vo.
                                                                     86 D

BAKER, WILLIAM.
A Practical compendium of the office of Coroner.   1851.
12mo.   52 D

BALDWIN, ARCHBISHOP OF CANTERBURY.
The itinerary of archbishop Baldwin through Wales A.D.
MCLXXXVIII.   By Giraldus De Barri.   Translated into
English by Sir R. C. Hoare.   2 vols.   1806   4to.   94 D

BALDWIN, EDWARD THOMAS.
A concise treatise upon law of Bankruptcy.   1879.   12mo.   160 F
The same.   4th ed.   1884.   12mo.   64 A
The same.   5th ed.   1887.   12mo.   64 A

BALDWIN, SAMUEL.
A Survey of the British Customs.   1770.   4to.   157 B

BALE, JOHN, BISHOP OF OSSORY.
Kynge Johan, a play in two parts.   Edited by J. P. Collier.
[Camden Society, vol. 2.]   1838.   8vo.   85 A
Select works of John Bale, containing The Examinations of
Lord Cobham, William Thorpe, and Anne Askewe, and the
Image of both churches.   Edited by Rev. Henry Christmas.
Cambridge, 1849.   8vo.   77 E

BALL, JAMES.
The popular conveyancer, with concise precedents.   1877.   8vo.
                                                                    163 G

BALL, THOMAS and FRANCIS BEATTY.
Reports of cases in the high court of chancery in Ireland, 1807–
1814.   2 vols.   1821–24.   8vo.   15 C

BALL, William.

An Appendix to the abridgment of the statutes of Ireland, containing an abridgment of the several acts passed 1793–1797. 5 vols. Dublin, 1794–97. 4to.　　158 B

An Index to the acts passed in Ireland, 1799–1800. Dublin, 1804. folio.　　32 G

BALL, William Edmund.

Leading cases on the law of Torts. 1884. 8vo.　　11 H

Principles of Torts and Contracts, a short digest of the common law, chiefly founded upon the works of Addison. 1880. 8vo.　　64 F

BALLOT.

The Ballot act, 1872. By G. A. R. Fitzgerald. 2nd ed. 1876. 12mo.　　52 A

The Ballot act, 1872. By W. C. Glen. 1873. 12mo. 160 C

[BALLOW, Henry.]

A Treatise of Equity. 1737. folio.　　155 D

The same, with the addition of marginal references and notes by John Fonblanque. 2 vols. 1793–94. 8vo.　　155 B

The same. 5th ed. 2 vols. 1820. 8vo.　　155 B

BANBURY, Oxfordshire.

The history of Banbury, including copious historical and antiquarian notices of the neighbourhood. By Alfred Beesley. 1841. 8vo.　　92 E

BANBURY PEERAGE.

The law of adulterine bastardy, with a report of the Banbury case. By Sir N. H. Nicolas. 1836. 8vo.　　52 A

BANC, Court in.

Practice of Court in Banc. By P. E. Vizard. 1880. 8vo. 52 A

BANCROFT, Hubert Howe.

The Bancroft library as material for Pacific States history. [1883.] [Pamphlets, vol. 30.]　　144 B

A Brief account of the literary undertakings of Hubert Howe Bancroft. 1883. [Pamphlets, vol. 30.]　　144 B

BANDA AND KIRWEE BOOTY.

Banda and Kirwee Booty. 10 vols. 1865–66. folio. **145 E**

> 1 and 2. Return of Official Correspondence presented to Parliament, 1863, 1864 and 1865.
> 3. Correspondence furnished by Military Department of India Office.
> 4. Correspondence furnished by Political Department of India Office.
> 5. Despatches from the London Gazette. Diary of Lord Canning. Extracts from Returns relative to the Mutiny, Nos. 1, 3, 4, presented to Parliament.
> 6. Extracts from Returns, Nos. 6, 7, 8 ; and Correspondence relative to Lord Clyde's Memorandum, &c.
> 7. Order of Reference. Minutes of Proceedings. Pleadings. Proofs.
> 8. Proofs. Miscellaneous Documents.
> 9 and 10. Proceedings and Arguments, 1st to 26th day. Judgment of the Right Hon. Stephen Lushington, D.C.L.

The Duke's Wink, or prize-money defalcations. By Tom Brown Agonistes. [Rev. Alfred Kinloch.] Tunbridge Wells, 1884. [Pamphlets, vol. 39.] **144 C**

The Petition of Alfred Kinloch, of Tunbridge Wells, in the County of Kent, on behalf of himself, and all other the persons who are entitled to share in the Booty of Banda and Kirwee. With Appendix. 1882. 4to. **145 E**

Affidavit of Alfred Kinloch. 1882. 4to. **145 E**

Three pamphlets on the Banda and Kirwee Booty. By Alfred Kinloch. **145 E**

> 1. The case of the Banda and Kirwee Booty. 1864.
> 2. Military claims for Booty of War. Tunbridge Wells, 1875.
> 3. A Letter to the Lords Commissioners of Her Majesty's Treasury, by one present at the captures of Banda and Kirwee, on the Prize Claims of the late Sir G. C. Whitlock's force. 1874.

BANK NOTES.

See BANKING and BILLS OF EXCHANGE. **78 D & 9 I**

BANK OF ENGLAND.

The bank charter act in the crisis of 1847, with an examination of certain passages in Mr. Disraeli's Life of Lord George Bentinck, 1854. [Pamphlets, vol. 9, pt. 1.] **144 A**

History of the Bank of England, its times and traditions. By John Francis. 3rd ed. 2 vols. [1848.] 8vo. **91 C**

The names and descriptions of the proprietors of unclaimed dividends on Bank Stock and on the public funds transferable at the Bank of England. 1805. 8vo. **134 I**

The same. 1808. 8vo. **134 I**

The same. 1823. 8vo. **134 I**

The unclaimed dividend books of the Bank of England. n d. 8vo. **134 I**

BANK OF ENGLAND—*continued.*

Report from committee of secrecy on Bank of England charter, with minutes of evidence. 1832. folio. **153 A**

BANKING AND BANKERS.

The Banking Almanac, directory, year book and diary for 1880, 1882, 1886–1889. 6 vols. 1880–89. **146 B**

The practice of Banking. By John Hutchison. 3 vols. 1880–87. 8vo. **78 D**

A Treatise on Banking law. By J. D. Walker. 2nd ed. 1885. 8vo. **78 D**

Law relating to Bankers and banking companies. By James Grant. 4th ed. 1882. 8vo. **78 D**

The history, law, and practice of Banking. By C. M. Collins. 1881. 8vo. **78 D**

Bank note reform, with suggestions for a new banking act. By J. K. Greig. 1880. [Pamphlets, vol. 30.] **144 B**

A Law manual for Bankers. By W. B. Wedgwood and I. S. Homans. New York, 1867. 8vo. **59 G**

A Century of Banking in Dundee from 1764 to 1864. By C. W. Boase. 2nd ed. containing memoranda concerning Scotch and English banking during the period. Edinburgh, 1867. 8vo. **78 D**

Report from the secret committee on Joint Stock Banks, with minutes of evidence and appendix. 1836. folio. **153 A**

A Few words on joint-stock banking in London. 1836. [Pamphlets, vol. 5.] **144 A**

BANKRUPTCY ARRANGEMENTS AND COMPOSITIONS.

See ARRANGEMENTS WITH CREDITORS. **12 I**

BANKRUPTCY COSTS.

Costs in Bankruptcy of proceedings under town and country fiats. By Francis Gregg. 2nd ed. 1838. Bound with F. Gregg's Bankruptcy. 1838. 12mo. **160 E**

Costs in Bankruptcy. By Francis Gregg. 1826. [Jacob's Tracts, vol. 8.] **144 E**

See also COSTS. **9 F**

BANKRUPTCY LAW AND PRACTICE.

The law of Bankruptcy. By G. Y. Robson. 6th ed. 1887. 8vo. **12 I**

BANKRUPTCY LAW—*continued.*

Law and practice of Bankruptcy. By L. Y. Lee and H. Wace.
3rd ed. 1887. 8vo. **12 I**

Bankruptcy law and practice. By H. W. Hart. 3rd ed. 1887.
8vo. **12 I**

The Bankruptcy act 1883 with notes. By W. Hazlitt and R.
Ringwood. 2nd ed. by R. Ringwood. 1887. 12mo. **64 A**

The student's guide to Bankruptcy. By John Indermaur.
2nd ed. 1887. 12mo. . . . **64 A**

The student's Bankruptcy. By A. Gibson and A. Weldon.
1887. 8vo. · **64 A**

The law and practice in Bankruptcy. By R. V. Williams and
W. V. Williams. 4th ed. 1886. 8vo. **12 I**

The Bankruptcy act 1883 and rules 1886. By M. D.
Chalmers and E. Hough. 2nd ed. 1886. 8vo. **12 I**

The law and practice under the Bankruptcy act 1883. By
C. L. Samson. 1884. 8vo. **12 I**

The law and practice in Bankruptcy. By E. C. Willis. 1884.
8vo. **12 I**

The Student's guide to the law and practice under the Bankruptcy act 1883. By W. J. S. Scott. 1883. 12mo. **64 A**

The Student's guide to the law of Bankruptcy. By J. F.
Haynes. 1883. 8vo. **64 A**

Judgment in re Dolphy, delivered in the Spanish Town
bankruptcy court, by Mr. Justice Bruce, April 23, 1874.
[Pamphlets, vol. 30.] · **144 B**

The law and practice in Bankruptcy, relative to public and
private meetings, meetings for the audit, dividend, and
certificate. By F. Gregg. 1826. [Jacob's Tracts, vol. 8.]
144 E

The judgment of Court of Demerara in case of Odwin v.
Forbes on plea of the English certificate of Bankruptcy in
bar in a foreign jurisdiction to the suit of a foreign creditor
as confirmed in appeal. By J. Henry. 1823. 8vo. **55 D**

The Solicitor's guide and Tradesman's instructor concerning
Bankrupts. 6th ed. 1808. See S. Turner's Epitome of
practice. 1809. 8vo. **163 B**

The statutes at large concerning Bankrupts. 1765. 12mo.
160 F

The laws relating to Bankrupts brought home to the present
time. By Thomas Davies. 1744. folio. · **156 C**

See also ARCHBOLD, BRETT, BULLEY and BUND, CHRISTIAN,
COOKE, CULLEN, DEACON, DORIA and MACRAE, EDEN,

BANKRUPTCY LAW—*continued.*

GOODINGE, GREEN, GREGG, JOEL, KENDALL, MONTAGU,
MONTAGU and AYRTON, MOORE, RIBTON, ROCHE and
HAZLITT, SHELFORD, SMITH, J. W., STEWART, and WHIT-
MARSH. **160 D E F**

BANKRUPTCY LAW, DIGESTS OF.

Index to all the reported cases decided in the several courts
of Equity in England . . . relating to Bankruptcy from the
earliest period. See Chitty's Index, 4th ed., vol. 1, 1883,
pp. 199–1042, and vol. 8, 1889, pp. 8153–8187. **14 D**

A Digest of the reported decisions of the Court of Bankruptcy
from 1756 to the present time. See Fisher's Digest, vol. 1,
1884, pp. 657–1506. **14 E**

A Digested Index to the common law reports relating to
Conveyancing and Bankruptcy from 1558 to the present
time. By E. Chitty and F. Forster. 1841. 8vo. **14 F**

BANKRUPTCY PRACTICE OF COUNTY COURTS.

List of county courts, distinguishing such as have bankruptcy
jurisdiction, and shewing to which courts those not having
such jurisdiction are attached for bankruptcy purposes.
See C. L. Samson's Bankruptcy, 1884, pp. 370–386. **12 I**

See also COUNTY COURTS and BANKRUPTCY LAW. **12 H I**

BANKRUPTCY REFORM.

An Analysis of the bill now depending in Parliament for the
consolidation and amendment of the Bankrupt law. By R.
H. Eden. 1823. [Jacob's Tracts, vol. 1.] **144 E**

An 'article' for Lord Brougham's Bankruptcy digest, being
remarks upon a recent letter. By a Practical Man. 1849.
[Pamphlets, vol. 6.] **144 A**

Bankruptcy and credit trade. By Sir George Stephen. 1852.
[Pamphlets, vol. 8.] **144 A**

Bankruptcy and Insolvency. Practical observations. By
John Laidman. 1847. [Pamphlets, vol. 6.] **144 A**

Bankruptcy. An Inquiry into the principle upon which the
law should be based. By A. E. Penn and F. E. Lamb.
Privately printed. 1883. [Pamphlets, vol. 30.] **144 B**

Bankruptcy, its cause and remedy. Suggestions. By Louis
M. Bergtheil. 1879. [Pamphlets, vol. 30.] **144 B**

Bankruptcy law reform. By a Registrar of the Court of
Bankruptcy, London. 1859. [Pamphlets, vol. 10.] **144 A**

BANKRUPTCY REFORM—*continued.*

Bankruptcy law reform. [By Joseph Rayner.] [1860 or 1861.] [Pamphlets, vol. 13.] **144 A**

Bankruptcy legislation and defaulters in the legal profession. Prize essays. The prizes offered by Sir Henry Peek, Bart., M.P. 1879. 8vo. **78 B**

Bankruptcy reform in a series of letters to Sir Robert Peel. By Cecil Fane. 1838. [Law Tracts, vol. 6.] **144 E**

Bankruptcy reform in a series of letters to Wm. Hawes, Esq. By C. Fane. Letters i. ii. iii. iv. 1848. [Pamphlets, vol. 6.] **144 A**

Considerations on the origin, progress, and present state of the English bankrupt laws. 1818. 8vo. **160 F**

The Courts of Bankruptcy and Review. 1834. 8vo. **160 F**

A Few hints on consideration of system of Bankruptcy, as administered by the commissioners. 1831. [Jacob's Tracts, vol. 11.] **144 F**

First report from select committee of House of Lords appointed to inquire into Bankruptcy and Insolvency, with minutes of evidence. 1849, and Report of Commissioners appointed to inquire into fees, funds, and establishments of Court of Bankruptcy, with minutes of evidence. 1854. folio. **153 A**

Imprisonment for debt and bankruptcy with a suggestion. By a Barrister. 1869. [Pamphlets, vol. 30.] **144 B**

Inquiries respecting the courts of commissioners of Bankrupts, and Lord Chancellor's Court. By Basil Montagu. 1825. [Jacob's Tracts, vol. 4.] **144 E**

A Letter addressed to Viscount Melbourne by Cecil Fane relative to the jurisdiction of the Court of Bankruptcy, in cases of contempt. 1837. [Pamphlets, vol. 2.] **144 A**

A Letter to Lord Lyndhurst upon the bankrupt law consolidation act 1849, from A Barrister. 1849. [Pamphlets, vol. 6.] **144 A**

Letters on the Bankrupt laws to E. B. Sugden, Esq. Letters ii. and iii. By Basil Montagu. 1829. [Jacob's Tracts, vol. 8.] **144 E**

Letters to Sir Edward Sugden on the court of commissioners and court of review. By Basil Montagu. 1834. [Jacob's Tracts, vol. 11.] **144 F**

Observations on a bill before Parliament for the consolidation and amendment of the laws relating to Bankrupts. By J. S. M. Fonblanque. 1824. [Jacob's Tracts, vol. 4.] **144 E**

BANKRUPTCY REFORM—*continued.*

On what principle should a Bankrupt law be founded ?   1866.
[Pamphlets, vol. 30.]   144 B

Practical suggestions on the law of Bankruptcy.   By Edward
Lawrance.   1859.   [Pamphlets, vol. 10.]   144 A

Reform of the Bankrupt court.   By a Commissioner of Bankrupts.   1829.   8vo   160 F

Reform of the Bankrupt Court.   By C. S. Cullen.   2nd ed.
1830.   [Jacob's Tracts, vol. 8.]   144 E

Reform of the laws relating to bankruptcy and insolvency.
By B. H. Abrahall.   1861.   [Pamphlets, vol. 13.]   144 A

Remarks on the 514th section of the bankruptcy and insolvency
bill.   By William Ford.   1860.   [Pamphlets, vol. 13.]   144 A

A Review of 'the report from the select committee of the
House of Commons' on the Bankruptcy Act 1861.   By
John Laidman.   1867.   [Pamphlets, vol. 30.]   144 B

Some observations upon the bill for the improvement of the
Bankrupt laws.   By Basil Montagu.   1822.   [Jacob's
Tracts, vol. 4.]   144 E

The statutes relating to Bankrupts, and a letter to Sir
Samuel Romilly on the revision of the Bankrupt law, and
the ' Report of the select committee of the House of
Commons on the operation of the bankrupt laws.'   By W.
D. Evans.   1818.   8vo.   160 F

Suggestions for some alteration of the present state of the
Bankrupt law.   By Francis Gregg.   1831.   [Jacob's Tracts,
vol. 8.]   144 E

Thoughts upon the abolition of the punishment of death in
cases of bankruptcy.   By Basil Montagu.   1821.   144 F

BANKRUPTCY REPORTS.

Bankruptcy and Insolvency Reports.   1853–1854.   1 vol.
1855.   8vo.   8 B

BANKRUPTCY RULES.

Rules and orders in Bankruptcy.   1828–1880.   7 vols.   1845–80.
12mo.   53 F

BANKRUPTS.

An alphabetical list of applicants for the benefit of the Bankrupt act (passed August 19, 1841) within the southern
district of New York.   New York, 1843.   8vo.   59 A

BANKRUPTS—*continued.*

The Bankrupt Directory from December 1820 to April 1843.
By George Elwick. 1843. 8vo. **140 H**

. The Bankrupts' Register from Jan. 1, 1831, to Jan. 31, 1832,
Jan. 1, 1842, to Dec. 1848. 8 vols. 1831–48. 4to. **140 H**

Dictionnaire des Faillites prononcées par les tribunaux de
Paris. 1848–1863. Paris, 1863. 4to. **140 H**

The Gazette of Bankruptcy, from October 19, 1861, to July
29, 1863. 3 vols. folio. **140 H**

List of Bankrupts, dividends and certificates, 1771–1799.
By Wm. Bailey. 2nd ed. 1799. 8vo. **140 G**

A List of Bankrupts, with their dividends, certificates &c.
from Jan. 1, 1786, to June 24, 1806. By Wm. Smith. 1806.
8vo. **140 H**

List of Bankrupts, with their. dividends, certificates &c. from
July 1, 1817, to July 1, 1819. 1819. 8vo. **140 H**

Perry's Bankrupt and Insolvent gazette. 1826–1889. 64 vols.
1826–89. 12mo. and 8vo. **75 A–E**

The Weekly Bankrupt List, from February 11, 1811, to
December 28, 1812. folio. **140 H**

BANKS, SIR JACOB.

A Letter from Sir J. B[an]ks to W. B[enso]n, Esq. S.O., concerning a late contract, that was endeavour'd to be establish'd
by a certain bold officer in Sweden, to the utter undoing of
the board of works in that kingdom. 1719. [Grimaldi's
Tracts, vol. 2.] **118 B**

BANKS, THOMAS CHRISTOPHER.

The dormant and extinct Baronage of England, or an historical and genealogical account of the lives of the English
nobility from the Norman conquest. 4 vols. 1807–37.
4to. **127 J**

Ecce Homo. The mysterious heir, or Who is Mr. Walter
Howard? an interesting question addressed to the Duke
of Norfolk. [By T. C. Banks.] 1815. Bound with C.
Howard's Historical anecdotes. 1769. 8vo. **80 B**

History of the ancient noble family of Marmyun, their singular
office of King's Champion by the tenure of the baronial
manor of Scrivelsby, also other dignitorial tenures. 1817.
4to. **79 H**

A History of dormant and extinct peerage of England from

BANKS, Thomas Christopher—*continued.*

Norman Conquest, including the regal families anterior to the House of Brunswick. vol. I. 1812. 8vo.   **124 G**

Honores Anglicani, or titles of honour of the English nobility. 1812. folio.   **125 H**

The Stirling Peerage, comprising an account of the resumption of the titles by the present Earl of Stirling, to which is prefixed an epitome of the genealogy of the noble family of Alexander. 1826. 8vo.   **127 J**

BANNING, Henry Thomas.

The law of Marriage Settlements. 1884. 8vo.   **13 H**

A Concise treatise on the statute law of the Limitation of Actions, with references to English and American cases and to the French Code. 1877. 8vo.   **10 G**

BANNISTER, Saxe.

Statements and documents relating to proceedings in New South Wales in 1824, 1825, and 1826, intended to support an appeal to the King by the attorney general of the colony. Cape Town, 1827. 8vo.   **78 B**

See also Aborigines.

BANNS OF MATRIMONY.

The proper time for publication of Banns of Matrimony in the morning service. By C. S. Greaves. 1867. 8vo.   **172 D**

BARBA, Alvarez Alonzo.

The Art of Metals. Translated by the Earl of Sandwich. 1669. See Treatises upon metals. 1738. 12mo.   **118 A**

BARBADOS.

Laws of Barbados, 1666–1863. 2 vols. 1855–64. 8vo.   **36 D**

The same. New ed. 1666–1874. 2 vols. 1875. 8vo.   **36 D**

Laws of Barbados. 1874–1889. 11 vols. 1875-88. 8vo.   **36 D**

BARBARIANS, Laws of the.

A Succinct account of the civil regulations comprised in the laws of the Barbarians. See B. Barrett's The Code Napoléon, vol. 1, 1811, pp. cxlvii–cccix.   **55 C**

See also Lindenbruck.

BARBER, WILLIAM HENRY.

The case of Mr. W. H. Barber, convicted in 1844 of a supposed guilty knowledge of certain will forgeries. By Archibald Michie. Sydney, 1847. 8vo. [Pamphlets, vol. 17.] **144 B**

The royal pardon vindicated, in a review of the case between Mr. W. H. Barber and the Incorporated Law Society. By Sir G. Stephen. 2nd ed, 1851. [Pamphlets, vol. 30.] **114 B**

BARBEYRAC, JEAN.

Les devoirs de l'homme et du citoien tels qu'ils lui sont prescrits par la loi naturelle, traduits du Latin du Baron de Pufendorf. Cinquième éd. 2 vols. in 1. Amsterdam, 1735. 12mo. **48 F**

Histoire des anciens traitez, ou recueil des traitez répandus dans les auteurs Grecs et Latins depuis les tems les plus reculez jusques à l'Empereur Charlemagne. 2 parts in 1 vol. Amsterdam, 1739. folio. **116 I**

BARETTI, GIUSEPPE.

A Dictionary, Spanish and English, and English and Spanish. 2nd ed. 1778. folio. **123 H**

The same. Another ed. 1807. 8vo. **123 B**

A New Dictionary of the Italian and English languages, based upon that of Baretti. Compiled by John Davenport and Guglielmo Comelati. 2 vols. 1860. 8vo. **123 B**

BARGAIN AND SALE.

Dissertation on and precedents of Bargain and Sale. See Bythewood and Jarman's Conveyancing, 3rd ed., vol. 3, 1842, pp. 216–267. **53 D**

See also C. Fearne's Works, 1797, pp. 1–34. **175 C**

BARGRAVE, JOHN, D.D.

Pope Alexander VII. and the College of Cardinals. With a catalogue of Dr. Bargrave's museum. Edited by J. C. Robertson. [Camden Society, vol. 92.] 1867. 8vo. **85 C**

BARKER, HENRY.

A Manual on the registration of deeds and other assurances in Yorkshire. 1885. 8vo. **13 B**

BARLOW, Rev. Frederic.
The complete English peerage. 2 vols. 1772–73. 8vo. **126 C**
The same. 2nd ed. 2 vols. 1775. 8vo. , **126 C**

BARNABEE'S JOURNAL.
Barnabæ Itinerarium, or Barnabee's Journal. 7th ed., to which are prefixed an account of the author [Richard Brathwait], a bibliographical history of the former editions of the work and illustrative notes. [By Joseph Haslewood.] 1818. 12mo. **118 A**

BARNARDISTON, Thomas.
Reports of cases determined in the Court of Chancery, April 25, 1740, to May 9, 1741. 1742. folio. **74 B**
Reports of cases determined in the Court of King's Bench, 1726–1734. 2 vols. 1744. folio. **74 B**

BARNES, Henry.
Notes of Cases in points of practice taken in the Court of Common Pleas at Westminster from 1732 to 1756 inclusive. 2 vols. 1754–56. 8vo.
The same. 2nd ed., to which is added a continuation of cases to the end of the reign of George the Second. 1772. 4to.
The same. 3rd ed. 1790. 8vo. **6 A**

BARNES, Rev. Joshua.
The history of that most victorious monarch, Edward III., with the life and death of his son Edward, sirnamed the Black Prince. Cambridge, 1688. folio. , **114 H**

BARNES, Ralph.
An Inquiry into equity practice and the law of real property, with a view to legislative revision. 1827. [Jacob's Tracts, vol. 6.] **144 E**
Report of the case of The Queen v. The president and chapter of the cathedral church of St. Peter in Exeter, regarding the deanery of Exeter, in the Queen's Bench. 1841. [Pamphlets, vol. 2.] **144 A**

BARNEWALL, Richard Vaughan and J. L. Adolphus.
Reports of cases in the Court of King's Bench, 1830–1834. 5 vols. 1831–35. 8vo. . . **4 B**

BARNEWALL, R. V. and E. H. ALDERSON.
Reports of cases in the Court of King's Bench, 1817–1822.
5 vols. 1818–22. 8vo. **4 B C**

BARNEWALL, R. V. and C. CRESSWELL.
Reports of cases in the Court of King's Bench,. 1822–1830.
10 vols. 1823–32. 8vo. **4 C D**

BARONETAGES.
The Baronetage of England. 1806. 12mo. **125 A**
The Baronettage of England. By Arthur Collins. 2 vols.
1720. 12mo. **125 B**
The Baronetage of England. By John Debrett. editions 1,
3, 4, 5, 6, 6 rewritten and 7. 13 vols. 1808–35. 12mo. **125 B**
Debrett's Illustrated baronetage and knightage for 1866, 1868,
and 1884–1889. 8 vols. 1866–89. 8vo. **125 B C**
The same, for the year 1879. 1879. 8vo. **124 E**
The Baronetage of England, or history of English baronets
and such baronets of Scotland as are of English families.
By Rev. Wm. Betham. 4 vols. 1801–1804. 4to. **127 I**
Baronetage of the British empire. By R. Broun. 1841.
12mo. **125 A**
The English baronets. By Thomas Wotton. 3 vols. 1727.
12mo. **124 B**
The same. Another ed. 4 vols in 5. 1741. 8vo. **125 C**
The same. Edited by E. Kimber and R. Johnson. 3 vols.
1771. 8vo. **125 C**
A Genealogical and heraldic history of the extinct and dor-
mant Baronetcies of England. By John Burke and J. B.
Burke. 1838. 8vo. **125 E**
The New baronetage of England. 2 vols. 1804. 12mo. **125 B**
A New baronetage of England. By John Almon. 3 vols.
1769. 12mo. **124 B**
The present baronetage of the United Kingdom for the years
1818–1821, 1831, 1832, 1834, 1835, 1837–1841, 1843 and
1844. 15 vols. 1818–44. 12mo. **218 B–D**
See also PEERAGES.

BARONIES.
Baronia Anglica, an history of. land-honors and baronies, and
of tenure in capite. By T. Madox. 1736. folio. **126 I**
Proceedings, precedents, and arguments on claims and con-
troversies concerning baronies by writ and other honours.
By Arthur Collins. 1734. folio. **125 H**

BARRETT, BRYANT.
The Code Napoléon, verbally translated from the French.
2 vols. 1811. 8vo. **55 C**

[BARRETT, EATON STANNARD.]
All the Talents, a satirical poem, in three dialogues. By
Polypus. [E. S. Barrett.] 6th ed. 1807. 8vo. **118 B**

BARRETT-LENNARD, THOMAS.
The position in law of Women. 1883. 8vo. **172 D**

BARRINGTON, DAINES.
Observations on the more ancient statutes, with a proposal for
new modelling the statutes. 3rd ed. 1769. 4to. **158 A**

BARRINGTON, SIR JONAH.
Historic memoirs of Ireland, comprising secret records of the
national convention, the rebellion, and the Union. 2nd ed.
2 vols. 1833. 4to. **114 G**

BARRISTERS.
The Inns of Court calendar, a record of the members of the
English bar. By Charles Shaw. 1877. 8vo. **80 F**
The same. 2nd ed. 1878. 8vo. **80 F**
Men at the bar, a biographical hand-list of members of Inns of
Court. By Joseph Foster. 2nd ed. 1885. 4to. **80 F**
Observations on the Chancery Bar. 1816. [Jacob's Tracts,
vol. 5.] **144 E**
A Synopsis of the members of the English bar. By James
Whishaw. 1835. 8vo. **80 F**
Thoughts of a junior on his position and his prospects, with a
few hints to reformers. 1852. [Pamphlets, vol. 17.] **144 B**
The truth about the bar and about the solicitors, being an
appeal from the factious in both professions to the discreet
in each and to all serious men. By Innes Lincoln, Esq.
[Louis De Souza.] 1882. [Pamphlets, vol. 30.] **144 B**

BARRON, ARTHUR and T. J. ARNOLD.
Reports of cases of controverted elections before committees
of the House of Commons, and of cases upon appeal from
the decisions of revising barristers in the Court of Common
Pleas, 1843–1846. 1846. 8vo. **66 A**

BARRON, ARTHUR and ALFRED AUSTIN.
Reports of cases of controverted elections in the fourteenth
Parliament of the United Kingdom. 1844. 8vo.   **66 A**

[BARROW, GEORGE.]
Loyalty and freedom, or the constitution and laws the rights
of Britons. Preston, n.d. 4to.   **78 G**

BARROW, JOHN HENRY.
The Mirror of Parliament, January 29, 1828, to July 1837.
38 vols. 1828–37. folio.
Second Series, November 15, 1837, to October 7, 1841.
24 vols. 1838–41. 8vo.   **256 E F**

BARRY, WILLIAM WHITTAKER.
Forms and precedents in Conveyancing, with introduction and
practical notes. 1872. 8vo.   **163 G**
The law and practice of benefit building, and freehold land
societies. 1866. 12mo.   **161 A**
The statutory jurisdiction of the Court of Chancery. 1861.
8vo.   **161 B**
Treatise on the practice of Conveyancing. 1865. 8vo. **163 G**

BARTER, WILLIAM GEORGE THOMAS.
Homer and English Metre.   An essay on translating the Iliad
and Odyssey, with a literal rendering of first book of the
Odyssey, and specimens of the Iliad. 1862. 8vo.   **83 C**
Life, Law and Literature ; essays. 1863. 8vo.   **83 C**

BARTLETT, WILLIAM and HENRY CHAPMAN.
A Handy-book for Investors, comprising a sketch of the rise,
progress, and present character of every species of investment. 1869. 12mo.   **169 D**

BARTOLUS DE SAXO FERRATO.
Lectura in Infortiatum.   Venetiis, 1471.   folio.   **118 H**

BARTON, CHARLES.
Elements of Conveyancing, to which are prefixed an essay
on that science and cursory remarks on its study and
practice. 6 vols. 1802–1805. 8vo.   **164 B**

BARTON, CHARLES—*continued*.

An Historical treatise of a suit in equity. 1796. 12mo. **167 B**

A Supplement to Mr. Barton's Precedents in Conveyancing. By S. F. T. Wilde. 3rd ed. 3 vols. 1826. 8vo. **13 G**

See also POWELL, J. J.

BASALTES.

The natural history of the Basaltes in northern counties of Ireland. By Rev. Wm. Hamilton. Dublin, 1790. 8vo. **95 E**

BASINGSTOKE, HAMPSHIRE.

History of Basingstoke. See B. B. Woodward's History of Hampshire, vol. 3, 1869, pp. 208–238. **88 G**

A Sketch of the history of Holy Ghost chapel at Basingstoke, to which is added The Ruins of a Temple, a poem. By J. J. 2nd ed. Basingstoke, 1808. 12mo. **88 A**

BASLE, COUNCIL OF.

Decreta concilii Basiliensis. [Basileæ, 1499.] 8vo. **118 A**

BASTARDY.

The law and practice of orders of affiliation and proceedings in bastardy. By T. W. Saunders. 9th ed. by T. W. Saunders and W. E. Saunders. 1888. 12mo. **9 A**

BASUTOLAND.

British Basutoland proclamations and the more important of the notices. 1888. 12mo. **37 B**

BATEMAN, JOHN.

The great landowners of Great Britain and Ireland. 4th ed. 1883. 8vo. **134 I**

BATEMAN, JOSEPH.

The general Highway Acts. 2nd ed. by W. N. Welsby. 1863. 12mo. **168 F**

The general Turnpike road act 3 Geo. IV. cap. 126. 2nd ed. and Supplement. 2 vols. 1823. 12mo. **176 G**

The same. 3rd ed. 1836. 12mo. **176 G**

The laws of the Excise. 1843. 8vo. **168 B**

A Practical treatise on the law of Auctions. 4th ed. by Rolla Rouse. 1863. 12mo. **160 C**

BATEMAN, Joseph—*continued.*
The same. 5th ed. by Rolla Rouse. 1874. 12mo. **160 C**
The same. 6th ed. by O. Smith and P. F. Evans. 1882.
12mo. **9 A**

BATEMAN, Rev. Thomas. See Agistment.

BATH, Order of the.
Observations introductory to an essay upon the Knighthood
of the Bath. By John Anstis. 1725. 8vo. **125 E**
Statutes of the most honourable order of the Bath 1784.
Bound with the preceding. 1725. 8vo. **125 E**

BATH, Somerset.
A Discourse of Bathe and the hot waters there, to which is
added, A century of observations fully declaring the nature
of the baths, with an account of the lives and character
of the physicians of Bath. By Thomas Guidott. 1676.
12mo. **118 A**
An Essay towards a description of Bath. By John Wood.
2nd ed. 2 vols. 1749. 8vo. **93 A**
Illustrated plan of the city of Bath, drawn and engraved by
J. Hollway. 1848. 12mo. **93 A**

BATTELY, Ven. John.
Antiquitates Rutupinæ, opus posthumum. [Edited by
T. Terry.] Oxoniæ, 1711. 8vo. **88 C**
The same. 2nd ed. Oxoniæ, 1745. 8vo. **88 C**
Antiquitates S. Edmundi Burgi ad annum MCCLXXII perductæ.
Oxoniæ, 1745. 8vo. **93 C**

BATTEN, Edmund.
A Practical treatise on the law relating to the specific performance of contracts. 1849. 8vo. **163 D**

BATTEN, Edmund Chisholm and Henry LUDLOW.
The jurisdiction, pleadings, and practice of the county courts
in equity, with a supplement including the law and practice
of partition. 1872. 8vo. **165 B**

BATTEN, John.
The Stannaries Act 1869, with notes. 1873. 12mo. **12 A**

BATTISTA, Giovan.
Il Consolato del Mare.   Venetia, 1612.   8vo.   118 E

BATTLE ABBEY, Sussex.
Custumals of Battle Abbey in the reigns of Edward I. and
Edward II. (1283–1312).   Edited by S. R. Scargill-Bird.
[Camden Society, n.s. vol. 41.]   1887.   8vo.   85 D

BATTLE OF THE BLOCKS.
The Battle of the Blocks, an heroic poem in three cantos.
By the author of The Fantoccini. [describes the duel fought
between George Canning and Lord Castlereagh on Putney
Heath, 21 Sep., 1809.]   1809.   8vo.   118 B

BATTLE, Trial by.
An Argument for construing largely the right of an appellee
of murder to insist on Trial by Battle, and also for abolishing
appeals.   By E. A. Kendall.   2nd ed.   1818.   8vo.   118 B
A Report of the proceedings against Abraham Thornton at
Warwick summer assizes 1817 for murder of Mary Ashford,
and subsequently in Court of King's Bench in an appeal of
said murder.   By J. Cooper.   Warwick, 1818.   8vo.   118 B

BAUGH, Robert.
A Map of the county of Shropshire.   1808.   folio.   19 D

BAWDWEN, Rev. William.
Dom. Boc. A translation of the record called Domesday so
far as relates to the counties of Middlesex, Hertford,
Buckingham, Oxford and Gloucester.   Doncaster, 1812.
4to.   89 F
Dom. Boc. A translation of the record called Domesday so
far as relates to the county of York, parts of Lancashire,
Westmoreland, and Cumberland, also the counties of
Derby, Nottingham, Rutland and Lincoln.   Doncaster,
1809.   4to.   94 C
Domesday book for the county of Dorset, with a translation.
1815.   folio.   87 H

BAWTRY AND THORNE, Yorkshire.
A Topographical history and description of Bawtry and
Thorne. By W. Peck. Doncaster, 1813. 4to.   ·94 C

BAXTER, WYNNE EDWIN.

The law and practice of the Supreme Court of Judicature.
1874. 12mo. . **169 F**

The same. 4th ed. 1880. 12mo. **169 F**

The same. 5th ed. 1883, and Supplement 1884. 2 vols.
1883–84. 12mo. **12 G**

BAY ISLANDS.

Laws of the Bay Islands 1852 to 1859. 1852–59. 4to. **36 B**

BAYLDON, J. S.

The art of valuing Rents and Tillages. 2nd ed. 1824.
8vo. **175 C**

The same. 9th ed. by J. C. Morton. 1876. 8vo. **11 E**

BAYLE, PIERRE.

A General dictionary historical and critical, in which a new
and accurate translation of that of Mr. Bayle is included
and interspersed with several thousand lives never before
published. By Rev. J. P. Bernard, Rev. T. Birch, and
other hands. 10 vols. 1734–41. folio. **122 H**

BAYLEY, JOHN.

Calendars of the proceedings in Chancery in the reign of
Queen Elizabeth, and examples of earlier proceedings in
that court, namely from the reign of Richard the Second to
that of Queen Elizabeth inclusive, from the originals in the
Tower. 3 vols. 1827–32. folio. **98 C**

The history and antiquities of the Tower of London, with
memoirs of royal and distinguished persons. 2nd ed.
1830. 8vo. **91 E**

BAYLEY, SIR JOHN.

The book of Common Prayer and administration of the Sacraments and other rites of the Church. 1816. 8vo. **77 E**

A Summary of law of bills of exchange, cash bills and promissory notes. 3rd ed. by W. E. Barnes. 1813. 8vo. **160 F**

The same. 5th ed. by Francis Bayley. 1830. 8vo. **160 F**

BAYLIS, THOMAS HENRY.

The rights, duties and relations of domestic servants and their
masters and mistresses. 3rd ed. 1860. 12mo. **172 D**

The same. 4th ed. 1873. 12mo. **53 A**

BAYLY, John Bethune.
Commentaries on laws of England in the order and compiled from the text of Blackstone. 1840. 8vo. **167 B**

BAZALGETTE, Charles N. and G. HUMPHREYS.
The law relating to County Councils. 3rd ed. by G. Humphreys. 1889. 8vo. **10 G**
The law relating to Local and Municipal government. Bound in 2 vols. 1885. 8vo. **10 G**

BEAL, Edward William.
The practice of court of general assessment sessions under Valuation Metropolis act, 1869, with forms. 1883. 8vo. **11 E**

BEAMES, John.
A Brief view of the writ of Ne Exeat Regno as an equitable process. 2nd ed. 1824. Bound with J. Beames's Equity Costs. 1840. 8vo. **52 D**
The elements of Pleas in Equity, with precedents of such pleas. 1818. 8vo. **167 B**
The general orders of the high court of Chancery from 1600 to the present period. 1815. 8vo. **161 B**
A Summary of doctrine of Courts of Equity with respect to Costs deduced from the leading cases. 1822. 8vo. **165 A**
The same. 2nd ed. 1840. 8vo. **52 D**
A Translation of Glanville, with notes. 1812. 8vo. **167 A**

BEARBLOCK, Rev. James.
A Treatise upon Tithes containing an estimate of every titheable article in common cultivation. 4th ed. ; with Observations on a pamphlet written by Rich. Flower recommending the abolition of tithes. 1813. 8vo. **176 E**
The same. 5th ed. 1818. 8vo. **176 E**

BEARCROFT, Rev. Philip.
An Historical account of Thomas Sutton and of his foundation in Charter-House. 1737. 8vo. **91 C**

BEASLEY, Thomas John.
Lectures relative to the profession of Attorney and Solicitor. Dublin, 1841. [Pamphlets, vol. 16.] **144 B**

BEASLEY, THOMAS JOHN—*continued.*
A Synopsis of proceedings in the Master's Office, under the
new rules. Dublin, 1837. 8vo.
The same. 3rd ed. 1843. 8vo.

BEATSON, ROBERT.
A Chronological register of both houses of the British Parliament from 1708 to 1807. 3 vols. 1807. 8vo. **134 B**
A Political index to histories of Great Britain and Ireland,
or a complete register of the hereditary honours, public offices,
and persons in office. 3rd ed. 3 vols. 1806. 8vo. **124 G**
The same. Modernised by Joseph Haydn. 1851. 8vo. **124 G**

BEATTIE, JAMES.
The Minstrel, or the progress of genius, with some other poems.
Edinburgh, 1807. 12mo. **83 A**
The Minstrel, with some other poems by J. Beattie, and Mis-
cellanies by James Hay Beattie, with an account of his life
and character by J. Beattie. 2 vols. 1799. 12mo. **83 A**

BEATTY, FRANCIS.
Reports of cases in the high court of chancery in Ireland.
1813–1830. Dublin, 1847. 8vo. **15 C**

BEAUFORT, REV. DANIEL AUGUSTUS.
Memoir of a map of Ireland, illustrating the topography of
that kingdom. 1792. 4to. **95 F**

BEAUFOY, MARK.
Nautical and hydraulic experiments, with numerous scientific
miscellanies. vol. 1. 1834. 4to. **78 H**

BEAUMONT, GEORGE DUCKETT BARBER.
The law of Fire and Life Insurance. 1833. 8vo. **169 A**
Observations on the code for real property, proposed by James
Humphreys, Esq. 1827. [Jacob's Tracts, vol. 5.] **144 E**

BEAUMONT, JOSEPH, BARRISTER.
The law and practice of Bills of Sale. 1855. 12mo. **160 G**

7

BEAUMONT, JOSEPH, SOLICITOR.
Agricultural holdings and law of distress. 1883. 8vo.   **160 B**

BEAVAN, CHARLES.
Ordines Cancellariæ, being a selection of general orders of
Court of Chancery from 1814 to 1852. 1853. 12mo.   **161 E**
Reports of cases in the Rolls Court from Michaelmas 1838 to
June 1866, with a general index by C. W. Chute.   36 vols.
1840–69. 8vo.   **2 A–C**

BEAWES, WYNDHAM.
Lex mercatoria rediviva, or a complete code of commercial
law, being a general guide to all men of business. 5th ed.
by Thomas Mortimer. 1792. folio.   **78 H**

BEC, ABBEY OF.
The history of the royal abbey of Bec, near Rouen in Nor-
mandy. By Dom. John Bourget. Translated from the
French. 1779. 12mo.   **84 A**

BECCARIA, CÆSARE BONESANA, MARQUIS OF.
Βεκκαριου περι αδικηματων και ποινων παρα Χαριλαου Π.
Σοφιανοπωλου. Beccaria on Crimes and punishments.
Translated into modern Greek by Charilaus P. Sophiano-
polos. 2nd ed. Athens, 1842. 8vo.   **56 C**
Dei delitti e delle pene. Nuova edizione. 1801. 12mo. **56 C**
The same. Another ed. Livorno, 1828. 8vo.   **56 C**

BECCARIA, GIOVANNI BATTISTA.
A Treatise upon artificial Electricity. Translated from the
original Italian. 1776. 4to.   **78 G**

BECHUANALAND.
British Bechuanaland proclamations and the more important
of the notices. 1885–1888. Cape Town, 1887–89. 8vo. **37 B**

BECKET, THOMAS À.
Materials for the history of Thomas Becket. Edited by
J. C. Robertson. 7 vols. 1875–85. 8vo.   **102 F**
Thomas Saga Erkibyskups. A life of archbishop Thomas
Becket in Icelandic. Edited by E. Magnusson. 2 vols.
1875–83. 8vo   **102 F**

BECKINGTON, Thomas.
Letters of Bishop Beckington and others written in the reigns
: of Henry. V. and Henry VI. Edited by Cecil Monro.
[Camden Society, vol. 86.] 1863. 8vo. 85 C
Memorials of the reign of King Henry VI.; official corre-
spondence of Thomas Bekynton. Edited by George
.Williams. 2 vols. 1872. 8vo. 102 D

BECKWITH, William.
Letter to Sir Samuel Romilly on the necessity of an enquiry into
causes of delay in chancery proceedings, and of arrears
of appeals in the House of Lords. 1810. 8vo. 83 H

BECON, Thomas.
The early works of Thomas Becon, being the Treatises published by him in the reign of Henry VIII. Catechism with
other pieces written by him in the reign of Edward VI.
Prayers and other pieces. Edited by Rev. John Ayre.
3 vols. Cambridge, 1843–44. 8vo. 77 E

BÉDARRIDE, Jassuda.
Droit Commercial, Commentaire du code de commerce. Livre
I. Titres 1, 2. Des Commerçants, et Des livres de com-
merce. 1 vol. Titres 3, 4. Des Sociétés. 2 vols. Titre 5.
Des bourses de commerce, agents de change et courtiers. 1
vol. Titre 6. Des Commissionnaires. 1 vol. Titre 7. Des
Achats et Ventes. 1 vol. Titre 8. De la lettre de change,
des billets à ordre et de la prescription. 2 vols. Livre II.
Du Commerce Maritime. 5 vols. Livre III. Traité des
faillites et banqueroutes ou commentaire de la loi du 28
Mai, 1838. 4me éd. 3 vols. Livre IV. De la juridiction
commerciale. 1 vol. 17 vols. Paris, 1854–64. 8vo. 58 B

BEDE, The Venerable.
Chronicon sive de sex hujus sæculi ætatibus ; Historia ecclesiastica gentis Anglorum. See Monumenta Historica Britannica. 1848. folio. 99 B

BEDELL, Right Rev. William.
A True relation of the life and death of Wm. Bedell, lord
bishop of Kilmore. Edited by T. W. Jones. [Camden
Society, n.s. vol. 4.] 1872. 8vo. 85 C

7—2

BEDFORD, Edward Henslowe.

Digest of preliminary examination questions in Latin grammar, arithmetic, &c. with answers. 2nd ed. 1882. 8vo. **168 A**

Final examination guide to the law of Probate and Divorce. 2nd ed. 1882. 12mo. **64 E**

Intermediate examination guide. 2 vols. 1872–74. 8vo. **168 A**

Intermediate examination guide to Book-keeping. 2nd ed. 1875. 12mo. **160 G**

BEDFORD, House of.

An Account of Woburn with memoirs of the late Francis, Duke of Bedford. [By J. D. Parry.] Woburn, 1818. 8vo. **86 B**

Anecdotes of the house of Bedford from the Norman conquest to the present period. [1796.] 8vo. **80 B**

BEDFORD LEVEL.

Bedford Level acts. 5 vols. 1663–1818. folio. **19 D**

A Collection of laws which form the constitution of the Bedford Level corporation, with an introductory history thereof. By C. N. Cole. 2nd ed. 1803. 8vo. **86 B**

The history of the drainage of the Bedford Level. By S. Wells. 2 vols. 1820–28. 8vo. **86 B**

Regulations of the Governor, bailiffs and conservators of Bedford Level Corporation. By R. Bevill. 1821. 8vo. **86 B**

BEDFORDSHIRE.

Bedford and its neighbourhood. By D. G. C. Elwes. Bedford, 1881. 12mo. **86 B**

A Concise topographical account of the county of Bedfordshire. By Rev. D. Lysons and S. Lysons. 1813. 4to. **86 G**

Delineations of Bedfordshire. By E. W. Brayley and J. Britton. 1801. 8vo. **86 B**

Regimental records of the Bedfordshire militia. 1759 to 1884. By Sir J. M. Burgoyne. 1884. 12mo. **86 B**

See also Bray, W. and Willis, B.

BEESLEY, Alfred.

The history of Banbury, including historical and antiquarian notices of the neighbourhood. 1841. 8vo. **92 E**

BELFAST, Antrim.

Historical collections relative to Belfast from earliest period to the union with Great Britain. Belfast, 1817. 8vo. **95 E**

BELGIUM.

The Belgian traveller, or a complete guide through the United Netherlands. By E. Boyce. 4th ed. 1819. 12mo. **84 A**

The land system of Belgium. By E. de Laveleye. See Land tenure in various countries, 1881, pp. 443–495. **78 B**

See also CODES.

BELL, SIR CHARLES.

The Hand, its mechanism and vital endowments as evincing design. 1833. 8vo. **77 B**

BELL, EVANS.

The Mysore reversion 'an exceptional case.' 2nd ed. 1866. 8vo. **78 C**

BELL, GEORGE JOSEPH.

Commentaries on laws of Scotland, in relation to mercantile and maritime law, moveable and heritable rights and bankruptcy. 6th ed. by P. Shaw. 2 vols. 1858. 8vo. **55 F**

Principles of the Law of Scotland. 3rd ed. 1833. 8vo. **175 D**

The same. 7th ed. by W. Guthrie. Edinburgh, 1876. 8vo. **55 F**

BELL, HENRY NUGENT.

The Huntingdon peerage, comprising a detailed account of the evidence and proceedings connected with the recent restoration of the earldom ; with a history of the illustrious house of Hastings. 1820. 4to. **127 J**

BELL, ROBERT.

A Dictionary of the law of Scotland. 3rd ed. by William Bell. 2 vols. Edinburgh, 1826. 8vo. **175 D**

Treatise on Election Laws, as they relate to Representation of Scotland. Edinburgh, 1812. 4to. **157 B**

BELL, SYDNEY SMITH.

Cases decided in the House of Lords on appeal from the courts of Scotland. 1842–1850. 7 vols. Edinburgh, 1843–52. 8vo. **15 A**

BELL, THOMAS.

Crown cases reserved for consideration and decided by the judges of England, 1858–1860. 1861. 8vo. **1 H**

BELL, WILLIAM.
A Dictionary and digest of the law of Scotland. New ed. by George Ross. 1861. 8vo.   175 D
The same. Rewritten by George Watson. 1882. 8vo. 55 F

BELLARMINO, ROBERTO.
Disputationes de controversiis Christianæ fidei, adversus hujus temporis hæreticos. 3 vols. Paris, 1608. folio.   77 F

BELT, ROBERT.
A Supplement to the Reports in Chancery of Francis Vesey. 2nd ed. 1825. 8vo.   3 G

BELTZ, GEORGE FREDERICK. See BRYDGES, Sir S. E.

BELZA, STANISLAW.
Wynagrodzenie za Prowadzenie Spraw. [Remuneration for the management of legal business.] Warszawa, 1887. 12mo.
    55 C

BENEDICT OF PETERBOROUGH.
The chronicle of the reigns of Henry II. and Richard I. A.D. 1169–1192, known commonly under the name of Benedict of Peterborough. Edited by Rev. Wm. Stubbs. 2 vols. 1867. 8vo.   102 C

BENENDEN, KENT.
The parish of Benenden, Kent, its monuments, vicars, and persons of note. Also a reprint of a rare pamphlet entitled This Winter's Wonders, dated 1673. By Rev. F. Haslewood. Privately printed. Ipswich, 1889. 8vo.   88 C

BENGAL.
Bengal Acts, 1862–1888. 8 vols. 1862–88. 8vo.   33 A
Bengal Law Reports, vols. 13, 14 and 15. 1874–1875. 3 vols. Calcutta, 1874–75. 8vo.   38 F
Calcutta Gazette, 1868–1888. 132 vols. 1868–88. 4to.
Charter establishing supreme court of judicature in Bengal. 1774. 8vo.   38 A
A Description of the roads in Bengal and Bahar. By James Rennell. 1778. 12mo.   84 A
The digest of Indian Law Reports. A compendium of the rulings of the High Court of Calcutta from 1862, and of the

BENGAL—*continued.*

Privy Council from 1831, to 1876. By D. Sutherland. 1877. 8vo.   **38 F**

Full bench rulings of the High Court of Bengal. Edited by L. A. Goodeve. 2 vols. Calcutta, 1865–74. 8vo.   **38 F**

General rules and circular orders of the High Court of Judicature in Bengal. Calcutta, 1881. 8vo.   **38 B**

Memoirs relative to the state of India. By Warren Hastings. New ed. 1786. 8vo.   **78 B**

The regulations of the Bengal Code. By C. D. Field. Calcutta, 1875. 8vo.   **38 C**

Reports of cases in the High Court of Judicature in Bengal in its original civil side. Edited by W. M. Bourke. Calcutta, 1867. 8vo.   **38 B**

Summary of statements and arguments submitted to the president of the Board of Control. By William Theobald. 1857. [Pamphlets, vol. 19.]   **144 B**

See also EAST INDIA COMPANY and INDIA.

BENJAMIN, JUDAH PHILIP.

The law of sale of personal property with references to the American decisions and to the French code and civil law. 1868. 8vo.   **174 D**

The same. 2nd ed. 1873. 8vo.   **174 D**

The same. 3rd ed. by A. B. Pearson and H. F. Boyd. 1883. 8vo.   **53 E**

The same. 4th ed. by A. B. Pearson-Gee and H. F. Boyd. 1888. 8vo.   **11 C**

BENLOE, GULIELME and GULIELME DALISON.

Les reports de G. Benloe des divers pleadings et cases en le court del Comon-bank 1532–1579; and, Les reports des divers special cases adjudge en le court del Comon-Bank 1546–1574, colligees par G. Dalison. 1689. folio.   **74 B**

BENNET, WILLIAM HEATH.

A Dissertation on the nature of the various proceedings in the Master's office in the Court of Chancery. 1834. 8vo. **161 B**

A Practical treatise on appointment and duties of a Receiver under the High Court of Chancery. 1849. 8vo.   **175 B**

BENNETT, JAMES.

The history of Tewkesbury. Tewkesbury, 1830. 8vo. **87 F**

BENNETT, Sir John.
Sir John Bennett and the Ward of Cheap : the legality of the
right of veto, claimed by the mayor and aldermen of London
on the election of a new alderman, considered.   By Walter
Rye.   Norwich, 1877.   [Pamphlets, vol. 30.]   **144 B**

BENTHAM, George.
Observations on Registration Bill now pending before House
of Commons.   1831.   [Jacob's Tracts, vol. 10.]   **144 E**

BENTHAM, Rev. James.
The history and antiquities of the conventual and cathedral
church of Ely.   Cambridge, 1771.   4to.   **86 G**
Supplement with memoirs of the late Rev. James Bentham.
By William Stevenson.   Norwich, 1817.   4to.   **86 G**
Life of Rev. James Bentham.   See J. P. Malcolm's Lives of
topographers and antiquaries.   1815.   4to.   **79 H**

BENTHAM, Jeremy.
Defence of Usury, shewing the impolicy of the present legal
restraints on the terms of pecuniary bargains, in a series of
letters to a friend.   2nd ed.   1790.   12mo.   **78 B**
The elements of the art of Packing as applied to Special juries,
particularly in cases of libel law.   1821.   8vo.   **78 C**
Indications respecting Lord Eldon, including history of the
pending judges'-salary-raising measure.   1825.   [Jacob's
Tracts, vol. 1.]   **144 E**
Traités de législation civile et pénale, ouvrage extrait des
manuscrits de M. Jérémie Bentham.   Par Ét. Dumont.   1858.
8vo.   **78 C**
A Treatise on judicial evidence, extracted from the manuscripts
of J. Bentham, by M. Dumont ; translated into English.
1825.   8vo.   **78 C**

BENTLY, William.
The history of the famous town of Halifax in Yorkshire, with
Revenge upon revenge, or an historical account of the
tragical practices of Sir John Eland upon the persons of
Sir Robert Beaumont and his allies.   1712.   12mo.   **94 A**

BENWELL, James Benjamin.
New Formulæ in valuation of annuities.   1830.   8vo.   **144 F**

BERCHUYS, Abrahamus Van.

Specimen Juridicum de juribus quæ in omni societate valent. Groningæ, 1820. [Latin Tracts.] **118 E**

BEREBLOCK, John.

Commentarii sive ephemeræ actiones rerum illustrium Oxonii gestarum in adventu serenissimæ principis Elizabethæ. Per J. B. See Oxford Historical Society, vol. 8, 1887, pp. 111–150. **85 F**

BERGENROTH, Gustav Adolph.

Calendar of letters, despatches, and state papers relating to the negotiations between England and Spain preserved in the archives at Simancas and elsewhere, 1485–1525. 3 vols. 1862–68. 8vo. **97 F**

BERKELEY FAMILY.

Berkeley manuscripts. Abstracts and extracts of Smyth's Lives of the Berkeleys, illustrative of ancient manners and the constitution. By T. D. Fosbroke. 1821. 4to. **87 F**

Case of W. F. Berkeley claiming to be Earl of Berkeley. See Peerage Cases, second series, vol. 1, pp. 228–289. **124 I**

Case on behalf of Sir M. F. F. Berkeley, K.C.B., claiming the title of Baron of Berkeley, with the evidence, arguments of counsel and judgments. 3 vols. 1858–62. folio. **124 J**

Minutes of evidence taken before committee for privileges on Earl of Berkeley's pedigree in 1799. 2 vols. 1811. folio. **124 J**

Minutes of evidence taken before the committee for privileges to whom the petition of W. F. Berkeley claiming the dignity of Baron de Berkeley was referred. 1829. See Peerage Evidence, vol. 3, pp. 207–475. **124 J**

BERKELEY, Gloucestershire.

A Copious history of the castle and parish of Berkeley. By T. D. Fosbroke. 1821. 4to. **87 F**

BERKSHIRE.

A Concise topographical account of the county of Berkshire. By Rev. D. Lysons and S. Lysons. 1813. 4to. **86 B**

Delineations of Berkshire. By E. W. Brayley and J. Britton. 1801. 8vo. **86 B**

Further observations upon the White Horse and other antiquities in Berkshire. By Rev. F. Wise. Oxford, 1742. 8vo. **86 B**

BERKSHIRE—*continued*.

A history of Berkshire. By Lieut.-Col. Cooper King. 1887. 8vo. **86 B**

The history of Newbury, including twenty-eight parishes in Berks. [By J. Bunny.] Speenhamland, 1839. 8vo. **86 B**

A Letter to Dr. Mead concerning some antiquities in Berkshire. By Rev. F. Wise. Oxford, 1738. 8vo. **86 B**

The Poll of the freeholders of Berks, on an election of two representatives in Parliament. Windsor, 1818. 8vo. **107 J**

The visitation of Berkshire, 1664–1666. By Elias Ashmole. Edited by W. C. Metcalf. Exeter, 1882. 4to. **86 B**

See also CLARKE, W. N. and WILLIS, B.

BERMUDA.

Acts of legislature of Islands of Bermuda, 1690–1883. By R. Gray. 2 vols. 1884. 8vo. **36 G**

Acts of legislature of Islands of Bermuda in force at end of year 1860. By J. H. Darrell. New York, 1862. 8vo. **36 G**

Bermuda Acts, 1857–1888. 9 vols. 1859–88. folio. **36 G**

BERNARDUS MORLANENSIS.

The poem called De contemptu mundi. See Satirical poets of the twelfth century, vol. 2, 1872, pp. 3–102. **102 E**

BERRY, WILLIAM.

County genealogies. Pedigrees of Essex families. 1839. folio. **126 I**

County genealogies. Pedigrees of Hertfordshire families. 1842. folio. **126 I**

County genealogies. Pedigrees of the families in the county of Hants. 1833. folio. **126 I**

County genealogies. Pedigrees of the families in the county of Kent. 1830. folio. **126 I**

County genealogies. Pedigrees of the families in the county of Sussex. 1830. folio. **126 I**

The history of the Island of Guernsey, with particulars of the islands of Alderney, Serk, and Jersey. 1815. 4to. **94 F**

BERWICK-UPON-TWEED.

The history of Berwick upon Tweed. By John Fuller. Edinburgh, 1799. 8vo. **92 D**

History of Berwick-upon-Tweed. By Frederick Sheldon. 1849. 8vo. **92 D**

BEST, William Mawdesley. /

· An Exposition of the practice relative to the Right to Begin and the Right to Reply in trials by jury and in appeals at Quarter Sessions. 1837. 8vo. **167 D**

Quintilian's Institutes of Oratory, book v., chap. vii., concerning witnesses, containing his rules for their judicious examination and cross-examination, translated with notes. 1836. [Law Tracts, vol. 6.] **144 D**

A treatise on presumption of law and fact with the theory and rules of presumptive or circumstantial proof in criminal cases. 1844. 8vo. **174 C**

A treatise on the principles of the law of Evidence with elementary rules for conducting the examination and cross-examination of witnesses. 3rd ed. 1860. 8vo. **167 D**

The same. 5th ed. 1870. 8vo. **167 D**

The same. 6th ed. by J. A. Russell. 1875. 8vo. **167 D**

The same. 7th ed. by J. M. Lely. 1883. 8vo. **9 I**

BEST, William Mawdesley and G. J. P. SMITH.

Reports of cases in the Courts of Queen's Bench and Exchequer Chamber. 1861–1864. 5 vols. 1862–66. 8vo. , **4 D**

BETHAM, Rev. William.

Genealogical tables of the sovereigns of the world from the earliest to the present period. 1795. folio. **125 H**

See also BARONETAGES.

BETHAM, Sir William.

Dignities feudal and parliamentary, and the constitutional legislature of the United Kingdom. vol. i. 1830. 8vo. **116 B**

Irish antiquarian researches. 2 vols. 1826–27. 8vo. **95 E**

BETTING.

The law of Betting. By G. H. Stutfield. 1884. 8vo. **10 B**

The law of horses, including the law of wagers and gaming. By G. H. H. Oliphant. 4th ed. 1882. 8vo. . **10 B**

BEVEN, Thomas.

Principles of the law of negligence. 1889. 8vo. **11 A**

BEVER, Thomas.

The history of the legal polity of Roman state, and of rise, progress, and extent of Roman laws. 1781. 4to. **113 G**

BEVERLEY, YORKSHIRE.

Beverlac, or the antiquities and history of Beverley. By George Poulson. 2 vols. in 1. 1829. 4to.   **94 C**

The history and antiquities of the town and minster of Beverley. By George Oliver. Beverley, 1829. 4to. **95 G**

BEVILL, ROBERT. See BEDFORD LEVEL.

BIBLE.

A complete concordance to the holy scriptures of the old and new testament. By A. Cruden. roth ed. 1831. 4to. **77 G**

Cyclopædia Bibliographica. By James Darling, Subjects Holy Scriptures. 1859. 4to.   **82 F**

A Dictionary of the Bible. Edited by Wm. Smith. 3 vols. 1863. 8vo.   **77 E**

. The Holy Bible according to the authorised version, with notes explanatory and practical. By Rev. G. D'Oyly and Rev. R. Mant. 3 vols. Oxford, 1817. 4to.   **77 G**

Sacred history of the old and new testament. By Wm. Whiston. 6 vols. 1745–46. 8vo.   ·   **77 A**

Synopsis criticorum aliorumque Sacræ Scripturæ interpretum et commentatorum. A Matthæo Polo, ex recensione Johannis Leusden. 5 vols. Ultrajecti, 1684–86. folio. **77 H**

BIBLIOGRAPHY.

American catalogue of books, or English guide to American literature. 1856. 8vo.   ·   **82 B**

The best books, or reader's guide to the choice of the best available books. A contribution towards classified bibliography. By W. S. Sonnenschein. 1887. 8vo.   **82 D**

The Bibliographer's manual of English literature. By W. T. Lowndes. 2 vols. 1834. 8vo.   **82 G**

The same, new ed. revised and enlarged with an appendix relating to the books of literary and scientific societies, by H. G. Bohn. 11 parts in 6 vols. 1857–64. 8vo.   **82 G**

A Bibliographical account of works relating to English topography. By Wm. Upcott. 3 vols. in 4. 1818. 4to. **82 I**

Bibliographie instructive ou traité de la connoissance des livres rares et singuliers. Par G. F. De Bure, le jeune. 7 vols. 1763–68, and Supplement ou catalogue des livres du cabinet de feu M. Louis Jean Gaignat. 2 vols. 1769. 9 vols. ⸱. Paris, 1763–69. 8vo.   ·   **82 A**

BIBLIOGRAPHY—*continued.*

Bibliotheca Britannica, or a general index to British and foreign literature. By Robert Watt, M.D. 4 vols. Edinburgh, 1824. 4to. **82 F**

Bibliotheca Cornubiensis. By G. C. Boase and W. P. Courtney. 3 vols. 1874–82. 4to. **82 F**

Bibliotheca Heraldica Magnæ Britanniæ. An analytical catalogue of books on genealogy, heraldry, nobility, knighthood, and ceremonies. By T. Moule. 1822. 8vo. **82 C**

British topography, or an account of what has been done for illustrating topographical antiquities of Great Britain and Ireland. By Richard Gough. 2 vols. 1780. 4to. **82 I**

A Catalogue of early English miscellanies formerly in the Harleian library. Edited by W. C. Hazlitt. [Camden Society, vol. 87.] 1864. 8vo. **85 C**

A Catalogue of the royal and noble authors of England. By Horace Walpole. New ed. 1796. 8vo. **82 C**

A Chronological list of books and single papers relating to subjects of the rate of mortality, annuities, and life assurance. [By Lewis Pocock.] 2nd ed. 1842. 8vo. **82 B**

A Critical dictionary of English literature, and British and American authors. By S. A. Allibone. 3 vols. 1859–71. 4to. **82 F**

Cyclopædia Bibliographica, a library manual of theological and general literature and guide to books. By James Darling. 1854. 4to. **82 F**

Cyclopædia Bibliographica. Subjects, Holy Scriptures. By James Darling. 1859. 4to. **82 F**

Essai de bibliographie du droit canonique. See G. Phillips's Du droit ecclésiastique, 1852, pp. 341–524. **77 C**

Handbook to the popular, poetical, and dramatic literature of Great Britain, from the invention of printing to the restoration. By W. C. Hazlitt. 1867. 8vo. **82 H**

Hints on catalogue titles and on index entries. By C. F. Blackburn. 1884. 8vo. **82 D**

An index to Periodical literature. By W. F. Poole. 3rd ed. brought down to January 1882, and Supplement from January 1, 1882, to January 1, 1887. 2 vols. 1882–88. 4to. **82 F**

The lawyer's reference manual of law books and citations. By C. C. Soule. Boston, 1883. 8vo. **82 D**

The Library companion. By Rev. T. F. Dibdin. 2nd ed. 2 vols. 1825. 8vo. **82 C**

Manuel du libraire et de l'amateur de livres. Par J. C. Brunet.

BIBLIOGRAPHY—*continued.*

Quatrième éd. 5 tomes. 1842–44. Supplément par P. Deschamps et G. Brunet. 2 tomes. 1878–80. 7 tomes. Paris, 1842–80. 8vo. **82 G**

Reminiscences of a literary life. By Rev. T. F. Dibdin. 2 vols. 1836. 8vo. **82 C**

The reporters arranged and characterized. By J. W. Wallace. 4th ed. by F. F. Heard. Boston, 1882. 8vo. **82 D**

A Short view of legal Bibliography. By R. W. Bridgman. 1807. 8vo. **82 C**

See ANONYMS, CATALOGUES, and LIBRARIES.

BICESTER, OXFORDSHIRE.

Audit rolls of Bicester priory, copies of original papers, memoranda, &c., illustrative of the history of Bicester. See J. Dunkin's Oxfordshire, vol. 2, 1823, pp. 219–260. **92 F**

The history and antiquities of Bicester. By John Dunkin. 1816. 8vo. **92 E**

Parochial antiquities attempted in the history of Ambrosden and Burcester. By White Kennett. New ed. 2 vols. Oxford, 1818. 4to. **92 F**

BIDDLE, JOHN.

A Table of references to unrepealed public general acts, arranged in the alphabetical order of their short or popular titles. 1864. 8vo. **31 E**

The same. 2nd ed. 1869, and Supplement, 1870. 2 vols. 1869–70. 8vo. **31 E**

BIDEFORD, DEVONSHIRE.

An Essay towards a history of Bideford. By John Watkins. Exeter, 1792. 8vo. **87 C**

BIGELOW, MELVILLE MADISON.

Elements of law of Torts. Cambridge, 1889 12mo. **64 E**

An Index of the cases overruled . . . by the courts of America, England, and Ireland, from the earliest period to the present time. Boston, 1873. 8vo. **14 F**

BIGG, JAMES.

Collection of public general statutes consolidating provisions usually introduced into acts relating to cemeteries, commissioners, companies &c. 2nd ed. 1877. 12mo. **9 C**

BIGG, JAMES—*continued.*

A Collection of the public general acts for the regulation of
: Railways. 11th ed. 1865. 12mo.   **175 A**

The same. 13th ed. 1875. 12mo.   **175 A**

Minutes of proceedings in Parliament respecting public and
private bills, committees, &c. 1856. 12mo.   **173 B**

BIGLAND, JOHN.

A Topographical and historical description of the county of
York. 1819. 8vo.   **94 B**

BIGLAND, RALPH.

Historical, monumental, and genealogical collections relative
to the county of Gloucester. 2 vols. 1791–92. folio. **88 H**

Observations on marriages, baptisms, and burials, as preserved
in parochial registers. 1764. 4to.   **127 I**

See also FOSBROKE, T. D.

BILLER, GEORGE.

Rhymes, reasons, and recollections, from the commonplace
books of a Sexagenarian. 1876. 12mo.   **78 A**

See also AURICULAR CONFESSION.

BILLS OF EXCHANGE.

A Digest of the law of Bills of Exchange. By M. D. Chalmers. 3rd ed. 1887. 8vo.   **9 I**

A Handy book on the law of Bills of Exchange. By J. W.
Smith. 1887. 12mo.   **52 G**

The law of Bills of Exchange. By Sir J. B. Byles. 14th ed.
by M. B. Byles and A. K. Loyd. 1885. 8vo.   **9 I**

The Bills of Exchange act 1882. By Aviet Agabeg and
W. F. Barry. 1883. 8vo.   **52 G**

Notes on the Bills of Exchange bill. By M. D. Chalmers.
1882. [Pamphlets, vol. 33.]   **144 C**

A Compendium of the laws on Bills of Exchange and other
commercial negotiable instruments of England, Germany,
and France. By H. D. Jencken. 1880. 8vo.   **9 I**

Points of difference between English and foreign systems of
law regarding Bills of Exchange and their relative merits.
By M. D. Chalmers. 1880. [Pamphlets, vol. 30.] **144 B**

Association for reform and codification of law of nations.
Report of special committee on codification of laws of Bills
of Exchange. 1875. [Pamphlets, vol. 33.]   **144 C**

BILLS OF EXCHANGE—*continued.*

In Chancery. Ooddeen *v.* Oakeley. Judgment of the lords justices of appeal. 1862. [Pamphlets, vol. 21.] **144 B**

Commentaries on the law of Bills of Exchange, foreign and inland, in England and America. By Joseph Story. 4th ed. by E. H. Bennett. Boston, 1860. 8vo. **59 E**

Advice concerning Bills of Exchange. By John Marius. 4th ed. 1684. See G. Malynes's Lex Mercatoria. 3rd ed. 1686. folio. **118 G**

See also BAYLEY, CHITTY, CUNNINGHAM, HOBLER, KYD, LAWES, and LOVELASS. **160 G**

BILLS OF LADING.

The contract of affreightment as expressed in Bills of Lading. By J. E. Scrutton. 1886. 8vo. **10 D**

A Practical treatise on charter-parties and Bills of Lading. By Edward Lawes. 1813. 8vo. **161 F**

See also SHIPPING. **11 F**

BILLS OF SALE.

The Bills of Sale acts 1878 and 1882, with an epitome of the law as affected by the acts. By Herbert Reed. 7th ed. 1889. 8vo. **11 E**

The form of Bills of Sale given as security for the payment of money. (Bills of Sale act, 1882.) By S. Buckmaster. 1887. 8vo. **11 E**

The Bills of Sale acts 1878 and 1882. By E W. Fithian. 2nd ed. 1884. 12mo. **11 E**

The law relating to Bills of Sale. By S. C. Macaskie. 1882. 8vo. **11 E**

A Concise practical treatise on the law of Bills of Sale. By John Indermaur. 1882. 12mo. **64 F**

The law of Bills of Sale. By G. E. Lyon and J. H. Redman. 3rd ed. 1881. 8vo. **11 E**

A Treatise on Bills of Sale. By F. C. J. Millar and J. R. Collier. 4th ed. by F. C. J. Millar. 1877. 12mo. **53 G**

See also BEAUMONT, BYRNE, GUIRY, and WILSON. **160 G**

BILLS, PRIVATE AND PUBLIC.

Alphabetical list of the Private bills 1853–1858, 1861–1889. 3 vols. 1853–89. 12mo. **146 D**

Private Bill legislation and provisional orders. Handbook for the use of solicitors and engineers. By L. L. Macassey. 1887. 8vo. **12 A**

BILLS, PRIVATE AND PUBLIC—*continued.*

A History of Private Bill legislation. By Frederick Clifford.
2 vols. 1885–87. 8vo. **83 H**

The Locus Standi of petitioners against Private Bills in Parliament. By J. M. Smethurst. 3rd ed. 1876. 12mo. **53 A**

Practice of the Court of Referees on Private Bills in parliament, with reports of cases as to the locus standi of petitioners, during the sessions 1867–72. By F. Clifford and P. S. Stephens. 2 vols. 1870–73. 8vo. **66 C**

Cases decided during the sessions 1873–88 by the Court of Referees on Private Bills in parliament. By F. Clifford, A. G. Rickards, and M. J. Michael. 4 vols. in 3. 1877–89. 8vo. **66 C**

Private Bill legislation. Can anything be now done to improve it ? By Alexander Pulling. 1859. [Pamphlets, vol. 11.] **144 A**

Report from the select committee on Private Bills, with the minutes of evidence. 1846. folio. **153 E**

The manner of proceeding on Bills in the House of Commons. By George Bramwell. 1837. 4to. **156 C**

A Manual of the practice of Parliament in passing public and private Bills. 1827. 12mo. **173 B**

Practical instructions on the passing of private bills through both Houses of Parliament. By A Parliament Agent. 1825. 8vo. **173 C**

The manner how statutes are enacted in Parliament by passing of bills. By William Hakewil. 1641. 12mo. **48 D**

See also BIGG, BRISTOWE, ELLIS, FRERE, HALCOMB, LUMLEY, SHERWOOD, VIZARD, and WEST. **173 B C**

BINGHAM, PEREGRINE.

The law and practice of Judgments and Executions, including Extents at the suit of the Crown. 1815. 8vo. **169 E**

Reports of cases in the Court of Common Pleas and other courts, 1822–1834. 10 vols. 1824–34. 8vo. **6 A**

New cases in the Court of Common Pleas and other courts, 1834–1840. 6 vols. 1835–41. 8vo. **6 A B**

BINNELL, ROBERT.

A Description of the river Thames, &c., with the City of London's jurisdiction and conservacy thereof proved, with a description of fish caught in the Thames or sold in London. 1758. 12mo. **92 B**

BIOGRAPHY.

The annual Biography and Obituary for the years 1818, 1820, 1821, 1823, 1825 and 1826. 6 vols. 1818–26. 8vo. **81 A**

Biographia Britannica. 2nd ed. by Andrew Kippis. 5 vols. [As far as the name Fastolff.] 1778–93. folio. **79 I**

The Biographical treasury; a dictionary of universal biography. By S. Maunder. 11th ed. 1859. 12mo. **81 B**

A Brief Biographical dictionary. By Rev. Charles Hole. 2nd ed. 1866. 12mo. **81 B**

A Classical dictionary, containing a copious account of all the proper names mentioned in ancient authors. By Rev. John Lempriere. 20th ed. 1844. 8vo. **84 C**

A Critical dictionary of English literature, containing thirty thousand biographies and literary notices. By S. A. Allibone. 3 vols. Philadelphia, 1859–71. 4to. **82 F**

A Dictionary of biography, comprising the most eminent characters of all ages, nations and professions. By R. A. Davenport. 1831. 8vo. **81 B**

Dictionary of Greek and Roman biography and mythology. Edited by Wm. Smith. 3 vols. 1864. 8vo. **81 I**

Dictionary of national biography. Edited by Leslie Stephen. 20 vols. 1885–89. 8vo. [In progress.] **79 E**

Dictionnaire universel des contemporains, contenant toutes les personnes notables de la France et des pays étrangers. Par G. Vapereau. Troisième édition. 1865. 4to. **81 E**

The general Biographical dictionary. New ed. by Alexander Chalmers. 32 vols. 1812–17. 8vo. **79 C D**

An Historical, genealogical and poetical dictionary, containing the lives and actions of all great men. 1703. 12mo. **79 A**

The history of the Worthies of England. By Thomas Fuller. New ed. by John Nichols. 2 vols. 1811. 4to. **79 H**

The lives and characters of the most illustrious persons, British and foreign, who died in the years 1711 and 1712. 2 vols. 1713–14. 8vo. **81 A**

Men of the time, a biographical dictionary of eminent living characters of both sexes. 6th ed. 1865, 7th ed. 1868, 8th ed. 1872, 9th ed. 1875, 10th ed. 1879, 11th ed. 1884, and 12th ed. 1887. 7 vols. 1865–87. 8vo. **81 D E**

A new and general biographical dictionary, containing an account of lives and writings of most eminent persons in every nation. 11 vols. 1761–62. 8vo. **79 C**

Public characters of 1798–1809. 10 vols. 1799–1809. 8vo. **81 C**

See AUTOBIOGRAPHY, BRANTÔME, and ENCYCLOPÆDIAS.

BIRCH, JOHN.

Military memoir of Colonel John Birch, written by Roe, his secretary, with an historical and critical commentary by the late Rev. John Webb. Edited by Rev. T. W. Webb. [Camden Society, n.s. vol. 7.] 1873. 8vo. **85 C**

BIRD, G.

The practising scrivener and modern conveyancer; being a collection of choice presidents. 1729. folio. **157 C**

BIRD, HENRY PEALE.

Defence of Mr. H. P. Bird in answer to the charges preferred against him by his late partner, Mr. Barclay Farquharson Watson. 1854. [Pamphlets, vol. 17.] **144 B**

BIRD, JAMES BARRY.

The new pocket conveyancer. 3rd ed. 2 vols. 1816. 12mo. **164 D**

The same. 5th ed. 2 vols. 1830. 12mo. **164 D**

BIRKETT, PERCIVAL.

Malvern Hills: historical sketch. 1882. 8vo. **93 F**

A Short history of rights of common upon the Forest of Dartmoor and the commons of Devonshire. 1885. 8vo. **87 C**

The value of open spaces and recreation grounds in thickly populated districts. 1884. [Pamphlets, vol. 36.] **144 C**

BIRMINGHAM.

An Appeal to the public on the subject of the riots in Birmingham, to which are added, Strictures on 'a pamphlet entitled 'Thoughts on the late riot at Birmingham.' By Joseph Priestley. Birmingham, 1791. 8vo. **93 E**

The Birmingham corporation (consolidation) act 1883. By E. O. Smith and C. A. Carter. 1883. 8vo. **93 E**

An History of Birmingham to the end of the year 1780. By W. Hutton. Birmingham, 1781. 8vo. **93 E**

Old and new Birmingham, a history of the town and its people. By R. K. Dent. Birmingham, 1880. 4to. **94 G**

BIRTHS, DEATHS, AND MARRIAGES.

The law concerning the registration of Births and Deaths in England and Wales and at sea. By A. J. Flaxman. 1875. 8vo. **11 E**

BIRTHS, DEATHS, AND MARRIAGES.—*continued*.

Lists of non-parochial registers and records in the custody of the Registrar General of births, deaths and marriages. 1859. folio. **100 H**

Observations on Lord John Russell's bill for registering births, deaths and marriages in England. By James Yates. 1836. [Law Tracts, vol. 5.] **144 E**

Report of the commissioners appointed to inquire into the state, custody, and authenticity of registers or records of births or baptisms, deaths or burials and marriages, in England and Wales, other than the parochial registers. 1838. folio. **100 H**

BISHOP, JOEL PRENTISS.

Commentaries on the Criminal law. 2nd ed. 2 vols. Boston, 1858–59. 8vo. **59 C**

The same. 3rd ed. 2 vols. Boston, 1865. 8vo. **59 C**

Commentaries on the law of marriage and divorce. 4th ed. 2 vols. Boston, 1864. 8vo. **59 G**

The first book of the Law ; explaining the nature, sources, books, and practical applications of legal science. Boston, 1868. 8vo. **59 F**

BISHOP, THE BOY.

Two sermons preached at St. Paul's, temp. Henry VIII., and at Gloucester, temp. Mary. Edited by J. G. Nichols. [Camden Society, n.s. vol. 14.] 1875. 8vo. **85 D**

BISHOPS' RIGHT TO VOTE.

The grand question, concerning the bishops' right to vote in Parliament in cases capital, stated and argued, from the Parliament-rolls and the history of former times. [By Edward Stillingfleet.] 1680. 12mo. **48 C**

BISSET, ANDREW.

Practical treatise on law of Estates for life. 1842. 8vo. **167 D**

Practical treatise on law of Partnership. 1847. 8vo. **173 D**

BITTLESTON, ADAM HENRY.

Practice under the Judicature acts. 1876. 8vo. **169 F**

Reports in chambers, Q.B. division. 1884. 8vo. **4 D**

BITTON, THOMAS DE.
: Account of the executors of Thomas, Bishop of Exeter, 1310.
. Edited by Ven. W. H. Hale and Rev. H. T. Ellacombe.
[Camden Society, n.s. vol. 10.] 1874. 8vo. **85 D**

BLACK, JEREMIAH SULLIVAN.
: Reports of decisions in the supreme court of the United
States, 1861 to 1862. See S. F. Miller's Reports, vol. 4.
~ Washington. 1875. 8vo. **57 C**

BLACK, WILLIAM HENRY.
A Comparative account of works produced and moneys received by the commissioners on the public records during
two periods of five years before and five years after March
12, 1831. 1837. 8vo. **97 I**
History and antiquities of the worshipful company of Leather-
sellers of the City of London. 1871. folio. **92 G**

BLACKBURN, CHARLES FRANCIS.
Hints on catalogue titles and on index entries, with a rough
vocabulary of terms and abbreviations. 1884. 8vo. **82 D**

BLACKBURN, COLIN.
A Treatise on the effect of the contract of sale, on the legal
rights of property and possession in goods, wares and
merchandize. 1845. 8vo. **163 D**
The same. 2nd ed. by J. C. Graham. 1885. 8vo. **9 E**

BLACKHEATH, KENT.
. The Hundred of Blackheath. By H. H. Drake. 1886. folio.
. **89 H**

BLACKPOOL, LANCASHIRE.
A Description of Blackpool in Lancashire. By W. Hutton.
3rd ed. 1817. 12mo. **89 A**
. An Historical and descriptive account of Blackpool. By Rev.
Wm. Thornber. Poulton, 1837. 12mo. **89 A**

BLACKSTONE, HENRY.
Reports of Cases in the Courts of Common Pleas and Exchequer Chamber, from Easter Term, 1788, to Hilary Term,
1796. 2nd ed. 2 vols. 1793–96. folio.
The same. 3rd ed. 2 vols. 1801. 8vo. **6 B**

BLACKSTONE, Sir William.

An Analysis of the laws of England, 3rd ed., to which is prefixed An introductory discourse on the study of the law. Oxford, 1758. 12mo.   **166 F**

The same. 5th ed. Oxford, 1762. 12mo.   **166 F**

An Argument in the Exchequer Chamber on giving judgment in the case of Perrin and another against Blake. 1772. See F. Hargrave's Law Tracts, 1787, pp. 487–510.   **144 G**

The biographical history of Sir William Blackstone, and a catalogue of all his works, with a nomenclature of Westminster Hall. By a Gentleman of Lincoln's Inn. [D. Douglas.] 1782. 8vo.   **79 C**

Commentaries on the laws of England. 4 vols. Oxford, 1765–69. 4to.   **156 B**

The same. 8th ed. 4 vols. Oxford, 1778. 8vo.   **166 F**

The same. 12th ed., with notes and additions by Edward Christian [with portraits of eminent judges]. 4 vols. London, 1793–95. 8vo.   **118 E**

The same. 14th ed. by Edward Christian. 4 vols. 1803. 8vo.   **166 F**

The same. 16th ed., with notes by J. T. Coleridge. 4 vols. 1825. 8vo.   **166 F**

The same. New ed. by Joseph Chitty. 4 vols. 1826. 8vo.   **166 G**

The same. Edited by J. L. Wendell from the 21st London edition. 4 vols. New York, 1852–50. 8vo.   **166 G**

The same. New ed. by R. M. Kerr. 4 vols. 1857. 8vo. **166 G**

The same. New ed. by R. M. Kerr. 4 vols. 1862. 8vo. **166 G**

Commentaires sur les loix Angloises de M. Blackstone. Traduits de l'Anglois par M. D. G . . . [de Gomicourt] sur la quatrième édition d'Oxford. 6 tomes. Bruxelles, 1774–76. 12mo.   **166 E**

An Analysis of Blackstone's Commentaries in a series of questions. By Barron Field. 1811. 8vo.   **166 F**

Remarks critical and miscellaneous on the Commentaries of Sir William Blackstone. By James Sedgwick. 2nd ed. 1807. 4to.   **156 B**

A Vindication of the Commentaries of Sir W. Blackstone from some strictures contained in ' Remarks on the Commentaries of Sir W. Blackstone,' by James Sedgwick. By Wm. Henry Rowe. 1805. 8vo.   **166 F**

A Translation of all the Greek, Latin, Italian and French quotations which occur in Blackstone's Commentaries on the laws of England. By J. W. Jones. 1823. 8vo.   **166 F**

BLACKSTONE, SIR WILLIAM—*continued.*
Law Tracts. 2 vols. Oxford, 1762. 8vo. **144 F**
Reports of cases in courts of Westminster Hall from 1746 to
1779. 2nd ed. by C. H. Elsley. 2 vols. 1828. 8vo. **4 D**
Tracts chiefly relating to the antiquities and laws of England.
3rd ed. Oxford, 1771. 4to. **144 G**
A Treatise on the law of descents in fee simple. Oxford,
1759. [Law Tracts, vol. 1.] **144 E**
See also AIRD, BLICKENSDERFER, KERR, STEPHEN, and
WARREN.

BLAGG, JOHN WARD.
The law as to Public Meeting. 1888. 12mo. **11 D**

BLANCH, WILLIAM HARNETT.
Ye parish of Camerwell; a brief account of the parish of
Camberwell, its history and antiquities. 1877. 8vo. **89 E**

BLANCKLEY, THOMAS RILEY.
A Naval expositor shewing and explaining the words and
terms of art belonging to ships. 1750. 4to. **78 G**

BLANDFORD, DORSET.
A Brief account of the dreadful fire at Blandford-Forum,
Dorset, with a Sermon preached at Blandford June 4, 1735,
and A serious address to the inhabitants of that town. By
Malachi Blake. 3rd ed. 1736. 12mo. **87 D**

BLANEFORDE, HENRY.
Johannis De Trokelowe et Henrici De Blaneforde, mona-
chorum S. Albani, Chronica et annales. Edited by H. T.
Riley. 1866. 8vo. **101 G**

BLASHFIELD, JOHN MARRIOT.
An Account of the history and manufacture of ancient and
modern terra cotta. 1855. [Pamphlets, vol. 40.] **144 C**
Examples of vases, tazzas, pateræ &c. manufactured in terra
cotta. 1853. 4to. **78 G**

BLASPHEMY.
Should the existing law as to Blasphemy be amended, and if
so, in what direction? By W. B. Odgers. 1883. [Pam-
phlets, vol. 31.] **144 C**
See also ASPLAND, L. M.

BLATCHFORD, Samuel.

Reports of cases in prize, in the circuit and district courts of the United States, for the southern district of New York, 1861–1865. New York, 1866. 8vo. **57 A**

BLENHEIM, Oxfordshire.

Description of Blenheim. See A. Rimmer's Pleasant spots around Oxford, 1878, pp. 206–249. **92 E**

The Oxford university and city guide, to which is added a guide to Blenheim. New ed. Oxford, 1837. 12mo. **92 E**

BLESSINTON, Charles John, 1 Earl of.

A Rental of parts of the estates of the late Earl of Blessinton, situate in the counties of Tyrone, Dublin and Kilkenny, to be sold 23 November, 1846. 1846. folio. **95 H**

BLEWERT, William.

Tables for calculating the value of stocks and annuities, and for a ready despatch of business in the public funds. 4th ed. [n.d.] 12mo. **146 E**

BLEWITT, Reginald James.

The Court of Chancery, a satirical poem. 1827. 8vo. **118 C**

BLICKENSDERFER, Ulric.

Blackstone's Elements of Law, &c., with analytical charts, tables and legal definitions. 1889. 8vo. **64 E**

BLIGH, Richard.

Reports of cases heard in the House of Lords on appeals and writs of error, 1819–1821. 4 vols. 1823–27. 8vo. **1 A**

New reports of cases heard in the House of Lords on appeals and writs of error, 1827–1837. 11 vols. 1829–37. 8vo. **1 A**

BLITHBURY, Suffolk.

An Historical account of Blithbury. By Thomas Gardner. 1754. 4to. **93 B**

BLOCKADE.

The law of Blockade, as contained in the report of eight cases in the high court of Admiralty, on the blockade of the coast of Courland, 1854. By J. P. Deane. 1855. 8vo. **55 A**

See also INTERNATIONAL LAW. **55 A B**

BLOME, RICHARD.

Britannia, or a geographical description of the kingdoms of England, Scotland and Ireland, with the isles and territories thereto belonging. 1673. folio. **86 G**

BLOMEFIELD, REV. FRANCIS.

Collectanea Cantabrigiensia, or collections relating to Cambridge, university, town and county. 1750. 8vo. **86 D**

An Essay towards a topographical history of the county of Norfolk: continued by Rev. Charles Parkin. 2nd ed. 11 vols. 1805–10. 8vo. **92 C**

The history of the ancient city and burgh of Thetford. Fersfield, 1739. 4to. **92 D**

The history of the city and county of Norwich. 2 vols. 1806. 8vo. **92 C**

BLONDE OF OXFORD.

The romance of Blonde of Oxford and Jehan of Dammartin. By Philippe De Reimes, a trouvère of the thirteenth century. Edited by M. Le Roux De Lincy. [Camden Society, vol. 72.] 1858. 8vo. **85 B**

BLORE, THOMAS.

History of the manor and manor-house of South Winfield in Derbyshire in a letter to the Earl of Leicester. 2nd ed. 1816. 4to. **87 B**

BLOUNT, CHARLES.

Janua Scientiarum, or a compendious introduction to geography, chronology, government, history, phylosophy. 1684. 12mo. **118 A**

BLOUNT, THOMAS.

Fragmenta antiquitatis, or ancient tenures of land and jocular customs of manors. Enlarged by Josiah Beckwith, with additions by H. M. Beckwith. 1815. 4to. **157 F**

The same. 4th ed. by W. C. Hazlitt. 1874. 8vo. **13 B**

NOMO-ΛΕΞΙΚΟΝ. A law dictionary. 1670. folio. **123 G**

BLOXAM, REV. JOHN ROUSE.

Magdalen College and King James II. 1686–1688, a series of documents edited by the Rev. J. R. Bloxam, D.D. [Oxford Historical Society, vol. 6.] Oxford, 1886. 8vo. **85 F**

BLOXAM, REV. JOHN ROUSE—*continued.*
Register of the demies, instructors in grammar and in music, chaplains, clerks and choristers of St. Mary Magdalen college, Oxford, from the foundation to A.D. 1857. 7 vols. 1853–1881, and Index 1885. 8 vols. 1853–85. 8vo. **92 E**

BLOXAM, RICHARD.
Regulations to be observed in conduct of business at chambers of Master of Rolls and Vice-Chancellors. 1857. 8vo. **161 C**

BLUNDELL, BEZER.
The case of Mr. Blundell, F.S.A. (Legalis) as detailed to the House of Peers by Lord Brougham, July 3, 1863, with the judgment delivered by the Court of Queen's Bench on Mr. Blundell's case. 1882. [Pamphlets, vol. 31.] **144 C**

BLUNT, JOHN ELIJAH.
A History of the establishment and residence of the Jews in England, with an enquiry into their civil disabilities. 1830. [Jacob's Tracts, vol. 7.] **144 E**

BLUNT, REV. JOHN HENRY.
The book of Church law, being an exposition of the legal rights and duties of the parochial clergy and the laity of the Church of England. Revised by W. G. F. Phillimore. 1872. 12mo. **166 A**
The same. 2nd ed. 1876, and 3rd ed. 1882. 12mo. **166 A**
The same. 4th ed. 1885. 12mo. **52 C**
The same. 5th ed. 1888. 12mo. **9 C**

BLYTH, ERNEST EGBERT.
An Analysis of Snell's Principles of Equity, with notes thereon. 1885, and 3rd ed. 1889. 8vo. **64 C**

BOASE, CHARLES WILLIAM.
A Century of banking in Dundee, from 1764 to 1864. 2nd ed. Edinburgh, 1867. 8vo. **78 D**

BOASE, REV. CHARLES WILLIAM.
Historic towns. Oxford. 2nd ed. 1887. 8vo. **92 E**
Register of the rectors and fellows, scholars, exhibitioners and bible clerks of Exeter college, Oxford, with illustrative documents and a history of the college. Oxford, 1879. 4to. **92 F**

BOASE, Rev. Charles William—*continued.*

Register of the University of Oxford. Vol. 1 (1449–63; 1505–71). Edited by the Rev. C. W. Boase. [Oxford Historical Society, vol. 1.] Oxford, 1885. 8vo. **85 F**

See also RANKE, LEOPOLD VON.

BOASE, George Clement and W. P. COURTNEY.

Bibliotheca Cornubiensis: a catalogue of the writings of Cornishmen, and of works relating to the county of Cornwall, with biographical memoranda and copious literary references. 3 vols. 1874–82. 4to. **82 F**

BOBBIN, Tim.

The works of Tim Bobbin, Esq. [John Collier] in prose and verse, with a memoir of the author. By John Corry. Rochdale, 1819. 8vo. **118 C**

BODMAN, James.

A Concise history of Trowbridge. Bristol, 1814. 12mo. **93 F**

BODMIN CHURCH, Cornwall.

Receipts and expenses in the building of Bodmin church, A.D. 1469 to 1472. Edited by Rev. J. J. Wilkinson. [Camden Society, n.s. vol. 14.] 1875. 8vo. **85 D**

BÖETHIUS, Hector.

The buik of the croniclis of Scotland ; or a metrical version of the history of Hector Boece, by Wm. Stewart. Edited by W. B. Turnbull. 3 vols. 1858. 8vo. **101 A B**

Scotorum historiæ a prima gentis origine, cum aliarum et rerum et gentium illustratione non vulgari: præmissa epistola nuncupatoria. [Paris,] 1526. folio. **113 F**

BOHN, Henry George.

Catalogue of the pictures, miniatures and art books collected during the last fifty years by H. G. Bohn. Privately printed. 1884. 8vo. **118 E**

A Dictionary of quotations from the English poets. 1882. 8vo. **83 C**

The question of unreciprocated foreign copyright in Great Britain. 1851. 8vo. **83 I**

BOHUN, WILLIAM.

Cursus Cancellariæ, or the course of proceedings in the high court of Chancery. 1715. 12mo. **161 B**

Institutio Legalis, or an introduction to study and practice of laws of England. 3rd ed. 1724. 12mo. **162 F**

The law of Tithes. 2nd ed. 1731. 12mo. **176 E**

The practising attorney, containing the business of an attorney in all its branches. 2nd ed. 1726. 12mo. **162 F**

The same. 4th ed. 2 vols. 1737. 12mo. **162 F**

Privilegia Londini, or the rights, liberties, privileges, laws and customs of the City of London. 3rd ed. 1723. 8vo. **91 B**

BOLLE FAMILY.

Anecdotes of the family of Bolle. See Rev. C. Illingworth's Account of parish of Scampton, 1810, pp. 43–65. **118 G**

BOLTON, LANCASHIRE.

Bolton-le-Moors and the townships in the parish. By P. A. Whittle. Bolton, 1855. 8vo. **89 B**

BOLTON, SOLOMON.

The extinct peerage of England. 1769. 8vo. **125 C**

BOLTON, THOMAS HENRY.

The Tithe acts. 1886. 12mo. **11 H**

BOMBAY.

Bombay acts 1862 to 1888. 8 vols. 1862–88. 8vo. **33 B**

The Bombay Government Gazette, 1868–1888. 122 vols. 1868–88. folio.

Bombay high court reports 1862–1869. 6 vols. Bombay, 1870. 8vo. **38 F**

Cases illustrative of Oriental law decided in supreme court at Bombay. By Sir T. E. Perry. 1853. 8vo. **38 C**

Charter dated December 8, 1823, establishing supreme court of judicature at Bombay. 1823. 8vo. **38 A**

Papers on the police of Bombay. See W. H. Morley's Analytical digest, vol. 2, 1849, pp. 453–545. **38 C**

BONA NOTABILIA.

A Brief treatise of Bona Notabilia. By George Lawton. York, 1825. 8vo. **94 A**

See also EXECUTORS.

BONAPARTE, Napoléon.

Histoire de Napoléon, d'après Norvins, Ségur, Capefigue, &c.
15e édition.　Bruxelles, 1842.　24mo.　　　**79 A**

Ought France to worship the Bonapartes?　1863.　[Pam-
phlets, voL 31.]　　　**144 C**

BOND, John James.

Handy-book of rules and tables for verifying dates of historical events, &c.　1869.　12mo.　　　**125 A**

BOND, Thomas.

Topographical and historical sketches of the boroughs of East
and West Looe.　1823.　8vo.　　　**87 A**

BONDS.

Dissertation on and precedents of Bonds.　See Bythewood
and Jarman's Conveyancing, 4th ed., voL 2, 1885, pp. 267–
368.　　　**13 D**

The law of money securities.　By C. Cavanagh.　2nd ed.
1885.　8vo.　　　**11 A**

The laws on negotiable securities.　By H. D. Jencken.　1880.
8vo.　　　**11 A**

The practice in the Court of Bankruptcy relating to Bonds.
By Scrope Ayrton.　1840.　12mo.　　　**160 G**

A Substitute for Sir J. Campbell's summary law for obtaining
judgments on bonds, bills and notes.　By An Attorney.
1835.　[Law Tracts, vol. 8.]　　　**144 E**

BONE, Samuel Vallis.

Precedents in Conveyancing, with an introduction and practical notes.　4 vols. in 2.　1838–40.　8vo.　　　**163 G**

BONNEY, Rev. Henry Kaye.

Historic notices in reference to Fotheringay.　Oundle, 1821.
8vo.　　　**92 D**

BOOKBINDING.

The art of bookbinding.　By J. W. Zaehnsdorf.　1880.　8vo.　**82 B**

BOOK-KEEPING.

A Practical treatise on solicitors' book-keeping by double
entry.　By R. H. Richardson.　3rd ed.　1885.　8vo.　**9 A**

BOOK-KEEPING—*continued.*

. Solicitors' Book-keeping by double entry on the triple column
system. By G. J. Kain. 10th ed. 1884. 12mo.   **9 A**

. The civil service book-keeping. Book-keeping no mystery,
its principles popularly explained. By An experienced
Book-keeper. 2nd ed. 1870. 12mo.   **160 G**

See also BEDFORD, INGLIS, MACKENZIE, OKE, and PRICE.
     160 G

BOOTE, RICHARD.

An Historical treatise of an action or suit at law, and of the
proceedings used in the King's Bench and Common Pleas,
from the original process to judgment. 1766. 8vo. **163 A**

The same. 4th ed. 1805. 8vo.   **163 A**

The same. 5th ed. by W. Ballantine. 1814. 8vo.   **163 A**

The same. 6th ed. by J. A. 1823. 8vo.   **163 A**

BOOTH, GEORGE.

The nature and practice of Real Actions in their writs and
process, original and judicial. 2nd ed. 1811. 8vo. **174 F**

BOOTHBY, BENJAMIN.

A Synopsis of the law relating to Indictable Offences. 2nd
ed. by L. Temple. 1854. 8vo.   **169 A**

BOOTHROYD, BENJAMIN.

The history of ancient borough of Pontefract, containing an interesting account of its castle. Pontefract, 1807. 8vo. **94 B**

BORCHOLTEN, JOHANNES.

Commentaria in quatuor institutionum juris civilis libros.
Geneva, 1640. 4to.   **48 F**

BORLACE, EDMOND.

Latham Spaw in Lancashire, with some remarkable cases and
cures effected by it. 1670. 12mo.   **89 A**

BORLASE, REV. WILLIAM.

Antiquities, historical and monumental, of the county of
Cornwall, with a vocabulary of the Cornu-British language.
2nd ed. 1769. folio.   **87 G**

The natural history of Cornwall. Oxford, 1758. folio. **87 G**

Observations on the ancient and present state of the Islands
of Scilly. Oxford, 1756. 4to.   **86 F**

BOROSCHNAY, Carl Von.
Das Rumänische Handels-Gesetz-Buch vom Jahre 1887. Bukarest, 1887. 12mo. **55 C**

BOROUGH COURT.
Borough Court rules. By P. S. Carey. 1841. 8vo. **160 G**

BOROUGH-ENGLISH.
The custom of Borough-English. See C. I. Elton's Tenures of Kent, 1867, pp. 162–176. **10 B**
See also Descents and Gavelkind.

BOROUGH, Sir John.
Notes of the treaty carried on at Ripon between King Charles I. and the Covenanters of Scotland, A.D. 1640. [Camden Society, vol. 100.] 1869. 8vo. **85 C**
The soveraignty of the British seas proved by records, history, and the municipal laws of this kingdom. 1686. See G. Malynes's Lex Mercatoria. 3rd ed. 1686. folio. **118 G**

BOROUGHS.
An Historical treatise of cities and burghs or boroughs. By Robert Brady. New ed. 1777. 8vo. **84 C**
The history of the boroughs and municipal corporations of the United Kingdom. By H. A. Merewether and A. J. Stephens. 3 vols. 1835. 8vo. **84 C**
History of the boroughs of Great Britain. [By T. H. B. Oldfield.] 2nd ed. 2 vols. 1794. 8vo. **84 C**
Plans of the municipal boroughs of England and Wales, showing their boundaries and division into wards. 1837. folio. **19 D**
Reports from commissioners on proposed division of counties and boundaries of boroughs. 4 vols. 1832. folio. **153 A**
Returns relative to the 120 smallest boroughs at present returning members to parliament. 1832. folio. **153 A**

BORSARI, Luigi.
Il codice Italiano di procedura civile annotato. Torino, 1865. 8vo. **56 D**
La pratica del codice di procedura civile Italiano ossia Formolario degli atti giudiziari più importanti nei procedimenti civili e commerciali. Torino, 1867. 8vo. **56 D**

BORTHWICK, WILLIAM.

An Inquiry into the origins and limitations of the feudal dignities of Scotland. Edinburgh, 1775. 12mo. **125 B**

BOSANQUET, JOHN BERNARD and C. PULLER.

. Reports of Cases argued and determined in the Courts of Common Pleas, and Exchequer Chamber, and in the House of Lords, 1796–1804. 3 vols. 1800–1804. folio.

The same. 3rd ed. 3 vols. 1826. 8vo. **6 B**

New reports of cases in the Court of Common Pleas and other courts, 1804–1807. 2nd ed. 2 vols. 1826. 8vo. **6 B**

BOSANQUET, SAMUEL RICHARD.

The new rules of Pleading. 1835. 12mo. **163 B**

The Tithes commutation act, with explanatory and practical notes. 1837. 12mo. **176 E**

BOSMERE, HAMPSHIRE.

A Topographical account of the hundred of Bosmere. By C. J. Longcroft. 1857. 4to. **88 B**

BOSTON, LINCOLNSHIRE.

Collections for a topographical and historical account of Boston. By Pishey Thompson. 1820. 4to. **90 G**

BOSWELL, EDWARD.

The civil division of the county of Dorset, containing lists of the principal civil magistrates and officers, and a complete Nomina villarum. Sherborne, 1795. 8vo. **87 D**

BOTT, EDMUND.

Decisions of Court of King's Bench upon laws relating to the Poor. 3rd ed. by Francis Const. 2 vols. 1793, and. 6th ed. by J. T. Pratt. 2 vols. 1827. 8vo. **174 A**

BOTTOMRY. See INSURANCE and SHIPPING.

BOUCHER, REV. JONATHAN.

Boucher's Glossary of archaic and provincial words. Edited by Rev. Joseph Hunter, with large additions by Joseph Stevenson. [As far as the word Blade.] 1833. 4to. **123 D**

BOUCHETTE, Joseph.

The British dominions in North America, or a description of
Lower and Upper Canada, New Brunswick, Nova Scotia,
the islands of Newfoundland, Prince Edward, and Cape
Breton. 2 vols. 1832. 4to. **84 D**

A topographical dictionary of the province of Lower Canada.
1832. 4to. **84 D**

. BOUNDARIES.

The law of Boundaries and Fences. By A. J. Hunt. 3rd
ed. by A. Brown. 1884. 12mo. **9 A**

De Finium regundorum actione, eruditorum examini submittit
Johannes Schorer. Traiecti ad Rhenum, 1740. [Latin
Tracts.] **118 E**

BOURDIN, Mark A.

The land tax. 3rd ed. by S. Bunbury. 1885. 12mo. **10 E**

BOURGET, John.

The history of the royal abbey of Bec, near Rouen, in Normandy. 1779. 12mo. **84 A**

BOURKE, Robert.

Decisions of C. S. Lefevre, speaker of the House of Commons,
on points of order, rules of debate, and the general practice
of the House. 2nd ed. 1857. 12mo. **66 B**

BOURKE, Walter M.

Reports of cases in the high court of judicature Bengal in its
original civil side. Calcutta, 1867. 8vo. **38 B**

BOUTELL, Rev. Charles.

Heraldry, historical and popular. 3rd ed. 1864. 8vo.
124 H

BOUVIER, John .

Institutes of American law. 4 vols. 1854. 8vo. **59 A**

A Law dictionary adapted to the constitution and laws of the
United States of America, to which is added Kelham's
Dictionary of the Norman and old French language. 11th
ed. 2 vols. Philadelphia, 1862. 8vo. **59 F**

BOWDITCH, JAMES.
A Series of letters addressed to Thomas Le Breton, Her
Majesty's attorney general, on the state of the laws of the
Channel Islands. 1844. 8vo. **94 F**

BOWEN, HENRY STORER.
Outlines of Specific Performance. 1886. 12mo. **64 E**

BOWER, GEORGE SPENCER and WALTER WEBB.
The law relating to electric lighting. 2nd ed. 1889. 12mo.
9 H

BOWLES, JOHN.
Considerations on the respective rights of judge and jury,
particularly upon trials for libel. 2nd ed. 1791. [Tracts
on law of libel, vol. 4.] **144 F**
A Letter to the Right Hon. C. J. Fox occasioned by his
motion in the House of Commons respecting Libels. 2nd
ed. 1792, and A second letter. 1792. [Tracts on law of
libel, vol. 4.] **144 F**

BOWLES, REV. WILLIAM LISLE and J. G. NICHOLS.
Annals and antiquities of Lacock Abbey, with memorials of
the foundress Ela, Countess of Salisbury, . . . including
notices of the monasteries of Bradenstoke, Hinton and Farley.
1835. 8vo. **93 F**

[BOWMAN, E.]
The English Pleader, being a select collection of various
precedents of declarations, pleas, and issues. By a Gentleman of Lincoln's Inn. 1734. 12mo. **173 E**

BOWYER, GEORGE.
Commentaries on the modern Civil law. 1848. 8vo. **63 F**
A Dissertation on the statutes of the cities of Italy ; and a
translation of the pleading of Prospero Farinacio in defence
of Beatrice Cenci and her relatives. 1838. 8vo. **83 J**

BOYCE, EDMUND.
The Belgian traveller, or a complete guide through the United
Netherlands. 4th ed. 1819. 12mo. **84 A**

BOYD, ALEXANDER CHARLES.
The Merchant Shipping laws. 1876. 8vo. **175 F**

BOYD, Hugh Fenwick and A. B. PEARSON.
The Factors' acts (1823 to 1877). 1884. 8vo. **10 A**

BOYD, Robert.
The office, powers and jurisdiction of His Majesty's Justices of
the Peace and Commissioners of supply. 2 vols. Edinburgh, 1787. 4to. **155 B**

BOYER, Abel.
Le dictionnaire royal, François-Anglois et Anglois-François.
Nouvelle édition, par Louis Du Mitaud. 2 tomes. 1816.
4to. **123 E**
The Political state of Great Britain from 1712–1732. 38 vols.
1714–32. 8vo. **143 D–F**

BOYLE, Herbert Edward.
Précis of an Action at common law. 1881. 8vo. **160 A**

BOYLE, Robert.
The philosophical works of Robert Boyle By Peter Shaw,
M.D. 3 vols. 1725. 8vo. **78 E**

BOYLE, William Robert Augustus.
A Practical treatise on law of Charities. 1837. 8vo. **161 F**

BRABROOK, Edward William.
The law relating to Industrial and Provident Societies, to
which are added, the law of France on the same subject and
remarks on trades unions. 1869. 12mo. **169 A**

BRACTON, Henricus de.
Bracton and his relation to the Roman law. By C. Gülterbock.
Translated by B. Coxe. Philadelphia, 1866. 8vo. **63 F**
De legibus et consuetudinibus Angliæ libri quinque. 1569.
folio. **49 G**
The same. Another ed. 1640. 4to. **49 G**
The same. Edited by Sir Travers Twiss. 6 vols. 1878–83.
8vo. **102 F G**

BRADBY, James.
A Treatise on the law of Distresses. 1808. 12mo. **165 G**

BRADFORD, JOHN.
    The writings of John Bradford, preb. of St. Paul's, Martyr.
    1555. Edited by A. Townsend. Cambridge, 1848. 8vo.

                                                        77 D

BRADSHAW, GEORGE.
    Bradshaw's Railway companion, containing the times of de-
    parture, fares &c. of the railways in England. Manchester,
    1842. 12mo.   **118 A**
    Bradshaw's Railway manual, shareholders' guide and directory,
    for the years 1866, 1868–1872, 1878–1888. 17 vols. 1866–
    88. 12mo.   **146 A B**
    Railway maps of England and Wales. 1845–72. folio. **19 D**

BRADY, REV. JOHN.
    Clavis Calendaria, or a compendious analysis of the calendar,
    illustrated with ecclesiastical, historical, and classical anec-
    dotes. 3rd ed. 2 vols. 1815. 8vo.   **85 G**

BRADY, JOHN HENRY.
    Plain instructions to executors and administrators, with a
    supplement containing an elaborate fictitious will. 3rd ed.
    1830. 8vo.   **168 B**

BRADY, ROBERT.
    An Historical treatise of cities and burghs, or boroughs. 2nd
    ed. 1704. 4to.   **84 F**
    The same. New ed. 1777. 8vo.   **84 C**
    An Introduction to the old English history in three several
    tracts. The First, An answer to Mr. Petyt's Rights of the
    Commons asserted, and to a book intituled Jani Anglorum
    facies nova. The Second, An answer to a book intituled
    Argumentum Antinormanicum, much upon the same sub-
    ject. The Third, The exact history of the succession of
    the Crown of England. 1684. folio.   **115 H**

BRAITHWAITE, THOMAS WOLFE.
    Manual of times of procedure in chancery. 1864. 8vo. **161 B**
    Oaths in chancery. 1854, and 2nd ed. 1864. 12mo. **173 B**
    Oaths in Supreme Court of Judicature. 1876. 12mo. **173 B**
    The same. 4th ed. 1881. 12mo.   **53 B**
    The record and writ practice of the Court of Chancery. 1858.
    8vo   **53 F**

BRAMSTON, Rev. John.
Witham in olden time. Two lectures delivered at the Witham
Literary Institution. Chelmsford, 1855. 12mo.   87 E

BRAMSTON, Sir John.
The autobiography of Sir John Bramston, K.B. Edited by
Lord Braybrooke. [Camden Soc. vol. 32.] 1845. 8vo. 85 A

BRAMWELL, George.
An Analytical table of the private statutes passed between
1727 and 1834. 2 vols. 1813–35. 8vo.   31 E

BRAND, Rev. John.
The history and antiquities of Newcastle-upon-Tyne. 2 vols.
1789. 4to.   .   93 G
Life of Rev. John Brand. See J. P. Malcolm's Lives of
Topographers and Antiquaries. 1815. 4to.   79 H

BRANDENBURGH, House of. See Jacob, Rev. A.

BRANDON, Woodthorpe.
The customary law of Foreign Attachment, and practice of
Mayor's Court of City of London therein. 1861. 8vo. 52 H
Notes of practice of the Mayor's Court of the City of London
in ordinary actions. 1864. 8vo.   172 D

BRANDT, Frederick.
Games, Gaming, and Gamesters' law. 1871. 8vo.   10 B

BRANNON, George.
The pleasure-visitor's companion in surveying the Isle of
Wight. Wootton, 1833. 12mo.   88 A

BRANTINGHAM, Thomas de, Bishop of Exeter.
Issue roll, containing payments made out of his Majesty's
Revenue in 44 Edw. III., A.D. 1370. Translated by F.
Devon. 1835. 4to.   98 A

BRANTÔME, Pierre de Bourdeilles, Seigneur de.
Les vies des dames galantes de son temps. 2 tomes. Leyde
et Amsterdam, 1666–90. 12mo.   79 A

BRANTÔME, P. DE BOURDEILLES, SEIGNEUR DE—*cont.*

Les vies des dames illustres de France de son temps. Leyde, 1699. 12mo. **79 A**

Les vies des hommes illustres et grands capitaines estrangers de son temps. 2 tomes. Leyde, 1699. 12mo. **79 A**

Les vies des hommes illustres et grands capitaines François de son temps. 4 tomes. Leyde, 1699. 12mo. **79 A**

BRASSEUR, ISIDORE.

Grammar of the French language. 17th ed. 1863. 12mo. **255 H**

BRATHWAIT, RICHARD. See BARNABEE'S JOURNAL.

BRAY, EDWARD.

The principles and practice of Discovery. 1885. 8vo. **9 G**

BRAY, REGINALD.

Concise directions for obtaining Lord Chancellor's orders for election and removal of Coroners of counties. 1831. 8vo. **164 G**

Sketch of a bill to promote the extinction of certain manorial tenures and customs in England. 1835. 12mo. **164 F**

BRAY, WILLIAM.

Sketch of a tour into Derbyshire and Yorkshire; including part of the counties of Buckingham, Warwick, Leicester, Nottingham, Northampton, Bedford, and Hertford. 2nd ed. 1783. 8vo. **87 A**

BRAYLEY, EDWARD WEDLAKE.

A Concise account, historical and descriptive, of Lambeth Palace. 1806. 4to. **91 G**

Delineations, historical and topographical, of the Isle of Thanet and Cinque Ports. 2 vols. 1817–18. 8vo. **88 D**

Delineations, topographical, historical, and descriptive, of Kent. 2 vols. 1808. 8vo. **88 D**

The history and antiquities of the abbey church of St. Peter Westminster. Illustrated by J. P. Neale. 2 vols. 1818–23. folio. **91 H**

Topographical history of Surrey. 5 vols. 1850. 4to. **93 D**

BRAYLEY, Edward Wedlake—*continued.*
The same. Revised and edited by Edward Walford. 4 vols.
[1878 &c.] 4to. **93 G**
London and Middlesex, or an historical, commercial, and descriptive survey of the metropolis of Great Britain. By
E. W. Brayley, Rev. J. Nightingale and J. N. Brewer.
4 vols. in 5. 1810–16. 8vo. **90 B**

BRAYLEY, Edward Wedlake and John BRITTON.
Delineations, topographical, historical, and descriptive, of Bed-
fordshire, Berkshire, and Buckinghamshire. 1 vol. bound
in 3 vols. 1801. 8vo. **86 B**
Delineations . . . of Cambridgeshire, Cheshire, and Cornwall.
1 vol. bound in 3 vols. 1801. 8vo. **86 E**
Delineations . . . of Cumberland, the Isle of Man, and
Derbyshire. 1 vol. bound in 2 vols. 1802. 8vo. **87 A**
The history of the ancient palace and late Houses of Parlia-
ment at Westminster. 1836. 8vo. **91 F**

BREACH OF PRIVILEGE.
Speech of J. W. Freshfield, Esq., M.P. in the House of Commons, August 1, 1839. 1839. [Pamphlets, vol. 28.] **144 B**

BREACH OF PROMISE.
Breach of promise, its history and social considerations. By
C. J. MacColla. 1879. 12mo. **78 A**
See Husband and Wife and Marriage.

BREAD.
Report from select committee on existing regulations relative
to making and sale of Bread. 1821. folio. **153 A**
What should be the price of Bread? and how can it be regulated? By J. H. James. 1855. [Pamphlets, vol. 10.]
144 A

BRECKNOCKSHIRE.
A History of the county of Brecknock. By Theophilus Jones.
2 vols. Brecknock, 1805–1809. 4to. **95 G**

BRENT, John.
Canterbury in the olden time. 2nd ed. 1879. 8vo. **88 C**

BRENTANO, Lujo.
On the history and development of gilds, and the origin of trade-unions. 1870. 8vo. **78 B**

BRETHERTON, Edward.
Manual of laws affecting qualification and registration of Parliamentary Voters, with practice of revising courts. 1863. 8vo. **166 D**

BRETT, Thomas.
The Bankruptcy act 1883 with notes. 1884. 12mo. **160 E**
Leading cases in Modern Equity. 1887. 8vo. **64 D**
See also CLERKE, A. St. J.

BREWER, James Norris.
A Topographical and historical description of the county of Oxford. 1819. 8vo. **92 E**

BREWER, Thomas. See CARPENTER, John.

BREWSTER, Rev. John.
The parochial history and antiquities of Stockton upon Tees. Stockton, 1796. 4to. **87 D**

BRICE, Andrew.
The Mobiad, or battle of the voice, an heroi-comic poem sportively satirical, being a description of an Exeter election. By Democritus Juvenal, vulgarly Andrew Brice. Exon, 1770. 8vo. **87 C**

BRICE, Seward.
The doctrine of Ultra Vires, being an investigation of the principles which limit the capacities, powers, and liabilities of Corporations. 1874. 8vo. **169 D**
The same. 2nd ed. 1877. 8vo. **9 F**

BRICKDALE, Matthew Inglett Fortescue.
The leases and sales of settled estates act [19 & 20 Vict. cap. 120] with notes, and a supplement containing the amending act 21 & 22 Vict. c. 77. 1861. 12mo. **175 E**

BRIDGES.
The law relating to Highways and Bridges. By W. C. Glen and A. Glen. 1883. 8vo. **10 B**

BRIDGES—*continued.*

The law of Highways in England and Wales, including bridges and locomotives. By Thomas Baker. 1880. 8vo. **52 H**

BRIDGES, JOHN.

The history and antiquities of Northamptonshire compiled from the manuscript collections of J. Bridges. By Rev. Peter Whalley. 2 vols. Oxford, 1791. folio. **92 H**

BRIDGES, WILLIAM THOMAS.

A Handy book for Justices of the Peace. 2nd ed. 1879. 12mo. **170 A**

BRIDGEWATER TREATISES.

The Bridgewater Treatises on the power, wisdom, and goodness of God, as manifested in the Creation. 12 vols. 1833–36. 8vo. **77 B**

BRIDGMAN, SIR JOHN.

Reports of Sir John Bridgman [in the Court of Common Pleas, 1613–1621]. 1659. folio. **74 B**

BRIDGMAN, SIR ORLANDO.

Conveyances being select precedents of deeds and instruments concerning the most considerable estates in England. 1682. folio. **118 F**

The same. 3rd ed. 1699. folio. **157 C**

The same. 5th ed. 2 vols. bound in 1. 1725. folio. **157 C**

Reports of judgments by Sir O. Bridgman. 1660–1667. Edited by Saxe Bannister. 1823. 8vo. **6 B**

BRIDGMAN, RICHARD ORLANDO.

A Digest of the reported cases on points of practice and pleading in Courts of Equity in England and Ireland, with Supplement by R. Scott. 2 vols. 1824–32. 8vo. **63 B**

BRIDGMAN, RICHARD WHALLEY.

An Analytical Digested index of the Reported Cases in the several courts of Equity, as well Chancery as Exchequer, and in the High Court of Parliament, distinctly showing the various points therein adjudged. 2 vols. 1805. 8vo.

The same. 3rd ed. with Supplement by Robert Scott. 4 vols. 1822–32. 8vo. **63 B**

Reflections on the study of the law. 1804. 12mo. **171 A**

BRIDGMAN, RICHARD WHALLEY—*continued.*

A Short view of legal bibliography. 1807. 8vo.   **82 C**

Thesaurus Juridicus : containing the Decisions of the several Courts of Equity, and of the High Court of Parliament, upon Petitions and Appeals, from the Revolution to Easter Term 1798. Vols. 1 and 2 [no more published]. 1799–1800. 8vo.

BRIDLINGTON, YORKSHIRE.

Historical sketches of Bridlington. By J. Thompson. Bridlington, 1821. 12mo.   **94 A**

BRIGHT, JOHN.

Letter to John Bright, Esq., M.P. By W. L. Sargent, one of his constituents. 1861. [Pamphlets, vol. 13.]   **144 A**

BRIGHT, JOHN EDWARD.

The law of Husband and Wife as respects property. 2 vols. 1849. 8vo.   **52 H**

BRIGHT, REV. JOHN SHENTON.

A History of Dorking and the neighbouring parishes. 1884. 8vo.   **93 D**

BRIGHTLY, FREDERICK CHARLES.

Bankrupt law of United States. Philadelphia, 1869. 8vo.   **59 B**

A Digest of decisions of Federal courts from organisation of the government to 1868. Philadelphia, 1868. 8vo.   **59 C**

BRIGHTON, SUSSEX.

An Epitome of Brighton, topographical and descriptive. By Richard Sickelmore. Brighton, [1815]. 12mo.   **93 E**

BRIMHAM ROCKS, YORKSHIRE.

An Historical and descriptive account of Brimham Rocks. 2nd ed. Ripon, 1839. 12mo.   **94 A**

[BRINDLEY, JAMES.]

The history of Inland Navigations, particularly those of the Duke of Bridgwater in Lancashire and Cheshire. 1766, and 2nd ed. 1769. 12mo.   **86 A**

BRISTOL, GLOUCESTERSHIRE.

The Bristol charities from the farther report of the Commissioners for enquiring concerning charities, with introductions and notes. By a Barrister. 1822. 12mo. **88 A**

The Bristol memorialist. By William Tyson. Bristol, 1823. 8vo. **88 A**

Bristol. The city charters, containing the original institution of mayors, recorders, sheriffs, and all other officers whatsoever, as also of a Common-council and the ancient laws and customs of the city. Bristol, 1736. 4to. **87 F**

The Childe of Bristow, a poem by John Lydgate. Edited by C. Hopper. [Camden Soc., vol. 73.] 1859. 8vo. **85 B**

A Chronological outline of the history of Bristol. By John Evans. Bristol, 1824. 4to. **87 F**

Historic towns. Bristol. By Wm. Hunt. 1887. 8vo. **88 A**

The history of Bristol, civil and ecclesiastical. By John Corry and Rev. John Evans. 2 vols. Bristol, 1816. 8vo. **87 F**

The Maire of Bristowe is Kalendar. By Robert Ricart, town clerk of Bristol 18 Edward IV. Edited by L. T. Smith. [Camden Soc., n.s. vol. 5.] 1872. 8vo. **85 C**

Mathews's Complete Bristol guide. 7th ed. Bristol, 1828. 12mo. **88 A**

Memoirs, historical and topographical, of Bristol and its neighbourhood. By Rev. Samuel Seyer. 2 vols. Bristol, 1821–23. 4to. **87 F**

The Poll-book, being a list of the freeholders and freemen who voted at the last election for the city and county of Bristol. Bristol, 1739. 8vo. **107 J**

A Popular history of Bristol. By George Pryce. Bristol, 1861. 8vo. **87 F**

Restoration of the church of St. Mary, Redcliffe, Bristol : An appeal by the vicar, with an abstract of reports by Messrs. Britton and Hosking. Bristol, 1842. 4to. **87 F**

BRISTOL, SIR JOHN, 1 EARL OF.

The Earl of Bristol's Defence of his negotiations in Spain. Edited by S. R. Gardiner. [Camden Society, vol. 104.] 1871. 8vo. **85 C**

BRISTOWE, JOHN SYER.

A Treatise on the theory and practice of Medicine. 6th ed. 1887. 8vo. **78 E**

BRISTOWE, LEONARD SYER and W. I. COOK.
The law of charities and mortmain. 1889. 8vo. **9 B**

BRISTOWE, SAMUEL BOTELER.
Private bill legislation. 1859. 12mo. **173 B**

BRITISH MUSEUM.
An Act for purchase of museum, or collection of Sir Hans
Sloane, and of Harleian collection of manuscripts, and other
acts and rules relating to British Museum. 1768. 12mo. **92 A**

Acts and votes of parliament relating to the British Museum,
with the statutes and rules thereof. 1805. 8vo. **92 A**

Handbook to the library of the British Museum. By Richard
Sims. 1854. 8vo. **82 H**

Regulations for the general security of the Museum. By
E. A. Bond. 1879. 8vo. **92 A**

Some observations upon the recent addition of a reading room
to British Museum. By Wm. Hosking. 1858. folio. **92 G**

Strictures on the minutes of evidence taken before the select
committee on the British Museum. By Edward Edwards.
1836. [Law Tracts, vol. 4.] **144 E**

Catalogue of Arundel MSS. 2 vols. 1834–41. folio. **81 H**

Catalogue of Burney MSS. 2 vols. 1840–41. folio. **81 H**

Catalogue of manuscript maps, charts and plans of topographical drawings. 2 vols. 1844. 8vo. **81 G**

Catalogue of MS. music. [By T. Oliphant.] 1842. 8vo. **81 G**

Catalogue of manuscripts formerly in the possession of Francis
Hargrave. 1818. 4to. **82 I**

Catalogue of MSS. of King's library, and an appendix to catalogue of Cottonian library. By D. Casley. 1734. 4to. **118 F**

Catalogue of MSS. preserved in British Museum hitherto undescribed. By Rev. S. Ayscough. 2 vols. 1782. 4to. **82 I**

Catalogus codicum manuscriptorum orientalium. 4 vols. 1838–
47. folio. **81 H**

List of additions to the manuscripts in British Museum, 1836–
1845. 2 vols. 1843–50. 8vo. **81 G**

Catalogue of maps, prints, &c., forming geographical and
topographical collection attached to library of George III.
1829. folio. **81 H**

The same. Another ed. 2 vols. 1829. 8vo. **81 G**

Catalogue of printed books in the British Museum. vol. 1.
Letter A. 1841. folio. **81 H**

BRITISH MUSEUM—*continued.*

Librorum impressorum qui in Museo Britannico adservantur, Catalogus. 7 vols. in 8 vols. 1813–19. 8vo. **82 H**

A List of books of reference in reading room of British Museum. 1859. 8vo. **82 H**

The same. 3rd ed. revised. 1889. 8vo. **82 H**

BRITTON OR BRETON, JOHN LE.

Britton. Containing the antient Pleas of the Crown. Translated by Robert Kelham. 1762. 8vo. **53 C**

Britton. The French text carefully revised, with an English translation and notes. By F. M. Nichols. 2 vols. Oxford, 1865. 8vo. **167 A**

See also D. Houard's Coutumes Anglo-Normandes, vol. 4, 1776, pp. 1–462. **40 A**

BRITTON, JOHN.

The Britton testimonial. An account of a public dinner given to John Britton at Castle hotel, Richmond, with preface by T. E. Jones. 1846. [Pamphlets, vol. 16.] **144 B**

A Dictionary of the architecture and archæology of the middle ages. 1838. 8vo. **123 C**

Essay on topographical literature, with accounts of sources, objects, and uses of national and local records and glossaries of words used in ancient writings. n.d. 4to. **85 I**

Memoir of John Aubrey, F.R.S. 1845. 4to. **79 H**

A Topographical and historical description of the county of Lancaster. 1815. 8vo. **89 B**

See also BRAYLEY, E. W.

BROCAS FAMILY.

The family of Brocas, of Beaurepaire and Roche Court. By Montagu Burrows. 1886. 8vo. **79 H**

BRODERIP, WILLIAM JOHN and PEREGRINE BINGHAM.

Reports of cases in the Court of Common Pleas and other courts, 1819–1822. 3 vols. 1820–22. 8vo. **6 C**

BRODRICK, GEORGE CHARLES.

English land and English landlords. An enquiry into the origin and character of the English land system, with proposals for its reform. 1881. 8vo. **83 J**

BRODRICK, George Charles—*continued.*

Memorials of Merton college, with biographical notices of the wardens and fellows. [Oxford Historical Society, vol. 4.] Oxford, 1885. 8vo. **85 F**

BROKERS. See Agency.

BROMLEY, Henry.

A Catalogue of engraved British portraits, from Egbert the Great to the present time. 1793. 4to. **127 J**

BROMLEY, Kent.

Outlines of the history and antiquities of Bromley. By John Dunkin. Bromley, 1815. 8vo. **88 C**

BROMPTON, John, Abbot of Jervaux.

Chronicon ab anno Domini 588 usque annum Domini 1198. See Scriptores Decem Hist. Angl. vol. 1, 1652, pp. 725–1284. **114 H**

BROOKE or BROOKESWORTHE, Ralphe.

A Catalogue and succession of the kings, princes, dukes, &c. of England since the Norman conquest. 1619. folio. **127 J**

The same. 2nd ed. 1622. folio. **127 J**

A Discoverie of certain errours in the much commended Britannia, 1594, very prejudiciall to the discentes and successions of the auncient nobilitie of this realm. To which is added, The learned Mr. Camden's Answer to this book. 1723. 8vo. **84 B**

BROOKE, Richard.

The office and practice of a Notary of England as connected with mercantile instruments. 1839, and 3rd ed. by Leone Levi. 1867. 8vo. **173 A**

The same. 4th ed. by Leone Levi. 1876. 8vo. **11 A**

BROOKE, Sir Robert.

La Graunde Abridgement. 1576 and 1586. 4to. **158 D**

The reading of Robert Brooke upon the stat. of Magna Charta, chap. 16. 1641. [Law Tracts and Arguments.] **144 F**

Some new cases written out of the great abridgement. Composed by and translated into English by John March. 1651. 12mo. **48 B**

BROOKE, William Graham.
The Public Worship regulation act, 1874, with notes. 1874.
12mo. **166 B**

Six judgments of the judicial committee of the privy council
in ecclesiastical cases, 1850–1872, with an historical introduction. 1872. 8vo. **50 B**

BROOM, Herbert.
Commentaries on the Common law, designed as introductory
to its study. 1856. 8vo. **161 F**
The same. 5th ed. 1875, and 6th ed. 1880. 8vo. **161 F**
The same. 7th ed. by W. F. A. Archibald and H. W. Greene.
1884, and 8th ed. by the same. 1888. 8vo. **64 A**
Constitutional law viewed in relation to common law and
exemplified by cases. 1866. 8vo. **163 D**
The same. 2nd ed. by G. L. Denman. 1885. 8vo. **64 B**
The Philosophy of Law. 2nd ed. 1878. 12mo. **63 G**
The same. 3rd ed. by J. C. H. Flood. 1883. 12mo. **63 G**
A Selection of Legal Maxims, classified and illustrated.
2nd ed. 1848. 8vo. **172 D**
The same. 3rd ed. 1858, and 4th ed. 1864. 8vo. **172 D**
The same. 6th ed. by H. F. Manisty and C. Cagney. 1884.
8vo. **64 E**

BROOM, Herbert and E. A. Hadley.
Commentaries on laws of England. 4 vols. 1869. 8vo. **167 A**

BROUGHAM, Henry Peter, 1 Baron.
A Bibliographical list of Lord Brougham's publications. By
the author of 'The handbook of fictitious names.' [Ralph
Thomas.] Privately printed. 1873. 12mo. **82 B**
The British constitution, its history, structure, and working.
1861. 8vo. **116 B**
An Inquiry into the colonial policy of the European powers.
2 vols. Edinburgh, 1803. 8vo. **116 B**
Is allegiance by birth affected in England by naturalization
in France? Opinions of M. Cremieux and others on Lord
Brougham's application in the year 1848 for French letters
of naturalization. By M. D. Hill. Bristol, 1869. [Pamph-
lets, vol. 31.] **144 C**
The life and times of Henry Lord Brougham written by himself. 3 vols. 1872–71. 8vo. **80 C**

BROUGHAM, H. P., 1 BARON—*continued.*

Life of Lord Brougham. See Lord Campbell's Lives of the lord chancellors, vol. viii., 1869, pp. 213–596. **79 G**

Misrepresentations in Campbell's Lives of Lyndhurst and Brougham. Corrected by St. Leonards. 1869. 8vo. **79 G**

Lord Brougham's acts and bills from 1811 to the present time. Collected and arranged by Sir J. E. Eardley-Wilmot. 1857. 8vo. **83 J**

Present state of the law. Speech in the House of Commons on Thursday, February 7, 1828. 1828. 8vo. **116 B**

The same. 2nd ed. 1828. [Pamphlets, vol. 2.] **144 A**

Speech in the House of Lords on Friday, May 12, 1848, on legislation and the law. 1848. 8vo. **83 J**

BROWN, ARCHIBALD.

An Epitome and analysis of Savigny's treatise on obligations in Roman law. 1872. 8vo. **63 G**

The law of Fixtures. 1871, and 2nd ed. 1872. 12mo. **168 E**

The same. 3rd ed., embracing the Agricultural holdings act 1875. 1875. 12mo. **168 E**

The same. 4th ed. 1881. 8vo. **10 A**

A New law dictionary and institute of the whole law. 2nd ed. 1880. 8vo. **64 E**

The practice of Supreme Court under Judicature acts 1873 to 1883, with forms of all proceedings. 1883. 8vo. **169 F**

See also SNELL, E. H. T.

BROWN, CORNELIUS.

The annals of Newark-upon-Trent, comprising the history, curiosities, and antiquities. 1879. 4to. **92 E**

BROWN, H. ROWLAND.

The beauties of Lyme Regis, Charmouth, the land-slip and their vicinities, topographically and historically considered. Lyme Regis, [1860]. 12mo. **87 C**

BROWN, JOSIAH.

Reports of Cases upon Appeals and Writs of Error determined in the High Court of Parliament, from the year 1701 to 1779. 7 vols. 1779–83. folio.

The same. Another ed. 7 vols. Dublin, 1784–89. 8vo.

The same. 2nd ed. with notes and many additional cases brought down to the year 1800. By T. E. Tomlins. 8 vols. 1803. 8vo. **1 A B**

BROWN, Mungo Ponton.
General synopsis of the decisions of the Court of Session from
its institution until November 1827. 4 vols. 1829. 4to.

BROWN, Rawdon.
Calendar of state papers and manuscripts relating to English
affairs existing in the archives and collections of Venice
and in other libraries of Northern Italy, 1202–1558. 8 vols.
1864–84. 8vo.   97 F G

BROWN, Thomas.
Miscellanea Aulica : or a collection of State-Treatises never
before publish'd. 1702. 12mo.   145 B

BROWN, Sir Thomas, M.D.
Life of Sir T. Brown. See J. P. Malcolm's Lives of Topographers and Antiquaries. 1815. 4to.   79 H

BROWN, William, Clerk of Court of Common Pleas.
The clerk's Tutor in Chancery. 2nd ed. 1694. 12mo. 49 D
The entring clerk's Introduction, being a collection of such
precedents of pleadings with process as are generally used
in every days practice. 3rd ed. 1702. 12mo.   49 C
The entring clerk's Vade Mecum, being an exact collection of
precedents for declarations and pleadings in most actions.
2nd ed. 1695. 12mo.   49 C
Formulae bene Placitandi. A Book of Entries, containing
variety of choice Precedents of Counts, Declarations, &c.
In two parts. 2nd ed. 1675. folio.
Modus transferendi status per recorda. A complete collection
of choice precedents for Fines upon writs of covenant, and
common recoveries upon writs of entry in the post in all
cases. . . . 1698. 12mo.   168 D
The same reprinted. 1700. 12mo.   168 D
The same. 6th ed. 1725. 12mo.   168 D

BROWN, William, of the Inner Temple.
Reports of cases in the High Court of Chancery, from 18 Geo.
III. 1778 to 34 Geo. III. 1794, during the time of Lord
Chancellor Thurlow. 4 vols. 1785–95. folio.
The same. 5th ed. by R. Belt. 4 vols. 1820. 8vo. 2 C D

BROWN, William, of Gray's Inn.
  The law of limitation as to real property. 1869. 8vo. 53 A

BROWNE, Arthur.
  A Compendious view of the civil law and of the law of the
    admiralty. 2nd ed. 2 vols. 1802. 8vo.   48 F

BROWNE, George.
  The principles and practice of the court for Divorce and
    Matrimonial causes. 1864. 8vo.   166 A
  The same. 2nd ed. 1868. 8vo.   166 A
  The same. 4th ed. 1880. 8vo.   52 E
  The same. 5th ed. by L. D. Powles. 1889. 8vo.   12 D
  The principles and practice of the Court of Probate in con-
    tentious and non-contentious business. 1873. 8vo.   174 C
  The same. 2nd ed. by L. D. Powles. 1881. 8vo.   12 D

BROWNE, George Lathom.
  A Treatise on the Companies act 1862, with special reference
    to winding-up. 1867. 8vo.   169 D
  Reports of trials for murder by poisoning. By G. L. Browne
    and C. G. Stewart. 1883. 8vo.   50 B

BROWNE, John.
  The practice of Court of Chancery. 2 vols. 1830. 12mo.
                                                         161 B

BROWNE, John Hutton Balfour.
  The law of railway companies. By J. H. B. Browne and
    H. S. Theobald. 1881. 8vo.   175 A
  The same. 2nd ed. 1888. 8vo.   11 D
  The law of Usages and Customs. 1875. 8vo.   11 I
  On the compulsory purchase of the undertakings of companies
    by corporations. 1876. 8vo.   52 C
  Practice before the railway commissioners. 1876. 8vo. 12 A
  The principles of the law of Rating of hereditaments in the
    occupation of companies. 1875. 8vo.   175 B
  The same. 2nd ed. by J. H. B. Browne and D. N. McNaughton.
    1886. 8vo.   11 D
  A Treatise on the law of Carriers. 1873. 8vo.   52 B

BROWNE, J. H. B. and W. H. MACNAMARA.
Reports of Cases decided by the Railway Commissioners.
vols. iv. to vi. 1885–89. 8vo. **3 C**

BROWNE, RICHARD GEORGE MACKLEY.
Admiralty procedure against merchant ships and cargoes.
1887. 8vo. **12 D**

BROWNING, WILLIAM ERNST.
An Exposition of the laws of marriage and divorce. 1872.
8vo. **10 H**
The practice and procedure of the court for Divorce and
Matrimonial causes. 1862. 12mo. **166 A**

BROWNING, W. E. and VERNON LUSHINGTON.
Reports of cases in the Court of Admiralty, and on appeal to
the Privy Council, 1863–1865. 1 vol. 1868. 8vo. **8 A**

BROWNLOW, RICHARD.
Brownlow Latine Redivivus. A Book of Entries of Declara-
tions, Informations, &c. contained in the Declarations and
Pleadings of Richard Brownlow, unskilfully turned into
English and printed in the years 1653 and 1654, now pub-
lished in Latin, their original language. 1693. folio.

BROWNLOW, RICHARD and JOHN GOLDESBOROUGH.
Reports of divers choice cases in law [in the Common Pleas
1589–1624]. Part 1, 3rd ed. 1675. Part 2, 2nd ed. 1675.
2 parts. 1675. 4to. **74 B**

BRUCE, WILLIAM DOWNING.
An Act to facilitate proof of title to, and conveyance of, real
estates . . . with notes and references. 1862. 8vo. **170 C**

BRUNET, JACQUES CHARLES.
Manuel du Libraire. 4me éd. 5 vols. 1842–44, and Supplément. Par P. Deschamps et G. Brunet. 2 vols. 1878–80.
7 vols. Paris, 1842–80. 8vo. **82 G**

BRUNSWICK, HOUSE OF.
History of most serene house of Brunswick-Lunenburgh in all
the branches thereof, from its origin to death of Queen
Anne. By D. J. [David Jones.] 1715. 8vo. **79 B**
See also JACOB, REV. A.

BRYAN, MICHAEL.
Dictionary of painters and engravers, biographical and critical.
New ed. by R. E. Graves and W. Armstrong. 2 vols.
1886–89. 8vo. **79 H**

BRYCE, JAMES.
The American Commonwealth. 3 vols. 1888. 8vo. **116 F**

BRYDALL, JOHN.
Camera regis, or a short view of London. 1676. 12mo. **91 B**
Decus et Tutamen, or a prospect of the laws of England.
1679. 12mo. **48 D**
Jus imaginis apud Anglos, or the law of England relating to
the nobility and gentry. 1675. 12mo. **48 D**
Non compos mentis, or the law relating to natural fools, mad
folks, and lunatick persons. 1700. 12mo. **48 D**

BRYDGES, SIR SAMUEL EGERTON.
A Review of the Chandos peerage case adjudicated 1803, and
of the pretensions of Sir S. E. Brydges, Bart. to designate
himself per legem terræ Baron Chandos of Sudeley. By
G. F. Beltz. 1834. 8vo. **124 F**

BUCHANAN, WILLIAM.
A Historical and genealogical essay upon the family and
surname of Buchanan. Glasgow, 1723. 8vo. **79 B**

BUCK, JOHN WILLIAM.
Cases in Bankruptcy, 1816–1820. 1 vol. 1820. 8vo. **8 B**

BUCKHOUNDS, ROYAL.
The hereditary masters of the royal buckhounds. See M.
Burrows's The family of Brocas, 1886, pp. 247–264. **79 H**

BUCKINGHAM, GEORGE, 1 DUKE OF.
Documents illustrating impeachment of Duke of Buckingham
in 1626. Edited by S. R. Gardiner. [Camden Society,
n.s. vol. 45.] 1889. 8vo. **85 E**
The fate of favourites exemplified in the fall of Villiers, Duke
of Buckingham, 1734. [Grimaldi's Tracts, vol. 1.] **118 B**

BUCKINGHAM, JOHN, 1 DUKE OF.

A Character of John Sheffield, late Duke of Buckinghamshire, with an account of the pedigree of the Sheffield
family. *1729*. [Grimaldi's Tracts, vol. 3.]   **118 B**

BUCKINGHAMSHIRE.

A Concise topographical account of Buckinghamshire. By
Rev. D. Lysons and S. Lysons. 1813. 4to.   **86 B**

Delineations of Buckinghamshire. By E. W. Brayley and
J. Britton. 1801. 8vo.   **86 B**

The history and antiquities of the county of Buckingham.
By George Lipscomb. 4 vols. 1847. 4to.   **86 G**

The history and antiquities of the town, hundred and deanery
of Buckingham. By Browne Willis. 1755. 4to.   **86 C**

History and topography of Buckinghamshire. By James
Joseph Sheahan. 1862. 8vo.   **86 C**

See BAWDWEN, REV. W., BRAY, W. and WILLIS, B.

BUCKLAND, REV. WILLIAM.

Geology and mineralogy considered with reference to natural
theology. 2 vols. 1836. 8vo.   **77 B**

BUCKLE, HENRY THOMAS.

History of Civilisation in England. vol. 1. 3rd ed. 1861.
vol. 2. 2nd ed. 1864. 2 vols. 1861–64. 8vo.   **116 G**

[BUCKLER, REV. BENJAMIN.]

Stemmata Chicheleana, or a genealogical account of some of
the families derived from Thomas Chichele. Oxford, 1765.
4to.   **127 J**

BUCKLEY, HENRY BURTON. .

The law and practice under the Companies acts 1862, 1867,
1870, and other acts relating to Joint Stock companies.
1873. 8vo.   **169 D**

The same. 2nd ed. 1875, and 3rd ed. 1879. 8vo.   **169 D**

The same. 4th ed. 1883. 8vo.   **52 C**

The same. 5th ed. 1887. 8vo.   **9 D**

BUCKNILL, JOHN CHARLES.

Notes on asylums for insane in America. 1876. 12mo.   **78 A**

BUDDHISM.

Buddhism, its history and tenets. See T. A. Wise's Paganism in Caledonia, 1884, pp. 141–196. **85 I**

BUILDING.

The law relating to Buildings, building leases, and building contracts. By Alfred Emden. 2nd ed. 1885. 8vo. **9 B**

A Digest of cases relating to the construction of buildings. By E. S. Roscoe. 2nd ed. 1883. 8vo. **9 B**

On Building Contracts. A legal handbook for architects, builders, and building owners. By E. Jenkins and J. Raymond. 1873. 12mo. **9 B**

Are Building Leases a fraud? A surveyor's thoughts upon a question of the day. By John McLaren. n.d. [Pamphlets, vol. 31.] **144 C**

Laxton's builders' price book for 1869. By William Laxton. 51st ed. 1869. 12mo. **146 E**

See also SARGANT, C. H.

BUILDING SOCIETIES.

The acts relating to Building Societies. By E. A. Wurtzburg. 1886. 8vo. **9 B**

The directory of Building Societies. Compiled by Horace Kent and V. M. Braund, 1885–6. 1885. 12mo. **146 D**

The law and practice of Building and Land Societies. By H. F. A. Davis. 3rd ed. 1884. 8vo. **9 B**

The law of Building Societies. By A. Scratchley and E. W. Brabrook. 2nd ed. 1882. 12mo. **9 B**

See also BARRY, JAMES, PRATT, ROUSE, and STONE. **161 A**

BULLAR, JOHN.

An Historical and picturesque guide to the Isle of Wight. Southampton, 1806. 12mo. **88 A**

BULLEN, EDWARD and S. M. LEAKE.

Precedents of Pleadings in actions in the superior courts of common law. 1860, and 2nd ed. 1863. 8vo. **173 E**

The same. 3rd ed. 1868. 8vo. **53 C**

The same. 4th ed. adapted to the present practice in the Q.B. division of the high court. Part 1 by T. J. Bullen and Cyril Dodd. 1882. Part 2 by T. J. Bullen and C. W. Clifford. 1888. 2 vols. 1882–88. 8vo. **12 E**

BULLER, Sir Francis.
An Institute of the law relative to trials at Nisi Prius. New
ed. by Arthur Onslow. 1789. 8vo. **173 A**
An Introduction to the law relative to trials at Nisi Prius.
2nd ed. 1775, and 4th ed. 1785. 4to. **157 B**
The same. 5th ed. 1790, and 6th ed. 1793. 8vo. **173 A**
The same. 7th ed. by R. W. Bridgman. 1817. 8vo. **53 B**

BULLEY, John Frederick and J. W. W. Bund.
Manual of law and practice of Bankruptcy. 1870. 12mo. **160 E**

BULLINGBROOKE, Edward.
Ecclesiastical law, or the statutes, constitutions, canons, ru-
bricks and articles of the Church of Ireland. 2 vols.
Dublin, 1770. 4to. **77 F**

BULLINGER, Henry.
The Decades of H. Bullinger, minister of the church of Zurich.
Edited by Rev. Thomas Harding. 4 vols. Cambridge,
1849–52. 8vo. **77 E**

BULLINGTON, Oxfordshire.
The history and antiquities of hundreds of Bullington and
Ploughley. By John Dunkin. 2 vols. 1823. 4to. **92 F.**

BULLION, GOLD.
Report, with minutes of evidence and accounts, from select
committee on high price of gold bullion. 1810. 8vo. **78 D**
Observations on Report of bullion committee. By Sir John
Sinclair. 2nd ed. 1810. [Jacob's Tracts, vol. 13.] **144 F**

BULLOCK, H. A.
History of the Isle of Man. 1816. 8vo. **94 F**

BULLOCK, Stanley.
Practical working of Municipal corporation and public health
acts exemplified in case of Le Feuvre *versus* Lankester.
1854. [Pamphlets, vol. 9, pt. 2.] **144 A**

BULSTRODE, Edward.
Reports of divers resolutions and judgments given in the court
of King's Bench, 1609–1639. 2nd ed. 1688. folio. **74 B**

BUNBURY, WILLIAM.

Reports of Cases in the Court of Exchequer, from 1 Geo. I. to
14 Geo. II. Published by G. Wilson. 1755. folio.
The same. 2nd ed. Dublin, 1793. 8vo. **7 C**

BUND, JOHN WILLIAM WILLIS.

The law of compensation for unexhausted agricultural im-
provements. 2nd ed. 1883. 12mo. **160 B**
The law relating to the salmon fisheries of England and
Wales. 1873. 8vo. **10 A**

[BUNNY, J.]

The history and antiquities of Newbury and its environs,
including twenty-eight parishes situate in the county of
Berks. Speenhamland, 1839. 8vo. **86 B**

BUNYAN, JOHN.

The Pilgrim's Progress from this world to that which is to
come. Edited by Rev. R. Philip. [1843.] 8vo. **77 B**

BUNYON, CHARLES JOHN.

Law of Fire Insurance. 1867, and 2nd ed. 1875. 8vo. **169 A**
The same. 3rd ed. 1885. 8vo. **10 D**
The law of Life Assurance. 1854. 8vo. **169 A**
The same. 2nd ed. 1868. 8vo. **10 D**

BURDETT, SIR FRANCIS.

Biographical sketch of Sir Francis Burdett (extracted from
the Universal Magazine). 1807. 8vo. **79 C**
An Exposition of circumstances which gave rise to election of
Sir F. Burdett for city of Westminster. 1807. 8vo. **79 C**
A Full account of the proceedings at the Middlesex election.
2nd ed. 1804. 8vo. **79 C**
Memoirs of the life of Sir Francis Burdett. 1810. 8vo. **79 C**
The plan of Reform proposed by Sir F. Burdett correctly
reported in two speeches in parliament. 1809. 8vo. **79 C**
Sir F. Burdett to his constituents, denying power of House of
Commons to imprison people of England. 1810. 8vo. **79 C**
Sir F. Burdett's Address to the Prince Regent, as proposed
in House of Commons, 7 Jan. 1812. 1812. 8vo. **79 C**
The spirited address of Sir Francis Burdett to his constituents,

BURDETT, SIR FRANCIS—*continued.*

the electors of Westminster, previous to his re-election for
the new parliament. 1812. 8vo. **79 C**

See also YORK, FREDERICK, 1 DUKE OF.

BURDETT, HENRY C.

Burdett's Official Intelligence, being a carefully compiled
précis of information regarding British, American and
foreign stocks, 1882–1889. 8 vols. 1882–89. 4to. **142 D**

BURGE, WILLIAM.

Commentaries on colonial and foreign laws generally, and in
their conflict with each other and with the law of England.
4 vols. 1838. 8vo. **55 D**

Observations on the supreme appellate jurisdiction of Great
Britain, as exercised by the courts of the Queen in council
and the House of Lords. 1841. 8vo. **55 D**

The Temple Church, an account of its restoration and repairs.
1843. 8vo. **91 D**

BURGES, JAMES BLAND.

Considerations on the law of Insolvency, with a proposal for
a reform. 1783. 8vo. **169 A**

BURGESS, RIGHT REV. THOMAS.

The Arabick Alphabet, or an easy introduction to the reading
of Arabick. Newcastle, 1809. 12mo. **255 H**

Motives to study of Hebrew. 2nd ed. 1814. 12mo. **255 H**

BURGHERSH, SUSSEX.

Burghersh, or the pleasures of a country life. [By Richard
Sargent.] 1855. 8vo. **93 E**

BURGO, JOANNES DE.

Pupilla oculi. De septem sacramentorum administratione, de
decem preceptis decalogi, ceterisque ecclesiasticorum officiis.
Argentorati, [Strassburg.] 1514. 8vo. **118 B**

BURGOYNE, SIR JOHN MONTAGU.

Regimental records of the Bedfordshire militia from 1759 to
1884. 1884. 12mo. **86 B**

BURIAL.

The law of Burial, including all the burial acts and official regulations. By J. B. Little. 1888. 12mo.   **9 B**

The laws of Burials. By T. Baker. 5th ed. 1882. 8vo.   **9 B**

The law relating to Burial of the dead. By W. C. Glen and R. C. Glen. 4th ed. 1881. 8vo.   **52 B**

On the law relating to Burials. Notes on the consecration of burial grounds and churches. [By Thomas Falconer.] 2nd ed. Cardiff, 1876. [Pamphlets, vol. 31.]   **144 C**

The judgment delivered December 11, 1809, by Sir John Nicholl upon the admission of articles exhibited in a cause of offices promoted by Kemp against Wickes, clerk, for refusing to bury an infant child of two of his parishioners who had been baptised by a dissenting minister. 1810. [Jacob's Tracts, vol. 2.]   **144 E**

De Sepultura. By Sir H. Spelman. See Sir H. Spelman's English works, 2nd ed. 1727, part 1, pp. 173–190.   **78 H**

BURKE, EDMUND.

A Letter from Edmund Burke to a noble lord, on attacks made upon him and his pension, in House of Lords, by Duke of Bedford and Earl of Lauderdale. 14th ed. 1796. 8vo. **83 G**

The same. New ed. 1831. [Jacob's Tracts, vol. 12.]   **144 F**

Opinions on Reform. Edited by T. H. Burke. 1831. [Jacob's Tracts, vol. 12.]   **144 F**

Speech on American taxation. 4th ed. 1783. Speech on moving his resolutions for conciliation with the Colonies. 3rd ed. 1784. Speech on presenting to the House of Commons a plan for the better security of the independence of parliament. New ed. 1780. Speech at the Guildhall in Bristol upon certain points relative to his parliamentary conduct. 5th ed. 1782. Speech on motion made for papers relative to directions for charging Nabob of Arcot's private debts to Europeans on revenues of the Carnatic. 1785. Five pamphlets in 1 vol. 1783–85. 8vo.   **83 G**

Speech on Reform delivered in the House of Commons, 1782. 1831. [Jacob's Tracts, vol. 12.]   **144 F**

BURKE, JOHN.

A Genealogical and heraldic history of the extinct and dormant Baronetcies of England. By John Burke and J. B. Burke. 1838. 8vo.   **125 E**

A General and heraldic dictionary of the Peerage of England, extinct, dormant, and in abeyance. 1831. 12mo. **125 E**

BURKE, John—*continued.*

A Genealogical and heraldic history of the Commoners of Great Britain and Ireland. 4 vols. 1836–38. 8vo. **126 E**

BURKE, Sir John Bernard.

A Genealogical and heraldic dictionary of the landed gentry of Great Britain and Ireland. 2 vols. 1850, and Index vol. [n.d.], 4th ed. 1863, 4th ed. revised 1868, 5th ed. 2 vols. 1871, 5th ed. with supplement, 2 vols. 1875, 6th ed. 2 vols. 1879, 6th ed. with supplement, 2 vols. 1882. 13 vols. 1850–82. 8vo. **126 E F**

The same. 7th ed. 2 vols. 1886 8vo. **Hall**

Genealogical history of dormant, abeyant, forfeited, and extinct peerages of British Empire. New ed. 1883. 8vo. **125 E**

The General Armory of England, Scotland, Ireland, and Wales ; comprising a registry of armorial bearings from the earliest to the present time. 1878. 8vo. **Hall**

Royal descents and pedigrees of founders' kin. 1864. 8vo. **125 E**

Vicissitudes of families and other essays. 2nd ed. 1859, and second series, 1860. 2 vols. 1859–60. 8vo. **79 B**

See also Peerages.

BURLAMAQUI, Jean Jacques.

The principles of natural law. Translated into English by Thomas Nugent. 1748. 8vo. **48 E**

The same. 2nd ed. 2 vols. 1763. 8vo. **48 E**

BURN, Jacob Henry.

A Descriptive catalogue of the London traders', tavern, and coffee-house tokens, current in the seventeenth century, presented to the Corporation library by H. B. H. Beaufoy. 1853, and 2nd ed. 1855. 8vo. **91 E**

BURN, John Ilderton.

A Practical treatise or compendium of the law of Marine Insurances. 1801. 12mo. **169 C**

BURN, John Southerden.

The Fleet registers, comprising the history of Fleet marriages, also notices of the May Fair, Mint and Savoy chapels. 1833. 8vo. **125 C**

BURN, JOHN SOUTHERDEN—*continued.*

The High Commission. Notices of the Court and its proceedings. 1865. 8vo. **116 C**

Livre des Anglois à Genève, with a few biographical notes.
1831. [Pamphlets, vol. 25.] **144 B**

BURN, REV. RICHARD.

Ecclesiastical law. 2 vols. 1763. 4to. **157 A**

The same. 2nd ed. 4 vols. 1767. 8vo. **166 B**

The same. 8th ed. by R. P. Tyrwhitt. 4 vols. 1824. 8vo.
166 B

The same. 9th ed. by R. Phillimore. 4 vols. 1842. 8vo. **52 F**

History of the Poor Laws, with observations. 1764. 8vo. **174 A**

The Justice of the Peace and parish officer. 7th ed. 3 vols.
1762, and 13th ed. 4 vols. 1776. 8vo. **170 A**

The same. 21st ed. by C. Durnford and J. King. 5 vols.
1810, and 28th ed. by J. Chitty and T. Chitty. 6 vols.
1837. 8vo. **170 A B**

The same. 30th ed. by J. B. Maule and others. 5 vols. in
10. 1869. 8vo. **12 A B**

BURNELL, HENRY BLOMFIELD.

The London (City) tithes act 1879, and the other tithes acts
affecting tithes in the City of London. 1880. 8vo. **11 H**

BURNET, GILBERT, BISHOP OF SALISBURY.

An Apology for the Church of England with relation to the
spirit of persecution for which she is accused. [By G. Burnet.]
n.d. [Tracts, 1688–89.] **118 E**

Bishop Burnet's History of his own time from Restoration of
King Charles II. to conclusion of treaty of peace at Utrecht
in reign of Queen Anne, with the author's life by the editor,
Thomas Burnet. 4 vols. 1818. 8vo. **115 F**

The history of the Reformation of the Church of England.
New ed. 3 vols. in 6. Oxford, 1816. 4to. **115 H**

BURNS, ROBERT.

The works of Robert Burns, with an account of his life and
a criticism on his writings, by James Currie, M.D. 2nd ed.
4 vols. 1801. 8vo. **83 D**

BURRELL, SIR WILLIAM.

Reports of cases determined by the Court of Admiralty,
1758–1774. Edited by R. G. Marsden. 1885. 8vo. **8 A**

[BURROUGHS, Samuel.]

History of the Chancery, relating to judicial power of that court, and the rights of the Masters. 1726. 12mo. **78 A**

The legal judicature in Chancery stated, with remarks on a late book [by Philip Yorke] intitled A discourse of the judicial authority belonging to the Master of the Rolls in the High Court of Chancery. 1727. 8vo. **161 B**

BURROW, Sir James.

Decisions of the Court of King's Bench upon settlement cases, 1732–1776. 2nd ed. 1786. 4to. **74 B**

The question concerning Literary Property, determined by court of King's Bench 20 April, 1769, in cause between Andrew Millar and Robert Taylor. 1773. 4to. **157 B**

Reports of cases adjudged in the Court of King's Bench, in time of Lord Mansfield, 1756 to 1772. 4 vols. 1766–76. folio.

The same. 3rd ed. 5 vols. 1777–80. folio.

The same. 4th ed. 5 vols. 1790. 8vo.

The same. 5th ed. With critical notes and observations. [By Mr. Serjeant Hill.] 5 vols. 1812. 8vo. **4 D E**

BURROWS, Montagu.

Historic towns. Cinque Ports. 2nd ed. 1888. 12mo. **88 D**

The register of the visitors of the University of Oxford, 1647–1658, with some account of the state of the University during the Commonwealth. [Camden Society, n.s. vol. 29.] 1881. 8vo. **85 D**

The family of Brocas, of Beaurepaire. 1886. 8vo. **79 H**

BURSTAL, Edward Kynaston.

Tabulated abstract of acts of parliament relating to Water undertakings, 1879–1887. 1888. 12mo. **11 I**

BURTON, John.

Monasticon Eboracense, or the ecclesiastical history of Yorkshire, also a short historical account of the parish of Hemingbrough. York, 1758. folio. **95 H**

BURTON, John Hill.

A Manual of law of Scotland. Edinburgh, 1839. 8vo. **55 G**

[BURTON, PHILIP.]

Cases with opinions of eminent counsel in matters of law, equity, and conveyancing. 2 vols. 1791. 8vo. **52 B**

The nature and extent of the business in the Office of Pleas in Lincoln's-Inn, both ancient and modern. 1770. 8vo. **168 B**

Practice of the Office of Pleas in the Court of Exchequer. By Philip Burton. 2 vols. 1791 8vɔ. **168 B**

BURTON, WALTER HENRY.

An Elementary compendium of the law of Real Property. 1828, and 4th ed. 1837. 8vo. **174 E**

The same. 6th ed. by E. P. Cooper. 1845. 8vo. **174 E**

The same. 8th ed. by E. P. Cooper. 1856. 8vo. **53 E**

BURY ST. EDMUND'S, SUFFOLK.

Antiquitates S. Edmundi Burgi ad annum MCCLXXII perductæ. Auctore Joanne Battely, S.T.P. Oxoniæ, 1745. 8vo. **93 C**

Historical and descriptive account of St. Edmund's Bury. By E. Gillingwater. St. Edmund's Bury, 1804. 12mo. **93 C**

An illustration of the monastic history and antiquities of St. Edmund's Bury. By Rev. Richard Yates. 1805. 4to. **93 G**

Wills and inventories from the registers of the Commissary of Bury St. Edmund's. Edited by Samuel Tymms. [Camden Society, vol. 49.] 1850. 8vo. **85 B**

BUSHBY, HENRY JEFFREYS.

A Manual of the practice of Elections in the United Kingdom. 3rd ed. 1868. 12mo. **166 C**

The same. 4th ed. by H. Hardcastle. 1874. 12mo. **166 C**

BUSWELL, JOHN.

An Historical account of the Knights of the Garter from 1350 to the present time. 1757. 8vo. **125 E**

BUTLER, CHARLES.

Horæ juridicæ subsecivæ, being a connected series of notes respecting the geography, chronology, and literary history of principal codes and original documents of Grecian, Roman, Feudal, and Canon law. 2nd ed. 1807. 8vo. **83 J**

See also LONDON INSTITUTION.

BUTLER, HILLARY.

The Mayor of Wigan, a tale, to which is added, The Invasion, a fable. 1760. 12mo. **118 C**

BUTLER, WILLIAM.

Exercises on the globes. 2nd ed. 1800. 12mo. **255 H**

BUTLER, WILLIAM ALLEN.

The revision of the statutes of the state of New York, and the revisers. New York, 1889. 8vo. **80 D**

BUTLIN, JOHN FRANCIS.

New and complete Examination guide and introduction to the Law. 1877. 8vo. **64 D**

BUTT, ISAAC.

The new law of Compensation to tenants in Ireland. Dublin, 1871. 8vo. **55 E**

BUTTERWORTH, ALEXANDER KAYE.

The law relating to Rates and Traffic on railways and canals. 1889. 8vo. **11 D**

BUTTERWORTH, HENRY.

Memoir of the late Henry Butterworth, F.S.A. 1861. [Pamphlets, vol. 16.] **144 B**

BUXTON, DERBYSHIRE.

A Handbook to the Peak of Derbyshire, and to the use of the Buxton mineral waters, or Buxton in 1854. By W. H. Robertson. 1854. 8vo. **87 A**

The history of Buxton, and visitor's guide to the curiosities of The Peak. By A. Jewitt. 1811. 8vo. **87 A**

The natural history of the medicinal waters of Buxton and Matlock. By Erasmus Darwin. See James Pilkington's Derbyshire, vol. 1, 1803, pp. 205–275. **87 A**

BYE-LAWS.

An essay on Bye-laws, with an appendix containing model bye-laws. By W. G. Lumley. 1877. 8vo. **52 B**

See also CORPORATIONS and LOCAL GOVERNMENT. .

BYLES, JOHN BARNARD.

Observations on the Usury laws, and on the effect of the recent alterations. 1845. 12mo. **53 H**

Practical treatise of law of bills of exchange, promissory notes, bank-notes and checks. 2nd ed. 1834. 12mo. **160 G**

The same. 9th ed. 1866. 8vo. **160 G**

The same. 13th ed. by M. B. Byles. 1879. 8vo. **52 G**

The same. 14th ed. by M. B. Byles and A. K. Loyd. 1885. 8vo. **9 I**

Sophisms of free trade and popular political economy examined. By A Barrister. [J. B. Byles.] 1849. 12mo. **78 A**

BYNKERSHOEK, CORNELIUS VAN.

Observationum juris Romani libri quatuor. In quibus plurima juris civilis aliorumque auctorum loca explicantur et emendantur. Francof., 1723. 4to. **49 F**

Opuscula varii argumenti, his inscriptionibus : I. Prætermissa ad L. 2 D. de Orig. Juris. II. De rebus mancipi et nec mancipi. III. De jure occidendi, vendendi, et exponendi liberos apud veteres Romanos. IV. De cultu religionis peregrinæ apud veteres Romanos. V. De captatoriis institutionibus. VI. De legatis pœnæ nomine. Lugduni Batavorum, 1719. 4to. **49 F**

Opuscula varii argumenti, nunc primum collecta cum præfatione D. Francisci Caroli Conradi. 2 vols. Halæ, 1729. 4to. **49 F**

BYRNE, JAMES PETER.

The law and practice respecting Bills of Sale. 2nd ed. Dublin, 1870. 12mo. **160 G**

BYTHEWOOD, WILLIAM MEECHAM.

A Selection of precedents forming a system of Conveyancing, with dissertations and practical notes. 2nd ed. with additional precedents and notes by Thomas Jarman, and index by George Sweet. 11 vols. 1829–36. 8vo. **163 F**

The same. 2nd ed. by James Stewart and W. P. Parken. 9 vols. 1834. 8vo. **163 F**

The same. 3rd ed. vols. 1–7 and 9 by G. Sweet, vol. 8, part 1, by W. Stokes, and vol. 11 by G. Sweet and A. Bisset. 10 vols. 1839–61. 8vo. **53 D**

The same. 4th ed. by L. G. G. Robbins. 7 vols. 1884–90. 8vo. **13 D**

CABABÉ, MICHAEL.

Attachment of debts in the high court of justice and in the county courts. 1881. 12mo. **169 C**

The same. 2nd ed. 1888. 12mo. **12 F**

Interpleader in the high court of justice and in the county courts. 1881. 12mo. **169 C**

The same. 2nd ed. 1888. 12mo. **12 E**

The principles of Estoppel. An essay. 1888. 12mo. **9 H**

CABABÉ, MICHAEL and CHARLES GREGSON ELLIS.

Reports of actions tried in the Q.B. division of the high court of justice from 1882 to 1885. vol. 1. 1885. 8vo. **4 E**

CABINET LAWYER.

The Cabinet Lawyer: a popular digest of the laws of England. By J. W. [John Wade.] 22nd ed. 1867. 12mo. **171 B**

The same. 25th ed. with supplements. 1886. 12mo. **10 E**

CAERNARVON, THE RECORD OF.

Registrum vulgariter nuncupatum, 'The Record of Caernarvon.' [Edited by Sir Henry Ellis.] 1838. folio. **99 D**

CÆSARIAN OPERATION.

Coroner's inquest on a woman called Rebecca Boner, on whom the Cæsarian operation had been performed at Woodbridge, Suffolk. 1833. [Pamphlets, vol. 3.] **144 A**

CAICOS ISLANDS.

Laws of Caicos Island, 1799–1860. By A. J. Duncombe. 1862. 8vo. **36 B**

See also TURKS AND CAICOS ISLANDS. **36 B**

CALAIS.

The chronicle of Calais in the reigns of Henry VII. and Henry VIII. to the year 1540. Edited by J. G. Nichols. [Camden Society, vol. 35.] 1846. 8vo. **85 A**

CALDECOTT, THOMAS.

Reports of cases relative to the duty and office of a justice of the peace, 1776–1785. 1786. 4to. **74 B**

CALDWELL, JAMES STAMFORD.

The law of Arbitration. 1817. 8vo. **160 B**

CALDWELL, JOHN STAMFORD.
Results of reading. 1843. 8vo.   **83 I**

CALENDAR, THE.
The book of days, a miscellany of popular antiquities in connection with the calendar. Edited by Robert Chambers. 2 vols. 1869–81. 8vo.   **85 G**
Clavis Calendaria, or a compendious analysis of the Calendar. By John Brady. 3rd ed. 2 vols. 1815. 8vo.   **85 G**
See also ALMANACS and CHRONOLOGY.

CALENDARS AND COURT GUIDES.
Boyle's court and country guide, 1794, 1798–1800, 1802, 1804, 1805, 1808–1889. 91 vols. 1794–1889. 12mo. **215 A–G**
British court and parliamentary guide. By Wm. Robson. For 1832, 1834–1838 and 1842. 1832–42. Bound with Robson's Directory. 7 vols. 1832–42. 4to.   **54 B**
The British imperial calendar, 1812, 1814–1820, 1822–1850, 1875 and 1876. 39 vols. 1812–76. 12mo. **218 D–G**
Civil service calendar, containing official regulations and instructions for candidates. By Wm. Bussell. 1887. 8vo. **255 H**
The Constitutional Year-Book for 1886, 1887 and 1889. 3 vols. 1886–89. 12mo.   **146 F**
The Court and City kalendar, or gentleman's register, containing Rider's Almanack, New and exact lists of both Houses of Parliament, Court and City register, Lists of the Army and Navy, 1756, 1765, 1766. 3 vols. 1756–66. 12mo.   **217 A**
The Court and City Register, 1744–46, 1748–55, 1757–64, 1767, 1768, 1772, 1774, 1776–83, 1785–89, 1791, 1793, 1795, 1796, 1798, 1799, 1801, 1804, 1805, 1806, 1809, 1810. 48 vols. 1744–1810. 12mo.   **217 A–D**
The Court calendar and a list of the public offices and officers, ecclesiastical and civil, employed in His Majesty's Government, with an exact list of the Lords Spiritual and Temporal, 1742, 1744, 1747. 3 vols. 1742–47. 12mo. **217 A**
The English Registry. By John Exshaw. 1768, 1779–89, 1791, 1792, 1795, 1799, 1803, 1805, 1807–16, 1825, 1827–29, 1833, 1838. 34 vols. Dublin, 1768–1838. 12mo. **141 A–C**
Gentleman's Register, 1749. 2nd ed. 1749. 12mo. **218 A**
The London Calendar, 1786, 1794, 1797, 1803, 1808–1816, 1818 and 1820. 15 vols. 1786–1820. 12mo.   **213 A–C**

CALENDARS AND COURT GUIDES—*continued.*

The polite intelligencer, 1806. 1806. 12mo. **218 H**

The Racing Calendar for the year 1830. By Edward and James Weatherby. 1831. 12mo. **146 C**

Robson's Royal court guide. 1839. 12mo. **218 H**

The royal blue book, 1823, 1824, 1829, 1831, 1832, 1834, 1837–1841, 1843–1889. 59 vols. 1823–89. 12mo. **215 & 216**

The royal kalendar, 1767, 1769–1771, 1773–1775, 1777, 1778, 1781–1786, 1788–1889. 117 vols. 1767–1889. 12mo. **217**

The royal Naval and Military calendar, and national record for 1821. By George Mackenzie. 1821. 12mo. **146 C**

The Schoolmaster's calendar and handbook of examinations and open scholarships, 1889. 1889. 12mo. **255 H**

Thompson's New royal court guide. 1844. 12mo. **218 H**

The upper ten thousand, a handbook of the titled, landed and official classes, 1875 to 1889. 15 vols. 1875–89. 12mo. **125 D**

Webster's Royal Red Book, April 1849. 1849. 12mo. **218 H**

Who's Who in 1870, 1873, 1876, 1877 and 1879 to 1889. 15 vols. 1870–89. 12mo. **126 D**

CALENDARS OF SOCIETIES AND UNIVERSITIES.

The Cambridge University Calendar, 1801–1889. 89 vols 1801–89. 12mo. **135 D–G**

The Dublin University Calendar, 1861, 1886. 2 vols. Dublin 1861–86. 12mo. **137 H**

The Incorporated Law Society's [Ireland] Calendar, 1886, 1887. 2 vols. Dublin, 1886–87. 12mo. **136 I**

The Durham University Calendar, with Almanack, 1881–1889. 9 vols. Durham, 1881–89. 12mo. **137 H**

St. David's College, Lampeter. The Calendar, 1881–2. Lampeter, 1881. 12mo. **137 H**

The Institute of Chartered Accountants in England and Wales. List of members and charter of incorporation 1881, 1883–1886, 1889. 6 vols. 1881–89. 8vo. **142 D**

The Society of Accountants and Auditors. List of members extracts from the articles and bye-laws. 1888, 1889 2 vols. 1888–89. 12mo. **142 D**

Register of fellows and associates of the Institute of Chemistry of Great Britain and Ireland, 1878–81, 1885, 1889. 6 vols. 1878–89. 8vo. **146 C**

The registers of Pharmaceutical Chemists, and Chemists and Druggists, 1869–1889. 21 vols. 1869–89. 8vo. **140**

CALENDARS OF SOCIETIES—*continued.*

The Calendar of the City of London College, 1887–1890.
3 vols. 1887–89. 8vo.   **137 H**

Charter, bye-laws, and list of members of the Institution of
Civil Engineers, 1867, 1873, 1879, 1881, 1883, 1885, 1887–
1889. 9 vols. 1867–89. 8vo.   **146 C**

The Dentist's Register, 1879 and 1881–1888. 9 vols. 1879–
88. 8vo.   **140 F**

The Incorporated Law Society's Calendar for the years 1881–
1890, with three supplements, 1885, 1887 and 1889. 13 vols.
1881–90. 12mo.   **134 G**

The London University Calendar for the year MDCCCXXXII.
1831. 12mo.   **136 A**

The London University [i.e. University of London] Calendar,
1850, 1851, 1854, 1857–1859, and 1861–1866. 12 vols.
1850–66. 12mo.   **136 A**

University of London. The Calendar, 1867–1890. 23 vols.
1867–89. 12mo.   **136 A B**

The College of State Medicine, London. Calendar for 1889–
90. 1889. 12mo.   **146 C**

Catalogue of fellows, and licentiates of Royal College of
Physicians. 1833, 1835, 1872. 3 vols. 1833–72. 8vo. **146 C**

Statistical Society. Council and officers, list of fellows, rules
&c. 1874. 8vo.   **146 E**

Calendar of the Royal College of Surgeons of England. 1876,
1884–1889. 7 vols. 1876–89. 8vo.   **146 C**

University College, London. Calendar 1853, 1856–1864,
1866–1889. 31 vols. 1854–88. 12mo.   **137 G**

Owens College, Manchester. Calendar for 1876–1877, 1886–
1890. 5 vols. Manchester, 1876–89. 12mo.   **137 H**

The Victoria University Calendar, 1887. Manchester, 1887.
12mo.   **137 H**

Oxford University Calendar, 1810, 1813–1828, 1830, 1838–
1889. 70 vols. 1810–89. 12mo.   **135 A–C**

CALFHILL, JAMES.
An Answer to John Martiall's Treatise of the Cross. Edited
by Rev. Richard Gibbings. Cambridge, 1846. 8vo. **77 D**

CALIFORNIA.
Compiled laws of California, containing all the acts passed
1850–53. By S. Garfielde and F. A. Snyder. Benicia,
1853. 8vo.   **59 B**

CALIFORNIA—*continued.*

Legal titles to mining claims and water rights in California. By Gregory Yale. San Francisco, 1867. 8vo. **60 B**

The practice act of California. By H. J. Labatt. San Francisco, 1856. 8vo. **59 B**

The statutes of California passed at fifth session of legislature at cities of Benicia and Sacramento, January to May 1854; and at sixth session of legislature at city of Sacramento, January to May 1855. 2 vols. 1854–55. 8vo. **59 B**

CALLIS, ROBERT.

Reading upon the statute 23 H. VIII. cap. 5, of Sewers. 1647. 8vo. **48 F**

The same. 2nd ed. 1685 and 1686. 2 vols. 8vo. **48 F**

The same. 4th ed. by W. J. Broderip. 1824. 8vo. **53 G**

CALTHROP, SIR HENRY.

Reports of special cases touching several customes and liberties of the City of London. 1670. 12mo. **49 A**

CALVERT, FREDERIC.

A Treatise upon the law respecting parties to suits in equity. 1837. 8vo. **161 C**

CALVERT, M.

History of Knaresborough. Knaresborough, 1844. 8vo. **94 A**

CALVINUS, OR KAHL, JOANNES.

Lexicon juridicum juris Cæsarei simul et canonici, feudalis item civilis criminalis theoretici ac practici. Genevæ, 1670. folio. **123 H**

CAMBERWELL, SURREY.

Ye parish of Camerwell: a brief account of the parish of Camberwell, its history and antiquities. By W. H. Blanch. 1877. 8vo. **89 E**

CAMBRIDGE, COLLEGES IN UNIVERSITY OF.

Masters' History of college of Corpus Christi, with a continuation to present time. By John Lamb. 1831. 4to. **86 D**

Alumni Etonenses, or a catalogue of the provosts and fellows of Eton college and King's college, Cambridge, from 1443 to 1797. By T. Harwood. Birmingham, 1797. 4to. **79 H**

CAMBRIDGE, COLLEGES IN UNIVERSITY OF—*continued.*

The case of the President of Queens' college, Cambridge, determined in Court of Chancery by Lord Eldon. Edited by Charles Bowdler. 1821. [Jacob's Tracts, vol. 2.] **144 E**

History of the College of St. John the Evangelist, Cambridge. By T. Baker. Edited by J. E. B. Mayor. 2 vols. Cambridge, 1869. 8vo. **86 D**

Statutes for the college of St. John the Evangelist in the University of Cambridge. Cambridge, 1885. 8vo. **86 D**

See also FRAMLINGHAM.

CAMBRIDGE, UNIVERSITY OF.

Annals of Cambridge. By C. H. Cooper. 3 vols. Cambridge, 1842–45. 8vo. **86 D**

The architectural history of the University of Cambridge. By R. Willis and J. W. Clark. 4 vols. Cambridge, 1886. 4to. **86 D**

Athenæ Cantabrigienses. By C. H. Cooper and Thompson Cooper. 2 vols. Cambridge, 1858–61. 8vo. **80 H**

Calendar, 1801–1889. 89 vols. 1801–89. 12mo. **135 D–G**

A Calendar of chief officers in University of Cambridge from earliest time. See J. Le Neve's Fasti Ecclesiæ Anglicanæ, vol. 3, 1854, pp. 597–704. **80 H**

Cambridge University Commission. Report of Her Majesty's Commissioners appointed to inquire into state, discipline, studies, and revenues of University and Colleges of Cambridge : with evidence, and appendix. 1852. folio. **154 E**

Enquiries and observations respecting the University library. By Basil Montagu. Cambridge, 1805. 8vo. **144 F**

Graduati Cantabrigienses sive catalogus exhibens nomina eorum quos gradu quocunque ornavit Academia Cantabrigiensis. Cantabrigiæ, 1823. 8vo. **80 H**

The same. New ed. Cantabrigiæ, 1856. 8vo. **80 H**

The same. New ed. Cantabrigiæ, 1873. 8vo. **80 H**

History of the university and colleges of Cambridge. By George Dyer. 2 vols. 1814. 8vo. **86 C**

The history of the University of Cambridge. By Thomas Fuller. New ed. by James Nichols. 1840. 8vo. **86 C**

The history of the University of Cambridge, from the Conquest to 1634. By Thomas Fuller. Edited by Rev. M. Prickett and T. Wright. Cambridge, 1840. 8vo. **86 C**

A history of the University of Cambridge, its colleges, halls, and public buildings. 2 vols. 1815. 4to. **86 G**

CAMBRIDGE, UNIVERSITY OF—*continued.*

Memorabilia Cantabrigiæ, or an account of the different colleges in Cambridge. By J. Wilson. 1803. 8vo.   **86 C**

Memorials of Cambridge. By C. H. Cooper. New ed. 3 vols. Cambridge, 1860–66. 4to.   **86 D**

Ordinationes Academiæ Cantabrigiensis. 1877. 8vo.   **146 F**

The Poll for election of a representative in Parliament for University of Cambridge, 26–27 November, 1822. By Henry Gunning. 2nd ed. Cambridge, 1822. 8vo.   **107 J**

The Poll for election of a representative in Parliament for University of Cambridge, 9–11 May, 1827. By Henry Gunning. Cambridge, 1827. 8vo. [Jacob's Tracts, vol. 7.]   **144 E**

The privileges of the University of Cambridge. By George Dyer. 2 vols. 1824. 8vo.   **86 C**

The University of Cambridge from the earliest times to the accession of Charles the First. By J. B. Mullinger. 2 vols. Cambridge, 1873–84. 8vo.   **86 E**

See also BLOMEFIELD, REV. F. and CANTALUPE, N.

CAMBRIDGESHIRE.

A Concise topographical account of the county of Cambridge. By Rev. D. Lysons and S. Lysons. 1808. 4to.   **86 D**

Delineations of Cambridgeshire. By E. W. Brayley and J. Britton. 1801. 8vo.   **86 E**

The Fenland past and present. By S. H. Miller and S. B. J. Skertchley. Wisbech, 1878. 8vo.   **89 C**

History of county of Cambridge. By E. Carter, first printed in 1754; reprinted by Wm. Upcott. 1819. 8vo.   **86 C**

The Poll for the election of two representatives in Parliament for the county of Cambridge on Thursday, Sept. 14, 1780. Cambridge, 1780. 8vo.   **107 J**

See also WILLIS, B.

CAMDEN SOCIETY.

Publications of the Camden Society. [All of which are catalogued under their respective authors and subjects.] 151 vols. 1838–89. 8vo.   **85 A–E**

A Descriptive catalogue of the works of the Camden Society. By J. G. Nichols. 1862. 8vo.   **85 C**

Catalogue of the first series of the works of the Camden Society, in numerical order; and general index as far as the word Baudouin. By Henry Gough. 1881. 8vo.   **85 C**

CAMDEN, WILLIAM.

Annales rerum Anglicarum et Hibernicarum, regnante Elizabetha. Lug. Batavorum, 1625. 12mo. **115 D**

Britannia ; sive florentissimorum regnorum Angliæ, Scotiæ,
Hiberniæ et Insularum adjacentium ex intima antiquitate
chorographica descriptio. 1586. 12mo. **118 A**

The same. Translated newly into English by Philémon
Holland. 1637. folio. **84 F**

The same. Translated from the edition published by the author
in MDCVII. Enlarged by the latest discoveries by Richard
Gough. 3 vols. 1789. folio. **84 H**

A Description of Yorkshire. n.d. 8vo. **94 B**

The origin of Surnames. See Sir W. Dugdale's Ancient
usage of Arms, 1812, pp. 208–248. **125 H**

See also BROOKE, RALPHE.

CAMERON, PETER HAY.

The law of intestate succession in Scotland. 1870. 8vo. **55 F**

CAMPBELL, GORDON.

An Analysis of Austin's Lectures on Jurisprudence, or the
philosophy of positive law. 1877. 12mo. **63 F**

CAMPBELL, JOHN.

A political survey of Britain : being a series of reflections on
the situation, lands, inhabitants, revenues, colonies, and commerce of this island. 2 vols. 1774. 4to. **115 H**

CAMPBELL, JOHN, 1 BARON.

Life of John, Lord Campbell. Edited by his daughter, the
Hon. Mrs. Hardcastle. 2nd ed. 2 vols. 1881. 8vo. **80 D**

The lives of the chief justices of England, from the Norman
Conquest till the death of Lord Tenterden. 3 vols. 1849–
57. 8vo. **79 G**

The lives of the lord chancellors and keepers of the great
seal of England. 3rd ed. 8 vols. 1848–69. 8vo. **79 G**

Misrepresentations in Campbell's Lives of Lyndhurst and
Brougham. Corrected by St. Leonards. 1869. 8vo. **79 G**

Reports of cases determined at Nisi Prius in the Courts of
King's Bench and Common Pleas and on the home circuit.
1807–1816. 4 vols. 1809–16. 8vo. **8 D**

CAMPBELL, ROBERT.
> The law of Negligence. 1871, and 2nd ed. 1878. 8vo. **172 G**
> The law relating to the sale of goods and commercial agency.
> 1881. 8vo. **10 B**

CANADA.
> Across Canada : a report on its agricultural resources. By
> Wm. Fream. Ottawa, 1886. [Canadian Pamphlets.] **84 B**
> British America. Arguments against a union of the provinces
> reviewed with further reasons for confederation. By the
> Hon. J. McCully, Q.C. 1867. [Pamphlets, vol. 31.] **144 C**
> British North American Almanac and annual record for 1864.
> Edited by J. Kirby. Montreal, 1864. 8vo. **195 A**
> Canada Directory for 1857–58. Montreal, 1858. 8vo. **195 B**
> The Canadian Dominion Directory for 1871. Montreal, 1871.
> 8vo. **195 B**
> Canadian forests. By H. B. Small. Montreal, 1884. [Cana-
> dian Pamphlets.] **84 B**
> The city of Brantford, province of Ontario, Canada. Brant-
> ford, 1886. [Canadian Pamphlets.] **84 B**
> Dominion of Canada. A guide book for intending settlers.
> 7th ed. Ottawa, 1886. [Canadian Pamphlets.] **84 B**
> Dominion of Canada. Industries and manufactures. By
> H. B. Small. Ottawa, 1885. [Canadian Pamphlets.] **84 B**
> Mineral resources of the Dominion of Canada. Ottawa, 1882.
> [Canadian Pamphlets.] **84 B**
> Province of Nova Scotia. Information for intending settlers.
> Ottawa, 1886. [Canadian Pamphlets.] **84 B**
> The reward of loyalty. By Sir John Dalrymple Hay. Edin-
> burgh, 1862. [Pamphlets, vol. 20.] **144 B**
> St. John and the province of New Brunswick. St. John, 1884.
> 12mo. **84 B**
> A sketch of Gaspesia. Ottawa, 1885. 12mo. **84 B**
> A sketch of the county of Welland, Ontario. Welland, 1886.
> [Canadian Pamphlets.] **84 B**
> Standard atlas of Dominion of Canada. 1878. folio. **Hall**
> Statistical account of Upper Canada, compiled with a view
> to a grand system of emigration in connexion with a reform
> of the poor laws. By R. Gourlay. 3 vols. 1822. 8vo. **84 B**
> Successful emigration to Canada. By Henry Tanner. Ot-
> tawa, 1885. [Canadian Pamphlets.] **84 B**
> See also BOUCHETTE, JOSEPH.

CANADA, Law of.

The civil code of Lower Canada. By Thomas McCord. Montreal, 1867. 12mo. **60 E**

Legal directory for lawyers and business men with a synopsis of the collection laws of each state and Canada. By J. H. Hubbell. New York, 1881. 8vo. **59 F**

The new municipal manual for Upper Canada. By R. A. Harrison. Toronto, 1859. 8vo. **60 E**

The registry laws affecting lands in Upper Canada. By Wm. Sladden. Toronto, 1857. 8vo. **60 E**

A System of Conveyancing comprising the principles, forms, and laws which regulate the transfer of property in Canada. By J. W. Hancock. Toronto, 1861. 8vo. **59 C**

Queen's Bench and Practice court reports, 1844–1862. 21 vols. Toronto, 1858–62. 8vo. **60 D**

Reports of cases adjudged in the courts of Chancery of Upper Canada, 1849–1861. 8 vols. Toronto, 1861–62. 8vo. **60 E**

Reports of cases decided in the Court of Common Pleas of Upper Canada, 1850–1862. 11 vols. Toronto, 1852–62. 8vo. **60 D E**

A Digest of reports of all cases determined in the Queen's Bench and Practice courts for Upper Canada, 1823–1851. By R. A. Harrison. Toronto, 1852. 8vo. **60 E**

The consolidated statutes for Upper Canada. Toronto, 1859. 8vo. **34 C**

The consolidated statutes of Canada. 1859. 8vo. **34 C**

Revised statutes of Canada. 2 vols. 1887. 8vo. **34 C**

Statutes of Canada, 1857–1889. 35 vols. 1857–89. 8vo. **34 B C**

Index to statutes in force in Lower Canada at end of session of 1856. By G. W. Wicksteed. Toronto, 1857. 8vo. **34 C**

Table of the provincial statutes and ordinances of Lower Canada. By G. W. Wicksteed. Toronto, 1857. 8vo. **34 C**

CANALS.

The law of Canals. By R. G. Webster. 1885. 8vo. **9 B**

History of canals. See F. Clifford's History of private bill legislation, vol. 1, 1885, pp. 33–43. **83 J**

A General history of inland navigation foreign and domestic. By J. Phillips. 5th ed. 1809. 8vo. **84 B**

Inland navigation, or select plans of the several navigable canals in Great Britain. By J. Cary. 1795. 4to. **84 F**

Account of river and canal navigations. See John Aikin's

171

CANALS—*continued.*

A description of the country round Manchester, 1795, pp. 105–145. **88 F**

The history of inland navigations, particularly those of the Duke of Bridgwater in Lancashire and Cheshire. [By James Brindley.] 1766. And Essays which have been lately wrote, some to establish, others to prevent a navigable canal being made from Witton Bridge to Knutsford, Macclesfield, Stockport, and Manchester. 1766. 12mo. **86 A**

See also RAILWAYS and WATER. **11 D & I**

CANCER.

On the geographical distribution of Cancer in England and Wales. By A. Haviland. 1869. [Pamphlets, vol. 32.] **144 C**

CANDY, GEORGE.

The jurisdiction, process and practice in the Mayor's Court, London. 1879. 8vo. **53 A**

CANNING, GEORGE.

The grand vizier unmasked, or remarks on the supposed claims of Mr. Canning to public confidence, in an appeal to the British parliament and people. 1827. [Jacob's Tracts, vol. 7.] **144 E**

The political life of George Canning from September 1822 to August 1827. By A. G. Stapleton. 2nd ed. 3 vols. 1831. 8vo. **79 C**

Speech to his constituents at Liverpool at the celebration of his fourth election. 1820. [Pamphlets, vol. 27.] **144 B**

See also BATTLE OF THE BLOCKS.

CANON LAW.

The regal power of the Church, or the fundamentals of the Canon law: a dissertation. By the Rev. E. G. Wood. Cambridge, 1888. 8vo. **77 C**

The English church canons of 1604, with historical introduction. By Rev. C. H. Davis. 1869. 8vo. **77 C**

Du droit ecclésiastique dans ses sources, considérées au point de vue des éléments législatifs qui les constituent. Par le Docteur Phillips, traduit par l'Abbé Crouzet. Paris, 1852. 8vo. **77 C**

A Collection of the laws and canons of the Church of England

CANON LAW—*continued.*

from its first foundation to the reign of King Henry VIII. Translated into English by John Johnson, M.A. New ed. 2 vols. Oxford, 1850–51. 8vo. **77 C**

The history of church laws in England from A.D. 602 to A.D. 1850. By E. Muscutt. 1851. 8vo. **77 C**

De ratione studii juris canonici in Belgio nuper instaurati. Per R. Winssingerum. 1825. [Latin Tracts.] **118 E**

Histoire du droit canon pour servir d'introduction à l'étude du droit canonique. Par M. Durand. Lyon, 1770. 12mo. **77 C**

Zegeri Bernardi Van-Espen Jus ecclesiasticum universum cæteraque scripta omnia, editio novissima, selectis adnotationibus Joannis Petri Gibert nuperrime aucta et illustrata. 10 vols. bound in 5. Venetiis, 1769. folio. **77 H**

Ordo judiciorum sive methodus procedendi in negotiis et litibus in foro ecclesiastico-civili Britannico et Hibernico. By Thomas Oughton. 2 vols. 1738. 4to. **77 F**

Repertorium Canonicum, or an abridgment of the ecclesiastical laws of this realm consistent with the temporal. By John Godolphin. 2nd ed. 1680. 8vo. **77 F**

Corpus juris canonici emendatum et notis illustratum, Gregorii XIII. Pont. Max. jussu editum, indicibus et appendice Pauli Lancelotti adauctum. 1650. 4to. **77 F**

Jus pontificium novum sive analytica postremi juris ecclesiastici enarratio. Authore Francisco Zypæo. Coloniæ Agrippinæ, 1620. 8vo. **118 B**

Tractatus de jurisdictione per et inter judicem ecclesiasticum et secularem exercenda, Doctoris Martæ, jurisconsulti Neapolitani. Moguntiæ, 1609. folio. **77 F**

Institutiones Juris Canonici ab Joan. Paulo Lancelotto Perusino conscriptæ. Editio ultima. Lugduni, 1606. 4to. **77 F**

Compendium juris Canonici Petri Ravennatis. Lugd., 1521. 8vo. **118 B**

Collection of treatises on Canon Law. Printed by Nicholas Du Pré for Geliert Du Pré. Paris, 1512. 4to. **118 E**

See also AYLIFFE, J., BUTLER, C., CALVINUS, COLQUHOUN, P. M. DE, ECCLESIASTICAL LAW, FULBECKE, W., GIBSON, E., LEUNCLAVIUS, MASCARDUS and TUDESCHIS.

CANTALUPE, NICHOLAS and RICHARD PARKER.

The history and antiquities of the University of Cambridge. 1721. 8vo. **86 C**

CANTERBURY, Archbishops and Cathedral of.

Actus pontificum Cantuariensis ecclesiæ, autore Gervasio Dorobernensi. See Scriptores Decem Hist. Angl., 1652, pp. 1629–1684. **114 H**

Chronica Willielmi Thorni monachi S. Augustini Cantuariæ. See Scriptores Decem Hist. Angl., 1652, pp. 1757–2296. **114 H**

Epistolæ Cantuarienses, the letters of the prior and convent of Christ Church, Canterbury, from 1187 to 1199. Edited by Rev. William Stubbs. 1865. 8vo. **102 B**

Historia monasterii S. Augustini Cantuariensis. By Thomas of Elmham. Edited by C. Hardwick. 1858. 8vo. **101 B**

The history and antiquities of the Cathedral Church of Canterbury and the once adjoining monastery. By the Rev. Mr. J. Dart. 1726. folio. **89 H**

Literæ Cantuarienses. The letter books of the monastery of Christ Church, Canterbury. Edited by J. B. Sheppard. 3 vols. 1887–89. 8vo. **102 H**

Matthæi Parker de antiquitate Britannicæ ecclesiæ et privilegiis ecclesiæ Cantuariensis cum archiepiscopis ejusdem LXX. . . . Samuele Drake, S.T.P. 1729. folio. **85 I**

Mediæval letters relating to the priory of Christ Church, Canterbury. [Camden Soc. n.s. vol. 19.] 1877. 8vo. **85 D**

A Repertory of the endowments of vicarages in the dioceses of Canterbury and Rochester. By A. C. Ducarel. 2nd ed. 1782. 8vo. **88 D**

A Selection from the wills of eminent persons proved in the Prerogative Court of Canterbury, 1495–1695. [Camden Society, vol. 83.] 1863. 8vo. **85 C**

See also LYNDEWODE, W.

CANTERBURY, City of.

An Account of the two cases of controverted elections of the City of Canterbury. By Henry Clifford. 1797. 8vo. **166 E**

The antiquities of Canterbury, or a survey of that ancient citie. By William Somner. 1640. 8vo. **88 C**

The Canterbury Guide. 3rd ed. 1830. 8vo. **88 D**

Canterbury in the olden time. By John Brent. , 2nd ed. 1879. 8vo. **88 C**

Translation of the several charters &c. granted by Edward IV., Henry VII., James I., and Charles II. to the citizens of Canterbury. By A Citizen. [C. R. Bunce.] Canterbury, 1791. 8vo. **88 D**

CANTERBURY, City of—*continued.*

A Walk in and about the city of Canterbury. By William Gostling, M.A. New ed. Canterbury, 1825. 8vo. **88 C**

CAPE OF GOOD HOPE.

Statutes, 1854–1888. 9 vols. 1854–88. folio. **36 G**

Votes and Proceedings of the Legislative Council, 1880–1888. 44 vols. 1880–88.

See also AFRICA, SOUTH.

CAPGRAVE, JOHN.

The Chronicle of England. Edited by Rev. F. C. Hingeston. 1858. 8vo. **101 A**

Liber de illustribus Henricis. Edited by Rev. F. C. Hingeston. 1858. 8vo. **101 B**

[CARACCIOLI, CHARLES.]

The antiquities of Arundel. 1766. 8vo. **80 A**

CARDIGANSHIRE.

An Essay on the value of the mines late of Sir Carbery Price. By Wm. Waller. 1698. 12mo. **94 E**

The history and antiquities of the county of Cardigan. By S. R. Meyrick. 1808. 4to. **94 D**

CARE, HENRY.

English liberties, or the free-born subject's inheritance ; containing Magna Charta and several other statutes. 4th ed. by W. N. [W. Nelson.] 1719. 12mo. **49 C**

CAREW, GEORGE.

Precedents of bills of costs for obtaining grants of probate and letters of administration. 1869. 8vo. **165 A**

CAREW, GEORGE, 1 BARON.

Letters from George Lord Carew to Sir T. Roe, 1615–1617. Edited by John Maclean. [Camden Society, vol. 76.] 1860. 8vo. **85 B**

See also CECIL, SIR ROBERT.

CAREW, SIR GEORGE.

Calendar of the Carew manuscripts in the archiepiscopal library at Lambeth, 1515–1624. Edited by Rev. J. S. Brewer and Wm. Bullen. 6 vols. 1867–73. 8vo. **97 E**

CAREW, RICHARD.

The survey of Cornwall and an epistle concerning the excel-
lencies of the English tongue. 1769. 4to. **86 F**

Carew's Survey of Cornwall ; to which are added Notes illustrative of its history and antiquities, by Thomas Tonkin,
now first published from the original manuscripts by Francis
Lord de Dunstanville. 1811. 4to. **86 F**

CAREY, PETER STAFFORD.

Borough Court Rules. 1841. 8vo. **160 G**

CARHAMPTON, SOMERSET.

History of the hundred of Carhampton in the county of
Somerset. By James Savage. Bristol, 1830. 8vo. **93 B**

CARKESSE, CHARLES.

The act of Tonnage and Poundage and rates of merchandize
with the further subsidy &c. and all other duties relating
to His Majesty's Customs. 1726. folio. **158 D**

CARLISLE, CUMBERLAND.

A Brief historical account of Carlisle cathedral. See Sir W.
Dugdale's History of St. Paul's Cathedral. 1716. **92 H**

The case of the Duke of Portland respecting two leases lately
granted by the Lords of the Treasury to Sir James Lowther,
Bart. [of the forest of Inglewood and soccage of the castle of
Carlisle.] 6th ed. 1768. 8vo. **87 A**

Historic towns. Carlisle. By M. Creighton. 1889. 12mo. **87 A**

The history and antiquities of Carlisle. By Samuel Jefferson.
Carlisle, 1838. 4to. **87 G**

Substance of a letter on the subject of a scheme recently
concluded between the dean and chapter of Carlisle and the
ecclesiastical commissioners for the transfer and future
management of the capitular estates. 1853. [Pamphlets,
vol. 9, pt. 1.] **144 A**

CARLISLE, NICHOLAS.

Concise description of the endowed grammar schools in
England and Wales. 2 vols. 1818. 8vo. **84 D**

Topographical dictionary of England. 2 vols. 1808. 4to. **84 F**

Topographical dictionary of Ireland. 1810. 4to. **95 F**

Topographical dictionary of Wales. 1811. 4to. **94 D**

CARNATIC, Nabob of the.

Case on the petitions of the Nabob of the Carnatic to the King and the two houses of Parliament. See Hargrave's Juridical Arguments, vol. 2, 1799, pp. 375–391. **144 G**

CARNEGIE, Andrew.

Triumphant democracy, or fifty years' march of the republic. 1886. 12mo. **78 B**

CARNEIRO, Manuel Borges.

Direito civil de Portugal. 3 vols. bound in 1 vol. Lisboa, 1826–28. 8vo. **39 B**

CAROLINE, Queen Consort of George IV.

The exclusion of the Queen from the Liturgy historically and legally considered. By A Barrister. [Walker Skirrow.] 3rd ed. 1821. [Jacob's Tracts, vol. 1.] **144 E**

CARPENTER, John.

Memoir of the life and times of John Carpenter, town clerk of London and founder of the City of London school. By Thomas Brewer. 1856. 8vo. **79 B**

CARPENTERS, Company of.

An Historical account of the Company of Carpenters of the City of London. By E. B. Jupp. 1848. 8vo. **89 E**

CARPENTERY.

Elementary principles of Carpentery. By T. Tredgold. 2nd ed. 1828. 4to. **78 G**

CARPMAEL, Alfred and Edward CARPMAEL.

Patent laws of the world, collected, edited, and indexed. 1885, and Supplement 1889. 2 vols. 1885–89. 8vo. **11 B**

CARPMAEL, William.

The law of Patents for inventions familiarly explained for the use of inventors and patentees. 2nd ed. 1836, 4th ed. 1846, and 6th ed. 1860. 8vo. **173 E**

CARR, Joseph W. Comyns.

The Abbey church of St. Alban's. 1877. 4to. **88 G**

CARR, Sir John.

My pocket book or hints for 'A ryghte merrie and conceitede'
tour in quarto to be called 'The Stranger in Ireland' in
1805. By a Knight Errant. [Edward Dubois.] 3rd ed.,
to which is added a correct report of the trial of Carr
v. Hood and Sharpe. 1808. 12mo. **118 B**

CARRÉ, Guillaume Louis Julien.

Lois de la procédure civile et administrative. 4me éd. Par
Adolphe Chauveau. 9 vols. Paris, 1862–63. 8vo. **58 B**

CARRIBEE ISLANDS.

Acts of Assembly of the Charibbee Leeward Islands. 1690–
1760. 2 vols. in 1. 1734–64. folio. **36 F**

The history of the Caribby Islands, viz. Barbados, St. Christophers, St. Vincents, &c., in all XXVIII., with a Caribbian
vocabulary. By John Davies. 1666. 4to. **84 E**

See also Nevis, Laws of, 1862, pp. 461–473. **36 F**

CARRICKFERGUS, Antrim.

The history and antiquities of Carrickfergus. By Samuel
M'Skimin. 3rd ed. Belfast, 1829. 8vo. **95 E**

CARRIERS.

The law of Carriers of goods and passengers by land and internal navigation. By W. H. Macnamara. 1888. 8vo. **9 B**

The law relating to carriage of goods by sea. By T. G. Carver.
1885. 8vo. **9 B**

Law relating to goods and passenger traffic on railways, canals,
and steamships. By E. B. Ivatts. 1883. 8vo. **9 B**

The law of Carriers. By J. H. B. Browne. 1873. 8vo. **52 B**

Law of Inland Carriers as regulated by Railway and Canal
traffic act, 1854. By E. Powell. 2nd ed. 1861. 8vo. **161 A**

A Practical treatise on the law of Carriers. By T. Chitty
and L. Temple. 1856. 8vo. **161 A**

Railway carrying and carriers law, the liabilities and non
liabilities of railways, carriers and others, as to goods,
luggage, passengers, &c. By Charles Nash. 1846. [Pam-
phlets, vol. 21.] **144 B**

See Bailments, Negligence, Railways, and Shipping.

CARRIGHAN, TERENTIUS.

The Chancery student's guide in the form of a didactic poem, setting forth in metrical verse the outline and leading features of a chancery suit. 1850. 12mo. **118 A**

A Letter concerning the doctrines and practice of the Court of Chancery. 1826. [Jacob's Tracts, vol. 5.] **144 E**

CARRINGTON, FREDERICK AUGUSTUS and A. V. KIRWAN.

Reports of cases argued and ruled at Nisi Prius 1843–1853. 3 vols. 1845–53. 8vo. **8 D**

CARRINGTON, F. A. and J. R. MARSHMAN.

Reports of cases argued and ruled at Nisi Prius 1841–1842. 1 vol. 1843. 8vo. **8 E**

CARRINGTON, F. A. and JOSEPH PAYNE.

Reports of cases argued and ruled at Nisi Prius 1823–1841. 9 vols. 1825–41. 8vo. **8 E**

CARTE, THOMAS.

Catalogue des rolles Gascons, Normans et François, conservés dans les archives de la Tour de Londres. 2 vols. in 1. 1743. folio. **99 B**

Report to the Master of the Rolls upon the Carte and Carew papers in the Bodleian and Lambeth libraries. [By T. D. Hardy and J. S. Brewer.] 1864. 8vo. **97 H**

CARTER, EDMUND.

The history of the county of Cambridge. 1819. 8vo. **86 C**

[CARTER, SAMUEL.]

Lex Custumaria, or a treatise of Copyhold estates. 1696. 12mo. **49 C**

Reports of several special cases in the Court of Common Pleas, 1664–1675. By S. C., of the Inner Temple. 1688. folio. **74 B**

CARTHEW, THOMAS.

Reading on the law of Uses. See Collectanea Juridica, vol. 1, 1791, pp. 369–377. **144 G**

Reports of Cases adjudged in the Court of King's Bench, from 3 James II. to 12 William III. 1728. folio.

The same. 2nd ed. 1741. folio. **74 C**

CARTWRIGHT, JOHN.
Reasons for Reformation. 1809. 8vo. **118 B**

CARTWRIGHT, THOMAS, BISHOP OF CHESTER.
The diary of Dr. Thomas Cartwright. August 1686 to Oct. 1687. Edited by Rev. Joseph Hunter. [Camden Society, vol. 22.] 1843. 8vo. **85 A**

CARVER, THOMAS GILBERT.
Law relating to carriage of goods by sea. 1885. 8vo. **9 B**

CARY, SIR GEORGE.
Reports or causes in Chancery out of the labours of Master William Lambert. 1650. 12mo. **49 B**
The same. New ed. 1820. 12mo. **49 B**

CARY, HENRY.
The law of Juries and Jurors. 1826. 12mo. **169 G**
The law of Partnership. 1827. 8vo. **173 D**

CARY, JOHN.
Inland navigation, or select plans of the several navigable canals throughout Great Britain. 1795. 4to. **84 F**

CASES.
Cases and opinions. See BURTON, PHILIP.
Cases argued and decreed in Chancery in the reign of Charles II. and James II. 3 parts in 1 vol. 1735. folio. **74 B**
Cases in equity abridged. Abridgment of cases in equity, alphabetically digested under proper titles. Vol. 1, 5th ed. 1793. Vol. 2, 2nd ed. 1769. 2 vols. 1793–69. folio. **74 C**
Cases in law and equity. See GILBERT, SIR JEFFREY.
Cases temp. Hardwicke. See HARDWICKE, EARL OF.
Cases temp. King. See SELECT CASES.
Cases temp. Talbot. See TALBOT.

CASEY, JAMES JOSEPH.
The Justices' manual, with the Justices' statute and notes thereon. Melbourne, 1872. 8vo. **55 D**

CASLEY, DAVID.

A catalogue of the manuscripts of the King's library, an appendix to the catalogue of the Cottonian library and 150 specimens of the manner of writing in different ages from the third to the fifteenth century. 1734. 4to. **118 F**

CASTLE, EDWARD JAMES.

The law of Commerce in time of war. 1870. 8vo. **55 A**

A Practical treatise on the law of Rating. 1879. 8vo. **175 B**

The same. 2nd ed. 1886. 8vo. **11 D**

CASTLE, HENRY JAMES.

Practical remarks on the principles of Rating, as applied to the proper and uniform assessment of railways, gas-works, &c. 1869. 8vo. **175 B**

Practical remarks upon the Union Assessment Committee act, 1862. 1863. 8vo. **176 G**

CASWALL, ALFRED.

A Treatise on Copyholds and copyhold enfranchisement. 3rd ed. 1841. 12mo. **164 F**

CATALOGUES, LEGAL.

A Catalogue of law books, published or for sale by Banks and Brothers. New York, 1889. 12mo. **82 A**

A Catalogue of the common and statute law books of this realm. Collected by Thomas Bassett. 1682. 12mo. **118 A**

Catalogues of the best editions of law books. By Henry Butterworth. 1836, 1845, and 1850. 12mo. **82 A**

Bibliotheca Legum. By J. Clarke. New ed. 1819. 12mo. **82 A**

Catalogue of modern law books. By C. Hunter. 1818. 12mo. **82 A**

Catalogues of law books published and for sale by Little and Brown, 1843 and 1867. Boston, 1843–67. 12mo. **82 A**

A Catalogue of modern law books. By A. Maxwell. 1833. A general catalogue of law books. By W. Maxwell. 1850, and Catalogues of modern law books. By W. Maxwell and Son. 1867 and 1885. 3 vols. 1833–85. 12mo. **82 A**

A Catalogue of modern law books sold by Richards & Co. 1835. 12mo. **82 A**

CATALOGUES, LEGAL—*continued.*

Catalogues of modern law books. By H. G. Stevens and R. W. Haynes. 1868 and 1881. 12mo. **82 A**

Catalogues of modern law books. By V. & R. Stevens and G. S. Norton. 1840 and 1848. 12mo. **82 A**

A Catalogue of modern law books sold by Stevens & Sons. 1833. 12mo. **82 A**

A Complete catalogue of modern law books, with a selection of such old works as are still of value. By H. G. Sweet. 1882, and 2nd ed. 1883. 2 vols. 1882–83. 8vo. **82 B**

Catalogues of the common and statute law books of the realm. By J. Walthoe, 1715, 1720, and 1725. 3 vols. bound in 1. 1715–25. 12mo. **118 A**

Bibliotheca legum Angliæ. Part 1.—A catalogue of the common and statute law books of this realm. By John Worrall, 1732, 1736, and 1788. Part 2.—A general account of the laws and law writers of England from the earliest times to the reign of Edward III. By E. Brooke. **1788,** and Supplement 1800. 4 vols. 1732–1800. 12mo. **82 A**

A Register of law publications published from Hilary term 1788 to Hilary term, 1792. See Collectanea Juridica, vol. 1, 1791, pp. [1–32], and vol. 2, 1792, pp. [1–26]. **144 G**

CATALOGUES, LIBRARY AND MISCELLANEOUS.

Advocates, College of. Catalogue of the library 1818 and Catalogue of the library sold by auction April 1861. 2 vols. 1818–61. 8vo. **82 C**

Antiquaries, Society of. A catalogue of the library. 1816. 4to. **82 I**

Athenæum Library, Liverpool. A catalogue of the library. By G. Burrell. Liverpool, 1820. 8vo. **82 B**

Birmingham Law Society. Catalogue of the library. Birmingham, 1873. 8vo. **82 B**

Bodleian Library. Catalogue of the Dodsworth manuscripts. By Rev. Joseph Hunter. 1838. 8vo. **82 B**

Bodleian library. Catalogue of the books and manuscripts bequeathed by Francis Douce. Oxford, 1840. folio. **81 H**

Bohn, Henry George. A catalogue of the pictures, miniatures, and art books collected during the last fifty years by H. G. Bohn. Privately printed. 1884. 8vo. **118 E**

Bristol Law Society. Catalogue of books in the library. 1871, and new ed. 1889. Bristol, 1871–89. 8vo. **82 B**

CATALOGUES, LIBRARY—*continued.*

Caius College, Cambridge. Catalogue of manuscripts in the library. By Rev. J. J. Smith. Cambridge, 1849. 8vo. **82 B**

Chetham Library. Bibliotheca Chethamensis. Edidit Joannes Radcliffe. 2 vols. Mancunii, 1791. 8vo. **82 C**

College of Arms. Catalogue of the Arundel manuscripts in the College of Arms. Not published. 1829. 8vo. **118 F**

Corpus Christi College, Cambridge. Catalogus librorum manuscriptorum quos Collegio Corporis Christi legavit Matthæus Parker. 1722. folio. **81 H**

The same. New ed. 1777. 4to. **82 I**

Dulau and Co. Catalogue of French books. By Dulau and Co., 37 Soho Square, London. n.d. 12mo. **82 B**

Dutch Church, Austin Friars. Catalogue of books, manuscripts, letters, &c. belonging to the Dutch Church, Austin Friars, London, deposited in library of Corporation of City of London. [By W. H. Overall.] 1879. 8vo. **82 C**

Faculty of Procurators, Glasgow. Catalogue of the books in the library. Glasgow, 1887. 8vo. **82 D**

Glasgow Public Library. Catalogue of Stirling's and Glasgow public library. Glasgow, 1888. 8vo. **82 D**

Goode, Very Rev. William. Catalogue of his important and valuable library. 1869. 8vo. **82 B**

Gray's Inn Library. Catalogue of the books. By W. R. Douthwaite. 1872. First supplement 1874. Second supplement 1878, and New ed. of catalogue by W. R. Douthwaite. 1888. 8vo. **82 D**

Gresham College. Catalogue of books, pictures, prints, &c. presented by Mrs. Lætitia Hollier to, and also of books and music in, Gresham College. 1872. 8vo. **82 C**

Guildhall Library. A catalogue of the library. [By Edward Tyrrell.] 1828. A Catalogue. [By Wm. Herbert.] 1840. Catalogue with an alphabetical list of authors. 1859, and 15 supplements 1860–1879. 5 vols. 1828–79. 8vo. **82 B**

Guildhall Library. Catalogue of the library. 1889. 8vo. **82 F**

Guildhall Library. Catalogue of sculpture, paintings, . . . and other works of art belonging to the Corporation, with books not included in the catalogue of the Guildhall library. 2 vols. 1867–68. 8vo. **82 B**

Guildhall Library. A catalogue of engraved portraits . . . and [other] works of art exhibited at the opening of the new library and museum, Nov. 1872. Edited by W. H. Overall. 1872. 8vo. **82 B**

CATALOGUES, LIBRARY—*continued*.

Hardwicke, Philip Yorke, 2 Earl of. Catalogue of manuscripts in possession of Earl of Hardwicke. 1794. 4to.   **82 I**

Hartley, Leonard Lawrie. Catalogue of his library. By J. C. Anderson. 3 vols. 1885–87. 8vo.   **82 C**

Hartwell House, Bucks. A catalogue of the law library. By W. H. McAlpine. 1865. 8vo.   **82 C**

Harvard University, Massachusetts. A catalogue of the law library. Cambridge, 1834, and 2nd ed. 1841. 8vo.   **82 B**

Heber, Richard. Bibliotheca Heberiana, parts 4, 6, 7, 8, and 11. 5 vols. 1834–36. 8vo.   **82 B**

Hoare Library. Catalogue of the Hoare library at Stourhead, co. Wilts. By J. B. Nichols. Printed for private use. 1840. 8vo.   **82 G**

Home Office. Catalogue of the library. 1852. 8vo.   **82 B**

House of Commons. Catalogue of library. 1830. folio.   **81 H**

Incorporated Law Society. Catalogues of the books in the library. 1841, 1851 and 1869. 2 vols. 1841–69. 8vo.   **82 B**

India. A catalogue of maps of the British possessions in India and other parts of Asia. 2 parts in 1 vol. 1870–72. 8vo.   **82 D**

Inner Temple. Catalogue of the library. 1833. 8vo.   **82 D**

Kerslake, Thomas. Catalogue of books. 1849. 8vo.   **82 B**

Lambeth Palace. A catalogue of the archiepiscopal manuscripts in the library at Lambeth palace. By H. J. Todd. 1812. folio.   **81 H**

Lincoln's Inn Library. Catalogue of the printed books. 1835. Catalogue of printed books. By W. H. Spilsbury. 1859, and Supplements to the catalogue, being the additions to the library, 1859 to 1881. 1 vol. [1862–81.] 8vo.   **82 D**

Lincoln's Inn Library. Catalogue of the manuscripts. By Rev. Joseph Hunter. 1838. 8vo.   **82 D**

Lincoln's Inn Library. Catalogue of books on foreign law, founded on the collection presented by C. P. Cooper. 1849. 8vo.   **82 D**

Lincoln's Inn Library. Specimen of a catalogue of the books on foreign law lately presented by C. P. Cooper. 1847. 8vo.   **82 D**

Liverpool Law Society. Catalogue of the contents of the library. Liverpool, 1880. 8vo.   **82 B**

London Institution. Catalogues of the library. 2 vols. in 1 vol. 1813–30, and 4 vols. 1835–52. 8vo.   **82 D**

CATALOGUES, LIBRARY—*continued.*

London Library. Catalogue. By J. G. Cochrane. 2nd ed. 1847. 8vo. **82 C**

Manchester Law Society. Catalogues of the library. Manchester, 1854 and 1881. 8vo. **82 B**

Melbourne Public Library. Catalogue of the library. 1861. 8vo. **82 D**

Middle Temple. Catalogue of the library. 1845. Catalogue of the library. [By Rev. J. H. Rowlatt.] 1863. Supplement to the catalogue. 1877, and Catalogue of the library. [By John Hutchinson.] 1880. 8vo. **82 D**

New York State Library. Catalogue of the general library. 2 vols. 1856–61. Catalogue of the law library. 2 vols. 1856–65, and Catalogue of the maps, manuscripts, engravings, coins, &c. 1857. Albany, 1856–65. 8vo. **82 C**

Ouvry, Frederic. Catalogue of his important library of manuscripts and printed books. 1882. 8vo. **82 C**

Parker, John Henry. A Catalogue of books in divinity. Oxford, 1837. 8vo. **82 A**

Patent Office. Catalogue of the library. 2 vols. 1857–58, and New ed. 2 vols. 1881–83. 8vo. **82 I**

Quaritch, Bernard. A General catalogue. 1877. 8vo. **82 H**

Record Office. Catalogue of the library. 1869, and 2nd ed. 1881. 8vo. **82 C**

Rodd, Thomas. A catalogue of books relating to Ireland. 1849. 12mo. **82 B**

Royal Asiatic Society. A Descriptive catalogue of historical manuscripts in Arabic and Persian languages preserved in the library. By W. H. Morley. 1854. 8vo. **82 A**

Royal Institution. A Catalogue of the library. By Wm. Harris. 1809. 8vo. **82 A**

Salt, William. Catalogue of his extensive and valuable library and important collection of manuscripts and ancient deeds. 1868. 8vo. **82 B**

Signet Library. Catalogue of the law books in the library. By Wm. Ivory. Edinburgh, 1856. **82 D**

Signet library. Catalogue of the printed books. [By D. Laing and T. G. Law.] 2 vols. Edinburgh, 1871–82. 8vo. **82 I**

Stowe Library. Catalogue of the collections of portraits and manuscripts, removed from Stowe House, Bucks, sold in London, March and June 1849. 1849. 8vo. **82 G**

Victoria, Supreme Court of. Catalogue of the library. 1861, and 2nd ed. 1873. And Catalogue of books recently added to the library. 1864. Melbourne, 1861–73. 8vo. **82 D**

CATECHISM.

A Biblical Catechism, introductory to, or explanatory of, the church catechism. By A Lay member of the Church of England. [John Stow.] 1841. 12mo. **77 A**

CATHEDRALS.

Monasticon Anglicanum. By Sir Wm. Dugdale. New ed. 6 vols. in 8. 1817–30. folio. **85 H I**

A Survey of the cathedrals [of England and Wales]. By Browne Willis. 3 vols. bound in 2. 1742. 4to. **84 D**

CATHRALL, WILLIAM.

The history of North Wales, to which is prefixed, a review of the history of Britain from the Roman period to the Saxon heptarchy. 2 vols. Manchester, 1828. 4to. **94 E**

CATTLE PLAGUE.

The Cattle Plague. By H. S. Constable. 3rd ed. York, 1866. 8vo. [Pamphlets, vol. 27.] **144 B**

The law relating to the cattle plague. By E. W. Cox. 1866. 12mo. **161 A**

[CATTON, CHARLES.]

The English peerage, or a view of ancient and present state of English nobility. 3 vols. 1789–90. folio. **126 I**

CAUSE LISTS.

Chancery and Rolls cause lists, 1832–1882. 50 vols. 1832–82. folio. **Hall**

Chancery Division sittings in chambers, 1883–1888. 12 vols. 1883–88. folio. **Hall**

King's Bench, Queen's Bench, Common Pleas, and Exchequer cause lists, 1832–1859. 16 vols. 1832–59. folio. **Hall**

Common Law cause lists and sittings at Nisi Prius, 1832–1882. 51 vols. 1832–82. folio. **Hall**

New Trials and special papers, Common Law, 1870–1888. 10 vols. 1870–88. folio. **Hall**

Lists of Summonses, 1880–88. 26 vols. 1880–88. folio. **Hall**

Daily cause lists, 1883–1888. 12 vols. 1883–88. folio. **Hall**

Court of Review, lists of petitions. 1832–1848. 4 vols. 1832–48. folio. **Hall**

Privy Council, House of Lords, Probate, &c. cause lists, 1847–1888. 30 vols. 1847–88. folio. **Hall**

CAUSES CÉLEBRES.
Causes Célèbres et Interessantes, avec les jugemens qui les
ont décidées.   Par M***, Avocat au Parlement.   [Gayot
de Pitaval.]   13 tomes.   Paris, 1735–38.   12mo.   **51 A B**
The same.   Rédigées de nouveau par M. Richer, ancien Avocat
au Parlement.   Tomes 1, 3–8, 10–14, 17–22.   18 vols.
Amsterdam, 1772–88.   12mo.   **51 B C**

CAUSTON, HENRY KENT STAPLE.
The Howard papers, with a biographical pedigree and criticism.
1862.   8vo.   **80 B**

CAUTHERLEY, CHARLES.
Costs in the county court.   1886.   8vo.   **9 F**

CAVANAGH, CHRISTOPHER.
The law and procedure of summary judgment on specially
indorsed writ under order XIV.   1887.   8vo.   **12 E**
The law of Money Securities.   1879.   8vo.   **172 F**
The same.   2nd ed.   1885.   8vo.   **11 A**
Principles and precedents of modern conveyancing.   1882.
8vo.   **13 D**

CAVE, EDWARD.
Description of the rise and progress of the Gentleman's
Magazine, with anecdotes of the projector and his early
associates.   By John Nichols.   See Gentleman's Magazine
Index, vol. 3, 1821, pp. iii–lxxx.   **128 G**

CAVENDISH FAMILY.
Memoirs of the family of Cavendish.   By White Kennet,
D.D.   1708.   8vo.   **79 B**

CAXTON, WILLIAM.
The statutes of Henry VII. in exact facsimile, from the very
rare original printed by Caxton in 1489.   Edited by John
Rae.   1869.   4to.   **114 G**

CECIL, SIR ROBERT.
Letters from Sir Robert Cecil to Sir George Carew.   Edited
by J. Maclean.   [Camden Soc. vol. 88.]   1864.   8vo.   **85 C**

CELLINI, BENVENUTO.

The life of B. Cellini, written by himself. Translated by T. Nugent. [Autobiography, vols. 14 and 15.] 2 vols. 1828. 12mo. **79 A**

CENCI, BEATRICE. See BOWYER, GEORGE.

CENSUS.

Abstract of the answers and returns of the Population of Great Britain, 1811, 1821, and 1831. 5 vols. 1812–33. folio.
153 B

Comparative account of the Population of Great Britain in the years 1801, 1811, 1821, and 1831. 1831. folio. **153 B**

Digest of the English census of 1871. Edited by James Lewis. 1873. 8vo. **78 G**

Inconsistencies of the English census of 1861 with the registrar-general's reports. By W. L. Sargant. 1865. [Pamphlets, vol. 26.] **144 B**

CERTIORARI.

The law as to Certiorari. See Fisher's Digest, vol. 2, 1884, pp. 2–38. **14 E**

CERVANTES, MIGUEL DE.

El ingenioso hidalgo Don Quijote de la Mancha, con la vida de Cervantes. Por D. M. F. De Navarrete. Paris, 1855. 8vo. **83 B**

CEYLON.

Ceylon Ordinances, 1857–1889. 9 vols. 1857–89. 4to & 8vo. **37 E**

A Collection of legislative acts of the government of Ceylon, 1796–1852. 2 vols. Colombo, 1853–54. **37 E**

Institutes of the laws of Ceylon. By H. B. Thomson. 2 vols. 1866. 8vo. **37 E**

The legislative enactments of Ceylon. [1799–1870.] 1874. 8vo. **37 E**

The proper system of railroads for Ceylon. By William Morris. 1860. [Pamphlets, vol. 13.] **144 A**

CHADWICK, SAMUEL.

Examples of Administration Bonds for the Court of Probate. 1861. 8vo. **12 D**

CHAFFERS, WILLIAM.

Hall marks on gold and silver plate. 1863. 8vo. **78 C**

Marks and monograms on pottery and porcelain, with short historical notices of each manufactory. 1863. 8vo. **78 C**

CHALMERS, ALEXANDER.

A History of the colleges, halls, and public buildings attached to the university of Oxford including the lives of the founders. Oxford, 1810. 4to. **92 F**

CHALMERS, GEORGE.

Opinions of eminent lawyers on various points of English jurisprudence chiefly concerning the colonies, fisheries, and commerce of Great Britain. 1858. 8vo. **55 E**

CHALMERS, MACKENZIE DALZELL.

The Bills of Exchange act, 1882. [45 & 46 Vict. c. 61.] With explanatory notes. 1882. 8vo. **160 G**

A Digest of the law of bills of exchange, promissory notes and cheques. 1878, and 2nd ed. 1881. 8vo. **160 G**

The same. 3rd ed. 1887. 8vo. **9 I**

The negotiable instruments act, 1881. Calcutta, 1882. 8vo. **38 D**

The Bankruptcy act and rules, 1883, with a commentary. By M. D. Chalmers and E. Hough. 1884. 8vo. **160 F**

The same. 2nd ed. 1886. 8vo. **12 I**

CHALMERS, REV. THOMAS.

On the power, wisdom, and goodness of God as manifested in the adaptation of external nature to the moral and intellectual constitution of man. 2 vols. 1833. 8vo. **77 B**

CHAMBERLAIN, HENRY.

A New and compleat history and survey of the cities of London and Westminster, the borough of Southwark and parts adjacent. [1770.] folio. **92 H**

CHAMBERLAIN, JOHN.

Letters written by John Chamberlain during the reign of Queen Elizabeth. Edited from the originals by Sarah Williams. [Camden Society, vol. 79.] 1861. 8vo. **85 C**

CHAMBERLAINSHIP.

Claims to the dignity or office of Lord Great Chamberlain of England. See Peerage Cases, first series, pp. 52–75, and third series vol. 2, pp. 1–11.   **124 I**

CHAMBERLAYNE, EDWARD and JOHN CHAMBER-LAYNE.

Angliæ Notitia; or the present state of England, 1669–1673, 1676, 1677, 1679, 1682, 1684, 1687, 1692, 1694, 1700, 1702, 1704, 1707, 1708, 1710, 1716, 1718, 1723, 1726–1729, 1735–1737, 1741, 1743, 1745, 1748, 1755. 36 vols. 1669–1755. 8vo.   **143 A–C**

CHAMBERS, CHARLES HARCOURT.

A Treatise on Leases. 1819. 8vo.   **172 A**

CHAMBERS, GEORGE FREDERICK.

The Churchwarden's Guide. 11th ed. [1888.] 12mo.   **9 C**

A Digest of the law relating to Commons and open spaces. 1877. 4to.   **157 A**

A Digest of the law relating to Public Health and local government. 6th ed. 1874; and 8th ed. 1881. 8vo.   **157 A**

A Digest of the law relating to public Libraries and Museums and literary institutions. 3rd ed. 1889. 8vo.   **10 G**

A Handbook for Public Meetings. 1878. 12mo.   **175 A**

The same. 2nd ed. 1886. 8vo.   **11 D**

The law relating to Highways and Bridges, to which is added the law relating to the Lighting of rural parishes. 1878. 4to.   **157 A**

The law relating to Rates and Rating. 1878. 4to.   **157 A**

The same. 2nd ed. 1889. 8vo.   **11 D**

CHAMBERS, JOHN.

A General history of Malvern. Worcester, 1817. 8vo.   **93 F**

CHAMBERS, JOHN DAVID.

A Complete dictionary of the law and practice of Elections of members of parliament. 1837. 12mo.   **166 C**

Practical treatise on jurisdiction of Court of Chancery over the persons and property of Infants. 1842. 8vo.   **52 I**

CHAMBERS, Judges'.

Practice at Judges' Chambers with forms of summonses and orders. By W. F. A. Archibald and P. E. Vizard. 2nd ed. 1886. 8vo. **12 G**

The practice at the judges' chambers and in the district registries. By W. E. Coe. 1876. 12mo. **12 G**

Forms of practical proceedings in Chambers of Master of the Rolls and Vice-chancellors. By E. W. Cox. 3rd ed. by John Biddle. 1863. 12mo. **161 B**

A Handy Book for the common law judges' chambers. By G. H. Parkinson. 1861. 12mo. **169 E**

A Manual of chancery chamber practice. By C. P. Cooper. 1853. Bound with O. D. Tudor's Chancery practice. 1852. 12mo. **161 B**

Speech of William Tooke, Esq., M.P., on the presentation of a petition respecting Judges' Chambers, Serjeants' Inn, in the House of Commons. 1833. [Pamphlets, vol. 34.] **144 C**

Debate on the presentation of a petition respecting Judges' Chambers, Serjeants' Inn, in the House of Commons. 1832. [Pamphlets, vol. 3.] **144 A**

See also BITTLESTON, A. H. and BLOXAM, R.

CHAMBERS, Robert.

The book of days, a miscellany of popular antiquities in connection with the calendar. 2 vols. 1869–81. 8vo. **85 G**

CHAMBERS, Sir Robert.

A Treatise on Estates and Tenures. 1824. 8vo. **13 A**

CHAMBERS, Thomas and A. T. T. PETERSON.

The law of Railway Companies. 1848. 8vo. **175 A**

CHAMPERTY.

The law of Maintenance and Champerty. By W. J. Tapp. 1861. 12mo. **53 A**

CHAMPNESS, William Swain.

An Insurance dictionary, being a practical explanation of the technical, medical, legal and scientific terms used in Insurance business. 1879. 12mo. **122 B**

CHANCE, Henry.

A Treatise on Powers. 2 vols. 1831 8vo. **174 C**

CHANCELLOR, EDWIN BERESFORD.
Historical Richmond. 1885. 8vo.   **93 D**

CHANCELLORS, LORDS.
The lives of the Lord Chancellors. By John Lord Campbell. 3rd ed. 8 vols. 1848–69. 8vo.   **79 G**
The lives of all the lords chancellors, lords keepers, and lords commissioners of the great seal of England, to the present time. 2 vols. 1708. 8vo.   **79 G**
The lives of lord chancellors and keepers of great seal of Ireland. By J. R. O'Flanagan. 2 vols. 1870. 8vo. **79 G**
A Catalogue of lords chancellors, keepers of the great seal, masters of the rolls, and principal officers of the high court of chancery. By T. D. Hardy. 1843. 8vo.   **80 E**
On the lord chancellors and keepers of the seal in the reign of King John. See E. Foss's Grandeur of the law. 1842. 8vo.   **80 E**
A letter to Lord Cottenham on the Separation of the judicial and political functions of the Lord Chancellor. By Basil Montagu. 1836. [Chancery Pamphlets, vol. 1.]   **144 A**
See also DUGDALE, SIR W. and JUDGES.

CHANCERY, COURT OF.
Arguments proving from antiquity the dignity, power, and jurisdiction of the Court of Chancery. See Special cases in Chancery, 3rd ed. 1736, vol. 1, pp. 1–45.   **74 G**
The chancery compensation to the six clerks, sworn clerks, agents, and record keeper under 5 & 6 Vict. cap. 103. 2 parts. 1845–46. [Pamphlets, vol. 3.]   **144 A**
A Discourse of the judicial authority belonging to the office of Master of the Rolls in the court of chancery. [By Philip Yorke, Earl of Hardwicke.] 1727. 8vo.   **49 E**
A History of the Court of Chancery. By Joseph Parkes. 1828. 8vo.   **83 I**
Lettres sur la cour de la Chancellerie et quelques points de la jurisprudence Anglaise. Par C. P. Cooper. Paris, 1830. 8vo.   **63 G**
Report of the commissioners appointed to inquire into constitution of accountant general's department of Court of Chancery. 1864. folio.   **153 B**
Report of the commissioners appointed to inquire into practice of Chancery, with minutes of evidence and appendices. 2 vols. 1826. folio.   **153 B**

CHANCERY, COURT OF—*continued.*

Reports of the commissioners appointed to inquire into process, practice, and system of pleading in Court of Chancery, 1852–1856. 3 vols. 1852–56. folio. **153 B**

A View of the Court of Chancery. By W. L. Wellesley. 1830. 8vo. **118 C**

Vindication of jurisdiction of Court of Chancery, with judgment given by King James on occasion of controversy between Lord Chancellor Ellesmere and Lord Coke. See Collectanea Juridica, vol. 1, 1791, pp. 20–78. **144 G**

See also BAYLEY, J., BLEWITT, R. J., BURROUGHS, S. and CARRIGHAN, T.

CHANCERY DECREES, JUDGMENTS, AND ORDERS.

The judgments, orders, and practice of the supreme court, chiefly in respect to actions assigned to the Chancery division. By L. L. Pemberton. 4th ed. 1889. 8vo. **12 F**

Morgan's Chancery acts and orders. 6th ed. by G. O. Morgan and E. A. Wurtzburg. 1885. 8vo. **12 F**

Forms of decrees, judgments, and orders in the high court of justice and courts of appeal, having especial reference to the Chancery division. By Sir H. W. Seton. 4th ed. 2 vols. in 3 vols. 1877–79. 8vo. **12 G**

Rules and orders of the Court of Chancery, 1828–1880. 7 vols. 1845–80. 12mo. **53 F**

The consolidated general orders of the Court of Chancery. 1860. 8vo. **52 C**

The statutes and orders relating to practice and pleading in the Court of Chancery 1813 to 1847. By S. S. Toulmin. 1847. 8vo. **173 G**

General orders, rules, means, and suggestions for the remedy of sundry abuses in the high court of chancery. Edited by A. H. Rawlins. 1831. [Jacob's Tracts, vol. 11.] **144 F**

An Order of the Court of Chancery made by Philip Lord Hardwicke, relating to the fees of the officers of the said court. 1744. 12mo. **49 F**

Rules and orders of the High Court of Chancery for regulating practice of said court. 4th ed. 1739. 12mo. **49 D**

A Collection of Chancery orders. 1669. 12mo. **49 D**

See BEAMES, J., BEAVAN, C., COX, H., DANIELL, E. R., SANDERS, G. W. and TUDOR, O. D. **161 B**

CHANCERY FOLIO.

Report of proceedings at the public meeting of law writers on Lord Cranworth's new order abolishing the old chancery folio. By J. R. Taylor. 1854. [Pamphlets, vol. 14.] **144 A**

CHANCERY FORMS.

Daniell's Chancery Forms. 4th ed. by Charles Burney. 1885. 8vo. **12 F**

Forms of claims and defences in the courts of the Chancery division of the high Court of Justice. By C. S. Drewry. 1876. 12mo. **52 B**

Forms of practical proceedings in the Court of Chancery. By H. Ayckbourn. New ed. 1873. 12mo. **52 B**

CHANCERY FUNDS.

The supreme court funds rules, with forms of orders in use in the chancery registrar's office. By M. M. Mackenzie and C. A. White. 1884. 8vo. **12 G**

Practice under the Chancery funds act, 1872. By L. Field and E. C. Dunn. 1873. 8vo. **12 G**

CHANCERY LANE.

Correspondence on the contemplated improvement of widening the north end of Chancery Lane. Compiled by John Robert Taylor. 1850, and 2nd ed. 1850, and Additional correspondence 1850. [Pamphlets, vol. 7.] **144 A**

CHANCERY LAW AND PRACTICE.

The Annual Practice, 1889–90. By T. Snow, C. Burney and F. A. Stringer. 1889. 8vo. **12 F**

Daniell's Chancery Practice. 6th ed. by L. Field and others. 2 vols. in 3 vols. 1882–84. 8vo. **12 F**

An Epitome of the Equity practice. By Archibald Brown. 4th ed. 1884. See E. H. T. Snell's Principles of Equity, 7th ed. 1884, pp. 631–812. **64 D**

Practice and procedure in Chancery actions. By S. Peel. 3rd ed. 1883. 8vo. **52 B**

Practice of the Chancery Division. By F. Evans. 1881. 8vo. **52 B**

The record and writ practice of the Court of Chancery. By T. W. Braithwaite. 1858. 8vo. **53 F**

The practice of the court of Chancery. 2nd ed. 1809. See S. Turner's Epitome of practice. 1809. 8vo. **163 B**

CHANCERY LAW—*continued.*

The practical register in Chancery. n.d. 8vo.   **161 D**

The same. New ed. by John Wyatt. 1800. 8vo.   **161 D**

The solicitor's compleat guide in the practice of the High Court of Chancery. By A Solicitor of the Court. 2 vols. 1776. 12mo.   **161 E**

The history and practice of the Court of Chancery. By lord chief baron Gilbert. 1758. 8vo.   **161 C**

The clerk's tutor in Chancery. By Wm. Brown. 2nd ed. 1694. 12mo.   **49 D**

The practice of the high Court of Chancery, with the reports of many cases wherein relief hath been there had, and where denied. 1672. 12mo.   **49 A**

See BARRY, BOHUN, BRAITHWAITE, BROWNE, J., BURROUGHS, CALVERT, GRANT, GRAY, HADDAN, HANDS, HARRISON, HINDE, JARMAN, KENNEDY, MADDOCK, NEWLAND, SMITH, J. S., TOTHILL, TURNER and VEAL.   **161 B–E**

See also ABRIDGMENTS, COSTS IN CHANCERY, DIGESTS and EQUITY.

CHANCERY PETITIONS.

The law and practice relating to Petitions in chancery and lunacy. By S. E. Williams. 1880. 8vo.   **11 B**

CHANCERY REFORM.

Abstract of a bill for reformation of Court of Chancery. 1831. [Jacob's Tracts, vol. 8.]   **144 E**

The abuses and remedies of Chancery. By George Norburie. See Hargrave's Law Tracts, 1787, pp. 425–448.   **144 G**

Chancery delays and their remedy, addressed to the suitor. By R. M. Hume. 1830. [Jacob's Tracts, vol. 8.]   **144 E**

Chancery delays. By C. E. Lewis. 1860. [Pamphlets, vol. 17.]   **144 B**

Considerations on reform in chancery. By An Equity Draftsman. 1842. [Chancery Pamphlets, vol. 2.]   **144 A**

Considerations suggested by the report made to His Majesty respecting the Court of Chancery. [By Lord Redesdale.] 2nd ed. 1826. [Chancery Pamphlets, vol. 1.]   **144 A**

The Court of Chancery, its inherent defects. By A Solicitor. 1849. Pamphlets, vol. 17.]   **144 B**

Courts of Equity. Speech of J. W. Freshfield in the House of Commons. 1839. [Chancery Pamphlets, vol. 2.]   **144 A**

The delay in the Masters' offices in Chancery and the remedy.

CHANCERY REFORM—*continued.*

CHANCERY REFORM—*continued.*

Observations on necessity for continuous proceedings in offices of Masters in Chancery. By Samuel Miller. 1848. [Pamphlets, vol. 6.] **144 A**

The present state of the Court of Chancery and appellate jurisdiction of the House of Lords. By A. H. Lynch, M.P. 1836. [Chancery Pamphlets, vol. 1.] **144 A**

Propositions as to chancery reform. 1830. [Pamphlets, vol. 17.] **144 B**

Reform of the Court of Chancery. By George Spence. 1830. [Pamphlets, vol. 17.] **144 B**

Some observations on the projected improvements in the Court of Chancery. By Wm. Courtenay. 1828. [Jacob's Tracts, vol. 11.] **144 F**

A Speech, delivered in the House of Commons, on the 16th December 1830, upon the Court of Chancery, by Sir Edward B. Sugden. 1831. [Jacob's Tracts, vol. 8.] **144 E**

Speeches of George Spence in the House of Commons, 17 June and 20 Dec. 1830. n.d. [Law Tracts, vol. 4.] **144 E**

Strictures on orders for regulation of practice and proceedings in Court of Chancery issued by the Lord Chancellor, 3 April 1828. 1829. [Jacob's Tracts, vol. 8.] **144 E**

Substance of a speech by Lord Langdale in House of Lords on better administration of justice in Court of Chancery. 1836. [Jacob's Tracts, vol. 11.] **144 E**

Substance of a speech by Thomas Pemberton in House of Commons on recommitment of bill for facilitating the administration of justice in Court of Chancery. 1840. [Chancery Pamphlets, vol. 2.] **144 A**

Suggestions for improvement of mode of taking evidence and administration of justice generally in Court of Chancery. By N. F. Edwards. 1859. [Pamphlets, vol. 17.] **144 B**

Suggestions for reform in proceedings in Chancery. By W. A. Garratt. 1837. [Chancery Pamphlets, vol. 2.] **144 A**

Suggestions for reform of Court of Chancery and appellate jurisdiction of House of Lords. By Christopher Temple, Q.C. 1850. [Pamphlets, vol. 7.] **144 A**

See also BARNES, R., BECKWITH, W., COOPER, C. P., MONTAGU, B. and SPENCE, G.

CHANDLER, PELEG W.

American criminal trials. 2 vols 1841–44. 12mo. **59 D**

CHANDLER, RICHARD.

The life of William Waynflete, Bishop of Winchester. 1811. 8vo. **80 C**

CHANDOS PEERAGE.

Argument at law, for the title of James Brydges, third and last Duke of Chandos, to the manor of Villiers in Queen's county in Ireland. See Hargrave's Juridical Arguments, vol. 1, 1797, pp. 88–292, and Appendix pp. v–xxi. **144 G**

A Review of the Chandos peerage adjudicated 1807. By G. F. Beltz. 1834. 8vo. **124 F**

CHANNEL ISLANDS.

An Account of the island of Jersey. By W. Plees. 1817. 8vo. **94 F**

An Authentic narrative of the oppressions of the islanders of Jersey; to which is prefixed a succinct history of that island. [By Dr. Shebbeare.] 2 vols. 1771. 8vo. **94 F**

A Brief description and historical notices of the Island of Jersey. New ed. Jersey, 1832. 12mo. **94 F**

The British Press and Jersey Times Royal Almanac for the year 1879 with tourist's guide and complete directory. Jersey, 1878. 12mo. **94 F**

Cæsarea, or an account of Jersey. By Philip Falle and Philip Morant. 1797. 8vo. **94 F**

The Channel Islands. By D. T. Ansted and R. G. Latham. 2nd ed. 1865. 8vo. **94 F**

Documens relatifs à l'île de Guernesey. 1814. 8vo. **94 F**

Histoire de l'érection originelle, de l'avancement et augmentation du havre de la ville de St. Pierre Port à Guernesey. Oxon, 1755. 8vo. **94 F**

An Historical account of Guernsey. By Thomas Dicey. 1751. 12mo. **94 F**

The history of Guernsey, with particulars of Alderney, Serk and Jersey. By Wm. Berry. 1815. 4to. **94 F**

History of the Channel Islands. See R. M. Martin's History of the British colonies, vol. 5, 1835, pp. 459–517. **116 C**

In the Privy Council. Cases of the States of the Island of Jersey and of certain of the ratepayers and householders of the said island and of Edward Nicolle, Esq. and others. 1852. folio. **95 H**

The laws, customs and privileges and their administration in Jersey. By A. J. Le Cras. 1839. 12mo. **94 F**

CHANNEL ISLANDS—*continued.*

Remarques et animadversions sur l'approbation des lois et coustumier de Normandie usitées es jurisdictions de Guernezé. Par Thomas Le Marchant. 2 vols. in 1 vol. Guernesey, 1826. 8vo. **94 F**

See also BOWDITCH, J. and WARNER, REV. R.

CHANNEL RAILWAY.

The Channel Railway, tube or tunnel; the advantages considered of constructing and laying a submarine tube as a means of communication across the channel. By P. J. Bishop. 1876. [Pamphlets, vol. 31.] **144 C**

CHAN-TOON, BARRISTER-AT-LAW.

Nature and value of Jurisprudence. 2nd ed. 1889. 8vo. **63 G**

CHAPEL ROYAL.

The old cheque-book of the Chapel Royal from 1561 to 1744. Edited by E. F. Rimbault. [Camden Society, n.s. vol. 3.] 1872. 8vo. **85 C**

CHAPMAN, THOMAS.

The practice of the court of King's Bench with bills of costs in the court. 2nd ed. 1831. 12mo. **162 F**

CHAPPLE, WILLIAM.

A Review of part of Risdon's Survey of Devon containing the general description of that county. Exeter, 1785. 8vo. **87 B**

CHARACTER.

Outlines of character. By Robert Maugham. 2nd ed. 1823. 8vo. **78 A**

CHARITIES.

Abstract of returns of Charitable Donations for benefit of poor persons made by ministers and churchwardens of several parishes and townships in England and Wales, 1786–1788. 2 vols. 1816. folio. **159 E**

The Charities register and digest, with an introduction by C. S. Loch. 2nd ed. 1884. 8vo. **134 I**

The same. 3rd ed. 1889. 8vo. **134 I**

Reports of the commissioners for inquiring concerning Charities in England and Wales, 1819–1838. 37 vols. 1819–38.

CHARITIES—*continued.*

Analytical digests. 2 vols. in 1, 1832–35, and Index, 2 vols. 1827–40. 40 vols. 1819–40. folio. **154 A–E**

Reports of the Charity commissioners for England and Wales, 1854–1888. 3 vols. 1854–88. folio. **154 E**

CHARITY AND MORTMAIN.

The law of charities and mortmain being a third ed. of Tudor's Charitable Trusts. By L. S. Bristowe and W. I. Cook. 1889. 8vo. **9 B**

The law of Charitable Bequests with an account of the Mortmain and Charitable uses act 1888. By A. D. Tyssen. 1888. 8vo. **9 B**

Dissertation on and precedents of Mortmain. See Bythewood and Jarman's Conveyancing, 4th ed., vol. 4, 1887, pp. 1–96. **13 D**

The law of charitable trusts. By R. E. Mitcheson. 1887. 8vo. **52 B**

The law relating to Charities. By F. M. Whiteford. 1878. 8vo. **52 B**

An Address to the Lords Spiritual and Temporal shewing cause ' why the [Charitable Trusts] bill should not pass into a law.' 1846. [Pamphlets, vol. 18.] **144 B**

The proposed alteration of the law of charitable trusts contained in the Dissenters' Chapels bill. By J. C. Evans. 1844. [Pamphlets, vol. 18.] **144 B**

Observations on the necessity of a legislative measure for the protection and superintendence of endowed public charities. By James Hine. 1842. [Pamphlets, vol. 10.] **144 A**

A Practical treatise of the law of Mortmain and Charitable uses and trusts. By Leonard Shelford. 1836. 8vo. **53 B**

Select Cases determined in Chancery, by Lord Hardwicke, on the statute of Mortmain. See Collectanea Juridica, vol. 1, 1791, pp. 433–457. **144 G**

See BOYLE, W. R. A., DUKE, G., FINLASON, W. F., FRANCIS, P., HIGHMORE, A. and RAWLINSON, J. **161 F**

See also Chitty's Index, 4th ed., vol. 2, 1885, pp. 1143–1262. **14 D**

CHARKE, CHARLOTTE.

A Narrative of the life of Mrs. Charlotte Charke, written by herself. [Autobiography, vol. 1.] 1827. 12mo. **79 A**

CHARLES I., KING OF ENGLAND.

History of Charles the First and the English revolution. By M. Guizot, translated by A. R. Scoble. new ed. 2 vols. 1854. 8vo. **115 C**

The life and martyrdom of King Charles I. By David Lloyd. 1668. 4to. **79 H**

The reign of King Charles the First. By E. Phillips. See Sir R. Baker's Chronicle, 8th ed. 1684, pp. 431–586. **114 G**

Charles I. in 1646. Letters of King Charles the First to Queen Henrietta Maria. Edited by John Bruce. [Camden Society, vol. 63.] 1856. 8vo. **85 B**

Collection of all remonstrances and other remarkable passages between Charles I. and his high court of parliament, Dec. 1641–March 1643. By Edward Husband. 1643. 8vo. **49 D**

Collection of all the publicke orders &c. of both Houses of Parliament, March 1642–December 1646. By Edward Husband. 1646. folio. **158 B**

Commentarii de rebellione Anglicana ab anno 1640 usque ad annum 1685, autore Roger Manley. 1686. 12mo. **115 D**

Debates in the House of Commons in 1625. Edited by S. R. Gardiner. [Camden Society, n.s. vol. 6.] 1873. 8vo. **85 C**

Diary of the marches of the royal army during the great civil war kept by R. Symonds. Edited by C. E. Long. [Camden Society, vol. 74.] 1859. 8vo. **85 B**

The Hamilton papers, being selections from original letters in the possession of the Duke of Hamilton and Brandon, relating to the years 1638–1650. [Camden Society, n.s. vol. 27.] 1880. 8vo. **85 D**

Historical collections, 1618 to 1640. By John Rushworth. 2 vols. 1682–80. folio. **115 I**

The indictment, arraignment, tryal and judgment of twenty-nine regicides, the murtherers of Charles I. . . . October 1660. 1724. 8vo. **51 E**

Letters shewing the designs of the Papists against the royal martyr King Charles the First and the Protestant religion. 1688. [Tracts, 1688–89.] **118 E**

Memorials of the English affairs from the beginning of the reign of Charles the First to the Restoration. By Bulstrode Whitelocke. A new ed. 4 vols. Oxford, 1853. 8vo. **115 C**

Notes of the treaty carried on at Ripon between King Charles I. and the Covenanters of Scotland A.D. 1640. By

CHARLES I., KING OF ENGLAND—*continued*.

Sir J. Borough. Edited by J. Bruce. [Camden Society, vol. 100.] 1869. 8vo. **85 C**

A Secret negotiation with Charles the First. 1643–1644. Edited by B. M. Gardiner. [Camden Society, n.s. vol. 31.] 1883. 8vo. **85 D**

Verney papers. Notes of proceedings in the Long Parliament temp. Charles I. Edited by J. Bruce. [Camden Society, vol. 31.] 1845. 8vo. **85 A**

See also AIRY, BIRCH, CLARENDON, RICHELIEU, SAVILE, and STATE PAPERS.

CHARLES II., KING OF ENGLAND.

The first thirteen years of the reign of King Charles the Second. By E. Phillips. See Sir R. Baker's Chronicle, 8th ed., 1684, pp. 587–750. **114 G**

History of Richard Cromwell and the restoration of Charles II. By M. Guizot. Translated by A. R. Scoble. 2 vols. 1856. 8vo. **115 C**

An Exact abridgment of all the trials which have been published since the year 1678, relating to the Popish and pretended Protestant plots. By P. N. 1690. 12mo. **118 B**

Five letters of King Charles II. communicated by the Marquis of Bristol. [Camden Society, vol. 87.] 1864. 8vo. **85 C**

Gesta Britannorum, or a succinct chronologie of the actions and exploits, battails and other passages which have happened from 1660 until 1661. By George Wharton. 1661. 12mo. **118 A**

Letters addressed from London to Sir Joseph Williamson while plenipotentiary at the congress of Cologne, 1673 and 1674. Edited by W. D. Christie. [Camden Society, n.s. vols. 8 and 9.] 2 vols. 1873–74. 8vo. **85 C**

Memoirs of Great Britain and Ireland from 1681 to 1692. By Sir John Dalrymple. 2nd ed. 2 vols. 1771–73. 4to. **114 F**

Moneys received and paid for secret services of Charles II. and James II., 1679 to 1688. Edited by J. G. Akerman. [Camden Society, vol. 52.] 1851. 8vo. **85 B**

Occasional discourses on the affairs of the two last reigns. See Lord Delamer's Works. 1694, 8vo. **83 A**

The Popish damnable plot against our religion and liberties, fairly laid open and discovered in the breviats of threescore

CHARLES II., KING OF ENGLAND—*continued.*
> and four letters and papers of intelligence 1680, and 24 other tracts on the same subject all bound together. 1679–80. 4to. **144 G**

See also AIRY, O. and AMOS, A.

CHARLES V., EMPEROR OF GERMANY.
> The history of the reign of the Emperor Charles V. By Wm. Robertson, D.D. [vols. 3–5 of his Works.] 3 vols. 1824. 8vo. **116 F**

CHARLETON, WALTER. See STONEHENGE.

CHARLEY, WILLIAM THOMAS.
> The new system of practice and pleading under the Supreme Court of Judicature acts. 1875. 12mo. **169 F**
> The same. 3rd ed. 1877. 12mo. **169 F**
> Real Property acts with explanatory notes. 1874, and 3rd ed. 1876. 12mo. **174 F**
> Reports of cases in supreme court of judicature illustrative of new system of practice and pleading. 3 vols. in 1. 1876–81. 8vo. **53 C**

CHARLTON, LIONEL.
> The history of Whitby and of Whitby Abbey. York, 1779. 4to. **94 C**

CHARNOCK, RICHARD.
> Digest of the various decisions distinguishing what defences may be given in evidence under the general issue and what must be specially pleaded. 1837. Bound with G. B. Mansel's Limitation. 1839. 12mo. **172 A**

CHARNWOOD FOREST, LEICESTERSHIRE.
> The history and antiquities of Charnwood Forest. By T. R. Potter. 1842. 4to. **90 G**

CHARTERHOUSE, LONDON.
> Charterhouse prize exercises, 1814 to 1832. 1833. 8vo. **83 C**
> Historical account of T. Sutton and of his foundation in Charter-House. By Rev. P. Bearcroft. 1737. 8vo. **91 C**

CHARTERPARTIES.
The contract of affreightment as expressed in charterparties. By T. E. Scrutton. 1886. 8vo.   **10 D**

A Practical treatise on Charter-Parties of affreightment. By Edward Lawes. 1813. 8vo.   **161 F**

CHARTER ROLLS.
Calendarium rotulorum chartarum et inquisitionum ad quod damnum. Edited by J. Caley. 1803. folio.   **98 C**

Rotuli chartarum in turri Londinensi asservati 1199–1216 accurante T. D. Hardy. 1837. folio.   **98 B**

CHARTERS, ANCIENT.
Formulare Anglicanum; or a collection of ancient charters and instruments from the Norman conquest to Henry VIII. By Thomas Madox. 1702. folio.   **85 I**

Of antient deeds and charters. See Sir H. Spelman's English works, 2nd ed., 1727, part 2, pp. 233–256.   **78 H**

See also AYLOFFE, SIR J. and CARTE, T.

CHASTER, ALBERT WILLIAM.
The powers, duties, and liabilities of executive officers. 1886. 8vo.   **168 B**

The same. 3rd ed. 1888. 8vo.   **9 I**

CHATHAM, WILLIAM, 1 EARL OF. See ALMON, JOHN.

CHATTERTON, THOMAS.
The works of T. Chatterton. Edited by Robert Southey and Joseph Cottle. 3 vols. 1803. 8vo.   **83 E**

CHAUNCY, SIR HENRY.
The historical antiquities of Hertfordshire with the original of counties, hundreds, &c. 1700. folio.   **88 H**

The same reprinted. 2 vols. Bishop's Stortford, 1826. 8vo.   **88 C**

Life of Sir Henry Chauncy. See J. P. Malcolm's Lives of Topographers. 1815. 4to.   **79 H**

CHELSEA, MIDDLESEX.
The Chelsea charities, 1862. Report of the committee of the vestry. 1863. folio.   **91 G**

CHELSEA—*continued*.

An Historical and topographical description of Chelsea and
its environs. By Thomas Faulkner. 1810. 8vo. **89 D**

The village of palaces, or chronicles of Chelsea. By the Rev.
A. G. L'Estrange. 2 vols. 1880. 8vo. **89 D**

CHELTENHAM, GLOUCESTERSHIRE.

Guide to Cheltenham and its environs. n.d. 12mo. **88 A**

New historical description of Cheltenham and its vicinity.
By S. Y. Griffith. Cheltenham, 1826. 4to. **88 G**

CHEMISTRY.

Chemistry considered with reference to natural theology. By
Wm. Prout. 2nd ed. 1834. 8vo. **77 B**

CHEPPING WYCOMBE, BUCKINGHAMSHIRE.

Charters and grants relating to the borough of Chepping
Wycombe. Wycombe, 1817, and London, 1817. [With
cases and opinions of counsel and many manuscript notes.]
2 vols. in 1 vol. 1817. 4to. **118 F**

CHERRY, RICHARD ROBERT.

The Irish land law and land purchase acts, 1881, 1885, and
1887, with the rules and forms issued under each act.
Dublin, 1888. 8vo. **55 E**

CHESHIRE.

A Concise topographical account of the county of Cheshire.
By Rev. Daniel Lysons and Samuel Lysons. 1806. 4to.
86 F

Delineations of Cheshire. By E. W. Brayley and J. Britton.
1801. 8vo. **86 E**

East Cheshire, past and present. By J. P. Earwaker. 2 vols.
1877–80. 4to. **87 G**

Historical antiquities in two books . . . the second containing
particular remarks concerning Cheshire, with a transcript of
Doomsday-Book so far as it concerneth Cheshire. By Sir
Peter Leycester. 1673. 4to. **87 G**

The history of Cheshire, containing King's Vale-Royal entire,
with considerable extracts from Sir Peter Leycester's Antiquities of Cheshire. 2 vols. Chester, 1778. 8vo. **86 E**

CHESHIRE—*continued*.

The history of the county palatine and city of Chester. By George Ormerod. 2nd ed. by Thomas Helsby. 3 vols. 1882. folio. **86 H**

The history of the county palatine of Chester. By J. H. Hanshall. Chester, 1817. 4to. **86 F**

Seasonable considerations on a navigable canal intended to be cut from river Trent at Wilden Ferry, Derbyshire, to river Mersey, with Supplement. 1766. 8vo. **87 A**

A Survey of the counties of Lancashire, Cheshire, &c. 1797. 8vo. **89 B**

A Topographical survey of the county of Chester. By Wm. Tunnicliff. Bath, 1789. 8vo. **93 A**

See also AIKIN, J., DODDRIDGE, SIR J., HUME, A., LEIGH, C., PENNANT, T. and WILLIS, B.

CHESTER.

History of the city of Chester. By Joseph Hemingway. 2 vols. Chester, 1831. 8vo. **86 E**

CHESTERFIELD, DERBYSHIRE.

Some observations upon the law of Ancient Demesne, with suggestions as to origin of families of Brewer, Brito, Hardwick, and Cavendish, the ancient Lords of the manor of Chesterfield. By Pym Yeatman. 1884. 8vo. **87 B**

CHESTERFIELD, PHILIP DORMER, 4 EARL OF.

Miscellaneous writings, to which are prefixed memoirs of his life. By M. Maty. 2nd ed. 4 vols. 1779. 8vo. **83 B**

CHETHAM, HUMPHRY.

Bibliotheca Chethamensis. 2 vols. Mancunii, 1791. 8vo. **82 C**

The last will of H. Chetham, of Clayton, in the county of Lancaster, Esq., dated December 16, 1651, whereby he founded and endowed an hospital and library in Manchester. Manchester, n.d. 4to. **88 F**

CHICHELEANA, STEMMATA.

Stemmata Chicheleana, or a genealogical account of some of the families derived from Thomas Chichele. [By Rev. Benjamin Buckler.] Oxford, 1765. 4to. **127 J**

CHICHESTER, SUSSEX.

The history of Chichester, with notes on the county of Sussex. By Alexander Hay. Chichester, 1804. 8vo. **93 E**

CHILD, SIR JOSIAH.

A new discourse of Trade. 4th ed. [1698.] 12mo. **78 A**

CHILDREN.

The law as applicable to the criminal offences of children. By T. W. Saunders and W. E. Saunders. 1887. 12mo. **52 E**

The laws relating to young children. By C. C. M. Baker. 1885. 8vo. **10 C**

The laws affecting juvenile offenders. By F. H. Lascelles. 1870. 8vo. **170 C**

Observations on the natural right of a father to the custody of his children and to direct their education. By James Ram. 1828. [Jacob's Tracts, vol. 11.] **144 F**

The laws concerning parents and children and the interests of infants. See Laws of Women, 1777, pp. 349–449. **178 C**

See also INFANTS.

CHILDREY, JOSHUA, D.D.

Britannia Baconica, or the natural rarities of England, Scotland, and Wales historically related, according to the precepts of the Lord Bacon. 1661. 12mo. **86 A**

CHINA.

An Authentic account of an embassy from the king of Great Britain to the emperor of China. By Sir G. Staunton. 2 vols. 1797. 4to. **84 F**

The Chinese: a general description of China and its inhabitants. By J. F. Davis. New ed. 1840. 8vo. **84 A**

The Chinese commercial guide. By S. W. Williams. 5th ed. Hongkong, 1863. 8vo. **78 A**

Our interests in China. A letter to Earl Russell. By H. N. Lay. 1864. [Pamphlets, vol. 25.] **144 B**

Le Saint Edit, étude de littérature Chinoise. Préparée par A. T. Piry. Shanghai, 1879. 4to. **83 J**

A Succinct account of the civil regulations comprised in the Ta Tsing Leu Lee. See B. Barrett's The Code Napoléon, vol. 1, 1811, pp. xlviii–lxxx. **55 C**

CHINA—*continued.*

Ta Tsing Leu Lee ; being the fundamental laws of the penal code of China. Translated by Sir G. T. Staunton. 1810. 4to.   **83 J**

CHIPPENHAM, WILTSHIRE.

Records of Chippenham. By F. H. Goldney. 1889. 8vo. **93 F**

CHISHOLM, JOHN C.

Manual of Coal Mines regulation act 1887. 1888. 8vo. **9 C**

CHITTY, EDWARD.

A Digested index to the common law reports relating to conveyancing and bankruptcy from 1558 to the present time. By E. Chitty and F. Foster. 1841. 8vo.   **14 F**

An Index to all Reported Cases decided in several Courts of Equity in England and Ireland, the Privy Council, and the House of Lords ; and to Statutes on or relating to principles, pleading, and practice of Equity and Bankruptcy ; from the earliest period. 2nd ed. 4 vols. 1837. 8vo.

The same. 3rd ed. brought down to 1853 by J. Macaulay. 4 vols. 1853. 8vo.   **14 D**

The same. 4th ed. with a selection of Irish cases. By W. F. Jones and H. E. Hirst. 9 vols. 1883–89. 8vo. **14 D**

CHITTY, HENRY.

A Treatise on law of descents. 1825. 8vo.   **165 G**

CHITTY, JOSEPH.

A Collection of Statutes of practical utility with notes thereon. 2 vols. in 4 parts. 1828–37. 8vo.   **176 A**

The same. 2nd ed. by W. N. Welsby and E. Beavan. 4 vols. in 5 vols. 1851–54. 8vo.   **176 A**

The same. 3rd ed. by W. N. Welsby and E. Beavan. 4 vols. in 8 vols. 1865. 8vo.   **176 A B**

The same. 4th ed. by J. M. Lely. 6 vols. 1880 ; and Annual Continuations, 1881–1889. By J. M. Lely. 3 vols. 9 vols. 1880–89. 8vo.   **70 I**

A Concise view of principles, object, and utility of Pleadings, and practice as to amendments pending trials at Nisi Prius and before sheriffs. 2nd ed. 1835. 8vo. **173 F**

CHITTY, JOSEPH—*continued.*

The law of bills of exchange, checks on bankers, promissory notes, and bank-notes. 1799. 8vo. **160 G**

The same. 2nd ed. 1807, and 8th ed. 1833. 8vo. **160 G**

The same. 10th ed. by J. A. Russell and D. Maclachlan. 1859. 8vo. **160 G**

The same. 11th ed. by J. A. Russell. 1878. 8vo. **160 G**

A Practical treatise on Criminal law with a copious collection of precedents. 4 vols. 1816. 8vo. **165 E**

The same. 2nd ed. 4 vols. 1826. 8vo. **165 E**

A Practical treatise on law of nations relative to legal effect of war on commerce of belligerents and neutrals. 1812. 8vo. **55 A**

A Practical treatise on Medical Jurisprudence. part 1. 1834. 8vo. **172 E**

A Practical treatise on Pleading and on parties to and forms of actions with precedents. 2 vols. 1809. 8vo. **173 F**

The same. 6th ed. by Joseph Chitty and Thomas Chitty. 3 vols. 1836–37. 8vo. **173 F**

A Practical treatise on Stamp laws. 1829. 12mo. **175 G**

The same. 2nd ed. by J. W. Hulme. 1841. 12mo. **175 G**

The practice of the law in all its departments. 3 vols. 1833–35. 8vo. **167 B**

Reports of cases principally on practice and pleading determined in the Court of King's Bench, 1770–1822. 2 vols. 1820–23. 8vo. **4 E**

A Summary of the practice of the courts of King's Bench and Common Pleas and Exchequer. 1832. 12mo. **162 A**

Treatise on laws of Commerce and Manufactures and contracts relating thereto. 4 vols. 1820–24. 8vo. **13 G**

A Treatise on the Game laws and on Fisheries, with a copious collection of precedents. 3 vols. 1812–16. 8vo. **168 F**

CHITTY, JOSEPH, JUNIOR.

Practical treatise on law of Contracts. 1826. 8vo. **163 D**

The same. 9th ed. by J. A. Russell. 1871. 8vo. **163 D**

The same. 11th ed. by J. A. Russell. 1881. 8vo. **52 C**

The same. 12th ed. by J. M. Lely and N. Geary. 1890. 8vo. **9 E**

Precedents in Pleading with copious notes on pleading practice and evidence. 3rd ed. by T. Chitty, L. Temple, R. G. Williams, and C. Jeffery. 2 vols. 1868. 8vo. **173 F**

CHITTY, Thomas.

Forms of practical proceedings in the courts of King's Bench, Common Pleas and Exchequer of Pleas. 2nd ed. 1835, 6th ed. 1847, 7th ed. 1856, and 10th ed. 1866. 12mo. **162 D**

Forms of practical proceedings in the Queen's Bench, Common Pleas and Exchequer divisions of the high court of justice. 11th ed. by T. W. Chitty. 1879. 12mo. **12 E**

Forms of practical proceedings in the Queen's Bench division of the high court of justice. 12th ed. by T. W. Chitty. 1883. 12mo. **12 E**

CHITTY, Tompson and Leofric TEMPLE.

A Practical treatise on the law of Carriers of goods and passengers. 1856. 8vo. **161 A**

CHIVALRY.

Memoirs of ancient chivalry. Translated from the French of M. [de la Curne] de St. Palaye, by the translator of the life of Petrarch [Mrs. Susannah Dobson]. 1784. 8vo. **125 C**

See also HERALDRY.

CHOLERA.

Cholera prospects compiled from personal observation in the East. By T. Fox, M.D. 1865. [Pamphlets, vol. 25.] **144 B**

CHOLMELEY, William.

The request and suit of a true-hearted Englishman, 1553. Edited by W. J. Thoms. [Camden Society, vol. 55.] 1853. 8vo. **85 B**

CHRISTIAN, Edmund Brown Viney.

The lays of a limb of the law. By the late John Popplestone. Edited by E. B. V. Christian. 1889. 12mo. **78 B**

CHRISTIAN, Edward.

The origin, progress and present practice of the Bankrupt law in England and Ireland. 2 vols. 1812–14. 8vo. **160 D**

The same. 2nd ed. 2 vols. 1818. 8vo. **160 D**

Practical instructions for suing out and prosecuting a Commission of Bankrupt. 1816. 8vo. **160 D**

The same. 2nd ed. 1820. 8vo. **160 D**

14

CHRISTIANITY.

The Christian manual, or of the life and manners of true Christians. By John Woolton, D.D., bishop of Exeter. Cambridge, 1851. 12mo. **77 D**

A Dissertation exhibiting a general view of the rise, progress and corruptions of Christianity. By Rev. Richard Whately. See Encyclopædia Britannica, 8th ed. vol. 1, 1860, pp. 447–545. **147 A**

Extracts from the article headed 'Christian Ethics and the Ethics of Christ' published in the 'Theological Review' of September 1864, also from an article in the 'Westminster Review.' n.d. [Pamphlets, vol. 27.] **144 B**

What I believe. By Leon Tolstoi, translated from the Russian by Constantine Popoff. 1885. 12mo. **77 A**

See also BELLARMINO, R. and MILLER, REV. C.

CHRIST'S HOSPITAL, LONDON.

Charges and orders for the several officers of Christ's Hospital 1784 and 1785. [1785.] 12mo. **92 A**

A History of the royal foundation of Christ's hospital with memoirs of eminent Blues. By the Rev. Wm. Trollope. 1834. 4to. **89 F**

CHRONICLES AND MEMORIALS.

Chronicles and Memorials of Great Britain and Ireland during the middle ages. Published under the direction of the Master of the Rolls. [All of which are catalogued under their respective authors and subjects.] 223 vols. 1858–89. 8vo. **101 & 102**

CHRONOLOGY.

Blair's Chronological tables revised and enlarged, comprehending the chronology and history of the world from the earliest times to the Russian treaty of peace, April 1856. By J. W. Rosse. 1856. 12mo. **116 D**

The Chronological historian, containing a regular account of all material transactions from the invasion of the Romans to the death of King George the First. By Mr. Salmon. 2nd ed. 1733. 12mo. **116 E**

The chronology of history. By Sir N. H. Nicolas. 1833. 12mo. **116 D**

The Handbook of the year 1868. A register of facts, dates, and events. By G. H. Townsend. 1869. 8vo. **146 C**

Haydn's Dictionary of Dates and universal information relating to all ages and nations. 19th ed. by B. Vincent. 1889. 8vo. **134 I**

CHRONOLOGY—*continued.*

Manual of dates. By G. H. Townsend. 1862. 8vo. **134 I**

Notitia historica, containing tables, calendars and miscellaneous information for use of historians, antiquaries and legal profession. By Sir N. H. Nicolas. 1824. 8vo. **116 E**

See also ASPIN, J., BETHAM, REV. W. and BOND, J. J.

CHURCH BUILDING AND LEASES.

The law of the building of churches, parsonages and schools; and of the divisions of parishes and places. By C. F. Trower. 1874. 8vo. **9 B**

Report from the select committee on Church Leases with the minutes of evidence. 1839. folio. **153 D**

CHURCH OF ENGLAND.

Church courts and church discipline. By R. I. Wilberforce. 1843. 8vo. **77 B**

A Church Dictionary. By W. F. Hook, D.D. 10th ed. 1867. 8vo. **77 E**

The Church question in England. A speech not delivered in the House of Lords, but addressed to their Lordships during the vacation. 1860. [Pamphlets, vol. 15.] **144 B**

De non temerandis ecclesiis, churches not to be violated, a tract of the rights and respects due unto the Church. By Sir H. Spelman. 7th ed. See Sir H. Spelman's English works, 2nd ed. 1727, part 1, pp. 1–36. **78 H**

The duty of a Conservative government towards the clergy and the church in their present relations with the state. By Rev. Charles Miller. 1841. [Pamphlets, vol. 5.] **144 A**

Four reports from the commissioners appointed to consider the state of the Established Church with reference to ecclesiastical duties and revenues, 1835–1836, and the draft of a fifth report, 1837. 1835–37. folio. **153 D**

A Letter to the Earl of Derby upon a public speech delivered in the House of Lords by the Lord bishop of Exeter on the Church discipline bill. By A. J. Stephens. 1856. [Pamphlets, vol. 10.] **144 A**

Observations on the modern clergy and present state of the church. By Rev. C. Lucas. Devizes, [1820]. 8vo. **118 E**

The Official year-book of the Church of England 1883–1885. 3 vols. 1883–5. 8vo. **146 E**

The old constitution and present establishment in Church and

CHURCH OF ENGLAND—*continued.*

State honestly asserted. By A Person of honour. 1718.
[Grimaldi's Tracts, vol. 1.]   **118 B**

The Option : being an enquiry into the grounds of the claim
made by the Archbishop on all consecrated and translated
Bishops, of the disposal of any preferment belonging to
their respective sees that he shall make choice of. See Collectanea Juridica, vol. 2, 1792, pp. 296–331.   **144 G**

Places of worship and schools sites bill. Speech by G. O.
Morgan. Wrexham, [1870.] [Pamphlets, vol. 38.] **144 C**

A Plan of church reform. By Lord Henley. 1832. [Jacob's
Tracts, vol. 12.]   **144 F**

Treason in the Church, an intercepted letter from O'Connell
to a member of the common council of London. 1839.
[Pamphlets, vol. 5.]   **144 A**

A Vindication of the Church of England and the penal laws
from the exceptions raised against them in a late pamphlet.
1688. [Tracts, 1688–9.]   **118 E**

See also BACON, J., BEDE, BURNET, CANON LAW, CANTER-
BURY, ECCLESIASTICAL LAW, ECTON, GIBSON, E., HALE,
W. H., MALLORY, J., PRIDEAUX, H. and PRYNNE, W.

CHURCH OF IRELAND.

The Church in Ireland. A second chapter of contemporary
history. By T. Andrews. 1869. [Pamphlets, vol. 34.] **144 C**

The Irish church. An address delivered in 1864 by Sir
H. M. Cairns. 3rd ed. 1868. [Pamphlets, vol. 34.] **144 C**

Letter to John Bright, Esq., M.P., respecting the Irish Church.
By Henry, Earl Grey. 1868. [Pamphlets, vol. 34.] **144 C**

The statutes, constitutions, canons, rubricks, and articles of
the Church of Ireland digested under proper heads. By E.
Bullingbrooke. 2 vols. Dublin, 1770. 4to.   **77 F**

CHURCHER'S COLLEGE, PETERSFIELD, HANTS.

The history of Churcher's College. [By Nathaniel Atcheson.]
1823. 8vo.   **88 A**

CHURCHILL, CAMERON.

The office and duties of the Sheriff. 1879. 8vo.   **53 G**
The same. 2nd ed. 1882. 8vo.   **11 F**

CHURCH-LANGTON, LEICESTERSHIRE.

The history of the rise and progress of the charitable foundations at Church-Langton with the different deeds of trust.
By Rev. William Hanbury. 1767. 8vo.   **89 C**

CHURCHWARDENS.

The Churchwarden's Guide. By G. F. Chambers. 11th ed. [1888.] 12mo.   **9 C**

A Practical guide to the duties of Churchwardens. By C. G. Prideaux. 15th ed. 1886. 12mo.   **9 C**

The Churchwarden's guide. By C. W. Lovesy. 8th ed. 1871.   **161 F**

Clergyman's legal handbook and Churchwarden's guide. By J. M. Dale. 5th ed. 1869. 12mo.   **9 C**

CHUTE, CHALONER WILLIAM.

Equity under the Judicature act, or the relation of equity to common law. 1874. 12mo.   **167 B**

See also BEAVAN, C.

CICERO, MARCUS TULLIUS.

Cicero, a drama. By N. T. Moile. 1847. 8vo.   **83 C**

The history of the life of Marcus Tullius Cicero. By Conyers Middleton. 2 vols. 1741. 4to.   **80 I**

The republic of Cicero reprinted from the third edition of Cardinal Mai (Rome, 1846), and translated with notes by G. G. Hardingham. 1884. 8vo.   **83 H**

See also CLASSICS.

CINQUE PORTS.

Charters of the Cinque Ports, two ancient towns and their members. Translated into English with annotations by Samuel Jeake. 1728. folio.   **89 G**

Cinque Ports. By M. Burrows. 2nd ed. 1888. 12mo. **88 D**

Delineations of the Isle of Thanet and the Cinque Ports. By E. W. Brayley. 2 vols. 1817–18. 8vo.   **88 D**

See also DOVER and KENT.

CIRCUITS, JUDGES'.

Circuits of the Judges 1838–89. 2 vols. 1838–89. folio. **Hall**

Letter to Lord Chelmsford on the Circuit System. By George Atkinson. [Pamphlets, vol. 31.]   **144 C**

CIRCUMSTANTIAL EVIDENCE.

Essay on the principles of circumstantial evidence, illustrated by numerous cases. By Wm. Wills. 4th ed. by A. Wills. 1862. 8vo.   **52 G**

See also BEST, W. M. and EVIDENCE.

CIRENCESTER, Richard of.

The itinerary of Richard of Cirencester, with an account of that author and his works. See W. Stukeley's Itinerarium Curiosum, vol. 2, 1776, pp. 79–177. **85 I**

Speculum historiale de gestis regum Angliæ (447–1066). Edited by J. E. B. Mayor. 2 vols. 1863–69. 8vo. **101 I**

CIVIL GOVERNMENT.

An Essay upon civil government. By A. M. Ramsay. 1732. 12mo. **49 E**

A treatise concerning Civil Government in three parts. By Josiah Tucker. 1781. 8vo. **49 E**

CIVIL LAW. See Roman Law.

CIVIL SERVICE.

The Civil Service. By W. R. Smee. [Paris, 1861.] [Pamphlets, vol. 14.] **144 A**

Civil Service calendar, 1887 : containing official regulations and instructions for candidates. By Wm. Bussell. 1887. 8vo. **255 H**

Civil Service Directory, 1889, containing a list of all the public departments, and the officials. 1889. 8vo. **255 H**

The same, 1890. 1890. 8vo. **Hall**

CIVILISATION.

History of civilisation in England. By H. T. Buckle. vol. 1. 3rd ed. 1861. vol. 2. 2nd ed. 1864. 2 vols. 1861–64. 8vo. **116 G**

CLAIMS AND DEFENCES.

Forms of Claims and Defences in Chancery division of high court of justice. By C. S. Drewry. 1876. 8vo. **52 B**

CLAIMS, Court of.

History, jurisdiction and practice of the Court of Claims of the United States. By William Richardson. Washington, 1882. [Pamphlets, vol. 31.] **144 C**

CLANCY, James.

A Treatise of the rights, duties, and liabilities of Husband and Wife at law and in equity. 3rd ed. 1827. 8vo. **168 G**

CLAPHAM, Rev. Samuel.
A Collection of the several points of Sessions Law alphabetically arranged. 2 vols. 1818. 8vo.   175 D

CLARENDON, Edward, 1 Earl of.
The history of the Rebellion and civil wars in England ; with
An historical view of the affairs of Ireland. New ed. by
Bulkeley Bandinel. 8 vols. Oxford, 1826. 8vo. 115 E
The life of Edward Earl of Clarendon written by himself.
Oxford, 1759. folio.   79 I
The proceedings in House of Commons touching impeach-
ment of Edward, Earl of Clarendon. 1700. 12mo. 50 B
State papers containing the materials from which the History
of the Rebellion was composed. 3 vols. Oxford, 1767–86.
folio.   115 I

CLARK, Rev. Andrew.
Register of the University of Oxford. vol. 2, parts 1–4. [1571–
1622.] Edited by A. Clark. [Oxford Hist. Soc. vols. 10–
12 and 14.] Oxford, 1887–89. 8vo.   85 F
Survey of the antiquities of the city of Oxford, composed in
1661–66 by Anthony Wood. Edited by A. Clark. vol. 1.
[Oxford Hist. Soc. vol. 15.] Oxford, 1889. 8vo.   85 F

CLARK, Charles.
A Digested index to all the reports in House of Lords, from
commencement of series by Dow in 1814, to end of eleven
volumes of House of Lords Cases. 1868. 8vo.   1 D
House of Lords cases on appeals and writs of error and claims
of peerages, 1850–1866. 9 vols. 1853–66. 8vo.   1 C D
A Summary of Colonial law, the practice of the Court of
appeals from the Plantations, and of the laws and their
administration in all the colonies. 1834. 8vo.   55 D

CLARK, Charles and William FINNELLY.
Reports of cases heard in the House of Lords on appeals and
writs of error, 1831–1846. 12 vols. 1835–47. 8vo. 1 B C
House of Lords Cases on appeals and writs of error. 1847–
1850. 2 vols. 1849–51. 8vo.   1 C

CLARK, Edwin Charles.
Analysis of Criminal liability. Cambridge, 1880. 12mo. 52 E
Early Roman law. The regal period. 1872. 12mo.   63 E

CLARK, HUGH.

A Concise history of Knighthood containing the religious and military orders which have been instituted in Europe. 2 vols. in 1 vol. 1784. 8vo. **125 E**

The arms of the nobility of England, Scotland, and Ireland. Engraved by H. Clark and T. Wormull, 1778, and The peerage of the nobility of England, Scotland, and Ireland. By H. Clark and T. Wormull. 1779. 12mo. **123 A**

CLARK, LATIMER.

Mr. Latimer Clark, C.E., A sketch of his life and work. By H. T. Humphreys. 1882. [Pamphlets, vol. 31.] **144 C**

CLARK, THOMAS.

Perpetuation or extinction of the Ecclesiastical jurisdiction in temporal concerns. 1840. 8vo. **166 B**

CLARKE, SIR EDWARD.

Allcard v. Skinner: speech for defendant. 1887. 8vo. **51 G**

The law of Extradition with the conventions upon the subject existing between England and foreign nations. 1867, and 2nd ed. 1874. 12mo. **168 D**

The same. 3rd ed. 1888. 8vo. **10 A**

CLARKE OR CLERKE, FRANCIS.

The practice of the court of Admiralty of England. 1722. 12mo. **160 A**

The same. Edited by E. Simpson. 1743. 12mo. **160 A**

Praxis [in Curiis Ecclesiasticis] per T. Bladen edita et recognita. Editio secunda. 1684. 8vo. **49 C**

CLARKE, G. R.

The history and description of the town and borough of Ipswich. Ipswich, 1830. 8vo. **93 C**

CLARKE, REV. GEORGE SOMERS.

Hebrew Criticism and Poetry with Appendixes of readings and interpretations of the four greater prophets. 1810. 8vo. **77 B**

CLARKE, HENRY W.

The history of tithes from Abraham to Queen Victoria. 1887. 8vo. **78 B**

CLARKE, JAMES.

A Survey of the lakes of Cumberland, Westmoreland, and
Lancashire, with an account of the adjacent country, and a
sketch of the border laws.   1787.   folio.   **86 H**

CLARKE, MARY COWDEN.

The complete concordance to Shakespeare, being a verbal
index to all the passages in the dramatic works of the poet.
New and revised ed.   1881.   8vo.   **83 F**

CLARKE, SAMUEL, D.D.

A collection of papers which passed between the late learned
Mr. Leibnitz and Dr. Clarke in the years 1715 and 1716,
relating to the principles of natural philosophy and religion,
to which are added Letters to Dr. Clarke concerning liberty
and necessity, also Remarks upon a book entituled A philosophical enquiry concerning human liberty.   By Samuel
Clarke, D.D.   1717.   12mo.   **78 A**

CLARKE, STEPHEN REYNOLDS.

The new Lancashire gazetteer, or topographical dictionary.
1830.   8vo.   **89 B**
The new Yorkshire gazetteer.   1828.   8vo.   **94 B**

CLARKE, WILLIAM NELSON.

Parochial topography of the hundred of Wanting with other
miscellaneous records relating to the county of Berks.
Oxford, 1824.   4to.   **86 B**

[CLARKSON, CHRISTOPHER.]

The history of Richmond in the county of York.   Richmond,
1814.   12mo.   **94 A**

CLASSICS, GREEK AND LATIN.

A Classical dictionary containing a copious account of all the
proper names mentioned in ancient authors.   By Rev. John
Lempriere.   20th ed.   1844.   8vo.   **84 C**
The Classics for the Million, being an epitome in English of
the works of the principal Greek and Latin authors.   By
Henry Grey.   2nd ed.   1881.   8vo.   **83 C**
Poetæ Minores Græci, accedunt etiam Observationes Radulphi
Wintertoni in Hesiodum.   Cantabrigiæ, 1684.   12mo. **47 E**
Poetriarum Octo Erinnæ, Myrus, Myrtidis, Corinnæ, Tele-

CLASSICS, GREEK AND LATIN—*continued.*

sillæ, Praxillæ, Nossidis, Anytæ, fragmenta et elogia
Græce et Latine; accedit Gottfridi Olearii dissertatio de
poetriis Græcis. Cura et studio Io. Christiani Wolfii.
Hamburgi, 1734. 4to.   **47 G**

Æschyli Choephoroe ex recensione Porsoniana, adjecti sunt
Choephoron Chorici Cantus sicut dispositi sunt in tentamine V. R. Caroli Burneii. Glasguæ, 1814. 24mo. **47 E**

Euripidis Opera omnia. 9 vols. Glasguæ, 1821.   8vo. **46 J**

Homeri Ilias. 2 vols. in 1. Lipsiæ, 1839. 12mo.   **47 E**

Phædri Augusti Cæsaris Liberti Fabularum Æsopiarum libri
quinque; interpretatione et notis illustravit Petrus Danet.
Parisiis, 1675. 4to.   **47 G**

Sapphus Poetriæ Lesbiæ Fragmenta et elogia, cura et studio
Jo. Christiani Wolfii. Hamburgi, 1733. 4to.   **47 F**

Poetæ Latini Rei Venaticæ, scriptores et Bucolici Antiqui,
videlicet Gratii Falisci atque M. Aurelii Olympii Nemesiani,
Cynegeticon, Halieuticon, et De Aucupio; itidem Bucolica
M. Aurelii Olympii Nemesiani et Calpurnii, quibus accedunt Gerardi Kempheri Observationes in tres priores Calpurnii Eclogas. Lugd. Bat., 1728, 4to.   **118 F**

Scriptores Latini in usum Delphini, cum notis variorum, variis
lectionibus, conspectu codicum et editionum et indicibus
locupletissimis, cura et impensis A. J. Valpy.   141 vols.
1819–30. 8vo.   **46 A–J**

	Vols.		Vols.
Apuleius. 6 vols.	69–74	Persius. 1 vol.	14
Aulus Gellius. 3 vols.	64–66	Phædrus. 2 vols.	38–39
Aurelius Victor. 1 vol.	123	Plautus. 5 vols.	125–129
Ausonius. 2 vols.	55–56	Plinius (Senior). 12 vols.	87–98
Boethius. 1 vol.	54		
Cæsar. 4 vols.	9–12	Pompeius Festus. 2 vols.	82–83
Catullus. 2 vols.	41–42		
Cicero. 13 vols.	129–141	Propertius. 2 vols.	45–46
Claudianus. 3 vols.	24–26	Prudentius. 4 vols.	67–70
Cornelius Nepos. 1 vol.	38	Quintus Curtius. 3 vols.	78–80
Dictys Cretensis et Dares Phrygius. 1 vol.	81		
Eutropius. 1 vol.	27	Sallustius. 3 vols.	14–16
Florus. 2 vols.	39–40	Statius. 4 vols.	61–64
Horatius. 5 vols.	75–79	Suetonius. 4 vols.	84–87
Justinus. 3 vols.	43–45	Tacitus. 8 vols.	16–23
Juvenalis. 3 vols.	12–14	Terentius. 4 vols.	57–60
Livius. 21 vols.	98–118	Tibullus. 2 vols.	42–43
Lucretius. 4 vols.	49–52	Valerius Maximus. 3 vols.	52–54
Manilius. 3 vols.	118–120		
Martialis. 3 vols.	47–49	Velleius Paterculus. 2 vols.	35–36
Ovidius. 9 vols.	27–35		
Panegyrici Veteres. 5 vols.	120–124	Virgilius. 8 vols.	1–8

CLASSICS, GREEK AND LATIN—*continued.*

C. Julii Cæsaris rerum ab se gestarum Commentarii. De bello Gallico libri viii. . . . Pictura totius Galliæ per Jucundum Veronensem ex descriptione Cæsaris. Veterum Galliæ locorum . . . ac fluviorum brevis descriptio. Lutetiæ, 1544. 12mo. **47 E**

C. Julii Cæsaris et A. Hirtii de rebus à C. Julio Cæsare gestis Commentarii cum C. Jul. Cæsaris fragmentis. 1759. 12mo. **47 E**

C. Julii Cæsaris de Bellis Gallico et Civili-Pompeiano, nec non A. Hirtii aliorumque de bellis Alexandrino, Africano, et Hispaniensi Commentarii ex optima Elzeviriana editione expressi. Aeræ, 1804. 12mo. **47 E**

Cato et Varro. Libri de re rustica, M. Catonis Lib. I. M. Terentii Varronis Lib. III. per Petrum Victoriū, ad veterum exemplarium fidem, suæ integritati restituti. Paris, 1543. 12mo. **118 A**

Catulli, Tibulli et Propertii Opera. Birminghamiæ, 1772. 4to. **47 H**

Eutropii epitome Belli Gallici ex Suetonii Tranquilli monumentis quæ desiderantur. In C. Julii Cæsaris commentarios de bello Gallico et civili, Henrici Glareani poetæ laureati Annotationes. Lutetiæ, 1544. 12mo. **47 E**

Flaccus, Calpurnius. Declamationes, curante Petro Burmanno. Lugd. Bat., 1720. 4to. **47 G**

Justinus, Marcus Junius. De historiis Philippicis et totius mundi originibus, interpretatione et notis illustravit Petrus Josephus Cantel. Parisiis, 1677. 4to. **47 F**

D. Junii Juvenalis Satiræ, interpretatione ac notis illustravit Ludovicus Prateus. Parisiis, 1684. 4to. **47 F**

A. Persii Flacci Satiræ, interpretatione ac notis illustravit Ludovicus Prateus. Parisiis, 1684. 4to. **47 F**

Caii Plinii Secundi Naturalis historiæ libri xxxvii., interpretatione et notis illustravit Joannes Harduinus. 5 vols. Paris, 1685. 4to. **47 F**

Quinctilian. De institutione oratoria libri duodecim recogniti et emendati per Petrum Burmannum. Lugd. Bat., 1720. 4to. **47 G**

Quinctilian. Declamationes XIX. majores et quæ ex CCCLXXXVIII. supersunt CXLV. minores. Curante Petro Burmanno. Lugd. Bat., 1720. 4to. **47 G**

Cl. Salmasii de re militari Romanorum Liber, opus posthumum. Lugd. Bat., 1657. 4to. **47 G**

C. Suetonii Tranquilli Opera omnia quæ extant, interpreta-

CLASSICS, Greek and Latin—*continued.*

tione et notis illustravit Augustinus Babelonius. Parisiis, 1684. 4to. **47 G**

Tacitus. Opera interpretatione perpetua et notis illustravit Julianus Pichon. 4 vols. Paris, 1682-87. 4to. **47 F**

Terence. Comœdiæ. Birminghamiæ, 1772. 4to. **47 H**

Virgil. Georgica in quinque linguas conversa. 1827. folio. **47 I**

CLAUSES CONSOLIDATION ACTS.

Collection of public general statutes consolidating provisions usually introduced into acts relating to cemeteries, commissioners, companies, &c. By James Bigg. 2nd ed. 1877. 12mo. **9 C**

The Consolidation acts of 1845 and 1847. By George Tayler. 3rd ed. 1857. 8vo. **163 D**

The Railway clauses, companies' clauses, and lands' clauses Consolidation Acts with notes. By R. P. Collier. 1845. 12mo. **175 B**

CLAYBROOK, Leicestershire.

The history and antiquities of Claybrook. By Rev. Aulay Macaulay. 1791. 8vo. **89 C**

CLAYTON, John.

Reports and pleas of assises at Yorke ; with some presidents usefull for pleaders at the assises. 1651. 12mo. **48 B**

CLAYTON, William Clayton.

Elements of Conveyancing with practical illustrations and select forms, 1855. 8vo. **163 G**

CLEAVELAND, John.

The banking system of the state of New York. 2nd ed. by G. S. Hutchinson. New York, 1864. 8vo. **59 B**

CLERGY LISTS.

Bosworth's Clerical Guide. 1887. 8vo. **75 J**

Clergy list 1841-1889, 49 vols. 1841-89. 8vo. **75 F-J**

Clerical Guide or ecclesiastical directory. 2nd ed. 1822, 3rd ed. 1829, and 4th ed. 1836. 3 vols. 1822-36. 8vo. **76 G**

Crockford's Clerical directory, 1868, 1872, 1874, 1876, 1878-1889. 16 vols. 1868-89. 8vo. **76 F G**

CLERGY, THE.

Ecclesiastical cases relating to the rights of the parochial clergy. By E. Stillingfleet. 2 vols. 1702–4. 8vo. **49 E**

Instructions for the use of candidates for holy orders, and of the parochial clergy. By Christopher Hodgson. 4th ed. 1829. 8vo. **52 F**

The rights of the Clergy of England. By William Nelson. 2nd ed. 1715. 12mo. **48 F**

See also ECCLESIASTICAL LAW.

CLERK, JOHN:

The law and practice of Elections and election committees. 1857. 12mo. **166 C**

CLERK, JOHN FREDERIC and W. H. B. LINDSELL.

The law of Torts. 1889. 8vo. **11 H**

CLERKE, AUBREY ST. JOHN.

The Conveyancing Act 1881, with Vendor and Purchaser Act 1874, and Solicitors' Remuneration Act 1881 with notes. By A. St. J. Clerke and T. Brett. 1881. 12mo. **164 E**

The same. 2nd ed. 1882, and Supplement containing The Conveyancing Act 1882. 2 vols. 1882. 12mo. **64 B**

The same. 3rd ed. 1889. 12mo. **13 G**

The law relating to Sales of land. By A. St. J. Clerke and H. M. Humphry. 1885. 8vo. **13 H**

CLERKENWELL, MIDDLESEX.

The discovery of the Jesuits' college at Clerkenwell in March 1627–1628. Edited by J. G. Nichols, and Supplementary note. [Camden Society, vols. 55 and 73.] 2 vols. 1853–59. 8vo. **85 B**

History and description of the parish of Clerkenwell. By T. Cromwell. 1828. 8vo. **89 D**

The history of Clerkenwell. By the late W. J. Pinks, with additions by E. J. Woods. 2nd ed. 1881. 8vo. **89 E**

CLERMONT, THOMAS, 1 BARON.

Sir John Fortescue, Knight, his life, works, and family history. 2 vols. Printed for private distribution. 1869. 4to. **79 I**

CLEVEDON, SOMERSET.

Chillcott's Clevedon new guide. 7th ed. Bristol, 1856. 12mo. **93 A**

CLEVELAND, YORKSHIRE.

The history and antiquities of Cleveland. By J. W. Ord. 1846. 4to. **94 D**

The history of Cleveland. By Rev. John Graves. Carlisle, 1808. 4to. **94 D**

CLIFFORD, FREDERICK.

History of private bill legislation. 2 vols. 1885–87. 8vo. **83 I**

Practice of the Court of Referees, on private bills in parliament, with reports of cases as to the Locus Standi of petitioners, 1867 to 1872. By F. Clifford and P. S. Stephens. 2 vols. 1870–73. 8vo. **66 C**

Cases decided during the sessions 1873–1888 by the Court of Referees on Private Bills in Parliament. By F. Clifford, A. G. Rickards and M. J. Michael. 4 vols. in 3. 1877–89. 8vo. **66 C**

CLIFFORD, HENRY.

A Report of the two cases of controverted elections of the borough of Southwark in 1796, to which are added an account of the two subsequent cases of the city of Canterbury. 1797. 8vo. **166 E**

CLIFFORD, SIR THOMAS and ARTHUR CLIFFORD.

A Topographical and historical description of the parish of Tixall in the county of Stafford. Paris, 1817. 4to. **93 B**

CLIFT, HENRY.

A New Book of Declarations, Pleadings, Verdicts, Judgments, and Judicial Writs; with the Entries thereupon; digested and published by Sir Charles Ingleby. 2nd ed. 1719. folio.

CLIFTON, GLOUCESTERSHIRE.

Chillcott's New guide to Clifton and the Hotwells. 13th ed. Bristol. n.d. 12mo. **88 A**

CLITHEROE, LANCASHIRE.

An History of the parish of Whalley and honor of Clitheroe. By Rev. T. D. Whitaker. 3rd ed. 1818. 4to. **88 F**

CLIVE, ROBERT, 1 BARON.

The opinions of several eminent counsel touching Lord Clive's jaghire or rent, 1764. See Collectanea Juridica, vol. 1, 1791, pp. 246–262.   **144 G**

CLODE, CHARLES MATHEW.

The administration of justice under Military and Martial law. 1872. 8vo.   **83 H**

The early history of the Guild of Merchant Taylors of the fraternity of St. John the Baptist, London. Privately printed. 2 vols. 1888. 8vo.   **89 E**

Memorials of the guild of Merchant Taylors and of its associated charities and institutions. Privately printed. 1875. 8vo.   **89 E**

The Military forces of the Crown ; their administration and government. 2 vols. 1869. 8vo.   **83 H**

The statutory powers of Her Majesty's principal secretary of state for the war department. Ordnance Branch. 1879. 8vo.   **83 H**

CLODE, WALTER.

The law and practice of Petition of right. 1887. 8vo.   **11 C**

The law relating to Tenement Houses and Flats for residential or business purposes. 1889. 8vo.   **10 B**

CLUB LAW AND CLUBS.

Wertheimer's law relating to clubs. 2nd ed. by A. W. Chaster. 1889. 8vo.   **9 C**

Club law and the law of unregistered friendly societies. By Dominick Daly. 2nd ed. 1889. 12mo.   **9 C**

Club Cases. By A. F. Leach. 1879. 8vo.   **9 C**

The Club directory, a general guide to the London and county clubs, and those of Scotland, Ireland, and British colonial possessions. By G. J. Ivey. 2nd ed. 1880. 8vo.   **Hall**

[CLUBBE, REV. JOHN.]

The history and antiquities of the ancient villa of Wheatfield in the county of Suffolk, 1758. Bound with Morant's Colchester. 1748. 8vo.   **88 G**

CLUN, SHROPSHIRE.

A Concise account of ancient documents relating to the honor, forest, and borough of Clun in Shropshire. Privately printed. Shrewsbury, 1858. 8vo.   **93 A**

CLUTTERBUCK, ROBERT.
History of Herts. 3 vols. 1815–27. folio. **88 H**

COAL MINES.
The Coal Mines regulation act 1887. By M. W. Peace. 1888.
8vo. **9 C**

Manual of the Coal Mines regulation act 1887. By J. C.
Chisholm. 1888. 8vo. **9 C**

The Coal Mines regulation act 1872. By M. W. Peace. 1872.
12mo. **172 F**

Maps and sections to accompany the Report of the Royal
Coal Commission. 1871. folio. **84 H**

A Treatise on the Coal mines of Durham and Northumberland. By J. H. H. Holmes. 1816. 8vo. **87 E**

England's grievance discovered in relation to the coal trade.
By Ralph Gardiner. London, 1655. Newcastle, reprinted
1796. 8vo. **92 D**

See also MINES and TAPPING, T.

COATES, REV. CHARLES.
The history and antiquities of Reading. 1802. 4to. **86 G**

COBBETT, PITT.
Leading cases and opinions on International Law. 1885.
8vo. **55 A**

COCKAYNE, REV. THOMAS OSWALD.
Leechdoms, wortcunning and starcraft of early England.
3 vols. 1864–66. 8vo. **102 A**

COCKBURN, SIR ALEXANDER JAMES EDMUND.
Charge in the case of The Queen against Thomas Castro
otherwise Arthur Orton otherwise Sir Roger Tichborne.
2 vols. 1874–75. 8vo. **118 E**

The Queen v. T. Castro. Proceedings on the trial at bar before the Lord Chief Justice, Mr. Justice Mellor, Mr. Justice
Lush and a special jury. Summing up January 29, 1874,
in Westminster Hall. 1874. folio. **49 H**

Charge to the grand jury at the Central Criminal Court in the
case of The Queen against Nelson and Brand. Edited by
F. Cockburn. 1867. 8vo. **50 B**

COCKBURN, Sir Alexander J. E.—*continued.*

On Nationality or the law relating to subjects and aliens, considered with a view to future legislation. 1869. 8vo. **11 A**

Our Judicial System. A letter to the lord high chancellor on the proposed changes in the judicature of the country. 1870. [Pamphlets, vol. 34.] **144 C**

Cases of controverted elections determined in the eleventh parliament of the United Kingdom. By A. E. Cockburn and W. C. Rowe. 1833. 8vo. **66 A**

COCKBURN, Rev. William.

The Clerk's Assistant in the practice of the ecclesiastical courts. 4th ed. Dublin. 1792. 8vo. **166 B**

[COCKIN, William.]

The art of delivering written language, or an essay on reading. [By W. C.] 1775. 8vo. **78 B**

CODES.

Argentine Republic. Códigos y leyes usuales de la República Argentina. Cuarta edition. Felix Lajouane, editor. 2 vols. Buenos Ayres, 1888. 8vo. **55 C**

Austria. General civil code for all the German hereditary provinces of the Austrian monarchy. Translated by J. M. Chevalier De Winiwarter. Vienna, 1866. 8vo. **55 C**

Belgium. Code Napoléon, seul texte du code civil officiel pour la Belgique. Par A. Delebecque et J. B. Hoffman. Quatrième édition. Bruxelles, 1881. 24mo. **55 C**

Belgium. Les Neuf Codes en vigueur en Belgique, suivis de leurs modifications. Paris, 1834. 24mo. **55 C**

Denmark. The Danish laws or the code of Christian V., translated for the use of the English inhabitants of the Danish settlements in America. 1756. 12mo. **55 C**

Egypt. Concordance des códes Égyptiens mixte et indigène avec le code Napoléon. Par Joseph Aziz. Première partie. Code civil. Alexandrie, 1886. 4to. **55 C**

England. Le Droit Anglais codifié. Par Arthur Pavitt. Paris, 1885. 8vo. **166 F**

England. An English code, its difficulties and the modes of overcoming them; a practical application of the science of Jurisprudence. By Sheldon Amos. 1873. 8vo. **63 F**

England. A Letter to the lord chancellor on expediency of proposal to form a new civil code for England. By John Reddie. 1828. [Jacob's Tracts, vol. 9.] **144 E**

CODES—*continued*.

France. Codes Français et lois usuelles. Par H. F. Rivière. 16me éd. 2 vols. Paris, 1888. 8vo. **55 C**

France. Les Codes Français collationnés sur les textes officiels. Par L. Tripier. 15me éd. Paris, 1864. 8vo. **58 G**

France. Cours de Code Napoléon. Par C. Demolombe. 20 vols. Paris, 1860–63. 8vo. **58 C**

France. Les Codes Français expliqués par leurs motifs, par des exemples et par la jurisprudence. Par J. A. Rogron. 5me éd. 2 vols. Paris, 1863. 4to. **40 I**

France. Les Codes Annotés de Sirey. Edition entièrement refondue par P. Gilbert. 3 vols. Paris, 1862–63. 8vo. **58 G**

France. Les Six Codes précédés de la charte constitutionnelle et de ses lois organiques. Paris, 1828. 8vo. **40 I**

France. The civil laws of France, supplemented by notes, illustrative of analogy between rules of Code Napoléon and leading principles of Roman law. By D. M. Aird. 1875. 12mo. **55 C**

France. Code Napoléon, being the French civil code literally translated. By R. S. Richards. [1850.] 8vo. **55 C**

France. Le droit civil Français, suivant l'ordre du Code. Par C. B. M. Toullier, continué et complété par J. B. Duvergier. 16me éd. 7 vols. Paris, [1846–48.] 8vo. **58 E F**

France. Le droit civil Français, suivant l'ordre du code civil. Livre troisième, titres vi–xi. Par J. B. Duvergier. 6 vols. Paris, 1835–43. 8vo. **58 C D**

France. The Code Napoléon, verbally translated from the French. By Bryant Barrett. 2 vols. 1811. 8vo. **55 C**

France. The French code of commerce as revised to the end of 1886 rendered into English. By Sylvain Mayer. 1887. 8vo. **55 C**

France. French mercantile law, with a new translation of the code of commerce. By N. Argles. 1882. 8vo. **55 C**

France. The French code of commerce and most usual commercial laws with a commentary, and a glossary of French judicial terms. By Leopold Goirand. 1880. 8vo. **55 C**

France. Commentaire du code de commerce et de la législation commerciale. Par J. Alauzet. 4 tomes. Paris, 1856–57. 8vo. **58 A B**

France. Les Codes Criminels interprétés par la jurisprudence et la doctrine, suivis d'un formulaire. Par R. De Villargues. Deuxième édition. Paris, 1864. 8vo. **40 H**

France. Théorie du code pénal. Par C. Adolphe et F. Hélie. 4me éd. 7 vols. Paris, 1861–63. 8vo. **58 A**

CODES—*continued.*

France. Traité de l'instruction criminelle, ou théorie du code d'instruction criminelle. Par J. Hélie. 9 vols. Paris, 1845–60. 8vo.   58 D

France. Code Penal, ou Recueil des principales ordonnances, édits et declarations sur les crimes et délits. 4me éd. Paris, 1777. 12mo.   40 I

See also BÉDARRIDE, J. and TROPLONG, R. T.

Germany. The criminal code of the German empire, translated with prolegomena and a commentary. By Geoffrey Drage. 1885. 12mo.   55 C

Greece and Rome. Horæ juridicæ subsecivæ. By Charle Butler. 2nd ed. 1807. 8vo.   83 J

Holland. Commercial code of the Netherlands. Rotterdam, 1880. 12mo.   55 C

India. The Anglo-Indian Codes. Edited by W. Stokes. 3 vols. 1887–89. 8vo.   38 D

India. The law of India. By Andrew Lyon. vol. 1. The Codes. 1873. 8vo.   38 D

India. The code of civil procedure 1882 as modified up to 1st July 1888. Calcutta, 1888. 8vo.   33 F

India. Commentaries on the code of civil procedure. By J. H. Nelson. 2nd ed. Madras, 1878. 8vo.   38 C

India. Code of criminal procedure, 1882. 1888. 8vo. 33 F

India. The code of criminal procedure. By H. T. Prinsep. 4th ed. Calcutta, 1873. 8vo.   38 C

India. Indian criminal codes. By Fendall Currie. 4th ed. 1872. 8vo.   38 C

India. An Analysis of the Indian penal code. By J. Cutler and E. F. Griffin. 1869. 8vo.   38 B

India. A Copy of the penal code prepared by the Indian law commissioners. Hertford, 1851. 8vo.   38 A

Italy. Codice civile del Regnod'Italia. Torino, 1865. 8vo. 56 C

Italy. Il codice Italiano di procedura civile. Annotato per cura del Cavaliere Luigi Borsari. Torino, 1865. 8vo. 56 D

Italy. La pratica del codice di procedura civile Italiano. Per cura di Luigi Borsari. Torino, 1867. 8vo.   56 D

Lower Canada. The civil code of Lower Canada. By Thomas McCord. Montreal, 1867. 12mo.   60 E

New York State. The codes of New York 1869. The penal code of New York 1869, and The civil code of New York 1870. By T. L. M. Browne. [Pamphlets, vol. 36.] 144 C

CODES—*continued.*

New York State. The proposed codification of our common law. By J. C. Carter. 1884. [Pamphlets, vol. 31.]   **144 C**

Prussia. The Frederician code, or a body of law for the dominions of the King of Prussia. Translated from the French. 2 vols. Edinburgh, 1761. 8vo.   **55 C**

Russia. The grand instructions to the commissioners appointed to frame a new code of laws for the Russian empire, translated from the original Russian. By M. Tatischeff. 1768. 8vo.   **55 C**

Saint Lucia. Code of civil procedure. 1881. 8vo.   **36 E**

Spain. Código de Comercio, decretado sancionado y promulgado en 30 de Mayo de 1829. Edicion oficial. Madrid, 1829. 8vo.   **39 E**

Spain. Código de las costumbres marítimas de Barcelona, hasta aquí vulgarmente llamado Libro del Consulado. Por D. Antonio de Capmany, y de Monpalau. Madrid, 1791. 4to.   **39 E**

COE, WILLIAM EDWARD.

The practice at the judges' chambers and in the district registries. 1876. 12mo.   **12 G**

COGGESHALL ABBEY, SUSSEX.

Radulphi de Coggeshall Chronicon Anglicanum. Edited by J. Stevenson. 1875. 8vo.   **102 F**

COGNOVITS.

The law of warrants of attorney and cognovits. By B. C. Robinson. 1844. 12mo.   **177 D**

See also Fisher's Digest, vol. 7, 1884, pp. 474–503.   **14 E**

COINS.

A List of coins lent for exhibition by F. K. Glover at opening of new library and museum of corporation of London. 1872. 8vo   **82 C**

Records of Roman history as exhibited on the Roman coins. By Francis Hobler. 2 vols. 1860. 4to.   **113 G**

COKE, SIR EDWARD.

A Book of Entries containing perfect precedents of all matters concerning practical part of laws of England in actions real, personal, and mixt and in appeals. 1614. folio.

The same. 2nd ed. 1671. folio,   **48 I**

COKE, SIR EDWARD—*continued.*

The Compleate Copyholder. 1644. 12mo.   **48 B**

Letter of the council to Sir Thomas Lake relating to the proceedings of Sir E. Coke at Oatlands. [Camden Society, vol. 87.] 1864. 8vo.   **85 C**

The life of Sir Edward Coke. By C. W. Johnson. 2 vols. 1837. 8vo.   **80 D**

Les Reports de divers Resolutions et Judgements donnes avec graund deliberation, per les tresreverendes judges et sages de la ley. [temp. Eliz. et Jac. I.] 11 parts in 4 vols. 1601–15. folio.

The twelfth Part of the Reports of Sir Edward Coke, of divers Resolutions and Judgments, &c. 1656. folio.

[Part 13.] Certain select Cases in law reported by Sir Edward Coke, late Lord Chief Justice of England &c.; translated out of a manuscript written with his own hand. 1659. folio.

The reports of Sir E. Coke. 2nd ed. [13 parts in 1 vol.] 1680. folio.

Les reports de E. Coke [with references by Edward Chilton]. 13 parts, in 4 vols. 1797. folio.

The reports of Sir E. Coke in thirteen parts complete. Revised and translated by George Wilson. 7 vols. Dublin, 1793. 8vo.

The same. New ed. by J. H. Thomas and J. F. Fraser. 6 vols. 1826. 8vo.   **4 E**

The reports of Sir E. Coke in verse. 3rd ed. by J. Worrall. With a life of Sir E. Coke. 1826. 12mo.   **79 A**

An exact abridgment in English of the Eleven books of reports of Sir E. Coke. By Sir T. Ireland. 3rd impression. 1657 and 1666. 12mo.   **48 B**

Un perfect table a touts les severall livers del Reportes de Sir Edward Coke. Compose & collect per Thomam Ashe. 1606. 12mo.   **49 A**

The first part of the Institutes of the lawes of England : or, a commentarie upon Littleton, not the name of a Lawyer onely, but of the Law it selfe. 2nd ed. 1629. 4to.   **155 C**

The same. 13th ed. Also Three learned tracts of the same author, with the Treatise of the old tenures, the whole revised and corrected by Francis Hargrave, and also an Analysis of Littleton written by an Unknown Hand in 1658–9, but never before published. 1775. folio.   **155 D**

The same. 14th ed. by Francis Hargrave and Charles Butler. 1789. folio.   **155 D**

COKE, Sir Edward—*continued.*

The same. 15th ed. by F. Hargrave and C. Butler. 2 vols. 1794. 8vo. **176 E**

The same. 16th ed. by F. Hargrave and C. Butler. 3 vols. 1809. 8vo. **176 E**

The same. 19th ed. by C. Butler. 2 vols. 1832. 8vo. **13 A**

A Systematic arrangement of Lord Coke's First institute of the laws of England on the plan of Sir Matthew Hale's analysis. By J. H. Thomas. 3 vols. 1818. 8vo. **176 E**

An Analysis of Coke on Littleton. Comprised in a series of questions. By George Fisk. 2 vols. 1824. 8vo. **176 D**

An Exact abridgment of the Lord Coke's Commentaries upon Littleton. By Sir H. Davenport. 1652. 12mo. **48 B**

An Abridgment of the first part of my Ld Coke's Institutes with some additions. 1714. 12mo. **48 B**

The second part of the Institutes of the lawes of England containing the Exposition of many ancient and other Statutes. 3rd ed. 1669. folio. **155 C**

The same. 6th ed. 1681. folio. **155 C**

The third part of the Institutes of the lawes of England : concerning High Treason and other Pleas of the Crown and Criminall Causes. 1644. folio. **155 C**

The same. 3rd ed. 1660 and 4th ed. 1669. folio. **155 C**

The same. 6th ed. 1680. folio. **155 C**

The fourth part of the Institutes of the laws of England. 1644. folio. **155 C**

The same. 5th ed. 1671, and 6th ed. 1681. folio. **155 C**

Three law tracts. I. The compleat copyholder. II. A reading on 27 Edward the First called the statute De Finibus levatis. III. A treatise of Bail and Mainprize to which are added, The old tenures, also some notes to Coke's commentary upon Littleton. By William Hawkins. 1764. 8vo. **144 F**

COKER, Rev. John.

A Survey of Dorsetshire, containing the antiquities and natural history of that county. 1732. folio. **87 G**

COLCHESTER, Essex.

Colchester. By Rev. E. L. Cutts. 1888. 8vo. **87 E**

The history and antiquities of Colchester. By Rev. Philip Morant. 2nd ed. London, 1768, reprinted Chelmsford, 1815. Bound with Rev. P. Morant's History of Essex, vol. 2. 1816. folio. **88 G**

COLCHESTER, ESSEX.—*continued.*

The history and description of Colchester. [By Joseph Strutt.] 2 vols. bound in 1. Colchester, 1803. 8vo. **87 E**

History and description of town and borough of Colchester. By Thomas Cromwell. 2 vols. 1825. 8vo. **87 E**

COLE, CHARLES NALSON.

A Collection of laws which form the constitution of the Bedford Level Corporation, with an introductory history thereof. 1761, and 2nd ed. 1803. 8vo. **86 A**

COLE, HENRY.

Documents illustrative of English history in the thirteenth and fourteenth centuries, selected from the records of the department of the Queen's Remembrancer of the Exchequer. 1844. folio. **99 E**

Record commission. Letters on the conduct of C. P. Cooper, the secretary, and on the general management of the commission. 1836. 8vo. **97 I**

COLE, HENRY WARWICK.

On the domicil of Englishmen in France. 1857. 8vo. **166 A**

Saint Augustine, a poem in eight books. Edinburgh, 1877. 8vo. **83 H**

COLE, JESSE.

Bills of Costs in Chancery. 1846. 8vo. **165 A**

COLE, RICHARD HENRY.

The law and practice as to particulars and conditions of sale. 1879. 8vo. **13 H**

COLE, WILLIAM ROBERT.

The law and practice in Ejectment. 1857. 8vo. **9 H**

The law relating to Criminal Informations and informations in the nature of Quo Warranto. 1843. 12mo. **168 G**

COLEMAN, E.

Bills of costs in chancery of plaintiff and defendant. 2nd ed. 1857. 12mo. **165 A**

COLENSO, Right Rev. John William.
Bishop Colenso's Fallacies [of Parts 1 and 2]. By Thomas
De Meschin. 1863. [Pamphlets, vol. 18.]   **144 B**

[COLERIDGE, Henry Nelson.]
Six months in the West Indies in 1825. 2nd ed. 1826.
8vo.   **84 A**

COLIGNY, Gaspard de.
Gasparis Colinii Castellonii, magni quondam Franciæ amiralii,
Vita. 1575. 12mo.   **118 A**

COLLATERAL CONSANGUINITY.
An Essay on Collateral Consanguinity. See Blackstone's
Law Tracts, 3rd ed. 1771, pp. 131–198.   **144 G**
See also Descents.

COLLECTANEA JURIDICA.
Collectanea Juridica : consisting of tracts relative to the law
and constitution of England. [Collected by Francis Hargrave.] 2 vols. 1791–92. 8vo.   **144 G**

COLLEGE OF ARMS.
A History of the College of Arms and the lives of all the
kings, heralds and pursuivants from the reign of Richard
III. By Rev. Mark Noble. 1805. 4to.   **127 J**
Catalogue of the Arundel manuscripts in the College of Arms.
Not published. 1829. 8vo.   **118 F**

COLLEGES.
The law as to colleges. See J. Grant's Law of corporations,
1850, pp. 529–551.   **52 D**
Notitia Monastica, or an account of all the colleges and hos-
pitals founded before 1540. By the Right Rev. Thomas
Tanner. Cambridge, 1787. folio.   **85 I**

COLLES, Richard.
Reports of cases upon appeals and writs of error, in Court of
parliament 1697–1709. 1 vol. Dublin, 1789. 8vo.   **1 D**

COLLETTE, Charles Hastings.
Popish Infallibility. A lecture delivered at St. Luke's parish
room, Bath. 1883. [Pamphlets, vol. 34.]   **144 C**

COLLETTE, CHARLES HASTINGS—*continued.*

Sacramental confession, priestly absolution and indulgences. Rome's system of 'The Sacrament of Penance,' practically explained and proved to be a modern invention and a system of priestcraft. 1885. 8vo. **77 B**

COLLIER DOCK, ISLE OF DOGS.

Collier Dock, Isle of Dogs. Act passed 6 George IV., sess. 1825, cap. cxix. with an index of matter and alphabetical list of owners and occupiers. 1825. 4to. **89 F**

COLLIER, JOHN.

The works of Tim Bobbin, Esq. [John Collier] in prose and verse, with a memoir of the author by John Corry. Rochdale, 1819. 8vo. **118 B**

COLLIER, ROBERT PORRETT.

The law relating to Mines. 1849. 12mo. **172 F**

The railway clauses, companies' clauses, and lands' clauses, consolidation Acts, with notes. 1845. 12mo. **175 B**

COLLIERIES.

The law of Collieries. By J. C. Fowler. 4th ed. by J. C. Fowler and D. Lewis. 1884. 12mo. **9 C**

Minutes of evidence &c. on petition of proprietors of collieries in South Wales taken before a committee of House of Commons May and June 1810. Newport, [1810]. [Jacob's Tracts, vol. 13.] **144 F**

See also COAL MINES.

COLLINS, ARTHUR.

The Baronettage of England. 2 vols. 1720. 12mo. **125 A**

The English baronage, or an historical account of the lives and actions of our nobility. vol. 1. 1727. 4to. **127 I**

The peerage of England, or an historical and genealogical account of the present nobility. 1 vol. in 2. 1709. 8vo. **126 A**

The same. 2nd ed. 2 vols. in 3. 1710–14. 8vo. **126 A**

The same. 3rd ed. 2 vols. 1714. 8vo. **126 A**

The same. 4th ed. 2 vols. 1717. 8vo. **126 A**

The same on an extended scale. 4 vols. 1735. 8vo. **126 A**

The same. 2nd ed. 4 vols. 1741, and Supplement 2 vols. 1750, 6 vols. 1741–50. 8vo. **126 A B**

COLLINS, ARTHUR—*continued.*

The same. 3rd ed. 5 vols. in 6. 1756. 8vo. **126 B**

The same. 4th ed. 7 vols. 1768. 8vo. **126 B**

The same. 5th ed. with supplement by B. Longmate. 9 vols. 1779–84. 8vo. **126 B C**

The same. [6th ed.] Continued to the present time by Sir Egerton Brydges. 9 vols. 1812. 8vo. **126 C**

Proceedings, precedents, and arguments on claims and controversies concerning baronies by writ and other honours. 1734. folio. **125 H**

COLLINS, CHARLES M'CARTHY.

History, law, and practice of Banking. 1881. 8vo. **78 D**

COLLINS, GEORGE WILLIAM.

The Stamp laws considered with a view to their influence on the admission of deeds and other writings in evidence. 1841. 8vo. **175 G**

COLLINS, JOHN.

An Introduction to merchants accompts containing seven distinct questions on accompts. 1675. See G. Malynes's Lex Mercatoria. 3rd ed. 1686, folio. **118 G**

COLLINSON, GEORGE DALE.

The law concerning idiots, lunatics, and other persons non compotes mentis. 2 vols. 1812. 8vo. **172 B**

COLLINSON, REV. JOHN.

The history and antiquities of the county of Somerset. 3 vols. Bath, 1791. 4to. **93 G**

COLLISIONS AT SEA.

The law of Collisions at sea. By A. G. Marsden. 2nd ed. 1885. 8vo. **11 F**

The Admiralty law of collisions at sea. By Richard Lowndes. 1867. 8vo. **160 A**

Admiralty court cases on the Rule of the Road. By William Holt. 1867. 8vo. **160 A**

'De concursu navium' dissertatio pro gradu doctoris in legibus habita. F. G. Raikes. 1881. [Pamphlets, vol. 31.] **144 C**

See also SHIPPING. **11 F**

COLLYER, JOHN.

The law of Partnership, 1832, and 2nd ed. 1840. 8vo. **173 D**

Reports of cases decided in the Court of Chancery, by Sir J. L. Knight Bruce. 1844-1846. 2 vols. 1845-47. 8vo. **2 D**

COLOGNE, TREATY OF.

A Complete series of letters from Sir Leoline Jenkins and Sir Joseph Williamson, ambassadors and plenipotentiaries at the treaty of Cologn in the years 1673-74. See W. Wynne's Life of Sir Leoline Jenkins, vol. 1, 1724, pp. 1-346. **79 I**

COLONIAL LAW.

Chapters on the law relating to the Colonies. By C. J. Tarring. 1882. 8vo. **55 D**

Opinions of eminent lawyers on various points of English jurisprudence chiefly concerning the colonies, . . . of Great Britain. By George Chalmers. 1858. 8vo. **55 E**

Commentaries on colonial and foreign laws generally, and in their conflict with each other and with the law of England. By Wm. Burge. 4 vols. 1838. 8vo. **55 D**

Summary of Colonial law, practice of Court of appeals from the Plantations, and of the laws and their administration in all the colonies. By Charles Clark. 1834. 8vo. **55 D**

The laws of the British colonies in the West Indies and other parts of America concerning pr pert and manumission of slaves. By J. H. Howard. 2 vols. y1827. 8vo. **55 D**

A Digest of the laws relating to shipping, navigation, commerce, and revenue in the British colonies in America and the West Indies. By Wm. Earnshaw. 1819. 8vo. **55 D**

A review of laws of United States of North America, British provinces, and West India Islands. 1790. 8vo. **55 D**

See also the names of the different colonies.

COLONIAL OFFICE LIST.

The Colonial Office List 1868, 1869, 1871-1889. 21 vols. 1868-89. 8vo. **142 F**

COLONIES.

The charters of the British colonies in America. n.d. 8vo. **118 C**

Emigration to the British Colonies of North America, Australia, New Zealand, the Cape of Good Hope and Natal. By John Bate. 1862. [Pamphlets, vol. 18.] **144 B**

COLONIES—*continued.*

History of the British colonies. By R. M. Martin. 5 vols. 1835. 8vo.   **116 C**

An Inquiry into the colonial policy of the European powers. By Lord Brougham. 2 vols. Edinburgh, 1803. 8vo. **116 B**

Letter to the Right Hon. Benjamin Disraeli, M.P., on the present relations of England with the colonies. By C. B. Adderley. 1861. [Pamphlets, vol. 18.]   **144 B**

Parliamentary government in the British colonies. By Alpheus Todd. 1880. 8vo.   **116 C**

A View of constitution of British colonies in North America and the West Indies at time the civil war broke out on continent of America. By A. Stokes. 1783. 8vo.   **55 D**

COLOSSEUM, LONDON.

A Description of the Colosseum as reopened in 1845. 18th ed. 1846. 8vo.   **92 B**

COLQUHOUN, PATRICK.

Treatise on the Police of the Metropolis. 5th ed. 1797, and 6th ed. 1800. 8vo.   **83 I**

COLQUHOUN, PATRICK MAC CHOMBAICH DE.

Summary of Roman Civil law, illustrated by commentaries on and parallels from the Mosaic, Canon, Mohammedan, English and Foreign law. 4 vols. 1849–60. 8vo. **63 F**

COLTMAN, FRANCIS JOSEPH.

Registration Cases in Common Pleas and Q.B. divisions and court of appeal, 1879–1885. 1 vol. 1886. 8vo.   **6 C**

COLUMBIA, BRITISH.

Ordinances, 1868–1871. 1868–71. folio.   **34 G**

Consolidated statutes. Victoria, 1877. 4to.   **34 G**

Statutes 1872–1889. 9 vols. Victoria, 1872–89. 4to. **34 G**

The Statutes up to and including the year 1888. vol. 1. Consolidated Acts, 1888. Victoria, 1888. 4to.   **34 G**

COLYAR, HENRY ANSELM DE.

A Treatise on the law of guarantees and of principal and surety. 1874. 8vo.   **52 H**

The same. 2nd ed. 1885. 8vo.   **11 C**

COMBERBACH, ROGER.
The report of several cases in the court of King's Bench at
Westminster, 1685–1698. 1724. folio. **74 C**

COMENIUS, JOHN AMOS.
Orbis sensualium pictus. J. A. Comenius's Visible World, or
a nomenclature and pictures of all the chief things that are
in the world, in above 150 copper cuts, written in Latin and
High-Dutch. Translated by Charles Hoole. 11th ed.
1728. 12mo. **118 A**

COMINES, FELIPE DE.
Las memorias de Felipe de Comines, Señor de Argenton, de
los hechos y empresas de Luis Undecimo y Carlos
Octavo, reyes de Francia. Traducidas de Frances con
escolios proprios por Don Ivan Vitrian. 2 vols. in 1.
Amberes, 1643. 4to. **79 H**

COMMENDAMS.
Case of Commendams before Privy Council in 1616. See
Collectanea Juridica, vol. 1, 1791, pp. 1–19. **144 G**
Case of Commendams in House of Lords, 1695. See Stilling-
fleet's Ecclesiastical cases, part 2, 1704, pp. 437–466. **49 E**

COMMERCE.
Annals of Commerce. By D. Macpherson. 4 vols. 1805.
4to. **78 G**
Assimilation of English and foreign commercial law. By H.
D. Jencken. 1873. [Pamphlets, vol. 31.] **144 C**
The Commercial Law Annual for 1873. 1873. 8vo. **146 E**
A Dictionary of commerce and commercial navigation. By
J. R. M'Culloch. 1882. 4to. **78 G**
Dictionnaire universel de commerce. Par Jacques Savary
des Bruslons. 4 tomes. Geneve, 1742. folio. **78 H**
An Historical and chronological deduction of the origin of
Commerce. By Adam Anderson. 2 vols. 1764. folio. **78 H**
Local courts and tribunals of commerce. By R. M. Pank-
hurst. Manchester, 1866. [Pamphlets, vol. 27.] **144 B**
Observations of a solicitor on the right of the public to form
limited liability partnerships, and on the theory, practice
and cost of commercial charters. By E. W. Field. 1854.
[Pamphlets, vol. 9, part 2.] **144 A**

COMMERCE—*continued.*

Report and suggestions addressed to the mercantile community of the United Kingdom by the London committee of merchants. 1852. [Pamphlets, vol. 8.] **144 A**

The universal cambist and commercial instructor. By P. Kelly. 2nd ed. 2 vols. in 1. 1821. 4to. **78 G**

COMMERCIAL LAW.

The law of Commerce in time of war. By E. J. Castle. 1870. 8vo. **55 A**

International commercial law. By Leone Levi. 2nd ed. 2 vols. 1863. 8vo. **55 A**

A Series of commercial forms. By G. Crabb. Edited by J. T. Christie. 5th ed. by L. Shelford. 2 vols. 1859. 8vo. **13 D**

The commercial system and stamp laws of Great Britain. By Ayling Chamberlain. 1841. [Pamphlets, vol. 21.] **144 B**

The laws of Commerce and Manufactures, and the contracts relating thereto. By J. Chitty. 4 vols. 1820-24. 8vo. **13 G**

A Practical treatise on law of nations relative to legal effect of war on commerce. By J. Chitty. 1812. 8vo. **55 A**

Commercial and Notarial precedents. By Joshua Montefiore. 1802. 4to. **157 B**

Lex mercatoria rediviva, or a complete code of commercial law, being a general guide to all men of business. By Wyndham Beawes. 5th ed. by T. Mortimer. 1792. folio. **78 H**

De jure maritimo et navali, or a treatise of affairs maritime and of commerce. By Charles Molloy. 10th ed. 2 vols. 1778. 8vo. **172 E**

See also MERCANTILE LAW. **10 I**

COMMON BENCH REPORTS.

Common Bench Reports 1845–1856, with a general index by John Scott. 19 vols. 1846–58. 8vo. **6 C D**

Common Bench Reports, new series 1856–1865. 20 vols. 1857–66. 8vo. **6 E F**

COMMON LAW, COURTS OF.

Six reports by the commissioners appointed to enquire into the practice and proceedings of the superior courts of Common Law, 1829–1834. 5 vols. 1829–34. folio. **153 B C**

First and Second reports of commissioners for inquiring into

COMMON LAW, COURTS OF—*continued*.

practice and system of pleading in superior courts of common law 1851 and 1853. 1 vol. 1851–53. folio. **153 C**

Common law commission. Proposed regulations and forms as to process, arrest, and bail in the superior courts of common law. 1829. [Jacob's Tracts, vol. 9.] **144 E**

COMMON LAW FORMS.

Chitty's Forms of practical proceedings in the Queen's Bench division of the high court of justice. 12th ed. by T. W. Chitty. 1883. 8vo. **12 E**

Forms of declarations, pleadings, and other proceedings in the superior courts of common law. By Henry Greening. 2nd ed. 1853. 12mo. **162 D**

Forms of practical proceedings chiefly intended as an appendix to the practice of the Court of King's Bench. By William Tidd. 8th ed. 1840. 8vo. **163 B**

COMMON LAW PRACTICE.

The Annual Practice, 1889–90. By T. Snow, C. Burney, and F. A. Stringer. 1889. 8vo. **12 F**

Chitty's Archbold's Practice of the Queen's Bench division of the high court of justice. 12th ed. by T. W. Chitty. 2 vols. 1885. 8vo. **12 E**

Country solicitor's practice. By W. F. A. Archibald. 1881. 8vo. **12 E**

Rules and orders of the courts of common law, 1828–1880. 7 vols. 1845–80. 12mo. **53 F**

Suggestions for some further improvements in the administration of the common law. By J. C. Day. 1877. [Pamphlets, vol. 32.] **144 C**

The common law procedure acts. By J. C. Day. 4th ed. 1872. 8vo. **52 B**

Lush's Practice of the superior courts of law at Westminster, in actions and proceedings over which they have a common jurisdiction. 3rd ed. by Joseph Dixon. 2 vols. 1865. 8vo. **52 B**

The new practice, pleading, and evidence in the Courts of common law at Westminster. By J. F. Archbold. 1853. 12mo. **162 D**

The practice of country attornies and their agents in the courts of law at Westminster with forms. By J. F. Archbold. 2nd ed. 2 vols. 1844. 12mo. **163 B**

COMMON LAW PRACTICE—*continued.*

A Summary of practice of courts of King's Bench and Common Pleas and Exchequer. By J. Chitty. 1832. 12mo. **162 A**

Country attorney's guide to practice of courts of King's Bench, Common Pleas, and Exchequer. 2nd ed. 1829. 8vo. **162 E**

Attorney's Practice epitomised, or the method, times, and expences of proceedings in the courts of King's Bench and Common Pleas. New ed. 1805. See Turner's Epitome of practice. 1809. 8vo. **163 B**

The Common Law common-plac'd. By Giles Jacob. 2nd ed. 1733. folio. **156 C**

A General abridgment of the Common Law. By Knightly D'Anvers. 2 vols. 1705–22. folio. **156 C**

Practical register of rules, orders and observations concerning the practice of the Common Law in the courts at Westminster. By William Style. 4th ed. 1707. 12mo. **49 F**

The practical part of the law, shewing the office of an attorney and a guide for solicitors in all the courts of Westminster. 3rd ed. 1702. 12mo. **49 F**

The Common law epitomized. By W. Glisson and A. Gulston. 2nd ed. 1679. 12mo. **49 C**

Praxis utriusque banci. The ancient and modern practice of the two superior courts at Westminster, and the practice of the Sheriffs' Court, London. 1674. 12mo. **49 C**

Gregories Moot-book, being a survey of the general titles of the common law. By William Hughes. 1663. 8vo. **63 C**

The body of the common law of England. By E. W. [Edmond Wingate.] 1655. 12mo. **49 C**

The elements of the common lawes of England. By Sir F. Bacon. 1635–36. 8vo. **49 C**

See BAGLEY, BOOTE, CROMPTON, FINLASON, GARDINER, GRAY, KIME, SELLON, STEPHEN and TIDD.

See also ABRIDGMENTS, ACTIONS, COSTS IN COMMON LAW and DIGESTS.

COMMON LAW PRINCIPLES.

Commentaries on the Common law, designed as introductory to its study. By Herbert Broom. 8th ed. by W. F. A. Archibald and H. W. Greene. 1888. 8vo. **64 A**

Principles of the Common law. By John Indermaur. 5th ed. 1888. 8vo. **64 A**

A Manual of Common Law. By J. W. Smith. 10th ed. by J. Trustram. 1887. 12mo. **64 B**

COMMON LAW PRINCIPLES—*continued.*

The Student's guide to the principles and practice of the Common Law. By John Indermaur. 1886. 8vo. **64 A**

Introductory lecture on the study of the Common Law, delivered by Joseph Napier in the theatre of the Royal Dublin Society 9 Nov. 1839. Dublin, 1839. 8vo. **144 G**

The history and analysis of the Common law of England. By Sir Matthew Hale. 5th ed. by C. Runnington. 2 vols. 1794. 8vo. **170 E**

Maximes of reason, or the reason of the common law of England. By Edmond Wingate. 1658. folio. **49 H**

COMMON LAW REPORTS.

Reports of cases in all the superior courts of common law, Easter term 1853 to Michaelmas term 1855. 3 vols. in 5 vols. 1853–55. 8vo. **65 A**

COMMON PLEAS.

The practice of Court of Common Pleas in personal actions and ejectment. By J. F. Archbold. 2 vols. 1829. 12mo. **162 A**

The new Instructor Clericalis, stating the authority, jurisdiction, and modern practice of the Court of Common Pleas. By John Impey. 7th ed. 1826. 8vo. **161 G**

The history and practice of the Court of Common Pleas. By Lord chief baron Gilbert. 2nd ed. 1761. 8vo. **163 C**

Practical register of Common Pleas. 1743. 12mo. **163 A**

Rules, orders and notices in the Court of Common Pleas from 1456 to 1747. 2nd ed. 1747. 12mo. **162 G**

See also COMMON LAW PRACTICE, HARRISON, J., PEACOCK, R. and RICHARDSON, R.

COMMONS AND COMMONERS.

Rights of common and other prescriptive rights. By Joshua Williams. 1880. 8vo. **9 D**

A Digest of the law relating to commons and open spaces. By G. F. Chambers. 1877. 4to. **157 A**

The law relating to profits à prendre and rights of common. By J. E. Hall. 1871. 8vo. **9 D**

Treatise on Commons. By C. I. Elton. 1868. 12mo. **52 B**

Six essays on Commons preservation : containing a legal and historical examination of manorial rights and customs, with a view to the preservation of commons near great towns. By J. M. Maidlow, W. P. Beale, F. O. Crump, H. H. Hocking, R. Hunter, E. H. Lockhart. 1867. 8vo. **52 C**

16

COMMONS AND COMMONERS—*continued.*

The acts for facilitating the inclosure of commons in England
and Wales. By G. W. Cooke. 4th ed. 1864. 8vo. **52 I**

The law of commons and commoners, with the learning of
prescriptions in general. 2nd ed. 1720. 12mo. **163 C**

See also BIRKETT, P., FINLAISON, J. and WOOLRYCH, H. W.

COMMON-WEALTH.

The Common-Wealth's friend, or an exact and speedie course
to justice and right. By John March. 1651. 12mo. **48 A**

Leviathan, or the matter, forme, and power of a Common-
Wealth ecclesiasticall and civill. By Thomas Hobbes of
Malmesbury. Oxford, 1881. 8vo. **78 D**

A relation of some abuses which are committed against the
Common-Wealth. Edited by Sir F. Madden. [Camden
Society, vol. 61.] 1855. 8vo. **85 B**

See also ADAMS, R., CROMWELL, O. and STATE PAPERS.

COMPANIES, LAW OF.

The law of Companies considered as a branch of the law of
Partnership. By Sir N. Lindley. 5th ed. 1889. 8vo. **9 D**

The law and practice of joint stock and other Companies. By
Lord Thring. 5th ed. by J. M. Rendel. 1889. 8vo. **9 D**

Companies acts 1862–1883, with analytical references. By
A. Pulbrook. 11th ed. 1889. 12mo. **9 D**

Company precedents for use in relation to companies subject
to the Companies acts 1862 to 1883 . . . with notes. By
F. B. Palmer. 4th ed. 1888. 8vo. **9 D**

The law and practice under the Companies acts 1862 to 1886.
By H. B. Buckley. 5th ed. 1887. 8vo. **9 D**

Dissertation on and precedents relating to Companies. See
Bythewood and Jarman's Conveyancing, 4th ed. vol. 4,
1887, pp. 320–373 and 516–597. **13 D**

Private Companies, their formation and advantages. By F. B.
Palmer. 6th ed. 1887. 12mo. **9 D**

The law and practice relating to joint stock companies. By
C. E. H. Chadwyck Healey. 2nd ed. 1886. 8vo. **9 D**

A Summary of the law of Companies. By T. E. Smith. 3rd
ed. 1885. 8vo. **64 B**

The law of joint stock Companies. By H. Hurrell and C. G.
Hyde. 1883. 8vo. **52 C**

Report of the case of Twycross v. Grant . . . and an intro-

COMPANIES, LAW OF—*continued.*

duction and notes, containing notices of the previous cases on the subject. By W. F. Finlason. 1877. 8vo. **51 E**

Observations on the object and effect of section 38 of the Companies Act 1867. By A Solicitor. 1877. [Pamphlets, vol. 32.] **144 C**

Remarks on the act of parliament 18 & 19 Vict. cap. 133 for the formation of companies with limited liability. By Edward Moss. 1856. [Pamphlets, vol. 10.] **144 A**

A View of the existing law affecting unincorporated joint stock companies. By John George, 1825. [Jacob's Tracts, vol. 7.] **144 E**

See Chitty's Index, vol. 2, 1885, pp. 1337–1721; and Fisher's Digest, vol. 2, 1884, pp. 298–814. **14 D E**

See also BROWNE, J. H. B., COX, E. W., DIGBY, K. E., LUDLOW, J. M. and WORDSWORTH, C.

COMPANIES, WINDING UP.

The practice and forms in winding up Companies. By Alfred Emden. 3rd ed. 1889. 8vo. **9 D**

Winding-up forms. By F. B. Palmer. 1885. 8vo. **9 D**

A Treatise on the Companies Act 1862 with special reference to winding-up. By G. L. Browne 1867. 8vo. **169 D**

A Manual on the winding up of companies by the Court of Chancery. By J. S. Taylor. 1865. 12mo. **169 D**

COMPANIONAGE.

Debrett's Baronetage, knightage and companionage, 1884–1889. 6 vols. 1884–89. 8vo. **125 C**

COMPENSATION.

The law and practice of Compensation. By S. Woolf and J. W. Middleton. 1884. 8vo. **9 D**

The principles of the law of Compensation. By C A. Cripps. 2nd ed. 1884. 8vo. **9 D**

The law of Compensation. By Eyre Lloyd. 5th ed. 1882. 8vo. **52 B**

The law of Compensation by arbitration and by jury under the Lands and railways clauses acts. By Charles Wordsworth. 2nd ed. 1867. 8vo. **163 D**

Compensation to land and house owners payable by public companies. By T. D. Ingram. 1864. 8vo. **163 C**

16—2

COMPOSITION.

Dissertation on and precedents of Composition. See Bythewood and Jarman's Conveyancing, 4th ed. vol. 2, 1885,
pp. 369–581. **13 D**

Arrangements between debtors and creditors under the Bankruptcy act 1861, with an introduction and notes and two
supplements. By J. P. De Gex and R. H. Smith. 2 vols.
1867–69. 8vo. **165 G**

Proposal for an act for facilitating deeds of composition
by insolvent traders. By Scrope Ayrton. 1833. [Law
Tracts, vol. 5.] **144 E**

A Summary of the law of Composition with creditors. By
Basil Montagu. 1823. 8vo. **165 G**

See also ARRANGEMENTS WITH CREDITORS, FORSYTH, W.,
GRIFFITH, W. D. and HOLLAND, T. E.

COMYN, ROBERT BUCKLEY.

A Treatise on the law of Landlord and Tenant. 2nd ed. by
George Chilton, junior. 1830. 8vo. **170 D**

COMYN, SAMUEL.

The law of Contracts and Promises as settled in the action of
Assumpsit. 2nd ed. 1824. 8vo. **163 D**

COMYNS, SIR JOHN.

Digest of laws of England. 5 vols. 1762–67. folio. **156 E**

The same. Continued down to present time by A Gentleman
of the Inner Temple. 5 vols. 1783. 8vo. **155 B**

The same. 5th ed., to which is added, A Digest of the cases
at Nisi Prius ; by A. Hammond. 8 vols. 1822. 8vo. **14 B C**

Reports of Cases in the Courts of King's Bench, Common
Pleas, and Exchequer ; with some special cases in the
Court of Chancery and before the Delegates, in the reigns
of K. William, Q. Anne, K. George I. and II. 1744. folio.

The same. 2nd ed. by S. Rose. 2 vols. 1792. 8vo. **4 E**

COMYNS, W. H.

Exercises on a series of Abstracts of title. 1873. 8vo. **160 A**

The same. 2nd ed. 1876. 8vo. **160 A**

The same. 4th ed. by A. J. Parker. 1884. 8vo. **13 A**

CONCANEN, Matthew Junior.

Observations on the use and abuse of the practice of the law. 3rd ed. [n.d.] [Law Tracts, vol. 2.] **144 E**

The history and antiquities of the parish of St. Saviour's, Southwark. By M. Concanen junior and Aaron Morgan. 1795. 8vo. **93 C**

CONDÉ, Louis, Prince of.

The life of Louis, prince of Condé, surnamed the Great. By Lord Mahon. 1845. 8vo. **79 B**

CONDITIONS OF SALE.

The law relating to Particulars and Conditions of Sale on a sale of land. By W. F. Webster. 1889. 8vo. **13 H**

Dissertation on and precedents of Conditions of Sale. See Bythewood and Jarman's Conveyancing, 4th ed. vol. 2, 1885, pp. 582–835. **13 D**

The law as to conditions of sale. By R. H. Cole. 1879. 12mo. **13 H**

CONFESSION.

Confession, a doctrinal and historical essay. By B. L. Desanctis, translated from the eighteenth Italian edition by M. H. G. Buckle. 1878. 12mo. **77 B**

See also COLLETTE, C. H.

CONFLICT OF LAWS.

Cases illustrative of the conflict between laws of England and Scotland with regard to marriage, divorce and legitimacy. By H. Prater. 1835. [Law Tracts, vol. 6.] **144 E**

See also BURGE, W. and INTERNATIONAL LAW.

CONIGRAVE, John Fairfax.

South Australia, a sketch of its history and resources. 2nd ed. Adelaide, 1886. 8vo. **84 B**

CONINGSBY, Sir Thomas.

Journal of the siege of Rouen 1591. Edited by J. G. Nichols. [Camden Society, vol. 39.] 1847. 8vo. **85 B**

CONKLING, Alfred.

Admiralty jurisdiction, law and practice of Courts of United States. 2nd ed. 2 vols. Albany, 1857. 8vo. **59 B**

The organisation, jurisdiction and practice of the courts of the United States. 4th ed. Albany, 1864. 8vo. **60 A**

CONNOR, Henry and James Anthony LAWSON.
Reports of cases in the high court of chancery, 1841–1843.
2 vols. Dublin, 1842–44. 8vo. **15 C**

CONOLLY, John.
An Inquiry concerning the indications of Insanity. 1830.
8vo. **172 B**

CONSET, Henry.
The practice of the spiritual or ecclesiastical courts, with a
brief discourse of the structure and manner of forming the
libel or declaration. By H. C. 1685. 4to. **49 F**
The same. 2nd ed. 1702. 8vo. **49 F**

CONSTABLES.
Snowden's Police Officer's Guide. 8th ed. by T. H. Lees.
1885. 12mo. **12 B**
The office of Constable comprising the laws relating to Con-
stables. By J. W. Willcock. 1827. 8vo. **163 D**
The office of Constable. By J. Ritson. 1815. 8vo. **163 D**
The office of Constables. By Sir Francis Bacon. 1610. See
G. Jacob's Complete parish officer. 1754. 12mo. **173 B**
See also Justice of the Peace.

CONSTITUTIONAL HISTORY AND LAW.
Introduction to the study of the law of the constitution. By
A. V. Dicey. 3rd ed. 1889. 8vo. **116 E**
The English parliament in its transformations through a
thousand years. By Rudolf Gneist, translated by R. J.
Shee. 1886. 8vo. **116 E**
The law and custom of the Constitution. Part I., Parliament.
By Sir W. R. Anson. Oxford, 1886. 8vo. **116 E**
Constitutional law viewed in relation to common law and
exemplified by cases. By Herbert Broom. 2nd ed. by
G. L. Denman. 1885. 8vo. **64 B**
Parliamentary history of England, from passing of the
Reform bill of 1832. By John Raven. 1885. 8vo. **116 B**
Leading cases in constitutional law briefly stated. By E.
C. Thomas. 2nd ed. 1885. 8vo. **64 B**
The constitutional history of England from the accession of
Henry VII. to the death of George II. By Henry Hallam.
new ed. 3 vols. 1884. 12mo. **116 D**
The constitutional history of England in its origin and

CONSTITUTIONAL HISTORY AND LAW—*continued*.

development. By Rev. Wm. Stubbs. 3 vols. 1883–84. 12mo.   **116 D**

English constitutional history from the Teutonic conquest to the present time. By T. P. Taswell-Langmead. 2nd ed. 1880. 8vo.   **116 E**

Manual of constitutional history. By F. Fulton. 1875. 8vo.   **116 C**

The constitutional history of England since the accession of George the Third. By Sir T. E. May. 3rd ed. 3 vols. 1871. 12mo.   **116 D**

Cases and opinions on constitutional law, and various points of English jurisprudence. By W. Forsyth. 1869. 8vo.   **63 F**

Constitutionalism of the future, or Parliament the mirror of the nation. By James Lorimer. 2nd ed. 1867. 8vo.   **116 E**

The government of England, its structure and its development. By W. E. Hearn. 1867. 8vo.   **116 E**

The British constitution, its history, structure and working. By Lord Brougham. 1861. 8vo.   **116 B**

The history of the unreformed parliament and its lessons. By Walter Bagehot. [1860.] [Pamphlets, vol. 15.]   **144 B**

A Manual of the English constitution, with a review of its rise and present state. By D. Rowland. 1859. 8vo.   **116 B**

The English constitution in the reign of Charles the Second. By Andrew Amos. 1857. 8vo.   **116 E**

The text-book of the Constitution. Magna Charta, the Petition of Right and the Bill of Rights. By E. S. Creasy. 1848. 8vo.   **116 E**

The constitution of England, or an account of the English government. By J. L. De Lolme. New ed. by W. H. Hughes. 1834. 8vo.   **116 F**

The book of rights, or constitutional acts and parliamentary proceedings affecting civil and religious liberty in England. By Edgar Taylor. 1833. 12mo.   **118 E**

The dogmas of the constitution. Four lectures on the theory and practice of the constitution delivered at King's College, London. By J. J. Park. 1832. 8vo.   **78 B**

An Address on the representative constitution of England. By H. A. Merewether. 1830. [Pamphlets, vol. 4.]   **144 A**

The constitution of Great Britain and Ireland, civil and ecclesiastical. By Francis Plowden. 1802. 8vo.   **116 E**

The parliamentary or constitutional history of England. By Several Hands. 2nd ed. 24 vols. 1761–63. 8vo.   **256 A**

CONSTITUTIONAL HISTORY AND LAW—*continued.*

The Constitution of England. By Sir J. Gilbert. See Sir
J. Gilbert's Reports, 1760, pp. 447–468.   **74 D**

The difference between an absolute and limited monarchy.
By Sir John Fortescue. 3rd ed. 1724. 8vo.   **48 E**

An Enquiry into the measures of submission to the supream
authority, and of the grounds upon which it may be lawful
for subjects to defend their religion, lives and liberties. By
Gilbert Burnet. [n.d.] [Tracts, 1688-89.]   **118 E**

See also BARROW, G., COX, H., SEDGWICK, T., STUART, G.,
URQUHART, D. and VAN HEYTHUYSEN, F. M.

CONSULS.

British consular jurisdiction in the East. By C. J. Tarring.
1887. 8vo.   **55 D**

Consul's manual. By L. Joel. 1879. 8vo.   **52 C**

See also BATTISTA, G. and FYNN, R.

CONTAGIOUS DISEASES ACTS.

Motion for repeal of Contagious Diseases Acts. Speech of
Dr. Lyon Playfair in House of Commons May 24, 1870.
1870. [Pamphlets, vol. 32.]   **144 C**

Third report on the operation of the Contagious Diseases Acts.
1870. [Pamphlets, vol. 32.]   **144 C**

CONTEMPORARY REVIEW.

Contemporary Review. vols. 21–56. 36 vols. 1873–89.
8vo.   **130 F–H**

CONTI, ARMAND DE BOURBON, PRINCE OF.

The works of A. de Bourbon, Prince of Conti, with a short
account of his life. 1713. 8vo.   **79 B**

CONTINGENT REMAINDERS AND CONTINGENCIES.

An Essay on the learning of contingent remainders, and
executory devises. By C. Fearne. 10th ed. by J. W. Smith.
2 vols. 1844. 8vo.   **13 H**

Contingencies with a double aspect. See R. Preston's
Tracts, 1797, pp. 67-77.   **163 G**

CONTRABAND OF WAR.

What is contraband of war and what is not. By Joseph
Moseley. 1861. 12mo.   **55 A**

See also INTERNATIONAL LAW.   **55 A B**

CONTRACTS.

A Treatise on the law of Contracts and upon the defences to actions thereon. By Joseph Chitty, jun. 12th ed. by J. M. Lely and N. Geary. 1890. 8vo. **9 E**

Principles of Contract. By Sir F. Pollock. 5th ed. 1889. 8vo. **9 E**

Principles of the English law of Contract and of agency in its relation to contract. By Sir W. R. Anson. 5th ed. 1888. 8vo. **64 B**

Law of Contracts. By J. I. C. Hare. Boston, 1887. 8vo. **59 C**

Selection of Cases on the English law of Contract. By G. B. Finch. 1886. 8vo. **52 C**

Law of Contracts. By J. W. Smith. 8th ed. by V. T. Thompson. 1885. 8vo. **9 E**

The effect of Contract of sale. By Lord Blackburn. 2nd ed. by J. C. Graham. 1885. 8vo. **9 E**

Law of Contracts. By C. G. Addison. 8th ed. by H. Smith. 1 vol. in 2 vols. 1883. 8vo. **9 E**

Principles of Torts and Contracts. By W. E. Ball. 1880. 8vo. **64 F**

Outline of Contract. By J. A. Shearwood. 1879. 8vo. **64 B**

Digest of Contracts. By S. M. Leake. 1878. 8vo. **9 E**

Rudimentary treatise on the law of Contracts for works and services. By David Gibbons. 3rd ed. 1875. 12mo. **163 E**

The law of Contracts. By T. Parsons. 4th ed. 2 vols. Boston, 1860. 8vo. **59 B**

The law of Contracts as settled in the action of Assumpsit. By S. Comyn. 2nd ed. 1824. 8vo. **163 D**

Essay upon the law of Contracts and Agreements. By J. J. Powell. 2 vols. 1790. 8vo. **163 D**

CONTRACTS, SPECIFIC PERFORMANCE OF.

Specific Performance of contracts. By Sir E. Fry. 2nd ed. by the author and W. D. Rawlins. 1881. 8vo. **9 E**

Outlines of Specific Performance. By H. S. Bowen. 1886. 12mo. **64 E**

The student's guide to Specific Performance and mortgages. By J. Indermaur and C. Thwaites. 1886. 8vo. **64 E**

A Practical treatise on the law relating to the Specific Performance of contracts. By E. Batten. 1849. 8vo. **163 D**

CONVERSION AND RECONVERSION.

A Treatise of Conversion 1696. 12mo. **49 C**

CONVERSION AND RECONVERSION—*continued*.

See Chitty's Index, vol. 2, 1885, pp. 1794–1842.   **14 D**

See Watson's Compendium, vol. 1, 1886, pp. 105–124.   **12 G**

See also TORTS.   **11 H**

CONVEYANCES, FRAUDULENT.

Treatise on the statutes of Elizabeth against fraudulent conveyances, the bills of sale acts 1878 and 1882, and the law of voluntary disposition of property. By H. W. May. 2nd ed. by S. W. Worthington. 1887. 8vo.   **13 I**

The law relating to fraudulent conveyances. By A. J. Hunt. 1872. 8vo.   **164 E**

The construction of the statutes 13 Eliz. cap. 5 and 27 Eliz. cap. 4 relating to voluntary and fraudulent conveyances. By William Roberts. 1800. 8vo.   **164 E**

CONVEYANCING ACTS.

The Conveyancing acts 1881, 1882 . . . and the Settled Land acts 1882 to 1887. By E. P. Wolstenholme and R. O. Turner. 5th ed. 1889. 8vo.   **13 G**

The Conveyancing and Settled Land acts, with other recent acts. By H. J. Hood and H. W. Challis. 3rd ed. 1889. 8vo.   **13 G**

The Conveyancing Acts . . . with notes. By A. St. J. Clerke and T. Brett. 3rd ed. 1889. 12mo.   **13 G**

A Short epitome of the principal statutes relating to Conveyancing. By G. N. Marcy. 4th ed. 1885. 12mo.   **64 C**

Statutes affecting the practice of conveyancing. By T. C. Williams. 1884. 8vo.   **13 G**

The Conveyancing acts 1881 and 1882, also the Solicitors' remuneration act 1881, with notes. By Meryon White. 1883. 12mo.   **64 B**

The recent Conveyancing statutes and the construction they have received from the courts. By C. E. B. Bowker. Hanley, 1883. [Pamphlets, vol. 32.]   **144 C**

The Conveyancing acts 1881, 1882, and the Solicitors' remuneration act 1881, with tables of costs and precedents. By J. S. Rubinstein. 4th ed. 1882. 8vo.   **64 B**

The Conveyancing act 1881 and the Vendor and Purchaser act 1874 with notes. By W. M. Harris and T. Clarkson. 1882. 8vo.   **163 G**

See also REAL PROPERTY STATUTES.

CONVEYANCING PRECEDENTS AND PRACTICE.

Index to precedents in Conveyancing. By W. A. Copinger. 1872. 8vo.   **13 F**

Precedents in Conveyancing with dissertations and notes. By W. M. Bythewood, T. Jarman and G. Sweet. 4th ed. by L. G. G. Robbins. 7 vols. 1884–90. 8vo.   **13 D**

A Handbook of practical forms. By H. Moore. Edited by T. L. Mears. 2nd ed. 1890. 8vo.   **13 F**

Prideaux's Precedents in Conveyancing. 14th ed. by F. Prideaux and J. Whitcombe. 2 vols. 1889. 8vo.   **13 F**

Concise precedents in Conveyancing. By G. Sweet. 4th ed. by C. C. Tucker and G. Cave. 2 vols. 1886. 8vo.   **13 F**

Davidson's Precedents and forms in conveyancing. 5 vols. in 8 vols. 1873–85. 8vo.   **13 E**

Concise precedents in Conveyancing. By M. G. Davidson. 14th ed. 1885. 12mo.   **13 E**

Conveyancing on short lines. By H. T. Frend. 1885. 8vo. **53 C**

Rouse's Practical Man. 16th ed. 1884. 12mo.   **13 G**

Precedents in Conveyancing. By T. Key and H. W. Elphinstone. 2nd ed. 2 vols. 1883. 8vo.   **13 F**

Common precedents in Conveyancing. By H. M. Humphry. 2nd ed. 1882. 8vo.   **13 F**

Hayes' Concise Conveyancer, with precedents. 4th ed. by W. B. Coltman. 1882. 8vo.   **13 E**

Principles and precedents of modern Conveyancing. By C. Cavanagh. 1882. 8vo.   **13 D**

Every-day Precedents in Conveyancing. By T. Wilkinson. 3rd ed. 1881. 8vo.   **13 F**

The Draftsman : containing a collection of concise precedents and forms in Conveyancing. By J. H. Kelly. 2nd ed. 1881. 12mo.   **13 F**

Deacon's Legal Handbook. By M. Lloyd and M. H. Jones. [n.d.] 12mo.   **13 F**

Practical Conveyancer. By Rolla Rouse. 3rd ed. 2 vols. 1867. 8vo.   **13 G**

Principles of conveyancing explained and illustrated by concise precedents. By H. Lewis. 1863. 8vo.   **53 D**

Selection of precedents. By F. Housman. 1861. 8vo. **53 C**

Crabb's Precedents in Conveyancing. Edited by J. T. Christie. 5th ed. by L. Shelford. 2 vols. 1859. 8vo.   **13 D**

Concise precedents in modern Conveyancing. By W. Hughes. 2nd ed. 3 vols. 1855–57. 8vo.   **13 E**

CONVEYANCING PRECEDENTS—*continued.*

A Complete manual of short conveyancing. By H. L. Prior.
1857. 8vo. **13 G**

The attorney's and solicitor's new pocket-book, and conveyancer's assistant. By F. C. Jones. 7th ed. by Rolla Rouse.
2 vols. 1850. 12mo. **13 G**

Shipman's Attorney's new pocket-book, notary's manual, and
conveyancer's assistant. By E. H. Cameron. 3rd ed. by
G. S. Allnutt. 1849. 8vo. **13 G**

Supplement to Mr. Barton's precedents in Conveyancing. By
S. F. T. Wilde. 3rd ed. by C. Barton, jun. 3 vols. 1826.
8vo. **13 G**

The Attorney's compleat Pocket-Book, containing above four
hundred precedents in law, equity and conveyancing. By
the author of The Attorney's practice epitomized. 5th ed.
2 vols. 1764. 12mo. **164 D**

The Compleat Clark, containing the best forms of all sorts of
presidents for conveyances and assurances. By J. H. 3rd
ed. 1671. 8vo. **118 E**

See also ATKINSON, S., BALL, J., BARRY, W. W., BIRD, G.,
BIRD, J. B., BONE, S. V., BRIDGMAN, SIR O., CLAYTON,
W. C., COVERT, N., HORSMAN, G., HUTTON, SIR R.,
MARTIN, T., MILL, J., POWELL, J. J., PRINCE, J. H. and
SHEPPARD, W.

CONVEYANCING PRINCIPLES.

The Student's Conveyancing. By J. Gibson and R. McLean.
2nd ed. by the Authors and A. Weldon. 1888. 8vo. **64 B**

The law of real property : chiefly in relation to conveyancing.
By H. W. Challis. 1885. 8vo. **64 E**

A Practical introduction to conveyancing. By H. W. Elphinstone. 3rd ed. 1884. 8vo. **13 A**

Principles of Conveyancing. By H. C. Deane. 2nd ed. 1883.
8vo. **13 A**

A Concise treatise on the law and practice of Conveyancing.
By Richard Hallilay. 1883. 12mo. **64 B**

Manual of the practice of Conveyancing. By G. W. Greenwood. 7th ed. by H. Greenwood. 1882. 8vo. **13 A**

Observations upon and a suggested form of act for the amendment of the law of Real Property and Conveyancing. By
W. D. Jeans. 1879. [Pamphlets, vol. 37.] **144 C**

Principles of conveyancing. By C. Watkins. 8th ed. by H.
H. White. 1838. 8vo. **52 D**

Systems of registration and conveyancing. A lecture delivered

CONVEYANCING PRINCIPLES—*continued*.

at King's College, London, October 30, 1832. By John
James Park. 1833. [Law Tracts, vol. 5.] **144 E**

A Lecture delivered at the Incorporated Law Society on the
principles and practice of Conveyancing. By S. F. T.
Wilde. 1833. [Pamphlets, vol. 3.] **144 A**

Notes respecting registration and the extrinsic formalities of
conveyances. By C. P. Cooper. 1831. 8vo. **63 G**

The law of real property and the practice of conveyancing.
By William Hayes. 1825. [Jacob's Tracts, vol. 1.] **144 E**

Six letters on Mr. Preston's Practical treatise on Conveyancing. By a West Country Attorney. 1816. 8vo. **163 G**

Practical points or Maxims in conveyancing. By A late
eminent Conveyancer, to which are added Critical observations on the various and essential parts of a Deed. By the
late J. Ritson. 1804. 8vo. **163 G**

An Analysis of the theory and practice of conveyancing. See
Collectanea Juridica, vol. 2, 1792, pp. 415–470. **144 G**

The art of conveyancing explained. [By R. Gardiner.] 2nd ed.
2 vols. 1698. 8vo. **49 E**

See also ATKINSON, S., BARRY, W. W., BARTON, C., CLAYTON,
W. C., HERNE, J., HUGHES, W., LILLY, J., NEWMAN, W.,
PERKINS, J., ROWE, W. H., SMITH, E., STEWART, J. and
WOOD, W.

See also REAL PROPERTY.

CONVICTIONS.

Law and practice of summary convictions. By W. Paley.
6th ed. by W. H. Macnamara. 1879. 8vo. **12 B**

Summary convictions. By T. J. Arnold. 1860. 8vo. **170 A**

Law of Convictions. By W. A. Hulton. 1835. 12mo. **164 F**

See also SUMMARY JURISDICTION.

CONVICTS.

The present aspect of the Convict question. By Sir Walter
Crofton. 1864. [Pamphlets, vol. 25.] **144 B**

The Purgatory of prisoners, or an intermediate stage between
the prison and the public. By Rev. Orby Shipley. 1857.
8vo. **78 C**

Synopsis of Charles Pearson's intended lecture upon prison
discipline. 1849. [Pamphlets, vol. 6.] **144 A**

Transportation and convict discipline considered. By Z. P.
Pocock. 1847. [Pamphlets, vol. 5.] **144 A**

CONYBEARE, Charles Augustus Vansittart.

Parliamentary elections corrupt and illegal practices prevention Acts 1854 to 1883, with notes. 1884. 8vo. **166 C**

The married women's property act 1882, with the acts of 1870 and 1874. By C. A. V. Conybeare and W. R. St. Clair Andrew. 2nd ed. 1883. 8vo. **10 H**

COODE, George.

On legislative expression or the language of the written law. 1845. [Pamphlets, vol. 21.] **144 B**

COOKE, Charles Wallwyn Radcliffe.

The Agricultural holdings act 1875. 1876. 8vo. **160 B**

COOKE, Edward.

The law and practice of the Court for relief of Insolvent debtors. 1827, and 2nd ed. 1839. 8vo. **169 A**

Suggestions submitted to the legislature for putting an end to all private Trusts and for establishing a general Court of Trusts. 1843. 8vo. **176 F**

[COOKE, Sir George.]

Reports and cases of practice in the Court of Common Pleas. By a late Eminent Hand. 1742. folio. **74 C**

Rules, orders and notices in the Court of Common Pleas at Westminster. 1742. folio. **74 C**

COOKE, George Alexander.

Topographical and statistical description of the county of Lancaster. [1825.] 12mo. **89 A**

COOKE, George Wingrove.

The acts for facilitating the enclosure of Commons in England and Wales. 1853, and 3rd ed. 1856. 8vo. **168 G**

The same. 4th ed. 1864. 8vo. **52 I**

The law of Copyhold Enfranchisement. 1853. 12mo. **164 G**

Law of agricultural tenancies. 1850. 8vo. **160 B**

The same. New ed. by G. T. Goldney and W. R. Griffiths. 1882. 8vo. **52 B**

The law of Defamation. 1844. 12mo. **175 G**

COOKE, James Richard and J. C. ALCOCK.

Reports of cases in the court of King's Bench in Ireland. 1833-1834. 1 vol. Dublin, 1834. 8vo. **15 C**

COOKE, JOHN.

The manor and parish of Hendon, drawn and engraved by John Cooke, with an index or book of reference to the map. 1796. 4to.   **89 E**

COOKE, REV. JOHN and REV. JOHN MAULE.

An Historical account of the royal hospital for seamen at Greenwich. 1789. 4to.   **88 E**

COOKE, WILLIAM.

Compendious system of Bankrupt laws. 1785. 8vo. **160 D**
The same. 7th ed. by G. Roots. 2 vols. 1817. 8vo. **160 D**

COOKE, SIR WILLIAM FOTHERGILL.

Authorship of the practical electric telegraph of Great Britain. By Rev. T. F. Cooke. 1868. 8vo.   **78 C**
The electric telegraph, was it invented by Professor Wheatstone? 2 vols. 1857–56. 8vo.   **78 C**

COOPER, CHARLES HENRY.

Annals of Cambridge. 3 vols. 1842–45. 8vo,   **86 C**
Memorials of Cambridge. 3 vols. 1860–66. 4to.   **86 D**
Athenæ Cantabrigienses, 1500–1609. By C. H. Cooper and T. Cooper. 2 vols. 1858–61. 8vo.   **80 H**

COOPER, CHARLES PURTON.

A Brief account of some of the most important proceedings in parliament relative to the defects in the administration of justice in Court of Chancery, House of Lords and Court of Commissioners of Bankrupt. 1828. 8vo.   **78 C**
The Delay in offices of masters in chancery, and the remedy. 1849, and 2nd ed. 1849. [Pamphlets, vol. 17.]   **144 B**
The House of Lords as a court of appeal. 1850. [Pamphlets, vol. 7.]   **144 A**
Lettres sur la cour de la Chancellerie et quelques points de la Jurisprudence Angloise. 2nd ed. 1828. 8vo.   **63 G**
The same, avec une introduction par M. P. Royer-Collard. Paris, 1830. 8vo.   **63 G**
A Manual of chancery chamber practice. 1853. Bound with O. D. Tudor's Chancery practice. 1852. 12mo.   **161 B**
Notes respecting Registration and the extrinsic formalities of Conveyances. Part I. 1831. 8vo.   **63 G**

COOPER, CHARLES PURTON—*continued.*

Reports of cases in Chancery decided by Lord Cottenham, commencing 7th July 1846. 2 vols. 1846–48. 8vo. **2 D**

Reports of some cases in Courts of the Lord Chancellor, Master of the Rolls, and Vice Chancellor, 1837–1838. 1 vol. 1838–1841. 8vo **2 D**

Select cases decided by Lord Brougham in the Court of Chancery in 1833 and 1834. 1 vol. 1835. 8vo. **2 D**

See also RECORD COMMISSION and RECORDS.

COOPER, GEORGE.

Cases in the Court of Chancery during the time of Lord Chancellor Eldon, 1815. 1 vol. 1815. 8vo. **2 D**

COOPER, HERBERT STONEHEWER.

Our new colony Fiji, its history, progress, and resources. 1882. 8vo. **84 G**

COOPER, THOMAS, BISHOP OF WINCHESTER.

An Answer in defence of the truth against the Apology of private mass. Edited by Rev. Wm. Goode. Cambridge, 1850. 12mo. **77 D**

COOPER, WILLIAM DURRANT.

Proofs of age of Sussex families, temp. Edw. II. to Edw. IV. 1860. 8vo. **93 E**

The Oxenbridges of Brede place, Sussex, and Boston, Massachusetts. 1860. 8vo. **93 E**

COOTE, HENRY CHARLES.

Common form practice of Court of Probate in granting probates and letters of administration. 1858. 12mo. **174 D**

The same. 2nd ed. 1859, and 5th ed. 1866. 8vo. **174 D**

Common form practice of High Court of Justice in granting Probates and Administrations. 8th ed. 1878. 8vo. **174 D**

The same. 9th ed. 1883. 8vo. **53 E**

The same. 10th ed. by T. H. Tristram. 1888. 8vo. **12 D**

New practice of court of admiralty. 1860. 8vo. **160 A**

The practice of the high court of Admiralty : also the practice of judicial committee of Privy Council in Admiralty appeals. 2nd ed. and supplement. 1868–69. 8vo. **52 A**

The practice of the Ecclesiastical Courts. 1847. 8vo. **52 F**

The Romans of Britain. 1878. 8vo. **113 C**

COOTE, RICHARD HOLMES.

The law of Mortgage 1821, and 2nd ed. 1837. 8vo. **172 G**

The same. 3rd ed. by the author and Richard Coote. 1850. 8vo. **172 G**

The same. 4th ed. by W. W. Mackeson. 1880. 8vo. **53 B**

The same. 5th ed. by W. W. Mackeson and H. A. Smith. 2 vols. 1884. 8vo. **13 C**

Letter on proposed General Registry. 1829. 12mo. **174 F**

COPINGER, WALTER ARTHUR.

Index to precedents in conveyancing and to common and commercial forms. 1872. 8vo. **13 F**

The law of Copyright in works of literature and art. 1870. 8vo. **164 G**

The same. 2nd ed. 1881. 8vo. **9 E**

On the custody and production of title deeds and other documentary evidence at law in equity and in matters of conveyancing. 1875. 8vo. **13 I**

Tables of stamp duties from 1815 to the present time, on conveyances, mortgages, and settlements. 1878. 8vo. **11 G**

The law of Rents with special reference to the sale of land in consideration of a rent charge or chief rent. By W. A. Copinger and J. E. C. Munro. 1886. 8vo. **11 E**

COPYHOLDS.

Treatise on Copyhold, customary freehold, and ancient demesne tenure. By J. Scriven. 6th ed. by Archibald Brown. 1882. 8vo. **13 B**

Treatise on the law of Copyholds and customary tenures of land. By C. Elton. 1874. 12mo. **13 B**

A Succinct treatise on the Copyhold acts. By James Cuddon. 1865. 8vo. **13 B**

A Treatise on Copyholds. By C. Watkins. New ed. by R. S. Vidal. 2 vols. 1826. 8vo. **13 A**

Opinions on a surrender of Copyhold, and Lord Loughborough's argument in C.P. on fines payable on admission to Copyhold estates. See Collectanea Juridica, vol. 2, pp. 258–261 and 340–346. **144 G**

Considerations on the question whether tenants by copy of court roll according to the custom of the manor, though not at the will of the lord, are freeholders qualified to vote in elections for knights of the shire. See Blackstone's Law Tracts, 3rd ed. 1771, pp. 199–240. **144 G**

COPYHOLDS—*continued.*

The complete Copyholder. By Sir Edward Coke. 1764. See Coke's Law Tracts, 1764, pp. 1–220. **144 F**

See also BRAY, R., CARTER, S., CASWALL, A., FISHER, R. B. and SANDERS, F. W. **164 F**

COPYHOLDS, ENFRANCHISEMENT OF.

Law and Practice on Enfranchisements and Commutations. By A. Brown. 1888. 8vo. **13 B**

Dissertation on and precedents of Enfranchisement of Copyholds. See Bythewood and Jarman's Conveyancing, 4th ed. vol. 2, 1885, pp. 862–911. **13 D**

Copyhold enfranchisement manual. By Rolla Rouse. 3rd ed. 1866. 8vo. **13 B**

Law of Copyholds, in reference to the Enfranchisement and Commutation of manorial rights, and the Copyhold acts. By Leonard Shelford. 1853. 12mo. **13 B**

The law and practice of Copyhold Enfranchisement. By G. W. Cooke. 1853. 12mo. **164 G**

Schedule and award for the enfranchisement of copyhold lands. By R. Bray. 1835. [Law Tracts, vol. 3.] **144 E**

COPYRIGHT.

The law of Artistic Copyright. By Reginald Winslow. 1889. 8vo. **9 E**

Dissertation on and precedents of Copyright. See Bythewood and Jarman's Conveyancing, 4th ed. vol. 4, 1887, pp. 664–782 and 834–854. **13 D**

The law relating to works of literature and art. By J. Shortt. 2nd ed. 1884. 8vo. **9 E**

The law relating to Copyright and trade marks. By J. H. Slater. 1884. 8vo. **9 E**

Suggestions for the improvement of the law of Copyright. By T. A. Romer. 1883. [Pamphlets, vol. 32.] **144 C**

The law of Copyright. By W. A. Copinger. 2nd ed. 1881. 8vo. **9 E**

The law of property in intellectual productions in Great Britain and the United States. By E. S. Drone. Boston, 1879. 8vo. **59 C**

Copyright and Patent laws of the United States, 1790 to 1868. By S. D. Law. 2nd ed. New York, 1867. 12mo. **60 A**

Suggestions on the Copyright (Works of art) bill now pend-

COPYRIGHT—*continued.*

ing in the House of Commons. By D. R. Blaine. 1861..
[Pamphlets, vol. 13.] **144 A**

The question of unreciprocated foreign Copyright in Great
Britain. By H. G. Bohn. 1851. 8vo. **83 I**

The law of Copyright in England and America. By G. T.
Curtis. Boston, 1847. 8vo. **59 C**

The case of Saunders *v.* Smith before the vice-chancellor and
on appeal before the lord chancellor, with notes. By G.
M. Crawford. 1839. 8vo. **51 E**

Enquiries respecting the proposed alteration of the law of
Copyright, as it affects authors and the universities. By
Basil Montagu. 1813. 8vo. **144 F**

The cases of the appellants and respondents [A. and J.
Donaldson *v.* T. Becket and others] in the cause of Literary
Property before the House of Lords, with notes. By A
Gentleman of the Inner Temple. 1774. 4to. **157 B**

See also BURROW, SIR J., FRASER, J., GODSON, R., MACFIE,
R. A., PHILLIPS, C. P. and UNDERDOWN, E. M.

CORBETT, UVEDALE and EDMUND ROBERT DANIELL.

Reports of cases of controverted elections in the sixth parliament of the United Kingdom. 1821. 8vo. **66 A**

CORDERY, ARTHUR.

The law relating to Solicitors of the supreme court of judicature. 1878. 8vo. **53 G**
The same. 2nd ed. 1888. 8vo. **11 G**

CORDERY, JOHN GRAHAM.

The Iliad of Homer. Translated by J. G. Cordery. 2 vols.
1871. 8vo. **83 C**

CORFE CASTLE, DORSET.

An Historical and architectural description of Corfe Castle.
By A Near Resident. Poole, 1829. Bound with Sydenham's History of Poole. 1839. 8vo. **87 D**

CORK.

Ancient and present state of county and city of Cork. By
Charles Smith. 2nd ed. 2 vols. Dublin, 1774. 8vo. **95 E**
Reports of proceedings at the special commissions (1867) for
the county and city of Cork in cases of high treason and
treason-felony. Dublin, 1871. 8vo. **50 A**

CORN.

Chronicon Preciosum, or an account of the price of Corn for the last 600 years. [By Wm. Fleetwood. 1707.] See W. Fleetwood's Works, 1737, pp. 379–434.   **77 H**

Dispersion of the gloomy apprehension of late repeatedly suggested from the decline of our corn trade. By Rev. John Howlett. 1797. 8vo.   **144 G**

Letter to electors of Bridgenorth upon the Corn laws. By W. W. Whitmore, M.P. 1826. [Jacob's Tracts, vol. 7.]   **144 E**

See also T. Tooke's High and low prices, vol. 2, 1823. 8vo. **73 D**

CORNER, RICHARD JAMES and A. B. CORNER.

Practice of the crown side of the court of Queen's Bench. 1844. 8vo.   **52 E**

CORNISH, WILLIAM FLOYER.

Treatise on Purchase Deeds of freehold estates and leasehold property. New ed. by G. Horsey. 1855. 8vo.   **175 A**

CORNWALL, COUNTY AND DUCHY OF.

Bibliotheca Cornubiensis. A catalogue of the writings of Cornishmen and of works relating to the county of Cornwall. By G. C. Boase and W. P. Courtney. 3 vols. 1874–82. 4to.   **82 F**

Case between Sir Wm. Clayton and the Duchy of Cornwall, and the history of the constitution of the Duchy. By John Haines. 1834–35. 8vo.   **87 A**

A Complete parochial history of the county of Cornwall. [Edited by Joseph Polsue.] 4 vols. 1867–72. 4to. **86 F**

A Concise topographical account of Cornwall. By Rev. Daniel Lysons and Samuel Lysons. 1814. 4to.   **86 G**

Delineations of Cornwall. By E. W. Brayley and J. Britton. 1801. 8vo.   **86 E**

Facsimile of part of Domesday book relating to Cornwall. By Sir Henry James. Southampton, 1861. folio.   **86 H**

An Historical survey of the county of Cornwall, to which is added a complete heraldry of the same. By C. S. Gilbert. 2 vols. 1817–20. 4to.   **86 F**

The history of Cornwall. By Richard Polwhele. 7 vols. bound in 2 vols. 1816–1808. 4to.   **86 F**

An Inquiry into tenure of conventionary estates in assessionable manors parcel of Duchy of Cornwall. See J. Manning's Exchequer Practice, 2nd ed. 1827, pp. 356–394.   **168 B**

CORNWALL, County and Duchy of—*continued.*

A Map of the county of Cornwall from an actual survey made
by Thomas Martyn. 1748. 8vo. **87 A**

Mineralogia Cornubiensis. A treatise on minerals, mines and
mining. By W. Pryce. 1778. folio. **87 G**

See also BORLASE, REV. W., CAREW, R., DODDRIDGE, SIR J.,
HALCOMB, J.,HEATH, R., OLIVER, REV. G., PYCROFT, J. W.,
SPARGO, T. and THOMAS, C.

CORNWALL, James.

Tables to the modern printed presidents of pleadings, writs
and returns of writs &c. at the common law ; being a continuation from Mr. Townsend's Tables down to this time.
1705. folio. **157 C**

CORONERS.

Office and duty of Coroners. By John Jervis. 5th ed. by
R. E. Melsheimer. 1888. 8vo. **9 F**

On Coroners, a paper read at the Bristol Law Students' Society,
3 February 1885. By E. M. Harwood. Bristol, 1885.
[Pamphlets, vol. 39.] **144 C**

Remarks on the proposals for amendment of the law of
coroners' inquests. By E. L. Hussey. Oxford, 1884.
[Pamphlets, vol. 32.] **144 C**

The Coroner's Court, its uses and abuses. By J. J. Dempsy.
1858. [Pamphlets, vol. 10.] **144 A**

A Practical compendium of the office of Coroner. By Wm.
Baker. 1851. 12mo. **52 D**

See also BRAY, R., GREENWOOD, W. and IMPEY, J.

CORPORATIONS.

The Municipal Corporations Act, 45 & 46 Vict. cap. 50. By
Sir C. Rawlinson. 8th ed. by T. Geary. 1883. 8vo. **9 F**

The law relating to Municipal Corporations. By T. J. Arnold.
3rd ed. by S. G. Johnson. 1883. 8vo. **9 F**

An Investigation of the principles which limit the capacities,
powers, and liabilities of Corporations. By Seward Brice.
2nd ed. 1877. 8vo. **9 F**

Law of private corporations aggregate. By J. K. Angell and
S. Ames. 8th ed. by J. Lathrop. Boston, 1866. 8vo. **59 C**

The law of Corporations aggregate and sole. By James
Grant. 1850. 8vo. **52 C**

CORPORATIONS—*continued.*

First report of the commissioners appointed to inquire into the municipal corporations in England and Wales, with appendices. 4 vols. 1835. folio. **153 C**

Report of the commissioners appointed to report and advise upon the boundaries and wards of certain boroughs and corporate towns (England and Wales). 2 vols. 1837. folio. **154 E**

See KYD, S., SAUNDERS, T. W., STONE, S. and WILLCOCK, J. W. **164 G**

See also BOROUGHS.

CORRUPT PRACTICES.

The Corrupt and illegal practices prevention act 1883. By J. C. Carter. 1883. 12mo. **166 D**

Corrupt practices at parliamentary elections. By Lewis Emanuel. 2nd ed. 1881. [Pamphlets, vol. 36.] **144 C**

Suggestions for an organization for restraint of corruption at elections. By W. D. Christie. 1864. [Pamphlets, vol. 25.] **144 B**

See also CONYBEARE, C. A. V. and ELECTIONS.

CORRY, JOHN.

The history of Bristol civil and ecclesiastical. By J. Corry and Rev. John Evans. 2 vols. Bristol, 1816. 8vo. **87 F**

The history of Lancashire. 2 vols. 1825. 4to. **88 F**

CORT, C. F.

Tribute to learning, fame, science and genius. 1834. 4to. **83 I**

CORVINUS, JOHANNES ARNOLDUS.

Enchiridium, seu institutiones imperiales, digestæ per Erotemata. Editio tertia. Amsterodami, 1649. 12mo. **48 A**

CORY, ISAAC PRESTON.

Practical treatise on Accounts, with a plan for amendment of law of partnership. 1839, and 2nd ed. 1839. 8vo. **160 A**

CORYTON, JOHN.

The law of Letters-Patent for sole use of inventions in United Kingdom of Great Britain and Ireland. 1855. 8vo. **173 E**

COSIN, CHARLES.

The names of the Roman Catholics and others who refus'd
to take the oaths to His late Majesty King George. 1745,
and 2nd ed. 1746. 8vo. **49 C**

COST-BOOK SYSTEM.

The Readwin prize essay on the Cost book, its principles and
practice as applicable to mining. By Thomas Tapping.
2nd ed. 1854. 8vo. **164 G**

The gold companies and the Cost-book system. By J. N.
Higgins. 1853. [Pamphlets, vol. 9, part 1.] **144 A**

COSTS, BILLS OF.

Precedents of bills of costs in the chancery, queen's bench,
probate, divorce, and admiralty divisions of the high court
of justice. By W. F. Summerhay and T. Toogood. 6th
ed. by T. Toogood. 1889. 8vo. **9 F**

Guide to the preparation of bills of costs in all the divisions
of the high court of justice. By T. W. Pridmore. 8th ed.
by C. W. Scott. 1887. 8vo. **9 F**

Models of bills of costs in the common law, chancery, and
probate, divorce and admiralty divisions of the high court
of justice. By A. T. Layton. 2nd ed. 1884. 8vo. **9 F**

Precedents of bills of costs. By T. Farries. 2nd ed. 1867.
12mo. **165 A**

Bills of costs between attorney and agent. By E. W. Gilbert.
3rd ed. 1847. 8vo. **165 A**

COSTS IN ADMIRALTY.

See ADMIRALTY JURISDICTION, and COSTS, BILLS OF.

COSTS IN BANKRUPTCY.

Costs in bankruptcy and liquidation under the Bankruptcy
act 1869. By John Scott. [1873.] 12mo. **165 A**

Costs in bankruptcy. By O. Richards. 1844. 12mo. **165 A**

Costs in bankruptcy of proceedings under town and country
fiats. By Francis Gregg. 2nd ed. 1838. Bound with
F. Gregg's Bankruptcy. 1838. 12mo. **160 E**

Costs in bankruptcy. By Francis Gregg. 1826. [Jacob's
Tracts, vol. 8.] **144 E**

See also BANKRUPTCY LAW, and COSTS, BILLS OF.

COSTS IN CHANCERY.

Costs in the chancery division of the high court of justice. By G. O. Morgan and E. A. Wurtzburg. 1882. 8vo. **9 F**

A Book of chancery costs. By W. Shaen and E. K. Greville. 2nd ed. by J. J. Bunning. 1870. 8vo. **165 A**

Bill of costs in chancery for plaintiff and defendant. By Jesse Cole. 1846. 8vo. **164 G**

A Summary of the doctrine of courts of equity with respect to costs. By John Beames. 2nd ed. 1840. 8vo. **52 D**

See COLEMAN, E., FARREN, G. and HARSTON, E. F. B. **165 A**

See also CHANCERY LAW, and COSTS, BILLS OF.

COSTS IN COMMON LAW.

The law of Costs in an action in the Queen's Bench division and in the court of appeal. By W. E. Gordon. 1884. 8vo. **9 F**

Costs in the high court of justice. By John Scott. 4th ed. 1880. 8vo. **9 F**

Costs under the Judicature acts 1873 and 1875, with precedents of taxed bills. By John Scott. 1876. 12mo. **165 A**

A Practical treatise on the law of Costs, in suits and proceedings in all the courts of Common Law, civil and criminal. By Walker Marshall. 2nd ed. 1862. 12mo. **52 D**

A Treatise on the law of Costs in actions and other proceedings in the courts of Common Law at Westminster. By John Gray. 1853. 8vo. **52 D**

The new book of Costs in the superior courts of Common Law at Westminster. By E. T. Dax. 1847. 8vo. **52 D**

Bills of costs as allowed on taxation, in the courts of Queen's Bench, Common Pleas and Exchequer. 4th ed. 1840. 12mo. **165 A**

Bills of costs and allowances in the Court of King's Bench. 3rd ed. 1816. 8vo. **165 A**

See EVANS, J., HARSTON, E. F. B., HULLOCK, J., LE RICHE, E. W., PALMER, J., SAYER, J. and WICKSTEAD, J.

See also COMMON LAW PRACTICE, and COSTS, BILLS OF.

COSTS IN CONVEYANCING.

Solicitors' remuneration order. The solicitors' remuneration act 1881, the general order made thereunder, and a Digest of decisions and opinions on points and questions which have arisen in practice. 1889. 8vo. **9 F**

COSTS IN CONVEYANCING—*continued.*

Conveyancing costs under The Solicitors' remuneration act 1881. By J. S. Rubinstein. 4th ed. 1888. 8vo.　　9 F

Conveyancing costs under the act 44 & 45 Vict. cap. 44. By W. Halliwell. 2nd ed. 1886. 8vo.　　9 F

Solicitors' Remuneration Act 1881, and the general order made thereunder.. By P. F. Evans. 1883. 8vo.　**164 G**

Conveyancing costs. By O. Richards. 1844. 12mo. **165 A**

See also COSTS, BILLS OF.

COSTS IN COUNTY COURTS.

County Court Costs. By C. Cautherley. 1886. 8vo.　9 F

See also COSTS, BILLS OF and COUNTY COURTS.

COSTS IN CROWN OFFICE.

The taxation of costs in the Crown office. By F. H. Short. 1879. 8vo.　　9 F

See also COSTS, BILLS OF and CROWN OFFICE.

COSTS IN PARLIAMENT.

Parliamentary costs. By E. Webster. 4th ed. by C. Cavanagh. 1881. 8vo.　　9 F

The parliamentary solicitor's assistant, containing a selection of bills of costs in the House of Lords and House of Commons. By John Palmer. 1823. 4to.　　**157 B**

See also COSTS, BILLS OF.

COSTS IN PROBATE.

Precedents of bills of costs for obtaining grants of probate and administrations. By G. Carew. 1869. 8vo.　　**165 A**

A Book of Costs in the common law, probate and divorce courts. By E. W. Le Riche. 1860. 8vo.　　**165 A**

See also COSTS, BILLS OF and PROBATE.

COTTAGE LIFE.

The economy of cottage life. By C. G. Pattisson. 1847. [Pamphlets, vol. 13.]　　**144 A**

COTTON.

Cultivation of cotton in Texas. Advantages of free labour. By J. De Cordova. 1858. [Pamphlets, vol. 12.]　**144 A**

COTTON—*continued.*

History and statistics of Cotton. See J. D. B. De Bow's Industrial resources of the southern and western states, vol. I, 1853, pp. 114–243. **84 D**

On the cultivation of Cotton in Italy. By G. Devincenzi. 1862. [Pamphlets, vol. 18.] **144 B**

The supply of Cotton from India. By F. C. Brown. 1863. [Pamphlets, vol. 18.] **144 B**

COTTON, BARTHOLOMÆUS DE.

Historia Anglicana (A.D. 449–1298), necnon ejusdem Liber de archiepiscopis et episcopis Angliæ. Edited by H. R. Luard. 1859. 8vo. **101 D**

COTTON, SIR ROBERT.

Catalogue of manuscripts in Cottonian library deposited in British Museum. By Joseph Planta. 1802. folio. **98 C**

Cottoni Posthuma. Divers choice pieces of Sir Robert Cotton. By James Howel. 1679. 12mo. **84 A**

An Exact abridgement of the records in the Tower of London from the reign of King Edward II. unto King Richard III. Revised by Wm. Prynne. 1657. folio. **99 B**

The same reprinted. 1679. folio. **99 B**

A Report from the Committee appointed to view the Cottonian library. 1732. Bound with Lists of law officers, 1730–33. folio. **118 G**

COTTU, CHARLES.

On the administration of criminal justice in England, and the Spirit of the English government. Translated from the French. 1822. 8vo. **165 F**

COULSON, HENRY J. W. and U. A. FORBES.

The law relating to Waters, sea, tidal and inland. 1880. 8vo. **11 I**

COUNCILS.

Concilia Magnæ Britanniæ et Hiberniæ a synodo Verolamiensi A.D. 446 ad Londinensem A.D. 1717. A Davide Wilkins. 4 vols. 1737. folio. **113 H**

Jani Anglorum facies nova, or several monuments of antiquity touching the great councils of the kingdom. 1680. 12mo. **49 D**

COUNSEL.

Counsel's retainers. By E. B. G. [G. B. Ellis.] 1888. 12mo. **9 F**

The duties and license of Counsel. By Thomas Wright. 1842. [Pamphlets, vol. 16.] **144 B**

A Letter to the vice-chancellor of England upon his resolution to abolish the practice of adjourning his court by reason of the absence of leading counsel. By C. P. Cooper. 2nd ed. 1850. [Pamphlets, vol. 7.] **144 A**

See also ADVOCACY and BARRISTERS.

COUNTIES.

Reports on proposed division of counties and boundaries of boroughs. 4 vols. 1832. folio. **153 A**

Reports on proposed division of Counties mentioned in schedule (F) of the Reform bill. 1832. folio. **153 A**

COUNTY COUNCILS.

The law relating to County Councils. By C. N. Bazalgette and G. Humphreys. 3rd ed. by G. Humphreys. 1889. 8vo. **10 G**

A Manual for returning officers for use at the first election of county councillors in January 1889. By F. R. Parker. 1889. 8vo. **10 G**

The election of County Councils under the local government act 1888. By F. R. Parker. . 1888. 8vo. **10 G**

The Local government act, the County electors act 1888, the Municipal corporations act 1882, with notes. By W. C. Ryde and E. L. Thomas. 1888. 8vo. **10 G**

The Councillors' handbook. By N. Herbert and A. F. Jenkin. 1888. 8vo. **10 G**

Greater London and its government. By George Whale. 1888. 8vo. **10 G**

COUNTY COURTS DIRECTORIES.

Index to the parishes, townships, hamlets and places contained within the districts of the several county courts in England and Wales. 3rd ed. 1880. folio. **84 F**

The same. 4th ed. 1889. folio. **Hall**

The London county courts directory. By H. W. Brider. 2nd ed. 1876. 4to. **Hall**

COUNTY COURTS PRACTICE.

A Complete practice of the County Courts. By G. Pitt-Lewis. 4th ed. 2 vols. 1890. **12 H**

The annual County Courts practice, 1890. By G. W. Heywood. 2 vols. 1890. 8vo. **12 H**

Archbold's County Court Practice. 10th ed. by C. A. White. 1889. 8vo. **12 H**

Stephen's County Court acts, orders and practice. By Henry Stephen and R. A. Stephen. 1889. 8vo. **12 H**

County courts act 1888. By C. E. Lloyd. 1888. 8vo. **12 H**

The practice of County Courts. By J. E. Davis. 6th ed. by S. M. Rhodes. 1887. 8vo. **12 H**

A County courts formulist. By R. A. Dale. 1887. 8vo. **12 H**

Jurisdiction and practice of county courts. By G. W. Heywood. 4th ed. 1886. 8vo. **165 B**

County Court statutes 1846 to 1882. By G. M. Wetherfield and F. Wetherfield. 2nd ed. 1886. 8vo. **165 B**

Pollock's Practice of the County Courts. 9th ed. by H. Nicol and H. C. Pollock. 1880. 8vo. **52 E**

Consolidated county court orders and rules. 1875. 4to. **157 C**

Rules, orders and forms for regulating the practice of the county courts. 1868. 8vo. **165 C**

See also MOSELY, J., RUMSEY, A., SWEET, J. and WILL, J. S.

COUNTY COURTS PRACTICE IN EQUITY.

The jurisdiction and practice of the County courts in equity. By E. C. Batten and H. Ludlow. 1872. 8vo. **165 B**

The jurisdiction and practice of the County Courts in equity. By J. E. Davis. 1872. 8vo. **165 B**

Precedents of pleadings in equity in the county courts. By P. M. Leonard. 1869. 8vo. **165 C**

Equitable jurisdiction of the County Courts. By C. E. Pollock and H. Nicol. 1865. 8vo. **165 B**

County courts equitable jurisdiction bill, 1865. A letter to John Arthur Roebuck, Esq., M.P., Q.C. By Vigil. 1865. [Pamphlets, vol. 25.] **144 B**

COUNTY COURTS REFORM.

County Court reform upon the basis of the second report of the Judicature commission. By G. M. Wetherfield. 2nd ed. 1872. [Pamphlets, vol. 32.] **144 C**

COUNTY COURTS REFORM—*continued.*

County Courts, their past, present, and future. By W. O. Boyes. Barnet, 1885. [Pamphlets, vol. 39.] **144 C**

County courts, what they are and what they should be. By Edmund Pooley. 1882. [Pamphlets, vol. 32.] **144 C**

A Letter to the attorney-general, Sir W. Webb Follett, M.P., suggesting amendments in proposed new County Courts bill. By W. J. Neale. 1844. [Pamphlets, vol. 20.] **144 B**

Local courts not the remedy for the defects of the law. By B. Boothby. 1844. [Pamphlets, vol. 20.] **144 B**

Lord Brougham's Local Courts bill examined. By H. B. Denton. 1833. 12mo. **165 C**

On the county courts' extension bill, with a proposal for a cheap and simple substitute in the superior courts of Westminster. By G. Becke. 1850. [Pamphlets, vol. 20.] **144 B**

On the working of the County Courts. By Vigil. 1861. [Pamphlets, vol. 20.] **144 B**

Remarks on operation of County Courts act 9 & 10 Vict. cap. 95. By S. Joyce. 1850. [Pamphlets, vol. 20.] **144 B**

See also FALCONER, T.

COUNTY COURTS, REPORTS IN.

Reports of Cases in the New County Courts, from 1849–1851. By W. H. Roberts, H. Leeming and J. E. Wallis. vol. 1, parts 1 to 5. 1849–51. 8vo. **68 A**

Reports of County Courts cases and appeals decided by all the superior courts, and of decisions in the county courts, with cases in bankruptcy. New series. 1860–1888. 18 vols. 1861–88. 8vo. **68 A**

COUNTY FAMILIES.

The county families of the United Kingdom. By Edward Walford. 3rd ed. 1865, 5th ed. 1869, and for the years 1872, 1875, 1876, and 1879 to 1889. 16 vols. 1865–89. 8vo. **126 F G**

COURT-HAND.

Court-Hand Restored : or, the student's assistant, in reading old deeds, charters, records, &c. By A. Wright. 4th ed. 1815. 4to. **78 G**

COURTS BARON AND COURTS LEET.

Complete Court-Keeper or land-steward's assistant. By Giles Jacob. 8th ed. by A Barrister. 1819. 8vo. **165 C**

COURTS BARON AND COURTS LEET—*continued.*

Practical treatise on copyhold tenure, with the methods of holding Courts-Leet, Courts-Baron, and other courts. By R. B. Fisher. 2nd ed. 1803. 8vo.　　　　**164 F**

The authority, jurisdiction and method of keeping county courts, Courts-Leet and Courts-Baron. By William Greenwood. 9th ed. 1730. 8vo.　　　　**165 C**

The practice of Courts-Leet and Courts-Baron published from the manuscripts of Sir William Scroggs. 4th ed. 1728. 12mo.　　　　**165 C**

See also GURDON, T., POWELL, R. and SHEPPARD, W.

COURTS MARTIAL.

The constitution and practice of Courts Martial. By T. F. Simmons. 6th ed. 1873. 8vo.　　　　**53 A**

See also MILITARY LAW and NAVAL LAW.

COURTS OF JUSTICE.

L'Authoritie et jurisdiction des courts de la Majestie de la Roygne. By Richard Crompton. 1637. 12mo.　　　**49 D**

The booke called The diversity of courts. By Andrew Horne. Translated by Wm. Hughes. 1768. 12mo.　　　**49 E**

History of Courts. See Historical law tracts, 2nd ed. 1761, pp. 207–282.　　　　**144 F**

Jurisdiction of Courts, being fourth part of Institutes of laws of England. By Sir E. Coke. 6th ed. 1681. folio. **155 C**

Outlines of jurisdiction of all courts in England and Wales. By Robert Maugham. 1838. 12mo.　　　　**170 F**

Table of courts in England and Wales for recovery of debts. See C. F. Trower's Law of debtor and creditor, 1860, pp. 441–499.　　　　**52 E**

When and where should our courts sit? By J. W. Smith and J. Trail. 1861. [Pamphlets, vol. 17.]　　　**144 B**

COVENANTS.

Law of Covenants. By G. B. Hamilton. 1888. 8vo. **13 B**

The law of Covenants. By T. Platt. 1829. 8vo. **13 B**

History of promises and covenants. See Historical law tracts, 2nd ed. 1761, pp. 59–78.　　　　**144 F**

[COVENTRIE, SIR WILLIAM.]

The Character of a Trimmer : his opinion of I. The laws and government. II. Protestant Religion. III. The Papists. IV. Foreign affairs. 1688. [Tracts, 1688–89.] **118 E**

COVENTRY, Thomas.

Mortgage Precedents. 1826. 8vo. **172 G**

Observations on the title to lands derived through Inclosure acts. See Law Journal Tracts, 1825-26, pp. 33-80. **144 G**

On conveyancers' evidence. 1832. 8vo. **167 E**

Treatise on the Stamp laws relating to deeds and assurances. vol. 1. 1833. 8vo. **175 G**

Analytical digested index to Common Law Reports, from time of Henry III. to reign of George III. By T. Coventry and S. Hughes. 2 vols. 1827. 8vo. **63 B**

COVENTRY, Walter of.

Historical collections of Walter of Coventry. Edited by Wm. Stubbs. 2 vols. 1872-73. 8vo. **102 E**

COVENTRY, Warwickshire.

Illustrative papers on the history and antiquities of Coventry By Thomas Sharp. Reprinted with corrections and additions by W. G. Fretton. [Birmingham], 1871. 4to. **94 G**

COVERDALE, Myles.

Writings and translations of Myles Coverdale. Edited by Rev. G. Pearson. 2 vols. Cambridge, 1844-46. 8vo. **77 C**

COVERT, Nicholas.

The Scrivener's guide, being choice forms of precedents. 3rd ed. by William Bohun. 2 vols. 1716. 12mo. **164 D**

The same. 5th ed. 2 vols. 1740. 12mo. **164 D**

COWELL, Herbert.

Hindu law, being a treatise on law administered to Hindus by British courts in India. Calcutta, 1871. 8vo. **38 B**

History and constitution of the courts and legislative authorities in India. Calcutta, 1872. 8vo. **38 B**

Law reports. Indian appeals. vols. ii.-xvi. 1874-1889. 15 vols. 1875-89. 8vo. **1 F G**

Supplemental Indian appeals decided between March 1872 and November 1873, and not reported in Moore's Indian Appeals. 1880. 8vo. **1 F**

The Indian digest, being a complete index to reported cases of high courts established in India. By H. Cowell and J. V. Woodman. Calcutta, 1870. 8vo. **38 C**

COWELL, Rev. John.

The Interpreter, containing the genuine signification of obscure
words used in the lawes of this realm. Enlarged by Thomas
Manley. 1672, and 2nd ed. 1684. folio.

The same. New ed. 1727. folio. **123 G**

COWPER, Henry.

Reports of cases adjudged in the court of King's Bench ; from
1774 to 1778. Dublin, 1794. 8vo.

The same. 2nd ed. 2 vols. 1800. 8vo. **4 E F**

COWPER, William.

Poems. By William Cowper ; with a sketch of his life by
John Newton. 2 vols. 1833. 8vo. **83 G**

COX, Edward William.

Digest of all the cases decided relating to magistrates, parochial, ecclesiastical, election, municipal and criminal law,
1856–1869. 1870. 8vo. **63 D**

Digest of all the cases decided relating to the Criminal law,
from 1856 to 1867. 1867. 12mo. **63 D**

Forms of practical proceedings in chambers of the Master of
the Rolls and the Vice-chancellors. 1857. 12mo. **161 B**

The same. 3rd ed. by John Biddle. 1863. 12mo. **161 B**

Law relating to the Cattle Plague. 1866. 12mo. **161 A**

New law and practice of Joint Stock companies. 4th ed.
1857, and 6th ed. 1862. 12mo. **169 D**

Principles of Punishment as applied in administration of
criminal law by judges and magistrates. 1877. 8vo. **175 A**

Reports of all cases decided by all superior courts relating
to magistrates, municipal and parochial law, 1859–1888.
14 vols. 1862–89. 8vo. **1 G**

Reports of all cases decided by superior courts of law and
equity relating to law, of joint-stock companies. 1864–1872.
5 vols. 1867–73. 8vo. **8 I**

Reports of cases in criminal law in all the courts in England
and Ireland. 1843 to 1890. 16 vols. 1846–90. 8vo. **1 H I**

New law and practice of Registration and Elections. By E.
W. Cox and S. G. Grady. 10th ed. 1868. 12mo. **166 E**

The same. 13th ed. by S. G. Grady. 1880. 12mo. **166 E**

Criminal law consolidation acts. By E. W. Cox and T. W.
Saunders. 3rd ed. 1870. 12mo. **165 D**

COX, HOMERSHAM.

Antient parliamentary elections, a history showing how parliaments were constituted and representatives of the people elected in antient times. 1868. 8vo. **116 E**

History of reform bills 1866 and 1867. 1868. 8vo. **116 E**

Institutions of English government. 1863. 8vo. **116 E**

Law and science of ancient lights. 2nd ed. 1871. 8vo. **10 G**

Orders, statutes and regulations affecting practice of Court of Chancery with notes. 1861. 8vo. **161 B**

COX, REV. JOHN CHARLES.

Notes on churches of Derbyshire. 4 vols. 1875–79. 8vo. **87 B**

COX, SAMUEL COMPTON.

Cases in the Courts of Equity from 1783 to 1796 inclusive. 2 vols. 1816. 8vo. **2 D**

COXE, REV. WILLIAM.

Historical tour in Monmouthshire, with views by Sir R. C. Hoare. 2 vols. 1801. 4to. **92 C**

[COZENS, ZACHARIAH.]

A Tour through the Isle of Thanet and some other parts of East Kent. 1793. 4to. **88 E**

CRABB, GEORGE.

Conveyancer's assistant, or a series of precedents in conveyancing and commercial forms. 2 vols. 1835. 12mo. **164 E**

The same. Edited by J. T. Christie. 5th ed. by L. Shelford. 2 vols. 1859. 8vo. **13 D**

Digest and index of all the statutes from Magna Charta to 1846. 4 vols. 1841–47. 8vo. **31 D**

The law of Real Property. 2 vols. 1846. 8vo. **174 E**

CRACROFT, BERNARD.

Trustee's guide, a synopsis of the ordinary powers of trustees in regard to investments. 12th ed. 1876. 8vo. **11 I**

CRAIG, RICHARD DAVIS.

Legal and equitable rights and liabilities as to trees and woods. 1866. 8vo. **11 I**

CRAIG, Richard Davis and T. J. PHILLIPS.

Reports of cases in Court of Chancery during time of Lord Chancellor Cottenham, 1840–41. 1 vol. 1842. 8vo. **2 D**

CRAIG, Sir Thomas.

Jus Feudale, tribus libris comprehensum, quod, praeter Jus Commune Longobardicum, Feudales Angliae Scotiaeque Consuetudines complectitur ; cum praefatione L. Menckenii. Lipsiae, 1716. 4to.

The same. 3rd ed. by J. Baillie. Edinburgh, 1732. folio. **48 H**

Scotland's Soveraignty asserted, being a dispute concerning Homage. Translated from the Latin with an account of the author by George Ridpath. 1695. 8vo. **114 A**

CRANCH, William.

Reports of decisions in the Supreme court of the United States, 1800 to 1815. 9 vols. See B. R. Curtis's Reports, vols. 1, 2, 3. Boston, 1855. 8vo. **57 B**

CRANMER, Thomas, Archbishop of Canterbury.

Miscellaneous writings and letters. Edited by Rev. J. E. Cox. Cambridge, 1846. 8vo. **77 E**

Two contemporary biographies of Cranmer. Edited by J. G. Nichols. [Camden Society, vol. 77.] 1859. 8vo. **85 B**

Writings and disputations relative to the sacrament of the Lord's Supper. Edited by Rev. J. E. Cox. Cambridge, 1844. 8vo. **77 E**

CRAVEN, Yorkshire.

The history and antiquities of the deanery of Craven. By T. D. Whitaker. 2nd ed. 1812. folio. **95 H**

CRAWFORD, George Morland.

Copyright in law reports. The case of Saunders v. Smith, before the Vice Chancellor and on appeal before the Lord Chancellor, with notes. 1839. 8vo. **51 E**

CRAWFURD, George.

Genealogical history of royal family of the Stewarts, to which are prefixed a general description of Shire of Renfrew and a deduction of noble and ancient families, proprietors there for upwards of 400 years. Edinburgh, 1710. folio. **113 F**

The peerage of Scotland. Edinburgh, 1716. folio. **127 J**

CRAWLEY, CHARLES.
The law of life insurance with a chapter on accident insurance.
1882. 8vo. **10 D**

CREASEY, JAMES.
Sketches illustrative of the topography and history of New
and Old Sleaford. Sleaford, 1825. 8vo. **89 C**

CREASY, SIR EDWARD SHEPHERD.
First platform of International law. 1876. 8vo. **55 A**
The text-book of the Constitution. Magna Charta, the Peti-
tion of Right, and the Bill of Rights. 1848. 8vo. **116 E**

CREATION AND DELUGE.
An attempt to explain philosophically Mosaical account of
creation and deluge. By P. Howard. 1797. 4to. **77 G**
See also ROBINSON, REV. T.

CREDIT.
Credit pernicious. By Archibald Rosser. 2nd ed. 1834.
[Pamphlets, vol. 3.] **144 A**
Paper and Credit. By W. R. Smee. [Paris, 1861.] [Pam-
phlets, vol. 14.] **144 A**
Remarks suggested by the present state of trade and credit.
1840. [Pamphlets, vol. 3.] **144 A**

CREICHTON, JOHN.
The memoirs of Captain John Creichton. By Jonathan Swift.
1827. [Autobiography, vol. 20.] 1827. 12mo. **79 A**

CREIGHTON, REV. MANDELL.
Historic Towns. Carlisle. 1889. 12mo. **87 A**

CREW, SIR THOMAS.
Proceedings and debates of House of Commons in sessions
of parliament Jan. to March 1628. 1707. 12mo. **48 C**

CRICKLADE CASE.
Report of the Cricklade case; comprehending proceedings in
courts of law, before select committee of Commons and in
both Houses of Parliament. By S. Petrie. 1785. 8vo. **66 B**

CRIMINAL CONSPIRACIES.

The law of criminal conspiracies and agreements. By R. S. Wright. 1873. 8vo.   **52 E**

CRIMINAL LAW, HISTORY AND REFORM OF.

Penological and preventive principles with special reference to Europe and America. By Wm. Tallack. 1889. 8vo. **78 C**

A History of the Criminal law of England. By Sir James Fitzjames Stephen. 3 vols. 1883. 8vo.   **52 E**

On the admission of the evidence of persons charged with criminal offences. By Joseph Addison. 1883. [Pamphlets, vol. 32.]   **144 C**

The state of the Criminal law. By A. H. Elworthy. 1875. [Pamphlets, vol. 32.]   **144 C**

Observations on the province and function of laymen in the administration of criminal justice. By W. F. Finlason. n.d. [Pamphlets, vol. 32.]   **144 C**

Defects in criminal administration and legislation of Great Britain and Ireland. By Wm. Tallack. 1872. 8vo. **78 C**

Crime and criminals. Is the gaol the only preventive? By Alexander Pulling. 1863. [Pamphlets, vol. 18.]   **144 B**

Charge to the grand jury of Kingston-upon-Hull. By Samuel Warren. 2nd ed. 1854. [Pamphlets, vol. 9, pt. 1.] **144 A**

Charge to the grand jury of Birmingham on the connexion between disease and crime. By M. D. Hill. 1854. [Pamphlets, vol. 9, part 1.]   **144 A**

Laws of debtor and creditor as they are, and as they ought to be. By P. Healey. 1849. [Pamphlets, vol. 6.] **144 A**

Suggestions for improvement of portions of Criminal law cognizable before justices out of sessions. By Wm. Foote. 2nd ed. 1843. 12mo.   **165 D**

Letter to Benjamin Hawes, Esq., M.P., and chairman of Metropolitan police committee from Mr. Serjeant Adams. 1838. [Pamphlets, vol. 5.]   **144 A**

On the administration of criminal justice in England. By C. Cottu. 1822. 8vo.   **165 F**

Thoughts on executive justice, with respect to our criminal laws, particularly on the circuits. By a sincere wellwisher to the public. [Martin Madan.] 2nd ed. 1785. 12mo. **118 B**

Considerations on criminal law. [By Henry Dagge.] 1772. 8vo.   **165 F**

History of the criminal law. See Historical law tracts, 2nd ed. 1761, pp. 1–57.   **144 F**

CRIMINAL LAW PRACTICE AND EVIDENCE.

Roscoe's Digest of the law of evidence in criminal cases. 11th ed. by H. Smith and G. G. Kennedy. 1890. 8vo. **9 H**

Precedents of Indictments. By T. W. Saunders and W. E. Saunders. 2nd ed. 1889. 8vo. **12 C**

A Digest of the criminal law. By Sir J. F. Stephen. 4th ed. 1887. 8vo. **52 E**

Pleading and evidence in criminal cases. By J. F. Archbold. 20th ed. by W. Bruce. 1886. 8vo. **12 C**

A Digest of cases relating to criminal law, 1756–1883. By John Mews. 1884. 8vo. **14 F**

A Digest of the law of criminal procedure in indictable offences. By Sir J. F. Stephen and H. Stephen. 1883. 8vo. **52 E**

Procedure and evidence relating to indictable offences, and certain rules and maxims of the criminal law. By S. Prentice. 1882. 8vo. **52 E**

Police code and manual of the criminal law. By C. E. H. Vincent. 1881. 8vo. **12 B**

A Practical treatise on criminal law. By Joseph Chitty. 2nd ed. 4 vols. 1826. 8vo. **165 E**

The third part of the Institutes of the lawes of England: concerning High Treason and other pleas of the Crown and Criminall Causes. By Sir E. Coke. 6th ed. 1680. folio. **155 C**

See also BOOTHBY, B., COX, E. W., SLEIGH, W. C., STARKIE, T. and WOOLRYCH, H. W.

CRIMINAL LAW PRINCIPLES.

A General view of the Criminal law of England. By Sir J. F. Stephen. 2nd ed. 1890. 8vo. **52 E**

Principles of the Criminal law. By S. F. Harris. 5th ed. by A. Agabeg. 1889. 8vo. **64 C**

A Sketch of the Criminal Law. By W. S. Shirley. 2nd ed. by C. S. Hunter. 1889. 8vo. **64 B**

A Selection of leading cases in the Criminal law. By W. S. Shirley. 1888. 8vo. **64 B**

Hints on Criminal law. By T. F. Uttley. 1888. 8vo. **64 C**

Epitome of criminal law. By J. C. Harrison. 2nd ed. 1885. 8vo. **64 C**

A Guide to Criminal law. By C. Thwaites. 1885. 8vo. **64 C**

An Analysis of Criminal Liability. By E. C. Clark. Cambridge, 1880. 12mo. **52 E**

CRIMINAL LAW PRINCIPLES—*continued.*

Crimes and misdemeanors. By Sir W. O. Russell. 5th ed. by S. Prentice. 3 vols. 1877. 8vo. **9 G**

Principles of punishment as applied in administration of Criminal law. By E. W. Cox. 1877. 8vo. **175 A**

Commentaries on the Criminal law. By J. P. Bishop. 3rd ed. 2 vols. Boston, 1865. 8vo. **59 C**

Outlines of criminal law comprising public wrongs. By Robert Maugham. 1837. 12mo. **170 F**

Dei delitti e delle pene. Di Cesare Beccaria. Nuova edizione. Livorno, 1828. 8vo. **56 C**

See also EDEN, W., MASCARDUS and PULTON, F.

CRIMINAL LAW STATUTES.

Criminal law consolidation acts. By E. W. Cox and T. W. Saunders. 3rd ed. 1870. 12mo. **165 D**

Criminal law consolidation and amendment acts of the 24 & 25 Vict. By C. S. Greaves. 2nd ed. 1862. 12mo. **165 D**

Consolidated Criminal Statutes of England and Ireland passed in last session of parliament. By J. F. Archbold. 1861. 12mo. **165 D**

Criminal law consolidation statutes. By J. E. Davis. 1861. 12mo. **165 D**

Alphabetical arrangement of Mr. Peel's acts. By A Barrister. 1827. 12mo. **165 D**

The same. 2nd ed. 1830. 12mo. **165 D**

An Abridgment of penal statutes. By Wm. Addington. 2nd ed. 1782. 4to. **158 B**

CRIPPS, CHARLES ALFRED.

Principles of the law of Compensation in reference to the Lands clauses consolidation acts. 1881. 8vo. **163 D**

The same. 2nd ed. 1884. 8vo. **9 D**

CRIPPS, HENRY WILLIAM.

The law relating to the Church and the Clergy. 2nd ed. 1850, and 4th ed. 1863. 8vo. **166 B**

The same. 6th ed. 1886. 8vo. **9 C**

Reports of new cases decided in the Chancery, Common law and Ecclesiastical courts. 1846–1849. 1 vol. 1849. 8vo. **8 G**

CRISP, JOHN.

The Conveyancer's guide or the law student's recreation, a poem. 3rd ed. 1832. 8vo.　　　　　　　　　**118 A**

CROKE, ALEXANDER.

A Report of case of Horner against Liddiard upon question of what consent is necessary to marriage of illegitimate minors, 1799, with an essay upon theory and history of laws relating to illegitimate children. 1800. 8vo.　　**51 E**

CROKE, SIR GEORGE.

Notes of the judgment delivered in the case of ship money. [Camden Society, n.s. vol. 14.] 1875. 8vo.　　　　**85 D**

Reports of select cases in the courts of King's Bench and Common Bench 1582–1641 written in French. Revised and published in English by Sir H. Grimston. 2nd ed. 3 vols. 1669. folio.　　　　　　　　　　　　　　　**74 C**

[CROKER, JOHN WILSON.]

Theatrical Tears, a poem occasioned by Familiar Epistles to Frederick J[one]s, Esq. 1807. Bound with Attorney's Guide. 1807. 12mo.　　　　　　　　　　　**118 A**

CROKER, THOMAS CROFTON.

Legends of the lakes, or sayings and doings at Killarney. 2 vols. 1829. 12mo.　　　　　　　　　　　**83 A**

Narratives illustrative of the contests in Ireland in 1641 and 1690. [Camden Society, vol. 14.] 1841. 8vo.　　**85 A**

CROMPTON, CHARLES and JOHN JERVIS.

Reports of cases in the Courts of Exchequer and Exchequer Chamber, 1830–1832. 2 vols. 1832–33. 8vo.　　**7 C**

CROMPTON, CHARLES and ROGER MEESON.

Reports of cases in the Courts of Exchequer and Exchequer Chamber 1832–1834. 2 vols. 1834–35. 8vo.　　**7 C**

CROMPTON, CHARLES, R. MEESON and H. ROSCOE.

Reports of cases in the Courts of Exchequer and Exchequer Chamber 1834–1835. 2 vols. 1835–36. 8vo.　　**7 C**

CROMPTON, George.

Practice common-placed or rules and cases of practice in courts of King's Bench and Common Pleas methodically arranged. 2 vols. 1780. 8vo.   162 E

The same. 2nd ed. by B. J. Sellon. 2 vols. 1798. 8vo.   162 E

CROMPTON, Richard.

L'Authoritie et jurisdiction des courts de la Majestie de la Roygne. 1637. 12mo.   49 D

Star-chamber cases, collected for the most part out of Mr. Crompton his booke, entituled The jurisdiction of divers courts. 1641. [Law tracts and arguments, 1641.]   144 F

CROMWELL, Oliver.

History of Oliver Cromwell and the English Commonwealth. By M. Guizot, translated by A. R. Scoble. 2 vols. 1854. 8vo.   115 C

Memoirs of the protectorate-house of Cromwell. By Mark Noble. 2 vols. Birmingham, 1784. 8vo.   80 B

An Act for the security of His Highness the Lord Protector his person and continuance of the nation in peace and safety 1656, and 36 other acts, petitions, proclamations &c. bound together. 1656–57. folio.   158 D

Letter from Earl of Manchester to House of Lords, giving an opinion on conduct of O. Cromwell. Edited by S. R. Gardiner. [Camden Society, n.s. vol. 31.] 1883. 8vo. 85 D

Prestwich's Respublica ; or a display of the honors of the Commonwealth under the protectorship of Oliver Cromwell. 1787. 4to.   127 J

The quarrel between Earl of Manchester and Oliver Cromwell, an episode of the English civil war. Edited by J. Bruce and D. Masson. [Camden Society, n.s. vol. 12.] 1875. 8vo.   85 D

See also ADAMS, R. and STATE PAPERS.

CROMWELL, Richard.

History of Richard Cromwell and the Restoration of Charles II. By M. Guizot, translated by A. R. Scoble. 2 vols. 1856. 8vo.   115 C

CROMWELL, Thomas Kitson.

History and description of the ancient town and borough of Colchester. 2 vols. 1825. 8vo.   87 E

CROMWELL, Thomas Kitson—*continued*.
History and description of parish of Clerkenwell, with engravings by J. and H. S. Storer. 1828. 8vo. **89 D**

CROSS, Francis.
Hints to all about to rent, buy or build house property. 4th ed. 1854. 12mo. **168 G**

CROSS, John.
Law of lien and stoppage in transitu. 1840. 8vo. **10 G**

CROSS, The.
An Answer to John Martiall's Treatise of the Cross. By James Calfhill. Edited by Rev. Richard Gibbings. Cambridge, 1846. 8vo. **77 C**
The 12 stations of the Cross as appointed August 20, 1384, by Pope John, [in Latin with Italian preface, n.d.]. Bound at end of Psalmista secundum morem curie Romane. 1499. 12mo. **118 B**

CROSSLEY, John Thomas and William MARTIN.
The intellectual calculator, or manual of practical arithmetic. 68th ed. n.d. 12mo. **255 H**

CROWN DEBTS.
The law of judgments and crown debts as they affect real property. By F. Prideaux. 4th ed. 1856. 12mo. **13 B**
See Elphinstone and Clark's Searches, 1887, pp. 78–90. **13 H**
See also Exchequer, Extents and Prerogative.

CROWN LEASES.
Account of all manors, messuages, lands, tenements and hereditaments in different counties of England and Wales held by lease from the crown. 1787. folio. **98 B**

CROWN OFFICE PRACTICE.
Practice on Crown side of Queen's Bench division. By F. H. Short and F. H. Mellor. 1890. 8vo. **12 E**
Crown office rules and forms 1886. By F. H. Short. 1886. 8vo. **52 E**
The taxation of costs in the Crown office. By F. H. Short. 1879. 8vo. **9 F**

CROWN OFFICE PRACTICE—*continued.*

The practice of the Crown Office of the Court of Queen's Bench. By J. F. Archbold. 1844. 12mo.   165 D

The law and practice in proceedings on the Crown side of the Court of Queen's Bench. By S. G. Grady and C. H. Scotland. 1844. 12mo.   165 D

See also CORNER, R. J., FOSTER, M., GUDE, R., HANDS, W., HAWKINS, W. and MATTHEWS, R.

CROYDON, SURREY.

The history and antiquities of Croydon. By Rev. D. W. Garrow. Croydon, 1818. 8vo.   93 C

Some account of the town, church and archiepiscopal palace of Croydon. By [Andrew Coltee] Ducarel. 1783. 4to.   93 D

CRUDEN, ALEXANDER.

A Complete concordance to holy scriptures of old and new testament, and to the Apocrypha. 10th ed. 1831. 4to. 77 G

CRUISE, WILLIAM.

A Digest of the Laws of England respecting Real Property. 3rd ed. 6 vols. 1824. 8vo.

The same. 4th ed. by H. H. White. 7 vols. 1835. 8vo.   14 B

Essay on nature and operation of Fines and Recoveries.   2nd ed.   2 vols. in 1.   1786.   8vo.   168 D

The same.   3rd ed.   2 vols.   1794.   8vo.   168 D

An Essay on Uses.   1795.   8vo.   176 G

The origin and nature of dignities or titles of honor, containing all the cases of peerage.   2nd ed.   1823.   8vo.   124 G

CRUMP, FREDERIC OCTAVIUS.

The English law of Sale and Pledge by factors and agents. 1868.   8vo.   168 D

Principles of law relating to Marine Insurance and General Average in England and America.   1875.   8vo.   169 B

See also COMMONS.

CRUTTWELL, REV. CLEMENT.

Tours through the whole island of Great Britain.   6 vols. 1806.   8vo.   86 A

CRYSTAL PALACE, SURREY.

Guide to the Crystal palace and park.   By Samuel Phillips. 2nd ed.   1854.   12mo.   93 C

CUDDON, James.
A Succinct treatise on Copyhold acts. 1865. 8vo. **13 B**

CULLEN, Archibald.
Principles of the Bankrupt law. 1800. 8vo. **160 F**

CULLUM, Rev. Sir John.
The history and antiquities of Hawsted and Hardwick in
the county of Suffolk. 2nd ed. 1813. 4to. **93 G**

CUMBERLAND.
A Concise topographical account of Cumberland. By Rev.
Daniel Lysons and Samuel Lysons. 1816. 4to. **86 G**
Delineations of Cumberland. By E. W. Brayley and J. Brit-
ton. 1802. 8vo. **87 A**
An Essay towards a natural history of Westmoreland and
Cumberland. By Thomas Robinson. 1709. 12mo. **93 F**
History and antiquities of Westmoreland and Cumberland.
By J. Nicolson and R. Burn. 2 vols. 1777. 4to. **94 G**
History of Cumberland. By R. S. Ferguson. 1890. 8vo. **87 A**
History of Cumberland. By W. Hutchinson. 2 vols. Car-
lisle, 1794. 4to. **87 G**
Jollie's Cumberland guide and directory. Carlisle, 1811.
8vo. **87 A**
See also BAWDWEN, Rev. W., CLARKE, J., GREENWICH,
WEST, T. and WILKINSON, Rev. J.

CUMIN, Patrick.
Manual of civil law : containing a translation of, and commentary on, the fragments of the XII. tables and the Institutes
of Justinian . . . and the text of the fragments of Ulpian
and of selections from Paul's Receptæ sententiæ. 2nd ed.
1865. 8vo. **63 G**

CUNNINGHAM, John.
Law relating to parliamentary and municipal elections and
petitions. 1877. 12mo. **166 E**
The same. 3rd ed. by C. T. Giles. 1885. 8vo. **9 H**

CUNNINGHAM, John and M. W. MATTINSON.
A Selection of precedents of Pleading under the Judicature
acts in the common law divisions. 1878. 8vo. **173 E**

CUNNINGHAM, JOHN and M. W. MATTINSON—*cont.*

A Selection of precedents of Pleading under the Judicature
acts in the Queen's Bench and Chancery divisions. 2nd ed.
by M. W. Mattinson and S. C. Macaskie. 1884. 8vo. **12 E**

CUNNINGHAM, TIMOTHY.

History and antiquities of four Inns of Court and of nine Inns
of Chancery, also of Serjeants' Inn and Scroop's Inn, &c.
Extracted from Dugdale's Origines Juridiciales. [By T.
Cunningham.] 1780. 8vo. **91 D**

History and antiquities relative to origin of government,
beginning of laws, antiquity of our laws in England &c.
Extracted from Dugdale's Origines Juridiciales. [By T.
Cunningham.] 1780. 8vo. **91 D**

History of our customs, aids, subsidies, national debts and
taxes. 1764, and 2nd ed. 1771. 8vo. **78 D**

Law dictionary, or general abridgment of the law; containing not only the explanation of the terms, but also the
law itself. 2 vols. 1764. folio. **123 G**

Law of bills of exchange, promissory notes, bank-notes and
insurances. By A Gentleman of the Middle Temple. 1760.
8vo. **160 G**

The same. By T. Cunningham. 6th ed. 1778. 8vo. **160 G**

The law of Simony. 1784. 8vo. **175 G**

The laws concerning Tithes. 3rd ed. 1748. 8vo. **176 E**

Reports of cases argued and adjudged in Court of King's
Bench, in the 7th–10th George II., during time of Lord
Chief Justice Hardwicke; to which is prefixed, a proposal
for rendering laws of England clear and certain. 2nd ed.
1770. folio. **74 C**

CUNYNGHAME, HENRY.

The law of Electric lighting. 1883. 8vo. **52 G**

CURRAN, JOHN PHILPOT.

Recollections of Curran and some of his contemporaries. By
Charles Phillips. 2nd ed. 1822. 8vo. **79 G**

CURRENCY.

On the alterations in the currency. See T. Tooke's High and
low prices, vol. 1, 1823. 8vo. **78 C**

CURRIE, FENDALL.

The Indian criminal codes. 4th ed. 1872. 8vo. **38 C**

CURRIE, JAMES.

The works of Robert Burns with an account of his life and a criticism on his writings. 2nd ed. 4 vols. 1801. 8vo. **83 D**

CURSON, HENRY.

Compendium of laws and government of Great Britain and Ireland and dominions thereunto belonging. 2nd ed. 1716. 12mo. **170 F**

CURTEIS, WILLIAM CALVERLEY.

Reports of cases in the Ecclesiastical courts at Doctors' Commons 1834–1844. 3 vols. 1840–44. 8vo. **8 G**

CURTIS, BENJAMIN ROBBINS.

Reports of decisions in the Supreme Court of the United States, with digest 1790 to 1854. 22 vols. Boston, 1855–56. 8vo. **57 B**

CURTIS, GEORGE TICKNOR.

An Inquiry into the Albany and Susquehanna railroad litigations of 1869. New York, 1871. [Pamphlets, vol. 29.] **144 B**

The law of Copyright. Boston, 1847. 8vo. **59 C**

The law of Patents for useful inventions in the United States of America. Boston, 1849. 8vo. **60 A**

The same. 3rd ed. Boston, 1867. 8vo. **60 A**

CURTIS, REV. JOHN.

A Topographical history of the county of Leicester. Ashby-de-la-Zouch, 1831. 8vo. **89 C**

CUSSANS, JOHN EDWIN.

History of Hertfordshire. 3 vols. 1870-81. folio. **89 H**

CUST, REGINALD JOHN.

The West Indian incumbered estates acts. 1859. 12mo. **38 D**

The same. 2nd ed. with supplement. 2 vols. 1865–74. 12mo. **38 D**

CUSTOM AND CUSTOMARY TENURES.

Custom and tenant right. By C. Elton. 1882. 8vo. **13 B**

Dissertations on early law and custom. By Sir H. S. Maine. 1883. 8vo. **83 I**

CUSTOM AND CUSTOMARY TENURES—*continued.*

Fragmenta antiquitatis or ancient tenures of land and jocular customs of manors. By Thomas Blount. 4th ed. by W. C. Hazlitt. 1874. 8vo. **13 B**

Law of customary tenures of land. By C. Elton. 1874. 8vo. **13 B**

Usages and Customs. By J. H. B. Browne. 1875. 8vo. **11 I**

See also KENNETT, RIGHT REV. W.

CUSTOMS, HISTORY AND LAW OF THE.

The laws of the Customs. By F. J. Hamel. 1876. 8vo. **9 G**

The laws of the Customs. By J. G. Walford. 1846. 8vo. **52 E**

History of our customs. By T. Cunningham. 2nd ed. 1771. 8vo. **78 D**

The report from committee of House of Commons appointed to enquire into frauds and abuses in the Customs 1733. Bound with Lists of law officers 1730–33. folio. **118 G**

Schedules and tables relative to the proposed consolidation of the Customs. n.d. 4to. **156 C**

See also BALDWIN, S., CARKESSE, C., HUME, J. D. and POPE, C.

CUTLER, JOHN.

The international law of navigable rivers. 1863. [Pamphlets, vol. 21.] **144 B**

The law of Naturalisation. 1870. 12mo. **11 A**

The law of Voluntary Settlements. 1869. 12mo. **175 E**

Reports of Patent Cases 1884–1889, and Digest of Patent Cases 1884–1889. 7 vols. 1884–90. 8vo. **76 H**

An Analysis of the Indian penal code (act XLV. of 1860). By J. Cutler and E. F. Griffin. 1869. 8vo. **38 B**

CUTTER, CHARLES A.

Rules for a printed dictionary catalogue. [Report on public libraries in the United States, part 2.] Washington, 1876. 8vo. **82 C**

CUTTS, REV. EDWARD LEWES.

Historic towns. Colchester. 1888. 8vo. **87 E**

CYPRUS.
Ordinances of the island of Cyprus 1880–1883 and 1885–1889. 2 vols. 1880–89. 8vo. **37 D**

DAFFORNE, RICHARD.
The merchants mirrour ; or directions for the perfect ordering and keeping of his accounts. 1684. See G. Malynes's Lex Mercatoria. 1686. folio. **118 G**

[DAGGE, HENRY.]
Considerations on Criminal law. 1772. 8vo. **165 F**

DAGGENHAM BREACH, ESSEX.
An Account of the stopping of Daggenham Breach. By John Perry. 1721. 8vo. **87 E**

DALE, CHARLES W. M. and R. C. LEHMANN.
Digest of cases overruled . . . in the English courts, from 1756 to 1886 inclusive. 1887. 8vo. **14 F**

DALE, JAMES MURRAY.
The clergyman's legal handbook, or compendium of clerical and parochial law. 2nd ed. 1859. 12mo. **166 A**
The same. 4th ed. 1866. 12mo. **166 A**
The same. 5th ed. by C. C. M. Dale. 1869. 12mo. **9 C**
Legal Ritual. The judgments delivered by Privy Council and Dean of Arches in recent cases of Martin v. Mackonochie, and Elphinstone v. Purchas, and Hebbert v. Purchas. A guide for incumbents, churchwardens and parishioners. 1871. 12mo. **53 F**

DALE, RICHARD AUSTEN.
A County Courts formulist. 1887. 8vo. **12 H**

DALE, ROBERT.
An exact catalogue of nobility of England. 1697. 12mo. **123 A**

DALE, SAMUEL.
The history and antiquities of Harwich and Dovercourt. 1730. 8vo. **87 E**
Life of S. Dale. See J. P. Malcolm's Lives of Topographers and Antiquaries, 1815. 4to. **79 H**

DALLAS, ALEXANDER JAMES.
Reports of decisions in the Supreme court of the United
States 1790 to 1800. 3 vols. See B. R. Curtis's Reports,
vol. I. Boston, 1855. 8vo. **57 B**

DALLAWAY, JAMES.
History of the western division of county of Sussex. Continued and completed by Rev. E. Cartwright. 2 vols. in 3.
1815–30. 4to. **94 G**

DALRYMPLE, ALEXANDER.
A Reply to a ' Letter from Andrew Stuart to the directors of
the East India Company.' 1779. 4to. **38 A**

DALRYMPLE, SIR JOHN.
An Essay towards a general history of Feudal property in
Great Britain. 4th ed. Dublin, 1759. 12mo. **49 F**
Memoirs of Great Britain and Ireland from dissolution of last
parliament of Charles II. until the sea battle off La Hogue.
2nd ed. 2 vols. 1771–73. 4to. **114 F**

D'ALTON, JOHN.
History of county of Dublin. Dublin, 1838. 8vo. **95 F**
Memoirs of Archbishops of Dublin. Dublin, 1838. 8vo. **80 C**

DALTON, MICHAEL.
The Countrey Justice, containing the practice of the Justices
of the Peace out of their sessions. 1626. folio. **156 C**
The same. Edited by W. Nelson. 1727. folio. **156 C**
Officium Vicecomitum. The office and authority of Sheriffs.
1623. folio. **156 C**
The same. 1670 and 1682. folio. **156 C**

DALY, DOMINICK.
Club law and the law of unregistered friendly societies. 2nd
ed. 1889. 12mo. **9 C**

DAMAGES.
Mayne's Treatise on Damages. 4th ed. by J. D. Mayne and
L. Smith. 1884. 8vo. **9 G**
A Treatise on the measure of Damages. By T. Sedgwick.
4th ed. by H. D. Sedgwick. New York, 1868. 8vo. **59 D**
Law of Damages. By J. Sayer. 1770. 8vo. **165 G**
See also NASMITH, D.

DAMASCUS.

A Journey to Damascus through Egypt, Nubia, Arabia
Petræa, Palestine, and Syria. By Viscount Castlereagh.
2 vols. 1847. 8vo. **84 B**

DANIEL, EDWARD MORTON.

Law of patents, designs, and trade marks. 1884. 8vo. **53 B**

DANIEL, WILLIAM THOMAS SHAW.

Bradford Law Students' Society. Inaugural address delivered
12 April 1875. Bradford, 1875. [Pamphlets, vol. 31.] **144 C**

The history and origin of the Law Reports. 1884. 8vo. **83 I**

Law reporting. A letter to Sir Roundell Palmer, having
particular reference to scheme of law reporting recommended
by committee appointed at meeting of the bar held Dec. 2,
1863. 1864. [Pamphlets, vol. 25.] **144 B**

A Letter to Sir Roundell Palmer on the present system of
Law reporting, its evils and a suggested remedy. [1863.]
[Pamphlets, vol. 20.] **144 B**

DANIELL, EDMUND ROBERT.

Considerations on reform in chancery. By An Equity Draftsman. 1842. [Chancery Pamphlets, vol. 2.] **144 A**

Practical observations on new orders for regulation of practice
and proceedings of Court of Chancery. 1841. 8vo. **161 C**

Reports of cases on the equity side of the Court of Exchequer
1817–1820. 1 vol. 1824. 8vo. **7 D**

The practice of the high Court of Chancery with some practical observations on the pleadings in that court. 3 vols.
1837–41. 8vo. **161 B**

The same. 2nd ed. by T. E. Headlam. 2 vols. 1845–51.
8vo. **161 C**

The same. 3rd ed. by T. E. Headlam. 2 vols. 1857. 8vo. **161 C**

The same. 4th ed. by L. Field and E. C. Dunn. 2 vols. in 3.
1865–67. 8vo. **161 C**

The same. 5th ed. by L. Field and E. C. Dunn. 2 vols. in 3.
1871. 8vo. **12 F**

The practice of the Chancery division of the high court of
Justice. 6th ed. by L. Field, E. C. Dunn, and T. Ribton.
2 vols. in 3. 1882–84. 8vo. **12 F**

Forms of pleadings and proceedings in the high court of
Chancery, with references to Daniell's Chancery practice.
By L. Field, E. C. Dunn and J. Biddle. 1867. 8vo. **161 B**

DANIELL, EDMUND ROBERT—*continued.*
The same. 2nd ed. by J. Biddle. 1871. 8vo.   **161 B**
Forms and precedents of proceedings in the Chancery division
of the high court of Justice. By L. Field, E. C. Dunn and
J. Biddle. 3rd ed. by W. H. Upjohn. 1879. 8vo.   **12 F**
The same. 4th ed. by C. Burney. 1885. 8vo.   **12 F**

DANSEY, REV. WILLIAM.
Horæ Decanicæ Rurales. An attempt to illustrate the name,
title, origin, appointment, and functions of Rural Deans.
2nd ed. 2 vols. 1844. 8vo.   **83 H**

DANSON, FREDERICK MAXWELL and J. H. LLOYD.
Reports of cases relating to commerce, manufactures &c. in
courts of common law 1828–1829. 1 vol. 1830. 8vo.   **4 F**

DANUBIAN PRINCIPALITIES.
Wallachia and Moldavia. Correspondence of D. Bratiano
with Lord Dudley C. Stuart, M.P., on the Danubian principalities. 1853. [Pamphlets, vol. 9, pt. 2.]   **144 A**

D'ANVERS, KNIGHTLEY.
A General abridgment of the Common Law. vol. 1, 1705.
vol. 2, 2nd ed. 1722. 2 vols. 1705–22. folio.   **156 C**

DARBY, J. G. N. and F. A. BOSANQUET.
A Practical treatise on the statutes of limitations in England
and Ireland. 1867. 8vo.   **53 A**

DARELL, REV. WILLIAM.
History of Dover Castle. 1797. 4to.   **88 E**

DARLING, JAMES.
Cyclopædia Bibliographica : a library manual of theological
and general literature. [Part 1. Authors.] 1854. 4to. **82 F**
Cyclopæd:- Bibliographica. [Part 2.] Subjects. Holy
Scripture 1850 4to.   **82 F**

DARLINGTON, HAYWARD RADCLIFFE.
The Railway and Canal traffic acts 1854 to 1888, with notes,
orders, rules, forms, fees, &c. 1889. 8vo.   **11 C**

DART, REV. JOHN.

History and antiquities of cathedral church of Canterbury and once adjoining monastery. 1726. folio. **89 H**

Life of J. Dart. See J. P. Malcolm's Lives of Topographers and Antiquaries. 1815. 4to. **79 H**

Westmonasterium ; or the history and antiquities of abbey church of St. Peter's Westminster, to which is added, Westminster Abbey, a poem. 2 vols. [1742.] folio. **91 H**

DART, JOSEPH HENRY.

Compendium of law and practice of Vendors and Purchasers of real estate. 2nd ed. 1852. 8vo. **177 A**

The same. 3rd ed. 1856. 8vo. **177 A**

The same. 4th ed. by the Author and W. Barber. 2 vols. 1871. 8vo. **177 A**

The same. 5th ed. by the Author and W. Barber. 2 vols. 1876. 8vo. **53 H**

The same. 6th ed. by W. Barber, R. B. Haldane and W. R. Sheldon. 2 vols. 1888. 8vo. **13 H**

DARTMOOR, DEVONSHIRE.

A Short history of the rights of common upon the Forest of Dartmoor and the commons of Devonshire. By Percival Birkett. 1885. 8vo. **87 C**

DAVENANT, CHARLES.

Discourses on the publick revenues and on the trade of England. Part 1. 1698. 12mo. **49 D**

DAVENPORT, SIR HUMPHREY.

An Exact abridgement of the Lord Coke's Commentaries upon Littleton. 1652. 12mo. **48 B**

DAVENPORT, JOHN MARRIOTT.

County of Oxford. Notes upon the jurisdiction of county justices within city of Oxford. 1872. 8vo. **92 E**

Lord lieutenant and high sheriff, correspondence upon the question of precedence. 1871. 8vo. **92 E**

Lords lieutenant and high sheriffs of Oxfordshire 1086–1868. Oxford, 1868. 8vo. **92 E**

Memorandum as to oaths and statutory declarations &c. Oxford, 1873. 8vo. **53 B**

DAVENPORT, JOHN MARRIOTT—*continued*.

Notes as to Oxford Castle. 1877. 8vo.   **92 E**

Oxfordshire annals. Oxford, 1869. 8vo.   **92 E**

· Oxfordshire militia. Sketch of the history of the regiment.
Oxford, 1869. 8vo.   **92 E**

DAVENPORT, RICHARD ALFRED.

Dictionary of biography comprising most eminent characters
of all ages, nations and professions. 1831. 8vo.   **81 B**

DAVIDSON, CHARLES.

Concise precedents in Conveyancing. 6th ed. by C. Davidson
and M. B. Stapylton. 1865. 12mo.   **164 E**

The same. 9th ed. by C. Davidson. 1874. 12mo.   **164 E**

The same. 11th ed. by C. Davidson and H. T. S. Dicey.
1879. 12mo.   **164 E**

The same. 13th ed. by M. G. Davidson. 1883. 12mo.   **53 E**

The same. 14th ed. by M. G. Davidson. 1885. 12mo.   **13 E**

Davidson's Precedents and forms in conveyancing. vol. 1.
Introduction and Common forms in conveyancing. 2nd ed.
by C. Davidson and T. C. Wright. 1855. 8vo.   **164 A**

The same. 3rd ed. by C. Davidson, T. C. Wright and
J. Waley. 1860. 8vo.   **164 A**

The same. 4th ed. by C. Davidson and T. C. Wright. 1874.
8vo.   **164 B**

The same. 5th ed. by T. C. Wright and J. K. Darley. 1885.
8vo.   **13 E**

Davidson's Precedents and forms in conveyancing. vol. 2.
Agreements and Conveyances on Sales and Mortgages.
2nd ed. by C. Davidson, T. C. Wright and J. Waley. 1858.
8vo.   **164 A**

The same. 3rd ed. in two parts. Part 1 by C. Davidson,
T. C. Wright and J. Waley, 1864, and Part 2 by C.
Davidson, T. C. Wright, J. Waley and T. Key. 1869.
8vo.   **164 A**

The same. 4th ed. in two parts. Part 1 by C. Davidson,
T. C. Wright and J. K. Darley, 1877, and Part 2 by
C. Davidson and T. Key, 1881.   **13 E**

Davidson's Precedents and forms in conveyancing. vol. 3.
Settlements. 2nd ed. by C. Davidson, T. C. Wright and
J. Waley. 1861. 8vo.   **164 A**

The same. 3rd ed. by C. Davidson, J. Waley, and T. Key.
2 vols. 1873. 8vo.   **13 E**

DAVIDSON, CHARLES—*continued.*

Davidson's Precedents and forms in conveyancing. vol. 4. Wills and Appointments of new trustees. 2nd ed. by C. Davidson, T. C. Wright and J. Waley. 1864. 8vo. **164 A**

The same. 3rd ed. by C. Davidson and T. Key. 1880. 8vo. **13 E**

Davidson's Precedents and forms in conveyancing. vol. 5. Leases and Miscellaneous instruments. 2nd ed. by C. Davidson, T. C. Wright, J. Waley and J. Whitehead. 1865. 8vo. **164 A**

The same. 3rd ed. by C. Davidson and M. G. Davidson. 2 vols. 1876–78. 8vo. **13 E**

DAVIES, REV. DAVID PETER.

A New historical and descriptive view of Derbyshire. Belper, 1811. 8vo. **87 C**

DAVIES, EDWARD.

A Letter to Sir Henry Halford touching some points of the evidence and observations of counsel on a commission of lunacy on Mr. Edward Davies. By G. M. Burrows. 1830. [Jacob's Tracts, vol. 7.] **144 E**

DAVIES, GEORGE CHRISTOPHER.

The handbook to the rivers and broads of Norfolk and Suffolk. 9th ed. 1887. 8vo. **92 C**

DAVIES, JOHN, OF KIDWELLY.

The history of the Caribby Islands, viz. Barbados, St. Christophers, St. Vincents &c. in all XXVIII, with a Caribbian vocabulary. 1666. 4to. **84 E**

DAVIES, SIR JOHN, ATTORNEY GENERAL, IRELAND.

A Report of cases and matters in law in the King's courts in Ireland. Dublin, 1762. 8vo. **15 D**

DAVIES, JOHN, OF THE ROLLS CHAPEL OFFICE.

A Collection of the most important cases respecting Patents of invention and the rights of Patentees. 1816. 8vo. **76 H**

DAVIES, REV. JOHN SILVESTER.

A History of Southampton, partly from the MS. of Dr. Speed in the Southampton archives. 1883. 8vo. **88 B**

DAVIES, R. RICE.
A Handy book of the land assessed and income tax laws.
1864. 8vo. 53 H

DAVIES, ROWLAND, DEAN OF ROSS.
Journal from March 8, 1688–9, to September 29, 1690. Edited
by Richard Caulfield. [Camden Society, vol. 68.] 1857.
8vo. 85 B

DAVIES, THOMAS.
The laws relating to Bankrupts brought home to the present
time. 1744. folio. 156 C

DAVIS, REV. CHARLES HENRY.
The English church canons of 1604; with historical introduction and notes. 1869. 8vo. 77 C

DAVIS, HENRY FREDERICK ALEXANDER.
Law of building and freehold land societies in England, Scot-
land and Ireland. 1870, and 2nd ed. 1874. 12mo. 161 A
The same. 3rd ed. 1884. 12mo. 9 B
A Manual of the law relating to industrial and provident
societies. 1869. 8vo. 10 C

DAVIS, JAMES EDWARD.
The Criminal law consolidation statutes. 1861. 12mo. 165 D
The jurisdiction of county courts in equity. 1872. 8vo. 165 B
The Labour Laws. 1875. 8vo. 170 C
Manual of law of Registration and Elections. 1868. 12mo. 166 E
The Master and Servant act 1867. 1868. 12mo. 172 D
The practice and evidence in actions in the County Courts.
2nd ed. 1857. 8vo. 165 B
The same. 5th ed. 1874, and Supplement 1876. 2 vols.
1874–76. 8vo. 165 B
The same. 6th ed. by S. M. Rhodes. 1887. 8vo. 12 H

[DAVIS, JOHN.]
Origines Divisianæ, or the Antiquities of the Devizes in some
familiar letters to a friend. 1754. 12mo. 93 F

DAVIS, JOHN CHANDLER BANCROFT.
Cases adjudged in the Supreme Court of the United States,
1882 to 1888. 24 vols. New York, 1884–89. 8vo. 57 E

DAVIS, JOHN FRANCIS.
The Chinese, a general description of China and its inhabitants. New ed. 1840. 8vo. **84 A**

DAVIS, PETER STEVENSON.
Analytical index of cases decided in supreme court, court of mines, and in vice-admiralty court of colony of Victoria, 1871–1883. Melbourne, 1885. 8vo. **55 D**

DAVISON, HENRY and HERMAN MERIVALE.
Reports of cases in the Court of Queen's Bench and upon writs of error to the Exchequer chamber, 1843–1844. 1 vol. 1844. 8vo. **4 F**

DAVISON, WILLIAM.
Life of W. Davison, secretary of state to Queen Elizabeth. By N. H. Nicolas. 1823. 8vo. **79 C**

DAX, EDWARD THOMAS.
The new book of costs in the superior courts of common law at Westminster. 1847. 12mo. **52 D**

DAX, THOMAS.
Letter to Baron Lyndhurst on The appellate jurisdiction of the House of Lords, The arrears of business in the common law courts, The local courts bill, The registry courts and trials of controverted elections. 2nd ed. 1842. 8vo. **55 D**
The practice in the offices of the masters on the plea side of the superior common law courts. 1844. 12mo. **53 A**
The practice on the plea side of the Court of Exchequer. 1831. 8vo. **168 B**

DAY, JOHN CHARLES FREDERIC SIGISMUND.
The Common law procedure acts and other statutes relating to the practice of the superior courts of Common law. 1861. 12mo. **161 G**
The same. 2nd ed. 1863, and 3rd ed. 1868. 12mo. **161 G**
The same. 4th ed. 1872. 8vo. **52 C**
Suggestions for some further improvements in the administration of the common law. 1877. [Pamphlets, vol. 32.] **144 C**

DAY, JOSEPH.
An Address to the attorneys at law and solicitors, practising in Great Britain, and to the public, upon the proceedings

DAY, JOSEPH—*continued.*
of a committee of the London Law Club, relative to a bill
proposed to be presented to Parliament for the incorporating
and better regulation of practitioners. 1796. 8vo. **160 C**

DEACON, EDWARD ERASTUS.
The law and practice of Bankruptcy. 3rd ed. by A. G
Langley. 2 vols. 1864. 12mo. **160 E**
Practical treatise on the Game laws. 1831. 8vo. **168 F**
Reports of cases in Bankruptcy. 1835–1840. 4 vols. 1837–41.
8vo. **8 B**

DEACON, EDWARD ERASTUS and EDWARD CHITTY.
Reports of cases in Bankruptcy. 1832–1835. 4 vols. 1833–37.
8vo. **8 B**

DEAN FOREST, GLOUCESTERSHIRE.
The laws of the Dean Forest and hundred of Saint Briavels.
By J. G. Wood. 1878. 8vo. **87 F**

DEANE, CHRISTOPHER PAGE.
Manual of the law concerning the retailing of intoxicating
drinks. 1887. 8vo. **12 C**

DEANE, HENRY CHARLES.
Principles of Conveyancing. An elementary work for the
use of students. 1874. 8vo. **163 G**
The same. 2nd ed. 1883. 8vo. **13 A**

DEANE, JAMES PARKER.
The act for amendment of the laws with respect to Wills,
with notes. 1852. 8vo. **177 D**
The law of Blockade as contained in report of eight cases in
court of Admiralty on blockade of coast of Courland, 1854
1855. 8vo. **55 A**
Reports of cases decided in the Ecclesiastical courts at Doctors'
Commons 1855–1857. 1 vol. 1858. 8vo. **8 G**

DEANE, LANCASHIRE.
A Curious description of the parish of Deane. See P. A.
Whittle's Bolton, 1855, pp. 323–353. **89 B**

DEARN, Thomas Downs Willmott.

Historical, topographical and descriptive account of the Weald of Kent. Cranbrook, 1814. 8vo. **88 E**

DEARSLEY, Henry Richard.

Crown Cases reserved for consideration and decided by the judges of England 1852–1856. 1 vol. 1856. 8vo. **1 H**

DEARSLEY, Henry Richard and Thomas Bell.

Crown cases reserved for consideration and decided by the judges of England 1856–1858. 1 vol. 1858. 8vo. **1 H**

DEATH, Punishment of.

The deterrent influence of capital punishment. By Thomas Beggs. 2nd ed. 1868. [Pamphlets, vol. 31.] **144 C**

Facts relating to the punishment of death in the metropolis. By E. G. Wakefield. 1831. 12mo. **78 A**

The law of homicide and of capital punishment. A debate in the English Parliament, June 12, 1877. 1878. [Pamphlets, vol. 31.] **144 C**

On the effects of capital punishment as applied to forgery and theft. 1818. [Montagu's Law Tracts.] **144 F**

The opinions of different authors upon the punishment of death. Selected by Basil Montagu. 1809. 8vo. **78 A**

DEBACH, Suffolk.

How the parish of Debach borrowed £400 and refused to pay it all back. [By Ralph Thomas.] 1879. [Pamphlets, vol. 32.] **144 C**

DE BODE, Clement, Baron.

An Address to members of House of Commons, with a copy of the petition to be presented to the House, concerning his claims for indemnification under treaties made between Great Britain and France in 1814, 1815 and 1818. 1833. [Pamphlets, vol. 5.] **144 A**

Statement for counsel's opinion, and opinions of eleven French jurisconsults concerning the indemnity due to the Baron de Bode under convention No. 7 of the conventions of 1815 and 1818. 1845. [Pamphlets, vol. 16.] **144 B**

DE BOW, James Dunwoody Brownson.

Industrial resources of the Southern and Western states. 4 vols. New Orleans, 1853. 8vo. **84 D**

DEBRETT, JOHN.

The Baronetage of England. Editions 1, 3, 4, 5, 6, 6 rewritten, and 7. 13 vols. 1808–35. 12mo. **125 B**

Illustrated baronetage and knightage of the United Kingdom for
1866, 1868, and 1884–1889. 8 vols. 1866–89. 8vo. **125 B C**

The same for 1879. 1879. 8vo. **124 E**

Illustrated House of Commons and the Judicial Bench, 1871,
and 1880 to 1889. 11 vols. 1871–89. 8vo. **134 B**

Peerage of England, Scotland and Ireland. Editions 1 to 20,
43 vols., 1802–34; and the editions for 1838, 1840, 1866,
1879, 1882, and 1884 to 1889. 54 vols. 1802–89. 12mo.
and 8vo. **124 C–E**

DEBTS AND DEBTORS.

Attachment of debts in high court of justice and in county
courts. By M. Cababé. 2nd ed. 1888. 12mo. **12 F**

Observations on proposed changes in the law of Debtor and
Creditor. By C. T. Swanston. 1868. [Pamphlets, vol.
32.] **144 C**

Law of debtor and creditor. By C. F. Trower. 1860. 8vo. **52 F**

Remarks on the present state of the law of debtor and
creditor, with suggestions for its improvement. By T. T.
à Beckett. 1844. [Pamphlets, vol. 3.] **144 A**

Debtors' laws, with a word to their victims. 1838. 8vo. **78 B**

A Letter on bill for more convenient recovery of small debts
in England and Wales, pointing out its impracticability
and impolicy. By W. 1821. [Jacob's Tracts, vol. 1.] **144 E**

Enquiries respecting the insolvent debtors bill, with the
opinions of Dr. Paley, Mr. Burke and Dr. Johnson, upon
imprisonment for debt. By Basil Montagu. 2nd ed.
1816. [Montagu's Law Tracts.] **144 F**

The law for surrender of effects and for personal liberation of
prisoners for debt. By J. P. Smith. 1814. 8vo. **169 A**

Account of the Society for discharge and relief of persons
imprisoned for small debts throughout England and Wales.
By James Neild. 3rd ed. 1808. 8vo. **84 B**

Imprisonment for debt unconstitutional and oppressive. By
Edward Farley. 1788. 8vo. **78 B**

History of Securities upon land for payment of debt, of
execution against moveables and land for payment of debt,
of personal execution for payment of debt, and of execution
for obtaining payment after the death of the debtor. See

DEBTS AND DEBTORS—*continued.*

Historical Law Tracts, vol. 2, 2nd ed. 1761, pp. 145–172, and 313–387. **144 F**

A Treatise on the action of Debt, from the original manuscript of Lord chief baron Gilbert. 1760. 8vo. **74 D**

See also ARRANGEMENTS WITH CREDITORS and ASSETS.

DE BURE, GUILLAUME FRANÇOIS, LE JEUNE.

Bibliographie instructive, ou traité de la connoissance de livres rares et singuliers. 7 vols. 1763–68, and Supplement ou catalogue des livres du cabinet de feu M. Louis J. Gaignat. 2 vols. 1769. 9 vols. Paris, 1763–69. 8vo. **82 A**

DE BURGH, WILLIAM.

Elements of Maritime International law. 1868. 8vo. **55 A**

DECCAN PRIZE CASE.

The proceedings and memorials in the Deccan Prize Case 1821–1833. 5 vols. 1823–33. folio and 4to. **145 F**

DECIMAL ASSOCIATION.

Decimal Association (formed June 12, 1854). Proceedings with an introduction by Professor De Morgan and notes. 1854. 8vo. **78 G**

International Association for obtaining a uniform decimal system of measures, weights and coins. Third report of the council 1859. [Pamphlets, vol. 12.] **144 A**

Memorial on decimal weights presented to Benjamin Disraeli, M.P., chancellor of Her Majesty's Exchequer. 1859. [Pamphlets, vol. 12.] **144 A**

On the metrical system of weights and measures and the desirableness of its universal adoption. By Rev. J. S. Porter. 1859. [Pamphlets, vol. 12.] **144 A**

The plan, objects and progress of International Association for obtaining a uniform decimal system of measures, weights and coins. By S. Brown. 1858. [Pamphlets, vol. 12.] **144 A**

DEE, JOHN.

The private diary of John Dee, and the catalogue of his library of manuscripts. Edited by J. O. Halliwell. [Camden Society, vol. 19.] 1842. 8vo. **85 A**

DEE RIVER, Cheshire.

Acts relating to navigation of river Dee with the bye laws, orders and rules of company of proprietors of Undertaking for recovering and preserving navigation of river Dee. 2 vols. 1773 and 1840. 12mo. **86 E**

DEEDS AND TITLE DEEDS.

Rules for the interpretation of deeds. By H. W. Elphinstone, R. F. Norton and J. W. Clark. 1885. 8vo. **9 G**

The custody and production of title deeds. By W. A. Copinger. 1875. 8vo. **13 I**

Treatise on purchase deeds. By W. F. Cornish. New ed. by G. Horsey. 1855. 8vo. **175 A**

Rules for the construction of statutes, deeds, and wills. By Basil Montagu. 1836. 12mo. **176 C**

The forms of deeds and documents in England and France compared and exemplified. By Charles Okey. 1835. [Pamphlets, vol. 1.] **144 A**

The stamp laws relating to deeds and assurances. By Thomas Coventry. vol. 1. 1833. 8vo. **175 G**

The law relative to Title-Deeds and other documents. By Robert Dixon. 2 vols. 1826. 8vo. **176 F**

Of antient deeds and charters. See Sir H. Spelman's English works, 2nd ed. 1727, part 2, pp. 233–256. **78 H**

The law of common assurances touching deeds in general. By Wm. Sheppard. 1669. folio. **49 G**

DEEDS, Registration of.

Dissertation on Registry and precedents of memorials &c. See Bythewood and Jarman's Conveyancing, 4th ed. vol. 6, 1890, pp. 1–25. **13 D**

A Manual on the registration of deeds and other assurances in Yorkshire. By H. Barker. 1885. 8vo. **13 B**

Forms of memorials, certificates, and affidavits, as used at the Yorkshire registries of deeds. By J. E. Dibb. 3rd ed. 1871. 8vo. **178 F**

Observations on the statutes for registering deeds. By J. Rigge. 1798. 8vo. **13 B**

See also Land Title and Transfer.

DEERING, Charles.

Nottinghamia vetus et nova ; or an historical account of the ancient and present state of the town of Nottingham. Nottingham, [1751.] 4to. **92 E**

DEFAMATION.

Law of Defamation. By G. W. Cooke. 1844. 12mo. **175 G**

See also LIBEL and SLANDER.

DE FERRIERE, CLAUDE JOSEPH.

La Science parfaite des Notaires, ou le parfait Notaire. Nouvelle édition par F. B. De Visme. 2 vols. Paris, 1771. 4to. **40 D**

DE FOE, DANIEL.

The history of the Union between England and Scotland, to which is prefixed, A life of Daniel De Foe. By George Chalmers. 1786. 4to. **113 F**

DE GEX, JOHN PETER.

Reports of cases in bankruptcy 1844–1848. 1 vol. 1852. 8vo. **8 B**

DE GEX, J. P., F. FISHER and H. C. JONES.

Reports of cases heard by Lord Chancellor and court of appeal in Chancery 1859–1862. 4 vols. 1861–70. 8vo. **2 D**

DE GEX, J. P. and H. C. JONES.

Reports of cases heard by Lord Chancellor and court of appeal in Chancery 1857–1859. 4 vols. 1858–61. 8vo. **2 D E**

DE GEX, J. P., H. C. JONES and R. H. SMITH.

Reports of cases heard by Lord Chancellor and court of appeal in Chancery 1862–1865. 4 vols. 1865–73. 8vo. **2 E**

DE GEX, J. P., S. MACNAGHTEN and A. GORDON.

Reports of cases heard by the Lord Chancellor and the court of appeal in Chancery 1851–1857. 8 vols. 1853–64. **2 E F**

DE GEX, J. P. and J. SMALE.

Reports of cases decided in the Court of Chancery by Sir J. L. Knight Bruce and Sir James Parker 1846–1852. 5 vols. 1849–53. 8vo. **2 F**

DE GEX, J. P. and R. H. SMITH.

Arrangements between Debtors and Creditors under the Bankruptcy act 1861, with an introduction and notes and Two Supplements. 3 vols. 1867–69. 8vo. **165 G**

DEGGE, Sir Simon.
  The parson's counsellor. 1676. 12mo.   49 B
  The same. 3rd ed. 1681 and 4th ed. 1685. 12mo.   49 B
  The same. 7th ed. by C. Ellis. 1820. 8vo.   52 F

DE GUIGNES, Joseph.
  Histoire générale des Huns, des Turcs, des Mogols, et des
    autres Tartares Occidentaux, &c. Précédée d'une introduc-
    tion contenant des tables des Princes qui ont regné dans
    l'Asie. 4 vols. in 5. Paris, 1756–58. 4to.   113 E

DE LA CROIX, Peter Firmin.
  A Review of the constitutions of principal states of Europe
    and of United States of America. Translated from the
    French. 2 vols. 1792. 8vo.   .   113 C

DELAMER, Henry, 2 Baron.
  The works of Henry late Lord Delamer. 1694. 8vo.   83 A

DELANE, William Frederick Augustus.
  A Collection of decisions in courts for revising lists of electors
    for Berkshire . . . cities of London and Westminster and
    boroughs of Abingdon &c. 2nd ed. 1836. 12mo.   66 B

DELAUNE, Thomas.
  Angliæ Metropolis, or the present state of London. 1690.
    12mo.   91 B

DELIVERY, Law of.
  A Treatise on Stoppage in transitu and incidentally of
    Delivery. By John Houston. 1866. 8vo.   11 G
  See also Sale, Law of.

DE LOLME, John Louis.
  The Constitution of England ; or, an account of the English
    government. New ed. 1790. 8vo.   · ·   116 F
  The same. New ed. by W. H. Hughes. 1834. 8vo.   116 F

DE MERVILLE, Pierre.
  La Coutume de Normandie reduite en maximes selon le sens
    litteral et l'esprit de chaque article. 1707. 4to.   40 A

DE MESCHIN, Thomas.
Bishop Colenso's Fallacies [of parts 1 and 2]. 1863. [Pamphlets, vol. 18.] **144 B**
Case of T. De Meschin, of the Inner Temple barrister. Privately printed. 1866. [Pamphlets, vol. 32.] **144 C**
Plan for recording judicial decisions. 1864. [Pamphlets, vol. 25.] **144 B**

DE MOLEYNS, Thomas.
The landowner's and agent's practical guide. 5th ed. Dublin, 1866. 8vo. **55 E**

DEMOLOMBE, Jean Charles Florent.
Cours de Code Napoléon. 20 vols. Paris, 1860–63. 8vo. **58 C**
De la publication des effets et de l'application des lois en général. 2me éd. Paris, 1860. 8vo. **58 C**
Traité de l'absence. 2me éd. Paris, 1860. 8vo. **58 C**
Traité de la distinction des biens. 2me éd. 2 vols. Paris, 1861. 8vo. **58 C**
Traité de l'adoption et de la tutelle officieuse ; de la puissance paternelle. 2me éd. Paris, 1861. 8vo. **58 C**
Traité de la Minorité de la tutelle et de l'émancipation de la Majorité. 2me éd. 2 vols. Paris, 1861. 8vo. **58 C**
Traité de la Paternité et de la Filiation. 2me éd. Paris, 1860. 8vo. **58 C**
Traité des donations entre-vifs et des testaments. 2me éd. 3 vols. Paris, 1863. 8vo. **58 C**
Traité des servitudes ou services fonciers. 3me éd. 2 vols. Paris, 1863. 8vo. **58 C**
Traité des Successions. 2me éd. 5 vols. Paris, 1862. 8vo. **58 C**
Traité du Mariage et de la séparation de corps. 2me éd. 2 vols. Paris, 1860–61. 8vo. **58 C**

DE MORGAN, Augustus.
The book of almanacs, by which ⌐ie almanac may be found for every year up to A.D. 2000. 1851. 8vo. **107 E**
Decimal Association (formed June 12, 1854). Proceedings with an introduction and notes. 1854. 8vo. **78 G**

DE MOTTEVILLE, Madame Françoise Langlois.
Memoir on the life of Henrietta Maria. Edited by M. G. Hanotaux. [Camden Soc. n.s. vol. 31.] 1883. 8vo. **85 D**

DE MOUNTENEY, Barclay.
The case of a Détenu. 1838. [Pamphlets, vol. 3.] **144 A**

DEMPSEY, J. Maurice.
Our ocean highways, a condensed universal route book by sea, by land and by rail. 1870. 8vo. **84 A**

DENFORD, Berkshire.
The Denford question with the law upon it and the decision of the court of King's Bench with remarks. By William James. Reading, 1813. 8vo. **163 G**

DENHAM, Sir John.
Poems and translations with The Sophy, a tragedy. 1668. 8vo. **83 A**

DENHOLM, James.
The history of the city of Glasgow and suburbs, to which is added, A sketch of a tour to the principal Scotch and English lakes. 3rd ed. Glasgow, 1804. 8vo. **95 C**

DENISART, Jean Baptiste.
Collection de décisions nouvelles et de notions relatives à la Jurisprudence actuelle. 9me éd. 4 vols. 1777. 4to. **40 F**

DENISON, Charles Marsh and C. H. SCOTT.
The practice and procedure of the House of Lords in English, Irish and Scotch appeal cases. 1879. 8vo. **12 A**

DENISON, Stephen Charles.
Crown cases reserved for consideration and decided by the judges of England 1844 to 1852. By S. C. Denison and R. R. Pearce. 2 vols. 1850–52. 8vo. **1 H**

DENMARK.
British Scandinavian Society. 'Danish' and 'Norse.' A paper read before the Society. By Andrew Johnston. 1875. [Pamphlets, vol. 32.] **144 C**
The Danish laws or the code of Christian V., translated. 1756. 12mo. **55 C**
Defence for the full hereditary right according to the Lex Regia of the kings and royal house of Denmark, especially

DENMARK—*continued.*

Prince Christian and his spouse. By C. F. Wegener. Copenhagen, 1853. [Pamphlets, vol. 9, pt. 1.]   **144 A**

Deliberation or decision ? being a translation from the Danish of the reply given by Herr Raaslöff to the accusations preferred against him on the part of the Danish cabinet. 1861. [Pamphlets, vol. 14.]   **144 A**

Germany, Denmark and the Scandinavian question. 1861. [Pamphlets, vol. 14.]   **144 A**

The rise, progress and present state of the Northern governments. By John Williams. 2 vols. 1777. 4to.   **113 F**

[DENNE, REV. SAMUEL.]

The history and antiquities of Rochester and its environs. Rochester, 1772. 12mo.   **88 C**

The same. 2nd ed. Enlarged by W. Wildash. Rochester, 1817. 8vo.   **88 C**

DENT, ROBERT K.

Old and New Birmingham, a history of the town and its people. Birmingham, 1880. 4to.   **94 G**

DERBY, DERBYSHIRE.

Collection of fragments illustrative of history and antiquities of Derby. By R. Simpson. 2 vols. Derby, 1826. 8vo. **87 C**

History of Derby from remote ages of antiquity to year MDCCXCI. By Wm. Hutton. 2nd ed. 1817. 8vo. **87 C**

See also ADAM, W.

DERBY, EDWARD GEOFFREY, 14 EARL OF.

How shall we vote ? or an inquiry into the principal measures of Lord Derby's administration. 1859. [Pamphlets, vol. 12.]   **144 A**

DERBY, JOHN, ALDERMAN OF LONDON.

The Will of John Derby [referring to property in the parish of St. Dionis Backchurch] and Copy of a grant to John Derby of property in Philpot Lane. [1877.] folio.   **91 G**

DERBYSHIRE.

A Concise topographical account of the county of Derby. By Rev. D. Lysons and S. Lysons. 1817. 4to.   **87 B**

DERBYSHIRE—*continued.*

A Delineation of Strata of Derbyshire forming surface from Bolsover in the East to Buxton in the West. By White Watson. Sheffield, 1811. 8vo. **87 B**

The history and gazetteer of the county of Derby : the materials collected by the publisher, Stephen Glover. Edited by Thomas Noble. 2 vols. Derby, 1831–33. 4to. **87 B**

History of Derbyshire. By J. Pendleton. 1886. 8vo. **87 B**

A New historical and descriptive view of Derbyshire. By Rev. D. P. Davies. Belper, 1811. 8vo. **87 A**

Notes on the churches of Derbyshire. By J. C. Cox. 4 vols. 1875–79. 8vo. **87 B**

Seasonable considerations on a navigable canal intended to be cut from river Trent at Wilden Ferry, Derbyshire, to river Mersey, with Supplement. 1766. 8vo. **87 A**

Sketch of a tour into Derbyshire and Yorkshire. By William Bray. 2nd ed. 1783. 8vo. **87 A**

Survey of the counties of Derbyshire &c. 1797. 8vo. **89 B**

A View of the present state of Derbyshire, with an account of its most remarkable antiquities. By James Pilkington. 2nd ed. 2 vols. 1803. 8vo. **87 A**

See also ADAM, W., AIKIN, J. and ASHBOURN.

DERBYSHIRE, MINERALOGY OF.

The compleat mineral laws of Derbyshire, taken from the originals. 1734. 12mo. **87 A**

The Derbyshire miners' glossary. By James Mander. 1824. 8vo. **87 B**

The Derbyshire mining customs and Mineral court act 1852. By Thomas Tapping. 1854. 12mo. **172 F**

The High Peak mineral customs and Mineral court act 1851, with notes. By Thomas Tapping. 1851. 12mo. **172 F**

The liberties, laws and customs of the lead mines of Wirksworth. By T. Houghton. 2nd ed. Derby, 1729. 12mo. **87 A**

Mineralogy of Derbyshire. By J. Mawe. 1802. 8vo. **87 A**

The rhymed chronicle of Edward Manlove concerning the liberties and customs of the lead mines within the Wapentake of Wirksworth. 2nd ed. by T. Tapping. 1851. 8vo. **87 A**

DE RUVIGNY FAMILY.

Henri, first Marquis De Ruvigny and Henri De Ruvigny, Earl of Galway. See Rev. C. D. A. Agnew's Protestant exiles from France, vol. 1, 1871, pp. 122–219. **80 G**

DERWENTWATER, James, 3 Earl of.

A Report from committee to whom all books and papers relating to sale of estate of James late Earl of Derwentwater were referred. 1732. folio. **118 G**

The speech of the Lord high steward upon proceeding to judgment against James, Earl of Derwentwater, and others [for high treason]. 1715. folio. **118 G**

DESANCTIS, Luigi.

Confession: a doctrinal and historical essay. Translated from the eighteenth Italian edition by M. H. G. Buckle. 1878. 12mo. **77 B**

DESBOROUGH HUNDRED, Bucks.

The history and antiquities of the hundred of Desborough. By T. Langley. 1797. 4to. **86 B**

DESCENTS.

The law of Descents. By C. Watkins. 4th ed. by J. Williams. 1837. 8vo. **13 B**

The law of Descents. By H. Chitty. 1825. 8vo. **165 G**

The debate in the House of Commons upon corruption of blood. By B. M. [Basil Montagu.] 1814. 8vo. **144 F**

The law of descents in fee simple. See Blackstone's Law Tracts, vol. 1, 1762, pp. 167–263. **144 F**

DE VILLARGUES, Rolland.

Les Codes Criminels interprétés par la jurisprudence et la doctrine, suivis d'un formulaire. 2me éd. Paris, 1864. 8vo. **40 H**

DEVISES.

Essay on the learning of contingent remainders and executory devises. By C. Fearne. 10th ed. by J. W. Smith. 2 vols. 1844. 8vo. **13 H**

An Essay upon the learning of Devises. By J. J. Powell. 3rd ed. with a treatise on the construction of Devises. 2 vols. 1827. 8vo. **178 C**

A Short treatise on Family Settlements and Devises. By Thomas Keatinge. 1810. 8vo. **175 E**

Opinions on a devise of a real and personal estate. See Collectanea Juridica, vol. 2, 1792, pp. 255–257. **144 G**

DEVISES—*continued.*

Case on devise of real and personal estate, with Mr. Peere Williams's opinion. See Collectanea Juridica, vol. 1, 1791, pp. 473–475. **144 G**

An Historical account of the original and nature as well as the law of Devises and Revocations. By Lord chief baron Gilbert. 1756. 12mo. **178 A**

See also EXECUTORS, LEGACIES and WILLS.

DEVIZES, WILTSHIRE.

Chronicles of the Devizes, a history of the castle, parks, and borough of that name. By James Waylen. 1839. 8vo. **93 F**

Origines Divisianæ ; or, the Antiquities of the Devizes in some familiar letters to a friend. [By John Davis.] 1754. 12mo. **93 F**

DEVONSHIRE.

An Alphabetical register of divers persons who have given towards the relief of the poor of the county of Devon. By R. Izacke. 1736. 8vo. **87 C**

The chorographical description or survey of the county of Devon. By Tristram Risdon. 1811. 8vo. **87 D**

Collections towards a description of the county of Devon. By Sir William Pole. 1791. 8vo. **87 D**

A Concise topographical account of the county of Devon. By Rev. D. Lysons and S. Lysons. 1822. 4to. **86 G**

Danmonii Orientales Illustres, or the Worthies of Devon. By John Prince. New ed. 1810. 4to. **79 H**

Devonshire parishes, or the antiquities of twenty-eight parishes in the archdeaconry of Totnes. By C. Worthy. 2 vols. Exeter, 1887–1889. 8vo. **87 D**

Historic collections relating to the monasteries in Devon. By Rev. George Oliver. Exeter, 1820. 8vo. **87 C**

The history of Devonshire. By Rev. Richard Polwhele. 3 vols. bound in 1. 1797–96. folio. **86 H**

A History of Devonshire, with sketches of its leading worthies. By R. N. Worth. 1886. 8vo. **87 D**

A Review of part of Risdon's Survey of Devon ; containing the general description of that county, with corrections and additions. By Wm. Chapple. Exeter, 1785. 8vo. **87 B**

See also HAMILTON, A. H. A., OLIVER, G., PYCROFT, J. W., SPARGO, T. and THOMAS, C.

DEVONSHIRE, WILLIAM, 2 DUKE OF.

Sermon preach'd at funeral of Wm. Duke of Devonshire in church of All-Hallows in Derby, Septemb. 5th, MDCCVII. By White Kennet, D.D. 1708. 8vo. **79 B**

DIALOGUE.

An Essay on Dialogue, particularly on the application of that form of writing to matters of law. See E. Wynne's Dialogues, 2nd ed., vol. I, 1785, pp. I–XCI. **170 F**

A Genuine Dialogue, facetious and pathetic, amorous and political, full of strange and surprizing adventures. By the Author of the Curious Maid. [M. Prior.] 1736. Bound with South Sea Scheme. 1732. 12mo. **118 B**

The Surveiors Dialogue very profitable for all men to peruse, especially lords of mannors, stewards of mannor-courts, tenants, farmers and husbandmen. [By G. Norden.] 4th ed. 1738. 8vo. **49 E**

DIBB, JOHN EDWARD.

Forms of memorials, certificates and affidavits as used at the Yorkshire registries of deeds. 3rd ed. 1871. 12mo. **178 E**

DIBDIN, REV. THOMAS FROGNALL.

The library companion, or the young man's guide and the old man's comfort in the choice of a library. 2nd ed. 2 vols. 1825. 8vo. **82 C**

Reminiscences of a literary life. 2 vols. 1836. 8vo. **82 C**

DICETO, RADULPHUS DE.

Abbreviationes Chronicorum et Ymagines historiarum. See Scriptores Decem Hist. Angl. vol. I, pp. 429–720. **114 H**

Historical works. Edited by Rev. Wm. Stubbs. 2 vols. 1876. 8vo. **102 F**

DICEY, ALBERT VENN.

The law of Domicil as a branch of the law of England, stated in the form of rules. 1879. 8vo. **9 G**

Lectures introductory to the study of the law of the constitution. 1885, and 3rd ed. 1889. 8vo. **116 E**

Rules for selection of parties to an action. 1870. 8vo. **11 A**

DICEY, THOMAS.

Historical account of Guernsey. 1751. 12mo. **94 F**

DICKENS, JOHN.
Reports of cases in the Court of Chancery [1559–1798].
Revised by John Wyatt. 2 vols. 1803. 8vo. **2 F**

[DICKINSON, SIR JOHN NODES.]
Practical proposals for a thorough reform of our judicial
system and an entire reconstruction of the whole law. By
An Outsider. 1867, and Further Proposals. By An Outsider. 1871. 8vo. **170 F**

DICKSON, LOTHIAN SHEFFIELD.
Why he did it ; or the true reasons for the displacement of an
old officer, at the instance of the Earl of Wilton, by major
general Peel, M.P., late secretary for war, addressed to the
British army. 6th ed. 1861. [Pamphlets, vol. 13.] **144 A**

DICKSON, R. W.
General view of the agriculture of Lancashire. Edited by
W. Stevenson. 1815. 8vo. **89 B**

DICKSON, WILLIAM GILLESPIE.
The law of Evidence in Scotland. 2nd ed. by John Skelton.
2 vols. Edinburgh, 1864. 8vo. **175 D**

DIGBY, SIR KENELM.
Journal of a voyage into the Mediterranean. Edited by John
Bruce. [Camden Society, vol. 96.] 1868. 8vo. **85 C**

DIGBY, KENELM EDWARD.
An Introduction to the history of the law of real property.
2nd ed. 1876. 8vo. **83 I**
Sale and transfer of shares in companies. 1868. 12mo. **169 D**

DIGESTION.
The function of Digestion considered with reference to natural
theology. By Wm. Prout. 2nd ed. 1834. 8vo. **77 B**

DIGESTS OF CASES.
In all the Courts. The Law Reports. Digest of cases from
1865 to 1889. 5 vols. 1882–90. 8vo. **73 F**

DIGESTS OF CASES—*continued.*

In all the Courts. Digest of reported decisions 1870–1880.
By T. W. Chitty and J. Mews. 2 vols. 1880. 8vo. **14 F**

In all the Courts. Law Magazine and Review and quarterly
digest of all reported cases. 1875–1889. 14 vols. 1876–
89. 8vo. **137 E F**

In all the Courts. The Complete annual digest of every
reported case 1883–1889. By Alfred Emden. 7 vols.
1884–90. 8vo. **14 F**

In all the Courts. A Digest of all the reported decisions of
the superior courts 1884–1889. By John Mews. 2 vols.
1889–90. 8vo. **14 E**

See also LAW JOURNAL REPORTS, LAW TIMES REPORTS,
TIMES LAW REPORTS, WEEKLY NOTES and WEEKLY
REPORTER.

Admiralty. See Fisher's Digest, vol. 6, pp. 1167–1772. **14 E**

See also ADMIRALTY LAW, DIGESTS OF.

Bankruptcy. Digest of all reported cases decided under the
Bankruptcy act 1883. By C. F. Morrell. 1888. 8vo. **14 F**

See also BANKRUPTCY LAW, DIGESTS OF.

Common Law. Digest of reported decisions of courts of
common law . . . 1756–1883. Founded on Fisher's Digest. By John Mews. 7 vols. 1884. 8vo. **14 E**

See also COVENTRY, T., EVANS, D. T., FREEMAN, K.,
HAMMOND, A., HARRISON, R. T., JEREMY, H., MOORE,
J. B., MORRIS, R., PRATT, W. T. and TOMLINS, T. E.

Conveyancing. Digested index to common law reports
relating to conveyancing, from 1558 to present time. By
E. Chitty and F. Foster. 1841. 8vo. **14 F**

Criminal Law. Digest of cases relating to Criminal law
1756–1883. By John Mews. 1884. 8vo. **14 F**

See COX, E. W., SLEIGH, W. A. W. and TOMLINS, H. N.

Divorce. Digest of decisions in divorce matters during the
last four years. By L. D. Powles. 1884. 8vo. **12 D**

See also Fisher's Digest, vol. 4, 1884, pp. 125–286. **14 E**

Ecclesiastical. Digest of cases decided in the court of Arches,
Prerogative court of Canterbury and Consistory court of
London. By A. Waddilove. 1849. 8vo. **63 D**

See COX, E. W., JEREMY, H., MADDY, E. and PRATT, W. T.

See also Fisher's Digest, vol. 3, 1884, pp. 614–820. **14 E**

Election. See COX, E. W. and WORDSWORTH, C. F. F.

Equity, House of Lords and Privy Council. Index to all
reported cases decided in several courts of Equity in Eng-

DIGESTS OF CASES—*continued.*

land and Ireland, Privy Council and House of Lords from the earliest period. By Edward Chitty. 4th ed. by W. F. Jones and H. E. Hirst. 9 vols. 1883–89. 8vo. **14 D**

Equity &c. Index to the modern reports in chancery 1689–1805. 2nd ed. 1807. 8vo. **63 B**

Equity &c. Index to all reports in House of Lords, from 1814 to 1866. By Charles Clark. 1868. 8vo. **1 D**

See also BRIDGMAN, R. O., BRIDGMAN, R. W., FREEMAN, K., JAGOE, J., JEREMY, H. and PRATT, W. T.

India. Analytical digest of cases decided in supreme courts of judicature in India, in courts of East India Co. and on appeal by Her Majesty in Council. By W. H. Morley. 3 vols. 1851–52. 8vo. **38 C**

India. The Indian digest, being a complete index to reported cases of high courts established in India. By H. Cowell and J. V. Woodman. Calcutta, 1870. 8vo. **38 C**

India. Digest of Indian law reports, a compendium of rulings of high court of Calcutta from 1862 and Privy Council from 1831 to 1876. By D. Sutherland. 1877. 8vo. **38 F**

Ireland. Digest of cases in the court of appeal, high court of justice and court of bankruptcy in Ireland. Reported in the Law Reports (Ireland) vols. i.–xx. 1878–1888. By W. Green and R. Manders. Dublin, 1890. 8vo. **17 I**

Ireland. Analytical digest of reported cases in several courts of common law in Ireland. By C. P. Archer. Dublin, 1842. 8vo. **15 F**

Magisterial, Municipal and Parochial. The Justice of the Peace Digest of cases reported during the years 1862 to 1882. By R. C. Glen. 1887. 4to. **68 G**

See also COX, E. W.

Nisi Prius. Digest of cases at Nisi Prius. By A. Hammond. See Sir J. Comyns's Digest, vol. 5, 1822, pp. 365–640. **14 B**

See also JEREMY, H., MANNING, J. and PRATT, W. T.

Overruled Cases. Digest of cases overruled, not followed, disapproved . . . in the English courts from 1756 to 1886 inclusive. By C. W. M. Dale and R. C. Lehmann. 1887. 8vo. **14 F**

Overruled Cases. Index of cases overruled . . . by the courts of America, England and Ireland from the earliest period. By M. M. Bigelow. Boston, 1873. 8vo. **14 F**

See also Chitty's Index, vol. 8, 1889, pp. 8236–8368. **14 D**

Patent Cases. Digest of Patent Cases reported in vols. 1–6

DIGESTS OF CASES—*continued.*

of The Reports of Patent Cases. 1884–1889. 3 vols.
1887–90. 8vo. **76 H**

Probate. Digest of decisions in probate matters during the
last four years. By L. D. Powles. 1884. 8vo. **12 D**

See also Fisher's Digest, vol. 7, 1884, pp. 927–1053. **14 E**

Scotland. Digest of House of Lords cases decided on appeal
from Scotland 1709 to 1864. By J. B. Kinnear. 1865.
8vo. **55 F**

See also SHAW, P.

Victoria. Analytical index of cases decided in supreme court,
court of mines and in vice-admiralty court of Victoria
1871–1883. By P. S. Davis. Melbourne, 1885. 8vo. **55 D**

DIGNITIES.

Book of dignities containing rolls of the official personages of
the British empire. By J. Haydn. 1851. 8vo. **124 G**

Court register and statesman's remembrancer containing a series
of all the great officers. By W. Sliford. 1741. 8vo. **124 G**

The same, corrected to June 3, 1782. By W. M. [Sir W.
Musgrave.] 1782. 8vo. **124 G**

Dignities feudal and parliamentary and the constitutional
legislature of the United Kingdom. By Sir W. Betham.
vol. 1. 1830. 8vo. **116 B**

A Dissertation on the history of hereditary dignities. By W.
F. Finlason. 1869. 8vo. **124 G**

The laws of honour, or a compendious account of the ancient
derivation of all titles, dignities, offices, &c. [By J. Le
Neve.] 1726. 12mo. **125 B**

A Manual of dignities, privilege and precedence. By C. R.
Dodd. 1843. 12mo. **124 G**

Murray's Official handbook of church and state. By Samuel
Redgrave. 1852. 12mo. **125 A**

The origin and nature of Dignities, containing all the cases of
peerage. By Wm. Cruise. 2nd ed. 1823. 8vo. **124 G**

A Political index to the histories of Great Britain and Ireland,
or a complete register of the hereditary honours, public
offices and persons in office. By Robert Beatson. 3rd ed.
3 vols. 1806. 8vo. **124 G**

DILAPIDATIONS.

Dilapidations, a text-book for architects and surveyors. By
B. Fletcher. 3rd ed. 1883. 8vo. **9 G**

DILAPIDATIONS—*continued.*

The law of dilapidations and nuisances. By David Gibbons.
2nd ed. 1849. 8vo. **52 E**

Royal Institute of British Architects. Report of the Select
committee on Dilapidations &c. 1844. 12mo. **165 G**

See also ELMES, J., GRADY, S. G. and MORRIS, T. **165 G**

DILWORTH, THOMAS.

A New and complete description of the terrestrial and celestial
globes. 2nd ed. 1794. 8vo. **255 H**

DINGLEY, THOMAS.

History from marble, compiled in the reign of Charles II.
Edited by J. G. Nichols. [Camden Society, vols. 94 and
97.] 2 vols. 1867–68. 8vo. **85 C**

DIPLOMACY.

See DUMONT, J. and TREATIES.

DIPLOMATIC REVIEW.

The Diplomatic Review, books 1 to 6. 25 vols. bound in 7.
1855–77. folio, 4to. and 8vo. **143 G**

DIPROSE, JOHN.

Some account of the parish of Saint Clement Danes, past and
present. 2 vols. 1868–76. 8vo. **89 D**

DIRECTORIES, ENGLISH, IRISH AND SCOTCH.

Bedfordshire (Kelly). 1854, 1864, 1869, 1877, 1885. 5 vols.
1854–85. 8vo. **196 F G**

Berkshire (Kelly). 1854, 1864, 1869, 1877, 1883, 1887. 6 vols.
1854–87. 8vo. **196 F G**

Birmingham with its suburbs (Kelly). 1860, 1864–65, 1867–
69, 1871–72, 1874–76, 1878–80, 1882–84, 1888. 18 vols.
1860–88. 8vo. **197 C D**

Bristol (Kelly). 1856, 1861, 1863, 1866, 1870, 1875, 1879,
1883, 1885. 9 vols. 1856–85. 8vo. **197 B C**

Bristol (Slater). 1880. 8vo. **197 F**

Buckinghamshire (Kelly). 1854, 1864, 1869, 1877, 1883,
1887. 6 vols. 1854–87. 8vo. **196 F G**

DIRECTORIES—*continuea.*

Cambridgeshire (Kelly). 1858, 1864, 1865, 1869, 1875, 1879, 1883. 7 vols. 1858–83. 8vo. **196 G**

Cheshire (Kelly). 1857, 1864. 2 vols. 1857–64. 8vo. **196 G**

Chester (Slater). 1880. 8vo. **197 F**

Cornwall (Kelly). 1856, 1873, 1883. 3 vols. 1856–83. 8vo. **197 A**

Cumberland (Kelly). 1858. 8vo. **197 A**

Derbyshire (Kelly). 1855, 1864, 1876, 1881. 4 vols. 1855–81. 8vo. **197 A & 196 G**

Devonshire (Kelly). 1856, 1866, 1873, 1883. 4 vols. 1856–83. 8vo. **197 A–C**

Dorsetshire (Kelly). 1859, 1864, 1875, 1880, 1885. 5 vols. 1859–85. 8vo. **197 A**

Dublin (Wilson). 1788, 1799, 1803, 1805, 1807–16, 1825, 1827–29, 1833, 1838. 20 vols. Dublin, 1788–1838. 12mo. **141 A–C**

Dublin, 1835–37, 1839–49. 14 vols. 1835–49. 12mo. **141 C D**

Durham (Kelly). 1858, 1879. 2 vols. 1858–79. 8vo. **197 A**

Edinburghshire. 1867–68. Edinburgh, 1867. 8vo. **197 F**

England and Wales. Commercial (Pigot), containing 280 principal Cities &c. 1822–23. 1822. 8vo. **54 A**

England and Wales (Pigot). 3 vols. 1830–36. 8vo. **54 A**

England and Wales (Municipal Corporations). 1866, 1878, 1880. 3 vols. 1866–80. 8vo. **194 E**

England and Wales (Magisterial and Official). 1878. 8vo. **194 E**

Essex (Pigot). 1834. 8vo. **54 A**

Essex (Kelly). 1845, 1855, 1859, 1862, 1866, 1871, 1874, 1878, 1882, 1886. 10 vols. 1845–86. 8vo. **196 E F**

Essex. Stratford, West Ham, Forest Gate & Plaistow (Kelly). 1889–90. 1889. 12mo. **194 A**

Essex. Walthamstow, Leyton, Leytonstone and Snaresbrook (Kelly). 1889–90. 1889. 12mo. **194 A**

Gloucestershire (Kelly). 1856, 1863, 1870, 1879, 1885, 1889. 6 vols. 1856–89. 8vo. **197 B C**

Great Britain and Ireland. London and 84 other cities and towns (Holden). 1805, 1808. 4 vols. 1805–8. 8vo. **54 A**

Great Britain and Ireland (Thom). 1862, 1863. 2 vols. 1862–63. 8vo. **194 D**

Hampshire (Kelly). 1859, 1864, 1875, 1880, 1885, 1890. 6 vols. 1859–90. 8vo. **197 A**

DIRECTORIES—*continued.*

Herefordshire (Kelly). 1856, 1863, 1870, 1879, 1885. 5 vols.
1856–85. 8vo. **197 B C**

Hertfordshire (Pigot). 1834. 8vo. **54 A**

Hertfordshire (Kelly). 1845, 1855, 1859, 1862, 1866, 1871,
1874, 1878, 1882, 1886. 10 vols. 1845–1886. 8vo. **196 E F**

Hull (Kelly). 1857, 1861, 1872, 1879, 1885. 5 vols. 1857–
85. 8vo. **197 C & E**

Huntingdonshire (Kelly). 1854, 1864, 1869, 1877, 1890.
5 vols. 1854–90. 8vo. **196 F G**

Ireland (Thom). 1850–1890. 41 vols. Dublin, 1850–90.
8vo. **141 D–H & 142 A**

Kent (Pigot). 1834. 8vo. **54 A**

Kent (Kelly). 1845, 1855, 1859, 1862, 1866, 1871, 1874,
1878, 1882, 1886. 10 vols. 1845–86. 8vo. **196 E F**

Kent. Beckenham (Kelly). 1889–90. 1889. 12mo. **194 A**

Kent. Blackheath, Lee, Lewisham and Greenwich (Kelly).
1889. 1889. 12mo. **194 A**

Kent. Bromley, Chislehurst and Bickley (Kelly). 1889–90.
1889. 12mo. **194 A**

Kent. Sydenham and Forest Hill (Kelly). 1889. 1889.
12mo. **194 A**

Lancashire. Liverpool and Manchester (Kelly). 1858, 1864,
1873, 1881, 1887. 5 vols. 1858–87. 8vo. **197 B**

Lancashire. Liverpool & Manchester (Slater). 1858. 8vo. **197 A**

Manchester (Pigot). 1821. 8vo. **197 A**

Leicestershire (Kelly). 1855, 1864, 1876, 1881, 1888. 5 vols.
1855–88. 8vo. **197 A & 196 G**

Lincolnshire (Kelly). 1861, 1868, 1876, 1885, 1889. 5 vols.
1861–89. 8vo. **197 B**

London (Kent). 1766, 1796, 1807, 1808, 1819, 1823, 1826.
7 vols. 1766–1826. **196 B**

London (Lowndes). 1780, 1787, 1792. 3 vols. 1780–92.
8vo. **196 B**

London. Post Office annual directory. 1801, 1804, 1807,
1809–10, 1812–15. 9 vols. 1801–15. 12mo. **196 A**

London. Post Office London directory. 1816–21, 1823–36.
20 vols. 1816–36. 12mo. **196 A**

London. Kelly's Post Office London directory. 1837–1890.
69 vols. 1837–90. 8vo. **54 B–H**

London (Johnstone). 1817. 8vo. **54 A**

DIRECTORIES—*continued.*

London (Pigot). 1822–23, 1834, 1838, 1840. 5 vols. 1822–40. 8vo.   **54 A**

London (Robson). 1824, 1828, 1830, 1833–38, 1842. 11 vols. 1824–42. 8vo.   **54 A B**

London, City of (Baldwin). 1760, 1770, 1783. 3 vols. 1760–83. 12mo.   **196 B**

London, City of (Collingridge). 1871–72, 1875–90. 18 vols. 1871–90. 8vo.   **196 C D**

London, Suburban (Kelly). 1860, 1863, 1865, 1868, 1872, 1876, 1880, 1884, 1888. 9 vols. 1860–88. 8vo.   **196 D**

London, Suburban. Camden Town and Kentish Town (Hutchings and Crowsley). 1873, 1876, 1877, 1879, 1880, 1882. 3 vols. 1873–82. 12mo.   **196 B**

London, Suburban. Camden and Kentish Towns (Kelly). 1889–90. 1889. 12mo.   **194 A**

London. Suburban. Chelsea, Pimlico and Belgravia (Kelly). 1889. 1889. 12mo.   **194 A**

London, Suburban. Hackney, Homerton, Dalston, Old Ford and Bow (Kelly). 1889. 1889. 12mo.   **194 A**

London, Suburban. Kennington, Battersea and South Lambeth (Kelly). 1889. 1889. 12mo.   **194 A**

London, Suburban. Kensington, Notting Hill, Brompton and Knightsbridge (Kelly). 1889. 1889. 12mo.   **194 A**

London, Suburban. Kilburn and Willesden (Kelly). 1889. 1889. 12mo.   **194 A**

London, Suburban. Marylebone and St. John's Wood (Kelly). 1889. 1889. 12mo.   **194 A**

London, Suburban. Paddington, Bayswater and Kensal Green (Kelly). 1889. 1889. 12mo.   **194 A**

Man, Isle of (Pigot). 1837. 8vo.   **197 F**

Middlesex (Pigot & Co.). 1834. 8vo.   **54 A**

Middlesex (Kelly). 1845, 1855, 1859, 1862, 1866, 1871, 1874, 1878, 1882, 1886. 10 vols. 1845–86. 8vo.   **196 E F**

Middlesex. Barnet, Finchley, Hendon and District (Kelly). 1889–90. 1889. 12mo.   **194 B**

Middlesex. Ealing, Acton, Hanwell, Gunnersbury and Chiswick (Kelly). 1889–90. 1889. 12mo.   **194 B**

Middlesex. Hampstead and Highgate (Hutchings and Crowsley). 1873, 1876, 1877, 1879, 1880, 1882. 3 vols. 1873–82. 12mo.   **196 B**

Middlesex. Hampstead and Highgate (Kelly). 1889–90. 1889. 12mo.   **194 B**

DIRECTORIES—*continued.*

Middlesex. Highbury, Stoke Newington, Stamford Hill and Upper and Lower Clapton (Kelly). 1889. 1889. 12mo.
194 B

Middlesex. Highgate, Holloway and Tufnell Park (Kelly). 1889–90. 1889. 12mo. **194 B**

Middlesex. Hornsey, Wood Green, Crouch End and Finsbury Park (Kelly). 1889–90. 1889. 12mo. **194 B**

Middlesex. Twickenham and Teddington (Kelly). 1889–90. 1889. 12mo. **194 B**

Middlesex. West Kensington, Shepherd's Bush, Fulham and Hammersmith (Kelly). 1889–90. 1889. 12mo. **194 B**

Monmouthshire (Kelly). 1871, 1884. 2 vols. 8vo. **197 B**

Monmouthshire (Slater). 1880. **197 F**

Norfolk (Kelly). 1858, 1865, 1869, 1875, 1879, 1883, 1888. 7 vols. 1858–88. 8vo. **196 G**

Northamptonshire (Kelly). 1854, 1864, 1869, 1877, 1885. 5 vols. 1854–85. 8vo. **196 F G**

Northumberland (Kelly). 1858, 1873, 1879. 3 vols. 1858–79. 8vo. **197 A**

Nottinghamshire (Kelly). 1855, 1864, 1876, 1881, 1888. 5 vols. 1855–88. 8vo. **197 A 196 G**

Oxfordshire (Kelly). 1854, 1864, 1869, 1877, 1883, 1887. 6 vols. 1854–87. 8vo. **196 F G**

Rutland (Kelly). 1855, 1864, 1876, 1881, 1888. 5 vols. 1855–88. 8vo. **197 A & 196 G**

Scotland (Oliver & Boyd). 1822, 1838–1890. 54 vols. Edinburgh, 1822–90. 12mo. **136 C–F**

Scotland (Pigot & Co.). 1837. 8vo. **197 F**

Scotland (Slater). 1867, 1878, 1886. 3 vols. 1867–86. 8vo. **197 F**

Sheffield (Kelly). 1857, 1861, 1865, 1867, 1871, 1877, 1881. 7 vols. 1857–81. 8vo. **197 D E**

Shropshire (Kelly). 1856, 1863, 1870, 1879, 1885. 5 vols. 1856–85. 8vo. **197 B C**

Shropshire (Slater). 1880. **197 F**

Somerset (Kelly). 1861, 1866, 1875, 1883, 1889. 5 vols. 1861–89. 8vo. **197 C**

Staffordshire (Kelly). 1860, 1864, 1868, 1872, 1876, 1880, 1884, 1888. 8 vols. 1860–88. 8vo. **197 C**

Suffolk (Kelly). 1858, 1865, 1869, 1875, 1879, 1883, 1888. 7 vols. 1858–88. 8vo. **196 G**

DIRECTORIES—*continued.*

Surrey (Pigot & Co.). 1834. 8vo.   **54 A**

Surrey (Kelly). 1845, 1855, 1859, 1862, 1866, 1871, 1874,
1878, 1882, 1886. 10 vols. 1845–86. 8vo.   **196 E F**

Surrey. Brixton, Clapham, Herne Hill and Tulse Hill (Kelly).
1889–90. 1889. 12mo.   **194 B**

Surrey. Camberwell, Peckham, Nunhead, Dulwich and Denmark Hill (Kelly). 1889–90. 1889. 12mo.   **194 B**

Surrey. Croydon, South Norwood, &c. (Kelly). 1890. 1889.
12mo.   **194 B**

Surrey. Norwood and Streatham (Kelly). 1890. 1889.
12mo.   **194 B**

Surrey. Penge and Anerley (Kelly). 1889–90. 1889.
12mo.   **194 B**

Surrey. Richmond, Kew, Mortlake and Sheen (Kelly).
1889–90. 1889. 12mo.   **194 B**

Surrey. Wandsworth, Putney, Tooting, Merton, Barnes and
Roehampton (Kelly). 1889. 1889. 12mo.   **194 B**

Sussex (Pigot & Co.). 1834. 8vo.   **54 A**

Sussex (Kelly). 1845, 1855, 1859, 1862, 1866, 1871, 1874,
1878, 1882, 1886. 10 vols. 1845–86. 8vo.   **196 E F**

Wales, North (Slater). 1880.   **197 F**

Wales, South (Kelly). 1871. 8vo.   **197 B**

Wales, South (Slater). 1880. 8vo.   **197 F**

Warwickshire (Kelly). 1860, 1864, 1868, 1872, 1876, 1880,
1884, 1888. 8 vols. 1860–88. 8vo.   **197 C**

Westmoreland (Kelly). 1858, 1873. 2 vols. 1858–73. 8vo.
                                                    197 A

Wiltshire (Kelly). 1859, 1864, 1875, 1880, 1885. 5 vols.
1859–85. 8vo.   **197 A**

Worcestershire (Kelly). 1860, 1864, 1868, 1872, 1876, 1880,
1884, 1888. 8 vols. 1860–88. 8vo.   **197 C**

Worcestershire (Littlebury). 1873. 8vo.   **197 E**

Yorkshire. North and East Ridings (Kelly). 1857, 1872,
1879. 3 vols. 1857–79. 8vo.   **197 E**

Yorkshire. West Riding (Kelly). 1857, 1861, 1867, 1871,
1877, 1881. 6 vols. 1857–81. 8vo.   **197 E F**

DIRECTORIES, FOREIGN AND COLONIAL.

Annuaire général du commerce, ou almanach des 500,000
adresses de Paris, des départements et des pays étrangers.
1846, 1867, 1868. 4 vols. 1846–68. 8vo.   **194 E**

DIRECTORIES, FOREIGN AND COLONIAL—*continued.*

Bengal, North-West Provinces, Punjab &c. (Thacker). 1868, 1878. 2 vols. Calcutta, 1868–78. 8vo.   **195 D**

Bombay. 1867, 1868, 1874. 3 vols. Bombay, 1867–74. 8vo.   **195 C**

Boston. 1856, 1858. 2 vols. Boston, 1856–58. 8vo. **195 A**

Canada. 1857–58, 1871. 2 vols. Montreal, 1858–71. 8vo.   **195 B**

Colonial ; including Sydney, Melbourne and New Zealand. 1862. 8vo.   **195 D**

European. 1866. 2 vols. 1866. 8vo.   **195 A**

Indian and Colonial (Street). 1867, 1871, 1873, 1875–76, 1880–81, 1882–83. 6 vols. 1867–82. 8vo.   **195 C**

Madras. 1868. Madras, 1868. 8vo.   **195 C**

Melbourne (Sands). 1859, 1860. 2 vols. Melbourne, 1859–60. 8vo.   **195 D**

New South Wales (Official). 1882, 1886–87. 2 vols. 1882–87. 8vo.   **195 E**

New Zealand (Wise & Co.). 1880–81, 1883–84. 2 vols. Dunedin, 1880–83. 8vo.   **195 F**

Sydney (Sands). 1864. 4th ed. 1864. 8vo.   **195 D**

United States (Zell). 1881. 3rd ed. 1881. 8vo.   **195 F**

Victoria (Official). 1871–72, 1880, 1884–85. 3 vols. 1871–84. 8vo.   **195 E**

DIRECTORIES OF TRADES.

Brewers and Maltsters (Kelly). 1877. 8vo.

Building Trades (Kelly). 1870, 1874, 1879, 1886. 4 vols. 1870–86. 8vo.

Cabinet and Upholstery Trades (Kelly). 1877. 8vo.

Carriers, stage coaches and coasting vessels. 1796, 1808, 1819, 1823, 1826. Issued with Kent's Directories. 5 vols. 1796–1826. 12mo.   **196 B**

Chemists and Druggists (Kelly). 1869, 1870, 1874, 1880. 4 vols. 1869–80. 8vo.

Companies, Joint Stock. 1865–1869. 5 vols. 1865–69. 8vo.   **194 D**

Engineers, and Iron and Metal Trades (Kelly). 1870, 1874, 1878, 1886. 4 vols. 1870–86. 8vo.

Grocery, and Oil and Color Trades (Kelly). 1872, 1875. 2 vols. 1872–75. 8vo.

DIRECTORIES OF TRADES—*continued.*

Leather Trades (Kelly). 1871, 1875, 1886. 3 vols. 1871–86. 8vo.

Markets, Guide to the (Kelly). 1868. 8vo.

Merchants and Manufacturers (Kelly). 1877. 1882. 1888. 3 vols. 1877–88. 8vo.

Merchants, Manufacturers and Shippers of Great Britain and the Continent. 1882. 8vo.

Merchants and Manufacturers in Birmingham, Carlisle, Hull, Leeds, Liverpool, Newcastle and Sheffield (Pigot). 1837. 8vo.

Stationers, Printers &c. (Kelly). 1872, 1876, 1880. 3 vols. 1872–80. 8vo.

Manufacturers of Textile Fabrics (Kelly). 1880. 8vo.

Watch and Clock Trades, Goldsmiths and Jewellers (Kelly). 1872, 1875, 1880. 3 vols. 1872–80. 8vo.

DIRECTORS.

The shareholders' and directors' legal companion. By F. B. Palmer. 10th ed. 1890. 12mo. **9 D**

The directory of directors. 1880–89. By Thomas Skinner. 9 vols. 1880–89. 12mo. **146 D**

DISCLAIMER.

Dissertation on and precedents of Disclaimer. See Bythewood and Jarman's Conveyancing, 4th ed. vol. 2, 1885, pp. 836–861. **13 D**

DISCOVERY.

The principles and practice of Discovery. By Edward Bray. 1885. 8vo. **9 G**

The law relating to Discovery. By W. S. Sichel and W. Chance. 1883. 8vo. **9 G**

Law of Discovery. By C. J. Peile. 1883. 8vo. **52 F**

A Letter to James Wigram, K.C., on the production of documents on motion before the hearing. By W. H. Bosanquet. 1836. [Jacob's Tracts, vol. 12.] **144 F**

See also HARE, T., KERR, W. W., PETHERAM, W. C., WIGRAM, J. and WILLIS, J. W.

D'ISRAELI, BENJAMIN.

The case of The Queen *v.* D'Israeli, with an argument in vindication of the practice of the bar. By Joseph Stammers. 1838. [Pamphlets, vol. 27.] **144 B**

DISSENTERS.

Law relating to Protestant Nonconformists and their places of worship. By A. Winslow. 1886. 12mo.　　　**9 C**

Parliamentary debates on the Dissenters' Chapels bill 7 & 8 Vict. cap. 45. 1844. 8vo.　　　**77 B**

Strictures on the Dissenters' Chapels bill. By Richard Matthews. 1844. [Pamphlets, vol. 18.]　　　**144 B**

Report of the Clough case in the Court of Exchequer in Ireland, April 1836. By A. J. Macrory. Dublin, 1836. [Jacob's Tracts, vol. 13.]　　　**144 F**

Report of the Wolverhampton meeting house case, 'Attorney-General and Mander *v.* Pearson,' before Lord Cottenham. 1836. [Law Tracts, vol. 4.]　　　**144 E**

The history, opinions, and present legal position of the English Presbyterians. [By Thomas Falconer.] 1834. [Law Tracts, vol. 4.]　　　**144 E**

A Letter to the vice-chancellor of England, in reply to his remarks relative to the British and Foreign Unitarian Association, delivered in pronouncing his judgement in the case of the Attorney-General *v.* Shore and others. By James Yates. 1834. [Law Tracts, vol. 4.]　　　**144 E**

Sketch of the history of the Regium donum, and parliamentary grant, to poor dissenting ministers of England and Wales. By T. Rees. 1834. [Law Tracts, vol. 4.] **144 E**

See also HEWLEY, LADY S.

DISTRESS.

The law of Distress. By A. Oldham and A. L. T. Foster. 2nd ed. 1889. 8vo.　　　**9 G**

A Guide to the law of Distress for rent. By R. T. Hunter. 1888. 8vo.　　　**9 G**

The law and practice of Distresses and Replevin. By Lord chief baron Gilbert. 4th ed. by W. J. Impey. 1823. 12mo.　　　**165 G**

The law of Distresses. By J. Bradby. 1808. 12mo. **165 G**

The modern practice of Distress and Replevin. By An Old Practitioner. 1776. 12mo.　　　**165 G**

A Treatise of Distresses, Replevins and Avowries. 3rd ed. 1746, and 4th ed. 1761. 12mo.　　　**166 A**

A Methodical treatise of Replevins, Distresses, &c. 2nd ed. 1739. 12mo.　　　**175 C**

DISTRICT REGISTRIES.

The practice in the district registries in the Queen's Bench division, high court of justice. By W. F. A. Archibald and P. E. Vizard. 2nd ed. 1886. 12mo. **12 G**

DISTRICT VISITING. •

Report of the district visitors of the Liberty of the Rolls District Visiting Society, with a pastoral letter from the incumbent [Rev. T. R. Redwar] to the parishioners. 1865. [Pamphlets, vol. 26.] **144 B**

DIVIDENDS UNCLAIMED.

See BANK OF ENGLAND.

DIVINITY.

Some thoughts concerning a proper method of studying divinity. By Wm. Wotton. See J. H. Parker's Catalogue of books in divinity, 1837, pp. i–xxiii. **82 A**

DIVORCE.

The principles and practice of the court for Divorce and Matrimonial causes. By George Browne. 5th ed. by L. D. Powles. 1889. 8vo. **12 D**

The procedure in Divorce and Matrimonial causes and matters. By T. W. H. Oakley. 3rd ed. 1889. 8vo. **12 D**

A Divorce and Probate Manual. By W. J. Dixon. 1886. 12mo. **64 E**

An Epitome of the laws of Probate and Divorce. By J. C. Harrison. 3rd ed. 1886. 8vo. **64 E**

Law practice and procedure in Divorce. By W. J. Dixon. 1883. 8vo. **12 D**

Student's Guide to law and practice of courts of Probate and Divorce. By J. F. Haynes. 2nd ed. 1882. 8vo. **64 E**

Digest of law and practice of court for Divorce and Matrimonial causes. By R. A. Pritchard and W. T. Pritchard. 3rd ed. by J. G. Witt and W. T. Pritchard. 1874. 8vo. **12 D**

Commentaries on the law of marriage and divorce. By J. P. Bishop. 4th ed. 2 vols. Boston, 1864. 8vo. **59 G**

Constant-Fidelis-Amandi Wannaar, Hagæ-Comitani, Capitis de Divortiis et Repudiis accurata explicatio. 1820. [Latin Tracts on Civil and Canon Law.] **118 E**

DIVORCE—*continuea.*

See also F. Clifford's History of private bill legislation, vol.
I, 1885, pp. 387–443.   83 I

See also BROWNING, W. E., ERNST, W., INDERWICK, F. A.,
IRELAND, J., MACQUEEN, J. F., MORGAN, H. D., POYNTER,
T. and SWABEY, M. C. M.

DIXON, HENRY HALL.

The law of the Farm, including the agricultural customs of
England and Wales. 1858. 12mo.   168 D

The same. 2nd ed. 1863. 12mo.   168 D

The same. 4th ed. by H. Perkins. 1879. 8vo.   10 A

DIXON, JOSEPH.

The law of Partnership. 1866. 8vo.   173 D

DIXON, ROBERT.

The law relative to Title-Deeds and other documents. 2 vols.
1826. 8vo.   176 F

Observations on the proposed new code relating to real
property. 1827. [Jacob's Tracts, vol. 5.]   144 E

DIXON, WILLIAM JOHN.

A Divorce and Probate manual. 1886. 12mo.   64 E

Law, practice and procedure in Divorce and other matrimonial
causes. 1883. 8vo.   12 D

Probate and administration law. 1880. 8vo.   174 C

The same. 2nd ed. 1885. 8vo.   12 D

DOCTORS' COMMONS.

Catalogue of the books in the library of the College of
Advocates, 1818, and Catalogue of the library sold by
auction, April 1861. 2 vols. 1818–61. 8vo.   82 C

Doctors' Commons, its courts and its registries. By G. J.
Foster. 3rd ed. 1871. 8vo.   52 F

On the reform of the testamentary jurisdiction, issued by the
committee of proctors in Doctors' Commons. 1853. [Pamph-
lets, vol. 9, part 2.]   144 A

DOD, CHARLES ROGER.

Electoral facts from 1832 to 1852 impartially stated. 1852,
and 2nd ed. 1853. 12mo.   134 B

DOD, CHARLES ROGER—*continued.*

A Manual of dignities, privilege and precedence. 1843.
12mo. **124 G**

The parliamentary companion. 1837, 1838, 1840, 1841,
1843–61, 1863–90. 56 vols. 1837–90. 12mo. **134 A**

Peerage, Baronetage and Knightage of Great Britain and
Ireland, 1883 to 1890. 8 vols. 1883–90. 12mo. **127 H**

DODD, CHARLES EDWARD.

Doubtful questions in the law of Elections stated and can-
vassed. 1826. [Jacob's Tracts, vol. 6.] **144 E**

DODD, JOHN THEODORE.

The settled land act 1882. 1883. 12mo. **175 E**

The settled land act 1884. 1884. 12mo. **175 E**

DODD, PHILIP WILLIAM and G. H. BROOKS.

The law and practice of the Court of Probate, contentions
and common form. 1865. 8vo. **174 C**

DODD, STEPHEN.

Historical and topographical account of town of Woburn, its
abbey and vicinity. Woburn, 1818. 12mo. **86 B**

DODDRIDGE, SIR JOHN.

A Compleat parson, or a description of advowsons or church-
living. 1641. [Law Tracts, 1641.] **144 F**

Historical account of ancient and modern state of principality
of Wales, dutchy of Cornwall, and earldom of Chester.
1630, and 2nd ed. 1714. 8vo. **94 E**

A Treatise of particular estates. 1794. 12mo. See W. Noy's
Maxims, 1794, pp. 117–136. **49 F**

DODINGTON, GEORGE BUBB.

Diary. [Autobiography, vol. 3.] 1827. 12mo. **79 A**

DODSON, JOHN.

Reports of cases in the high court of Admiralty. 1811–1822.
2 vols. 1815–28. 8vo. **8 A**

DODSWORTH, ROGER.

A Catalogue of the manuscripts, written or collected by Roger
Dodsworth, in the Bodleian library. By Rev. Joseph Hunter.
1838. 8vo. **82 B**

See also DUGDALE, SIR W.

DODSWORTH, WILLIAM.

A Guide to the cathedral church of Salisbury. 3rd ed. Salisbury, 1792. 12mo.   **93 F**

DOGS.

Law relating to Dogs. By F. Lupton. 1888. 8vo.   **9 G**

DOLLOND, JOHN.

Life. By John Kelly. 3rd ed. 1808. 4to.   **81 F**

DOMAT, JEAN.

Civil law in its natural order : with the publick law. Translated by William Strahan. 2 vols. 1722. folio.   **48 H**

The same. 2nd ed. 2 vols. 1737. folio.   **48 H**

DOMEIER, EDWARD AUGUSTUS.

Descriptive road book of Germany. 1830. 12mo.   **84 A**

DOMESDAY BOOK.

Domesday book for county of Dorset with a translation. By Rev. William Bawdwen ; to which are prefixed, A dissertation on Domesday book and some account of the copy of that record in library of dean and chapter at Exeter. By Rev. John Hutchins. 1815. folio.   **87 H**

Domesday book illustrated. By R. Kelham. 1788. 8vo. **97 I**

Domesday book, seu liber censualis Wilhelmi primi regis Angliæ, inter archivos regni in domo capitulari Westmonasterii asservatus. [Edited by A. Farley.] 2 vols. 1783. folio.   **98 D**

A general introduction to Domesday book with indexes of the tenants in chief and under tenants at the time of the survey. By Sir Henry Ellis. 2 vols. 1833. 8vo.   **97 I**

Libri censualis vocati Domesday-Book Additamenta ex codic. antiquiss. ; Exon Domesday ; Inquisitio Eliensis ; Liber Winton. ; Boldon Book. Edited by Sir H. Ellis. 1816. folio.   **98 D**

Libri censualis vocati Domesday-Book Indices. Accessit dissertatio generalis de ratione hujusce libri. By Sir H. Ellis. 1816. folio.   **98 D**

Translation of Domesday so far as relates to counties of Middlesex, Hertford, Buckingham, Oxford and Gloucester. By Rev. Wm. Bawdwen. Doncaster, 1812. 4to.   **89 F**

DOMESDAY BOOK—*continued.*

Translation of Domesday so far as relates to county of York, parts of Lancashire, Westmoreland and Cumberland, also the counties of Derby, Nottingham, Rutland, and Lincoln. By Rev. Wm. Bawdwen. Doncaster, 1809. 4to.   **94 C**

See also EYTON, REV. R. W., GALE, R., HENSHALL, REV. S., MORTON, J., READER, W., WARNER, REV. R. and WYND-HAM, H. P.

DOMESTIC RELATIONS.

The law of the Domestic Relations. By W. P. Eversley. 1885. 8vo.   **10 C**

See also HUSBAND AND WIFE, INFANCY and MASTER AND SERVANT.

DOMICIL.

The law of Domicil. By A. V. Dicey. 1879. 8vo.   **9 G**

On the Domicil of Englishmen in France. By H. W. Cole. 1857. 8vo.   **166 A**

The law of Domicil. By R. Phillimore. 1847. 8vo.   **52 F**

The law of Domicil. See J. Henry's Case of Odwin v. Forbes, 1823, pp. 181–209.   **55 D**

DOMINICA, ISLAND OF.

The history of the island of Dominica. By Thomas Atwood. 1791. 8vo.   **84 B**

Laws of the Island of Dominica, 1763–1859. 2 vols. Dominica, 1858–60. 4to.   **36 F**

Dominica Acts, 1860–1888. 4 vols. 1860–88. folio.   **36 F**

DONALDSON, THOMAS LEVERTON.

Pompeii, illustrated with picturesque views, engraved by W. B. Cooke. 2 vols. in 1. 1827. folio.   **81 H**

DONCASTER, YORKSHIRE.

The history and antiquities of Doncaster and its vicinity. By Edward Miller. Doncaster, [1804.] 4to.   **94 D**

The history and topography of the deanery of Doncaster. By Rev. Joseph Hunter. 2 vols. 1828. folio.   **94 H**

See also J. Wainwright's Yorkshire, 1829, pp. 1–151.   **94 C**

DONNELL, ROBERT.

Practical guide to law of tenant compensation and farm purchase under Irish land act. Dublin, 1871. 8vo.   **55 E**

DONNELLY, Ross.
Minutes of cases in the court of Chancery, 1836–37. 1 vol.
1837. 8vo. **2 F**

DORIA, Adair Andrew and D. C. MACRAE.
The law and practice in Bankruptcy. 2 vols. 1861–63,
and new ed. by A. A. Doria. 1873. 12mo. **160 E**

DORKING, Surrey.
A History of Dorking and the neighbouring parishes. By
Rev. J. S. Bright. 1884. 8vo. **93 D**

DORNE, John.
Daily ledger of John Dorne, 1520. [Oxford Historical
Society, vols. 5 & 16.] Oxford, 1885–89. 8vo. **85 F**

DORSETSHIRE.
The civil division of the county of Dorset. By Edward
Boswell. Sherborne, 1795. 8vo. **87 D**
Domesday book for the county of Dorset, with a translation.
By Rev. William Bawdwen. 1815. folio. **87 H**
The history and antiquities of Dorset. By John Hutchins.
3rd ed. by W. Shipp and J. W. Hodson. 4 vols. 1861–73.
folio. **87 H**
The Poll for the county of Dorset, taken at the general
election in May 1807. By G. Frampton. Dorchester,
1807. 8vo. **107 J**
Survey of Dorset. By Rev. John Coker. 1732. folio. **87 G**

DOUCE, Francis.
Catalogue of printed books and manuscripts bequeathed by
F. Douce to Bodleian library. Oxford, 1840. folio. **81 H**
Catalogue of Lansdowne MSS. in British Museum. [By
F. Douce and Sir H. Ellis.] 2 parts in 1 vol. 1812–19.
folio. **98 C**

DOUGAL, Frederick Henry.
Index register to next of kin, heirs at law, legatees &c. since
1698. 5th ed. [1881.] 8vo. **134 I**
The same. [6th ed. 1882] and 8th ed. 1888. 8vo. **134 I**

DOUGLAS CAUSE.
Arguments of the Lord Chancellor, and Lord Chief Justice
of the King's Bench, in the Douglas cause, in the House of
Lords, February 27, 1769. See Collectanea Juridica, vol. 2,
1792, pp. 386–404. **144 G**

[DOUGLAS, D.]

The biographical history of Sir William Blackstone and a
catalogue of all his works with a Nomenclature of Westminster Hall. By A Gentleman of Lincoln's Inn [D. Douglas].
1782. 8vo. **79 C**

DOUGLAS, GEORGE.

Proceedings of a general court martial held at Guernsey on
Captain George Douglas, 16th regiment. By H. S. Douglas.
1849. [Pamphlets, vol. 32.] **144 C**

DOUGLAS, LADY JANE.

Letters of Lady Jane Douglas. 1767. 8vo. **80 C**

DOUGLAS, JONATHAN PERCY.

A Run through South Wales, viâ the London and North-
Western railway. Shrewsbury, [1868]. 12mo. **94 E**

DOUGLAS, SIR ROBERT.

The Baronage of Scotland. vol. 1. Edinburgh, 1798.
folio. **125 H**
Peerage of Scotland. Edinburgh, 1764. folio. **125 H**
The same. 2nd ed. by J. P. Wood. 2 vols. Edinburgh,
1813. folio. **125 H**

DOUGLAS, ROBERT R.

Alphabetical reference index to recent and important maritime
law decisions. 1888. 8vo. **11 F**

DOUGLAS, SYLVESTER, LORD GLENBERVIE.

The history of the cases of controverted elections, 1774-1776.
2nd ed. 4 vols. 1802. 8vo. **66 A**
Reports of Cases in the Court of King's Bench. 1783. folio.
The same. 2nd ed. 1786, and 3rd ed. 1790. 8vo.
The same. 4th ed. by Mr. Serjeant Frere and H. Roscoe.
4 vols. 1813-31. 8vo. **4 F**

DOUTHWAITE, WILLIAM RALPH.

Catalogue of the books in the library of Gray's Inn. 2 vols.
1872-78. 8vo. **82 D**
The same. [New ed.] 1888. 8vo. **82 D**
Gray's Inn, its history and associations. 1886. 8vo. **91 D**
Gray's Inn. Notes illustrative of its history and antiquities.
1876. 8vo. **91 D**

DOVEDALE, DERBYSHIRE.

History and topography of Ashbourn, the valley of the Dove and adjacent villages. Ashbourn, 1839. 8vo. **87 B**

DOVER, KENT.

Harbours of refuge. By F. R. A. Glover. 1859. 8vo. **78 B**

The history of Dover and of Dover Castle with a short account of the Cinque Ports. By Rev. John Lyon. 2 vols. in 1. Dover, 1813–14. 4to. **88 E**

History of Dover Castle. By Rev. William Darell. 1797. 4to. **88 E**

A Report on the corporation of Dover with a brief history of Dover harbour. Dover, 1835. 4to. **88 E**

DOVERCOURT, ESSEX.

The history and antiquities of Harwich and Dovercourt. Collected by Silas Taylor, enlarged by Samuel Dale. 1730. 8vo. **87 E**

DOW, PATRICK.

Reports of cases upon appeals and writs of error in the House of Lords. 1813–1818. 6 vols. 1814–19. 8vo. **1 D**

DOW, PATRICK and CHARLES CLARK.

Reports of cases upon appeals and writs of error in the House of Lords. 1827–1832. 2 vols. 1830–32. 8vo. **1 D**

DOWELL, STEPHEN.

History and explanation of stamp duties and stamp laws at present in force in United Kingdom. 1873. 8vo. **78 D**

A History of taxation and taxes in England from earliest times to year 1885. 2nd ed. 4 vols. 1888. 8vo. **78 D**

The Income Tax laws at present in force in the United Kingdom. 1874. 12mo. **168 G**

The same. 2nd ed. 1885. 8vo. **10 C**

A sketch of the history of Taxes in England. vol. 1 to the civil war 1642. 1876. 8vo. **78 D**

· DOWER.

The law of Dower. By C. H. Scribner. 2 vols. Philadelphia, 1867. 8vo. **59 D**

The law of Dower. By J. J. Park. 1819. 8vo. **52 F**

DOWER—*continued.*

Remarks on the best method of Barring Dower. By J. H. Prince. 1805. [Pamphlets, vol. 27.] **144 B**

See also Fisher's Digest, vol. 4, 1884, pp. 333–342. **14 E**

See also HUSBAND AND WIFE.

DOWLING, ALFRED SEPTIMUS.

Reports of cases in King's Bench practice court, with points of practice decided in Courts of Common Pleas and Exchequer 1830–1841. 9 vols. 1833–42. 8vo. **4 F G**

Reports of cases in King's Bench practice court with points of practice decided in Courts of Common Pleas and Exchequer. New Series 1841–1843. By A. S. Dowling and V. Dowling. 2 vols. 1843–44. 8vo. **4 G**

DOWLING, A. S. and JOHN JAMES LOWNDES.

Reports of cases in Queen's Bench practice court with points of pleading and practice decided in Courts of Common Pleas and Exchequer 1843–1849. 7 vols. 1845–51. 8vo. **4 G H**

DOWLING, JAMES and ARCHER RYLAND.

Reports of cases in the Court of King's Bench 1822–1827. 9 vols. 1822–31. 8vo. **4 H**

D'OYLY FAMILY.

A Biographical, historical, genealogical and heraldic account of the house of D'Oyly. By W. D. Bayley. 1845. [Grimaldi's Tracts, vol. 3.] **118 B**

D'OYLY, REV. GEORGE and REV. RICHARD MANT.

The Holy Bible according to the authorised version with notes. 3 vols. Oxford, 1817. 4to. **77 F**

DRAGE, GEOFFREY.

The criminal code of the German empire : translated with prolegomena and a commentary. 1885. 12mo. **55 C**

DRAINAGE.

The history of imbanking and draining of divers fens and marshes both in foreign parts and in this kingdom. By Wm. Dugdale. 2nd ed. by C. N. Cole. 1772. folio. **85 I**

See also SEWERS and WATERS.

DRAKE, FRANCIS.

Eboracum, or the history and antiquities of the city of York. 1736. folio. **95 H**

Life of Francis Drake. See J. P. Malcolm's Lives of Topographers. 1815. 4to. **79 H**

DRAKE, SIR FRANCIS.

Sir Francis Drake's memorable service done against the Spaniards in 1587. By Robert Leng. Edited by Clarence Hopper. [Camden Society, vol. 87.] 1864. 8vo. **85 C**

DRAKE, HENRY HOLMAN.

The Hundred of Blackheath. 1886. folio. **89 H**

DRAPERS' COMPANY.

Reports of deputations who in pursuance of resolutions of the court of assistants of the Drapers' Company visited the estates of the company in the county of Londonderry. 1829. 8vo. **95 F**

Another ed. 1841. 8vo. **95 F**

DRAYTON, MICHAEL.

Notes upon Drayton's Polyolbion. See J. Selden's Works vol. 3, 1726, pp. 1727–1878. **115 I**

DREAM, THE.

The Dream. [1688. A poem.] [Tracts, 1688–89.] **118 E**

DRESS.

Gossip on Dress, or half-an-hour's amusement. 1863. [Pamphlets, vol. 18.] **144 B**

The philosophy of dress, with a few notes on national costumes. 1864. [Pamphlets, vol. 25.] **144 B**

DREWRY, CHARLES STEWART.

A Concise treatise on the principles of Equity Pleading with precedents. 1858. 12mo. **173 E**

Forms of claims and defences in the Chancery division of the high Court of Justice. 1876. 12mo. **52 B**

Law and practice of Injunctions. 1849. 8vo. **169 A**

New practice of the Court of Chancery. 1856. 12mo, **161 E**

DREWRY, CHARLES STEWART—*continued*.

Observations on points relating to amendment of law of patents. 1839. [Law Tracts, vol. 6.] **144 E**

Reports of cases decided in Court of Chancery 1852–1859, by Sir R. T. Kindersley. 4 vols. 1853–60. 8vo. **2 F G**

DREWRY, CHARLES STEWART and JOHN JACKSON SMALE.

Reports of cases decided in Court of Chancery 1859–1865, by Sir R. T. Kindersley. 2 vols. 1862–67. 8vo. **2 G**

DRINK.

Manual of the law concerning the retailing of intoxicating drinks. By C. S. Deane. 1887. 8vo. **12 C**

Law of sales of food, drinks and medicines. Edited by A Barrister and Magistrate. 1875. 12mo. **168 E**

DRONE, EATON S.

Law of property in intellectual productions in Great Britain and the United States. Boston, 1879. 8vo. **59 C**

DROPSY.

On the geographical distribution of dropsy in England and Wales. By A. Haviland. 1869. [Pamphlets, vol. 32.] **144 C**

DRURY, ROBERT.

Adventures during fifteen years' captivity on the island of Madagascar. [Autobiography, vol. 2.] 1827. 12mo. **79 A**

DRURY, WILLIAM B.

Reports of cases in Chancery 1843–1844. Dublin, 1851. 8vo. **15 D**

Select cases in Chancery 1858–1859. Dublin, 1860. 8vo. **15 D**

DRURY, W. B. and FREDERICK WILLIAM WALSH.

Reports of cases in the Court of Chancery 1837–1840. 2 vols. Dublin, 1839–42. 8vo. **15 D**

DRURY, W. B. and ROBERT RICHARD WARREN.

Reports of cases in the Court of Chancery 1841–1843. 4 vols. Dublin, 1843–46. 8vo. **15 D**

DU BARRI, Marie Jeanne, Countess.
Memoirs. [Autobiography, vols. 5–8.] 4 vols. 1830–31.
12mo. **79 A**

DUBLIN.
Chartularies of St. Mary's abbey, Dublin, with the register of
its house at Dunbrody and Annals of Ireland. Edited by
J. T. Gilbert. 2 vols. 1884. 8vo. **102 H**
Dublin Gazette, 1862–1889. 57 vols. 1862–89. 8vo. **Hall**
Dublin University calendar, 1861, 1886. 2 vols. Dublin,
1861–86. 12mo. **137 H**
History of church of St. Patrick near Dublin. By W. M.
Mason. Dublin, 1819. 4to. **95 F**
A History of city of Dublin. By J. T. Gilbert. 2 vols.
Dublin, 1854–59. 8vo. **95 E**
History of city of Dublin. By J. Warburton, Rev. G. White-
law, and Rev. R. Walsh. 2 vols. 1818. 4to. **95 F**
History of county of Dublin. By J. D'Alton. Dublin, 1838.
8vo. **95 F**
History of Dublin. By W. Harris. 1766. 8vo. **95 E**
The memoirs of the Archbishops of Dublin. By John D'Alton.
Dublin, 1838. 8vo. **80 C**
Practice of the Court of Record of the borough of Dublin.
By W. P. Pike. Dublin, 1842. 12mo. **55 E**
Register of the abbey of St. Thomas, Dublin. Edited by
John T. Gilbert. 1889. 8vo. **102 I**
Report of Her Majesty's commissioners appointed to inquire
into state, discipline, studies, and revenues of University of
Dublin, and of Trinity College ; with appendices. Dublin,
1853. folio. **154 E**
Report of proceedings at a visitation holden in Trinity college
Dublin to hear appeals of G. F. Shaw and Robert Car-
michael, fellows of the college. By J. F. Waller. Dublin,
1858. 8vo. **95 E**
Rules, bye laws and prospectus of classes of Dublin law
institute. Dublin, 1840–41. [Pamphlets, vol. 16.] **144 B**
The Society of King's Inns, Dublin, its origin and progress.
By W. F. Littledale. 1859. [Pamphlets, vol. 14.] **144 A**

[DUBOIS, Edward.]
My pocket book, or hints for ' a ryghte merrie and conceitede '
tour, in quarto, to be called ' The Stranger in Ireland ' in-
1805. By a Knight Errant [Edward Dubois]. 3rd ed.
1808. 12mo. **118 B**

DUBOURDIEU, Rev. John.
Statistical survey of Antrim. 2 vols. 1812. 8vo. **95 E**

DU CANGE, Charles Dufresne, Seigneur.
Glossarium ad scriptores mediæ et infimæ Latinitatis. Editio
nova. 6 vols. Paris, 1733–36. folio. **123 H**
Glossarium novum, seu supplementum ad auctiorem Glossarii
Cangiani editionem ; collegit et digessit D. P. Carpentier.
4 vols. Paris, 1766. folio. **123 H**
The Testimonies of Du Fresne. See Appendix to Sir John
Fortescue's De laudibus legum Angliæ, 2nd ed. 1741.
folio. **115 H**

DUCAREL, Andrew Coltée.
History of royal hospital and collegiate church of St. Katharine near Tower of London. 1782. 4to. **89 F**
Life of A. C. Ducarel. See J. P. Malcolm's Lives of Topographers. 1815. 4to. **79 H**
Repertory of endowments of vicarages in dioceses of Canterbury and Rochester. 2nd ed. 1782. 8vo. **88 D**
Some account of the town, church and archiepiscopal palace
of Croydon. 1783. 4to. **93 D**

DUCK, Stephen.
Poems on several subjects. 7th ed. with some account of the
life of the author. 1730. 12mo. **83 C**

DUDLEY, John, 1 Viscount and T. CUNNINGHAM.
The law of a Justice of Peace and parish officer. 3 vols.
1769. 4to. **156 B**

DUELS.
. The charge of Sir Francis Bacon touching Duels, upon an
information in the Star-chamber against Priest and Wright.
See Bacon's Works, vol. 6, 1826, pp. 108–137. **78 F**
The Duello or single combat. See J. Selden's Works, vol. 3,
1726, pp. 49–84. **115 I**

DUER, John.
The law and practice of Marine Insurance. 2 vols. New
York, 1845–46. 8vo. **59 E**

DUFOUR, Gabriel.
Traité général de Droit Administratif appliqué. 2me éd.
7 vols. Paris, 1854–57. 8vo. **58 C**

DUGDALE, Sir William.

The ancient usage in bearing arms; with additions by T. C.
Banks. 1812. folio. **125 H**

Antiquities of Warwickshire. 1656. folio. **94 G**

The same. 2nd ed. by W. Thomas. 2 vols. 1730. folio.
94 H

The Baronage of England. 2 vols. 1675–76. folio. **125 H**

A Small specimen of the many mistakes in Sir W. Dugdale's
Baronage. By Richard Rawlinson. Monmouth, 1801.
[Grimaldi's Tracts, vol. 3.] **118 B**

History of imbanking and draining of divers fens and marshes
both in foreign parts and in this kingdom. 2nd ed. by
C. N. Cole. 1772. folio. **85 I**

History of St. Paul's cathedral; likewise an historical account
of the cathedrals and chief collegiate churches in Province
of York. 2nd ed. by E. Maynard. 1716. folio. **92 H**

The same. New ed. by H. Ellis. 1818. folio. **92 H**

Life, diary and correspondence. Edited by Wm. Hamper.
1827. 4to. **79 I**

Life of Sir W. Dugdale. See J. P. Malcolm's Lives of Topographers. 1815. 4to. **79 H**

Monasticon Anglicanum; sive Pandectæ Cœnobiorum Bene-
dictinorum &c. Per R. Dodsworth et G. Dugdale. 3 vols.
1682–61–73. folio. **85 H**

The same. Translated into English, with considerable additions. 1718. folio. **85 H**

Additional volumes by John Stevens. 2 vols. 1722–23.
folio. **85 H**

Monasticon Anglicanum. New ed. by J. Caley, H. Ellis and
B. Bandinel. 6 vols. in 8 vols. 1817–30. folio. **85 H I**

Origines juridiciales, or historical memorials of the English
laws . . . also A Chronologie of the lord chancelors . . .
and serjeants at law. 2nd ed. 1671. folio. **125 H**

See also Cunningham, T.

DUHIGG, Bartholomew Thomas.

History of the King's Inns; or an account of the legal body in
Ireland, from its connexion with England. Dublin, 1806.
8vo. **95 E**

DUKE, George.

The law of charitable uses. 1676. folio. **49 G**

The same. Edited by R. W. Bridgman. 1805. 8vo. **161 F**

DUKES, THOMAS FARMER.
Antiquities of Shropshire, Shrewsbury. 1844. 4to. 93 G

DULWICH COLLEGE, SURREY.
Dulwich College and the endowed schools commissioners. A tract for the times. By J. R. Adams. 1873. [Pamphlets, vol. 33.] 144 C
See also GALER, A. M.

DUMONT, JEAN.
Corps universel diplomatique du droit des gens ; contenant un recueil des traitez d'alliance, de paix &c. faits en Europe, depuis le règne de Charlemagne, jusques à présent. 8 vols. 1726–31. Supplement : Histoire des anciens traitez depuis les tems les plus reculez, jusques à Charlemagne. Par M. Barbeyrac. 1 vol. 1739. Recueil des traitez &c. continué par M. Rousset. 1 vol. 1739. Cérémonial diplomatique des cours de l'Europe, recueilli en partie par Dumont, mis en ordre et augmenté par M. Rousset. 2 vols. 1739. 12 vols. Amsterdam, 1726–39. folio. 116 H I

DUMONT, PIERRE ÉTIENNE LOUIS.
A Treatise on judicial evidence, extracted from the manuscripts of Jeremy Bentham. 1825. 8vo. 78 C

DUNCAN, JAMES ARCHIBALD.
The annual review of mercantile cases for the years 1885–1886. 2 vols. 1886–87. 8vo. 172 F

DUNCAN, JOHN MORISON.
Treatise on the parochial ecclesiastical law of Scotland. Edinburgh, 1864. 8vo. 55 G

DUNCOMBE, ALFRED JOHN.
Laws of the Turks and Caicos islands 1799–1860. 1862. 8vo. 36 B

DUNCOMBE, GILES.
Tryals per pais : or the law of England concerning juries by Nisi Prius &c. 4th ed. with a farther treatise of evidence. 1702. 12mo. · 169 G
The same. 5th ed 1718, 6th ed. 1725, and 7th ed. 1739. 12mo. 169 G

DUNCUMB, Rev. John.

Collections towards the history and antiquities of the county of Hereford. [With continuation by W. H. Cooke.] 3 vols. in 4. Hereford, 1804-12-82. 4to.   **88 G**

DUNDEE, Forfarshire.

Burgh laws of Dundee, with the history, statutes and proceedings of the guild of merchants and fraternities of craftsmen. By A. J. Warden. 1872. 8vo.   **95 C**

A Century of banking in Dundee from 1764 to 1864. By C. W. Boase. 2nd ed. Edinburgh, 1867. 8vo.   **78 D**

DUNKIN, John.

The history and antiquities of Bicester, with an inquiry into the history of Alchester. 1816. 8vo.   **92 E**

Outlines of history and antiquities of Bromley in Kent and An investigation of antiquities of Holwood Hill in the parish of Keston. By A. J. Kempe. Bromley, 1815. 8vo.   **88 C**

Oxfordshire: the history and antiquities of the hundreds of Bullington and Ploughley. 2 vols. 1823. 4to.   **92 F**

DUNSFORD, Martin.

Historical memoirs of the town and parish of Tiverton. Exeter, 1790. 4to.   **87 D**

DUNSTABLE, Bedfordshire.

Annales prioratus de Dunstaplia, A.D. 1-1297. See Annales Monastici, vol. 3, 1866, pp. 1-420.   **102 A**

DUNSTAN, Saint.

Memorials of Saint Dunstan, archbishop of Canterbury. Edited by Rev. Wm. Stubbs. 1874. 8vo.   **102 E**

DUNWICH, Suffolk.

Historical account of Dunwich. By T. Gardner. 1754. 4to.   **93 B**

DURAND DE MAILLANE, Pierre Toussaint.

Histoire du droit canon pour servir d'introduction à l'étude du droit canonique. Lyon, 1770. 12mo.   **77 C**

DURHAM.

Durham University calendar 1881–1889. 9 vols. 1881–89. 12mo. **137 H**

The general election poll for knights of the shire to represent in Parliament the county palatine of Durham. 1790. Newcastle upon Tyne, 1790. 4to. **107 J**

Historia ecclesiæ Dunhelmensis. By Symeon of Durham. Edited by Thomas Arnold. 1882. 8vo. **102 G**

History and antiquities of Durham. By Robert Surtees. 4 vols. 1816–40. folio. **87 H**

History and antiquities of North Durham, [completing Surtees' History of Durham.] By Rev. James Raine. 1852. folio. **88 H**

History and antiquities of Durham. By Wm. Fordyce. 2 vols. Newcastle. [1857.] 4to. **87 E**

History and antiquities of Durham. By Wm. Hutchinson. 3 vols. 1785–94. 4to. **87 D**

Registrum Palatinum Dunelmense. The register of Richard De Kellawe 1311–1316. Edited by Sir T. D. Hardy. 4 vols. 1873–78. 8vo. **102 E**

View of the county palatine of Durham. By E. Mackenzie and M. Ross. 2 vols. Newcastle, 1834. 4to. **87 E**

See also GREENWICH, HOLMES, J. H. H., SYKES, J. and WALLIS, J.

DURHAM, COURT OF CHANCERY OF.

The practice of Court of Chancery of county palatine of Durham. By a Solicitor of that court [Martin Williamson]. Sunderland, 1807. 8vo. **166 A**

DURNFORD, CHARLES and EDWARD HYDE EAST.

Reports of Cases in the Court of King's Bench from Mich. Term 26 Geo. III. to Trin. Term 40 Geo. III. 8 vols. 1787–1800. folio.

The same. 4th ed. [entitled Term Reports]. 8 vols. 1794–1802. 8vo. **5 I**

DUTCH LANGUAGE.

Grand Dictionnaire Hollandois et François. Par P. Maurin. 4me éd. Rotterdam, 1768. 4to. **123 C**

See also MINSHEU, J.

DUTCH LAW.

Commercial code of the Netherlands. 1880. 12mo. **55 C**

Simon Van Leewen's Commentaries on Roman-Dutch law revised by C. W. Decker. Translated from the Dutch by J. G. Kotzé. 2 vols. 1881–86. 8vo. **55 D**

Institutes of Holland, or manual of law, practice and mercantile law. By J. Van Der Linden. Translated by Henry Juta. Cape Town, 1884. 8vo. **55 D**

Judicial, practical and mercantile guide, translated from the Dutch of J. Van Der Linden. 1814. 8vo. **55 D**

The land system of Holland. By E. de Laveleye. See Systems of land tenure, 1881, pp. 443–495. **78 B**

See also GROTIUS, H.

DUVERGIER, JEAN BAPTISTE.

Droit civil Français, suivant l'ordre du code civil. Livre 3me, titres vi–xi. 6 vols. Paris, 1835–43. 8vo. **58 C D**

DWARRIS, SIR FORTUNATUS.

A General treatise on Statutes, their rules of construction and the proper boundaries of legislation and of judicial interpretation. 2nd ed. by W. H. Amyot. 1848. 8vo. **176 C**

A Letter addressed to the Lord high Chancellor of England on his proposed scheme for the consolidation of the statute law. 1853. [Pamphlets, vol. 23.] **144 B**

DYCE SOMBRE, DAVID OCHTERLONY.

In the prerogative court of Canterbury. Dyce Sombre against Troup, Solaroli (intervening), and Prinsep, and the Hon. East India Company (also intervening). In the goods of D. O. Dyce Sombre, Esq., deceased. vol. I. Scripts— Pleadings . . . and Exhibits. [1856.] folio. **49 I**

Mr. Dyce Sombre's Refutation of the charge of lunacy brought against him in court of chancery. Paris, 1849. 8vo. **118 B**

DYER, GEORGE.

History of the university and colleges of Cambridge. 2 vols. 1814. 8vo. **86 C**

Privileges of university of Cambridge, with observations on its history, antiquities, &c. 2 vols. 1824. 8vo. **86 C**

DYER, SIR JAMES.

Les Reports des divers select matters et resolutions en le

DYER, Sir James—*continued.*

several regnes de le roys Hen. 8 et Edw. 6 et le roignes Mar. et Eliz. 1672. folio. **74 C**

The same, translated by J. Vaillant. 3 vols. 1794. 8vo. **4 H**

EADMER, Monk of Canterbury.

Historia Novorum in Anglia, et Opuscula duo de vita Sancti Anselmi. Edited by M. Rule. 1884. 8vo. **102 H**

EADWIG, King of England.

Inquiry into life and character of King Eadwig. See J. Allen's Royal Prerogative, 1849, pp. 217–268. **83 I**

EAGLE, Francis King and Edward YOUNGE.

Collection of reports of cases, statutes and ecclesiastical laws, relating to tithes. 4 vols. 1826. 8vo. **65 A**

EAGLE, William.

The law of Tithes. 2 vols. 1830. 8vo. **176 E**

The statute of 2 & 3 William IV. c. 100, relating to moduses and exemptions from tithes. 1834. [Jacob's Tracts, vol. 11.] **144 F**

EARDLEY-WILMOT, Sir John Eardley.

Lord Brougham's acts and bills, with a review, showing their results upon the amendment of the law. 1857. 8vo. **83 J**

EARL MARSHAL, Office of.

The office of Earl Marshal of England. See C. Howard's Historical Anecdotes, 1769, pp. 138–201. **80 B**

EARLY CLOSING.

Early closing on Saturdays. Correspondence compiled by J. R. Taylor. 1855. [Pamphlets, vol. 13.] **144 A**

EARNSHAW, William.

Digest of laws (from 1660 to 1819) relating to shipping, navigation, commerce and revenue, in the British colonies in America and the West Indies, including laws for abolition of slave trade. 1819. 8vo. **55 D**

EARTH.

A New theory of the Earth. By Wm. Whiston. 4th ed.
1725. 12mo. **77 A**

The scriptural history of the earth and of mankind. By
Philip Howard. 1797. 4to. **77 G**

EARWAKER, Rev. John Parsons.

East Cheshire past and present, or a history of the hundred of
Macclesfield. 2 vols. 1877–80. 4to. **87 G**

EASEMENTS.

Law of Easements. By C. J. Gale. 6th ed. by G. Cave.
1888. 8vo. **9 G**

Law of Easements. By J. L. Goddard. 3rd ed. 1884.
8vo. **9 G**

An Analytical summary of the law of Easements. By W. O.
·Morris. Dublin, 1869. 12mo. **166 A**

The American law of Easements and Servitudes. By Emory
Washburn. 2nd ed. Boston, 1867. 8vo. **59 D**

See also Air, Lights and Waters.

EAST, Sir Edward Hyde.

Notes of cases decided in the supreme court of judicature at
Fort William in Bengal. See W. H. Morley's Analytical
Digest, vol. 2, 1851, pp. 1–243. **38 C**

Reports of cases in the Court of King's Bench 1800–1812.
16 vols. 1801–14. 8vo. **4 I & 5 A**

Treatise of the Pleas of the Crown. 2 vols. 1803. 8vo. **53 C**

EAST INDIA COMPANY.

Dacoitee in excelsis; or the spoliation of Oude by the East
India Company, faithfully recounted. [By Samuel Lucas.]
1857. 8vo. **78 C**

A Reply to a 'Letter from Andrew Stuart to the directors
of the East India Company.' By Alexander Dalrymple.
1779. 4to. **38 A**

Report of debate at East-India house, at a special general
court of proprietors of East-India stock, relative to compen-
sations to be granted to the Company's maritime officers.
1834. [Pamphlets, vol. 5.] **144 A**

Restoration of King of Tanjore considered. 1777. 4to. **38 A**

Copies of papers relative to restoration of King of Tanjore.
5 vols. 1777. 4to. **38 A**

EAST INDIA COMPANY—*continued.*
Treaties and grants from country powers to East India Co. respecting their presidency of Fort St. George, Fort William and Bombay, 1756–1772. 1774. 4to.   **38 A**

EASTER SEPULCHRES.
Easter Sepulchres, their object, nature and history. By Alfred Heales. 1869. 4to.   **85 I**

EASTERN COUNTIES RAILWAY.
Sections of the intended Eastern Counties Railway from London to Norwich and Yarmouth. 1835. folio.   **19 D**

EASTERN QUESTION.
The Eastern question and the Paris treaty of 1856. By Blue Pamphlet. 1871. [Pamphlets, vol. 33.]   **144 C**
A Letter to Lord Palmerston showing the importance of opening Suez Canal and futility of Euphrates railway. By An Old Indian. 1857. [Pamphlets, vol. 10.]   **144 A**
See also URQUHART, D.

EASTMEAD, REV. WILLIAM.
Historia Rievallensis; containing the history of Kirkby Moorside with a dissertation on the animal remains in the recently discovered cave at Kirkdale. 1824. 8vo.   **94 B**

ECCLESIASTICAL BENEFICES AND REVENUES.
A Book of the valuations of all the ecclesiastical preferments in England and Wales. 1680. 12mo.   **49 A**
Liber Regis, vel Thesaurus rerum ecclesiasticarum. By John Bacon. 1786. 4to.   **100 G**
Observations on the law and practice of sequestration of ecclesiastical benefices. By Rev. H. B. Wilson. 1836. [Pamphlets, vol. 1.]   **144 A**
Report of commissioners appointed to inquire into ecclesiastical revenues of England and Wales. 1835. folio.   **153 D**
Taxatio ecclesiastica Angliæ et Walliæ, auctoritate P. Nicholai IV. circa A.D. 1291. [Edited by T. Astle, Rev. J. Ayscough, and J. Caley.] 1802. folio.   **99 C**
Valor Ecclesiasticus temp. Henry VIII. auctoritate regia institutus [A.D. 1535 cum] appendice et indicibus. [Edited by John Caley.] 6 vols. 1810–14. folio.   **98 D**
See also ECTON, J.

ECCLESIASTICAL COMMISSIONERS.

Acts relating to the ecclesiastical commissioners for England. 3rd ed. with supplement. 1844–45. 8vo.   **77 A**

Orders in council ratifying schemes of the ecclesiastical commissioners for England, 1836–1862. 15 vols. 1843–63. 8vo.   **77 A**

General index to the first six volumes ending October 1848, and general index, made up to the end of the year 1854. 2 vols. 1848–55. 8vo.   **77 A**

The argument of N. Fuller in the case of T. Lad and R. Mansell his clients, wherein it is plainly proved that the ecclesiastical commissioners have no power by their commission to imprison or to fine any of his Majesties subjects or to put them to the oath ex officio. 1641. [Law Tracts and Arguments, 1641.]   **144 F**

ECCLESIASTICAL COURTS.

Considerations on Ecclesiastical courts' reform in reference to the government bill now before the House of Commons. By Harvey Gem. 1844. [Law Tracts, vol. 8.]   **144 E**

Letter to Robert Monsey, Baron Cranworth, on constitution of ecclesiastical courts. By A. J. Stephens. 1853. 12mo. **166 A**

The special and general reports made by commissioners appointed to inquire into practice and jurisdiction of Ecclesiastical Courts in England and Wales. 1832. folio.   **153 C**

The spiritual courts. See Law Journal Tracts, 1825–6, pp. 1–9.   **144 G**

See also HOLLAND, S. L.

ECCLESIASTICAL DIGNITARIES.

Fasti Ecclesiæ Anglicanæ, or a calendar of the principal ecclesiastical dignitaries in England and Wales. By John Le Neve. Continued by T. D. Hardy. 3 vols. Oxford, 1854. 8vo.   **80 H**

ECCLESIASTICAL HISTORY.

Registrum epistolarum Fratris Johannis Peckham. Edited by C. T. Martin. 3 vols. 1882–85. 8vo.   **102 G H**

The repressor of over much blaming of the clergy. By R. Pecock. Edited by C. Babington. 2 vols. 1860. 8vo. **101 D**

See also ABBEYS, CANTERBURY ARCHBISHOPS OF, CHURCH OF ENGLAND, MONASTERIES and REFORMATION.

ECCLESIASTICAL LAW.

A Summary of the law and practice in the Ecclesiastical Courts. By T. E. Smith. 3rd ed. 1888. 8vo. **64 C**

Practical treatise on law relating to the Church and the Clergy. By H. W. Cripps. 6th ed. by C. A. Cripps. 1886. 8vo. **9 C**

The book of Church law. By J. H. Blunt. 4th ed. 1885. 12mo. **9 C**

Ecclesiastical law of the Church of England. By Sir R. Phillimore. 3 vols. 1873–76. 8vo. **9 C**

Privy Council tracts, edited by a Judicial Committee, a handy book of privy council law in ecclesiastical cases and patent cases. 1872. 8vo. **77 B**

American ecclesiastical law. By R. H. Tyler. Albany, 1866. 8vo. **59 D**

Practical treatise of the laws relating to the clergy. By A. J. Stephens. 2 vols. 1848. 8vo. **9 C**

The practice of ecclesiastical courts. By H. C. Coote. 1847. 8vo. **52 F**

Statutes relating to ecclesiastical and eleemosynary institutions. By A. J. Stephens. 2 vols. 1845. 8vo. **31 E**

Ecclesiastical law. By Rev. Richard Burn. 9th ed. by Robert Phillimore. 4 vols. 1842. 8vo. **52 F**

A Practical arrangement of ecclesiastical law. By F. N. Rogers. 1840. 8vo. **166 A**

The Ecclesiastical legal guide to archbishops, bishops and their secretaries, the clergy, patrons of benefices, solicitors, parish officers, &c. By a Barrister. Part 1. 1839. 8vo. **166 B**

The parson's counsellor with the law of tithes. By Sir Simon Degge. 7th ed. by C. Ellis. 1820. 8vo. **52 F**

A System of English Ecclesiastical law. By Richard Grey. 3rd ed. 1735. 12mo. **49 F**

See also CANON LAW and CLERGY, THE.

See also BROOKE, W. G., CLARK, T., CLARKE, F., COCKBURN, REV. W., CONSET, H., DALE, J. M., DUNCAN, J. M., FLOYER, P.,GIBSON,E., HARDING, G. R. and LAW, REV. J. T.

ECCLESIASTICAL POLITY AND TERMS.

The works of Mr. Richard Hooker, in eight books of ecclesiastical polity. 1666. folio. **77 F**

Glossary of ecclesiastical terms. See Register of S. Osmund, vol. 2, 1884, pp. 161–206. **102 H**

ECHYNGHAM FAMILY.

Echyngham of Echyngham. By S. Hall. 1850. 8vo. **80 C**

ECONOMICS AND ECONOMIC HISTORY.

Analysis of the principles of Economics. By Patrick Geddes. 1885. [Pamphlets, vol. 39.] **144 C**

The English village community examined in its relations to the manorial and tribal systems, an essay in economic history. By F. Seebohm. 2nd ed. 1883. 8vo. **83 H**

ECTON, JOHN.

Liber valorum et decimarum, being an account of the valuations and yearly tenths of all such ecclesiastical benefices in England and Wales as now stand chargeable with the payment of first-fruits and tenths. 1711. 8vo. **118 B**

Thesaurus rerum ecclesiasticarum, being an account of the valuations of all the ecclesiastical benefices in the several dioceses in England and Wales. 1742. 4to. **100 G**

EDDIS, ARTHUR SHELLY.

Principles of the administration of assets in payment of debts. 1880. 8vo. **12 F**

EDEN, ROBERT.

Jurisprudentia philologica, sive elementa juris civilis, secundum methodum et seriem institutionum Justiniani. Oxonii, 1744. 4to. **155 B**

EDEN, ROBERT HENLEY.

Analysis of the bill for consolidation and amendment of bankrupt law. 1823. [Jacob's Tracts, vol. I.] **144 E**

The law of Injunctions. 1821. 8vo. **169 A**

Observations upon the bill for consolidation and amendment of bankrupt laws. 1824. [Jacob's Tracts, vol. I.] **144 E**

Practical treatise on Bankrupt law. 1825. 8vo. **160 D**

The same. 3rd ed. 1832. 8vo. **160 D**

Reports of cases in Court of Chancery from the original manuscripts of Lord Chancellor Northington. 2nd ed. 2 vols. 1827. 8vo. **2 G**

EDEN, WILLIAM.

Four letters to the Earl of Carlisle. 3rd ed. 1780. 12mo. **78 A**

Principles of penal law. [By Wm. Eden.] 1771. 8vo. **165 F**

EDINBURGH.

Cassell's Old and new Edinburgh, its history, its people and its places. By James Grant. 3 vols. 1880–83. 4to. **95 D**

Edinburgh Gazette. 1862–89. 49 vols. 1862–89. folio. **Hall**

The story of the University of Edinburgh during its first 300 years. By Sir A. Grant. 2 vols. 1884. 8vo. ' **95 D**

EDINBURGH REVIEW.

The Edinburgh Review, or critical journal. 1802–1889. 170 vols. 1802–89, and general index to vols. 1–140. 5 vols. 1813–74. 175 vols. 1802–89. 8vo. **255 A–G**

EDMONDS, Frederic.

Memorial and petition to secretary of state, in the matter of revision ordered by him of defective coroner's inquest on body of Jacob Curnow Millett. 1871. 8vo. **50 B**

EDMONDSON, Joseph.

Baronagium genealogicum : or the Pedigrees of the English peers. 6 vols. in 3. 1764–84. folio. **124 I**

Companion to peerage of Great Britain and Ireland. 1776. Bound with Edmondson's Peerage. 1785. 8vo. **125 C**

Complete body of Heraldry. 2 vols. 1780. folio. **124 I**

Historical and genealogical account of family of Greville, including the history and succession of Earls of Warwick and some account of Warwick Castle. 1766. 8vo. **80 C**

The present peerages . . . the plates of arms revised by Joseph Edmondson. 1785. 8vo. **125 C**

EDMONTON, Middlesex.

The history and antiquities of the parish of Edmonton. By Wm. Robinson. 1819. 8vo. **89 D**

EDMUNDS, Lewis.

The law and practice of letters patent for inventions. 1890. 8vo. **11 B**

EDUCATION.

Education acts 1870–1880. By H. Owen. 15th ed. 1881. 8vo. **9 H**

Education acts 1870–1880. By W. C. Glen. 6th ed. 1881. 8vo. **52 F**

EDUCATION—*continued.*

Education. A lecture delivered at the Witham Literary Institution. 1845. [Pamphlets, vol. 5.] **144 A**

The Education journal, or magazine of general instruction. 1836. folio. **78 H**

Observations on the present system of Education. 10th ed. 1845. [Pamphlets, vol. 5.] **144 A**

Ragged schools in relation to government grants for education : authorized report of conference held at Birmingham. By Charles Ratcliff. 1861. [Pamphlets, vol. 15.] **144 B**

Some thoughts concerning Education. By John Locke. See J. Locke's Works, vol. 9, 1823, pp. 1–205. **78 E**

See also MILLER, REV. C.

EDWARD THE CONFESSOR.

Lives of Edward the Confessor. Edited by H. R. Luard. 1858. 8vo. **101 A**

See also AILREDUS.

EDWARD I., II. AND III., KINGS OF ENGLAND.

Account of the expenses of John of Brabant and Thomas and Henry of Lancaster, A.D. 1292–3. Edited by Joseph Burtt. [Camden Society, vol. 55.] 1853. 8vo. **85 B**

Adæ Murimuth Continuatio Chronicarum. [1303–1347.] Robertus De Avesbury De gestis mirabilibus regis Edwardi Tertii. Edited by E. M. Thompson. 1889. 8vo. **102 I**

Chronicles of the reigns of Edward I. and Edward II. Edited by Rev. Wm. Stubbs. 2 vols. 1882–83. 8vo. **102 G**

History of Edward I. By W. Prynne. 1670. folio. **115 I**

History of Edward the Third, with the life and death of his son Edward the Black Prince. By Rev. Joshua Barnes. Cambridge, 1688. folio. **114 H**

Édouard III et les bourgeois de Calais, ou les Anglais en France. Par M. Guizot. Edited by Rev. A. C. Clapin. 1890. 12mo. **83 C**

See also FROISSART, SIR J., LINGARD, REV. J., MARTYN, W., STATE PAPERS and TURNER, S.

EDWARD IV., KING OF ENGLAND.

A Chronicle of first 13 years of reign of Edward the Fourth. By John Warkworth, D.D. Edited by J. O. Halliwell. [Camden Society, vol. 10.] 1839. 8vo. **85 A**

EDWARD IV., KING OF ENGLAND—*continued*.

Historie of the arrivall of Edward IV. in England and the finall recouerye of his kingdomes from Henry VI. Edited by John Bruce. [Camden Society, vol. 1.] 1838. 8vo. **85 A**

The most pleasant song of Lady Bessy, the eldest daughter of Edward the Fourth, and how she married Henry the Seventh. With notes by T. Heywood. 1829. 8vo. **83 C**

Three books of P. Vergil's English history, comprising reigns of Henry VI., Edward IV. and Richard III. Edited by Sir H. Ellis. [Camden Soc., vol. 29.] 1844. 8vo. **85 A**

See also LINGARD, REV. J., MARTYN, W., STATE PAPERS and TURNER, S.

EDWARD V., KING OF ENGLAND.

Grants &c. from the Crown during the reign of Edward the Fifth. Edited by J. G. Nichols. [Camden Society, vol. 60.] 1854. 8vo. **85 B**

See also LINGARD, REV. J., MARTYN, W., STATE PAPERS and TURNER, S.

EDWARD VI., KING OF ENGLAND.

History of England from fall of Wolsey to defeat of Spanish Armada. By J. A. Froude. 12 vols. 1858–70. 8vo. **115 B**

See also GODWIN, F., LINGARD, REV. J., MARTYN, W., STATE PAPERS and TURNER, S.

EDWARDS, CHARLES JOHNSTON.

The law of Execution upon judgments and orders of the Chancery and Queen's Bench divisions of the high court of justice. 1888. 8vo. **12 E**

EDWARDS, EDWIN.

Jurisdiction of court of Admiralty of England. 1847. 8vo. **160 A**

EDWARDS, JOHN WILLIAM and W. F. HAMILTON.

The law of Husband and Wife. 1883. 8vo. **52 H**

EDWARDS, MORTON.

A Guide to modelling in clay and wax and for terra cotta. 1879. 12mo. **78 A**

EDWARDS, THOMAS.

Reports of cases in the high court of Admiralty. 1808–1812.
1 vol. 1812. 8vo. **8 A**

Reports of the leading decisions in the High Court of Admiralty in cases of vessels sailing under British licenses. 1812.
[Pamphlets, vol. 29.] **144 B**

EDWARDS, WILLIAM DOUGLAS.

Compendium of law of property in land. 1888. 8vo. **11 D**

EGERTON, LORD FRANCIS.

The Egerton papers. A collection of documents chiefly illustrative of times of Elizabeth and James I. from original
manuscripts property of Lord Francis Egerton. Edited by
J. P. Collier. [Camden Society, vol. 12.] 1840. 8vo. **85 A**

EGYPT.

Concordance des codes Égyptiens avec le code Napoléon.
Par J. Aziz. Première partie. Code civil. Alexandrie,
1886. 4to. **55 C**

The law of liquidation of Egypt. By Sir Sherston Baker.
2nd ed. 1884. [Pamphlets, vol. 39.] **144 C**

EJECTMENT.

The law of landlord and tenant, including the law of Ejectment. By J. H. Redman and G. E. Lyon. 3rd ed. 1886.
12mo. **10 E**

The law and practice in Ejectment. By W. R. Cole. 1857.
8vo. **9 H**

Principles and practice of action of Ejectment and resulting
action for mesne profits. By John Adams. 4th ed. 1846.
8vo. **166 C**

Action of Ejectment. By C. Runnington. 1781. 12mo. **166 C**

The law and modern practice of Ejectments. By A Gentleman of the Inner Temple. 1779. 8vo. **166 C**

The law and practice of Ejectment. [By Sir Jeffrey Gilbert.]
1734. 12mo. **166 C**

See also LANDLORD AND TENANT.

ELAND, SIR JOHN.

Revenge upon revenge, or an historical account of the tragical
practices of Sir John Eland of Eland upon the persons of
Sir Robert Beamont and his allies. 1708. See W. Bentley's
History of Hallifax, 1712, pp. 107–174. **94 A**

ELDON, JOHN, 1 EARL OF.

Eldoniana, a familiar poetical dialogue between a Reformer and a Chancery barrister in Westminster Hall. By Rev. J. W. Fea. 1826. [Jacob's Tracts, vol. 3.] **144 E**

Five minutes' examination of an article in the last number of the Edinburgh Review respecting the judicial character of Lord Eldon. By A Barrister. 1823. [Jacob's Tracts, vol. 1.] **144 E**

Indications respecting Lord Eldon, including history of the pending judges'-salary-raising measure. By Jeremy Bentham. 1825. [Jacob's Tracts, vol. 1.] **144 E**

Judgment of Lord Chancellor Eldon on the petition of Wellesley v. the Duke of Beaufort, delivered at Westminster Hall. 1827. [Jacob's Tracts, vol. 6.] **144 E**

The public and private life of Lord Chancellor Eldon with selections from his correspondence. By Horace Twiss. 2nd ed. 3 vols. 1844. 8vo. **79 G**

See also Campbell's Lord Chancellors, vol. 7. 1850. 8vo. **79 G**

ELECTION.

The law of Election. See Chitty's Index, vol. 3, 1886, pp. 2085–2116. **14 D**

See also Watson's Equity, vol. 1, 1886, pp. 176–185. **12 G**

ELECTION AGENT.

The powers, duties and liabilities of an Election Agent. By F. R. Parker. 1885. 8vo. **9 H**

ELECTION COMMITTEES.

Handbook of the practice of Election committees. By P. B. Sharkey. 2nd ed. 1866. 12mo. **166 D**

ELECTIONS, PARLIAMENTARY AND MUNICIPAL.

The law relating to parliamentary and municipal elections. By John Cunningham. 3rd ed. 1885. 8vo. **9 H**

Rogers on Elections. 14th ed. by J. C. Carter. 2 vols. 1885. 12mo. **52 F**

Guide to election law, and the law and practice of election petitions. By C. Leigh and H. D. Le Marchant. 4th ed. by G. Anderson and C. E. Ellis. 1885. 8vo. **166 C**

The parliamentary election acts for England and Wales. By J. M. Lely and W. D. I. Foulkes. 1885. 8vo. **166 D**

ELECTIONS, PARLIAMENTARY AND MUNICIPAL—*continued.*

The practice at parliamentary elections. By Daniel Ward. 1885. 12mo. **166 E**

Management of parliamentary and municipal elections. By M. W. Mattinson and S. C. Macaskie. 1884. 12mo. **166 D**

Law and practice of registration and elections. By E. W. Cox and S. G. Grady. 13th ed. by S. G .Grady. 1880. 12mo. **166 E**

The Franchise, a manual of registration and election law and practice. By William Leader. 1879. 12mo. **166 C**

The law and practice of election petitions. By Henry Hardcastle. 1874. 12mo. **166 C**

Ancient parliamentary elections. A history showing how parliaments were constituted in ancient times. By Homersham Cox. 1868. 8vo. **116 E**

The middle classes and the borough franchise. By H. W. Cole. 1866. [Pamphlets, vol. 35.] **144 C**

Electoral abuses considered, and a remedy suggested. By A Defeated Candidate. [1859.] [Pamphlets, vol. 10.] **144 A**

Joint possession of county and borough franchise. Report of cases of Capell and Burton appellants, and Overseers of Aston respondents, in Court of Common Pleas. By G. E. Denne. 2nd ed. 1850. [Pamphlets, vol. 7.] **144 A**

The register of parliamentary contested elections. By H. S. Smith. 1841. 12mo. **134 B**

The law of parliamentary elections from the issuing of the writ to the return of the members. By Basil Montagu and W. J. Neale. 1839. 12mo. **166 D**

Examen du système électoral Anglais, depuis l'acte de réforme, comparé au système électoral Français. Par A. Jollivet. Paris, 1835. 12mo. **166 D**

Laws concerning election of members of parliament with determinations of House of Commons thereon. By A Gentleman of the Inner Temple. 1768. 12mo. **166 C**

The same. New ed. 1774, and 6th ed. 1780. 12mo. **166 C**

Determinations of House of Commons, concerning elections. 1741. 12mo. **166 C**

See also ANSTEY, T. C., BELL, R., BRETHERTON, E., BUSHBY, K. J., CHAMBERS, J. D., CLERK, J., DAVIS, J. E., DELANE, W. F. A., DODD, C. E., GLANVILLE, J., HANDS, W., HARE, T., HEYWOOD, S., PICKERING, P. A., WARREN, S. and WORDSWORTH, C. F. F.

ELECTRIC LIGHTING.

Law relating to electric lighting. By G. S. Bower and W. Webb. 2nd ed. 1889. 12mo. **9 H**

Law of electric lighting. By H. Cunynghame. 1883. 8vo. **52 G**

The Electric lighting act 1882 and the rules issued under the act. By J. V. V. Fitzgerald. 1882. 8vo. **166 E**

See also F. Clifford's History of private bill legislation, vol. 1, 1885, pp. 231–247. **83 I**

ELECTRIC TELEGRAPH AND ELECTRICITY.

Treatise upon the law of telegraphs. By W. L. Scott and M. P. Jarnagin. Boston, 1868. 8vo. **60 B**

Authorship of the practical electric telegraph of Great Britain. By Rev. T. F. Cooke. 1868. 8vo. **78 C**

The electric telegraph, was it invented by Professor Wheatstone? By W. F. Cooke. 2 vols. 1857–56. 8vo. **78 C**

Plan and description of the original electro-magnetic telegraph. By Wm. Alexander. 1851. 8vo. **78 C**

A Treatise upon artificial electricity. Translated from the Italian of Giambatista Beccaria. 1776. 4to. **78 G**

ELEGIT.

Procedure on Elegit and Equitable Execution with forms. By F. Stone. 1882. 12mo. **12 F**

See also EXECUTION.

ELIZABETH, QUEEN OF ENGLAND.

Ancient biographical poems on Queen Elizabeth and others. Edited by J. P. Collier. [Camden Society, vol. 61.] 1855. 8vo. **85 B**

Annales rerum Anglicarum et Hibernicarum regnante Elizabetha. Autore Guil. Camdeno. Lug. Batavorum, 1625. 12mo. **115 D**

Annals of the first four years of the reign of Queen Elizabeth. By Sir John Hayward. Edited by John Bruce. [Camden Society, vol. 7.] 1840. 8vo. **85 A**

Catalogue of exhibition of Armada and Elizabethan relics, held in theatre royal Drury Lane, London. By W. H. K. Wright. Plymouth, 1888. 8vo. **78 C**

Contemporary notes of occurrences, written by John Stowe in the reign of Queen Elizabeth. [Camden Society, n.s. vol. 28.] 1880. 8vo. **85 D**

ELIZABETH, QUEEN OF ENGLAND—*continued.*

Elizabethan Oxford. Reprints of rare tracts. Edited by Charles Plummer. [Oxford Historical Society, vol. 8.] Oxford, 1887. 8vo. **85 F**

The grand reception and entertainment of Queen Elizabeth at Oxford in 1592. [Oxford Historical Society, vol. 8.] Oxford, 1887. 8vo. **85 F**

Historical collections, or an exact account of the proceedings of the four last parliaments of Q. Elizabeth. By Heywood Townshend. 1680. folio. **115 H**

Household expenses of the Princess Elizabeth during her residence at Hatfield, October 1, 1551, to September 30, 1552. Edited by Viscount Strangford. [Camden Society, vol. 55.] 1853. 8vo. **85 B**

Injunctions given by the Queenes Majestie concerning both the clergie and laity of this realme 1559, printed 1641. [Law Tracts and Arguments, 1641.] **144 F**

Letters of Queen Elizabeth and King James VI. of Scotland. Edited by John Bruce. [Camden Society, vol. 46.] 1849. 8vo. **85 B**

The progresses and public processions of Queen Elizabeth. By John Nichols. New ed. 3 vols. 1823. 4to. **114 E**

Sir F. Walsingham's Letter to Monsieur Critoy concerning the Queen's proceedings against both Papists and Puritans. n.d. 8vo. [Tracts, 1688-9.] **118 E**

See also CHAMBERLAIN, J., EGERTON, LORD F., FROUDE, J. A., LINGARD, REV. J., MARY QUEEN OF SCOTS, STATE PAPERS and TURNER, S.

ELLIS, ARTHUR LEE.

Trustees' guide to Investments. 1887, and 2nd ed. 1889. 12mo. **176 F**

The same. 3rd ed. 1889. 12mo. **11 I**

ELLIS, ARTHUR MACKAY.

A Guide to the house tax acts. 1885. 8vo. **10 B**

A Guide to the income tax acts. 1885. 12mo. **168 G**

The same. 2nd ed. 1886. 12mo. **10 C**

ELLIS, CHARLES.

Law of fire & life insurance & annuities. 1832. 8vo. **169 A**

The same. 2nd ed. 1846. 8vo. **52 I**

ELLIS, Charles Thomas.
Practical remarks and precedents of proceedings in parliament on bills. 1802, and 2nd ed. 1810. 8vo.   **173 B**

[ELLIS, George Beloe.]
Counsel's Retainers. By E. B. G. [G. B. Ellis.] 1888. 12mo.   **9 F**

ELLIS, Sir Henry.
A General introduction to Domesday book with indexes of the tenants in chief and under tenants at the time of the survey. 2 vols. 1833. 8vo.   **97 I**

Libri censualis vocati Domesday-Book Indices. Accessit dissertatio generalis de ratione hujusce libri. 1816. folio. **98 D**

Libri censualis vocati Domesday-Book Additamenta ex codic. antiquiss. Exon' Domesday. Inquisitio Eliensis. Liber Winton'. Boldon Book. 1816. folio.   **98 D**

ELLIS, Thomas Flower and C. BLACKBURN.
Reports of cases in the Courts of Queen's Bench and Exchequer Chamber 1852–1858. 8 vols. 1853–59. 8vo.   **5 A**

ELLIS, T. F., C. BLACKBURN and F. ELLIS.
Reports of cases in the Courts of Queen's Bench and Exchequer Chamber 1858. 1 vol. 1860. 8vo.   **5 B**

ELLIS, Thomas Flower and Francis ELLIS.
Reports of cases in the Courts of Queen's Bench and Exchequer Chamber 1858–1861. 3 vols. 1863–67. 8vo.   **5 B**

ELLWOOD, Thomas.
The history of the life of Thomas Ellwood written by himself. [Autobiography, vol. 20.] 1827. 12mo.   **79 A**

ELMER, Joseph.
The practice in Lunacy under commissions and inquisitions. New ed. 1857. 12mo.   **172 B**
The same. 4th ed. 1864, and 5th ed. 1872. 12mo.   **172 B**
The same. 6th ed. 1877. 12mo.   **10 G**

ELMES, James.
A Practical treatise on ecclesiastical and civil Dilapidations. 3rd ed. 1829. 8vo.   **165 G**
A Topographical dictionary of London and its environs. 1831. 8vo.   **92 B**

ELOCUTION AND ELOQUENCE.

Elocution, voice and gesture illustrated by annotated pieces. By Rupert Garry. 1888. 12mo.   **78 B**

Reflections on the decline of Eloquence in England. By · Henry Somner. 1833. [Pamphlets, vol. 5.]   **144 A**

ELPHINSTONE, Howard Warburton.

A Practical introduction to Conveyancing. 2nd ed. 1881. 8vo.   **163 G**

The same. 3rd ed. 1884. 8vo.   **13 A**

On searches, containing a concise treatise on the law of judgments . . . as affecting land. By H. W. Elphinstone and J.W. Clark. 1887. With appendix entitled, The land charges registration and searches act 1888. 1889. 8vo.   **13 H**

Rules for the interpretation of deeds. By H. W. Elphinstone, R. F. Norton and J. W. Clark. 1885. 8vo.   **9 G**

ELSTOB, Elizabeth.

The rudiments of grammar for the English-Saxon tongue, first given in English : with an Apology for the study of Northern antiquities. 1715. 8vo.   **123 B**

ELSYNGE, Henry.

The ancient method and manner of holding parliaments in England. 3rd ed. 1675. 12mo.   **48 D**

The same. 4th ed. 1679, and new ed. 1768. 12mo.   **48 D**

Notes of the debates in the House of Lords. 1621. Edited by S. R. Gardiner. [Camden Society, vol. 103.] 1870. 8vo.   **85 C**

Notes of the debates in the House of Lords. 1624 and 1626. Edited by S. R. Gardiner. [Camden Society, n.s. vol. 24.] 1879. 8vo.   **85 D**

ELTON, Charles Isaac.

Custom and Tenant-right. 1882. 12mo.   **13 B**

Law of copyholds and customary tenures. 1874. 12mo.   **13 B**

The tenures of Kent. 1867. 8vo.   **10 B**

Treatise on commons and waste lands. 1868. 12mo.   **52 B**

ELWES, Dudley George Cary.

Bedford and its neighbourhood. Bedford, 1881. 8vo.   **86 B**

History of the castles, mansions and manors of Western Sussex. 3 parts in 1 vol. 1876–79. folio.   **93 D**

ELY, Cambridgeshire.

Historical account of Wisbech and of the origin of the royal franchise of the Isle of Ely. By W. Watson. Wisbech, 1827. 8vo. **86 D**

The history and antiquities of the conventual and cathedral church of Ely. By James Bentham, and Supplement by Wm. Stevenson. 2 vols. 1771–1817. 4to. **86 G**

EMDEN, Alfred.

A Digest of all reported cases not contained in the 'Law Reports' for the year 1883. 1884. 8vo. **14 F**

The Complete annual digest of every reported case 1883–1889. 7 vols. 1884–90. 8vo. **14 F**

The law relating to building, building leases and building contracts. 1882. 8vo. **161 A**

The same. 2nd ed. 1885. 8vo. **9 B**

The practice in winding-up companies. 1883. 8vo. **169 E**

The same. 2nd ed. 1888. 8vo. **52 C**

The same. 3rd ed. 1889. 8vo. **9 D**

A Complete collection of practice statutes, orders and rules from 1275 to 1885. By A. Emden and E. R. Pearce-Edgcumbe. 1885. 8vo. **176 B**

The same. 2nd ed. 1886. 8vo. **71 I**

EMERIGON, Balthazard Marie.

Traité des assurances et des contrats à la grosse. 2 vols. Marseille, 1783. 4to. **58 G**

The same. Translated by S. Meredith. 1850. 8vo. **169 B**

EMERSON, Thomas.

A Concise treatise on the courts of law of the City of London. 1794. 8vo. **91 E**

EMERTON, Wolseley Partridge.

Abridgment of Adam Smith's Inquiry into the nature and causes of the wealth of nations. Oxford, 1881. 12mo. **78 D**

EMIGRATION.

Emigration to the British colonies of North America, Australia, New Zealand, Cape of Good Hope and Natal, showing their extent, products, resources and the inducements they each offer to emigrants. By John Bate. 1862. [Pamphlets, vol. 18.] **144 B**

EMIGRATION—*continued*.

The national importance of Emigration. By C. H. Bagot.
1863. [Pamphlets, vol. 18.]   **144 B**

Remarks on Emigration with a draft of a bill. By N. W.
Senior. 1831. 8vo.   **78 D**

Report of a public meeting of the National colonial emigration society. 1863. [Pamphlets, vol. 18.]   **144 B**

Steam communication with the Cape of Good Hope, Australia
and New Zealand suggested as the means of promoting
emigration to those colonies. By Frederick Jerningham.
1848. [Pamphlets, vol. 6.]   **144 A**

See also GOURLAY, R.

EMPIRICKS.

An Historical account of the proceedings of the royal college
of physicians of London against Empiricks. By Charles
Goodall. 1684. 8vo.   **91 B**

EMPLOYERS.

Employers and employed. By W. C. Spens and R. T.
Younger. 1887. 8vo.   **9 H**

The duty and liability of Employers. By W. H. Roberts and
G. Wallace. 3rd ed. 1885. 8vo.   **9 H**

The labour laws. By J. E. Davis. 1875. 8vo.   **170 C**

See also MASTER and SERVANT.   **10 H**

ENCYCLOPÆDIAS.

Chambers's Encyclopædia, a dictionary of universal knowledge.
New ed. 5 vols. 1888–90. 8vo. [In progress.]   **122 D**

The Cyclopædia. By A. Rees. 45 vols. 1819. 4to.   **147 C–F**

Cyclopædia, or an universal dictionary of arts and sciences.
By E. Chambers. With Supplement by A. Rees. 5 vols.
1791. folio.   **158 F**

Dictionnaire universel d'histoire et de géographie. Par M.
N. Bouillet. 20me éd. Paris, 1864. 8vo.   **122 C**

Dictionnaire universel François et Latin, vulgairement appelé
Dictionnaire de Trévoux. Nouvelle éd. 8 vols. Paris,
1776. folio.   **122 G**

Encyclopædia Britannica. 8th ed. with Index. 22 vols.
Edinburgh, 1853–60. 4to.   **147 A B**

The same. 9th ed. with Index. 25 vols. Edinburgh,
1875–89. 4to.   **122 E–G**

Enquire within upon everything. [By Robert Kemp Philp.]
43rd ed. 1871. 8vo.   **146 E**

ENCYCLOPÆDIAS—*continued.*

The great historical, geographical and poetical dictionary, collected from the best historians. 1694. folio. **122 H**

Haydn's Dictionary of Dates. 19th ed. 1889. 8vo. **134 I**

Hazell's Annual for 1890 : a cyclopædic record of men and topics of the day. Edited by E. D. Price. 1890. 12mo. **Hall**

The London Encyclopædia. or universal dictionary of science, art, literature and practical mechanics. 22 vols. 1836. 8vo. **122 A B**

The new American Cyclopædia, a popular dictionary of general knowledge. By G. Ripley and C. A. Dana. 16 vols. New York, 1860–63. 8vo. **122 C D**

Treasury of Knowledge, and library of reference. By Samuel Maunder. New ed. by B. B. Woodward. 1859 12mo. **78 A**

ENDERBIE, PERCY.

Cambria triumphans : or, Brittain in its perfect lustre, shewing the origin and antiquity of that illustrious nation . . . with the coats of arms of the nobility. 1661. folio. **95 H**

ENFIELD, MIDDLESEX.

The history and antiquities of Enfield. By Wm. Robinson. 2 vols. in 1. 1823. 8vo. **89 D**

ENFIELD, WILLIAM.

Essay towards history of Liverpool. 1774 folio. **89 G**

ENGLAND, ANTIQUITIES AND TOPOGRAPHY OF.

Bacon's New large scale ordnance atlas of the British Isles with plans of towns. 1883. 4to. **Hall**

Bibliographical account of the works relating to English topography. By W. Upcott. 4 vols. 1818. 8vo. **82 I**

The book of British topography. By J. P. Anderson. 1881. 8vo. **82 H**

The border antiquities of England and Scotland. [By Sir Walter Scott.] 2 vols. 1814. 4to. **95 G**

Britannia Baconica, or the natural rarities of England, Scotland and Wales. By J. Childrey. 1661. 12mo. **86 A**

Britannia, or a chorographical description of England, Scotland and Ireland. By William Camden. Enlarged by Richard Gough. 3 vols. 1789. folio. **84 H**

Britannia, or a geographical description of the Kingdoms of

ENGLAND, ANTIQUITIES AND TOPOGRAPHY OF—*continued.*

England, Scotland and Ireland. By Richard Blome. 1673. folio.   **86 G**

British curiosities in art and nature, an account of rarities both ancient and modern. 2nd ed. 1828. 12mo.   **86 A**

British Topography. By R. Gough. 2 vols. 1780. 4to.   **82 I**

Cambria triumphans : or Brittain in its perfect lustre. By Percy Enderbie. 1661. folio.   **95 H**

Churton's English county calendar, containing a concise description of each county. 1847. 8vo.   **86 A**

Collectanea Curiosa ; or miscellaneous tracts relating to the history and antiquities of England and Ireland, the Universities of Oxford and Cambridge, and a variety of other subjects. By J. Gutch. 2 vols. Oxford, 1781. 8vo. **84 C**

Description of the direct and cross roads in England and Wales. By D. Paterson. 18th ed. 1829. 8vo.   **86 A**

The English counties delineated, or a description of England. By T. Moule. 2 vols. 1837. 4to.   **84 F**

Essays upon several subjects concerning British antiquities. By H. Home. 3rd ed. Edinburgh, 1763. 12mo.   **84 A**

Historical antiquities in two books, the first treating in general of Great Britain and Ireland. By Sir Peter Leycester. 1673. 4to.   **87 G**

The history of North Wales, and a review of the history of Britain from Roman period to Saxon heptarchy. By William Cathrall. 2 vols. Manchester, 1828. 4to. **94 E**

Index villaris, or an alphabetical table of all the cities, market towns, parishes, villages and private seats in England and Wales. By John Adams. 1680. folio.   **85 I**

The itinerary of John Leland the antiquary. 2nd ed. 9 vols. in 5. Oxford, 1745. 8vo.   **86 A**

Joannis Lelandi antiquarii, de rebus Britannicis, Collectanea, ex autographis descripsit ediditque Tho. Hearnius. 5 vols. Oxonii, 1715. 8vo.   **86 A**

Notitia Parliamentaria, or an history of the counties, cities and boroughs in England and Wales. By Browne Willis. vol. I. 1715. 8vo.   **84 B**

Observations on Monsieur de Sorbier's Voyage into England. By Thomas Sprat. 1665. 12mo.   **118 A**

Ordnance Survey of England and Wales ; one inch scale. 110 maps. 2 vols. 1805–66. folio.

New Ordnance Survey of England and Wales ; one inch scale. 179 maps. 1865–89. folio.

ENGLAND, ANTIQUITIES AND TOPOGRAPHY OF—*continued.*
A Political survey of Britain. By John Campbell. 2 vols.
1774. 4to. **115 H**
A Relation or rather a true account of the Island of England
about the year 1500. Translated from the Italian by C. A.
Sneyd. [Camden Society, vol. 37.] 1847. 8vo. **85 A**
A Statistical account of the British empire. By J. R.
McCulloch. 2 vols. 1837. 8vo. **84 G**
Stockdale's Parliamentary guide, or members' and electors'
complete companion, being an historical account of the
several cities, counties and boroughs in Great Britain.
1784. 8vo. **84 B**
The Theatre of the empire of Great Britaine. By John Speed.
New ed. 1676. folio. **85 I**
A Topographical dictionary of England. By Nicholas Carlisle.
2 vols. 1808. 4to. **84 F**
Topographical dictionary of England, with historical descrip-
tions. By S. Lewis. 5 vols. 1831. 4to. **84 F**
Tours through the whole island of Great Britain. By Rev.
C. Cruttwell. 6 vols. 1806. 8vo. **86 A**
The travels through England of Dr. Richard Pococke during
1750, 1751 and later years. Edited by J. J. Cartwright.
[Camden Society, n.s. vols. 42 & 44.] 2 vols. 1888–89.
8vo. **85 E**
Villare Anglicum : or a view of the townes of England. Col-
lected by the appointment of Sir Henry Spelman. 1656.
8vo. **86 A**
See ABBEYS, ANTIQUITIES, ATLASES and BOROUGHS.

ENGLAND, HISTORY OF.
Angliæ Notitia ; or the present state of England, 1669–1755.
By E. and J. Chamberlayne. 36 vols. 1669–1755. 8vo.
143 A–C
Annales of England. Containing the reignes of Henry the
Eight, Edward the Sixt, Queene Mary. By Francis Godwyn.
1630. 4to. **114 F**
Bishop Burnet's History of his own time [1660–1713]. 4 vols.
1818. 8vo. **115 F**
British history of Geoffrey of Monmouth in twelve books.
Translated from the Latin by Aaron Thompson. New ed.
by J. A. Giles. 1842. 8vo. **115 A**
Chronicle of the kings of England. A.C. 55–A.D. 1660. By
Sir Richard Baker. 8th ed. 1684. folio, **114 G**

ENGLAND, HISTORY OF—*continued.*

Chronicle or history of England [1189-1558]. By Richard
Grafton. 2 vols. 1809. 4to.   **114 G**

Chronicles of England, France, Spain and the adjoining
countries, 1326–1399. By Sir John Froissart. Translated
by Thomas Johnes. 2 vols. 1857. 8vo.   **115 A**

Chronicles of England, Ireland and Scotland, first collected
by R. Holinshed, W. Harrison, and others, continued to the
year 1586 by John Hooker, alias Vowell, and others.
3 vols. in 2. 1586-87. folio.   **114 H**

Classical and pre-historic influences upon British history. By
S. Bannister. 2nd ed. 1871. [Pamphlets, vol. 33.]   **144 C**

Collection of scarce and valuable tracts, selected from public
and private libraries, particularly that of Lord Somers.
2nd ed. by Walter Scott. 13 vols. 1809-15. 4to.   **113 G**

Conference about the next succession to crown of England.
[By Robert Parsons.] 1681. 12mo.   **48 D**

[The Cronycle of Englonde with the fruyt of tymes. The
descrypcyon of Englonde, Walys, Scotlond and Irelonde.]
Enprynted by Julyan Notary. 1515. Bound with Higden's
Polychronicon, 1527. folio.   ·   **114 G**

England defenceless since the declaration of Paris. Pamphlets
by David Urquhart. 1860-74. [Urquhart's Pamphlets,
vol. 2, part 1.]   **143 G**

The English, Scotch and Irish historical libraries, giving a
short view and character of most of our historians, with an
account of our records, &c. By Right Rev. W. Nicolson.
3rd ed. 1736. folio.   **115 I**

The half century, its history, political and social. By W.
Wilks. 1852. 12mo.   **116 E**

A Help to English history. By Peter Heylyn. Now first
published by Paul Wright. 1773. 8vo.   **113 A**

Historia Majoris Britanniæ. Per Joannem Majorem. Editio
nova. Edimburgi, 1740. 4to.   **115 H**

Historiæ Anglicanæ Scriptores X. By Roger Twysden.
2 vols. 1652. folio.   **114 H**

Historical notes, 1509-1714. By F. S. Thomas. 2 vols.
1856. 8vo.   **99 A**

Historical questions exhibited in the Morning Chronicle in
January 1818 ; enlarged, corrected and improved. 1818.
[Jacob's Tracts, vol. 1.]   **144 E**

Historical view of the English government from settlement
of Saxons in Britain to accession of the House of Stewart.
By John Millar. 2nd ed. 1790. 4to.   **114 F**

ENGLAND, HISTORY OF—*continued.*

The historie and lives of twentie Kings of England (William the First to Henry the Eighth). By William Martyn. 1615. 4to. **114 E**

History from marble, compiled in the reign of Charles II. By T. Dingley. Edited by J. G. Nichols. [Camden Society, vols. 94 and 97.] 2 vols. 1867–68. 8vo. **85 C**

History made easy : an epitome of English History. By John Gibson. 1882. 8vo. **116 E**

History of England A.C. 55 to A.D. 1688. By David Hume. New ed. 6 vols. 1830. 8vo. **115 F**

History of England 1713–1783. By Lord Mahon. 4th ed. 7 vols. 1853–54. 8vo. **115 G**

History of England A.C. 55 to A.D. 1688. By Rev. John Lingard. 4th ed. 13 vols. 1837–38. 12mo. **115 D**

History of England 1688–1760. By T. G. Smollett. New ed. 4 vols. 1830. 8vo. **115 F**

History of England during the Middle Ages. By Sharon Turner. 2nd ed. 5 vols. 1825. 8vo. **115 E**

History of England from the accession of James the Second. By Lord Macaulay. 5 vols. 1860–61. 8vo. **115 G**

History of England from fall of Wolsey to death of Elizabeth. By J. A. Froude. 12 vols. 1858–70. 8vo. **115 B**

History of England in 1688. By Rapin de Thoyras. Translated by N. Tindal. 2nd ed. 2 vols. 1732–33. folio. **115 I**

History of England in the eighteenth century. By W. E. H. Lecky. 6 vols. 1883–87. 8vo. **116 G**

History of England principally in the seventeenth century. By Leopold Von Ranke. Edited by C. W. Boase and G. W. Kitchin. 6 vols. Oxford, 1875. 8vo. **115 F**

History of Normandy and of England. By Sir Francis Palgrave. 4 vols. 1851–64. 8vo. **115 A**

History of our own times, 1837–1880. By Justin McCarthy. 4 vols. 1881. 8vo. **116 G**

History of the English people, 449–1815. By J. R. Green. 4 vols. 1885–86. 8vo. **115 C**

History of the Norman conquest of England. By E. A. Freeman. 6 vols. 1877–79. 8vo. **115 A B**

History of the reigns of Henry VIII., Edward VI., Mary and Elizabeth. By Sharon Turner. 2nd ed. 4 vols. 1827–29. 8vo. **115 E**

The history of the Union between England and Scotland. By Daniel De Foe. 1786. 4to. **113 F**

ENGLAND, HISTORY OF—*continued.*

An Introduction to the old English history. By Robert
Brady. 1684. folio.   115 H

Jani Anglorum facies altera and England's Epinomis. See
J. Selden's Works, vol. 2, 1683, pp. 969–1032.   115 I

Memoirs of Great Britain and Ireland. By Sir John
Dalrymple. 2nd ed. 2 vols. 1771–73. 4to.   114 F

The memoirs of Sir James Melvil, containing an impartial
account of the most remarkable affairs of state, 1558–1625.
By George Scott. 1683. folio.   114 G

Monstrelet's Chronicles of England, France, Spain and the
adjoining countries. Translated by Thomas Johnes. 2 vols.
1840. 8vo.   115 A

The new state of England. By Guy Meige. 1691, 3rd ed.
1699, 4th ed. 1702. 3 vols. 1699–1702. 12mo.   143 C

The present state of Great Britain and Ireland. By Guy
Meige. 1707, 1711, 1716, 1718, 1723, 1728, 1731, 1738,
1742, 1745, 1748. 11 vols. 1707–48. 12mo.   143 C D

Original papers containing the secret history of Great Britain,
1660–1714. By James Macpherson. 2nd ed. 2 vols.
1776. 4to.   114 F

The political state of Great Britain from 1712 to 1732. By
Abel Boyer. 38 vols. 1714–32. 8vo.   143 D-F

Reports of the commissioners on historical manuscripts with
appendixes and indexes. 19 vols. 1870–90. folio and
8vo.   98 F & 99 F

A Representation of the threatening dangers impending over
Protestants in Great Britain before the coming of the Prince
of Orange. [By Robert Ferguson.] 1689. [Tracts, 1688–
89.]   118 E

Revolutions in English history. By Rev. Robert Vaughan.
3 vols. 1859–63. 8vo.   115 G

Synopsis of English history from the earliest times to 1870.
By Stacey Grimaldi. 2nd ed. 1871. 12mo.   116 E

Treasury of history. By S. Maunder. 1858. 12mo.   116 D

Triumphant democracy, or fifty years' march of the republic.
By A. Carnegie. 1886. 12mo.   78 B

See ANGLO-SAXON HISTORY, CHRONOLOGY, CONSTITU-
TIONAL HISTORY, GREAT BRITAIN AND IRELAND,
RECORD COMMISSION, RECORDS and STATE PAPERS.

See also the names of all the Sovereigns.

ENGLAND, LANGUAGE OF.

Critical pronouncing dictionary of the English language. By
John Walker. New ed. by T. Young. 1863. 8vo. **123 B**

The Derbyshire miner's glossary. By James Mander. Bakewell, 1824. 8vo. **87 B**

Dictionary of the English language. By Noah Webster.
2 vols. 1864. 4to. **123 D**

Dictionary of the English language. By R. G. Latham.
2 vols. in 4 vols. 1866–70. 4to. **123 D**

Dictionary of the English language. By Samuel Johnson.
Corrected by Rev. J. H. Todd. 2nd ed. 3 vols. 1827.
4to. **123 D**

Etymological dictionary of the English language. By Rev.
W. W. Skeat. 2nd ed. Oxford, 1884. 4to. **123 E**

The Globe dictionary. 1873. 8vo. **123 B**

Glossary of Anglo-Norman and Gascon words. See Black
book of the Admiralty, vol. 4, 1876, pp. 147–197. **102 D**

Glossary of Anglo-Norman, Saxon and early English words.
See Munimenta Gildhalliæ Londoniensis, vol. 2, part 2,
1860, pp. 691–778, and vol. 3, 1862, pp. 287–372. **101 C**

Glossary of Lancashire words and phrases. See Tim Bobbin's
Works, 1819, pp. 67–96. **118 B**

Glossary of obscure or obsolete words and phrases. See J.
Capgrave's Chronicle of England, 1858, pp. 375–413. **101 A**

Glossary of obsolete English words. See Political poems and
songs, vol. 2, 1861, pp. 301–341. **101 C**

Glossary of old English words. See Chronicle of Robert of
Gloucester, vol. 2, 1887, pp. 881–982. **102 I**

Glossary of old English words. See Pecock's Repressor,
vol. 2, 1860, pp. 627–683. **101 D**

Glossary of old English words. See Polychronicon Ranulphi
Higden, vol. 9, 1886, pp. 1–176. **102 B**

Glossary to explain the original, the acceptation and obsolete-
ness of words and phrases. See Kennett's Parochial Antiquities, vol. 2, 1818, 4to. **92 F**

Imperial dictionary of the English language. By John
Ogilvie. New ed. by Charles Annandale. 4 vols. 1882–
83. 4to. **123 E**

New dictionary of the English language combining explanation with etymology. By Charles Richardson. New ed.
2 vols. 1858. 4to. **123 E**

New English dictionary on historical principles. Edited by
J. A. H. Murray. vol. 1. Oxford, 1888. 4to. [In progress.] **123 F**

ENGLAND, LANGUAGE OF—*continued.*

The new world of words, or a general English dictionary. By Edward Phillips. 4th ed. 1678. folio. **123 G**

Nuttall's Standard Dictionary of the English Language. New ed. by Rev. James Wood. 1886. 8vo. **Hall**

A Short introduction to English grammar with critical notes. [By Robert Lowth.] New ed. 1795. 12mo. **255 H**

See also ANGLO-SAXON LANGUAGE, ARCHAIC AND PROVINCIAL WORDS and MINSHEU, J.

ENGLAND, LAW AND GOVERNMENT OF.

New commentaries on the laws of England. By H. J. Stephen. 11th ed. by A. Brown. 4 vols. 1890. 8vo. **10 E**

Another copy. 4 vols. 1890. 8vo. **64 C**

Commentaries on the present laws of England. By Thomas Brett. 2 vols. 1890. 8vo. **64 C**

The Cabinet Lawyer : a popular digest of the laws of England. By J. W. [John Wade.] 25th ed. 1886. 12mo. **10 E**

Henrici De Bracton, De legibus et consuetudinibus Angliæ, Libri quinque. Edited by Sir Travers Twiss. 6 vols. 1878–83. 8vo. **102 F G**

History of modern English law. By Sir R. K. Wilson. 1875. 12mo. **170 F**

A Code of English law (principles and practice). By F. R. Syms. 1870. 12mo. **170 F**

History of English law from time of the Saxons to end of reign of Elizabeth. By John Reeves. New ed. by W. F. Finlason. 3 vols. 1869. 8vo. **170 E**

Commentaries on the laws of England. By H. Broome and E. A. Hadley. 4 vols. 1869. 8vo. **167 A**

The historical method of studying English law. By M. H. Cookson. 1866. [Pamphlets, vol. 35.] **144 C**

Britton. The French text carefully revised with an English translation and notes. By F. M. Nichols. 2 vols. Oxford, 1865. 8vo. **167 A**

A Compendium of English and Scotch law. By James Paterson. Edinburgh, 1860. 8vo. **55 F**

Certaine considerations upon the government of England. By Sir Roger Twysden. Edited by J. M. Kemble. [Camden Society, vol. 45.] 1849. 8vo. **85 B**

Ancient laws and institutes of England. [Edited by B. Thorpe.] 1840. folio. **99 B**

An introductory lecture upon the study of English law de-

ENGLAND, LAW AND GOVERNMENT OF—*continued.*
livered in the University of London. By Andrew Amos.
1829. [Jacob's Tracts, vol. 7.] **144 E**

A Digest of the laws of England. By Sir John Comyns.
5th ed. 8 vols. 1822. 8vo. **14 B C**

A Translation of Glanville with notes. By John Beames.
1812. 8vo. **167 A**

The grounds and maxims and an analysis of the English laws.
By W. Noy. 6th ed. by C. Barton. 1794. 12mo. **49 F**

An Institute of the laws of England, or the laws of England
in their natural order according to common use. By Thomas
Wood. 10th ed. 1772. folio. **155 D**

An Analysis of the Laws of England. See Blackstone's Law
Tracts, 3rd ed. 1771, pp. 1–130. **144 G**

A Proposal for rendering the laws of England clear and
certain. By T. Cunningham. 2nd ed. 1770. folio. **74 C**

An Introduction to the knowledge of the laws and constitution
of England. By A Gentleman of the Middle Temple.
1763. 12mo. **170 F**

Doctor and Student : or dialogues between a doctor of
divinity, and a student in the laws of England. By C. St.
German. 16th ed., to which are now restored Thirteen
chapters on the power and jurisdiction of the parliament.
1761. 12mo. **48 D**

The grounds and rudiments of law and equity, alphabetically
digested. By A Gentleman of the Middle Temple. 1749,
and 2nd ed. 1751. folio. **155 C**

Animadversions upon the present laws of England. 1750.
8vo. **83 I**

Leges Marchiarum or Border laws. By Most Rev. William
Nicolson. 1747. 8vo. **95 C**

An Historical and political discourse of the laws and government of England. Collected from manuscript notes of
J. Selden, by N. Bacon. 4th ed. 1739. folio. **78 H**

Institutio legalis, or an introduction to study and practice of
laws of England. By W. Bohun. 3rd ed. 1724. 12mo. **162 F**

Les termes de la ley : or certain difficult and obscure words
and termes of the laws of this realm, now in use, expounded
and explained. [By W. Rastal.] 1721. 12mo. **48 D**

Decus et Tutamen, or a prospect of the laws of England. By
John Brydall. 1679. 12mo. **48 D**

Origines Juridiciales, or historical memorials of the English
laws, courts of justice . . . also A Chronologie of the lord

ENGLAND, LAW AND GOVERNMENT OF—*continued.*

chancelors . . . and serjeants at law. By Sir W. Dugdale. 2nd ed. 1671. folio.　　　　　　　　　　**125 H**

De Republica Anglorum. The maner of gouernement of the realme of England. By Sir T. Smyth. 1584. 12mo.　**48 D**

Institutions, or princypal groundes of the lawes and statutes of Englande. 1556. 12mo.　　　　　　　　　**118 A**

See CODES, CONSTITUTIONAL HISTORY and FEUDAL LAW.

See also BLACKSTONE, SIR W., CARE, H., CURSON, H., FLETA, FORTESCUE, SIR J., FRANCILLON, J., FULBECKE, W., HARGRAVE, F., PETERSDORFF, C., SARGENT, R., SPELMAN, SIR H., SPENCE, G., WOODDESON, R. and WYNNE, E.

ENGLAND, LITERATURE OF.

A Bird's-eye view of English literature from the seventh century to the present time. By H. Grey 1884. 8vo.　**83 A**

See also ANONYMS, BIBLIOGRAPHY CATALOGUES and LIBRARIES.

ENGLAND, PUBLIC DEPARTMENTS OF.

Notes of materials for the history of public departments. By F. S. Thomas. 1846. folio.　　　　　　　　**99 E**

ENGLAND, ROYAL FAMILIES OF.

A Catalogue and succession of the kings, princes, dukes &c. of England since the Norman conquest. By Ralph Brooke. 2nd ed. 1622. folio.　　　　　　　　　**127 J**

The catalogue of honor, or tresury of true nobility peculiar and proper to the Isle of Great Britaine. By Thomas Milles. 1610. folio.　　　　　　　　　　　**126 I**

A Collection of all the wills now known to be extant of the kings and queens of England, from William I. to Henry VII. exclusive. By John Nichols. 1780. 4to.　**114 D**

A Genealogy of the kings of England and their issue from William the Conqueror to the present time. By Richard Mitchell. 1817. 12mo.　　　　　　　　　**125 A**

General history of House of Guelph to accession of George I. By A. Halliday. 1821. 4to.　　　　　　　**114 G**

The glory of regality ; an historical treatise of the anointing and crowning of the kings and queens of England. By Arthur Taylor. 1820. 8vo.　　　　　　　**116 B**

The history of the Royal family, or a succinct account of the marriages and issue of all the kings and queens of England.

ENGLAND, ROYAL FAMILIES OF—*continued.*

[An anonymous abridgment of F. Sandford's Genealogical history, 1707.] 1741. 12mo. **115 D**

Le Livere de Reis de Brittanie, e Le Livere de Reis de Engletere. Edited by John Glover. 1865. 8vo. **102 B**

The royal families of England anterior to the House of Brunswick. See T. C. Banks's Dormant and extinct peerage, vol. 1, pp. 1–145. **124 F**

The succession to the English crown, a historical sketch. By Alfred Bailey. 1879. 8vo. **116 B**

ENGLISH, HENRY SCALE.

Laws of Pews or seats in churches. 1826. 8vo. **173 E**

ENGRAVERS AND ENGRAVINGS.

Dictionary of painters and engravers, biographical and critical. By Michael Bryan. New ed. by R. E. Graves and W. Armstrong. 2 vols. 1886–89. 8vo. **79 H**

A Selection from collection of engravings belonging to and exhibited by Alfred Morrison at opening of new library and museum of corporation of London. 1872. 8vo. **82 B**

ENLARGEMENT OF LONG TERMS.

Dissertation on and precedents of Enlargement of Long Terms. See Bythewood and Jarman's Conveyancing, 4th ed. vol. 2, 1885, pp. 912–923. **13 D**

ENTRIES.

Book of special Entries of declarations, pleadings, issues, verdicts, judgments and judicial process in such actions as are now in use. By Sir Thomas Robinson. 1684. folio.

A Book of Entries. By Edward Coke. 2nd ed. 1671. folio. **48 I**

A Collection of Entries of declarations, barres, replications, rejoynders, issues, verdicts, judgments, executions, proces, continuances, essoynes and divers other matters. By Wm. Rastell. 1670. folio.

Intrationum Liber, omnibus legum Angliæ studiosis apprime necessarius. H. Smythe. 1546. folio.

See also ASTON, R., BROWN, W., BROWNLOW, R., CLIFT, H., HANSARD, J., LEVINZ, SIR C., LILLY, J., MALLORY, J., VIDIAN, A. and WINCH, SIR H.

EPIGRAMS.

The Anglo-Latin satirical poets and epigrammatists of the twelfth century. Edited by T. Wright. 2 vols. 1872. 8vo. **102 E**

Anytæ Tegeatidis Epigrammata. 1734. 4to. **47 G**

Marci Valerii Martialis Epigrammata ex editione Bipontina cum notis et interpretatione in usum Delphini. 2 vols. 1823–22. 8vo. **46 D**

See also English hexameter translations, 1847, pp. 38–57. **83 A**

EPITAPHS.

Ancient funeral monuments of Great Britain and Ireland. By John Weever. 1767. 4to. **85 G**

History from marble compiled in the reign of Charles II. By T. Dingley. [Camden Society, vols. 94 and 97.] 2 vols. 1867–68. 8vo. **85 C**

EPPING FOREST, Essex.

Epping Forest Commission. The Rolls of Court of Attachments of royal forest of Waltham, 1713 to 1848 ; and Miscellaneous presentments and regulations at forest courts recorded before 1713. 4 vols. in 2. 1873. 4to. **87 G**

The forest of Essex, its history, laws, administration and ancient customs. By W. R. Fisher. 1887. 8vo. **87 F**

EQUITABLE ASSURANCE SOCIETY.

The deed of settlement of the Society for equitable assurances on lives and survivorships. 1777. 8vo. **78 B**

The deed of settlement of the Society for equitable assurances on lives and survivorships with bye-laws, orders, reports, and 9 addresses by W. Morgan. 1833. 8vo. **78 C**

A Short account of the Society for equitable assurances on lives and survivorships. 1829. [Pamphlets, vol. 30.] **144 B**

EQUITABLE EXECUTION.

Procedure on elegit and equitable execution. By F. Stone. 1882. 12mo. **12 F**

EQUITABLE MORTGAGES AND RECOVERIES.

Equitable Mortgages. By S. Miller. 1844. 8vo. **172 G**

Judgment creditor after execution v. Equitable mortgagee. The objections to Lord Cottenham's Dictum in Whitworth v. Gaugain briefly examined. By W. F. Browell. 1844. [Pamphlets, vol. 21.] **144 B**

EQUITABLE MORTGAGES.—*continued.*

Case on validity of Equitable Recoveries; with opinions of counsel thereon. 1790. See Collectanea Juridica, vol. 1, 1791, pp. 214–245. **144 G**

EQUITY.

Manual of principles of equity. By John Indermaur. 2nd ed. 1890. 8vo. **64 C**

The principles of Equity. By E. H. T. Snell. 9th ed. by A. Brown. 1889. 8vo. **64 D**

Aids to Equity, intended to assist the student in reading Snell's Principles of Equity. By A. Gibson and A. Weldon. 4th ed. 1890. 8vo. **64 C**

A Manual of Equity jurisprudence. By J. W. Smith. 14th ed. by J. Trustram. 1889. 12mo. **64 C**

A Practical exposition of the principles of Equity. By H. A. Smith. 2nd ed. 1888. 8vo. **64 D**

Student's Equity. By A. Gibson and R. McLean. 1887. 8vo. **64 C**

Practical compendium of equity. By W. W. Watson. 2nd ed. 2 vols. 1886. 8vo. **12 G**

Commentaries on equity jurisprudence as administered in England and America. By Joseph Story. 13th ed. by M. M. Bigelow. 2 vols. 1886. 8vo. **59 D**

Introduction to principles of equity. By J. A. Shearwood. 1885. 8vo. **64 D**

The equitable jurisdiction of the Court of Chancery. By G. Spence. 2 vols. 1846–49. 8vo. **52 G**

Introductory lecture on Equity delivered in the theatre of the Royal Dublin Society. By Echlin Molyneux. Dublin 1839. 8vo. **144 G**

What are Courts of Equity? A lecture delivered at King's college, London. By John James Park. 1832. [Law Tracts, vol. 5.] **144 E**

Practice of Court of Exchequer upon proceedings in equity. By D. B. Fowler. 2nd ed. 2 vols. 1817. 8vo. **168 B**

Epitome of practice on equity side of Court of Exchequer. By Samuel Turner. 1806. See S. Turner's Epitome, 1809, 8vo. **163 B**

See also ADAMS, J., BALLOW, H., BARTON, C., CHUTE, C. W., FONBLANQUE, J., FRANCIS, R., GOLDSMITH, G., GRIFFITH, W., HAYES, W., HAYNES, F. O., HOME, H., JEREMY, G., ROBERTS, T. A., SMITH, J. S. and UNDERHILL, A.

EQUITY CASES ABRIDGED.
A General Abridgment of Cases in Equity, argued and adjudged in the High Court of Chancery. By A Gentleman
of the Middle Temple. 4th ed. 2 vols. 1756. folio.
The same. vol. 1. 5th ed. vol. 2. 2nd ed. 2 vols. 1793–
69. folio. **74 C**

EQUITY PLEADING.
Commentaries on equity pleading. By Joseph Story. 8th
ed. by I. F. Redfield. Boston, 1870. 8vo. **59 D**
Concise treatise on principles of equity pleading with pre-
cedents. By C. S. Drewry. 1858. 12mo. **173 E**
Pleadings in suits in the Court of Chancery by English bill.
By J. Mitford. 5th ed. by J. W. Smith. 1847. 8vo. **173 G**
A Digest of pleading in equity. By Basil Montagu. 1824.
8vo. **173 G**
See also BEAMES, J., LEWIS, K., LUBÉ, D. G., MAYNE, J. D.,
VAN HEYTHUYSEN, F. M. and WELFORD, R. G.

EQUITY REPORTS.
Reports of cases in the Court of Chancery from Easter term
1853 to Michaelmas term 1855. 3 vols. in 4. 1854–55.
8vo. **65 A**

ERASMUS, DESIDERIUS.
Colloquia Familiaria. Basileæ, 1524. 12mo. **118 A**

ERCK, JOHN CAILLARD.
A Repertory of inrolments on the patent rolls of Chancery
in Ireland, commencing with the reign of King James I.
Dublin, 1846. 8vo. **99 A**

ERDESWICK, SAMPSON.
Survey of Staffordshire, containing antiquities of that county
with additions by Rev. T. Harwood. 1820. 8vo. **93 B**

ERLE, TWYNIHOE WILLIAM.
The Jury laws and their amendment. 1882. 8vo. **83 I**
On the present system of summoning special juries in London
and Middlesex. 1865. [Pamphlets, vol. 25.] **144 B**

ERLE, SIR WILLIAM.
The law relating to trade unions. 1869. 8vo. **11 I**

ERNST, WILLIAM.
A Treatise of Marriage and Divorce. 1879. 8vo. **172 D**

ERRORS AND WRITS OF ERROR.

Concerning Writs of Error in criminal cases. See Hargrave's
Juridical Arguments, vol. 1, 1797, pp. 403–410. **144 G**

The law and practice of Writs of Error. 1781. 8vo. **167 D**

The law of Errors and writs of error. 1703. 12mo. **167 D**

ERSKINE, JOHN.

Principles of law of Scotland. 5th ed. 1777. 8vo.

The same. 7th ed. 1791, and 12th ed. 1827. 8vo.

The same. New ed. by J. G. Smith. 1860. 8vo. **55 F**

The same. 14th ed. by W. Guthrie, 1870, and 16th ed. by
W. Guthrie. 1881. 8vo. **55 F**

The same. 17th ed. by N. M. [Norman Macpherson.] 1886.
8vo. **55 F**

ERSKINE, THOMAS, 1 BARON.

Speeches on subjects connected with liberty of the press and
against constructive treasons. Collected by James Ridgway.
4 vols. 1810. 8vo. **83 G**

Speeches on miscellaneous subjects. 1812. 8vo. **83 G**

Speeches of Thomas Lord Erskine, with memoir of his life.
By Edward Walford. 2 vols. 1870. 8vo. **83 G**

See also Lord Campbell's Lord Chancellors, vol. 6, 1850,
pp. 353–679. **79 G**

ESCHEAT AND FORFEITURE.

The law of Escheat and Forfeiture. See Watson's Compendium of Equity, 2nd ed. vol. 1, 1886, pp. 186–191. **12 G**

ESPEN, ZEGER BERNARD VAN.

Jus ecclesiasticum universum cæteraque scripta omnia. Editio
novissima adnotationibus J. P. Gibert nuperrime aucta et
illustrata. 10 vols. in 5. Vénetiis, 1769. folio. **77 H**

ESPINASSE, ISAAC.

The defects in general and statute law which require revision
of legislature, particularly such as relate to office of justice
of peace. 1827. [Jacob's Tracts, vol. 5.] **144 E**

Digest of the law of actions and trials at Nisi Prius. 2nd ed.
2 vols. 1793. 8vo. **173 A**

The same. 4th ed. 2 vols. 1812. 8vo. **173 A**

Reports of cases argued and ruled at Nisi Prius 1793–1807.
6 vols. 1796–1811. 8vo. **8 E**

ESSAYS.

Essaies. Religious meditations. Places of perswasion and disswasion, seène and allowed. By Francis Bacon. 1598. 12mo. **118 A**

Life, law and literature, essays on various subjects. By W. G. Barter. 1863. 8vo. **83 C**

Specimen Essays, comprising hints on Composition, punctuation &c. and Twelve Essays. By John Gibson and F. R. Burrows. 1881. 8vo. **255 H**

ESSAYS AND REVIEWS.

Judgment of Lords of judicial committee of Privy Council upon appeals of Williams *v.* Lord Bishop of Salisbury and Wilson *v.* Fendall from the Court of Arches. 1864. [Pamphlets, vol. 26.] **144 B**

ESSEX, COUNTY OF.

Historical account of the part of Essex within twelve miles of London. See Rev. Daniel Lysons's Environs of London, vol. 4, 1796, pp. 53–287 and 646–653. **89 F**

The history and antiquities of Essex. By N. Salmon. 1740. folio. **88 G**

The history and antiquities of Essex. By Rev. Philip Morant. 1768. Reprinted. 2 vols. Chelmsford, 1816. folio. **88 H**

The history and topography of Essex. By Thomas Wright. 2 vols. in 3. 1836. 4to. **87 F**

History of Essex. By E. Ogborne. 1814. 4to. **87 F**

Holiday notes in East Anglia, a selection of articles on holiday resorts in Norfolk, Suffolk and Essex. 1886. 12mo. **92 C**

List of names of gentlemen and other freeholders that voted for knights of the shire for county of Essex, 1722. 1724. 8vo. **107 J**

New and complete history of Essex. By A Gentleman. [P. Muilman.] 6 vols. Chelmsford, 1770–72. 8vo. **87 E**

Pedigrees of Essex families. By W. Berry. 1839. folio. **126 I**

Poll for a knight of the shire to represent the county of Essex, taken at Chelmsford, 13–14 Dec. 1763. 1764. 8vo. **107 J**

Poll for knights of the shire to represent the county of Essex, taken at Chelmsford, 7th May, 1734. 1738. 8vo. **107 J**

Speculi Britanniæ pars, an historical description of the county of Essex. By John Norden. 1594. Edited by Sir H. Ellis. [Camden Society, vol. 9.] 1840. 8vo. **85 A**

Another copy. 1840. 8vo. **87 E**

See also NEWCOURT, R.

ESSEX, EARLS OF.

Ancient biographical poems on the Earls of Essex. Edited by J. P. Collier. [Camden Soc. vol. 61.] 1855. 8vo.　　**85 B**

Memoir and trial of Robert Earl of Essex. See Criminal Trials, vol. 1, 1832, pp. 277–388.　　**51 D**

An Account of the death of the Earl of Essex. n.d. 8vo. [Tracts, 1688–89.]　　**118 E**

Essex papers. Edited by Osmund Airy. vol. 1. 1672–1679. [Camden Society, n.s. vol. 47.] 1890. 8vo.　　**85 E**

Murder will out, or a clear and full discovery that the Earl of Essex did not feloniously murder himself, but was barbarously murthered by others. By Henry Danvers 1689. [Tracts, 1688–89.]　　**118 E**

ESTATES.

The law of Estates. See Watson's Compendium of Equity, 2nd ed. vol. 1, 1886, pp. 192–247.　　**12 G**

Practical treatise on the law of Estates for life. By Andrew Bisset. 1842. 8vo.　　**167 D**

Treatise on the disposition and conveyance of lands entailed. By John Tamlyn. 1835. 8vo.　　**167 B**

A Series of letters to a man of property on the sale, purchase, leasing, settlement and devising of estates. By Sir E. B. Sugden. 5th ed. 1829. 8vo.　　**167 D**

An Elementary treatise on Estates. By Richard Preston. 2 vols. 1820–27. 8vo.　　**167 D**

A Treatise on Estates and Tenures. By Sir Robert Chambers. 1824. 8vo.　　**13 A**

Estates executed, executory, vested and contingent. See R. Preston's Tracts, 1797, pp. 47–66.　　**163 G**

A Treatise of particular estates. 1794. See W. Noy's Maxims, 1794, pp. 117–136.　　**49 F**

A Treatise concerning estates tayle and discents of inheritance. By N. N. 1641. [Law tracts, 1641.]　　**144 F**

ESTIENNE, H. AND R.
See STEPHANUS, H. AND R.

ESTOPPEL.

The principles of Estoppel. By M. Cababé. 1888. 12mo. **9 H**

The law of Estoppel. By L. F. Everest and E. Strode. 1884. 8vo.　　**9 H**

ETCHING.

Liverpool Art Club. Collection illustrative of the history and practice of Etching. Sent and catalogued by James Anderson Rose. Liverpool, 1874. [Pamphlets, vol. 33.] **144 C**

ETHICS.

Essays in Jurisprudence and Ethics. By Frederick Pollock. 1882. 8vo. **63 F**

On Mr. Spencer's Data of Ethics. By Malcolm Guthrie. 1884. 8vo. **78 C**

ETIENNE DE ROUEN.

The 'Draco Normannicus' of Etienne de Rouen. See Chronicles of the reigns of Stephen, Henry II. and Richard, vol. 2, 1885, pp. 589–781. **102 H**

ETON, BUCKS.

Alumni Etonenses, or a catalogue of the provosts and fellows of Eton college and King's college, Cambridge, from 1443 to 1797. By T. Harwood. Birmingham, 1797. 4to. **79 H**

The architectural history of the colleges of Cambridge and Eton. By R. Willis and J. W. Clark. 4 vols. Cambridge, 1886. 4to. **86 D**

History of Eton College. By H. C. M. Lyte. 1875. 8vo. **86 C**

Rambles round Eton and Harrow. By A. Rimmer. 1882. 8vo. **86 C**

See also WINDSOR.

EUCLID.

Les elemens d'Euclide. Par le P. Dechalles. Nouvelle ed. par M. Ozanam. Paris, 1730. 12mo. **255 H**

Elements of Euclid ; printed from text of Robert Simson. Corrected by Samuel Maynard. 1839. 12mo. **255 H**

The philosophical and mathematical commentaries of Proclus on the first book of Euclid's Elements. Translated by T. Taylor. 2 vols. 1792. 4to. **78 G**

EUER, SAMPSON.

Doctrina Placitandi, ou l'art et science de bon pleading. [By Sampson Euer.] 1677. 4to.

A System of Pleading ; including a translation of the Doctrina Placitandi of S. Euer. By A Gentleman of the Middle Temple. 1771. 4to. **156 A**

EUGENE, FRANCIS, PRINCE OF SAVOY.
Memoirs written by himself. [Autobiography, vol. 18.]   1830.
12mo.   **79 A**

EUROPE.
The annals of Europe for the years 1739, 1740, 1742 and
1743.   5 vols.   1740–45.   8vo.   **113 A**
Chronological history of European states, from treaty of
Nimeguen in 1678 to 1794; also Biographical sketches of
the sovereigns, statesmen, warriors, patriots, &c.   By Rev.
Charles Mayo.   Bath, 1795.   folio.   **115 I**
A Compleat history of Europe, or a view of the affairs thereof
from 1643 to 1712.   15 vols.   1706–13.   8vo.   **113 A**
European and American excursions and tours.   By Thomas
Cook.   1865.   [Pamphlets, vol. 25.]   **144 B**
The general history of Europe contained in the historical and
political Monthly Mercuries from Nov. 1688 to Dec. 1699.
By J. Phillips.   10 vols.   1692–99.   8vo.   **116 A**
History of Europe from 1789 to 1815.   By Sir A. Alison.
7th ed.   20 vols.   1847–48.   12mo.   **113 B**
History of Europe from 1815 to 1852.   By Sir A. Alison.
9 vols.   1853–59.   8vo.   **113 B C**
History of modern Europe to 1763 in a series of letters from
a nobleman to his son.   [By William Russell.]   New ed.
with a continuation to 1825.   6 vols.   1827.   8vo.   **113 C**
An Inquiry into colonial policy of European powers.   By Lord
Brougham.   2 vols.   Edinburgh, 1803.   8vo.   **116 B**
An Inquiry into origin of laws and political institutions of
modern Europe.   By George Spence.   1826.   8vo.   **113 C**
Introduction to the literature of Europe in the fifteenth, six-
teenth and seventeenth centuries.   By Henry Hallam.
4th ed.   3 vols.   1854.   8vo.   **116 C**
The Monethly Account, Number 4, January 1688 or 1689.
[Tracts, 1688–89.]   [Eleven articles describing Italy and
other European countries and cities.]   **118 E**
The Prophecy of Bishop Usher concerning a most dreadful
persecution that would fall on the Protestant churches of
Europe.   1688.   [Tracts, 1688–89.]   **118 E**
Fielding's Regal tables, or genealogical descent of all the
sovereign princes in Europe.   1786.   Bound with Fielding's
Peerage.   1786.   12mo.   **124 B**
Review of the constitutions of principal states of Europe.   By
P. F. De La Croix.   2 vols.   1792.   8vo.   **113 C**

EUROPE—*continued.*

The royal families of Europe and royal family alliances (from the Spectator, January 3, 1863, and January 2, 1864). 1863-64. 4to. **114 H**

Table of the foreign mercantile laws and codes in force in the principal states of Europe and America. By Charles Lyon-Caen. Translated by N. Argles. 1876. 8vo. **55 C**

A View of society in Europe in its progress from rudeness to refinement. By G. Stuart. Edinburgh, 1778. 4to. **115 H**

View of the state of Europe during the Middle ages. By Henry Hallam. 5th ed. 3 vols. 1829. 8vo. **116 C**

EUROPEAN ASSURANCE SOCIETY.

Arbitration acts, 1872–75. Minutes of proceedings before the arbitrators, 1872–78. 4 vols. 1872–79. folio. **145 D**

Minutes of proceedings on appeal, 1875–79. folio. **145 D**

Award of the arbitrator F. S. Reilly dated 2 September 1879. 1879. folio. **145 D**

EUROPEAN MAGAZINE.

The European Magazine and London Review, 1782–1826. 89 vols. 1782–1826. 8vo. **252 A–E**

EVANS, DANIEL THOMAS.

Law Digest, a general index to the reports and statutes, 1855–1872. 9 vols. 1855–73. 8vo. **63 D**

EVANS, REV. EVAN.

Some specimens of the poetry of the antient Welsh bards, translated into English. 1764. 8vo. **83 J**

EVANS, FRANK.

Practice of the Chancery division. 1881. 8vo. **52 B**

EVANS, JOHN, ATTORNEY-AT-LAW.

Costs in actions not above £20 in contract and not above £5 in tort in the superior courts. 1859. 12mo. **165 A**

EVANS, JOHN, PRINTER.

Chronological outline of history of Bristol and stranger's guide through its streets. Bristol, 1824. 4to. **87 F**

EVANS, PATRICK FLEMING.
The Solicitors' remuneration act 1881, and the general order
made thereunder. 1883. 8vo. **164 G**

EVANS, WILLIAM.
A Treatise upon the law of principal and agent, in contract
and tort. 1878. 8vo. **53 E**
The same. 2nd ed. 1888. 8vo. **11 C**

EVANS, SIR WILLIAM DAVID.
Collection of statutes connected with general administration of
the law. 2nd ed. by A. Hammond. 8 vols. 1823. 8vo. **176 B**

EVELYN, JOHN.
The charters of the City of London which have been granted
since the Conquest. By J. E. 1745. 12mo. **92 A**

EVEREST, LANCELOT FEILDING.
The defence of insanity in criminal cases. 1887. [Pamphlets,
vol. 39.] **144 C**
The law of Estoppel. By L. F. Everest and Edmund Strode.
1884. 8vo. **9 G**

EVERSLEY, WILLIAM PINDER.
The law of domestic relations. 1885. 8vo. **10 C**

EVESHAM, WORCESTERSHIRE.
Chronicon abbatiæ de Evesham ad annum 1418. Edited by
Rev. W. D. Macray. 1863. 8vo. **101 I**
The history and antiquities of the abbey and borough of
Evesham. By W. Tindal. Evesham, 1794. 4to. **93 F**
The history of Evesham. By G. May. 1834. 8vo. **93 F**
A Short account of the history and antiquities of Evesham.
By E. J. Rudge. Evesham, 1820. 8vo. **93 F**

EVIDENCE.
Roscoe's Digest of law of Evidence in criminal cases. 11th
ed. by H. Smith and G. G. Kennedy. 1890. 8vo. **9 H**
A Digest of the law of Evidence. By Sir J. F. Stephen.
5th ed. 1887. 8vo. **9 I**
A Treatise on the law of Evidence. By J. P. Taylor. 8th
ed. 2 vols. 1885. 8vo. **9 I**

EVIDENCE—*continued.*

Principles and practice of law of Evidence. By E. Powell. 5th ed. by J. Cutler and E. F. Griffin. 1885. 8vo. **9 I**

Digest of Evidence on trial of actions at Nisi Prius. By H. Roscoe. 15th ed. by M. Powell. 2 vols. 1884. 8vo. **9 I**

Principles of the law of Evidence. By W. M. Best. 7th ed. by J. M. Lely. 1883. 8vo. **9 I**

On the admission of the evidence of persons charged with criminal offences. By Joseph Addison. 1883. [Pamphlets, vol. 32.] **144 C**

Digest of the Scottish law of Evidence. By John Kirkpatrick. Edinburgh, 1882. 8vo. **55 F**

The law of Evidence as administered in England and applied to India. By Joseph Goodeve. New ed. by L. A. Goodeve. Calcutta, 1871. 8vo. **38 C**

The law of Evidence. By Simon Greenleaf. 3 vols. Boston, 1863–60. 8vo. **59 E**

The principles of circumstantial evidence. By W. Wills. 4th ed. 1862. 8vo. **52 G**

An Examination of Mr. Pitt Taylor's thesis ' on the expediency of passing an act to permit defendants in criminal courts and their wives or husbands to testify on oath.' By Francis Worsley. 1861. [Pamphlets, vol. 13.] **144 A**

Rules of law respecting admission of extrinsic evidence in aid of interpretation of wills. By Sir James Wigram. 4th ed. 1858. 8vo. **52 G**

A Few brief remarks on Lord Denman's bill for improving the law of Evidence. By J. J. Lowndes. 1843. [Pamphlets, vol. 18.] **144 B**

A Treatise on judicial evidence extracted from the manuscripts of Jeremy Bentham. By M. Dumont. Translated into English. 1825. 8vo. **78 C**

An Analysis of medical evidence. By J. G. Smith. 1825. 8vo. **172 E**

The philosophy of Evidence. By Daniel McKinnon. 1812. [Jacob's Tracts, vol. 2.] **144 E**

The theory of Evidence. [By Henry, Earl Bathurst.] 1761. 8vo. **167 D**

See also CHARNOCK, R., COLLINS, G. W., COVENTRY, T., DICKSON, W. G., FIELD, C. D., GILBERT, SIR J., GRESLEY, R. N., HARE, T., NORTON, J. B., PEAKE, T., PHILLIPS, S. M. and STARKIE, S.

EVOLUTION.

On Mr. Spencer's Formula of Evolution as an exhaustive statement of the changes of the universe. By M. Guthrie. 1879. 8vo. **78 C**

EWALD, ALEXANDER CHARLES.

Our public records, a brief handbook to the national archives. 1873. 8vo. **98 A**

EXAMINATIONS.

The Schoolmaster's calendar and handbook of examinations and open scholarships. 1889. 12mo. **255 H**

Digest of questions asked at final pass examination of articled clerks on all the subjects, with answers. By R. Hallilay. 15th ed. 1889. 8vo. **64 C**

Student's Digest, containing a collection of questions set at all the final examinations of the Law Society in recent years. By A. Gibson and A. Weldon. 1888. 8vo. **64 C**

Digest of questions asked at final examination of articled clerks on law of probate and divorce. By R. Hallilay. 1888. 8vo. **64 E**

Digest of probate, divorce, bankruptcy, admiralty, ecclesiastical and criminal law. By T. B. Napier and R. M. Stephenson. 1888. 8vo. **64 E**

Aids to the Final. By Albert Gibson and Arthur Weldon. 6th ed. 1888. 12mo. **64 D**

Self-Preparation for the Final Examination. By John Indermaur. 5th ed. 1887. 8vo. **64 D**

Intermediate law examination made easy. A complete guide to Stephen's Commentaries. By A. Gibson. 7th ed. 1887. 8vo. **64 D**

Digest of questions set in bar and solicitors' final examinations. By J. A. Shearwood. 2nd ed. 1884. 8vo. **64 D**

The honours examination digest. By J. F. Haynes and T. A. Nelham. 1883. 8vo. **64 D**

The London Matriculation Course. By John Gibson. 1883. 8vo. **255 G**

Intermediate guide. By H. W. Purkis. 1883. 12mo. **64 D**

Aids to the Intermediate, being a short guide to Stephen's Commentaries on the laws of England (8th edition). By Albert Gibson. 1881. 12mo. **64 A**

A Digest of the examination questions in common law, con-

EXAMINATIONS—*continued*.

veyancing, equity, bankruptcy and criminal law. By Robert Maugham. 8th ed. 1861. 12mo. **168 A**

Middle class and non-gremial examinations. Cui bono? By A. H. Wratislaw. 1860. [Pamphlets, vol. 13.] **144 A**

See ANDERSON, C. H., BEDFORD, E. H. and BUTLIN, J. F.

EXCELLING, THE LOVE OF.

The private tutor, or thoughts upon the love of excelling and the love of excellence. [By Basil Montagu.] 1820. 8vo. **78 C**

EXCHANGE.

Dissertation on and precedents of Exchange. See Bythewood and Jarman's Conveyancing, 4th ed. vol. 2, 1885, pp. 924–937. **13 D**

EXCHANGES.

The stile of Exchanges containing both their law and custom. By John Scarlett. 2nd ed. 1684. 12mo. **49 A**

EXCHEQUER COURT AND PRACTICE.

On the origin of the title and office of Cursitor-Baron of the Exchequer. By Edward Foss. 1855. Bound with E. Foss's Grandeur of the law. 1842. 8vo. **80 E**

Attorney's practice in the Exchequer of Pleas. By George Price. 1831. 12mo. **168 B**

A Treatise on the Court of Exchequer. By George Price. 1827. 8vo. **168 B**

The practice of the Court of Exchequer. Revenue branch. By James Manning. 2nd ed. 1827. 8vo. **168 B**

The practice in the Office of Pleas of the Court of Exchequer epitomized. 1806. See Turner's Epitome. 1809. 8vo. **163 B**

Treatise on Court of Exchequer. By a late Lord Chief Baron of that court. [Sir Jeffrey Gilbert.] 1758. 12mo. **168 B**

The practice of the Exchequer Court. By Sir Thomas Fanshaw. 1658. 12mo. **48 B**

See also BURTON, P. and DAX, T.

EXCHEQUER REPORTS.

Reports of cases in the courts of Exchequer and Exchequer Chamber 1847–1856. 11 vols. 1849–56. 8vo. **7 D E**

EXCHEQUER ROYAL.

Analysis of contents of Rubeus Liber Feodorum or red book of the Exchequer. By Rev. Joseph Hunter. 1838. 8vo. **82 B**

Antient kalendars and inventories of the treasury of His Majesty's Exchequer. Edited by Sir F. Palgrave. 3 vols. 1836. 8vo. **99 A**

Considerations for regulating the Exchequer. By Christopher Vernon. 1642. 12mo. **48 B**

Documents illustrative of English history in the thirteenth and fourteenth centuries selected from records of department of Queen's Remembrancer of the Exchequer. By Henry Cole. 1844. folio. **99 E**

History and antiquities of Exchequer of kings of England from Norman conquest to 1327. By Thomas Madox. 2nd ed. 2 vols. 1769. 4to. **103 F**

Index to records called the Originalia and memoranda on the lord treasurer's remembrancer's side of the Exchequer. By Edward Jones. 2 vols. 1795. folio. **98 E**

Index to various repertories, books of orders and decrees and other records preserved in the Court of Exchequer. By Adam Martin. 1819. 8vo. **99 A**

Issue roll, containing payments made out of His Majesty's Revenue in 1370. By Thomas de Brantingham. Translated by F. Devon. 1835. 4to. **98 A**

Issues of the Exchequer, being a collection of payments made out of His Majesty's revenue from Henry III. to Henry VI. inclusive. Edited by F. Devon. 1837. 8vo. **98 A**

Issues of the Exchequer, being payments made out of His Majesty's revenue during the reign of King James I. Edited by F. Devon. 1836. 8vo. **98 A**

Nonarum Inquisitiones in Curia Scaccarii temp. Edw. III. [Edited by G. Vanderzee.] 1807. folio. **98 C**

Rotuli Scaccarii regum Scotorum. The exchequer rolls of Scotland A.D. 1264–1436. 4 vols. Edinburgh, 1878–80. 8vo. **99 B**

Testa de Nevill sive Liber Feodorum in Curia Scaccarii temp. Hen. III. et Edw. I. [Edited by J. Caley and W. Illingworth.] 1807. folio. **98 B**

EXCISE.

Laws of the Excise. By J. Bateman. 1843. 8vo. **168 B**

The spirit of the general letters and orders issued by the Board of Excise from 1700 to 1827 inclusive. By W. Hersee. 1829. 8vo. **168 B**

EXCISE—*continued.*
Acts relating to the Excise. 1781–1820. folio. **156 D**
Tables of the duties, allowances, bounties and drawbacks of
Excise. n.d. 4to. **156 D**

EXCOMMUNICATION.
Report of the cause between Wm. Beaurain and Sir Wm.
Scott for unlawfully excommunicating the plaintiff, tried in
the Court of King's Bench, Guildhall, London, 6 March
1813. 1814. 8vo. **50 A**

EXECUTION.
Treatise on law of Execution in high court and inferior courts.
By T. K. Anderson. 1889. 8vo. **12 E**
The law of Execution upon judgments and orders of Chancery
and Queen's Bench divisions of high court of justice. By
C. J. Edwards. 1888. 8vo. **12 E**
The law of Executions as affecting land. By H. W. Elphin-
stone and J. W. Clark. 1887. 8vo. **13 H**
Procedure on elegit and equitable execution. By F. Stone.
1882. 12mo. **12 F**
Law of Executions. By Sir Jeffrey Gilbert. 1763. 12mo. **168 B**
See also BINGHAM, P. and DEBTS.

EXECUTIVE OFFICERS.
The powers, duties and liabilities of Executive Officers. By
A. W. Chaster. 3rd ed. 1888. 8vo. **9 I**

EXECUTORS.
A Compendium of the law relating to executors and adminis-
trators. By W. G. Walker. 2nd ed. by W. G. Walker and
E. J. Elgood. 1888. 8vo. **9 I**
Solicitors' reports to residuary legatees as to the executors'
management of their testators' estates. By Frederick Wood.
1887. 8vo. **9 I**
Practical advice to testators and executors. By W. Phippen.
7th ed. 1886. 8vo. **13 I**
Law of Executors. By S. C. Macaskie. 1881. 8vo. **52 H**
The law of Executors and Administrators. By Sir E. V.
Williams. 8th ed. by R. L. V. Williams and W. V. V.
Williams. 2 vols. 1879. 8vo. **9 I**
The office and duty of Executors. By T. Wentworth. 14th
ed. by H. Jeremy. 1829. 8vo. **52 G**

EXECUTORS—*continued*.

Examination of authorities on question, whether executors
having a power to sell can make a good conveyance of
legal estate in the land without concurrence of heir-at-law ?
See Law Journal Tracts, 1825–26, pp. 115–128. **144 G**

Of the several remedies of executors for the recovery of rent.
By A Member of the Inner Temple. See Law Journal
Tracts, 1825–26, pp. 129–149. **144 G**

On the claim of executors to the residue of their testators'
personal estate. By J. B. Parry. See Law Journal Tracts,
1825–26, pp. 1–32. **144 G**

The Orphan's legacy. By J. Godolphin. 4th ed. 1701.
8vo. **48 G**

See also BRADY, J. H., HUDSON, J. C., PRITCHARD, T. S.
and TOLLER, S.

EXECUTORY DEVISES AND LIMITATIONS.

An Essay on the learning of Executory Devises. By C.
Fearne. 10th ed. 2 vols 1844. 8vo. **13 G**

An Inquiry into the soundness of certain points relative to
executory limitations lately impeached. By A Licentiate.
See Law Journal Tracts, 1825–26, pp. 81–96. **144 G**

EXETER, DEVONSHIRE.

Alphabetical register of divers persons who have given towards the relief of the poor of the city and county of Exon.
By R. Izacke. 1736. 8vo. **87 C**

The antique description and account of the city of Exeter.
By John Vowell, alias Hoker. Exon, 1765. 8vo. **87 C**

Description of the Guildhall, Exeter. By Rev. George Oliver
and Pitman Jones. Exeter, 1853. 12mo. **87 C**

Exeter. By E. A. Freeman. 1887. 8vo. **87 C**

History and description of city of Exeter and its environs.
By A. Jenkins. Exeter, 1806. 8vo. **87 C**

The history of Exeter. By Rev. George Oliver. Exeter,
1821. 8vo. **87 C**

Letters and papers of John Shillingford, mayor of Exeter,
1447–50. Edited by S. A. Moore. [Camden Society,
n.s. vol. 2.] 1871. 8vo. **85 C**

Letters to Her Majesty's Attorney-general on the mal-practices
in the Crown courts at Exeter. By Charles Bird. Exeter,
1842. [Pamphlets, vol. 18.] **144 B**

The Mobiad, or battle of the voice, being a description of an

EXETER—*continued.*

Exeter election. By Democritus Juvenal, vulgarly Andrew Brice. Exon, 1770. 8vo.   87 C

Remarkable antiquities of the city of Exeter, originally collected by Richard Izacke. 3rd ed. continued to the year 1724, by Samuel Izacke. 1734. 8vo.   87 C

Report of case of The Queen *v.* President and chapter of cathedral church of St. Peter in Exeter, in Queen's Bench. By R. Barnes. 1841. [Pamphlets, vol. 2.]   144 A

EXETER, THOMAS BITTON, BISHOP OF.

Account of the executors of Thomas, bishop of Exeter, 1310. Edited by Ven. W. H. Hale and Rev. H. T. Ellacombe. [Camden Society, n.s. vol. 10.] 1874. 8vo.   85 D

EXHIBITIONS, OF 1851 AND 1862, IN LONDON.

Exhibition of the Works of Industry of all nations, 1851. Official descriptive and illustrated catalogue of the Great Exhibition, 1851. 4 vols. 1851–52. 8vo.   142 C

Exhibition of the Works of Industry of all nations, 1851. Reports by the Juries on the subjects in the 30 classes into which exhibition was divided. 2 vols. 1852. 8vo. 142 C

The same. 1852. 8vo.   142 C

How to double the value of the Great Exhibition to exhibitors and the world. By A Non-exhibitor. 1862. [Pamphlets, vol. 19.]   144 B

International Exhibition, 1862. Illustrated catalogue of the industrial department. 2 vols. 1862. 8vo.   142 C

International Exhibition, 1862. Kingdom of Italy. Official descriptive catalogue. 1862. 8vo.   142 C

EXTENTS.

The law and practice of Extents. See W. Tidd's Practice, 9th ed. vol. 2, 1828, pp. 1042–1089.   163 B

The law and practice of Extents in chief and in aid. By Edward West. 1817. 8vo.   168 D

Report of the case of The King against Bebb and others on an Extent, with an appendix of some cases and records in extents which have not been before printed. By T. B. Hughes. 1811. 8vo.   50 B

Old and new Extent. See Historical law tracts, 2nd ed. 1761, pp. 403–426.   144 F

EXTRADITION.

Law of Extradition. By Sir E. Clarke. 3rd ed. 1888. 8vo. **10 A**

K. I. ΚΥΡΙΑΚΟΥ περὶ ἐκδόσεως ἐγκληματίων [On the extradition of criminals. By C. J. Kyriacos.] Athens, 1885. 8vo. **55 A**

L'Extradition. Recueil renfermant in extenso tous les traités conclus jusqu'au 1er Janvier 1883 entre les nations civilisées. Par F. J. Kirchner. 1883. 8vo. **10 A**

The law of Extradition international and inter-state. By S. T. Spear. Albany, 1879. 8vo. **59 E**

EYNESBURY, Hunt‾

The history and antiquities of Eynesbury and St. Neots. By Rev. G. C. Gorham. 2 vols. 1824. 8vo. **88 C**

EYTON, Rev. Robert William.

Antiquities of Shropshire. 12 vols. 1854–60. 8vo. **93 A**

Domesday studies, an analysis and digest of the Somerset survey and of the Somerset gheld inquest of A.D. 1084. 2 vols. 1880. 8vo. **93 B**

Domesday studies, an analysis and digest of the Staffordshire survey. 1881. 4to. **93 B**

Notes on Domesday. 1880. [Pamphlets, vol. 32.] **144 C**

FABLES.

Lessing's Fabeln in Prosa und Versen. In vier Büchern. Düben, 1860. 12mo. **83 B**

Phædri Augusti Cæsaris Liberti Fabularum Æsopiarum libri quinque ; .interpretatione et notis illustravit Petrus Danet. Parisiis, 1675. 4to. **47 G**

FACCIOLATI, Jacopo.

Totius Latinitatis Lexicon consilio et cura Jacobi Facciolati, opera et studio Ægidii Forcellini lucubratum. Edidit Jacobus Bailey. 2 vols. 1828. 4to. **123 G**

FACTORS' ACTS.

The new Factors' act annotated. By A. B. Pearson-Gee. 1890. 8vo. **10 A**

The law of mercantile agents, or the Factors' act 1889. By M. Moloney. 1890. 12mo. **10 A**

The sale of goods, including the Factors' act 1889. By M. D. Chalmers. 1890. 8vo. **10 B**

FACTORS' ACTS—*continued.*

Factors' acts 1823 to 1877. By H. F. Boyd and A. B. Pearson. 1884. 8vo.   10 A

The English law of Sale and Pledge by factors and agents. By F. O. Crump. 1868. 8vo.   168 D

Law of principal and factor. Statement of its defects and the remedy. 1842. [Pamphlets, vol. 21.]   144 B

Law relating to principal and factor. Resolutions of a general meeting of merchants, bankers and others, and 2 reports of Committee for conducting proceedings in Parliament. 1823–26. 8vo.   153 E

Report from select committee [of House of Commons] on law relating to Agents or Factors &c. 1823. folio.   153 E

Law relating to Principal and Factor. Address delivered by Mr. Freshfield to select committee of House of Commons. 2nd ed. 1823. 8vo.   153 E

FACTORY ACTS.

Factory and workshop act 1878. By A. Redgrave. 1878. 8vo.   10 A

The English factory legislation. By Ernst Edler Von Plener. Translated by F. L. Weinmann. 1873. 12mo.   78 A

The Factory acts. By H. C. Oats. 1862. 12mo.   168 D

The Factory controversy, a warning against meddling legislation. By Harriet Martineau. Manchester, 1855. [Pamphlets, vol. 33.]   144 C

FACTS.

A Treatise on Facts, as subjects of inquiry by a jury. By James Ram. 1861. 8vo.   52 H

See also EVIDENCE.   9 H I

FAIRMAN, WILLIAM.

The Stocks examined and compared ; or, a guide to purchasers in the public funds. 5th ed. 1808. 8vo.   144 F

FALCONER, THOMAS.

The history, opinions and present legal position of English Presbyterians. [By T. Falconer.] 1834. [Law Tracts, vol. 4.]   144 E

List of county court judges. Note on the abolition of certain franchise gaols. [By T. Falconer.] 1865. 8vo.   80 F

FALCONER, THOMAS—*continued.*

On County Courts, local courts of record, and on changes
proposed to be made in such courts, in second report of
judicature commissioners. 1873. 8vo.　　　　**165 B**

On law relating to Burials.　Notes on consecration of burial
grounds and churches. [By T. Falconer.] 2nd ed.　Cardiff, 1876. [Pamphlets, vol. 31.]　　　　**144 C**

On Probate Courts.　1850. [Pamphlets, vol. 7.]　　**144 A**

Remarks on the Testamentary jurisdiction bill.　1854. [Pam-
phlets, vol. 12.]　　　　**144 A**

FALCONER, THOMAS and EDWARD H. FITZHERBERT.

Cases of controverted elections determined in committees of
the House of Commons, 1835–1839.　1839.　8vo.　**66 A**

FALCONER, WILLIAM.

A New universal dictionary of the Marine ; to which is annexed
a vocabulary of French sea-phrases and terms of art.
Edited by William Burney.　1815.　4to.　　　　**123 D**

FALKLAND ISLANDS.

Laws and ordinances of the Falkland Islands, 1853–1857.
1858.　8vo.　　　　**37 F**

The same.　1843–1884.　1884.　folio.　　　　**37 F**

FALLE, PHILIP.

Cæsarea, or an account of Jersey.　2nd ed.　1734.　8vo.　**94 F**

The same.　Another ed. by P. Morant.　1797.　4to.　**94 F**

FAMILIAR WORDS.

Familiar Words, effect of their misuse on the character of men
and the fate of nations.　By David Urquhart. [Urquhart's
Pamphlets, vol. 5.]　　　　**143 G**

FAMILIES, VICISSITUDES OF.

Vicissitudes of families and other essays.　By Sir Bernard
Burke.　2nd ed.　1859.　8vo.　　　　**79 B**

Vicissitudes of families.　By Sir B. Burke.　Second series.
1860.　8vo.　　　　**79 B**

FAMILY HISTORY.

How to write the history of a family, a guide for the
genealogist.　By W. P. W. Phillimore.　1887.　8vo.　**124 G**

FANSHAW, Sir Thomas.
Practice of the Exchequer court. 1658. 12mo. **48 B**

FANTOSME, Jordan.
Chronicle of the war between English and Scotch in 1173
and 1174. See Chronicles of reigns of Stephen, Henry II.
and Richard I. vol. 3, 1886, pp. 201–377. **102 H**

FAREHAM QUAY, Hampshire.
Candid review of facts in litigation between Peter Barfoot
and others with Bishop of Winchester concerning right of
Fareham quay. 1788. 8vo. **88 A**

FARLEY, Edward.
Imprisonment for debt unconstitutional and oppressive. 1788.
8vo. **78 B**

FARM LAW AND FARMING.
Law of the Farm. By H. H. Dixon. 4th ed. by H. Perkins.
1879. 8vo. **10 A**
Practical suggestions as to instruction in farming in Canada
and the United States of America and Tasmania. 17th ed.
[n.d.] [Pamphlets, vol. 39.] **144 C**

FARMER, John.
The history of ancient town and once famous Abbey of
Waltham, Essex. To which is added The history of Abbies
abridg'd from year 977 to their dissolution, and down to
reign of Queen Elizabeth. 1735. 8vo. **87 E**

FARMER, John S.
Americanisms old and new. A dictionary of words, phrases
and colloquialisms peculiar to the United States, British
America, The West Indies &c. &c. 1889. 8vo. **123 C**

FARNFIELD, William Henry.
Law of Pilotage on the river Thames. 1874. 12mo. **176 E**

FARREN, Edwin James.
Historical essay on rise and early progress of doctrine of life
contingencies in England. 1844. 8vo. **78 B**

FARREN, GEORGE.

Observations on importance in purchases of land &c. of ascertaining rates or laws of mortality among Europeans by chronic diseases and hot climates : illustrations of progress of mania, melancholia, craziness and demonomania as displayed in Shakespeare's characters of Lear, Hamlet, Ophelia and Edgar. 1826. 8vo. **78 C**

A Treatise of Life Assurance. 1823. 8vo. **169 A**

FARREN, GEORGE, JUNIOR.

Bills of costs in chancery. 1841. 12mo. **165 A**

A Key to the Statutes affected by the enactments of reigns of Geo. IV. & Wm. IV. 1837. 12mo. **176 C**

FARRIES, THOMAS.

Precedents of bills of costs. 2nd ed. 1867. 12mo. **165 A**

FARWELL, GEORGE.

Concise treatise on Powers. 1874. 8vo. **13 C**

FAULKNER, THOMAS.

Historical and topographical account of Fulham, including hamlet of Hammersmith. 1813. 8vo. **89 E**

Historical and topographical description of Chelsea and its environs. 1810. 8vo. **89 D**

History and antiquities of Hammersmith. 1839. 8vo. **89 D**

History and antiquities of Kensington, and catalogue of pictures in the palace. 1820. 4to. **89 E**

FAUX, WILLIAM.

Memorable days in America, being a journal of a tour to the United States. 1823. 8vo. **84 D**

FAVERSHAM, KENT.

History and antiquities of abbey and church of Faversham. By John Lewis. 1727. 4to. **88 E**

History of Faversham. By E. Jacob. 1774. 8vo. **88 D**

FAWCETT, JOHN HENRY.

Treatise on court of Referees in Parliament, and reports of cases decided in that court during last session. 1866. 8vo. **66 A**

FAWCETT, William Mitchell.
The law of Landlord and Tenant. 1871. 8vo. **170 C**

FEARNE, Charles.
An Essay on the learning of Contingent Remainders and Executory Devises. 1772. 8vo. **175 C**
The same. 2nd ed. 1773, and 3rd ed. 1776. 8vo. **175 C**
The same. vol. 1. Of Contingent Remainders. 5th ed. 1795; vol. 2. Of Executory Devises. 4th ed. by J. J. Powell. 1795. 2 vols. 1795. 8vo. **175 C**
The same. 6th ed. by Charles Butler. 1809. 8vo. **175 C**
The same. 9th ed. by Charles Butler. 1831. 8vo. **175 C**
The same. 10th ed. by J. W. Smith. 2 vols. 1844. 8vo. **13 H**
Posthumous works ; consisting of A Reading on statute of inrolments, Arguments in the case of General Stanwix, and A collection of cases and opinions ; selected from the author's manuscripts. By T. M. Shadwell. 1797. 8vo. **175 C**

FEES.
An Exact table of fees of all the courts at Westminster. 3rd ed. 1697. 12mo. **48 C**
Reports from select committee on Fees in Courts of law and equity, with minutes of evidence. 1847–50. folio. **153 D**

FELL, Walter William.
The law of Mercantile Guaranties and of principal and surety in general. 2nd ed. 1820. 8vo. **174 C**

FELTHAM, John.
A Tour through the island of Mann in 1797 and 1798. Bath, 1798. 8vo. **94 F**

FENCES.
The law of boundaries and fences. By A. J. Hunt. 3rd ed. by A. Brown. 1884. 12mo. **9 A**
The law of party walls and fences. By H. W. Woolrych. 1845. 8vo. **11 I**

FENIAN CONSPIRACY.
Report of proceedings for trial of Thomas Luby, Clarke and others for treason-felony. Dublin, 1866. 8vo. **50 A**
. Report of trial of Robert Kelly, for murder of head-constable

FENIAN CONSPIRACY—*continued.*

Talbot, at City of Dublin Commission court, October 1871. Dublin, 1873. 8vo. **50 A**

Report of trials of A. M. Sullivan and R. Pigott, for seditious libels on the government, at County of Dublin Commission. By T. P. Law. Dublin, 1868. 8vo. **50 A**

Report of trials of T. F. Burke and others for high treason, at special commission, Dublin, 1867. By W. G. Chamney. Dublin, 1869. 8vo. **50 A**

Reports of proceedings at the special commissions (1867), for county and city of Cork, and county and city of Limerick, in cases of high treason and treason-felony, and of trials for treason-felony, at summer assizes 1867, for counties of Clare and Kerry. Dublin, 1871. 8vo. **50 A**

FENN, CHARLES.

Compendium of the English and foreign funds, debts and revenues of all nations ; banks, railways, mines and the principal joint-stock companies. 9th ed. 1867. 8vo. **168 F**

The same. 12th ed. by R. L. Nash. 1876. 8vo. **168 F**

The same. 14th ed. by R. L. Nash. 1889. 8vo. **10 A**

FENNING, DANIEL and JOSEPH COLLYER.

A New system of Geography, or a general description of the whole known world. 4th ed. 2 vols. 1772–73. folio. **158 F**

FENS, THE.

The Fenland past and present. By S. H. Miller and S. B. J. Skertchley. Wisbech, 1878. 8vo. **89 C**

The Fens. By W. Marshall. 1879. [Pamphlets, vol. 33.] **144 C**

History of imbanking and draining of fens and marshes. By Sir W. Dugdale. 2nd ed. by C. N. Cole. 1772. folio. **85 I**

A Mapp of ye great levell of ye Fenns. 1685. folio. **86 H**

See also BEDFORD LEVEL, LYNN and WISBECH.

FENTON, RICHARD.

Historical tour through Pembrokeshire. 1811. 4to. **94 D**

FEOFFMENT.

Dissertation on and precedents of Feoffment. See Bythewood and Jarman's Conveyancing, 3rd ed. vol. 4, pp. 37–69. **53 D**

Certain observations concerning a deed of feoffment. By T. H., Gent. See W. Noy's Maxims, 1794, pp. 137–160. **49 F**

FERDINAND AND ISABELLA.
History of the reign of Ferdinand and Isabella the Catholic of Spain. By W. H. Prescott. 7th ed. revised. 2 vols. 1851. 8vo.   **113 C**

FERGUSON, James
A short account of the life of James Ferguson, F.R.S. written by himself. [Autobiography, vol. 19.] 1826. 12mo.   **79 A**

FERGUSON, James F.
Remarks on the Limitation of Actions bill intended for Ireland, with extracts from ancient records relating to advowsons of churches in Ireland. Dublin, 1843. 8vo.   **144 G**

FERGUSON, Richard Saul.
A History of Cumberland. 1890. 8vo.   **87 A**

FERGUSSON, James.
Reports of some recent decisions by the Consistorial Court of Scotland in actions of divorce. 1817. 8vo.   **175 D**

FERRAR, John.
The history of Limerick and An essay on Castle Connell Spa, on water in general and cold bathing. 1787. 8vo.   **95 E**

FEUDAL LAW.
A Succinct account of the civil regulations comprised in the Assises of Jerusalem. See The Code Napoléon, translated by B. Barrett, vol. 1, 1811, pp. cccx–ccclvii.   **55 C**

Historical treatise on Feudal law and constitution and laws of England. By F. S. Sullivan. 2nd ed. by G. Stuart. 1776. 4to.   **157 B**

History of privilege which an heir-apparent in a feudal holding has to continue possession of his ancestor. See Historical Law Tracts, 2nd ed. 1761, pp. 173–186.   **144 F**

An Essay towards a general history of Feudal property in Great Britain. By Sir John Dalrymple. 4th ed. Dublin, 1759. 12mo.   **49 F**

The original growth, propagation and condition of feuds and tenures by knight-service in England. See Sir H. Spelman's English works, vol. 2, 1727, pp. 1–46.   **78 H**

See also BUTLER, C., CRAIG, SIR T. and MASCARDUS, J.

FIELD, BARRON.
Analysis of Blackstone's Commentaries on the laws of England
in a series of questions. 1811. 8vo. **166 F**

FIELD, CHARLES DICKINSON.
Chronological table of, and index to, the Indian statute-book
from the year 1834 : with a general introduction to the
statute law of India. 1870. 4to. **38 F**
Landholding, and the relation of landlord and tenant, in
various countries. 2nd ed. Calcutta, 1885. 8vo. **10 E**
The law of Evidence, with especial reference to courts of British
India not established by royal charter. 1867. 8vo. **38 D**
The same. 2nd ed. Calcutta, 1873. 8vo. **38 D**
Regulations of Bengal code. Calcutta, 1875. 8vo. **38 C**

FIELD, DAVID DUDLEY.
Draft outlines of an international code. New York, 1872.
8vo. **55 A**

FIELD, EDWIN WILKINS.
Edwin Wilkins Field. A memorial sketch. By Thomas
Sadler, Ph.D. 1872. 8vo. **79 B**
Observations of a Solicitor on defects in the Equity courts.
1840. [Chancery Pamphlets, vol. 2.] **144 A**
Recent and future law reforms. Judicial procedure a single
and inductive science. By E. W. F. 1843. [Pamphlets,
vol. 20.] **144 B**

FIELD, LEONARD and EDWARD C. DUNN.
The practice of the Court of Chancery under The Court of
Chancery Funds Act 1872. 1873. 8vo. **12 G**
Forms and precedents of pleadings and proceedings in court
of Chancery with references to fourth edition of Daniell's
Chancery Practice. By L. Field, E. C. Dunn and J. Biddle.
2 parts in 1 vol. 1867–68. 8vo. **161 C**
The same. 2nd ed. by John Biddle, with references to fifth
edition of Daniell's Chancery Practice. 1871. 8vo. **161 C**

FIELD, WILLIAM.
Historical and descriptive account of town and castle of
Warwick and of neighbouring spa of Leamington. War-
wick, 1815. 4to. **93 F**

FIELDING, HENRY.

An Enquiry into the causes of the late increase of Robbers, &c. with some proposals for remedying this growing evil. 2nd ed. 1751. 12mo. **118 A**

FIELDING, JOHN.

New peerage of England, Scotland and Ireland, 3 editions, 1786, 1790 and 1791. 3 vols. 1786–91. 12mo. **124 B**

Regal tables, or genealogical descent of all the sovereign princes in Europe, 1786. Bound with Fielding's Peerage. 1786. 12mo. **124 B**

FIELDING, SIR JOHN.

Account of the origin and effects of a police set on foot by Duke of Newcastle in 1753, upon a plan presented by the late Henry Fielding. 1758. 8vo. **118 B**

Extracts from such of the penal laws as particularly relate to the peace and good order of this metropolis. New ed. 1762. 8vo. **165 F**

A Plan for preventing robberies within twenty miles of London. 1755. 8vo. **118 B**

A Plan of the universal register office established in the year 1749. 6th ed. 1753. 8vo. **118 B**

FIJI.

Fiji Ordinances, 1875–1878, 1881, 1888. 4 vols. Levuka, 1875–89. folio. **35 G**

Our new colony Fiji, its history, progress and resources. Edited by H. S. Cooper. 1882. 8vo. **84 G**

FILACER'S OFFICE.

The Filacer's office in the Court of King's Bench. By John Trye. 1684. 12mo. **49 B**

FILANGIERI, GAETANO.

The Science of Legislation. Translated from the Italian by William Kendall. 1792. 8vo. **170 F**

FILMER, SIR ROBERT.

Observations concerning the original and various forms of Government. 1696. 12mo. **48 C**

Patriarcha, or natural power of kings. 1680. 12mo. **48 C**

FINANCE.

Barker's Trade and finance annual, 1886–1887. 2nd ed.
1887. 8vo. **134 I**

Financial Register and stock exchange manual, 1873, 1876.
2 vols. 1873–76. 8vo. **146 E**

The state of the nation with respect to its public funded debt,
revenue and disbursements comprized in the [seven] reports
of the select committee on Finance appointed by the House
of Commons. 1798. 8vo. **78 D**

FINCH, GERARD BROWN.

A Selection of cases on the English law of contract. 1886.
8vo. **52 C**

FINCH, SIR HENEAGE.

Reports of cases decreed in the high court of Chancery during
the time Sir Heneage Finch was Lord Chancellor, 1673–
1680. [Edited by W. Nelson.] 1725. folio. **74 C**

FINCH, SIR HENRY.

Law, or a discourse thereof in foure books. 1627, and Another
ed. 1678. 12mo. **48 B**

FINE ROLLS.

Excerpta e rotulis finium in Turri Londinensi asservatis,
Henrico Tertio Rege 1216–1272. Cura Caroli Roberts.
2 vols. 1835. 8vo. **99 A**

Fines sive pedes finium in Curia domini regis 1195–1214.
Edited by Rev. J. Hunter. 2 vols. 1835–44. 8vo. **98 A**

Rotuli de oblatis et finibus in turri Londinensi asservati
tempore regis Johannis. Accurante T. D. Hardy. 1835.
8vo. **98 A**

FINES AND RECOVERIES.

A Succinct view of the operation of Fines and Recoveries.
By J. W. Smith. 1846. 12mo. **168 D**

Fines and Recoveries by tenant in tail. See R. Preston's
Tracts, 1797, pp. 26–41. **163 G**

Essay on the nature and operation of Fines and Recoveries.
By Wm. Cruise. 3rd ed. 2 vols. 1794. 8vo. **168 D**

A Reading on 27 Edward I. the statute De Finibus Levatis.
See Coke's Law Tracts, 1764, pp. 221–278. **144 F**

The present practice of Fines and Recoveries with the theory
belonging to each. 1751. 8vo. **168 E**

FINES AND RECOVERIES—*continued.*

Modus transferendi status per recorda. A complete collection of choice precedents for Fines upon writs of covenant and common recoveries upon writs of entry in the post in all cases. By Wm. Brown. 6th ed. 1725. 12mo. **168 D**

See also HANDS, W., MANBY, R., MILLER, D. and WILSON, G.

FINLAISON, JOHN.

Sketch of the law relating to public rights over Wastes and Common Lands with some practical observations on the Wimbledon Common question. 1867. 8vo. **163 C**

FINLASON, WILLIAM FRANCIS.

A Brief and practical exposition of the law of Charitable Trusts. 1860. 12mo. **161 F**

The Common law procedure acts of 1852 & 1854 with notes. 1855. 12mo. **161 G**

A Dissertation on the history of hereditary dignities, with special reference to the case of the Earldom of Wiltes 1869. 8vo. **124 G**

Exposition of our Judicial system and Civil procedure as reconstructed under the Judicature acts. 1877. 12mo. **169 F**

A Few words on the Law as it was, as it is and as it ought to be with special reference to county courts, suits and actions at law. 1850. [Pamphlets, vol. 7.] **144 A**

History and effects of laws of Mortmain. 1853. 8vo. **161 F**

The history, constitution and character of Judicial committee of Privy Council considered as a judicial tribunal especially in ecclesiastical cases. 1878. 8vo. **174 C**

The history, objects and advantages of the Assizes. 1877. [Pamphlets, vol. 29.] **144 B**

The history of law of Tenures of land in England and Ireland. 1870. 8vo. **176 E**

Martial law as allowed by law of England in time of rebellion, with practical illustrations drawn from official documents in the Jamaica case. 1866. 8vo. **53 A**

Report of the case of The Queen *v.* Gurney and others in the Court of Queen's Bench. 1870. 8vo. **51 G**

Report of the case of Twycross *v.* Grant with notices of the previous cases on the liabilities of promoters of companies. 1877. 8vo. **51 E**

Selection of leading cases on pleading and parties to actions with practical notes. 1847. 8vo. **173 F**

FIRE INSURANCE.

The laws of Insurance, fire, life, accident and guarantee. By
J. B. Porter. 2nd ed. 1887. 8vo.   10 D

The law of Fire Insurance. By C. J. Bunyon. 3rd ed. 1885.
8vo.   10 D

Digest of Fire Insurance decisions in the courts of Great
Britain and North America. By H. A. Littleton and J. S.
Blatchley. 2nd ed. New York, 1868. 8vo.   59 F

FISHBOURNE, ERNEST HENRY.

The Thames conservancy. 1882. 12mo.   11 H

FISHER, RICHARD BARNARD.

Practical treatise on Copyhold tenure, with the methods of
holding courts-leet, courts-baron and other courts. 2nd ed.
1803. 8vo.   164 F

FISHER, RICHARD SWAINSON.

The progress of the United States of America from the earliest
periods ; geographical, statistical and historical. New York,
1854. 8vo.   84 E

FISHER, ROBERT ALEXANDER.

Digest of reported cases in the House of Lords and Privy
Council, and in courts of Common Law, Divorce, Probate,
Admiralty and Bankruptcy. 5 vols. 1870. 8vo.   14 E

The same. New ed. by J. Mews. 7 vols. 1884. 8vo.   14 E

Stamp act of 1870, with notes. 1871. 8vo.   175 G

FISHER, WILLIAM RICHARD.

The forest of Essex, its history, laws, administration and
ancient customs. 1887. 8vo.   87 F

The law of Mortgage. 1856. 8vo.   172 F

The same. 2nd ed. 2 vols. 1868, and 3rd ed. 2 vols.
1876. 8vo.   172 F

The same. 4th ed. 1884. 8vo.   13 C

FISHERY LAWS.

A Handy book of the Fishery Laws. By G. C. Oke. 2nd
ed. by J. W. W. Bund. 1884. 12mo.   10 A

Fishery laws of the United Kingdom. By James Paterson.
2nd ed. 1873. 8vo.   52 H

FISHERY LAWS—*continued.*

The law relating to the Salmon fisheries of England and Wales. By J. W. W. Bund. 1873. 8vo.   **10 A**

The laws relating to Salmon Fisheries in Great Britain. By Thomas Baker. 2nd ed. 1868. 12mo.   **168 E**

FISHMONGERS' COMPANY.

The Fishmongers' Pageant on Lord Mayor's day, 1616. By John Gough Nichols. 1844. folio.   **91 H**

FISK, GEORGE.

An Analysis of Coke on Littleton comprised in a series of questions. 2 vols. 1824. 8vo.   **176 D**

FITHIAN, EDWARD WILLIAM.

Bills of sale acts 1878 and 1882. 2nd ed. 1884. 12mo. **11 E**

FITZGERALD, GERALD AUGUSTUS ROBERT.

Ballot act 1872 with an introduction. 1872. 12mo.   **160 C**

The same. 2nd ed. 1876. 12mo.   **52 A**

The law relating to public health and local government. 1876. 8vo.   **174 G**

FITZGERALD, JOHN VESEY VESEY.

The Electric Lighting act 1882 and the rules issued under the act. 1882. 8vo.   **166 E**

The Public Health act 1875 with notes. 1875. 12mo.   **174 G**

The same. 5th ed. 1886. 8vo.   **174 G**

FITZ-GIBBONS, JOHN.

The reports of several cases in the Court of King's Bench, with some special cases in the Courts of Chancery, Common Pleas and Exchequer, 1727–1732. 1732. folio.   **74 C**

FITZHERBERT, ANTHONY.

La Graunde Abridgement. 1577. folio.   **158 D**

The New Natura Brevium. 1652. 12mo.   **49 C**

The same. 1687. 12mo.   **49 C**

The same. 7th ed., with a Commentary containing notes and observations on the most remarkable and useful writs, by Lord Chief Justice Hale. 1730. 4to.   **156 A**

The same. 8th ed. 1755. 4to.   **156 A**

The same. 9th ed. 2 vols. 1794. 8vo.   **178 D**

FITZHERBERT, NICHOLAS.

Oxoniensis in Anglia Academiæ descriptio. Romæ, 1602.
See Oxford Historical Society, vol. 8, 1887, pp. 1–32. **85 F**
See also J. Leland's Itinerary, vol. 9, 1744, pp. 103–130. **86 B**

FITZ-WARINE, FULK.

The legend of Fulco Fitz-warin. See R. de Coggeshall's
Chronicon Anglicanum, 1875, pp. 275–415. **102 F**

FIXTURES, LAW OF.

The law of Fixtures. By A. Amos and J. Ferard. 3rd ed.
by C. A. Ferard and W. H. Roberts. 1883. 8vo. **10 A**
Law of Fixtures. By A. Brown. 4th ed. 1881. 8vo. **10 A**
The law of Fixtures with reference to real property and
chattels of a personal nature. By S. G. Grady. 3rd ed.
1876. 12mo. **165 G**

FLANAGAN, STEPHEN WOULFE and C. KELLY.

Reports of cases in Chancery in the Rolls Court 1840–1842.
Dublin, 1843. 8vo. **15 D**

FLATS, LAW OF.

The law relating to Tenement Houses and Flats for residential
or business purposes. By W. Clode. 1889. 8vo. **10 B**

FLAXMAN, ARTHUR JOHN.

The law concerning the registration of births and deaths in
England and Wales, and at sea. 1875. 8vo. **11 E**
The law of parliamentary and municipal registration. 3rd ed.
1885. 8vo. **53 F**

FLEET PRISON AND REGISTERS.

The Œconomy of the Fleete : or, an apologeticall answeare
of Alexander Harris (late warden there) unto XIX articles
sett forth against him by the prisoners. Edited by Augustus
Jessopp. [Camden Soc. n.s. vol. 25.] 1879. 8vo. **85 B**
The Fleet registers, comprising the history of Fleet marriages.
By J. S. Burn. 1833. 8vo. **125 C**

FLEETWOOD, GEORGE.

Letter from George Fleetwood to his father, giving an account
of the battle of Lutzen. Edited by Sir Philip De M. G
Egerton. [Camden Society, vol. 39.] 1847. 8vo. **85 D**

FLEETWOOD, WILLIAM, BISHOP OF ELY.
A Compleat collection of the sermons, tracts and pieces of all kinds that were written by Dr. William Fleetwood. 1737. folio. **77 H**
The life and miracles of St. Wenefrede. [By William Fleetwood.] 2nd ed. 1713. 8vo. **79 B**

FLEMING, CHARLES and J. TIBBINS.
Royal dictionary, English and French and French and English. 2 vols. Paris, 1879–85. 4to. **123 F**

FLEMING, J.
Tables: comprising sinking fund tables, loan repayment, annuity and compound interest tables. 1886. 8vo. **11 H**

FLEMING, REV. ROBERT.
The Rise and fall of the Papacy. 1849. 8vo. **77 B**

FLEMISH LANGUAGE.
Dictionnaire Flamend et François. Par F. Halma. Amsterdam, 1710. 4to. **123 C**

FLETA.
Fleta: seu, commentarius juris Anglicani . . . Accedit tractatulus vetus de agendi excipiendique formulis Gallicanus, Fetassavoir dictus; subjungitur etiam Joannis Seldeni ad Fletam dissertatio historica. 2nd ed. 1685. 4to. **49 G**
Fleta, seu commentarius juris Anglicani. Liber primus antiqua placita coronæ continens. 1735. folio. **49 G**
See also D. Houard's Coutumes Anglo-Normandes, vol. 3, 1776. 8vo. **40 A**

FLETCHER, BANISTER.
Dilapidations; a text-book for architects and surveyors, in tabulated form. 3rd ed. 1883. 8vo. **9 G**
Light and Air; a text-book for architects and surveyors. 2nd ed. 1886. 12mo. **10 G**

FLOOD, JOHN CHARLES HENRY.
Law relating to wills of personal property. 1877. 8vo. **13 I**
The pitfalls of testators. A few hints about the making of wills. 1884. 8vo. **13 I**

FLORENCE.

The history of Florence. See Machiavel's Works 1680, pp. 1–189. **113 G**

FLOYER, PHILIP.

The Proctor's practice in the ecclesiastical courts. 1744. 12mo. **166 B**

FLÜGEL, JOHANN GOTTFRIED.

Flügel's Complete dictionary of the German and English languages adapted to the English student. By C. A. Feiling, A. Heimann and John Oxenford. New ed. 2 vols. 1861. 8vo. **123 C**

FLUX, WILLIAM.

Law to regulate the Sale of Poisons. 1869. 12mo. **53 C**

FOARD, JAMES THOMAS.

A Treatise on the law of merchant shipping and freight. 1880. 8vo. **53 G**

FŒLIX, JEAN JACQUES GASPARD.

Traité du droit international privé, ou du conflit des lois des différentes nations en matière de droit privé. 3me éd. par C. Demangeat. 2 vols. Paris, 1856. 8vo. **55 B**

FOLEY, ROBERT.

Laws relating to the Poor. 3rd ed. 1751. 12mo. **174 A**
The same. 4th ed. 1758. 12mo. **174 A**

FOLKARD, HENRY COLEMAN.

The pawnbrokers', factors' and merchants' guide to the law of loans and pledges. 1873. 8vo. **53 B**
The law of slander and libel (founded on the treatise of the late Mr. Starkie). 4th ed. 1876. 8vo. **11 F**

FOLLETT, THOMAS LISLE.

Elements of the science of good government. 1833. [Jacob's Tracts, vol. 13.] **144 F**

FONBLANQUE, John.
A Treatise of Equity. [By Henry Ballow] with the addition ot marginal references and notes by John Fonblanque. 2 vols. 1793–94, and 5th ed. 2 vols. 1820. 8vo. **155 B**

FONBLANQUE, John William Martin.
Reports of cases in the several courts of the Commissioners in Bankruptcy. 1849–1852. 1 vol. 1852. 8vo. **8 B**

FONTHILL, Wiltshire.
Delineations of Fonthill and its abbey. By John Rutter. 1823. folio. **94 H**

FOOD.
Law of sales of food, drinks and medicines. Edited by A Barrister and Magistrate. 1875. 12mo. **168 E**

FOOTE, John Alderson.
Foreign and domestic law : concise treatise on private international jurisprudence. 1878. 8vo. **55 A**

FOOTE, William.
Suggestions for the improvement of portions of the criminal law cognizable before justices out of sessions. 2nd ed. 1843. 12mo. **165 D**

FORBES, James David.
A Dissertation exhibiting a general view of the progress of Mathematical and Physical science, principally from 1775 to 1850. See Encyclopædia Britannica, 8th ed. vol. 1, pp. 796–996. **147 A**

FORBES, Urquhart Atwell.
The law relating to trustee and post-office savings banks. 1878. 12mo. **11 E**
The law of savings banks since 1878. 1884. 12mo. **11 E**

FORD, Charles.
Handbook on oaths. 3rd ed. 1879. 12mo. **53 B**
The same. 5th ed. 1889. 12mo. **12 G**
The Solicitors' acts with notes. 2nd ed. 1877. 8vo. **160 C**

FORD, Douglas Morey.
Solicitors as advocates. 1881. 8vo. **11 G**

FORDUN, John de.
Scotichronicon, cum supplementis et continuatione Walteri
Boweri, insulæ Sancti Columbæ abbatis. Curâ Walteri
Goodall. 2 vols. Edinburghi, 1759. folio. **114 H**

FORDYCE, William.
History and antiquities of the county of Durham. 2 vols.
Newcastle, [1857.] 4to. **87 E**

FOREIGN ENLISTMENT ACT.
The Foreign enlistment act. By F. W. Gibbs. 1863.
[Pamphlets, vol. 18.] **144 B**

FOREIGN JUDGMENTS, AND LAW.
The law and practice relating to foreign judgements and parties
out of the jurisdiction. By F. T. Piggott. 2nd ed. 1884.
8vo. **10 D**
Commentaries on colonial and foreign laws generally and in
their conflict with each other and with the law of England.
By Wm. Burge. 4 vols. 1838. 8vo. **55 D**
See also Codes, Henry, J. and International Law.

FOREIGN OFFICE LIST.
The Foreign Office list, forming a complete British diplomatic
and consular handbook. Compiled by Edward Hertslet.
1867, 1869–1890. 27 vols. 1867–90. 8vo. **142 E F**

FORESTS AND FOREST LAWS.
Historical inquiries concerning forests and forest laws with
remarks upon the New Forest. By Percival Lewis. 1811.
4to. **88 B**
Manual of jurisprudence for forest officers. By B. H. Baden-
Powell. Calcutta, 1882. 8vo. **38 D**
Number II. of a selection of leading statutes, containing : The
Forest Charter and four other acts. By Henry Greening.
1842. 8vo. **176 B**
Treatise of the Forest laws. By John Manwood. 4th ed.
By Wm. Nelson. 1717. 8vo. . **52 H**

FORESTALLING.

Inquiry into laws of Forestalling, Regrating and Ingrossing. By W. Illingworth. 1800. 12mo. **168 E**

FORFEITURE.

The law of Escheat and Forfeiture. See Watson's Compendium of Equity, 2nd ed. vol. 1, 1886, pp. 186–191. **12 G**

Dissertation on and precedents of Forfeiture. See Bythewood and Jarman's Conveyancing, 3rd ed. vol. 4, 1840, pp. 70–104. **53 D**

Some considerations on law of Forfeiture for high treason. [By C. Yorke.] 4th ed. Edinburgh, 1778. 12mo. **168 E**

FORREST, ROBERT.

Reports of cases in the court of Exchequer 1800–1801. 1 vol. 1802. 8vo. **7 E**

FORSYTH, ROBERT.

The Beauties of Scotland. 5 vols. Edinburgh, 1805–1808. 8vo. **95 D**

FORSYTH, WILLIAM.

Cases and opinions on Constitutional law, and various points of English Jurisprudence. 1869. 8vo. **63 F**

History of trial by jury. 1852. 8vo. **83 I**

Hortensius. An historical essay on the office and duties of an advocate. 3rd ed. 1879. 8vo. **83 H**

Law relating to composition and arrangements with creditors. 3rd ed. 1854. 8vo. **165 G**

Law relating to custody of infants in cases of difference between parents or guardians. 1850. 8vo. **169 A**

FORTESCUE FAMILY.

A History of the family of Fortescue in all its branches. By Thomas (Fortescue) Lord Clermont. Printed for private distribution. 1869. 4to. **79 I**

FORTESCUE, JOHN, 1 BARON.

Reports of select cases in all the courts of Westminster Hall 1695–1738 ; also the opinion of all the judges of England relating to the grandest prerogative of the Royal family, and some observations relating to the prerogative of a Queen Consort. 1748. folio. **74 D**

FORTESCUE, SIR JOHN.

De laudibus legum Angliæ [in Latin with English translation by Robert Mulcaster]. Hereto are added the two Sums of Sir Ralph de Hengham commonly called Hengham Magna and Hengham Parva ; with notes by John Selden. 1672. 12mo. **49 D**

The same. [Translated and edited by Francis Gregor.] 1737, and 2nd ed. 1741. folio. **115 H**

The same with notes by A. Amos. 1825. 8vo. **170 F**

The difference between an absolute and limited monarchy. 1714. 8vo. **48 F**

The same. 3rd ed. 1724. 8vo. **48 F**

The works of Sir John Fortescue. Collected and arranged by Thomas (Fortescue) Lord Clermont. Printed for private distribution. 1869. 4to. **79 I**

FORTNIGHTLY REVIEW.

The Fortnightly Review, 1873 to 1889. 34 vols. 1873–89. 8vo. **131 B–F**

FORTUNE, E. F. THOMAS.

Epitome of the stocks and public funds, English, Foreign and American. 17th ed. by D. M. Evans. 1856. 12mo. **168 E**

National life annuities ; comprising all the tables, and every necessary information contained in the act of parliament for granting the same. 1808. 8vo. **144 F**

FOSBROKE, REV. THOMAS DUDLEY.

Berkeley manuscripts. Abstracts and extracts of Smyth's Lives of the Berkeleys ; with a copious history of the castle and parish of Berkeley. 1821 4to. **87 F**

An Original history of the city of Gloucester, including the original papers of Ralph Bigland. 1819. folio. **88 H**

The same. Another ed. 1819. 4to. **87 F**

FOSS, EDWARD.

Biographia Juridica. A biographical dictionary of judges of England from the Conquest to present time. 1870. 8vo. **80 E**

The Grandeur of the Law. A list of members of present House of Lords ; whose ancestors have occupied the judicial seat in England. 1842. 4to. **80 E**

The judges of England, with sketches of their lives ; and mis-

FOSS, EDWARD—*continued.*
cellaneous notices connected with courts at Westminster
from time of the Conquest. 9 vols. 1848–64. 8vo. **80 E**

The lineage of Sir Thomas More. 1842. Bound with E.
Foss's Grandeur of the Law. 1842. 4to. **80 E**

On the lord chancellors and keepers of the seal in the reign of
King John. 1847. Bound with E. Foss's Grandeur of the
Law. 1842. 4to. **80 E**

On the origin of the title and office of Cursitor-Baron of the
Exchequer. 1855. Bound with E. Foss's Grandeur of the
Law. 1842. 8vo. **80 E**

Tabulæ Curiales, or tables of the superior courts of Westminster
Hall, showing the judges who sat in them from 1066 to
1864. 1865. 8vo. **80 E**

FOSTER, EDWARD JOHN.
The law of joint ownership and partition of real estate. 1878.
8vo. **13 B**

FOSTER, FRANK, i.e. DANIEL PUSELEY.
Number One ; or, The way of the world. 1862. 8vo. **195 D**

FOSTER, GEORGE JARVIS.
Doctors' Commons : its courts and registries, with a treatise
on Probate Court business. 1868. 8vo. **174 C**

The same. 2nd ed. 1869. 8vo. **174 C**

The same. 3rd ed. 1871. 8vo. **52 F**

FOSTER, JOSEPH.
Alumni Oxonienses : the members of the University of Oxford, 1715–1886 : their parentage &c. with a record of their
degrees. 4 vols. Oxford, 1888. 8vo. **80 G**

Men-at-the-bar, a biographical hand-list of the members of
the various inns of court. 2nd ed. 1885. 4to. **80 F**

The peerage, baronetage and knightage of the British Empire
1880, 1881, 1882 and 1883. 6 vols. 1880–83. 4to. **124 H**

FOSTER, SIR MICHAEL.
A Report of some proceedings on the commission for trial of
the rebels in 1746 in county of Surrey and of other crown
cases. With discourses upon a few branches of the Crown
Law. Dublin, 1767. 8vo. **49 F**

The same. 2nd ed. London, 1776. 8vo. **1 H**

FOSTER, THOMAS CAMPBELL.
Treatise on writ of Scire Facias. 1851. 8vo. **175 D**

FOSTER, THOMAS CAMPBELL and W. F. FINLASON.
Reports of cases decided at Nisi Prius, 1856–1867. 4 vols.
1860–67. 8vo. **8 F**

FOTHERINGAY, NORTHAMPTONSHIRE.
Historic notices in reference to Fotheringay. By Rev. H.
K. Bonney. Ouhdle, 1821. 8vo. **92 D**

FOUGASSES, THOMAS DE.
The generall historie of the magnificent state of Venice. Englished by W. Shute. 2 vols. in 1. 1612. folio. **113 G**

FOULKES, WILLIAM DECIMUS INGLETT.
Smith's Action at law, and an elementary view of proceedings
in an action in supreme court. 3rd ed. 1884. 12mo. **64 A**

FOUNTAINHALL, SIR JOHN LAUDER, LORD.
Decisions of Lords of council and session 1678 to 1712,
also transactions of Privy Council, of Criminal Court, and
Court of Exchequer. 2 vols. Edinburgh, 1759–61. folio.

FOWLER, DAVID BURTON.
The practice of the Court of Exchequer upon proceedings in
equity. 2 vols. 1795. 8vo. **168 B**
The same. 2nd ed. 2 vols. 1817. 8vo. **168 B**

FOWLER, JOHN COKE.
Collieries and Colliers, a handbook of the law and leading
cases relating thereto. 1861. 12mo. **161 F**
The same. 2nd ed. 1869, and 3rd ed. 1872. 12mo. **161 F**
The same. 4th ed. by J. C. Fowler and David Lewis. 1884.
12mo. **9 D**

FOX, CHARLES JAMES.
Biographical memoirs and anecdotes of the late Charles James
Fox. 1806. 8vo. **79 C**

FOX, ROBERT.
The history of Godmanchester in the county of Huntingdon.
1831. 8vo. **88 C**

FOXE, John.

Narratives of the days of the Reformation. Edited by J. G. Nichols. [Camden Society, vol. 77.] 1860. 8vo. **85 B**

FRAMLINGHAM, Suffolk.

The history of Framlingham, including brief notices of the masters and fellows of Pembroke Hall in Cambridge. By the late Robert Hawes, with considerable additions and notes by Robert Loder. Woodbridge, 1798. 4to. **93 B**

FRANCE, History of.

Catalogue des rolles Gascons, Normans et François, conservés dans les archives de la Tour de Londres. Par Thomas Carte. 2 vols. in 1. 1743. folio. **99 B**

Chronicles containing an account of the cruel civil wars between the houses of Orleans and Burgundy from 1400 to 1467. By E. de Monstrelet and continued by others to 1516. Translated by T. Johnes. 2 vols. 1840. 8vo. **115 A**

Chronological history of France. By the Sieur De Mezeray. Translated by John Bulteel. 1683. folio. **113 H**

Chronologique de l'histoire de France. Par F. E. de Mezeray. Nouvelle éd. 4 vols. Amsterdam, 1740. 4to. **113 E**

Considérations sur les principaux événements de la révolution Française. La Directoire. Par Madame De Staël. Edited by Victor Oger. 2nd ed. 1882. 12mo. **83 C**

Genealogy of royal family of France. 1825. folio. **126 I**

Historical sketch of the French bar from its origin to the present day. By A. Young. Edinburgh, 1869. 8vo. **79 B**

A History of France. By G. W. Kitchin. 2nd ed. 3 vols. Oxford, 1881–85. 12mo. **113 E**

A Letter of several French ministers fled into Germany, upon account of persecution in France, to such of their brethren in England as approved the King's declaration touching liberty of conscience. [n.d.] [Tracts, 1688–89.] **118 E**

Memoirs of the Duke of Sully. New ed. 5 vols. 1819. 8vo. **80 A**

The monarchy of France in its rise, progress and fall. By W. Tooke. 1855. 8vo. **113 E**

Petite histoire du peuple Français. Par Paul Lacombe. Edited by Jules Bué. 10th ed. [n.d.] 12mo. **83 C**

Protestant exiles from France in reign of Louis XIV. By Rev. D. C. A. Agnew. 2nd ed. 3 vols. 1871–74. 8vo. **80 G**

FRANCE, HISTORY OF—*continued.*

Récits d'histoire de France. Par J. Michelet. Edited by
A. Esclangeon. Part I. From the earliest times to the
battle of Rocroy. 1889. 12mo. **83 C**

Recueil de documents sur les exactions, vols et cruautés des
armées Prussiennes en France. Bordeaux, 1871. 8vo. **78 C**

1685–1885. In memory of the revocation of the edict of
Nantes, 24th October, 1685. By M. Gwynne-Griffith. [n.d.]
[Pamphlets, vol. 40.] **144 C**

See also COMINES, F. DE and ENGLAND, HISTORY OF.

FRANCE, LANGUAGE OF.

Dictionnaire de la langue Française. Par E. Littré. 5 vols.
Paris, 1881. 4to. **123 F**

Dictionnaire François et Hollandois. Par P. Marin. 4me éd.
Amsterdam, 1762. 4to. **123 C**

Le dictionnaire royal François-Anglois et Anglois-François.
Par M. Boyer. Nouvelle éd. par Louis du Mitaud. 2 vols.
1816. 4to. **123 E**

Dictionnaire universel François et Latin vulgairement appelé
Dictionnaire de Trévoux. Nouvelle éd. 8 vols. Paris, 1771.
folio. **122 G**

General French and English and English and French dictionary. By A. Spiers. 2 vols. [n.d.] 8vo. **123 E**

Glossary of obsolete French words. See Britton, edited by
F. M. Nichols, vol. 2, 1865, pp. 363–384. **167 A**

Glossary of obsolete French words. See Du Cange's Glossarium, vol. 10, 1766. folio. **123 H**

Glossary of Old French and Gothic words. See Chronicles
of Robert of Brunne, vol. 2, 1887, pp. 769–846. **102 I**

A Grammar of the French language. By Isidore Brasseur.
17th ed. 1863. 12mo. **255 H**

Grammatical exercises English and French. By M. Porny.
6th ed. 1789. 12mo. **255 H**

The Public Examination French Grammar. By John Gibson.
2nd ed. 1883. 8vo. **255 H**

Royal dictionary, English and French and French and
English. By Professors Fleming and Tibbins. 2 vols.
Paris, 1879–85. 4to. **123 F**

A Vocabulary of French sea-phrases and terms of art. See
Falconer's Marine Dictionary. 1815. 4to. **123 D**

See also FURETIÈRE, A. and MINSHEU, J.

FRANCE, LAW OF.

Nationality, domicile and residence in France; decree of October 2, 1888, concerning foreigners. By Thomas Barclay. 1888. 8vo.   **55 C**

French law of marriage and conflict of laws that arises therefrom. By E. Kelly. 1885. 8vo.   **55 C**

The lunacy law of France. See G. L. Harrison's Legislation on insanity, 1884, pp. 1025–1039.   **59 G**

The land system of France. By T. E. C. Leslie. See Systems of Land tenure, 1881, pp. 291–312.   **78 B**

Experiences of an English buyer of land in France. 1876. [Pamphlets, vol. 35.]   **144 C**

The law of France on industrial and provident societies. See Brabrook's Industrial Societies, 1869, pp. xxxii–xxxvii and 89–104.   **169 A**

Dictionnaire législatif et réglementaire des Chemins de Fer. Par G. Palaa. Paris, 1864. 8vo.   **40 H**

Lois de la procédure civile et administrative. Par G. L. J. Carré. 4me éd. Par C. Adolphe. 9 vols. Paris, 1862–63. 8vo.   **58 B**

Répertoire de législation et de jurisprudence en matière de Brevets d'Invention. Par A. Huard. Paris, 1863. 12mo.   **58 F**

Journal de jurisprudence commerciale et maritime. Par MM. Girod et Clariond. 16 vols. bound in 2. Marseille, 1820–37. 8vo.   **58 F**

Concise digest of the law, usage, and custom relating to commercial and civil intercourse of subjects of Great Britain and France. By C. H. Okey. 4th ed. 1834. 8vo.   **55 C**

Recueil général des anciennes lois Françaises, depuis l'an 420 jusqu'à la révolution de 1789. Par MM. Jourdan, Decrusy, Isambert, avec Table par MM. Isambert, Decrusy, Taillandier. 29 vols. Paris, 1822–33. 8vo.   **58 A**

The law of France respecting Foreigners. See J. Henry's Case of Odwin v. Forbes, 1823, pp. 209–250.   **55 D**

Nouveau code des Prises, ou Recueil des edits, declarations, lettres patentes &c. sur la course et l'administration des Prises, depuis 1400 jusqu'à l'établissement du Conseil des Prises. Par M. Lebeau. 3 vols. Paris, An 7–9 [1798–1800]. 4to.   **40 H**

Institution au droit François. Par G. Argou. 11me éd. Par A. G. Boucher d'Argis. 2 vols. 1787. 12mo.   **58 F**

Collection de décisions nouvelles et de notions relatives à la jurisprudence actuelle. Par J. B. Denisart. 9me éd. 4 vols. Paris, 1777. 4to.   **40 F**

FRANCE, LAW OF—*continued.*

Maximes du droit public François. 2 vols. Paris, 1772. 12mo. **58 F**

Traité des Fiefs. Par C. Pocquet. 5me éd. Paris, 1771. 4to. **58 G**

Nouveau commentaire sur les ordonnances des mois d'Août 1669 et Mars 1673 ensemble sur l'edit du mois de Mars 1673 touchant les Epices. Par M * * *. Nouvelle éd. Paris, 1761. 12mo. **58 F**

Nouveau commentaire sur l'ordonnance de la Marine du mois d'Août 1681. Par René Josué Valin. 2 vols. La Rochelle, 1760. 4to. **40 E**

L'Art de proceder en justice, ou la science des moyens judiciels necessaires pour découvrir la verité. Par M. L. Lasseré. Paris, 1677. 8vo. **58 G**

See also BÉDARRIDE, J., CODES, DEMOLOMBE, J. C. F., POTHIER, R. J. and TROPLONG, R. T.

FRANCE, LITERATURE OF.

About, Edmond. La Fille du Chanoine, La Mère de la Marquise, Trente et Quarante, Le Roi des Montagnes. Edited by Rev. P. H. E. Brette and Gustave Masson. 7th ed. 1880. 12mo. **83 C**

Bonnechose, Émile De. Lazare Hoche. Edited by Henri Bué. 10th ed. 1882. 12mo. **83 C**

Chateaubriand, F. R. de, Viscount. Les Aventures du dernier Abencerage. Edited by A. Roulier. 1880. 12mo. **83 C**

Corneille, Pierre. Le Cid, tragédie en cinq actes et en vers. 5me éd. Bielefeld, 1860. 24mo. **83 A**

Corneille, Pierre. Commentaires sur le théatre de Pierre Corneille, et autres morceaux intéressans. vols. 2 and 3. 1774. 24mo. **83 A**

D'Aubigné, Jean Henri Merle. Histoire de Bayart. Edited by Jules Bué. New ed. 1881. 12mo. **83 C**

De Witt, Madame Henriette. Derrière les Haies. Edited by Paul De-Bussy. 7th ed. 1882. 12mo. **83 C**

Dumas, Alexandre. La Tulipe Noire. Edited by Paul Blouet. 1882. 12mo. **83 C**

Feuillet, Octave. Le Roman d'un jeune homme pauvre. Edited by H. Bué. 1890. 12mo. **83 C**

Halévy, Ludovic. L'Abbé Constantin. Edited by George Petilleau. 2nd ed. 1888. 12mo. **83 C**

FRANCE, Literature of—*continued.*

Maistre, Xavier de. Les Prisonniers du Caucase. Edited by I. H. B. Spiers. 1888. 12mo.   **83 C**

Maistre, Xavier de. Voyage autour de ma Chambre. Edited by Jules Bué. 2nd ed. 1882. 12mo.   **83 C**

Malot, Hector. Capi et sa troupe. Épisode de ' sans famille.' Edited by F. Tarver. 2nd ed. 1889. 12mo.   **83 C**

Malot, Hector. Sous Terre. Épisode de ' sans famille.' Edited by A. Dupuis. 1890. 12mo.   **83 C**

Mérimée, Prosper. Colomba. Edited by Rev. P. H. E. Brette. 2nd ed. 1882. 12mo.   **83 C**

Musset, Alfred de. Selections from the prose and poetical works of Alfred de Musset. Edited by Gustave Masson. 2nd ed. 1880. 12mo.   **83 C**

Ponsard, François. Le Lion Amoureux. Edited by H. J. V. De Candole. 2nd ed. 1880. 12mo.   **83 C**

Pressensé, Madame E. de. Rosa. Edited by Gustave Masson. 2nd ed. 1881. 12mo.   **83 C**

Saintine, X. B. Picciola. Edited by Paul Baume. 2 vols. 1880–81. 12mo.   **83 C**

Scribe, Eugène. Bertrand et Raton, ou l'art de conspirer. Comédie en cinq actes. Edited by Jules Bué. 6th ed. 1881. 12mo.   **83 C**

Sévigné, Marie de Rabutin Chantal, Marquise de. Letters of Madame de Sévigné to her daughter and her friends. 9 vols. 1811. 12mo.   **83 A**

Töpffer, Rodolphe. Le Presbytère. La Bibliothèque de mon Oncle. Edited by Rev. P. H. E. Brette and G. Masson. 1873. 12mo.   **83 C**

Villemain, Abel François. Lascaris, ou les Grecs du xvᵉ siècle. Edited by A. Dupuis. 2nd ed. 1875. 12mo.   **83 C**

See also GUIZOT, G., LAMARTINE, A. DE, LE SAGE, A. R., MICHELET, J., MIRABAUD, J. B. DE, MOLIÈRE, J. B. P., MONTESQUIEU, C. DE S., RABELAIS, F., RACINE, J., ROCHEFOUCAULD, F., SAND, G. and ZOLA, E.

FRANCILLON, James.

Lectures elementary and ·familiar on English law. First series. 1860. 8vo.   **170 G**

FRANCIS, John.

History of the Bank of England, its times and traditions. 3rd ed. 2 vols. [n.d.] 8vo.   **91 C**

FRANCIS, PHILIP.
The law of Charities. 1854. 12mo. **161 F**

FRANCIS, SIR PHILIP, K.C.B.
Memoirs of Sir Philip Francis, K.C.B., with correspondence
and journals. By J. Parkes and H. Merivale. 2 vols.
1867. 8vo. **80 B**

FRANCIS, RICHARD.
Maxims of Equity ; to which is added the Case of the Earl
of Coventry concerning the defective execution of powers.
1728, and 2nd ed. 1739. folio. **155 D**

FRANCISCAN FRIARS IN ENGLAND.
Monumenta Franciscana. Edited by J. S. Brewer and Richard
Howlett. 2 vols. 1858–82. 8vo. **101 A**

FRANCISCO, FRAY.
El hecho de los tratados del matrimonio pretendido por el
Principe de Gales con la serenissima Infante de Espana
Maria. Narrative of the Spanish marriage treaty. Edited
and translated by S. R. Gardiner. [Camden Society, vol.
101.] 1869. 8vo. **85 C**

FRASER, HUGH.
Law of Libel in its relation to the Press. 1889. 8vo. **11 F**

FRASER, SIMON.
Reports of proceedings before select committees of House
of Commons in cases of controverted Elections, 1790–92.
2 vols. 1791–93. 8vo. **66 A**

FRAUD, LAW OF.
A Treatise on the law of Fraud. By W. W. Kerr. 2nd ed.
1883. 8vo. **10 A**
A Treatise on the Statute of Frauds. By W. F. Agnew. 1876.
8vo. **10 A**
A General treatise on principles and practice by which courts
of equity are guided as to prevention or correction of Fraud.
By J. E. Hovenden. 2 vols. 1825. 8vo. **168 E**
A Treatise on the Statute of Frauds. By William Roberts.
1805. 12mo. **168 E**
See also CONVEYANCES, FRAUDULENT.

FREEHOLD.

The seisin of the freehold. By J. Williams. 1878. 8vo. **53 G**

Opinions on an estate in fee simple defeasible on leaving no issue. See Collectanea Juridica, vol. 2, pp. 277–291. **144 G**

FREEHOLD LAND SOCIETIES.

The law of building and freehold land societies. By H. F. A. Davis. 3rd ed. 1884. 12mo. **9 B**

FREEMAN, EDWARD AUGUSTUS.

Historic Towns. Exeter. 1887. 8vo **87 C**

The history of the Norman conquest of England, its causes and its results. 6 vols. 1877–79. 8vo. **115 A B**

FREEMAN, KENNETT.

Repertorium Juridicum ; an index to all the cases in the year-books, entries, reports and abridgments in law and equity. By A Barrister of the Middle Temple. 1742. folio.

The same. New ed. by T. E. Tomlins. 2 vols. 1788. 8vo. **63 D**

FREEMAN, RICHARD.

Cases argued and decreed in the high court of Chancery, from 1676 to 1706. Revised by T. Dixon. 1742. folio. **74 D**

Reports of cases in the Court of Chancery, 1660–1706. 2nd ed. by J. E. Hovenden. 1823. 8vo. **2 G**

Reports of cases in courts of King's Bench and Common Pleas 1670 to 1683. Revised by T. Dixon. 1742. folio. **74 D**

FREE-TRADE.

Sophisms of free-trade and popular political economy examined. By A Barrister [J. B. Byles]. 1849. 12mo. **78 A**

FREND, ALFRED BLACKBURNE.

Exposition of conduct of George Rooper, relative to certain slanderous expressions uttered by him, and affecting character of A. B. Frend. 1848. [Pamphlets, vol. 6.] **144 A**

FREND, HENRY TYRWHITT.

Perexigua, or land transfer and other conveyancing on short lines. 1885. 8vo. **53 C**

Precedents of instruments relating to the transfer of land to railway companies. By H. T. Frend and T. H. Ware. 2nd ed. with a treatise upon lands clauses consolidation acts. By D. Sturges and T. L. M. Browne. 1866. 8vo. **53 F**

FRERE, CHARLES.
The practice of committees of the House of Commons, with
reference especially to private bills. 1846. 8vo. **173 C**

FRESHFIELD, JAMES WILLIAM.
Law relating to Principal and Factor. Address delivered by
Mr. Freshfield to select committee of House of Commons.
2nd ed. 1823. folio. **153 E**
Speech in House of Commons on Breach of Privilege. 1839.
[Pamphlets, vol. 28.] **144 B**
Speech in House of Commons on Courts of Equity. 1839.
[Chancery Pamphlets, vol. 2.] **144 A**

FRIENDLY SOCIETIES.
Club law and the law of unregistered friendly societies. By
Dominick Daly. 2nd ed. 1889. 12mo. **9 C**
Law of Friendly Societies. By J. T. Pratt. 10th ed. by
E. W. Brabrook. 1881. 12mo. **10 A**

FROISSART, SIR JOHN.
Chronicles of England, France, Spain and the adjoining
countries, 1326–1399. Translated by Thomas Johnes.
2 vols. 1857. 8vo. **115 A**

FROST, CHARLES.
Notices relative to the early history of the town and port of
Hull. 1827. 4to. **94 D**

FROUDE, JAMES ANTHONY.
The English in Ireland in the eighteenth century. 3 vols.
1887. 12mo. **115 D**
History of England from the fall of Wolsey to the defeat of
the Spanish Armada. 12 vols. 1858–70. 8vo. **115 B**

FRY, DANBY PALMER.
Law relating to Vaccination. 5th ed. 1872. 12mo. **176 G**
Union assessment committee acts. 7th ed. by R. C. Glen
and A. D. Lawrie. 1887. 12mo. **11 I**

FRY, EDWARD.
A Treatise on the specific performance of contracts, including
those of public companies. 1858. 8vo. **163 D**
The same. 2nd ed. by the author and W. D. Rawlins. 1881.
8vo. **9 E**

FULBECKE, WILLIAM.

A Parallele, or conference of the civil law, the canon law, and the common law of this realme of England. 1618. 8vo. **48 E**

FULHAM, MIDDLESEX.

An Historical and topographical account of Fulham. By Thomas Faulkner. 1813. 8vo. **89 E**

FULKE, WILLIAM.

A Defence of the translations of the Holy Scriptures into the English tongue, against the cavils of Gregory Martin. Edited by Rev. C. H. Hartshorne. Cambridge, 1843. 8vo. **77 D**

Stapleton's Fortress overthrown. A rejoinder to Martiall's reply. A discovery of the dangerous rock of the Popish church commended by Sanders. Edited by Rev. Richard Gibbings. Cambridge, 1848. 8vo. **77 D**

FULLER, JOHN.

The history of Berwick upon Tweed, including a short account of the villages of Tweedmouth and Spittal. Edinburgh, 1799. 8vo. **92 D**

FULLER, THOMAS.

The history of the University of Cambridge and of Waltham Abbey, with the Appeal of injured innocence unto the religious, learned and ingenuous reader, in a controversy betwixt Peter Heylin and the author. New ed. by James Nichols. 1840. 8vo. **86 C**

The history of the University of Cambridge from the conquest to the year 1634. Edited by the late Rev. Marmaduke Prickett and Thomas Wright. 1840. 8vo. **86 C**

The history of the worthies of England. New ed. by John Nichols. 2 vols. 1811. 4to. **79 H**

The holy state and the profane state. New ed. with notes by James Nichols. 1841. 8vo. **80 B**

Life of Thomas Fuller. See J. P. Malcolm's Lives of topographers. 1815. 4to. **79 H**

FULTON, FORREST.

Manual of constitutional history containing fundamental principles and leading cases in constitutional law. 1875. 8vo. **116 C**

FUNDS, THE.

Compendium of the English and foreign funds. By C. Fenn. 14th ed. by R. L. Nash. 1889. 8vo.   **10 A**

Epitome of the stocks and public funds. By E. F. T. Fortune. 17th ed. by D. M. Evans. 1856. 12mo.   **168 E**

The law relating to the public Funds. By J. J. Wilkinson. 1839. 12mo.   **168 F**

The laws relating to English and foreign funds, shares and securities. By William Royle. 1875. 8vo.   **168 F**

The stocks examined and compared, or a guide to purchasers in the public funds. By Wm. Fairman. 5th ed. 1808. 8vo.   **144 F**

See also FINANCE.

FUNERAL MONUMENTS.

Ancient funeral monuments of Great Britain, Ireland and the islands adjacent, whereunto is prefixed a discourse on funeral monuments. By John Weever. 1767. 4to.   **81 F**

FURETIÈRE, ANTOINE.

Dictionnaire universel, contenant generalement tous les mots François tant vieux que modernes et les termes des sciences et des arts. 2me éd. par B. de Bauval. La Haye, 1701. folio. [2 vols. only, containing A to N.]

FURLEY, ROBERT.

History of the Weald of Kent, with an outline of the early history of the county. 2 vols. in 3. 1871–74. 8vo. **88 E**

FURNEAUX, REV. PHILIP.

Letters to Mr. Justice Blackstone concerning his Exposition of the act of toleration and some positions relative to religious liberty. 2nd ed. 1771. 8vo.   **77 B**

FURNESS, LANCASHIRE.

Antiquities of Furness. By T. West. 1774. 4to.   **88 F**

The same. New ed. by Wm. Close. 1813. 8vo.   **89 B**

FYNN, ROBERT.

British consuls abroad, their origin, rank and privileges, duties, jurisdiction and emoluments. 3rd ed. 1851. 12mo. **163 D**

GABBETT, JOSEPH.
Digested abridgment of statute law of England and Ireland, to the year 1811. 2 vols. Dublin, 1812. 8vo. **63 B**

GACHES, LOUIS.
Town councillors & burgesses manual. 1875. 8vo. **176 F**

GAGE, JOHN.
History and antiquities of Hengrave in Suffolk. 1822. 4to. [Bound with Cullum's Hawsted, 1813.] **93 G**
The history and antiquities of Suffolk. Thingoe hundred. 1838. folio. **93 H**

GAIGNAT, LOUIS JEAN.
Catalogue des livres du cabinet de feu M. Louis Jean Gaignat. 2 vols. Paris, 1769. 8vo. **82 A**

GAILL, ANDREAS.
Practicarum observationum, tam ad processum judiciarium præsertim imperialis cameræ, quam causarum decisiones pertinentium, libri duo. De pace publica et proscriptis sive bannitis imperii, libri II. De Pignorationibus, liber singularis. De manuum injectionibus, sive arrestis imperii, tractatus. Editio postrema. Coloniæ Agrippinæ, 1621. 4to.

GAIMAR, GEOFFREY.
Lestorie des Engles solum la translacion Maistre Geffrei Gaimar. Edited by Sir T. D. Hardy and C. T. Martin. 2 vols. 1888–89. 8vo. **102 I**

GAINSBOROUGH, LINCOLNSHIRE.
The history and antiquities of Gainsburgh. By Adam Stark. 1817. 8vo. **89 C**

GAIUS, THE JURIST.
Commentaries on the Roman law ; with an English translation and annotations. By F. Tomkins and W. G. Lemon. 1869. 8vo. **63 E**
Commentaries ; translated with notes by J. T. Abdy and B. Walker. 2nd ed. Cambridge, 1874. 8vo. **63 E**
Elements of Roman law summarized. A concise digest of the matter contained in Institutes of Gaius and Justinian. By S. F. Harris. 1875. 8vo. **63 E**
Elements of Roman law ; with a translation and commentary by Edward Poste. 2nd ed. Oxford, 1875. 8vo. **63 E**

GALE, Charles James.
Reports of cases in the Court of Exchequer. 1835–1836. 2 vols.
1836–38. 8vo. **7 E**
A Treatise on the law of Easements. By C. J. Gale and
T. D. Whatley. 1839. 8vo. **166 A**
The same. 2nd ed. by C. J. Gale. 1849. 8vo. **166 A**
The same. 5th ed. by D. Gibbons. 1876. 8vo. **52 F**
The same. 6th ed. by G. Cave. 1888. 8vo. **9 G**

GALE, Charles James and Henry DAVISON.
Reports of cases in court of Queen's Bench and Exchequer
Chamber. 1841–1843. 3 vols. 1842–43. 8vo. **5 B**

GALE, Roger.
Registrum Honoris de Richmond; exhibens terrarum et
villarum, quæ quondam fuerunt Edwini Comitis infra Rich-
mundshire, descriptionem, ex libro Domesday in thesauria
domini regis. 1722. folio. **95 H**

GALE, Samuel.
History of cathedral church of Winchester. Begun by Henry
late Earl of Clarendon and continued by Samuel Gale.
1715. 8vo. **88 A**

GALER, Allan Maxey.
Norwood & Dulwich : past and present. 1890. 4to. **93 D**

GALFRIDUS ANGLICUS.
Promptorium parvulorum sive clericorum, lexicon Anglo-
Latinum princeps. Edited by Albert Way. [Camden
Society, vols. 25, 54, 89.] 3 vols. 1843–65. 8vo. **85 A–C**

GALLISON, John.
Reports of cases in Circuit Court of United States for first
circuit 1812 to 1815. 2nd ed 2 vols. Boston, 1845.
8vo. **57 A**

GALLOWAY.
The history of Galloway. By Rev. William Mackenzie.
2 vols. Kirkcudbright, 1841. 8vo. **95 C**

GALWAY.
History of Galway. By J. Hardiman. Dublin, 1820. 4to. **95 F**

GAMBELLONA, ANGELUS.

Finis commentariorum seu lectura super institutionibus Justinianis. Lugd., 1524. folio.

GAMBIA.

Laws and ordinances of the British settlements in the Gambia and their dependencies 1843–1867. 1868. folio.   **37 D**

Ordinances of the settlement on the river Gambia from 15th Sept. 1879 to 30th Dec. 1885. Compiled by Francis Smith. vols. 2 and 3. 1886–87. folio.   **37 D**

Rules of the court of civil and criminal justice of the settlement on the River Gambia. 1877. folio.   **37 C**

GAMBIER, EDWARD JOHN.

Treatise on Parochial Settlements. 1828. 8vo.   **175 E**

GAME LAWS AND LICENSES.

Handy book of the Game laws. By G. C. Oke. 3rd ed. by J. W. W. Bund. 1881. 8vo.   **10 A**

Game Licenses. Year 1869–70. Names and addresses of all persons who have taken out licenses in the United Kingdom. 1869. folio.   **156 B**

The game laws. By J. Locke. 5th ed. 1866. 12mo. **52 H**

A Treatise on the Game laws and on Fisheries. By Joseph Chitty. 3 vols. 1812–16. 8vo.   **168 F**

See also DEACON, E. E., LEIGH, P. B., NELSON, W. and PATERSON, J.   **168 F**

GAMES AND GAMING.

Games, gaming and gamesters' law. By F. Brandt. 1871. 8vo.   **10 B**

The gamester's law ; wherein is treated of unlawful games. 2nd ed. 1711. 12mo.   **48 C**

See also BETTING.

GAOLS.

Facts and arguments in favour of a more frequent delivery of gaols. By Lord Western. 1842. [Pamphlets, vol. 18.] **144 B**

List of county court judges. Note on the abolition of certain franchise gaols. [By T. Falconer.] 1865. 8vo.   **80 F**

GARDINER, Ralph.

England's grievance discovered in relation to the coal trade, with map of the river of Tine and situation of the town and corporation of Newcastle. London, 1655. Newcastle, re-printed, 1796. 8vo. **92 D**

[GARDINER, Robert.]

Ars Clericalis : the art of conveyancing explained. By R. G. 2nd ed. 2 vols. 1698. 8vo. **49 E**

Instructor Clericalis. The first part directing clerks both in the court of King's Bench and Common Pleas. By R. G. 6th ed. 1721, and 7th ed. 1727. 12mo. **163 B**

The New Retorna Brevium collected from the many printed law books extant concerning the retorn of writs. By R. G. 1707, and 3rd ed. 1738. 12mo. **178 D**

GARDINER, Right Rev. Stephen.

Oration on true obedience, with Bishop Bonner's preface. Edited by B. A. Heywood. 1870. 12mo. **78 A**

GARDNER, Thomas.

Historical account of Dunwich, Blithburgh, Southwold, with remarks on some places contiguous. 1754. 4to. **93 B**

GARFIELDE, S. and F. A. SNYDER.

Compiled laws of the State of California, containing all the acts passed. 1850–53. Benicia, 1853. 8vo. **59 B**

GARROW, Rev. David William.

History and antiquities of Croydon, to which is added a sketch of the life of John Whitgift, lord archbishop of Canterbury. Croydon, 1818. 8vo. **93 C**

GARRY, Rupert.

Elocution, voice and gesture illustrated by annotated pieces. 1888. 12mo. **78 B**

GARTER, Order of the.

An Historical account of the knights of the Garter from 1350 to the present time. By John Buswell. 1757. 8vo. **125 E**

History of the order of the Garter. By Elias Ashmole. 1715. 8vo. **125 E**

See also Pote, J.

GAS.

The law relating to Gas and Water. By W. H. Michael and J. S. Will. 3rd ed. 1884. 8vo.   **10 B**

See also F. Clifford's History of private bill legislation, vol. I, 1885, pp. 203–231.   **83 I**

GAVELKIND.

Tenures of Kent. By C. I. Elton. 1867. 8vo.   **10 B**

Common law of Kent, or Customs of Gavelkind, with decisions concerning Borough English. By T. Robinson. New ed. by J. D. Norwood. Ashford, 1858. 8vo.   **10 B**

A History of Gavelkind. By C. Sandys. 1851. 8vo. **10 B**

A Treatise of Gavelkind, both name and thing. By Wm. Somner. 2nd ed. 1726. 8vo.   **81 F**

The history of Gavel-kind with the etymology thereof. By Silas Taylor. 1663. 8vo.   **118 A**

GAZETTEERS.

The Edinburgh gazetteer or geographical dictionary. 6 vols. Edinburgh, 1822. 8vo.   **84 G**

Gazetteer of territories under government of East India company and of native states on continent of India. By E. Thornton. 4 vols. 1854. 8vo.   **84 G**

General dictionary of geography, forming a complete gazetteer. By A. K. Johnston. New ed. 1882. 8vo.   **Hall**

Imperial gazetteer, a general dictionary of geography. Edited by W. G. Blackie. 2 vols. 1856. 4to.   **84 E**

The universal gazetteer, or short view of the several nations of the world. By Mr. Salmon. 10th ed. 1777. 8vo. **84 A**

GEARE, EDWARD ARUNDEL.

The investment of trust funds. 1886. 8vo.   **53 H**

The same. 2nd ed. 1889. 8vo.   **11 I**

GEARY, WILLIAM NEVILL MONTGOMERIE.

Law of theatres and music halls. 1885. 8vo.   **11 H**

GENEALOGY.

Bibliotheca heraldica Magnæ Britanniæ. By Thomas Moule. 1822. 8vo.   **82 C**

Calendarium genealogicum, Henry III. and Edward I. Edited by Charles Roberts. 2 vols. 1865. 8vo.   **96 B**

GENEALOGY—*continued.*

Collectanea topographica et genealogica. [Edited by J. G. Nichols.] 8 vols. 1834-43. 8vo. **127 I**

County Genealogies. (Kent, Sussex, Hants, Essex, Herts.) By W. Berry. 5 vols. in 4. 1830-42. folio. **126 I**

Fielding's Regal tables, or genealogical descent of all the sovereign princes in Europe. 1786. 12mo. [Bound with Fielding's Peerage, 1786.] **124 B**

Genealogical tables of the sovereigns of the world. By Rev. Wm. Betham. 1795. folio. **125 H**

The genealogist's guide to printed pedigrees. By G. W. Marshall. 1879. 8vo. **124 H**

Historical and genealogical dictionary. 1703. 12mo. **79 A**

How to write the history of a family, a guide for the genealogist. By W. P. W. Phillimore. 1887. 8vo. **124 G**

Index to pedigrees and arms contained in Heralds' visitations and other genealogical manuscripts in British Museum. By Richard Sims. 1849. 8vo. **124 H**

Manual for the genealogist, topographer, antiquary and legal professor. By Richard Sims. 2nd ed. 1861. 8vo. **124 G**

Royal descents and pedigrees of founders' kin. By Sir J. B. Burke. 1864. 8vo. **125 E**

The sphere of gentry : an historical and genealogical work of arms and blazon. By S. Morgan. 1661. folio. **118 F**

See also BURKE, J., BURKE, SIR J. B., COUNTY FAMILIES and GRIMALDI, S.

GENERAL AVERAGE.

The law of General Average. By Richard Lowndes. 4th ed. 1888. 8vo. **10 B**

See also AVERAGE.

GENERAL ISSUE.

An Inquiry into the principles of pleading the general issue. By A. J. P. Lutwyche. 1838. 12mo.

See also CHARNOCK, R.

GENEVA.

Illustrated guide of Geneva. Geneva, 1888. 12mo. **84 A**

Livre des Anglois à Geneve, with a few biographical notes. By J. S. Burn. 1831. [Pamphlets, vol. 25.] **144 B**

GENT, Thomas.
Life of Thomas Gent. See J. P. Malcolm's Lives of Topographers. 1815. 4to. 79 H

GENTLEMAN'S MAGAZINE.
The Gentleman's Magazine, or monthly intelligencer, 1731-
1880. 247 vols. 1731-1880. 8vo. **127, 128, & 129**
General index, 1731-1786. By S. Ayscough. 2 vols. 1818;
general index, 1786-1818, with introduction descriptive of
rise and progress of the magazine. By John Nichols.
2 vols. 1821. 4 vols. 1818-21. 8vo. **128 G**
List of plates and woodcuts, 1731-1818, and an alphabetical
index thereto. [By C. St. Barbe, junior.] 1821. 8vo. **128 G** '
Index to the obituary and biographical notices, 1731-1780.
By R. H. Farrar. 3 vols. 1886-91. 8vo. **128 G**

GENTLEMEN PENSIONERS, Band of.
Curialia, part ii., containing a Memoir regarding the band
of gentlemen pensioners. By S. Pegge. 1784. 4to. **83 J**

GENTOO LAWS.
A Code of Gentoo laws, or ordinations of the Pundits. By
N. B. Halhed. 1781. 4to. **38 A**

GEOFFREY OF MONMOUTH.
British history; in twelve books. Translated by Aaron Thompson. New ed. by J. A. Giles. 1842. 8vo. **115 A**

GEOGRAPHY.
La Cosmographie universelle recueillie de chasque bon autheur
et approuvé, tant des historiens, comme de ceux qui ont
descrit les lieux particuliers. Par Sebastian Munster.
Bale, 1552. folio. **118 H**
Dictionary of geography. By A. K. Johnston. New ed.
1882. 8vo. **Hall**
Dictionary of Greek and Roman geography. Edited by Wm.
Smith. 2 vols. 1854-57. 8vo. **84 C**
Dictionary of the various countries, places and principal
natural objects in the world. By J. R. M'Culloch. New
ed. by F. Martin. 4 vols. in 2. 1866. 8vo. **84 G**
Exercises on the globes. By W. Butler. 2nd ed. 1800.
12mo. **255 H**
The gallery of nature, a pictorial and descriptive tour through
creation. By Thomas Milner. New ed. 1855. 8vo. **84 D**

GEOGRAPHY—*continued.*

Geography made easy, a manual of geography prepared on a new principle. By John Gibson. 1882. 12mo.　　**84 A**

Glossary of geographical names. See Chronica Rogeri de Hoveden, vol. 4, 1871, pp. 199–241.　　**102 C**

A Manual of modern geography. By J. Gregory. 2nd ed. 1740. 12mo.　　**84 A**

A New and complete description of the terrestrial and celestial globes. By T. Dilworth. 2nd ed. 1794. 8vo.　　**255 H**

A new system of geography, or a general description of the whole known world. By D. Fenning and J. Collyer. 4th ed. 2 vols. 1772–73. folio.　　**158 F**

The new universal geographical and historical grammar, being an improvement and continuation of Salmon's and Guthrie's grammars. 1777. 8vo.　　**84 A**

Our ocean highways. By J. M. Dempsey. 1870. 8vo.　**84 A**

The treasury of geography. By S. Maunder and W. Hughes. New ed. 1860. 12mo.　　**84 A**

Universal pocket companion. 3rd ed. 1760. 12mo.　**84 A**

See also ATLASES, ENGLAND ANTIQUITIES AND TOPO-GRAPHY OF and GAZETTEERS.

GEOLOGY.

The gallery of nature, a pictorial and descriptive tour through creation. By Thomas Milner. New ed. 1855. 8vo.　**84 D**

Geology & mineralogy considered with reference to natural theology. By Rev. W. Buckland. 2 vols. 1836. 8vo.　**77 B**

GEOMETRY.

A Treatise of practical Geometry. By David Gregory. 10th ed. Edinburgh, 1787. 8vo.　　**255 H**

See also EUCLID and HUTTON, C.

GEORGE I. II. AND III., KINGS OF ENGLAND.

Answer to Shepheard the Assassine's speech, to which is added An account of the treasonable sermon of Edward Bisse, Incumbent of St. George's parish near Bristol. 1718. [Grimaldi's Tracts, vol. 2.]　　**118 B**

History of England, 1688–1760. By T. G. Smollett. New ed. 4 vols. 1830. 8vo.　　**115 F**

History of England from the peace of Utrecht to the peace of Versailles, 1713–1783. By Lord Mahon. 4th ed. 7 vols. 1853–54. 8vo.　　**115 G**

GEORGE I. II. AND III., KINGS OF ENGLAND—*continued.*

History of England in the eighteenth century. By W. E. H. Lecky. 6 vols. 1883–87. 8vo.   **116 G**

A Letter touching the late rebellion, and what means led to it, and of the Pretender's title. By Philalethes. 1717. [Grimaldi's Tracts, vol. 1.]   **118 B**

The names of the Roman Catholics and others who refus'd to take the oaths to his late Majesty King George. By Charles Cosin. 2nd ed. 1746. 8vo.   **49 C**

Political memoranda of Francis, 5th Duke of Leeds. Edited by O. Browning. [Camden Society, n.s. vol. 35.] 1884. 8vo.   **85 D**

The resigners vindicated, or the defection reconsidered, in which the designs of all parties are set in a true light. By A Gentleman. [George Sewell.] 3rd ed. 1718. [Grimaldi's Tracts, vol. 2.]   **118 B**

Titles and honours conferred by kings George I. and II. in Great Britain and Ireland. Collected by John Philipps. 1728. [Grimaldi's Tracts, vol. 1.]   **118 B**

See also STATE PAPERS.

GEORGE IV., KING OF ENGLAND.

A Report of the trial, 'The King *v.* John and Leigh Hunt,' for a libel on the Prince Regent. 1812. 12mo.   **118 B**

The R.——L Mystery, or The secrets of an illustrious family, a poem. By Town Talk. 1812. 12mo.   **118 B**

GERMANY.

A Descriptive road book of Germany. By E. A. Domeier. 1830. 12mo.   **84 A**

Germany and Italy. 2nd enlarged ed. translated from the German. 1859. [Pamphlets, vol. 10.]   **144 A**

Germany, Denmark and the Scandinavian question. 1861. [Pamphlets, vol. 14.]   **144 A**

A Handbook for travellers in Southern Germany. 3rd ed. 1843. 8vo.   **84 A**

Letters and other documents illustrating the relations between England and Germany at the commencement of the thirty years' war. Edited by S. R. Gardiner. [Camden Society, vols. 90 and 98.] 2 vols. 1865–68. 8vo.   **85 C**

Who is the real enemy of Germany? 1868. [Pamphlets, vol. 33.]   **144 C**

GERMANY, Language of.

Flugel's Complete dictionary of the German and English languages. New ed. 2 vols. 1861. 8vo. **123 C**

Glossary of Low-German words. See Black book of the Admiralty, vol. 4, 1876, pp. 241–262. **102 D**

See also MINSHEU, J.

GERMANY, Law of.

Allgemeines Deutsches Handelsgesetzbuch. 1884. 8vo. **55 C**

The criminal code of the German empire, translated by G. Drage. 1885. 12mo. **55 C**

The lunacy law of Germany. See G. L. Harrisson's Legislation on Insanity, 1884, pp. 1042–1091. **59 G**

See also GAILL, A. and LAMPADIUS, J.

GERVASE OF CANTERBURY.

Historical works. Edited by Rev. Wm. Stubbs. 2 vols. 1879–80. 8vo. **102 G**

Tractatus de combustione et reparatione Dorobornensis ecclesiæ. Imaginationes de discordiis inter monachos Cantuarienses et Archiepiscopum Baldewinum. Chronica de tempore regum Angliæ, Stephani, Hen. II. et Ricardi I. Vitæ Dorobornensium archiepiscoporum. See Scriptores Decem Hist. Angl., 1652, pp. 1289–1684. **114 H**

GERVASIUS TILBURIENSIS.

A Correct copy of ancient dialogue concerning Exchequer ascribed to Gervasius Tilburiensis. See T. Madox's History of the Exchequer, vol. ii., pp. 329–452. **103 F**

Excerpta ex otiis imperialibus. See R. De Coggeshall's Chronicon Anglicanum, 1875, pp. 417–449. **102 F**

GESENIUS, FRIEDRICH HEINRICH WILHELM.

A Hebrew and English lexicon of the Old Testament including the Biblical Chaldee ; from the Latin of William Gesenius. 25th ed. by E. Robinson. Boston, 1888. 8vo. **123 B**

GIANT'S CAUSEWAY.

A Guide to the Giant's Causeway. By Rev. G. N. Wright. 1823. 12mo. **95 E**

GIBBON, EDWARD.

The history of the decline and fall of the Roman empire.
New ed. with some account of the life and writings of the
author, by Alexander Chalmers. 1831. 8vo. **113 D**

GIBBONS, DAVID.

Law of dilapidations and nuisances. 1838. 8vo. **165 G**

The same. 2nd ed. 1849. 8vo. **52 E**

Lex temporis. A treatise on the law of Limitation and Prescription. 1835. 12mo. **172 A**

Rudimentary treatise on the law of Contracts for works and
services. 3rd ed. 1875. 12mo. **163 E**

GIBBS, FREDERICK WAYMOUTH.

The Foreign enlistment act. 2nd ed. 1863. [Pamphlets,
vol. 18.] **144 B**

Recognition; a chapter from history of North American and
South American states. 1863. [Pamphlets, vol. 16.] **144 B**

GIBRALTAR.

Gibraltar ordinances, 1867–88. 5 vols. 1867–88. folio. **37 D**

History of Gibraltar. See R. M. Martin's History of the
British colonies, vol. 5, 1835, pp. 1–102. **116 C**

GIBSON, ALBERT.

Aids to Equity: intended to assist the student in reading
Snell's Principles of Equity. 1881. 8vo. **167 C**

The same. 3rd ed. by A. Gibson and Arthur Weldon. 1887.
8vo. **64 C**

The same. 4th ed. by A. Gibson and Arthur Weldon. 1890.
8vo. **64 C**

Aids to the Final. 3rd ed. 1885. 12mo. **168 A**

The same. 6th ed. by A. Gibson and A. Weldon. 1888.
12mo. **64 D**

The same. 7th ed. by A. Gibson and A. Weldon. 1890.
12mo. **64 D**

Aids to the Intermediate. 1881. 12mo. **64 D**

Gibson's Law Notes, a monthly magazine for law students
and others. 1882–1889. 8 vols. 1882–89. 8vo. **62 G**

Intermediate law examination made easy. A complete guide
to Stephen's Commentaries. 2nd ed. 1880. 8vo. **168 A**

The same. 7th ed. by A. Gibson and A. Weldon. 1887.
8vo. **64 D**

GIBSON, ALBERT—*continued.*

The same. 8th ed. by A. Gibson and A. Weldon. 1890. 8vo. **64 D**

The Student's Conveyancing. By A. Gibson and R. McLean. 1885. 8vo. **64 B**

The same. 2nd ed. by the Authors and A. Weldon. 1888. 8vo. **64 B**

Student's Equity. By A. Gibson and R. McLean. 1887. 8vo. **64 C**

Student's Practice of the courts. By A. Gibson and R. McLean. 1882. 8vo. **163 C**

The same. 4th ed. by the Authors and A. Weldon. 1889. 8vo. **64 E**

Intermediate examination digest. By A. Gibson and A. Weldon. 1887. 8vo. **64 C**

The same. 2nd ed. 1890. 8vo. **64 C**

Student's Bankruptcy. By A. Gibson and A. Weldon. 1887. 8vo. **64 A**

Student's Criminal and magisterial law. By A. Gibson and A. Weldon. 1890. 8vo. **64 C**

Student's Digest : containing a collection of questions set at all the final (pass) examinations of the Law Society in recent years. By A. Gibson and A. Weldon. 1888. 8vo. **64 C**

Student's probate, divorce and admiralty. By A. Gibson and A. Weldon. 1887. 8vo. **64 E**

The Student's Statute Law. By A. Gibson and A. Weldon. 1886. Supplements. 1887–90. 8vo. **64 F**

GIBSON, EDMUND.

Codex juris ecclesiastici Anglicani : or the statutes, constitutions, canons, rubricks and articles of the Church of England, methodically digested under their proper heads with a commentary. 2nd ed. 2 vols. Oxford, 1761. folio. **77 H**

GIBSON, JOHN.

History of Glasgow. Glasgow, 1777. 8vo. **95 C**

GIBSON, JOHN, M.A.

Geography made easy. 1882. 8vo. **84 A**

History made easy. 1882. 8vo. **116 E**

London Matriculation Course. 1883. 8vo. **255 H**

Public Examination French Grammar. 1883. 8vo. **255 H**

Public Examination Latin Grammar. 1883. 8vo. **255 H**

GIBSON, JOHN, M.A.—*continued.*

Specimen Essays, comprising hints on composition, punctuation, &c. and twelve essays.   By John Gibson and F. R. Burrows.   1881.   8vo.   255 G

GIBSON, WILLIAM SIDNEY.

A brief memoir of Lord Lyndhurst.   1866, 2nd new ed.   1869.   8vo.   79 G

GIFFARD, JOHN WALTER DE LONGUEVILLE.

Reports of cases adjudged in court of Chancery by Vice Chancellor Sir John Stuart 1858–1865.   5 vols.   1860–71.   8vo.   2 G

GIFFORD, JOHN.

The Complete English lawyer.   By a Student of the Inner Temple.   [n.d.]   8vo.   171 B
The same.   By John Gifford.   5th ed.   1821.   8vo.   171 B
The same.   15th ed.   1828.   8vo.   171 B

GIFFORD, WILLIAM.

Memoir of Wm. Gifford, written by himself.   [Autobiography, vol. 20.]   1827.   12mo.   79 A

GILBERT, CHARLES SANDOE.

Historical survey of the county of Cornwall, with a complete heraldry of the same.   2 vols.   1817–20.   4to.   86 F

GILBERT, E. W.

Bills of costs between attorney and agent.   3rd ed.   1847.   8vo.   165 A

GILBERT, SIR JEFFRAY.

Cases in law and equity in the King's Bench and Chancery in the twelfth and thirteenth years of Queen Anne during the time of Lord chief justice Parker.   With two treatises, the one on the Action of Debt, the other on the Constitution of England.   1760.   8vo.   74 D
Historical account of the original and nature as well as the law of Devises and Revocations.   By a late Learned Judge. 1739.   12mo.   178 A
The same.   New ed.   By the late Lord Chief Baron Gilbert. 1756.   12mo.   178 A

GILBERT, Sir Jeffray—*continued.*

History and practice of Court of Common Pleas. By a late
Learned Judge. 1737. 12mo. **163 C**

The same. 2nd ed. by the late Lord Chief Baron Gilbert.
1761. 12mo. **163 C**

The history and practice of the high court of Chancery. 1758.
8vo. **161 C**

Law and practice of Ejectment. [By Sir J. Gilbert.] 1734.
12mo. **166 C**

Law of Distresses and Replevins. 1757. 12mo. **165 G**

The same. 2nd ed. by A Barrister. 1780. 12mo. **165 G**

The same. 4th ed. by W. J. Impey. 1823. 12mo. **165 G**

The law of Evidence. By a late Learned Judge. Dublin, 1754.
12mo. **167 F**

The same. London, 1756, and 4th ed. 1777. 8vo. **167 F**

The same considerably enlarged by Capel Lofft, to which is
prefixed, Some account of the author; his Abstract of
Locke's Essay; and his Argument in a case of homicide in
Ireland. 4 vols. 1791–96. 8vo. **167 F**

The same. 6th ed. by James Sedgwick. 1801. 8vo. **167 F**

The law of Executions, to which are added The history
and practice of the Court of King's Bench and some
cases touching wills of lands and goods. 1763. 12mo.
168 B

The law of Uses and Trusts, together with, A treatise of dower.
1734. 12mo. **176 G**

The same. 3rd ed. by E. B. Sugden. 1811. 8vo. **176 G**

Reports of Cases in Equity argued and decreed in the Courts
of Chancery and Exchequer, chiefly in the reign of K.
George I. To which are added some Select Cases in
Equity heard and determined in the Court of Exchequer
in Ireland. 1734. folio.

The same. 2nd ed. 1742. folio. **74 D**

Treatise of Tenures. 3rd ed. 1757. 12mo. **176 D**

The same. 4th ed. by Charles Watkins. 1796. 8vo. **176 D**

Treatise on the Court of Exchequer. By a late Lord Chief
Baron of that court. 1758. 12mo. **168 B**

GILBERT, John Thomas.

Chartularies of St. Mary's abbey, Dublin; with the register
of its house at Dunbrody and Annals of Ireland. 2 vols.
1884. 8vo. **102 H**

GILBERT, John Thomas—*continued*

Historic and municipal documents of Ireland A.D. 1172–1320. 1870. 8vo. . **102 D**

History of the City of Dublin. 2 vols. Dublin, 1854–59. 8vo. **95 E**

Register of abbey of St. Thomas, Dublin. 1889. 8vo. **102 I**

GILL, Harry.

Mr. Harry Gill's Comments and observations upon the various transactions in which he has been engaged with the Birmingham manufacturers from 1806 to 1827. Privately printed. 1844. [Pamphlets, vol. 16.] **144 B**

GILL, Joseph.

Epitome of law and practice of court for relief of insolvent debtors. 1836. 12mo. **169 A**

GILLING WEST, Yorkshire.

The history of Yorkshire. Wapentake of Gilling West. By G. H. De S. N. Plantagenet-Harrison. 1885. folio. **94 H**

GILLINGWATER, Edmund.

Historical account of town of Lowestoft and a general account of Island of Lothingland. 1790. 4to. **93 B**

Historical and descriptive account of St. Edmund's Bury. Saint Edmund's Bury, 1804. 12mo. **93 C**

GIRALDUS CAMBRENSIS.

Giraldi Cambrensis Opera. Edited by J. S. Brewer and J. F. Dimock. 7 vols. 1861–77. 8vo. **101 D E**

The itinerary of Archbishop Baldwin through Wales 1188. Translated by Sir R. C. Hoare. 2 vols. 1806. 4to. **94 D**

GISBORNE, Thomas.

Essays on Agriculture. 2nd ed. 1854. 12mo. **83 J**

GLANVILLA, Ranulphus de.

Tractatus de legibus et consuetudinibus regni Angliæ tempore regis Henrici Secundi cum MSS. Harl. Cott. Bodl. et Mill. collatus. Edited by John Rayner. 1780. 12mo. **49 B**

A Translation of Glanville with notes. By John Beames. 1821. 8vo. **167 A**

GLANVILLE, JOHN.

Reports of certain cases determined and adjudged by the Commons in Parliament in the years 1623 and 1624, with An Historical account of the ancient right of determining cases upon controverted elections. 1775. 8vo.   **66 A**

The voyage to Cadiz in 1625. Edited by Rev. A. B. Grosart. [Camden Society, n.s. vol. 32.] 1883. 8vo.   **85 D**

GLASGOW.

History of city of Glasgow and suburbs. By James Denholm. 3rd ed. Glasgow, 1804. 8vo.   **95 C**

History of Glasgow. By J. Gibson. 1777. 8vo.   **95 C**

GLASTONBURY ABBEY, SOMERSET.

Glastonbury abbey, its history and ruins. By Rev. J. Williamson. Wells, 1865. 8vo.   **93 A**

GLEIG. REV. GEORGE ROBERT.

The history of the British empire in India. 4 vols. 1830-35. 12mo.   **116 D**

GLEN, ALEXANDER.

Law of county government. 1890. 8vo.   **10 G**

The rivers pollution prevention act 1876, with notes. 1876. 8vo.   **11 E**

GLEN, REGINALD CUNNINGHAM.

The Justice of the Peace. Digest of cases reported 1862 to 1882, with an alphabetical index. 1887. 4to.   **68 G**

The local government and public health orders relating to urban, rural and port sanitary authorities and joint hospital boards. 1884. 8vo.   **172 B**

GLEN, ROBERT GEORGE.

Manual of laws affecting medical men. 1871. 8vo.   **10 I**

GLEN, WILLIAM CUNNINGHAM.

The acts regulating duties of justices of the peace out of sessions with respect to indictable offences and summary convictions, known as Jervis's acts. 2nd ed. 1861. 12mo. **169 G**

The same. 3rd ed. 1868, and 5th ed. 1884. 12mo. **169 G**

The same. 6th ed. by A. H. Bodkin and E. G. Douglas 1887. 12mo.   **12 C**

28—2

GLEN, William Cunningham—*continued.*

Ballot act 1872, with notes. 1873. 12mo.   **160 C**

Burial board acts of England and Wales. 1858. 12mo. **161 A**

The same. 2nd ed. 1869. 12mo.   **161 A**

The same. 4th ed. 1881. 12mo.   **52 B**

The consolidated and other orders of the poor law commissioners and the poor law board. 4th ed. 1859. 12mo. **174 B**

The same. 9th ed. 1883. 8vo.   **174 B**

Elementary education acts. 3rd ed. 1873. 12mo.   **166 B**

The same. 6th ed. by R. C. Glen. 1881. 8vo.   **52 F**

Law of Highways. 1860, and 2nd ed. 1865. 12mo. **168 F**

The same. New ed. by W. C. Glen and A. Glen. 1883. 8vo.   **10 B**

The law relating to the public health and local government. 1858, and 5th ed. 1869. 12mo.   **174 G**

The same. 10th ed. by W. C. Glen and A. Glen. 1888. 8vo.   **11 D**

The law relating to the removal of Nuisances injurious to health. 1858. 12mo.   **173 B**

Parliamentary registration manual. 2nd ed. 1868, and 4th ed. 1885. 12mo.   **173 B**

Small Tenements Rating acts and Parish vestries and vestry clerks acts. 4th ed. 1866. 12mo.   **175 B**

The statutes in force relating to the Poor, Parochial Unions and Parishes. 2 vols. 1857–66. 8vo.   **174 B**

The same. New ed. 3 vols. 1873–79. 8vo.   **11 B**

GLISSON, William and Anthony GULSTON.

The common law epitomized. 2nd ed. 1679. 12mo. **49 C**

GLOUCESTER.

Account of the Cathedral of Gloucester. Published by the Society of Antiquaries. 1809. folio.   **91 H**

Historia et cartularium monasterii Sancti Petri Gloucestriæ. Edited by W. H. Hart. 3 vols. 1863–67. 8vo. **102 A**

The history and antiquities of Gloucester. By Samuel Rudder. Cirencester, 1781. 8vo.   **87 F**

A L st of the freemen who polled at the contested election of a member to serve in Parliament for the city of Gloucester. Gloucester, 1816. 8vo.   **107 J**

An Original history of the city of Gloucester including the original papers of the late Ralph Bigland. By Rev. T. D. Fosbroke. 1819. 4to.   **87 F**

GLOUCESTER, ROBERT OF.

The metrical chronicle of Robert of Gloucester. Edited by
W. A. Wright. 2 vols. 1887. 8vo.   **102 I**

GLOUCESTERSHIRE.

The ancient and present state of Gloucestershire. By Sir Robert
Atkyns. 2nd ed. 1768. folio.   **88 H**

A Collection of coats of arms borne by the nobility and
gentry of the county of Glocester. [By Sir George
Naylor.] 1792. 4to.   **88 G**

Collection relative to the county of Gloucester. By Ralph
Bigland. 2 vols. 1791–92. folio.   **88 H**

The laws of Dean Forest and hundred of Saint Briavels. By
J. G. Wood. 1878. 8vo.   **87 F**

A New history of Gloucestershire. By Samuel Rudder. Cirencester, 1779. folio.   **88 H**

Topographical survey of counties of Somerset, Gloucester, &c.
By Wm. Tunnicliff. Bath, 1789. 8vo.   **93 B**

Translation of Domesday, so far as it relates to Gloucestershire. By Rev. Wm. Bawdwen. 1812. 4to.   **89 F**

The visitation of the county of Gloucester 1682–1683. Edited
by T. F. Fenwick and W. C. Metcalfe. Privately printed.
Exeter, 1884. 4to.   **87 F**

GLOVER, FREDERICK ROBERT AUGUSTUS.

Harbours of refuge not 'dangerous decoys,' 'ship traps' nor
'wrecking pools.' 1859. 8vo.   **78 B**

GLOVER, STEPHEN.

The history and gazetteer of the county of Derby. Edited
by Thomas Noble. 2 vols. Derby, 1831-33. 4to. **87 B**

GLOVER, WILLIAM.

Lord Brougham's Law Reforms, and courts of local jurisdiction. 2nd ed. 1834. [Jacob's Tracts, vol. 11.]   **144 F**

GLYN, THOMAS CHRISTOPHER and R. S. JAMESON.

Cases in Bankruptcy 1821-28. 2 vols 1824-28. 8vo. **8 C**

GNEIST, RUDOLF.

English parliament in its transformations through a thousand
years. Translated by R. J. Shee. 1886. 8vo.   **116 E**

GODALMING, Surrey.

Eleven tracts relating to Mary Tofts, the rabbit woman of
Godalming. 1726–27. 8vo. **118 B**

GODBOLT, John.

Reports of certain cases arising in the severall courts of record
at Westminster in the raignes of Q. Elizabeth, K. James
and the late King Charles. 1653. 8vo. **74 D**

GODDARD, John Leybourn.

A Treatise on the law of Easements, 1871, and 2nd ed. 1877.
8vo. **166 A**

The same. 3rd ed. 1884. 8vo. **9 G**

GODEFRIDUS, Prior Wintoniensis.

Epigrammata Godefridi Prioris. See Satirical poets of twelfth
century, vol. 2, 1872, pp. 103–155. **102 E**

GODEFROI, Henry.

A Digest of the principles of the law of trusts and trustees.
1879. 8vo. **53 H**

The law of railway companies. By Henry Godefroi and John
Shortt. 1869. 8vo. **53 F**

GODMANCHESTER, Huntingdonshire.

The history of Godmanchester. By Robert Fox. 1831.
8vo. **88 C**

GODOLPHIN, John.

The Orphan's legacy ; or, a testamentary abridgment in three
parts : I. Of last wills and testaments ; II. Of executors
and administrators ; III. Of legacies and devises. 3rd ed.
1685. 8vo. **48 G**

The same. 4th ed. 1701. 8vo. **48 G**

Repertorium canonicum, or an abridgment of the ecclesiastical
laws of this realm consistent with the temporal. 1678,
and 2nd ed. 1680. 8vo. **77 F**

A View of the Admiral jurisdiction. 1661. 12mo. **49 B**

GODSON, Richard.

Practical treatise on the law of Patents for inventions and of
Copyright, with two supplements. 1823–35. 8vo. **173 E**

The same. 2nd ed. with a supplement. 1844. 8vo. **173 E**

GODWIN, Francis, Bishop of Hereford.
Annales of England, containing the reignes of Henry the
Eighth, Edward the Sixt, Queene Mary. Englished, cor-
rected and inlarged by Morgan Godwyn. 1630. 4to. **114 F**

GOETHE, Johann Wolfgang Von.
Aus meinem Leben. Wahrheit und Dichtung. 2 vols. Stutt-
gart, 1861. 12mo. **83 B**
The same. Another ed. Stuttgart, 1875. 12mo. **83 B**
English hexameter translations from Schiller, Göthe, Homer
&c. 1847. 8vo. **83 A**

GOIRAND, Leopold.
The French code of commerce, with a commentary. 1880.
8vo. **55 C**

GOLD.
The gold companies and the cost-book system. By J. N.
Higgins. 1853. [Pamphlets, vol. 9, pt. 1.] **144 A**
The gold discoveries. By W. R. Smee. [Paris, 1861.]
[Pamphlets, vol. 14.] **144 A**
Gold ; or legal regulations for the standard of gold and silver
wares in different countries of the world. Translated from
the German by Mrs. Brewer, with notes by E. W. Streeter.
1877. 8vo. **78 B**
Hall marks on gold and silver plate. By William Chaffers.
1863. 8vo. **78 C**
See also Bullion.

GOLD COAST COLONY.
Analytical index to the ordinances regulating the civil and
criminal procedure of the Gold Coast Colony. By S. Smith.
1888. 8vo. **37 D**
Ordinances of the Gold Coast, 1878–1880, 1884–1886 and
1888. 2 vols. 1878–88. folio. **37 D**
Ordinances of the Gold Coast and Gold Coast Colony in force
April 7th, 1887. 1887. 8vo. **37 D**

GOLDNEY, Frederick Hastings.
Records of Chippenham relating to the borough from 1554
to 1889. Privately printed. 1889. 8vo. **93 F**

GOLDONI, CARLO.

Un Curioso accidente, commedia in tre atti. Edited by Rev.
A. C. Clapin. 1890. 12mo. **83 B**

Life of Goldoni. [Autobiography, vols. 9 and 10.] 2 vols.
[n.d.] 12mo. **79 A**

GOLDSMITH, GEORGE.

Doctrine and practice of Equity. 5th ed. 1862. 12mo. **167 B**
The same. 6th ed. 1871. 12mo. **167 B**

GOOD, JOHN.

Measuring made easy, or the description and use of Coggeshall's sliding-rule. Corrected by J. Atkinson, Sen. 1760.
12mo. **255 H**

GOODALL, CHARLES.

The royal college of physicians of London, founded and
established by law as appears by letters patent &c.; and
An historical account of the college's proceedings against
Empiricks. 1684. 8vo. **91 B**

GOODEVE, JOSEPH.

The law of Evidence as administered in England and applied
to India. New ed. by L. A. Goodeve. Calcutta, 1871.
8vo. **38 C**

Shall we transfer our lands by register? A letter to the Lord
Chancellor on the contemplated transfer of land by register.
1854. [Pamphlets, vol. 9, pt. 2.] **144 A**

GOODEVE, LOUIS ARTHUR.

Full bench rulings of the High Court of Bengal. 2 vols.
Calcutta, 1865–74. 8vo. **38 F**

Modern law of personal property, 1887. 8vo. **64 F**

Modern law of real property. 1883. 8vo. **64 F**

The same. 2nd ed. 1885. 8vo. **64 F**

Railway passengers and railway companies, their duties, rights
and liabilities. 1876. 12mo. **175 B**

The same. 2nd ed. 1885. 8vo. **11 D**

GOODEVE, THOMAS MINCHIN.

Abstract of reported cases relating to Letters Patent for
Inventions 1876, and Appendix 1878. 2 vols. 1876–78.
8vo. **173 E**

GOODEVE, THOMAS MINCHIN—*continued.*

The same. (Bringing the cases down to the end of the year
1883.) 1884. 8vo. **76 H**

GOODINGE, THOMAS.

Law against Bankrupts, or a treatise wherein statutes against
bankrupts are explained. 2nd ed. 1701. 12mo. **160 E**

GOODS, SALE OF.

The sale of goods, including] the Factors act, 1889. By
M. D. Chalmers. 1890. 8vo. **10 B**

Digest of law relating to the sale of goods. By W. C. A. Ker.
1888. 8vo. **10 B**

Law relating to the sale of goods and commercial agency.
By R. Campbell. 1881. 8vo. **10 B**

GOODWILL.

Law of Goodwill. By C. E. Allan. 1889. 8vo. **10 B**

Law of trade marks, including a chapter on Goodwill. By
L. B. Sebastian. 3rd ed. 1890. 8vo. **11 H**

GOODWIN, FREDERICK.

The XII. Tables. 1886. 8vo. **63 F**

GORDON, WILLIAM EDWARD.

The law of costs in an action in the Queen's Bench division
and in the court of appeal. 1884. 8vo. **9 F**

GÖRGEI, ARTHUR

A Short account of General Georgey's surrender to the
Russians. By C. D. B. Zabrocki. Bradford, 1851. [Pam-
phlets, vol. 9, pt. 1.] **144 A**

GORHAM, REV. GEORGE CORNELIUS.

History and antiquities of Eynesbury and St. Neot's, Hunts ;
and of St. Neot's, Cornwall. 2 vols. 1824. 8vo. **88 C**

The case of the Rev. G. C. Gorham against the Bishop of
Exeter. By E. F. Moore. 1852. 8vo. **50 A**

A Review of the Gorham case in its aspects, moral and legal,
with a critical examination of the judgment. By J. D.
Chambers. 1850. [Pamphlets, vol. 7.] **144 A**

GOSPEL, The.

Thoughts on the Gospel of Jesus Christ. By A Lay Member of the Church of England. [John Stow.] Greenwich, 1846. 8vo. 77 C

GOSSET, J. A.

Practical guide to account stamp duty, Customs and inland revenue act 1881. 1887. 8vo. 11 G

GOSTLING, Rev. William.

A Walk in and about the city of Canterbury. New ed. Canterbury, 1825. 8vo. 88 C

GOTHIC LANGUAGE.

Linguarum veterum septentrionalium thesaurus. Auctore G. Hickesio. 2 vols. Oxoniæ, 1705. folio. 123 G

GOUDSMIT, Joel Emmanuel.

The Pandects; a treatise on the Roman law, and upon its connection with modern legislation. Translated from the Dutch by R. De Tracy Gould. 1873. 8vo. 63 E

GOUGH, Henry.

Catalogue of first series of works of Camden Society in numerical order and General index down to the word Baudouin. 1881. 8vo. 85 C

General index to the publications of The Parker Society. Cambridge, 1855. 8vo. 77 E

A Manual of practice in the office of Land Registry. 1862. 12mo. 53 A

[GOUGH, Richard.]

British topography, or an historical account of what has been done for illustrating the topographical antiquities of Great Britain and Ireland. 2 vols. 1780. 4to. 82 I

History and antiquities of Pleshy. 1803. 4to. 87 F

Some account of the alien priories and of such lands as they are known to have possessed in England and Wales. 2 vols. 1779. 12mo. 84 A

Life of Richard Gough. See J. P. Malcolm's Lives of topographers. 1815. 4to. 79 H

GOULDESBOROUGH, John.

Reports or collection of choice cases and matters agitated in all the Courts at Westminster, 1586–1602. Edited by W. S., of the Inner Temple. 1653. 4to. **74 D**

GOURLAY, Robert.

Statistical account of Upper Canada ; compiled with a view to a grand system of emigration in connexion with a reform of the poor laws. 3 vols. 1822. 8vo. **84 B**

GOVER, William Henry.

Hints as to advising on title and practical suggestions for perusing and analysing abstracts. 1889. 8vo. **13 I**

GOVERNMENT.

The difference between an absolute and limited monarchy. By Sir John Fortescue. 3rd ed. 1724. 8vo. **48 F**

Direct legislation by the people versus Representative government. Translated from the original Swiss pamphlets, by Eugene Oswald. 1869. 8vo. [Pamphlets, vol. 35.] **144 C**

Elements of the science of good government. By T. L. Follett. 1833. [Jacob's Tracts, vol. 13.] **144 F**

An Essay upon Civil Government. By the Chevalier Ramsay. 1732. 12mo. **49 E**

A Letter to John Bull, Esq. from his second cousin Thomas Bull. By the late Rev. W. Jones. Reprinted. [n.d.] [Pamphlets, vol. 9, pt. 1.] **144 A**

Observations concerning the original and various forms of Government. By Sir R. Filmer. 1696. 12mo. **48 C**

Speech delivered at the town hall, Leeds. By Sir C. W. Dilke. 1871. [Pamphlets, vol. 32.] **144 C**

Two treatises of Government. By John Locke. See J. Locke's Works, vol. 5, 1823, pp. 207–487. **78 E**

A Treatise concerning Civil Government. By Josiah Tucker. 1781. 8vo. **49 E**

A Treatise concerning the nature of Government. 1703. 8vo. **49 E**

Whitelockes notes uppon the kings writt for choosing members of parlement xiii Car. II ; being disquisitions on the government of England by king, lords and commons. Published by Charles Morton. 2 vols. 1766. 4to. **114 F**

See also CONSTITUTIONAL HISTORY.

GOW, Neil.

The law of Partnership. 3rd ed. 1830. 8vo.   **173 D**

Reports of cases at Nisi Prius in the Court of Common Pleas 1818–1820, and on the Oxford circuit 1818–1820. 1 vol. 1828. 8vo.   **8 F**

GRADY, Standish Grove.

The diminution of the Poor Rate by improved legislation and a more just distribution of the burden. 2nd ed. 1862. 12mo.   **174 B**

The Hindoo law of inheritance. 1868. 8vo.   **38 B**

The law of Fixtures, to which is added the law of Dilapidations. 2nd ed. 1866. 12mo.   **165 G**

The same. 3rd ed. 1876. 12mo.   **165 G**

The Mahommedan law of inheritance and contract. 1869. 8vo.   **38 B**

The law and practice in proceedings on the Crown side of the Court of Queen's Bench. By S. G. Grady and C. H. Scotland. 1844. 12mo.   **165 D**

GRAFTON, Richard.

Chronicle or history of England, to which is added a table of the bailiffs, sheriffs and mayors of the City of London from 1189 to 1558. 2 vols. 1809. 4to.   **114 G**

GRAGLIA, C.*

A New pocket dictionary of the Italian and English languages, with a compendious elementary Italian grammar. 15th ed. by C. T. 1829. 12mo.   **123 B**

GRAMMAR SCHOOLS.

Concise description of endowed grammar schools in England and Wales. By N. Carlisle. 2 vols. 1818. 8vo.   **84 D**

Grammar schools considered with reference to a case lately decided by the Lord Chancellor. By A Barrister. [Saxe Bannister.] 1820. [Jacob's Tracts, vol. 2.]   **144 E**

GRANT, Family of.

Mémoires historiques, généalogiques, politiques, militaires &c. &c. de la maison de Grant. Par Charles Grant, Vicomte De Vaux. 1796. 8vo.   **79 B**

GRANT, Alexander.

Reports of cases in Courts of Chancery of Upper Canada. 1849–1861. 8 vols. Toronto, 1861–62. 8vo.   **60 E**

GRANT, SIR ALEXANDER.
The story of the University of Edinburgh during its first
three hundred years. 2 vols. 1884. 8vo.   **95 D**

GRANT, HARDING.
Advice to Trustees, and to those who appoint to that office.
1830. 8vo.   **176 G**
The practice of the Court of Chancery. 2 vols. 1826, and 4th
ed. 2 vols. 1837. 12mo.   **161 E**

GRANT, JAMES, BARRISTER-AT-LAW.
The law relating to bankers and banking. 1856. 8vo. **160 C**
The same. 2nd ed. by R. A. Fisher. 1865. 8vo.   **160 C**
The same. 3rd ed. by R. A. Fisher. 1873. 8vo.   **160 C**
The same. 4th ed. by C. C. M. Plumptre. 1882. 8vo. **78 D**
The law of Corporations in general. 1850. 8vo.   **52 C**

GRANT, JAMES, OF THE 62ND REGIMENT.
Cassell's Old and new Edinburgh, its history, its people and
its places. 3 vols. 1880–83. 4to.   **95 D**

GRANTHAM.
Collections for history of town and soke of Grantham. By
Edmund Turnor. 1806. 4to.   **90 G**

GRANTS.
Dissertation on and precedents of Grants. See Bythewood
and Jarman's Conveyancing, 3rd ed., vol. 4, 1840, pp.
105–174.   **53 D**

GRAVES, REV. JOHN.
History of Cleveland. Carlisle, 1808. 4to.   **94 D**

GRAVESEND, KENT.
History of town and parishes of Gravesend and Milton. By
Robert Pocock. Gravesend, 1797. 8vo.   **88 D**

GRAVESEND, RICHARD.
Account of the executors of Richard, bishop of London 1303.
Edited by Ven. W. H. Hale and Rev. H. T. Ellacombe.
[Camden Society, n.s. vol. 10.] 1874. 8vo.   **85 D**

GRAY, George Godfrey.
The right to lateral support from land and buildings. 1886.
8vo. **53 A**

GRAY, John.
Country attorney's practice in conducting actions in superior
courts of law at Westminster. 1836. 12mo. **163 B**
The same. 9th ed. by Wm. Paterson. 1869. 12mo. **163 B**
The country solicitor's practice in the High Court of Chancery.
1837. 12mo. **161 E**
The law of costs in the courts of common law at Westminster.
1853. 8vo. **52 D**

GRAY, John Chipman.
Restraints on the alienation of property. 1883. 8vo. **13 C**

GRAY'S INN.
Gray's Inn, its history and associations. By W. R. Douthwaite.
1886. 8vo. **91 D**
The Gray's-Inn Journal. By A. Murphy. 2 vols. in 1. 1756.
12mo. **78 A**
Gray's Inn. Notes illustrative of its history and antiquities.
By W. R. Douthwaite. 1876. 8vo. **91 D**
See also À Beckett, A. W.

GREAT BRITAIN AND IRELAND, Chronicles and
Memorials of, during the Middle Ages. 228 vols.
1858–90. 8vo. **101 & 102**

1. Capgrave. The Chronicle of England. Edited by F. C.
Hingeston. 1858. **101 A**
2. Chronicon Monasterii de Abingdon. Edited by J. Stevenson.
2 vols. 1858. **101 A**
3. Lives of Edward the Confessor. Edited by H. R. Luard. 1858.
101 A
4. Monumenta Franciscana. Edited by J. S. Brewer and R. Howlett. 2 vols. 1858–82. **101 A**
5. Fasciculi Zizaniorum Magistri Jo. Wyclif cum Tritico. Ascribed
to Thomas Netter. Edited by W. W. Shirley. 1858. **101 A**
6. The Buik of the Croniclis of Scotland ; or, a metrical version of
the History of Hector Boece, by W. Stewart. Edited by W.
B. Turnbull. 3 vols. 1858. **101 A B**
7. Capgrave. Liber de illustribus Henricis. Edited by F. C.
Hingeston. 1858. **101 B**
8. Elmham. Historia Monasterii S. Augustini Cantuariensis.
Edited by C. Hardwick. 1858. **101 B**

GREAT BRITAIN AND IRELAND—*continued.*

9. Eulogium (historiarum sive temporis) : Chronicon ab orbe condito usque ad A.D. 1366. A Monacho quodam Malmesburiensi exaratum. Accedunt continuationes duæ, &c. Edited by F. S. Haydon. 3 vols. 1858–63.   101 B

10. Historia Regis Henrici Septimi, à B. Andrea conscripta ; necnon alia quædam ad eundem Regem spectantia. Edited by J. Gairdner. 1858.   101 B

11. Memorials of Henry the Fifth, King of England. Edited by C. A. Cole. 1858.   101 B

12. Munimenta Gildhallæ Londoniensis ; Liber Albus, Liber Custumarum, et Liber Horn. Edited by H. T. Riley. 3 vols. in 4. 1859–62.   101 C

13. Chronica Johannis de Oxenedes. Edited by Sir H. Ellis. 1859.   101 C

14. Political Poems and Songs relating to English history, Edw. III.-Ric. III. Edited by T. Wright. 2 vols. 1859–61.   101 C

15. Bacon, R. Opera inedita. Edited by J. S. Brewer. 1859.   101 C

16. Bartholomæi de Cotton Historia Anglicana (449–1298). Edited by H. R. Luard. 1859.   101 D

17. Brut y Tywysogion, or Chronicle of the Princes of Wales. Edited by J. Williams ab Ithel. 1860.   101 D

18. Royal and Historical Letters during the reign of Henry IV. Edited by F. C. Hingeston. 1860.   101 D

19. The Repressor of overmuch blaming of the Clergy. By R. Pecock. Edited by C. Babington. 2 vols. 1860.   101 D

20. Annales Cambriæ. Edited by J. Williams ab Ithel. 1860.   101 D

21. Giraldus Cambrensis. Opera. Vols. 1–4 edited by J. S. Brewer. Vols. 5–7 edited by J. F. Dimock. 7 vols. 1861–77.   101 D E

22. Letters and Papers illustrative of the Wars of the English in France during the reign of Henry VI. Edited by J. Stevenson. 2 vols. in 3. 1861–64.   101 E

23. Anglo-Saxon Chronicle. Edited with a Translation by B. Thorpe. 2 vols. 1861.   101 E

24. Letters and Papers illustrative of the reigns of Richard III. and Henry VII. Edited by J. Gairdner. 2 vols. 1861–63.   101 E

25. Grosseteste. Epistolæ. Edited by H. R. Luard. 1861.   101 F

26. Descriptive Catalogue of Materials relating to the History of Great Britain and Ireland to the end of the reign of Henry VII. By Sir T. D. Hardy. vols. 1–4. 1862–71.   101 F

27. Royal and other Historical Letters illustrative of the reign of Henry III. Edited by W. W. Shirley. 2 vols. 1862–66.   101 F

28. Chronica Monasterii S. Albani. Edited by H. T. Riley. 12 vols. 1863–76.   101 G H

     (i.) Thomæ Walsingham Historia Anglicana. 2 vols.

     (ii.) Willelmi Rishanger et quorundam anonymorum Chronica et Annales. 1259–1307.

     (iii.) Johannis de Trokelowe et Henrici de Blaneforde Chronica et Annales. 1259–1296, 1307–1324, 1392–1406.

     (iv.) Walsingham. Gesta Abbatum Monasterii Sancti Albani. 3 vols.

     (v.) Johannis Amundesham. Annales Monasterii S. Albani. 1421–1440. 2 vols.

GREAT BRITAIN AND IRELAND—*continued.*

(vi.) Registra Johannis Whethamstede, Willelmi Albon et Willelmi Wallingforde. 2 vols.

(vii.) Ypodigma Neustriæ a Thoma Walsingham.

29. Chronicon Abbatiæ de Evesham, ad annum 1418. Edited by W. D. Macray. 1863.   101 H

30. Ricardi de Cirencestria Speculum historiale de gestis Regum Angliæ. Edited by J. E. B. Mayor. 2 vols. 1863–69. 101 H

31. Year Books of the reigns of Edward I. and III. Edited and translated by A. J. Horwood and L. O. Pike. vols. 1–10. 1863–89.   101 I & 102 A

32. Narrative of the Expulsion of the English from Normandy, 1449–1450. Edited by J. Stevenson. 1863.   102 A

33. Historia et Cartularium Monasterii Sancti Petri Gloucestriæ. Edited by W. H. Hart. 3 vols. 1863–67.   102 A

34. Neckam. De Naturis rerum libri duo. With the Poem De laudibus Divinæ Sapientiæ. Edited by T. Wright. 1863. 102 A

35. Leechdoms, wortcunning, and starcraft of Early England. Edited by O. Cockayne. 3 vols. 1864–66.   102 A

36. Annales Monastici. Edited by H. R. Luard. 5 vols. 1864–69. 102 A

37. Magna Vita S. Hugonis episcopi Lincolniensis. Edited by J. F. Dimock. 1864.   102 A

38. Chronicles and Memorials of the Reign of Richard I. Edited by W. Stubbs. 2 vols. 1864–65.   102 B

39. Recueil des Croniques et anchiennes istories de la Grant Bretaigne. Par J. de Waurin. Edited by W. Hardy. vols. 1–4. 1864–84. 102 B

40. A Collection of the Chronicles and Ancient Histories of Great Britain, &c. By John de Waurin. Translated by W. Hardy and E. L. C. P. Hardy. vols. 1, 2. 1864–87.   102 B

41. Higden, R. Polychronicon ; with English translation of John Trevisa, &c. Edited by C. Babington and J. R. Lumley. 9 vols. 1865–86.   102 B

42. Le Livere de Reis de Brittanie e le livere de Reis de Engletere. [By Peter of Ickham (?)] Edited by J. Glover. 1865. 102 B

43. Chronica Monasterii de Melsa. Auctore Thoma de Burton. Accedit continuatio ad annum 1406. Edited by E. A. Bond. 3 vols. 1866–68.   102 C

44. Matthæi Parisiensis Historia Anglorum ; sive, ut vulgo dicitur, Historia Minor. Edited by Sir F. Madden. 3 vols. 1866–69. 102 C

45. Liber Monasterii de Hyda. A.D. 455–1023. Edited by E. Edwards. 1866.   102 C

46. Chronicum Scotorum. A Chronicle of Irish Affairs to A.D. 1135. With Supplement to 1150. Edited with a translation by W. M. Hennessy. 1866.   102 C

47. The Chronicle of Pierre de Langtoft, in French verse. Edited by T. Wright. 2 vols. 1866–68.   102 C

48. The War of the Gaedhil with the Gaill, or the Invasions of Ireland by the Danes and other Norsemen. Edited by J. H. Todd. 1867.   102 C

49. Gesta Regis Henrici Secundi Benedicti abbatis. Chronicle of the reigns of Henry II. and Richard I. 1169–1192. Edited by W. Stubbs. 2 vols. 1867.   102 C

GREAT BRITAIN AND IRELAND—*continued.*

50. Munimenta Academica, or Documents illustrative of Academical Life and Studies at Oxford. By H. Anstey. 2 vols. 1868. **102 C**

51. Rogeri de Houedene Chronica. Edited by W. Stubbs. 4 vols. 1868–71. **102 C**

52. Willelmi Malmesbiriensis De gestis Pontificum Anglorum libri v. Edited by N. E. S. A. Hamilton. 1870. **102 C**

53. Historic and Municipal Documents of Ireland, 1172–1320. Edited by J. T. Gilbert. 1870. **102 D**

54. Annals of Loch Cé, A Chronicle of Irish affairs from A.D. 1014– A.D. 1590. Edited by W. M. Hennessy. 2 vols. 1871. **102 D**

55. Monumenta Juridica. The Black book of the Admiralty. Edited by Sir T. Twiss. vols. 1–4. 1871–76. **102 D**

56. Memorials of the reign of Henry VI. Official Correspondence of Thomas Bekynton, Secretary to Henry VI., and Bishop of Bath and Wells. Edited by G. Williams. 2 vols. 1872. **102 D**

57. Matthæi Parisiensis Chronica Majora. Edited by H. R. Luard. 7 vols. 1872–84. **102 D**

58. Memoriale fratris Walteri de Coventria, the Historical Collections of Walter of Coventry. Edited by W. Stubbs. 2 vols. 1872– 73. **102 E**

59. The Anglo-Latin Satirical Poets and Epigrammatists of the Twelfth Century. Edited by T. Wright. 2 vols. 1872. **102 E**

60. Materials for a History of the Reign of Henry VII. Edited by W. Campbell. 2 vols. 1873–77. **102 E**

61. Historical Papers and Letters from the Northern Registers. Edited by J. Raine. 1873. **102 E**

62. Registrum Palatinum Dunelmense. The Register of Richard de Kellawe, 1311–1316. Edited by T. D. Hardy. 4 vols. 1873–78. **102 E**

63. Memorials of Saint Dunstan, Archbishop of Canterbury. Edited by W. Stubbs. 1874. **102 E**

64. Chronicon Angliæ, ab Anno Domini 1328 usque ad Annum 1388, auctore monacho quodam Sancti Albani. Edited by E. M. Thompson. 1874. **102 E**

65. Thómas Saga Erkibyskups. A Life of Archbishop Thomas Becket in Icelandic. Edited by E. Magnússon. 2 vols. 1875–84. **102 E**

66. Radulphi de Coggeshall Chronicon Anglicanum. Edited by J. Stevenson. 1875. **102 F**

67. Materials for the History of Thomas Becket, Archbishop of Canterbury. Vols. 1–6 edited by J. C. Robertson. Vol. 7 edited by J. B. Sheppard. 7 vols. 1875–85. **102 F**

68. Radulphi de Diceto Decani Lundoniensis opera historica. The Historical Works of R. de Diceto. Edited by W. Stubbs. 2 vols. 1876. **102 F**

69. Roll of the proceedings of the King's Council in Ireland, A.D. 1392–93. Edited by J. Graves. 1877. **102 F**

70. Henrici de Bracton de Legibus et Consuetudinibus Angliæ. Edited by Sir T. Twiss. 6 vols. 1878–83. **102 F G**

71. The Historians of the Church of York and its Archbishops. Edited by J. Raine. vols. 1, 2. 1879–86. **102 G**

72. Registrum Malmesburiense. The Register of Malmesbury Abbey. Edited by J. S. Brewer and C. T. Martin. 2 vols. 1879–80. **102 G**

GREAT BRITAIN AND IRELAND—*continued.*

73. The Historical Works of Gervase of Canterbury. Edited by W. Stubbs. 2 vols. 1879-80. 102 G

74. Henrici Archidiaconi Huntendunensis Historia Anglorum. The History of the English, by Henry, Archdeacon of Huntingdon. Edited by T. Arnold. 1879. 102 G

75. Symeonis Monachi opera omnia. 2 vols. 1882-85. 102 G

76. Chronicles and Memorials of the reigns of Edward I. and Edward II. Edited by W. Stubbs. 2 vols. 1882-83. 102 G

77. Registrum Epistolarum fratris Joannis de Peckham. Edited by C. T. Martin. 3 vols. 1882-86. 102 G

78. Vetus Registrum Sarisberiense. The Register of S. Osmund. Edited by W. H. R. Jones. vols. 1, 2. 1883-84. 102 H

79. Cartularium Monasterii de Rameseia. Edited by W. H. Hart and Rev P. A. Lyons. vols. 1, 2. 1884-86. 102 H

80. Chartularies of St. Mary's Abbey, Dublin. Edited by J. T. Gilbert. 2 vols. 1884-85. 102 H

81. Eadmeri Historia Novorum in Anglia. Edited by M. Rule. 1884. 102 H

82. Chronicles of the Reigns of Stephen, Henry II. and Richard I. Edited by R. Howlett. vols. 1-4. 1884-89. 102 H

83. Chronicon Abbatiæ Rameseiensis. Edited by W. D. Macray. 1886. 102 H

84. Roger de Wendover. Flowers of History. Edited by H. G. Hewlett. 3 vols. 1886-89. 102 H

85. Letter Book of the Monastery of Christ Church, Canterbury. Edited by J. B. Sheppard. 3 vols. 1887-89. 102 H

86. Robert of Gloucester. Metrical Chronicle. Edited by W. A. Wright. 2 vols. 1887. 102 I

87. Chronicles of Robert of Brunne. Edited by F. J. Furnivall. 2 vols. 1887. 102 I

88. Icelandic Sagas. Edited by G. Vigfusson. vols. 1, 2. 1887. 102 I

89. Tripartite Life of S. Patrick. Edited by Whitley Stokes. 2 vols. 1887. 102 I

90. Willelmi Malmesburiensis Monachi De Gestis Regum Anglie libri quinque. Edited by W. Stubbs. 2 vols. 1887-89. 102 I

91. Lestoire des Engles solum Geffrei Gaimar. Edited by T. D. Hardy, continued and translated by C. T. Martin. 2 vols. 1888-89. 102 I

92. Chronicle of Henry Knighton, Canon of Leicester. Edited by J. R. Lumby. vol. 1. 1889. 102 I

93. Chronicle of Adam Murimuth, with the Chronicle of Robert of Avesbury. Edited by E. M. Thompson. 1889. 102 I

94. Register of the Abbey of St. Thomas, Dublin. Edited by J. T. Gilbert. 1889. 102 I

95. Flores Historiarum, per Matthæum Westmonasteriensem collecti. Edited by H. R. Luard. 3 vols. 1890. 102 I

96. Annals and Memorials of St. Edmund's Abbey. Edited by T. Arnold. vol. 1. 1890. 102 I

GREAVES, CHARLES SPRENGEL.

Criminal law consolidation and amendment acts of the 24 & 25 Vict. with notes. 1861, and 2nd ed. 1862. 12mo. **165 D**

GREAVES, CHARLES SPRENGEL—*continued.*

A Letter to Lord John Russell on the amendment of the quarter sessions &c. &c. 1839. [Pamphlets, vol. 4.] **144 A**

The proper time for the publication of Banns of Matrimony in the morning service. 1867. 8vo. **172 D**

GREECE.

Dictionary of Greek and Roman biography and mythology. Edited by Wm. Smith. 3 vols. 1864. 8vo. **81 G**

Dictionary of Greek and Roman geography. Edited by Wm. Smith. 2 vols. 1854–57. 8vo. **84 D**

History of Greece. By G. Grote. 12 vols. 1854–57. 8vo. **113 D**

History of Herodotus. By G. Rawlinson. 4 vols. 1858–60. 8vo. **113 D**

GREECE, LANGUAGE OF.

Dictionnaire Grec moderne Français. Par F. D. Dehèque. Paris, 1825. 12mo. **123 B**

Græcum Lexicon Manuale primum a Benjamine Hederico institutum. Editio nova. 1825. 4to. **123 F**

A Greek-English lexicon. By H. G. Liddell, D.D., and R. Scott, D.D. 5th ed. Oxford, 1861. 4to. **123 F**

Joannis Scapulæ Lexicon Græco-Latinum. Editio nova accurata. Lugduni, 1663. folio.

Lehrbuch der neugriechischen Sprache. Von W. v. Ludemann. Leipzig, 1826. 8vo. **255 H**

Thesaurus Græcæ linguæ. Ab H. Stephano. 5 vols. 1573. folio.

See also MINSHEU, J.

GREECE, LAW OF.

Succinct account of the civil regulations comprised in the laws of Solon. See The Code Napoléon, translated by D. Barrett, vol. 1, 1811, pp. xcii–cxv. **55 C**

See also BUTLER, C.

GREEN, EDWARD.

The spirit of the Bankrupt laws. 3rd ed. by a late commissioner. 1776. 12mo. **160 E**

The same. 4th ed. by a late commissioner. 1780. 8vo. **160 E**

GREEN, John Richard.
History of English people. 4 vols. 1885–86. 8vo. 115 C

GREEN, Samuel Swett.
Library Aids. New York, 1883. 12mo. 82 B

GREEN, Valentine.
The history and antiquities of the city and suburbs of Worcester. 2 vols. in 1. 1796. 4to. 95 G
Survey of city of Worcester. Worcester, 1764. 8vo. 93 F

GREEN, William.
Digest of cases reported in the Irish Reports, 1867–1877. Dublin, 1879. 8vo. 17 I
Digest of cases reported in the Law Reports (Ireland), vols. i–xx, 1878–1888. By W. Green and R. Manders. Dublin, 1890. 8vo. 17 I

GREENE, John.
The priviledges of the lord mayor and aldermen of the City of London. 1708, and 2nd ed. 1722. 8vo. 92 B

GREENE, Joshua.
A Digested index of the cases determined in the Court of Admiralty. 1818. 8vo. 63 C

GREENE, Thomas Whitcombe.
An Analysis and summary of the institutes of Roman law. 1870. 12mo. 63 E
The same. 2nd ed. 1872, and 3rd ed. 1875. 12mo. 63 E
A Site for Her Majesty's superior courts at the Temple. 1862. [Pamphlets, vol. 17.] 144 B

GREENE, William.
Index to the laws of Mauritius in force on 1st August 1879. 5th ed. Mauritius, 1879. 8vo. 37 F

GREENING, Henry.
Collection of forms of Declarations and other Pleadings usually prepared in attornies' offices. 1837. 12mo. 162 D
Forms of declarations, pleadings and other proceedings in the

GREENING, HENRY—*continued.*
> superior courts of common law. 2nd ed. 1853. 12mo.
> **162 D**
> Number II. of a selection of leading statutes, containing : The
> Forest Charter and 4 other acts. 1842. 8vo. **176 B**

GREENLEAF, SIMON.
> Law of evidence. 3 vols. 1863–60. 8vo. **59 E**

GREENOCK, RENFREWSHIRE.
> History of the town of Greenock. By Daniel Weir. Greenock,
> 1829. 8vo. **95 C**
> See also GLASGOW.

GREENWICH, KENT.
> Account of legacies, gifts, rents, fees &c. appertaining to church
> and poor of parish of St. Alphege, Greenwich. By John
> Kimbell. 1816. 4to. **88 E**
> Bye-Laws, rules, orders and directions for the better govern-
> ment of His Majesty's royal hospital for seamen at Green-
> wich. 1776. 4to. **88 E**
> Historical account of royal hospital for seamen at Greenwich.
> By Rev. John Cooke and Rev. John Maule. 1789. 4to.
> **88 E**
> The palace and the hospital, or chronicles of Greenwich. By Rev.
> A. G. L'Estrange. 2 vols. 1886. 8vo. **88 D**
> Plans of the estates belonging to Greenwich hospital in Cum-
> berland, Northumberland and Durham. 1805. folio. **86 H**
> Reports of the proceedings of Sir G. Colpoys and others on
> viewing estates of Greenwich hospital in Cumberland, North-
> umberland and Durham. 2 vols. 1805–23. folio. **87 G**

GREENWOOD, GEORGE WRIGHT.
> Manual of practice of conveyancing. 2nd ed. 1858, and
> 3rd ed. by G. W. Greenwood and H. Horwood. 1865.
> 12mo. **164 D**
> The same. 6th ed. by H. Greenwood. 1881. 12mo. **164 D**
> The same. 7th ed. by H. Greenwood. 1882. 12mo. **13 A**

GREENWOOD, HARRY.
> Recent real property statutes. 1878. 8vo. **174 F**
> The same. 2nd ed. 1884. 8vo. **13 G**

GREENWOOD, HENRY CHARLES and T. C. MARTIN.
Magisterial and Police guide. 1874. 8vo.   **172 C**
The same. 2nd ed. 1880. 8vo.   **172 C**
The same. 3rd ed. by T. C. Martin. 1890. 8vo.   **12 C**

GREENWOOD, JAMES.
A Concise handbook of the laws relating to medical men.
1882. 8vo.   **10 H**

GREENWOOD, THOMAS.
Cathedra Petri. A political history of the great Latin patriarchate. 4 vols. 1861. 8vo.   **77 C**

GREENWOOD, WILLIAM.
Βουλευτήριον ; or practical demonstrations of county judicatures : wherein is amply explained the judicial and minis-
terial authority of sheriffs, coroners, &c. 5th ed. 1675,
and 7th ed. revised by J. Wilkinson. 1703. 12mo. **165 C**
The same. 9th ed. 1730. 12mo.   **165 C**

GREGG, FRANCIS.
Costs in Bankruptcy. 1826. [Jacob's Tracts, vol. 8.] **144 E**
Costs in Bankruptcy of proceedings under town and country
fiats. 2nd ed. 1838. Bound with Gregg's Bankruptcy,
1838. 12mo.   **160 E**
The law and practice in bankruptcy as connected with the
official assignees. 1838. 12mo.   **160 E**
The law and practice in Bankruptcy relative to public and
private meetings, meetings for the audit and dividend and
the certificate. 1826. [Jacob's Tracts, vol. 8.] **144 E**
Suggestions for some alterations of the present state of the
Bankrupt law. 1831. [Jacob's Tracts, vol. 8.] **144 E**

GREGO, JOSEPH.
Alexandra Palace, Catalogue of the exhibition of pictures,
drawings, and engravings, illustrative of British field sports,
Muswell Hill, 1881. 4to.   **78 C**

[GREGORY, ARTHUR.]
Gregorie's Moot book : being a survey of the general titles of
the common law with the cases thereof. Much enlarged
by W. Hughes. 1663. 4to.   **63 C**

GREGORY, David.
Practical geometry. 10th ed. Edinburgh, 1787. 8vo. **255 H**

GREGORY, George.
The life of Thomas Chatterton. 1803. 8vo. **83 E**

GREGORY, J.
Manual of modern geography. 2nd ed. 1740. 12mo. **84 A**

GREGORY, William.
Chronicle of London. Edited by James Gairdner. [Camden Society, n.s. vol. 17.] 1876. 8vo. **85 D**

GREGSON, Matthew.
Portfolio, Second edition with additions of Fragments relative to the history and antiquities of the county palatine and duchy of Lancaster. Liverpool, 1824. folio. **89 G**

GRENADA.
Laws of Grenada 1766–1875. 1875. 8vo. **36 D**
Laws of Grenada 1766–1852. Edited by W. Snagg. Grenada, 1852. 8vo. **36 D**
Grenada Acts 1857–72. 3 vols. 1857–72. 8vo. **36 E**
Ordinances of Grenada 1878–89. 4 vols. 1878–89. 4to. **36 E**

GRESHAM, Sir Thomas.
The last will and testament of Sir Thomas Gresham dated 5 July 1575, and, An act for the establishing of an agreement between Sir Henry Nevill and Dame Anne Gresham for the better performing of the last will of Sir Thomas Gresham. 1581. 8vo. **118 B**

GRESLEY, Richard Newcombe.
A Treatise on the law of Evidence in the courts of equity. 1836. 8vo. **167 F**

GREVILLE FAMILY.
Historical and genealogical account of the noble family of Greville. By J. Edmondson. 1766. 8vo. **80 C**

GREY FRIARS OF LONDON.
Chronicle of the Grey Friars of London. Edited by J. G. Nichols. [Camden Society, vol. 53.] 1852. 8vo. **85 B**

GREY FRIARS OF LONDON—*continued.*
The rise, progress and suppression of the Convent of the Grey
Friars in London. See Rev. Wm. Trollope's History of
Christ's hospital, 1834, pp. 6–29, 36, 41, 43. **89 F**

GREY, HENRY.
A Bird's-eye view of English literature from the seventh
century to the present time. 1884. 8vo. **83 A**
The Classics for the Million, being an epitome in English of
the works of the principal Greek and Latin authors. 2nd
ed. 1881. 8vo. **83 C**
A Key to the Waverley novels in chronological sequence,
with index of the principal characters. 1884. 8vo. **83 A**

GREY, RICHARD.
System of English ecclesiastical law. 3rd ed. 1735. 12mo. **49 F**

GREY OF WILTON, WILLIAM, 13 OR 14 BARON.
A Commentary of the services and charges of Wm. Lord
Grey of Wilton, K.G. By his son Arthur Lord Grey of
Wilton, K.G. Edited by Sir P. De M. G. Egerton.
[Camden Society, vol. 40.] 1847. 8vo. **85 B**

GRIFFIN, RALPH.
Abstract of reported cases relating to letters patent for
inventions, 1884–1886. 1887. 8vo. **76 H**
Patent cases decided by the comptroller-general and law
officers of the crown in 1887. 1888. 8vo. **76 H**

GRIFFITH, EDWARD.
Cases of supposed exemption from poor rates, claimed on the
ground of extra-parochiality, with a sketch of the ancient
history of parish of St. Andrew, Holborn. 1831. 8vo. **89 D**

GRIFFITH, GUALTER CRADDOCK.
A Digest of the stamp duties. 7th ed. 1874. 12mo. **175 G**
The same. 9th ed. 1886. 12mo. **11 G**

GRIFFITH, JOHN RICHARD.
The married women's property act. 1871. 8vo. **172 D**
The same. 3rd ed. 1875. 8vo. **172 D**
The same 5th ed. by S. W. Bromfield. 1883. 8vo. **10 H**

GRIFFITH, Samuel Young.
Griffith's New historical description of Cheltenham and its
vicinity. Cheltenham, 1826. 4to. **88 G**

GRIFFITH, William Brandford.
Ordinances of settlement on the Gold Coast and of Gold
Coast colony, in force April 7th, 1887. 1887. 8vo. **37 D**

GRIFFITH, William Downes.
Treatise on arrangements with creditors. 1865. 12mo. **165 G**

GRIFFITHS, Frederick Augustus.
Notes on military law, proceedings of courts martial, &c.
Woolwich, 1841. 12mo. **172 F**

GRIMALDI, Rev. Alexander Beaufort.
A Catalogue of paintings, drawings and engravings by and
after Wm. Grimaldi. Privately printed. 1873. 8vo. **118 C**
A Catalogue of printed books, pamphlets, articles &c. composed, edited or translated by writers bearing the name of
Grimaldi, from 1498 to 1883. Privately printed. 1883.
8vo. **118 C**

GRIMALDI, Stacey.
Lectures on the sources from which pedigrees may be traced
from the Norman conquest to the present time. 1835.
[Law Tracts, vol. 7.] **144 E**
Miscellaneous writings, prose and poetry, from printed and
manuscript sources. Edited by Rev. A. B. Grimaldi.
Privately printed. 4 parts in 2 vols. 1874–84. 8vo. **118 C**
Origines Genealogicæ ; or the sources whence English genea-
logies may be traced, from the Conquest to the present
time. 1828. 4to. **127 J**
Rotuli de dominabus et pueris et puellis de donatione regis
in XII comitatibus anno 31 Regis Henrici II. 1185.
Curante S. Grimaldi. 1830. 4to. **103 F**
Synopsis of English history, from the earliest times to the
year 1870. 2nd ed. 1871. 12mo. **116 E**

GRINDAL, Most Rev. Edmund.
Remains. Edited by Rev. W. Nicholson. Cambridge, 1843.
8vo. **77 D**

GRIQUALAND WEST.

Statute law of the territory of Griqualand West. 2 vols.
Cape Town, 1875–77. **36 G**

GROCERS' COMPANY.

Some account of Company of Grocers of City of London.
By J. B. Heath. Not published. 1829. 8vo. **89 E**

GROCYN, WILLIAM.

Linacre's Catalogue of books belonging to W. Grocyn in
1520, with his accounts as executor, followed by a memoir
of W. Grocyn. See Oxford Hist. Soc. vol. xvi. pp. 317–
380. **85 E**

GROSE, FRANCIS and THOMAS ASTLE.

The Antiquarian repertory : a miscellaneous assemblage of
topography, history, biography, customs and manners.
New ed. 4 vols. 1807–1809. 4to. **85 I**

GROSSETESTE, RIGHT REV. ROBERT.

Roberti Grosseteste, episcopi quondam Lincolniensis, Epistolæ. Edited by H. R. Luard. 1861. 8vo. **101 F**

GROSVENOR, SIR ROBERT.

The controversy between Sir R. Scrope and Sir R. Grosvenor
in the Court of Chivalry, 1385–1390. By Sir N. H. Nicolas.
Privately printed. 2 vols. 1832. 4to. **118 F**

GROTE, GEORGE.

History of Greece. 12 vols. 1854–57. 8vo. **113 D**

GROTIUS, HUGO.

De jure belli ac pacis libri tres, accesserunt annotata in
epistolam Pauli ad Philemonem, dissertatio de mari libero
et libellus singularis de æquitate, indulgentia et facilitate,
quem Nicolaus Blancardus è codice auctoris descripsit, nec
non Joann. Frid. Gronovii v. c. notæ in totum opus de jure
belli ac pacis. Amstelodami, 1689. 8vo. **48 E**

The same. Amstelædami, 1712. 8vo. **48 E**

The same. 2 vols. Amstelædami, 1735. 8vo. **48 E**

His three books treating of the rights of war and peace.
Translated by Wm. Evats. 1682. folio. **48 H**

GROTIUS, HUGO—*continued.*
The same. Translated by Rev. A. C. Campbell. 3 vols.
Pontefract, 1814. 8vo.   ·   **48 E**
The introduction to Dutch jurisprudence of Hugo Grotius.
Rendered into English by C. Herbert. 1845. 8vo. **55 D**
Select theses on the laws of Holland and Zeeland, being a
commentary of Hugo Grotius' Introduction to Dutch Juris-
prudence. By D. G. Van Der Keesel. Translated from
the Latin by C. A. Lorenz. 2nd ed. 1868. 8vo. **55 D**

GROUND-RENTS.
Ground-Rents and building leases. By C. H. Sargant. 1886.
12mo. **11 E**

GRUEBER, ERWIN.
Roman law of damage to property. 1886. 8vo. **63 E**

GRUNDY, JOHN.
The stranger's guide to Hampton Court palace and gardens.
1847. 12mo. **89 D**

GUARANTEES.
The law of guarantees and of principal and surety. By
H. A. De Colyar. 2nd ed. 1885. 8vo. **11 C**
See also FELL, W. W. and THEOBALD, W. **174 C**

GUARDIAN AND WARD.
The law of the domestic relations including guardian and
ward. By W. P. Eversley. 1885. 8vo. **10 C**
See also INFANCY.

GUARDIAN, THE.
The Guardian. 6th ed. 2 vols. 1734. 12mo. **83 A**

GUDE, RICHARD.
The practice of the Crown side of the Court of King's Bench
and the practice of the Sessions. 2 vols. 1828. 8vo. **165 F**

GUELPH, HOUSE OF.
General history of the house of Guelph or royal family of
Great Britain to the accession of King George the First.
By Andrew Halliday. 1821. 4to. **114 G**

GUERNSEY. See CHANNEL ISLANDS.

GUIANA, British.
Ordinances of British Guiana, 1856–1889. 12 vols. 1856–89.
folio and 4to. **36 B**

GUIDOTT, Thomas.
A Discourse of Bath and the hot waters there, to which is
added, A century of observations more fully declaring the
nature of the baths, with an account of the lives and character
of the physicians of Bath. 1676. 12mo. **118 A**

GUIGNES, Joseph de.
Histoire générale des Huns, des Turcs, des Mogols, et des
autres Tartares Occidentaux &c., précédée d'une introduction contenant des tables chronol. et historiques des
Princes qui ont regné dans l'Asie. 4 vols. in 5. Paris,
1756–58. 4to. **113 E**

GUILDFORD, Surrey.
A Description of the hospital of the Blessed Trinity in Guildford, erected and endowed by George Abbot, lord archbishop
of Canterbury. Guildford, 1777. 8vo. **79 B**

GUILDS.
On the history and development of Gilds and the origin of
trade-unions. By L. Brentano. 1870. 8vo. **78 B**

GUILLIM, John.
Display of Heraldrie. 3rd ed. 1638. 4to. **125 H**
The same. 6th ed. 1724. folio. **125 H**

GUIRY, Michael Grace.
The Bills of Sale acts 1878 and 1882. 1882. 8vo. **160 G**
Municipal corporations act 1882. Municipal elections act
1884, and Ballot act 1872. 1884. 8vo. **52 C**

GUIZOT, François Pierre Guillaume.
Alfred le Grand, ou l'Angleterre sous les Anglo-Saxons.
Edited by H. Lallemand. 3rd ed. 1881. 12mo. **83 C**
Édouard III et les bourgeois de Calais, ou les Anglais en
France. Edited by Rev. A. C. Clapin. 1890. 12mo. **83 C**
Guillaume le Conquérant, ou l'Angleterre sous les Normands.
Edited by A. J. Dubourg. 7th ed. 1878. 12mo. **83 C**
History of Charles I. and the English revolution. Translated
by A. R. Scoble. New ed. 2 vols. 1854. 8vo. **115 C**

GUIZOT, François Pierre Guillaume—*continued.*
History of Oliver Cromwell and the English Commonwealth.
Translated by A. R. Scoble. 2 vols. 1854. 8vo. **115 C**
History of Richard Cromwell and the Restoration of Charles II.
Translated by A. R. Scoble. 2 vols. 1856. 8vo. **115 C**

GUNNING, Frederic.
A Practical treatise on the law of Tolls. 1833. 8vo. **176 F**

GUNPOWDER PLOT.
The Gunpowder Plot. By D. Jardine. 1835. 12mo. **51 D**
A True and perfect relation of the whole proceedings against
the late most barbarous traitors, Garnet a Jesuite, and his
confederates. 1606. 8vo. **51 D**

GURDON, Thornhagh.
History of high court of parliament and history of Court baron
and Court leet. 2 vols. 1731. 8vo. **49 E**

GURWOOD, John.
The despatches of the Duke of Wellington during his various
campaigns in India, Denmark, Portugal, Spain, The Low
Countries and France from 1799 to 1818. New ed. 12 vols.
1837–38. 8vo. **114 A B**
The general orders of the Duke of Wellington in Portugal,
Spain and France from 1809 to 1814, in the Low Countries
and France in 1815, and in France, army of occupation, from
1816 to 1818. 1837. 8vo. **114 A**

GUSTAVUS ADOLPHUS.
Letters relating to the mission of Sir Thomas Roe to Gustavus
Adolphus. 1629–30. Edited by S. R. Gardiner. [Camden
Society, n.s. vol. 14.] 1875. 8vo. **85 D**

GUTCH, Rev. John.
Collectanea Curiosa ; or, miscellaneous tracts relating to the
history and antiquities of England and Ireland, the Universities of Oxford and Cambridge and a variety of other
subjects. 2 vols. Oxford, 1781. 8vo. **84 C**
See also Wood, Anthony À.

GÜTERBOCK, Carl.
Bracton and his relation to the Roman law. Translated by
B. Coxe. Philadelphia, 1866. 8vo. **63 F**

GUTHRIE, Malcolm.
On Mr. Spencer's Data of Ethics. 1884. 8vo.   **78 C**
On Mr. Spencer's Formula of Evolution as an exhaustive statement of the changes of the universe. 1879. 8vo. **78 C**
On Mr. Spencer's Unification of Knowledge. 1882. 8vo. **78 C**

GUTHRIE, William.
Complete history of English peerage. 2 vols in 1. 1763. 4to.
127 J

GUY, William Augustus.
Principles of forensic medicine. 2nd ed. 1861. 12mo. **172 E**

GUYLFORDE, Sir Richard.
Pylgrymage of Sir R. Guylforde to the Holy Land, A.D. 1506. Edited by Sir H. Ellis. [Camden Soc. vol. 51.] 1851. 8vo.
85 B

GWEDIR FAMILY.
The history of the Gwedir family. By Sir John Wynne. 1770. 8vo. ·   **79 B**

GWILLIM, Sir Henry.
A Collection of acts and records of parliament with reports of cases respecting Tithes. 2nd ed. by C. Ellis. 4 vols. 1825. 8vo.   **65 A**

GWYNN, John.
London and Westminster improved, illustrated by plans, to which is prefixed A discourse on public magnificence with Observations on the state of arts and artists in this kingdom. 1766. 4to.   **89 F**

GWYNNE, Thomas.
The law relating to the duties on Probates and Letters of Administration in England and Inventories of personal estates in Scotland and on Legacies and Successions to personal estates in Great Britain. 2nd ed. 1836. 8vo. **174 D**

GYLL, Gordon Willoughby James.
History of the parish of Wraysbury, Ankerwycke priory and Magna Charta Island with the history of Horton and the town of Colnbrook, Bucks. 1862. 4to.   **86 B**

HABÈAS CORPUS.

Report of the proceedings in the cases of Ameer Khan and Hashmadad Khan. By C. C. .Macrae. Calcutta, 1870. [Pamphlets, vol. 29.] **144 B**

See also Fisher's Digest, vol. 3, 1884, pp. 2011–2025. **14 E**

HACKNEY, MIDDLESEX.

An Act for taking down the church and tower belonging to the parish of Saint John at Hackney, and for building another church and tower. 1803. 8vo. **89 D**

History and antiquities of parish of Hackney. By Wm. Robinson. 2 vols. 1842–43. 8vo. **89 D**

HADDAN, THOMAS HENRY.

Outlines of the administrative jurisdiction of the Court of Chancery. 1862. 12mo. **161 D**

Remarks on legal education with reference to the suggested introduction of legal studies into the University of Oxford. 1848. [Pamphlets, vol. 7.] **144 A**

HADDOCK FAMILY.

Correspondence of the family of Haddock 1657–1719. Edited by E. M. Thompson. [Camden Society, n.s. vol. 31.] 1883. 8vo. **85 D**

HAGGARD, JOHN.

Reports of cases in the Consistory Court of London, 1789–1821. 2 vols. 1822. 8vo. **8 G**

Reports of cases in the Ecclesiastical Courts, 1827–1833. 4 vols. 1829–33. 8vo. **8 G**

Reports of cases in the high court of Admiralty, 1822–1838. 3 vols. 1825–40. 8vo. **8 A**

HAINES, JOHN.

Case between Sir Wm. Clayton and the Duchy of Cornwall, and,The history of the constitution of the Duchy of Cornwall. 1834–35. 8vo. **87 A**

HAKEWIL, WILLIAM.

The libertie of the subject against the pretended power of impositions. 1641. 12mo. **48 D**

The manner how statutes are enacted in parliament by passing of bills. 1641. 12mo. **48 D**

HAKEWIL, WILLIAM—*continued.*
Modus tenendi parliamentum ; or, the old manner of holding
parliaments in England. 1671. 12mo. **48 D**

HAKEWILL, JAMES.
History of Windsor and its neighbourhood. 1813. 4to. **86 G**

HALCOMB, JOHN.
A Practical treatise of passing Private Bills through both
Houses of Parliament. 1836, and Supplement, 1838. 2 vols.
1836–38. 8vo. **173 B**
Report of the trials and subsequent proceedings in causes of
Rowe *v.* Grenfell, Rowe *v.* Brenton and another, and Doe
(dem. Carthew) *v.* Brenton, relative to claims made by
Lessees of Duke of Cornwall to Copper Mines within Dutchy
Lands, and involving question of Title to lands and estates
of the tenants. 1826. [Jacob's Tracts, vol. 10.] **144 E**

HALE, SIR MATTHEW.
Considerations touching the amendment or alteration of lawes.
See Hargrave's Law Tracts, 1787, pp. 249–289. **144 G**
A Discourse concerning the courts of King's Bench and
Common Pleas. See Hargrave's Law Tracts, 1787, pp.
357–376. **144 G**
Discourse touching provision for the Poor. 1716. 12mo. **144 F**
Historia Placitorum Coronæ. History of Pleas of the Crown,
with notes by S. Emlyn. 2 vols. 1736. folio. **155 E**
The same. New ed. by G. Wilson. 2 vols. 1778. 8vo. **53 C**
The history and analysis of the common law of England. By
A Learned Hand [Sir M. Hale]. 1713. 12mo. **170 E**
The same. 2nd ed. 1 vol. 1716, and 5th ed. by C. Run-
nington. 2 vols. 1794. 12mo. **170 E**
Jurisdiction of the Lords House, or Parliament considered
according to ancient records. 1796. 8vo. **127 I**
The original institution, power, and jurisdiction of parliaments.
1707. 12mo. **49 E**
Pleas of the Crown : or, a summary of the principal matters
relating to that subject. 5th ed. 1716. 12mo. **144 F**
Preface to Rolle's Abridgment published 1668. See Collectanea Juridica, vol. 1, 1791, pp. 263–282. **144 G**
The primitive origination of mankind considered and examined
according to the light of nature. 1677. folio. **78 H**

HALE, Sir Matthew—*continued*.

Short treatise touching sheriffs accompts. To which is added, A tryal of witches at assizes held at Bury St. Edmonds, March 1664, before Sir Matthew Hale. 1683. 12mo.   **49 E**

The same. Another ed. 1716. 12mo.   **144 F**

A Treatise in three parts. 1. De jure maris et brachiorum ejusdem. 2. De portibus maris. 3. Concerning the customs of goods imported and exported. See Hargrave's Law Tracts, 1787, pp. 1–248.   **144 G**

See also S. A. Moore's History of the Foreshore, 1888, pp. 318–413.   **11 E**

See also HERBERT, Sir E.

HALE, William Hale.

A Series of precedents and proceedings in criminal causes extending from 1475 to 1640 illustrative of the discipline of the Church of England. 1847. 8vo.   **155 B**

HALHED, Nathaniel Brassey.

A Code of Gentoo laws, or ordinations of the Pundits, from a Persian translation made from the original written in the Shanscrit language. 1776 and 1781. 4to.   **38 A**

HALIBURTON, Thomas Chandler.

An Historical and statistical account of Nova Scotia. 2 vols. Halifax, 1829. 8vo.   **84 B**

HALIFAX, George, 1 Marquess of.

Letters to his brother Henry Savile, envoy at Paris, and vice-chamberlain to Charles II. and James II. Edited by W. D. Cooper. [Camden Soc., vol. 71.] 1858. 8vo.   **85 B**

HALIFAX, Yorkshire.

The history and antiquities of the parish of Halifax. By Rev. John Watson. 1775. 4to.   **94 C**

The history of the famous town of Halifax in Yorkshire. By William Bently. 1712. 12mo.   **94 A**

HALKETT, Lady Anne.

The autobiography of Anne Lady Halkett. Edited by J. G. Nichols. [Camden Soc., n.s. vol. 13.] 1875. 8vo.   **85 D**

HALKETT, SAMUEL and REV. JOHN LAING.

A Dictionary of the anonymous and pseudonymous literature of Great Britain. 4 vols. Edinburgh, 1882–88. 8vo. **82 E**

HALL, FREDERICK JAMES and PHILIP TWELLS.

. Reports of cases in court of Chancery during time of Lord Chancellor Cottenham, 1849–50. 2 vols. 1850–51. 8vo. **2 G**

HALL, JOHN EDWARD.

A Treatise on the law relating to profits à prendre and rights of common. 1871. 8vo. **9 D**

HALL, ROBERT GREAM.

Essay on rights of the crown and privileges of the subject in seashores of the realm. 2nd ed. by R. L. Loveland. 1875. 8vo. **53 G**

The same. 3rd ed. by S. A. Moore. 1888. 8vo. **11 E**

Observations on the inexpediency of a general metropolitan registry for deeds and other assurances affecting lands in England & Wales. 1834. [Jacob's Tracts, vol. 11.] **144 F**

HALL, SPENCER.

Echyngham of Echyngham. 1850. 8vo. **80 C**

HALL, THEODORE HALL.

Law of Allotments, being a treatise on law relating to allotment of land for the labouring poor. 1886. 8vo. **9 A**

HALL, WILLIAM CHAMPAIN.

Legal forms compiled for the use of attorneys and solicitors. 1865. 12mo. **164 E**

HALL, WILLIAM EDWARD.

Treatise on international law. 2nd ed. 1884. 8vo. **55 B**

HALLAM, HENRY.

The constitutional history of England from accession of Henry VII. to death of George II. New ed. 3 vols. 1884. 12mo. **116 D**

Introduction to literature of Europe in fifteenth, sixteenth and seventeenth centuries. 4th ed. 3 vols. 1854. 8vo. **116 C**

View of the state of Europe during the Middle Ages. 5th ed. 3 vols. 1829. 8vo. **116 C**

HALLAMSHIRE, YORKSHIRE.
The history and topography of the parish of Sheffield. By
Joseph Hunter. New ed. with additions by Rev. A. Gatty.
1869. folio. **95 H**

HALLIDAY, SIR ANDREW.
A General history of the house of Guelph, or royal family of
Great Britain, to the accession of King George the First.
1821. 4to. **114 G**
A Letter to Lord Robert Seymour : with a Report of the
number of lunatics and idiots in England and Wales. 1829.
[Jacob's Tracts, vol. 7.] **144 E**

HALLILAY, RICHARD.
The articled clerks' hand-book. 1859. 8vo. **160 C**
The same. 4th ed. by G. Badham. 1873. 8vo. **64 A**
Treatise on law and practice of Conveyancing. 1883. 12mo.
64 B
View of proceedings in an action in Chancery division of
high court of justice including practice on appeal. 2nd ed.
1884. 12mo. **64 A**
Digest of questions asked at final examination of articled
clerks on law of Probate and Divorce. 1888. 8vo. **64 E**
Digest of the examination questions in conveyancing, common
law and equity, from 1836 with answers. 1856. 8vo. **168 A**
The same. 13th ed. by H. W. Purkis. 1884. 8vo. **64 D**
The same. 14th ed. by R. Hallilay. 1886. 8vo. **64 D**
The same. 15th ed. by R. Hallilay. 1889. 8vo. **64 D**

HALLIWELL, JAMES ORCHARD.
A Dictionary of archaic and provincial words, obsolete phrases,
proverbs and ancient customs from the fourteenth century.
5th ed. 2 vols. 1865. 8vo. **123 B**
An Historical account of the New Place, Stratford-upon-Avon,
the last residence of Shakespeare. 1864. folio. **94 H**

HALLIWELL, WILLIAM.
Handy-book of Conveyancing costs. 1882. 8vo. **165 A**
The same. 2nd ed. 1886. 8vo. **9 F**

HALL-MARKS.
Hall-marks on gold and silver plate. By W. Chaffers. 1863.
8vo. **78 C**

HALMA, François.
Dictionnaire Flamand et François. 1710. 8vo.   123 C

HAMEL, Felix Hargrave.
International law in connexion with municipal statutes relating
to the commerce, rights and liabilities of the subjects of
neutral states pending foreign war. 1863. 12mo.   55 A

HAMEL, Felix John.
Laws of the customs with commentary. 1854. 8vo.   165 F
The same. 1876. 8vo.   9 G

HAMILTON FAMILY.
The Hamilton Palace Collection. Illustrated priced catalogue.
1882. 4to.   118 F
Hamilton Papers ; being selections from original letters in
the possession of the Duke of Hamilton and Brandon, re-
lating to the years 1638–1650. Edited by S. R. Gardiner.
[Camden Society, n.s. vol. 27.] 1880. 8vo.   85 D
An Inquiry into the pedigree, descent and public transactions
of the chiefs of the Hamilton Family. By Wm. Aiton.
Glasgow, 1827. 8vo.   80 C
Memoirs of the house of Hamilton, corrected. [By Dr.
Hamilton of Bardowie.] Edinburgh, 1828. 8vo.   80 C
Reply to the misstatements of Dr. Hamilton of Bardowie in
his late 'Memoirs of the house of Hamilton, corrected,'
respecting the descent of his family. [By J. Riddell.]
Edinburgh, 1828. 8vo.   80 C

HAMILTON, Alexander Henry Abercromby.
Quarter Sessions from Queen Elizabeth to Queen Anne ;
illustrations of local government and history chiefly of the
county of Devon. 1878. 8vo.   78 B

HAMILTON, Charles.
The Hedaya, or guide, a commentary on the Mussalman
laws. 2nd ed. by S. G. Grady. 1870. 8vo.   38 D

HAMILTON, Gawayne Baldwin.
The law of Covenants. 1888. 8vo.   13 B
The Trustee Acts, containing trustee act 1850, trustee exten-
sion act 1852 and trustee act 1888. 1889. 8vo.   11 I

HAMILTON, LEONIDAS.
Mexican law, a compilation of Mexican legislation and Mexican mining law annotated. 1882. 8vo. **55 C**

HAMILTON, THOMAS.
Annals of the Peninsular campaigns from 1808 to 1814. 3 vols. 1829. 12mo. **114 C**

HAMILTON, REV. WILLIAM.
Letters concerning the northern coast of the county of Antrim, with the natural history of the basaltes in the northern counties of Ireland. Dublin, 1790. 8vo. **95 E**

HAMMERSMITH, MIDDLESEX.
An Account of Fulham, including the Hamlet of Hammersmith. By Thomas Faulkner. 1813. 8vo. **89 E**
The history and antiquities of parish of Hammersmith. By Thomas Faulkner. 1839. 8vo. **89 D**

HAMMICK, JAMES THOMAS.
The Marriage law of England. 1873. 12mo. **172 D**
The same. 2nd ed. 1887. 12mo. **10 H**

HAMMOND, ANTHONY.
Analytical Index to Term Reports, and others, during reign of George III. and IV. 2nd ed. 2 vols. 1827. 8vo. **63 C**
Digest of cases at Nisi Prius. See Sir J. Comyn's Digest, vol. 5, 1822, pp. 365–640. **14 B**

HAMMOND, NATHANIEL.
The elements of Algebra in a new and easy method 3rd ed. 1764. 8vo. **255 H**

HAMPDEN, RIGHT REV. RENN DICKSON.
Report of the case of the Rt. Rev. R. D. Hampden, Lord Bishop Elect of Hereford. By R. Jebb. 1849. 8vo. **50 A**

HAMPER, WILLIAM.
The life, diary, and correspondence of Sir William Dugdale sometime Garter principal King of arms. 1827. 4to. **79 I**

HAMPSHIRE.

Χοιροχωρογραφία sive Hoglandiæ Descriptio. By M. C. 1709. 12mo.   **118 C**

Description of Hogland : with its dedication : imitated in English. By Pen-Men-Maur. 1711. 12mo.   **118 C**

General history of Hampshire. By B. B. Woodward, T. C. Wilks and C. Lockhart. 3 vols. [1861–69.] folio.   **88 G**

Hampshire Repository, or historical, economical and literary miscellany. 2 vols. 1799–1801. 8vo.   **88 A**

History, gazetteer and directory of Hampshire and Isle of Wight. By W. White. Sheffield, 1859. 8vo.   **88 A**

Pedigrees of the families in the county of Hants. By William Berry. 1833. folio.   **126 I**

Poll for the election of one knight for the county of Southampton. 1780. 8vo.   **107 K**

Poll for the election of two knights for the county of Southampton, taken at Winchester, June 1790. By G. Hollis. Romsey, 1791. 8vo.   **107 K**

A Topographical account of the hundred of Bosmere, including the parishes of Havant, Warblington and Hayling. By C. J. Longcroft. 1857. 8vo.   **88 B**

See also WARNER, REV. R.

HAMPSON, SIR GEORGE FRANCIS.

Treatise on liabilities of Trustees. 2nd ed. 1830. 8vo. **176 F**

HAMPSTEAD.

Records of the manor, parish and borough of Hampstead. Edited by F. E. Baines. 1890. 4to.   **89 E**

The topography and natural history of Hampstead. By John James Park. 1818. 8vo.   **89 E**

HAMPTON COURT PALACE.

Historical catalogue of the pictures in royal collection at Hampton Court, with an account of the state rooms. By Ernest Law. 1881. 8vo.   **89 D**

The stranger's guide to Hampton Court palace and gardens. By John Grundy. 1847. 12mo.   **89 D**

The stranger's guide to Hampton Court palace and gardens. By Wm. Willshire. 1869. 12mo.   **89 D**

HANBURY, Rev. William.
The history of the rise and progress of the charitable foundations at Church-Langton. 1767. 8vo. **89 C**

HANCOCK, John Webster.
A System of Conveyancing, comprising the principles, forms
and laws which regulate the transfer of property in Canada.
Toronto, 1861. 8vo. **59 C**

HAND, The.
The hand, its mechanism and vital endowments as evincing
design. By Sir Charles Bell. 1833. 8vo. **77 B**

HANDS, William.
Law of Patents for inventions. 1808. 8vo. **173 E**
Treatise on Fines and Recoveries. 1807. 8vo. **168 D**
The same. 3rd ed. 1817. 8vo. **168 D**
The proceedings on Election petitions. 1812. 8vo. **166 C**
Solicitor's assistant in Court of Chancery. 1809. 8vo. **161 C**
The Solicitor's practice on the Crown side of the court of
King's Bench. 1803. 8vo. **162 F**

HANGING AND HANGMAN.
Hanging not punishment enough for murtherers, highway
men and house-breakers ; offered to the consideration of
the two Houses of Parliament, 1701. Reprinted 1812.
[Montagu's Law Tracts.] **144 F**
Origin of thirteen pence halfpenny as hangman's wages. See
S. Pegge's Anecdotes, 1818, pp. 331–348. **83 H**

HANNINGTON, Charles Mepham.
Registration made easy, or a concise plan for a general register.
1831. 12mo. **174 F**

HANOVER.
The Prussian state trial for high treason of the Hanoverian
minister of state, Count Adolphus Platen zu Hallermund.
1868. [Pamphlets, vol. 37.] **144 C**

HANSARD, George.
A Treatise on the law relating to aliens and denization and
naturalization. With supplement. 1844–46. 8vo. **52 A**

HANSARD, JOHN.

A Book of Entries of Declarations and other Pleadings in the most usual Actions in the Court of King's Bench, to which are added Appeals of Murder and Mayheme. 1685. folio.

HANSARD'S DEBATES.

The Parliamentary history of England, from the earliest period [1066] to the year 1803. [Compiled by Wm. Cobbett.] 36 vols. 1806–20. 8vo. **109 A & 110 A**

Cobbett's [afterwards Hansard's] Parliamentary debates, 1803–1820. 41 vols. 1804–20. 8vo. **110 B–D**

New series, 1820–1830. 25 vols. 1820–30. 8vo. **110 D E**

Third series, 1830–1890. 343 vols. 1831–90. 8vo.

110 E–112 H

General Index to the first and second series, 1803–1830. Edited by Sir John Philippart. 1834. 8vo. **112 I**

General Indexes, 1851–87. 5 vols. 1851–87. 8vo. **112 I**

HANSE TOWNS.

The ancient sea laws of the Hanse Towns taken out of a French book intitled Les Us et Coutumes de la Mer, 1686. See G. Malynes's Lex Mercatoria, 3rd ed. 1686, folio. **118 G**

HANSHALL, J. H.

History of County Palatine of Chester. Chester, 1817. 4to. **86 F**

HANSON, ALFRED.

Acts relating to Probate, legacy and succession duties with copious notes. 2nd ed. 1870. 12mo. **176 D**

The same. 3rd ed. 1876. 8vo. **11 G**

Revenue acts of 1880 and 1881 so far as they relate to the new death duties. 1883. 8vo. **11 G**

HARBOURS OF REFUGE.

Harbours of refuge not 'dangerous decoys,' 'ship traps' nor 'wrecking pools.' By F. R. A. Glover. 1859. 8vo. **78 B**

HARDCASTLE, HENRY.

Law and practice of Election petitions. 1874. 12mo. **166 C**

Rules which govern the construction and effect of statutory law. 1879. 8vo. **53 H**

HARDCASTLE, MARY SCARLETT.
Life of Lord Campbell. 2nd ed. 2 vols. 1881. 8vo. **80 D**

HARDIMAN, JAMES.
The history of the town and county of the town of Galway.
Dublin, 1820. 4to. **95 F**
Inquisitionum in officio rotulorum Cancellariæ Hiberniæ
asservatarum repertorium. [Edited by J. Hardiman.]
2 vols. Dublin, 1826-29. folio. **98 B**

HARDING, GEORGE ROGERS.
Acts and orders relating to Joint Stock Companies. Brisbane,
1887. 8vo. **55 D**
Acts and orders relating to the Jurisdiction, Practice and
Pleading of the Supreme Court of Queensland (exclusive
of its criminal jurisdiction). Brisbane, 1885. 8vo. **55 D**
Acts and orders relating to the jurisdiction, practice and
pleading of the supreme court of Queensland (on the crown
side). Brisbane, 1887. 4to. **55 D**
Handy book of ecclesiastical law. 2nd ed. 1862. 12mo. **166 B**
Settled Land act of 1886 and the rules of court made thereunder. Brisbane, 1889. 8vo. **55 D**
Acts and rules relating to Insolvency. By G. R. Harding
and P. Macpherson. Brisbane, 1887. 8vo. **55 D**

HARDINGHAM, GEORGE GATTON.
The Republic of Cicero. Reprinted from the 3rd ed. of
Cardinal Mai (Rome, 1846) and translated with notes.
1884. 8vo. **83 H**

HARDINGHAM, GEORGE GATTON MELHUISH.
Trade Marks : notes on the British, foreign and colonial laws
relating thereto. 1881. 8vo. **55 B**

HARDOUIN, JEAN.
Nummi antiqui populorum et urbium illustrati. Paris, 1684.
4to. **113 G**

HARDRES, SIR THOMAS.
Reports of cases adjudged in the court of Exchequer, 1655–
1669. 1693. folio. **74 D**

HARDWICK, SUFFOLK.

The history and antiquities of Hawsted and Hardwick. By Rev. Sir John Cullum. 2nd ed. 1813. 4to.   93 G

HARDWICKE, PHILIP, 2 EARL OF.

Cases in court of King's Bench, 1733–38, temp. Earl Hardwicke. By T. Lee. 2nd ed. 1815. 8vo.   5 B

Catalogue of manuscripts in possession of Earl Hardwicke. 1794. 4to.   82 I

A Discourse of the judicial authority belonging to the office of Master of the Rolls in the court of chancery. [By Philip Yorke, Earl of Hardwicke.] 1727. 8vo.   49 D

Order of the Court of Chancery made by Philip Lord Hardwicke relating to the fees of the officers of the said court. 1744. 12mo.   49 F

Reports in court of Chancery, 1736–39, temp. Earl Hardwicke. By M. J. West. 1827. 8vo.   3 I

Reports in court of King's Bench, 1734–36, temp. Earl Hardwicke. By T. Cunningham. 2nd ed. 1770. folio. 74 C

Reports in King's Bench and Chancery, 1733–45, temp. Earl Hardwicke. By Wm. Ridgeway. 1794. 8vo.   5 H

Select cases, determined in Chancery by Lord Hardwicke, on the Statute of Mortmain. See Collectanea Juridica, vol. 1, 1791, pp. 433–457.

HARDY, SIR THOMAS DUFFUS.

Annual reports of the deputy keeper of the public records. 14 vols. 1862–78. 8vo.   100 A-C

Catalogue of lords chancellors, keepers of the great seal, masters of the rolls and principal officers of the high court of chancery. 1843. 8vo.   80 F

Descriptive catalogue of materials relating to history of Great Britain and Ireland. 3 vols. in 4. 1862–71. 8vo. 101 F

Report to the Master of the Rolls upon the documents in the archives and public libraries of Venice. 1866. 8vo. 97 H

Syllabus (in English) of the documents relating to England and other kingdoms contained in the collection known as 'Rymer's Fœdera,' 1066–1654. 3 vols. 1869–85. 8vo. 97 H

Report to the Master of the Rolls upon the Carte and Carew papers in the Bodleian and Lambeth libraries. By T. D. Hardy and J. S. Brewer. 1864. 8vo.   97 H

See also LE NEVE, J. and RECORD COMMISSION.

HARDY, WILLIAM.

Annual reports of the deputy keeper of the public records.
8 vols. 1879–86. 8vo.   **100 D E**

The charters of the Duchy of Lancaster. Translated and
edited by W. Hardy. 1845. 8vo.   **89 B**

A Collection of the chronicles and ancient histories of Great
Britain, now called England, by John De Wavrin. Translated by W. Hardy. 2 vols. 1864–87. 8vo.   **102 B**

HARE, J. I. CLARK.

The law of Contracts. Boston, 1887. 8vo.   **59 C**

American Leading Cases, being select decisions of American
courts in several departments of law with especial reference
to mercantile law. By J. I. C. Hare and H. B. Wallace.
4th ed. 2 vols. Philadelphia, 1857. 8vo.   **59 F**

HARE, THOMAS.

The development of the wealth of India. 1861. [Pamphlets,
vol. 14.]   **144 A**

Election of representatives, parliamentary and municipal.
4th ed. 1873. 12mo.   **166 C**

On an organisation of the metropolitan elections. 1865.
[Pamphlets, vol. 26.]   **144 B**

Reports of cases adjudged in the Court of Chancery, 1841–
1853. 11 vols. 1843–58. 8vo.   **2 H**

Treatise on Discovery of evidence. 1836. 8vo.   **165 G**

The same. 2nd ed. by S. Hare. 1877. 12mo.   **165 G**

HARGRAVE, FRANCIS.

Catalogue of manuscripts formerly in possession of F. Hargrave, deposited in British Museum. 1818. 4to.   **82 I**

Collectanea Juridica : consisting of tracts relative to the law
and constitution of England. [Collected by Francis Hargrave.] 2 vols. 1791–92. 8vo.   **144 G**

Collection of tracts relative to the law of England, from
manuscripts, now first edited. 1787. 8vo.   **144 G**

Juridical arguments & collections. 2 vols. 1797–99. 4to. **144 G**

Opinion of Mr. Hargrave on case of Duke of Athol in respect
to Isle of Mann. 1788. 8vo.   **94 F**

HARGRAVE, JOHN FLETCHER.

Treatise on the Thellusson act 39 and 40 Geo. III. c. 98, with
practical observations upon trusts for accumulation. 1842.
8vo.   **176 E**

HARLE, William Lockey.

Argument on the inutility of the distinction between barrister and attorney, addressed to the Lord Chancellor. 1851. [Pamphlets, vol. 8.]   **144 A**

A Career in the Commons, or letters to a young member of parliament on the conduct and principles necessary to constitute him an enlightened and efficient representative. 1850. 8vo.   **78 B**

HARLEIAN LIBRARY, Manuscripts and Miscellany.

Catalogue of early English miscellanies formerly in the Harleian library. Edited by W. C. Hazlitt. [Camden Society, vol. 87.] 1864. 8vo.   **85 C**

Catalogue of the Harleian manuscripts in the British Museum. Edited by H. Wanley, D. Casley, Rev. R. Nares and others. 4 vols. 1808–12. folio.   **98 C**

The Harleian miscellany ; a collection of pamphlets and tracts selected from the library of Edward Harley, Second Earl of Oxford, with annotations by the late William Oldys and some additional notes. With two supplemental volumes by Thomas Park. 10 vols. 1808–13. 4to.   **113 F**

HARLEIAN SOCIETY.

Harleian Society's Publications. Registers of baptisms, marriages and burials. 14 vols. 1877–89. 8vo.

1, 4. Parish of Saint Peeters upon Cornhill, London, 1538–1774. Edited by G. W. G. L. Gower. 2 vols. 1877–79. 8vo.   **90 E**

2. Canterbury Cathedral, 1564–1878. Edited by Robert Hovenden. 1878. 8vo.   **88 E**

3. Parish of Saynte De'nis Backchurch, London, 1538–1754. Edited by J. L. Chester. 1878. 8vo.   **90 E**

5. Parish of St. Mary Aldermary, London, 1558–1754. Edited by J. L. Chester. 1880. 8vo.   **90 E**

6. Parish of St. Thomas the Apostle, London, 1558–1754. Edited by J. L. Chester. 1881. 8vo.   **90 E**

7. Parish of St. Michael, Cornhill, London, 1546–1754. Partly edited by J. L. Chester. 1882. 8vo.   **90 E**

8. Parishes of St. Antholin, Budge Row, London, 1538–1754, and of St. John Baptist on Wallbrook London, 1682–1754. Edited by J. L. Chester and G. J. Armytage. 1883. 8vo.   **90 E**

9, 10, 13. Parish of St. James, Clarkenwell, Christenings and Marriages 1551–1754. Edited by Robert Hovenden. 3 vols. 1884–88. 8vo.   **90 E**

11, 14. Parish of St. George, Hanover Square. Marriages 1725–1809. Edited by J. K. Chapman. 2 vols. 1886–89.   **90 F**

12. Parish of Stourton, Wiltshire, 1570–1800. Edited by Rev. J. H. Ellis. 1887. 8vo.   **93 F**

HARLEY, LADY BRILLIANA.

Letters of Lady B. Harley with introduction and notes by
T. T. Lewis. [Camden Soc., vol. 58.] 1853. 8vo. **85 B**

HARPSFIELD, NICHOLAS.

Treatise on the pretended divorce between Henry VIII. and
Catharine of Arragon. Edited by N. Pocock. [Camden
Society, n.s. vol. 21.] 1878. 8vo. **85 D**

HARRIS, ELLIS.

A Table showing at a glance the incidence of the English
Death Duties. 1890. 8vo. **11 G**

HARRIS, GEORGE.

The four books of Justinian's Institutions translated into
English with notes. 3rd ed. Oxford, 1811. 4to. **48 G**

HARRIS, GEORGE, LL.D., F.S.A.

The autobiography of George Harris of the Middle Temple.
Printed for private circulation. 1888. 8vo. **80 C**

Principia Prima Legum ; or, an enunciation and analysis of
the elementary principles of Law, in its several departments.
Part 1. [1865.] 8vo. **63 F**

HARRIS, REV. JOHN.

History of Kent. vol. 1. [all published.] 1719. folio. **89 H**

HARRIS, RICHARD.

Before trial : what should be done by client, solicitor and
counsel, with a treatise on the defence of insanity. 1886.
12mo. **176 F**

Hints on Advocacy; conduct of cases civil and criminal. 6th
ed. 1882. 8vo. **52 A**

The same. 9th ed. 1889. 8vo. **11 G**

HARRIS, SEYMOUR FREDERICK.

Elements of Roman law summarized. Digest of matter contained in Institutes of Gaius and Justinian. 1875. 8vo. **63 E**

Principles of the Criminal law. 1877. 8vo. **165 D**

The same. 2nd ed. by the Author and F. P. Tomlinson. 1881.
8vo. **165 D**

The same. 3rd ed. by the Author and A. Agabeg. 1884.
8vo. **64 C**

HARRIS, Seymour Frederick—*continued.*
The same. 4th ed. by A. Agabeg. 1886. 8vo.   **64 C**
The same. 5th ed. by A. Agabeg. 1889. 8vo.   **64 C**

HARRIS, Walter.
History and antiquities of the city of Dublin, with an history of the cathedrals of Christ Church and St. Patrick. Dublin, 1766. 8vo.   **95 E**

HARRIS, William Manning and Thomas CLARKSON.
The Conveyancing act 1881 and the Vendor and purchaser act 1874 with notes. 1882. 8vo.   **163 G**

HARRISON, George H. de S. N. Plantagenet.
History of Yorkshire. Wapentake of Gilling West. 1875. 8vo.   **95 H**

HARRISON, George L.
Legislation on Insanity. A collection of all the lunacy laws of the states and territories of the United States, to the year 1883 inclusive ; also the laws of England on Insanity, legislation in Canada on private houses, and portions of the lunacy laws of Germany, France, &c. Privately printed. Philadelphia, 1884. 8vo.   **59 G**

HARRISON, James Carter.
Epitome of laws of Probate and Divorce. 1880. 8vo. **174 D**
The same. 2nd ed. 1883, and 3rd ed. 1886. 8vo. **64 E**
An Epitome of the Criminal law. 1882. 8vo. **165 D**
The same. 2nd ed. 1885. 8vo. **64 C**
A Selection of Statutes for students. 1885. 8vo. **64 F**

HARRISON, Joseph.
The accomplish'd practiser in the High Court of Chancery. 1741. 8vo. **161 D**
The same. Newly arranged by John Newland. 2 vols. in 1. 1808. 8vo. **161 D**
Present practice of court of Common Pleas. 1761. 8vo. **162 E**
Present practice of court of King's Bench. 1761. 8vo. **162 E**

HARRISON, Octavian Baxter Cameron.
Practice of sheriffs' court of City of London. 1860. 8vo. **12 A**

HARRISON, ROBERT ALEXANDER.
The new municipal manual for Upper Canada. Toronto,
1859. 8vo. **60 E**
Digest of reports of all cases in the Queen's Bench and
Practice Courts for Upper Canada, 1823–51. By R. A.
Harrison and J. L. Robinson. Toronto, 1852. 8vo. **60 E**

HARRISON, SAMUEL BEALEY.
Analytical digest of all the reported cases determined in
House of Lords and several courts of Common Law, both
in Banc and Nisi Prius, 1756–1827. 2 vols. 1828. 8vo.
The same. 2nd ed. 3 vols. 1835, with Addenda. 2 vols.
1837. 5 vols. 1835–37. 8vo.
The same. 3rd ed. by R. T. Harrison. 4 vols. 1844. 8vo. **63 C**

HARRISON, SAMUEL BEALEY and F. L. WOLLASTON.
Reports of cases in the Court of King's Bench and in the
Bail Court, 1835–1836. 2 vols. 1836–37. 8vo. **5 B**

HARRISON, WILLIAM.
Chief rents and other rent charges. 1884. 8vo. **11 E**

HARROGATE, YORKSHIRE.
The new Harrogate guide. 4th ed. 1825. 12mo. **94 A**
The waters of Harrogate and its vicinity. By Adam Hunter.
5th ed. 1838. 8vo. **94 A**

HARROW, MIDDLESEX.
Rambles round Eton and Harrow. By A. Rimmer. 1882.
8vo. **86 C**

HARSTON, EDWARD FRENCH BUTTEMER.
Scale of costs and fees in chancery and common law divisions
of high court of justice rearranged. 1878. 8vo. **165 A**

HART, HENRY GEORGE.
New annual Army list, 1841–1890. 50 vols. 1841–1890.
8vo. **133 E–G**
New [quarterly] Army list, Feb. 1839 to Oct. 1890 (imperfect). 87 vols. 1839–1890. 8vo. **210 F–211 D**

HART, Henry Wyatt.
Bankruptcy law and practice. 2nd ed. 1884. 8vo. 160 D
The same. 3rd ed. 1887. 8vo. 12 I

HARTLEPOOL, Durham.
History of Hartlepool. By Sir Cuthbert Sharp. Durham,
1816. 8vo. 87 E

HARTWELL, Bucks.
Ædes Hartwellianæ, or notices of the manor and mansion of
Hartwell. By W. H. Smyth. Printed for private circu-
lation. 1851. 4to. 86 G
Catalogue of the law library at Hartwell House. By W. H.
McAlpine. 1865. 8vo. 82 C
The cycles of celestial objects continued at the Hartwell
observatory to 1859. By W. H. Smyth. Printed for
private circulation. 1860. 4to. 86 G

HARVEY, Daniel Whittle.
A Letter to the burgesses of Colchester, containing a plain
statement of proceedings before benchers of Inner Temple
upon his application to be called to the bar and upon his
appeal to the judges. 1822. 8vo. 78 B
Proceedings in a cause Harvey versus Andrew, tried at Chelms-
ford 17 March 1810 by a special jury before Mr. Justice
Heath. 2nd ed. 1832. 8vo. 78 B
Report of proceedings on investigation before benchers of
Inner Temple upon application of D. W. Harvey, M.P. to
be called to the bar. Chelmsford, 1834. 8vo. 78 B
The speech and reply of D. W. Harvey, M.P. in the House of
Commons on moving for leave to bring in a bill to empower
the Court of King's Bench to regulate the admission of
students and barristers. 1832. 8vo. 78 B
Observations and strictures upon the speech and reply of
D. W. Harvey. By C. Stokes. 1832. 8vo. 78 B

HARVEY, Gabriel.
Letter book of Gabriel Harvey, A.D. 1573–1580. Edited
by E. J. L. Scott. [Camden Society, n.s. vol. 33.] 1884.
8vo. 85 D

HARVEY, Rev. Thomas.
A Letter to the lord bishop of London on the case of the Rev.
Thomas Harvey, ex-British Chaplain at Antwerp. By An
Officiating Parish Priest. 1846. [Pamphlets, vol. 5.] 144 A

HARWICH, Essex.

The history of Harwich and Dovercourt. Collected by Silas Taylor, enlarged by Samuel Dale. 1730. 8vo. **87 E**

HARWOOD, A. A.

The law and practice of United States naval courts-martial. New York, 1867. 8vo. **59 G**

HARWOOD, John Augustus.

Acts and ordinances of legislative council of the Straits Settlements, 1867–1886. 2 vols. 1886. 8vo. **37 F**

HARWOOD, Thomas.

Alumni Etonenses ; or, a catalogue of the provosts and fellows of Eton college and King's college, Cambridge, 1443 to 1797, with an account of their lives and preferments. Birmingham, 1797. 4to. **79 H**

HASLAM, John.

Medical jurisprudence as it relates to Insanity according to the law of England. 1817. 8vo. **172 B**

HASLEWOOD, Rev. Francis.

The parish of Benenden, Kent ; its monuments, vicars and persons of note, also a reprint of an exceedingly rare pamphlet entitled This Winter's Wonders, dated 1673. Privately printed. Ipswich, 1889. 8vo. **88 C**

HASTED, Edward.

The history and topographical survey of the county of Kent. 4 vols. Canterbury, 1778–99. folio. **89 H**

Hasted's History of Kent continued to the present time. Part 1, the Hundred of Blackheath. By H. H. Drake. 1886. folio. **89 H**

Life of Edward Hasted. See J. P. Malcolm's Lives of Topographers and Antiquaries. 1815. 4to. **79 H**

HASTINGS, Sussex.

Ross's Hastings and St. Leonards guide. 4th ed. [n.d.] 12mo. **93 E**

HASTINGS FAMILY.

The Huntingdon peerage, comprising a detailed account of the evidence and proceedings connected with the recent restoration of the earldom, with a history of the illustrious house of Hastings. By H. N. Bell. 1820. 4to. **127 J**

HASTINGS, SYDNEY.

Riots, a concise statement of the law relating thereto. 1886. 12mo. **11 E**

A Treatise on Torts and the legal remedies for their redress. 1885. 8vo. **64 E**

HASTINGS, WARREN.

Letters containing a correct and important elucidation on the subject of Mr. Hastings's impeachment. 1790. 8vo. **78 B**

Memoirs relative to the state of India. New ed. 1786. 8vo. **78 B**

HATHERLEY, WILLIAM PAGE, 1 BARON.

A Memoir of W. P. Wood, baron Hatherley, with selections from his correspondence. Edited by W. R. W. Stephens. 2 vols. 1883. 8vo. **79 G**

Truth and its counterfeits. A lecture by Sir W. P. Wood before the Young Men's Christian Association in Exeter hall, November 11, 1856. [Pamphlets, vol. 23.] **144 B**

See also HEMMING, G. W. and A. E. MILLER.

HATSELL, JOHN.

A Collection of cases of privilege of parliament from the earliest records to the year 1628. 1776. And Precedents of proceedings in the House of Commons. 1781. 2 vols. in 1. 1776–81. 4to. **114 D**

The same. 2nd ed. 3 vols. 1785. 4to. **114 D**

HATTON FAMILY.

Correspondence of the family of Hatton ; being chiefly letters addressed to Christopher, first Viscount Hatton, A.D. 1601–1704. Edited by E. M. Thompson. [Camden Society, n.s. vols. 22 and 23.] 2 vols. 1878. 8vo. **85 D**

[HATTON, EDWARD.]

A New view of London, or an ample account of that city. 2 vols. 1708. 8vo. **92 B**

HAUGHTON, GRAVES CHAMNEY.
Institutes of Hindu law, or the ordinances of Menu translated
by Sir Wm. Jones and collated with the Sanscrit text by
G. C. Haughton. 3rd ed. by S. G. Grady. 1869. 8vo.   38 B

HAULTAIN, CHARLES.
The new Navy list, Nov. 1841 to Aug. 1845.   5 vols.   1841–
45.   8vo.   133 H

HAWES, ROBERT.
The history of Framlingham, including brief notices of the
masters and fellows of Pembroke Hall in Cambridge.   With
considerable additions and notes by Robert Loder.   Woodbridge, 1798.   4to.   93 B

HAWKE, MICHAEL.
The grounds of the lawes of England.   1657.   12mo.   49 B

HAWKINS, FRANCIS VAUGHAN.
Concise treatise on construction of wills.   1863.   8vo.   13 I

HAWKINS, WILLIAM.
A Summary of the Crown law.   1770.   12mo.   165 D
A Treatise of the Pleas of the Crown.   2 vols.   1716–21.
folio.
The same.   2nd ed.   2 vols. in 1.   1724–26.   folio.   155 E
The same.   4th ed.   2 vols.   1762.   folio.   155 E
The same.   6th ed. by Thomas Leach.   2 vols.   1777–87.
8vo.   174 A
The same.   8th ed. by J. Curwood.   2 vols.   1824.   8vo.   53 C

HAWLES, SIR JOHN.
The Englishman's right; a dialogue between a barrister at law
and a juryman.   1764.   [Tracts on Libel, vol. 1.]   144 F

HAWSTED, SUFFOLK.
History and antiquities of Hawsted and Hardwick.   By Rev.
Sir John Cullum.   2nd ed.   1813.   4to.   93 G

HAY, ALEXANDER.
The history of Chichester with notes on the county of Sussex
Chichester, 1804.   8vo.   93 E

HAY, WILLIAM.

Decisions of supreme courts of England and Scotland on liability of proprietors, masters and servants for reparation of injuries arising from accidents and the negligence of parties. Edinburgh, 1860. 8vo. **172 A**

HAYDN, JOSEPH.

Book of Dignities, containing rolls of the official personages of the British empire. 1851. 8vo. **124 G**

Dictionary of Dates relating to all ages and nations, for universal reference. 1841, and 6th ed. 1853. 8vo. **146 F**

The same. 13th ed. by B. Vincent. 1868. 8vo. **146 F**

The same. 18th ed. by B. Vincent. 1885. 8vo. **146 F**

The same. 19th ed. by B. Vincent. 1889. 8vo. **134 I**

HAYES, EDMUND.

Reports of cases in the court of Exchequer in Ireland. 1830–1832. Dublin, 1837. 8vo. **15 D**

HAYES, EDMUND and THOMAS JONES.

Reports of cases in the court of Exchequer in Ireland. 1832–1834. Dublin, 1843. 8vo. **15 D**

HAYES, WILLIAM.

The concise conveyancer, or short precedents with practical remarks. 2nd ed. by W. B. Coltman. 1864. 8vo. **164 D**

The same. 3rd ed. by W. B. Coltman. 1869. 8vo. **53 C**

The same. 4th ed. by W. B. Coltman. 1882. 8vo. **13 E**

Doctrine of Equity. 1836. [Jacob's Tracts, vol. 11.] **144 F**

Free trade in land. Comments on the speech of Professor Fawcett at Brighton as respects some passages in reply to the letters of ' A Hertfordshire Incumbent' and others in the *Times*. 1868. [Pamphlets, vol. 33.] **144 C**

Letter to Andrew Amos, Esq. occasioned by a lecture lately delivered by him as professor of English law in the University of London. [n.d.] [Jacob's Tracts, vol. 7.] **144 E**

Letter to the Right Hon. Robert Peel on the law of real property and the practice of conveyancing. 1825. [Jacob's Tracts, vol. 1.] **144 E**

A short introduction to Conveyancing. 1834. 12mo. **164 D**

The same. 3rd ed. 1837. 12mo. **164 D**

The same. 5th ed. 2 vols. 1840. 8vo. **53 C**

HAYES, WILLIAM—*continued*.
Concise forms of Wills with practical notes. By W. Hayes
and Thomas Jarman. 1835. 12mo. **178 A**
The same. 3rd ed. 1840. 12mo. **178 A**
The same. 9th ed. by J. W. Dunning. 1883. 8vo. **131**

HAYNES, FREEMAN OLIVER.
Fusion, a lecture in which the question of uniting and blending
into one, the courts and systems of law and equity is con-
sidered. 1873. [Pamphlets, vol. 33.] **144 C**
Outlines of Equity. 1858, and 3rd ed. 1873. 12mo. **167 B**
The same. 5th ed. 1880. 12mo. **64 C**

HAYNES, JOHN FREDERICK.
The Practice of the chancery division of the high court of
justice. 1879. 8vo. **52 B**
Student's Guide to law and practice of courts of Probate and
Divorce. 2nd ed. 1882. 8vo. **64 E**
Student's guide to law of Bankruptcy. 1883. 8vo. **64 A**
The Student's Leading cases. 2nd ed. 1884. 8vo. **64 E**
The Student's Statutes. 1875, and 2nd ed. 1881. 8vo. **176 B**
The same. 4th ed. 1889. 8vo. **64 F**
The honours examination digest. By J. F. Haynes and
T. A. Nelham. 1883. 8vo. **64 C**

HAYWARD, ABRAHAM.
Report of the proceedings before the judges as visitors of the
Inns of Court on the appeal of A. Hayward, Q.C. 1848, and
Remarks on a late decision of the judges as visitors of the
Inns of Court. By Charles Neate. 1848. 8vo. **78 B**

HAYWARD, SIR JOHN.
Annals of first four years of reign of Queen Elizabeth. Edited
by John Bruce. [Camden Soc., vol. 7.] 1840. 8vo. **85 A**

HAZLITT, WILLIAM and RICHARD RINGWOOD.
The Bankruptcy act 1883 with notes. 1884. 12mo. **64 A**
The same. 2nd ed. by R. Ringwood. 1887. 12mo. **64 A**

HAZLITT, William Carew.

Catalogue of early English miscellanies formerly in the Harleian library. [Camden Society, vol. 87.] 1864. 8vo.
85 C

Handbook to the popular poetical and dramatic literature of Great Britain from the invention of printing to the restoration. 1867. 8vo.
82 H

HEALES, Alfred.

Easter Sepulchres, their object, nature and history. 1869. 4to.
85 I

HEALEY, Charles Edward Hely Chadwyck.

Law and practice relating to joint stock companies, with precedents and notes. 1875. 8vo.
169 D

The same. 2nd ed. 1886. 8vo.
9 D

HEALTH.

Essays on health culture. By G. Jaeger. Translated and edited by L. R. S. Tomalin. 1887. 8vo.
78 A

Manual for medical officers of health. By Edward Smith. 1872. 12mo.
172 E

Report of a public meeting, to consider the best method of extending the operations of the Metropolitan Association for improving the dwellings of the industrious classes. [1854.] [Pamphlets, vol. 9, pt. 1.]
144 A

See also Public Health.

HEARN, William Edward

The government of England, its structure and its development. 1867. 8vo.
116 E

HEARNE, Thomas.

A Collection of curious discourses written by eminent antiquaries upon several heads in our English antiquities. 2 vols. 1771. 8vo.
85 G

The same. Another ed. 2 vols. 1773. 8vo.
85 G

Life of Thomas Hearne. See J. P. Malcolm's Lives of Topographers and Antiquaries. 1815. 4to.
79 H

Remarks and collections of T. Hearne (July 4, 1705–Dec. 14, 1712). Edited by C. E. Doble. [Oxford Hist. Soc., vols. 2, 7 & 13.] 3 vols. Oxford, 1885–89. 8vo.
85 F

HEART DISEASE.

On the geographical distribution of heart disease in England and Wales. By Alfred Haviland. 1869. 8vo. [Pamphlets, vol. 32.] **144 C**

HEATH, CHARLES.

The excursion down the Wye from Ross to Monmouth. 1799. 8vo. **92 C**

Historical and descriptive accounts of the ancient and present state of the town of Monmouth. Monmouth, 1804. 4to. **92 C**

HEATH, JOHN BENJAMIN.

Some account of the worshipful company of Grocers of the City of London. Not published. 1829. 8vo. **89 E**

HEATH, ROBERT.

Natural and historical account of Islands of Scilly, and a general account of Cornwall. 1750. 8vo. **87 A**

HEATH, SIR ROBERT.

Speech in the case of Alexander Leighton in the Star Chamber, June 4, 1630. Edited by S. R. Gardiner. [Camden Society, n.s. vol. 14.] 1875. 8vo. **85 D**

HEBREW LANGUAGE.

A Hebrew and English lexicon of the Old Testament. From the Latin of Wm. Gesenius. 25th ed. by E. Robinson. Boston, 1888. 8vo. **123 B**

Hebrew Criticism and Poetry. By Rev. G. S. Clarke. 1810. 8vo. **77 B**

Motives to the study of Hebrew. By Right Rev. T. Burgess. 2nd ed. 1814. 12mo. **255 H**

The scholars instructor, an Hebrew grammar. By Israel Lyons. 2nd ed. Cambridge, 1757. 8vo. **255 H**

See also MINSHEU, J.

HEBREWS, THE EPISTLE TO THE.

Reflections on the Epistles of St. Paul, and on that to the Hebrews, with scriptural illustrations. By A lay member of the Church of England. [John Stow.] 1847. 8vo. **77 B**

HEDERICUS, Benjamin.
Græcum lexicon manuale, labore Sam. Patricii, cura J. A. Ernesti atque iterum recensitum a T. Morell. Editio nova, cui accedit magnus verborum numerus ex schedis P. H. Larcheri. 1825. 4to.   123 F

HEINECCIUS, Johann Gottlieb.
Opera. 8 vols. Geneva, 1744–48. 4to.   47 G H

HEIRSHIP.
History of the privilege which an heir-apparent in a feudal holding has, to continue the possession of his ancestor; and History of the limited and universal representation of heirs. See Historical law tracts, 2nd ed. 1761, pp. 173–186 and 389–402.   144 F

HESCH, P. J.
Memoirs of John Caspar Lavater, with a brief memoir of his widow. 1842. 12mo.   79 A

HÉLIE, Faustin.
Traité de l'instruction criminelle, ou théorie du code d'instruction criminelle. 9 vols. Paris, 1845–60. 8vo.   58 D

HELIGOLAND.
Heligoland Ordinances, 1864–1888. 1864–88. folio.   37 D
History of Heligoland. See R. M. Martin's History of the British colonies, vol. 5, 1835, pp. 544–549.   116 C

HEMINGWAY, Joseph.
History of city of Chester from its foundation to present time. 2 vols. Chester, 1831. 8vo.   86 E

HEMMING, George Wirgman and A. E. MILLER.
Reports of cases adjudged in Court of Chancery before Sir W. P. Wood, 1862–1865. 2 vols. 1864–66. 8vo.   2 I

HEMSLEY, William Botting.
The gallery of Marianne North's paintings of plants and their homes, Royal gardens, Kew. Descriptive catalogue. 3rd ed. 1883. 12mo.   93 C

HENDON, MIDDLESEX.

A Catalogue of all the demesne lands of William Duke of Powis deceased in the parish and manor of Hendon [with many manuscript notes]. 1756. 8vo. **118 B**

The manor and parish of Hendon, drawn and engraved by John Cooke, with an index to the map. 1796. 4to. **89 E**

New map of the whole manor and parish of Hendon. By Francis Whishaw. 1828. 4to. **89 E**

Book of reference to the new map . . . with an index of the names of owners of lands and tenements in Hendon. By Francis Whishaw. 1828. 4to. **89 E**

HENGHAM, SIR RALPH DE.

The Summs of Sir Ralph de Hengham, commonly called Hengham Magna and Hengham Parva. See Appendix to Sir John Fortescue's De laudibus legum Angliæ, 2nd ed. 1741. folio. **115 H**

HENGRAVE, SUFFOLK.

The history and antiquities of Hengrave. By John Gage. 1822. 4to. [Bound with Cullum's Hawsted, 1813.] **93 G**

HENRIETTA MARIA, QUEEN CONSORT OF CHARLES I.

Memoir by Madame De Motteville on the life of Henrietta Maria. Edited by M. G. Hanotaux. [Camden Society, n.s. vol. 31.] 1883. 8vo. **85 D**

See also CHARLES I.

HENRY I., II., III., IV., V. AND VI., KINGS OF ENGLAND.

Johannis Capgrave Liber de illustribus Henricis. Edited by Rev. F. C. Hingeston. 1858. 8vo. **101 B**

The flowers of history, by Roger de Wendover, A.D. 1154–1235 Edited by H. G. Hewlett. 3 vols. 1886–89. 8vo. **102 H**

Gesta Regis Henrici Secundi Benedicti Abbatis. Edited by Wm. Stubbs. 2 vols. 1867. 8vo. **102 C**

Pipe Rolls: the Great Rolls of the Pipe, for the years 1155–1158. Edited by Rev. J. Hunter. 1844. 8vo. **98 A**

Rotuli de dominabus et pueris et puellis de donatione regis in XII comitatibus anno 31 Regis Henrici II. 1185. Curante Stacey Grimaldi. 1830. 4to. **103 F**

Thomas Agnellus De morte et sepultura Henrici Regis Angliæ Junioris. See R. de Coggeshall's Chronicon Anglicanum, 1875, pp. 263–273. **102 E**

HENRY I., II., III., IV., V. AND VI., KINGS OF ENGLAND—
continued.

Calendarium genealogicum, Henry III. and Edward I. Edited
by Charles Roberts. 2 vols. 1865. 8vo.   **96 B**

The chronicle of William De Rishanger of the Barons' wars.
Edited by J. O. Halliwell. [Camden Society, vol. 15.]
1840. 8vo.   **85 A**

History of Henry III. By W. Prynne. 1670. folio.   **115 I**

Royal and other historical letters illustrative of the reign of
Henry III. Edited by Rev. W. W. Shirley. 2 vols.
1862-66. 8vo.   **101 F**

Short view of the long life and raigne of Henry the Third.
Presented to King James, 1627. [Law Tracts and Arguments, 1641.]   **144 F**

An English chronicle of the reigns of Richard II., Henry IV.,
Henry V. and Henry VI. written before the year 1471.
Edited by Rev. J. S. Davies. [Camden Society, vol. 64.]
1856. 8vo.   **85 B**

Royal and historical letters during the reign of Henry IV.
Edited by Rev. F. C. Hingeston. 1860. 8vo.   **101 D**

Memorials of Henry the Fifth, king of England. Edited by
C. A. Cole. 1858. 8vo.   **101 B**

Historie of the arrivall of Edward IV. in England and the
finall recouerye of his Kingdome from Henry VI. Edited
by J. Bruce. [Camden Soc., vol. 1.] 1838. 8vo.   **85 A**

Letters and papers illustrative of the wars of the English in
France during reign of Henry VI. Edited by Rev. J.
Stevenson. 2 vols. in 3. 1861–64. 8vo.   **101 E**

Memorials of the reign of King Henry VI. Official correspondence of Thomas Bekynton. Edited by George
Williams. 2 vols. 1872. 8vo.   **102 D**

The reign of Henry VI. By Polydore Vergil. See Camden
Society, vol. 29, 1844, pp. 1–112.   **85 A**

See also LINGARD, REV. J., MARTYN, W., STATE PAPERS
and TURNER, S.

HENRY VII. AND VIII., KINGS OF ENGLAND.

A London chronicle during the reigns of Henry VI. and
Henry VIII. Edited by C. Hopper. [Camden Society,
vol. 73.] 1859. 8vo.   **85 B**

Rutland papers. Original documents illustrative of the courts
and times of Henry VII. and Henry VIII. Edited by
W. Jerdan. [Camden Society, vol. 21.] 1842. 8vo. **85 A**

Bull of Pope Innocent VIII. on the marriage of Henry VII.

HENRY VII. AND VIII., KINGS OF ENGLAND—*continued.*
with Elizabeth of York. Communicated by J. P. Collier.
[Camden Society, vol. 39.] 1847. 8vo. **85 B**

Historia regis Henrici Septimi, a Bernardo Andrea Theolosate
conscripta. Edited by James Gairdner. 1858. 8vo. **101 B**

The history of the reigne of King Henry the Seventh. By
Francis Bacon. 1629. 4to. **114 F**

Letters and papers illustrative of the reigns of Richard III.
and Henry VII. Edited by James Gairdner. 2 vols.
1861–63. 8vo. **101 E**

Materials for a history of the reign of Henry VII. Edited
by Rev. Wm. Campbell. 2 vols. 1873–77. 8vo. **102 E**

The most pleasant song of Lady Bessy, the eldest daughter
of King Edward IV., and how she married King Henry VII.
With notes by Thomas Heywood. 1829. 8vo. **83 C**

The statutes of Henry VII. in exact facsimile from the very
rare original, printed by Caxton in 1489. Edited by John
Rae. 1869. 4to. **114 G**

The history of the reign of Hènry the Eighth. By Sharon
Turner. 2nd ed. 2 vols. 1827. 8vo. **115 E**

Observations on statutes of Reformation parliament in reign
of Henry VIII. By Andrew Amos. 1859. 8vo. **116 E**

State papers during the reign of King Henry VIII. 11 vols.
1830–52. 4to. **103 F**

Statutes which have beene made in the time of the most
victorious reigne of King Henry the Eight. Imprinted at
London by Thomas Marshe. 1575. folio. **158 B**

A Treatise on the pretended divorce between Henry VIII.
and Catharine of Arragon. By N. Harpsfield. Edited by
N. Pocock. [Camden Soc., n.s. vol. 21.] 1878. 8vo. **85 D**

See also FROUDE, J. A., GODWIN, F., LINGARD, REV. J.,
MARTYN, W. and STATE PAPERS.

HENRY, ARCHDEACON OF HUNTINGDON.
Historia Anglorum. The history of the English from A.C.
55 to A.D. 1154. Edited by T. Arnold. 1879. 8vo. **102 G**

See also Monumenta Historica Britannica. 1848. folio. **99 B**

HENRY, JABEZ.
The judgment of the Court of Demerara in the case of Odwin
v. Forbes . . . with a treatise on the difference between
personal and real statutes, and its effect on foreign judgments and contracts, marriages and wills. 1823. 8vo. **55 D**

HENRY, JARDINE.

The government annuity tables embracing the values of annuities on single and two joint lives at 3, 4, 5, and 6 per cent. per annum for every combination of age and sex. 2 vols. 1859. 8vo.   160 B

HENSHALL, REV. SAMUEL and JOHN WILKINSON.

Domesday, or an actual survey of South Britain by the commissioners of William the Conqueror, completed in the year 1086, faithfully translated with an introduction, notes and illustrations, comprehending the counties of Kent, Sussex and Surrey, 1799. 4to.   88 E

HERALDRY.

The ancient usage in bearing Arms. By Sir W. Dugdale. With additions by T. C. Banks. 1812. folio.   125 H

Bibliotheca heraldica Magnæ Britanniæ. By Thomas Moule. 1822. 8vo.   82 C

The British herald, or cabinet of armorial bearings of the nobility and gentry of Great Britain and Ireland. By Thomas Robson. 3 vols. Sunderland, 1830. 4to.   127 J

A Complete body of Heraldry. By Joseph Edmondson. 2 vols. 1780. folio.   124 I

Copper Plates of the coats-of-arms of the English peers. See Catton's Peerage, vol. 3. 1790. folio.   126 I

Display of Heraldry. By John Guillim. 6th ed. 1724. folio.   125 H

The General Armory of England, Scotland, Ireland and Wales. By Sir J. B. Burke. 1878. 8vo.   Hall

Heraldry, historical and popular. By C. Boutell. 3rd ed. 1864. 8vo.   124 H

Heraldry in miniature, containing the arms, crests, supporters and mottos of the peers and peeresses of England, Scotland and Ireland, likewise the arms of the present baronets of England. 1781. 12mo.   124 B

Index to the pedigrees and arms contained in Heralds' Visitations in British Museum. By R. Sims. 1849. 8vo. 124 H

On Heraldry and its connection with Gothic architecture. By W. L. Donaldson. 1837. [Pamphlets, vol. 25.]   144 B

The Sphere of Gentry deduced from the principles of nature, an historical and genealogical work of Arms and Blazon. By Sylvanus Morgan. 1661. folio.   118 G

Symbola Scotica, or an attempt to elucidate some of the

HERALDRY—*continued.*

more obscure armorial bearings, principally the mottoes used by many of the Scottish families. See S. Pegge's Anecdotes, 1818, pp. 213–268. **83 H**

HERAUD, JOHN ABRAHAM.

The legend of St. Loy, with other poems. 1820. 8vo. **83 C**

A practical epitome and exposition of the whole stamp law and duties. 1824. 12mo. **175 G**

HERBERT, SIR EDWARD.

The Lord chief justice Herbert's Account examined by W(illiam) A(twood), wherein it is shewn that those authorities in law whereby he would excuse his judgment in Sir Edward Hales his case are very unfairly cited and as ill applied. 1689. [Law Tracts, 1688–89.] **118 E**

Some animadversions upon a book writ by Sir Edw. Herbert, entituled, A short account of the authorities in law upon which judgment was given in Sir Edward Hale's case. See Atkins's Tracts, 2nd ed., 1741, pp. 291–318. **144 F**

Speech of lord chancellor Jefferies on occasion of creating Sir Edward Herbert lord chief justice of the King's Bench. See Collectanea Juridica, vol. 2, 1792, pp. 405–409. **144 G**

HERBERT, NICHOLAS and AUSTIN FLEEMING JENKIN.

The councillor's handbook, a practical guide to the election and business of a county council. 1888. 8vo. **10 G**

HERBERT, THOMAS.

The law on Adulteration, being The sale of food and drugs acts 1875 and 1879 with notes. 1884. 12mo. **9 A**

HERBERT, WILLIAM.

Antiquities of the Inns of Court and Chancery, with a concise history of the English law. 1804. 8vo. **91 D**

Lambeth Palace, illustrated by a series of views representing its most interesting antiquities in buildings, portraits, stained glass &c. 1806. 4to. **91 G**

HERBERT OF CHERBURY, EDWARD, 1 BARON.

The life of Edward Lord Herbert of Cherbury, written by himself. [Autobiography, vol. 18.] 1830. 12mo. **79 A**

HEREFORD.

The ancient customs of the city of Hereford, with translations of the earlier city charters and grants. By Richard Johnson. 1868. 4to.   88 B

HEREFORD, WALTER, 1 VISCOUNT.

Ancient biographical poems on Viscount Hereford and others. Edited by J. P. Collier. [Camden Society, vol. 61.] 1855. 8vo.   85 B

HEREFORDSHIRE.

Alphabetical list of Poll for county of Hereford, taken at Widemarsh on July 15–21, 1802. Hereford, 1802. 8vo.   107 J

Collections towards history and antiquities of the county of Hereford. By Rev. J. Duncumb. [With continuations by W. H. Cooke.] 3 vols. in 4. 1804-12-82. 4to.   88 G

The excursion down the Wye from Ross to Monmouth. By Charles Heath. 1799. 8vo.   92 C

Introductory sketches towards a topographical history of the county of Hereford. By Rev. John Lodge. Kington, 1793. 8vo.   88 B

HERNE, JOHN.

Law of Conveyances. 1656, and 2nd ed. 1658. 12mo.   48 C

The Pleader, containing perfect presidents of declarations and proceedings in all kinds of actions. 1657. folio.   49 G

HERODOTUS.

Herodoti Halicarnassensis Historia ex editione Jacobi Gronovii. 9 vols. in 4. Glasguæ, 1771. 12mo.   46 J

History of Herodotus. By G. Rawlinson. 4 vols. 1858–60. 8vo.   113 D

HERON, DENIS CAULFEILD.

The principles of Jurisprudence. 1873. 8vo.   63 G

HERSEE, WILLIAM.

The spirit of the general letters and orders issued by the Board of Excise from 1700 to 1827 inclusive. 1829. 8vo.   168 B

HERTFORD.

History of the ancient town and borough of Hertford. By Lewis Turnor. Hertford, 1830. 8vo.   88 C

HERTFORDSHIRE.

Copy of Poll for knights of shire for Herts, taken at Hertford, April 22nd, 1784. 1784. 8vo. 107 J

Copy of Poll for knights of shire for Herts, taken at Hertford, June 23rd, 1790. 1790. 8vo. 107 J

Copy of Poll for knights of shire for Herts, taken at Hertford, July 10th & 12th, 1802. 1802. 8vo. 107 J

Copy of Poll for knights of shire for Herts, taken at Hertford, Feb. 11th and 12th, 1805. 1805. 8vo. 107 J

Historical account of the part of Herts within twelve miles of London. See Rev. Daniel Lysons's Environs of London, vol. 4, 1796, pp. 1–51. 89 F

History and antiquities of Herts. By Robert Clutterbuck. 3 vols. 1815–27. folio. 88 H

History of Hertfordshire. By J. E. Cussans. 3 vols. 1870–81. folio. 89 H

History of Herts. By N. Salmon. 1728. folio. 88 H

Pedigrees of Hertfordshire families. By W. Berry. 1842. folio. 126 I

See also BAWDWEN, REV. W., BRAY, W., CHAUNCY, SIR H., NEWCOURT, R. and PENNANT, T.

HERTSLET, LEWIS and SIR EDWARD HERTSLET.

British and foreign state papers 1812–1881. 72 vols. 1841–88. 8vo. 117 A-I

Complete collection of treaties and conventions between Great Britain and foreign powers. 18 vols. 1840–90. 8vo. 145 B-D

Treaties and tariffs regulating the trade between Great Britain and foreign nations in force on the 1st January 1875. Turkey. 1875. 8vo. 145 D

See also FOREIGN OFFICE LIST.

HERTZBERG, EBBE.

Grundtrækkene i den ældste Norske Proces. Kristiania, 1874. 8vo. 55 C

HESSE, GRAND DUCHY OF.

A Report on the tenure of land in the grand duchy of Hesse. By R. B. D. Morier. See Systems of land tenure, 1881, pp. 394–441. 78 B

HETLEY, SIR THOMAS.

Reports of cases taken as they were argued by most of the Kings sergeants at the Common Pleas bars, 1627–1631. 1657. folio.   74 D

HEWLETT, WILLIAM OXENHAM.

Notes on dignities in the peerage of Scotland which are dormant or which have been forfeited. 1882. 8vo.   124 H

HEWLEY, LADY SARAH.

Full report of hearing in House of Lords in May and June 1839 on appeal of trustees, with judgment of the Vice-Chancellor 23 Dec. 1833, the judgment of Lord Lyndhurst 5 Feb. 1836, the case of the appellants, the case of the respondents. 1839. 8vo.   51 F

Historical defence of trustees of Lady Hewley's Foundations. By Rev. J. Hunter. 1834. [Law Tracts, vol. 3.]   144 E

Lady Hewley's Charities. Observations on the case of the Attorney general v. Shore and others. By J. S. Stock. 1836. [Law Tracts, vol. 3.]   144 E

Letter to Vice Chancellor of England in reply to His Honour's Remarks relative to British and Foreign Unitarian Association delivered in pronouncing judgment in case of Attorney general v. Shore and others. By James Yates. 1834. [Law Tracts, vol. 3.]   144 E

A Plain statement of trusts and recent administration of Lady Hewley's charities. By T. W. Tottie. 1834. [Law Tracts, vol. 3.]   144 E

Substance of speech of C. P. Cooper as counsel for Rev. Charles Wellbeloved in suit of Attorney general v. Shore. 1834. [Law Tracts, vol. 3.]   144 E

HEXAMETERS.

English hexameter translations from Schiller, Göthe, Homer, Callinus and Meleager. 1847. 8vo.   83 A

Hexametrical Experiments, or a version of four of Virgil's pastorals done in a structure of verse similar to that of the original Latin. 1838. 4to.   83 J

HEYLIN, PETER.

A Help to English history, containing a succession of all the kings of England, the kings and princes of Wales, the kings and lords of Man, the Isle of Wight, as also of all the dukes,

HEYLIN, Peter—*continued.*
   marquesses, earls and bishops thereof.   1670, 1671, 1675,
   1680, 1709, 1773.   6 vols.   1670–1773.   12mo.   **113 A**
   Life of P. Heylyn.   By George Vernon.   1682.   12mo.   **79 A**
   See also Fuller, T.

HEYWOOD, Benjamin Arthur.
   The Irish Church.   An address delivered in 1864 by Sir H.
   M. Cairns, with a postscript, statistics and notes by B. A.
   Heywood.   3rd ed.   1868.   [Pamphlets, vol. 34.]   **144 C**
   The royal supremacy in matters ecclesiastical in pre-reforma-
   tion times.   Bishop Gardiner's Oration on true obedience.
   Edited by B. A. Heywood.   1870.   12mo.   **78 A**
   A Vacation tour at the Antipodes through Victoria, Tasmania,
   New South Wales, Queensland, and New Zealand in 1861–
   1862.   1863.   8vo.   **84 B**

HEYWOOD, George Washington.
   Common law and equity practice of county courts.   1870.
   12mo.   **165 B**
   The jurisdiction and practice of the county courts.   4th ed.
   1886.   8vo.   **165 B**

HEYWOOD, Samuel.
   Digest of law respecting county elections.   2nd ed.   1812.
   8vo.   **166 C**
   Digest of so much of the law respecting borough elections as
   concerns cities and boroughs in general.   1797.   8vo.   **166 C**

HEYWORTH, Lawrence.
   Glimpses at the origin, mission and destiny of man.   1851.
   12mo.   **78 A**

HICKES, Rev. George.
   Linguarum Vett. Septentrionalium Thesaurus grammatico-
   criticus et archæologicus.   6 parts in 2 vols.   Oxoniæ, 1705.
   folio.   **123 G**

HIGDEN, Ranulph.
   Polycronycon.   Englysshed by John de Trevisa.   Imprented
   in Southwerke by Peter Treveris.   1527.   folio.   **114 G**
   The same.   Edited by C. Babington and J. R. Lumley.
   9 vols.   1865–86.   8vo.   **102 B**

HIGGS, JOSEPH.

Guide to Justices, being modern English precedents for direction of Justices of peace. 1734. 12mo. **170 A**

HIGH COMMISSION.

The High Commission. Notices of the Court and its proceedings. By J. S. Burn. 1865. 8vo. **116 C**

HIGHGATE, MIDDLESEX.

Some account of free grammar school of Highgate and of its founder Sir R. Cholmeley. By I. G. 1822. 8vo. **89 D**

HIGHMORE, ANTHONY.

Digest of the doctrine of Bail in civil and criminal cases. 1783. 8vo. **160 C**

Law of Idiocy and Lunacy. 1807. 12mo. **172 B**

Pietas Londinensis, the history, design and present state of the various public charities in and near London. 1814. 8vo. **92 B**

Succinct view of the history of Mortmain. 1787, and 2nd ed. 1809. 8vo. **161 F**

HIGHMORE, NATHANIEL JOSEPH.

Summary proceedings in Inland Revenue cases in England and Wales. 1882. 12mo. **169 A**

The same. 2nd ed. 1887. 12mo. **10 D**

HIGHWAYS.

The law relating to Highways. By W. C. Glen. New ed. by W. C. Glen and A. Glen. 1883. 8vo. **10 B**

The law of Highways. By J. T. Pratt. 12th ed. by S. Prentice. 1881. 8vo. **10 B**

The law of Highways. By T. Baker. 1880. 8vo. **52 H**

The law relating to Highways and Bridges. By G. F. Chambers. 1878. 4to. **157 A**

The law of Highways. By J. K. Angell and T. Durfee. 2nd ed. by G. F. Choate. Boston, 1868. 8vo. **59 E**

The law of Highways in England and Wales. By Leonard Shelford. 3rd ed. 1862. 12mo. **168 G**

See also BATEMAN, J. and SPEARMAN, R. H.

HILL, CHARLES.

Sunday, its influence on health and national prosperity. 2nd
ed. 1877. Le Dimanche. . . . Genève, 1876. KYPIAKH.
. . . Athens, 1878. Continental Sunday labour. A warning to the English nation. 1877. The Bible on the
Sabbath. 1876. Sunday laws. A paper read at the
Social Science congress. 1878. [all six in 1 vol.] 1876–
78. 12mo. **77 A**

HILL, JAMES.

The law relating to trustees. 1845. 8vo. **53 I**

HILL, MATTHEW DAVENPORT.

Charge to grand jury of Birmingham on connexion between
disease and crime. 1854. [Pamphlets, vol. 9, pt. 1.] **144 A**
Is allegiance by birth affected in England by naturalization
in France ? Opinions of M. Crémieux and others on Lord
Brougham's application in 1848 for French letters of natu-
ralization. Bristol, 1869. [Pamphlets, vol. 31.] **144 C**
Report of a charge delivered to grand jury of borough of
Birmingham. 1848. [Pamphlets, vol. 6.] **144 A**

HILLIARD, FRANCIS.

The American law of real property. 3rd ed. 2 vols. New
York, 1855. 8vo. **60 B**
The law of Mortgages, being a general view of the English
and American law upon that subject. 2nd ed. 2 vols.
Boston, 1856. 8vo. **59 G**
The law of remedies for Torts or private wrongs. Boston,
1867. 8vo. **60 B**
The law of sales of personal property. 2nd ed. Philadelphia,
1860. 8vo. **60 B**
The law of Torts. 2 vols. Boston, 1859. 8vo. **60 B**

HINDE, ROBERT.

Modern practice of Court of Chancery. 1785. 8vo. **161 C**

HINDERWELL, THOMAS.

The history and antiquities of Scarborough. 3rd ed. Scarborough, 1832. 8vo. **94 B**

HINDLE, FREDERICK GEORGE.

Legal status of licensed victuallers. 1883. 8vo. **12 C**

32—2

HINDMARCH, WILLIAM MATTHEWSON.

The law relating to Patent privileges for the sole use of inventions. 1846. 8vo.   **173 E**

HINDU LAW.

Hindu law and usage. By J. D. Mayne. 1878. 8vo.   **38 D**

A Chart of Hindu family inheritance. By Almaric Rumsey. 2nd ed. 1877. 8vo.   **38 B**

Hindu law, being a treatise on law administered exclusively to Hindus by British courts in India. By Herbert Cowell. Calcutta, 1871. 8vo.   **38 B**

A Selection of leading cases on the Hindu law of inheritance. By J. B. Norton. 2 vols. Madras, 1870–71. 8vo.   **38 B**

Institutes of Hindu law. Translated by Sir W. Jones. 3rd ed. by S. G. Grady. 1869. 8vo.   **38 B**

Hindoo law of inheritance. By S. G. Grady. 1868. 8vo. **38 B**

A Digest of Hindu law. Book 1, Inheritance. By R. West and J. G. Buhler. Bombay, 1867. 8vo.   **38 B**

A Manual of Hindoo law as prevailing in Madras. By T. L. Strange. 2nd ed. Madras, 1863. 8vo.   **38 B**

Vivada Chintamani : a succinct commentary on the Hindoo law prevalent in Mithila. From the original Sanscrit of Vachaspati Misra. By Pross'onno Coomar Tagore. Calcutta, 1863. 8vo.   **38 A**

Hindu Law ; principally with reference to such portions of it as concern the administration of justice in the King's Courts in India. By Sir Thomas Strange. 3rd ed. with an introduction by J. D. Mayne. Madras, 1859. 8vo.   **38 B**

Succinct account of civil regulations comprised in ordinances of Menu. See B. Barrett's Code Napoléon, vol. 1, 1811, pp. xx–xlvii.   **55 C**

See also BENGAL, BOMBAY, INDIA and MADRAS.

HINTON, JOHN HOWARD.

The history and topography of the United States. 2 vols. 1830–32. 4to.   **84 F**

HISTORICAL MANUSCRIPTS.

Reports of commissioners on historical manuscripts ; with appendixes and indexes. 19 vols. 1870–90. folio & 8vo.   **98 F & 99 F**

HISTORICAL REGISTER.

The Historical Register, containing an impartial relation of all transactions, foreign and domestic, from 1714–1735. 22 vols. 1724–36. 8vo.   **256 H**

HISTORY, Universal.

Eulogium historiarum sive temporis : Chronicon ab orbe condito usque ad A.D. 1490. Edited by F. S. Haydon. 3 vols. 1858–63. 8vo. **101 B**

Flores Historiarum. The Creation to A.D. 1326. Edited by H. R. Luard. 3 vols. 1890. 8vo. **102 I**

The Flowers of History. By Roger de Wendover. 1154–1235. Edited by H. G. Hewlett. 3 vols. 1886–89. 8vo. **102 H**

Lavoisne's Complete Atlas, exhibiting an accurate account of origin, descent and marriages of all royal families from beginning of the world to 1822. 3rd ed. 1822. folio. **125 H**

Matthæi Parisiensis monachi Sancti Albani Chronica Majora. Edited by H. R. Luard. 7 vols. 1872–83. 8vo. **102 D E**

Universal history from earliest account of time, compiled from original authors. 7 vols. in 9. 1736–44. folio. **113 H**

See also CHRONOLOGY and HOFMANN, J. J.

HOARE, Sir Richard Colt.

Ancient history of North Wiltshire. 1819. folio. **93 H**

Ancient history of South Wiltshire. 1812. folio. **93 H**

Catalogue of the Hoare library at Stourhead, co. Wilts. By J. B. Nichols. Printed for private use. 1840. 8vo. **82 G**

The itinerary of Archbishop Baldwin through Wales, 1188. By Giraldus De Barri. Translated into English by Sir R. C. Hoare. 2 vols. 1806. 4to. **94 D**

The history of modern Wiltshire. By Sir R. C. Hoare and others. 6 vols. in 4. 1822–44. folio. **94 H**

HOBART, Sir Henry.

Reports in the reign of K. James I. with some few cases in the reign of Q. Elizabeth. 1641. 4to.

The same. 3rd ed. 1671. folio.

The same. 4th ed. 1678. folio. **74 D**

HOBBES, Thomas.

Hobbs's Tripos in three discourses : the first, human nature ; the second, de corpore politico ; the third, of liberty and necessity. 3rd ed. 1684. 12mo. **78 A**

Leviathan, or the matter, forme and power of a Common-Wealth ecclesiastical and civil. 1651. folio. **118 G**

The same. New ed. Oxford, 1881. 8vo. **78 D**

HOBLER, Francis.

Familiar exercises between an attorney and his articled clerk
on principles of laws of Real Property. 1831. 12mo. **174 E**

The same. 2nd ed. 1838. 12mo. **174 E**

Liber Mercatoris, or the Merchant's manual, being a concise
treatise on bills of exchange. 1838. 12mo. **160 G**

Records of Roman history as exhibited on the Roman coins.
2 vols. 1860. 4to. **113 G**

HODGES, William, Attorney-at-Law.

Historical account of Ludlow Castle. 1794. 8vo. **93 A**

HODGES, William, Barrister-at-Law.

Law of railways and railway companies. 1847. 8vo. **175 B**

The same. 3rd ed. by C. M. Smith. 1863. 8vo. **175 B**

The same. 6th ed. by J. M. Lely. 1876. 8vo. **175 B**

The same. 7th ed. by J. M. Lely. 2 vols. 1888. 8vo. **11 D**

Reports of cases in the Court of Common Pleas. 1835–1837.
3 vols. 1836–39. 8vo. **6 F G**

HODGSON, Christopher.

Account of augmentation of small livings by ' The Governors
of the bounty of Queen Anne for the augmentation of the
maintenance of the poor clergy,' with supplement. 1826–35.
8vo. **100 G**

The same. 2nd ed. with supplement. 1845–64. 8vo. **100 G**

Instructions for the use of candidates for holy orders, and of
the parochial clergy. 4th ed. 1829. 8vo. **166 B**

The same. 8th ed. 1860. 8vo. **53 F**

HODGSON, Rev. John.

A History of Northumberland in three parts. 7 vols. Newcastle, 1858–35. 4to. **92 D**

HOFFMAN, David.

A Course of Legal Study. 2nd ed. 2 vols. Baltimore, 1836.
8vo. **170 G**

HOFMANN, Johann Jacob.

Lexicon Universale, historiam sacram et profanam omnis
ævi omniumque gentium, chronologiam, geographiam,
genealogiam, mythologiam omnemque antiquitatem, etc.
explanans. 4 vols. Lugd. Bat., 1698. folio. **145 E**

HOGAN, DENIS.
An Appeal to the public and a farewell address to the army, including some strictures upon the general conduct of our military force. 10th ed. 1808. 8vo. **118 B**

HOGAN, WILLIAM.
Reports of cases in the Rolls Court in Ireland, 1816–1834. 2 vols. Dublin, 1828–38. 8vo. **15 D**

HOLBORN, LONDON.
Statement respecting present unequal, oppressive and illegal assessment of the land tax in the Holborn division of county of Middlesex, 1852. [Pamphlets, vol. 8.] **144 A**
See also GRIFFITH, E.

HOLBOURNE, SIR ROBERT.
Readings upon the statute 25 Edw. III. cap. 2, being the Statute of Treasons. 1681. 12mo. **49 B**

HOLDERNESS, YORKSHIRE.
The history and antiquities of the seigniory of Holderness. By George Poulson. 2 vols. Hull, 1840–41. 4to. **94 C**

HOLDSWORTH, EDWARD.
Muscipula sive Kambromyomachia. 1709. 12mo. **118 C**

HOLDSWORTH, WILLIAM ANDREWS.
Handy book of Parish law. 3rd ed. 1872. 12mo. **173 B**
The same. 9th ed. 1883. 12mo. **11 A**

HOLE, REV. CHARLES.
Brief biographical dictionary. 2nd ed. 1866. 12mo. **81 B**

HOLINSHED, RALPH.
Chronicles of England, Ireland and Scotland, first collected by R. Holinshed, W. Harrison and others, continued to the year 1586 by John Hooker alias Vowell and others. 3 vols. in 2. 1586–87. folio. **114 H**

HOLLAND.
The Belgian traveller, or a complete guide through the United Netherlands. By E. Boyce. 4th ed. 1819. 12mo. **84 A**

HOLLAND—*continued.*

The rise of the Dutch republic, a history. By J. L. Motley.
New ed. 3 vols. 1869. 8vo. 113 D

The rise, progress and present state of the Northern governments. By John Williams. 2 vols. 1777. 4to. 113 F

A View of the Dutch trade in all the states, empires and
kingdoms in the world ; translated from the French of
Monsieur Huet. 2nd ed. 1722. 12mo. 78 A

HOLLAND, Spencer Langton.

Summary of Ecclesiastical Courts commission's report : and
of Dr. Stubbs' historical reports ; with a review of the
evidence before the commission. 1884. 12mo. 77 B

HOLLAND, Thomas Erskine.

Elements of Jurisprudence. 3rd ed. Oxford, 1886. 8vo. 63 F

The same. 4th ed. Oxford, 1888. 8vo. 63 F

Essay upon Composition Deeds. 1864. 12mo. 165 G

Essays upon the form of the law. 1870. 8vo. 170 F

The Institutes of Justinian. Oxford, 1873. 12mo. 63 E

The same. 2nd ed. Oxford, 1881. 12mo. 63 E

The University of Oxford in the twelfth century. See Oxford
Historical Soc., vol. 16, 1890, pp. 137–192. 85 E

Select titles from the digest of Justinian. By T. E. Holland
and C. L. Shadwell. Oxford, 1881. 8vo. 63 E

HOLLIDAY, John.

The life of William, late Earl of Mansfield. 1797. 4to. 79 H

HOLMES, J. H. H.

A Treatise on the coal mines of Durham and Northumberland.
1816. 8vo. 87 E

HOLROYD, Edward.

Law of Patents for inventions. 1830. 8vo. 173 E

Observations upon the case of Abraham Thornton, shewing
the danger of pressing presumptive evidence too far.
3rd ed. 1819. 8vo. 118 B

HOLT, Edward Hallett.

Handy book on the registration of title and transfer of land.
1876. 8vo. 10 E

HOLT, Francis Ludlow.

Reports of cases at Nisi Prius in court of Common Pleas and
on northern circuit. 1815–1817. 1 vol. 1818. 8vo. **8 F**

A System of the Shipping and Navigation laws of Great
Britain. 2 vols. 1820. 8vo. **175 F**

HOLT, John.

General view of agriculture of county of Lancaster drawn up
for consideration of Board of Agriculture. 1795. 8vo. **89 A**

HOLT, Sir John.

Modern cases in the court of Queen's Bench in the second
and third years of Queen Anne, in the time when Sir John
Holt sate chief justice there. 3rd ed. reviewed by W. B.
1733. folio. **74 D**

A Report of all the cases determined by Sir John Holt,
1688–1710, during which time he was lord chief justice of
England. 1738. folio. **74 D**

HOLT, William.

Admiralty court cases on the Rule of the Road as laid down
by the articles and regulations now in force under order in
council for preventing collisions at sea. 1867. 8vo. **160 A**

HOLTHOUSE, Henry James.

A New Law dictionary, to which is added, an outline of an
action at law and of a suit in equity. 2nd ed. 1846.
12mo. **171 A**

HOLYWELL, Flintshire.

The history of the parishes of Whiteford and Holywell. By
Thomas Pennant. 1796. 4to. **95 G**

HOME, Henry, Lord Kames.

Essays upon several subjects concerning British antiquities.
3rd ed. Edinburgh, 1763. 12mo. **84 A**

Historical law tracts. [By Henry Home, Lord Kames.]
2 vols. Edinburgh, 1758. 8vo. **144 F**

The same. 2nd ed. 1 vol. Edinburgh, 1761. 8vo. **144 F**

Principles of Equity. 3rd ed. 2 vols. 1778. 8vo. **167 C**

HOMER.

English hexameter translations from Schiller, Göthe, Homer
&c. 1847. 8vo. **83 A**

HOMER—*continued.*

Homeri Ilias.   2 vols. in 1.   Lipsiæ, 1839.   12mo.   **47 E**

The Iliad of Homer.   Translated by J. G. Cordery.   2 vols.
1871.   8vo.   **83 C**

The Iliad of Homer.   Translated by Mr. Pope.   6 vols. in 3.
1715–20.   folio.   **83 J**

See also BARTER, W. G. T.

HONDURAS, BRITISH.

A Collection of the Ordinances of British Honduras, 1858–
1889.   9 vols.   Belize, 1858–89.   folio.   **36 A B**

Consolidated digest of the laws, 1765–1857.   Belize, 1857.
folio.   **36 A**

Consolidated laws.   1887.   8vo.   **36 B**

Laws in force on 31 Dec. 1881.   2 vols. in 1.   1882.   8vo.   **36 B**

HONE, WILLIAM.

The three trials of Wm. Hone for publishing three parodies,
viz.   The late John Wilkes's catechism.   The political
litany and The sinecurist's creed ; on three ex-officio informations at Guildhall, London, December 18–20, 1817.
1818.   8vo.   **51 G**

HONG KONG.

Hong Kong laws, 1841–1855.   Hong Kong, 1856.   folio. **37 E**

Ordinances of Hong Kong, 1844–1865.   1866.   8vo.   **37 E**

Ordinances of Hong Kong, 1857–1880, 1884.   5 vols.   Hong
Kong, 1857–84.   folio and 8vo.   **37 E**

HONOR.

Honor military and civill.   By Sir W. Segar.   1602. folio. **126 I**

Honores Anglicani ; or, titles of honour of the English nobility.
By T. C. Banks.   1812.   folio.   **125 H**

Honores Anglicani ; or, titles of honour the temporal nobility of
the English nation.   By Simon Segar.   1712.   12mo. **125 A**

Titles of Honor.   By J. Selden.   3rd ed.   1672.   folio. **126 I**

A Treatise of Honour military and civil according to the laws
and customs of England.   By John Logan.   See J. Guillim's
Display of heraldry, 6th ed.   1724, folio.   **125 H**

See also DIGNITIES and MILLES, T.

HOOD, Henry John and Henry William CHALLIS.

' The Conveyancing Acts, 1881 and 1882, with a commentary : containing also the Settled Land Act, 1882, and the Married Women's Property Act, 1882 : to which is prefixed a short treatise on the law of Real Property in relation to Conveyancing, by H. W. Challis. 1882. 8vo. **164 A**

The same. 2nd ed. 1884. 8vo. **164 A**

The same. 3rd ed. 1889. 8vo. **13 G**

HOOK, Walter Farquhar.

A Church dictionary. 10th ed. 1867. 8vo. **77 C**

The Queen and her chaplain. Dr. Hook's Protestant sermon (on the text Hear the church) as preached by him at the chapel royal before Queen Victoria and for which he was dismissed his chaplaincy. [1837.] [Pamphlets, vol. 5.] **144 A**

HOOKER, Richard.

The works of Richard Hooker in eight books of ecclesiastical polity, with an account of his life and death. 1666. folio.
    . **77 F**

HOOKER, Sir William Jackson.

Kew gardens, or a popular guide to the royal botanic gardens of Kew. 10th ed. 1851. 12mo. **93 C**

HOOPER, Right Rev. John.

Early writings. Edited by Rev. S. Carr. Cambridge, 1843. 8vo. **77 D**

Later writings ; with his letters and other pieces. Edited by Rev. C. Nevinson. Cambridge, 1852. 8vo. **77 D**

HOPE, Sir Thomas.

Scotch Law Practicks. 1726. 12mo.

HOPKINS, Manley.

A Handbook of Average, to which is added a chapter on Arbitration. 3rd ed. 1868. 8vo. **160 C**

The same. 4th ed. 1884. 8vo. **9 A**

HOPWOOD, Charles Henry and F. J. COLTMAN.

Registration cases in the Court of Common Pleas, 1868–1878. 2 vols. 1873–79. 8vo. **6 G**

HOPWOOD, CHARLES HENRY and F. A. PHILBRICK.
Registration cases in the Court of Common Pleas, 1863–1867.
1 vol. 1868. 8vo. **6 G**

HORATII, THE.
The Horatii, a tragedy. [By I. H. Wright.] 1846. [Pamphlets, vol. 23.] **144 B**

HORN, HENRY and EDWIN TYRRELL HURLSTONE.
Reports of cases in the Courts of Exchequer and Exchequer Chamber, 1838–1839. 1 vol. 1840. 8vo. **7 F**

HORNE, ANDREW.
La Somme appelle Mirroir des Justices vel speculum justiciariorum. 1642. 12mo. **49 E**
The book called the Mirrour of Justices with the booke called the Diversity of Courts. Both translated by W[illiam] H[ughes]. 1646. 12mo. **49 E**
The same. Another ed. 1768. 12mo. **49 E**

HORRY, SIDNEY CALDER.
The laws relating to Licensed Victuallers. 1837. 12mo. **172 A**

HORSES, LAW OF.
The law of Horses. By G. H. H. Oliphant. 4th ed. by C. E. Lloyd. 1882. 8vo. **10 B**
Horse warranty on the purchase and sale of horses. By F. H. Lascelles. 2nd ed. 1881. 8vo. **10 B**
The laws relative to Horses. 1825. 8vo. **168 G**

HORSFIELD, REV. THOMAS WALKER.
The history and antiquities of Lewes and its vicinity. 1824. 4to. **93 E**
The history, antiquities and topography of the county of Sussex. 2 vols. Lewes, 1835. 4to. **94 G**

HORSMAN, GILBERT.
Precedents in Conveyancing. 3 vols. 1744. folio. **157 D**
The same. 3rd ed. 2 vols. 1768. folio. **157 D**
The same. 4th ed. 3 vols. 1785. 8vo. **163 E**

HORTICULTURE.
The library of agricultural and horticultural knowledge.
3rd ed. 1834. 8vo. 83 J

HORWOOD, RICHARD.
Plan of the cities of London and Westminster, the borough
of Southwark and parts adjoining, shewing every house
[mounted on 3 sheets, in 3 cases]. 1799. 4to. 89 F

HOSKING, WILLIAM.
Some observations upon the recent addition of a reading room
to the British Museum. 1858. folio. 92 G

HOUARD, DAVID.
Dictionnaire de la Coutume de Normandie. 4 vols. Rouen,
1780-82. 4to. 40 B
Traités sur les coutumes Anglo-Normandes, publiés en Angle-
terre, depuis le onzième jusqu'au quatorzième siècle. 4 vols.
Rouen, 1776. 4to. 40 A

HOUCK, LOUIS.
The law of navigable Rivers. Boston, 1868. 8vo. 60 B

HOUGH, RIGHT REV. JOHN.
Table-Talk and papers of Bishop Hough, 1703–1743. By
Rev. W. D. Macray. See Oxford Hist. Soc. vol. 16, 1890,
pp. 381–416. 85 F

HOUGHTON, THOMAS.
Rara avis in terris : or the compleat Miner, in two books ; the
first containing the liberties, laws and customs of the lead
mines of Wirksworth, Derbyshire ; the second teacheth the
art of Dialling and Levelling. Derby, 1729. 12mo. 87 A
The same. 2nd ed. 1738. 12mo. 118 A

HOUSE OF COMMONS PRACTICE.
Decisions of C. S. Lefevre, speaker of the House of Commons,
on points of order, rules of debate, and general practice of
the House. By R. Bourke. 2nd ed. 1857. 8vo. 66 B
See also BILLS, PRIVATE AND PUBLIC.

HOUSE OF LORDS CASES.

Reports of cases in the House of Lords on appeals and writs of error, claims of peerage and divorces, 1847–1866. 11 vols. 1849–66, and Digested index. By C. Clark. 1868. 12 vols. 1849–68. 8vo.   1 C D

HOUSE OF LORDS PRACTICE.

Practice of House of Lords in English, Scotch and Irish appeal cases under Appellate Jurisdiction act 1876. By C. M. Denison and C. H. Scott. 1879. 8vo.   12 A

Appeal Practice of supreme court of Judicature and House of Lords. By Locock Webb. 1877. 8vo.   12 A

The practice in the House of Lords. By John Palmer. 1830. 8vo.   ·   52 H

See also APPEAL PRACTICE.

HOUSE PROPERTY AND HOUSE TAX.

The law relating to Tenement Houses and Flats for residential or business purposes. By W. Clode. 1889. 8vo.   10 B

Handbook of house property. By E. L. Tarbuck. 4th ed. 1887. 12mo.   10 B

Guide to house tax acts. By A. M. Ellis. 1885. 8vo.   10 B

Reports of tax cases under the act 37 Vict. cap. 16, and under the Taxes management act, vol. i. 1875–1883. 1884. 8vo.
                                         68 B

Hints to all about to rent, buy or build house property. By F. Cross. 4th ed. 1854. 12mo.   168 G

HOUSES OF PARLIAMENT.

The history of the ancient palace and late Houses of Parliament at Westminster. By E. W. Brayley and John Britton. 1836. 8vo.   91 F

On the proposed site of the new Houses of Parliament. By C. Fowler. 1836. [Pamphlets, vol. 5.]   144 A

HOUSMAN, FRANCIS.

Selection of precedents in conveyancing. 1861. 8vo. 53 C

HOUSTON, JOHN.

Treatise on the law of Stoppage in Transitu and incidentally of retention and delivery. 1866. 8vo.   11 G

HOVEDEN, ROGER.
Chronica. Edited by W. Stubbs. 4 vols. 1868–71. 8vo.
102 C

HOVENDEN, JOHN EYKYN.
The principles and practice by which Courts of Equity are guided as to the prevention or remedial correction of fraud. 2 vols. 1825. 8vo. **168 E**
A Supplement to Vesey Junior's Reports of cases in Chancery. 2 vols. 1827. 8vo. **3 I**

HOWARD, BENJAMIN CHEW.
Reports of decisions in the Supreme court of the United States, 1843–1854. 24 vols. See B. R. Curtis's Reports, vols. 14–21, Boston, 1855–56; and S. F. Miller's Reports, 4 vols. Washington, 1874–75. 8vo. **57 B C**

HOWARD FAMILY.
Historical anecdotes of some of the Howard family. By Charles Howard. 1769. 8vo. **80 B**
The Howard papers, with a biographical pedigree and criticism. By H. K. S. Causton. 1862. 8vo. **80 B**
See also BANKS, T. C.

HOWARD, JOHN HENRY.
The laws of the British colonies in the West Indies and other parts of America, concerning real and personal property and manumission of slaves. 2 vols. 1827. 8vo. **55 D**

HOWARD, PHILIP.
The scriptural history of the earth and of mankind compared with the cosmogonies, chronologies and original traditions of ancient nations. 1797. 4to. **77 G**

HOWEL, JAMES.
Cottoni Posthuma. Divers choice pieces of that renowned antiquary Sir Robert Cotton. 1679. 12mo. **84 A**

HOWELL, THOMAS BAYLY and T. J. HOWELL.
A Complete collection of State Trials and proceedings for high treason and other crimes and misdemeanors from the earliest period to the year 1820. 33 vols. 1816–26, and General index by David Jardine. 1 vol. 1828. 34 vols. 1816–28. 8vo. **50 I J**

HOWGRAVE, Francis.
An Essay of the ancient and present state of Stamford. Stamford, 1726. 8vo.   89 C

HOWLETT, Rev. John.
Dispersion of the gloomy apprehensions, of late suggested, from the decline of our corn trade. 1797. 8vo.   144 G
Enclosures, a cause of improved agriculture, of plenty and cheapness of provisions, of population, and of both private and national wealth. 1787. 8vo.   144 G
Enquiry concerning the influence of tithes upon agriculture, whether in the hands of clergy or laity. 1801. 8vo. 144 G
Enquiry into the influence which enclosures have had upon the population of this kingdom. 2nd ed. 1786. 8vo. 144 G
Essay on population of Ireland. 1786. 8vo.   144 G
Examination of Mr. Pitt's speech, in the house of Commons, on Friday, February 12, 1796, relative to the condition of the poor. 1796. 8vo.   144 G
The insufficiency of the causes to which the increase of our poor and of the poor rates have been commonly ascribed; the true one stated. 1788. 8vo.   144 G

HUARD, Adrien.
Répertoire de législation et de jurisprudence en matière de Brevets d'Invention. Paris, 1863. 12mo.   58 F

HUBBACK, John.
The evidence of Succession to real and personal property and peerages. 1844. 8vo.   53 H

HUBBELL, J. H.
Legal directory for lawyers and business men, with a synopsis of the collection laws of each state and Canada. New York, 1881. 8vo.   59 F

HUDSON, Corrie.
Guide to making and proving wills. 1876. 8vo.   13 I
Practical guide to payment of legacy and succession duties. 2nd ed. 1867. 8vo.   176 D
The same. 5th ed. 1878. 8vo.   176 D
The same. 6th ed. by A. T. Layton. 1884. 8vo.   176 D
The same. 8th ed. by A. T. Layton. 1890. 8vo.   11 G

HUDSON, John C.

The executor's guide. New ed. [1870.] 12mo. **52 G**

HUDSON, William.

Treatise on Court of Star-Chamber. See Collectanea Juridica, vol. 2, 1792, pp. 1–240. **144 G**

HUDSON, William Elliot and John BROOKE.

Reports of cases in the courts of King's Bench and Exchequer Chamber in Ireland, 1827–1831. 2 vols. Dublin, 1829–46. 8vo. **15 E**

HUDSON'S BAY.

Papers presented to the committee appointed to inquire into the state and condition of the countries adjoining to Hudson's Bay. 1749. folio. **37 G**

HUET, Peter Daniel.

A View of the Dutch trade in all the states, empires and kingdoms in the world. 2nd ed. 1722. 12mo. **78 A**

HUGGINS, Hastings Charles.

Laws of Nevis, 1681 to 1861. 1862. 8vo. **36 F**

HUGH DE AVALON.

Magna vita S. Hugonis episcopi Lincolniensis. Edited by Rev. J. F. Dimock. 1864. 8vo. **102 A**

HUGHES, David.

The law relating to Insurance. 1828. 8vo. **169 A**

HUGHES, Thomas Bridges.

Report of the case of the King against Bebb and others on an Extent, with an appendix of some cases and records in Extents not before printed. 1811. 8vo. **50 B**

HUGHES, William, Barrister, Gray's Inn.

An Exact abridgment of publick acts and ordinances of Parliament, 1640 to 1656. 1657. 4to. **158 D**

The Grand Abridgment of the Law continued ; or, a collection of the principal cases and points of the Common Law of

33

HUGHES, WILLIAM—*continued.*
England, contained in all the reports extant, from the first
of Elizabeth, to this present, by way of common-place.
[vol. 1 only.] 1660. 4to.   63 C
See also GREGORY, A. and HORNE, A.

HUGHES, WILLIAM, BARRISTER, LINCOLN'S INN.
Concise precedents in modern conveyancing. 2nd ed. 3 vols.
1855–57. 8vo.   13 E
The new Stamp act 13 & 14 Vict. cap. 97 with practical notes.
1850. 12mo.   175 G
The practice of Conveyancing. 2 vols. 1856–57. 12mo.
                                                            164 E
The practice of Sales of Real Property with precedents of
forms. 2nd ed. 2 vols. 1849–50. 12mo.   174 D

HUGHES, WILLIAM, F.R.G.S.
The treasury of geography, physical, historical, descriptive
and political. New ed. 1860. 12mo.   84 A

HUGHSON, DAVID, i.e. EDWARD PUGH.
An Epitome of the privileges of London including Southwark.
1816. 12mo.   92 A
London : being an accurate history and description of the
British metropolis and its neighbourhood to thirty miles
extent. 6 vols. 1806–1809. 8vo.   89 C

HUGUENOT REFUGEES.
Protestant exiles from France, or the Huguenot refugees and
their descendants in Great Britain and Ireland. By Rev.
D. C. A. Agnew. 2nd ed. 3 vols. 1871–74. 8vo. 80 G

HULL, HUGH MUNRO.
Index to the statutes of Tasmania. 1826–1877. Hobart
Town, 1877. 8vo.   35 E

HULL, YORKSHIRE.
A Collection of statutes relating to the town of Kingston-
upon-Hull and the county of the same town. By Wm.
Woolley. 1830. 8vo.   94 B
A Copy of the Poll, taken at the guild-hall in the town of
Kingston-upon-Hull, on 12th and 13th Oct. 1774. Hull,
1774. 8vo.   107 K

HULL, YORKSHIRE—*continued.*

The history of the town and county of Kingston upon Hull. By Rev. John Tickell.   Hull, 1798.   4to.   **94 D**

Notices relative to the early history of the town and port of Hull.   By Charles Frost.   1827.   4to.   **94 D**

HULLOCK, JOHN.

The law of Costs in civil actions and criminal proceedings. 1796, and 2nd ed.   2 vols. in 1.   1810.   8vo.   **165 A**

HULTON, WILLIAM ADAM.

Treatise on law of Convictions.   1835.   12mo.   **164 F**

HUMAN NATURE AND UNDERSTANDING.

A Treatise of human nature. By David Hume. Edited by T. H. Green and T. H. Grose. New ed. 2 vols. 1886. 8vo.   **78 E**

An Essay concerning human understanding. By John Locke. 4th ed.   1700.   folio.   **78 H**

Abstract of Mr. Locke's Essay on human understanding. By Sir Jeffray Gilbert. 1788. 8vo.   **80 C**

See also HOBBES, T. and MALEBRANCHE, N.

HUMANITY.

Humanity and humanitarianism with special reference to the prison system of Great Britain and the United States. By William Tallack.   1871.   8vo.   **78 C**

HUME, REV. ABRAHAM.

Ancient Meols : or, some account of the antiquities found near Dove Point, on the sea-coast of Cheshire. 1863. 8vo. **86 E**

HUME, DAVID.

Essays, moral, political and literary. Edited by T. H. Green and T. H. Grose. New ed. 2 vols. 1882. 8vo.   **78 E**

The history of England from the invasion of Julius Cæsar to the Revolution in 1688. New ed. 6 vols. 1830. 8vo. **115 F**

The life of David Hume, written by himself. [Autobiography, vol. 4.]   1826.   12mo.   **79 A**

A Treatise of human nature and dialogues concerning natural religion. Edited by T. H. Green and T. H. Grose. New ed.   2 vols.   1886.   8vo.   **78 E**

33—2

HUME, James Deacon.
  The laws of the Customs. 1825. 8vo.   165 F
  The same. With supplements. 1836. 8vo.   165 F

HUME, Robert Montagu.
  Chancery delays and their remedy. 1830. [Jacob's Tracts,
    vol. 8.]   144 E
  A Letter on the delay in the Masters' offices in Chancery and
    the remedy, addressed to the suitors. 1832. [Chancery
    Pamphlets, vol. 1.]   144 A

HUME, Sophia.
  An Exhortation to the inhabitants of the province of South
    Carolina to bring their deeds to the light of Christ in their
    own consciences. Bristol, 1751. 12mo.   118 C

HUMPHREYS, James.
  Observations on the actual state of the English laws of real
    property, with the outlines of a code. 1826. 8vo.   83 I
  A Contre-projet to the Humphreysian code. By John James
    Park. 1828. 8vo.   83 J

HUMPHRY, Hugh McNab.
  Common precedents in Conveyancing. 1881. 8vo.   163 G
  The same. 2nd ed. 1882. 8vo.   13 F
  See also CLARKE, A. St. J.

HUMPHRY, William Wood.
  Contributory remarks on a general registry, with an appendix
    containing the questions and plan of the real property com-
    missioners. 1830. [Jacob's Tracts, vol. 10.]   144 E

HUNDREDS AND HUNDRED ROLLS.
  Account of the ancient division of the English nation into
    hundreds and tithings. By G. Sharp. 1784. 12mo. 78 A
  Rotuli Hundredorum temp. Hen. III. et Edw. I. in Turr.
    Lond. et in curia receptæ Scaccarii Westm. asservati.
    Edited by W. Illingworth. 2 vols. 1812–18. folio. 98 E

HUNGARY.
  A Short account of General Georgey's surrender to the Rus-
    sians. By C. D. B. Zabrocki. Bradford, 1851. [Pamphlets,
    vol. 9, pt. 1.]   144 A

HUNT, ARTHUR JOSEPH.

The law relating to boundaries and fences. 1866, and 2nd ed.
1870. 12mo. **161 A**

The same. 3rd ed. by A. Brown. 1884. 12mo. **9 A**

The law relating to Fraudulent Conveyances, under the statutes
of Elizabeth and the bankrupt acts. 1872. 8vo. **164 E**

HUNT, WILLIAM.

Collection of cases on Annuity act, with an epitome of the practice relative to enrolment of memorials. 1794. 8vo. **160 B**

The same. 2nd ed. 1796. 8vo. **160 B**

HUNT, REV. WILLIAM.

Historic towns : Bristol. 1887. 8vo. **88 A**

HUNTER, ADAM.

The waters of Harrogate and its vicinity. 5th ed. 1838.
8vo. **94 A**

HUNTER, REV. JOSEPH.

The Attorney general versus Shore. An historical defence of
the trustees of Lady Hewley's Foundations and of the claims
upon them of the Presbyterian ministry of England. 1834.
[Law Tracts, vol. 3.] **144 E**

Hallamshire. The history and topography of the parish of
Sheffield. 1819. folio. **95 H**

The same. New ed. by Rev. A. Gatty. [n.d.] folio. **95 H**

The history and topography of the deanery of Doncaster.
2 vols. 1828. folio. **94 H**

Three catalogues describing the contents of The Red Book of
the Exchequer, of the Dodsworth manuscripts in the Bodleian library, and of the manuscripts in the library of Lincoln's
Inn. 1838. 8vo. **82 B**

HUNTER, RICHARD T.

Guide to law of distress for rent. 1888. 8vo. **9 G**

HUNTER, SYLVESTER JOSEPH.

An Elementary view of the proceedings in a suit in equity.
1858. 12mo. **167 C**

The same. 6th ed. by G. W. Lawrance. 1873. 12mo. **167 C**

Observations on real property law reform. 1860. [Pamphlets,
vol. 15.] **144 B**

HUNTER, WILLIAM ALEXANDER.

Introduction to Roman law. 3rd ed. 1885. 12mo. 63 E

A Systematic and historical exposition of Roman law in the order of a code ; embodying the institutes of Gaius and the institutes of Justinian. Translated into English by J. A. Cross. 1876. 8vo. 63 E

The same. 2nd ed. 1885. 8vo. 63 E

The same. 4th ed. 1887. 8vo. 63 E

HUNTINGDON, COUNTY OF.

The visitation of the county of Huntingdon under the authority of Wm. Camden by his deputy Nicholas Charles, A.D. MDCXIII. Edited by Sir Henry Ellis. [Camden Society, vol. 43.] 1849. 8vo. 85 B

Another copy 1849. 8vo. 88 C

HURLSTONE, EDWIN TYRRELL and F. J. COLTMAN.

Reports of cases in the Courts of Exchequer and Exchequer Chamber, 1862–65. 3 vols. 1863–66. 8vo. 7 E

HURLSTONE, EDWIN TYRRELL and JOHN GORDON.

Exchequer Reports, 1854–56. 2 vols. 1855–56. 8vo. 7 D E

HURLSTONE, EDWIN TYRRELL and J. P. NORMAN.

Reports of cases in the Courts of Exchequer and Exchequer Chamber, 1856–62. 7 vols. 1857–62. 8vo. 7 E F

HURRELL, HENRY and CLARENDON GOLDING HYDE.

The law of joint stock companies. 1883. 8vo. 52 C

HURTLEY, THOMAS.

Concise account of some natural curiosities in the environs of Malham in Craven, Yorkshire. 1786. 8vo. 94 B

HUSBAND AND WIFE.

The rights and liabilities of husband and wife. By J. F. Macqueen. 3rd ed. by J. C. Russell and R. B. Russell. 1885. 8vo. 10 C

Law of husband and wife. By M. Lush. 1884. 8vo. 10 C

A Digest of the law of husband and wife as it affects property. By Ralph Thicknesse. 1884. 8vo. 10 C

The Wife-beaters' manual, a guide to husbands' connubial cor-

HUSBAND AND WIFE—*continued.*

rections. By Henry Romeike. Edited by C. W. Barker. 1884. [Pamphlets, vol. 38.] **144 C**

The law of husband and wife. By J. W. Edwards and W. F. Hamilton. 1883. 8vo. **52 H**

The law of husband and wife as respects property. By J. E. Bright. 2 vols. 1849. 8vo. **52 H**

Observations on the doctrine applicable to the separate use and non-anticipation clauses as carried out in the case of Tullett *v.* Armstrong. By B. Blundell. 1839. [Law Tracts, vol. 6.] **144 E**

The mutual rights of husband and wife. By R. Mence. 1838. [Law Tracts, vol. 6.] **144 E**

Observations respecting the question how far a contingent or reversionary interest of husband and wife in her right in personal estate is assignable during the coverture. By T. Canning. 1820. [Jacob's Tracts, vol. 1.] **144 E**

Of the interest of the husband in the real and personal estates and chattels real and personal of the wife. See Collectanea Juridica, vol. 2, 1792, pp. 410–414. **144 G**

Baron and Feme. A treatise of the common law concerning husbands and wives. 1700. 12mo. **168 G**

The same. 3rd ed. 1738. 12mo. **168 G**

See also CLANCY, J., POTHIER, R. J., PRATER, H., REDMAN, J. H. and ROPER, R. S. D.

HUSBAND, EDWARD.

Collection of all remonstrances, and other remarkable passages between Charles I. and his high court of parliament, Dec. 1641–March 1643. 1643. 8vo. **49 D**

Collection of all the publicke orders &c. of both Houses of Parliament, March 1642–December 1646. 1646. folio. **158 B**

HUTCHINS, REV. JOHN.

Dissertation on Domesday book ; and some account of the copy of that record in the library of the dean and chapter at Exeter. 1815. folio. **87 H**

The history and antiquities of the county of Dorset, with a copy of Domesday book and the Inquisitio Gheldi for the county. 2 vols. 1774. folio. **86 H**

The same. 2nd ed. [by R. Gough and J. B. Nichols.] 4 vols. 1796–1815. folio. **86 H**

The same. 3rd ed. by W. Shipp and J. W. Hodson. 4 vols. 1861–73. folio. **87 H**

HUTCHINSON, ROGER.
Works. Edited by J. Bruce. Cambridge, 1842. 8vo. **77 D**

HUTCHINSON, WILLIAM.
The history and antiquities of the county palatine of Durham.
3 vols. Newcastle. 1785–94. 4to. **87 D**
The history of the county of Cumberland and some places
adjacent. 2 vols. Carlisle, 1794. 4to. **87 G**
View of Northumberland, with an excursion to abbey of Mail-
ross in Scotland. 2 vols. in 1. Newcastle, 1778. 4to. **92 D**

HUTCHISON, JOHN.
The practice of Banking. 3 vols. 1880–87. 8vo. **78 D**

HUTTEN, LEONARD.
The antiquities of Oxford. A dissertation. See Oxford
Historical Society, vol. 8, 1887, pp. 35–108. **85 F**

HUTTON, CHARLES.
The compendius measurer, being a brief treatise on Mensuration and practical geometry, with an introduction to decimal
and duodecimal arithmetic. 2nd ed. 1790. 12mo. **255 H**

HUTTON, HENRY DIX.
Handy book of farm tenure and purchase under the Landlord
and tenant (Ireland) act 1870. 3rd ed. 1872. 8vo. **55 E**

HUTTON, SIR RICHARD.
Reports containing many choice cases, judgments and resolu-
tions in points of law. 2nd ed. 1682. folio. **74 D**
The young clerk's guide. 2nd ed. 1650. 12mo. **48 A**
The same. 6th ed. 1653. 12mo. **48 A**

HUTTON, WILLIAM.
The Court of Requests. With a memoir. Edinburgh, 1840.
[Law Tracts, vol. 7.] **144 E**
A Description of Blackpool. 3rd ed. 1817. 12mo. **89 A**
An History of Birmingham to the end of the year 1780. Bir-
mingham, 1781. 8vo. **93 E**
The history of Derby from the remote ages of antiquity to the
year MDCCXCI. 2nd ed. 1817. 8vo. **87 C**

HYDE ABBEY, HAMPSHIRE.

Liber monasterii de Hyda and a chartulary of the abbey of
Hyde in Hampshire A.D. 455–1023. Edited by Edward
Edwards. 1866. 8vo.   **102 C**

HYDE, EDGAR.

The Indian succession act. 1865. 8vo.   **38 D**

HYDRAULIC EXPERIMENTS.

Nautical and hydraulic experiments.   By Colonel Mark
Beaufoy. vol. 1. 1834. 4to.   **78 H**

IBBOTSON, HORATIO WALTER.

The Legal Prompter; being a compilation for immediate
reference to Statutes most in use. 1860. 12mo.   **176 C**

ICELANDIC GLOSSARY AND SAGAS.

Glossary of Icelandic words.   See Thomas Saga Erkibyskups,
vol. 2, 1883, pp. 297–584.   **102 E**
Icelandic Sagas and other historical documents, relating to
settlements and descents of the Northmen on British Isles.
Edited by G. Vigfusson. vols. 1, 2. 1887. 8vo.   **102 I**

IDIOCY.

The law concerning idiots, lunatics and persons of unsound
mind. By C. P. Phillips. 1858. 12mo.   **172 B**
The law concerning idiots, lunatics and other persons non
compotes mentis. By G. D. Collinson. 2 vols. 1812.
8vo.   **172 B**
See also INSANITY and LUNACY.

ILLEGITIMACY.

A Report of the case of Horner against Liddiard upon the
question of what consent is necessary to the marriage of
illegitimate minors; with an essay upon laws relating to
illegitimate children. By A. Croke. 1800. 8vo.   **51 E**

ILLINGWORTH, REV. CAYLEY.

Topographical account of parish of Scampton in county of
Lincoln. 1810. 4to.   **118 G**

ILLINGWORTH, WILLIAM.

An Inquiry into the laws respecting Forestalling, Regrating, and Ingrossing. 1800. 12mo.   168 E

Observations on the public records of the four courts at Westminster. 1831. 8vo.   97 I

ILLUSTRATED LONDON NEWS.

The Illustrated London News, 1868–1873. 12 vols. 1868–73. folio.   156 F & 157 F

ILLUSTRATED TIMES.

The Illustrated Times, 1861–1867, 1870, 1871. 9 vols. 1861–71. folio.   155 F & 156 F

IMBANKING.

The history of imbanking and draining of divers fens and marshes both in foreign parts and in this kingdom. By Wm. Dugdale. 2nd ed. by C. N. Cole. 1772. folio.   85 I

See also BEDFORD LEVEL, SEWERS and WATERS.

IMPEY, JOHN.

The Modern Pleader. 1794. 8vo.   173 F

The same. 2nd ed. 1814. 8vo.   173 F

The new Instructor Clericalis, stating the authority, jurisdiction, and modern practice of the Court of Common Pleas. 4th ed. 1794. 8vo.   161 G

The same. 7th ed. 1826. 8vo.   161 G

The new Instructor Clericalis, stating the authority, jurisdiction and modern practice of the court of King's Bench. 1782. 8vo.   161 G

The same. 9th ed. 1818, and 10th ed. 1823. 8vo. 161 G

The practice of office of Sheriff and Under Sheriff, also the practice of office of Coroner. 3rd ed. 1812. 8vo.   175 E

IMPEY, WALTER J.

The general Stamp act 55 Geo. III. cap. 184, with notes of cases decided on the Stamp laws. 1823. 12mo.   175 G

Law and practice of the writ of Mandamus. 1826. 8vo. 172 D

INCLOSURES.

Enclosures, a cause of improved agriculture, of cheapness of provisions, of population and of both private and national wealth. By Rev. John Howlett. 1787. 8vo.   144 G

INCLOSURES—*continued.*

Enquiry into the influence which enclosures have had upon the population of this kingdom. By Rev. John Howlett. 2nd ed. 1786. 8vo. **144 G**

History of Inclosures. See F. Clifford's History of private bill legislation, vol. 1, pp. 13–28 and 493–503. **83 I**

See also COMMONS and COVENTRY, T.

INCOME TAX.

A Full analysis of the Income tax acts. By W. T. Pratt. 5th ed. by D. Ward. 1887. 12mo. **10 C**

A Guide to the Income tax acts. By A. M. Ellis. 2nd ed. 1886. 12mo. **10 C**

Income tax laws. By S. Dowell. 2nd ed. 1885. 8vo. **10 C**

Reports of tax cases under 37 Vict. cap. 16 and under the Taxes management act. vol. 1, 1875–1883. 1884. 8vo. **68 B**

Handy book of land assessed and income tax laws. By R. R. Davies. 1864. 8vo. **53 H**

Occupation, or a glance at the property and income tax. By R. G. Arrowsmith. 1854. [Pamphlets, vol. 21.] **144 B**

The Income tax act 5 & 6 Vict. c. 35 By John Paget. 1842. 12mo. **168 G**

Observations &c. upon the act for taxing income. 1799. 12mo. **168 G**

INCUMBRANCES.

Concise view of law relating to priority of incumbrances. By W. G. Robinson. 1873. 8vo. **11 C**

A Practical treatise of Assets, Debts and Incumbrances. By James Ram. 1832. 8vo. **160 C**

INDEMNITY.

Dissertation on and precedents of Indemnity. See Bythewood and Jarman's Conveyancing, 4th ed. vol. 2, 1885, pp. 938–970. **13 D**

See also GUARANTEES.

INDERMAUR, JOHN.

A Concise practical treatise on the law of bills of sale. 1882. 12mo. **64 F**

Epitome of leading common law cases. 1873. 8vo. **171 C**

The same. 6th ed. 1886. 8vo. **64 B**

INDIA, History and Geography of—*continued.*

Charters establishing the supreme courts of judicature in India.
[n.d.] 8vo.   38 A

Des Sentiments de justice et d'humanité de l'Angleterre dans
la question Indienne. Paris, 1857. 8vo.   78 C

The development of the wealth of India. By Thomas Hare.
1861. [Pamphlets, vol. 14.]   144 A

The familiar epistles of Mr. John Company to Mr. John Bull.
1858. [Pamphlets, vol. 19.]   144 B

Gazetteer of territories under government of East India
Company and of native states on continent of India. By
E. Thornton. 4 vols. 1854. 8vo.   84 G

The Highlands of India, vol. 2, being a chronicle of field sports
and travels in India. By D. J. F. Newall. 1887. 8vo. 84 B

The Hindoos. 2 vols. 1834–35. 12mo.   116 D

The history of British India. By James Mill. 2nd ed. 6 vols.
1820. 8vo.   116 B

The history of British India from 1805 to 1835. By H. H.
Wilson. 3 vols. 1848. 8vo.   116 B

The history of India. By Wm. Robertson, D.D. [vol. 9 of
his Works]. 1824. 8vo.   116 F

The history of the British empire in India. By Rev. G. R.
Gleig. 4 vols. 1830–35. 12mo.   116 D

India Reform. No. IV. The native states of India. [1853.]
[Pamphlets, vol. 9, pt. 1.]   144 A

Memorandum of the improvements in the administration
of India during the last thirty years. 1858. [Pamphlets,
vol. 10.]   144 A

Pamphlets on India. By David Urquhart. 1843–78. [Urqu-
hart's Pamphlets, vol. 2.]   143 G

A President in council the best government for India. 1858.
[Pamphlets, vol. 19.]   144 B

Report by general committee of the Fund for relief of sufferers
by Mutiny in India, dated 15 February 1858. [Pamphlets,
vol. 10.]   144 A

Suggestions for reconstruction of government of India. By
J. T. Mackenzie. 1857. [Pamphlets, vol. 10.]   144 A

Taylor's Students' Manual of Indian history and the Edinburgh Review. 1877. [Pamphlets, vol. 34.]   144 C

The trade and commerce of India. By J. T. Mackenzie.
1859. [Pamphlets, vol. 14.]   144 A

See also East India Company and Hastings, W.

INDIA, Law of.

The law of India. By Andrew Lyon. 2 vols. 1873. 8vo. **38 D**

Commentaries on the transfer of property act 1882. By H. H. Shephard and K. Brown. Madras, 1887. 8vo. **38 D**

Law of limitation in India. By H. H. Shephard. 2nd ed. Madras, 1883. 8vo. **38 D**

Manual of Jurisprudence for forest officers. By B. H. Baden-Powell. Calcutta, 1882. 8vo. **38 D**

The negotiable instruments act 1881. By M. D. Chalmers. Calcutta, 1882. 8vo. **38 D**

Punjab customary law. By C. L. Tupper. 3 vols. Calcutta, 1881. 8vo. **38 C**

The tenure of land in India. By Sir George Campbell. See Systems of land tenure, 1881, pp. 213–289. **78 B**

Indian Registration act 1871. By Carr Stephen. 4th ed. Calcutta, 1877. 8vo. **38 B**

Law of evidence as administered in England and applied to India. By J. Goodeve. New ed. Calcutta, 1871. 8vo. **38 C**

Limitation of civil suits in British India. By N. H. Thomson. 2nd ed. Calcutta, 1870. 8vo. **38 B**

The Hedaya, or guide : a commentary on the Mussalman laws. Translated by C. Hamilton. 2nd ed. 1870. 8vo. **38 D**

Indian Criminal law and procedure. By M. H. Starling. 1869. 8vo. **38 C**

Indian succession act. By Edgar Hyde. 1865. 8vo. **38 D**

Personal property in the East Indies, in what cases subject to, or exempt from legacy and residue duty. By J. B. Alcock. With supplement. 1850–51. 12mo. **38 D**

See also Bengal, Bombay, Codes, Cowell, H., Digests of Cases, Field, C. D., Hindu Law, Madras, Mohammedan Law and Norton, J. B.

INDIA LIST. See Army Lists.

INDIA, Statutes of.

Acts of government of India, 1834–50. 1840–52. folio. **33 H**

Indian acts, 1834–1889. 34 vols. 1834–89. 8vo. **33 C–F**

Legislative acts of the governor-general of India in council, 1834–1867. By Wm. Theobald. 5 vols. 1868, and Continuation to 1869. 2 vols. 1869–70. 7 vols. Calcutta, 1868–70. 8vo. **33 G**

Narrative of the course of legislation during the years 1860–1869. Calcutta, 1861–69. 8vo. **33 G**

INDIA, STATUTES OF—*continued.*
Chronological table of, and index to, Indian statute-book from
1834. By C. D. Field. 2 vols. 1870–72. 4to. **38 F**
Index to the acts of Indian legislatures, 1834–1866. By
R. Damodhur. Bombay, 1867. 8vo. **33 G**

INDIANS.
Remarks on the Indians of North America in a letter to an
Edinburgh Reviewer. By Philadelphus. [Saxe Bannister.]
1822. [Jacob's Tracts, vol. 2.] **144 E**

INDICTABLE OFFENCES.
See CRIMINAL LAW PRACTICE.

INDUSTRIAL SOCIETIES.
The law relating to industrial and provident societies. By
H. F. A. Davis. 1869. 8vo. **10 C**

INFANCY.
Treatise on law and practice relating to Infants. By A. H.
Simpson. 2nd ed. by E. J. Elgood. 1890. 8vo. **10 C**
Commentaries on the law of Infancy and the law of Coverture.
By R. H. Tyler. Albany, 1868. 8vo. **59 E**
Law relating to Custody of Infants in cases of difference
between parents or guardians. By W. Forsyth. 1850.
8vo. **169 A**
The jurisdiction of court of Chancery over infants. By J. D.
Chambers. 1842. 8vo. **52 I**
The law relating to infants. By W. Macpherson. 1842.
8vo. **52 I**
Letter to the Lord Chancellor on Infant custody bill. By
Pearce Stevenson. 1839. [Law Tracts, vol. 6.] **144 E**

INFORMATIONS.
Informations criminal and Quo Warranto. By John Shortt.
1887. 8vo. **10 C**
The law and practice relating to Criminal Informations and
informations in the nature of Quo Warranto. By W. Cole.
1843. 12mo. **168 G**

INGLIS, WILLIAM.
Book-keeping. [n.d.] 12mo. **160 G**

INGRAM, Rev. James.
Memorials of Oxford. 3 vols. Oxford, 1834–37. 4to. 92 F

INGRAM, Thomas Dunbar.
Compensation to land and house owners payable by railway
and other public companies. 1864. 8vo. 163 C

INGROSSING.
Inquiry into laws of Forestalling, Regrating, and Ingrossing.
By W. Illingworth. 1800. 12mo. 168 E

INGS, Edward.
The act for the abolition of Arrest on mesne process in civil
actions. 1840. 12mo. 160 C

INHERITANCE.
Observations on the law of Inheritance with the act for the
amendment thereof 3 & 4 W. IV. c. 106. By John Tamlyn.
1834. [Law Tracts, vol. 5.] 144 E

INJUNCTIONS.
A Treatise on the law and practice of Injunctions. By W.
W. Kerr. 3rd ed. 1888. 8vo. 10 C
The law and practice of injunctions. By W. Joyce. 2 vols.
1872. 8vo. 10 C
Law of Injunctions. By C. S. Drewry. 1849. 8vo. 169 A
Law of Injunctions. By R. H. Eden. 1821. 8vo. 169 A

INLAND REVENUE CASES.
Summary proceedings in inland revenue cases. By N. J.
Highmore. 2nd ed. 1887. 12mo. 10 D

INNER TEMPLE.
Catalogue of printed books and manuscripts in library of the
Inner Temple. 1833. 8vo. 82 E
Masters of the bench of the Inner Temple 1450–1883, and
masters of the Temple 1540–1883. [not published.] 1883.
8vo. 80 F
Students admitted to the Inner Temple, 1571–1625. 1868.
8vo. 80 F

INNER TEMPLE—*continued.*

See also ADDISON, C. G., HARVEY, D. W., HAYWARD, A. and INNS OF COURT.

INNES, JAMES.

Idea Juris Scotici; or, a summary view of the Laws of Scotland. 1733. 4to.

INNKEEPERS.

Law of Horses, including law of Innkeepers &c. By G. H. H. Oliphant. 4th ed. by C. E. Lloyd. 1882. 8vo. **10 B**

The law relating to innkeepers. By C. H. M. Wharton. 1876. 8vo. **10 D**

The liability of Innkeepers. By F. C. Moncreiff. 1874. 12mo. **169 A**

The laws relating to Inns, Hotels and Alehouses. By J. W. Willcock. 1829. 12mo. **169 A**

INNOCENT VIII.

Bull of Pope Innocent VIII. on the marriage of Henry VII. with Elizabeth of York. Edited by J. P. Collier. [Camden Society, vol. 39.] 1847. 8vo. **85 B**

INNS OF COURT AND CHANCERY.

Antiquities of the Inns of Court and Chancery. By William Herbert. 1804. 8vo. **91 D**

A Guide to the Inns of Court and Chancery. By R. R. Pearce. 1855. 8vo. **91 D**

The history and antiquities of the four Inns of Court and 9 Inns of Chancery extracted from Dugdale's Origines Juridiciales. [By T. Cunningham.] 1780. 8vo. **91 D**

The Inns of Court and Chancery, and historical memoranda. By E. R. P. [E. R. Pickering.] [1859.] 8vo. **91 D**

The Inns of Court and legal education. By C. T. Saunders. 1875. [Pamphlets, vol. 33.] **144 C**

Lecture on the early history and academic discipline of Inns of Court and Chancery. By J. F. Macqueen. 1851. [Pamphlets, vol. 9, part 1.] **144 A**

Picturesque views with an historical account of the Inns of Court in London and Westminster. By Samuel Ireland. 1800. 8vo. **91 D**

See also BARRISTERS, CATALOGUES, LIBRARY, GRAY'S INN, INNER TEMPLE and LINCOLN'S INN.

INQUISITION.

Discorso dell' origine, forma, leggi ed uso dell' officio dell' inquisitione, nella città e dominio di Venetia. Del Paolo dell' ordine de' Servi [i.e. father Paul Sarpi]. 1639. 8vo. 118 A

INROLMENTS.

Posthumous works of Charles Fearne, consisting of A Reading on statute of inrolments &c. selected from the author's manuscripts, by T. M. Shadwell. 1797. 8vo. 175 C

INSANITY.

Crime and insanity, their causes, connexion and consequences, how distinguished and how treated by human legislation. By C. M. Burnett. 1832. [Pamphlets, vol. 9, pt. 1.] 144 A

The defence of insanity in criminal cases. By L. R. Everest. 1887. [Pamphlets, vol. 39.] 144 C

The defence of Insanity. See R. Harris's Before Trial, 1886, pp. 210–291. 176 F

Insanity and the lunacy laws. By William Wood. 1879. [Pamphlets, vol. 34.] 144 C

The medical jurisprudence of insanity. By Isaac Ray. 4th ed. Boston, 1860. 8vo. 59 G

Remarks on the plea of Insanity and on the management of criminal lunatics. By Wm. Wood, M.D. 1851. [Pamphlets, vol. 9, part 1.] 144 A

See also CONOLLY, J., HARRISON, G. L., HASLAM, J., MORISON, SIR A., PRICHARD, J. C. and TUKE, D. H.

INSOLVENCY.

Rules and orders in insolvency, 1828–1861. 3 vols. 1845-61. 12mo. 53 F

The statutes for the relief of Insolvent Debtors. By Leonard Shelford. 1856. 12mo. 169 A

The practice of Insolvency under the Protection acts. By D. C. Macrae. 1852. 12mo. 169 A

Observations on the Insolvent Debtors act: miscalled 'An act for relief of insolvent debtors.' By Wm. Jones. 1827. [Jacob's Tracts, vol. 5.] 144 E

A Letter to Wm. Jones, Esq. occasioned by his Observations on the Insolvent Debtors act. By Henry Dance. 1827. [Jacob's Tracts, vol. 5.] 144 E

See also BURGES, J. B., COOKE, E., GILL, J., KENDALL, J., LAW, W. J. and NICHOLLS, J.

INSURANCE.

Essay on Insurances, explaining nature of various kinds of Insurance practised by different commercial states of Europe. By Nicolas Magens. 2 vols. 1755. 4to.   **157 A**

Handy Assurance Directory. By Wm. Bourne. 3rd ed. 1889. 8vo.   **134 I**

Hints to the agents and friends of assurance offices. By R. Christie and W. Newmarch. 1852. [Pamphlets, vol. 9, pt. 1.]   **144 A**

The Insurance Blue Book and insurance companion, 1878–82, 1884–5. 4 vols. 1878–84. 8vo.   **146 E**

The Insurance Cyclopædia. By Cornelius Walford. 5 vols. [Aba-Han. all published.] 1871–78. 8vo.   **122 A**

Insurance dictionary, being a practical explanation of technical terms used in insurance business. By W. S. Champness. 1879. 12mo.   **122 B**

The Insurance Year Book, 1886. 1886. 8vo.   **146 E**

INSURANCE, LAW OF.

A Popular statement of the law of Insurance. By C. F. Morrell. 1883. 12mo.   **169 A**

A Treatise on the law of Insurance. By Willard Phillips. 5th ed. 2 vols. New York, 1867. 8vo.   **59 F**

A Treatise on law of Insurance. By Samuel Marshall. 5th ed. by Wm. Shee. 1865. 8vo.   **169 B**

A Treatise on Insurances. By B. M. Emerigon. Translated by S. Meredith. 1850. 8vo.   **169 B**

The law of Insurance. By D. Hughes. 1828. 8vo.   **169 A**

Complete digest of theory, laws and practice of Insurance. By John Weskett. 1781. 4to.   **157 C**

See also F. Clifford's History of private bill legislation, vol. 2, 1887, pp. 562–624.   **83 I**

See also ACCIDENT INSURANCE, FIRE INSURANCE, LIFE INSURANCE and MARINE INSURANCE.

INTEREST TABLES.

Interest tables at 5 per cent. By J. King. 1880. 8vo.   **134 J**

Tables of simple interest at 5, 4½, 4, 3½, 3 and 2½ per cent. per annum. By James Laurie. 32nd ed. [n.d.] 8vo.   **Hall**

INTERNATIONAL LAW.

Commentaries upon International Law. By Sir Robert Phillimore. 3rd ed. 4 vols. 1879–89. 8vo.   **55 B**

INTERNATIONAL LAW—*continued.*

Elements of International Law. By H. Wheaton. 3rd English ed. by A. C. Boyd. 1889. 8vo. 55 B

Selected cases, statutes and orders illustrative of the principles of Private International law. By Horace Nelson. 1889. 8vo. 55 A

Lectures on International Law in time of peace. By J. N. Pomeroy. Edited by T. S. Woolsey. 1886. 8vo. 55 B

A Digest of the international law of the United States. By F. Wharton. 3 vols. Washington, 1886. 8vo. 59 E

Leading cases and opinions on International law. By Pitt Cobbett. 1885. 8vo. 55 A

Treatise on international law. By W. E. Hall. 2nd ed. Oxford, 1884. 8vo. 55 B

Commentaries on the Conflict of Laws. By Joseph Story. 8th ed. by M. M. Bigelow. Boston, 1883. 8vo. 55 A

Foreign and domestic law : a treatise on private international jurisprudence. By J. A. Foote. 1878. 8vo. 55 A

First platform of International law. By Sir E. S. Creasy. 1876. 8vo. 55 A

Commentaries on the law of Nations. By W. O. Manning. New ed. by S. Amos. 1875. 8vo. 55 B

Juridical review of case of the British Barque 'Springbok.' By L. Gessner. [1873 or 1874.] [Pamphlets, vol. 34.] 144 C

Brief on behalf of owners of cargo of British Barque 'Springbok' as submitted 18 Aug. 1873 to mixed commission on British and American claims under treaty of Washington, 1871. By W. M. Evarts. [1873.] Privately printed. [Pamphlets, vol. 34.] 144 C

Draft outlines of an international code. By David Dudley Field. New York, 1872. 8vo. 55 A

Kent's commentary on international law. Edited by J. T. Abdy. 1866. 8vo. 55 A

Shall England uphold the capture of private property at sea? By A Lawyer. 1866. 8vo. [Pamphlets, vol. 26.] 144 B

International commercial law. By Leone Levi. 2nd ed. 2 vols. 1863. 8vo. 55 A

International law in connexion with municipal statutes relating to the commerce, rights and liabilities of the subjects of neutral states pending foreign war. By F. H. Hamel. 1863. 12mo. 55 A

Traité du droit international privé, ou du conflit des lois des différentes nations en matière de droit privé. Par J. J. G.

INTERNATIONAL LAW—*continued*.

Fœlix. 3me éd. par C. Demangeat. 2 vols. Paris, 1856. 8vo. **55 B**

Observations on feasibility of forming an International Council and armed executive for adjusting national disputes and obviating necessity of war. By A Solicitor. 1855. [Pamphlets, vol. 14.] **144 A**

The laws of war affecting commerce and shipping. By H. B. Thomson. 1854. [Pamphlets, vol. 9, pt. 2.] **144 A**

Right of search as between France, America & Great Britain. By D. C. Moylan. 1843. [Pamphlets, vol. 4.] **144 A**

The rights of War and Peace, including the law of nature and of nations. Translated from Latin of Grotius, by Rev. A. C. Campbell. 3 vols. Pontefract, 1814. 8vo. **48 E**

Practical treatise on law of nations relative to legal effect of war on commerce of belligerents and neutrals. By J. Chitty. 1812. 8vo. **55 A**

The Duke of Newcastle's Letter to Monsieur Michell in answer to Prussian memorial respecting capture of vessels and property of neutral powers in time of war. 1753. See Collectanea Juridica, vol. 1, 1791, pp. 129–166. **144 G**

See also CUTLER, J., DE BURGH, W., PUFENDORF, S., SAVIGNY, F. V., TWISS, SIR T., VATTEL, E. DE, WARD, H. W., WARD, R., WESTLAKE, J., WHEATON, H. and WOOLSEY, T. D.

INTERPLEADER.

Interpleader in the high court of justice and in the county courts. By M. Cababé. 2nd ed. 1888. 12mo. **12 E**

The practice of interpleader by sheriffs and high bailiffs. By D. Warde. 1887. 8vo. **12 E**

Practical treatise of law of Interpleader. By H. A. Simon. 1842. 12mo. [Bound with E. Lawes's Bills of Exchange. 1842.] **160 G**

INTERROGATORIES.

The law relating to interrogatories. By W. S. Sichel and W. Chance. 1883. 8vo. **9 G**

Law and practice relating to discovery by Interrogatories. By William Comer Petheram. 1864. 8vo. **169 C**

Digest of rules and practice as to Interrogatories for examination of witnesses. By J. W. Willis. 1816. 8vo. **169 C**

See also DISCOVERY.

INTESTACY.

Principles of the law of Succession to deceased persons. By
T. R. Potts. 1888. 8vo. **11 G**

The law's disposal of a person's estate who dies without will.
By P. Lovelass. 11th ed. by N. Gow. 1823. 8vo. **177 D**

The law of the distribution of the personal estates of intestates.
By F. Mascall. 1818. 8vo. **52 H**

Of the disposition or administration of intestates goods. By
John Selden. See J. Selden's Tracts, 1683, folio. **114 G**

INVENTIONS.

Counsel to inventors of improvements in the useful arts. By
Thomas Turner. 1850. 12mo. **78 A**

See also PATENTS.

INVESTMENTS.

The law relating to the Investment of trust money. By J. S.
Vaizey. 1890. 8vo. **11 I**

The Investment of trust funds. By E. A. Geare. 2nd ed.
1889. 8vo. **11 I**

Trustee's guide to Investments. By A. L. Ellis. 3rd ed.
1889. 12mo. **11 I**

Burdett's Official Intelligence, being a carefully compiled
précis of information regarding British, American and
foreign stocks, 1882–1890. 9 vols. 1882–90. 4to. **142 D**

Vade mecum for Investors for 1886, compiled from official
sources. By F. C. Mathieson. 1885. 12mo. **134 J**

Investors' Manual. vols. 5–8, 10–13 & 15. 9 vols. 1875–
85. folio. **Hall**

A Synopsis of the ordinary powers of trustees in regard to
Investments. By B. Cracroft. 12th ed. 1876. 8vo. **11 I**

Handy-book for Investors, a sketch of the rise, progress and
present character of every species of Investment. By W.
Bartlett and H. Chapman. 1869. 12mo. **169 D**

A Treatise on Investments. By R. A. Ward. 2nd ed. 1852.
8vo. **169 D**

INWOOD, WILLIAM.

Tables for purchasing of estates, for renewing of leases, and for
valuing reversionary estates. 7th ed. 1837. 12mo. **176 D**

The same. 20th ed. 1875. 12mo. **176 D**

The same. 22nd ed. 1884. 12mo. **134 I**

IONIAN ISLANDS.
History of the Ionian Islands. See R. M. Martin's History
of the British colonies, vol. 5, 1835, pp. 295–458. **116 C**

IPSWICH, SUFFOLK.
An Account of the gifts and legacies that have been given
and bequeathed to charitable uses in the town of Ipswich.
Ipswich, 1747. 8vo. **93 C**
The history and description of the town and borough of
Ipswich. By G. R. Clarke. Ipswich, 1830. 8vo. **93 C**
The Poll for bailives of Ipswich, taken September 8, 1754.
Ipswich, 1754. 8vo. **107 J**
The Poll for members of Parliament for the borough of Ipswich,
taken September 9, 1780. Ipswich, [n.d.] 8vo. **107 J**

IRELAND, ANTIQUITIES AND TOPOGRAPHY OF.
Antiquities of Ireland. By Edward Ledwich. Dublin, 1790.
4to. **95 F**
Atlas to accompany the second report of the Railway Com-
missioners, Ireland. 1838. folio. **19 D**
Giraldi Cambrensis Opera. Edited by J. F. Dimock. vol. 5.
Topographia Hibernica et Expugnatio Hibernica. 1867.
8vo. **101 E**
Irish antiquarian researches. By Sir William Betham. 2 vols.
Dublin, 1826–27. 8vo. **95 E**
Leigh's New pocket road book of Ireland. 3rd ed. 1835.
12mo. **95 E**
Letters concerning the northern coast of the county of Antrim ;
with natural history of basaltes in northern counties of
Ireland. By Rev. W. Hamilton. Dublin, 1790. 8vo. **95 E**
Memoir of a map of Ireland illustrating the topography of
that kingdom. By D. A. Beaufort. 1792. 4to. **95 F**
Plans and sections of the several lines of Railway in Ireland,
laid out under the direction of the Commissioners. 2 vols.
1837. folio. **19 D**
Reports upon boundaries of cities and boroughs in Ireland in
respect to election of members to serve in parliament. 1832.
folio. **153 A**
Statistical account ; or, parochial survey of Ireland. By
W. S. Mason. 3 vols. Dublin, 1814–19. 8vo. **95 F**
Topographical dictionary of Ireland. By Nicholas Carlisle.
1810. 4to. **F**

IRELAND, HISTORY OF.

An Account of Ireland, statistical and political.   By Edward
Wakefield.   2 vols.   1812.   4to.   **95 F**

The annals of loch Cé : a chronicle of Irish affairs A.D. 1014
to A.D. 1590.   Edited by W. M. Hennessy.   2 vols. 1871.
8vo.   **102 D**

Annual reports of the deputy keeper of the public records in
Ireland.   3 vols.   1869–86.   8vo.   **100 F**

The case of Ireland's being bound by acts of parliament in
England stated.   By William Molyneux. 1719. 12mo. **48 C**

The Celtic records of Ireland, an analysis of Dr. O'Donovan's
edition of The annals of the four masters.   Dublin, 1852.
8vo.   **97 I**

Chronicum Scotorum : a chronicle of Irish affairs from the
earliest times to 1135 and from 1141 to 1150.   Edited by
W. M. Hennessy.   1866.   8vo.   **102 C**

The English in Ireland in the eighteenth century.   By J. A.
Froude.   3 vols.   1887.   12mo.   **115 D**

An Essay on the population of Ireland.   By Rev. John
Howlett.   1786.   8vo.   **144 G**

Historic memoirs of Ireland, comprising secret records of the
national convention, the rebellion and the Union.   By Sir
Jonah Barrington.   2nd ed.   2 vols.   1833   4to.   **114 G**

Historical notes relating to Ireland, 1509–1625.   By F. S.
Thomas.   1856.   8vo.   **99 A**

Ireland before and after the Union with Great Britain.   By
R. M. Martin.   3rd ed.   1848.   8vo.   **95 E**

The Irish State Trial.   By Henry Crompton.   1881. [Pam-
phlets, vol. 34.]   **144 C**

A Letter to the Right Hon. Chichester Fortescue, M.P., on
the state of Ireland.   By John, Earl Russell.   4th ed. 1868.
[Pamphlets, vol. 34.]   **144 C**

Narratives illustrative of the contests in Ireland in 1641 and
1690.   Edited by T. C. Croker. [Camden Society, vol. 14]
1841.   8vo.   **85 A**

Records of Ireland, and their application to professional purposes.   By T. J. Beasley. 1842. [Lectures &c. Ireland.] **144 G**

A Repertory of inrolments on patent rolls of Chancery in
Ireland commencing with reign of King James I.   By J. C.
Erck.   Dublin, 1846.   8vo.   **99 A**

Reports of commissioners of national education in Ireland
from 1834 to 1848 inclusive.   Dublin, 1848.   8vo.   **95 E**

Short history of the Irish people down to date of plantation of

IRELAND, HISTORY OF—*continued.*

Ulster. By A. G. Richey. Edited by R. R. Kane. Dublin, 1887. 8vo.   115 C

The ultimate remedy for Ireland. [By Rowley Lascelles.] 1831. [Lectures &c. Ireland.]   144 G

The war of the Gaedhill with the Gaill, or the invasion of Ireland by the Danes and other Norsemen. Edited by J. H. Todd. 1867. 8vo.   102 C

The work of the Irish leagues. The speech of Sir Henry James, Q.C., M.P., replying in the Parnell commission inquiry. [1890.] 12mo.   115 D

See also CHRONOLOGY, CONSTITUTIONAL HISTORY, ENGLAND HISTORY OF, RECORD COMMISSION, RECORDS and STATE PAPERS.

[IRELAND, JOHN.]

Nuptiæ Sacræ ; or, an inquiry into the scriptural doctrine of Marriage and Divorce, addressed to the two Houses of parliament. 1821. [Jacob's Tracts, vol. 2.]   144 E

IRELAND, LANGUAGE OF.

Glossary of Irish and Irish-Latin words. See Tripartite life of S. Patrick, vol. 2, 1887, pp. 639–666.   102 I

Glossary of old Irish words. See Chronicum Scotorum, 1866, pp. 351–356.   102 C

See also Giraldus Cambrensis, vol. 5, 1867, pp. 413–435. 101 E

IRELAND, LAW OF.

History of land tenure in Ireland. By W. E. Montgomery. Cambridge, 1889. 8vo.   55 E

The Irish land law and land purchase acts 1881, 1885 and 1887. By R. R. Cherry. Dublin, 1888. 8vo.   55 E

The land law (Ireland) act 1881, and Landlord and tenant act 1870, with the rules to both acts. By George M'Dermot. 2nd ed. Dublin, 1881. 8vo.   55 E

The tenure of land in Ireland. By M. Longfield. See Systems of land tenure, 1881, pp. 1–92.   78 B

The new law of Compensation to tenants in Ireland. By Isaac Butt. Dublin, 1871. 8vo.   55 E

The Chancery (Ireland) act 1867 with the orders, schedules and tables of fees. Dublin, 1868. 8vo.   55 E

The landowner's and agent's practical guide. By Thomas de Moleyns. 5th ed. Dublin, 1866. 8vo.   55 E

IRELAND, Law of—*continued.*

Report of sub-committee of Incorporated Society of attorneys and solicitors of Ireland specially appointed to inquire into state of office for registry of deeds in Ireland. Dublin, 1862. [Pamphlets, vol. 16.] **144 B**

General orders of the equity side of the Court of Exchequer in Ireland. Dublin, 1844. 8vo. **55 E**

Remarks on the Limitation of Actions bill intended for Ireland; with short extracts from ancient records relating to advowsons of churches in Ireland. By J. F. Ferguson. Dublin, 1843. [Lectures &c. Ireland.] **144 G**

Comparative view of differences between English and Irish statute and common law. By W. T. Ayres. 2 vols. Dublin, 1780. 8vo. **170 G**

See also BEASLEY, T. J., DONNELL, R., HUTTON, H. D., PIKE, W. P. and STODDART, SIR J.

IRELAND, SAMUEL.

Picturesque views, with an historical account of the Inns of Court. 1800. 8vo. **91 D**

IRELAND, SIR THOMAS.

An Exact abridgment in English of the Eleven books of reports of Sir Edward Cook. Third impression. 1657, and 1666. 12mo. **48 B**

IRELAND, WILLIAM HENRY.

England's Topographer ; or, a new and complete history of the county of Kent. 4 vols. 1828–30. 8vo. **88 E**

IRISH CHANCERY REPORTS.

Reports of cases in the High Court of Chancery, Court of Appeal in Chancery, Rolls Court, the Landed Estates Court, and Court of Bankruptcy and Insolvency in Ireland, 1850–1866. 17 vols. Dublin, 1852–67. 8vo. **16 H I**

IRISH CIRCUIT REPORTS.

Reports of cases on six circuits in Ireland taken during the assizes 1841–1843. Dublin, 1843. 8vo. **15 E**

IRISH COMMON LAW REPORTS.

Reports of cases in the Courts of Queen's Bench, Common Pleas, Exchequer, Exchequer Chamber, and Court of Criminal Appeal, 1849–1866. 17 vols. Dublin, 1852–67. 8vo. **15 G–I**

IRISH EQUITY REPORTS.

Cases in the High Court of Chancery, the Rolls Court, and the Equity Exchequer, 1838–1850. 13 vols. Dublin, 1839–52. 8vo.   **16 G**

IRISH JURIST.

Irish Jurist. 1861–66. 5 vols. Dublin, 1862–66. 4to. **139 G**

IRISH LAW REPORTS.

Irish law reports in the court of Queen's Bench, Common Pleas and Exchequer of Pleas from 1838 to 1850. 13 vols. Dublin, 1839–52. 8vo.   **15 G**

IRISH LAW TIMES.

The Irish Law Times, and Solicitors' Journal, 1867–1889. 23 vols. Dublin, 1868–89. 4to.   **138 A–E**

IRISH RECORD PUBLICATIONS.

Ancient laws of Ireland. [Edited by W. Neilson Hancock, Rev. Thaddeus O'Mahony, and Alexander George Richey.] Vols. 1 to 4. Dublin, 1865–79. 8vo.   **99 A**

Vol. 1. Introduction to Senchus Mor, and . . . [the] law of distress.
2. Senchus Mor: pt. 2. Law of distress (completed); laws of hostage-sureties, fosterage, saer-stock tenure, daer-stock tenure, and of social connexions.
3. Senchus Mor (conclusion); being the *. . . customary law, and the Book of Arcill.
4. 'Of taking lawful possession,' and certain other Brehon law tracts.

IRISH REPORTS.

The Irish Reports; containing reports of cases in the superior courts in Ireland. Common Law Series, 1867–1878. 10 vols. Dublin, 1868–78. 8vo.   **15 I**

The same. Equity Series, 1867–1878. 11 vols. Dublin, 1868–78. 8vo.   **16 I**

Digest of cases in the Superior Courts in Ireland, reported in the Irish Reports, from Hilary term, 1867, to Michaelmas term, 1877. Compiled by Wm. Green. Dublin, 1879. 8vo.   **17 I**

IRISH SOCIETY, THE.

Concise view of the origin of the honourable society of the governor and assistants of London of the new plantation in Ulster called The Irish Society. 1822. 8vo. **95 E**

The same. Another ed. 1832. 8vo.   **95 E**

IRISH SOCIETY, THE—*continued.*
Reports of the deputations to Ireland in the years 1815, 1825–1827, and 1832. 1815–32. 8vo.   **95 F**

IRON.
The invention of grooved rollers for manufacture of bar iron. By David Mushet. 1855. [Pamphlets, vol. 25.]   **144 B**
Observations shewing the real value of rolled iron for free trade. By R. Cort. 1860. [Pamphlets, vol. 14.]   **144 A**

IRVING, DAVID.
Introduction to study of Civil Law. 4th ed. 1837. 8vo. **63 F**

ISÆUS.
Speeches of Isæus in causes concerning law of succession to property at Athens. By Wm. Jones. 1779. 4to.   **83 J**

ISAMBERT, FRANÇOIS ANDRÉ.
Recueil Général des Anciennes Loix Françaises, depuis l'an 420 jusqu'à la Révolution de 1789 ; avec notes de concordance et table par MM. Jourdan, Decrusy, Isambert, Armet et Taillandier. 29 vols. Paris, 1822–33. 8vo.   **58 A**

ISLEWORTH, MIDDLESEX.
The history and antiquities of the parish of Isleworth. By G. J. Aungier. 1840. 8vo.   **89 D**
Istleworth-Syon's Peace, containing certain articles of agreement made between Algernoone, Earl of Northumberland, lord of the manor of Istleworth-Syon, and others of the one part and Sir Thomas Ingram and others copyhold tenants of the said manor of the other part. 1800. 8vo.   **89 D**

ISLINGTON, MIDDLESEX.
The history, topography and antiquities of the parish of St. Mary, Islington. By John Nelson. 1811. 4to.   **89 E**
An Inaugural address, delivered in the theatre of the Islington Literary and Scientific Society, on the opening of the new building. Thursday, Nov. 16, 1837. By J. J. J. Sudlow. 1837. [Pamphlets, vol. 5.]   **144 A**

ITALY.
The case of the war in Italy stated. 1718. [Grimaldi's Tracts, vol. 2.]   **118 B**

ITALY—*continued.*

A Dissertation on statutes of cities of Italy, and a translation of pleading of Prospero Farinacio in defence of Beatrice Cenci and her relatives. By G. Bowyer. 1838. 8vo. **83 J**

Germany and Italy. 2nd enlarged ed. translated from the German. 1859. [Pamphlets, vol. 10.] **144 A**

International Exhibition, 1862. Kingdom of Italy. Official descriptive catalogue. 1862. 8vo. **142 C**

The Monethly Account, Number 4, January 1688 or 1689. [Tracts, 1688–9.] [Eleven articles describing Italy and other European countries and cities.] **118 E**

Report to the Master of the Rolls upon the documents in the archives and public libraries of Venice. 1866. 8vo. **97 H**

'Villa Volpicelli,' or the shut school. By H. B. Hamilton. 1853. [Pamphlets, vol. 23.] **144 B**

ITALY, LANGUAGE OF.

New dictionary of the Italian and English languages. By J. Davenport and G. Comelati. 2 vols. 1860. 8vo. **123 B**

New pocket dictionary of the Italian and English languages. With a compendious elementary Italian grammar. By C. Graglia. 15th ed. by C. I. 1829. 12mo. **123 B**

See also MINSHEU, J.

ITALY, LAW OF.

Rivista penale di dottrina, legislazione e giurisprudenza. Diretta dall' avvocato Luigi Lucchini. 8 vols. Padova, 1874–78. 8vo. **56 E**

Giornale del Foro, pubblicazione Romana di giurisprudenza teorico-pratica. 2 vols. Roma, 1873–75. 8vo. **56 C**

Dei Diritti degli Autori di opere dell' ingegno, studi teorico-pratici sulla legislazione Italiana in rapporto colle leggi delle altre nazioni. Dell' avvocato Moise Amar. Torino, 1874. 8vo. **56 E**

Annali della giurisprudenza Italiana. Raccolta generale delle decisioni delle corti di cassazione e d' appello &c. 8 vols. in 10. Firenze, 1867–74. 8vo. **56 G**

Raccolta ufficiale delle leggi e dei decreti del regno d' Italia. 28 vols. 1861–70. Supplementare. 9 vols. 1861–69. 37 vols. Torino, 1861–70. 8vo. **56 D E**

Collezione delle sentenze della Corte di Cassazione del regno, 1860–70. 11 vols. Genova, 1860–70. 4to. **56 F**

Annali di giurisprudenza. Raccolta di decisioni della corte

ITALY, Law of—*continued.*

suprema di cassazione, delle corti regie di Firenze e di Lucca e dei tribunali di prima istanza, per opera di una società di giureconsulti Toscani. 6 vols. 1860–65. 8vo.   56 F

Sullo studio giuridico prelezione. Da B. C. Zappala. Catania, 1863. 8vo.   56 C

Autorità degl' Italiani su la scienza del diritto. Da B. C. Zappalà. Catania, 1862. 8vo.   56 C

Raccolta degli atti del governo della luogotenenza generale del re in Sicilia. Palermo, 1862. 8vo.   56 C

Raccolta degli atti del governo dittatoriale e prodittatoriale in Sicilia (1860). Palermo, 1861. 8vo.   56 C

Raccolta degli atti del governo di sua maestà il Re di Sardegna 1828, 1829, 1830, 1859 and 1860. 11 vols. Torino, 1846–60. 8vo.   56 C

Raccolta di regi editti, proclami, manifesti ed altri provvedimenti de' magistrati ed uffizi. 37 vols. in 14. [vols. 29 and 30 missing.] Torino, 1814–37. 8vo.   56 A

The same. Serie V. 22 vols. [vol. 1. missing.] Torino, 1838–58. 8vo.   56 B

Edict of the grand duke of Tuscany for the reform of criminal law in his dominions. Warrington, 1789. 8vo.   56 C

See also Codes. ·

ITALY, Literature of.

Amicis, Edmondo de. Novelle. Edited by Rev. A. C. Clapin. 1890. 12mo.   83 B

Carcano, Giulio. Memorie d' un Fanciullo, Il cappellano della rovella. Edited by Rev. A. C. Clapin. 1890. 12mo. 83 B

Goldoni, Carlo. Un Curioso Accidente. Edited by Rev. A. C. Clapin. 1890. 12mo.   83 B

Maffei, Scipione. Merope. Edited by Rev. A. C. Clapin. 1890. 12mo.   83 B

IVATTS, Edmund B.

Carriers' Law, relating to goods and passenger traffic on railways, canals and steam ships. 1883. 8vo.   9 B

IVEY, George James.

The Club directory, a general guide to the London and county clubs, and those of Scotland, Ireland and British colonial possessions. 1879. 8vo.   134 I

The same. 2nd ed. 1880. 8vo.   Hall

IZACKE, RICHARD.

An Alphabetical register of divers persons who have given towards the relief of the poor of the county of Devon and city of Exon. 1736. 8vo. **87 C**

Remarkable antiquities of the city of Exeter. 3rd ed. continued to 1724, by Samuel Izacke. 1734. 8vo. **87 C**

JACOB, REV. ALEXANDER.

Complete English peerage, to which is prefixed A succinct history of the house of Brunswic Brandenburgh, Saxe-Gotha and Mecklenburgh. 2 vols. 1766. folio. **125 H**

JACOB, EDWARD, F.S.A.

History of town and port of Faversham. 1774. 8vo.. **88 D**

JACOB, EDWARD, BARRISTER-AT-LAW.

Reports of cases in the court of Chancery during the time of Lord Chancellor Eldon, 1821–1822. 1 vol. 1828. 8vo. **2 H**

JACOB, EDWARD and JOHN WALKER.

Reports of cases in court of Chancery during time of Lord Chancellor Eldon, 1819–1821. 2 vols. 1821–23. 8vo. **2 I**

JACOB, GILES.

City liberties ; or, the rights and privileges of freemen of London. 1732. 8vo. **92 B**

Common Law common-plac'd. 2nd ed. 1733. folio. **156 C**

The compleat Court-Keeper, or land-steward's assistant. 3rd ed. 1724. 12mo. **165 C**

The same. 6th ed. 1764. 12mo. **165 C**

The same. 7th ed. 1781. 12mo. **165 C**

The same. 8th ed. by A Barrister. 1819. 12mo. **165 C**

The complete Parish Officer. 13th ed. 1754. 8vo. **173 B**

Every man his own lawyer ; or, a summary of the laws of England. 10th ed. by J. R. 1788. 8vo. **170 G**

Lex Mercatoria ; or, the merchant's companion, containing all the laws and statutes relating to merchandize. 1718. 8vo. **172 F**

A New law dictionary. 4th ed. 1739. folio. **122 G**

The same. 10th ed. corrected and enlarged by J. Morgan 1782. folio. **122 G**

The statute law common-plac'd ; or, a general table to the Statutes. 5th ed. 1748. 12mo. **176 C**

JAEGER, Gustav.

Essays on health culture. Translated and edited by L. R. S. Tomalin. Revised ed. 1887. 8vo. **78 A**

JAGOE, John.

Index to reported cases not over-ruled or obsolete, and to statutes, rules and orders relating to principles, pleading and practice of courts of equity in England and Ireland, from the earliest time to 1850. 2 vols. 1851. 8vo. **63 B**

JAMAICA.

Acts of Assembly passed in the island of Jamaica, 1681–1754. 1756. folio. **35 G**

Acts of Assembly passed in the island of Jamaica, 1681–1769. 2 vols. in 1. Kingston, 1787. folio. **35 G**

Acts of Assembly passed in the island of Jamaica, 1770–1788. 2 vols. Kingston, 1786–89. 4to. **36 A**

The continuation of the laws of Jamaica, 1695. 1698. folio. **35 G**

A Digest of the laws of Jamaica, 1681–1868. By James Minot. 2 vols. Jamaica, 1865–69. 8vo. **36 A**

The handbook of Jamaica for 1882. Compiled by A. C. Sinclair and L. R. Fyfe. Kingston, 1882. 8vo. **84 B**

The history of Jamaica. [By Edward Long.] 3 vols. 1774. 4to. **84 E**

The laws of Jamaica, 1857–1889. 12 vols. Kingston, 1857–89. 4to. **36 A**

The laws of Jamaica, 1683 and 1684 ; to which is added A short account of the island. By F. H. 2 vols. in 1. 1683–84. 12mo. **55 D**

Slave law of Jamaica with proceedings and documents relative thereto. 1828. 8vo. **55 D**

The statutes and laws of the Island of Jamaica. Revised ed. by Hon. C. Ribton Curran. 12 vols. 1889. 4to. **36 A**

JAMES I., King of England.

A Booke of Proclamations published since the beginning of His Majesty's reigne. 1609. folio. **49 H**

A Compleat history of the lives and reigns of Mary Queen of Scotland, and of James the Sixth, King of Scotland. By William Sanderson. 1656. 4to. **114 E**

Correspondence of King James VI. of Scotland with Sir Robert Cecil and others in England, during the reign of

JAMES I., KING OF ENGLAND—*continued.*

Queen Elizabeth. Edited by J. Bruce. [Camden Society, vol. 78.] 1861. 8vo. **85 B**

The Fortescue papers, consisting chiefly of letters relating to state affairs. Collected by John Packer. Edited by S. R. Gardiner. [Camden Society, n.s. vol. 1.] 1871. 8vo. **85 C**

Historical collections of private passages of state, weighty matters in law and remarkable proceedings, 1618 to 1640. By John Rushworth. 2 vols. 1682–80. folio. **115 I**

Inquiry into the genuineness of a letter dated February 3rd, 1613, and signed 'Mary Magdeline Davers.' [Camden Society, vol. 87.] 1864. 8vo. **85 C**

Letters and other documents illustrating the relations between England and Germany at the commencement of the thirty years' war. Edited by S. R. Gardiner. [Camden Society, vols. 90 and 98.] 2 vols. 1865–68. 8vo. **85 C**

Letters of Queen Elizabeth and King James VI. of Scotland. Edited by J. Bruce. [Camden Society, vol. 46.] 1849. 8vo. **85 B**

Parliamentary debates in 1610. Edited from the notes of A member of the House of Commons. By S. R. Gardiner. [Camden Society, vol. 81.] 1862. 8vo. **85 C**

The progresses, processions and magnificent festivities of James the First. By John Nichols. 4 vols. 1828. 4to. **114 E**

See also EGERTON, LORD F., ELSYNGE, H., FRANCISCO, F. and STATE PAPERS.

JAMES II., KING OF ENGLAND.

Bishop Burnet's History of his own time, from the restoration of Charles II. to the peace of Utrecht in the reign of Queen Anne. 4 vols. 1818. 8vo. **115 F**

The Crisis; or, a discourse representing, from the most authentick records, the just causes of the late happy Revolution. With some seasonable remarks on the danger of a Popish Successor. By Richard Steele. 1714. 8vo. **49 F**

The debate between the Houses of Lords and Commons at the conference held 1688, relating to the word Abdicated and the vacancy of the throne. 1695. 12mo. **48 C**

An Enquiry into the present state of affairs, and in particular whether we owe allegiance to the king in these circumstances? [By G. Burnet.] 1689. 8vo. [Tracts, 1688–9.] **118 E**

An Exact abridgment of all the trials which have been published since the year 1678 relating to the Popish and pretended Protestant plots. By P. N. 1690. 12mo. **118 B**

JAMES II., KING OF ENGLAND—*continued.*

Extracts from the life of James II. as written by himself. See
J. Macpherson's Secret history of Great Britain, 2nd ed. 1776,
vol. 1, pp. 16–262.   114 F

The history of England from the accession of James the Second.
By Lord Macaulay. 5 vols. 1860–61. 8vo.   115 G

A Letter to a member of the Convention. [By William
Sherlock.] [n.d.] ; and An Answer of a Letter to a member
of the Convention. [n.d.] [Tracts, 1688–9.]   118 E

Magdalen college and King James II. 1686–1688. A series
of documents collected and edited by The Rev. J. R.
Bloxam, D.D. [Oxford Historical Society, vol. 6.] Oxford,
1886. 8vo.   85 F

Memoirs of Great Britain and Ireland from dissolution of
last parliament of Charles II. until the sea battle of La
Hogue. By Sir John Dalrymple. 2nd ed. 2 vols. 1771–
73. 4to.   114 F

Moneys received and paid for secret services of Charles II.
and James II. 1679 to 1688. Edited by J. Y. Akerman.
[Camden Society, vol. 52.] 1851. 8vo.   85 B

Occasional discourses on the affairs of the two last reigns.
See Lord Delamer's Works. 1694. 8vo.   83 A

A Representation of the threatening dangers impending over
Protestants in Great Britain before the coming of the Prince
of Orange. [By R. Ferguson.] 1689. [Tracts, 1688–9.] 118 E

Three Letters :   I. A Letter from a Jesuit at Liege to a Jesuit
at Fribourg giving an account of the happy progress of
religion in England.   II. A Letter from the Reverend
Father Petre, Jesuit, written to the Reverend Father la Chese
touching the present affairs of England.   III. The Answer
of the Reverend Father la Chese to a Letter of the Reverend
Father Petre upon the method or rule he must observe with
His Majesty for the conversion of his Protestant subjects.
1688. [Tracts, 1688–9.]   118 E

JAMES FREDERICK EDWARD, THE PRETENDER.

What if this marriage should prove true ? or what if it should
not ? In a Dialogue between Whig and Tory. 1718.
[Grimaldi's Tracts, vol. 2.]   118 B

JAMES, SIR HENRY.

Facsimile of part of Domesday book relating to Cornwall.
Southampton, 1861. folio.   86 H

Facsimiles of national manuscripts from William the Con-

JAMES, SIR HENRY—*continued.*

queror to Queen Anne. 4 vols. Southampton, 1865–68.
folio. **99 E**

Facsimiles of national manuscripts of Scotland. Part 1.
Southampton, 1867. folio. **100 H**

JAMES, SIR HENRY, Q.C. M.P.

The work of the Irish leagues. The speech of Sir Henry
James replying in the Parnell commission inquiry. [1890.]
12mo. **115 D**

JAMES, JAMES HENRY.

On the right and cost of redeeming property mortgaged to
benefit building societies and freehold land societies. 1854.
12mo. **161 A**

Redemption of mortgages in building societies. The judgment of the Lord Chancellor considered in the suit of
Fleming *v.* Self, with full report.' 1855. 12mo. **161 A**

What should be the price of bread ? and how can it be regulated ? 1855. [Pamphlets, vol. 10.] **144 A**

JAMES, PROSSER.

Vichy and its therapeutical resources. 1883. 8vo. **84 A**

JAMES, WILLIAM.

The Denford question with the law upon it, and the decision
of the court of King's Bench. Reading, 1813. 8vo. **163 G**

JAMES, WILLIAM ROBERTS.

Charters and other documents relating to the King's town
and parish of Maidstone, with notes. 1825. 8vo. **88 C**

JAMIESON, JOHN.

Jamieson's Dictionary of the Scottish language abridged by
John Johnston. A new ed. by John Longmuir. Edinburgh,
1867. 8vo. **123 B**

JANE, QUEEN OF ENGLAND.

The chronicle of Queen Jane and of two years of Queen Mary,
and especially of the rebellion of Sir Thomas Wyat. Written by a resident in the Tower of London. Edited by
J. G. Nichols. [Camden Society, vol. 48.] 1850. 8vo. **85 B**

JANSONIUS, JOANNES.
Novus Atlas, sive theatrum orbis terrarum in quo tabulæ et
descriptiones omnium regionum totius universi exhibentur.
6 vols. Amstelodami, 1656–58. folio. **84 H**

JARDINE, DAVID.
Criminal Trials. 2 vols. 1832–35. 12mo. **51 D**
General index to the collection of State Trials compiled by
T. B. Howell and T. J. Howell. 1828. 8vo. **50 J**
A Reading on the use of Torture in the criminal law of
England previously to the Commonwealth. 1837. 8vo. **78 C**

JARMAN, HENRY.
New practice of the Court of Chancery. 1853. 12mo. **161 E**
The same. 3rd ed. 1864. 12mo. **161 E**

JARMAN, THOMAS.
A Treatise on Wills. 2 vols. 1844. 8vo. **178 B**
The same. 2nd ed. by E. P. Wolstenholme and S. Vincent.
2 vols. 1855. 8vo. **178 B**
The same. 3rd ed. by E. P. Wolstenholme and S. Vincent.
2 vols. 1861. 8vo. **53 I**
The same. 4th ed. by S. Vincent. 2 vols. 1881. 8vo. **13 I**
See also BYTHEWOOD, W. M., HAYES, W. and POWELL, J. J.

JAY, WILLIAM.
Recollections of William Jay, of Bath; with occasional
glances at some of his contemporaries and friends. By
Cyrus Jay. 1859. 8vo. **79 B**

JEAFFRESON, JOHN CORDY.
A Book about lawyers. 2nd ed. 2 vols. 1867. 8vo. **79 G**

JEAKE, SAMUEL.
Charters of the Cinque Ports, two ancient towns and their
members. Translated into English. 1728. folio. **89 G**
The great and ancient charter of the Cinque Ports. [Trans-
lated into English by S. Jeake.] 1682. 12mo. **88 D**

JEBB, RICHARD.
Report of the case of the Rt. Rev. R. D. Hampden, D.D.,
in Hereford cathedral, the Ecclesiastical courts and the
Queen's Bench. 1849. 8vo. **50 A**

JEBB, ROBERT.
Cases chiefly relating to the criminal and presentment law decided by the twelve judges of Ireland, 1822–1840. Dublin, 1841. 8vo. **15 E**

JEBB, ROBERT and RICHARD BOURKE.
Reports of cases in the court of Queen's Bench in Ireland, 1841–1842. Dublin, 1843. 8vo. **15 E**

JEBB, ROBERT and ARTHUR R. SYMES.
Reports of cases in the courts of Queen's Bench and Exchequer chamber in Ireland, 1838–1841. 2 vols. 1840–1842. 8vo. **15 E**

JEFFERSON, SAMUEL.
History and antiquities of Carlisle. Carlisle, 1838. 4to. **87 G**

JENCKEN, HENRY DIEDRICH.
Compendium of the laws on bills of exchange, promissory notes, cheques, and other commercial negotiable instruments of England, Germany and France. 1880. 8vo. **9 I**
The laws of negotiable securities. 1880. 8vo. **11 A**

JENKINS, ALEXANDER.
The history and description of the city of Exeter and its environs. Exeter, 1806. 8vo. **87 C**

JENKINS, DAVID.
Eight centuries of reports ; or, eight hundred cases solemnly adjudged in the Exchequer chamber, or upon writs of error. 2nd ed. by A Gentleman of the Middle Temple. 1734. folio. **74 E**
The works of that grave and learned lawyer, Judge Jenkins, prisoner in Newgate, upon divers statutes concerning the liberty of the subject. 1648. 12mo. **48 A**

JENKINS, EDWARD and JOHN RAYMOND.
On Building contracts. A legal handbook for architects, builders and building owners. 1873. 8vo. **52 A**

JENKINS, SIR LEOLINE.
The life of Sir Leoline Jenkins, judge of the high court of Admiralty. By William Wynne. 2 vols. 1724. folio. **79 I**

JEPSON, ARTHUR.

The lands clauses consolidation acts. 1880. 8vo.   10 E

JEREMY, GEORGE.

A Treatise on the Equity jurisdiction of the high Court of
Chancery. 1828. 8vo.   167 C

JEREMY, HENRY.

Analytical digest of reports of cases decided in courts of
Common Law and Equity, of Appeal and Nisi Prius, and
in the Ecclesiastical Courts, 1838–1849. 4 vols. 1839–50.
8vo.   63 C

See also PRATT, W. T.

JERSEY. See CHANNEL ISLANDS.

JERUSALEM.

The fall of Jerusalem. By Rev. H. H. Milman. New ed.
1865. 8vo.   83 A
Jerusalem explored, being a description of the ancient and
modern city. By E. Pierotti. Translated by T. G. Bonney.
vol. 1, text. vol. 2, plates. 2 vols. 1864. folio.   77 H
The Temple at Jerusalem, a paper read before Jews' College
Literary Society. By M. N. Adler. 1887. 8vo.   84 B

JERVIS, SIR JOHN.

All the new rules, from 1 Will. IV. to 2 Vict. ; and an appen-
dix of statutes of general reference in relation to pleading
and practice. 4th ed. 1839. 8vo.   163 B
A Practical treatise on the office and duties of Coroners.
1829. 12mo.   164 G
The same. 2nd ed. by W. N. Welsby. 1854. 12mo. 164 G
The same. 3rd ed. by C. W. Lovesy. 1866. 12mo. 164 G
The same. 4th ed. by R. E. Melsheimer. 1880. 12mo. 52 D
The same. 5th ed. by R. E. Melsheimer. 1888. 12mo. 9 F
See also GLEN, W. C.

JEUDWINE, JOHN WYNNE.

Agricultural holdings act 1883. 2nd ed. 1883. 8vo. 9 A
The Time Tables for the high court of justice and for the
county court. 2nd ed. 1884. 8vo.   169 G

JEVONS, William Stanley.
Pure logic ; or, the logic of quality apart from quantity ; with remarks on Boole's system, and on the relation of logic and mathematics. 1864. 12mo. **78 A**

JEWEL, Right Rev. John.
An Apology of private mass. An anonymous Popish treatise against Bishop Jewel. Edited by Rev. Wm. Goode. Cambridge, 1850. 12mo. **77 D**
The works of John Jewel, bishop of Salisbury. Edited by Rev. John Ayre. 4 vols. Cambridge, 1845–50. 8vo. **77 E**

JEWITT, ARTHUR.
The history of Buxton, and visitor's guide to the curiosities of The Peak. 1811. 8vo. **87 A**

JEWITT, Llewellynn.
A History of Plymouth. 1873. 4to. **87 D**

JEWS, The.
The case of David Salomons, Esq., being his address to the court of aldermen on applying for admission as alderman of the Ward of Portsoken, October 15, 1844. Revised by himself. 1844. [Pamphlets, vol. 23.] **144 B**
History of the establishment and residence of the Jews in England, with an enquiry into their civil disabilities. By J. E. Blunt. 1830. [Jacob's Tracts, vol. 7.] **144 E**
Progress of Jewish emancipation since 1829. 1848. [Pamphlets, vol. 6.] **144 A**
A Succinct account of the civil regulations comprised in the Jewish law. See B. Barrett's Code Napoléon, vol. 1, 1811, pp. viii–xix. **55 C**
The works of Flavius Josephus, the learned and authentic Jewish historian. Translated by William Whiston. 1844. 8vo. **113 E**
See also Moses.

JOANNES DE OXENEDES.
Chronica. Edited by Sir H. Ellis. 1859. 8vo. **101 C**

JOANNES HAGUSTALDENSIS.
Historia de gestis regum Anglorum. See Historiæ Anglicanæ Scriptores X., vol. 1, 1652, pp. 258–283. **114 H**

JOCELIN DE BRAKELOND.

Chronica Jocelini de Brakelonda, de rebus gestis Samsonis, Abbatis monasterii Sancti Edmundi. Nunc primum typis mandata curante J. G. Rokewode. [Camden Society, vol. 13.] 1840. 8vo. 85 A

JOEL, JONATHAN EDMONDSON.

Manual of bankruptcy and bills of sale law. 1884. 8vo. 160 F

JOEL, LEWIS.

A Consul's manual and shipowner's and shipmaster's practical guide in their transactions abroad. 1879. 8vo. 52 C

JOHN, KING OF ENGLAND.

A Description of the Patent Rolls in the Tower of London; with an itinerary of King John. By T. D. Hardy. 1835. 8vo. 98 A

Kynge Johan, a play in two parts. By John Bale. Edited by J. P. Collier. [Camden Society, vol. 2.] 1838. 8vo. 85 A

Rotuli de Liberate ac de Misis et Præstitis regnante Johanne. Accurante T. D. Hardy. 1844. 8vo. 98 A

Rotulus Cancellarii, vel antigraphum magni rotuli pipæ de tertio anno regni regis Johannis. [Edited by J. Hunter.] 1833. 8vo. 99 A

See also FINE ROLLS, LINGARD, REV. J., MARTYN, W. and TURNER, S.

JOHNES, ARTHUR JAMES.

Consequences of the government measures now pending on Bankruptcy and imprisonment for debt. 1869. With postscript. [Pamphlets, vol. 30.] 144 B

Observations on the impracticable character of the provisions of the act for conferring Admiralty jurisdiction on the County Courts. 1868. [Pamphlets, vol. 32.] 144 C

Remarks on the late report from select committee on Bankruptcy act. Carnarvon, 1866. [Pamphlets, vol. 30.] 144 B

Should law of imprisonment for debt in superior courts be abolished or amended ? 1868. [Pamphlets, vol. 34.] 144 C

Suggestions for a reform of the Court of Chancery, by a union of the jurisdictions of Equity and Law. 1834. 8vo. 161 C

JOHNSON, ANDREW.

Trial of A. Johnson before the senate of the United States on impeachment for high crimes and misdemeanors. 3 vols. Washington, 1868. 8vo. 59 E

JOHNSON, Cuthbert William.
The life of Sir Edward Coke, with memoirs of his contemporaries. 2 vols. 1837. 8vo. **80 D**

JOHNSON, Henry Robert Vaughan.
Reports of cases adjudged in the high Court of Chancery, before Sir William Page Wood, 1858–1860. 1860. 8vo. **2 I**

JOHNSON, H. R. V. and George Wirgman HEMMING.
Reports of cases in the Court of Chancery, before Sir W. P. Wood. 1859–1862. 2 vols. 1861–63. 8vo. **2 I**

JOHNSON, James.
A View of the jurisprudence of the Isle of Man. Edinburgh, 1811. 8vo. **55 D**

JOHNSON, James and John Henry JOHNSON.
The Patentee's Manual, being a treatise on the law and practice of letters patent, especially intended for the use of patentees and inventors. 4th ed. 1879. 8vo. **173 E**
The same. 5th ed. 1884. 8vo. **11 B**

JOHNSON, John.
A Collection of the laws and canons of the Church of England from its first foundation to the reign of King Henry VIII. Translated into English. New ed. by John Baron. 2 vols. Oxford, 1850–51. 8vo. **77 C**

JOHNSON, Richard.
The ancient customs of the city of Hereford, with translations of the earlier city charters and grants. 1868. 8vo. **88 B**

JOHNSON, Rev. Samuel.
The works of the late Reverend Mr. Samuel Johnson. 2nd ed. 1713. folio. **77 H**

JOHNSON, Samuel, LL.D.
A Dictionary of the English language, with a history of the language and an English grammar. With corrections by Rev. J. H. Todd. 2nd ed. 3 vols. 1827. 4to. **123 D**
Plays of William Shakespeare, with corrections and illustrations of various commentators. 8 vols. 1768. 8vo. **83 G**

JOHNSON, SAMUEL, LL.D.—*continued.*
The Rambler, March 20, 1750, to March 14, 1752. 208 numbers. 4 vols. in 2. 1791. 8vo. **83 D**
The works of Samuel Johnson, LL.D. 11 vols. Oxford, 1825. 8vo. **83 E**

JOHNSON, WILLIAM.
Reports of cases adjudged in the Court of Chancery of New York, 1814–1823. 7 vols. Albany, 1816–24. 8vo. **57 A**

JOHNSTON, ALEXANDER KEITH.
Dictionary of geography, descriptive, physical, statistical and historical. 2nd ed. 1855. 8vo. **84 G**
The same. New ed. 1882. 8vo. **Hall**

JOHNSTON, GEORGE.
Proceedings of a general court martial, held at Chelsea Hospital, May and June 1811, for the trial of Lieut.-Col. George Johnston, on a charge of mutiny exhibited against him for deposing William Bligh, Captain General and Governor of New South Wales. 1811. 8vo. **50 B**

JOHNSTONE, REV. JAMES.
Anecdotes of Olave the Black, King of Man ; with XVIII Eulogies on Haco, King of Norway, by Snorro Sturlson, poet to that monarch. 1780. 12mo. **118 A**

JOINT OWNERSHIP.
The law of joint ownership and partition of real estate. By E. J. Foster. 1878. 8vo. **13 B**

JOLLIE, F.
Jollie's Cumberland guide and directory. Carlisle, 1811. 8vo. **87 A**

JOLLIVET, ADOLPHE.
Examen du système électoral Anglais, depuis l'acte de réforme, comparé au système électoral Français. 1835. 12mo. **166 D**

JONES, CHARLES JAMES.
On the collection and recovery of Rent-Charge. 2nd ed. 1849. 12mo. **53 F**

[JONES, DAVID.]

The history of the most serene house of Brunswick-Lunenburgh in all the branches thereof from its origin to the
death of Queen Anne. 1715. 8vo. **79 B**

JONES, EDWARD.

Index to records called the Originalia and Memoranda on
the lord treasurer's remembrancer's side of the Exchequer
2 vols. 1795. folio. **98 E**

JONES, EDWARD C.

Reports of cases decided in the Court of Common Pleas of
Upper Canada, 1850–1862. 11 vols. Toronto, 1852–62.
8vo. **60 D E**

JONES, FREDERICK CONINGESBY.

Jones's Attorney's and Solicitor's new pocket book and conveyancer's assistant. 6th ed. by Thomas Coventry. 2 vols.
1826. 12mo. **164 D**
The same. 7th ed. by Rolla Rouse. 2 vols. 1850. 8vo. **13 G**

JONES, HERBERT GEORGE.

The Court of Exchequer and the county courts. A letter to
Lord Chelmsford on the late extraordinary judgment of the
Court of Exchequer in the case of Furber v. Sturmey. 1858.
[Pamphlets, vol. 10.] **144 A**

JONES, INIGO.

Life of Inigo Jones. See J. P. Malcolm's Lives of Topo-
graphers and Antiquaries. 1815. 4to. **79 H**
The most notable antiquity of Great Britain, vulgarly called
Stone-Heng, restored. 1725. folio. **95 G**

JONES, JOHN.

De libellis famosis ; or, the law of libels. 1812. 8vo. **172 A**
The history of Wales. 1824. 8vo. **94 E**

JONES, JOHN WINTER.

A Translation of all the Greek, Latin, Italian and French
quotations which occur in Blackstone's Commentaries on
the laws of England. 1823. 8vo. **166 F**

JONES, LEONARD AUGUSTUS.
Index to legal periodical literature. Boston, 1888. 8vo. **82 F**
A Treatise on the law of Mortgages of real property. 2 vols.
Boston, 1878. 8vo. **59 G**

JONES, THEOPHILUS.
A History of the county of Brecknock. 2 vols. Brecknock,
1805–9. 4to. **95 G**

JONES, SIR THOMAS.
The reports of several special cases adjudged in the Courts of
King's Bench and Common Pleas at Westminster in the
reign of King Charles II. 2nd ed. 1729. folio. **74 D**

JONES, THOMAS.
Reports of cases in the court of Exchequer in Ireland, 1834–
38. 2 vols. · Dublin, 1838–47. 8vo. **15 E**

JONES, THOMAS and HENRY CAREY.
Reports of cases in the court of Exchequer in Ireland, 1838–
39. Dublin, 1839. 8vo. **15 E**

JONES, THOMAS and EDMOND DIGGES LA TOUCHE.
Reports of cases in the high court of Chancery, 1844–46.
3 vols. Dublin, 1846–49. 8vo. **15 E**

JONES, SIR WILLIAM, M.P.
Les reports de divers special cases cy bien in le court de
banck le roy, come le common-banck in Angleterre, 1620–
1641. 1675. folio. **74 D**

JONES, SIR WILLIAM, JUDGE OF COURT OF BENGAL.
An Essay on the law of Bailments. 1781. 8vo. **160 C**
The same. 3rd ed. by Wm. Nichols. 1823. 8vo. **160 C**
The same. 4th ed. by W. Theobald. 1833. 8vo. **9 A**
Institutes of Hindu law verbally translated from the original
Sanscrit. Calcutta, 1796. 8vo. **38 B**
The same. 3rd ed. by S. G. Grady. 1869. 8vo. **38 B**
The speeches of Isæus in causes concerning the law of suc-
cession to property at Athens, with a prefatory discourse,
notes, and a commentary. 1779. 4to. **83 J**

JONES, WILLIAM HANBURY.
The law of Uses. 1862. 8vo. **176 G**

JOSEPHUS, FLAVIUS.
Works. Translated by W. Whiston. 1844. 8vo. **113 E**

JOYCE, WILLIAM.
The law and practice of Injunctions in equity and at common law. 2 vols. 1872. 8vo. **10 C**

JUDGES' CHAMBERS. See CHAMBERS, JUDGES'.

JUDGES OF ENGLAND AND IRELAND.
Biographica Juridica. A biographical dictionary of the judges of England from the Conquest to the present time. By Edward Foss. 1870. 8vo. **80 E**

Chronicle of the law officers of Ireland from the earliest period, also a chronological table of the law officers from reign of Queen Elizabeth to present time, with an outline of legal history of Ireland. By C. J. Smyth. 1839. 8vo. **80 F**

The Grandeur of the Law. A list of members of the present House of Lords, whose ancestors have occupied the judicial seat in England. By Edward Foss. 1842. 4to. **80 E**

The judges of England, with sketches of their lives ; and miscellaneous notices connected with courts at Westminster from the time of the Conquest. By Edward Foss. 9 vols. 1848–64. 8vo. **80 E**

List of county court judges [1847–64]. [By Thomas Falconer.] 1865. 8vo. **80 F**

Lists, accounts and tables of fees of the officers and servants belonging to the Judges of the several courts in Westminster Hall and the circuits, the associates and clerks of assize ; presented to the House of Commons pursuant to their orders of 23 March 1729 and 4 March 1730, and A report from the Committee to whom the several lists were referred. 1730–32. folio. **118 G**

The lives of the chief justices of England from the Norman conquest till the death of Lord Tenterden. By John Lord Campbell. 3 vols. 1849–57. 8vo. **79 G**

Strictures on the lives and characters of the most eminent lawyers of the present day, including those of the lord chancellor and the twelve judges. [By Edward Wynne.] 1790. 8vo. **80 F**

JUDGES OF ENGLAND AND IRELAND—*continued.*
Table of the Judges of England, 1837–1887. Compiled by R. J. Block. 1887. 8vo.   **80 F**

Tabulæ Curiales ; or, tables of the superior courts of Westminster Hall, showing the judges who sat in them from 1066 to 1864. By Edward Foss. 1865. 8vo.   **80 E**

Triumphs of Justice over unjust judges. Originally printed in 1681 for Benjamin Harris, reprinted for J. J. Franklin. [1817.] 8vo.   **118 B**

See also CHANCELLORS, LORDS.

JUDGMENTS.
The law and procedure of summary judgment on specially indorsed writ under order xiv. By C. Cavanagh. 1887. 8vo.   **12 E**

On searches, containing a concise treatise on the law of judgments as affecting land. By H. W. Elphinstone and J. W. Clark. 1887. 8vo.   **13 H**

The practice on signing judgment. By H. H. Walker. 1879. 8vo.   **12 E**

Plans for recording judicial decisions. By Thomas De Meschin. 1864. [Pamphlets, vol. 25.]   **144 B**

The practice of registering judgments. By J. Pask. 1859. 8vo.   **13 B**

The law of judgments. By F. Prideaux. 4th ed. 1856. 8vo.   **13 B**

The science of Legal Judgment. By James Ram. 1834. 8vo.   **169 E**

A Second book of judgements in real, personal and mixt actions and upon the statute. By George Townesend. 1674. 12mo.   **49 E**

See also CHANCERY DECREES.

JUDICATURE, SUPREME COURT OF.
Student's Practice of the courts. By A. Gibson and R. M'Lean. 4th ed. by the authors and A. Weldon. 1889. 8vo.   **64 E**

Wilson's Practice of the Supreme Court of Judicature. 7th ed. by C. Burney, M. M. Mackenzie and C. A. White. 1888. 8vo.   **12 G**

A Manual of the practice of the Supreme Court of Judicature in the Queen's Bench and Chancery Divisions. By John Indermaur. 5th ed. 1888. 8vo.   **64 E**

JUDICATURE, SUPREME COURT OF—*continued.*

The Supreme Court of Judicature acts. By R. W. Andrews and A. B. Stoney. 4th ed. 1885. 8vo.   **12 G**

The Judicature acts and rules 1873–83. By W. E. Baxter. 5th ed. 1883, and Supplement 1884. 2 vols. 1883–84. 12mo.   **12 G**

Judicature acts 1873 and 1875. By J. M. Lely and W. D. I. Foulkes. 4th ed. 1883. 8vo.   **12 G**

Hints on Practice, or practical notes on the Judicature acts, orders, rules and regulations of the Supreme Court. By A. R. Whiteway. 2nd ed. 1883. 8vo.   **52 I**

See AYCKBOURN, H., BITTLESTON, A. H., BROWN, A., CHARLEY, W. T., PARKER, F. R. and ROGERS, A.

See also CHANCERY LAW AND PRACTICE, and COMMON LAW PRACTICE.

JUDICIAL SYSTEM.

An Exposition of our Judicial system and civil procedure as reconstructed under the judicature acts. By W. F. Finlason. 1877. 12mo.   **169 F**

Our Judicial system. A letter to the Lord High Chancellor on the proposed changes in the judicature of the country. By Sir A. E. Cockburn. 1870. [Pamphlets, vol. 34.]   **144 C**

Practical proposals for a thorough reform of our judicial system, and an entire reconstruction of the whole law. By An Outsider. [Sir J. N. Dickinson.] 1867, and Further Proposals. 1871. . 8vo.   **170 F**

Recent and future law reforms. Judicial procedure a single and inductive science. By E. W. F. [E. W. Field]. 1843. [Pamphlets, vol. 20.]   **144 B**

JUNIUS.

The trial of John Almon, bookseller, for selling Junius's Letter to the K——. 1770. [Tracts on libel, vol. 3.]   **144 F**

JUNIUS, FRANCISCUS.

Etymologicum Anglicanum, ex autographo descripsit et accessionibus permultis auctum edidit Edwardus Lye. Præmittuntur vita auctoris et grammatica Anglo-Saxonica. Oxonii, 1743. folio.   **123 G**

JUNNER, ROBERT GORDON.

Practice before railway commissioners. 1874. 8vo.   **12 A**

JUPP, EDWARD BASIL.
An Historical account of the Worshipful company of Carpenters of the City of London. 1848. 8vo.   89 E

JURIDICAL REVIEW.
The Juridical Review, a journal of legal and political science.
1889–1890. 2 vols. Edinburgh, 1889–90. 8vo.   131 H

JURIES.
An Appeal to the citizens of London against the alledged
lawful mode of packing special juries. By T. J. Wooler.
1817. [Pamphlets, vol. 27.]   144 B

The dark side of trial by jury. By Joseph Brown. 1859.
[Pamphlets, vol. 12.]   144 A

Debates in both Houses of Parliament on the bill for removing
doubts respecting the functions of juries in cases of libel.
1792. [Tracts on Libel, vol. 4.]   144 F

The elements of the art of packing as applied to special juries.
By Jeremy Bentham. 1821. 8vo.   78 C

The Englishman's right ; a dialogue between a barrister at
law and a juryman. By Sir John Hawles. 1764. [Tracts
on Libel, vol. 1.]   144 F

An Enquiry into the extent of the power of juries on trials of indictments or informations for publishing criminal writings or
libels. [By F. Maseres.] 1792. [Tracts on Libel, vol. 2.] 144 F

The grand-jury-man's oath and office explained. A dialogue
between a barrister at law and a grand-jury-man. 1680.
[Tracts on Libel, vol. 1.]   144 F

A Guide to English juries. 1682. 12mo.   49 A

History of trial by jury. By Wm. Forsyth. 1852. 8vo. 83 I

Is trial by jury worth keeping ? By Graham Willmore. 1850.
[Pamphlets, vol. 7.]   144 A

The juryman's guide. By Sir G. Stephen. 1845. 12mo. 52 I

Observations on the rights and duties of juries in trials for
libels. By J. Towers. 1784. [Tracts on Libel, vol. 2.] 144 F

Proposal for amending the law affecting juries and jurymen.
By Serjeant Pulling. 1865. [Pamphlets, vol. 35.]   144 C

The rights of juries vindicated. The speeches of the dean of
St. Asaph's counsel in the Court of King's Bench, Westminster, in shewing cause why a new trial should be granted.
1785. [Tracts on Libel, vol. 3.]   144 F

The security of Englishmen's lives, or the trust, power and
duty of grand juries of England explained. [By Lord
Somers.] A new ed. 1771. [Tracts on Libel, vol. 1.] 144 F

JURIES—*continued.*

Unanimity in trial by jury defended. By George Rochfort Clarke. 1859. [Pamphlets, vol. 12.] **144 A**

See also ASTRY, SIR J., CARY, H., DUNCOMBE, G. and ERLE, T. W.

JURISPRUDENCE.

The nature and value of Jurisprudence. By Chan-Toon. 2nd ed. 1889. 8vo. **63 G**

The elements of Jurisprudence. By T. E. Holland. 4th ed. Oxford, 1888. 8vo. **63 F**

Elements of Law considered with reference to principles of general jurisprudence. By William Markby. 3rd ed. Oxford, 1885. 8vo. **63 G**

Essays in Jurisprudence and Ethics. By Frederick Pollock. 1882. 8vo. **63 F**

Outlines of Jurisprudence. By B. R. Wise. Oxford, 1881. 12mo. **63 G**

Principles of Jurisprudence. By D. C. Heron. 1873. 8vo. **63 G**

An English code, its difficulties and the modes of overcoming them ; a practical application of the science of Jurisprudence. By Sheldon Amos. 1873. 8vo. **63 F**

A Systematic view of the science of Jurisprudence. By Sheldon Amos. 1872. 8vo. **63 F**

The institutes of Law : a treatise of the principles of Jurisprudence, as determined by Nature. By James Lorimore. Edinburgh, 1872. 8vo. **63 G**

On identity of method in the search for truth. Jurisprudence. By John Tozer. [n.d.] [Pamphlets, vol. 35.] **144 C**

The study of Jurisprudence. By R. M. Pankhurst. [n.d.] [Pamphlets, vol. 35.] **144 C**

Jurisprudence. By C. S. M. Phillipps. 1863. 8vo. **63 F**

The Province of Jurisprudence determined. By John Austin. 2nd ed. by Sarah Austin. 1861. 8vo. **63 F**

Lettres sur la cour de la Chancellerie et quelques points de la Jurisprudence Angloise. Par C. P. Cooper. 2nd ed. Paris, 1830. 8vo. **63 G**

A Treatise of Universal Jurisprudence. By J. P. Thomas. 2nd ed. 1829. 8vo. **63 G**

Elements of Jurisprudence treated of in the preliminary part of a course of lectures on the laws of England. [By Richard Wooddeson.] 1783. 4to. **63 F**

JURISPRUDENCE—*continued.*

Richardi Zouchei elementa Jurisprudentiæ, definitionibus, regulis et sententiis selectioribus juris civilis illustrata. Amstelodami, 1652. 12mo.   **48 A**

See also LAW.

JURIST.

The Jurist, containing reports of cases determined in law and in equity, 1837–1854. 18 vols. in 31. 1838–55. 4to. **67 A-E**

The same. New Series, 1855–1866. 12 vols. in 24. 1856–67. 4to.   **67 F-I**

The Jurist; or, quarterly journal of jurisprudence and legislation. 3 vols. 1827–32. 8vo.   **140 B**

JUSTICE.

Justice and its miscarriages, with observations upon the necessity of appointing a minister of justice. By John Turner. 1861. [Pamphlets, vol. 19.]   **144 B**

See also LASSERÉ, L. DE.

JUSTICE OF THE PEACE, THE.

The Justice of the Peace. 1837–1890. 54 vols. 1837–90. 4to.   **68 B-G**

Digest of cases reported during the years 1862 to 1882. Compiled by R. C. Glen. 1887. 4to.   **68 G**

JUSTICES OF THE PEACE.

The Justices' Manual; or, guide to the ordinary duties of a justice of the peace. By S. Stone. 25th ed. by G. B. Kennett. 1889. 12mo.   **12 C**

The Justices' Note-Book. By W. K. Wigram. 5th ed. by W. S. Shirley. 1888. 8vo.   **12 B**

The acts regulating duties of justices of the peace out of sessions with respect to indictable offences &c. known as Jervis's acts. By W. C. Glen. 6th ed. by A. H. Bodkin and E. G. Douglas. 1887. 12mo.   **12 C**

Stone's practice for justices of the peace, justices' clerks and solicitors at petty and special sessions. 9th ed. by W. H. Macnamara. 1882. 8vo.   **12 B**

Justice of the peace and parish officer. By R. Burn. 30th ed. by J. B. Maule. 5 vols. in 10. 1869. 8vo.   **12 A B**

Justice of the peace and parish officer. By J. F. Archbold. 4 vols. 1859–55. 12mo.   **170 B**

JUSTICES OF THE PEACE—*continued.*

The defects in general and statute law which require revision of the legislature, particularly such as relate to the office of justice of peace. By I. Espinasse. 1827. [Jacob's Tracts, vol. 5.]   **144 E**

The law of a Justice of Peace and parish officer. By John lord viscount Dudley and Ward, and T. Cunningham. 3 vols. 1769. 4to.   **156 B**

The Justice's Case law, being a concise abridgment of all the cases of Crown law relating to Justices of peace digested. 1731. 12mo.   **169 G**

A Catalogue of the names of all His Majesties Justices of the Peace in commission in the several counties throughout England and Wales. Carefully collected by S. N., Esquire. 1680. 4to.   **78 G**

The complete justice. 1668. 12mo.   **48 A**

The office of a justice of peace. 1662. 12mo.   **48 A**

A Manuall : or, analecta, being a compendious collection out of such as have treated of the office of justices of the peace. 1642. 12mo.   **48 A**

See also ARNOLD, T. J., BOYD, R., BRIDGES, W. T., CALDE-COTT, T., DALTON, M., HIGGS, J., HORNE, A., SHEPPARD, W., WILLIAMS, T. W., WINGATE, E. and YOUNG, W.

JUSTINIAN.

Analysis of M. Ortolan's Institutes of Justinian, including the history and generalisation of Roman law. By T. L. Mears. 1876. 12mo.   **63 E**

Bartoli de Saxo Ferrato Lectura in Infortiatum. [vol. 2 of Justinian's Pandects.] Venetiis, 1471. folio.   **118 G**

Codicis Dn. Justiniani Repetitæ Prelectiones Libri XII. Accursii commentariis, et multorum veterum ac recentiorum jurisprudentum maxime Antonii Contii ; accesserunt his Chronici Canones . . . collecti et digesti, eodem Antonio Contio auctore. Parisiis, 1576. folio.

The four books of Justinian's Institutions, translated into English with notes. By George Harris. 3rd ed. Oxford, 1811. 4to.   **48 G**

The Institutes of Justinian, edited as a recension of the institutes of Gaius. By T. E. Holland. 2nd ed. Oxford, 1881. 12mo.   **63 E**

The Institutes of Justinian, translated in English. By J. B. Moyle. 2nd ed. Oxford, 1889. 8vo.   **63 E**

JUSTINIAN—*continued.*

The Institutes of Justinian, with English translation and notes. By T. C. Sandars. 8th ed. 1888. 8vo. **63 E**

Institutiones juris civilis cum omnibus Sylvestri Aldobrandini annotationibus hactenus impressis, quibus hac novissima editione accesserunt præclaræ Francisci Cornelli Brixiani annotationes. Venetiis, 1580. 12mo. **118 A**

Institutionum libri quatuor. Lugd. Batav. 1670. 12mo. **48 C**

Institutionum, libri quattuor ; with introductions, commentary, and excursus. By J. B. Moyle. 2nd ed. Oxford, 1890. 8vo. **63 E**

Pandectæ Justinianæ in novum ordinem digestæ cum legibus codicis et novellis quæ jus Pandectarum confirmant, explicant aut abrogant. Nova editio. 3 vols. Lugduni, 1782. folio.

Quinquaginta decisiones quæ a secundo libro codicis usque ad nonum diffusæ sunt. Per D. Petrum Franciscum Linglois. Antverpiæ, 1661. folio. **48 H**

Select titles from the digest of Justinian. Edited by T. E. Holland and C. L. Shadwell. Oxford, 1881. 8vo. **63 E**

See also EDEN, R., GAIUS, GAMBELLONA, A. and ROMAN LAW.

KAIN, GEORGE JAMES.

Solicitors' book-keeping by two methods, single-column and double-column. [n.d.] 8vo. **160 G**

Solicitors' book-keeping by double entry. 10th ed 1884. 8vo. **9 A**

KATCHENOVSKY, PROFESSOR.

Prize law : particularly with reference to the duties and obligations of Belligerents and Neutrals. Translated from the Russian by Frederic Thomas Pratt. 1867. 8vo. **55 A**

KAY, EDWARD EBENEZER.

Reports of cases in the Court of Chancery, 1853–1854. 1 vol. 1854. 8vo. **2 I**

KAY, EDWARD EBENEZER and HENRY R. V. JOHNSON.

Reports of cases in the Court of Chancery, 1854–1858. 4 vols 1855–59. 8vo. **2 I**

KAY, JOSEPH.

The law relating to Shipmasters and Seamen. 2 vols. 1875. 8vo. **175 F**

KEANE, DAVID DEADY and JAMES GRANT.

Registration cases in the Court of Common Pleas, 1854–1862.
1 vol. 1863. 8vo. **6 G**

KEARSLEY, GEORGE.

Kearsley's Complete peerage of England, Scotland and Ireland,
1791, 1796, 1799, 1802, 1804, 1809. 12 vols. in 9. 1792–
1809. 12mo. **123 A**

Tax Tables for 1808, 1809, 1810, 1811, 1812, 1820, 1822,
1825, 1826, 1829, 1832. 11 vols. 1808–32. 12mo. **176 D**

KEATINGE, THOMAS.

A Short treatise on Family Settlements and Devises. 1810.
8vo. **175 E**

KEBLE, REV. JOHN.

Sermons, academical and occasional. 1847. 8vo. **77 B**

KEBLE, JOSEPH.

Reports in the court of King's Bench at Westminster from
1660 to 1678. 3 vols. 1685. folio. **74 D**

The statutes at large in paragraphs and sections or numbers
from Magna Charta to 1680. 1681. folio. **158 E**

KEEN, BENJAMIN.

Reports of cases in Chancery, in the Rolls Court during the
time of Lord Langdale, 1836–1839. 2 vols. 1837–39.
8vo. **3 A**

KEESSEL, DIONYSIUS GODEFRIDUS VAN DER.

Select theses on the laws of Holland and Zeeland, being a
commentary of Hugo Grotius' Introduction to Dutch Jurisprudence. Translated from the original Latin by C. A.
Lorenz. 2nd ed. with a biographical notice of the author,
by J. de Wal. 1868. 8vo. **55 D**

KEILWEY, ROBERT.

Reports d'ascuns cases aux temps Henry VII et Henry VIII,
qui ne sont comprises deins les livres des terms et ans de
mesmes les Roys; seligès hors des papieres de Robert
Keilwey, par Jean Croke; ovesque les Reports d'ascuns
cases, prises per Guilleaume Dallison et per Guilleaume
Bendloe. La tierce édition. 1688. folio. **74 D**

KELHAM, ROBERT.

A Dictionary of the Norman or old French language; to which are added, The laws of William the Conqueror. 1779. 8vo. 123 B

Domesday book illustrated: containing an account of that antient record, and a translation of the difficult passages, with occasional notes. 1788. 8vo. 97 I

See also BOUVIER, J.

KELLAWE, RICHARD DE.

Registrum Palatinum Dunelmense. The register of Richard de Kellawe, lord palatine and bishop of Durham, 1311-1316. Edited by Sir T. D. Hardy. 4 vols. 1873-78. 8vo. 102 E

KELLY, EDMOND.

French law of marriage and conflict of laws that arises there-from. 1885. 8vo. 55 C

KELLY, JAMES BIRCH.

Practical treatise on law of life annuities. 1835. 8vo. 160 B
Summary of history and law of Usury. 1835. 8vo. 176 G

KELLY, JAMES HENRY.

The Draftsman. 1873. 12mo. 164 D
The same. 2nd ed. 1881. 12mo. 13 F

KELLY, JOHN.

The life of John Dollond, F.R.S., inventor of the achromatic telescope. 3rd ed. 1808. 4to. 81 F

KELLY, PATRICK.

The universal cambist and commercial instructor, being a treatise on the exchanges, monies, weights and measures of all trading nations and their colonies. 2nd ed. 2 vols. in 1. 1821. 4to. 78 G

KELLY, RICHARD J.

The law of Newspaper Libel. 1889. 12mo. 11 F

KELSEYE, GILES DE.

Copy will of Giles de Kelseye; also English translation thereof. [Referring to property in the parish of St. Dionis Back-church.] 1877. folio. 91 G

KELYNG, Sir John.

A Report of divers cases in Pleas of the Crown in the reign of the late King Charles II. 1708. folio. **74 D**

KELYNGE, William.

A Report of cases in Chancery, the King's Bench, &c., 1731–1736. 1764. folio. **74 E**

KEMBLE, John Mitchell.

Codex diplomaticus Ævi Saxonici. 6 vols. 1839–48. 8vo. **115 A**

The Knights Hospitallers in England. Edited by Rev. L. B. Larking, with an historical introduction by J. M. Kemble. [Camden Society, vol. 65.] 1857. 8vo. **85 B**

KEMP, William.

Kemp's Nine daies wonder: performed in a daunce from London to Norwich. Edited by the Rev. A. Dyce. [Camden Society, vol. 11.] 1840. 8vo. **85 A**

KENDAL, Westmoreland.

The annals of Kendal, being a historical and descriptive account of Kendal and its environs. By C. Nicholson. Kendal, 1832. 8vo. **93 F**

KENDALL, Edward Augustus.

An Argument for construing largely the right of an appellee of murder to insist on trial by battle; and also for abolishing appeals. 2nd ed. 1818. 8vo. **118 B**

KENDALL, John.

A Manual of the law and practice in Bankruptcy and Insolvency. 2nd ed. 1849. 12mo. **160 E**

KENILWORTH, Warwickshire.

A Concise history and description of Kenilworth Castle. By Henry Sharpe. 22nd ed. Warwick, 1835. 12mo. **93 E**

KENNEDY, Gilbert George and J. S. SANDARS.

The law of land drainage and sewers. 1884. 8vo. **11 E**

KENNEDY, Lewis and T. B. GRAINGER.

The present state of the Tenancy of Land in Great Britain. 1828. 8vo. **170 E**

KENNEDY, THOMAS.
  The code of practice of the Court of Chancery. 2nd ed.
  . 2 vols. 1845–53. 12mo.   161 E

KENNEDY, WILLIAM.
  Annals of Aberdeen from the reign of King William the Lion.
  . . 2 vols. 1818. 4to.   95 D

KENNETT, BASIL.
  Of the Law of Nature and Nations. Eight books. Written
  . in Latin by the baron Puffendorf. Done into English by
     Basil Kennett. 3rd ed. 1717. folio.   48 H
  . Romæ antiquæ notitia ; or, the antiquities of Rome. 13th
     ed. 1763. 8vo.   .   113 D

KENNETT, RIGHT REV. WHITE.
  A Glossary to explain the original, the acceptation and obso-
     leteness of words and phrases and to shew the rise, practice
     and alteration of customs, laws and manners. 1816. .[At
     end of J. Dunkin's History of Bicester. 1816. 4to.] 92 E
  Life of White Kennet. See J. P. Malcolm's Lives of Topo-
  . graphers and Antiquaries. 1815. 4to.   79 H
  Parochial antiquities attempted in the history of Ambrosden,
     Burcester and other adjacent parts in the counties of Oxford
     and Bucks. Oxford, 1695. 4to.   92 F
  The same. New ed. 2 vols. Oxford, 1818. 4to.   92 F
  . A Sermon preach'd at the funeral of William Duke of Devon-
     shire, with some memoirs of the family of Cavendish. 1708.
     8vo.   79 B

KENNINGTON, SURREY.
  Manor of Kennington, Surrey, parcel of the possessions of the
     Duchy of Cornwall. Petitions to the Crown and the
     Houses of Lords and Commons from copyholders of manor
     of Kennington, praying for an enfranchisement of their
  . copyhold estates. Durham, 1854. [Pamphlets, vol. 10.]
                                                                 144 A
KENNY, COURTNEY STANHOPE.
  History of law of England as to effects of Marriage on property
     and on wife's legal capacity. 1879. 8vo.   172 D

KENSINGTON, MIDDLESEX.
  . History and antiquities of Kensington. By Thomas Faulkner.
  . 1820. 4to.   89 E

KENSINGTON, MIDDLESEX—*continued.*

Kensington picturesque and historical. By W. J. Loftie. 1888. 8vo. **89 E**

KENT.

Account of the Weald of Kent. By T. D. W. Dearn. Cranbrook, 1814. 8vo. **88 E**

Delineations, topographical, historical and descriptive of Kent. By E. W. Brayley. 2 vols. 1808. 8vo. **88 D**

Domesday translated, with an introduction and notes ; comprehending the counties of Kent, Sussex and Surrey. By Rev. S. Henshall and John Wilkinson. 1799. 4to. **88 E**

England's Topographer ; or, a new and complete history of the county of Kent. By W. H. Ireland. 4 vols. 1828–30. 8vo. **88 E**

Historical account of the part of Kent within twelve miles of London. See Rev. Daniel Lysons's Environs of London, vol. 4, 1796, pp. 289–569 and 653–661. **89 F**

The history and topographical survey of Kent. By Edward Hasted. 4 vols. Canterbury, 1778–99. folio. **89 H**

Hasted's History of Kent continued to the present time. Part 1, the Hundred of Blackheath. By H. H. Drake. 1886. folio. **89 H**

History, gazetteer and directory of the county of Kent. By Samuel Bagshaw. 2 vols. Sheffield, 1847. 8vo. **88 D**

The history of Kent. By John Harris. vol. 1. [no more published.] 1719. folio. **89 H**

History of the Weald of Kent, with an outline of the early history of the county. By Robert Furley. 2 vols. in 3. 1871–74. 8vo. **88 E**

House of Commons. Minutes of evidence given before select committee of railway bills on North Kent lines, by South Eastern, North Kent (Vignoles') and London and Croydon railway companies. 1845. folio. **89 G**

The monuments and painted glass of upwards of one hundred churches chiefly in the eastern part of Kent. By Rev. Philip Parsons. Canterbury, 1794. 4to. **88 E**

Papers relating to proceedings in the county of Kent, 1642–1646. Edited by R. Almack. [Camden Society, vol. 61.] 1855. 8vo. **85 B**

Pedigrees of the families in the county of Kent. By William Berry. 1830. folio. **126 I**

KENT—*continued.*

A Perambulation of Kent, containing the description, hystorie and customes. By Wm. Lambarde. 1596. 8vo. **88 D**

Poll for knights of the shire to represent the county of Kent; taken at Maidstone, on 15th and 16th of May, 1734. 1734. 8vo. **107 I**

The same, taken at Maidstone, on 1st and 2nd of May, 1754. 1754. 8vo. **107 J**

The same, taken on Pennenden Heath, on 28, 29, and 30th of June, 1790. Rochester, 1791. 8vo. **107 J**

The same, taken on Penenden Heath, on 13th to 22nd of July, 1802. Canterbury, 1803. 8vo. **107 K**

The same. Another ed. 1804. 8vo. **107 K**

Proceedings principally in the county of Kent, in connection with the parliaments called in 1640. Edited by Rev. L. B. Larking. [Camden Society, vol. 80.] 1862. 8vo. **85 C**

Repertorium ecclesiasticum parochiale Londinense, an ecclesiastical parochial history of the diocese of London. By Richard Newcourt. 2 vols. 1708–1710. folio. **92 G**

A Tour through the Isle of Thanet and some other parts of East Kent. [By Zachariah Cozens.] 1793. 4to. **88 E**

Villare Cantianum ; or, Kent surveyed and illustrated. By Thomas Philipott. To which is added an historical catalogue of the high sheriffs of Kent. Collected by John Philipott. 1659. 4to. **88 E**

KENT, JAMES.

Commentaries on American law. 10th ed. by Wm. Kent. 4 vols. Boston, 1860. 8vo. **59 A**

The same. 11th ed. by G. F. Comstock. 4 vols. Boston, 1866. 8vo. **59 A**

Kent's Commentary on International law. Edited by J. T. Abdy. 1866. 8vo. **55 A**

KENYON, LLOYD, 1 BARON.

The life of Lloyd, first Lord Kenyon, lord chief justice of England. By George Thomas Kenyon. 1873. 8vo. **80 D**

See also Lord Campbell's Lives of the Chief Justices, vol. 3, 1857, pp. 1–93. **79 G**

Notes of cases in the Court of King's Bench. Arranged for the press by J. W. Hanmer, 1753–59. 2 vols. 1819–25. 8vo. **5 B**

Two arguments before Lord Chancellor Loughborough in the

KENYON, LLOYD, 1 BARON—*continued.*
case of Myddleton against Lord Kenyon and others. See
Hargrave's Juridical Arguments, vol. 1, 1797, pp. 293–365,
and Appendix pp. xxii–xxv. **144 G**

KER, WALTER CHARLES ALAN.
Digest of law relating to Sale of Goods. 1888. 8vo. **10 B**

KERR, ROBERT MALCOLM.
An Action at law ; being an outline of jurisdiction of superior
courts at common law. 2nd ed. 1857. 12mo. **160 A**
The same. 3rd ed. by Bassett Smith. 1861. 12mo. **160 A**
Commentaries on the laws of England. By Sir W. Blackstone,
adapted to the present state of the law by R. M. Kerr.
4 vols. 1857. 8vo. **166 G**
The same. 3rd ed. 4 vols. 1862. 8vo. **166 G**

KERR, ROBERT MALCOLM NAPIER.
The Student's Blackstone. 9th ed. 1885. 12mo. **166 G**
The same. 10th ed. 1887. 12mo. **166 G**
The same. 11th ed. 1890. 12mo. **64 C**

KERR, WILLIAM WILLIAMSON.
The law of Fraud and Mistake as administered in courts of
equity. 1868. 8vo. **168 E**
The same. 2nd ed. 1883. 8vo. **10 A**
A Treatise on the law and practice as to Receivers appointed
by the Court of Chancery. 1869. 8vo. **175 B**
The same. 2nd ed. 1882. 8vo. **11 E**
The law and practice of Injunctions. 1867. 8vo. **169 A**
The same. 2nd ed. 1878. 8vo. **169 A**
The same. 3rd ed. 1888. 8vo. **10 C**
A Treatise on the law of Discovery. 1870. 8vo. **165 G**

KERRY.
The ancient and present state of the county of Kerry. By
Charles Smith. Dublin, 1774. 8vo. **95 E**

KEW GARDENS, SURREY.
Guide to the royal botanic gardens and pleasure grounds, Kew.
By Daniel Oliver. 29th ed. 1881. 12mo. **93 C**

KEW GARDENS, SURREY—*continued.*

Kew Gardens ; or, a popular guide to the royal botanic
gardens of Kew. By Sir W. J. Hooker. 10th ed. 1851.
12mo. **93 C**

See also HEMSLEY, W. B.

KEY, THOMAS and H. W. ELPHINSTONE.

Precedents in Conveyancing. 2 vols. 1878. 8vo. **164 D**

The same. 2nd ed. 2 vols. 1883. 8vo. **53 D**

The same. 3rd ed. by T. Key. 2 vols. 1890. 8vo. **13 F**

KEYSER, HENRY.

The law relating to transactions on the Stock Exchange.
1850. 12mo. **176 D**

KIDD, JOHN.

On the adaptation of external nature to the physical condition
of man. 4th ed. 1836. 8vo. **77 B**

KIDDINGTON, OXFORDSHIRE.

The history and antiquities of Kiddington. By Rev. Thomas
Warton. 3rd ed. 1815. 4to. **92 E**

KILBURNE, RICHARD.

Life of Richard Kilburne. See J. P. Malcolm's Lives of Topographers and Antiquaries. 1815. 4to. **79 H**

KILLARNEY, LAKES OF.

Legends of the lakes ; or, sayings and doings at Killarney.
By T. C. Croker. 2 vols. 1829. 12mo. **83 A**

KIMBELL, JOHN.

An Account of the legacies, gifts, rents, fees &c. appertaining
to the church and poor of the parish of St. Alphege, Greenwich. 1816. 4to. **88 E**

KIMBER, EDWARD.

The peerage of England. 1766. 12mo. **124 B**

The same. 2nd ed. 1769. 12mo. **124 B**

The peerage of Ireland. 1768. 12mo. **124 B**

The peerage of Scotland. 1767. 12mo. **124 B**

KIMBER, EDWARD—*continued.*

The baronetage of England. [a new ed. of Wootton's Baronetage.] By Edward Kimber and Richard Johnson. 3 vols. 1771. 8vo. **125 C**

KIME, WILLIAM THOMAS.

Practical hints and memoranda for the use of persons engaged in conducting proceedings in the courts of law at Westminster. 1848. 12mo. **162 G**

KING, CHARLES COOPER.

A History of Berkshire. 1887. 8vo. **86 B**

KING, DANIEL.

The history of Chester. By George Ormerod, with a republication of King's Vale Royal. 2nd ed. by Thomas Helsby. 3 vols. 1882. folio. **86 H**

KING, SIR JOHN.

A Memoir of the life and death of Sir John King, knight. Written by his father in 1677, and now first printed. Edited by George Henry Sawtell. 1855. 8vo. **79 B**

KING, JOSEPH.

Interest tables calculated at five per cent. 1880. 8vo. **134 I**

KING'S BENCH PRACTICE.

Practice of court of King's Bench, with bills of costs in the court. By T. Chapman. 2nd ed. 1831. 12mo. **162 F**

Collection of forms and entries which occur in practice in courts of King's Bench and Common Pleas in personal actions and ejectment. By J. F. Archbold. 1825. 12mo. **162 D**

Rules and orders of the court of King's Bench, from 1604 to 1811. By R. Peacock. 1811. 8vo. **162 G**

A Discourse concerning the courts of King's Bench and Common Pleas. See Hargrave's Law Tracts, 1787, pp. 357–376. **144 G**

A Discourse against the jurisdiction of the King's Bench over Wales by process of latitat. [circa 1745.] See Hargrave's Law Tracts, 1787, pp. 377–423. **144 G**

The practising attorney; or, new King's Bench guide. 1779. 12mo. **163 A**

KING'S BENCH PRACTICE—*continued.*

The Attorney's practice in the Court of King's Bench. By
Robert Richardson. 6th ed. 2 vols. 1776. 12mo. **163 A**

Digest of adjudged cases in the court of King's Bench from
the Revolution to the present period. By a Gentleman of
Lincoln's Inn. 1775. folio. **156 D**

History and practice of the court of King's Bench. See Sir
J. Gilbert's Law of Executions, 1763, pp. 305–369. **168 B**

Rules, orders and notices in the court of King's Bench from
1604 to 1747. [By Sir George Cooke.] 2nd ed. 1747.
12mo. **162 G**

See GARDINER, R., HARRISON, J. and IMPEY, J.

See also COMMON LAW PRACTICE and CROWN OFFICE
PRACTICE.

KING'S BENCH PRISON.

A Description of the King's Bench prison. 4th ed. [n.d.]
12mo. **118 A**

Sketches from St. George's Fields. By Giorgione di Castel
Chiuso. [Peter Bailey.] 1820, and Second series. 1821.
2 vols. 1820–21. 12mo. **118 A**

KING'S COLLEGE HOSPITAL.

Rules and regulations of the King's College Hospital, Portugal street, Lincoln's Inn, and 11th annual report. 1850.
[Pamphlets, vol. 7.] **144 A**

The same. 22nd annual report. 1861. [Pamphlets, vol. 14.]
144 A

KING'S COUNCIL AND COURT.

An Essay upon the original authority of the King's Council.
By Sir Francis Palgrave. 1834. 8vo. **97 I**

Rotuli Curiæ Regis. Rolls and records of the court held before the King's justiciars or justices, 1195 to 1199. Edited
by Sir F. Palgrave. 2 vols. 1835. 8vo. **99 A**

KING'S INNS, DUBLIN.

History of the King's Inns ; or, an account of the legal body
in Ireland from its connexion with England. By B. T.
Duhigg. Dublin, 1806. 8vo. **95 E**

The society of King's Inns, Dublin : its origin and progress.
By W. F. Littledale. 1859. [Pamphlets, vol. 14.] **144 A**

KINGSTON, Surrey.

The charters of the town of Kingston upon Thames. Translated into English by George Roots. 1797. 8vo. **93 C**

KINGSTON, Duchess of.

Case of the Dutchess of Kingston's will made in France, with the opinion of Mons. Target thereon. 1789. See Collectanea Juridica, vol. 1, 1791, pp. 323–331. **144 G**

KINLOCH, Rev. Alfred.

See BANDA AND KIRWEE BOOTY.

See also St. John Colbran's Guide to Tunbridge Wells, 2nd ed. 1884, pp. 1–151. [By Rev. A. Kinloch.] **88 D**

KINNEAR, John Boyd.

Digest of House of Lords cases decided on appeal from Scotland, 1709 to 1864; with glossary of Scottish law terms. 1865. 8vo. **55 F**

A Practical treatise on the law of Bankruptcy in Scotland. 2nd ed. 1869. 8vo. **55 F**

KIPPIS, Andrew.

Biographia Britannica; or, the lives of the most eminent persons who have flourished in Great Britain and Ireland from the earliest ages to the present times. 2nd ed. 5 vols. 1778–93. folio. [no more published.] **79 I**

KIRBY, John.

The Suffolk traveller. 2nd ed. 1764. 8vo. **93 C**

KIRBY, Rev. William.

On the power, wisdom and goodness of God as manifested in the creation of animals and in their history, habits and instincts. 2nd ed. 2 vols. 1835. 8vo. **77 B**

KIRCHNER, F. J.

L'Extradition. Recueil renfermant in-extenso tous les traités conclus jusqu'au 1er Janvier, 1883, entre les nations civilisées, et donnant la solution précise des difficultés qui peuvent surgir dans leur application; avec une préface de Georges Lachaud. Publié sous les auspices de C. E. Howard Vincent. 1883. 8vo. **10 A**

KIRKBY MOORSIDE, YORKSHIRE.

Historia Rievallensis ; containing the history of Kirkby Moorside, with a dissertation on the animal remains in the recently discovered cave at Kirkdale. By Rev. William Eastmead. 1824. 8vo. **94 B**

KIRKPATRICK, HENRY CLARE.

Report of the action for libel brought by Rev. Robert O'Keeffe against Cardinal Cullen. 1874. 8vo. **50 B**

KIRKPATRICK, JOHN.

Digest of the Scottish law of Evidence. Edinburgh, 1882. 8vo. **55 F**

KITCHIN, GEORGE WILLIAM.

A History of France. 2nd ed. 3 vols. Oxford, 1881-85. 12mo. **113 E**

See also RANKE, LEOPOLD VON.

KITCHIN, JOHN.

Le Court Leete et Court Baron. 1585. 12mo. **49 B**
The same. Another ed. 1607. 12mo. **49 B**
The same in English. 4th ed. 1663. 12mo. **49 B**
The same. 5th ed. 1675. 12mo. **49 B**

KNAPP, JEROME WILLIAM.

Reports of cases before the committees of the Privy Council, 1829–1836. 3 vols. 1831–36. 8vo. **1 D**

KNAPP, JEROME WILLIAM and EDWARD OMBLER.

Cases of controverted elections in the twelfth parliament of the United Kingdom, 1834–1835. 1837. 8vo. **66 A**

KNARESBOROUGH, YORKSHIRE.

The history of Knaresborough. By M. Calvert. Knaresborough, 1844. 8vo. **94 A**

KNAVE'S CALENDAR.

The Knave's Calendar ; or, a step towards the duty of a legislator. 1799. 8vo. **118 B**

KNIGHT SERVICE.

The original growth, propagation and condition of feuds and tenures by knight service in England. See Sir H. Spelman's English works, vol. 2, 1727, pp. 1–46. **78 H**

KNIGHTAGES.

Calendar of knights ; containing lists of knights bachelors, British knights of foreign orders, also knights of the Garter, Thistle, Bath, St. Patrick, and the Guelphic and Ionian orders from 1760. By Francis Townsend. 1828. 8vo.   125 E

See also DEBRETT, J. and DOD, C. R.

KNIGHTHOOD.

A Concise history of knighthood, containing the religious and military orders which have been instituted in Europe. By Hugh Clark. 2 vols. in 1.   1784. 8vo.   125 E

An Inquiry into the history of feudal and obligatory knight-hood in England. By F. M. Nichols. 1863. 4to.   126 I

See also BATH, GARTER, and MOULE, T.

KNIGHTON, HENRY.

Chronica de eventibus Angliæ a tempore Regis Edgari usque mortem Regis Ricardi Secundi.   See Scriptores Decem Hist. Angl., 1652, pp. 2511–2742.   114 H

Chronicon Henrici Knighton, vel Cnitthon, Monachi Leyces-trensis. Edited by J. R. Lumby. vol. 1. 1889. 8vo. 102 I

KNIGHTS HOSPITALLERS.

The knights hospitallers in England. Edited by Rev. L. B. Larking. [Camden Society, vol. 65.]   1857. 8vo.   85 B

KNIGHTS TEMPLARS.

The history of the Knights Templars, the Temple church and the Temple. By C. G. Addison.   1842. 8vo.   91 D

KNOWLEDGE.

On Mr. Spencer's Unification of Knowledge. By Malcolm Guthrie.   1882. 8vo.   78 C

The treasury of knowledge. By Samuel Maunder. New ed. 1859. 12mo.   78 A

KNOX, JOHN.

The historie of the Reformation of the Church of Scotland ; with some treatises conducing to the history. Edited by David Buchanan.   1644. folio.   113 F

KÖE, JOHN HERBERT and SAMUEL MILLER.
The law and practice in Bankruptcy. 2nd ed. 2 vols. 1844.
8vo.   52 A

KORAN, THE.
The Koran, commonly called The Alcoran of Mohammed.
Translated from the original Arabic by George Sale. A
new ed. 2 vols. 1825. 8vo.   77 B

KOTZEBUE, AUGUSTUS VON.
Sketch of the life and literary career of Augustus Von Kotzebue; with the journal of his exile to Siberia. Written by
himself. [Autobiography, vols. 11 and 12.] 2 vols. 1827.
12mo.   79 A

KYD, STEWART.
The law of Awards. 2nd ed. 1799. 8vo.   160 B
The law of bills of exchange and promissory notes. 3rd ed.
1795. 8vo.   160 G
The law of Corporations. 2 vols. 1793-94. 8vo.   164 G

KYRIACOS, C. J.
Περὶ ἐκδόσεως ἐγκληματίων. [On the extradition of criminals.]
Athens, 1885. 8vo.   55 A

KYTELER, ALICE.
A Contemporary narrative of the proceedings against Dame
Alice Kyteler, prosecuted for sorcery in 1324, by Richard
de Ledrede, bishop of Ossory. Edited by T. Wright. [Cam-
den Society, vol. 24.] 1843. 8vo.   85 A

LABATT, HENRY J.
Practice act of California. San Francisco, 1856. 8vo.   59 B

LABOUCHERE, HENRY.
'Mea Culpa:' Mr. Labouchere penitent. By Argus. [n.d.]
8vo.   144 G

LABOUR.
Labour disputes before magistrates. By J. R. Sayer and
S. Savill. 1888. 8vo.   9 H
The labour laws. By J. E. Davis. 1875. 8vo.   170 C

LABOUR—*continued.*

On the beneficial employment of the surplus labouring classes in the winter season of the year. By James Dean. 1845. [Pamphlets, vol. 19.] **144 B**

Report from the Poor Law Commissioners, on an enquiry into the Sanitary condition of the Labouring Population of Great Britain. 1842. 8vo. **159 A**

Local Reports on the Sanitary condition of the Labouring Population of England. 1842. 8vo. **159 A**

Reports on the Sanitary condition of the Labouring Population of Scotland. 1842. 8vo. **159 A**

The rights of the Operatives asserted. By W. S. V. Sankey. 1838. [Pamphlets, vol. 27.] **144 B**

See also MASTER AND SERVANT.

LACKINGTON, JAMES.

Memoirs of the forty-five first years of life of J. Lackington. [Autobiography, vol. 13.] 1830. 12mo. **79 A**

LACOCK ABBEY, WILTSHIRE.

Annals and antiquities of Lacock Abbey. By Rev. W. L. Bowles. 1835. 8vo. **93 F**

LACOMBE, PAUL.

Petite histoire du peuple Français. Edited by Jules Bué. 10th ed. [n.d.] 12mo. **83 C**

LACTANTIUS, LUCIUS CŒLIUS.

Opera commentariis illustrata a Tho. Spark, A.M. ex Æde Christi Oxonii. 1684. 8vo. • **47 F**

LAGOS.

Analytical index to the ordinances regulating the civil and criminal procedure of the colony of Lagos. By Smalman Smith. 1888. 8vo. **37 D**

Table of offences in their relation to jurisdiction of district commissioners of colony of Lagos. By E. H. Richards. 1889. 8vo. **37 D**

LAIRD, FRANCIS CHARLES.

Topographical and historical description of the county of Rutland. 1818. 8vo. **92 F**

37—2

LAKE, SIR EDWARD.

Diary in the years 1677–1678. Edited by G. P. Elliott.
[Camden Society, vol. 39.] 1846. 8vo. **85 B**

Sir Edward Lake's account of his interview with Charles I. on
being created a baronet. Edited by T. P. Langmead.
[Camden Society, vol. 73.] 1859. 8vo. **85 B**

LAKES, THE.

Guide to the lakes. By T. West. 7th ed. 1799. 8vo. **87 A**

Select views in Cumberland, Westmoreland, and Lancashire.
By Rev. Joseph Wilkinson. 1821. folio. **91 H**

Sketch of a tour to principal Scotch and English lakes. See
J. Denholm's History of Glasgow, 1804, pp. 441–608. **95 C**

Survey of lakes of Cumberland, Westmoreland, and Lancashire.
By James Clarke. 1787. folio. **86 H**

LAMARTINE, ALPHONSE DE.

Christophe Colomb. Edited by R. A. C. Clapin. 1882.
12mo. **83 C**

LAMB, JOHN.

The Phenomena and Diosemeia of Aratus. Translated into
English verse, with notes. 1848. 8vo. **83 C**

LAMBARD, WILLIAM.

The duties of Constables, Borsholders, Tythingmen, and such
other low and lay ministers of the Peace. Whereunto be
adjoyned the severall offices of church ministers and churchwardens, &c. 1619. 12mo. [Bound with Eirenarcha,
1619.] **48 C**

Eirenarcha, or the office of the Justices o the Peace, in foure
books. 1619. 12mo. **48 C**

Life of William Lambarde. See J. P. Malcolm's Lives of
Topographers and Antiquaries. 1815. 4to. **79 H**

A Perambulation of Kent, containing the description, hystorie,
and customes of that shyre. 1596. 8vo. **88 D**

LAMBERT, B.

The History and survey of London and its environs. 4 vols.
1806. 8vo. **90 A**

LAMBERT, WILLIAM.

Reports, or causes in Chancery collected by Sir George Cary
out of the labours of W. Lambert. 1650. 12mo. **49 B**

The same. New ed. 1820. 12mo. **49 B**

LAMBETH PALACE AND PARISH.

A Catalogue of the archiepiscopal manuscripts in the library at Lambeth palace. By H. J. Todd. 1812. folio. **81 H**

The history and antiquities of the parish of Lambeth and the archiepiscopal palace. By T. Allen. 1827. 4to. **93 D**

Lambeth Palace illustrated by a series of views representing its most interesting antiquities. A concise account historical and descriptive. By W. Herbert and E. W. Brayley. 1806. 4to. **91 G**

LAMPADIUS, JACOBUS.

De Republica Romano-Germanica liber unus. Cum annotatis Hermanni Conringii. Helmestadt, 1671. 8vo. **113 C**

LAMPETER.

The Charters and statutes of Saint David's College in the county of Cardigan. 1879. 8vo. **94 E**

The Calendar of St. David's College, Lampeter, 1881–2. Lampeter, 1881. 12mo. **137 H**

LANCASHIRE.

Charters of the Duchy of Lancaster. Translated and edited by Wm. Hardy. 1845. 8vo. **89 B**

The county palatine of Lancaster. Surveyed by Wm. Yates, engraved by Thomas Billinge. 1786. 4to. **88 F**

Ducatus Lancastriæ. Pars I. Calendarium inquisitionum post mortem &c. temp. regum Edw. I. ad Car. I. Partes II., III., IV. A calendar to the pleadings, depositions &c. from Henry VII. to 1603. Edited by R. J. Harper, J. Caley and W. Minchin. 4 parts in 3 vols. 1823–34. folio. **99 C**

General view of the agriculture of Lancashire. Drawn up for the consideration of the Board of Agriculture from communications of Mr. John Holt. 1795. 8vo. **89 A**

General view of the agriculture of Lancashire. Drawn up by R. W. Dickson, revised and prepared for the press by W. Stevenson. 1815. 8vo. **89 B**

The history of inland navigations ; particularly those of the Duke of Bridgwater, in Lancashire and Cheshire. [By James Brindley.] 2 parts in 1 vol. 1766. 8vo. **86 A**

History of Lancashire. By J. Corry. 2 vols. 1825. 4to. **88 F**

A Map of the county palatine of Lancaster from an accurate survey made in the years 1828 and 1829. By G. Hennet. 1830. 4to. **88 F**

LANCASHIRE—*continued.*

The natural history of Lancashire. By Charles Leigh. Oxford, 1700. folio.   **89 G**

The new Lancashire gazetteer ; or, topographical dictionary. By S. R. Clarke. 1830. 8vo.   **89 B**

Portfolio of fragments relative to the history and antiquities of Lancashire. By Matthew Gregson. 2nd ed. 1824. folio.   **89 G**

Potts's Discovery of witches in the county of Lancaster, 1613. Reprinted, with an introduction and notes, by James Crossley. 1845. 8vo.   **89 B**

A Survey of the counties of Lancashire, Cheshire, Derbyshire, &c., with a general account of the river and canal navigations within those districts. 1797. 8vo.   **89 B**

Topographical and historical description of the county of Lancaster. By John Britton. 1815. 8vo.   **89 B**

Topographical and statistical description of the county of Lancaster. By G. A. Cooke. [1825.] 12mo.   **89 A**

A Topographical survey of the county of Lancaster. By Wm. Tunnicliff. Bath, 1789. 8vo.   **93 B**

See also AIKIN, J., BAINES, E., BAWDWEN, REV. W., COLLIER, J., LAKES, THE, PRESTON and WHITAKER, REV. T. D.

LANCASTER.

An Historical and descriptive account of the town of Lancaster. Lancaster, 1807. 8vo.   **89 A**

The history and antiquities of the town of Lancaster. By Rev. Robert Simpson. Lancaster, 1852. 8vo.   **89 B**

LANCASTER CHANCERY PRACTICE.

Lancaster chancery practice. By T. Snow and H. Winstanley. 1885. 8vo.   **12 H**

Statutes, orders, and rules of court of chancery of county palatine of Lancaster. By T. Snow and H. Winstanley. 1880. 8vo.   **12 H**

The Chancery of the County Palatine of Lancaster, its practice and modes of procedure. By J. W. Winstanley. Liverpool, 1855. 8vo.   **170 C**

The jurisdiction, practice and proceedings of the Court of Chancery of the county palatine of Lancaster. By J. J. Aston. 1852. 8vo.   **170 C**

LANCASTER COMMON PLEAS PRACTICE.

The practice and procedure of the court of Common Pleas at Lancaster. By J. Walton. 1870. 12mo. **170 C**

The practice of the court of Common Pleas at Lancaster in personal actions and ejectment. By Wm. Wareing. 1836. 12mo. **170 C**

Rules of the Court of Common Pleas of the county palatine of Lancaster. Preston, 1835. 12mo. **170 C**

[LANCELOT, CLAUDE.]

A New method of learning with facility the Latin tongue, with a treatise on Latin poetry. Translated and improved from the French of the Messieurs de Port Royal by T. Nugent. New ed. 2 vols. 1816. 8vo. **255 H**

LANCELOTTUS, JOANNES PAULUS.

Corpus Juris Canonici emendatum et notis illustratum, Gregorii XIII. Pont. Max. jussu editum, indicibus et appendice adauctum. 1650. 4to. **77 F**

Institutiones juris canonici, quibus jus pontificium singulari methodo libris quatuor comprehenditur. Lugduni, 1606. 4to. **77 F**

LAND DRAINAGE.

The law of land drainage and sewers. By G. G. Kennedy and J. S. Sanders. 1884. 8vo. **11 E**

The Land Drainage Act 1861 with practical notes and forms. By Theodore Thring. 1862. 12mo. **170 C**

LAND LAWS.

The Land Laws. By Frederick Pollock. 2nd ed. 1887. 8vo. **83 J**

Land in fetters ; or, the history and policy of the laws restraining the alienation and settlement of land in England. By T. E. Scrutton. 1886. 8vo. **83 J**

The reform of the land laws. By John Davy. 1886. [Pamphlets, vol. 39.] **144 C**

Landholding, and the relation of landlord and tenant, in various countries. By C. D. Field. 2nd ed. Calcutta, 1885. 8vo. **10 E**

Systems of land tenure in various countries. Edited by J. W. Probyn. New ed. 1881. 8vo. **78 B**

LAND LAWS—*continued.*

English land and English landlords. Enquiry into origin and character of the English land system, with proposals for its reform. By G. C. Brodrick. 1881. 8vo. **83 J**

Free trade in Land. Comments on the speech of Professor Fawcett at Brighton, as respects some passages in reply to the letters of 'A Hertfordshire Incumbent' and others in the *Times.* By Wm. Hayes. 1868. [Pamphlets, vol. 33.] **144 C**

The land laws of England discussed with reference chiefly to some recent writings of Professor Fawcett and others. By Two Barristers. Privately printed. 1867. [Pamphlets, vol. 35.] **144 C**

Remarks with reference to the land laws of England on some passages in J. S. Mill's Principles of political economy and Louis Blanc's Letters on England. 1867. [Pamphlets, vol. 35.] **144 C**

An Address to the landed gentry of England on the Land Bills before Parliament. 3 parts. 1859. [Pamphlets, vol. 11.] **144 A**

The Modern Land Steward. By the author of The new farmer's calendar. 1801. 8vo. **170 E**

The Land Purchaser's companion and the laws relating to tenants and tenures. 1733. 12mo. **170 E**

The duty and office of a Land Steward. By Edward Laurence. 2nd ed. 1731. 12mo. **170 E**

LAND, REGISTRATION OF.

Registration of title to land and how to establish it without cost or compulsion. By C. F. Brickdale. 1886. 8vo. **53 A**

Essay on the registration of titles. By John Topham. 1886. [Pamphlets, vol. 40.] **144 C**

A Radical scheme for a land act, and a land registration act. By M. A., barrister-at-law. [n.d.] [Pamphlets, vol. 39.] **144 C**

Handy book on the registration of title and transfer of land. By E. H. Holt. 1876. 8vo. **10 E**

Papers on the registration of titles to land. By W. S. Cookson. 1874. [Pamphlets, vol. 35.] **144 C**

Observations on registration of title with reference to the bill for the transfer of land. By A Solicitor of Lincoln's Inn of forty years' standing. 1862. [Pamphlets, vol. 35.] **144 C**

LAND, REGISTRATION OF—*continued.*

A Manual of practice in the office of Land Registry. By Henry Gough. 1862. 12mo. **53 A**

Liverpool Law Society. Remarks on the Title to landed estates bill, and the Registry of landed estates bill. Liverpool, 1859. [Pamphlets, vol. 11.] **144 A**

Registration of titles. By John Turner. 1859. [Pamphlets, vol. 23.] **144 B**

Thoughts on the present state and prospects of legal discontent in relation to the registration of titles. 1858. [Pamphlets, vol. 12.] **144 A**

A Few remarks upon the report of the commissioners appointed to consider the subject of the registration of titles. By G. T. Jenkins. 1857. [Pamphlets, vol. 12.] **144 A**

A Few words of explanation and advice to Landowners on the Bill for the registration of land. By A conveyancing Barrister. 2nd ed. 1857. [Pamphlets, vol. 11.] **144 A**

Shall we register our deeds? Answered by Sir Edward Sugden. 1852. [Pamphlets, vol. 8.] **144 A**

A Letter to a member of parliament on the proposed register bill. By A. B. 1831. [Law Tracts, vol. 5.] **144 E**

Extracts from the Register bill with notes explanatory of the mode of registration. 1831. 12mo. **174 F**

Letter on the subject of the proposed General Registry. By R. H. Coote. 1829. 12mo. **174 F**

Observations on the proposed establishment of a general register. By John Hodgkin. 1829. [Jacob's Tracts, vol. 10.] **144 E**

Arguments and materials for a register of estates. 1698. 8vo. **49 F**

A Proposal for the erecting of county registers for freehold lands. By E. B., Esquire. 1697. 8vo. **49 F**

A Treatise showing how useful, safe, reasonable, and beneficial the Inrolling and Registring of all conveyances of lands may be to the inhabitants of this kingdom. By a Person of great learning and judgment. [Sir Matthew Hale.] 2nd ed. 1695. 8vo. **49 F**

Reasons for a Registry: shewing briefly the great benefits and advantages that may accrew to this nation thereby. By a Well-wisher to the publick interest of the nation. 1678. 8vo. **49 F**

See also ASGILL, J., BENTHAM, G., BRUCE, W. D., HALL, R. G., HANNINGTON, C. M., HUMPHRY, W. W., PLOWDEN, F. and WILSON, R.

LAND REVENUE.

Observations on Crown land revenue. 1787. 8vo. **155 B**

Reports of surveyor-general of the Land Revenue 1797, 1802, 1806, 1809. Reprinted in 1 vol. 1812. folio. **159 E**

Report from select committee on Land Revenues of the Crown, with the minutes of evidence. 1834. folio. **153 D**

LAND, SALES OF.

The law relating to Sales of land. By A. St. J. Clerke and H. M. Humphry. 1885. 8vo. **13 H**

See also VENDORS and PURCHASERS.

LAND SOCIETIES.

The law and practice of Building and Land Societies. By H. F. A. Davis. 3rd ed. 1884. 8vo. **9 B**

LAND TAX.

Exposition of the land tax. By M. A. Bourdin. 3rd ed. 1885. 12mo. **10 E**

Equalisation of the land tax. A Statement respecting the present unequal, oppressive, and as it is believed illegal assessment of the Land Tax, in the Holborn division of the county of Middlesex. 1852. [Pamphlets, vol. 8.] **144 A**

Suggestions for an equitable adjustment of the land tax. 1830. [Pamphlets, vol. 5.] **144 A**

See also DAVIS, R. R. and MILLER, S.

LAND TITLE AND TRANSFER.

Land Transfer. Published by order of the bar committee. 1886. 8vo. **53 A**

Associated provincial law societies. Report of the committee to the members of the association, on the Land Titles and Transfer bill. Leeds, 1874. [Pamphlets, vol. 35.] **144 C**

Impediments to the transfer of land. By George Sweet. 1874. [Pamphlets, vol. 35.] **144 C**

Observations on the Land Titles and Transfer bill. By George Sweet. 1874. [Pamphlets, vol. 35.] **144 C**

Observations on transfer of land bill and other law bills in parliament. By Lord St. Leonards. 1870. 8vo. **170 C**

A Proposition to the Land Transfer commissioners. By Robert Wilson. 1868. 8vo. **170 C**

Transfer of Land act 25 & 26 Vict. c. 53. Office of land registry. General orders and forms. 1866. 8vo. **170 C**

LAND TITLE—*continued.*

The transfer of land act and the declaration of title act. By
E. N. Ayrton. 1863. 12mo. **53 A**

On the true remedies for the evils which affect the Transfer
of Land : a paper read before the Juridical Society, on
Monday the 24th March, 1862. By Joshua Williams.
1862. [Pamphlets, vol. 19.] **144 B**

Suggestions for an act to give an indefeasible title in land,
addressed to the Legislature. By E. N. Ayrton. 1857.
[Pamphlets, vol. 11.] **144 A**

A Letter to Sir Richard Bethell, M.P., Her Majesty's Solicitor
General, on the defects of the present system of transferring
land. By C. M. Roche. 1855. [Pamphlets, vol. 19.] **144 B**

Shall we transfer our lands by register ? By Joseph Goodeve.
1854. [Pamphlets, vol. 9, pt. 2.] **144 A**

The act for simplifying the transfer of property 7 & 8 Vict.
cap. 76, with general observations on the act. By John
Towgood. 1845. [Pamphlets, vol. 19.] **144 B**

A Letter to Lord Campbell on the subject of The Bill ' to
lessen the expense attending the transfer of freehold lands
of small value.' By George Fitch. 1843. [Pamphlets,
vol. 19.] **144 B**

A Dialogue between a Doctor of Laws and a Student, touching
the reasons why the ' Land Transfer Acts ' are not generally used. 2nd ed. [n.d.] [Pamphlets, vol. 39.] **144 C**

See also ATKINSON, R. W. and BRUCE, W. D.

LANDED GENTRY AND LANDOWNERS.

An Essay on the position of the British Gentry. By Rev.
John Hamilton Gray. See Burke's Landed Gentry, 4th ed.,
1863, pp. i–xviii. **126 E**

A Genealogical and heraldic dictionary of the landed gentry
of Great Britain and Ireland. By Sir J. B. Burke. 2 vols.
1850, and Index vol. [n.d.], 4th ed. 1863, 4th ed. revised
1868, 5th ed. 2 vols. 1871, 5th ed. with supplement,
2 vols. 1875, 6th ed. 2 vols. 1879, 6th ed. with supplement, 2 vols. 1882. 13 vols. 1850–82. 8vo. **126 E F**

The same. 7th ed. 2 vols. 1886. 8vo. **Hall**

The great landowners of Great Britain and Ireland. By John
Bateman. 4th ed. 1883. 8vo. **134 I**

Return of owners of land in England and Wales (exclusive of
the Metropolis), 1873. 2 vols. 1875. folio. **100 H**

Return of owners of lands and heritages in Scotland, 1872–
73. Edinburgh, 1874. folio. **100 H**

LANDED GENTRY—*continued.*

Return of owners of land of one acre and upwards in Ireland. Dublin, 1876. folio. **100 H**

LANDLORD AND TENANT.

Woodfall's law of Landlord and Tenant. 14th ed. by J. M. Lely. 1889. 8vo. **10 E**

A Concise view of the law of landlord and tenant. By J. H. Redman and G. E. Lyon. 3rd ed. 1886. 12mo. **10 E**

The law of landlord and tenant. By J. W. Smith. 3rd ed. by V. T. Thompson. 1882. 8vo. **10 E**

A Manual of the law of landlord and tenant. By H. Smith and T. S. Soden. 2nd ed. 1878. 8vo. **170 C**

The law of landlord and tenant. By J. F. Archbold. 3rd ed. 1864. 12mo. **170 C**

Tenant's law ; or, the laws concerning landlords, tenants, and farmers. 7th ed. 1718. 12mo. **170 E**

The same. 14th ed. 1753. 12mo. **170 E**

The same. 15th ed. 1760. 12mo. **170 E**

The same. 17th ed. 1777. 12mo. **170 E**

Landlord's law. By G. Meriton. 3rd ed. 1669. 12mo. **49 A**

See also COMYN, R. B., FAWCETT, W. M., KENNEDY, L., MATHEW, J. M., PAUL, J. and SHIPMAN, R.

LANDS CLAUSES CONSOLIDATION ACTS.

Principles of law of Compensation in reference to Lands clauses consolidation acts. By C. A. Cripps. 2nd ed. 1884. 8vo. **9 D**

The Lands clauses consolidation acts. By A. Jepson. 1880. 8vo. **10 E**

See also COLLIER, R. P., COMPENSATION, and FREND, H. T.

LANE, RICHARD.

Reports in the Court of Exchequer 1605–1612, being the first collections in that court extant. 1657. folio. **74 E**

LANE, THOMAS.

The student's guide through Lincoln's Inn, containing an account of that society. 2nd ed. 1805. 8vo. **91 D**

LANG, ANDREW.

Oxford : brief historical and descriptive notes. New ed. 1890. 8vo. **92 E**

LANGDALE, HENRY, 6 BARON.

Report of the proceedings respecting Rugby school, before Lord Langdale, master of the Rolls, with his lordship's judgment thereon.   Rugby, 1839.   8vo.   93 F

Substance of a speech delivered by Lord Langdale, in the House of Lords, on the 13th of June, 1836, on the motion made by the lord chancellor for the second reading of the bill for the better administration of justice in the high court of Chancery.   1836.   [Jacob's Tracts, vol. 11.]   144 F

LANGDALE, THOMAS.

A Topographical dictionary of Yorkshire.   Northallerton, 1809.   8vo.   94 B

LANGDELL, C. C.

A Selection of cases on sales of personal property.   Boston, 1872.   8vo.   60 B

LANGFORD, JOHN ALFRED, C. S. MACKINTOSH and J. C. TILDESLEY.

Staffordshire and Warwickshire, past and present.   2 vols. in 4. [1875–76.]   4to.   93 G

LANGHORNE, JOHN and WILLIAM LANGHORNE.

Plutarch's Lives, translated from the original Greek, with a life of Plutarch.   4th ed. by Rev. Francis Wrangham. 6 vols.   1826.   8vo.   80 A

LANGLEY, THOMAS.

The history and antiquities of the hundred of Desborough and deanery of Wycombe, in Buckinghamshire ; including the borough towns of Wycombe, and Marlow, and sixteen parishes.   1797.   4to.   86 B

LANGMEAD, THOMAS PITT TASWELL-.

English constitutional history, from the Teutonic conquest to the present time.   2nd ed.   1880.   8vo.   116 E

LANGTOFT, PIERRE DE.

The chronicle of Pierre de Langtoft, in French verse, from the earliest period to the death of King Edward I.   Edited by Thomas Wright.   2 vols.   1866–68.   8vo.   102 C

LANSDOWNE MANUSCRIPTS.
Catalogue of the Lansdowne manuscripts in the British
Museum. 2 parts in 1 vol. 1819. folio.   **98 C**

LAS CASES, DIEUDONNÉ, COMTE DE.
Genealogical, chronological, historical and geographical atlas,
exhibiting all the royal families in Europe. By Mr. Le
Sage. [D. Las Cases.] 1801. folio.   **125 H**

LASCELLES, FRANCIS HENRY.
Horse Warranty. The law relating to the purchase, sale,
letting and hiring of horses. 2nd ed. 1881. 12mo. **10 B**
The laws affecting Juvenile Offenders. 1870. 8vo.   **170 C**

LASSERÉ, LOUIS DE.
L'Art de proceder en justice, ou la science des moyens judiciels,
necessaires pour découvrir la verité ; tant en matiere civile
que criminelle. Paris, 1677. 4to.   **58 G**

LATCH, JEAN.
Plusiers tres-bons cases, come ils estoyent adjudgées es trois
premiers ans du raign du Roy Charles I, en la Court de
Bank le Roy, 1625–1628. Publiées par E. Walpoole. 1662.
folio.   **74 E**

LATERAL SUPPORT.
The law of Support and Subsidence. By H. L. Stephen.
1890. 12mo.   **9 B**
The right to Lateral Support from land and buildings. By
G. G. Gray. 1886. 8vo.   **53 A**

LATHAM, FRANCIS LAW.
The law of window lights. 1867. 8vo.   **10 G**

LATHAM, ROBERT GORDON.
A Dictionary of the English language. 2 vols. in 4. 1866–70.
4to.   **123 D**

LATHAM SPAW, LANCASHIRE.
Latham Spaw, with some remarkable cases and cures effected
by it. By E. Borlace. 1670. 12mo.   **89 A**

LATHOM HOUSE, LANCASHIRE.

A Journal of the siege of Lathom House, in Lancashire, defended by Charlotte de la Tremouille, countess of Derby, against Sir Thomas Fairfax and other parliamentarian officers, 1644. 1823. 12mo. **89 A**

LATIMER, HUGH.

Sermons and remains of Hugh Latimer, sometime bishop of Worcester, Martyr, 1555. Edited by Rev. G. E. Corrie. 2 vols. Cambridge, 1844–45. 8vo. **77 D**

LATIN LANGUAGE.

Ainsworth's Latin dictionary, improved by T. Morell, revised by J. Carey. 2nd ed. 2 vols. 1823. 4to. **123 E**

Catholicon Anglicum, an English-Latin wordbook, dated 1483. Edited by S. J. H. Herrtage. [Camden Society, n.s. vol. 30.] 1882. 8vo. **85 D**

Glossary of Latin words and expressions. See Chronicon Monasterii de Abingdon, vol. 2, 1858, pp. 421–473. **101 A**

Glossary of Latin words. See Capgrave's Liber de illustribus Henricis, 1858, pp. 255–264. **101 B**

Glossary of Mediæval Latin. See Munimenta Gildhalliæ Londoniensis, vol. 2, part 2, 1860, pp. 779–838, and vol. 3, 1862, pp. 373–407. **101 C**

Latin-English dictionary. By W. Smith. 1863. 8vo. **123 E**

Manipulus vocabulorum: a dictionary of English and Latin words, arranged in the alphabetical order of the last syllables. By Peter Levins. First printed A.D. 1570; now re-edited by H. B. Wheatley. [Camden Society, vol. 95.] 1867. 8vo. **85 C**

Promptorium parvulorum sive clericorum, lexicon Anglo-Latinum princeps. Auctore Fratre Galfrido Grammatico dicto. Edited by Albert Way. [Camden Society, vols. 25, 54, 89.] 3 vols. 1843–65. 8vo. **85 A B C**

Public Examination Latin Grammar. By John Gibson. 2nd ed. 1883. 8vo. **255 H**

See also Du CANGE, C. D., FACCIOLATI, J., LANCELOT, C., MINSHEU, J., SPELMAN, H. and STEPHANUS, R.

LATTEY, ROBERT THOMAS.

A Handy book on the practice and procedure before the judicial committee of the privy council. 1869. 8vo. **12 A**

LAUDERDALE FAMILY.

The Lauderdale papers, 1639–1679. Edited by O. Airy. [Camden Society, n.s. vols. 34, 37 and 38.] 3 vols. 1884–85. 8vo. **85 D**

Letters addressed to the Earl of Lauderdale. Edited by O. Airy. [Camden Society, n.s. vol. 31.] 1883. 8vo. **85 D**

LAURENCE, EDWARD.

The duty and office of a Land Steward. 2nd ed. 1731. 12mo. **170 E**

LAURIE, JAMES.

Tables of simple interest at 5, $4\frac{1}{2}$, 4, $3\frac{1}{2}$, 3 and $2\frac{1}{2}$ per cent. per annum, from 1 day to 12 years. [n.d.] 8vo. **Hall**

LAVATER, JOHN CASPAR.

Memoirs of J. C. Lavater, with a brief memoir of his widow. By P. J. Heisch. 1842. 12mo. **79 A**

LAVOISNE, C. V.

Complete genealogical, historical, chronological and geographical atlas. 3rd ed. 1822. folio. **125 H**

LAW.

The Legal Correspondent (part 1). By Fred. Wood. 1889. 8vo. **11 G**

Wynagrodzenie za Prowadzenie Spraw. [Remuneration for the management of legal business.] By Stanislaw Belza. Warszawa, 1887. 12mo. **55 C**

A Guide to the Legal Profession. By J. H. Slater. 1884. 8vo. **64 E**

The philosophy of Law. By Herbert Broom. 3rd ed. by J. C. H. Flood. 1883. 12mo. **63 G**

The tendency of the legislation of the nineteenth century to revert to that of the ninth. By A. J. King. 1883. [Pamphlets, vol. 35.] **144 C**

Bankruptcy legislation and defaulters in the legal profession. Prize essays. 1879. 8vo. **78 B**

The science of Law. By Sheldon Amos. 1874. 8vo. **63 F**

A Lecture delivered to the Otago Law Clerks' Association. By James Macassey. 1872. [Pamphlets, vol. 36.] **144 C**

Essays upon the form of the Law. By T. E. Holland. 1870. 8vo. **170 F**

LAW—*continued.*

Principia Prima Legum ; or, an enunciation and analysis of the elementary principles of Law. By G. Harris. Part I. [1865.] 8vo. **63 F**

On the Economy of the Law. By George Cochrane. 5th ed. 1863. [Pamphlets, vol. 17.] **144 B**

Traités de législation civile et pénale : ouvrage extrait des manuscrits de M. Jérémie Bentham. Par Ét. Dumont. 1858. 8vo. **78 C**

Address to the Mutual Law Association. By Charles Rann Kennedy. 1852. [Pamphlets, vol. 21.] **144 B**

Speech of Lord Brougham in the House of Lords, on Friday, May 12, 1848, on legislation and the law. 1848. 8vo. **83 G**

Horæ Juridicæ ; or, thoughts on the profession of the law. By W. D. Lewis. 1845. [Pamphlets, vol. 3.] **144 A**

On legislative expression ; or, the language of the written law. By George Coode. 1845. [Pamphlets, vol. 21.] **144 B**

Law and lawyers ; or, sketches and illustrations of legal history and biography. [By James Grant.] 2 vols. 1840. 8vo. **79 G**

The practice of the Law in all its departments. By J. Chitty. 3 vols. 1833–35. 8vo. **167 B**

The science of legal judgment. By James Ram. 1834. 8vo. **169 E**

The attorney and solicitor's complete assistant. Compiled by a Gentleman eminent in practice. 2 vols. 1768–67. 12mo. **164 E**

Reflections ; or, hints founded upon experience and facts touching the Law, lawyers, officers, and others concerned in the administration of justice. 1759. 12mo. **171 A**

The gentleman's assistant, tradesman's lawyer, and country-man's friend. 2nd ed. 1709. 12mo. **170 F**

The young lawyer's recreation, being a choice collection of cases, passages, and customs in the law. 1694. 12mo. **48 C**

Treatise enumerating the most illustrious families of England who have been raised to honour and wealth by the profession of the law. By H. Philipps. 1686. 12mo. **49 D**

See ADLINGTON, J. H., BERCHUYS, A. V., FINCH, SIR H., NORTH, R., SHEPPARD, W. and WILLIAMS, T.

See also LAWS.

LAW ADVERTISER.

The Law Advertiser, 1823–30. 8 vols. 1823–30. 4to. **139 G**

LAW AMENDMENT SOCIETY.

Society for promoting the amendment of the Law. Fifth annual report of council. 1848. [Pamphlets, vol. 20.] **144 B**

Eighteenth annual report of the council, for the session 1860-61 ; with a financial statement, the rules of the society, and a list of the council and members. 1861. [Pamphlets, vol. 20.] **144 B**

Report of the committee on equity on the law respecting lunacy. 1848. [Pamphlets, vol. 15.] **144 B**

Further report of committee on Equity on the Masters' offices. 1849. [Pamphlets, vol. 17.] **144 B**

The bar, the attorney, and the client. Second Report. [1854.] [Pamphlets, vol. 20.] **144 B**

The expediency of abolishing the practice of opening biddings in the court of Chancery. Read by Mr. Serjeant Woolrych at a General Meeting on Jan. 14th, 1861. [Pamphlets, vol. 20.] **144 B**

On some proposed amendments in the law relating to Procedure and Evidence on criminal trials. Read by Mr. Edgar at a General Meeting on Jan. 28th, 1861. [Pamphlets, vol. 20.] **144 B**

On the expediency of passing an act to permit defendants in criminal courts, and their wives or husbands, to testify on oath. Read by Mr. J. Pitt Taylor at a General Meeting on Feb. 11th, 1861. [Pamphlets, vol. 20.] **144 B**

Observations on the Bankruptcy and Insolvency bill. Read by Mr. A. Edgar and Mr. Wm. Hawes at a General Meeting on Feb. 25th, 1861. [Pamphlets, vol. 20.] **144 B**

European conventions with respect to Domicil. By Mr. Serjeant Woolrych, read at a General Meeting on Feb. 26th, 1863. [Pamphlets, vol. 20.] **144 B**

Report of the special committee on Convict Discipline. 1863. [Pamphlets, vol. 20.] **144 B**

The present state of the law of Copyright in Literature and the fine arts, with a view to its amendment. By Mr. Serjeant Burke. 1863. [Pamphlets, vol. 20.] **144 B**

On the sale of Benefices, in connection with 'Augmentation of Benefices bill.' By A. Waddilove. 1863. [Pamphlets, vol. 20.] **144 B**

LAW ASSOCIATION, METROPOLITAN AND PROVINCIAL.

Reports of the committee of management made to the annual general meetings, 1848–1863. 1 vol. 1848–63. 8vo. **70 B**

Circulars, 1852–1863. 2 vols. 1852–63. 8vo. **70 B**

LAW COURTS.

An Address to the legal world on the centralisation of the courts of law and equity. By R. A. Routh and C. W. Rowden. 1851, [Pamphlets, vol. 32.]　　144 C

The concentration of the courts and offices of law in London. [n.d.] [Pamphlets, vol. 32.]　　144 C

The Law Courts and new Houses of Parliament. Extracts from the evidence taken before the select committee of the House of Commons in 1841 and 1842, proving the necessity of removing the courts of law to the neighbourhood of the inns of court. 1843. [Pamphlets, vol. 8.]　　144 B

The same. With extracts from the evidence taken before the revised committee in 1845. 1853. [Pamphlets, vol. 9, pt. 1.]　　144 A

The new Houses of Parliament and the Law Courts. Are the law courts to remain at Westminster? By An old law reformer. [Harvey Gem.] Brighton, 1853. [Pamphlets, vol. 32.]　　144 C

Observations on the proposed concentration of the courts of justice in the vicinity of the Inns of Court. 1859. [Pamphlets, vol. 10.]　　144 A

Petition of the Society of Lincoln's Inn against the Courts of Justice Site bill. 1864. [Pamphlets, vol. 32.]　　144 C

A Review of the evidence taken before the select committee of the House of Commons on the proposal to remove the courts of law and equity from Westminster to the neighbourhood of the inns of court, with extracts from the evidence. 1842. [Pamphlets, vol. 4.]　　144 A

A Site for Her Majesty's superior courts at the Temple. By T. W. Greene. 1862. [Pamphlets, vol. 17.]　　144 B

Westminster Hall Courts. Facts for the consideration of parliament, before the final adoption of a plan perpetuating the courts of law on a site injurious and costly to the suitor. 1840. [Pamphlets, vol. 4.]　　144 A

When and where should our Courts sit? By J. W. Smith and J. Trail. 1861. [Pamphlets, vol. 17.]　　144 B

Where shall the new law courts be built? By An old law reformer. [Harvey Gem.] 1854. [Pamphlets, vol. 32.]　　144 C

LAW DICTIONARIES.

The Judicial Dictionary of words and phrases judicially interpreted. By F. Stroud. 1890. 8vo.　　123 F

Wharton's Law-Lexicon: forming an epitome of the law of England; and containing full explanations of the technical

LAW DICTIONARIES—*continued.*

terms and phrases thereof, both ancient and modern. 8th ed. by J. M. Lely. 1889. 8vo.   **10 E**

A Juridical glossary. By H. C. Adams. vol. 1, A to E. Albany, N.Y., 1886. 8vo.   **123 G**

A Dictionary of English law. By Charles Sweet. 1882. 8vo.   **123 G**

A New law dictionary and institute of the whole law. By A. Brown. 2nd ed. 1880. 8vo.   **64 E**

A Concise law dictionary. By H. N. Mozley and G. C. Whiteley. 1876. 8vo.   **64 E**

The Law Dictionary. By Sir T. E. Tomlins. 4th ed. by T. P. Granger. 2 vols. 1835. 4to.   **123 G**

A New Law Dictionary. By Giles Jacob. Corrected and enlarged by J. Morgan. 10th ed. 1782. folio.   **122 G**

Law Dictionary; or, General Abridgment of the Law. By T. Cunningham. 2 vols. 1764. folio.   **123 G**

The Interpreter; containing the genuine signification of obscure words used in the lawes of this realm. By Rev. John Cowel. New ed. 1727. folio.   **123 G**

NOMO-ΛΕΞΙΚΟΝ, a law dictionary. By Thomas Blount. 1670. folio.   **123 G**

See also BOUVIER, J., HOLTHOUSE, H. J., POTTS, T., RASTAL, W. and WHISHAW, J.

LAW JOURNAL.

The Law Journal: a weekly publication of notes of cases and legal news, 1866–1890. 26 vols. 1866–90. folio and 4to.   **18 A–D**

The Law Journal Notes of Cases decided in all the superior courts of law and equity, 1866–1890, and List of petitions and dividends in bankruptcy, 1866–1890. 26 vols. 1866–90. 4to.   **18 E F**

A Collection of Law Tracts, published in 1825 and 1826 in the Law Journal. [vol. 1 only.] [1830.] 4to.   **144 G**

LAW JOURNAL REPORTS.

The Law Journal Reports; comprising reports of cases in the courts of Chancery, King's Bench, Common Pleas, Exchequer of Pleas, and Exchequer Chamber, and cases connected with the office and duties of Magistrates, 1822–1831. 9 vols. 1823–31. 4to.   **18 G H**

The same. New Series, 1832–1890. 59 vols. in 140. 1832–90. 4to.   **18 H–20 G**

LAW JOURNAL REPORTS—*continued.*

An Analytical digest of the cases published in the Law Journal and other contemporary reports from 1822 to 1885. 13 vols. 1831–86. 4to.   **20 I**

The public general acts of Great Britain and Ireland, 1866–1890. 25 vols. Published for the proprietors of the Law Journal Reports. 1866–90. 4to.   **18 A B**

LAW LISTS.

The Law List 1775, 1777, 1779, 1780, 1782, 1783, 1785, 1787, 1789, 1790, 1792–1890. 109 vols. 1775–1890. 12mo.   **134 C–G**

The 'Law List' and the 'Incorporated Law Society's Calendar,' their earlier annual publication and improvement. By John Miller. 1883. [Pamphlets, vol. 34.]   **144 C**

Lists of attornies and solicitors admitted in pursuance of the late act for the better regulation of attornies and solicitors ; presented to the House of Commons pursuant to their orders of the 26 January 1729 and 22 February 1730. 2 vols. in 1. 1729–31. folio.   **118 G**

The London Law Directory. 1848. 12mo.   **136 A**

The Irish Law List 1878, 1879, 1880–1881, 1885. 4 vols. 1878–85. 8vo.   **136 I**

The Scottish Law List 1848, 1849, 1860–1890. 33 vols. Edinburgh, 1848–90. 12mo.   **136 G H**

The Law List of Australia for the years 1863, 1864, 1870, 1873, 1876, 1878, 1880, 1882, 1884–5, 1886–7. By R. H. Smith. 10 vols. Melbourne, 1863–87. 12mo.   **136 I**

New South Wales Law Almanac for 1888. Sydney, 1887. 12mo.   **136 I**

New Zealand law list. By G. B. Barton. Dunedin, 1877. 8vo.   **136 I**

The Ontario Legal Directory, a complete law list for the province of Ontario. By W. E. Hodgins. Toronto, 1879. 8vo.   **136 I**

Carlisle's Legal Directory ; containing a carefully prepared summary of the Commercial Laws of each State and Territory, together with the name and address of each certified attorney of the American Law Association, &c. By W. T. Carlisle. New York, 1881. 8vo.   **136 I**

Legal directory for lawyers and business men. By J. H. Hubbell. New York, 1881. 8vo.   **59 F**

Sharp and Alleman's Lawyer's and banker's directory for 1890. Philadelphia, 1890. 8vo.   **Hall**

LAW MAGAZINE AND LAW REVIEW.

The Law Magazine; or, quarterly review of Jurisprudence, June 1828–Feb. 1856. 55 vols. 1829–56. 8vo. **137 A–C**

The Law Review, and quarterly journal of British and foreign Jurisprudence, November 1844 to February 1856. 23 vols. 1845–56. 8vo. **137 C D**

The Law Magazine and Law Review, or quarterly journal of Jurisprudence, May 1856 to August 1890. 50 vols. 1856–90. 8vo. **137 D–F**

LAW QUARTERLY REVIEW.

The Law Quarterly Review. Edited by Frederick Pollock. 6 vols. 1885–90. 8vo. **131 G**

LAW REFORM.

An Alarm on the rights of the poor, and the property of the rich, in danger, from a supposed law reform. By George Strickland. 2nd ed. 1833. [Law Tracts, vol. 5.] **144 E**

The amalgamation of the two branches of the legal profession, considered with reference to contemplated law reforms. By C. T. Saunders. 1870. [Pamphlets, vol. 35.] **144 C**

Common sense versus common law. By Wm. Massey. 1850. 8vo. **78 B**

Considerations touching the amendment, or alteration of lawes. By Sir Matthew Hale. See Hargrave's Law Tracts, 1787, pp. 249–289. **144 G**

Copy of petition [of Thomas Clark] for legal and judicial reforms: presented to the House of Commons by George Grote, Feb. 2, 1841. 1841. folio. **118 G**

A Few words on the Law as it was, as it is, and as it ought to be; with special reference to county court suits and actions at law. By W. F. Finlason. 1850. [Pamphlets, vol. 7.] **144 A**

Fusion. A lecture in which the question of uniting and blending into one the courts and systems of law and equity is considered. By F. O. Haynes. 1873. [Pamphlets, vol. 33.] **144 C**

Fusion practicable; or, a letter to the lord chancellor of Great Britain, on the further assimilation of the jurisdiction of the superior courts of law and equity. By J. J. Aston. 1863. [Pamphlets, vol. 17.] **144 B**

Juridical Letters, addressed to The Right Hon. Robert Peel, in reference to the present crisis of Law Reform. By Eunómus. [John James Park.] 1830. 8vo. **170 F**

LAW REFORM—*continued.*

On jurisprudence and amendment of the law. By Sir J. P. Wilde. 1864. [Pamphlets, vol. 26.] **144 B**

Law Quibbles; or, a treatise of the evasions, tricks, turns, and quibbles commonly used in the profession of the Law; with an Essay on the amendment and reduction of the laws of England. 2nd ed. 1726, and 4th ed. 1736. 12mo. **170 F**

Law Reform in connection with the concentration of the courts and offices of justice. By F. D. Lowndes. Liverpool, 1865. [Pamphlets, vol. 35.] **144 C**

Law-reforming difficulties exemplified in a letter to Lord Brougham; accompanied by an analysis of a bill for the improvement of the law relating to the administration of deceased persons' estates. By T. T. à Beckett. 1849. [Pamphlets, vol. 6.] **144 A**

Letter from Lord Brougham to Sir J. Graham, on making and digesting of the law. 1849. [Pamphlets, vol. 6.] **144 A**

A Letter to the members of the new parliament on the defects in the general and statute law, which require the revision of the legislature. By I. Espinasse. 1827. [Jacob's Tracts, vol. 5.] **144 E**

Letters to John Bull, Esq., on lawyers and law reform. By Joshua Williams. 1857. 12mo. **170 F**

Observations on the great expence of prosecuting suits at law, with a plan proposing a remedy. See Collectanea Juridica, vol. 1, 1791, pp. 476–480. **144 G**

On the present unsettled condition of the Law, and its administration. By John Miller. 1839. 8vo. **170 F**

The patient, the physician and the fee. A law tract for the times. By A Student of fifty years' standing. 1877. [Pamphlets, vol. 36.] **144 C**

Practical proposals for a thorough reform of our Judicial System, and an entire reconstruction of the whole law. By An Outsider. [Sir J. N. Dickinson.] 1867, and Further Proposals. 1871. 8vo. **170 F**

Present state of the law. The speech of Henry Brougham, Esq., M.P., in the House of Commons, on Thursday, February 7, 1828. 2nd ed. 1828. [Pamphlets, vol. 2.] **144 A**

Proposals humbly offered to the parliament for remedying the great charge and delay of suits at law and in equity. By An Attorney. 7th ed. [n.d.] [Law Tracts, vol. 1.] **144 E**

Recent and future Law Reforms. By E. W. Field. 1843. [Pamphlets, vol. 20.] **144 B**

Reflections on certain parts of the law of England; with

LAW REFORM—*continued.*

suggestions for the improvement of the same. By G. Long.
[Jacob's Tracts, vol. 6.] **144 E**

Reform. By B. Montagu. 1827. [Montagu's Tracts.] **144 F**

Remarks on law expenses, with suggestions for reducing them.
By H. Dance. 1830. [Jacob's Tracts, vol. 8.] **144 E**

Remarks on law reform, addressed more particularly to the
general reader. By William Smith. 1840. [Law Tracts,
vol. 6.] **144 E**

A Revised code of national education, national Christianity,
social science, and law amendment ; or, a plea for the revival of the study of the Common Law. By C. Miller.
1862. [Pamphlets, vol. 27.] **144 B**

Several draughts of acts heretofore prepared by persons appointed to consider of the inconvenience, delay, charge, and
irregularity in law proceedings. 1653. 4to. **158 D**

Simplification of the Law. Practical Suggestions. By Sir
Henry Thring, K.C.B. 1875. [Pamphlets, vol. 35.] **144 C**

Suggestions as to reform in some branches of the law. By
James Stewart. 1842. 8vo. **170 F**

Suggestions for some alterations of the law, on the subjects
of Practice, Pleading and Evidence. By Edward Lawes.
1827. [Jacob's Tracts, vol. 9.] **144 E**

LAW REPORTING.

Cases and reports. Remarks upon the proposed alterations
in the system of Law Reporting. By J. H. Ramsay.
Privately printed. 1864. [Pamphlets, vol. 25.] **144 B**

A Letter to Sir Roundell Palmer, having particular reference
to the scheme of law reporting recommended by the committee appointed at the meeting of the bar Dec. 2, 1863.
By W. T. S. Daniel. 1864. [Pamphlets, vol. 25.] **144 B**

A Letter to Sir Roundell Palmer on the present system of
law reporting, its evils and a suggested remedy. By W. T.
S. Daniel. [1863.] [Pamphlets, vol. 20.] **144 B**

Mr. Purton Cooper's Memorandum of a proposal to analyze,
compress, and classify our reports. London, 1858. Reprinted Boulogne, 1860. [Pamphlets, vol. 15.] **114 B**

Nine letters to Mr. P. Cooper, in relation to his proposal
for analyzing, compressing, and classifying our reports.
Privately printed. 1858. [Pamphlets, vol. 15.] **144 B**

Our law-reporting system. Cannot its evils be prevented?
By Alexander Pulling. 1863. [Pamphlets, vol. 20.] **144 B**

LAW REPORTS, The.

The history and origin of the Law Reports, and the condition of the Reports on the 31st December, 1883. By W. T. S. Daniel. 1884. 8vo.   **83 J**

The Law Reports in all the Courts. Published under the authority of the Incorporated Council of Law Reporting for England and Wales, from 1865–1890. 212 vols., and Digests of cases 1865–1890. 6 vols. 1882–90. 218 vols. 1866–90. 8vo.   **72, 73 & 1 F G**

Another copy, except Indian Appeals. 201 vols. 1866–90. 8vo.   **61 & 62**

Admiralty and Ecclesiastical Cases, 1865–75. 4 vols. 1867–75. **73 B**

Appeal Cases :

Chancery Appeal Cases, 1865–75. 10 vols. 1866–75. **72 C**

English and Irish Appeal Cases and claims of peerage before House of Lords, 1866–75. 7 vols. 1866–75. **73 C D**

Appeal Cases before the House of Lords (English, Irish, and Scotch) and the Judicial Committee of the Privy Council, 1875–1890. 15 vols. in 16. 1876–90. **72 C D**

Scotch and Divorce Appeal Cases before the House of Lords, 1866–1875. 2 vols. 1869–75. **73 B**

Indian Appeals, 1873–1889. 16 vols. 1874–89, and Supplemental Appeals, 1872–73. 1880. **1 F G**

Privy Council Appeals, 1865–1875. 6 vols. 1867–75. **73 C**

Cases determined by the Chancery Division and by the chief judge in bankruptcy and by the Court of Appeal and in lunacy, 1875–1890. 45 vols. 1876–90. **72 F–I**

Court of Common Pleas, 1865–1875. 10 vols. 1866–75. **73 H**

Common Pleas Division, 1875–1880. 5 vols. 1876–80. **73 H I**

Cases determined by the court for Crown Cases Reserved, 1865–1875. 2 vols. 1872–1875. **73 B**

Equity Cases before the Master of the Rolls and the Vice-chancellors, 1865–1875. 20 vols. 1866–75. **72 D–F**

Court of Exchequer, 1865–1875. 10 vols. 1866–75. **73 I**

Exchequer Division, 1875–1880. 5 vols. 1876–80. **73 I**

Courts of Probate and Divorce, 1865–75. 3 vols. 1869–75. **73 D**

Probate Division, 1875–1890. 15 vols. 1876–90. **73 D**

Court of Queen's Bench, 1865–1875. 10 vols. 1866–75. **73 D E**

Queen's Bench Division, 1875–1890. 25 vols. 1876–90. **73 E–G**

Digest of cases, together with a digest of the important statutes, 1865–1885. 3 vols. 1882–86. **73 F**

Consolidated Current Index, 1886–1888. 1889. **73 F**

The Current Index of all cases reported in 'The Law Reports' and 'Weekly Notes,' 1889, 1890. 2 vols. 1889–90. **73 F**

LAW REPORTS, The (Ireland).

The Law Reports (Ireland), containing reports of cases argued and determined in the Court of Appeal, the High Court of

LAW REPORTS, THE (IRELAND)—*continued.*

· Justice, and the Court of Bankruptcy in Ireland, 1878–1890. 24 vols. Dublin, 1879–90. 8vo. **17 H I**

Digest of Cases reported in the Law Reports (Ireland), volumes i.–xx. Compiled by W. Green and R. Manders. Dublin, 1890. 8vo. · **17 I**

LAW REVIEW.

The Law Review and quarterly journal of British and foreign Jurisprudence, November 1844 to February 1856. 23 vols. 1845–56. 8vo. **137 C D**

LAW SCRUTINY.

The Law Scrutiny ; or, Attornies guide. 1807. 12mo. **118 A**

LAW SOCIETY, THE INCORPORATED.

Calendar for the years 1881–1890, and supplements 1885, 1887, and 1889. 13 vols. 1881–90. 8vo. **134 G**

Catalogues of the books in the library. 1841, 1851 and 1869. 3 vols. in 2. 1841–51–69. 8vo. **82 B**

Charter of incorporation, dated 22 December 1831, bye-laws made and ordained at a general meeting of the members 22 May 1832 and general regulations made by the committee of management. 1839. 8vo. **70 B**

Charter of incorporation, dated 26 February 1845, bye-laws made and ordained at a general meeting of the members 9 May 1845, general regulations made by the council, grant of arms, crest and supporters June 1845, and the statutes relating to attorneys and solicitors 6 & 7 Vict. c. 73 and 7 & 8 Vict. c. 86. 1845. 8vo. · **70 B**

Charter of Incorporation : Supplemental charter, bye-laws and regulations, 1872. 1879. 8vo. **70 B**

Copy of the deed of settlement of the Law Institution, dated 16 February, 1827. 1829. 8vo. **70 B**

The Incorporated Law Society and the Law Club. By J. R. Macarthur. 1883. [Pamphlets, vol. 34.] **144 C**

Official record of the entertainments given by the London members of the Incorporated Law Society in the Jubilee year 1887. 1887. 8vo. **70 B**

Proceedings and resolutions of the annual provincial meetings of the members of the Society, 1874–1890. 17 vols. 1874–90. 8vo. **70 B**

Proceedings at the third and fourth annual meetings of the

LAW SOCIETY, THE INCORPORATED—*continued.*
Law Institution, held 2 June 1829 and 7 June 1830. 1829–
30. 8vo. **70 B**
Prospectus of a law institution ; for a library &c. to be established in or near Chancery Lane. London, Jan. 23, 1825.
1825. 8vo. **70 B**
Reports made to the annual general meetings of the members
of the Incorporated Law Society, 1837–1890. 6 vols. 1837–
90. 8vo. **70 B**
See also LAW LISTS.

LAW SOCIETY (IRELAND), THE INCORPORATED.
Calendar and Law Directory for the years 1886, 1887. 2 vols.
Dublin, 1886–87. 8vo. **136 I**

LAW STUDENT'S ANNUAL.
The Law Student's Annual, 1882 and 1884. By J. A. Shearwood. 2 vols. 1882–84. 8vo. **64 D**

LAW STUDENTS' JOURNAL.
The Law Students' Journal, 1879 to 1890. Edited by J.
Indermaur and C. Thwaites. 12 vols. 1879–90. 8vo. **62 G**

LAW TIMES.
The Law Times, from April 1843 to October 1890. 89 vols.
1843–90. folio. **65 B–F**

LAW TIMES REPORTS.
The Law Times Reports, April 1843 to Nov. 1859. 34
vols. 1843-60. folio. **65 B, C**
The Law Times Reports. New Series. 1859–1890. 62
vols. 1860–90. 8vo. **17 A–F**
General index to Law Times Reports (n.s.). vols. 1 to 50.
Sept. 1859 to Aug. 1884. 5 vols. [n.d.] 8vo. **17 G**

LAW, ERNEST.
A Historical catalogue of the pictures in the royal collection
at Hampton Court; with an account of the state rooms.
1881. 8vo. **89 D**

LAW, REV. JAMES THOMAS.
The ecclesiastical statutes at large. 5 vols. 1847. 8vo. **31 D**

LAW, Rev. James Thomas—*continued.*

Forms of Ecclesiastical law ; or, the mode of conducting suits in the Consistory courts : being a translation of the first part of Oughton's Ordo Judiciorum. 1831. 8vo.   **166 B**

LAW, John.

Proposals and reasons for constituting a council of trade in Scotland. Glasgow, 1751. 12mo.   **114 A**

LAW, Samuel.

A Domestic Winter-Piece : or, a poem exhibiting a full view of the author's dwelling-place in the winter-season. Leeds, 1772. 12mo.   **83 C**

LAW, Stephen D.

Copyright and patent laws of the United States 1790 to 1868. 2nd ed.   New York, 1867. 12mo.   **60 A**

LAW, William John.

Comments on new scheme of Insolvency. 1843. 12mo. **169 A**

LAWES, Edward.

The declaration on bills of exchange, promissory notes &c. illustrated and explained. 1842. 12mo.   **160 G**

A Practical treatise on charter-parties of affreightment, bills of lading, and stoppage in transitu. 1813. 8vo.   **161 F**

Suggestions for some alterations of the law, on the subjects of Practice, Pleading, and Evidence ; and for some amendments of the statutes of frauds and limitations. 1827. [Jacob's Tracts, vol. 9.]   **144 E**

LAWRANCE, George Woodford.

Precedents of Deeds of Arrangement between debtors and their creditors. 1884. 8vo.   **165 G**

The same. 2nd ed. 1886. 8vo.   **52 E**

The same. 3rd ed. 1888. 8vo.   **12 I**

LAWRENCE, Basil Edwin.

History of the laws affecting the property of married women in England. 1884. 8vo.   **10 H**

LAWRENCE, Edwin.

The progress of a century : or, the age of iron and steam. 1886. 8vo.   **78 B**

LAWRENCE, Philip Henry.

Extracts from the court rolls of the manor of Wimbledon.
1866. 8vo. 93 C

LAWRENCE, William Beach.

The indirect claims of the United States, under the treaty of
Washington, of May 8, 1871, as submitted to the tribunal
of arbitration at Geneva. Providence, 1872. 8vo. 59 A

Notice sur la vie et les œuvres de M. W. B. Lawrence. Gand,
1876. [Pamphlets, vol. 35.] 144 C

LAWS.

De l'Origine des loix, des arts et des sciences et de leur progrès chez les anciens peuples. [Par A. Y. Goguet.] 3 vols.
in 2. Paris, 1758. 4to. 78 H

Direct legislation by the people, versus representative government; translated from the original Swiss pamphlets by
Eugene Oswald. 1869. [Pamphlets, vol. 35.] 144 C

Enchiridion Legum: a discourse concerning the beginnings,
nature, difference, progress and use of laws in general; and
in particular, of the common and municipal laws of England. 1673. 12mo. 49 A

Law as it relates to the economic condition of a people. By
J. A. Lawson. 1842. [Pamphlets, vol. 16.] 144 B

Petri Josephi De Ryckere Oratio de legum interpretatione.
1824. [Latin Tracts on civil and canon law.] 118 E

The Spirit of Laws. Translated from the French of M. De
Secondat, Baron De Montesquieu, by Thomas Nugent.
5th ed. 2 vols. 1773. 8vo. 49 G

Tractatus ex variis juris interpretibus, continet eos tractatus,
qui de cognitione et interpretatione juris, ac verborum
significatione summatim et in genere tractant; cum indicibus. 18 vols. in 13. Lugduni, 1549. folio.

See also Law.

LAWSON, John.

Lectures concerning Oratory delivered in Trinity college,
Dublin. 1759. 12mo. 78 A

LAWSON, William Norton.

Practice as to letters patent for inventions, copyright in designs,
and registration of trade marks; with the practice in actions
for infringement of patent. 1884. 8vo. 53 B

The same. 2nd ed. 1889. 8vo. 11 B

LAWTON, George.

A Brief treatise of Bona Notabilia ; with an account of the archiepiscopal courts of probate within the province of York, and of other courts of probate, in the counties of York and Nottingham. York, 1825. 8vo.   **94 A**

LAWYERS.

A Book about lawyers. By John Cordy Jeaffreson. 2nd ed. 2 vols. 1867. 8vo.   **79 G**

The Burning Shame ; or, punishment for bad lawyers, a custom peculiar to the borough of Newport in the Isle of Wight, a poem. By T. Nicholls. 1812. 12mo.   **118 C**

Law and lawyers ; or, sketches and illustrations of legal history and biography. [By James Grant.] 2 vols. 1840. 8vo.   **79 G**

Law students and young attorneys, their conduct and some of the conditions of professional success. By C. T. Saunders. Birmingham, 1866. [Pamphlets, vol. 27.]   **144 B**

The Lawyer and his profession. By J. O. Smith. 1860. 8vo.   **170 F**

The life of a lawyer, written by himself. [Sir James Stewart.] 1830. 8vo.   **79 B**

Lives of Eminent British Lawyers. By H. Roscoe. [n.d.] 8vo.   **79 B**

Coke, Sir Edward. 1–43.	Wilmot, Sir J. E. 229–240.
Selden, John. 43–59.	Blackstone, Sir W. 240–257.
Hale, Sir Matthew. 59–83.	Thurlow, Lord. 258–287.
Guilford, Lord. 83–113.	Ashburton, Lord. 287–306.
Jefferies, Lord. 113–139.	Jones, Sir Wm. 306–328.
Somers, Lord. 140–170.	Erskine, Lord. 329–391.
Mansfield, Lord. 171–228.	Romilly, Sir Samuel. 391–410.

Pseudo Lawyers. By F. A. Lewis. 1851. [Pamphlets, vol. 20.]   **144 B**

Some professional recollections by a former member of the council of the Incorporated Law Society. [Charles Reynolds Williams.] 1883. 8vo.   **80 G**

Strictures on the lives and characters of the most eminent lawyers of the present day. [By Edward Wynne.] 1790. 8vo.   **80 F**

Thoughts on present condition of legal practitioners. By One of the proscribed. 1834. [Law Tracts, vol. 5.]   **144 E**

Thoughts on the present state and prospects of legal discontent. No. VI. 1860. [Pamphlets, vol. 15.]   **144 B**

LAWYERS—*continued*

Westminster Hall ; or, professional relics and anecdotes of the bar, bench, and woolsack. [Compiled by Henry and Thomas Roscoe.] 3 vols. 1825. 12mo. **79 A**

LAWYER'S MAGAZINE.

The Lawyer's and Magistrate's Magazine; including an account of every important proceeding in the Courts at Westminster, 1790–1794. 6 vols. 1790–94. 8vo. **140 A**

LAXTON, WILLIAM.

Laxton's Builders' price book for 1869; the Metropolitan Buildings Act, with notes of cases and decisions in the superior courts. 51st ed. 1869. 12mo. **146 E**

LAYTON, ALFRED THOMAS.

Models of bills of costs. 2nd ed. 1884. 8vo. **9 F**

LEACH, ARTHUR FRANCIS.

Club cases, being considerations on the formation, management and dissolution of clubs. 1879. 8vo. **9 C**

Digest of law relating to probate duty. 1878. 8vo. **174 D**

LEACH, THOMAS.

Cases in Crown Law, determined by the twelve judges; by the court of King's Bench, and by Commissions of Oyer and Terminer, and general gaol delivery, 1730–88. 1789. 8vo.

The same. From 1730–1800. 3rd ed. 2 vols. 1800. 8vo.

The same. From 1730–1815. 4th ed. 2 vols. 1815. 8vo. **1 H**

LEADER, WILLIAM.

The Franchise, a manual of registration and election law and practice. 1879. 12mo. **166 C**

LEADING CASES.

American Leading Cases, being select decisions of American courts in several departments of law with especial reference to mercantile law. By J. I. C. Hare and H. B. Wallace. 4th ed. 2 vols. Philadelphia, 1857. 8vo. **59 F**

An Epitome of leading conveyancing and equity cases. By John Indermaur. 6th ed. 1887. 8vo. **64 B**

Leading cases and opinions on International law. By Pitt Cobbett. 1885. 8vo. **55 A**

LEADING CASES—*continued.*

Leading cases in Constitutional Law briefly stated. By E. C. Thomas. 2nd ed. 1885. 8vo. **64 B**

Leading cases made easy ; a selection of leading cases in the Common Law. By W. S. Shirley. 3rd ed. 1886. 8vo. **64 B**

Leading cases on Torts. By W. E. Ball. 1884. 8vo. **11 H**

Leading common law cases. By John Indermaur. 6th ed. 1886. 8vo. **64 B**

A Selection of cases on sales of Personal Property. By C. C. Langdell. vol. 1. Boston, 1872. 8vo. **60 B**

A Selection of cases on the English law of Contract. By G. B. Finch. 1886. 8vo. **52 C**

A Selection of leading cases in Equity. By F. T. White and O. D. Tudor. 6th ed. 2 vols. 1886. 8vo. **10 F**

A Selection of leading cases in the Criminal Law. By W. S. Shirley. 1888. 8vo. **64 B**

A Selection of leading cases on Mercantile and Maritime Law. By O. D. Tudor. 3rd ed. 1884. 8vo. **10 F**

A Selection of leading cases on the law relating to conveyancing. By O. D. Tudor. 3rd ed. 1879. 8vo. **10 F**

A Selection of leading cases on various branches of the law. By J. W. Smith. 9th ed. by R. H. Collins and R. G. Arbuthnot. 2 vols. 1887. 8vo. **10 F**

The Student's leading cases. By J. F. Haynes. 2nd ed. 1884. 8vo. **64 E**

LEAKE, STEPHEN MARTIN.

Digest of law of uses and profits of land. 1888. 8vo. **10 D**

Elementary digest of law of property in land. 1874. 8vo. **174 F**

Elements of law of Contracts. 1867. 8vo. **163 D**

The same. New ed. 1878. 8vo. **9 E**

LEAMINGTON.

Historical and descriptive account of town and castle of Warwick and of neighbouring spa of Leamington. By Wm. Field. Warwick, 1815. 4to. **93 F**

LEARNING.

Of the advancement and proficience of learning ; or, the partitions of sciences, IX bookes. By Francis Bacon, interpreted by G. Wats. Oxford, 1640. 4to. **78 G**

A Tribute to learning, fame, science and genius. By C. F. Cort. 1834. 4to. **83 J**

LEASES AND LEASEHOLDS.

Precedents of Leases for years. By J. M. Lely and W. A. Peck. 1889. 8vo. **13 C**

Dissertation on and precedents of Leases. See Bythewood and Jarman's Conveyancing, vol. 3, 1886, pp. 1–616. **13 D**

Unfair restraints upon dealings with leasehold property. By Thomas Colborne. 1883. [Pamphlets, vol. 35.] **144 C**

Ethics of Urban Leaseholds. [1879.] [Pamphlets, vol. 35.] **144 C**

Precedents of Leases, with practical notes. By John Andrews. 2nd ed. 1878. 12mo. **13 C**

The law of Leases. By T. Platt. 2 vols. 1847. 8vo. **13 C**

A Treatise on Leases and terms for years. By Charles Harcourt Chambers. 1819. 8vo. **172 A**

Opinions on terms in gross, and attendant on the inheritance. See Collectanea Juridica, vol. 2, 1792, pp. 267–276. **144 G**

An Essay on the learning respecting the creation and execution of Powers, and also respecting the nature and effect of Leasing Powers. By J. J. Powell. 1787. 8vo. **174 B**

LEATHERSELLERS' COMPANY.

History and antiquities of the Company of Leathersellers of the City of London. By W. H. Black. 1871. folio. **92 H**

LEBEAU, Monsieur.

Nouveau Code des Prises, ou Recueil des Edits, Déclarations, Lettres patentes &c. sur la course et l'administration des Prises, depuis 1400 jusqu'à l'établissement du Conseil des Prises. 3 vols. Paris, An 7–9 [1798–1800]. 4to. **40 H**

LE BLOND, Guillaume.

The military engineer; or, a treatise on the attack and defence of all kinds of fortified places. 1759. 8vo. **78 B**

LECKY, William Edward Hartpole.

A History of England in the eighteenth century. 8 vols. 1883–90. 8vo. **116 G**

LE CRAS, Abraham Jones.

. The laws, customs, and privileges, and their administration in the Island of Jersey. 1839. 12mo. **94 F**

LEDWICK, Rev. Edward.

Antiquities of Ireland. Dublin, 1790. 4to. **95 F**

A Statistical account of the parish of Aghaboe in the Queen's county, Ireland. Dublin, 1796. 8vo. **95 E**

LEE, SIR GEORGE.

Reports of cases in the Arches and Prerogative courts of Canterbury, containing the judgments of Sir George Lee, 1752–58. By J. Phillimore. 2 vols. 1833–32. 8vo. 8 H

LEE, JOHN YATE.

The evidence of Abstracts of title to real property. 1843. 8vo. 13 A

LEE, LAWFORD YATE.

The law and practice of bankruptcy and imprisonment for debt. 1871. 8vo. 160 D

The same. 2nd ed. by L. Yate Lee and Henry Wace. 1884. 8vo. 160 D

The same. 3rd ed. by L. Y. Lee and H. Wace. 1887. 8vo. 12 I

LEE, RICHARD.

A Treatise of captures in war. 2nd ed. 1803. 8vo. 55 A

LEE, THOMAS.

Cases in the Court of King's Bench at Westminster, 7–10 George II., during which time the late Lord chief justice Hardwicke presided in that court. 2nd ed. 1815. 8vo. 5 B

Dictionary of practice in civil actions in courts of King's Bench and Common Pleas. 2 vols. 1811–12. 8vo. 162 G

The same. 2nd ed. 2 vols. 1825. 8vo. 162 G

LEECHDOMS, SAXON.

Leechdoms, wortcunning, and starcraft of early England. Edited by Rev. Oswald Cockayne. 3 vols. 1864–66. 8vo. 102 A

LEEDS, YORKSHIRE.

The civil, ecclesiastical, literary, commercial, and miscellaneous history of Leeds &c. By E. Parsons. 2 vols. Leeds, 1834. 8vo. 94 B

Ducatus Leodiensis ; or, the topography of the town and parish of Leedes and parts adjacent. By Ralph Thoresby. 2nd ed. by T. D. Whitaker. Leeds, 1816. folio. 95 H

National exhibition of works of art at Leeds, 1868. Official catalogue. Leeds, 1868. 8vo. 94 A

A Summary view of the proposed canal from Leeds to Liverpool, and of its importance to the public. Leeds, 1770. 8vo. 94 A

LEEDS, Francis, 5 Duke of.
Political memoranda, [1774–1796]. Edited by Oscar Browning. [Camden Society, n.s. vol. 35.] 1884. 8vo. **85 D**

LEEMING, Henry and Richard Assheton CROSS.
General and quarter sessions of the peace; their jurisdiction and
practice in other than criminal matters. 1858. 8vo. **175 E**
The same. 2nd ed. by H. Lloyd and H. F. Thurlow. 1876.
8vo. **53 F**

LEES, James.
The laws of British Shipping and of marine assurance. 9th
ed. 1865, and 10th ed. 1877. 8vo. **175 F**

LEEUWEN, Simon van.
Commentaries on the Roman-Dutch law. Edited by C. W.
Decker, translated by J. G. Kotze. 2 vols. 1881–86.
8vo. **55 D**

LEEWARD ISLANDS.
Acts of the General Legislature of the Leeward Islands, 1877–
1888. 4 vols. 1877–88. folio. **36 E**
See also Antigua.

LEGACIES.
Treatise on the law of Legacies. By R. S. D. Roper. 4th
ed. by H. H. White. 2 vols. 1847. 8vo. **10 F**
Treatise on the law of Legacies. By Wm. Lowndes. 1824.
8vo. **172 A**
The Orphan's legacy. By John Godolphin. 4th ed. 1701.
8vo. **48 G**
See also Executors and Wills.

LEGACY DUTIES.
A Practical guide to the payment of Legacy and Succession
duties. By Corrie Hudson. 8th ed. by A. T. Layton.
1890. 8vo. **11 G**
Table showing at a glance the incidence of the English Death
Duties. By Ellis Harris. 1890. 8vo. **11 G**
Revenue acts of 1880 and 1881 so far as they relate to the
new Death Duties. By A. Hanson. 1883. 8vo. **11 G**
Acts relating to Probate, Legacy and Succession duties, with
copious notes. By A. Hanson. 3rd ed. 1876. 8vo. **11 G**
The law relating to Probate, Legacy and Succession duties in

39—2

LEGACY DUTIES—*continued.*

England, Ireland and Scotland. By Leonard Shelford. 2nd ed. 1861. 12mo. **176 D**

See also GWYNNE, T. and TREVOR, C. C.

LEGAL BIBLIOGRAPHY.

An Index to legal periodical literature. By L. A. Jones. Boston, 1888. 8vo. **82 F**

A Short view of legal bibliography. By R. W. Bridgman. 1807. 8vo. **82 C**

See also CATALOGUES, LEGAL.

LEGAL EDUCATION.

Advice on the study and practice of the Law. By Wm. Wright. 3rd ed. 1824. 8vo. **171 A**

A Course of Legal Study. By D. Hoffman. 2nd ed. 2 vols. Baltimore, 1836. 8vo. **170 G**

The first book of the Law ; explaining the nature, sources, books, and practical applications of Legal Science. By J. P. Bishop. Boston, 1868. 8vo. **59 F**

The Inns of Court and legal education. By C. T. Saunders. 1875. [Pamphlets, vol. 33.] **144 C**

A Letter to Henry Brougham, Esq., M.P., upon the present state of legal education. By G. B. Mansel. 1830. [Law Tracts, vol. 3.] **144 E**

Outlines of practical Law, being the law student's first book. By the Editors of the Law Chronicle. 1858. 8vo. **170 E**

A Popular and practical introduction to Law studies. By Samuel Warren. 3rd ed. 2 vols. 1863. 12mo. **171 A**

Reflections on the natural and acquired endowments requisite for the study of the Law. By Joseph Simpson. 5th ed. by M. Dawes. [n.d.] 12mo. **171 A**

Reflections on the study of the Law. By R. W. Bridgman. 1804. 8vo. **171 A**

Remarks on legal education with reference to the suggested introduction of legal studies into the University of Oxford. By T. H. Haddan. 1848. [Pamphlets, vol. 7.] **144 A**

Report from the select committee on Legal Education, with the minutes of evidence. 1846. folio. **153 D**

Studii legalis ratio ; or, directions for the study of the law. By Wm. Phillips. 1675. 12mo. **48 A**

The study and practice of the Law, considered in their various relations to society. By John Raithby. 2nd ed. 1816. 8vo. **170 G**

LEGAL FACETIÆ.

The Conveyancer's guide ; or, The law student's recreation, a poem. By John Crisp. 3rd ed. 1832. 8vo.   **118 A**

The Court of Chancery, a satirical poem. By Reginald James Blewitt. 1827. 8vo.   **118 C**

Eldoniana ; a familiar poetical dialogue between a reformer and a chancery barrister in Westminster Hall. By Rev. John W. Fca. 1826. [Jacob's Tracts, vol. 3.]   **144 E**

Fragmenta antiquitatis ; or, ancient tenures of land and jocular customs of manors. By Thomas Blount. 4th ed. by W. C. Hazlitt. 1874. 8vo.   **13 B**

The law scrutiny ; or attornies' guide. 1807. 12mo. **118 A**

The lays of a limb of the law. By the late John Popplestone. Edited by E. B. V. Christian. 1889. 12mo.   **78 B**

Leading cases made easy. A selection of leading cases in the common law, with notes. By W. S. Shirley. 1880. 8vo.   **64 B**

Legal facetiæ, satirical and humorous. By John Willock. 1887. 8vo.   **78 B**

The Pleader's Guide, a didactic poem, containing the conduct of a suit at law. By the late John Surrebutter, Esquire. [John Anstey.] 5th ed. 1808. 8vo.   **118 A**

A View of the Court of Chancery. By W. L. Wellesley. 1830. 8vo.   **118 C**

LEGAL FORMS.

Legal forms for common use. By J. W. Smith. 6th ed. 1875. 12mo.   **164 E**

Legal Forms, compiled for the use of attorneys and solicitors. By W. C. Hall. 1865. 12mo.   **164 E**

See also MOORE, H.

LEGAL MAXIMS.

A Selection of Legal Maxims classified and illustrated. By Herbert Broom. 6th ed. by H. F. Manisty and C. Cagney. 1884. 8vo.   **64 E**

Legal Maxims with observations and cases. By G. F. Wharton. 1865. 8vo.   **64 E**

The Grounds and Maxims, and an analysis of the English laws. By Wm. Noy. 6th ed. by C. Barton. 1794. 12mo.   **49 F**

Maxims and rules of the law of England. See C. Lofft's Reports of cases, 1776, pp. 9–43.   **74 E**

Maximes du droit public François. 2 vols. 1772. 12mo. **58 F**

See also BACON, SIR F., FRANCIS, R. and WINGATE, E.

LEGAL OBSERVER.

The Legal Observer, or journal of jurisprudence, Nov. 1830 to Dec. 1856. 52 vols. in 59. 1831–56. 8vo. **139 D–G**

LEGGETT, EUGENE.

A Treatise on the law of Bills of Lading. 1880. 8vo. **52 I**

LEGISLATURE AND LEGISLATION.

A Declaration of the people's natural right to a share in the legislature. By Granville Sharp. 2nd ed. 1775. 8vo. **49 D**

Essays on the spirit of legislation in the encouragement of agriculture, population, manufactures and commerce. Translated from the French. 1772. 8vo. **78 B**

The science of Legislation. By Gaetano Filangieri. Translated from the Italian by Wm. Kendall. 1792. 8vo. **170 F**

LEGITIMACY.

The law of marriage and legitimacy. By H. Weightman. 1871. 8vo. **53 A**

Practical treatise on the law of Marriage, Divorce and Legitimacy. By J. F. Macqueen. 2nd ed. 1860. 8vo. **166 A**

See also INFANCY.

LEHR, ERNEST.

Éléments de droit civil Russe. Paris, 1877. 8vo. **55 C**

LEIBNITZ, GOTFRIED WILHELM.

A Collection of papers which passed between the late learned Mr. Leibnitz and Dr. Clarke, in the years 1715 and 1716, relating to the principles of natural philosophy and religion. By S. Clarke. 1717. 12mo. **78 A**

LEICESTER.

History and antiquities of the ancient town of Leicester. By John Throsby. Leicester, 1791. 4to. **90 G**

Poll for members to represent the borough of Leicester in Parliament, March 22 to April 6, 1768. Leicester, 1768. 8vo. **107 K**

Poll for electing two burgesses to represent borough of Leicester in the ensuing Parliament, 23rd to 31st May, 1796. Leicester, 1796. 8vo. **107 K**

Poll for the election of two representatives in Parliament for the borough of Leicester, commenced June 13th, closed June 23rd, 1826. Leicester, 1826. 8vo. **107 K**

LEICESTER, Robert, 11 Earl of.

Correspondence of Robert Dudley, Earl of Leycester, during his government of the Low Countries, in 1585 and 1586. Edited by J. Bruce. [Camden Society, vol. 27.] 1844. 8vo. **85 A**

LEICESTERSHIRE.

The history and antiquities of the county of Leicester. By John Nichols. 4 vols. in 8. 1795–1811. folio. **89 H & 90 H**

Poll for a knight of the shire, to represent the county of Leicester, begun on the 12th of Jan. 1775, and continued till the 26th. Leicester, 1775. 8vo. **107 K**

Select views in Leicestershire, with descriptive and historical relations and a series of excursions to the villages and places of note in the county. By John Throsby. 2 vols. 1789–90. 4to. **89 C**

A Topographical history of the county of Leicester. By Rev. John Curtis. Ashby-de-la-Zouch, 1831. 8vo. **89 C**

See also BRAY, W.

LEIGH, Charles.

Life of Charles Leigh, M.D. See J. P. Malcolm's Lives of Topographers and Antiquaries, 1815, 4to. **79 H**

The natural history of Lancashire, Cheshire, and the Peak in Derbyshire ; with an account of the British, Phœnician, Armenian, Gr. and Rom. antiquities in those parts. Oxford, 1700. folio. **89 G**

LEIGH, Hon. Edward Chandos and L. W. CAVE.

Crown cases reserved for consideration and decided by the judges of England, 1861–1865. 1 vol. 1866. 8vo. **1 H**

LEIGH, Hon. E. C. and Henry D. LE MARCHANT.

A Guide to Election Law and the law and practice of election petitions. 1870, and 4th ed. by Y. Anderson and C. E. Ellis. 8vo. 1885. **166 C**

LEIGH, Patrick Brady.

The Game laws. 1831. 12mo. **168 F**

LEIGH PEERAGE.

A History of the claim of George Leigh to the dormant title of Baron Leigh of Stoneley in the county of Warwick. 2nd ed. 2 vols. 1832. 8vo. **124 F**

LELAND, John.

De rebus Britannicis Collectanea ex autographis descripsit ediditque Tho. Hearnius. 6 vols. Oxonii, 1715. 8vo. **86 A**

The itinerary of John Leland the antiquary. 2nd ed. 9 vols. in 5. Oxford, 1745. 8vo. **86 A**

LELY, John Mountney.

The annual continuations of Chitty's Statutes, 1881–1890. 3 vols. 1885–90. 8vo. **70 I**

Railway and Canal traffic. The regulation of railways act 1873, and other statutes. 1873. 8vo. **175 B**

The Judicature acts with notes, forming a practice of the Supreme Court. By J. M. Lely and W. D. I. Foulkes. 2nd ed. 1877. 12mo. **169 F**

The same. 3rd ed. 1881. 12mo. **169 F**

The same. 4th ed. 1883. 12mo. **12 G**

The Licensing acts, containing the law of the sale of liquors by retail and the management of licensed houses. By J. M. Lely and W. D. I. Foulkes. 1872. 12mo. **172 A**

The same. 2nd ed. 1874. 12mo. **172 A**

The parliamentary election acts for England and Wales. By J. M. Lely and W. D. I. Foulkes. 1885. 8vo. **166 D**

The Agricultural holdings act 1883 and other statutes. By J. M. Lely and Edward Robert Pearce. 1883. 8vo. **9 A**

Precedents of Leases for years. By J. M. Lely and W. A. Peck. 1889. 8vo. **13 C**

LE MARCHANT, Thomas.

Remarques et animadversions sur l'approbation des lois et coustumier de Normandie usitées ès jurisdictions de Guernezé. 2 vols. in 1. Guernesey, 1826. 8vo. **94 F**

LEMPRIERE, Rev. John.

A Classical dictionary, containing a copious account of all the proper names mentioned in ancient authors. 20th ed. 1844. 8vo. **84 C**

LE NEVE, John.

Fasti Ecclesiæ Anglicanæ; or, a calendar of the principal ecclesiastical dignitaries in England and Wales, and of the chief officers in the Universities of Oxford and Cambridge, from the earliest time to 1715. Corrected and continued by T. D. Hardy. 3 vols. Oxford, 1854. 8vo. **80 H**

LE NEVE, JOHN—*continued.*

The laws of honour ; or, a compendious account of the ancient derivation of all titles, dignities, offices, &c. [By John Le Neve.] 1726. 12mo. **125 B**

LENG, ROBERT.

Sir Francis Drake's memorable service done against the Spaniards in 1587. Now first edited by C. Hopper. [Camden Society, vol. 87.] 1864. 8vo. **85 C**

LEONARD, PATRICK MARCELLINUS.

Precedents of pleadings in equity in the county courts. 1869. 8vo. **165 C**

LEONARD, WILLIAM.

Reports and Cases of Law, argued and adjudged in the Courts at Westminster in the time of Elizabeth and James I. 4 parts in 1 vol. 1658–75. folio.

The same. 2nd ed. 4 parts in 2 vols. 1687. folio. **74 E**

LE RICHE, EDWARD W.

A Book of Costs in the common law and divorce courts. 1860. 8vo. **165 A**

LE SAGE, ALAIN RENÉ.

Le Diable Boiteux ; or, the Devil upon two sticks. Translated from the last edition at Paris. 1713. 12mo. **118 A**

Histoire de Gil Blas de Santillane. Nouvelle éd. vols. 2, 3, 4. Paris, 1787. 12mo. [vol. 1 missing.] **155 A**

LESLIE, SIR JOHN.

A Dissertation exhibiting a general view of the progress of Mathematical and Physical science, chiefly during the Eighteenth century. See Encyclopædia Britannica, 8th ed. vol. 1, pp. 691–793. **147 A**

LESSING, GOTTHOLD EPHRAIM.

Fabeln in Prosa und Versen. In vier Büchern. Düben, 1860. 12mo. **83 B**

L'ESTRANGE, REV. ALFRED GUY.

The palace and the hospital ; or, chronicles of Greenwich. 2 vols. 1886. 8vo. **88 D**

The village of palaces ; or, chronicles of Chelsea. 2 vols. 1880. 8vo. **89 D**

L'ESTRANGE, Sir Robert.

Tully's Offices in three books turned out of Latin into English. 5th ed. 1699. 12mo.   **78 A**

LETTERS.

Original letters of eminent literary men of the sixteenth, seventeenth and eighteenth centuries. Edited by Sir H. Ellis. [Camden Society, vol. 23.] 1843. 8vo.   **85 A**

LEUNCLAVIUS, Johannes.

Juris Græco-Romani tam canonici quam civilis tomi duo, Gr. et Lat., ex variis Europæ Asiæque bibliothecis eruti. Nunc primum editi curâ Marquardi Freheri. 2 vols. in 1. Francofurti, 1596. folio.   **118 G**

LEVI, Leone.

International commercial law. 2 vols. 1863. 8vo.   **55 A**

LEVINS, Peter.

Manipulus Vocabulorum : a dictionary of English and Latin words, arranged in the alphabetical order of the last syllables. First printed 1570 ; now re-edited by H. B. Wheatley. [Camden Society, vol. 95.] 1867. 8vo.   **85 C**

LEVINZ, Sir Cresswell.

Collection of select and modern Entries referring to the cases in his Reports. 1702. folio.

Reports en Bank le Roy, commençant en le 12 an de Roy Charles II, et fini en le 8 an de Will. III. 3 parts in 2 vols. 1702. folio.

The same. 2nd ed. translated into English by Mr. Serjeant Salkeld. 3 parts in 2 vols. 1722. folio.   **74 E**

LEVY, Matthias.

Shorthand notes and the practice relating to them. 1886. 8vo.   **11 F**

LEWES, Sussex.

The history and antiquities of Lewes and its vicinity. By Rev. T. W. Horsfield ; with the natural history of the district, by G. Mantell. Lewes, 1824. 4to.   **93 D**

LEWES, Sussex—*continued*.

A Poll, taken 5 and 6 July, 1802 ; for the election of members to represent the borough of Lewes in Parliament. Lewes, 1803. 12mo. **107 K**

The same. Taken 5 and 6 October, 1812. Lewes, 1812. 8vo. **107 K**

The same. Taken 7–10 June, 1826. Lewes, 1826. 8vo. **107 K**

LEWIN, Frederick Albert.

The law of Apportionment. 1869. 12mo. **9 A**

LEWIN, Sir Gregory Allnutt.

A Report of cases determined on the crown side on the Northern circuit, 1822–38. 2 vols. 1834–39. 12mo. **1 H**

LEWIN, Thomas.

A Practical treatise on the law of Trusts and Trustees. 1837, and 2nd ed. 1842. 8vo. **176 G**

The same. 6th ed. 1875. 8vo. **176 G**

The same. 7th ed. 1879. 8vo. **53 I**

The same. 8th ed. by F. A. Lewin. 1885. 8vo. **11 I**

LEWIS, Sir George Cornewall.

Remarks on the use and abuse of political terms. A new ed. by Sir R. K. Wilson. Oxford, 1877. 8vo. **78 B**

LEWIS, Hubert.

Principles of conveyancing explained and illustrated by concise precedents. 1863. 8vo. **53 D**

Principles of Equity drafting. 1865. 12mo. **167 C**

LEWIS, James.

Digest of the English census of 1871. 1873. 8vo. **78 G**

LEWIS, Rev. John.

The history and antiquities, as well ecclesiastical as civil, of the Isle of Tenet in Kent. 2nd ed. 1736. 4to. **88 E**

History and antiquities of the abbey and church of Favresham, in Kent ; of the adjoining priory of Davington, and Maison-Dieu of Ospringe, and parish of Bocton subtus le Bleyne. 1727. 4to. **88 E**

LEWIS, PERCIVAL.

Historical inquiries concerning forests and forest laws; with topographical remarks upon the ancient and modern state of the New Forest. 1811. 4to.　　　88 B

LEWIS, SAMUEL.

A Topographical dictionary of England, with historical and statistical descriptions, illustrated by maps of the different counties and islands. 5 vols. 1831. 4to.　　　84 F

LEWIS, THOMAS.

On the constitution, jurisdiction, and practice of the Sheriffs' courts of London. 1833. 8vo.　　　175 E

LEWIS, WILLIAM DAVID.

Can Remainders be too remote? 1844. [Pam., vol. 23.] 144 B
Horæ Juridicæ; or, thoughts on the profession of the law. 1845. [Pamphlets, vol. 3.]　　　144 A
The law of Perpetuity, or remoteness in limitations of estates; with supplement. 1843-49. 8vo.　　　53 C

LEY, SIR JAMES.

Reports of divers resolutions in law, arising upon cases in the Court of Wards and other courts at Westminster, 1608-1629; to which is added, a treatise of Wards and Liveries. 1659. folio.　　　74 E

LEYCESTER, SIR PETER.

Historical antiquities, in two books: the first treating in general of Great-Brettain and Ireland; the second containing particular remarks concerning Cheshire, with a transcript of Doomsday-Book so far as it concerneth Cheshire. 1673. 4to.　　　87 G
The history of Chester. By George Ormerod, with a republication of Leycester's Cheshire Antiquities. 2nd ed. by Thomas Helsby. 3 vols. 1882. folio.　　　86 H

LIBEL.

The law of Slander and Libel (founded on treatise of late Mr. Starkie). 5th ed. by H. C. Folkard. 1891. 8vo. 11 F
Law of Newspaper Libel. By R. J. Kelly. 1889. 12mo. 11 F
The law of Libel in its relation to the Press. By Hugh Fraser. 1889. 8vo.　　　11 F

LIBEL—*continued.*

The law of Libel. See A. Powell's Law affecting Printers, 2nd ed., 1889, pp. 131–185, and 261–274.　　　　**11 C**

A Digest of the law of Libel and Slander. By W. Blake Odgers. 2nd ed. 1887. 8vo.　　　　**11 F**

The law of anti-religious Libel. By Rev. J. B. White. Dublin, 1834. 8vo.　　　　**172 A**

Observations on practice of Court of Chancery in cases relating to libellous and immoral publications. 1823. [Jacob's Tracts, vol. 1.]　　　　**144 E**

De libellis famosis ; or, the law of libels. By J. Jones. 1812. 8vo.　　　　**172 A**

A Letter to the Right Hon. Charles James Fox, occasioned by his motion in the House of Commons respecting libels. By John Bowles. 2nd ed. 1792, and A second letter. By John Bowles. 1792. [Tracts on Libel, vol. 4.]　　**144 F**

Considerations on the respective rights of judge and jury, particularly upon trials for libel. By John Bowles. 2nd ed. 1791. [Tracts on Libel, vol. 4.]　　　　**144 F**

The deformity of the doctrine of libels ; with a view of the case of the dean of St. Asaph. By M. Dawes. 1785. [Tracts on Libel, vol. 3.]　　　　**144 F**

England's Alarm ! on the prevailing doctrine of libels, as laid down by the Earl of Mansfield. Also The celebrated dialogue between a gentleman and a farmer, written by Sir Wm. Jones, with Remarks thereon, and on the case of the Dean of St. Asaph. By M. Dawes. 1785. [Tracts on Libel, vol. 3.]　　　　**144 F**

A Letter to the jurors of Great Britain occasioned by an opinion of the Court of King's Bench in the case of the King and Woodfall. By George Rous. 2nd ed. 1785. [Tracts on Libel, vol. 3.]　　　　**144 F**

Discussions on the law of Libels as at present received. [By W. James Adair.] 1785. [Tracts on Libel, vol. 2.] **144 F**

Considerations on libel, suggested by Mr. Fox's notice in parliament of an intended motion on that subject. By John Leach. 2nd ed. [n.d.] [Tracts on Libel, vol. 2.]　　**144 F**

A Letter concerning libels, warrants, the seisure of papers and sureties for the peace or behaviour. [By John Almon.] 7th ed. 1771. [Tracts on Libel, vol. 1.]　　**144 F**

A Summary of the law of Libel in four letters signed Phileleutherus Anglicanus. 1771. [Tracts on Libel, vol. 1.] **144 F**

A Letter to Sir Richard Aston, Knt., containing a reply to his scandalous abuse and some thoughts on the modern

LIBEL—*continued.*

doctrine of libels. By Robert Morris. 2nd ed. 1770.
[Tracts on Libel, vol. 3.]   **144 F**

An Essay on the liberty of the press, chiefly as it respects
personal slander. [By T. Hayter.] 2nd ed. [1755.]
[Tracts on Libel, vol. 1.]   **144 F**

The doctrine of libels and the duty of juries fairly stated. By
The author of The excise scheme dissected, &c. 1752.
[Tracts on Libel, vol. 1.]   **144 F**

State law ; or, the doctrine of libels discussed and examined.
2nd ed. 1730. [Tracts on Libel, vol. 1.]   **144 F**

LIBERTY.

British Liberties, or the free-born subject's inheritance. 2nd
ed. 1767. 8vo.   **49 C**

English Liberties, or the free-born subject's inheritance. By
Henry Care. 4th ed. by W. N. 1719. 8vo.   **49 C**

Letters to Mr. Justice Blackstone concerning his Exposition
of the act of toleration and some positions relative to
religious liberty. By Rev. P. Furneaux. 2nd ed. 1771.
8vo.   **77 B**

The libertie of the subject against the pretended power of impositions. By Wm. Hakewil. 1641. 12mo.   **48 D**

Speeches of T. Erskine when at the bar on subjects connected
with the liberty of the press. 4 vols. 1810. 8vo.   **83 B**

The works of that grave and learned lawyer, Judge Jenkins,
prisoner in Newgate, upon divers statutes concerning the
liberty of the subject. 1648. 12mo.   **48 A**

LIBRARIES.

A Digest of the law relating to Public Libraries and Museums
and literary and scientific institutions. By G. F. Chambers.
3rd ed. 1889. 8vo.   **10 G**

Library Aids. By S. S. Green. New York, 1883. 12mo. **82 B**

The library companion ; or, the young man's guide and the
old man's comfort in the choice of a library. By Rev. T.
F. Dibdin. 2nd ed. 2 vols. 1825. 8vo.   **82 C**

Public libraries in the United States of America, their history,
condition and management. Special report. Department
of the interior, bureau of education. 2 parts. Washington,
1876. 8vo.   **82 C**

See also CATALOGUES, LIBRARY.

LIBRARY ASSOCIATION OF THE UNITED KINGDOM.

Transactions and proceedings of the meetings of the Library Association of the United Kingdom, 1877–1884. 5 vols. 1877–90. 8vo. **82 E**

Monthly notes, 1880–83. 4 vols. in 2. 1880–83. 8vo. **82 E**

The Library Chronicle : a journal of librarianship and bibliography. Edited by E. C. Thomas. 5 vols. 1884–88. 8vo. **82 E**

The Library : a magazine of bibliography and literature. Edited by J. Y. W. MacAlister. 2 vols. 1889–90. 8vo. **82 E**

LICENCES.

Dissertation on and precedents of Licences. See Bythewood and Jarman's Conveyancing, 4th ed., vol. 3, 1886, pp. 617–639. **13 D**

See also EASEMENTS and LEASES.

LICENSING ACTS AND LICENSED VICTUALLERS.

Intoxicating liquor licensing acts 1872, 1874. By J. Paterson. 7th ed. 1889. 12mo. **12 C**

A Manual of the law concerning the retailing of intoxicating drinks. By C. P. Deane. 1887. 8vo. **12 C**

The legal status of licensed victuallers. By F. G. Hindle. 1883. 8vo. **12 C**

On the laws regulating licenses for the sale of intoxicating liquors in England. By E. T. Payne. 1883. [Pamphlets, vol. 35.] **144 C**

The laws as to licensing. By G. C. Oke. 2nd ed. by W. C. Glen. 1874. 8vo. **53 A**

The laws relating to licensed victuallers. By S. C. Horry. 1837. 12mo. **172 A**

LICHFIELD, STAFFORDSHIRE.

A Short account of Lichfield cathedral. [By J. C. Woodhouse.] 4th ed. Lichfield, 1834. 8vo. **93 C**

LIDDELL, REV. HENRY GEORGE and REV. R. SCOTT.

Greek-English lexicon. 5th ed. 1861. 4to. **123 F**

LIEN.

A Treatise on the Lien of Attornies. By Whitley Stokes. 1860. 8vo. **10 G**

LIEN—*continued.*

Law of Lien and stoppage in transitu. By John Cross. 1840.
8vo.   10 G

A Summary of the law of Lien. By Basil Montagu. 1821.
8vo.   172 A

The law relative to the rights of Lien and stoppage in
transitu. By Richard Whitaker. 1812. 8vo.   172 A

See also Fisher's Digest, vol. 4, 1884, pp. 1856–1881.   14 E

LIFE ASSURANCE.

The law of insurance, fire, life, accident and guarantee. By
J. B. Porter. 2nd ed. 1887. 8vo.   10 D

The decisions in life assurance law. By A. Scratchley. 1887.
8vo.   10 D

Law of life insurance. By C. Crawley. 1882. 8vo.   10 D

The law of life assurance. By C. J. Bunyon. 2nd ed. 1868.
8vo.   10 D

A Treatise on the law of fire and life insurance. By J. K.
Angell. 2nd ed. Boston, 1855. 8vo.   59 E

Remarks on certain acts of the last session of parliament
affecting life assurance. By Frederick Chaplin. 1853.
[Pamphlets, vol. 9, pt. 2.]   144 A

See also BAILY, F., BEAUMONT, G. D. B., ELLIS, C., FARREN,
E. J., FARREN, G., KELLY, J. B. and POCOCK, L.

LIGHT.

Light and Air. By B. Fletcher. 2nd ed. 1886. 8vo. 10 G

A Digest of the law of Light. By E. S. Roscoe. 2nd ed
1886. 8vo.   10 G

Law and science of ancient lights. By H. Cox. 2nd ed.
1871. 8vo.   10 G

See also EASEMENTS, LATHAM, F. L. and YOOL, G. V.

LILLY, JOHN.

Collection of Modern Entries ; or, select pleadings in the courts
of King's Bench, Common Pleas, and Exchequer. 1723,
and 2nd ed. 1741. folio.

The same. 5th ed. 2 vols. 1791. 8vo.   173 F

The practical conveyancer. 3rd ed. 1742. folio.   157 E

The practical register ; or, a general abridgment of the law.
2 vols. 1719. folio.   157 E

LILLY, William.

William Lilly's History of his life and times, 1602 to 1681, written by himself to his worthy friend Elias Ashmole. [Autobiography, vol. 4.] 1829. 12mo. **79 A**

LIMERICK.

The history of Limerick, and An essay on Castle Connell Spa. By John Ferrar. Limerick, 1787. 8vo. **95 E**

Reports of proceedings at the special commission (1867) for the county and city of Limerick, in cases of high treason and treason-felony. Dublin, 1871. 8vo. **50 A**

LIMITATIONS.

The Statutes of Limitations. See Bythewood and Jarman's Conveyancing, 4th ed. vol. 1, 1884, pp. 1–62. **13 D**

A Manual of the statutes of Limitation. By James Walter. 4th ed. 1883. 8vo. **10 G**

The rule against perpetuities ; a treatise on remoteness in Limitations. By R. G. Marsden. 1883. 8vo. **11 B**

The law of Limitation as to real property. By William Brown. 1869. 8vo. **53 A**

See also ACTIONS, LIMITATION OF, DARBY, J. G. N., FERGUSON, J. F., GIBBONS, D. LEWIS, W. D. and MANSEL, G. B.

LINCOLN.

An Account of all the courts in the diocese of Lincoln. See R. Swan's Jurisdiction of the ecclesiastical courts, 1830, pp. 81–112. **78 C**

Roberti Grosseteste, episcopi quondam Lincolniensis, Epistolæ. Edited by H. R. Luard. 1861. 8vo. **101 F**

LINCOLN'S INN.

The case between Lincoln's Inn, the Court of King's Bench and Mr. T. J. Wooler, with a critical commentary. By Mr. Wooler. 1826. [Jacob's Tracts, vol. 3.] **144 E**

Lincoln's Inn, its ancient and modern buildings, with an account of the library. By W. H. Spilsbury. 2nd ed. 1873. 12mo. **91 D**

Return from the Society of Lincoln's Inn to the select committee of the House of Commons, appointed to enquire into the state of the public records of the Kingdom. 1801. 8vo. **97 I**

The student's guide through Lincoln's Inn. By Thomas Lane. 2nd ed. 1805. 8vo. **91 D**

See also CATALOGUES, LIBRARY, and INNS OF COURT.

LINCOLNSHIRE.

Chronicle of rebellion in Lincolnshire, 1470. Edited by J. G. Nichols. [Camden Soc., vol. 39.] 1847. 8vo. **85 B**

The history of the county of Lincoln. By Thomas Allen. 2 vols. 1833–34. 4to. **89 C**

See also FENS, THE.

LINDENBROG, FRIEDRICH.

Codex legum antiquarum : in quo continentur leges Wisigothorum ; edictum Theodorici Regis ; lex Burgundionum; lex Salica ; lex Alamanorum ; lex Baivvariorum ; decretum Tassilonis Ducis ; lex Ripuariorum ; lex Saxonum; Angliorum et Werinorum ; Frisionum ; Longobardorum ; constitutiones Siculæ sive Neapolitanæ; capitulare Karoli Magni et Hludowici Impp. Quibus accedunt Formulæ solennes priscæ publicorum privatorumque negotiorum, nunc primum editæ ; et Glossarium ; ex Bibliotheca Frid. Lindenbrogi. Francofurti, 1613. folio. **118 G**

[LINDESAY, PATRICK.]

The interest of Scotland considered with regard to its police, agriculture, trade, &c. 1733. 8vo. **114 A**

LINDLEY, SIR NATHANIEL.

The law of Companies considered as a branch of the law of Partnership. 5th ed. 1889. 8vo. **9 D**

A Treatise on the law of Partnership. 2 vols. 1860, and supplement, 1863. 3 vols. 1860–63. 8vo. **173 D**

The same. 2nd ed. 2 vols. 1867. 8vo. **173 D**

The same. 3rd ed. 2 vols. 1873. 8vo. **173 D**

The same. 4th ed. 2 vols. 1878. 8vo. **53 B**

The same. 5th ed. 1888. 8vo. **11 D**

LINDSAY, RALPH.

Etymology of Southwark. 3rd ed. 1839. 12mo. **93 C**

LINGARD, REV. JOHN.

History of England, from the first invasion by the Romans [to 1688]. 4th ed. 13 vols. 1837–39. 12mo. **115 D**

LINGLOIS, PETRUS FRANCISCUS.

Quinquaginta decisiones Imperatoris Justiniani, quæ a secundo libro codicis usque ad nonum diffusæ sunt. Antverpiæ, 1661. folio. **48 H**

LIPSCOMB, George.

The history and antiquities of the county of Buckingham. 4 vols. 1847. 4to. **86 G**

LISBON.

Short account of view of Lisbon now exhibiting in H. A. Barker's Panorama, Leicester Square. 1812. 12mo. **84 B**

LISET, Abraham.

Amphithalami; or, the accountant's closet, being an abridgment of merchants accounts. 1684. See G. Malynes's Lex Mercatoria, 3rd ed. 1686. folio. **118 G**

LITERATURE AND LITERARY MEN.

The cases of the appellants and respondents in the cause of Literary Property, before the House of Lords : wherein the decree of Lord Chancellor Apsley was reversed. By a Gentleman of the Inner Temple. 1774. 4to. **157 B**

Original letters of eminent literary men of the sixteenth, seventeenth, and eighteenth centuries. Edited by Sir Henry Ellis. [Camden Society, vol. 23.] 1843. 8vo. **85 A**

The question concerning Literary Property, determined by the court of King's Bench, in the cause between A. Millar and R. Taylor. By J. Burrow. 1773. 4to. **157 B**

The scientific and literary treasury. By Samuel Maunder. New ed. 1858. 12mo. **78 A**

A Summary of facts, drawn from the records of the Royal Literary Fund, and issued by the committee; together with a report of the proceedings at the last annual meeting, March 12, 1858. 1858. [Pamphlets, vol. 11.] **144 A**

A Treatise on the laws of Literary Property. By Robert Maugham. 1828. 8vo. **172 A**

See also ANONYMS, BIBLIOGRAPHY, CATALOGUES, COPYRIGHT and LIBRARIES.

LITTLE, James Brooke.

The Agricultural holdings act 1883 (46 & 47 Vict. cap. 61). 1884. **9 A**

The law of Allotments for the poor. 1887. 8vo. **9 A**

The law of Burial, including all burial acts and official regulations. 1888. 12mo. **9 B**

LITTLETON, EDWARD.

Les reports en le courts del Common Banck & Exchequer en le 2, 3, 4, 5, 6, 7 ans del reign de Roy Charles le I. 1683. folio.   74 E

LITTLETON, H. A. and J. S. BLATCHLEY.

Digest of Fire Insurance decisions in the courts of Great Britain and North America. 2nd ed. by S. G. Clarke. New York, 1868. 8vo.   59 F

LITTLETON, THOMAS.

Les Tenures du Monsieur Littleton. 1577. 12mo.   49 A
Tenures in English perused and amended. 1600. 12mo. 48 A
Tenures in French and English. 1671. 12mo.   48 A
See also COKE, SIR E.

LITTRÉ, MAXIMILIEN PAUL ÉMILE.

Dictionnaire de la langue Française. Et Supplément, par Marcel Devic. 5 tomes. Paris, 1881. folio.   123 F

LITURGIES AND PRAYERS.

ΒΙΒΛΟΣ ΤΗΣ ΔΗΜΟΣΙΑΣ ΕΥΧΗΣ [English Prayer-book in Greek]. Cambridge, 1665. 12mo.   118 A
The Book of Common Prayer. By Sir John Bayley 1816. 8vo.   77 E
The Book of Common Prayer with notes. By Right Rev. Richard Mant. 3rd ed. Oxford, 1825. 4to.   77 G
The Book of Common Prayer [with the Act for the Uniformity of Common Prayer]. 1724. folio.   77 H
Christian prayers and holy meditations. Collected by Henry Bull. [A.D. 1566.] Reprinted. Cambridge, 1842. 12mo. 77 D
Family prayers adapted from the Bible Psalms, and family and private prayers principally from the liturgy of the Church of England. By a lay-member of that Church [John Stow]. 1840. 8vo.   77 C
La Liturgia Ynglesa, o el Libro de Oracion Commun. Hispanizado por D. F. A. de Alvarado. 1707. 8vo. 77 B
Liturgies and occasional forms of prayer set forth in the reign of Queen Elizabeth. Edited by Rev. W. K. Clay. Cambridge, 1847. 8vo.   77 D
A Rational illustration of the Book of Common Prayer of the Church of England By Charles Wheatly. Oxford, 1810. 8vo.   77 B

LITURGIES AND PRAYERS—*continued.*

Thoughts on the Book of Common Prayer used in the Church of England. By a lay member of that Church [John Stow]. 2 vols. 1850–56. 12mo. **77 A**

Troubles connected with the Prayer Book of 1549. Edited by Nicholas Pocock. [Camden Society, n.s. vol. 37.] 1884. 8vo. **85 D**

Two liturgies, A.D. 1549 and A.D. 1552 ; with other documents set forth by authority in the reign of King Edward VI. Edited by Rev. J. Ketley. Cambridge, 1844. 8vo. **77 D**

LIVERPOOL.

Authentic copies of the several acts of parliament relative to the docks, port and harbour of Liverpool, and the lighthouses, &c. thereto belonging. Liverpool, 1804. 8vo. **89 B**

Catalogue of the contents of the library of the Incorporated Law Society of Liverpool. Liverpool, 1880. 8vo. **82 B**

A Catalogue of the library of the Athenæum, Liverpool. By George Burrell. Liverpool, 1820. 8vo. **82 B**

An Essay towards the history of Leverpool : drawn up from papers left by George Perry, and from other materials since collected. By Rev. Wm. Enfield. 2nd ed. 1774. folio. **89 G**

Liverpool Art Club. Collection illustrative of the history and practice of Etching. Lent and catalogued by James Anderson Rose. Liverpool, 1874. [Pamphlets, vol. 33.] **144 C**

The Liverpool guide, including a sketch of the environs. By W. Moss. 2nd ed. Liverpool, 1797. 8vo. **89 A**

Liverpool, its commerce, statistics, and institutions. By Henry Smithers. Liverpool, 1825. 4to. **88 F**

Memorials of Liverpool ; including a history of the Dock estate. By J. A. Picton. 2 vols. 1873. 8vo. **89 B**

A Statement of facts in support of the petition of the inhabitants of Liverpool and its vicinity for an adjournment of the assizes from Lancaster to Liverpool and Manchester. Liverpool, 1833. [Pamphlets, vol. 20.] **144 B**

A Summary view of the proposed canal from Leeds to Liverpool, and of its importance to the public. Leeds, 1770. 8vo. **94 A**

Two arguments in the Exchequer for the Corporation of Liverpool against the Corporation of London. See Hargrave's Juridical Arguments, vol. 1, 1797, pp. 471–510, and Appendix, pp. xxx–liii. **144 G**

LIVINGSTON, John.
United States law register and official directory. New York, 1860. 8vo. 59 F
The same. New York, 1868. 8vo. 59 F

LIVIUS, Titus.
The discourses of N. Machiavel upon the First decade of T. Livius. See N. Machiavel's Works, 1680, pp. 263–431. 113 G
See also Classics.

LLORENTE, Juan Antonio.
Leyes del Fuero-Juzgo, ó recopilacion de las leyes de los Wisi-Godos Españoles. Segunda edicion del texto Castellano, precede un discurso preliminar, y una declaracion de voces antiquadas. Madrid, 1792. 8vo. 39 C

LLOYD, Bartholomew Clifford and F. GOOLD.
Reports of cases in the high court of Chancery in Ireland, 1835. 1 vol. 1836. 8vo. 15 F
A Selection of cases in the high court of Chancery in Ireland, 1834–1836. Dublin, 1839. 8vo. 15 F

LLOYD, Clement Elphinstone.
The County Courts Act 1888. 1888. 8vo. 52 E

LLOYD, David.
Memoires of the lives, actions, sufferings, and deaths of those noble personages that suffered by death for the Protestant religion in our late intestine wars ; with the life and martyrdom of King Charles I. 1668. folio. 79 H

LLOYD, Eyre.
Law of Compensation under lands clauses, railways clauses consolidation acts and other acts. 1867. 8vo. 163 D
The same. 5th ed. 1882. 8vo. 52 C
The succession laws of Christian countries. 1877. 8vo. 11 G

LLOYD, John Horatio and W. N. WELSBY.
Reports of cases relating to commerce, manufactures, &c. determined in the courts of Common Law, 1829 and 1830. 1 vol. 1829–30. 8vo. 5 C

LLOYD, Morgan.

Legal handbook and complete manual of practical law forms.
[n.d.] 12mo. **13 F**

The law of Prohibition. 1849. 12mo. **174 D**

LOANS AND LOAN SOCIETIES.

The contract of Pawn. By F. Turner. 2nd ed. 1883. 8vo. **11 B**

The pawnbrokers', factors', and merchants' guide to the law
of loans and pledges. By H. C. Folkard. 1873. 8vo. **53 B**

Instructions for the establishment of Loan Societies. 1837.
8vo. **144 F**

LOCAL AND PERSONAL ACTS.

The Local and Personal Acts, from 1798 to 1890. 417 vols.
1798–1890. folio. **26 D–31 C**

An Index to the Local and Private Acts, 1801–1887. 3 vols.
1867–90. folio. **31 E**

Index to the Local and Personal, and Private acts, 1798–1839.
By Thomas Vardon. 1840. 8vo. **31 E**

LOCAL COURTS.

An Estimate of Mr. Brougham's Local Court bill. By An
Observer. 1830. [Jacob's Tracts, vol. 7.] **144 E**

A Letter to Sir F. Pollock, on the subject of Local Courts.
By Henry Manisty. 1843. [Pamphlets, vol. 3.] **144 A**

Local Courts and tribunals of commerce. By R. M. Pankhurst. Manchester, 1866. [Pamphlets, vol. 27.] **144 B**

Lords Lyndhurst, Brougham, and local courts. 1834. 12mo.
165 C

A Review of the objections taken by An 'Observer' and by
Mr. Raines to the Lord Chancellor's Bill for the establishment of courts of local jurisdiction. By Michael Quin.
1831. 12mo. **165 C**

See also County Courts Reform.

LOCAL GOVERNMENT.

The law relating to the Public Health and Local Government.
By W. C. Glen. 10th ed. by W. C. Glen and A. Glen.
1888. 8vo. **11 D**

History of local authorities. See F. A. Clifford's History of
Private Bill legislation, vol. 2, 1887, pp. 199–357. **83 I**

Fry's Union assessment committee acts. 7th ed. by R. C. Glen
and A. D. Lawrie. 1887. 12mo. **11 I**

LOGIC.

Logic. By Richard Whately, D.D. 1869. 12mo. 78 A

Pure logic ; or, the logic of quality apart from quantity. By
W. S. Jevons. 1864. 12mo. 78 A

LOLLARD DOCTRINES.

An Apology for Lollard doctrines, attributed to Wicliffe.
Edited by J. H. Todd. [Camden Society, vol. 20.] 1842.
8vo. 85 A

LONDON AND ITS ENVIRONS.

Angliæ Metropolis ; or, the present state of London. By
Thomas Delaune. 1690. 12mo. 91 B

Calendar of Wills proved and enrolled in the Court of Husting,
London, A.D. 1258–A.D. 1688. Edited by R. R. Sharpe.
2 vols. 1889–90. 8vo. 90 D

Camera Regis ; or, a short view of London. By John Brydall.
1676. 12mo. 91 B

The citizen's pocket chronicle, containing a digested view of
the history, antiquity, and temporal government of the City
of London. 1827. 12mo. 91 B

The City remembrancer : being historical narratives of the
great plague at London, 1665 ; great fire, 1666 ; and great
storm, 1703 ; with observations and reflections on the plague
in general, and historical accounts of the most memorable
plagues, fires and hurricanes. 2 vols. 1769. 8vo. 92 B

Commentaries on the history, constitution, and chartered
franchises of the City of London. By George Norton. 3rd
ed. 1869. 8vo. 91 E

The corporation of the city of London. See F. A. Clifford's
Private Bill legislation, vol. 2, pp. 358–432. 83 I

A Discourse of the true antiquity of London. See Stillingfleet's Ecclesiastical cases, second part. 1704. 8vo. 49 E

Ecclesiastical topography. A collection of one hundred views
of churches in the environs of London, accompanied with
descriptions. [Edited by Samuel Woodburn.] 2 vols. in 1.
1807–10. folio. 91 G

The environs of London, being an historical account of the
towns, villages and hamlets within twelve miles of that
capital. By Rev. D. Lysons. 4 vols. 1792–96. 4to. 89 F

The freemen of London's necessary and useful companion ;
or, the citizen's birth-right. 1703. 12mo. 92 A

LONDON AND ITS ENVIRONS—*continued.*

Greater London : a narrative of its history, its people, and its places. By Edward Walford. 2 vols. [1884.] 4to. **90 C**

Greater London and its government. By George Whale. 1888. 8vo. **10 G**

Handbook to the environs of London, alphabetically arranged. By James Thorne. 2 vols. 1876. 8vo. **89 C**

London. By W. J. Loftie. 1887. 8vo. **89 C**

The history and survey of London and its environs. By B. Lambert. 4 vols. 1806. 8vo. **90 A**

A History of London. By W. J. Loftie. 2nd ed. 2 vols. 1884. 8vo. **89 C**

The history of London from its foundation. By Wm. Maitland and others. 2 vols. 1756. folio. **92 H**

The ' Intelligence Quarterly' for London and Suburbs. 1887. 8vo. **91 F**

Leigh's New picture of London. Edited by S. C. 1818. 12mo. **92 B**

List of pupils of the City of London School who have proceeded to the Universities, 1844 to 1856. 1856. [Pamphlets, vol. 40.] **144 C**

Londinium Redivivum ; or, an ancient history and modern description of London. By J. P. Malcolm. 4 vols. 1802-7. 4to. **90 C**

London and Middlesex ; or, an historical, commercial, and descriptive survey of the metropolis of Great Britain. By E. W. Brayley, Rev. J. Nightingale and J. N. Brewer. 4 vols. in 5. 1810–16. 8vo. **90 B**

London and Westminster improved, illustrated by plans By John Gwynn. 1766. 4to. **89 F**

The London directory of 1677, the oldest printed list of the merchants and bankers of London. Reprinted. 1878. 12mo. **118 A**

London illustrated, a guide to the places of amusement, objects of interest and leading hotels. 1883. 8vo. **89 F**

London in the olden time, being a topographical and historical memoir of London, Westminster, and Southwark. By Wm. Newton. 1855. folio. **92 H**

Map of London, published by John Cassell. [n.d.] 4to. **92 G**

The names of all suche gentlemen of accompte as were residing within ye citie of London, liberties and suburbes thereof, 28 Novembris 1595. 8vo. **118 E**

A New history of London, including Westminster and Southwark. By John Noorthouck. 1773. 4to. **89 F**

LONDON ·AND ITS ENVIRONS—*continued.*

New remarks of London ; or, a survey of the cities of London and Westminster, of Southwark and part of Middlesex and Surrey. Collected by the Company of Parish Clerks. 1732. 12mo.   **91 B**

A New view of London, or an ample account of that city. [By Edward Hatton.] 2 vols. 1708. 8vo.   **92 B**

Old and new London, a narrative of its history, its people and its places. By Walter Thornbury and Edward Walford. 6 vols. 1879–85. 8vo.   **90 D**

Kelly's Post office guide to London. 1862. 8vo.   **92 B**

A Selection from the collection of views and drawings, illustrating topography of London, Westminster and Southwark, exhibited by J. E. Gardner at opening of new library and museum of corporation of London. 1872. 8vo.   **82 B**

Some account of London. By Thomas Pennant. 3rd ed. 1793. 4to.   **89 F**

A Survey of cities of London and Westminster and borough of Southwark. By John Rocque. 1751. folio.   **91 H**

A Survey of the cities of London and Westminster, and the borough of Southwark, written in 1698. By John Stow, corrected and enlarged in 1720, by John Strype. 6th ed. 2 vols. 1754–55. folio.   **92 H**

A Topographical dictionary of London and its environs. By James Elmes. 1831. 8vo.   **92 B**

See also BINNELL, R., BURN, J. H., CHAMBERLAIN, H., HORWOOD, R., HUGHSON, D., MORRIS, C., NEWCOURT, R., OVERALL, W. H., SCOTT, B., STORR, J. S. and WILKINSON, R.

LONDON BRIDGE.

Abstract of proceedings and evidence relative to London Bridge, taken from reports of a select committee of the House of Commons made in 1799, 1800 and 1801. 1819. 4to.   **91 G**

Chronicles of London Bridge. By An Antiquary. [Richard Thompson.] 1827. 8vo.   **91 C**

The conduct of the corporation of the City of London considered, in respect of the designs submitted to it, for rebuilding London Bridge, in a letter to G. H. Sumner. By An Architect. 1823. 8vo.   **91 C**

Report from the committee on the state of London Bridge, with minutes of evidence, 1821. folio.   **153 A**

LONDON CHARITIES.

The charities of London in 1861. By Sampson Low junior. 1862. 12mo. **92 B**

The same for the year 1875. Edited by Charles Mackeson. 1875. 12mo. **92 B**

The endowed charities of the City of London ; reprinted at large from seventeen reports of the commissioners for inquiring concerning charities. 1829. 8vo. **91 E**

Pietas Londinensis : the history, design, and present state of the various public charities in and near London. By Anthony Highmore. 1814. 8vo. **92 B**

Report of the Royal City Parochial Charities Commission, with four appendices. 4 vols. in 1. 1880. folio. **154 E**

See also CHARITIES.

LONDON CHARTERS.

The charters of the City of London, with acts of parliament and of common council relating to its government. See J. Noorthouck's History of London, 1773, pp. 773–873. **89 F**

The historical charters and constitutional documents of the City of London ; with an introduction and notes. By An Antiquary. [Walter de Gray Birch.] 1884. 4to. **91 F**

The pleadings, arguments, and other proceedings in the Court of Kings-Bench upon the Quo Warranto touching the charter of the City of London, with the judgment entred thereupon. 1696. folio. **91 G**

The royal charter of confirmation granted by King Charles II. to the City of London. Translated into English by S. G. [1680.] 12mo. **92 A**

See also EVELYN, J. and LUFFMAN, J.

LONDON CHRONICLES.

A Chronicle of London from 1089 to 1483, written in the fifteenth century. Edited by E. Tyrrell. 1827. 8vo. **89 F**

Chronicle of the Grey Friars of London. Edited by J. G. Nichols. [Camden Society, vol. 53.] 1852. 8vo. **85 B**

Croniques de London depuis l'an 44 Hen. III. jusqu'à l'an 17 Edw. III. Edited by G. J. Aungier. [Camden Society, vol. 28.] 1844. 8vo. **85 A**

A London chronicle during the reigns of Henry the Seventh and Henry the Eighth. Edited by Clarence Hopper. [Camden Society, vol. 73.] 1859. 8vo. **85 B**

See also GREGORY, W. and WRIOTHESLEY, C.

LONDON CITY COMPANIES.

See Carpenters Fishmongers, Grocers, Leather-sellers, Merchant Taylors and Scriveners.

LONDON GAZETTE.

The London Gazette, 1665–1890.   464 vols.   1665–1890.
folio.   41-45

Index to the orders in Council, proclamations, royal commissions of inquiry, and orders and notices of government departments, from January 1st, 1830, to December 31st, 1883. Compiled by A. Pulling.   1885.   8vo.   **45 H**

LONDON, Guildhall.

An Account of the monuments and pictures in Guildhall of City of London.   1827.   [City of London Tracts.]   **91 C**

Descriptive account of Guildhall of City of London, its history and associations.   By J. E. Price.   1886.   folio.   **92 H**

Munimenta Gildhallæ Londoniensis ; Liber Albus, Liber Custumarum, et Liber Horn.   Edited by H. T. Riley. 3 vols. in 4.   1859–62.   8vo.   **101 C**

LONDON, Health and Improvement of.

Burial-ground incendiarism.   The last fire at the bone-house in the Spa-fields Golgotha, or the minute anatomy of grave-digging in London.   By G. A. Walker.   1846. [Pamphlets, vol. 17.]   **144 B**

Centralization or Representation ?   A letter to the Metropolitan sanitary commissioners.   By J. T. Smith.   2nd ed. 1848.   [Pamphlets, vol. 6.]   **144 A**

London health and London traffic.   The embankment of the north side of the Thames between Blackfriars and Westminster bridges.   By T. L. Wood.   1859.   [Pamphlets, vol. 11.]   **144 A**

Proceedings at a public meeting held at the London Tavern 1 Dec. 1858 for the purpose of devising measures to diminish the overcrowding of the streets and provide improved dwellings for the working classes.   By C. Pearson.   1859. [Pamphlets, vol. 27.]   **144 B**

Prospectus of a design for various improvements in the Metropolis, principally about the Court.   By An Architect 1816.   8vo.   **91 B**

The question of Smithfield market fully considered.   By Clericus.   1837.   8vo.   **91 C**

Report of a public meeting to consider the best method of

LONDON, Health and Improvement of—*continued.*
extending operations of Metropolitan Association for improving dwellings of the industrious classes. List of Shareholders, &c. 1854. [Pamphlets, vol. 9, pt. 1.] **144 A**

The representation of the leaseholders and contractors interested in the houses and buildings in Pickett street, near Temple Bar, Skinner street, Fleet market and Snow hill; with the scheme of the proposed lottery. [n.d.] 8vo. **91 C**

LONDON HOSPITALS.

Account of the royal hospital and collegiate church of Saint Katherine, near the Tower of London. By J. B. Nichols. 1824. 4to. **89 F**

A History of the royal foundation of Christ's hospital. By Rev. Wm. Trollope. 1834. 4to. **89 F**

History of the royal hospital and collegiate church of St. Katherine, near the Tower of London, from its foundation in the year 1273. [By A. C. Ducarel.] 1782. 4to. **89 F**

Memoranda, references, and documents relating to the Royal Hospitals of the city of London. By J. F. Firth. 1836. 8vo. **91 C**

LONDON INSTITUTION.

Catalogue of the library, systematically classed : preceded by an historical and bibliographical account of the establishment. 4 vols. 1835–52. 8vo. **82 E**

The charter, act of parliament and bye-laws. 1832. 8vo. **82 E**

The inaugural oration spoken by Charles Butler, on the 4th November, 1815, at the ceremony of laying the first stone of the London Institution. 1816. 8vo. **82 E**

Introductory discourse delivered in amphitheatre of London Institution. By W. T. Brande. 1819. 8vo. **82 E**

LONDON LAWS AND CUSTOMS.

The customary law of the City of London. By W. Brandon. Part 1. The distribution of the personal estates of freemen dying intestate. 1845. [Pamphlets, vol. 20.] **144 B**

Practical treatise on laws, customs and regulations of city and port of London. By A. Pulling. 1842. 8vo. **91 E**

Orders for regulating the standing of carts for hire in the City of London. 1825. [City of London Tracts.] **91 C**

The laws and customs, rights, liberties and privileges of the City of London. 1765. 12mo. **92 A**

LONDON LAWS AND CUSTOMS—*continued.*

The same. 2nd ed. 1774. 12mo.   **92 A**

Privilegia Londini ; or, the rights, laws and customs of the City of London. By W. Bohun. 3rd ed. 1723. 8vo.   **91 B**

Lex Londinensis, or the city law : shewing the powers, customs and practice of all the courts. 1680. 12mo. **92 A**

The City law ; shewing the customes, franchises, liberties, priviledges of the city of London. 1658. 12mo.   **92 A**

See also CALTHROP, SIR H., EMERSON, T., FIELDING, SIR J., HUGHSON, D., JACOB, G. and NORTON, G.

LONDON MAYOR, SHERIFF AND CORPORATION.

Calendar of letters from the mayor and corporation of the City of London, circa A.D. 1350–1370. Edited by R. R. Sharpe. 1885. 8vo.   **91 F**

Correspondence between Mr. Alderman Venables and Mr. Coles respecting the office of Undersheriff of London and Middlesex. 1821. [Law Tracts, vol. 3.]   **144 E**

De antiquis legibus liber. Cronica maiorum et vicecomitum Londoniarum 1178 to 1274. Edited by T. Stapleton. [Camden Society, vol. 34.] 1846. 8vo.   **85 A**

The Livery triumphant. A letter to the Lord Mayor on his conduct respecting the late common hall, with the proceedings at large of the common hall. [n.d.] 12mo. **118 B**

Observations on the disputes at present arising in the Corporation of the City of London. By Alexander Pulling. 1847. [Pamphlets, vol. 35.]   **144 C**

A Reply to the statement of the court of rulers and assistants of the Fellowship, contained in the report of the Committee of controul over the coal and corn meters. 1818. [City of London Tracts.]   **91 C**

Some account of the citizens of London and their rulers from 1060 to 1867, and a calendar of the mayors and sheriffs from 1189 to 1867. By B. B. Orridge. 1867. 8vo. **91 C**

Two arguments in the Exchequer for the Corporation of Liverpool against the Corporation of London. See Hargrave's Juridical Arguments, vol. 1, 1797, pp. 471–510 and Appendix, pp. XXX–LIII.   **144 G**

See also GRAFTON, R., GREENE, J. and MILDMAY, SIR W.

LONDON, PARISHES IN CITY OF.

Brief notices of fabric and glebe of St. Mary Aldermary. By Rev. H. B. Wilson. 1840. [Pamphlets, vol. 1.] **144 A**

LONDON, PARISHES IN CITY OF—*continued.*

Correspondence and proceedings under the Union of benefices act, resulting in the order of council for removal of parish church of St. Dionis Backchurch and the sale of the site. 1878. By Rev. W. H. Lyall. [Pamphlets, vol. 37.] **144 C**

History of the parish of St. Laurence Pountney. By Rev. H. B. Wilson. 1831. 4to. **89 F**

A Letter to the parishioners of Saint Thomas the Apostle. By Rev. H. B. Wilson. [1850.] [Pamphlets, vol. 7.] **144 A**

Memorials of Temple Bar; with some account of Fleet Street, and the parishes of St. Dunstan and St. Bride. By T. C. Noble. 1869. 8vo. **89 D**

LONDON, PORT OF.

Abstract of laws and regulations relating to shipping in port of London. By C. Rowland. 2nd ed. 1843. 12mo. **92 A**

Minutes of the evidence taken at the Committees on the bill for rendering more commodious the Port of London. (City plan and Merchants plan.) 1799. folio. **91 G**

See also COLLIER DOCK.

LONDON SEWERS AND WATER SUPPLY.

Court of Sewers. A letter on the power of the Court to authorise in certain cases the demand of fees. By E. Mullins. 1836. 8vo. **118 B**

History of London water supply from creation of man to A.D. 1884. By A. Gladstone. 1884. [Pamphlets, vol. 38.] **144 C**

The London sewerage question. Some serious observations and suggestions upon the defective plan of sewerage proposed by the Metropolitan Board of Works. By G. R. Booth. [n.d.] [Pamphlets, vol. 11.] **144 A**

The Metropolis water supply and sewer questions answered; also considerations on the mineral water question. By G. P. Pond. 1879. [Pamphlets, vol. 38.] **144 C**

Report from the provisional directors of the London (Watford) Spring water company; and Mr. Hope's opening speech before the parliamentary committee. By J. R. Hope. 1852. [Pamphlets, vol. 9, pt. 2.] **144 A**

Report from select committee on supply of Water to the Metropolis, with minutes of evidence. 1821. folio. **153 A**

Reports on the results of a microscopical examination of the organic matters of waters supplied from the Thames and other sources. By Edwin Lankester and Peter Redfern. 1852. [Pamphlets, vol. 9, pt. 2.] **144 A**

LONDON SEWERS—*continued.*

Review of the report by the General Board of Health on the supply of water to the Metropolis. By S. C. Homersham. 1850. [Pamphlets, vol. 7.]   **144 A**

Standing orders of the Commissioners of Sewers of the City of London. 1806. [City of London Tracts.]   **91 C**

Substance of a Memorial presented by the Chartered gas light and coke company to the Commissioners of Sewers, London. [n.d.] [City of London Tracts.]   **91 C**

The water supply and main drainage of London. See F. A. Clifford's History of private bill legislation, vol. 2, pp. 36–198, and 334–348.   **83 I**

LONDON TITHES.

The tithes acts affecting the commutation and redemption of tithes in the City of London. By H. B. Burnell. 1880. 8vo.   **11 H**

Cases relating to the Tithes of the City of London. By T. G. Western. 1823. 8vo.   **66 A**

Important argument at the Mansion House, 8th Feb. 1823, before the Lord Mayor upon the Rev. Dr. Owen's application for a warrant for tithes, at 2*s.* 9*d.* in the pound upon rack-rental, under the statute of 37th Henry VIII. 1823. [City of London Tracts.]   **91 C**

LONDONDERRY.

Ordnance survey of the county of Londonderry. Vol. 1. Dublin, 1837. 8vo.   **95 F**

Reports of deputations who, in pursuance of resolutions of the Court of Assistants of the Drapers' Company, visited the estates of the company in the county of Londonderry. 1829. 8vo.   **95 F**

The same. Another ed. 1841. 8vo.   **95 F**

[LONG, EDWARD.]

The history of Jamaica ; or, general survey of the antient and modern state of that island. 3 vols. 1774. 4to.   **84 E**

LONG, GEORGE.

Reflections on certain parts of the law of England, with suggestions for the improvement of the same. 1827. [Jacob's Tracts, vol. 6.]   **144 E**

Law relative to sales of Personal Property. 1821. 8vo.   **174 E**

LONGCROFT, Charles John.

A Topographical account of the Hundred of Bosmere in the county of Southampton, including the parishes of Havant, Warblington and Hayling. 1857. 4to. **88 B**

LONGE REPORT.

En cest volume est conteinus le longe report de Anno Quinto Edwardi Quarti, ore novelment inprimée et corrigée. 1638. folio. **74 E**

LONGFIELD, Robert and J. F. TOWNSEND.

Reports of cases in the court of Exchequer in Ireland, 1841–1842. Dublin, 1843. 8vo. **15 F**

LONGMATE, Barak.

The peerage of England, Scotland and Ireland. 2 vols. in 1. 1813. 12mo. **123 A**

The pocket peerage of England, Scotland and Ireland, 1788, 1790, 1793, 1808, 1813. 10 vols. 1788-1813. 12mo. **123 A**

LOOE, Cornwall.

Report of the cases of the borough of West Looe ; with notes and cases illustrative of the general history of boroughs. By H. A. Merewether. 1823. 8vo. **87 A**

Topographical and historical sketches of the boroughs of East and West Looe. By T. Bond. 1823. 8vo. **87 A**

LOOSEY, Charles F.

Collection of the laws of Patent privileges of all the countries of Europe, the United States of N. America and the Dutch West Indies. Vienna, 1849. 8vo. **55 E**

LORD, Henry William.

The Highway of the Seas in time of war. 1862. 12mo. **55 A**

LORD LIEUTENANT.

Lord lieutenant and high sheriff, correspondence on question of precedence. By J. M. Davenport. 1871. 8vo. **92 E**

LORIMER, James.

Constitutionalism of the future ; or, Parliament the mirror of the nation. 2nd ed. 1867. 8vo. **116 E**

LORIMER, JAMES—*continued.*

Equal representation. A letter to Lord John Russell. 1859.
[Pamphlets, vol. 23.]   **144 B**

The institutes of Law : a treatise of the principles of Jurisprudence as determined by Nature. 1872. 8vo. .   **63 G**

LOUTH, LINCOLNSHIRE.

Notitiæ Ludæ, or notices of Louth. Louth, 1834. 8vo. **89 C**

LOUTH, JOHN.

The reminiscences of John Louth, archdeacon of Nottingham,
written in the year 1579. See Camden Society, vol. 77,
1859, pp. 1–59.   **85 B**

LOVELASS, PETER.

The law's disposal of a person's estate, who dies without will
or testament ; to which is added the disposal of a person's
estate by will and testament. 7th ed. 1792, and 9th ed.
1798. 8vo.   **177 D**

The same. 11th ed. by Niel Gow. 1823. 8vo.   **177 D**

The Trader's Safeguard ; or, a full explanation of the law
concerning bills of exchange, promissory notes and evidence
on a trial by jury. 3rd ed. 1796. 8vo.   **160 G**

LOVESY, CONWAY WHITHORNE.

The Churchwarden's guide. 8th ed. 1871. 12mo.   **161 F**

The law of Arbitration between masters and workmen. 1867.
12mo.   **160 B**

LOWE, LOUISA.

The Bastilles of England ; or, the lunacy laws at work. 1883.
8vo.   **78 C**

LOWER, MARK ANTONY.

A Compendious history of Sussex, topographical, archæological,
and anecdotical. 2 vols. 1870. 8vo.   **93 E**

Patronymica Britannica : a dictionary of the family names of
the United Kingdom. 1860. 8vo.   **127 I**

LOWESTOFT, SUFFOLK.

Historical account of Lowestoft, and a general account of
island of Lothingland. By E. Gillingwater. 1790. 4to. **93 B**

LOWNDES, JOHN JAMES and P. B. MAXWELL.
Bail Court cases, 1852–1854. vol. 1. parts 1–5. 1852–54.
8vo.   **5 C**

LOWNDES, J. J., P. B. MAXWELL and C. E. POLLOCK.
Reports of cases in Queen's Bench practice court, with points
of practice and pleading decided in courts of Common Pleas
& Exchequer, 1850–1851. 2 vols. 1851–52. 8vo. **5 B C**

LOWNDES, RICHARD.
The Admiralty law of collisions at sea. 1867. 8vo. **160 A**
The law of General Average (English and foreign). 1873.
8vo.   **168 F**
The same. 3rd ed. 1878. 8vo.   **52 H**
The same. 4th ed. 1888. 8vo.   **10 B**
A Treatise on law of Marine Insurance. 1881. 8vo. **169 B**
The same. 2nd ed. 1885. 8vo.   **10 D**

LOWNDES, WILLIAM.
Treatise on the law of Legacies. 1824. 8vo.   **172 A**

LOWNDES, WILLIAM THOMAS.
The bibliographer's manual of English literature. 2 vols. 1834.
8vo.   **82 G**
The same. New ed. revised and enlarged, with an appendix
relating to the books of literary and scientific societies, by
H. G. Bohn. 6 vols. 1864. 8vo.   **82 G**

LOWTH, ROBERT, D.D.
The life of William of Wykeham, bishop of Winchester. 3rd ed.
Oxford, 1777. 8vo.   **80 C**
A Short introduction to English grammar, with critical notes.
[By Robert Lowth.] New ed. 1795. 12mo.   **255 H**

LUBÉ, DENIS GEORGE.
Analysis of principles of Equity Pleading. 1823. 8vo. **173 G**

LUCAS, REV. CHARLES.
Observations on the modern clergy and the present state of
the church. Devizes, [1820]. 8vo.   **118 E**

LUCAS, Robert de Neufville.
The perils of Trusts and Trustees illustrated by unreported
cases founded in fact. 1860. 12mo. **176 F**

[LUCAS, Samuel.]
Dacoitee in excelsis ; or, the spoliation of Oude by the East
India Company, faithfully recounted. 1857. 8vo. **78 C**

LUCCHINI, Luigi.
Rivista penale di dottrina, legislazione e giurisprudenza. 8 vols.
Padova, 1874–78. 8vo. **56 E**

LUCIAN.
Lucian of Samosata, from the Greek ; with the comments and
illustrations of Wieland and others. By Wm. Tooke. 2 vols.
1820. 4to. **83 J**
The triumphs of the Gout, translated from the Greek. See
G. West's Odes of Pindar, 1749, pp. 229–278. **83 J**

LUDERS, Alexander.
Reports of proceedings in committees of the House of Commons upon controverted elections, 1785–1787. 3 vols. 1808–
1790. 8vo. **66 B**

LUDLOW, Shropshire.
Churchwardens' accounts of the town of Ludlow, 1540 to 1600.
Edited by T. Wright. [Camden Society, vol. 102.] 1869.
8vo. **85 C**
Historical account of Ludlow Castle. By Wm. Hodges.
Ludlow, 1794. 8vo. **93 A**

LUDLOW, Henry and Henry JENKYNS.
The law of Trade-Marks and Trade-Names. 1873. 8vo. **176 F**
The same. With supplement by J. Bryce. 1877. 8vo. **11 H**

LUDLOW, John Malcolm.
The Joint-Stock companies winding-up act 1848, and winding-
up amendment act 1849 ; with notes. 1850. 12mo. **169 D**

LUFFMAN, John.
The charters of London complete, also Magna Charta and
the Bill of Rights, with notes. 1793. 8vo. **91 B**

LUMLEY, BENJAMIN.

Parliamentary practice on passing Private Bills through the House of Commons, and the preliminary measures of the House of Lords, with Appendix. 1838–39. 8vo. **173 B**

LUMLEY, WILLIAM GOLDEN.

An Abridgment of the cases upon the subject of the Poor law. 2 vols. 1840–43. 8vo. **174 B**

An Essay on Bye-laws. 1877. 8vo. **52 A**

The law of annuities and rent charges. 1833. 8vo. **52 A**

The law of parochial assessments. 6th ed. 1872. 8vo. **173 B**

The same. 7th ed. by W. C. Glen. 1882. 8vo. **11 A**

The local board election manual. 4th ed. by A. Macmorran. 1886. 12mo. **10 G**

The new Sanitary laws. 1859. 12mo. **175 A**

The same. 3rd ed. by W. G. Lumley and E. Lumley. 1873. 8vo. **175 A**

The Nuisances removal and diseases prevention act of 1855. 2nd ed. 1860. 12mo. **173 B**

The Poor law election manual. 4th ed. 1877. 12mo. **174 B**

The same. 5th ed. 1886. 8vo. **11 C**

The Poor removal and Union chargeability act. 2nd ed. 1865. 12mo. **174 B**

The Public Health act 1875, annotated. By W. G. Lumley and Edmund Lumley. 1876. 8vo. **175 A**

The same. 3rd ed. by W. Patchett and A. Macmorran. 1887. 8vo. **11 D**

LUNACY.

The statutes relating to Lunacy. By J. F. Archbold. 3rd ed. by S. G. Lushington. 1890. 8vo. **10 H**

The law and practice of Lunacy. By H. M. R. Pope. 2nd ed. by J. H. Boome and V. De S. Fowke. 1890. 8vo. **10 H**

Handbook to the Lunacy acts amendment act 1889. By R. W. Partridge and E. Partridge. 1889. 8vo. **53 A**

Law and practice of petitions in Chancery and Lunacy. By S. E. Williams. 1880. 8vo. **11 B**

The practice in Lunacy. By Joseph Elmer. 6th ed. 1877. 8vo. **10 H**

Cause in lunacy. Reduction of the will of the late Colonel Maclean. 1861. [Pamphlets, vol. 20.] **144 B**

LUNACY—*continued*.

The laws of Lunacy and their crimes as they affect all classes of society. By Richard Saumarez. 1859. [Pamphlets, vol. 15.] **144 B**

Suggestions on law of Lunacy and lunatic asylums. By J. Leech. 2nd ed. 1852. [Pamphlets, vol. 9, part 2.] **144 A**

A Letter to the Lord Chancellor on a defect in the law regulating the custody of Lunatics. By C. P. Cooper. 3rd ed. 1849. [Pamphlets, vol. 6.] **144 A**

Society for promoting the amendment of the law. Report of the committee on equity on the law respecting Lunacy. 1848. [Pamphlets, vol. 15.] **144 B**

On the amendment of the law of Lunacy. A letter to Lord Brougham. By A Phrenologist [Thomas Tichborne]. 1843. [Pamphlets, vol. 20.] **144 B**

See also BRYDALL, J., COLLINSON, G. D., HALLIDAY, SIR A., HIGHMORE, A., LOWE, L., LUSHINGTON, S. G., PHILLIPS, C. P., SHELFORD, L. and WINSLOW, L. S.

LUPTON, FREDERICK.
Law relating to Dogs. 1888. 8vo. **9 G**

LUSH, MONTAGUE.
The law of husband and wife, within the jurisdictions of the Queen's Bench and Chancery divisions. 1884. 8vo. **10 C**

LUSH, ROBERT.
The practice of the superior courts of law at Westminster, in actions and proceedings over which they have a common jurisdiction. 1840. 12mo. **162 E**
The same. 2nd ed. by James Stephen. 1856. 12mo. **162 E**
The same. 3rd ed. by J. Dixon. 2 vols. 1865. 8vo. **52 B**

LUSHINGTON, GODFREY.
A Manual of Naval Prize law. 1866. 8vo. **172 G**

LUSHINGTON, SYDNEY GEORGE.
The Lunacy acts amendment act 1889. 1889. 8vo. **53 A**

LUSHINGTON, VERNON.
Reports of cases in the high court of Admiralty and on appeal to the Privy Council, 1859–1862. 1 vol. 1864. 8vo. **8 A**

LUTWYCHE, ALFRED JAMES PETER.

- Inquiry into principles of pleading general issue. 1838. 12mo.
- Reports of cases in the court of Common Pleas on appeal from the decisions of the revising barristers, 1843–1853. 2 vols. 1847–54. 8vo. **6 G**

LUTWYCHE, SIR EDWARD.

Un livre des entries contenant auxi un report des resolutions del court sur diverse exceptions prises as pleadings, et sur auters matters en ley, surdand en le courte de Common-Bank, 1682–1704. 2 vols. 1704. folio. **74 F**

Reports and entries of Sir E. Lutwyche in Court of Common Pleas, 1682–1704. By W. Nelson. 1718. folio. **74 F**

LUTZEN, BATTLE OF.

Letters from George Fleetwood to his father, giving an account of the battle of Lutzen. Edited by Sir P. D. M. G. Egerton. [Camden Society, vol. 39.] 1847. 8vo. **85 B**

LYDGATE, JOHN.

The Childe of Bristowe, a poem. Edited by Clarence Hopper. [Camden Society, vol. 73.] 1859. 8vo. **85 B**

Lydgate's verses on the kings of England. Edited by James Gairdner. [Camden Society, n.s. vol. 17.] 1876. 8vo. **85 D**

LYME, CHESHIRE.

The antiquities of Lyme and its vicinity. By W. Marriott. Stockport, 1810. 8vo. **86 E**

LYME REGIS, DORSET.

The beauties of Lyme Regis, Charmouth, and their vicinities. By H. R. Brown. Lyme Regis, [n.d.] 12mo. **87 C**

History of Lyme Regis. By G. Roberts. 1823. 12mo. **87 C**

LYNDEWODE, WILLIAM.

- Constitutiones legitime seu legatine regionis Anglicanæ, cum subtilissima interpretatione dñi Johannis de Athon. Paris, 1505. [Bound with Provinciale, 1525.] **118 F**

Provinciale, seu constitutiones Angliæ, cum summariis atque justis annotationibus. 1525. 4to. **118 F**

LYNDEWODE, WILLIAM—*continued.*

Provinciale (seu Constitutiones Angliæ) cum summariis atque eruditis annotationibus. Cui adjiciuntur Constitutiones Legatinæ Othonis et Othoboni, Cardinalium, cùm annotationibus Johannis de Athona. Oxoniæ, 1679. folio. **77 F**

LYNDHURST, JOHN SINGLETON, 1 BARON.

A Brief memoir of Lord Lyndhurst. By Wm. Sidney Gibson. 1866, and new ed. 1869. 8vo. **79 G**

Life of Lord Lyndhurst. By Sir T. Martin. 2nd ed. 1884. 8vo. **80 D**

Life of Lord Lyndhurst. See Lord Campbell's Lives of the lord chancellors, vol. viii., 1869, pp. 1–212. **79 G**

Misrepresentations in Campbell's Lives of Lyndhurst and Brougham. Corrected by St. Leonards. 1869. 8vo. **79 G**

LYNN, NORFOLK.

The history of Lynn. By Wm. Richards. 2 vols. Lynn, 1812. 8vo. **92 C**

LYON, ANDREW.

The law of India. 2 vols. 1873. 8vo. **38 D**

LYON, GEORGE EDWARD.

The law of bills of sale. 1873. 12mo. **160 G**

The same. 3rd ed. by G. E. Lyon and J. H. Redman. 1881. 12mo. **11 E**

LYON, REV. JOHN.

History of Dover and of Dover Castle, with a short account of the Cinque Ports. 2 vols. in 1. Dover, 1813–14. 4to. **88 E**

LYON-CAEN, CHARLES.

Table of the foreign mercantile laws and codes in force in the principal states of Europe and America. Translated by N. Argles. 1876. 8vo. **55 C**

LYONS, ISRAEL.

The scholars instructor, an Hebrew grammar. 2nd ed. Cambridge, 1757. 8vo. **255 H**

LYSONS, REV. DANIEL.

The Environs of London ; being an historical account of the towns, villages, and hamlets, within twelve miles of that capital. 4 vols. 1792–96. 4to. **89 F**

LYSONS, Rev. Daniel—*continued.*

An Historical account of those parishes in the county of Middlesex which are not described in the Environs of London. 1800. 4to.   **89 F**

Magna Britannia ; being a concise topographical account of the several counties of Great Britain. By Rev. Daniel Lysons and Rev. S. Lysons. 6 vols. in 9. 1813–22. 4to.

Vol. 1. Bedfordshire, Berkshire, Buckinghamshire.		**86 B**
Vol. 2. Cambridgeshire.		**86 D**
Cheshire.		**86 F**
Vol. 3. Cornwall.		**86 F**
Vol. 4. Cumberland.		**86 G**
Vol. 5. Derbyshire.		**87 B**
Vol. 6. Devonshire.		**86 G**

LYTE, Henry Churchill Maxwell.

A History of Eton college. 1875. 8vo.   **86 B**

A History of the University of Oxford, from the earliest times to the year 1530. 1886. 8vo.   **92 E**

LYTTELTON, George, 1 Baron.

The works of George Lord Lyttelton. By G. E. Ayscough. 3rd ed. 2 vols. 1776. 8vo.   **83 B**

MACALPIN, Daniel Rankin.

Law relating to money lenders and borrowers. 1880. 8vo.   **11 A**

McARTHUR, Charles.

The contract of marine insurance. 1885. 8vo.   **169 B**

The same. 2nd ed. 1890. 8vo.   **10 D**

McARTHUR, John.

Principles and practice of Naval Courts-Martial. 1792. 8vo.   **172 G**

MACASKIE, Stuart Cunningham.

The law of executors and administrators. 1881. 8vo.   **52 H**

The law relating to bills of sale. 1882. 8vo.   **11 E**

MACASSEY, Luke Livington.

Private Bill legislation and provisional orders. Handbook for the use of solicitors and engineers. 1887. 8vo.   **12 A**

The law relating to civil engineers, architects and contractors. By L. L. Macassey and J. A. Strahan. 1890. 8vo.   **9 B**

MACAULAY, Rev. Aulay.
The history and antiquities of Claybrook, in the county of
Leicester. 1791. 8vo.   89 C

MACAULAY, Thomas Babington, 1 Baron.
The history of England, from the accession of James II. 5 vols.
1860-61. 8vo.   115 G

McCARTHY, Justin.
A History of our own times, from accession of Queen Victoria
to general election of 1880. 4 vols. 1881. 8vo.   116 G

McCLELAND, Thomas.
Reports of cases in the courts of Exchequer and Exchequer
Chamber, 1824. 1 vol. 1825. 8vo.   7 F

McCLELAND, Thomas and Edward YOUNGE.
Reports of cases in the courts of Exchequer and Exchequer
Chamber, 1824-1825. 1 vol. 1827. 8vo.   7 F

MACCLESFIELD, Cheshire.
East Cheshire; or, a history of the hundred of Macclesfield.
By J. P. Earwaker. 2 vols. 1877-80. 4to.   87 G

MacCOLLA, Charles James.
Breach of Promise, its history and social considerations. 1879.
12mo.   78 A

McCORD, Thomas.
The civil code of Lower Canada. Montreal, 1867. 12mo. 60 E

McCULLAGH, James Samuel Gordon.
Procedure & practice in the County Courts. 3rd ed. 1890.
8vo.   12 H

McCULLOCH, John Ramsay.
Dictionary, geographical, statistical, and historical, of various
countries, places, and principal natural objects in the world.
New ed. by F. Martin. 4 vols. in 2. 1866. 8vo.   84 G
Dictionary of commerce and commercial navigation; with a
supplement containing the most recent information, by
A. J. Wilson. 1882. 4to.   78 G
Statistical account of British empire. 2 vols. 1837. 8vo. 84 G

McDERMOT, George.

The land law (Ireland) act 1881, and Landlord and tenant
act 1870 ; with the rules to both acts. 2nd ed. Dublin,
1881. 8vo.   55 E

MACDONALD, Alexander.

Handybook of the law relative to masters, workmen, servants
and apprentices. 1868. 8vo.   172 D

MACDONELL, John.

The law of master and servant. 1883. 8vo.   10 H
Reports of State Trials. New Series. Edited by John
Macdonell. vols. 1, 2. 1888–89. 8vo.   50 J

MACFIE, Robert Andrew.

Copyright and Patents for Inventions. Pleas and plans for
cheaper books and greater industrial freedom. 2 vols.
Edinburgh, 1879–83. 8vo.   83 I
The Patent question under free trade : a solution of difficulties
by abolishing or shortening the inventors' monopoly and
instituting national recompenses. 2nd ed. 1863. [Pamph-
lets, vol. 36.]   144 C

McHENRY, Luis Josef Antonio.

A New Spanish grammar. New ed. 1854. 12mo. 255 H

MACHIAVELLI, Niccolo.

Tutte le opere divise in V parti. 1550. 4to.   118 E
Works. Translated into English. 1680. folio.   113 G

MACHINERY.

A Statement of the law relating to Securities over Machinery.
By Andrew Tosh. Edinburgh, 1887. 12mo.   55 G

MACHYN, Henry.

The diary of Henry Machyn, 1550 to 1563. Edited by J. G.
Nichols. [Camden Society, vol. 42.] 1848. 8vo.   85 B

MACKAY, Hugh William Boyd.

Practical treatise on law of property. 1882. 8vo.   53 E

MACKENZIE, Eneas.

A Descriptive and historical account of Newcastle upon Tyne.
2 vols. Newcastle, 1827. 4to. **92 D**

An Historical, topographical, and descriptive view of the county
palatine of Durham. By E. Mackenzie and M. Ross.
2 vols. Newcastle, 1834. 4to. **87 E**

MACKENZIE, Sir George.

The institutions of the law of Scotland. 1694. 12mo. **55 G**

The same. 6th ed. Edinburgh, 1723. 12mo. **55 G**

The laws and customes of Scotland, in matters Criminal.
Edinburgh, 1678. 8vo.

The same. 2nd ed. 1699. folio.

Pleadings, in some remarkable cases, before the supreme courts
of Scotland, since the year 1661. Edinburgh, 1672. 4to.

The Works of. 2 vols. Edinburgh, 1716–22. folio. **79 I**

[MACKENZIE, Henry.]

The Man of feeling. New ed. 1800. 8vo. **83 A**

MACKENZIE, Montague Muir and C. A. WHITE.

The supreme court funds rules. 1884. 8vo. **12 G**

MACKENZIE, Thomas, Lord Mackenzie.

Studies in Roman Law, with comparative views of laws of
France, England, and Scotland. 2nd ed. 1865. 8vo. **63 E**

MACKENZIE, William.

A Concise and easy system of book-keeping for solicitors.
1858. 12mo. **160 G**

MACKENZIE, Rev. William.

The history of Galloway. 2 vols. 1841. 8vo. **95 C**

Index to all the Statute or Tynwald laws of the Isle of Man.
Douglas, 1861. 8vo. **32 B**

MACKINTOSH, Sir James.

A Dissertation exhibiting a general view of the progress of
Ethical Philosophy, chiefly during the Seventeenth and
Eighteenth centuries. See Encyclopædia Britannica, 8th
ed., vol. I, pp. 291–445. **147 A**

Memoirs of the life of Sir James Mackintosh. Edited by
his son R. J. Mackintosh. 2nd ed. 2 vols. 1836. 8vo. **80 C**

MACLACHLAN, David.

Law of Merchant Shipping. 2 vols. 1860–62. 8vo. **175 F**
The same. 2nd ed. 1875. 8vo. **175 F**
The same. 3rd ed. 1880. 8vo. **11 F**

MACLAURIN, Colin.

An Account of Sir Isaac Newton's philosophical discoveries, in four books. 1748. 4to. **78 G**
A Treatise of Algebra. 4th ed. 1779. 8vo. **255 H**

MACLAURIN, John, Lord Dreghorn.

Arguments and Decisions, in remarkable Cases, before the High Court of Justiciary, and other Supreme Courts, in Scotland. 1774. 4to.

MACLEAN, Charles Hope and G. ROBINSON.

Cases decided by the House of Lords on appeals and writs of error, 1839. 1 vol. 1840. 8vo. **15 B**

MACLEAN, Sir John.

Parochial and family history of deanery of Trigg Minor, in county of Cornwall. 3 vols. 1873–79. 4to. **86 F**

MACMORRAN, Alexander.

Orders issued by the Local Government Board and their predecessors, under acts relating to relief of the poor, &c. By A. Macmorran and S. G. Lushington. 1890. 8vo. **11 C**
The Poor law statutes from 1879 to 1889. By A. Macmorran and M. S. J. Macmorran. 1890. 8vo. **11 C**

MACNAGHTEN, Steuart and Alexander GORDON.

Reports of cases in Court of Chancery, during the time of Lord Chancellor Cottenham, 1849–1851. 3 vols. 1850–52. 8vo. **3 A**

MACNAMARA, William Henry.

A Digest of the law of Carriers of goods and passengers by land and internal navigation. 1888. 8vo. **9 B**

MACPHERSON, David.

Annals of commerce, manufactures, fisheries, and navigation. 4 vols. 1805. 4to. **78 G**

MACPHERSON, JAMES.

Original papers ; containing the secret history of Great Britain, from Restoration to accession of House of Hanover : with Extracts from the life of James II. as written by himself. 2nd ed. 2 vols. 1776. 4to. **114 F**

The poems of Ossian. Translated by James Macpherson. New ed. 2 vols. 1796. 8vo. **83 D**

MACPHERSON, WILLIAM.

The law relating to Infants. 1842. 8vo. **52 I**

The practice of the Judicial Committee of Her Majesty's Most Honorable Privy Council. 1860. 12mo. **174 C**

The same. 2nd ed. 1873. 8vo. **12 A**

MACQUEEN, JOHN FRASER.

A Lecture on the early history and academic discipline of the Inns of Court and Chancery, delivered before the benchers at Lincoln's Inn. 1851. [Pamphlets, vol. 9. pt. 1.] **144 A**

A Practical treatise on Divorce and Matrimonial jurisdiction under the act of 1857 and new orders. 1858. 8vo. **166 A**

The same. 2nd ed. 1860. 8vo. **166 A**

Practical treatise on the appellate jurisdiction of the House of Lords and Privy Council. 1842. 8vo. **52 H**

Reports of Scotch appeals and writs of error in the House of Lords, 1851–1865. 4 vols. 1855–66. 8vo. **15 B**

Rights and liabilities of Husband and Wife. 1849. 8vo. **168 G**

The same. 2nd ed. by S. Hastings and J. D. Davenport. 1872. 8vo. **168 G**

The same. 3rd ed. by J. C. Russell and R. B. Russell. 1885. 8vo. **10 C**

MACQUER, PHILIP.

A Chronological abridgment of Roman history from foundation of the city to extinction of the republic. Translated from the French by Thomas Nugent. 1760. 8vo. **113 D**

MACQUOID, GILBERT SAMUEL.

Jacobite songs and ballads, with notes. 1888. 8vo. **83 H**

Up and Down, Sketches of Travel. 1890. 8vo. **84 B**

MACRORY, EDMUND.

Reports of cases relating to letters patent for inventions, 1841–1851. 1 vol. 1855. 8vo. **76 H**

McSKIMIN, Samuel.
The history and antiquities of the county of the town of
Carrickfergus. 3rd ed. Belfast, 1829. 8vo. **95 E**

MAC SWINNEY, Robert Forster.
The law of mines, quarries, and minerals. 1884. 8vo. **10 I**

MADAGASCAR, Language of.
A Vocabulary of the Madagascar language. See Autobiography, vol. 2, 1826, pp. 321–330. **79 A**

[MADAN, Martin.]
Thoughts on executive justice, with respect to our criminal
laws, particularly on the circuits. By a sincere wellwisher
to the public. 2nd ed. 1785. 12mo. **118 B**

MADDOCK, Henry.
Reports of cases in the Court of the Vice Chancellor of
England, during the time of Sir Thomas Plumer and Sir
John Leach, 1815–1821. 5 vols. 1817–22. 8vo. **3 A**
A Treatise on the principles and practice of the High Court
of Chancery. 2nd ed. 2 vols. 1820. 8vo. **161 C**
The same. 3rd ed. 2 vols. 1837. 8vo. **161 C**

MADDOCK, Henry and Thomas Charles GELDART.
Reports of cases in the Courts of the Vice Chancellor of
England, during the time of Sir John Leach, 1821–1822.
1 vol. 1829. 8vo. **3 A**

MADDY, Edwin.
Digest of cases argued and determined in the Arches and
Prerogative courts of Canterbury, the Consistory court of
London, and the High Court of Delegates. 1835. 8vo. **63 D**

MADOX, Thomas.
Baronia Anglica : an history of land-honors and baronies, and
of tenure in capite, verified by records. 1736. folio. **126 I**
Firma burgi ; or, an historical essay concerning the cities,
towns, and buroughs of England. 1726. folio. **99 E**
Formulare Anglicanum ; or, a collection of ancient charters
and instruments of divers kinds, taken from the originals.
1702. folio. **85 I**

MADOX, THOMAS—*continued.*

The history and antiquities of the Exchequer of the Kings of England, from the Norman conquest to 1327 ; with a correct copy of the antient dialogue concerning the Exchequer, ascribed to Gervasiụs Tilburiensis. 1711. folio.   **99 B**

The same. 2nd ed. 2 vols. 1769. 4to.   **103 F**

MADRAS.

Acts of the council of the governor of Fort Saint George, for the purpose of making laws and regulations, 1862–1865. Madras, 1866. 8vo.   **33 G**

Annual reports of the Madras Presidency Administration, for the years 1870–72. 2 vols. Madras, 1872. 8vo.   **38 A**

Charter establishing supreme court of judicature at Madras, dated 26 Dec. 1800. 8vo.   **38 B**

Fort St. George Gazette, 1868–1889. 48 vols. 1868–89. folio.

Madras acts, 1862–1889. 6 vols. Madras, 1862–89. 8vo. **33 B**

A Manual of Hindoo law prevailing in the presidency of Madras. By T. L. Strange. Madras, 1863. 8vo.   **38 B**

The predecessors of the high court of Madras. By John Shaw. Madras, 1882. 8vo.   **80 F**

The regulations of the Government of Fort St. George in force at the end of 1847. By Richard Clarke. 1848. 4to. **33 H**

Report on administration of presidency of Madras, during the years 1875–79. 4 vols. Madras, 1877–79. 8vo. **38 A**

Statement by Sir Charles Trevelyan of the circumstances connected with his recall from the government of Madras. 1860. [Pamphlets, vol. 14.]   **144 A**

Statutes, acts and regulations in force in the Madras presidency on the 1st January 1875. By H. S. Cunningham. 2nd ed. Madras, 1875. 8vo.   **33 B**

MAGENS, NICOLAS.

Essay on Insurances, explaining the nature of various kinds of Insurance practised by different commercial states of Europe. 2 vols. 1755. 4to.   **157 A**

MAGISTERIAL LAW.

A Magisterial and Police guide. By H. C. Greenwood and T. C. Martin. 3rd ed. by T. C. Martin. 1890. 8vo. **12 C**

The practice of Magistrates' courts. By T. W. Saunders. 5th ed. 1882. 8vo.   **12 B**

MAGISTERIAL LAW—*continued.*

Oke's Magisterial Synopsis: a practical guide for magistrates, their clerks, solicitors and constables. 13th ed. by T. W. Saunders. 2 vols. 1881. 8vo. **12 C**

Oke's Magisterial Formulist: a complete collection of forms. 6th ed. by T. W. Saunders. 1881. 8vo. **12 C**

An Elementary treatise on Magisterial law. By W. S. Shirley. 1881. 12mo. **64 E**

The Magistrate's Assistant. By A County Magistrate [Dr. S. Glasse]. 3rd ed. Glocester, 1794. 8vo. **172 B**

See ROBINSON, W. and TOONE, W.

See also JUSTICE OF THE PEACE.

MAGNA CHARTA.

A Commentary on Magna Charta. See F. S. Sullivan's Lectures, 2nd ed., 1776, pp. 340–389. **157 B**

The Great Charter and Charter of the Forest, with other authentic instruments. With an introductory history of the charters. See Blackstone's Law Tracts, 3rd ed., 1771, pp. 281–353 and pp. i–lxxx. **144 G**

An Historical essay on the Magna Charta of King John. By Richard Thomson. 1829. 8vo. **114 D**

A History and defence of Magna Charta, with a discourse, containing a short account of rise and progress of national freedom ; and an essay on parliaments. 1769. 8vo. **114 D**

Magna Charta cum statutis, tum antiquis, tum recentibus, maximopere animo tenendis, nunc demum ad unum, tipis ædita, per Richardum Tottill. 1587. 12mo. **48 A**

Magna Charta ; or, the great charter commonly called the Bill of Rights, with notes. By A. H. Elworthy. [Pamphlets, vol. 36.] **144 C**

An Occasional discourse in vindication of Magna Charta, the articles in Latin and English on which it was founded and the Great Charter both in French and English. See Rev. S. Johnson's Works, 2nd ed., 1713, pp. 337–396. **77 H**

See also BROOKE, SIR R., CREASY SIR E. S. and LUFFMAN, J.

MAIDSTONE, KENT.

The charters and other documents relating to Maidstone, with notes. By W. R. James. 1825. 8vo. **88 C**

The history and antiquities of Maidstone. By Rev. Wm. Newton. 1741. 8vo. **88 C**

MAIDSTONE, KENT—*continued.*

The Poll for electing two burgesses, for the town and borough of Maidstone, Kent, to serve in a certain parliament, taken on 31st October, and 1st November, 1806. 1806. 8vo. **107 K**

The same. Taken 7–9 May, 1807. 1807. 8vo. **107 K**

The same. Taken 17 June, 1818. Maidstone, 1818. 8vo. **107 K**

The same. Taken 8 March, 1820. Maidstone, 1820. 8vo. **107 K**

The same. Taken June 10, 1826. Maidstone, 1826. 8vo. **107 K**

MAINE, SIR HENRY SUMNER.

Ancient law : its connection with the early history of society, and its relation to modern ideas. 1861. 8vo. **83 I**

The same. 4th ed. 1870. 8vo. **83 I**

Dissertations on early law and custom. 1883. 8vo. **83 I**

Village communities in the East and West. 1871. 8vo. **83 I**

MAINPRIZE.

A Treatise of Bail and Mainprize. See Sir Edward Coke's Three law tracts, 1764, pp. 279–303. **144 F**

MAINTENANCE.

The law of maintenance and champerty. By W. J. Tapp. 1861. 12mo. **53 A**

MAITLAND, WILLIAM.

The history of London from its foundation to the present time. 2 vols. 1756. folio. **92 H**

Life of William Maitland. See J. P. Malcolm's Lives of Topographers and Antiquaries, 1815. 4to. **79 H**

MAJOR, JOHN.

Historia Majoris Britanniæ tam Angliæ quam Scotiæ. Editio nova. Edinburgi, 1740. 4to. **115 H**

MALCOLM, JAMES PELLER.

Lives of topographers and antiquaries who have written concerning the antiquities of England, with portraits of the authors. 1815. 4to. **79 H**

Londinium redivivum ; or, an ancient history and modern description of London. 4 vols. 1802-7. 4to. **90 C**

MALDEN, CHARLES EDWARD and A. H. POYSER.

Digest of practice of Queen's Bench division. 1884. 8vo. **52 B**

MALEBRANCHE, NICOLAS.

An Examination of P. Malebranche's Opinion of seeing all things in God. See Locke's Works, vol. 9, 1823, pp. 211–255. **78 F**

Search after Truth, or a treatise of the nature of the human mind. Translated by Richard Sault. 1694. 8vo. **78 A**

MALHAM, YORKSHIRE.

A Concise account of some natural curiosities in the environs of Malham. By Thomas Hurtley. 1786. 8vo. **94 B**

MALICIOUS PROSECUTION.

The law relating to actions for malicious prosecution. By Herbert Stephen. 1888. 8vo. **12 C**

Sir H. Jenner's judgment in Panton *v.* Williams. 1840. [Pamphlets, vol. 1.] **144 A**

MALLORY, JOHN.

Modern Entries, in English : being a select collection of pleadings in the courts of King's Bench, Common Pleas and Exchequer : and also all kinds of Writs, original and judicial. 4th ed. 2 vols. 1791. 8vo.

Quare Impedit in two parts. Part 1. containing an abridgment of the law of the patronages of churches, &c. Part 2. containing precedents of pleadings. 1737. folio. **157 C**

MALMESBURY ABBEY, WILTSHIRE.

Registrum Malmesburiense. Register of Malmesbury abbey. Edited by J. S. Brewer. 2 vols. 1879–80. 8vo. **102 G**

MALMESBURY, WILLIAM OF.

De gestis pontificum Anglorum libri quinque. Edited by N. E. S. A. Hamilton. 1870. 8vo. **102 C**

De gestis regum Anglorum libri quinque ; Historiæ novellæ libri tres. Edited by W. Stubbs. 2 vols. 1887–89. 8vo **102 I**

MALT.

An Enquiry as to the practicability and policy of reducing the duties on Malt and Beer, and increasing those on British spirits. 1830. [Pamphlets, vol. 5.] **144 A**

See also MILLER, S.

MALTA.

History and description of the venerable and miraculous Icon of our blessed Lady of Philermos, patroness of the order of Malta. [n.d.] [Pamphlets, vol. 39.] **144 C**

History of Malta and Gozo. See R. M. Martin's History of the British colonies, vol. 5, 1835, pp. 103–294. **116 C**

Malta Ordinances, 1857–1873. 5 vols. 1857–73. folio. **37 D**

MALVERN, WORCESTERSHIRE.

History of Malvern. By John Chambers. 1817. 8vo. **93 F**

Malvern Hills ; historical sketch. By Percival Birkett. 1882. 8vo. **93 F**

MALYNES, GERARD.

Consuetudo, vel lex mercatoria ; or, the ancient law merchant in three parts, according to the essentials of traffick. 3rd ed. 1686. folio. **118 G**

MAN.

An Essay on Man, in four epistles, to Henry St. John, Lord Bolingbroke. By Alexander Pope. 1819. folio. **118 G**

Essays on the active powers of man. By Thomas Reid. Edinburgh, 1788. folio. **78 G**

Glimpses at the origin, mission, and destiny of man. By L. Heyworth. 1851. 12mo. **78 A**

Of Man. See T. Hobbes' Leviathan, 1881, pp. 4–125. **78 D**

On the adaptation of external nature to the physical condition of man. By John Kidd. 4th ed. 1836. 8vo. **77 B**

The primitive origination of mankind, considered and examined according to the light of nature. By Sir Matthew Hale. 1677. folio. **78 H**

The scriptural history of the earth, and of mankind. By Philip Howard. 1797. 4to. **77 G**

A Sketch of the natural laws of man. By G. Spurzheim. 1825. 12mo. **78 A**

MAN, ISLE OF, HISTORY AND ANTIQUITIES OF.

Account of Isle of Man. By W. Sacheverell. 1702. 12mo. **94 F**

An Account of the past and present state of the Isle of Man. By George Woods. 1811. 8vo. **94 F**

Anecdotes of Olave the Black, King of Man. By Rev. James Johnstone. 1780. 12mo. **118 A**

MAN, ISLE OF, HISTORY AND ANTIQUITIES OF—*continued.*

Delineations of Cumberland and the Isle of Man. By E. W.
Brayley and J. Britton. 1802. 8vo. **87 A**

General view of the agriculture of the Isle of Man. By Thomas
Quayle. 1812. 8vo. **94 F**

An Historical and statistical account of the Isle of Man. By
Joseph Train. 2 vols. Douglas, 1845. 8vo. **94 F**

The history and description of the Isle of Man. [By George
Waldron.] 2nd ed. 1744. 12mo. **94 F**

The history of the house of Stanley . . . to which is added a
description of the Isle of Man. Preston, 1793. 8vo. **80 A**

The history of Island of Man. By R. Rolt. 1773. 8vo. **94 F**

History of Isle of Man. By H. A. Bullock. 1816. 8vo. **94 F**

Isle of Mann and diocese of Sodor and Mann. Antient
and authentic records relating to the history and constitution of that island. By Rev. W. P. Ward. 1837. 8vo. **94 F**

Sketches of the coasts and islands of Scotland and Isle of
Man. By Lord Teignmouth. 2 vols. 1836. 12mo. **95 C**

A Tour through the island of Mann in 1797 and 1798. By
John Feltham. Bath, 1798. 8vo. **94 F**

A Tour through the Isle of Man ; with a review of the Manks
history. By David Robertson. 1794. 8vo. **94 F**

See also ATHOL, DUKES OF.

MAN, ISLE OF, LAWS OF.

Ancient ordinances and statute laws of the Isle of Man, 1422–
1820. By M. A. Mills. Douglas, 1821. 8vo. **32 A**

Index to all the statute, or Tynwald laws of the Isle of Man.
By Rev. W. Mackenzie. Douglas, 1861. 8vo. **32 B**

The report of the commissioners of enquiry for the Isle of
Man, 1792. 1805. folio. **95 H**

Statute laws of the Isle of Mann. Douglas, 1797. 8vo. **32 A**

The same. 1826–1832. By G. Geneste. 1834–1836. By
J. M. Jeffcott. 1839–1848. By James Gell. 1849–1853.
By J. Burman. 1853–1861. By J. C. Lamothe. 5 vols.
Douglas, 1832–62. 8vo. **32 B**

A View of the jurisprudence of the Isle of Man. By James
Johnson. Edinburgh, 1811. 8vo. **55 D**

MANBY, ROGER.

Law and practice of Fines and Recoveries. 1738. 12mo. **168 D**

MANBY, THOMAS.
· A Collection of the Statutes made in the reigns of King
Charles the I. and King Charles the II. 1667. folio. **158 D**

MANCETTER MARTYRS.
· The Mancetter martyrs, the sufferings and martyrdoms of Mr.
Robert Glover and Mrs. Joice Lewis. By Rev. B. Richings.
4th ed. 1860. 8vo. **79 B**

MANCHESTER.
Catalogues of the library of the Manchester Law Society.
1854 and 1881. 8vo. **82 B**
· Cathedral commission and the collegiate and cathedral and
parish church of Manchester. Manchester, 1853. [Pam-
phlets, vol. 9, pt. 1.] **144 A**
· The history of Manchester. By Rev. John Whitaker. 2 vols.
· 1771–75. 4to. **88 F**
The Manchester guide. Historical description of the towns of
Manchester and Salford. Manchester, 1804. 8vo. **89 A**
Manchester : its political, social, and commercial history.
· By James Wheeler. 1836. 8vo. **89 A**
Manchester rectory division bill. Report of the evidence
given before committee of House of Commons, with a full
report of speeches of counsel. Manchester, 1850. 8vo. **89 A**
Manchester vindicated, being a compleat collection of the
papers lately published in defence of that town in the
Chester Courant. [By Dr. Thomas Deacon.] Chester, 1749.
12mo. **89 A**
Memorials of Manchester streets. By R. W. Procter. Man-
chester, 1874. 4to. **89 G**
The trial of an indictment against Joseph Hanson, for a conspiracy to aid the weavers of Manchester in raising their
wages. 1809. 8vo. **51 E**
The whole proceedings before the coroner's inquest on the
body of John Lees, who died of sabre wounds at Manchester,
August 16, 1819 ; with an accurate plan of St. Peter's Field.
By J. A. Dowling. 1820. 8vo. **51 E**
See also AIKIN, J., CHETHAM, H. and PALMER, J.

MANCHESTER, EDWARD, 2 EARL OF.
A Letter from the Earl of Manchester to the House of Lords,
giving an opinion on the conduct of Oliver Cromwell.
Edited by S. R. Gardiner. [Camden Society, n.s. vol. 31.]
1883. 8vo. **85 D**

MANCHESTER, EDWARD, 2 EARL OF—*continued*.

The quarrel between the Earl of Manchester and Oliver Cromwell, an episode of the English civil war. Edited by J. Bruce and D. Masson. [Camden Society, n.s. vol. 12.] 1875. 8vo. **85 D**

MANDAMUS.

Informations (criminal and quo warranto), Mandamus, and Prohibition. By John Shortt. 1887. 8vo. **10 C**

Law and practice of the writ of Mandamus. By T. Tapping. 1848. 8vo. **53 A**

Law and practice of the writ of Mandamus. By W. J. Impey. 1826. 8vo. **172 D**

MANDER, JAMES.

The Derbyshire miners' glossary ; or, an explanation of the technical terms of the miners, used in the High Peak and Low Peak ; with the mineral laws and customs within those districts. Bakewell, 1824. 8vo. **87 B**

MANITOBA.

Consolidated statutes of Manitoba. 1880. 8vo. **34 D**

MANLEY, SIR ROGER.

Commentarii de rebellione Anglicana, ab anno 1640 usque ad annum 1685. 1686. 12mo. **115 D**

MANLOVE, EDWARD.

The rhymed chronicle of E. Manlove, concerning the liberties and customs of the lead mines within Wapentake of Wirksworth. 2nd ed. by T. Tapping. 1851. 8vo. **87 A**

MANNERS AND CUSTOMS.

Testamenta vetusta ; being illustrations from wills of manners, customs, &c. from the reign of Henry II. to the accession of Queen Elizabeth. By Sir N. H. Nicolas. 2 vols. 1826. 8vo. **114 D**

MANNING, JAMES.

Digest of the Nisi Prius reports. 2nd ed. 1820. 8vo. **63 D**

The practice of the court of Exchequer. Revenue branch. 2nd ed. 1827. 8vo. **168 B**

MANNING, James and T. C. GRANGER.
. Cases argued and determined in the court of Common Pleas,
. 1840–1845. 7 vols. 1841–46. 8vo. : 6 G H

MANNING, James, T. C. GRANGER and J. SCOTT.
Common Bench reports, 1845–49. 8 vols. 1846–51. 8vo. 6 C D

MANNING, James and Archer RYLAND.
Reports of cases in the court of King's Bench, 1827–1830.
5 vols. 1828–37. 8vo. 5 C

MANNING, James and John SCOTT.
Common Bench Reports, 1850. 1 vol. 1857. 8vo. 6 D

MANNING, Rev. Owen.
The history and antiquities of the county of Surrey, continued
to present time by W. Bray. 3 vols. 1804–14. folio. 93 H

MANNING, William Oke.
Commentaries on the law of Nations. New ed. by S. Amos.
1875. 8vo. 55 B

MANNINGHAM, John.
Diary of John Manningham of the Middle Temple and of
Bradbourne, Kent, 1602–1603. Edited by John Bruce.
[Camden Society, vol. 99.] 1868. 8vo. 85 C

MANNYNG, Robert, of Brunne.
The story of England. [in verse.] Edited by F. J. Furnivall.
2 vols. 1887. 8vo. 102 I

MANORS AND MANORIAL COURTS.
Select pleas in manorial and other seignorial courts. vol. 1.
Edited by F. W. Maitland. [Selden Society, vol. 2.] 1889.
8vo. 85 G
Tenures of land and customs of manors. By Thomas Blount.
New ed. by W. C. Hazlitt. 1874. 8vo. 13 B
The Surveior's dialogue, very profitable for all men to peruse,
especially lords of mannors, stewards of mannor courts,
tenants, farmers, and husbandmen. 4th ed. 1738. 8vo. 49 E
The law and customs of England relating to Manors. By
William Nelson. 1726. folio. 49 H

MANSEL, George Barclay.

Letter to Henry Brougham, Esq. M.P. upon present state
of legal education. 1830. [Law Tracts, vol. 3.] **144 E**

The practice upon Writ of Trial for debts not exceeding 20*l.*
before the sheriff. 1833. 12mo. **176 F**

A Treatise on law of Limitation. 1839. 12mo. **172 A**

MANSFIELD, William, 1 Earl of.

The life of William, late Earl of Mansfield. By John Holliday. 1797. 4to. **79 H**

See also Lord Campbell's Lives of the Chief Justices of England, vol. 2, 1849, pp. 302–584. **79 G**

MANSLAUGHTER AND MURDER.

Remarks on opinions of some of the most celebrated writers
on crown law, respecting distinction between manslaughter
and murder. By Granville Sharp. 1773. 12mo. **118 B**

MANT, Right Rev. Richard.

Book of Common Prayer. 3rd ed. Oxford, 1825. 4to. **77 G**

MANUFACTURES.

A Treatise on the laws of Commerce and Manufactures. By
Joseph Chitty. 4 vols. 1820–24. 8vo. **13 G**

See also **Macpherson, D.**

MANUSCRIPTS, National.

Facsimiles of the national manuscripts from William the Conqueror to Queen Anne. Selected under the direction of
the Master of the Rolls. 4 vols. Southampton, 1865–68.
folio. **99 E**

Facsimiles of the national manuscripts of Scotland. Part 1.
Southampton, 1867. folio. **100 H**

MANWOOD, John.

A Treatise of the lawes of the Forest. 1615. 8vo. **49 F**

The same. 4th ed. by W. Nelson. 1717. 8vo. **52 H**

MANZONI, Alessandro.

I Promessi Sposi, storia Milanese del secolo decimosettimo.
Firenze, 1845. 12mo. **83 B**

The same. Ottava edizione postuma colla vita dell'autore,
scritta da Giulio Carcano. Milano, 1878. 12mo. **83 B**

MAPES, WALTER.

Gualteri Mapes de nugis curialium distinctiones quinque.
Edited by Thomas Wright. [Camden Society, vol. 50.]
1850. 8vo. **85 B**

The Latin poems attributed to Walter Mapes. Collected
and edited by T. Wright. [Camden Society, vol. 16.]
1841. 8vo. **85 A**

MARCH, JOHN.

Actions for slander ; to which is added Awards and Arbitrements. 1647. 12mo. **48 A**

The Common-Wealth's friend ; or, an exact and speedie course
to justice and right. 1651. 12mo. **48 A**

Reports ; or, new cases, taken in the 15, 16, 17 and 18 years·
of King Charles the First. 2nd ed. 1675. 8vo. **5.C**

MARCY, GEORGE NICHOLS.

A Short epitome of the principal statutes relating to Conveyancing. 3rd ed. 1881, and 4th ed. 1885. 12mo. **64 C**

The law and practice of Originating Summons, with forms.
By G. N. Marcy and J. T. Dodd. 1889. 8vo. **12 F**

MARGARET, QUEEN OF ANJOU.

Letters of Queen Margaret in the reigns of Henry V. and
Henry VI. Edited by Cecil Monro. [Camden Society,
vol. 86.] 1863. 8vo. **85 C**

MARIN, PIERRE.

Dictionnaire complet François et Hollandois.. Amsterdam,
1710. 4to. **123 C**

The same. 4th ed. 2 vols. Amsterdam, 1762–68. 4to. **123 C**

MARINA, FRANCISCO MARTINEZ.

Ensayo histórico-crítico sobre la antigua legislacion y principales cuerpos legales de los reynos de Leon y Castilla.
Madrid, 1808. 4to. **39 C**

Juicio Crítico de la novísima recopilacion. Madrid, 1820.
8vo. **39 E**

MARINE INSURANCE.

The contract of Marine Insurance. By C. McArthur. 2nd ed.
1890. 8vo. **10 D**

MARINE INSURANCE—*continued.*

The law of Marine Insurance. By J. Arnould. 6th ed. by
D. Maclachlan. 2 vols. 1887. 8vo. **10 D**

A Practical treatise on the law of Marine Insurance. By
R. Lowndes. 2nd ed. 1885. 8vo. **10 D**

See also BURN, J. T., CRUMP, F. O., DUER, J., MARSHALL,
S., NEWSON, H., PARK, J. A. and PARKER, T.

MARINE SOCIETY.

The bye-laws and regulations of the Marine Society. 1772,
3rd ed. 1787, and 5th ed. 1809. 12mo. **118 A**

MARITIME LAW.

Maritime Legislation. By E. E. Wendt. 3rd ed. 1888.
8vo. **11 F**

Alphabetical reference index to recent and important maritime law decisions. By R. R. Douglas. 1888. 8vo. **11 F**

Digest of Maritime law. By W. T. Pritchard. 3rd ed.
2 vols. 1887. 8vo. **14 C**

A Selection of leading cases on Mercantile and Maritime Law.
By O. D. Tudor. 3rd ed. 1884. 8vo. **10 F**

The ancient sea laws of the Hanse Towns, taken out of a
French book intitled Les Us et Coutumes de la Mer, 1686.
See G. Malynes's Lex Mercatoria, 1686, folio. **118 G**

See also FALCONER, W., INTERNATIONAL LAW, MOLLOY,
C., PARSONS, T., SHIPPING LAW and VALIN, R. J.

MARIUS, JOHN.

Advice concerning bills of exchange. 2nd ed. 1670. 12mo. **49 A**

The same. 4th ed. 1684. See G. Malynes's Lex Mercatoria,
1686. folio. **118 G**

MARKBY, WILLIAM.

Elements of Law, considered with reference to principles of
general jurisprudence. Oxford, 1871. 12mo. **63 G**

The same. 3rd ed. Oxford, 1885. 8vo. **63 G**

MARLBOROUGH, JOHN, 1 DUKE OF.

The military life of John, Duke of Marlborough. By Archibald Alison. 1848. 8vo. **80 B**

MARMION, Family of.

History of noble family of Marmyun, their singular office of King's Champion· by the tenure of baronial manor of Scrivelsby. By T. C. Banks. 1817. 4to.   79 H

MARRIAGE.

The Marriage law of England. By J. T. Hammick. 2nd ed. 1887. 12mo.   10 H

French law of marriage and conflict of laws that arises there-from. By Edmond Kelly. 1885.· 8vo.   55 C

The relationships which bar marriage considered scripturally, socially, and historically. By C. J. Brown. Edinburgh, 1871. [Pamphlets, vol. 36.]   144 C

Commentaries on the law of marriage and divorce. By J. P. Bishop. 4th ed. 2 vols. Boston, 1864. 8vo.   59 G

Traités du contrat de Mariage. Par R. J. Pothier. 12me éd. par M. Bugnet. Paris, 1861. 8vo.   58 D

Traité du Mariage et de la séparation de corps. Par J. C. F. Demolombe. 2me éd. 2 vols. Paris, 1860–61. 8vo. 58 C

Du Contrat de Mariage et des droits respectifs des époux. Par R. T. Troplong. 4 vols. Paris, 1857. 8vo.   58 E

First report of commissioners appointed to inquire into state and operation of law of marriage as relating to prohibited degrees of affinity. 1848. folio.·   153 E

On law as to marriages abroad between English subjects within prohibited degrees. 1840. [Law Tracts, vol. 7.]   144 E

Two arguments before lord chancellor Thurlow in the case of Scott and wife against Vernon and others, on the effect of a legacy with condition restraining marriage without consent of legatee's natural mother. See Hargrave's Juridical Arguments, vol. 1, 1797, pp. 22–87.   144 G

On the construction of marriage articles and cross remainders, in case of Duke of Richmond, with opinion of Mr. Booth, argument of Mr. Wedderburn, and decree of lord chancellor Apsley. See Collectanea Juridica, vol. 2, 1792, pp. 347–380.   144 G

Concerning effect of sentences of courts ecclesiastical in cases of marriage, when offered in evidence in courts temporal. See Hargrave's Law Tracts, 1787, pp. 449–486.   144 G

See BROWNING, W. E., ERNST, W., GREAVES, C. S., IRELAND, J., KENNY, C. S., MARTIN, T., MORGAN, REV. H. D., POYNTER, T., PRATER, H., SANCHEZ, R. P. T., STODDART, SIR J. and SWINBURNE, H.

See also DIVORCE and HUSBAND AND WIFE.

MARRIAGE SETTLEMENTS.

The law of marriage settlements. By H. T. Banning. 1884. 8vo. **13 H**

The law of marriage settlements. By J. P. Peachey. 1860. 8vo. **53 H**

See also ATHERLEY, E. G. and SETTLEMENTS.

MARRIAGE WITH DECEASED WIFE'S SISTER.

Argument in relation to Levitical marriage law, particularly as affecting the question of marriage of a widower with his deceased wife's sister. By T. Binney. Abridged from the 4th ed. 1851. [Pamphlets, vol. 24.] **144 B**

The xviiith chapter of Leviticus not the marriage code of Israel. By J. P. Brown-Westhead. 1850. [Pamphlets, vol. 24.] **144 B**

Facts and opinions in favour of legalising marriage with a deceased wife's sister. [n.d.] [Pamphlets, vol. 24.] **144 B**

A Letter to the lord bishop of Exeter in reference to his speech in House of Lords against second reading of Earl St. Germans' bill for legalizing marriage with a deceased wife's sister. By W. C. Sleigh. 2nd ed. 1851. [Pamphlets, vol. 24.] **144 B**

Letters from the Right Rev. Bishop McIlvaine of Ohio, and other eminent persons in the United States of America, in favour of marriage with a deceased wife's sister. 1851. [Pamphlets, vol. 24.] **144 B**

Marriage law dialogues. A day too late, or a glance at the working of the marriage law of 1835. 4th ed. 1852. [Pamphlets, vol. 24.] **144 B**

Marriage with a deceased wife's sister considered in a letter to the Earl of Ellesmere. By Joseph Beaumont. 1851. [Pamphlets, vol. 24.] **144 B**

Marriage with a wife's sister. By E. B. Denison. 1851. [Pamphlets, vol. 24.] **144 B**

Marriages Bill. Speeches of the Earl of St. Germans and Viscount Gage in the House of Lords, Feb. 25, 1851. 1851. [Pamphlets, vol. 24.] **144 B**

Memorandum in relation to marriage with a deceased wife's sister. Compiled for private circulation. 1851. [Pamphlets, vol. 24.] **144 B**

Observations on the debate on the marriages bill in the House of Lords. 1851. [Pamphlets, vol. 24.] **144 B**

MARRIAGE WITH DECEASED WIFE'S SISTER— *continued.*

Opinions of eminent divines in favour of the lawfulness of marriage with a deceased wife's sister. 1851. [Pamphlets, vol. 24.]   144 B

A Short letter on the Bishop of Exeter's speech on the Marriage Bill. By E. B. Denison. 3rd ed. 1851. [Pamphlets, vol. 24.]   144 B

MARRIED WOMEN'S PROPERTY.

A Digest of the law of husband and wife as it affects property. By R. Thicknesse. 1884. 8vo.   10 C

History of the laws affecting property of married women in England. By B. E. Lawrence. 1884. 8vo.   10 H

Married women's property acts 1870, 1874 and 1882. By J. R. Griffith. 5th ed. by S. W. Bromfield. 1883. 8vo. 10 H

Married women's property acts. By C. A. V. Conybeare and W. R. St. Clair Andrew. 2nd ed. 1883. 12mo.   10 H

See also HUSBAND AND WIFE.

MARRIOTT, SIR JAMES.

Decisions in the court of Admiralty, during time of Sir G. Hay and of Sir J. Marriott, 1776–1779. 1 vol. 1801. 8vo. 8 A

Sir James Marriott's argument in giving judgment in the court of Admiralty in the case of the ship Columbus. See Collectanea Juridica, vol. 1, 1791, pp. 82–128.   144 G

MARRIOTT, WILLIAM.

The antiquities of Lyme and its vicinity. Stockport, 1810. 8vo.   86 E

MARSDEN, JOHN BENJAMIN.

The influence of the Mosaic code upon subsequent legislation. 1862. 8vo.   78 C

MARSDEN, REGINALD GODFREY.

The law of collisions at sea. 2nd ed. 1885. 8vo.   11 F

Reports of cases determined by court of Admiralty 1758–1774. by Sir W. Burrell, with extracts from records of court of Admiralty 1584–1839, and a collection of cases and opinions upon Admiralty matters 1701–1781. 1885. 8vo.   8 A

The rule against perpetuities, a treatise on remoteness in limitations. 1883. 8vo.   10 G

MARSHALL, CHARLES.
. Reports of cases in the Court of Common Pleas, 1813–1816.
2 vols. 1815–17. 8vo. **6 H**

MARSHALL, GEORGE WILLIAM.
Genealogist's guide to printed pedigrees. 1879. 8vo. **124 H**

MARSHALL, JOHN.
Analysis of Titles to land consolidation (Scotland) act 1868,
31 & 32 Vict. cap. ci. Edinburgh, 1869. 8vo. **55 F**

MARSHALL, SAMUEL.
The law of Insurance. 2 vols. 1802. 8vo. **169 B**
The same. 2nd ed. 2 vols. 1808. 8vo. **169 B**
. The same. 5th ed. by Wm. Shee. 1865. 8vo. **169 B**

MARSHALL, WALKER.
The law of Costs in all suits and proceedings in courts of
common law. 1860. 12mo. **165 A**
The same. 2nd ed. 1862. 12mo. **52 D**
The law relating to the duties of Railway Companies as
carriers of passengers and goods. 1862. 12mo. **175 B**

MARTA, PETRUS.
Digesta novissima totius Juris controversi scientiæ, ex omnibus
decisionibus universi Orbis, quæ huc usque impressæ fuêre.
6 vols. in 2. Coloniæ, 1622. folio.
Tractatus de Jurisdictione per et inter judicem ecclesiasticum
et secularem exercenda. Moguntiæ, 1690. folio. **77 F**

MARTEN, HENRY.
Familiar Epistles. [n.d.] [Tracts, 1688–9.] **118 C**

MARTENS, GEORGE FRÉDÉRIC DE.
Recueil de Traités des Puissances et États de l'Europe,
tant dans leur rapport mutuel que dans celui envers les
Puissances et Etats dans d'autres parties du globe, depuis
1761 jusqu'à 1801. 7 vols. Gottingue, 1817–1802. **145 A**
Supplément, depuis 1761 jusqu'à présent [1807], précédé de
Traités du 18ᵉ Siècle qui ne se trouvent pas dans le Corps
Universel Diplomatique de Mrs. Dumont et Rousset. 4 vols.
Gottingue, 1802–8. 8vo. **145 A**

MARTENS, George Frédéric de—*continuea*.

Nouveau Recueil de Traités . . . des Puissances et États de l'Europe, depuis 1808 jusqu'à 1830. 8 vols. in 9. Gottingue, 1817–31. 8vo.　　　　　　　　　　**145 A B**

MARTIALL, John.

An Answer to John Martiall's Treatise of the cross. By James Calfhill, D.D., bishop elect of Worcester. Edited by Rev. Richard Gibbings. Cambridge, 1846. 8vo.　　　**77 D**

Stapleton's Fortress overthrown. A rejoinder to Martiall's reply. A discovery of the dangerous rock of the Popish church commended by Sanders. By Wm. Fulke. Edited by Rev. Richard Gibbings. Cambridge, 1848. 8vo. **77 D**

MARTIN, Adam.

Index to various repertories, books of orders and decrees, and other records in Court of Exchequer. 1819. 8vo.　**99 A**

The same. Another copy [with many manuscript notes]. 1819. 8vo.　　　　　　　　　　　　　　　　**118 E**

MARTIN, Robert Montgomery.

History of the British colonies. 5 vols. 1835. 8vo. **116 C**

Ireland before and after the Union with Great Britain. 3rd ed. 1848. 8vo.　　　　　　　　　　　　　　**95 E**

MARTIN, Sir Theodore.

A Life of Lord Lyndhurst from letters and papers in possession of his family. 2nd ed. 1884. 8vo.　　**80 D**

MARTIN, Thomas, Barrister-at-Law.

Character of Lord Bacon, his life and works. 1835. 8vo. **79 B**

The Conveyancers' Recital-book. 1834. 12mo.　**164 E**

Martin's Practice of conveyancing, with forms. By Charles Davidson. 5 vols. 1844–41. 8vo.　　　　　**164 A**

MARTIN, Thomas, Chancellor of Winchester.

A Traictise declaryng and plainly prouyng that the pretended marriage of priestes and professed persones is no marriage. 1554. 8vo.　　　　　　　　　　　　　　**118 B**

MARTIN, Thomas, F.S.A.

The history of town of Thetford, in counties of Norfolk and Suffolk. Edited by Richard Gough. 1779. 4to.　**92 D**

MARTINDALE, J. B..

Martindale's American Law Directory. 1885–6. A complete directory of the practising lawyers of the United States and Canada. Chicago, 1885. 8vo. **59 F**

MARTYN, THOMAS.

A New and accurate map of the county of Cornwall, from an actual survey. 1748. 8vo. **87 A**

MARTYN, WILLIAM.

The historie and lives of twentie kings of England (William the First to Henry the Eighth). 1615. 4to. **114 E**

MARY, QUEEN OF ENGLAND.

Annales of England, containing the reignes of Henry VIII., Edward VI., Queen Mary. By Francis Godwin. 1630. 4to. **114 F**

The chronicle of Queen Jane and of two years of Queen Mary. By a resident in the Tower of London. Edited by J. G. Nichols. [Camden Society, vol. 48.] 1850. 8vo. **85 B**

History of England from fall of Wolsey to defeat of Spanish armada. By J. A. Froude. 12 vols. 1858–70. 8vo. **115 B**

History of the reigns of Edward VI., Mary and Elizabeth. By Sharon Turner. 2nd ed. 2 vols. 1829. 8vo. **115 E**

MARY, QUEEN OF SCOTS.

Accounts and papers relating to Mary Queen of Scots. Edited by A. J. Crosby and J. Bruce. [Camden Society, vol. 93.] 1867. 8vo. **85 C**

Compleat history of lives and reigns of Mary Queen of Scotland and of James VI. King of Scotland. By W. Sanderson. 1656. 4to. **114 E**

History of Scotland from the Reformation till the death of Queen Mary. By G. Stuart. 2 vols. 1782. 4to. **113 F**

Maria Stuart. Ein Trauerspiel. Von Schiller. Stuttgart, 1861. 12mo. **83 B**

Trial of Mary Queen of Scots. See N. T. Moile's State Trials, 1838, pp. 279–335. **83 H**

See also MELVIL, SIR J.

MARYLEBONE, MIDDLESEX.

A Topographical and historical account of the parish of St. Mary-Le-Bone. By Thomas Smith. 1833. 8vo. **89 E**

MARYLEBONE, MIDDLESEX—*continued.*

Topographical survey of the borough of St. Marylebone as incorporated and defined by act of parliament 1832. Engraved by B. R. Davies, from surveys and drawings by F. A. Bartlett, under direction of J. Britton. 1834. folio. **92 H**

MASCALL, FRANCIS.

A Digest of the law of the distribution of the personal estates of intestates. 1818. 8vo. **52 H**

MASCARDUS, JOSEPHUS.

De Probationibus. Conclusiones Probationum omnium, quæ in utroque foro quotidie versantur. 3 vols. Francofurti ad Mœnum, 1593–95. folio. **48 I**

MASON, WILLIAM MONCK.

The history and antiquities of the collegiate and cathedral church of St. Patrick, near Dublin, from its foundation in 1190. Dublin, 1819. 4to. **95 F**

MASON, WILLIAM POWELL.

Reports of cases in the Circuit court of the United States for the first circuit, 1816 to 1830. 2nd ed. 5 vols. Boston, 1836–51. 8vo. **57 A**

MASON, WILLIAM SHAW.

Statistical account; or, parochial survey of Ireland. 3 vols. Dublin, 1814–19. 8vo. **95 F**

MASS.

An Answer in defence of the truth against the Apology of private mass. By T. Cooper, published in 1562. With An Apology of private mass. An anonymous Popish treatise against Bishop Jewel. Edited by Rev. Wm. Goode. Cambridge, 1850. 12mo. **77 D**

MASSEY, WILLIAM.

Common sense versus common law. 1850. 8vo. **78 B**

MASTER AND SERVANT.

Law of Master and Servant. By C. M. Smith. 4th ed. 1885. 8vo. **10 H**

MASTER AND SERVANT—*continued.*

Notes on law of Master and Servant. By J. Paterson. 1885. 8vo. **10 H**

The law of Master and Servant. By J. Macdonell. 1883. 8vo. **10 H**

Laws concerning Masters and Servants. By a Gentleman of the Inner Temple. 1767. 12mo. **172 D**

See also BAYLIS, T. H., DAVIS, J. E., LOVESY, C. W., MACDONALD, A., PETERSDORFF, C. and SPIKE, E.

MASTERS OF THE ROLLS.

A Catalogue of Lords Chancellors, Keepers of the Great Seal, Masters of the Rolls, and principal officers of the high court of Chancery. By T. D. Hardy. 1843. 8vo. **80 E**

A Discourse of the judicial authority belonging to the office of Master of the Rolls in the court of chancery. [By Philip Yorke, Earl of Hardwicke.] 1727. 8vo. **49 D**

MASTERS' OFFICES.

The delay in offices of Masters in Chancery, and the remedy. By C. P. Cooper. 2nd ed. 1849. [Pamphlets, vol. 17.] **144 B**

Facts and suggestions respecting the Masters' Offices. 1841. [Chancery Pamphlets, vol. 2.] **144 A**

Observations regarding the office of Master in Chancery. By a Master's Clerk. 1831. [Jacob's Tracts, vol. 11.] **144 F**

The practice in offices of Masters on plea side of superior common law courts. By T. Dax. 1844. 12mo. **53 A**

Society for promoting the amendment of the law. Further report of the committee on Equity on the Masters' Offices. 1849. [Pamphlets, vol. 17.] **144 B**

A Treatise of the Maisters of the Chauncerie. [circa 1600.] See Hargrave's Law Tracts, 1787, pp. 291–319. **144 G**

See also BENNET, W. H., HUME, R. M. and MILLER, S.

MASTERS, REV. ROBERT.

History of the college of Corpus Christi in the University of Cambridge; with a continuation to the present time, by John Lamb. 1831. 4to. **86 D**

MASTIN, REV. JOHN.

The history and antiquities of Naseby, in the county of Northampton. Cambridge, 1792. 8vo. **92 D**

MATHEW, John Mee.
Manual of law of Landlord and Tenant. 1841. 8vo. **170 D**

MATLOCK, Derbyshire.
The Gem of the Peak ; or, Matlock Bath and its vicinity. By
William Adam. 3rd ed. 1843. 12mo. **87 A**

MATTHEWS, Richard.
Digest of law relating to offences punishable by Indictment
and Information in Crown office. 1833. 12mo. **165 F**
Strictures on the Dissenters' chapels bill. 1844. [Pamphlets,
vol. 18.] **144 B**

MATTINSON, Miles Walker and S. C. MACASKIE.
A Handbook of the law relating to the management of parliamentary and municipal elections. 1884. 12mo. **166 D**

MATY, Mathew.
Miscellaneous writings of the late P. D. Stanhope, Earl of
Chesterfield ; with memoirs of his life. 2nd ed. 4 vols.
1779. 8vo. **83 B**

MAUDE, Frederic Philip and C. E. POLLOCK.
Compendium of law of Merchant Shipping. 1853. 8vo. **175 F**
The same. 2nd ed. 1861, and 3rd ed. 1864. 8vo. **175 F**
The same. 4th ed. by C. E. Pollock and G. Bruce. 2 vols.
1881. 8vo. **11 F**

MAUGHAM, Robert.
The attorneys' hand-book. 1853. 12mo. **160 C**
A Digest of the examination questions in common law, con-
veyancing, equity, bankruptcy, and criminal law. 6th ed.
1855, and 8th ed. 1861. 12mo. **168 A**
The law of attornies, solicitors and agents. 1825. 8vo. **52 A**
Outlines of character. 2nd ed. 1823. 8vo. **78 A**
Outlines of criminal law, comprising public wrongs. 1837.
12mo. **170 F**
Outlines of law, comprising injuries to persons and property.
1837. 12mo. **170 F**
Outlines of the jurisdiction of all the courts in England and
Wales. 1838. 12mo. **170 F**

MAUGHAM, ROBERT—*continued.*
Outlines of the law of real property. 1842. 12mo.　**170 F**
Treatise on laws of Literary Property. 1828. 8vo.　**172 A**
Treatise on the principles of the Usury laws. 1824. 8vo.
　Bound with the preceding.　**172 A**

MAULE, GEORGE and WILLIAM SELWYN.
Reports of cases in the court of King's Bench, 1813–1817.
　6 vols. 1814–29. 8vo.　**5 C D**

MAUNDER, SAMUEL.
The Biographical treasury, a dictionary of universal biography.
　11th ed. with a supplement. 1859. 12mo.　**81 B**
The treasury of Geography, physical, historical, descriptive,
　and political. New ed. by W. Hughes. 1860. 12mo.　**84 A**
Scientific and Literary treasury. New ed. 1858. 12mo.　**78 A**
The treasury of History. New ed. 1858. 12mo.　**116 D**
The treasury of Knowledge and library of reference. New ed.
　by B. B. Woodward. 1859. 12mo.　**78 A**
The treasury of Natural History. 5th ed. 1858. 12mo.　**78 A**

MAURITIUS.
A Collection of ordinances passed by legislative council of
　Mauritius. 1857–1889. 15 vols. Mauritius, 1857–89.
　folio & 8vo.　**37 F**
Decisions of the supreme court, vice-admiralty court and
　bankruptcy court of Mauritius, 1861. By A. Piston. 2nd ed.
　1863. 4to.　**37 F**
Index to the laws of Mauritius in force August 1879. By
　W. Greene. 5th ed. Mauritius, 1879. 8vo.　**37 F**

MAWE, JOHN.
The mineralogy of Derbyshire ; with a description of the most
　interesting mines in the North of England, in Scotland, and
　in Wales : and an analysis of Mr. Williams's work, intitled
　The mineral kingdom. 1802. 8vo.　**87 A**

MAXIMS.
Moral Maxims and reflections. By the Duke of Rochefou-
　cault. Now made English. 1694. 12mo.　**83 A**

MAXWELL, SIR PETER BENSON.
On the interpretation of statutes. 2nd ed. 1883. 8vo.　**11 G**

MAY, GEORGE.
The history of Evesham. Evesham, 1834. 8vo. 93 F

MAY, HENRY WILLIAM.
Treatise on statutes of Elizabeth against fraudulent conveyances ; the bills of sale registration acts and the law of
voluntary dispositions of property. 1871. 8vo. 53 E
The same. 2nd ed. by S. W. Worthington. 1887. 8vo. 13 I

MAY, SIR THOMAS ERSKINE.
The constitutional history of England since the accession of
George III., 1760–1860. 2 vols. 1861–63. 8vo. 116 E
The same. 3rd ed. 3 vols. 1871. 12mo. 116 D
A Practical treatise on the law, privileges, proceedings, and
usage of Parliament. 2nd ed. 1851. 8vo. 173 C
The same. 6th ed. 1868. 8vo. 173 C
The same. 9th ed. 1883. 8vo. 12 A

MAYER, SYLVAIN.
The French code of commerce as revised to the end of 1886.
Rendered into English. 1887. 8vo. 55 C

MAYHEW, CHARLES JEREMIAH.
The law of Merger. 1861. 8vo. 13 C

MAYNE, JOHN DAWSON.
Equitable defences and replications under the Common Law
Procedure act 1854. 1854. 12mo. 167 C
A Treatise on Hindu law and usage. 1878. 8vo. 38 D
A Treatise on the law of Damages. 1856. 8vo. 165 F
The same. 2nd ed. by Lumley Smith. 1872. 8vo. 165 F
The same. 4th ed. by J. D. Mayne and L. Smith. 1884.
8vo. 9 G

MAYO, REV. CHARLES.
Chronological history of the European states, from 1678 to
1794 ; also Biographical sketches of the sovereigns, statesmen, warriors, patriots, &c. Bath, 1795. folio. 115 I

MAYOR'S COURT, LONDON.
The jurisdiction and practice of the Mayor's Court. By
L. E. Glyn, L. Probyn and F. S. Jackson. 1888. 8vo. 12 D

MAYOR'S COURT, LONDON—*continued.*

The practice and pleading in the Mayor's Court, London. By E. H. Railton and Rockingham Gill. 1888. 12mo. **12 D**

Epitome of the Notes of practice of the Mayor's Court. By W. Brandon. 1871. 8vo. **172 D**

Notes of practice of the Mayor's Court in ordinary actions. By W. Brandon. 1864. 8vo. **172 D**

See also ASHLEY, H., ATTACHMENT, CANDY, G. and YEAT-MAN, J. P.

MEARS, THOMAS LAMBERT.

Analysis of M. Ortolan's Institutes of Justinian, including the history and generalization of Roman law. 1876. 8vo. **63 E**

MEASURES.

The compendious measurer, being a brief treatise on Mensuration. By C. Hutton. 2nd ed. 1790. 12mo. **255 H**

The law relating to weights and measures. By G. C. Whiteley. 1879. 8vo. **11 I**

Measuring made easy, or the description and use of Coggeshall's sliding-rule. By J. Good. 1760. 12mo. **255 H**

See also DECIMAL ASSOCIATION.

MEAUX ABBEY, YORKSHIRE.

Chronica Monasterii de Melsa, auctore Thoma De Burton. Edited by E. A. Bond. 3 vols. 1866–68. 8vo. **102 C**

MECHANICS.

An Elementary treatise on Mechanics. By Wm. Whewell. 5th ed. Cambridge, 1836. 8vo. **78 C**

MECHANICS' INSTITUTES.

The rise and progress of Mechanics' Institutes in England. By J. R. Taylor. 1861. [Pamphlets, vol. 21.] **144 B**

MECKLENBURGH, HOUSE OF. See JACOB, REV. A.

MEDIA AND PERSIA, LAW AND HISTORY OF.

A Succinct account of the civil regulations comprised in the Zend Avesta. See B. Barrett's Code Napoléon, vol. 1, 1811, pp. lxxxi–xci. **55 C**

See also Rollin's Ancient History, vol. 2, 1851, pp. 1–153. **113 C**

MEDICAL DIRECTORIES.

The Dictionary of Medical Specialists. Edited by W. P. W. Phillimore. 1889. 12mo. **Hall**

The London and provincial medical directory, 1856, 1859, 1863, 1875 and 1878–1890. 17 vols. 1856–90. 8vo. **76 B C**

The Medical Register, 1859, 1860, 1862–1890. 31 vols. 1859–90. 8vo. **76 D E**

MEDICAL JURISPRUDENCE AND MEDICAL MEN.

The law relating to medical practitioners in England. By Joseph Craven. 1890. 12mo. **10 H**

A Manual of Medical Jurisprudence. By A. S. Taylor. 11th ed. 1886. 12mo. **10 H**

The student's guide to Medical Jurisprudence. By John Abercrombie. 1885. 8vo. **10 H**

Principles and practice of Medical Jurisprudence. By A. S. Taylor. 3rd ed. by T. Stevenson. 2 vols. 1883. 8vo. **10 I**

The laws relating to medical men. By James Greenwood. 1882. 8vo. **10 H**

A Manual of the laws affecting medical men. By R. G. Glenn. 1871. 8vo. **10 I**

An Exposition of the case of the assistant surgeons of the royal navy. By A Naval medical officer. 3rd ed. 1850. [Pamphlets, vol. 7.] **144 A**

An Exposure of the most nefarious and heartless system of swindling ever tolerated in any civilized community. By J. Teevan, B.A. 1847. [Pamphlets, vol. 5.] **144 A**

A Critical examination of Sir James Graham's bill, with practical views of the representation, incorporation, and organization of the medical profession. By John Forbes. 1845. [Pamphlets, vol. 21.] **144 B**

Introductory lecture on Medical Jurisprudence, delivered in the theatre of the Royal Dublin Society. By Thomas Brady. Dublin, 1839. [Lectures &c. Ireland.] **144 G**

A Practical treatise on Medical Jurisprudence. By J. Chitty. Part 1. 1834. 8vo. **172 E**

See also GUY, W. A., SMITH, JOHN G., WEIGHTMAN, H. and WILLCOCK, J. W.

MEDICINE.

A Treatise on the theory and practice of Medicine By J. S. Bristowe. 6th ed. 1887. 8vo. **78 E**

MEDICINE—*continued.*

Law of sales of food, drinks and medicines. Edited by
A Barrister and Magistrate. 1875. 12mo. **168 E**

The forbidden book, with new fallacies of the faculty: being
the Chrono-Thermalist; or, people's medical enquirer for
1850. [By Samuel Dickson.] 1850. 8vo. **78 E**

MEESON, ROGER and WILLIAM NEWLAND WELSBY.

Reports of cases in the courts of Exchequer and Exchequer
Chamber, 1836–1847. 16 vols. 1837–49. 8vo. **7 F G**

Meeson and Welsby's Reports. A general index to the
16 vols. By Edward Wise. 1849. 8vo. **7 G**

MEGGISON, HOLKER.

The administration of Assets in equity. 1832. 8vo. **160 C**

MEGONE, WILLIAM· BERNARD.

Reports of cases under the Companies acts, 1888–1890. 2 vols.
1890–91. 8vo. **8 I**

MELLIUS FREIRIUS, PASCHALIS JOSEPHUS.

Elenchus capitum titulorum et paragraphorum in Historia et
Institutionibus juris civilis et criminalis Lusitani. Conimbricæ, 1829. 8vo. **39 A**

Historiæ juris civilis Lusitani Liber singularis. Editio secunda.
Conimbricæ, 1827. 8vo. **39 A**

Institutiones juris civilis Lusitani cum publici tum privati.
4 vols. Conimbricæ, 1827–28. 8vo. **39 A**

Institutionum juris criminalis Lusitani Liber singularis.
Editio secunda. Conimbricæ, 1829. 8vo. **39 A**

MELSHEIMER, RUDOLPH EYRE and W. LAURENCE.

The law and customs of the London Stock Exchange. 1879.
12mo. **176 D**

The same. 2nd ed. by R. E. Melsheimer and S. Gardner.
1884. 8vo. **176 D**

The same. 3rd ed. by R. E. Melsheimer and S. Gardner.
1891. 8vo. **11 G**

MELVIL, SIR JAMES.

The memoires of Sir James Melvil; containing an impartial
account of the most remarkable affairs of state, 1558–1625.
Published by George Scott. 1683. folio. **114 G**

MEN OF THE TIME.

Men of the Time, a biographical dictionary of eminent living characters of both sexes. 6th ed. 1865, 7th ed. 1868, 8th ed. 1872, 9th ed. 1875, 10th ed. 1879, 11th ed. 1884, and 12th ed. 1887. 7 vols. 1865–87. 8vo. **81 D E**

MENDHAM, REV. JOSEPH.

Catalogue of the Mendham collection : being a selection of books and pamphlets from the library of the late Rev. Joseph Mendham. By John Nicholson. 1871, and Supplement 1874. 8vo. **82 B**

MERCANTILE LAW.

A Compendium of mercantile law. By J. W. Smith. 10th ed. by John Macdonell. 2 vols. 1890. 8vo. **10 I**

Elements of mercantile law. By T. M. Stevens. 1890. 12mo. **10 I**

The law of mercantile agents ; or, the Factors' act 1889. By M. Moloney. 1890. 12mo. **10 A**

The interpretation of mercantile agreements. By J. D. Wood. 1886. 8vo. **10 I**

Principles of mercantile law. By J. Slater. 1884. 8vo. **53 A**

A Selection of leading cases on mercantile and maritime law. By O. D. Tudor. 3rd ed. 1884. 8vo. **10 F**

Table of the foreign mercantile laws and codes in force in the principal states of Europe and America. By Charles Lyon-Caen. Translated by N. Argles. 1876. 8vo. **55 C**

Mercantile and maritime guide. By G. Willmore and E. Beedell. 1856. 8vo. **146 G**

Report and suggestions addressed to the mercantile community of the United Kingdom, by the London Committee of Merchants, and others. 1852. [Pamphlets, vol. 8.] **144 A**

The Merchant's Lawyer; or, the law of Trade in general. By a Gentleman of the Middle Temple [Timothy Cunningham]. 2 vols. 1761. 8vo. **172 E**

Lex Mercatoria ; or, the merchant's companion. By Giles Jacob. 1718. 8vo. **172 F**

See DUNCAN, J. A., HARE, J. I. C. and MALYNES, G.

See also AGENCY, COMMERCIAL LAW and MARITIME LAW.

MERCER, HENRY.

The late Captain Henry Mercer of the Royal Artillery, with an inquiry into the cause of his death. By A. H. H. Mercer. 2nd ed. Toronto, 1867. [Pamphlets, vol. 36.] **144 C**

MERCHANT TAYLORS' COMPANY AND SCHOOL.

The early history of the Guild of Merchant Taylors. By
C. M. Clode. Privately printed. 2 vols. 1888. 8vo. **89 E**

Excerpta e fastis scholæ Mercatorum Scissorum. By Rev.
J. A. Hessey. [1850.] 8vo. **89 E**

The history of Merchant Taylors' School. By Rev. H. B.
Wilson. 1814. 4to. **89 E**

Memorials of the guild of Merchant Taylors. By C. M. Clode.
Privately printed. 1875. 8vo. **89 E**

MEREWETHER, HENRY ALWORTH.

Address to the King, lords, and commons, on representative
constitution of England. 1830. [Pamphlets, vol. 4.] **144 A**

Report of the case of borough of West Looe ; with notes and
cases illustrative of general history of boroughs. 1823.
8vo. **87 A**

The history of the boroughs and municipal corporations of
the United Kingdom, from the earliest time. By H. A. Merewether and A. J. Stephens. 3 vols. 1835. 8vo. **84 D**

MERGER.

The Law of Merger. By C. J. Mayhew. 1861. 8vo. **13 C**

The Law of Merger. See R. Preston's Conveyancing, 3rd ed.
vol. 3, 1829, 8vo. **163 E**

Difference between Merger, remitter and extinguishment.
See R. Preston's Tracts, 1797, pp. 42–46. **163 G**

MERITON, GEORGE.

Landlord's law. 3rd ed. 1669. 12mo. **49 A**

MERIVALE, CHARLES.

History of the Romans under the empire. 7 vols. 1864–62.
8vo. **113 E**

MERIVALE, JOHN HERMAN.

Letter to Wm. Courtenay, Esq., on subject of the Chancery
Commission. 1827. [Jacob's Tracts, vol. 4.] **144 E**

Letters to a Chancery Reformer occasioned by the withdrawal
of the late bill for facilitating the administration of justice.
1841. [Chancery Pamphlets, vol. 2.] **144 A**

Reports of cases in the Court of Chancery, 1815–1817. 3 vols.
1817–19. 8vo. **3 A B**

MIDDLESEX REGISTRY.

Dissertation on the Middlesex registry and precedents of memorials &c. See Bythewood and Jarman's Conveyancing, 4th ed., vol. 6, 1890, pp. 1–9 and 20–25. **13 D**

Observations on the statutes for registering deeds. By J. Rigge. 1798. 8vo. **13 B**

MIDDLETON, CONYERS.

History of life of Marcus Tullius Cicero. 2 vols. 1741. 4to. **80 I**

MIDDLETON, EMPSON EDWARD.

Impeachment of modern Astronomy. 1879. 12mo. **78 B**

MIDDLETON, JAMES WILLIAM.

The Settled estates act 1877, with summary of practice. 1878. 12mo. **175 E**

Statutes relating to Settled estates. 3rd ed. 1882. 12mo. **13 H**

MIEGE, GUY.

The ancient sea laws of Oleron, Wisby, and the Hanse Towns, still in force; taken out of a French book intitled Les Us et Coutumes de la Mer. 1686. See G. Malynes's Lex Mercatoria, 3rd ed. 1686, folio. **118 G**

The new state of England. 1691, 3rd ed. 1699, 4th ed. 1702. 3 vols. 1699–1702. 12mo. **143 C**

The present state of Great Britain and Ireland. 1707, 1711, 1716, 1718, 1723, 1728, 1731, 1738, 1742, 1745, 1748. 11 vols. 1707–48. 12mo. **143 C D**

MILDMAY, SIR WILLIAM.

The method and rule of proceeding upon all elections, polls and scrutinies at common halls and wardmotes within the City of London. By W. M. 1743. 12mo. **91 B**

The same. By Sir W. Mildmay. New ed. 1819. 12mo. **91 B**

MILFORD HAVEN, PEMBROKESHIRE.

A Tour to Milford Haven. By Mary Morgan. 1795. 8vo. **94 E**

MILITARY ENGINEERING.

The military engineer; or, a treatise on the attack and defence of fortified places. By G. Le Blond. 1759. 8vo. **78 B**

44

MILITARY LAW.

Summary of military law. By P. Story. 1886. 8vo. **10 I**

The constitution and practice of courts martial. By T. F. Simmons. 6th ed. 1873. 8vo. **53 A**

Martial law as allowed by law of England in time of rebellion; with practical illustrations drawn from official documents in the Jamaica case. By W. F. Finlason. 1866. 8vo. **53 A**

Manual of military law for all ranks of the army, militia, and volunteer services. By J. K. Pipon and J. F. Collier. 3rd ed. 1863. 12mo. **172 F**

See also CLODE, C. M., GRIFFITHS, F. A., PRENDERGAST, H., SAMUEL, E. and TYTLER, A. F.

MILL, JAMES.

History of British India. 2nd ed. 6 vols. 1820. 8vo. **116 B**

MILL, JOB.

The present practice of Conveyancing; or, select precedents of conveyances. 1746. folio. **157 E**

MILL, JOHN STUART.

A Review of Mr. J. S. Mill's Essay 'On Liberty,' and an investigation of his claim to be considered the leading philosopher and thinker of the age. By A Liberal. 1867. [Pamphlets, vol. 36.] **144 C**

MILLAR, FREDERICK CHARLES JAMES and J. R. COLLIER.

A Treatise on bills of sale. 1858. 12mo. **160 G**

The same. 4th ed. by F. C. J. Miller. 1877. 12mo. **53 G**

MILLAR, JOHN.

Historical view of the English government from the settlement of the Saxons in Britain to the accession of the House of Stewart. 1790. 2nd ed. 4to. **114 F**

MILLER, REV. CHARLES.

The duty of a Conservative Government towards the clergy and the church, in their present relations with the state. 1841. [Pamphlets, vol. 5.] **144 A**

The Oxford examination statute examined by an examiner; or, a plea for moral philosophy and law. 1864. [Pamphlets, vol. 27.] **144 B**

MILLER, REV. CHARLES—*continued.*

The principles of Mr. Shaw Lefevre's Parochial assessments bill, and the Tithe commutation act, compared. 1839. [Law Tracts, vol. 6.] **144 E**

A Revised code of national education, national Christianity, social science, and law amendment ; or, a plea for the revival of the study of the Common Law. 1862. [Pamphlets, vol. 27.] **144 B**

The petition of Rev. C. Miller, respecting the Tithe Commutation act, presented to the House of Lords by the bishop of London, session 1840. 1841. [Pamphlets, vol. 5.] **144 A**

MILLER, DAVID.

Practical directions for acknowledging and levying Fines and for suffering and perfecting Common Recoveries. By D. M. 1822. 12mo. **168 D**

The same. By D. Miller. 2nd ed. 1825. 12mo. **168 D**

MILLER, EDWARD.

The history and antiquities of Doncaster and its vicinity. Doncaster, [1804.] 4to. **94 D**

MILLER, FREDERICK.

Saint Pancras past and present, being historical, traditional, and general notes of the parish. 1874. 8vo. **89 D**

MILLER, JOHN.

An Inquiry into the present state of the civil law of England. 1825. 8vo. **63 F**

On the present unsettled condition of the Law, and its administration. 1839. 8vo. **170 F**

MILLER, SAMUEL.

An Essay on the present state of the law respecting Equitable Mortgages by deposit of deeds. 1842. 8vo. **172 G**

The law of Equitable Mortgages. 1844. 8vo. **172 G**

The laws relating to the Land Tax. 1849. 8vo. **170 C**

Observations on the necessity for continuous proceedings in the offices of the Masters in Chancery. 1848. [Pamphlets, vol. 6.] **144 A**

Suggestions for a general equalization of the Land Tax, and the abolition of the income and real property taxes, and the malt duty. 1848. [Pamphlets, vol. 19.] **144 B**

MILLER, SAMUEL—*continued.*
Suggestions for a general equalization of the Land Tax, with
a view to provide the means of reducing the Malt duties.
3rd ed. 1843. 12mo.   170 C

MILLER, SAMUEL F.
Reports of decisions ·in Supreme Court of United States.
1855 to 1862. 4 vols. Washington, 1874–75. 8vo. 57 C

MILLER, SAMUEL HENRY and SYDNEY B. J. SKERTCHLY.
The Fenland past and present. Wisbeach, 1878. 8vo. 89 C

MILLES, THOMAS.
Catalogue of honor ; or, treasury of true nobility peculiar and
proper to the Isle of Great Britaine. 1610. folio. 126 I

MILLETT, JACOB CURNOW.
Memorial and petition of F. Edmonds to secretary of state, in
matter of revision ordered by him of defective coroner's
inquest on the body of J. C. Millett. 1871. 8vo. 50 B

MILLS, MARK ANTHONY.
Ancient ordinances and statute laws of the Isle of Man:
with copious extracts from several British statutes which
have reference thereto. Douglas, 1821. 8vo. 32 A

MILMAN, VERY REV. HENRY HART.
Annals of St. Paul's Cathedral. 2nd ed. 1869. 8vo. 89 E
The fall of Jerusalem. New ed. 1865. 8vo. 83 A

MILNE, JOSHUA.
The valuation of annuities and assurances on lives and survivorships. 2 vols. 1815. 8vo. 160 B

MILNER, REV. JOHN.
The history, civil and ecclesiastical, and survey of the antiquities, of Winchester. 2 vols. Winchester, 1809. 4to. 88 B

MILNER, REV. THOMAS.
The gallery of Nature : a pictorial and descriptive tour through
creation. New ed. 1855. 8vo. 84 D

MILNES, James.
Sectionum Conicarum elementa nova methodo demonstrata.
Editio tertia. Oxoniæ, 1723. 8vo. **255 H**

MILTON, John.
A Common-place book of John Milton, and a Latin essay
and Latin verses presumed to be by Milton. Edited by
A. J. Horwood. [Camden Society, n.s. vols. 16 and 16*.]
1876, 1877. 8vo. **85 D**
Original papers illustrative of the life and writings of John
Milton. Collected and edited by W. D. Hamilton. [Cam-
den Society, vol. 75.] 1859. 8vo. **85 B**
The works of John Milton, with a life of the author. By
Rev. John Mitford. 8 vols. 1863. 8vo. **83 G**

MILWARD, Charles Richard.
Reports of cases in the court of Prerogative in Ireland and
in Consistory court of Dublin, 1819–1842. Dublin, 1847.
8vo. **15 F**

MINES.
The Mining Manual for 1888. By W. R. Skinner. 1888.
8vo. **134 I**
The law of mines, quarries, and minerals. By R. F. Mac
Swinney. 1884. 8vo. **10 I**
The law of mines and minerals. By W. Bainbridge. 4th ed.
by A. Brown. 1878. 8vo. **10 I**
The law relating to mines, minerals, and quarries. By
A. Rogers. 2nd ed. 1876. 8vo. **10 I**
Some account of mines and the advantages of them to this
kingdom. 1721. 8vo. **84 A**
See Arundell, W., Collier, R. P., Hamilton, L., Pettus,
Sir J., Pryce, W. Tredinnick, R., Underhill, A.,
Waller, W. and Yale, G.
See also Coal Mines and Derbyshire, Mineralogy of,

MINOT, George.
The statutes at large and treaties of United States of America,
1845–1855. 2 vols. Boston, 1852–55. 8vo. **32 B**
The same. 1856–1859. By G. Minot and G. P. Sanger.
Boston, 1859. 8vo. **32 B**

MINOT, James.
A Digest of the laws of Jamaica, 1681–1868. 2 vols. Jamaica, 1865–69. 8vo. **36 A**

MINSHEU, John.
A Dictionary in Spanish and English, 1623. A Spanish grammar. 1623. Pleasant and delightful Dialogues in Spanish and English. 1623. [all 3 in 1 vol.] 1623. 4to. **122 G**

The guide into the tongues in these eleven languages, viz.: 1. English; 2. British or Welsh; 3. Low Dutch; 4. High Dutch; 5. French; 6. Italian; 7. Spanish; 8. Portuguez; 9. Latine; 10. Greeke; 11. Hebrew: also A Spanish dictionary with Latin and English. 1617. folio. **122 G**

MIRABAUD, Jean Baptiste De.
System of Nature; or, the laws of the moral and physical world. Translated by S. Wilkinson. 3 vols. 1820–21. 8vo. **83 B**

MIREHOUSE, John.
Practical treatise on law of Advowsons. 1824. 8vo. **52 A**
Practical treatise on law of Tithes. 2nd ed. 1822. 8vo. **176 E**

MIST'S WEEKLY JOURNAL.
The Original Weekly Journal, 1718–1725. 3 vols. 1718–25. folio. **19 D**

MISTAKE.
Law of fraud and mistake. By W. W. Kerr. 2nd ed. 1883. 8vo. **10 A**

MITCHELL, Richard.
A Genealogy of the kings of England and their issue from William I. to the present time. 1817. 12mo. **125 A**

MITCHESON, Richard Edmund.
Charitable trusts: the jurisdiction of the charity commission. 1887. 8vo. **52 B**

MITFORD, JOHN, 1 BARON REDESDALE.

Considerations suggested by The Report made to His Majesty under a commission, authorising the commissioners to make certain inquiries respecting the Court of Chancery. [By Lord Redesdale.] 1826. [Jacob's Tracts, vol. 3.]   **144 E**

The same. 2nd ed. 1826. [Chancery Pam., vol. 1.]   **144 A**

The pleadings in suits in the court of Chancery by English bill. [By John Mitford.] 1780. 8vo.   **173 G**

The same. By John Mitford. 3rd ed. 1814. 8vo.   **173 G**

The same. 5th ed. by J. W. Smith. 1847. 8vo.   **173 G**

MODELLING.

Guide to modelling in clay and wax, and for terra cotta. By Morton Edwards. 1879. 12mo.   **78 A**

MODERN REPORTS.

Modern Reports; or, select cases adjudged in the courts of King's Bench, Chancery, Common Pleas, and Exchequer. 5th ed. by Thomas Leach. 12 vols. 1796. 8vo.   **5 D**

MOHAMMEDAN LAW.

Moohummudan law of inheritance, and rights and relations affecting it. By A. Rumsey. 3rd ed. 1880. 8vo.   **38 B**

Chart of family inheritance, according to orthodox Moohummudan law, with an explanatory treatise. By A. Rumsey. 2nd ed. 1871. 8vo.   **38 B**

The Hedaya, or guide; a commentary on the Mussalman laws. By C. Hamilton. 2nd ed. by S. G. Grady. 1870. 8vo.   **38 D**

The Mahommedan law of inheritance and contract. By S. G. Grady. 1869. 8vo.   **38 B**

The Moohummudan law of sale. Selected and translated from the Arabic by N. B. E. Baillie. 1850. 8vo.   **38 B**

The Koran; commonly called the Alcoran of Mohammed. Translated from the original Arabic by George Sale. New ed. 1825. 8vo.   **77 B**

See also BENGAL, BOMBAY, INDIA and MADRAS.

MOHEDANUS, JOANNES.

Decisiones sacræ rotæ Romanæ. Marpurgi Cattorum, 1603. folio.   **48 H**

MOILE, Nicholas Thirning.
Cicero. A drama. 1847. 8vo.   **83 C**
State trials. Specimen of a new edition. 1838. 8vo. **83 H**

MOLIÈRE, Jean Baptiste Poquelin.
Œuvres. Par M. Bret. 6 vols. Paris, 1773. 8vo.   **83 B**

MOLLOY, Charles.
De jure maritimo et navali ; or, a treatise of affairs maritime
   and of commerce. 7th ed. 1722. 8vo.   **172 E**
The same. 9th ed. 2 vols. 1769. 8vo.   **172 E**
The same. 10th ed. 2 vols. 1778. 8vo.   **172 E**

·MOLLOY, Philip.
Reports of cases in the high court of Chancery in Ireland,
   1827 to 1831. 3 vols. Dublin, 1832–33. 8vo.   **15 G**

MOLONEY, Michael.
The law of Mercantile Agents. 1890. 12mo.   **10 A**

MOLYNEUX, William.
The case of Ireland's being bound by acts of parliament in
   England, stated. 1719. 12mo.   **48 C**

MONAGHAN.
History of the county of Monaghan. By E. P. Shirley. 1879.
   folio.   **95 G**

MONASTERIES.
The Ancren Riwle : a treatise on the rules and duties of
   monastic life. Edited and translated by James Morton.
   [Camden Society, vol. 57.] 1853. 8vo.   **85 B**
Annales Monastici. Edited by Rev. H. R. Luard. 5 vols.
   1864–69. 8vo.   **102 A**
Historic collections relating to the monasteries in Devon. By
   Rev. G. Oliver. Exeter, 1820. 8vo.   **87 C**
Mediæval letters relating to the priory of Christ Church,
   Canterbury. [Camden Soc., n.s. vol. 19.] 1877. 8vo. **85 D**
Monasticon dioecesis Exoniensis, with two supplements. By
   Rev. G. Oliver. 1846–54. folio.   **86 H**
Three chapters of letters relating to the suppression of monas-

MONASTERIES—*continued.*

    teries. Edited by T. Wright. [Camden Society, vol. 36.] 1843. 8vo.   **85 A**

    See also ABBEYS, ABERCONWAY, ABINGDON, BATTLE, BURY ST. EDMUNDS, CANTERBURY, DUBLIN, EVESHAM, GLOUCESTER, HYDE, RAMSEY and S. ALBANS.

MONCREIFF, FREDERICK CHARLES.

    The liability of Innkeepers. 1874. 12mo.   **169 A**

MONEY.

    Lombard Street. A description of the money market. By Walter Bagehot. 8th ed. 1882. 8vo.   **78 D**

    Money and taxation : an extra circulation guaranteed and the stamp taxes modified and adjusted. [n.d.] [Pamphlets, vol. 36.]   **144 C**

    Some considerations of the consequences of the lowering of interest, and raising the value of Money. See Locke's Works, vol. 5, 1823, pp. 1–206.   **78 F**

    Three lectures on the cost of obtaining money, and on some effects of private and government paper money. By N. W. Senior. 1830. 8vo.   **78 D**

    The Universal Cambist and commercial instructor. By P. Kelly. 2nd ed. 2 vols. in 1. 1821. 4to.   **78 G**

MONEY SECURITIES AND MONEY LENDERS.

    Law of money securities. By C. Cavanagh. 2nd ed. 1885. 8vo.   **11 A**

    Law relating to money lenders and borrowers. By D. R. Macalpin. 1880. 8vo.   **11 A**

    An Essay on money-lending, containing a defence of legal restrictions on the rate of interest. By F. Neale. 1826. [Jacob's Tracts, vol. 3.]   **144 E**

MONEY, UNCLAIMED.

    Gun's Index to advertisements for next of kin, heirs-at-law, legatees, and cases of unclaimed money. 1881. 8vo.   **134 I**

    Index register for next of kin, heirs at law, legatees, and of unclaimed property from 1754 to 1856. By C. W. De Bernardy. 1858. 8vo.   **134 I**

    Index register to next of kin, heirs-at-law, legatees, &c. since 1698. By F. H. Dougal. 8th ed. 1888. 8vo.   **134 I**

MONEY, UNCLAIMED—*continued.*

Index to heirs at law, next of kin, owners of unclaimed money, missing friends, and legatees and creditors in Chancery suits, who have been advertised for during the last 150 years. By Edward Preston. 4th ed. 1878. 8vo.   **134 I**

Supplement to the 4th ed. of Chambers's Index to next of kin. By S. H. Preston. 1888. 8vo.   **134 I**

The reliable next of kin annual. By C. H. Cowlishaw. 1886. 8vo.   **134 I**

Unclaimed money. A handy book for heirs at law, next of kin and persons in search of a clue to unclaimed money. By Edward Preston. 1878. 8vo.   **134 I**

Unclaimed money register. By C. W. De Bernardy. 1883. 12mo.   **134 I**

MONEY, WALTER.

The history of Newbury. 1887. 8vo.   **86 B**

MONMOUTH AND MONMOUTHSHIRE.

The excursion down the Wye from Ross to Monmouth. By Charles Heath. 1799. 8vo.   **92 C**

Historical and descriptive accounts of Monmouth. By Charles Heath. Monmouth, 1804. 4to.   **92 C**

An Historical tour in Monmouthshire. By Rev. William Coxe. 2 vols. 1801. 4to.   **92 C**

History of Monmouthshire. By D. Williams. 1796. 4to. **92 C**

A Tour through Monmouthshire and Wales. By H. P. Wyndham. 2nd ed. Salisbury, 1781. 4to.   **95 G**

MONMOUTH, JAMES, I DUKE OF.

Account of the proceedings against the rebels tried in the West of England in 1685, for taking arms under the Duke of Monmouth ; with a complete list of all the persons that suffered. 2nd ed. 1716. 12mo.   **115 D**

Original letters of Duke of Monmouth in Bodleian library. Edited by Sir G. Duckett. [Camden Society, n.s. vol. 31.] 1883. 8vo.   **85 D**

MONSTRELET, ENGUERRAND DE.

Chronicles containing an account of the cruel civil wars between the houses of Orleans and Burgundy, 1400 to 1467. By E. De Monstrelet, and continued by others to 1516. Translated by Thomas Johnes. 2 vols. 1840. 8vo.   **115 A**

MONTAGU, BASIL.

MONTAGU, BASIL—*continued.*

The private tutor ; or, thoughts upon the love of excelling and of excellence. [By B. Montagu.] 1820. 8vo.   78 C

Reform. 1827. [Montagu's Law Tracts.]   144 F

Reports of cases in Bankruptcy, 1829–1832. 1 vol. 1832. 8vo.   8 C

Rules for the construction of statutes, deeds, and wills. 1837. 12mo.   176 C

Some observations upon the bill for improvement of the Bankrupt laws. 1822. [Jacob's Tracts, vol. 4.]   144 E

The law of composition with creditors. 1823. 8vo.   165 G

Summary of law of Lien. 1821. 8vo.   172 A

Summary of law of Set-Off. 1801. 8vo.   175 E

Thoughts upon abolition of Punishment of Death, in cases of Bankruptcy. 1821. [Montagu's Law Tracts.]   144 F

Law of parliamentary elections. By B. Montagu and W. J. Neale. 1839. 12mo.   166 D

See also BACON, F.

MONTAGU, BASIL and SCROPE AYRTON.

Law and practice in Bankruptcy. 2 vols. 1837. 12mo.   160 E

Reports of cases in Bankruptcy, 1833–1838. 3 vols. 1834–39. 8vo.   8 C

MONTAGU, BASIL and RICHARD BLIGH.

Reports of cases in Bankruptcy, 1832–33. 1835. 8vo.   8 C

MONTAGU, BASIL and EDWARD CHITTY.

Reports of cases in Bankruptcy, 1838–40. 1840. 8vo.   8 C

MONTAGU, BASIL, E. C. DEACON and J. DE GEX.

Reports of cases in Bankruptcy, 1840–1844. 3 vols. 1842–45. 8vo.   8 C

MONTAGU, BASIL and JOHN MACARTHUR.

Reports of cases (in Bankruptcy) decided by the lord chancellor and vice-chancellor, 1826–1830. 1 vol. 1830. 8vo. 8 C

MONTAGU, MOSES.

Fifty sonnets on various subjects, with some account of that poem. For private circulation. 1860. 8vo.   83 D

Fifty more sonnets on various subjects. For private circulation. 1861. 8vo.   83 D

MONTAGUE, LADY MARY WORTLEY.
Letters of the Right Honourable Lady M—y W——y
M——e, written during her travels in Europe, Asia and
Africa. New ed. 1785. 12mo. **83 A**

MONTEFIORE, JOSHUA.
Commercial and Notarial precedents. 1802. 4to. **157 B**

MONTEITH, EARLDOM OF. See AIRTH PEERAGE.

MONTESQUIEU, CHARLES DE SECONDAT, BARON DE.
Œuvres. Nouvelle éd. 7 vols. 1769. 12mo. **83 A**
Œuvres. Nouvelle éd. 7 vols. in 6. 1777–75. 12mo. **83 A**
The spirit of laws. Translated from the French by Thomas
Nugent. 2nd ed. 2 vols. 1752. 8vo. **49 G**
The same. 5th ed. 2 vols. 1773. 8vo. **49 G**
The same. New ed. by M. D'Alembert. 2 vols. Cincinnati,
1873. 8vo. **83 H**

MONTFORT, SIMON DE.
The miracles of Simon De Montfort. See Camden Society,
vol. 15, 1840, pp. 67–110. **85 A**

MONTGOMERY, WILLIAM ERNEST.
History of land tenure in Ireland. 1889. 8vo. **55 E**

MONTHLY LAW MAGAZINE.
The Monthly Law Magazine and Political Review. 1838–
1841. 10 vols. 1838–41. 8vo. **140 B**

MONTHLY MERCURIES.
The general history of Europe contained in the historical
and political Monthly Mercuries, from November 1688 to
December 1699, done from the originals published at the
Hague, by J. Phillips. 10 vols. 1692–99. 8vo. **116 A**

MONTSERRAT.
Acts of assembly from 1668 to 1740. 1740. folio. **36 F**
Ordinances of Montserrat, 1857–1859, 1861–1863, 1865–1875,
1878–1885, 1887. 4 vols. 1857–87. folio. **36 F**

MOODY, WILLIAM.
Crown cases reserved for consideration and decided by the
judges of England, 1824–1844. 2 vols. 1837–44. 8vo. **1 H**

MOODY, WILLIAM and BENJAMIN HEATH MALKIN.
Reports of cases at Nisi Prius, 1826–1830. 1 vol. 1831.
8vo.   8 F

MOODY, WILLIAM and FREDERICK ROBINSON.
Reports of cases at Nisi Prius, 1830–1844. 2 vols. 1837–44.
8vo.   .   8 F

MOORE, EDMUND FITZ.
  The case of the Rev. G. C. Gorham against the Bishop of
    Exeter as heard and determined by the judicial committee
    of the Privy Council on appeal from the Arches Court of
    Canterbury 1852. 8vo.   50 A
  The cases of Westerton against Liddell, and Horne and
    others, and Beal against Liddell and Parke and Evans, as
    heard and determined by the Consistory court of London,
    the Arches court of Canterbury, and the judicial committee
    of the Privy Council. 1857. 8vo.   50 A
  Reports of cases heard and determined by the Judicial Com-
    mittee, and the Lords of the Privy Council, 1836–1862.
    15 vols. [n.d.] 8vo.   I D E
  The same. New Series 1862–1873. 9 vols. [n.d.] 8vo. I E
  Reports of cases heard and determined by the Judicial Com-
    mittee, and Privy Council, on appeal from the East Indies,
    1836–1872. 14 vols. [n.d.] 8vo.   I E F

MOORE, SIR FRANCIS.
  Cases [temp. Hen. VIII., Eliz. et Jac. I.] publié par Gefrey
    Palmer. 1663. folio.   .
  The same. 2nd ed. 1675. folio.   74 F

MOORE, HENRY.
  A Handbook of Practical Forms. 1886. 8vo.   53 D
  The same. 2nd ed. 1890. 8vo.   13 F
  Instructions for preparing abstracts of titles, with a collection
    of precedents. 3rd ed. 1873. 12mo.   160 A
  The same. 4th ed. by R. Merivale and N. Pearson. 1886.
    12mo.   .   13 A
  Practical forms of agreements. 1884. 8vo.   53 D
  The same. 2nd ed. by T. L. Mears. 1887. 8vo.   13 F

MOORE, JOHN.

Beauties of Dr. John Moore selected from his works; with a new account of the Doctor and his writings and notes. By Rev. F. Prevost and F. Blagdon. 1803. 12mo. **83 C**

MOORE, JOHN BAYLY.

Digested index to the Term Reports, containing all the points of law argued and determined in the Court of King's Bench, 1785 to 1814, and in the Court of Common Pleas, 1788 to 1815. 2 vols. 1816. 8vo. **63 D**

Reports of cases in Courts of Common Pleas and Exchequer Chamber, 1817–27. 12 vols. 1818–31. 8vo. **6 H I**

MOORE, JOHN BAYLY and JOSEPH PAYNE.

Reports of cases in the courts of Common Pleas and Exchequer Chamber, 1827–1831. 5 vols. 1828–32. 8vo. **6 I**

MOORE, JOHN BAYLY and JOHN SCOTT.

Cases in the courts of Common Pleas and Exchequer Chamber and in the House of Lords, 1831–1834. 4 vols. 1833–34. 8vo. **6 I**

MOORE, JONAS.

A Mapp of ye great levell of ye Fenns. 1685. folio. **86 H**

MOORE, STUART ARCHIBALD.

History of the Foreshore and the law relating thereto, with a hitherto unpublished treatise by Lord Hale, Lord Hale's 'De jure maris' and Hall's Essays on the rights of the Crown in the sea-shore. 1888. 8vo. **11 E**

MOORE, THOMAS.

Precedents in Bankruptcy, containing forms of petitions in all cases which occur in the prosecution of commissions of bankrupts. 2nd ed. 1789. 8vo. **160 F**

MORALITY.

The elements of morality including polity. By Wm. Whewell. 2 vols. 1845. 8vo. **77 B**

Essays on the principles of morality and natural religion. [By H. Home, Lord Kames.] Edinburgh, 1751. 12mo. **77 B**

On the morality of heathen philosophers. By J. S. Boone. See Charterhouse Prize Exercises, 1833, pp. 1–32. **83 C**

MORANT, Rev. Philip.

The history and antiquities of Colchester. 1748. folio. **88 G**

The same. 2nd ed. 1768. Reprinted Chelmsford, 1815. folio. Bound with Morant's History of Essex, vol. 2, 1816. **88 H**

The history and antiquities of the county of Essex. 2 vols. 1768. Reprinted Chelmsford, 2 vols. 1816. folio. **88 H**

Life of Philip Morant. See J. P. Malcolm's Lives of Topographers and Antiquaries, 1815, 4to. **79 H**

MORAYSHIRE.

Survey of province of Moray. Aberdeen, 1798. 8vo. **95 C**

MORE, John Schank.

Lectures on the law of Scotland. Edited by John McLaren. 2 vols. Edinburgh, 1864. 8vo. **55 F**

MORE, Sir Thomas.

The lineage of Sir Thomas More. By E. Foss. 1842. 4to. Bound with E. Foss's Grandeur of the law. 1842. **80 E**

MOREAU DE SAINT-MÉRY, Médéric Louis Elie.

Description de la partie Française de l'Isle Saint Domingue. 2 tomes. Philadelphie, 1797–98. 4to. **84 D**

MORGAN, George Osborn.

Chancery acts and orders. 1858. 12mo. **161 D**

The same. 5th ed. by G. O. Morgan and C. W. Chute. 1876. 8vo. **52 B**

The same. 6th ed. by G. O. Morgan and E. A. Wurtzburg. 1885. 8vo. **12 F**

Costs in Chancery, with an appendix of bills of costs. By G. O. Morgan and H. Davey. 1865. 8vo. **52 D**

Law of costs in the Chancery division of the high court of justice. By G. O. Morgan and E. A. Wurtzburg. 1882. 8vo. **9 F**

Places of worship and school sites bill. Speech delivered in House of Commons on moving second reading of the bill, 6 April, 1870. Wrexham, [n.d.] [Pamphlets, vol. 38.] **144 C**

MORGAN, Rev. Hector Davies.

The doctrine and law of Marriage, Adultery, and Divorce. 2 vols. Oxford, 1826. 8vo. **172 D**

MORGAN, JOHN.

The Attorney's Vade Mecum and client's instructor, treating of actions. 2 vols. 1787. 12mo. **163 A**

MORGAN, MARY.

A Tour to Milford Haven in 1791. 1795. 8vo. **94 E**

MORGAN, SYLVANUS.

The sphere of gentry, deduced from the principles of nature: an historical and genealogical work of arms and blazon. 1661. folio. **118 G**

MORGAN, WILLIAM.

Nine addresses delivered to the members of the Society for equitable assurances, 1793-1830. 1833. 8vo. **78 C**

MORISON, SIR ALEXANDER.

Lectures on Insanity for the use of students. Edited by his son. 5th ed. Edinburgh, 1856. 8vo. **172 B**

MORISON, JAMES.

A Biographical sketch of James Morison the hygeist. 1873. [Pamphlets, vol. 36.] **144 C**

MORLEY, WILLIAM HOOK.

Analytical digest of reported cases decided in supreme courts of judicature in India, 1774-1850. 3 vols. 1850-52. 8vo. **38 C**
Descriptive catalogue of historical manuscripts in Arabic and Persian, in library of Royal Asiatic Society. 1854. 8vo. **82 A**

MORRELL, CHARLES FRANCIS.

Digest of all reported cases decided under the Bankruptcy act 1883. 1888. 8vo. **14 F**
Popular statement of law of Insurance. 1883. 12mo. **169 A**
Reports of cases under the Bankruptcy act 1883, 1884-1890. 7 vols. 1885-91. 8vo. **8 D**

[MORRIS, CORBYN.]

Observations on the past growth and present state of the City of London. By the Author of A Letter from a Bystander. 1751. folio. **92 H**

45

MORRIS, RICHARD.
Analytical digest of selected Practice cases decided in the
Common Law courts, to 1847. 1847. 8vo. **63 D**

MORRIS, ROBERT.
Collection of precedents in conveyancing in relation to letters
patent for inventions. 1887. 8vo. **13 C**

MORRIS, THOMAS.
A Discourse upon Dilapidations. 1871. 12mo. **165 G**

MORRIS, WILLIAM O'CONNOR.
Summary of law of Easements. Dublin, 1869. 12mo. **166 A**

MORTGAGES.
Dissertation on and precedents of Mortgages. See Bythewood
and Jarman's Conveyancing, 4th ed., vol. 3, 1886, pp. 640–
1236. **13 D**
Student's guide to specific performance and mortgages. By
J. Indermaur and C. Thwaites. 1886. 8vo. **64 B**
Law of Mortgage. By R. H. Coote. 5th ed. 2 vols. 1884.
8vo. **13 C**
Law of Mortgage. By W. R. Fisher. 4th ed. 1884. 8vo. **13 C**
Precedents of mortgages. By J. Andrews. 1879. 8vo. **13 C**
Opinions of three eminent counsel on tacking prior and sub-
sequent Securities, and on 4 & 5 Wm. & Mary, c. 16, which
respects Frauds by Clandestine Mortgages. See Collectanea
Juridica, vol. 2, 1792, pp. 241–254. **144 G**
Case of Willoughby and Willoughby in Chancery on priority
of mortgage debts. See Collectanea Juridica, vol. 1, 1791,
pp. 337–366. **144 G**
History of securities upon land for payment of debt. See
Historical Law Tracts, 2nd ed. 1761, pp. 145–172. **144 F**
See ALDRED, P. F., COVENTRY, T., HILLIARD, F., JAMES,
J. H., JONES, L. A., POWELL, J. J. and ROUSE, R.
See also EQUITABLE MORTGAGES.

MORTIMER, THOMAS.
Every man his own Broker : or, a guide to Exchange Alley.
5th ed. 1762. 12mo. **118 B**

MORTLAKE, SURREY.

History of the Independents or Dissenters at Mortlake ; with an account of their chapel. By J. E. Anderson. 1888. 8vo. **93 C**

History of the parish of Mortlake. By J. E. Anderson. Privately printed. 1886. 8vo. **93 C**

MORTMAIN. See CHARITY.

MORTON, REV. JOHN.

The natural history of Northamptonshire ; with some account of the antiquities, and a transcript of Doomsday-book so far as it relates to that county. 1712. folio. **92 G**

MORTON, T. C.

A Practical treatise of the law of vendors and purchasers of chattels personal. 1836. 8vo. **177 B**

MOSELEY, JOSEPH.

Law of the new County Courts. 1847. 8vo. **165 C**

What is Contraband of war and what is not. 1861. 12mo. **55 A**

MOSELY, WILLIAM.

Reports of cases in the high court of chancery, 1726–1730. Dublin, 1793. 8vo. **74 F**

MOSES.

The influence of the Mosaic code upon subsequent legislation. By J. B. Marsden. 1862. 8vo. **78 C**

The moral system of Moses. By S. Pye. 1770. 4to. **77 G**

See also CREATION.

MOSLEY, SIR OSWALD.

History of the castle, priory, and town of Tutbury, in the county of Stafford. 1832. 8vo. **93 C**

MOSS, WILLIAM.

The Liverpool guide, including a sketch of the environs. 2nd ed. Liverpool, 1797. 8vo. **89 A**

MOSSOP, REV. J.

Elegant orations ancient and modern, for the use of schools. 1788. 12mo. **83 A**

MOTLEY, JOHN LOTHROP.
The rise of the Dutch Republic. New ed. 3 vols. 1869.
8vo. **113 D**

MOULE, THOMAS.
Bibliotheca Heraldica Magnæ Britanniæ, an analytical cata-
logue of books on genealogy, heraldry, nobility, knighthood
and ceremonies. 1822. 8vo. **82 C**
The English counties delineated; illustrated by a map of
London and by county maps. 2 vols. 1837. 4to. **84 F**

MOWNTAYNE, THOMAS.
The troubles of T. Mowntayne, rector of St. Michael, Tower-
Ryal in the reign of Queen Mary, written by himself. See
Camden Society, vol. 77, 1859, pp. 177–217. **85 B**

MOXON, THOMAS BOUCHIER.
English practical banking. 2nd ed. 1886. 8vo. **78 D**

MOYLE, JOHN BARON.
Imperatoris Justiniani institutionum libri quattuor. Oxford,
1883, and 2nd ed. Oxford, 1890. 8vo. **63 E**
The Institutes of Justinian, translated in English. Oxford,
1883, and 2nd ed. Oxford, 1889. 8vo. **63 E**

MOZLEY, HERBERT NEWMAN and G. C. WHITELY.
A Concise law dictionary. 1876. 8vo. **64 E**

[MUILMAN, PETER.]
A New and complete history of Essex, from a late survey.
6 vols. Chelmsford, 1770–72. 8vo. **87 E**

MUIRHEAD, JAMES.
Historical introduction to the private law of Rome. Edinburgh, 1886. 8vo. **63 E**

MULLINGER, JAMES BASS.
The University of Cambridge, from earliest times to accession
of Charles I. 2 vols. Cambridge, 1873–84. 8vo. **86 E**

MULLINS, EDWARD.
Court of Sewers: a letter on the power of the Court to authorise in certain cases the demand of fees. 1836. 8vo. **118 B**

MUNSTER, Sebastian.
La Cosmographie universelle recueillie de chasque bon autheur et approuvé tant des historiens comme de ceux qui ont descrit les lieux particuliers. Paris, 1552. folio. **118 G**

MURIMUTH, Adam.
Chronicle of A. Murimuth, with the Chronicle of Robert of Avesbury. Edited by E. M. Thompson. 1889. 8vo. **102 I**

MURPHY, Arthur.
The Gray's Inn Journal. 2 vols. in 1. 1756. 12mo. **78 A**
Works of Cornelius Tacitus; with an essay on the life and genius of Tacitus. 4 vols. 1793. 4to. **113 E**

MURPHY, Francis Stack and E. T. HURLSTONE.
Reports of cases in the court of Exchequer, 1836–1837. 1 vol. 1838. 8vo. **7 G**

MURRAY, David.
Some considerations in reference to the Limited owners (Scotland) bill 1888. Glasgow, 1888. 8vo. **55 E**

MURRAY, Sir Thomas.
Laws and acts of parliament of Scotland, 1424 to 1678. Edinburgh, 1681. folio. **30 G**

MURTON, Walter.
Wreck Inquiries. The law and practice relating to formal investigations into shipping casualties. 1884. 8vo. **53 I**

MUSCUTT, Edward.
History of church laws in England, from A.D. 602 to A.D. 1850. 1851. 8vo. **77 C**

MUSGRAVE, William.
Genuine memoirs of the life and character of Sir Robert Walpole, and of the family of Walpoles. 1732. 8vo. **79 B**

MUSGRAVE, Sir William.
The court register and statesman's remembrancer; containing a series of all the great officers. 1782. 8vo. **124 G**

MUSIC-HALLS.

Law of theatres and music-halls. By W. N. M. Geary. 1885.
8vo.   11 H

MUSNICKI, L. N. H.

Roxolana, the Podolian, a tale of the sixteenth century. 1850.
[Pamphlets, vol. 23.]   144 B

MYLNE, JAMES WILLIAM and R. D. CRAIG.

Reports of cases in the court of Chancery, 1835–1841.   5 vols.
1837–48.   8vo.   3 B

MYLNE, JAMES WILLIAM and BENJAMIN KEEN.

Reports of cases in the court of Chancery, 1832–1835.   3 vols.
1834–37.   8vo.   3 B

MYSORE.

The Mysore reversion, 'an exceptional case.'   By Major
Evans Bell.   2nd ed.   1866.   8vo.   78 C

MYTHOLOGY, GREEK AND ROMAN.

Dictionary of Greek and Roman biography and mythology.
Edited by Wm. Smith.   3 vols.   1864.   8vo.   81 I

NAMES.

The origin of surnames.   By W. Camden.   See Sir W.
Dugdale's Ancient usage of arms, 1812, pp. 208–248.   125 H
Patronymica Britannica : a dictionary of the family names of
United Kingdom.   By M. A. Lower.   1860.   8vo.   127 I

NAPIER, THOMAS BATEMAN.

Concise practice of Queen's Bench and Chancery divisions and
of Court of Appeal.   1884.   8vo.   64 E
Modern digest of law necessary to be known for Final Examination of Incorporated Law Society.   1887.   8vo.   64 E
Digest of subjects of probate, divorce, bankruptcy, admiralty,
ecclesiastical and criminal law.   By T. B. Napier and
R. M. Stephenson.   1888.   8vo.   64 E

NAPIER, SIR WILLIAM FRANCIS PATRICK.

History of the war in the Peninsula and in the South of France.
6 vols.   1832–40.   8vo.   114 C D

NASEBY, NORTHAMPTONSHIRE.
The history and antiquities of Naseby. By Rev. John Mastin.
Cambridge, 1792. 8vo. 92 D

NASH, THOMAS ARTHUR.
The life of Richard Lord Westbury, formerly Lord high
chancellor. 2 vols. 1888. 8vo. 80 D

NASH, TREADWAY RUSSEL.
Collections for the history of Worcestershire. 2nd ed. 2 vols.
1799. folio. 94 H

NASMITH, DAVID.
Institutes of English adjective law; an outline of law of
Evidence and measure of Damages. 1879. 12mo. 63 G
Institutes of English private law. 2 vols. 1875. 12mo. 63 G
Institutes of English public law. 1873. 12mo. 63 G

NATAL.
Blue book for the colony of Natal, 1863–1889. 32 vols.
Pietermaritzburg, 1863–90. folio. 37 B C
Laws and votes, 1857–1867. 5 vols. 1857–67. folio. 37 A
Laws, 1868–1889. 6 vols. 1868–90. folio. 37 A
Votes, 1868–85 and 1888–89. 11 vols. 1868–89. folio. 37 B A

NATIONAL DEBTS.
History of our customs, national debts and taxes. By Timothy
Cunningham. 2nd ed. 1771. 8vo. 78 D
On the constitutional and moral right or wrong of our
National Debt. By F. W. Newman. 1849. [Pamphlets,
vol. 27.] 144 B
The rights and duties of Property, with a plan for paying off
the national debt. By John Sangster. 1851. 12mo. 78 D
See also FINANCE and FUNDS, THE.

NATIONAL REVIEW.
The National Review, March 1883–February 1891. 16 vols.
1883–91. 8vo. 130 I J

NATIONALITY.
On Nationality, or the law relating to subjects and aliens,
considered with a view to future legislation. By Sir
A. J. E. Cockburn. 1869. 8vo. 11 A
See also ALIENS.

NATURAL HISTORY.

Appendix to contributions to Natural history. By James Simson. New York, 1878. [Pamphlets, vol. 36.] **144 C**

Caii Plinii Secundi Naturalis Historiæ libri XXXVII., interpretatione et notis illustravit Joannes Harduinus. 5 vols. Paris, 1685. 4to. **47 F**

The Gallery of Nature. By Rev. T. Milner. New ed. 1855. 8vo. **84 D**

Treasury of Natural history. By Samuel Maunder. 5th ed. 1858. 12mo. **78 A**

See also CHALMERS, REV. T. and MIRABAUD, J. B. DE.

NATURAL LAW.

The institutes of Law: a treatise of the principles of Jurisprudence as determined by Nature. By James Lorimer. Edinburgh, 1872. 8vo. **63 G**

A Sketch of the Natural laws of Man. By G. Spurzheim. 1825. 12mo. **78 A**

The rights of war and peace, including the law of nature and of nations. Translated from the Latin of Grotius by R. A. C. Campbell. 3 vols. Pontefract, 1814. 8vo. **48 E**

The principles of natural law. By J. J. Burlamaqui. Translated by T. Nugent. 2nd ed. 2 vols. 1763. 8vo. **48 E**

See also INTERNATIONAL LAW and PUFFENDORF, S.

NAVAL BIOGRAPHY AND CHRONOLOGY.

A Naval biographical dictionary. By W. R. O'Byrne. 1849. 8vo. **81 E**

Naval Biography. [1805.] 8vo. **81 B**

Naval chronology; or, an historical summary of naval and maritime events, from time of the Romans to treaty of peace 1802. By Isaac Schomberg. 5 vols. in 3. 1802. 8vo. **81 B**

NAVAL LAW AND NAVY.

Criminal law of the Navy. By T. Thring. 2nd ed. 1877. 8vo. **172 G**

Law and practice of United States naval Courts-Martial. By A. A. Harwood. New York, 1867. 8vo. **59 G**

Naval Prize law. By G. Lushington. 1866. 8vo. **172 G**

Regulations and instructions relating to His Majesty's Service at sea. 11th ed. 1772. 4to. **158 C**

NAVAL LAW AND NAVY—*continued.*

Extracts from the several treaties subsisting between Great Britain and other kingdoms and states, of such articles and clauses as relate to the duty and conduct of the commanders of the king of Great Britain's ships of war. 1741. 4to. **158 C**

See also KATCHENOVSKY and MCARTHUR, J.

NAVIGATION.

Nautical and hydraulic experiments. By Colonel Mark Beaufoy. Vol. 1. 1834. 4to. **78 H**

A Naval expositor, shewing and explaining the words and terms of art belonging to ships. By T. R. Blanckley. 1750. 4to. **78 G**

The whole history of Navigation from its original to 1704. See Locke's Works, vol. 10, 1823, pp. 357–512. **78 F**

See also CANALS and SHIPPING, LAW OF.

NAVY LISTS.

A List of the commissioned officers of His Majesty's fleet with the dates of their respective commissions and of the first commissions. 1826. 8vo. **133 H**

The Navy List. Published quarterly. Jan. 1829–Oct. 1890 (imperfect). 83 vols. 1829–90. 12mo. **213 A–G**

The new Navy List, Nov. 1841–Aug. 1845, by C. Haultain, Feb. 1846–Feb. 1853, by J. Allen. 15 vols. 1841–53. 8vo. **133 H**

The Royal Navy List, Jan. 1878–April 1881, by C. E. Warren and F. Lean ; July 1881–Oct. 1890, by F. Lean. 26 vols. 1878–90. 8vo. **133 H I**

[NAYLOR, SIR GEORGE.]

A Collection of coats of arms borne by the nobility and gentry of the county of Glocester. 1792. 4to. **88 G**

NE EXEAT REGNO.

A Brief view of the writ of Ne exeat regno. By John Beames. 2nd ed. 1824. 8vo. Bound with J. Beames's Equity Costs. 1840. **52 D**

NEALE, JOHN PRESTON.

The history and antiquities of the abbey church of St. Peter, Westminster. By E. W. Brayley, illustrated by J. P. Neale. 2 vols. 1818–23. folio. **91 H**

NEATE, CHARLES.

Remarks on a late decision of the judges as visitors of the Inns of Court. 1848. 8vo. Bound with A. Hayward's Report of proceedings, &c. 1848. **78 B**

NECKAM, ALEXANDER.

De naturis rerum libri duo; with the poem, De laudibus divinæ sapientiæ. Edited by T. Wright. 1863. 8vo. **102 A**

NEEDLER, CULVERWELL.

Debate of the House of Commons in January 1704 upon the great question, whether an action lies at common law for an elector who is denied his vote for members of parliament. 2nd ed. 1721. 8vo. **48 E**

NEGLIGENCE.

Law of Negligence. By Thomas Beven. 1889. 8vo. **11 A**
Law of Negligence. By H. Smith. 2nd ed. 1884. 8vo. **11 A**
Law of Negligence. By R. Campbell. 1878. 8vo. **172 G**
See also HAY, W. and SAUNDERS, T. W.

NEGOTIABLE SECURITIES.

The laws of Negotiable Securities : a condensed manual. By H. D. Jencken. 1880. 8vo. **11 A**
See also BILLS OF EXCHANGE.

NEILD, JAMES.

An Account of the Society for the discharge and relief of persons imprisoned for small debts throughout England and Wales; and Account of persons confined for debt in the various prisons of England and Wales. 1802. 8vo. **84 B**
The same. 3rd ed. 1808. 8vo. **84 B**

NELSON, HORACE.

Selected cases, statutes and orders illustrative of the principles of Private International law. 1889. 8vo. **55 A**

NELSON, HORATIO, 1 VISCOUNT.

Life, memoirs and anecdotes of the late Lord Nelson. 5th ed. 1805. 12mo. **79 C**
History of H.M.S. Victory. By W. J. L. Wharton. 1875. 12mo. **78 A**

NELSON, James Henry.
".·· Commentaries on the code of civil procedure (Act No. X. of
1877). 2nd ed. Madras, 1878. 8vo. **38 C**

NELSON, John.
· The history, topography and antiquities of the parish of
St. Mary, Islington. 1811. 4to. **89 E**

NELSON, William.
Laws of England concerning the game, of hunting, hawking,
fishing, and fowling. 3rd ed. 1736. 12mo. **168 F**
Lex maneriorum ; or, the law and customs of England re-
lating to manors and lords of manors. 1726. folio. **49 H**
The same. Another copy. **49 H**
Reports of special cases in Chancery in the reigns of Charles I.,
Charles II. and William III. 1717. 8vo. **3 B**
Rights of the clergy of England. 2nd ed. 1715. 8vo. **48 F**

NEVILLE, Ralph and Walter Henry MACNAMARA.
A Collection of the cases decided under The railway and canal
traffic act 1854, and Reports of cases decided by the Railway commissioners, 1855–1881. 3 vols. 1874–81. 8vo. **3 B**
See also BROWNE, J. H. B. and W. H. MACNAMARA.

NEVILLE, Sandford and W. M. MANNING.
Reports of cases in the court of King's Bench, 1832–1836.
6 vols. 1834–39. 8vo. **5 D E**

NEVILLE, Sandford and T. E. PERRY.
Reports of cases in the court of King's Bench and Exchequer
Chamber, 1836–1838. 3 vols. 1837–38. 8vo. **5 E**

NEVIS.
Laws 1681 to 1861. By H. C. Huggins. 1862. 8vo. **36 F**
· Ordinances, 1870–1888. 4 vols. 1870–88. folio. **36 F**

NEW BRUNSWICK.
Acts of general assembly, 1786–1846, 1848–1862, 1863–1870,
· 1872–1886, 1889, 1890. 13 vols. Fredericton, 1838–90.
· 4to. and 8vo. **34 H**
St. John and the province of New Brunswick. 3rd ed. St. John,
1884. 12mo. **84 B**

NEW BRUNSWICK—*continued.*

Statistical and practical observations relative to New Brunswick. By A. Wedderburn. Saint John, 1835. 4to. **84 E**

NEW FOREST, HAMPSHIRE.

Historical inquiries concerning forests, with topographical remarks upon the state of the New Forest. By Percival Lewis. 1811. 4to. **88 B**

History of the New Forest. See B. B. Woodward's History of Hampshire, vol. 3, pp. 1–88. **88 G**

The New Forest, its history and its scenery. By J. R. Wise. 1867. 8vo. **88 B**

NEW PRACTICE CASES.

New Practice Cases, 1844–1848. By R. G. Welford, A. Bittleston, P. Parnell, &c. 3 vols. 1847–49. 8vo. **5 E**

NEW REPORTS.

New Reports, containing cases decided in the courts of equity and common law, 1862–1865. 6 vols. 1863–65. 8vo. **3 C**

See also BOSANQUET, J. B. and C. PULLER.

NEW SOUTH WALES.

Acts and ordinances. By T. Callaghan. 3 vols. Sydney, 1844–52. 8vo. **35 D**

The augmentation of the license fees paid by the occupiers of the crown lands in the colony of New South Wales. By E. T. Hamilton. 1844. [Pamphlets, vol. 18.] **144 B**

Census of the colony of New South Wales, taken 7 April 1861. Sydney, 1862. folio. **37 G**

Collection of acts relating to transfer of land in New South Wales. By A. Oliver. Sydney, 1877. 8vo. **37 G**

Memorandum and articles of association of the incorporated Law Institute of New South Wales. Sydney, 1884. [Pamphlets, vol. 40.] **144 C**

New South Wales law almanac, 1888. 1887. 12mo. **136 I**

The private acts. 1832–1862. Sydney, 1863. folio. **35 D**

Public general statutes, 1824–1889. 16 vols. Sydney, 1861–90. folio. **35 D**

See also BANNISTER, S.

NEW YORK.

Address delivered before the New York State Bar Association. By S. Hand. Albany, 1878. [Pamphlets, vol. 36.] **144 C**

An alphabetical list of applicants for the benefit of the Bankrupt act (passed August 19, 1841), within the southern district of New York. New York, 1843. 8vo. **59 A**

Book of forms adapted to the code of procedure. Albany, 1865. 8vo. **60 C**

Charter and constitution of the Association of the Bar of the City of New York. 1873. Report of the library committee, to the Association. 1873. Report of the committee on extortions, to the Association. 1872, and Report of the committee on Law reporting, to the association. 1873. [all four in 1 vol.] New York, 1872–73. 8vo. **59 G**

Civil code of state of New York. Albany, 1865. 8vo. **60 C**

The code of criminal procedure of the state of New York. Albany, 1850. 8vo. **60 C**

Code of procedure of the state of New York ; with the revised rules of the courts. By J. Townshend. New York, 1867. 12mo. **60 C**

The code of procedure of the state of New York. 5th ed. New York, 1867. 32mo. **60 C**

Penal code of state of New York. Albany, 1865. 8vo. **60 C**

Political code of state of New York. Albany, 1859. 8vo. **60 C**

The same. Another ed. Albany, 1860. 8vo. **60 C**

Report of the special committee on railroads, appointed to investigate alleged abuses in the management of railroads chartered by the state of New York. 5 vols. Albany, 1880. 8vo. **60 A**

The revision of the statutes of the state of New York and the revisers. By W. A. Butler. New York, 1889. 8vo. **80 D**

Revised statutes of the state of New York. Edited by M. H. Throop. 7th ed. 3 vols. New York, 1882. 8vo. **32 D**

Rules and regulations in Bankruptcy adopted by the circuit and district courts of the United States for the southern district of New York, January 4th, 1842. New York, 1842. 8vo. **59 A**

Statutes at large of the state of New York. Edited by J. W. Edmonds. 6 vols. Albany, 1863–68. 8vo. **32 D**

NEW ZEALAND.

Ordinances of New Zealand, 1841–1853. 1 vol. Wellington, 1871. folio. **35 F**

NEW ZEALAND—*continued.*

Statement by Richard Oliver, minister for public works, 6 Aug. 1880. Wellington, 1880. folio. **37 G**

Statistics of New Zealand, for 1853–1857. Compiled from official records. Auckland, 1858. folio. **37 G**

Statutes of New Zealand, 1854–1890. 27 vols. Auckland and Wellington, 1854–90. folio and 4to. **35 F G**

NEWALL, DAVID JOHN FALCONER.

The Highlands of India, vol. 2, being a chronicle of field sports and travel in India. 1887. 8vo. **84 B**

NEWARK UPON TRENT, NOTTINGHAMSHIRE.

Annals of Newark-upon-Trent, comprising the history, curiosities, and antiquities. By C. Brown. 1879. 4to. **92 E**

NEWBURY, BERKSHIRE.

The history and antiquities of Newbury and its environs. [By J. Bunny.] Speenhamland, 1839. 8vo. **86 B**

The history of the ancient town and borough of Newbury. By Walter Money. 1887. 8vo. **86 B**

NEWBURY, WILLIAM OF.

Historia rerum Anglicarum, et continuatio ad annum 1298. See Chronicles of the reigns of Stephen, Henry II. and Richard I. Vols. 1 and 2. 1884–5. 8vo. **102 H**

NEWCASTLE UPON TYNE, NORTHUMBERLAND.

A Copy of the list of burgesses of the borough of Newcastle, delivered Sept. 7, 1835. Newcastle, 1835. 8vo. **107 K**

The same, delivered Sept. 5, 1836. Newcastle, 1836. 8vo. **107 K**

A Copy of the list of persons objected to as not being entitled to have their names retained on the burgess list of the borough of Newcastle. Newcastle, 1836. 8vo. **107 K**

A Copy of the list of persons who claim to have their names inserted on the burgess list of the borough of Newcastle. Newcastle, 1835. 8vo. **107 K**

A Copy of the ward list of burgesses of the borough of Newcastle. Newcastle, 1835. 8vo. **107 K**

The same. Newcastle, 1836. 8vo. **107 K**

NEWCASTLE UPON TYNE—*continued.*

A Descriptive and historical account of. Newcastle. By E. Mackenzie. Newcastle, 1827. 4to.   **92 D**

England's grievance discovered in relation to the coal trade, with the map of the river .Tine. By Ralph Gardiner. 1655. Reprinted, Newcastle, 1796. 8vo.   **92 D**

The history and antiquities of Newcastle upon Tyne. By John Brand. 2 vols. 1789. 4to.   **93 G**

NEWCOME, REV. PETER.

The history of the ancient and royal foundation called the Abbey of St. Alban. Part 1. 1793. 4to.   **88 B**

The same. Parts 1 and 2. 1795. 4to.   **88 B**

NEWCOURT, RICHARD.

Life of Richard Newcourt. See J. P. Malcolm's Lives of Topographers and Antiquaries. 1815. 4to.   **79 H**

Repertorium ecclesiasticum parochiale Londinense : an ecclesiastical parochial history of the diocese of London. 2 vols. 1708–1710. folio.   **92 G**

NEWFOUNDLAND.

Newfoundland acts, 1858–1859, 1862, 1865–1866, 1868–1879, 1881–1890. 16 vols. 1858–90. folio and 8vo.   **34 G**

NEWGATE CALENDAR.

Newgate Calendar, 1807, 1809, 1810, 1811, and 1812. 5 vols. 1807–12. 8vo.   **50 C**

Old Bailey Sessions Papers, Dec. 1824 to Oct. 1834 (imperfect). 8 vols. 1824–34. 4to.   **50 J**

NEWLAND, JOHN.

Practice of Court of Chancery. 2 vols. in 1. 1808. 8vo. **161 D**

The same. 2nd ed. 2 vols. 1819. 8vo.   **161 D**

NEWMAN, WILLIAM.

Complete theory of Conveyancing. 3 vols. 1781. folio. **157 E**

NEWNHAM, W. H.

Operations of the poor law amendment act in the county of Sussex. Reports of the auditor of the Uckfield union. 1836. 8vo.   **93 E**

NEWPORT, Isle of Wight.
. See Nicholls, T. and Wight, Isle of.

NEWSON, Harry.
A Digest of the law of Shipping and of marine insurance. 1879, and 2nd ed. 1883. 8vo. **175 G**
The law of salvage, towage, and pilotage. 1886. 8vo. **11 E**

NEWSPAPER LAW.
The law specially affecting printers, publishers and newspaper proprietors. By A. Powell. 2nd issue. 1889. 8vo. **11 C**
See also Copyright and Libel.

NEWSPAPERS.
The Newspaper press directory, 1879 and 1881 to 1890. 11 vols. 1879–90. 8vo. **146 G**

NEWTON, Sir Isaac.
An Account of Sir Isaac Newton's philosophical discoveries. By C. Maclaurin. 1748. 4to. **78 G**
Authentic memoirs of Sir Isaac Newton. See E. Turner's History of Grantham, 1806, pp. 157–186. **90 G**
Tables for renewing and purchasing of Leases, Annuities, and Reversions. 6th ed. 1808. 12mo. **176 D**

NEWTON, John.
Poems by William Cowper, with a sketch of his life. 2 vols. 1833. 8vo. **83 G**

NEWTON, Richard.
The Characters of Theophrastus, with a translation of the Greek into Latin. Oxford, 1754. 8vo. **78 B**

NEWTON, Rev. William.
The history and antiquities of Maidstone. 1741. 8vo. **88 C**

NEWTON, William.
London in the olden time ; being a topographical and historical memoir of London, Westminster, and Southwark. 1855. folio. **92 H**

NICHOLAS, Sir Edward.
The Nicholas papers. Correspondence of Sir E. Nicholas, secretary of state. Edited by G. F. Warner, vol. 1, 1641–1652. [Camden Society, n.s. vol. 40.] 1886. 8vo. **85 D**

NICHOLAS, Thomas.
Annals and antiquities of the counties and county families of Wales. 2 vols. 1872. 8vo. **94 E**

NICHOLL, Sir John.
Report of the judgment in Dew *v.* Clark, delivered by Sir John Nicholl in the Prerogative Court of Canterbury, Easter Term, 1826. By John Haggard. 1826. 8vo. **51 G**

NICHOLLS, James.
Practice in Insolvency in the courts of Bankruptcy. 2nd ed. By J. Nicholls and E. Doyle. 1845. 12mo. **169 A**

NICHOLLS, Thomas.
The Burning Shame ; or, punishment for bad lawyers, a custom peculiar to the borough of Newport in the Isle of Wight, a poem. 1812. 12mo. **118 C**

NICHOLS, Francis Morgan.
Britton. The French text revised, with English translation, introduction, and notes. 2 vols. Oxford, 1865. 8vo. **167 A**
An Inquiry into the history of feudal and obligatory knighthood in England. 1863. 4to. **126 I**

NICHOLS, John.
Collection of all the wills, now known to be extant, of the kings and queens of England, princes and princesses of Wales, and every branch of the blood royal, from the reign of William the Conqueror to that of Henry VII. exclusive. 1780. 4to. **114 D**
The history and antiquities of the county of Leicester. 4 vols. in 8. 1795–1811. folio. **89 H & 90 H**
The progresses and public processions of Queen Elizabeth. New ed. 3 vols. 1823. 4to. **114 E**
The progresses, processions, and magnificent festivities of King James I., his royal consort, family, and court. 4 vols. 1828. 4to. **114 E**

NICHOLS, JOHN BOWYER.

Account of the royal hospital and collegiate church of Saint Katharine, near the Tower of London. 1824. 4to. **89 F**

Catalogue of the Hoare Library at Stourhead, co. Wilts. Printed for private use. 1840. 8vo. **82 G**

NICHOLS, JOHN GOUGH.

Collectanea topographica et genealogica. [Edited by J. G. Nichols.] 8 vols. 1834–43. 8vo. **127 I**

A Descriptive catalogue of the works of the Camden Society. 1862. 8vo. **85 C**

The Fishmongers' Pageant on Lord Mayor's day 1616. 1844. folio. **91 H**

NICHOLSON, CORNELIUS.

The annals of Kendal, being a historical and descriptive account of Kendal and its environs. Kendal, 1832. 8vo. **93 F**

NICOL, HENRY and GEORGE WASHINGTON HEYWOOD.

The annual county courts practice, 1889. 2 vols. 1889. 8vo. **52 E**

The same. 1890. By G. W. Heywood. 2 vols. 1890. 8vo. **12 H**

NICOLAS, SIR NICHOLAS HARRIS.

The Chronology of History. 1833. 12mo. **116 D**

The controversy between Sir Richard Scrope and Sir Robert Grosvenor in the Court of Chivalry 1385–1390. vol. 1. A literal copy of the Roll, with documents illustrative of the suit. vol. 2. A history of the family of Scrope and biographical notices of the deponents. Privately printed. 2 vols. 1832. 4to. **118 F**

History of the earldoms of Strathern, Monteith, and Airth. 1842. 8vo. **124 F**

The law of adulterine bastardy, with a report of the Banbury case. 1836. 8vo. **52 A**

Life of William Davison, secretary of state to Queen Elizabeth. 1823. 8vo. **79 C**

Notitia Historica ; containing tables, calendars, and miscellaneous information, for the use of historians, antiquaries, and the legal profession. 1824. 8vo. **116 E**

NICOLAS, Sir Nicholas Harris—*continuea.*

Observations on the state of historical literature, with remarks on record offices and on the proceedings of the record commission. 1830, and Refutation to Mr. Palgrave's ' Remarks in reply to Observations on the state of historical literature.' Additional facts relative to the record commission. 1831. 8vo. [bound together.] **99 A**

Proceedings and ordinances of the Privy Council of England, 1386–1461. 6 vols. 1834–37. 8vo. **98 A**

Synopsis of peerage of England. 2 vols. 1825. 12mo. **124 F**

The same. Revised by Wm. Courthope. 1857. 8vo. **124 F**

Testamenta Vetusta ; being illustrations from wills, of manners, customs, &c., from the reign of Henry II. to the accession of Queen Elizabeth. 2 vols. 1826. 8vo. **114 D**

NICOLSON, Joseph and Richard BURN.

The history and antiquities of the counties of Westmoreland and Cumberland. 2 vols. 1777. 4to. **94 G**

NICOLSON, William, Bishop of Carlisle.

The English historical library ; giving a short view and character of most of our historians either in print or manuscript, with an account of our records, law-books, coins, &c. 2nd ed. 1714. folio. **115 I**

The English, Scotch and Irish historical libraries ; giving a short view and character of most of our historians . . . with an account of our records, &c. 3rd ed. 1736. folio. **115 I**

Leges Marchiarum ; or, border laws. 1705. 12mo. **95 C**

The same. Another ed. 1747. 12mo. **95 C**

NIGELLUS WIREKER, Præcentor of Canterbury.

The Speculum Stultorum and other works. See Satirical poets of the twelfth century, vol. 1, 1872, pp. 3–239. **102 E**

NIMEGUEN, The Peace of.

A Collection of all the acts, memorials, and letters, that pass'd in the negotiation of the Peace : with the treaties concluded at Nimeguen. 1679. 12mo. **113 A**

A Compleat series of letters from the ambassadors and mediators for the general peace at Nimeguen, 1675 to 1679. See W. Wynne's Life of Sir Leoline Jenkins, vol. 1, pp. 347–552, and vol. 2, pp. 1–642. **79 I**

NINETEENTH CENTURY.

The Nineteenth Century; a monthly review. March 1877–
Dec. 1890. 28 vols. 1877–90. 8vo. **132 H I**

NISBET, Sir John.

Some doubts and questions in the Law, especially of Scotland;
as also the Decisions of the Lords of Council and Session
1665–1677. Edinburgh, 1698. folio.

NISI PRIUS.

Roscoe's digest of the law of evidence on the trial of actions
at Nisi Prius. 15th ed. by M. Powell. 2 vols. 1884.
8vo. **9 H**

Abridgment of the law of Nisi Prius. By W. Selwyn. 13th ed.
2 vols. 1869. 8vo. **53 B**

Law of Nisi Prius. By J. F. Archbold. 2nd ed. 2 vols. 1845.
12mo. **173 A**

Law of Nisi Prius evidence in civil actions and arbitrations
and awards. By A. J. Stephens. 3 vols. 1842. 8vo. **173 A**

See also BULLER, Sir F., ESPINASSE, J. and MANNING, J.

NOBILITY.

A Catalogue of nobility. 1662. 12mo. **125 A**

An Historical and critical essay on the true rise of Nobility.
[By Maurice Shelton.] 1718. 8vo. **48 D**

Jus imaginis apud Anglos; or, the law of England relating to
the nobility and gentry. By J. Brydall. 1675. 12mo. **48 D**

A Treatise of the nobilitie of the realme, collected out of the
body of the common law. [By James Yorke?] 1642.
12mo. **48 D**

See also BROOKE, R., DIGNITIES, HONOR and PEERAGES.

NOBLE, Rev. Mark.

A History of the College of Arms; and the lives of all the
kings, heralds, and pursuivants, from the reign of Richard III.
1805. 4to. **127 J**

Memoirs of the protectorate-house of Cromwell. 2 vols.
Birmingham, 1784. 8vo. **80 B**

NOBLE, Theophilus Charles.

Memorials of Temple Bar; with some account of Fleet street
and the parishes of St. Dunstan and St. Bride. 1869.
8vo. **89 D**

NOLAN, Michael.

Laws for the relief and settlement of the Poor. 2 vols. 1805. 8vo. **174 B**

Substance of the speech of M. Nolan before a committee of the House of Commons upon the Shoreham road bill. 1811. [Jacob's Tracts, vol. 13.] **144 F**

NONCONFORMISTS.

The law relating to Protestant Nonconformists. By R. Winslow. 1886. 8vo. **9 C**

See also DISSENTERS.

NOORTHOUCK, John.

A New history of London, including Westminster and Southwark. 1773. 4to. **89 F**

[NORDEN, G.]

The Surveiors Dialogue very profitable for all men to peruse, especially lords of mannors, stewards of mannor-courts, tenants, farmers and husbandmen. 4th ed. 1738. 8vo. **49 E**

NORDEN, John.

· A Progress of piety whose jesses lead into the harbour of heavenly heart's ease. Cambridge, 1847. 12mo. **77 D**

Speculi Britanniæ pars ; an historical and chorographical description of the county of Essex, 1594. Edited by Sir H. Ellis. [Camden Society, vol. 9.] 1840. 8vo. **85 A**

The same. Another copy. **87 E**

NORFOLK.

Copy of the poll for knights of the shire for the county of Norfolk. Taken 12th–20th July, 1802. Norwich, 1802. 8vo. **107 K**

The same. Taken 19th–23rd May, 1817. Norwich, 1817. 8vo. **107 K**

An Essay towards a topographical history of Norfolk. By Rev. Francis Blomefield, continued by Rev. Charles Parkin. 2nd ed. 11 vols. 1805–10. 8vo. **92 C**

The handbook to the rivers and broads of Norfolk and Suffolk. By G. C. Davis. 9th ed. 1887. 8vo. **92 C**

Holiday notes in East Anglia ; being a selection of articles on the holiday resorts in Norfolk, Suffolk, and Essex. 1886. 12mo. **92 C**

NORFOLK—*continued.*

Icenia, sive Norfolciæ descriptio topographica. See Sir H.
Spelman's English works, 1727, part 2, pp. 133–162. **78 H**

Index monasticus ; or, the monasteries, colleges, and hospitals
formerly established in the diocese of Norwich. By Richard
Taylor. 1821. folio. **92 G**

Poppy-land papers descriptive of scenery on the East Coast.
By Clement Scott. 1886. 12mo. **92 C**

Popular county histories. A history of Norfolk. By Walter
Rye. 1885. 8vo. **92 C**

NORFOLK, DUKES OF.

Ancient biographical poems on the Duke of Norfolk and
others. Edited by J. P. Collier. [Camden Society, vol. 61.]
1855. 8vo. **85 B**

Memoir and trial of the Duke of Norfolk. See Criminal
Trials, 1832, pp. 121–245. **51 D**

NORMANDY, HISTORY OF.

The 'Draco Normannicus' of Etienne de Rouen. See
Chronicles of the reigns of Stephen, Henry II. and Richard,
vol. 2, 1885, pp. 589–781. **102 H**

Eadmeri Historia Novorum in Anglia. Edited by Martin
Rule. 1884. 8vo. **102 H**

Guillaume le Conquérant, ou l'Angleterre sous les Normands.
Par G. Guizot. Edited by A. J. Dubourg. 7th ed. 1878.
12mo. **83 C**

The history of Normandy and of England. By Sir Francis
Palgrave. 4 vols. 1851–64. 8vo. **115 A**

The history of the Norman conquest of England, its causes
and its results. By E. A. Freeman. 6 vols. 1877–79.
8vo. **115 A B**

Magni rotuli Scaccarii Normanniæ de anno ab incarnatione
Domini MCLXXXIIII, Willielmo filio Radulfi senescallo, quæ
extant. [Edited by Henry Petrie.] 1830. 4to. **103 F**

Narratives of expulsion of English from Normandy, 1449–1450.
Edited by Rev. J. Stevenson. 1863. 8vo. **102 A**

Rotuli Normanniæ in Turri Londinensi asservati, Johanne et
Henrico Quinto Angliæ regibus. Accurante T. D. Hardy.
1835. 8vo. **98 A**

Ypodigma Neustriæ, a Thoma Walsingham conscriptum.
Edited by H. T. Riley. 1876. 8vo. **101 H**

See also ENGLAND, HISTORY OF and ROUEN.

NORMANDY, Language of.

A Dictionary of the Norman or old French language. By
Robert Kelham. 1779. 8vo. **123 B**
See also France, Language of.

NORMANDY, Laws of.

Coutume de Normandie. Par M. Pesnelle. 3me éd. par
M. Roupnel. Rouen, 1759. 4to. **40 B**
La Coutume de Normandie reduite en maximes selon le sens
litteral et l'esprit de chaque article. Par Pierre De Mer-
ville. Paris, 1707. 4to. **40 A**
Commentaires du Droit Civil tant public que privé observé
au pays et duché de Normandie. Par Guillaume Terrien.
Rouen, 1654. folio. **157 F**
Coustumes du pais de Normandie, anciens ressors et enclaves
d'iceluy. Par Lambert Bailly. Paris, 1586. 4to. **118 F**
See also Houard, D., Le Marchant, T. and Routier, C.

NORTH, Marianne.

The gallery of Marianne North's paintings of plants and their
homes, Royal gardens, Kew. Descriptive catalogue. By
W. B. Hemsley. 3rd ed. 1883. 12mo. **93 C**

NORTH, Roger.

A Discourse on the study of the Laws. With notes by a
member of the Inner Temple. 1824. 12mo. **78 B**

NORTH-WEST TERRITORIES.

Journals of the Council of the North-West Territories of
Canada 1877–79, 1881, 1883–87. Regina, 1886–87. 8vo. **34 E**
Ordinances of the North-West Territories 1881, 1886, 1888
and 1890. 4 vols. Regina, 1882–90. 8vo. **34 E**

NORTHAMPTONSHIRE.

Calendar of wills relating to counties of Northampton and
Rutland, proved in court of archdeacon of Northampton,
1510 to 1652. Edited by W. P. W. Phillimore. [Index
Library, vol. 1.] 1888. 8vo. **124 H**
The history and antiquities of Northamptonshire, compiled
from the manuscript collections of J. Bridges. By Rev.
Peter Whalley. 2 vols. Oxford, 1791. folio. **92 H**

NORTHAMPTONSHIRE—*continued.*

The history and antiquities of the county of Northampton. By George Baker. 2 vols. 1822–30. folio. 93 H

The natural history of Northamptonshire, with some account of the antiquities ; and a transcript of Doomsday-book. By John Morton. 1712. folio. 92 G

See also BRAY, W. and PENNANT, T.

NORTHUMBERLAND.

History and antiquities of North Durham, as subdivided into shires of Norham, Island, and Bedlington, now united to Northumberland. By Rev. J. Raine. 1852. folio. 88 H

A History of Northumberland, in three parts. By Rev. John Hodgson. 7 vols. Newcastle, 1858–35. 4to. 92 D

The natural history and antiquities of Northumberland. By John Wallis. 2 vols. 1769. 4to. 92 D

Northumberland Poll-Book ; containing a list of freeholders who voted at the contested elections for Northumberland in 1747–8, 1774, and Feb. and March, 1826. Alnwick, 1826. 8vo. 107 K

Poll-Book of the contested election for Northumberland, June 20th to July 6th, 1826. Alnwick, 1827. 8vo. 107 K

Poll-Book of the contested election for the northern division of Northumberland, taken on the 10th and 11th of August, 1847. Alnwick, 1847. 8vo. 107 K

Poll-Book of the contested election for the southern division of Northumberland, on the 20th and 21st Dec. 1832. Newcastle-on-Tyne, 1833. 8vo. 107 K

A View of Northumberland. By W. Hutchinson. 2 vols. in 1. Newcastle, 1778. 4to. 92 D

See also GREENWICH, HOLMES, J. H. H. and SYKES, J.

NORTON, GEORGE.

Commentaries on the history, constitution, and chartered franchises of the City of London. 1829. 8vo. 91 E

The same. 3rd ed. 1869. 8vo. 91 E

Exposition of the privileges of City of London in regard to claims of Non-freemen to deal by wholesale within its jurisdiction. 1821. [City of London Tracts.] 91 C

NORTON, JOHN BRUCE.

The administration of justice in Southern India. Madras, 1853. 8vo. 38 B

NORTON, John Bruce—*continued.*

The law of evidence applicable to India. 8th ed. Madras, 1873. 8vo. **38 C**

A Selection of leading cases on the Hindu law of inheritance. 2 vols. Madras, 1870–71. 8vo. **38 B**

NORWAY.

British Scandinavian Society. 'Danish' and 'Norse.' A paper read before the Society. By A. Johnston. 1875. [Pamphlets, vol. 32.] **144 C**

Eighteen eulogies on Haco, King of Norway. By Snorro Sturlson, poet to that monarch. See Rev. J. Johnston's Anecdotes of Olave the Black. 1780. 12mo. **118 A**

Germany, Denmark, and the Scandinavian question. 1861. [Pamphlets, vol. 14.] **144 A**

Grundtrækkene i den ældste Norske Proces. Af Ebbe Hertzberg. Kristiania, 1874. 8vo. **55 C**

The rise, progress, and present state of the Northern governments. By John Williams. 2 vols. 1777. 4to. **113 F**

NORWICH.

. History of the city and county of Norwich. By Rev. Francis Blomefield. 2 vols. 1806. 8vo. **92 C**

Review of the arguments for removing Lent Assizes from Thetford to Norwich. By Vindex. Thetford, 1824. 8vo. **92 C**

NORWOOD, Surrey.

Norwood and Dulwich : past and present. By A. M. Galer. 1890. 4to. **93 D**

NOTARIES.

Office and practice of a Notary of England. By Richard Brooke. 5th ed. by G. Chambers. 1890. 8vo. **11 A**

Delle Opere che illustrano il notariato. Saggio di Vladimiro Dr. Pappafava. Zara, 1880. 8vo. **82 C**

A Law manual for Notaries and Bankers. By W. B. Wedgwood and I. S. Homans. New York, 1867. 8vo. **59 G**

Remarks upon Notarial evidence. By Alexander Ridgway. 1852. [Pamphlets, vol. 8.] **144 A**

See also De Ferriere, C. J., Montefiore, J. and West, W.

NOTCUTT, George Jarvis.

The factory and workshop acts. 1874. 12mo. **168 D**

NOTES AND QUERIES.

Notes and Queries : a medium of intercommunication for literary men, artists, antiquaries, &c., Nov. 1849–Dec. 1890. 82 vols. 1850–90. 8vo. **128 H I J & 129 H I**

General Indexes 1849-1885. 6 vols. 1856-86. 8vo. **129 I**

NOTES OF CASES.

Notes of cases in the Ecclesiastical and Maritime courts, 1841-1850. 7 vols. 1843-50. 8vo. **8 H**

NOTICES.

Dissertation on and precedents of Notices. See Bythewood and Jarman's Conveyancing, 4th ed. vol. 4, 1887, pp. 97–121. **13 D**

NOTTINGHAMSHIRE AND NOTTINGHAM.

The antiquities of Nottinghamshire. By Robert Thoroton. 2nd ed. by John Throsby. 3 vols. 1797. 4to. **92 E**

Nottinghamia vetus et nova ; or, an historical account of the ancient and present state of the town of Nottingham. By Charles Deering. Nottingham, [1751.] 4to. **92 E**

See BAWDWEN, REV. W., BRAY, W. and LOUTH, J.

See also RIVERS.

NOVA SCOTIA.

Historical and statistical account of Nova Scotia. By T. C. Haliburton. 2 vols. Halifax, 1829. 8vo. **84 B**

Journal and Proceedings of the House of Assembly of the Province of Nova Scotia, 1863–1867. 8 vols. Halifax, 1863–67. folio.

Law reports, containing decisions of the Bench of the supreme court in Nova Scotia, 1834-1841. By James Thomson. Halifax, 1853. 8vo. **. 55 E**

Revised statutes of Nova Scotia, 1st series, 1851. 2nd series, 1859. 3rd series, 1864. 3 vols. Halifax, 1851-64. 8vo. **34 F**

Statutes of Nova Scotia, 1851–1890. 12 vols. Halifax, 1852–90. 8vo. **34 F**

NOWELL, ALEXANDER.

A Catechism written in Latin ; together with the same translated into English by T. Norton. Edited by G. E. Corrie. Cambridge, 1853. 8vo. **77 D**

NOY, WILLIAM.

Reports and cases in the time of Queen Elizabeth, King James, and King Charles, 1559–1649. 1656. folio. **74 F**

Treatise of the principall Grounds and Maximes of the lawes of this kingdome. By W. N. 1641. [Law Tracts and Arguments, 1641.] **144 F**

The same. 6th ed. with an analysis of the English laws. By C. Barton. 1794. 12mo. **49 F**

NUCIUS, NICANDER.

The second book of the travels of Nicander Nucius. Edited by Rev. J. A. Cramer. [Camden Society, vol. 17.] 1841. 8vo. **85 A**

NUISANCES.

Law of nuisances. By E. W. Garrett. 1890. 8vo. **11 A**

Practical proceedings for the removal of nuisances. By T. Smith. 4th ed. 1867. 8vo. **53 B**

An Essay on waste, nuisance, and trespass. By G. V. Yool. 1863. 8vo. **11 I**

The Nuisances removal and diseases prevention act of 1855. By W. G. Lumley. 2nd ed. 1860. 12mo. **173 B**

Law relating to removal of nuisances injurious to health. By W. C. Glen. 1858. 12mo. **173 B**

Law of dilapidations and nuisances. By David Gibbons. 2nd ed. 1849. 8vo. **52 E**

See also PUBLIC HEALTH and TORTS. **11 D & 11 H**

NUMISMATICS.

A Descriptive catalogue of the London traders', tavern and coffee-house tokens current in the seventeenth century. By J. H. Burn. 2nd ed. 1855. 8vo. **91 E**

Joannis Harduini Nummi antiqui populorum et urbium illustrati. Paris, 1684. 4to. **113 G**

Numismata Anglo-Saxonica et Anglo-Danica breviter illustrata ab Andrea Fountaine. 1705. See G. Hickes' Thesaurus, 1705. folio. **123 G**

Records of Roman history as exhibited on the Roman coins. By Francis Hobler. 2 vols. 1860. 4to. **113 G**

Remarks on and descriptive catalogue of the ancient British coins. See Monumenta Historica Britannica, 1848, pp. cli-clxxiii. **99 B**

OAKLEY, Thomas William Henry.
Divorce practice. 1885. 8vo.   166 A
The same. 2nd ed. 1886. 8vo.   52 F
The same. 3rd ed. 1889. 8vo.   12 D

OATES, Henry Carne.
The Factory acts. 1862. 12mo.   168 D

OATHS.
Oaths and Affirmations in Great Britain and Ireland. By
F. A. Stringer. 1890. 12mo.   12 G
Handbook on Oaths. By Charles Ford. 5th ed. 1889.
12mo.   12 G
Oaths in the Supreme Court of Judicature. By T. V. Braith-
waite. 4th ed. 1881. 12mo.   53 B
Memorandum as to Oaths and statutory declarations &c. By
J. M. Davenport. Oxford, 1873. 8vo.   53 B
Oaths in Common Law. Forms of oaths, affirmations, decla-
rations and jurats. By Robert Cole. 1859. 12mo.   173 B
Extracts from acts of parliament relating to the oaths to be
taken by members of parliament. By E. B. S[ugden].
1829. [Jacob's Tracts, vol. 7.]   144 E
The book of Oaths, and the severall forms thereof, both
ancient and modern. 1649. 12mo.   48 B
The same. Another ed. 1689. 8vo.   48 B
Seven lectures concerning the obligation of promissory oaths.
By Robert Sanderson. 1655. 12mo.   48 B

OBEDIENCE.
Bishop Gardiner's Oration on true obedience. Edited by
B. A. Heywood. 1870. 12mo.   78 A

OBLIGATIONS.
An Epitome and analysis of Savigny's treatise on obligations
in Roman law. By A. Brown. 1872. 8vo.   63 G
Traité des obligations. Par R. J. Pothier. 2me éd. par
M. Bugnet. Paris, 1861. 8vo.   58 D

O'BYRNE, William Richard.
A Naval biographical dictionary. 1849. 4to.   81 E

OCKERBY, Horace.

The Book of Dignities ; containing lists of the official personages of the British Empire, &c. By Joseph Haydn, continued to the present time. 1890. 8vo. **124 G**

O'CONNELL, Daniel.

The judgment of Lord Denman in the case of O'Connell and others against the Queen, as delivered in the House of Lords, Sept. 4, 1844. Edited by D. Leahy. 1844. 8vo. **51 E**

Treason in the Church, an intercepted letter from O'Connell to a member of the Common-Council of London. 1839. [Pamphlets, vol. 5.] **144 A**

ODDIE, Henry Hoyle.

Recollections of the character of the late Henry Hoyle Oddie. Privately printed. 1830. [Pamphlets, vol. 26.] **144 B**

ODGERS, William Blake.

A Digest of the law of libel and slander. 1881. 8vo. **53 H**

The same. 2nd ed. 1887. 8vo. **11 F**

Should the existing law as to Blasphemy be amended, and if so, in what direction ? 1883. [Pamphlets, vol. 31.] **144 C**

O'DONOVAN, John.

The Celtic records of Ireland, an analysis of Dr. O'Donovan's edition of The annals of the four masters. Dublin, 1852. 8vo. **97 I**

O'FLANAGAN, James Roderick.

The lives of the lord chancellors and keepers of the great seal of Ireland. 2 vols. 1870. 8vo. **79 G**

OGBORNE, Elizabeth.

The history of Essex from the earliest period to the present time. 1814. 4to. **87 F**

OGILBY, John.

Itinerarium Angliæ ; or, a book of roads, containing the principal road-ways of England and Wales. 1675. folio. **85 I**

The traveller's pocket book ; or, Book of the roads. By J. Ogilby and Wm. Morgan. 21st ed. 1782. 12mo. **86 A**

OGILVIE, JOHN.

.· The Imperial dictionary of the English language. New ed. by
Charles Annandale. 4 vols. 1882–83. 4to.   **123 E**

OKE, GEORGE COLWELL.

. Handy book of Game and Fishery laws. 1861. 12mo. **168 F**

Handy book of Fishery laws. 2nd ed. with Supplement and
notes, by J. W. W. Bund. 1884. 12mo.   **10 A**

Handy book of Game laws. 3rd ed. with a Supplement by
J. W. W. Bund. 1881. 12mo.   **10 A**

Improved system of solicitor's book-keeping. 1849. 8vo.
    160 G

The laws as to Licensing Inns. 1872. 12mo.   **172 A**

The same. 2nd ed. by W. C. Glen. 1874. 8vo.   **53 A**

The laws of Turnpike Roads. 2nd ed. 1861. 12mo. **176 G**

The Magisterial Formulist ; being a complete collection of
forms and precedents in all cases out of quarter sessions
and in parochial matters. 2nd ed. 1856. 8vo.   **172 C**

The same. 3rd ed. 1862. 8vo.   **172 C**

The same. 6th ed. by T. W. Saunders. 1881. 8vo.   **12 C**

The Magisterial Synopsis : a practical guide for magistrates,
their clerks, attornies, and constables in all matters out of
quarter sessions. 6th ed. 1858. 8vo.   **172 C**

The same. 11th ed. 2 vols. 1872. 8vo.   **172 C**

The same. 13th ed. by T. W. Saunders. 2 vols. 1881. 8vo.
    12 C

OKEY, CHARLES HENRY.

Analyse de l'acte de Réforme du Parlement en Angleterre.
Revue par N. M. Thevenin. Paris, 1832. 12mo. **166 D**

A Concise digest of the law, usage, and custom relating to
commercial and civil intercourse of subjects of Great Britain
and France. 2nd ed. Paris, 1829. 8vo.   **55 C**

The same. 4th ed. 1834. 8vo.   **55 C**

Droit d'Aubaine de la Grande-Bretagne. Paris, 1830, and
2me éd. 1831. 12mo.   **160 B**

Droits, priviléges et obligations des étrangers dans la Grande-
Bretagne. 2me éd. revue par N. M. Thevenin. Paris, 1831.
12mo.   **160 B**

The forms of deeds and documents in England and France
compared. 1835. [Pamphlets, vol. 1.]   **144 A**

OLAVE THE BLACK, KING OF MAN.
Anecdotes of Olave the Black, King of Man. By Rev. James
Johnstone. 1780. 12mo. **118 A**

OLDFIELD, THOMAS HINTON BURLEY.
History of the boroughs of Great Britain. [By T. H. B. Oldfield.] 2nd ed. 2 vols. 1794. 8vo. **84 C**
History of the original constitution of Parliament, with the
present state of the representation. 1797. 8vo. **84 C**
The representative history of Great Britain and Ireland; a
history of House of Commons and of counties, cities, and
boroughs of United Kingdom. 6 vols. 1816. 8vo. **84 C**

OLDHAM, ARTHUR and ARTHUR LA TROBE FOSTER.
The law of Distress. 1886. 8vo. **52 F**
The same. 2nd ed. 1889. 8vo. **9 G**

[OLDYS, WILLIAM.]
The life of George Abbot, lord archbishop of Canterbury, with
the lives of his two brothers Robert Abbot lord bishop of
Salisbury and Sir Morris Abbot, Knt. lord mayor of London.
Guildford, 1777. 8vo. **79 B**

OLEARIUS, GOTTFRIDUS.
Dissertatio de poetriis Græcis. Hamburgi, 1734. 4to. Bound
with Sapphus Carmina. 1733. **47 G**

OLERON.
The ancient sea laws of Oleron taken out of a French book
intitled Les Us et Coutumes de la Mer, 1686. See G.
Malynes's Lex Mercatoria. 1686. folio. **118 G**

OLIPHANT, GEORGE HENRY HEWIT.
The law concerning Horses, Racing, Wagers and Gaming.
1847. 12mo. **168 G**
The same. 4th ed. by C. E. Lloyd. 1882. 8vo. **10 B**
Law of Pews in churches and chapels. 1853. 12mo. **173 E**

OLIVER, ALEXANDER.
A Collection of acts relating to the transfer of, or dealing with
land in New South Wales. Sydney, 1877. 8vo. **37 G**

OLIVER, DANIEL.
Guide to the royal botanic gardens and pleasure grounds,
Kew. 29th ed. 1881. 12mo. 93 C

OLIVER, REV. GEORGE, CANON OF PLYMOUTH.
Historic collections relating to the monasteries in Devon.
Exeter, 1820. 8vo. 87 C
The history of Exeter. Exeter, 1821. 8vo. 87 C
Monasticon Dioecesis Exoniensis, being a collection of records
and instruments illustrating the ancient conventual, colle-
giate, and eleemosynary foundations in Cornwall and Devon,
with two supplements. 1846-54. folio. 86 H
Description of the Guildhall, Exeter. By Rev. G. Oliver and
Pitman Jones. Exeter, 1853. 12mo. 87 C

OLIVER, REV. GEORGE, VICAR OF CLEE.
An Historical and descriptive account of the collegiate church
of Wolverhampton. Wolverhampton, 1836. 8vo. 93 C
The history and antiquities of the town and minster of
Beverley. Beverley, 1829. 4to. 95 G

OLIVER, WILLIAM ATKINSON.
A Practical manual of Shipping law. 1868. 12mo. 175 G
The same. 5th ed. 1874. 12mo. 175 G

OLYMPIC GAMES.
Odes of Pindar, with a dissertation on the Olympick Games.
By Gilbert West. 1749. 4to. 83 J

O'MALLEY, EDWARD LOUGHLIN and H. HARDCASTLE.
Reports of the decisions of the judges for the trial of election
petitions in England and Ireland pursuant to the Parliamentary elections acts 1868. 3 vols. 1870-81. 8vo. 66 B

ONTARIO.
Revised statutes. 2 vols. Toronto, 1877. 8vo. 34 D
Revised statutes. 1887. 2 vols. Toronto, 1887. 8vo. 34 D
Statutes of the province of Ontario, 41-53 Vict. 13 vols.
Toronto, 1878-90. 8vo. 34 D
See also CANADA.

ORATORY.

Elegant Orations, ancient and modern. By Rev. J. Mossop. 1788. 12mo.   83 A

· Lectures concerning Oratory, delivered in Trinity college, Dublin. By John Lawson. 1759. 12mo.   78 A

Quintilian's Institutes of oratory, book v. chap. vii. concerning witnesses. Translated with notes by W. M. Best. [Law Tracts, vol. 6.]   144 E

See also ELOCUTION.

ORD, JOHN WALKER.

The history and antiquities of Cleveland. 1846. 4to. 94 D

ORDER XIV.

The law of summary judgment on specially indorsed writ under order XIV. By C. Cavanagh. 1887. 8vo.   12 E

ORDNANCE SURVEY.

Ordnance Survey of England and Wales; one inch scale. 110 maps. 2 vols. 1805–66. folio.

New Ordnance Survey of England and Wales ; one inch scale. 216 maps. 1865–90. folio. [in progress.]

ORIENTAL LIFE.

Cases illustrative of Oriental life decided in H.M. supreme court at Bombay. By Sir T. E. Perry. 1853. 8vo. 38 C

See also BENGAL, BOMBAY, INDIA and MADRAS.

ORMEROD, GEORGE.

· The history of the county palatine and city of Chester, with a republication of King's Vale Royal and Leycester's Cheshire Antiquities. 3 vols. 1819. folio.   86 H

The same. 2nd ed. by T. Helsby. 3 vols. 1882. folio. 86 H

ORPHANS.

The case of Orphans consider'd from antiquity, with some remarks on our Courts of Wards, and why put down. 1725. 12mo.   49 F

See also INFANCY.

ORRERY, JOHN, 5 EARL OF.

Remarks on the life and writings of Jonathan Swift in a series of letters. 3rd ed. 1752. 8vo.   83 C

ORRIDGE, Benjamin Brogden.
Some account of the citizens of London and their rulers, from 1060 to 1867 ; and a calendar of the mayors and sheriffs from 1189 to 1867. 1867. 8vo.   91 C

ORTOLAN, Joseph Louis Elzéar.
Analysis of M. Ortolan's institutes of Justinian, including the history and generalization of Roman law. By T. L. Mears. 1876. 8vo.   63 E
Explication historique des Instituts de l'Empereur Justinien, précédée d'une généralisation du droit Romain. 7me éd. 3 vols. Paris, 1863. 8vo.   58 D
The history of Roman law. Translated by I. T. Prichard and D. Nasmith. 1871. 8vo.   63 E

OSENEY MONASTERY, Oxfordshire.
Annales Monasterii de Oseneia A.D. 1016–1347. [et] Chronicon vulgo dictum Chronicon Thomæ Wykes. See Annales Monastici, vol. 4, 1869, pp. 1–352.   102 A

OSMUND, St.
Vetus registrum Sarisburiense, alias dictum Registrum S. Osmundi episcopi. The register of S. Osmund. Edited by W. H. R. Jones. 2 vols. 1883–84. 8vo.   102 H

OSSIAN.
The Poems of Ossian. Translated by James Macpherson. New ed. 2 vols. 1796. 8vo.   83 C

OTHO AND OTHOBON.
Provinciale (seu Constitutiones Angliæ), auctore Gulielmo Lyndwood, cui adjiciuntur Constitutiones Legatinæ D. Othonis et D. Othoboni, cardinalium, cum annotationibus Johannis de Athona. Oxoniæ. 1679. 4to.   77 H

OTTO, Everard.
Thesaurus juris Romani, continens rariora meliorum interpretum opuscula, in quibus jus Romanum emendatur, explicatur, illustratur ; itemque classicis aliisque auctoribus haud raro lumen accenditur. 5 vols. Lugd. Bat., 1725–35. folio.   19 F

OTTO, WILLIAM T.
Cases argued and adjudged in the Supreme Court of the
United States, 1875–1882. 17 vols. Boston, 1876–83.
8vo. 57 D E

OUDE.
Dacoitee in excelsis ; or, the spoliation of Oude by the East
India Company, faithfully recounted. [By Samuel Lucas.]
1857. 8vo. 78 C

OUGHTON, THOMAS.
Forms of Ecclesiastical law ; or, the mode of conducting
suits in the Consistory courts : being a translation of the
first part of Oughton's Ordo Judiciorum. By Rev. J. T.
Law. 1831. 8vo. 77 F
Ordo judiciorum sive methodus procedendi in negotiis et
litibus in foro ecclesiastico-civili Britannico et Hibernico.
2 vols. 1738. 4to. 77 F

OVERALL, WILLIAM HENRY and H. C. OVERALL.
Analytical index to the series of records known as the
Remembrancia, preserved among the archives of the city of
London, A.D. 1579–1664. 1878. 8vo. 91 F

OVERBOROUGH, LANCASHIRE.
Antiquitates Bremetonacenses ; or, the Roman antiquities of
Overborough. By Rev. Richard Rauthmel. Kirkby Lons-
dale, 1824. 8vo. 89 A

OVERSEERS.
Manual for overseers . . . and vestry clerks. By H. Owen.
8th ed. 1887. 8vo. 11 A
See also PARISH LAW. 11 A

OWEN, HUGH and JOHN BRICKDALE BLAKEWAY.
A History of Shrewsbury. 2 vols. 1825. 4to. 92 F

OWEN, HUGH, JUNIOR.
Elementary education acts. 12th ed. 1876. 12mo. 166 B
The same. 15th ed. 1881. 12mo. 9 H
Manual for overseers, assistant·overseers, collectors of pocr
rates, and vestry clerks. 7th ed. 1884. 12mo. 173 B
The same. 8th ed. 1887. 8vo. 11 A

OWEN, THOMAS.
Reports in the King's Bench and Common Pleas, 1556-1615. 1656. folio.   74 F

OWEN, WILLIAM.
A Dictionary of the Welsh language, explained in English. 2 vols. 1803. 4to.   123 C

OWEN, WILLIAM and WILLIAM JOHNSTON.
A New and general biographical dictionary. 11 vols. 1761-62. 8vo.   79 C

OXENBRIDGE FAMILY.
The Oxenbridges of Brede place, Sussex, and Boston, Massachusetts. By W. D. Cooper. 1860. 8vo.   93 E

OXFORD, CITY AND UNIVERSITY OF.
Alumni Oxonienses : the members of the University of Oxford, 1715-1835 : with a record of their degrees. By Joseph Foster. 4 vols. Oxford, 1888. 8vo.   80 G
Alumni Oxonienses 1500-1714. By Joseph Foster. vol. I. [Abba-Dyve.] 1891. 8vo.   80 G
Calendar, 1810, 1813-1828, 1830, 1838-1890. 71 vols. 1810-90. 12mo.   135 A-C
A Calendar of the chief officers in the University of Oxford, from the earliest time. See J. Le Neve's Fasti Ecclesiæ Anglicanæ, vol. 3, 1854, pp. 463-595.   80 H
A Catalogue of all graduates and of all masters of arts and doctors of musick who have proceeded or been created in the University of Oxford, 1659-1782. Oxford, 1782. 8vo.   80 H
The same. New ed. 1659-1800. Oxford, 1801. 8vo. 80 H
The same. New ed. 1659-1850. Oxford, 1851. 8vo. 80 H
A Copy of the Poll for election of a member to represent University of Oxford, in Parliament. Taken in the Convocation House, 4th to 20th Jan. 1853. 1853. 12mo. 107 K
Corpus statutorum Universitatis Oxoniensis. Oxonii, 1768. 4to.   92 F
Historic towns. Oxford. By Rev. C. W. Boase. 2nd ed. 1887. 12mo.   92 E
Historical Register of the University of Oxford, with an alphabetical record of university honours and distinctions. Oxford, 1888. 8vo.   80 G

OXFORD, City and University of—*continued.*

History of the University of Oxford, its colleges, halls, and public buildings. [By W. Combe.] 2 vols. 1814. 4to. **92 G**

Memorials of Oxford. By Rev. James Ingram. 3 vols. Oxford, 1834–37. 4to. **92 F**

Notitia Oxoniensis Academiæ. 1675. 8vo. **80 H**

Observations on the Oxford press. See Blackstone's Law Tracts, 3rd ed., 1771, pp. 241–280. **144 G**

Oxford : brief historical and descriptive notes. By Andrew Lang. New ed. 1890. 8vo. **92 E**

The Oxford University and city guide. New ed. Oxford, 1837. 12mo. **92 E**

Oxford University Commission. Report of Her Majesty's Commissioners appointed to inquire into the state, discipline, studies, and revenues of the University and Colleges of Oxford : with evidence, and appendix. 1852. folio. **154 E**

Oxonia antiqua restaurata, containing upwards of 190 engravings by Joseph Skelton and others, the literary portion by members of the university. 2nd ed. by E. J. Carlos. 1843. 4to. **92 G**

Railway traveller's walk through Oxford. 1860. 12mo. **92 E**

Speech of G. J. Goschen on the Oxford University tests abolition bill. 1865. [Pamphlets, vol. 26.] **144 B**

Statuta Universitatis Oxoniensis. Oxonii, 1870. 8vo. **146 F**

Student's handbook to the university and colleges of Oxford. 7th ed. Oxford, 1883. 12mo. **135 C**

See also ACLAND, T. D., ANSTEY, REV. H., BURROWS, M., CHALMERS, A., DAVENPORT, J. M., GUTCH, REV. J., LYTE, H. C. M., MILLER, REV. C., POINTER, J., PYCROFT, J. W., RIMMER, A., SEWELL, R. C., TURNER, W. H. and WOOD, A.

OXFORD, Colleges in University of.

The case of visitation of colleges, in the House of Lords, in Exeter College case. See E. Stillingfleet's Ecclesiastical Cases, part 2, 1704, pp. 411–436. **49 E**

Register of the rectors and fellows of Exeter college, Oxford, with illustrative documents and a history cf the college. By Rev. C. W. Boase. Oxford, 1879. 4to. **92 F**

Register of the demies, instructors in grammar and in music, chaplains, clerks, and choristers of Saint Mary Magdalen college, Oxford, from the foundation to A.D. 1857. By Rev. J. R. Bloxam. 7 vols. 1853–81, and Index 1885. 8 vols. 1853–85. 8vo. **92 E**

OXFORD HISTORICAL SOCIETY.

Publications of the Oxford Historical Society. 17 vols. Oxford, 1885–90. 8vo. **85 F**

1, 10, 11, 12, 14. Register of the University of Oxford. Edited by Rev. C. W. Boase and Rev. A. Clark. 2 vols. in 5. 1885–89.

2, 7, 13. Remarks and collections of Thomas Hearne. Edited by C. E. Doble. 3 vols. 1885–89.

3. The early history of Oxford, 727–1100, preceded by a sketch of the mythical origin of the City and University. By James Parker. 1885.

4. Memorials of Merton College ; with biographical notices of the Wardens and Fellows. By Hon. G. C. Brodrick. 1885.

5, 16. Collectanea. First series. Edited by C. R. L. Fletcher. Second series. Edited by M. Burrows. 2 vols. 1885–90.

First series. Part i. The Stamford schism. Letters relating to Oxford in the 14th century. By H. H. Henson.

ii. The catalogue of the library of Oriel College in the 14th century. By C. L. Shadwell.

iii. The daily ledger of John Dorne, 1520. By F. Madan.

iv. All Souls' College *v.* Lady Jane Stafford, 1587. By the Editor.

v. The account book of James Wilding, 1682–8. By E. G. Duff.

vi. Dr. Wallis' letter against Mr. Maidwell, 1700. By T. W. Jackson.

Second series. Part i. The Oxford Market. By Rev. O. Ogle.

ii. The University of Oxford in the 12th century. By T. E. Holland.

iii. The Friars Preachers *v.* The University. By Rev. H. Rashdall.

iv. Notes on the Jews in Oxford. By A. Neubauer.

v. Linacre's catalogue of Grocyn's books, followed by a memoir of Grocyn. By the Editor.

vi. Table-talk and papers of Bishop Hough, 1703–1743. By Rev. W. D. Macray.

vii. Extracts from the ' Gentleman's Magazine ' relating to Oxford, 1731–1800. By F. J. Haverfield.

6. Magdalen College and King James II., 1686–8. A series of documents collected and edited by the Rev. J. R. Bloxam. 1886.

7. See No. 2.

8. Elizabethan Oxford. Reprints of rare tracts. Edited by Charles Plummer. 1887.

9. Letters of Richard Radcliffe and John James, of Queen's College, Oxford, 1755–83 ; with notes and appendices. Edited by Margaret Evans. 1888.

10, 11, 12. See No. 1.

13. See No. 2.

14. See No. 1.

OXFORD HISTORICAL SOCIETY—*continued.*

15, 17. 'Survey of the Antiquities of the City of Oxford,' composed
in 1661–6, by Anthony Wood. Edited by Andrew Clark.
vols. 1 & 2. 1889–90.

16. See No. 5.

17. See No. 15.

OXFORDSHIRE.

The natural history of Oxfordshire. By Robert Plot. Oxford, 1677. folio.   **92 G**

Oxfordshire: the history and antiquities of the hundreds of
Bullington and Ploughley. By J. Dunkin. 2 vols. 1823.
4to.   **92 F**

Parochial antiquities attempted in the history of Ambrosden,
Burcester and other adjacent parts in the counties of Oxford and Bucks. By Right Rev. White Kennett. New ed.
2 vols. Oxford, 1818. 4to.   **92 F**

A Topographical and historical description of the county of
Oxford. By J. N. Brewer. 1819. 8vo.   **92 E**

See also BAWDWEN, REV. W. and DAVENPORT, J. M.

PAGANISM.

History of Paganism in Caledonia. By T. A. Wise. 1884.
4to.   **85 I**

PAGE, JOHN.

Poem on the siege of Rouen. Edited by James Gairdner.
[Camden Society, n.s. vol. 17.] 1876. 8vo.   **85 D**

PAGET, JOHN.

The Income tax act 5 & 6 Vict. c. 35. 1842, 12mo.   **168 G**

PAINTERS AND PAINTINGS.

A Catalogue of paintings, drawings, and engravings by and
after Wm. Grimaldi. By Rev. A. B. Grimaldi. Privately
printed. 1873. 8vo.   **118 C**

Dictionary of painters and engravers, biographical and critical. By Michael Bryan. New ed. by R. E. Graves and
W. Armstrong. 2 vols. 1886–89. 8vo.   **79 H**

Dictionary of painters containing memoirs of the most eminent
professors of painting, from the year 1250. By Matthew
Pilkington. New ed. 2 vols. 1824. 4to.   **79 H**

PALAA, G.

Dictionnaire législatif et règlementaire des Chemins de Fer. Paris, 1864. 8vo. **40 H**

PALACE COURT.

The Palace Court in constitution and practice, with reasons for its abolition. By S. Abrahams. 1848. 8vo. **78 B**

PALEY, WILLIAM.

Law of Principal and Agent, chiefly with reference to mercantile transactions. 1812. 8vo. **174 C**

The same. 3rd ed. by J. H. Lloyd. 1833. 8vo. **174 C**

Law and practice of summary convictions by justices of the peace. 4th ed. by H. T. J. Macnamara. 1856. 8vo. **164 F**

The same. 6th ed. by W. H. Macnamara. 1879. 8vo. **12 B**

PALGRAVE, SIR FRANCIS.

The antient kalendars and inventories of the treasury of His Majesty's Exchequer. 2 vols. 1836. 8vo. **99 A**

Documents and records illustrating the history of Scotland, preserved in the treasury of Her Majesty's Exchequer. 1837. 8vo. **99 A**

Essay upon the original authority of the King's Council. 1834. 8vo. **97 I**

The history of Normandy and of England. 4 vols. 1851-64. 8vo. **115 A**

Parliamentary writs and writs of military summons. 2 vols. in 4. 1827-34. folio. **98 D**

The rise and progress of the English Commonwealth. Anglo-Saxon period. 2 vols. 1832. 4to. **114 E**

Rolls and records of the court held before the King's justiciars or justices, 1195 to 1199. 2 vols. 1835. 8vo. **99 A**

PALMER, FRANCIS BEAUFORT.

Conveyancing and other forms and precedents relating to Companies. 1877. 8vo. **169 D**

Company precedents. 2nd ed. 1881, and 3rd ed. 1884. 8vo. **169 D**

The same. 4th ed. 1888. 8vo. **52 C**

The same. 5th ed. 1891. 8vo. **9 D**

Private companies, their formation and advantages. 6th ed. 1887. 12mo. **9 D**

PALMER, Francis Beaufort—*continued.*

Shareholders' & Directors' legal companion. 1878. 12mo. **169 D**

The same. 10th ed. 1890. 12mo. **9 D**

Winding-up forms, a collection of forms relating to the winding-up of companies. 1885. 8vo. **9 D**

PALMER, Sir Gefrey.

Reports [in King's Bench and Common Bench, 1619–1629]; imprime et publie per l'original. 1678. folio. **74 F**

PALMER, John, Architect.

The history of the siege of Manchester by the King's forces, 1642, with the complaint of Lieut. col. John Rosworm against the inhabitants of Manchester, relative to that event. Manchester, 1822. 8vo. **89 B**

PALMER, John, Barrister-at-Law.

The attorney and agent's new table of Costs in the court of King's Bench, Common Pleas, and Exchequer of Pleas. 8th ed. 1818. 4to. **157 B**

The same. 10th ed. 1829, and supplement 1833. 4to. **157 B**

The parliamentary solicitor's assistant, containing a selection of bills of costs in the House of Lords and House of Commons. 1823. 4to. **157 B**

The practice in the House of Lords on appeals, writs of error and claims of peerage. 1830. 8vo. **52 H**

The practice on Appeals from the colonies to the Privy Council. 1831, with supplement 1834. [Jacob's Tracts, vol. 12.] **144 F**

PALMER, Samuel.

Index to the Times newspaper, 1842 to 1890. 49 vols. 1891–76 & 1868–91. 8vo. **134 H I**

PAPPAFAVA, Vladimiro.

Delle opere che illustrano il Notariato. Zara, 1880. 8vo. **82 C**

PARIS.

Galignani's Paris guide; or, stranger's companion through the French metropolis. 10th ed. 1822. 12mo. **84 A**

Panorama de Paris. Texte Français de L. Riga, texte Anglais de G. W. Yapp. Paris, 1857. folio. **84 H**

PARIS, MATTHEW.

Chronica Majora. Edited by H. R. Luard. 7 vols. 1872-83. 8vo.   **102 D E**

Historia Anglorum, item ejusdem Abbreviatio chronicorum Angliæ. Edited by Sir F. Madden. 3 vols. 1866-69. 8vo.   **102 C**

PARISH LAW.

Statutes in force relating to the Poor, Parochial Unions, and Parishes. vols. 1-3 by W. C. Glen, vol. 4 by A. Macmorran and M. S. J. Macmorran. 4 vols. 1873-90. 8vo. **11 C D**

Steer's Parish Law. 5th ed. by W. H. Macnamara. 1887. 8vo.   **11 A**

Handy book of parish law. By W. A. Holdsworth. 9th ed. 1883. 8vo.   **11 A**

Parochial assessments. By W. G. Lumley. 7th ed. 1882. 8vo.   **11 A**

Shaw's Parish law. By J. F. Archbold. 6th ed. by W. C. Glen. 1881. 8vo.   **11 A**

Law of the building of churches and of the divisions of parishes. By C. F. Trower. 1874. 12mo.   **9 B**

The Parish, its powers and obligations at law. By Toulmin Smith. 2nd ed. 1857. 8vo.   **53 B**

Observations on the present mode of valuing property for assessment to the parochial rates. By H. H. Carwardine. 1841. [Pamphlets, vol. 4.]   **144 A**

Parochial settlements an obstruction to poor law reform. By J. M. White. 1835. [Pamphlets, vol. 4.]   **144 A**

The principles of Mr. Shaw Lefevre's Parochial assessments bill, and the Tithe commutation act, compared. By Rev. C. Miller. 1839. [Law Tracts, vol. 6.]   **144 E**

See also AMOS, A., GAMBIER, E. J., JACOB, G. and PAUL, J.

PARISH REGISTERS.

Observations on marriages, baptisms, and burials as preserved in parochial registers. By Ralph Bigland. 1764. 4to. **127 I**

A Pamphlet shewing the necessity for some legislative provision for the better custody and preservation of old parish registers. Kendal, 1878. [Pamphlets, vol. 36.]   **144 C**

See also HARLEIAN SOCIETY.

PARK, JAMES ALLAN.

A System of the law of Marine Insurances. 1787. 8vo. **169 B**

PARK, James Allan—*continued.*
The same. 7th ed. 2 vols. 1817. 8vo.   **169 B**
The same. 8th ed. by F. Hildyard. 2 vols. 1842. 8vo. **169 B**

PARK, John James.
A Contre-projet to the Humphreysian code ; and to the projects of Redaction of Messrs. Hammond, Uniacke, and Twiss. 1828. 8vo.   **83 J**
The dogmas of the constitution. Four lectures on the theory and practice of the constitution, delivered at King's College, London. 1832. 8vo.   **78 B**
Juridical Letters, addressed to the Right Hon. Robert Peel, in reference to the present crisis of Law Reform. By Eunomus [John James Park]. 1830. 8vo.   **170 F**
Systems of registration and conveyancing. A lecture delivered at King's College, London, Oct. 30, 1832. 1833. [Law Tracts, vol. 5.]   **144 E**
The topography and natural history of Hampstead. Republished with additions and corrections. 1818. 8vo. **89 E**
A Treatise on the law of Dower. 1819. 8vo.   **52 F**
What are courts of Equity ? A lecture delivered at King's College, London. 1832. [Law Tracts, vol. 5.]   **144 E**

PARKER, Francis Edward.
Tributes of the Massachusetts Historical Society to Francis E. Parker. Privately printed. Cambridge, 1887. 8vo. **79 C**

PARKER, Frank Rowley.
An Analysis of the principal steps in a Bankruptcy proceeding. 1870. 4to.   **157 C**
Analytical index and digest of the Supreme Court of Judicature acts. Printed for private circulation. 1875. 8vo. **157 C**
The same. 2nd ed. 1883. 8vo.   **169 F**
The election of County Councils under the Local Government Act 1888. 1888. 8vo.   **10 G**
Manual for returning officers, for use at the first election of county councillors. 1889. 8vo.   **10 G**
Powers, duties, and liabilities of an election agent, and of a returning officer at a parliamentary election in England and Wales. 1885. 8vo.   **9 H**

PARKER, Matthew.

Catalogus librorum manuscriptorum in Bibliotheca collegii
Corporis Christi in Cantabrigia quos legavit Matthæus
Parker. 1722. folio.   81 H

The same. New ed. by J. Nasmith. 1777. 4to.   82 I

Correspondence of Matthew Parker, 1535–1575. Edited by
John Bruce and Rev. T. T. Perowne. Cambridge, 1853.
8vo.   77 E

De antiquitate Britannicæ Ecclesiæ et privilegiis ecclesiæ
Cantuariensis cum archiepiscopis ejusdem LXX . . .
Accurante Samuele Drake. 1729. folio.   85 I

PARKER SOCIETY.

Publications of the Parker Society. [All of which are catalogued under their respective authors and subjects.] 54 vols.
1841–53. 8vo. & 12mo.   77 D E

General Index to the publications of the Parker Society. By
Henry Gough. Cambridge, 1855. 8vo.   77 E

PARKER, Thomas, 1 Earl of Macclesfield.

Cases adjudged in the court of King's Bench concerning
settlements and removals, in the time when Lord Parker
sat chief justice there. 2nd ed. 1729. 8vo.   74 F

PARKER, Thomas.

The law of Shipping and Insurance, with a digest of adjudged
cases. 1775. 4to.   157 B

PARKER, Sir Thomas, Lord Chief Baron.

Reports of cases concerning the revenue in the Court of
Exchequer, 1743–1767. 1776. folio.   74 F

PARKES, Joseph.

A History of the Court of Chancery. 1828. 8vo.   83 I

Memoirs of Sir Philip Francis, K.C.B., with correspondence
and journals. By J. Parkes and H. Merivale. 2 vols. 1867.
8vo.   80 B

[PARKIN, Rev. Charles.]

. The history of Great Yarmouth. Lynn, 1776. 8vo.   92 C

PARKINSON, George Hewlings.

A Handy book for the common law judges' chambers. 1861.
12mo.   **169 E**

PARLIAMENT, History, Debates and Proceedings of.

A Discourse on the rise and power of parliaments. [By
Thomas Sheridan.] 1685. 12mo.   **49 A**

A History and defence of Magna Charta ; with an essay on
Parliaments, describing their origin in England. 1769.
8vo.   **114 D**

History, debates, and proceedings of both Houses of Parliament, 1743 to 1774. 7 vols. 1792. 8vo.   **256 A B**

Inquiry into the rise and progress of parliament, chiefly in
Scotland. By A. Wight. Edinburgh, 1784. 4to.   **114 F**

Miscellanea Parliamentaria, containing presidents and orders
of the House of Lords and Commons. By W. Petyt. 1680.
12mo.   **48 C**

Modus tenendi parliamentum, an ancient treatise on the mode
of holding the parliament in England. Edited by T. D.
Hardy. 1846. 8vo.   **98 A**

Of the public councils of this kingdom, and of affairs of war
and peace therein debated. See Collectanea Juridica, vol. 2,
1792, pp. 332–339.   **144 G**

The original institution, power, and jurisdiction of Parliaments.
By Sir Matthew Hale. 1707. 12mo.   **49 E**

Parliamentary history and review for 1826, part 2. 1827.
[Law Tracts, vol. 7.]   **144 E**

The Parliamentary Register; or, history of the proceedings
and debates of the House of Commons, 1774–1813. 129 vols.
1775–1813. 8vo.   **256 B–F**

The Parliamentary register ; or, history of the proceedings
and debates of the House of Commons of Ireland, 1781–
1797. 2nd ed. 17 vols. Dublin, 1784–1801. 8vo.   **255 G**

Rotuli Parliamentorum, ut et petitiones et placita in Parlia-
mento temp. Edw. I.—19 Hen. VII., [1278–1503.] 6 vols.
[n.d.] folio.   **98 B**

Index to the Rolls of Parliament 1278–1503. By Rev. J.
Strachey, Rev. J. Pridden and E. Upham. 1832. folio. **98 B**

The Times parliamentary debates, 1886–1890. House of
Commons. 16 vols. 1886–90. 4to.   **105 A**

The Times parliamentary debates, 1886–1890. House of
Lords. 5 vols. 1886–90. 4to.   **104 A**

PARLIAMENT, History of—*continued.*

See Barrow, J. H., Brady, R., Elsynge, H., Gurdon, T.,
Hakewil, W., Oldfield, T. H. B., Parry, C. H., Prynne,
W., Ryley, W. and Whitelocke, Sir B.

See also Constitutional History, Hansard's Debates
and Magna Charta.

PARLIAMENT, House of Commons.

The antient right of the commons of England asserted. By
William Petyt. 1680. 12mo.   48 C

A Career in the Commons ; or, letters to a young member of
parliament. By W. L. Harle. 1850. 8vo.   78 B

Journals of the House of Commons, 1547–1889. 144 vols. in
148. 1803–89. folio.   104 F–106 F

General Index, 1547–1865. 9 vols. 1803–68. folio. 109 B

Reports from committees of the House of Commons, which
have been printed by order of the House and are not inserted in the Journals, from 1715 to 1800. 15 vols. and
General Index. 1803. 16 vols. folio.   109 B C

A State of the proceedings in the House of Commons, with
relation to the impeached Lords. 1701. folio.   118 G

See also Boroughs, Elections and Needler, C.

PARLIAMENT, House of Lords.

Calendar of the journals of the House of Lords, 1509 to 1642
and 1660 to 1826. 2 vols. [n.d.] folio.   104 D

A Collection of the several Protests in the House of Lords, in
the session of parliament 1722 and 1723. 1723. folio. 118 G

A Complete collection of all the protests made in the House
of Lords, 1641–1745. 1745. 12mo.   49 D

The grandeur of the law. A list of the members of the
present House of Lords, whose ancestors have occupied the
judicial seat in England. By Edward Foss. 1842. 4to. 80 E

Journals of the House of Lords, 1509 to 1889. 121 vols. in
127. n.d.–1889. folio.   103 B–104 E

General index, 1509–1863. 7 vols. 1836–65. folio. 104 F

Jurisdiction of the Lords House ; or, Parliament considered
according to ancient records. By Sir M. Hale. Edited by
F. Hargrave. 1796. 8vo.   127 I

The order and manner of the sitting of the Lords as Peers of
the Realme. By Thomas Walkley. 1628. 8vo.   49 D

PARLIAMENT, HOUSE OF LORDS—*continued.*

Remembrances of methods and proceedings used in the House of Lords. By Henry Scobell; with The priviledges of the baronage of England. By John Selden. 1689. 12mo. **48 C**

Several proceedings and resolutions of House of Peers, in relation to the Lords impeached or charged. 1701. folio. **118 G**

PARLIAMENT, LAW AND PRIVILEGE OF.

Law, privileges, proceedings and usage of Parliament. By Sir T. E. May. 9th ed. 1883. 8vo. **12 A**

The privileges of the House of Commons. By C. R. Kennedy. 1840. [Pamphlets, vol. 28.] **144 B**

The recent proceedings in the House of Commons on the subject of Privilege. By T. Pemberton. 2nd ed. 1837, and 3rd ed. 1840. [Pamphlets, vol. 28.] **144 B**

Parliamentary Privileges. Considerations on the judgment of the Court of Queen's Bench in the late case of Stockdale *v.* Hansard. 1839. [Pamphlets, vol. 28.] **144 B**

Speech in the House of Commons, on Breach of Privilege. By J. W. Freshfield. 1839. [Pamphlets, vol. 28.] **144 B**

The judicial privilege of the Commons on controverted elections considered, and its partial abolition vindicated. By T. B. Rutherford. 1838. [Pamphlets, vol. 28.] **144 B**

The question of privilege raised by the decision in the case of Stockdale *v.* Hansard. By S. A. Ferrall. 1837. [Pamphlets, vol. 28.] **144 B**

Case of Mr. Perry's commitment by the House of Lords for a breach of privilege. See Hargrave's Juridical Arguments, vol. 2, 1799, pp. 183–220. **144 G**

A Collection of cases and records on Privilege of Parliament. 1764. 8vo. **114 D**

Cases in Parliament resolved and adjudged, upon petitions, and writs of error, 1694–1699. By Sir B. Shower. 3rd ed. 1740. folio. **74 G**

Lex Parliamentaria; or, a treatise of the law and customs of parliament. 2nd ed. [n.d.] 8vo. **48 C**

Lex Parliamentaria; or, a treatise of the law and custom of the parliaments of England. By G. P., Esq. [George Petyt.] 1690. 12mo. **48 C**

Memorials of method and manner of proceedings in Parliament in passing bills. By H. S. E. 1670. Bound with Hakewil's Modus Tenendi Parliamentum, 1671. 12mo. **48 D**

PARLIAMENT, LAW AND PRIVILEGE OF—*continued*.

A Collection of rights and priviledges of Parliament; with
the true and just Prerogatives of the kings of England.
By A Gentleman that wishes all happinesse and peace to
this distracted kingdome. 1643. 8vo.   **49 F**

The soveraigne power of parliaments and kingdomes. By
William Prynne. 1643. 8vo.   **48 D**

See also ANGLESEY, A., BILLS PRIVATE AND PUBLIC, CON-
STITUTIONAL HISTORY AND LAW and HATSELL, J.

PARLIAMENT, MEMBERS OF.

Biographical index to the present House of Commons. By
Joshua Wilson. 1808. 12mo.   **134 B**

Biographical index to the present House of Lords. By the
author of the ' Political index to the House of Commons.'
1808. 12mo.   **134 B**

Chronological register of both houses of British Parliament,
1708 to 1807. By R. Beatson. 3 vols. 1807. 8vo. **134 B**

Debrett's House of Commons and the Judicial Bench, 1871
and 1880 to 1890. 12 vols. 1871–90. 8vo.   **134 B**

Dod's Parliamentary Companion, 1837, 38, 40, 41, 1843–61,
1863–65, 1867–90. 55 vols. 1837–90. 12mo.   **134 A**

List of all the places in England and Wales that send
members to parliament; with the names of the members,
from 1660 to the present year. 1724. 12mo.   **124 A**

List of the lords spiritual and temporal and of the members
of the House of Commons. 1734–5. 12mo.   **124 A**

List of the lords spiritual and temporal as also of the knights
and commissioners of shires, citizens, and burgesses of the
first and second parliaments of George I., 1715–1727. 1719–
27. [Grimaldi's Tracts, vols. 1 and 2.]   **118. B**

The new House of Commons, with biographical notices of
its members and of nominated candidates. 1885. 12mo.
134 B

Return of the names and titles of all members of Parliament
of. England, Scotland and Ireland 1213–1874; with the
name of the constituency represented and date of return
of each. 2 vols. 1878, and Index to Part 1. Parliaments
of England 1213–1702. With appendix and corrigenda.
1888. 3 vols. 1878–88. folio.   **151 D**

Stockdale's Parliamentary guide; or, member's and elector's
complete companion. 1784. 8vo.   **84 B**

PARLIAMENTARY PAPERS.

Sessional papers printed by order of House of Commons, and Papers presented by Command, 1801–1888. [Containing Public Bills, Reports of Committees and Commissioners, Accounts and Papers, &c.] 4,780 vols. 1801–1889. folio & 8vo.   **Gallery**

Sessional papers printed by order of House of Lords, or presented by royal command, 1804–1888. 2,897 vols. 1804–1888. folio & 8vo.   **Gallery**

Classification of Parliamentary Reports, and a breviate of their contents : likewise tables of arrangement in volumes of the Accounts and other papers, and Bills, 1801–1826. 1830. folio.   **199 E**

General Index to the Bills printed by order of the House of Commons, 1801–1852. 1853. folio.   **199 E**

General Index to Bills, Reports, Accounts, and other papers printed by order of House of Commons, 1801–1826, 1832–1838, 1844–1889. 6 vols. 1829–90. folio.   **199 D**

General index to the Divisions of the House of Commons 1836–1857. 2 vols. 1855–57. folio.   **199 E**

General index to the Reports of public petitions 1833–1852. 1855. folio.   **199 E**

General Index to the Reports of Select Committees printed by order of the House of Commons, 1801–1852. 1853. folio.   **199 E**

General Index to Sessional Papers printed by order of House of Lords, 1801–1870. 2 vols. 1860–72. folio.   **199 E**

PARLIAMENTARY REFORM.

Equal Representation. A letter to Lord John Russell. By James Lorimer. 1859. [Pamphlets, vol. 23.]   **144 B**

Free Parliaments. The case of Ashby v. White. [n.d.] [Pamphlets, vol. 11.]   **144 A**

Handbook of Reform explaining true principles of political government and taxation. 1859. [Pamphlets, vol. 12.] **144 A**

Manhood suffrage combined with relative equality in representation ; a contribution towards parliamentary reform. By J. R. Stodart. [n.d.] [Pamphlets, vol. 15.]   **144 B**

Parliamentary Reform. An Essay. By Walter Bagehot. 1859. [Pamphlets, vol. 21.]   **144 B**

Proceedings at law between M. Ashby and W. White, in relation to an election at Aylesbury. 1721. 12mo.   **48 F**

Reasons for reformation. By J. Cartwright. 1809. 8vo. **118 B**

The redistribution, extension and purification of the elective

PARLIAMENTARY REFORM—*continued*.

franchise. By A Revising Barrister [Sir J. E. Wilmot.]
1853. [Pamphlets, vol. 9, pt. 2.] **144 A**

Several speeches against the bill for repealing the Triennial
Act, as they were spoken in the House of Commons. 1716.
folio. **118 G**

See CRICKLADE CASE, ELECTIONS, & STAPLETON, A. G.

PARLIAMENTARY WRITS.

Brevia Parliamentaria rediviva. By Wm. Prynne. 1662.
8vo. **97 I**

Parliamentary writs and writs of military summons. Edited
by Sir F. Palgrave. 2 vols. in 4. 1827–34. folio. **98 D**

PARRY, CHARLES HENRY.

The parliaments and councils of England chronologically
arranged from the reign of William I. to the revolution in
1688. 1839. 8vo **99 A**

PARRY, WILLIAM EDWARD.

Journal of a second voyage for the discovery of a North-West
passage from the Atlantic to the Pacific, performed in the
years 1821–23, in his Majesty's ships Fury and Hecla.
And Appendix. 2 vols. 1824–5. 4to. **84 F**

PARSONS, EDWARD.

The civil, ecclesiastical, literary, commercial, and miscellaneous
history of Leeds, Halifax, Huddersfield, Bradford, Wakefield,
Dewsbury, Otley, and the manufacturing district of Yorkshire. 2 vols. Leeds, 1834. 8vo. **94 B**

PARSONS, JAMES.

Exposition of principles of Partnership. 1889. 8vo. **59 G**

PARSONS, REV. PHILIP.

The monuments and painted glass of upwards of one hundred
churches chiefly in the eastern part of Kent ; with an appendix, containing the churches of Hadleigh and Lavenham
in Suffolk, and of Dedham in Essex. 1794. 4to. **88 E**

[PARSONS, ROBERT.]

An Answere to the Fifth part of reportes lately set forth by
Syr Edward Cooke, concerning the ancient and moderne

[PARSONS, ROBERT]—*continued.*

municipall lawes of England, which do apperteyne to spirituall power and jurisdiction. By a Catholick Devyne. [R. Parsons.] 1606. 12mo. **48 D**

A Conference about the next succession to the crown of England. Published by R. Doleman. [R. Parsons.] 1681. 12mo. **48 D**

PARSONS, THEOPHILUS.

Law of Contracts. 4th ed. 2 vols. Boston, 1860. 8vo. **59 B**

Treatise on Maritime Law. 2 vols. Boston, 1859. 8vo. **59 G**

PARTIES TO ACTIONS.

Treatise on rules for selection of parties to an action. By A. V. Dicey. 1870. 8vo. **11 A**

Practice of the superior courts of law at Westminster; with introductory treatises respecting parties to actions, &c. By R. Lush. 3rd ed. by J. Dixon. 2 vols. 1865. 8vo. **52 C**

Selection of leading cases on pleading and parties to actions. By W. F. Finlason. 1847. 8vo. **173 F**

PARTITION.

Dissertation on and precedents of Partition. See Bythewood and Jarman's Conveyancing, 4th ed., vol. 4, 1887, pp. 122–193. **13 D**

The partition acts 1868 and 1876. By W. G. Walker. 2nd ed. 1882. 8vo. **13 B**

The law of joint ownership and partition of real estate. By E. J. Foster. 1878. 8vo. **13 B**

PARTNERSHIP.

A Digest of the law of Partnership. By F. Pollock. 5th ed. 1890. 8vo. **11 B**

Exposition of principles of Partnership. By James Parsons. 1889. 8vo. **59 G**

Student's Guide to Trusts and Partnerships. By John Indermaur. 2nd ed. 1889. 8vo. **64 G**

A Treatise on the law of Partnership. By Sir N. Lindley. 5th ed. 1888. 8vo. **11 B**

Commentaries on the law of Partnership. By J. Story. 7th ed. by W. F. Wharton. 1881. 8vo. **11 B**

The law of Partnership. By J. Dixon. 1866. 8vo. **173 D**

PARTNERSHIP—*continued.*

Observations of a solicitor on the right of the public to form
Limited Liability Partnerships. By E. W. Field. 1854.
[Pamphlets, vol. 9, pt. 2.]   **144 A**

See also BISSET, A., CARY, H., COLLYER, J., GOW, N.,
MONTAGU, B., POTHIER, R. J. and WATSON, W.

PARTON, JOHN.

Some account of the hospital and parish of St. Giles in the
Fields, Middlesex. 1822. folio.   **92 G**

PARTRIDGE, RICHARD W. and ERNLE PARTRIDGE.

The Lunacy acts amendment act 1889. 1889. 8vo.   **53 A**

PARTY WALLS.

Law of party walls and fences. By H. W. Woolrych. 1845.
8vo.   **11 I**

See also BOUNDARIES.

PASK, JAMES.

The judgment law amendment acts relating to real property.
3rd ed. 1866. 8vo.   **13 B**

The practice of registering judgments. 1859. 8vo.   **13 B**

PATENT CASES, REPORTS OF.

Abstract of reported cases relating to letters patent for inventions. By T. M. Goodeve. 1884. 8vo.   **76 H**

Abstract of reported cases relating to letters patent for inventions, 1884–1886. By R. Griffin. 1887. 8vo.   **76 H**

Patent cases decided by the comptroller–general and law
officers of the crown in 1887. By R. Griffin. 1888. 8vo.
     76 H

Reports of Patent Cases, 1884–1890. By John Cutler. 7 vols.
1884–90, and Digest of Patent Cases, 1884–87. 8 vols.
1884–90. 8vo.   **76 H**

See also DAVIES, J., MACRORY, E. and WEBSTER, T.

PATENT OFFICE AND PATENTS.

Abridgements of specifications relating to patents for inventions. 103 vols. 1857–89. 12mo.   **108 A–L**

Catalogue of the Patent Office library. 2 vols. 1857–58, and
New ed. 2 vols. 1881–83. 8vo.   **82 I**

PATENT OFFICE AND PATENTS—*continued.*

A General index to the Repertory of patent inventions from 1815 to 1845. 1846, and Index of all Patents granted in England from 1815 to 1845 inclusive. 1849. 8vo. **108 L**

The Commissioners of Patents' Journal, 1854-1883. 45 vols. 1854-83. 8vo.

The Illustrated Journal of the Patent Office, 1884-1888. 9 vols. 1886-89. 8vo.

Official Journal of the Patent Office. 10 vols. 1884-88. 8vo.

Illustrated Official Journal (Patents). 3 vols. 1889-90. 8vo.

The Patent office library. By Peter Jensen. 1884. [Pamphlets, vol. 40.] **144 C**

PATENTS, LAW OF.

Law and practice relating to Letters Patent for Inventions. By Robert Frost. 1891. 8vo. **11 B**

A Digest of the law and practice of Letters Patent for Inventions. By C. Higgins. 2nd ed. by C. Higgins and G. Edwardes Jones. 1890. 8vo. **11 B**

Law and practice of Letters Patent for Inventions. By Lewis Edmunds. 1890. 8vo. **11 B**

Practice as to Letters Patent for Inventions ; with the practice in actions for infringement of patent. By W. N. Lawson. 2nd ed. 1889. 8vo. **11 B**

Patent laws of the world, collected, edited, and indexed. By A. Carpmael and E. Carpmael. 1885, and Supplement, 1889. 2 vols. 1885-9. 8vo. **53 B**

Patent laws of Latin-America (South and Central America). Translated by J. Géraud. Rio de Janeiro, 1888. 12mo. **55 C**

A Collection of precedents in Patents conveyancing. By Robert Morris. 1887. 8vo. **13 C**

Patentee's manual. By James Johnson and J. H. Johnson. 5th ed. 1884. 8vo. **11 B**

An Analysis of the Patents designs and trade mark act 1883, with remarks on its working. By A. V. Newton. 1883. [Pamphlets, vol. 36.] **144 C**

The Government Patent bill. By H. T. Woods. 1883. [Pamphlets, vol. 37.] **144 C**

Patent Monopoly as affecting the encouragement, improvement, and progress of sciences, arts, and manufactures. By Henry Dircks. 1869. [Pamphlets, vol. 37.] **144 C**

On the report of the Patent law commissioners. By Robert Wilson. 1865. [Pamphlets, vol. 26.] **144 B**

PATENTS, LAW OF—*continued.*

The law of Patents for inventions familiarly explained. By Wm. Carpmael. 6th ed. 1860. 8vo. **173 E**

Collection of the laws of Patent privileges of all the countries of Europe, the United States of N. America and the Dutch West Indies. By C. F. Loosey. Vienna, 1849. 8vo. **55 E**

Observations on points relating to amendment of law of patents. By C. S. Drewry. 1839. [Law Tracts, vol. 6.] **144 E**

See also ABEL, C. D., AGNEW, W. F., ARCHER, W. H., CORYTON, J., CURTIS, G. T., DANIEL, E. M., GODSON, R., HANDS, W., HINDMARCH, W. M., HOLROYD, E., HUARD, A., LAW, S. D., MACFIE, R. A., TERRELL, T., TURNER, T. and WAGGETT, J. F.

PATERSON, DANIEL.

A New and accurate description of all the direct and principal cross roads in England and Wales. 7th ed. 1786, and 15th ed. 1811. 8vo. **86 A**

The same. 18th ed. by E. Mogg. 1829. 8vo. **86 A**

PATERSON, JAMES.

A Compendium of English and Scotch law. Edinburgh, 1860. 8vo. **55 F**

Fishery laws of the United Kingdom. 2nd ed. 1873. 8vo. **52 H**

Game laws of the United Kingdom. 1861. 12mo. **168 F**

The intoxicating liquor licensing acts 1872, 1874. 3rd ed. 1874. 12mo. **172 A**

The same. 7th ed. 1889. 12mo. **12 C**

Notes on the law of master and servant. 1885. 8vo. **10 H**

PATERSON, NOEL HUNTINGDON.

A Manual of the usages of the Stock Exchange and of the law affecting the same. 1870. 12mo. **176 D**

PATON, THOMAS.

Law and practice in appeals from Scotland to the House of Lords. Edinburgh, 1858. 8vo. **55 G**

PATON, THOMAS S.

Reports of cases decided in the House of Lords upon appeal from Scotland, 1726 to 1821. 6 vols. Edinburgh, 1849-56. 8vo. **15 A**

PATRICK, St.

The tripartite life of S. Patrick ; with other documents relating
to that saint. Edited by Whitley Stokes. 2 vols. 1887.
8vo.   ·   **102 I**

PATTISON, Margaret Amanda.

The emigrant's vade mecum, or guide to the 'price grant' in
Venezuelan Guyana. 1868. 8vo.   **84 A**

PAUL, John.

Every landlord or tenant his own lawyer ; or, the whole law
respecting landlords, tenants, and lodgers. 4th ed. by
George Wilson. 1778. 12mo.   **170 D**
The same. 7th ed. by George Wilson. 1791. 12mo. **170 D**
The Parish officer's complete guide. 2nd ed. 1774. 8vo.
173 B

PAUL, St.

A Paraphrase and notes on the epistles of St. Paul to the
Galatians, Corinthians, Romans, Ephesians. With an Essay
for the understanding of St. Paul's epistles by consulting St.
Paul himself. See Locke's Works, vol. 8, 1823. 8vo. **78 F**
See also HEBREWS.

PAVING.

The law and practice as to paving of private streets. By
W. Spinks. 1887. 8vo.   **11 G**

PAVITT, Arthur.

Le Droit Anglais codifié. Paris, 1885. 8vo.   **166 F**

PAWN.

Contract of Pawn. By F. Turner. 2nd ed. 1883. 8vo. **11 B**
Pawnbrokers', factors', and merchants' guide to the law of
loans and pledges. By H. C. Folkard. 1873. 8vo. **53 C**
The law concerning Pawn-Brokers and Usurers. 2nd ed. 1775.
12mo.   **173 E**

PEACE, Maskell William.

The Coal Mines regulation act, 1872. 1872. 12mo. **172 F**
The Coal Mines regulation act, 1887, and the Truck acts,
1831 and 1887. 1888. 8vo.   **9 C**

PEACHEY, James Pearse.
The law of marriage and other family settlements. 1860.
8vo.   53 H

PEACOCK, Robert.
Rules and orders of the Court of Common Pleas from 1654 to
1811. 1811. 8vo.   162 G

PEAK OF DERBYSHIRE.
A Handbook to the Peak of Derbyshire. By W. H. Robert-
son. 1854. 12mo.   87 A
The history of Buxton and visitor's guide to the curiosities of
the Peak. By A. Jewitt. 1811. 8vo.   87 A
The natural history of Lancashire, Cheshire, and the Peak.
By Charles Leigh. Oxford, 1700. folió.   89 G
See also Adam, W. and Derbyshire, Mineralogy of.

PEAKE, Thomas.
Cases determined at Nisi Prius in the Court of King's Bench,
1790–1812. 3rd ed. 2 vols. 1820–29. 8vo.   8 F
Compendium of law of Evidence. 1801. 8vo.   167 F
The same. 2nd ed. 1804, and 3rd ed. 1808. 8vo.   167 F

PEARCE, Robert Rouviere.
A Guide to the Inns of Court and Chancery ; with notices of
their ancient discipline, rules, orders, and customs, readings,
masques, and entertainments. 1855. 8vo.   91 D

PEARSON, Anthony.
The great case of Tithes truly stated, clearly open'd, and fully
resolv'd. 1732. 12mo.   176 E

PEARSON-GEE, Arthur Beilby.
The new Factors' act annotated. 1890. 8vo.   10 A

PECK, Rev. Francis.
Academia tertia Anglicana ; or, the antiquarian annals of
Stanford in Lincoln, Rutland, and Northampton shires.
1727. folio.   89 G

PECK, WILLIAM.
A Topographical account of the Isle of Axholme. Vol. I.
[All published.] Doncaster, 1815. 4to. 90 G
A Topographical history of Bawtry and Thorne. With a
supplement. Doncaster, 1813–14. 4to. 94 C

PECKHAM, JOANNES DE.
Registrum epistolarum. Edited by C. T. Martin. 3 vols.
1882–86. 8vo. 102 G

PECKWELL, ROBERT HENRY.
Cases of controverted elections, 1802–1806. 2 vols. 1805–6.
8vo. 66 B

PECOCK, REGINALD, BISHOP OF CHICHESTER.
The repressor of over much blaming of the clergy. Edited
by C. Babington. 2 vols. 1860. 8vo. 101 D

PEDIGREES.
The genealogist's guide to printed pedigrees. By G. W.
Marshall. 1879. 8vo. 124 H
Royal descents and pedigrees of founders' kin. By Sir J. B.
Burke. 1864. 8vo. 125 E
See also GENEALOGY.

PEEK, FRANCIS.
Social wreckage, a review of the laws of England as they
affect the poor. 1883. 12mo. 78 A

PEEL, SIR ROBERT.
Alphabetical arrangement of Mr. Peel's acts. By A Barrister.
1827, and 2nd ed. 1830. 12mo. 165 D
Substance of the speech delivered by R. Peel in the House of
Commons in moving for leave to bring in a bill for the
better recovery of small debts. 1827. [Jacob's Tracts,
vol. 12.] 144 F

PEEL, SYDNEY.
A Concise treatise on the practice and procedure in Chancery
actions. 1878. 8vo. 161 D
The same. 3rd ed. 1883. 8vo. 52 B

PEERAGE CLAIMS.

Peerage Claims and Evidence. 35 vols. folio. **124 I J & 125 I**

Abergavenny. See Berkeley Peerage by tenure, vols. 1 and 3, 1858–62. **124 J**

Airlie. Peerage cases, 3rd series, vol. 1, pp. 1–32 ; and Peerage evidence, vol. 8. **124 I J**

Airth. Peerage evidence, vol. 14. **124 J**

Anglesey. Peerage cases, 3rd series, vol. 1, pp. 33–53 ; and Peerage evidence, vols. 3 and 14. **124 I J**

Annandale. Peerage cases, 3rd series, vol. 1, pp. 54–128 ; and Peerage evidence, vols. 3, 8, 14 and 22. **124 I J & 125 I**

Athenry. Peerage cases, 2nd series, vol. 1, pp. 153–174 ; and Peerage evidence, vol. 3. **124 I J**

Aylesford. Peerage evidence, vol. 23. **125 I**

Balfour of Burleigh. Peerage cases, 3rd series, vol. 1, pp. 129–163. **124 I**

Banbury. Peerage cases, 2nd series, vol. 1, pp. 176–203, 3rd series, vol. 1, pp. 194–261 ; and Peerage evidence, vols. 2 and 8. **124 I J**

Barnewall. Peerage cases, 1st series, pp. 1–8 ; and Peerage evidence, vol. 11. **124 I J**

Beaumont. Peerage cases, 2nd series, vol. 1, pp. 204–227 ; and Peerage evidence, vol. 21. **124 I & 125 I**

Belhaven. Peerage cases, 3rd series, vol. 1, pp. 262–273 ; and Peerage evidence, vol. 24. **124 I & 125 I**

Berners. Peerage cases, 2nd series, vol. 1, pp. 293–295, 3rd series, vol. 1, pp. 274–292 ; and Peerage evidence, vols. 3 and 9. **124 I J**

Borthwick. Peerage cases, 1st series, pp. 9–14 ; 3rd series, vol. 1, pp. 293–304 ; and Peerage evidence, vols. 9 and 11. **124 I J**

Botetourt. Peerage cases, 3rd series, vol. 1, pp. 305–310. **124 I**

Bowes. Peerage cases, 1st series, pp. 15–16 ; and 2nd series, vol. 1, pp. 295–296. **124 I**

Brandon. Peerage cases, 1st series, pp. 33–36 ; and Peerage evidence, vol. 3, pp. 50–57. **124 I J**

Braye. Peerage cases, 2nd series, vol. 1, pp. 297–360 ; and Peerage evidence, vols. 5, 11 and 14. **124 I J**

Broke. Peerage evidence, vol. 3, pp. 40–46. **124 J**

Buchan. Peerage cases, 2nd series, vol. 1, pp. 361–363. **124 I**

Buckhurst. Peerage evidence, vol. 24. **125 I**

Buttevant. Peerage evidence, vol. 9. **124 J**

Camoys. Peerage cases, 2nd series, vol. 1, pp. 364–467 ; and Peerage evidence, vol. 15. **124 I J**

Cassillis. Peerage cases, 1st series, pp. 37–48. **124 I**

Chandos. Peerage cases, 2nd series, vol. 1, pp. 468–470, 3rd series, vol. 1, pp. 311–352 ; and Peerage evidence, vol. 11. **124 I J**

Chesterfield. Peerage evidence, vol. 24. **125 I**

Clifford. Peerage cases, 1st series, pp. 49–51. **124 I**

Clinton. Peerage cases, 3rd series, vol. 1, pp. 353–363. **124 I**

Crawfurd. Peerage cases, 2nd series, vol. 2, pp. 1–483 ; 3rd series, vol. 1, pp. 364–375 ; and Peerage evidence, vol. 16. **124 I & 125 I**

De Balrath. Peerage cases, 3rd series, vol. 1, pp. 376–397. **124 I**

PEERAGE CLAIMS—*continued.*

PEERAGE CLAIMS—*continued.*

Townshend. Peerage evidence, vol. 21.   **125 I**

Tracy. Peerage cases, 2nd series, vol. 3, pp. 466-524.   **124 I**

Vaux. Peerage cases, 2nd series, vol. 3, pp. 525-569 ; and Peerage evidence, vol. 7.   **124 I J**

Wharton. Peerage cases, 1st series, pp. 416-542 ; 2nd series, vol. 3, pp. 570-628 ; and Peerage evidence, vol. 13.   **124 I J**

Wigtoun. Peerage cases, 1st series, pp. 543-563 ; and 3rd series, vol. 4, pp. 505-516.   **124 I**

Willoughby of Parham. Peerage cases, 3rd series, vol. 4, pp. 517-519 ; and Peerage evidence, vol. 3, pp. 58-63.   **124 I**

Zouche. Peerage cases, 3rd series, vol. 4, p. 520 ; and Peerage evidence, vol. 13.   **124 I J**

PEERAGE, THE.

Considerations concerning the bill now depending in Parliament, relating to the Peerage of Great Britain. 1719. [Grimaldi's Tracts, vol. 2.]   **118 B**

The evidence of Succession to real and personal property and peerages. By John Hubback. 1844. 8vo.   **53 H**

An Inquiry into the manner of creating peers. [By Richard West.] 2nd ed. 1719. 8vo.   **49 C**

The limitation of the Peerage, the security of the liberties of people of England. 1720. [Grimaldi's Tracts, vol. 2.]   **118 B**

The Old Whig. Numbers 1 and 2. On the state of the peerage, with remarks upon the Plebeian. [By Joseph Addison.] 1720. [Grimaldi's Tracts, vol. 2.]   **118 B**

Peerages by tenure. See Berkeley peerage by tenure, 3 vols. 1858-62. folio.   **124 J**

The Plebeians. By a Member of the House of Commons [Mr. Auditor Benson]. 6th ed. 1719. [Grimaldi's Tracts, vol. 2.]   **118 B**

The priviledges of the baronage of England. By John Selden. 1689. See H. Scobell's Remembrances, 1689. 12mo.   **48 C**

Reports from the Lords Committees touching the dignity of a Peer of the Realm. 5 vols. 1829. folio.   **153 D**

Some reflections upon a pamphlet called The Old Whig. [By Sir Robert Walpole.] 1719. [Grimaldi's Tracts, vol. 2.]   **118 B**

Stemmata Magnatum. Origin of the titles of some of the English nobility. See S. Pegge's Anecdotes, 1818, pp. 173-200.   **83 H**

See also DIGNITIES and HONOR.

PEERAGES, ENGLISH.

British compendium ; or, a particular account of the present
nobility. Editions 1–12. 21 vols. 1719–69. 12mo. **124 A**

A Catalogue and succession of the kings, princes, dukes,
marquesses, earls, and viscounts of England since Norman
conquest. By R. Brooke. 2nd ed. 1622. folio. **127 J**

Catalogue of honor ; or, treasury of true nobility peculiar and
proper to the Isle of Great Britaine. By Thomas Milles.
1610. folio. **126 I**

A Catalogue of nobility. 1662. 12mo. **125 A**

Compendium of British peerage. By C. White. 1825. 12mo.
125 A

A Complete English peerage. By Rev. Alexander Jacob.
2 vols. 1766. folio. **125 H**

The Complete English peerage. By Rev. Frederic Barlow.
2nd ed. 2 vols. 1775. 8vo. **126 C**

A Complete history of the English peerage. By William
Guthrie. 2 vols. in 1. 1763. 4to. **127 J**

Debrett's Peerage of England, Scotland, and Ireland. Editions
1 to 20, 43 vols. 1802–34 ; and the editions for 1838, 1840,
1866, 1879, 1882 and 1884 to 1890, 55 vols. 1802–90.
12mo. & 8vo. **124 C–E**

Dod's Peerage, baronetage, and knightage of Great Britain
and Ireland, 1883–1891. 9 vols. 1883–91. 12mo. **127 H**

The English peerage. [By Charles Catton.] 3 vols. 1789–
90. folio. **126 I**

An Exact catalogue of the nobility of England. By Robert
Dale. 1697. 12mo. **123 A**

The extinct peerage of England. By Solomon Bolton. 1769.
8vo. **125 C**

A Genealogical and heraldic dictionary of the peerage and
baronetage of the British Empire. By John Burke. 4th ed.
1832, 9th ed. by J. Burke and J. B. Burke, 1847, and the
editions for 1850, 1854, 1858, 1863, 1864, 1867–1872, 1874–
1890 by J. B. Burke. 30 vols. 1832–90. 8vo. **125 E–G**

A Genealogical history of the dormant, abeyant, forfeited, and
extinct peerages of the British empire. By Sir J. B. Burke.
New ed. 1883. 8vo. **125 E**

A List of the English, Scots, and Irish nobility. By Charles
Whitworth. 1765. 12mo. **125 A**

A New catalogue of the dukes &c. of England, Scotland, and
Ireland. By Thomas Walkly. 1658. 12mo. **125 A**

The new peerage. 3 vols. 1769 ; 2nd ed. 3 vols. 1778, and
3rd ed. 3 vols. 1785. 9 vols. 1769–85. 12mo. **125 A**

PEERAGES, ENGLISH—*continued.*

The peerage, baronetage, and knightage of the British Empire for 1880, 1881, 1882 and 1883. By Joseph Foster. 6 vols. 1880–83. 4to. **124 H**

The peerage of England. 2 vols. 1779. 12mo. **125 A**

Present peerage of the United Kingdom, 1807, 1808, 1810–1821, 1831, 1832, 1834, 1835, 1837–1841, 1843 and 1844. 25 vols. 1807–44. 12mo. Bound with the Imperial & Royal Calendars. **217 & 218**

Sams's Annual peerage of the British empire. Edited by A., E., and M. Innes. 2 vols. 1827. 12mo. **124 F**

Short view of the families of the present English nobility. By T. Salmon. 3rd ed. 1761. 12mo. **123 A**

A Synopsis of the peerage of England. By Sir N. H. Nicolas, revised by Wm. Courthope. 1857. 8vo. **124 F**

See ALMON, J., BANKS, T. C., CLARK, H., COLLINS, A., DUGDALE, SIR W., EDMONDSON, J., FIELDING, J., KEARSLEY, G., KIMBER, E., LODGE, E., LONGMATE, B., PLAYFAIR, W. and POLLARD, R.

See also DIGNITIES and HONOR.

PEERAGES, IRISH.

The Irish compendium ; or, rudiments of honour, 1st ed. 1722, 2nd ed. 1727, 3rd ed. 1735, 4th ed. 1745, and 5th ed. 1756. 5 vols. 1722–56. 12mo. **124 B**

Peerage of Ireland. By E. Kimber. 1768. 12mo. **124 B**

Peerage of Ireland. By J. Almon. 2 vols. 1768. 8vo. **124 F**

The peerage of Ireland. By John Lodge. 4 vols. 1754. 8vo. **124 F**

The same. Continued by Mervyn Archdall. 7 vols. Dublin, 1789. 8vo. **124 F**

A Short view of the families of the present Irish nobility. By Thomas Salmon. 1759. 12mo. **123 A**

See also PEERAGES, ENGLISH.

PEERAGES, SCOTTISH.

The nature and descent of ancient peerages connected with the state of Scotland. By George Wallace. 2nd ed. Edinburgh, 1785. 8vo. **124 F**

Notes on dignities in the peerage of Scotland which are dormant, or which have been forfeited. By W. O. Hewlett. 1882. 8vo. **124 H**

Peerage of Scotland. By E. Kimber. 1767. 12mo. **124 B**

PEERAGES, Scottish—*continued*.

The peerage of Scotland. By George Crawfurd. Edinburgh, 1716. folio.   **127 J**

Thoughts on the disqualifications of the eldest sons of the peers of Scotland to sit from that country in parliament By Alexander, Lord Saltoun. 2nd ed. 1789. 8vo. **124 F**

Rudiments of honour; or, the Scots compendium. Editions 1–8. 9 vols. 1720–1826. 12mo.   **125 A**

See also Douglas, Sir R. and Peerages, English.

PEERE WILLIAMS, William.

Reports of cases in the court of Chancery, and of some special cases adjudged in the Court of King's Bench, 1695 to 1735. Published with notes and references by his son, W. Peere Williams. 3 vols. 1740–49. folio.

The same. 4th ed. with additional references to proceedings in the Court, and to later cases, by S. C. Cox. 3 vols. 1787. 8vo.

The same. 5th ed. 3 vols. 1793. 8vo.

The same. 6th ed. with additional references. By J. B. Monro, W. L. Lowndes and J. Randall. 3 vols. 1826. 8vo.   **3 C**

PEGGE, Samuel.

Anonymiana ; or, ten centuries of observations on various authors and subjects. Compiled by a late very learned and reverend divine [Samuel Pegge]. 2nd ed. 1818. 8vo. **83 H**

Curialia Miscellanea ; or, anecdotes of old times, regal, noble, gentilitial, and miscellaneous. 1818. 8vo.   **83 H**

Curialia ; or, an historical account of some branches of the royal household, and A memoir regarding the King's honourable band of gentlemen pensioners. 1784. 4to. **83 J**

PEILE, Clarence John.

The law and practice of Discovery in the supreme court of justice. 1883. 8vo.   **52 F**

PEMBERTON, Loftus Leigh.

The Judgments and Orders of the court of appeal and high court of justice, chiefly in reference to actions assigned to the Chancery division. 1876. 8vo.   **169 E**

The same. 2nd ed. 1876, and 3rd ed. 1882. 8vo.   **169 E**

The same. 4th ed. 1889. 8vo.   **12 F**

PEMBERTON, Loftus Leigh—*continued.*
The practice in equity by way of Revivor and Supplement.
1867. 8vo. 53 F

PEMBROKESHIRE.
Historical tour through Pembrokeshire. By Richard Fenton.
1811. 4to. 94 D

PENDLETON, John.
History of Derbyshire. 1886. 8vo. 87 B

PENFOLD, Charles.
The justice of rating railway companies to the relief of the
poor considered. 1849. [Pamphlets, vol. 6.] 144 A
The principle of Rating railway, gas, water, and other com-
panies, land, tithes, buildings, and other properties liable to
be assessed towards the relief of the poor. 6th ed. by J. T.
Kershaw and W. Marshall. 1870. 8vo. 175 B
The same. 7th ed. by A. Glen. 1884. 8vo. 53 F

PENINSULAR WAR.
Annals of the Peninsular campaigns from 1808 to 1814. By
the author of 'Cyril Thornton' [Thomas Hamilton]. 3 vols.
1829. 12mo. 114 C
History of the war in the Peninsula and in the South of France.
By Sir W. F. P. Napier. 6 vols. 1832–40. 8vo. 114 C D
See also WELLINGTON, Arthur, 1 Duke of.

PENNANT, Thomas.
History of parishes of Whiteford and Holywell. 1796. 4to. 95 G
The journey from Chester to London. 1811. 8vo. 86 E
Life of T. Pennant. See J. P. Malcolm's Lives of Topographers
and Antiquaries. 1815. 4to. 79 H
Some account of London. 3rd ed. 1793. 4to. 89 F

PENNSYLVANIA.
The charters of the province of Pensilvania and city of Philadelphia, 1742. Philadelphia, 1742. folio. 156 C

PENNY, George.
Traditions of Perth during the last century. Perth, 1836.
8vo. 95 C

PEPYS, SAMUEL.

Diary and correspondence, with a life and notes by Richard, Lord Braybrooke. Deciphered, with additional notes, by Rev. Mynors Bright. 6 vols. 1875–79. 8vo.　　116 F

PERIODICALS.

An Index to legal periodical literature. By Leonard A. Jones. Boston, 1888. 8vo.　　82 F

An Index to periodical literature. By W. F. Poole. 3rd ed. brought down to January 1882, and the first Supplement, Jan. 1, 1882, to Jan. 1, 1887. 2 vols. 1882–88. 8vo. 82 F

An Index to the leading British reviews and magazines for 1882, 1883 and 1884. By W. M. Griswold. 1885. 8vo. 82 F

Bentley's Miscellany, vols. 43–64. 20 vols. 1858–68. 8vo. [vols. 45 and 50 missing.]　　254 A B

Blackwood's Edinburgh Magazine, April 1817 to Dec. 1890. 148 vols. 1817–90, and General Index to vols. 1 to 50. 1855. 8vo.　　250 & 251 A B

The British Critic, a new review, May 1793 to Dec. 1813. 42 vols. 1793–1813. 8vo.　　252 E–G

Fraser's Magazine. vols. 7 & 8, 1833. 2 vols. 1833. 8vo. [containing portraits of literary characters.]　　254 E

See also CONTEMPORARY REVIEW, FORTNIGHTLY REVIEW, and other leading reviews and magazines.

PERJURY.

Case on the effect of the King's pardon of perjury. See Hargrave's Juridical Arguments, vol. 2, 1799, pp. 221–271.
　　144 G

PERKINS, JOHN.

A Profitable booke, treating of the lawes of England. 1576. 12mo. Bound with Littleton's Tenures, 1577.　　49 A

The same, 1586, 1642, and 1657. 12mo.　　49 A

The same. 14th ed. 1757. 12mo.　　49 A

PERKS, WALTER.

The deeds of arrangement act 1887 (50 & 51 Vict. c. 57). 1888. 8vo.　　12 I

PERPETUITIES.

The rule against perpetuities. By R. G. Marsden. 1883. 8vo.　　10 G

PERPETUITIES—*continued.*

The law of perpetuity. By W. D. Lewis. 1843, and Supplement. 1849. 8vo. **53 C**

PERRAULT, CHARLES.

Les hommes illustres qui ont paru en France pendant ce siecle avec leurs portraits au naturel. 2 vols. Paris, 1696–1700 folio. **79 I**

PERRY, HENRY JAMES and J. W. KNAPP.

Cases of controverted elections in the eleventh parliament of the United Kingdom. 1833. 8vo. **66 B**

PERRY, JOHN.

An account of the stopping of Daggenham Breach ; containing also proposals for rendering the ports of Dover and Dublin commodious for entertaining large ships. 1721. 8vo. **87 E**

PERRY, SIR THOMAS ERSKINE.

Cases illustrative of oriental life, and application of English law to India, decided in H.M. supreme court at Bombay, [1841–1852.] 1853. 8vo. **38 C**

PERRY, THOMAS ERSKINE and HENRY DAVISON.

Reports of cases in the Court of Queen's Bench and Exchequer Chamber, 1838–1841. 4 vols. 1839–42. 8vo. **5 E**

PERRY'S GAZETTE.

Perry's Bankrupt monthly gazette, 1826–1887. 62 vols. 1826–87. 12mo. **75 A–E**

Perry's Bankrupt weekly gazette, vols. 61–63, 1888–1890. 3 vols. 1888–90. 4to. **75 E**

PERSONAL PROPERTY.

The student's guide to the law of real and personal property. By J. Indermaur and C. Thwaites. 2nd ed. 1889. 8vo. **64 E**

Law of Sale of Personal Property. By J. P. Benjamin. 4th ed. by A. B. Pearson-Gee and H. F. Boyd. 1888. 8vo. **11 C**

Principles of the law of Personal Property. By Joshua Williams. 13th ed. 1887. 8vo. **64 F**

Modern law of Personal Property. By L. A. Goodeve. 1887. 8vo. **64 F**

PERSONAL PROPERTY—*continued.*

A Compendium of the law of real and personal property. By J. W. Smith. 6th ed. by the Author and J. Trustram. 2 vols. 1884. 8vo.   11 C

A Concise abridgment of the law of Personal Property. By J. A. Shearwood. 1882. 8vo.   64 E

Law relating to wills of personal property. By J. C. H. Flood. 1877. 8vo.   13 I

Law of warranties and representations upon the sale of personal chattels. By T. W. Saunders. 1874. 12mo. 11 I

See also HILLIARD, F., HUBBACK, J., LANGDELL, C. C., LONG, G. and STORY, W. W.

PERTH.

Traditions of Perth during the last century. By George Penny. Perth, 1836. 8vo.   95 C

PERTH, JAMES, 4 EARL OF.

Letters from James Earl of Perth, to his sister, the Countess of Errol, and other members of his family. Edited by Wm. Jerdan. [Camden Society, vol. 33.] 1845. 8vo.   85 A

PERU.

History of the conquest of Peru. By W. H. Prescott. 6th ed. 2 vols. 1850. 8vo.   113 C

Narrative of a journey from Lima to Para across the Andes and down the Amazon. By W. Smyth and F. Lowe. 1836. 8vo.   84 E

PESHALL, REV. SIR JOHN.

The antient and present state of the city of Oxford. By Anthony à Wood, with additions by the Rev. Sir J. Peshall. 1773. 4to.   92 F

PESNELLE, MONSIEUR.

Coutume de Normandie. 3me éd. par M. Roupnel. Rouen 1759. 4to.   40 B

PETER, APSLEY PETRE.

Analysis and digest of the decisions of Sir George Jessel, late Master of the Rolls, 1873–1883. 1883. 8vo.   3 C

PETERBOROUGH.
Chronicon Petroburgense. Nunc primum typis mandatum,
curante Thomâ Stapleton. [Camden Society, vol. 47.]
1849. 8vo. **85 B**

PETERS, RICHARD.
Public statutes at large of United States of America, 1789–
1845. 8 vols. Boston, 1861–62. 8vo. **32 B**
Reports of decisions in the Supreme court of the United States,
1828 to 1842. 16 vols. in 8. See B. R. Curtis's Reports,
vols. 7–14. Boston, 1855. 8vo. **57 B**

PETERSDORFF, CHARLES.
Abridgment of cases in the courts of King's Bench, Common
Pleas, Exchequer, and at Nisi Prius, from 1660 to 1823.
15 vols. 1825–30. 8vo. **63 A**
Practical and elementary abridgment of the Common Law,
1824–1840. 5 vols. 1841–44. 8vo. **63 A**
Concise practical abridgement of the Common and Statute
Law. 2nd ed. 6 vols. 1861–64, and Supplement, 1863–
1870. 1870. 7 vols. 1861–70. 8vo. **14 C**
The same. Another copy. **63 A B**
Law students' and practitioners' commonplace book of law
and equity. By A Barrister. [C. Petersdorff.] 1871. 8vo.
14 C
Lectures on theory and practice of the laws of England delivered
at Lyon's Inn hall in 1828 and 1829. Vol. 1, containing
the first course. 1829. 8vo. **170 G**
A Practical compendium of the law of Master and Servant.
1876. 12mo. **172 D**
Practical precedents in Pleading. 1835. 8vo. **173 G**

PETGRAVE, EZEKIEL CHARLES.
A Code of the law of Principal and Agent, with a preface.
1876. [Pamphlets, vol. 29.] **144 B**
Manual of law of Principal and Agent. 1857. 12mo. **174 C**

PETHERAM, WILLIAM COMER.
The law and practice relating to discovery by Interrogatories
under Common law procedure act 1854. 1864. 12mo. **169 C**

PETITION OF RIGHT.
Law and practice of petition of right. By Walter Clode.
1887. 8vo. **11 C**

PETITIONS IN CHANCERY AND LUNACY.
Law and practice relating to Petitions in Chancery and
Lunacy. By S. E. Williams. 1880. 8vo.   **11 C**

PETRARCA, Francesco.
Mémoires pour la vie de François Pétrarque, tirés de ses
œuvres et des auteurs contemporains. [Par l'abbé de Sade.]
3 vols. Amsterdam, 1764–67. 4to.   **81 F**

PETRIE, Henry.
Magni Rotuli Scaccarii Normanniæ de anno MCLXXXIIII,
Willielmo filio Radulfi senescallo, quæ extant. [By Henry
Petrie.] 1830. 4to.   **103 F**

Monumenta historica Britannica ; or, materials for the history
of Britain from the earliest period. Vol. I, extending to
the Norman conquest. By H. Petrie and Rev. J. Sharpe;
completed by T. D. Hardy. 1848. folio.   **99 B**

PETRIE, Samuel.
Report of the Cricklade case ; comprehending proceedings in
courts of law, before select committee of Commons and in
both Houses of Parliament. 1785. 8vo.   **66 B**

PETTUS, Sir John.
Fodinæ Regales ; or, the history, laws, and places of the chief
mines and mineral works in England, Wales, and the
English pale in Ireland, as also of the Mint and Money.
1670. 4to.   **85 I**

PETTY BAG OFFICE.
Forms of writs and other proceedings on the common law side
of the Court of Chancery issuing out of the Petty Bag office.
By F. G. Abbott. 1849. 12mo.   **161 E**

PETTY SESSIONS.
Guide to the law and practice of petty sessions. By E. T.
Ayers. 1884. 8vo.   **12 B**

Stone's Practice for justices of the peace at petty and special
sessions. 9th ed. by W. H. Macnamara. 1882. 8vo.   **12 B**

[PETYT, George.]
Lex Parliamentaria : or, a treatise of the law and custom of
the Parliaments of England. By G. P., Esq. 1690. 12mo.
   48 C

PETYT, WILLIAM.

The antient right of the Commons of England asserted. 1680.
12mo. 48 C

Miscellanea Parliamentaria : containing presidents 1. Of
freedom from arrests. 2. Of censures. 1680. 12mo. 48 C

See also BRADY, R.

PEWS.

History and law of church seats, or pews. By A. Heales.
2 vols. 1872. 8vo. 53 B

Law of Pews in churches and chapels. By G. H. H. Oliphant.
1853. 12mo. 173 E

Laws respecting Pews, or seats in churches. By H. S. English.
1826. 8vo. 173 E

See also ECCLESIASTICAL LAW.

PHEAR, JOHN BUDD.

A Treatise on rights of water. 1859. 8vo. 53 I

PHILIPOTT, THOMAS.

Villare Cantianum ; or, Kent surveyed and illustrated ; with
an historical catalogue of the high sheriffs of Kent, collected
by John Philipott. 1659. 4to. 88 E

PHILIPPART, SIR JOHN.

General index to the first and second series of Hansard's
Parliamentary Debates, 1803–1830. 1834. 8vo. 112 I

PHILIPPS, HENRY.

Treatise enumerating the most illustrious families of England
who have been raised to honour and wealth by the profession of the law. 1686. 12mo. 49 D

PHILIPPS, JOHN.

Titles and honours conferred by King George I. and his
present Majesty in Great Britain and Ireland. 1728.
[Grimaldi's Tracts, vol. 1.] 8vo. 118 B

PHILIPPS, JOHN, BARRISTER-AT-LAW.

Election cases determined by committees of the House of
Commons, 1780–1781. 1782. 8vo. 66 B

PHILIPPS, WILLIAM.

Studii legalis ratio ; or, directions for the study of the law.
2nd ed. 1675. 12mo. 48 A

PHILIPS, JOSEPH.
Letters on Special Pleading, an introduction to the study of that branch of the law. 2nd ed. 1850. 12mo. **173 G**

PHILLIMORE, JOSEPH.
Reports of cases in the Arches and Prerogative Courts of Canterbury, containing the judgments of Sir G. Lee, 1752–1758. 2 vols. 1833–32. 8vo. **8 H**
Reports of cases in the Ecclesiastical Courts, 1809–1821. 3 vols. 1818–27. 8vo. **8 H**

PHILLIMORE, SIR ROBERT JOSEPH.
Commentaries upon international law. 4 vols. 1854–61, and 2nd ed. 4 vols. 1871–74. 8vo. **169 C**
The same. 3rd ed. 4 vols. 1879–89. 8vo. **55 B**
Ecclesiastical law of the Church of England. 2 vols. 1873, and Supplement 1876. 8vo. **9 C**
Judgment delivered by Sir Robert Phillimore in the cases of Martin *v.* Mackonochie and Flamank *v.* Simpson. By W. G. F. Phillimore. 1868. 8vo. **51 G**
The law of Domicil. 1847. 8vo. **52 F**

PHILLIMORE, WILLIAM PHILLIMORE WATTS.
The Dictionary of Medical Specialists. 1889. 12mo. **Hall**
How to write the history of a family, a guide for the genealogist. 1887. 8vo. **124 G**
The Index Library. 5 vols. 1888–90. 8vo. **124 H**

> 1. A Calendar of wills relating to the counties of Northampton and Rutland, 1510–1652. 1888. 8vo.
> 2, 5. A Calendar of Chancery proceedings in the reign of Charles I. 2 vols. 1889–90. 8vo.
> 3. Index nominum to the Royalist Composition Papers, first and second series. A to F. 1889. 8vo.
> 4. An Index to Signet Bills, 1584 to 1596, and 1603 to 1624, with a calendar of Writs of Privy Seal. 1890. 8vo.

PHILLIPPS, CHARLES SPENCER MARCH.
Jurisprudence. 1863. 8vo. **63 F**

PHILLIPPS, SAMUEL MARCH.
A Treatise on the law of Evidence. 1814. 12mo. **167 F**
The same, 9th ed. 2 vols. 1843. 8vo. **167 G**

PHILLIPS, Charles.
Recollections of Curran and some of his contemporaries. 2nd
ed. 1822. 8vo.   **79 G**

PHILLIPS, Charles Palmer.
The law concerning idiots, lunatics, and persons of unsound
mind. 1858. 8vo.   **172 B**
The law of Copyright in works of literature and art. 1863.
8vo.   **164 G**

PHILLIPS, Edward.
The new world of words ; or, a general English dictionary.
4th ed. 1678. folio.   **123 G**
The reign of Charles I. and the first thirteen years of Charles II.
See Sir R. Baker's Chronicle. 1684. folio.   **114 G**

PHILLIPS, George.
Du droit ecclésiastique dans ses sources, considérées au point
de vue des éléments législatifs qui les constituent. Traduit
par l'Abbé Crouzet. Paris, 1852. 8vo.   **77 C**
Versuch einer Darstellung der Geschichte des Angelsächsischen
Rechts. Göttingen, 1825. 8vo.   **55 C**

PHILLIPS, John.
General history of Europe contained in the historical and
political Monthly Mercuries 1688 to 1699. 10 vols. 1692–
99. 8vo.   **116 A**

PHILLIPS, John, Surveyor.
General history of inland navigation, containing a complete
account of the canals in England. 5th ed. 1809. 8vo. **84 B**

PHILLIPS, Samuel.
Guide to the Crystal Palace. 2nd ed. 1854. 12mo.   **93 C**

PHILLIPS, Thomas.
The history and antiquities of Shrewsbury ; with an appendix
containing several particulars relative to castles, monasteries,
&c. in Shropshire. Shrewsbury, 1779. 8vo.   **93 B**

PHILLIPS, Thomas Jodrell.
Reports of cases in the Court of Chancery, 1841–1849. 2 vols.
1847–49. 8vo.   **3 D**

PHILLIPS, WILLARD.
Treatise on the law of Insurance. 5th ed. 2 vols. New York,
1867. 8vo. 59 F

PHILOSOPHY.
An Account of Sir Isaac Newton's philosophical discoveries.
By Colin Maclaurin. 1748. 4to. 78 G
A Compendium of principles in philosophy and divinity. By
John Vizard. 1836. 12mo. 77 A
A Dissertation exhibiting a general view of the progress of
Metaphysical and Ethical Philosophy. By Dugald Stewart
and Sir James Mackintosh. See Encyclopædia Britannica,
8th ed., vol. 1, pp. 1–445. 147 A
Essays in Jurisprudence and Ethics. By Frederick Pollock.
1882. 8vo. 63 F
Essays on philosophical subjects. By Adam Smith. 1795.
4to. 78 G
Joh. Gottl. Heineccii Elementa Philosophiæ rationalis et
moralis, præmissa est Historia Philosophica. Editio quinta.
Genevæ, 1744. See Heineccii Opera, vol. 1. 47 G
M. T. Ciceronis Opera Philosophica. See Delphin Classics,
vols. 138, 139 and 140. 1830. 8vo. 46 J
The philosophical works of Robert Boyle. By Peter Shaw.
3 vols. 1725. 8vo. 78 F
The works of Francis Bacon. New ed. by Basil Montagu.
16 vols. 1825–34. 8vo. 78 E
The works of J. Locke. New ed. 10 vols. 1823. 8vo. 78 F
See also CLARKE, S. and GUTHRIE, M.

PHILPOT, JOHN.
The examinations and writings of John Philpot, archdeacon
of Winchester, martyr 1555. Edited by Rev. Robert Eden.
Cambridge, 1842. 8vo. 77 D

PHIPPEN, WILLIAM.
Practical advice to Testators and Executors. 6th ed. 1882.
12mo. 176 E
The same. 7th ed. 1886. 12mo. 13 I

PHRENOLOGY AND PHYSIOGNOMY.
Manual of Phrenology. [By James De Ville.] New ed. 1832.
12mo. 78 C

PHRENOLOGY AND PHYSIOGNOMY—*continued.*
Phrenological theory of treatment of criminals defended. By
M. B. Sampson. 1843. [Pamphlets, vol. 18.] 144 B
Phrenology ; or, the doctrine of the mind. By G. Spurzheim.
3rd ed. 1825. 8vo. 78 C
The Propensitorial Zodiac ; or, psychoneurology of the mental
faculties. By R. T. Stothard. 1870. 8vo. 78 C
A View of the philosophical principles of phrenology. By
G. Spurzheim. 3rd ed. [n.d.] 8vo. 78 C

PHYSICIANS, ROYAL COLLEGE OF.
Catalogue of fellows and licentiates of the Royal College of
Physicians 1833, 1835, 1872. 3 vols. 1833–72. 8vo. 146 C
See also GOODALL, C.

PHYSIOLOGY.
Animal and vegetable physiology considered with reference
to natural theology. By P. M. Roget. 2nd ed. 2 vols.
1834. 8vo. 77 B

PICKERING, EDWARD ROWLAND.
Popery, the Inquisition and the Jesuits, historical facts ex-
posing their profligate and dangerous tenets. [By E. R.
Pickering.] 1851. 12mo. 77 A
The Society of Staple Inn, Inns of Court, &c. and Chancery
and historical memoranda. By E. R. P. 1853, and
Another ed. [1859.] 8vo. 91 D

PICKERING, PERCIVAL ANDRÉ.
Remarks on a report from a select committee of the late
House of Commons on the publication of printed papers.
2nd ed. 1838. [Pamphlets, vol. 28.] 144 B
Remarks on Treating and other matters relating to the election
of members of parliament. 1849. 8vo. 166 D

PICTON, JAMES ALLANSON.
Memorials of Liverpool, historical and topographical. 2 vols.
1873. 8vo. 89 B

PICTURES.
Alexandra Palace. Catalogue of the exhibition of pictures,
drawings, and engravings, illustrative of British field sports.
By J. Grego. 1881. 4to. 78 C

PICTURES—*continued.*

The Hamilton Palace collection. Illustrated priced catalogue.
1882. 4to.   **118 I**

See also PAINTERS and PLANTS.

PIEROTTI, ERMETE.

Jerusalem explored, being a description of the ancient and
modern city. Translated by T. G. Bonney. Vol. 1, text;
vol. 2, plates. 2 vols. 1864. folio.   **77 H**

PIGGOTT, FRANCIS TAYLOR.

Foreign Judgments. [Part I.] Their effect in the English
courts. Part II. The effect of an English judgment abroad.
Service on absent defendants. 2 vols. 1879–81. 8vo. **169 E**

The same. 2nd ed. with chapters on the laws of the British
colonies, European and Asiatic nations, and the states and
republics of America. 1884. 8vo.   **10 D**

Principles of the law of Torts. 1885. 8vo.   **11 H**

PIGOT, GEORGE, 1 BARON.

Copies of papers relative to the arrest of Lord Pigot. 7 vols.
1777–79. 4to.   **38 A**

Defence of Lord Pigot. 2nd ed. 1778. 4to.   **38 A**

Original papers, with an authentic state of the proofs and
proceedings before the coroner's inquest assembled at
Madras upon the death of Lord Pigot on the 11th day of
May 1777. 1778. 4to.   **38 A**

PIGOTT, GILLERY and HUNTER RODWELL.

Reports of cases in the court of Common Pleas on appeal
from decisions of revising barristers, 1843–1845. 1846.
8vo.   **6 I**

PIGOTT, NATHANIEL.

Treatise of Common Recoveries. 1739. 12mo.   **175 C**

The same. 2nd ed. by a Serjeant at law [G. Wilson]. 1770.
8vo.   **175 C**

PIKE, WILLIAM PATRICKSON.

Practical precedents in civil bill process. Dublin, 1843,
and 2nd ed. Dublin, 1851. 12mo.   **55 E**

Practice of the court of record of the borough of Dublin.
Dublin, 1842. 12mo.   **55 E**

PILKINGTON, Right Rev. James.
Works. Edited by Rev. J. Scholefield. Cambridge, 1842.
8vo. 77 D

PILKINGTON, James.
View of the present state of Derbyshire; with an account of
its most remarkable antiquities. 2nd ed. 2 vols. 1803.
8vo. 87 A

PILKINGTON, Matthew.
General dictionary of painters, containing memoirs of the
most eminent professors of the art of painting from the
year 1250. New ed. 2 vols. 1824. 4to. 79 H

PILOTAGE.
The law of salvage, towage, and pilotage. By H. Newson.
1886. 8vo. 11 E

PINDAR.
Odes of Pindar. Translated from the Greek by Gilbert West.
1749. 4to. 83 J

PINKETT, Francis Frederick.
Numerical and alphabetical index of the ordinances of Sierra
Leone. 1887. folio. 37 D

PINKS, William John.
The history of Clerkenwell; with additions by the editor,
E. J. Wood. 2nd ed. 1881. 8vo. 89 E

PINTO, Antonio Joaquim de Gouvea.
Tratado regular e pratico de testamentos e successões.
Segunda edição. Lisboa, 1820. 8vo. 39 B

PIPON, James Kennard and J. F. COLLIER.
Manual of military law for all ranks of the army, militia and
volunteer services. 3rd ed. 1863. 12mo. 172 F

PIRY, A. Théophile.
Le Saint Edit, étude de littérature Chinoise. Shanghai, 1879.
4to. 83 I

PITT, RIGHT HON. WILLIAM.
Examination of Mr. Pitt's speech in the House of Commons, on Feb. 12, 1796, relative to the condition of the poor. By Rev. John Howlett. 1796. 8vo. **144 G**
Life of William Pitt. By Earl Stanhope. 4 vols. 1861–62. 8vo. **79 B**

PITT-LEWIS, GEORGE.
A Complete practice of the county courts. 2 vols. 1880, and 2nd ed. 2 vols. 1883–84. 8vo. **165 C**
The same. 3rd ed. Vol. I. [All published.] 1887. 8vo. **165 C**
The same. 4th ed. 2 vols. 1890. 8vo. **12 H**

PITT-TAYLOR, FRANK.
The Bankruptcy act 1869 and the Debtors act 1869 ; including the rules, orders, and forms. 1875. 12mo. **160 E**
The same. 2nd ed. 1880. 8vo. **160 E**
The Bankruptcy act 1883 and the Debtors act 1869 illustrated by notes. 1884. 12mo. **64 A**

PIUS IX., POPE OF ROME.
The letters apostolic of Pope Pius IX. considered with reference to the law of England and the law of Europe. By Travers Twiss. 1851. 8vo. **77 B**
See also ROME, CHURCH OF.

PIXLEY, FRANCIS WILLIAM.
Auditors, their duties and responsibilities. 1881. 8vo. **9 A**
The investigation of the accounts of commercial undertakings previous to their conversion into public companies. 1890. 8vo. **52 C**

PLAGUES.
The City remembrancer : being historical narratives of the great plague, at London, 1665 ; with observations and reflections on the plague in general, and historical accounts of the most memorable plagues. 2 vols. 1769. 8vo. **92 B**

PLANTS.
The gallery of Marianne North's paintings of plants and their homes, Royal gardens, Kew. Descriptive catalogue. By W. B. Hemsley. 3rd ed. 1883. 12mo. **93 C**

PLATE.

Hall marks on gold and silver plate. By W. Chaffers. 1863.
8vo. **78 C**

PLATO, THE PHILOSOPHER.

History of the restoration of Platonic theology by the latter
Platonists. See Commentaries of Proclus, vol. 2, 1792,
pp. 211–320. **78 G**

Menexenus, a dialogue of Plato. See G. West's Odes of
Pindar, 1749, pp. 279–315. **83 J**

Remarks on the life and writings of Plato. By Wm. Lowndes.
1827. [Jacob's Tracts, vol. 13.] **144 F**

PLATT, THOMAS.

The law of Covenants. 1829. 8vo. **13 B**

The law of Leases. 2 vols. 1847. 8vo. **13 C**

PLATTES, GABRIEL.

A Discovery of subterranean treasure. 1738. See A Collection of treatises upon metals. 1738. 12mo. **118 A**

PLAYFAIR, JOHN.

A Dissertation exhibiting a general view of the progress of
Mathematical and Physical science, since the revival of
letters in Europe. See Encyclopædia Britannica, 8th ed.
vol. 1, pp. 549–688. **147 A**

PLAYFAIR, WILLIAM.

British family antiquity illustrative of the origin and progress
of the rank, honours, and personal merit of the nobility of
the United Kingdom. 9 vols. in 18. 1809–11. 4to. **126 H I**

PLEADINGS.

Precedents of pleadings in personal actions. By E. Bullen
and S. M. Leake. 4th ed. Part 1 by T. J. Bullen and
C. Dodd. 1882. Part 2 by T. J. Bullen and C. W. Clifford.
1888. 2 vols. 1882–88. 8vo. **12 E**

Law of summary judgment on specially indorsed writ under
order XIV. By C. Cavanagh. 1887. 8vo. **12 E**

A Selection of precedents of Pleading under the Judicature
acts in the Queen's Bench and Chancery divisions. By
J. Cunningham and M. W. Mattinson. 2nd ed. by M. W.
Mattinson and S. C. Macaskie. 1884. 8vo. **12 E**

PLEADINGS—*continued.*

Forms of indorsements of writs of summons, pleadings, and other proceedings in the Queen's Bench division prior to trial. By G. B. Allen and W. B. Allen. 1883. 12mo. **12 E**

The principles of pleading in civil actions. By H. J. Stephen. 7th ed. by F. F. Pinder. 1866. 8vo. **173 G**

A Review of the ancient authorities upon pleading. See Morris and Finlason's Common law procedure act, 1853, pp. 1–216. **161 G**

The uses and abuses of Special Pleading; with suggestions for a change in the forms of procedure in the superior courts. By Wm. Corrie. 1850. [Pamphlets, vol. 21.] **144 B**

Selection of Leading cases on Pleading and parties to actions. By W. F. Finlason. 1847. 8vo. **173 F**

A Practical treatise on Pleading with precedents. By Joseph Chitty. 6th ed. by J. Chitty and T. Chitty. 3 vols. 1836–37. 8vo. **173 F**

The principles, object, and utility of Pleadings, and practice as to Amendments pending trials at Nisi Prius and before sheriffs. By Joseph Chitty. 2nd ed. 1835. 8vo. **173 F**

What is special pleading? A letter to Sir Thomas Denman in answer to this question. By William Theobald. 1832. [Law Tracts, vol. 5.] **144 E**

Pleader's assistant, containing a select collection of precedents of modern pleadings in the courts of King's Bench and Common Pleas, &c. 1786. 12mo. **174 A**

Method of pleading by rule and president. 1697. 12mo. **174 A**

Collection of special rules for Pleading in actions real, personal and mixt. 2nd ed. 1694. 12mo. **48 B**

Liber Placitandi. A book of special Pleadings; containing precedents of pleas in abatement, declarations &c. 1674. folio.

See Bosanquet, S. R., Bowman, E., Chitty, J. Junior, Clayton, J., Cornwall, J., Euer, S., Greening, H., Herne, J., Impey, J., Jervis, Sir J., Petersdorff, C., Philips, J., Robinson, C., Townesend, G., Wentworth, J. and Wilson, G.

See also Criminal Law Practice, Entries and Equity Pleading.

PLEAS OF THE CROWN.

A Treatise of the Pleas of the Crown. By Wm. Hawkins. 8th ed. by John Curwood. 2 vols. 1824. 8vo. **53 C**

PLEAS OF THE CROWN—*continued*.

A Treatise of the pleas of the Crown. By E. H. East. 2 vols.
1803. 8vo.   **53 C**

Britton. Containing the antient Pleas of the Crown. Translated by Robert Kelham. 1762. 8vo.   **53 C**

Fleta, seu commentarius juris Anglicani. Liber primus antiqua
placita coronæ continens. 1735. folio.   **49 G**

See also HALE, SIR M., SELDEN SOCIETY, STAUNDFORD, W.
and TREMAINE, SIR J.

PLEES, W.

An Account of the island of Jersey. Southampton, 1817.
8vo.   **94 F**

PLENER, ERNST EDLER VON.

The English factory legislation. Translated from the German
by F. L. Weinmann. 1873. 12mo.   **78 A**

PLESHY, ESSEX.

The history and antiquities of Pleshy. By G. R. [Richard
Gough.] 1803. 4to.   **87 F**

PLINIUS, CAIUS SECUNDUS.

Naturalis historiæ libri xxxvii., interpretatione et notis illustravit Joannes Harduinus. 5 vols. Paris, 1685. 4to.   **47 F**

See also Delphin Classics, vols. 87–96, 1826. 8vo.   **47 F G**

PLOT, ROBERT.

Natural history of Oxfordshire, an essay toward the natural
history of England. By R. P. Oxford, 1677. folio. **92 G**

Natural history of Staffordshire. Oxford, 1686. folio. **93 G**

PLOUGHLEY, OXFORDSHIRE.

History and antiquities of hundreds of Bullington and
Ploughley. By John Dunkin. 2 vols. 1823. 8vo. **92 F**

PLOWDEN, EDMUND.

Les Comentaires, ou les Reportes, de dyuers cases esteantes
matters in ley, en les temps des raygnes le Roye Edwarde
le size, le Roigne Mary, le Roy & Roigne Phillipp & Mary &
le Roigne Elizabeth. 2 parts in 1 vol. 1571–79. folio. **49 H**

The same. Translated into English ; to which are added the
Quæries of Mr. Plowden. 2 vols. 1816. 8vo.   **5 F**

PLOWDEN, EDMUND—*continued.*
Quæries, or a moot-book of choice cases. 1662. 12mo. **49·A**
See also ASHE, T.

PLOWDEN, FRANCIS.
The constitution of the United Kingdom of Great Britain and
Ireland civil and ecclesiastical. 1802. 8vo. **116 E**
Impartial thoughts upon the beneficial consequences of In-
rolling all deeds, wills and codicils affecting lands through-
out England and Wales. 1789. 8vo. **169 A**
The law of Usury and Annuities. 1797. 8vo. **176 G**
The principles and law of Tithing. 1806. 8vo. **176 F**

PLUMPTON, SIR EDWARD.
Plumpton correspondence. A series of letters, chiefly domes-
tick, written in the reigns of Edward IV., Richard III.,
Henry VII. and Henry VIII. Edited by T. Stapleton.
[Camden Society, vol. 4.] 1839. 8vo. **85 A**

PLUTARCH.
Les vies des hommes illustres. Traduites en François, avec
des remarques. [Vol. 1 only.] Paris, 1694. 4to. **80 I**
Plutarch's Lives. Translated with notes and a life of Plutarch
by John Langhorne and William Langhorne. 4th ed. by
Rev. Francis Wrangham. 6 vols. 1826. 8vo. **80 A**

PLYMOUTH, DEVONSHIRE.
History of Plymouth. By Llewellynn Jewitt. 1873. 4to. **87 D**

[POCOCK, LEWIS.]
A Chronological list of books and single papers relating to
the subjects of the rate of mortality, annuities and life
assurance. 1836. 8vo. **82 B**
The same. By L. Pocock. 2nd ed. 1842. 8vo. **82 B**

POCOCK, ROBERT.
History of the incorporated town and parishes of Gravesend
and Milton. Gravesend, 1797. 8vo. **88 D**
Memorials of the family of Tufton, earls of Thanet. [By
R. Pocock.] Gravesend, 1800. 8vo. **79 C**
Robert Pocock the Gravesend historian, naturalist, antiquarian,
botanist, and printer. By G. M. Arnold. 1883. 8vo. **79 C**

POCOCKE, RICHARD.
Travels through England during 1750, 1751, and later years.
Edited by J. J. Cartwright. [Camden Society, n.s. vols. 42
and 44.] 2 vols. 1888–89. 8vo.   85 E

POCQUET, CLAUDE.
Traité des Fiefs. 5me éd. Paris, 1771. 4to.   58 G

POETRY.
Ancient and modern poetry. See W. G. T. Barter's Essays,
1863, pp. 1–38.   83 C
The Anglo-Latin satirical poets and epigrammatists of the
twelfth century. Edited by T. Wright. 2 vols. 1872.
8vo.   102 E
A Dictionary of quotations from the English poets. By H. G.
Bohn. 1882. 8vo.   83 C
Historical, genealogical & poetical dictionary. 1703. 12mo. 79 A
Jacobite songs and ballads (selected), with notes. By G. S.
Macquoid. 1888. 8vo.   83 H
List of ryming words. See Chronicles of Robert of Brunne,
vol. 2, 1887, pp. 583–738.   102 I
Rhymes, reasons, and recollections from the common-place
books of a Sexagenarian. By G. Biller. 1876. 12mo. 78 A
Select poetry chiefly devotional of the reign of Queen
Elizabeth. Collected and edited by E. Farr. 2 vols.
Cambridge, 1845. 12mo.   77 D
Some account of the Sonnet. See M. Montagu's Fifty sonnets,
pp. ix–xvi, and Fifty more sonnets, pp. x–xii.   83 C
Three early English metrical romances, with an introduction
and glossary. Edited by John Robson. [Camden Society,
vol. 18.] 1842. 8vo.   85 A
See also PYPER, W,

POINTER, REV. JOHN.
Oxoniensis Academia ; or, the antiquities and curiosities of
the University of Oxford. 1749. 12mo.   92 E

POISONS.
Law to regulate the Sale of Poisons. By Wm. Flux. 1869.
12mo.   53 C
Reports of trials for Murder by Poisoning. By G. L. Browne
and C. G. Stewart. 1883. 8vo.   50 B
See also MEDICAL JURISPRUDENCE.

POLAND.
Die Ereignisse zu Warschau am 15. August 1831. Von
Johann Czynski. Zweibrücken, 1832. [Jacob's Tracts,
vol. 13.]   144 F
Letters addressed to Earl Russell respecting the late events
at Warsaw and in Poland. By George Mitchell. 1862.
[Pamphlets, vol. 21.]   144 B
The rise, progress, and present state of the Northern govern-
ments. By John Williams. 2 vols. 1777. 4to.   113 F

POLE, SIR WILLIAM.
Collections towards a description of the county of Devon.
1791. 8vo.   87 D

·

POLICE.
Magisterial and police guide. By H. C. Greenwood and
T. C. Martin. 3rd ed. by T. C. Martin. 1890. 8vo.   12 C
Police officer's guide. By R. L. Snowden. 8th ed. by T. H.
Lees. 1885. 8vo.   12 B
Police code and manual of the criminal law. By C. E. H.
Vincent. 1881. 8vo.   12 B
See also ADAMS, J., COLQUHOUN, P., FIELDING, H.,
FIELDING, SIR J. and STONE, J.

POLITICAL ECONOMY.
An Abridgment of Adam Smith's Inquiry into the nature
and causes of the wealth of nations. By W. P. Emerton.
Oxford. 1881. 8vo.   78 D
Four letters to the Earl of Carlisle. By Wm. Eden. 3rd ed.
with a fifth letter. 1780. 12mo.   78 A
An Inquiry into the nature and causes of the wealth of nations.
By Adam Smith. Edited by J. E. T. Rogers. 2nd ed.
2 vols. Oxford, 1880. 8vo.   78 D
Introductory lectures on political economy delivered in
Easter term 1831. By Richard Whately. 2nd ed. 1832.
8vo.   78 C
Mr. Samuel Smith, M.P., on National progress and poverty.
1884. [Pamphlets, vol. 37.]   144 C
Sophisms of free trade and popular political economy exa-
mined. By A Barrister [J. B. Byles]. 1849. 12mo. 78 A
See also NATIONAL DEBT and SENIOR, N. W.

POLITICAL EDUCATION.
A Fragment on Political Education. By George Whale.
1882. [Pamphlets, vol. 33.] **144 C**

POLITICAL SONGS.
The political songs of England from the reign of John to that
of Edward II. Edited and translated by T. Wright.
[Camden Society, vol. 6.] 1839. 8vo. **85 A**

POLITICAL TERMS.
Remarks on the use and abuse of political terms. By Sir
G. C. Lewis. New ed. by Sir R. K. Wilson. 1877. 8vo.
78 B

POLL BOOKS.
Poll Books. [Catalogued under the names of the counties and
boroughs.] 36 vols. 1722–1853. 8vo. & 12mo. **107 J K**

POLLARD, Robert.
The peerage of Great Britain and Ireland. Vol. 1. 1793.
4to. **127 J**

POLLEXFEN, Sir Henry.
Arguments and reports in some special cases [in all the courts,
1669–1685]. 1702. folio. **74 F**

POLLOCK, Charles Edward.
The practice of the County Courts. 1851. 8vo. **165 B**
The same. 6th ed. by C. E. Pollock and H. Nicol. 1868.
8vo. **165 B**
The same. 9th ed. by H. Nicol and H. C. Pollock. 1880.
8vo. **52 E**
Equitable jurisdiction of the County Courts. By C. E. Pollock
and H. Nicol. 1865. 8vo. **165 B**

POLLOCK, Frederick.
Digest of the law of Partnership. 1877. 8vo. **173 D**
The same. 3rd ed. 1884. 8vo. **173 D**
The same. 4th ed. with an essay on codification. 1888.
8vo. **53 B**
The same. 5th ed. 1890. 8vo. **11 B**
An Essay on Possession in the common law. By F. Pollock
and R. S. Wright. 1888. 8vo. **11 C**

POLLOCK, FREDERICK—*continued.*

Essays in Jurisprudence and Ethics. 1882. 8vo.   **63 F**

The land laws. 2nd ed. 1887. 8vo.   **83 J**

The law of Torts. 1887. 8vo.   **11 H**

Principles of Contract at law and in equity. 1876. 8vo. **163 E**

The same. 3rd ed. 1881. 8vo.   **163 E**

The same. 5th ed. 1889. 8vo.   **9 E**

See also LAW QUARTERLY REVIEW.

[POLSUE, JOSEPH.]

A Complete parochial history of the county of Cornwall.
4 vols. 1867–72. 4to.   **86 F**

POLWHELE, REV. RICHARD.

History of Cornwall. 7 vols. in 2. 1816–1808. 4to. **86 F**

History of Devonshire. 3 vols. in 1. 1797–96. folio. **86 H**

POMEROY, JOHN NORTON.

Lectures on international law in time of peace. Edited by
T. S. Woolsey. 1886. 8vo.   **55 B**

POMPEII.

Pompeii, illustrated with views. By T. L. Donaldson, engraved by W. B. Cooke. 2 vols. in 1. 1827. fólio. **81 H**

PONTEFRACT, YORKSHIRE.

The history of Pontefract. By· B. Boothroyd. Pontefract,
1807. 8vo.   **94 B**

POOLE, DORSET.

The history of the town and county of Poole. By John
Sydenham. 1839. 8vo.   **87 D**

POOLE, MATTHEW.

Synopsis criticorum aliorumque Sacræ Scripturæ interpretum
et commentatorum. 5 vols. Ultrajecti, 1684–86. folio.
   77 H

POOLE, WILLIAM FREDERICK.

Index to periodical literature. By W. F. Poole. 3rd ed.
1882, and the first Supplement, Jan. 1, 1882, to Jan. 1, 1887.
By W. F. Poole and W. J. Fletcher. 2 vols. 1882–1888.
4to.   **82 F**

POOR AND POOR LAW.

. The statutes in force relating to the Poor, &c. Vols. 1–3 by W. C. Glen, vol. 4 by A. Macmorran and M. S. J. Macmorran. 4 vols. 1873–90. 8vo.   **11 B C**

Orders issued by the Local Government Board, under the acts relating to the relief of the poor, &c. By A. Macmorran and S. G. Lushington. 1890. 8vo.   **11 C**

Poor law election manual. By W. G. Lumley. 5th ed. by W. C. Glen. 1886. 8vo.   **11 C**

The Poor Law. By J. F. Archbold. 14th ed. by W. C. Glen. 1885. 8vo.   **11 C**

Poor law orders. By W. C. Glen. 9th ed. 1883. 8vo. **174 B**

Social wreckage, a review of the laws of England as they affect the poor. By F. Peek. 1883. 12mo.   **78 A**

The Poor removal and Union chargeability act. By W. G. Lumley. 2nd ed. 1865. 12mo.   **174 B**

A Plea for the very poor, being the first general report of the Leicester Square Soup Kitchen. 1850. 8vo.   **78 B**

An Abridgment of the cases upon the subject of the Poor law. By W. G. Lumley. 2 vols. 1840–43. 8vo. **174 B**

Parochial settlements an obstruction to poor law reform. By J. M. White. 1835. [Pamphlets, vol. 4.]   **144 A**

Remarks on the Poor Law amendment act. By J. M. White. 1834. [Pamphlets, vol. 4.]   **144 A**

Instructions from the central board of Poor law commissioners to assistant commissioners. [1835.] See N. W. Senior's Pamphlets, 1831, &c. 8vo.   **78 D**

Laws for the relief and settlement of the Poor. By M. Nolan. 2 vols. 1805. 8vo.   **174 B**

See BOTT, E., BURN, REV. R., FOLEY, R., GRADY, S. G., HALE, SIR M., HOWLETT, REV. J., ROBINSON, W. and WILLCOCK, J. W.

See also PARISH LAW, RATING and SETTLEMENTS, PARISH.

POOR, HENRY V.

Manual of the Railroads of the United States and Directory of railway officials. 2 vols. 1888. 8vo.   **129 J**

POPE, ALEXANDER.

An Essay on Man, in four epistles to Henry St. John, Lord Bolingbroke. 1819. folio.   **118 G**

Iliad of Homer translated. 6 vols. in 3. 1715–20. folio. **83 I**

POPE, ALEXANDER—*continued*.
Letters to Atterbury in the Tower of London. Edited by J.
  G. Nichols. [Camden Society, vol. 73.] 1859. 8vo. **85 B**
The works of A. Pope; with the commentary and notes of
  William Warburton. 9 vols. 1770. 8vo. **83 E**

POPE, CHARLES.
The practical abridgment of the laws of Customsand Excise.
  6th ed. 1820. 8vo. **165 F**

POPE, HENRY MONTAGU RANDALL.
Law and practice of Lunacy. 1877. 8vo. **172 B**
The same. 2nd ed. by J. H. Boome and V. de S. Fowke.
  1890. 8vo. **10 H**

POPE, JOHN BUCKINGHAM.
Railway rates and radical rule. 1884. 12mo. **78 A**

POPE, SIR THOMAS.
The life of Sir T. Pope, founder of Trinity college, Oxford.
  By Thomas Warton. 1772. 8vo. **79 B**

POPHAM, SIR JOHN.
Reports and cases; with some remarkable cases by other
  learned pens since his death. 1656. folio.
The same. 2nd ed. 1682. folio. **74 F**

POPULATION.
Two lectures on Population delivered before the University
  of Oxford in Easter Term 1828. By N. W. Senior, with
  Correspondence between the author and Rev. T. R. Malthus.
  1831. 8vo. **78 D**
See also CENSUS.

PORCELAIN.
Marks and monograms on pottery and porcelain. By W.
  Chaffers. 1863. 8vo. **78 C**

PORNY, MARK ANTHONY.
Grammatical exercises English and French. 6th ed. 1789.
  12mo. **255 H**

PORTER, JAMES BIGGS.
Laws of fire, life, accident, and guarantee insurance. 1884.
8vo.   169 B
The same. 2nd ed. 1887. 8vo.   10 D

PORTLAND, WILLIAM HENRY, 3 DUKE OF.
The case of the Duke of Portland respecting two leases lately
granted by the Lords of the Treasury to Sir James Lowther,
Bart. [of the forest of Inglewood and soccage of the castle
of Carlisle]. 6th ed. 1768. 8vo.   87 A

PORTRAITS.
Catalogue of engraved British portraits from Egbert the Great
to present time. By H. Bromley. 1793. 4to.   127 J
A Collection of engraved portraits, catalogued and exhibited
by J. A. Rose, at the opening of the new library and
museum of the corporation of London, November 1872.
1872. 8vo.   82 B
Fraser's Magazine. Vols. 7 & 8. 2 vols. 1833. 8vo. [con-
taining portraits of literary characters.]   254 E

PORTUGAL, LANGUAGE OF.
A Dictionary of the Portuguese and English languages, in
two parts. By Anthony Vieyra. Transtagano, 2 vols.
1773. 4to.   123 G
See also MINSHEU, J.

PORTUGAL, LAW OF.
Direito civil de Portugal. Por M. B. Carneiro. 3 vols. in 1.
Lisboa, 1826–28. 8vo.   39 B
Ordenações e leis do reino de Portugal. Nona edição. 3 vols.
Coimbra, 1824. 8vo.   39 A
Tratado regular e pratico de testamentos e successões.
Por A. J. De Gouvea Pinto. Segunda edição. Lisboa,
1820. 8vo.   39 B
See also MELLIUS FREIRIUS, P. J.

POSSESSION.
An Essay on Possession in the common law. By F. Pollock
and R. S. Wright. 1888. 8vo.   11 C
The law of Possession. See W. Brown's Law of limitation as
to real property. 1869. 8vo.   53 A
See also SAVIGNY, F. C. VON and SCHOLLAERT, F. J.

POSTAGE STAMP, THE.

Opinions from the press upon the letter and parcels post and the adhesive stamp. By Patrick Chalmers. Wimbledon, 1883. [Pamphlets, vol. 37.]   **144 C**

The penny postage scheme of 1837, was it an invention or a copy? By P. Chalmers. 1881. [Pamphlets, vol. 37.] **144 C**

The position of Sir Rowland Hill made plain. By Patrick Chalmers. 1882. [Pamphlets, vol. 37.]   **144 C**

A Short review of the adhesive stamp. By Patrick Chalmers. 1883. [Pamphlets, vol. 40.]   .   .   **144 C**

Submission of the Sir Rowland Hill committee. 2nd ed. with Opinions from the press on 'The adhesive postage stamp.' By P. Chalmers. 1886. [Pamphlets, vol. 40.] **144 C**

POSTE, EDWARD.

Gaii institutionum juris civilis commentarii quatuor; or, Elements of Roman law by Gaius. Oxford, 1871. 8vo. **63 E**

The same. 2nd ed. Oxford, 1875. 8vo.   **63 E**

POSTLETHWAYT, MALACHY.

Great Britain's true system ; with an introduction relative to forming a new plan of British politicks. 1757. 8vo. **78 D**

POTE, JOSEPH.

The history and antiquities of Windsor Castle ; with an Appendix containing the names of the knights of the Garter, also an alphabetical index of all the plates of arms. Eton, 1749-62. 4to.   **86 B**

Registrum Regale sive Catalogus. I. Præpositorum utriusque collegii Regalis Etonensis et Cantabrigiensis. II. Sociorum Collegii Etonensis. III. Alumnorum e collegio Etonensi in Collegium Regale Cantabrig. per singulos annos cooptatorum. Etonæ, 1774. 8vo.   **79 H**

POTHIER, ROBERT JOSEPH.

Œuvres, annotées et mises en corrélation avec le code civil et la législation actuelle, par M. Bugnet. 12me éd. 11 vols. Paris, 1861-62. 8vo.   **58 D**

    1. Coutume d'Orléans.
    2. Eloge de Pothier. Traité des obligations. De la prestation des fautes.
    3. Traités du contrat de vente, Des retraits, Du contrat de constitution de rente.

POTHIER, ROBERT JOSEPH—*continued.*

4. Traités du contrat de louage, Du contrat de bail à rente, Du contrat de société, Des cheptels, Des contrats des louages maritimes, Du contrat de change.
5. Traités du prêt à usage, Du précaire, Du prêt de consomption, De l'usure, Des contrats de dépôt, De mandat d'assurance, De prêt à la grosse aventure, De jeu et de nantissement.
6. Traités du contrat de mariage, Douaire, Droit d'habitation, Garde noble et bourgeoise, Préciput légal des nobles.
7. Traités de la puissance du mari, de la communauté, des donations entre mari et femme.
8. Traités des successions, Donations testamentaires, Donations entre-vifs, Substitutions et des propres.
9. Traités des personnes et des choses, du domaine, de propriété, de la possession, de la prescription, de l'hypothèque, des fiefs, des cens, des champarts.
10. Traité de la procédure civile. Traité de la procédure criminelle.
11. Table générale des matières par ordre alphabétique.

Œuvres posthumes. 2 vols. Paris, 1777. 4to. **40 E**
A Treatise on the contract of Partnership ; with the civil code and code of commerce relating to that subject in the same order. Translated by O. D. Tudor. 1854. 8vo. **173 D**

POTTER, THOMAS ROSSELL.
History and antiquities of Charnwood Forest. 1842. 4to. **90 G**

POTTERY.
Marks and monograms on pottery and porcelain. By W. Chaffers. 1863. 8vo. **78 C**

POTTS, THOMAS.
Potts's Discovery of witches in the county of Lancaster, reprinted from the original edition of 1613 with an introduction and notes by James Crossley. 1845. 8vo. **89 B**

POTTS, THOMAS.
Compendious Law Dictionary, containing an explanation of the terms and the law itself. 1803. 12mo. **171 A**

POTTS, THOMAS RADFORD.
Principles of the law of Succession to deceased persons. 1888. 8vo. **11 G** .

POULSON, George.
Beverlac ; or, the antiquities and history of the town of Beverley. 2 vols. in 1. 1829. 4to.   **94 C**
The history and antiquities of the seigniory of Holderness. 2 vols. Hull, 1840–41. 4to.   **94 C**

POWELL, Arthur.
The law specially affecting printers, publishers, and newspaper proprietors. 2nd issue. 1889. 8vo.   **11 C**

POWELL, Edmund.
Principles and practice of the law of Evidence. 2nd ed. 1859. 12mo.   **167 F**
The same. 4th ed. by J. Cutler and E. F. Griffin. 1875. 12mo.   **167 F**
The same. 5th ed. by J. Cutler and E. F. Griffin. 1885. 12mo.   **9 I**
Law of inland carriers. 2nd ed. 1861. 8vo.   **161 A**

POWELL, John Joseph.
An Essay on Devises. 1788. 8vo.   **178 B**
The same. 3rd ed. by T. Jarman. 2 vols. 1827. 8vo.   **178 C**
An Essay on the learning respecting creation and execution of Powers, and also respecting nature and effect of Leasing Powers. 1787. 8vo.   **174 B**
Essay upon the law of contracts and agreements. 2 vols. 1790. 8vo.   **163 D**
The law of Mortgages. 1785. 8vo.   **172 G**
The same. 4th ed. 2 vols. 1799, and 6th ed. by T. Coventry. 2 vols. 1826. 8vo.   **172 G**
Original precedents in Conveyancing selected from the manuscript collection of the late J. J. Powell. Revised and corrected by Charles Barton. 6 vols. 1802. 8vo.   **163 G**

POWELL, Robert.
A Treatise of the antiquity, authority, uses and jurisdiction of the ancient Courts of Leet, or view of Franck-Pledge. 1642. 12mo.   **49 E**

POWELL, Thomas.
The Attourney's Academy ; or, the manner and forme of proceeding practically, upon any suite, plaint or action whatsoever, 1623. 8vo,   **49 C**

POWELL, THOMAS—*continued.*

The same. 3rd impression. 1630. 8vo. **49 C**

The Attornies Almanacke, provided and desired for the generall ease and daily use of all such as shall have occasion to remove any person, cause or record, from an inferiour court to any the higher courts at Westminster. 1627. 8vo. Bound with the preceding. **49 C**

The Repertorie of records remaining in the 4 treasuries on the receipt side at Westminster, the two remembrancers of the Exchequer. 1631. 8vo. **49 G**

POWER, DAVID, H. RODWELL and E. L. DEW.

Reports of the decisions of committees of the House of Commons in the trial of controverted elections, 1848–56. 2 vols. 1853–57. 8vo. **66 B**

POWERS.

Concise treatise on Powers. By G. Farwell. 1874. 8vo. **13 C**

Practical treatise of Powers. By Sir E. B. Sugden. 8th ed. 1861. 8vo. **13 C**

The language of Powers. See R. Preston's Tracts, 1797, pp. 84–92. **163 G**

See also CHANCE, H., FRANCIS, R. and POWELL, J. J.

POWLES, LOUIS DISTON.

A Digest of the decisions in probate and divorce matters during the last four years. 1884. 8vo. **12 D**

POYNTER, THOMAS.

A Concise view of the doctrine and practice of the ecclesiastical courts in Doctors' Commons on various points relative to the subject of Marriage and Divorce. 2nd ed. 1824. 8vo. **172 D**

PRATER, HENRY.

Cases illustrative of the conflict between the laws of England and Scotland with regard to marriage, divorce, and legitimacy. 1835. 8vo. **172 D**

An Essay upon the law respecting husband and wife. 1834. [Jacob's Tracts, vol. 12.] **144 F**

The same. 2nd ed. 1836. 8vo. **172 D**

PRATT, JOHN TIDD.

Abstract of all the printed acts of parliament for the establishment of Courts of Requests in England and Wales. 1824.
8vo.   175 C

Income Tax acts. 3rd ed. by J. Paterson. 1870. 12mo.
                                                    168 G

The same. 5th ed. by D. Ward. 1887. 12mo.   10 C

Law of Highways. 12th ed. by S. Prentice. 1881. 8vo. 10 B

Law relating to Friendly Societies in England and Wales.
1829. 12mo.   168 E

Law relating to Savings Banks. 6th ed. 1844. 12mo. 175 D

The property tax act (5 & 6 Vict. cap. 35) with explanatory
notes. 1842. 12mo. Bound with Paget's Income Tax.
1842.   168 G

The same. 2nd ed. 1843. 12mo.   168 G

A Summary of the Savings Banks in England, Scotland, Wales,
and Ireland. 1846. 8vo.   175 D

The Watching and Lighting act 3 & 4 Will. IV. cap. 90.
4th ed. by W. C. Glen. 1869. 12mo.   177 D

PRATT, WILLIAM TIDD.

Continuation of Jeremy's analytical digest of the reports of
cases decided in the courts of Common Law and Equity,
of Appeal and Nisi Prius, and in the Ecclesiastical courts,
1850–1854. 2 vols. 1851–55. 8vo.   63 C

Law relating to benefit building societies. 2nd ed. 1865.
12mo.   161 A

Law relating to friendly societies, and industrial and provident
societies. 7th ed. 1867. 12mo.   168 E

The same. 10th ed. by E. W. Brabrook. 1881. 12mo. 52 H

The same. 11th ed. by E. W. Brabrook. 1888. 12mo. 10 A

PRAYERS.

Private prayers, put forth by authority during the reign of
Queen Elizabeth. Edited by Rev. W. K. Clay. Cambridge, 1851. 8vo.   77 E

See also LITURGIES AND PRAYERS.

PRECEDENCY.

A Table of precedency of men, with notes containing authorities
upon which some parts are founded. [By C. G. Young.
n.d.] 8vo.   125 C

PRECEDENTS IN CHANCERY.

Precedents in Chancery, being a collection of cases argued and adjudged in the High Court of Chancery, 1689 to 1722. 1733. folio.

The same. 2nd ed. with notes and references by Thomas Finch. 1786. 8vo. **3 D**

PREMEDITATION.

La Premeditazione in rapporto alla psicologia, al diritto, alla legislazione comparata. Per B. Alimena. Torino, 1887. 8vo. **55 B**

PRENDERGAST, HARRIS.

The law relating to Officers in the Army. 1855. 12mo. **172 F**

PRENTICE, SAMUEL.

Procedure and evidence relating to indictable offences, and certain rules and maxims of criminal law. 1882. 8vo. **52 E**

The proceedings in an action in the Queen's Bench, Common Pleas and Exchequer divisions. 1877. 8vo. **160 A**

The same. 2nd ed. 1880. 8vo. **160 A**

PREROGATIVE, ROYAL.

An Exposition of the King's Prerogative. By Sir William Stanford. 1607. 12mo. **49 C**

Inquiry into the rise and growth of the Royal Prerogative in England. By John Allen. New ed. by B. Thorpe. 1849. 8vo. **83 I**

The opinion of all the judges of England relating to the grandest prerogative of the royal family, and some observations relating to the prerogative of a Queen Consort. See J. Fortescue's Reports of select cases, 1748, pp. 398–440. **74 C**

PRESBYTERIANS.

History, opinions, and present legal position of English Presbyterians. [By T. Falconer.] 1834. [Law Tracts, vol. 4.] **144 E**

See also DISSENTERS.

PRESCOTT, WILLIAM HICKLING.

History of the Conquest of Mexico. 6th ed. 2 vols. 1850. 8vo. **113 C**

PRESCOTT, William Hickling—*continued.*

History of the Conquest of Peru. 6th ed. 2 vols. 1850. 8vo.   **113 C**

History of the reign of Ferdinand and Isabella the Catholic of Spain. 7th ed. 2 vols. 1851. 8vo.   **113 C**

PRESCRIPTIVE RIGHTS.

Rights of Common and other prescriptive rights. By Joshua Williams. 1880. 8vo.   **9 D**

See also Easements and Limitations.

PRESS, The, Newspaper.

A Sketch of the political history of the past three years in connexion with The Press Newspaper, and the part it has taken on the leading questions of the time. 1856. [Pamphlets, vol. 11.]   **144 A**

PRESTON, Lancashire.

The Cobler of Preston, as it is acted at the Theatre Royal in Drury Lane. By C. Johnson. 2nd ed. 1716. 12mo. **118 C**

The Happiness of Retirement, in an epistle from Lancashire to a Friend at Court ; to which is added An Encomium on the town of Preston. 1733. 12mo.   **89 A**

The history of Preston together with the Guild Merchant and some account of the Duchy and County Palatine of Lancaster. 1822. 4to.   **88 F**

PRESTON, Richard.

Analysis of the first and best edition of Preston on estates, by way of question and answer. See Law Journal Tracts, 1825–6, pp. 151–273.   **144 G**

An Elementary treatise on Estates. 2 vols. 1820–27. 8vo.   **167 D**

An Essay in a course of lectures on Abstracts of Title. 2nd ed. 3 vols. 1823–24. 8vo.   **13 A**

Six letters on Mr. Preston's Practical treatise on Conveyancing. By A West Country Attorney. 1816. 8vo.   **163 G**

Tracts. 1797. 8vo.   **163 G**

1. The definition and nature of cross remainders.
2. Fines and recoveries by tenant in tail.
3. Difference between merger, remitter and extinguishment.
4. Estates executed, executory, vested and contingent.

PRESTON, Richard—*continued*.

    5. Contingencies with a double aspect.
    6. The succession by a parent to a child.
    7. The language of powers.

Treatise on Conveyancing with a view to its application to practice. 1806. 8vo.   **163 E**
The same. 2nd ed. 3 vols. 1813–16. 8vo.   **163 E**
The same. 3rd ed. 3 vols. 1819–29. 8vo.   **163 E**

PRESTON, Thomas.
School Board guide and teacher's manual. 1871. 12mo. **166 C**

PRESTWICH, Sir John.
Respublica ; or, a display of the honors of the Commonwealth under protectorship of O. Cromwell. 1787. 4to.   **127 J**

PRESUMPTIONS.
A Treatise on presumptions of law and fact, with the theory and rules of presumptive or circumstantial proof in criminal cases. By W. M. Best. 1844. 8vo.   **174 C**
See also Evidence.

PREVOST, Rev. Francis and F. BLAGDON.
Beauties of Dr. John Moore selected from his works; with account of the Doctor and his writings. 1803. 8vo. **83 C**

PRICE, Sir Carbery.
An Essay on the value of the mines late of Sir Carbery Price. By William Waller. 1698. 12mo.   **94 E**

PRICE, George.
Attorney's practice in Exchequer of Pleas. 1831. 12mo. **168 B**
Reports of cases in the Court of Exchequer, 1814–1824. 13 vols. 1816–28. 8vo.   **7 G H**
Treatise on the Court of Exchequer. 1827. 8vo.   **168 B**

PRICE, John Dutton.
A System of book-keeping adapted to the use of solicitors. 1829. 8vo.   **160 G**

PRICE, JOHN EDWARD.

Descriptive account of the Guildhall of the City of London,
its history and associations. 1886. folio. **92 H**

PRICE, RICHARD..

. Observations on reversionary payments ; on schemes for providing annuities for widows and for persons in old age;
also, Essays on life annuities and political arithmetic. 2nd
ed. 1772, and 5th ed. 2 vols. 1792. 8vo. **160 B**

PRICES.

Thoughts and details on the high and low prices of the last
thirty years. By Thomas Tooke. 2 vols. 1823. 8vo. **78 D**

PRICHARD, JAMES COWLES.

A Treatise on Insanity and other disorders affecting the mind.
1835. 8vo. **172 B**

PRIDEAUX, CHARLES GREVILLE.

· A Practical guide to the duties of Churchwardens in the execution of their office. 8th ed. 1857. 12mo. **161 F**

The same. 13th ed. 1875. 12mo. **161 F**

The same. 15th ed. 1886. 12mo. **9 C**

PRIDEAUX, FREDERICK.

The law of Judgments on crown debts as they affect real
property. 3rd ed. 1845. 12mo. **169 E**

The same.. 4th ed. 1856. 12mo. **13 B**

Precedents in Conveyancing ; with dissertations on its law and
practice. 3rd ed. 1858. 8vo. **164 B**

The same. 5th ed. 2 vols. 1866. 7th ed. 2 vols. 1873.
9th ed. 2 vols. 1876. 11th ed. 2 vols. 1882, and 12th ed.
2 vols. 1883. All 5 editions by F. Prideaux and J. Whitcomb. 10 vols. 1866–83. 8vo. **164 C**

The same. 13th ed. by F. Prideaux and J. Whitcomb. 2 vols.
1885. 8vo. **13 F**

The same. 14th ed. by F. Prideaux and J. Whitcomb. 2 vols.
1889. 8vo. **13 F**

· See also INDERMAUR, JOHN.

PRIDEAUX, HUMPHREY.

Ecclesiastical Tracts, viz. I. The validity of the orders of the Church of England. II. The justice of the present established law which gives the successor in any ecclesiastical benefice all the profits from the day of avoidance. III. An award of King Charles I. showing that personal tithes are still due by the law of the land. 2nd ed. 1716. 8vo. **77 B**

Letters to John Ellis sometime under-secretary of state, 1674–1722. Edited. by E. M. Thompson. [Camden Society, n.s. vol. 15.] 1875. 8vo. **85 D**

Life of Rev. Humphrey Prideaux, with several tracts and letters of his upon various subjects. 1748. 8vo. **79 B**

The original and right of Tithes truly stated, to which is annex'd, the draught of a Bill prepared 1691, for the restraining of pluralities of benefices with cure of souls ; with Reasons for the said bill. 1710. 12mo. **176 F**

The same. 2nd ed. 1736. 12mo. **176 F**

PRIDMORE, THOMAS WEBSTER.

Guide to the preparation of bills of costs. 6th ed. 1879, and 7th ed. 1884. 8vo. **165 A**

The same. 8th ed. by C. W. Scott. 1887. 8vo. **52 D**

The same. 9th ed. by C. W. Scott. 1891. 8vo. **9 F**

PRIESTCRAFT.

A Modest apology for Parson Alberoni governor to King Philip a minor, and universal curate of the whole Spanish monarchy ; the whole being a short but unanswerable defence of priestcraft. [By Thomas Gordon.] 2nd ed. 1719. [Grimaldi's Tracts, vol. 2.] **118 B**

PRIESTLY, JOSEPH.

An Appeal to the public on the subject of the riots in Birmingham, with Strictures on a pamphlet intitled, Thoughts on the late riot at Birmingham. Birmingham, 1791. 8vo. **93 E**

PRIMOGENITURE.

The law and custom of primogeniture. By G. C. Brodrick. See Systems of land tenure, 1881, pp. 93–168. **78 B**

The Succession laws of Christian countries, with special reference to the law of Primogeniture as it exists in England. By Eyre Lloyd. 1877. 8vo. **11 G**

PRIMOGENITURE—*continued.*

A Letter to Isaac Tomkins and Peter Jenkins on primogeniture. By Timothy Winterbottom. 2nd ed. 1835. [Law
Tracts, vol. 5.] **144 E**

PRINCE EDWARD ISLAND.

Acts of general assembly of Prince Edward Island, 1773–1890.
10 vols. Charlottetown, 1862–90. 8vo. **34 E**

Private and local acts of general assembly of Prince Edward
Island, 1773–1862. Charlottetown, 1862. 8vo. **34 E**

PRINCE, JOHN.

Danmonii Orientales Illustres; or, the worthies of Devon.
Exeter, 1701. folio. **79 I**

The same. New ed. 1810. 4to. **79 H**

PRINCE, JOHN HENRY.

A Further assistant to the practice of Conveyancing containing original practical remarks with precedents. 1813.
8vo. **163 G**

Remarks on the best method of barring dower. 1805.
[Pamphlets, vol. 27.] **144 B**

PRINCIPAL AND AGENT. See AGENCY.

PRINCIPAL AND SURETY. See GUARANTEES.

PRINSEP, HENRY THOBY.

Code of criminal procedure and other laws relating to procedure in the criminal courts of British India. 3rd ed.
Calcutta, 1869. 8vo. **38 C**

The same. 4th ed. Calcutta, 1873. 8vo. **38 C**

PRINTERS AND PRINTING.

The law specially affecting printers &c. By A. Powell. 2nd
issue. 1889. 8vo. **11 C**

A List of medals connected with printers and the art of
printing, exhibited by Wm. Blades at opening of new
library and museum of the corporation of London. 1872.
8vo. **82 B**

The origin and progress of printing. See T. Astle's Origin of
writing, 1803, pp. 213–228. **78 G**

PRIOR, HERMAN LUDOLPHUS.
A Complete manual of short conveyancing. 1857. 8vo. **13 G**

[PRIOR, MATTHEW.]
A Genuine dialogue facetious and pathetic, amorous and political, full of strange and surprizing adventures. By the Author of the Curious Maid. 1736. Bound with South Sea Scheme. 1732. 12mo. **118 B**

PRIORIES.
Some account of the alien priories and of such lands as they are known to have possessed in England and Wales. [By Richard Gough.] 2 vols. 1779. 12mo. **84 A**

PRISONS AND PRISONERS.
Dissertatio juridica inauguralis de religione et anxia judicum cura circa existimationem et vitam reorum ; quam . . . publico examini submittit F. P. Vegelin a Claerbergen. Franequeræ, 1757. [Latin Tracts on civil and canon law.] **118 E**

The prison acts of 1877 and 1865. By R. Anderson. 1878. 12mo. **53 E**

The Purgatory of prisoners ; or an intermediate stage between the prison and the public. By Rev. Orby Shipley. 1857. 8vo. **78 C**

Synopsis of Mr. Charles Pearson's intended lecture upon prison discipline. 1849. [Pamphlets, vol. 37.] **144 C**

See also DEBTS, NEILD, J. and TALLACK, W.

PRITCHARD, ROBERT ALBION and W. T. PRITCHARD.
A Digest of the law and practice of the court for Divorce and Matrimonial causes. 1859. 8vo. **166 A**

The same. 3rd ed. by J. G. Witt and W. T. Pritchard. 1874. 8vo. **12 D**

PRITCHARD, THOMAS SIRRELL.
Handy-book for executors and administrators. 1861. 12mo. **168 B**

The jurisdiction, practice, and procedure of the Quarter Sessions in judicial matters. 1875. 8vo. **175 E**

PRITCHARD, WILLIAM TARN.
Analytical digest of all reported cases determined by the Court of Admiralty. 1847. 8vo. **63 D**

PRITCHARD, WILLIAM TARN—*continued.*
The same. 2nd ed. by R. A. Pritchard and W. T. Pritchard.
2 vols. 1865. 8vo. **63 D**
The same. 3rd ed. by J. C. Hannen and W. T. Pritchard.
2 vols. 1887. 8vo. **14 C**

PRIVATE ACTS.
The private acts from 1700 to 1889. 208 vols. 1700–1889.
folio. **23 C–26 C**
See also ACTS OF PARLIAMENT, INDEXES OF.

PRIVATE BILLS.
See BILLS, PRIVATE AND PUBLIC and REFEREES, COURT OF.

PRIVY COUNCIL.
Acts of the Privy Council of England. New series, vols. 1
and 2, A.D. 1542–1550. Edited by J. R. Dasent. 2 vols.
1890. 8vo. **99 A**
History, constitution, and character of the Judicial committee
of the Privy Council considered as a judicial tribunal.
By W. F. Finlason. 1878. 8vo. **174 C**
The practice of the Judicial committee of the Privy Council.
By Wm. Macpherson. 2nd ed. 1873. 8vo. **12 A**
Handy book on the practice and procedure before the
Judicial committee of Privy Council. By R. T. Lattey.
1869. 12mo. **12 A**
Proceedings and ordinances of the Privy Council of England,
1386–1461. By Sir H. Nicolas. 6 vols. 1834–37. 8vo. **98 A**
An Essay upon the original authority of the King's Council.
By Sir F. Palgrave. 1834. 8vo. **97 I**
England's Glory ; or, an exact catalogue of the Lords of the
Privy Council. 1660. 12mo. **49 D**
See also APPEAL CASES and APPEAL PRACTICE.

PRIZE LAW.
Prize Law : particularly with reference to the duties and obligations of belligerents and neutrals. By Professor Katchenovsky. Translated by F. T. Pratt. 1867. 8vo. **55 A**
A Manual of Naval Prize law. By Godfrey Lushington.
1866. 8vo. **172 G**
See also BLATCHFORD, S.

PROBABILITY.

Du calcul des probabilités. Par C. F. De Bicquilley. Nouvelle éd. Paris, 1805. [Jacob's Tracts, vol. 13.] **144 F**

See also Encyclopædia Britannica, xix. 768-788. **122 F**

PROBATE, COURT OF.

Student's Probate, Divorce and Admiralty. By A. Gibson and A. Weldon. 2nd ed. 1891. 8vo. **64 E**

Coote's common form practice and Tristram's contentious practice and practice on motions and summonses in granting probates and administrations. 10th ed. by T. H. Tristram. 1888. 8vo. **12 D**

Epitome of the laws of Probate and Divorce. By J. C. Harrison. 3rd ed. 1886. 8vo. **64 E**

A Divorce and Probate manual. By W. J. Dixon. 1886. 12mo. **64 E**

Probate and administration, law and ·practice in common form and contentious business. By W. J. Dixon. 2nd ed. 1885. 8vo. **12 D**

Student's Guide to law and practice of courts of Probate and Divorce. By J. F. Haynes. 2nd ed. 1882 8vo. **64 E**

Principles and practice of the Court of Probate. By George Brown. 2nd ed. by L. D. Powles. 1881. 8vo. **12 D**

Examples of Administration Bonds for the Court of Probate. By Samuel Chadwick. 1861. 8vo. **12 D**

On Probate Courts. By Thomas Falconer. 1850. [Pamphlets, vol. 7.] **144 A**

See also DODD, P. W., LAWTON, G., POWLES, L. D., SWAN, R. and WEATHERLEY, E.

PROBATE DUTY.

Digest of the law relating to Probate Duty. By A. F. Leach. 1878. 8vo. **174 D**

See also LEGACY DUTIES.

PROBYN, JOHN WEBB.

Systems of land tenure in various countries : a series of essays published under the sanction of the Cobden Club. New ed. 1881. 8vo. **78 B**

PROCESS IN ABSENCE.

History of process in absence. See Historical law tracts, 2nd ed., 1761, pp. 295-312. **144 F**

PROCLUS, Diadochus.
The philosophical and mathematical commentaries of Proclus
on the first book of Euclid's Elements, and a translation
from the Grcek of Proclus's Theological Elements. By
T. Taylor. 2 vols. 1792. 4to. 78 G

PROCTER, Richard Wright.
Memorials of Manchester streets. Manchester, 1874. 4to.
89 G

PROFITS.
A Digest of the law of Uses and Profits of Land. By S. M.
Leake. 1888. 8vo. 10 D
A Treatise on the law relating to profits à prendre. By J. E.
Hall. 1871. 8vo. 52 B

PROHIBITION.
Informations, Mandamus, and Prohibition. By J. Shortt.
1887. 8vo. 10 C
Law of Prohibition. By M. Lloyd. 1849. 12mo. 174 D

PROMISSORY NOTES.
Commentaries on the law of promissory notes and checks on
banks and bankers. By J. Story. 6th ed. Boston, 1868.
8vo. 60 A
See also Bills of Exchange.

PROPERTY.
Popular Tables for ascertaining the value of lifehold, leasehold,
and church property. By C. M. Willich. 10th ed. 1887.
12mo. 134 J
Restraints on the alienation of property. By J. C. Gray.
1883. 8vo. 13 C
Law of property. By H. W. B. Mackay. 1882. 8vo. 53 E
Law relating to the priority of incumbrances and other rights
in property. By W. G. Robinson. 1873. 8vo. 11 C
A Handy book on property law in a series of Letters. By
Lord St. Leonards. 7th ed. 1863. 12mo. 53 E
Lord St. Leonards' Act to further amend the law of property,
with notes. By J. S. Vaizey. 1860. 12mo. 174 D
The rights and duties of property. By John Sangster. 1851.
12mo. 78 D

PROPERTY—*continued.*

The act for simplifying the transfer of property 7 & 8 Vict. cap. 76; with general observations on the act. By John Towgood. 1845. [Pamphlets, vol. 19.] **144 B**

History of Property. See Historical Law Tracts, 2nd ed., 1761, pp. 79–143. **144 F**

See also PERSONAL PROPERTY and REAL PROPERTY.

PROPERTY LAWYER.

The Property Lawyer. 12 vols. 1826–29. 8vo. **140 A**

The same. New Series. 3 vols. 1830. 8vo. **140 B**

PROSTITUTION.

A Comparative survey of laws in force for the prohibition, regulation, and licensing of Vice in England and other countries. By Sheldon Amos. 1877. 8vo. **177 C**

PROTESTANT RELIGION.

A Collection of white and black lists; or, a view of those gentlemen who have given their votes in Parliament for and against the Protestant religion. 1752. 12mo. **49 D**

Lists of foreign protestants and aliens resident in England 1618–1688. Edited by W. D. Cooper. [Camden Society, vol. 82.] 1862. 8vo. **85 C**

Memoires of the lives, actions, sufferings, and deaths of those noble, reverend, and excellent personages that suffered for the protestant religion in our late intestine wars. By David Lloyd. 1668. 4to. **79 H**

A New protestant litany. 1689. [Tracts, 1688–9.] **118 E**

Protestant exiles from France in the reign of Louis XIV. By Rev. D. C. A. Agnew. 2nd ed. 3 vols. 1871–74. 8vo. **80 G**

Rome's Master-Peece; or the grand conspiracy of the Pope and his Jesuited instruments to extirpate the Protestant religion, by kindling a civill war in Scotland &c. By Wm. Prynne. 2nd ed. 1644. 8vo. **118 E**

PROUT, WILLIAM.

Chemistry, meteorology, and the function of digestion considered with reference to natural theology. 2nd ed. 1834. 8vo. **77 B**

PROVIDENT SOCIETIES.

Law of friendly, industrial and provident societies. By W.
T. Pratt. 11th ed. by E. W. Brabrook. 1888. 12mo. **10 A**

The law relating to industrial and provident societies. By
H. F. A. Davis. 1869. 8vo. **10 C**

PRUSSIA.

The agrarian legislation of Prussia during the present century.
By R. B. D. Morier. See Systems of land tenure, 1881,
pp. 351–393. **78 B**

The Frederician Code ; or, a body of law for the dominions
of the king of Prussia. 2 vqls. Edinburgh, 1761. 8vo. **55 C**

See also GERMANY.

PRYCE, GEORGE.

A Popular history of Bristol, antiquarian, topographical, and
descriptive. Bristol, 1861. 8vo. **87 F**

PRYCE, WILLIAM.

Mineralogia Cornubiensis, a treatise on minerals, mines, and
mining, containing the theory and natural history of strata,
fissures, and lodes. 1778. folio. **87 G**

PRYNNE, WILLIAM.

Brevia Parliamentaria rediviva. 1662. 8vo. **97 I**

Catalogue of printed books, by W. Prynne. 1643. 8vo. **118 E**

Documents relating to the proceedings against W. Prynne in
1634 and 1637, with a biographical fragment by John
Bruce. Edited by S. R. Gardiner. [Camden Society, n.s.
vol. 18.] 1877. 8vo. **85 D**

The Doome of Cowardisze and Treachery ; or, a Looking-
Glasse for cowardly or corrupt Governours, and Souldiers.
1643. 8vo. **118 E**

The Falsities and Forgeries of the anonymous author of a
late pamphlet intituled, The Fallacies of Mr. William
Prynne, discovered and confuted, in a short View of his
Books. 1644. 8vo. **118 E**

History of King John, King Henry III. and King Edward I.
1670. folio. **115 I**

An Humble Remonstrance against the Tax of Ship-Money
lately imposed. Written in 1636. 1643. 8vo. **118 E**

Independency examined, unmasked, refuted, by twelve new
particular Interrogatories. 1644. 8vo. **118 E**

PRYNNE, WILLIAM—*continued.*

A Moderate Apology against a pretended Calumny. 1644.
8vo.   118 E

The Opening of Great Seal of England. 1643. 8vo.   118 E

The Popish Royall Favourite ; or, a full discovery of His
Majesties extraordinary favours to, and protections of
notorious Papists, Priests, Jesuits, &c. 1643. 8vo.   118 E

Rome's Master-Peece ; or the grand conspiracy of the Pope
and his Jesuited instruments to extirpate the Protestant
religion, by kindling a civill war in Scotland &c. 2nd ed.
1644. 8vo.   118 E

A Soveraign antidote to prevent, appease, and determine our
unnaturall and destructive civill warres and dissentions.
2nd Impression. 1642. 8vo.   118 E

The soveraigne power of parliaments and kingdomes. 1643.
8vo.   48 D

Twelve considerable serious questions touching Church Government. 1644. 8vo.   118 E

A Vindication of Psalme 105, v. 15 (Touch not mine anointed,
and doe my Prophets no harme), from some false Glosses
obtruded on it by Royalists. 3rd ed. 1644. 8vo.   118 E

A True and full Relation of the Prosecution, Arraignment,
Tryall, and Condemnation of Nathaniel Fiennes, late
Colonel and Governor of the City and Castle of Bristoll.
By W. Prynne and Clement Walker. 1644. 8vo.   118 E

PSALMS, THE.

A Concordance to the Psalter contained in the book of common
prayer. [n.d.] Bound with A. Cruden's Concordance.
10th ed. 1831. 4to.   77 G

Ψαλτηριον του Δαβιδ. [David's Psalms in Greek.] Cambridge;
1664. 12mo.   118 A

Psalterium secundum mores et consuetudinem sancte Romane
ecclesie vigilanti cura novissime impressum per Joannem
de Tridino dictum Tacuinus. Venetiis, 1499. 12mo. 118 B

A Version of the Psalms of David. By a Lay member of
the Church of England [John Stow]. 3rd ed. 1842.
12mo.   77 A

The whole book of Psalms collected into English metre. By
Thomas Sternhold, John Hopkins and others. 1724. folio.
Bound with Common Prayer. 1724. folio.   77 H

PSEUDONYMS. See ANONYMS.

PUBLIC HEALTH.

Law relating to Public Health.   By W. C. Glen and A. Glen. 10th ed.   1888.   8vo.   11 D

Public Health act, 1875, annotated.   By W. G. Lumley and E. Lumley.   3rd ed. by W. Patchett and A. Macmorran. 1887.   8vo.   11 D

A Digest of the law relating to Public Health.   By G. F. Chambers.   8th ed.   1881.   8vo.   157 A

Practical working of the Municipal corporation and public health acts exemplified in case of Le Feuvre *v.* Lankester. By S. Bullock.   1854.   [Pamphlets, vol. 9, pt. 2.]   144 A

Results of sanitary improvement.   By Southwood Smith. 1854.   [Pamphlets, vol. 9, pt. 1.]   144 A

See also BAKER, T., FITZGERALD, G. A. R., FITZGERALD, J. V. V., SAUNDERS, T. W. and SMITH, W. R.

PUBLIC LAW.

Civil law in its natural order : with the public law.   By Jean Domat.   Translated by Wm. Strahan.   2nd ed.   2 vols. 1737.   folio.   48 H

See also INTERNATIONAL LAW.

PUBLIC MEETINGS.

The law as to Public Meetings.   By J. W. Blagg.   1888. 12mo.   11 D

Handbook for Public Meetings.   By G. F. Chambers.   2nd ed. 1886.   8vo.   11 D

Handy book on the law and practice of Public Meetings. By J. W. Smith.   2nd ed.   1867.   12mo.   175 A

PUBLIC OFFICES.

First and Second reports of committee appointed to inquire into fees and emoluments of public offices.   1837.   folio.   153 D

PUBLISHERS.

The law specially affecting printers, publishers &c.   By A. Powell.   2nd issue.   1889.   8vo.   11 C

Appeal to the public against the monopoly of the large publishers.   By James Wildy.   1835.   [Pamphlets, vol. 4.]   144 A

PUFENDORF, SAMUEL.

Of the law of nature and nations.   Translated into English by Basil Kennet.   3rd ed.   1717.   folio.   48 H

PUFENDORF, SAMUEL—*continued.*

Les devoirs de l'homme et du citoien tels qu'ils lui sont prescrits par la loi naturelle. Traduits par Jean Barbeyrac. 5me éd. 2 vols. in 1. Amsterdam, 1735. 12mo. **48 F**

De officio hominis et civis juxta legem naturalem libri duo. Buddei historiam juris naturalis præmisit Tho. Johnson. Editio quarta. 1758. 8vo. **48 F**

PUGHE, WILLIAM OWEN.

A Dictionary of the Welsh language explained in English. 2 vols. in 1. Denbigh, 1832. 8vo. **123 C**

A Grammar of the Welsh language. 2nd ed. Denbigh, 1832. 8vo. · **123 C**

An Outline of the characteristics of the Welsh and its utility in connection with other ancient languages for developing the primitive speech of mankind. Denbigh, 1832. 8vo. Bound with the preceding. . **123 C**

PULBROOK, ANTHONY.

The Companies acts, 1862–83. 9th ed. 1886. 12mo. **169 D**

The same. 11th ed. 1889. 12mo. **9 D**

PULLING, ALEXANDER.

Crime and criminals. Is the gaol the only preventive? 1863. [Pamphlets, vol. 18.] **144 B**

Observations on disputes at present arising in the Corporation of City of London. 1847. [Pamphlets, vol. 35.] **144 C**

The order of the Coif. 1884. 8vo. **80 F**

Our law-reporting system. Cannot its evils be prevented? 1863. [Pamphlets, vol. 20.] **144 B**

· Practical treatise on the laws, customs, and regulations of the city and port of London. 1842. 8vo. **91 E**

Private bill legislation. Can anything be now done to improve it? [Pamphlets, vol. 11.] **144 A**

Proposals for amending the law affecting juries and jurymen. 1865. [Pamphlets, vol. 35.] **144 C**

Summary of law of attorneys and solicitors. 1849. 12mo. **160 C**

The same. 3rd ed. 1862. 8vo. **11 G**

PULLING, ALEXANDER, JUNIOR.

The current index of all cases reported in The Law Reports and Weekly Notes, 1886–1890. 3 vols. 1888–90. 8vo. **73 F**

PULLING, ALEXANDER, JUNIOR—*continued.*
Index to the orders in Council, proclamations, royal commissions of inquiry, and orders and notices of government departments, published in the London Gazette, January 1st, 1830, to December 31st, 1883. 1885. 4to. **45 H**

PULTON, FERDINANDO.
A Collection of sundrie statutes frequent in use ; with notes and references. 1632. folio. **158 E**
The same. Another ed. 1636. folio. **158 E**
De Pace regis et regni, viz. : A Treatise declaring which be the great and generall offences of the realme and the chiefe impediments of the peace of the king and the kingdome. 1610. folio. **155 E**
The same. Another ed. 1615. folio. **155 E**
Kalender ; or, table comprehending effect of all statutes from Magna Charta to 7 Jac. I. 1617. folio. **158 B**

PUNCH.
Punch. Vols. 50, 51, 58, 59, 64, 65, and 74–99. 1866–1890. 32 vols. in 16. 1866–90. 4to.

PUNJAB.
Opinions of the press in India on the Tenant right controversy in the Punjab. Lahore, 1869. 8vo. **38 B**
Punjab customary law. By C. L. Tupper. 3 vols. Calcutta, 1881. 8vo. **38 C**

PURCHASE DEEDS.
Dissertation on and precedents of Purchase Deeds. See Bythewood and Jarman's Conveyancing, 4th ed., vol. 5, 1888. 8vo. **13 D**
Treatise on Purchase Deeds of freehold estates and leasehold property. By W. F. Cornish. New ed. by G. Horsey. 1855. 8vo. **175 A**
Proposed reasons for the appeal to the Lords, from the decree of Chancery, in the cause of J. Fox, W. M. Pitt, and others, against Robert Mackreth. See Hargrave's Juridical Arguments, vol. 1, 1797, pp. 453–470 and 526–570. **144 G**

PURITY.
Purity Meetings, who hath bewitched you ? By Wilbraham Taylor. 1885. [Pamphlets, vol. 40.] **144 C**

PURKIS, HENRY WAKEHAM.
> The Intermediate Guide. 1883. 12mo.   **64 D**
> The Telegram, containing questions and answers in common law, conveyancing, and equity of articled clerks' examination, 1859–1864. 24 numbers. 1859–64. 8vo.   **168 A**

PUTNEY COLLEGE.
> Letter to Duke of Buccleuch on education at Putney College. By Rev. M. Cowie. 1849. [Pamphlets, vol. 6.]   **144 A**

PYCROFT, REV. JAMES.
> Twenty years in the church. An autobiography. 1859. 8vo.   **80 B**

PYCROFT, JAMES WALLIS.
> The claim to the foreshores of the sea coast and tidal rivers in the counties of Devon and Cornwall by Her Majesty's Commissioners of Woods and Forests examined and considered. Privately printed. 1854. 4to.   **118 F**
> A Short inquiry into the nature of the protection afforded by legislative incorporation in relation to the University and colleges of Oxford. 1851. [Pamphlets, vol. 8.]   **144 A**
> The same. 2nd ed. 1851. [Pamphlets, vol. 9, pt. 2.]   **144 A**

PYE, SAMUEL.
> The moral system of Moses. 1770. 4to. .   **77 G**

PYPER, WILLIAM.
> Gradus ad Parnassum; sive novus synonymorum, epithetorum, versuum, ac phrasium poeticarum thesaurus. Editio nova. Edinburgi, 1831. 8vo.   **47 F**

QUAKERS.
> A Collection of acts of parliament relative to those Protestant Dissenters usually called Quakers, from 1688. 1777. 12mo.   **175 A**

QUARE IMPEDIT.
> Quare Impedit in two parts. Part I. containing an abridgment of the law concerning the patronages of churches, &c. Part II. containing precedents of pleadings. By J. Mallory. 1737. folio.   **157 C**
> See also ECCLESIASTICAL LAW.

- QUARTER SESSIONS.
  The practice of the Court of Quarter Sessions. By J. F. Archbold. 4th ed. 1885. 8vo.   12 C
  A Vade Mecum of practice in appellate and civil cases at Quarter Sessions. By F. J. Smith. 1882. 12mo.   12 B
  Quarter sessions from Queen Elizabeth to Queen Anne. By A. H. A. Hamilton. 1878. 8vo.   78 B
  The general and quarter sessions of the peace. By H. Leeming and R. A. Cross. 2nd ed. by H. Lloyd and H. F. Thurlow. 1876. 8vo.   53 F
  A Letter to Lord John Russell on the amendment of the Quarter Sessions. By C. S. Greaves. 1839. [Pamphlets, vol. 4.]   144 A
  See also BEST, W. M. and PRITCHARD, T. S.

QUARTERLY REVIEW.
  The Quarterly Review, Feb. 1809–Oct. 1890.   163 vols.
  1812–90. 8vo.   132 A–G
  Indexes to vols. 1–159.   8 vols.   1819–85.   8vo.   132 G

QUAYLE, THOMAS.
  General view of agriculture of Isle of Man. 1812. 8vo. 94 F

QUEBEC.
  Orders in council and regulations having force of law in province of Quebec. 7 vols. Quebec, 1884–90. 8vo. 34 E
  Plan of a code of laws for the province of Quebec reported by the Advocate General. 1774. 12mo.   55 E

QUEENBOROUGH.
  Copy of charter of borough of Queenborough. [n.d.] 12mo. 88 D

QUEEN'S BENCH PRACTICE.
  Practice of the Queen's Bench division of high court of justice. By J. F. Archbold. 14th ed. 2 vols. 1885. 8vo. 12 E
  Digest of the practice of the Queen's Bench division. By C. E. Malden and A. H. Poyser. 1884. 8vo.   52 B
  Concise practice of Queen's Bench and Chancery divisions. By T. B. Napier. 1884. 8vo.   64 E
  Forms of practical proceedings in the Queen's Bench division of high court of justice. By T. Chitty. 12th ed. 1883. 8vo.   12 E

QUEEN'S BENCH PRACTICE—*continued.*

Archibald's Country solicitor's practice, a handbook of the practice in the Queen's Bench division of the high court of justice. By W. F. A. Archibald. 1881. 8vo.   **12 E**

See also COMMON LAW PRACTICE and CROWN OFFICE PRACTICE.

QUEEN'S BENCH REPORTS.

Queen's Bench Reports, 1841–1852. By J. L. Adolphus and T. F. Ellis. 18 vols. 1843–56. 8vo.   **5 F G H**

QUEENSLAND.

The Queensland Statutes, 1827–1888. Edited by A. Pain and J. L. Woolcock. 5 vols. Brisbane, 1889. 8vo. **35 E**

Queensland Statutes, 1860–1889. 13 vols. Brisbane, 1860–89. folio and 4to.   **35 E**

See also HARDING, G. R.

QUÉRARD, JOSEPH-MARIE.

A Martyr to bibliography : a notice of the life and works of J. M. Quérard, bibliographer. By Olphar Hamst [Ralph Thomas]. 1867. 8vo.   **82 B**

QUINTILIANUS, MARCUS FABIUS.

Declamationes XIX. majores et quæ ex CCCLXXXVIII. supersunt CXLV. minores. Curante Petro Burmanno. Lugd. Bat., 1720. 4to.   **47 G**

De institutione oratoria libri duodecim recogniti et emendati per Petrum Burmannum. Lugd. Bat., 1720. 4to. **47 G**

Institutes of oratory, book v. chap. vii. concerning witnesses. Translated by W. M. Best. 1836. [Law Tracts, vol. 6.] **144 E**

QUO WARRANTO.

Placita de Quo Warranto temporibus Edw. I. II. & III. in curia receptæ Scaccarii Westm. asservata. Edited by W. Illingworth. 1818. folio.   **98 C**

The proceedings in the Court of King's-Bench upon the Quo Warranto touching the charter of the City of London, with the judgment entred thereupon. 1696. folio.   **91 G**

RABELAIS, FRANÇOIS.

Works, translated by Sir Thomas Urquhart and Mr. Motteux. New ed. 2 vols. 1849. 12mo.   **118 B**

RACINE, Jean.
Œuvres complètes. Nouvelle éd. Paris, 1829. 8vo. **83 H**

RACING.
The law concerning Horses, Racing, Wagers, and Gaming.
By G. H. H. Oliphant. 4th ed. by C. E. Lloyd. 1882.
8vo. **10 B**

RAILTON, Ernest H. and Rockingham Gill.
Practice and pleading in the Mayor's Court, London. 1888.
12mo. **12 D**

RAILWAY AND CANAL CASES.
Cases relating to Railways and Canals, argued and adjudged
in the Courts of Law and Equity 1835 to 1854. By H. I.
Nicholl and others. 7 vols. 1840–55. 8vo. **3 D**
See also Neville, R.

RAILWAY COMMISSION PRACTICE.
Practice before the railway commissioners. By J. H. B. Browne.
1876. 8vo. **12 A**
The practice before the railway commissioners. By R. G.
Junner. 1874. 8vo. **12 A**

RAILWAYS.
Analysis of railways consisting of a series of reports on the
1,200 miles of projected railways in England and Wales,
now before Parliament. By F. Whishaw. 1837. 8vo. **78 C**
Bradshaw's Railway companion, containing the times of de-
parture, fares &c. of the railways in England. Manchester,
1842. 12mo. **118 A**
The broad and narrow gauge ; or, remarks on the report of
the Gauge Commissioners. By Henry Lushington. 1846.
[Pamphlets, vol. 21.] **144 B**
Dictionnaire législatif et réglementaire des Chemins de Fer.
Par G. Palaa. Paris, 1864. 8vo. **40 H**
History of railways. See F. Clifford's History of private bill
legislation, vol. 1, 1885, pp. 43–184. **83 I**
Railway Intelligence. January 1861 and January 1875. Com-
piled by Mihill Slaughter. 2 vols. 1861–75. 8vo. **146 B**
Railway rates and radical rule. By J. B. Pope. 1884. 12mo.
78 A

RAILWAYS—*continued.*

Railway revelations ; being letters on the subject of the proposed Direct London and Manchester railways. By T. Mulock. 1845. [Pamphlets, vol. 21.] **144 B**

The railway shareholder's manual, or practical guide to all the railways in the world. By Henry Tuck. 6th ed. 1845. 12mo. **118 A**

Robinson's Railway time and fare tables, containing correct time and fare tables of all the principal railways in Great Britain. 1841. 12mo. **118 A**

See also POOR, H. V.

RAILWAYS, LAW OF.

Law relating to public statutory undertakings comprising railway companies &c. By J. B. Street. 1890. 8vo. **11 G**

The Railway and Canal traffic acts 1854 to 1888, with notes, orders, &c. By H. R. Darlington. 1889. 8vo. **11 D**

The law relating to rates and traffic on railways and canals. By A. K. Butterworth. 1889. 8vo. **11 D**

The law of railways, railway companies, and investments. By Sir W. Hodges. 7th ed. by J. M. Lely. 2 vols. 1888. 8vo. **11 D**

The law of railway companies. By J. H. B. Browne and H. S. Theobald. 2nd ed. 1888. 8vo. **11 D**

Railway passengers and railway companies. By L. A. Goodeve. 2nd ed. 1885. 8vo. **11 D**

On some remarkable decisions affecting railway passengers. By F. K. Munton. 1883. [Pamphlets, vol. 37.] **144 C**

Railway carrying and carriers' law, the liabilities and non-liabilities of railways, carriers, and others as to goods, passengers, &c. By C. Nash. 1846. [Pamphlets, vol. 21.] **144 B**

Railway and land taxation, shewing the origin, progress, law, operation, and statistics of the poor and other rates, and their injustice and impolicy with reference to railways. By C. Nash. 1844. [Pamphlets, vol. 21.] **144 B**

See à BECKETT, T. T., BIGG, J., CHAMBERS, T., FREND, H. T., GODEFROI, H., LELY, J. M., MARSHALL, W., PENFOLD, C., REDFIELD, T. F., REDMAN, J. H., RIDDELL, H. and SHELFORD, L.

See also CARRIERS and RATING.

RAINE, REV. JAMES.

The history and antiquities of North Durham, as subdivided into the shires of Norham, Island, and Bedlington, now united to Northumberland. 1852. folio. **88 H**

RAITHBY, JOHN.
An Index to the statutes at large, from Magna Carta to 1809.
1814. 4to. 70 G
The same. Another ed. 3 vols. 1814. 8vo. 31 D
The study and practice of the law, considered in their various
relations to society, in a series of letters. 2nd ed. 1816.
8vo. 170 G

RALEIGH, SIR WALTER.
Documents relating to Sir W. Raleigh's last voyage. [Camden
Society, vol. 87.] 1864. 8vo 85 C
History of the World in five books. 1687. folio 113 H
The life of Sir W. Raleigh, Knight; with his trial at Win-
chester. [By John Shirley.] 1677. 12mo. 79 A
Trial of Sir Walter Raleigh. See Criminal Trials, 1832
pp. 389–520. 51 D

RAM, JAMES.
Observations on the natural right of a father to the custody of
his children and to direct their education. 1828. [Jacob's
Tracts, vol. 11.] 144 F
The science of Legal Judgment. 1834. 8vo. 169 E
Treatise of assets, debts, and incumbrances. 1832. 8vo. 160 C
Treatise on facts as subjects of inquiry by a jury. 1861. 8vo.
52 H

RAMSAY, ANDREW MICHAEL.
An Essay upon civil government. 1732. 12mo. 49 E

RAMSEY MONASTERY, HUNTINGDON.
Cartularium monasterii de Rameseia. Edited by W. H. Hart
and Rev. P. A. Lyons. 2 vols. 1884–86. 8vo. 102 H
Chronicon Abbatiæ Rameseiensis, a sæc. X. usque ad an.
circiter 1200. Cura W. D. Macray. 1886. 8vo. 102 H

RANKE, LEOPOLD VON.
A History of England principally in the seventeenth century.
Edited by C. W. Boase and G. W. Kitchin. 6 vols. Oxford,
1875. 8vo. 115 F
The Popes of Rome, their ecclesiastical and political history
during the sixteenth and seventeenth centuries. Translated
by Sarah Austin. 4th ed. 3 vols. 1866. 8vo. 113 C

RANKINE, JOHN.

The rights and burdens incident to the ownership of lands
and other heritages in Scotland. 2nd ed. 1884. 8vo. **55 F**

Treatise on the law of leases in Scotland. 1887. 8vo. **55 F**

RAPIN-THOYRAS, PAUL DE.

Acta Regia : being the account which M. Rapin de Thoyras
published of the History of England, grounded upon the
records in Rymer's Fœdera ; with an account of the grants
from the Crown to the nobility, 1087–1634. Translated by
S. Whatley. 1733. folio. **115 I**

History of England. [B.C. 53–A.D. 1689.] Translated by
N. Tindal. 2nd ed. 2 vols. 1732–33. folio. **115 I**

RASTELL, JOHN.

The Exposicions of the termes of the lawes of England, with
diures propre rules and principles of the lawe, as well out
of the bookes of maister Litleton, as of other. Gathered
both in French and English, for yong men very necessary,
whereunto are added the olde tenures. 1567. 12mo. **48 D**

The same. 1575. 12mo. **48 D**

Les termes de la Ley ; or, certaine difficulte and obscure
words and termes of the common lawes and statutes of this
realme now in use expounded and explained. [By John
Rastell.] Newly imprinted. 1636. 12mo. **48 D**

The same. New ed. by T[homas] B[lount]. 1667. 12mo.
48 D

The same. By T[homas] B[lount]. 1685. 12mo. **48 D**

The same. 1721. 8vo. **48 D**

RASTELL, WILLIAM.

A Collection of Entries of declarations, barres, replications,
rejoynders, issues, verdicts, judgments, executions, proces,
continuances, and divers other matters. 1670. folio.

A Collection of the statutes from 9 Henry III. to 23 Elizabeth,
under titles placed by order of alphabet. [1581.] 4to. **158 B**

RATING.

Principles of Rating practically considered. By E. Boyle and
G. H. Davies. 1890. 8vo. **11 D**

Urban Rating. By C. H. Sargant. 1890. 8vo. **11 E**

RATING—*continued.*

The law relating to Rates and Rating. By G. F. Chambers. 2nd ed. 1889. 8vo.   **11 D**

Practical treatise on the law of Rating. By E. J. Castle. 2nd ed. 1886. 8vo.   **11 D**

Principles of the law of Rating. By J. H. B. Browne. 2nd ed. 1886. 8vo.   **11 D**

Small Tenements Rating acts. By W. C. Glen. 4th ed. 1866. 12mo.   **175 B**

Observations on the present mode of valuing property for assessment to the parochial rates. By H. H. Carwardine. 1841. [Pamphlets, vol. 4.]   **144 A**

See also CASTLE, H. J., PENFOLD, C., ROSHER, G. B., RYDE, E. and RYDE, W. C.

RATTIGAN, WILLIAM HENRY.

De Jure Personarum ; or a treatise on the Roman law of persons. 1873. 8vo.   **63 F**

RAUTHMEL, REV. RICHARD.

Antiquitates Bremetonacenses ; or, the Roman Antiquities of Overborough. Kirkby Lonsdale, 1824. 8vo.   **89 A**

RAVEN, JOHN.

The parliamentary history of England from the passing of the Reform bill of 1832. 1885. 8vo.   **116 B**

RAVENNAS, PETRUS.

Compendium Juris Canonici. Lugd., 1521. 8vo.   **118 B**

RAWDON, MARMADUKE.

The life of Marmaduke Rawdon of York. Edited by Robert Davies. [Camden Society, vol. 85.] 1863. 8vo.   **85 C**

RAWLINSON, SIR CHRISTOPHER.

The Municipal Corporation act 5 & 6 Will. IV. c. 76 and the acts since passed for amending the same. 4th ed. by W. N. Welsby. 1863. 12mo.   **164 G**

The same. 6th ed. by T. Geary. 1874. 8vo.   **164 G**

The same. 8th ed. by T. Geary. 1883. 8vo.   **9 F**

RAWLINSON, GEORGE.

The history of Herodotus. 4 vols. 1858–60. 8vo.   **113 D**

RAWLINSON, James.
Guide to solicitors on taking instructions for Wills. 1874. 8vo.   **177 D**
Notes on the Mortmain acts. 1877. 8vo.   **161 F**

RAY, Isaac.
Medical jurisprudence of insanity. Boston, 1860. 8vo. **59 G**

RAYMOND, Robert, 1 Baron.
Reports of cases argued and adjudged in the courts of King's Bench and Common Pleas, in the reigns of William, Anne, Geo. I. and Geo. II., 1694–1734. 2 vols. 1743. folio.
The same. 3rd ed. 2 vols. 1775. folio.
The same. 4th ed. by J. Bayley. 3 vols. Dublin, 1792. 8vo.   **5 H**
The same. 5th ed. by C. J. Gale. Vol. 1. 1832. 8vo. **5 H**

RAYMOND, Sir Thomas.
Reports of divers special cases in the Courts of King's Bench, Common Pleas, and Exchequer, in the reign of King Charles II. 2nd ed. 1743. folio.   **74 F**

RAYNER, John.
Cases at large concerning Tithes. 3 vols. 1783. 8vo. **65 A**

READE, Sir William.
Copies of all papers recorded in the Heralds' College connected with the claim made in 1810 by Sir William Reade to the title of baronet. See Peerage Evidence, vol. 10. **124 J**

READER, William.
Domesday book for the county of Warwick, translated; with a brief dissertation on Domesday Book. Coventry, 1835. 4to.   **93 E**

READING.
The art of delivering written language ; or, an essay on reading. [By William Cockin.] 1775. 8vo.   **78 B**
Results of reading. By J. S. Caldwell. 1843. 8vo.   **83 I**

READING, Berkshire.
History and antiquities of Reading. By Rev. C. Coates. 1802. 4to.   **86 G**

REAL ASSETS.

Essay on Real Assets. By J. Williams. 1861. 8vo. **53 F**

REAL PRESENCE.

The substance of the argument, delivered before the judicial committee of the Privy Council, by A. J. Stephens, in the case of T. B. Sheppard against W. J. E. Bennett, clerk. 1872. 8vo. **51 F**

REAL PROPERTY.

Student's guide to law of real and personal property. By J. Indermaur and C. Thwaites. 2nd ed. 1889. 8vo. **64 F**

A Compendium of the law of property in land. By W. D. Edwards. 1888. 8vo. **11 D**

Principles of the law of real property. By Joshua Williams. 16th ed. 1887. 8vo. **64 F**

Modern law of real property. By L. A. Goodeve. 2nd ed. 1885. 8vo. **64 F**

Concise abridgment of the law of real property. By J. A. Shearwood. 3rd ed. 1885. 8vo. **64 F**

Compendium of the law of real and personal property. By J. W. Smith. 6th ed. by the author and J. Trustram. 2 vols. 1884. 8vo. **11 C**

The settlement of real estates. By Joshua Williams. 1879. 8vo. **13 H**

The law of joint ownership and partition of real estate. By E. J. Foster. 1878. 8vo. **13 B**

An Introduction to the history of the law of real property. By K. E. Digby. 2nd ed. 1876. 8vo. **83 I**

The law of Limitation as to real property. By William Brown. 1869. 8vo. **53 A**

The judgment law amendment acts relating to real property. By James Pask. 3rd ed. 1866. 8vo. **13 B**

Outlines of the law of real property. By Robert Maugham 1842. 12mo. **170 F**

A Digest of the law respecting real property. By W. Cruise 4th ed. 7 vols. 1835. 8vo. **14 B**

See BURTON, W. H., CRABB, G., HILLIARD, F., HOBLER, F. HUBBACK, J., LEAKE, S. M., ROSCOE, R., STEVENS, W. and WASHBURN, E.

See also CONVEYANCING PRECEDENTS, CONVEYANCING PRINCIPLES, JUDGMENTS and PROPERTY.

REAL PROPERTY REFORM.

A Contre-Project to the Humphreysian code. By John James Park. 1828. 8vo. **83 J**

An Essay on the reform of law of real property and practice of Conveyancing. By A Solicitor. 1871. 12mo. **174 F**

Facts and suggestions as to the law of real property. By N. T. Lawrence. 1880. [Pamphlets, vol. 37.] **144 C**

Letter on law of real property and practice of conveyancing. By W. Hayes. 1825. [Jacob's Tracts, vol. 1.] **144 E**

Letter to James Humphreys, Esq. on his proposal to repeal the laws of real property and substitute a new code. By E. B. Sugden. 1826. [Jacob's Tracts, vol. 4.] **144 E**

Observations on real property law reform. By S. J. Hunter. 1860. [Pamphlets, vol. 15.] **144 B**

Observations on the code for real property proposed by James Humphreys. By G. D. B. Beaumont. [Jacob's Tracts, vol. 5.] **144 E**

Observations on natural state of English laws of real property, with outlines of a code. By James Humphreys. 1826. 8vo. **83 I**

Observations on proposed new code relating to real property. By R. Dixon. 1827. [Jacob's Tracts, vol. 5.] **144 E**

Observations upon, and a suggested form of act for the amendment and simplification of the law of real property and conveyancing. By W. D. Jeans. Warrington, 1879. [Pamphlets, vol. 37.] **144 C**

Remarks on the expediency of framing a new code of laws for real property. By a Barrister of the Inner Temple. 1827. [Jacob's Tracts, vol. 5.] **144 E**

Reports made by the commissioners appointed to inquire into the law of England respecting Real Property 1829, 1830, 1832, 1833. 3 vols. 1829–33. folio. **153 E**

Suggestions sent to the commissioners appointed to inquire into the laws of Real Property. By John Tyrrell. [Not published.] 1829. 8vo. **174 F**

REAL PROPERTY STATUTES.

Real Property statutes. By H. Greenwood. 2nd ed. 1884. 8vo. **13 G**

Real Property acts, with explanatory notes. By W. T. Charley. 3rd ed. 1876, and Supplement. 1879. 12mo. **174 F**

The Real Property statutes passed in the reigns of king William IV. and queen Victoria. By L. Shelford. 7th ed. 1863. 8vo. **53 E**

REAL PROPERTY STATUTES—*continued.*

Acts relating to the law of Real Property passed in last session of parliament. By S. Atkinson. 1833. 8vo. **174 E**

See also CONVEYANCING ACTS and SUGDEN, SIR E.

RECEIVERS.

The law and practice as to receivers. By W. W. Kerr. 2nd ed. 1882. 8vo. **11 E**

The appointment and duties of a Receiver under the High Court of Chancery. By W. H. Bennet. 1849. 8vo. **175 B**

RECORD AND WRIT PRACTICE.

Record and writ practice of the Court of Chancery. By T. W. Braithwaite. 1858. 8vo. **53 F**

RECORD COMMISSION.

Comparative account of works produced and moneys received by the commissioners on the public records during two periods of five years before and five years after 12 March 1831. By Wm. Black. 1837. 8vo. **97 I**

Comparison between certain statements contained in the evidence given before the select committee upon the record commission and various documents illustrative of the matters referred to in such evidence. 1837. 8vo. **97 I**

A Leaf omitted out of the Record report, or some remarks upon the public records, contained in a Letter addressed to a member of parliament, 1837. Another leaf omitted out of the Record report, contained in a Second letter addressed to a member of parliament, 1837. A third leaf omitted out of the Record report, contained in a Third letter addressed to a member of parliament, 1837. [All by John Bruce.] 1 vol. 1837. 8vo. **97 I**

A Letter upon the report of the recent record committee. By Basil Montagu. 1837. 8vo. **97 I**

Letters from eminent historical writers relating to the publications of the Board of Commissioners on the public records. 1836. 8vo. **97 I**

Letters on the conduct of C. P. Cooper the secretary, and on the general management of the commission. By Henry Cole. 1835–6. 8vo. **97 I**

Observations, letters, and opinions of commissioners, on constitution and duties of record commission. 1836. 8vo. **97 I**

RECORD COMMISSION—*continued.*

Observations on the state of historical literature, with remarks on record offices and on the proceedings of the record commission. By N. H. Nicolas. 1830. 8vo.   **99 A**

Papers and documents relating to the evidence of certain witnesses examined before the select committee of the House of Commons appointed to inquire into the management and affairs of the record commission. [By C. P. Cooper.] 1837. 8vo.   **97 I**

Proceedings of the commissioners for the arrangement and preservation of the public records of the kingdom, 1806–1809, so far as relates to Scotland. 1808–9. folio.   **98 E**

Record commission, Scotland. Correspondence of C. P. Cooper, secretary to the Board, with Thomas Thomson, deputy clerk registrar. Memorial of R. Pitcairn, Writer to the Signet. Reports of deputy clerk registrar from 1822 to 1831 ; and 2 Reports by R. Pitcairn to C. P. Cooper. 1835. 8vo.   **97 I**

Refutation of Mr. Palgrave's 'Remarks in reply to Observations on the state of historical literature.' Additional facts relative to the record commission. By N. H. Nicolas. 1831. 8vo.   **99 A**

Reports [first and second] from the select committee appointed to inquire into the state of the public records of the kingdom. 1801. folio.   **98 E**

Reports from commissioners appointed to execute measures recommended by a select committee of House of Commons respecting the public records of the kingdom, 1800–1819; and Appendix, containing engraved Fac Similes inserted in the several works printed under commission, with explanations. 2 vols. 1819. folio.   **98 E**

Reports from the commissioners appointed to execute the measures recommended in an address of the House of Commons respecting the public records of Ireland, 1810–1825. 3 vols. 1819–25. folio.   **98 E**

Report, resolutions, and proceedings of the select committee of House of Commons appointed to inquire into management and affairs of Record Commission. 1837. 8vo.   **97 I**

Report to the king in council from the board of commissioners on the public records. 1837. 8vo.   **97 I**

The same, with Appendix. 1837. folio.   **98 E**

Rules for the guidance of Members of Parliament, in the management of select committees and preparation of reports. [Criticisms on the Record report.] 1837. 8vo.   **97 I**

RECORD COMMISSION PUBLICATIONS.

Publications of the Commissioners of Public Records. 136 vols. in 145. 1783–1875. folio & 8vo.

Acts of the Lords Auditors of Causes and Complaints, A.D. 1466–A.D. 1494. [Edited by T. Thomson.] 1839. folio.   98 C

Acts of the Lords of Council in Civil Causes, A.D. 1478–1495. [Edited by T. Thomson.] 1839. folio.   98 C

Acts of the Parliament of Scotland, from 1124 to 1707 ; and general index, with a supplement to the acts. [Edited by T. Thomson and C. Innes.] 12 vols. 1814–75. folio.   31 G

Ancient laws and institutes of England. [Edited by B. Thorpe.] 1840. folio.   99 B

Ancient laws and institutes of Wales. [Edited by A. Owen.] 1841. folio.   99 B

Calendarium Inquisitionum post mortem, sive Escaetarum, temp. Reg. Hen. III. ad Ric. III. ; cum appendice de quamplurimis aliis Inquisitionibus, a regno Hen. III. usque Jac. I. [Edited by J. Caley and J. Bayley.] 4 vols. 1806–28. folio.   98 C

Calendarium Rotulorum Patentium in Turri Londinensi. [Edited by Rev. S. Ayscough and J. Caley.] 1802. folio.   98 C

Calendars of Proceedings in Chancery, in the reign of Queen Elizabeth ; with examples of earlier proceedings in that court, from the reign of Ric. II. to that of Q. Elizabeth. [Edited by J. Bayley.] 3 vols. 1827–32. folio.   98 C

Catalogue of Harleian MSS. in the British Museum ; with indexes of persons, places, and matters. [By H. Wanley and others.] 4 vols. 1808–12. folio.   98 C

Catalogue of Lansdowne MSS. in the British Museum ; with indexes of persons, places, and matters. [By F. Douce and Sir H. Ellis.] 2 parts in 1 vol. 1812–19. folio.   98 C

Catalogue of MSS. in Cottonian Library, deposited in the British Museum. [By Joseph Planta.] 1802. folio.   98 C

Description of the Patent Rolls in the Tower of London ; with an Itinerary of King John. By T. D. Hardy. 1835. 8vo.   98 A

Documents and records illustrating the history of Scotland. Edited by Sir F. Palgrave. Vol. 1. 1837. 8vo.   99 A

Documents illustrative of English history in the thirteenth and fourteenth centuries. Edited by H. Cole. 1844. folio.   99 E

Domesday Book, seu liber censualis Wilhelmi primi regis Angliæ inter archivos regni in domo capitulari Westmonasterii asservatus. [Edited by A. Farley.] 2 vols. 1783. folio.   98 D

A General introduction to Domesday Book, with indexes of the tenants in chief and under tenants at the time of the survey. By Sir Henry Ellis. 2 vols. 1833. 8vo.   97 I

Libri censualis vocati Domesday-Book Additamenta ex codic. antiquiss. ; Exon Domesday ; Inquisitio Eliensis ; Liber Winton. ; Boldon Book. Edited by Sir H. Ellis. 1816. folio.   98 D

Libri censualis vocati Domesday-Book Indices. Accessit dissertatio de ratione hujusce libri. By Sir H. Ellis. 1816. folio.   98 D

Ducatus Lancastriæ. Pars I. Calendarium inquisitionum post mortem &c. temp. regum Edw. I. ad Car. I. Partes II., III., IV. A calendar to the pleadings, depositions &c. from Hen. VII. to 1603. Edited by R. J. Harper, J. Caley and W. Minchin. 4 parts in 3 vols. 1823–34. folio.   99 C

RECORD COMMISSION PUBLICATIONS—*continued*.

Essay upon the original authority of the King's Council. By Sir Francis Palgrave. 1834. 8vo.   **97 I**

Excerpta e rotulis finium in Turri Londinensi asservatis, 1216–1272. Cura C. Roberts. 2 vols. 1835. 8vo.   **99 A**

Fines sive pedes finium in Curia domini regis 1195–1214. Edited by Rev. J. Hunter. 2 vols. 1835–44. 8vo.   **98 A**

Handbook to the public records. By F. S. Thomas. 1853. 8vo. **98 A**

Historical notes, 1509–1714. By F. S. Thomas. 3 vols. 1856. 8vo.   **99 A**

Inquisitionum ad Capellam Domini Regis retornatarum, quæ in publicis Archivis Scotiæ adhuc servantur, abbreviatio. [Edited by T. Thomson.] 3 vols. 1811–16. folio.   **98 E**

Inquisitionum in Officio Rotulorum Cancellariæ Hiberniæ asservatarum repertorium. [Edited by James Hardiman.] 2 vols. 1826–29. folio.   **98 B**

Issue roll of Thomas de Brantingham, Containing payments made out of his Majesty's Revenue in 44 Edw. III., A.D. 1370 Translated by F. Devon. 1835. 4to.   **98 A**

Issues of the Exchequer, being a collection of payments made out of his Majesty's Revenue from Henry III. to Henry IV. inclusive. Edited by F. Devon. 1836. 8vo.   **98 A**

Issues of the Exchequer, being a collection of payments made out of his Majesty's Revenue during the reign of King James I. Edited by F. Devon. 1836. 8vo.   **98 A**

Kalendars (Antient) and inventories of the treasury of his Majesty's Exchequer. Edited by Sir F. Palgrave. 3 vols. 1836. 8vo. **99 A**

Magnum Rotulum Scaccarii, vel Magnum Rotulum Pipæ, de anno tricesimo-primo regni Henrici I. (ut videtur) ; quem plurimi hactenus laudarunt pro Rotulo quinti anni Stephani Regis. Edited by J. Hunter. 1833. 8vo.   **98 A**

Modus tenendi Parliamentum : ancient treatise on mode of holding the Parliament. Edited by T. D. Hardy. 1846. 8vo. **98 A**

Monumenta historica Britannica ; or, materials for the history of Britain from the earliest period. Vol. 1, extending to the Norman Conquest. By H. Petrie and Rev. J. Sharpe ; finally completed for publication by T. D. Hardy. 1848. folio. **99 B**

Nonarum Inquisitiones in Curia Scaccarii, temp. Edw. III. [Edited by G. Vanderzee.] 1807. folio.   **98 D**

Parliamentary writs and writs of military summons ; together with the records and muniments relating to Parliaments. Edited by Sir F. Palgrave. 2 vols. in 4. 1827–34. folio.   **98 D**

Pipe Rolls : the Great Rolls of the Pipe, 1155–1158 and 1189–1190. Edited by Rev. J. Hunter. 2 vols. 1844. 8vo.   **98 A**

Placita de Quo Warranto temp. Edw. I., II. & III. in Curia Receptæ Scaccarii Westm. asservata. [Edited by W. Illingworth.] 1818. folio.   **98 C**

Placitorum in Domo Capitulari Westmonasteriensi asservatorum abbreviatio, temp. regum Ric. I.–Edw. 11. [Edited by W. Illingworth.] 1811. folio.   **98 B**

Proceedings and ordinances of the Privy Council of England, 1386–1542. Edited by Sir H. Nicolas. 7 vols. 1834–37. 8vo. **98 A**

Registrum Magni Sigilli Regum Scotorum in archivis publicis asservatum, A.D. 1306–1424. [Edited by T. Thomson.] 1814. folio.   **98 E**

RECORD COMMISSION PUBLICATIONS—*continued.*

Registrum vulgariter nuncupatum 'The Record of Caernarvon;' e codice MS. Harleiano 696 descriptum. [Edited by Sir H. Ellis.] 1838. folio. 99 D

Rotuli Chartarum in Turri Londinensi asservati. Accurante T. D. Hardy. Vol. 1, pars 1, 1199–1216. 1837. folio. 98 B

Rotuli Curiæ Regis. Rolls and records of the Court held before the King's Justiciars or Justices, from 6 Rich. I. to 1 John. Edited by Sir F. Palgrave. 2 vols. 1835. 8vo. 99 A

Rotuli de Liberate ac de Misis et Præstitis, regnante Johanne. Cura T. D. Hardy. 1844. 8vo. 98 A

Rotuli de Oblatis et Finibus in Turri Londinensi asservati, tempore Regis Johannis. Accurante T. D. Hardy. 1835. 8vo. 98 A

Rotuli Hundredorum, temp. Hen. III. et Edw. I., in Turr' Lond' et in Curia Receptæ Scaccarii Westm. asservati. [Edited by W. Illingworth.] 2 vols. 1812–18. folio. 98 E

Rotuli Litterarum Clausarum in Turri Londinensi asservati, 1204–1227. Accurante T. D. Hardy. 2 vols. 1833–44. folio. 98 B

Rotuli Litterarum Patentium in Turri Londinensi asservati. Accurante T. D. Hardy. Vol. 1, 1201–1216. 1835. folio. 98 B

Rotuli Normanniæ in Turri Londinensi asservati, Johanne et Henrico quinto. Accurante T. D. Hardy. Vol. 1, de annis 1200–1205, necnon de anno 1417. 1835. 8vo. 98 A

Rotuli Scotiæ in Turri Londinensi et in Domo Capitulari Westmonasteriensi asservati, temp. Edw. I.–Hen. VIII. [Edited by Mr. Macpherson.] 2 vols. 1814–19. folio. 99 C

Rotuli selecti ad res Anglicas et Hibernicas spectantes, ex Archivis in Domo Capitulari West-Monasteriensi deprompti. Cura J. Hunter. 1834. 8vo. 98 A

Rotulorum originalium in Curia Scaccarii abbreviatio, temp. Regum Hen. III.–Edw. III. [Edited by H. Playford.] 2 vols. 1805–10. folio. 99 C

Rotulorum Patentium et Clausorum Cancellariæ Hiberniæ Calendarium. Vol. 1, pars 1, Hen. II.–Hen. VII. [Edited by E. Tresham.] 1828. folio. 98 B

Rotulus Cancellarii, vel Antigraphum Magni Rotuli Pipæ, de tertio anno regni Regis Johannis. 1833. 8vo. 99 A

Rymer, Thomas et Robert Sanderson. Fœdera, conventiones, litteræ, et cujuscunque generis acta publica, etc. ab 1066 ad 1383. Denuo aucta, et emendata, accurantibus A. Clarke, F. Holbrooke, et J. Caley. 4 vols. in 7. 1816–69. folio. 99 C

Syllabus (in English) of Rymer's Fœdera. By Sir T. D. Hardy. 3 vols. 1869–85. 8vo. 97 H

State papers during the reign of King Henry VIII. 11 vols. 1830–52. 4to. 103 F

Statutes of the realm from Magna Carta to the end of the reign of Queen Anne. 9 vols. in 13. 1810–28. Alphabetical Index, 1 vol. 1824. Chronological Index, 1 vol. 1828. 15 vols. 1810–28. folio. 99 D

Taxatio Ecclesiastica Angliæ et Walliæ, auctoritate P. Nicholai IV. circa A.D. 1291. [Edited by J. Caley.] 1802. folio. 98 B

Testa de Nevill: sive Liber Feodorum in Curia Scaccarii, temp. Hen. III. et Edw. I. [Edited by J. Caley and W. Illingworth.] 1807. folio. 98 E

RECORD COMMISSION PUBLICATIONS—*continued.*

Valor Ecclesiasticus temp. Hen. VIII. auctoritate regia institutus [A.D. 1535 cum] appendice et indicibus. [Edited by J. Caley.] 6 vols. 1810–14. folio. 98 D

RECORDS, PUBLIC.

Annual reports of the deputy keeper of the public records, 1840–1861. 7 vols. 1840–61. folio. 153 E

The same. 1862–1890. 25 vols. 1862–90. 8vo. 100 A–E

Annual reports of the deputy keeper of the public records in Ireland. 1869–1890. 4 vols. 1869–90. 8vo. 100 F

Classified index to the legal, ecclesiastical, civil, genealogical, topographical, and miscellaneous records &c. of Ireland. 1832. folio. 99 E

Commissions and abstract of annual reports of commissioners on public records of the kingdom. 1806. folio. 98 E

Index to records, called the Originalia and Memoranda on the lord treasurer's remembrancer's side of the Exchequer. By Edward Jones. 2 vols. 1795. folio. 98 E

An Index to the Records, with directions to the several places where they are to be found : and short explanations of the different kinds of Rolls, Writs, &c. [By Mr. Strachey.] 1739. 12mo. 97 I

Index to various repertories, books of orders and decrees, and other records preserved in the Court of Exchequer. By Adam Martin. [With manuscript notes.] 1819. 8vo. 118 E

Observations on the public records of the four courts at Westminster. By William Illingworth. 1831. 8vo. 97 I

Our public records, a brief handbook to the national archives. By A. C. Ewald. 1873. 8vo. 98 A

Papers relative to the project of building a general record office, with plans. By C. P. Cooper. 1835. 8vo. 97 I

Proposal for the erection of a general record office on the site of the Rolls estate. By C. P. Cooper. 1832. 8vo. 97 I

Records and record searching, a guide to the genealogist and topographer. By Walter Rye. 1888. 8vo. 124 G

Return from the Society of Lincoln's Inn to the select committee of the House of Commons appointed to enquire into state of public records of the kingdom. 1801. 8vo. 97 I

See also AYLOFFE, SIR J., BRITTON, J., COTTON, SIR R. NICOLSON, W. and POWELL, T.

RECOVERIES.
Case on the validity of Equitable Recoveries, with the opinions of several eminent counsel thereon. See Collectanea Juridica, vol. 1, 1797, pp. 214–245. **'144 G**
Common Recoveries, their nature and use. By N. Pigott. 2nd ed. by a Serjeant at law [G. Wilson]. 1770. 8vo. **175 C**
See also FINES and RECOVERIES.

RED HORSE IN WARWICKSHIRE.
Observations upon the White Horse ; with an account of the Red Horse. By Rev. F. Wise. Oxford, 1742. 8vo. **86 B**

REDACTION.
A Contre-projet to the Humphreysian code ; and to the projects of Redaction of Messrs. Hammond, Uniacke, and Twiss By J. J. Park. 1828. 8vo. **83 J**

REDFIELD, ISAAC FLETCHER
The law of Railways. 3rd ed. 2 vols. 1867. 8vo. **60 A**
The law of Wills. 2nd ed. 2 vols. 1867. 8vo. **60 B**

REDFORD, GEORGE and THOMAS HURRY RICHES.
The history of the ancient town and borough of Uxbridge. Uxbridge, 1818. 8vo. **89 D**

REDGRAVE, ALEXANDER.
The factory and workshop act 1878, with copious notes. 1878. 8vo. **10 A**

REDGRAVE, SAMUEL.
Murray's Official handbook of church and state. 1852. 12mo. **125 A**

REDMAN, JOSEPH HAWORTH.
Concise view of law of husband and wife. 1883. 12mo. **168 G**
The law affecting railway companies as carriers of goods and live stock. 1870. 12mo. **175 B**
The same. 2nd ed. 1880. 12mo. **53 F**
The law of arbitration and awards. 1872. 8vo. **160 B**
The same. 2nd ed. 1884. 8vo. **9 A**

REDMAN, Joseph Haworth—*continuea*.

Concise view of the law of landlord and tenant. By J. H.
Redman and G. E. Lyon. 1876. 12mo.   **170 C**

The same. 2nd ed. 1879. 12mo.   **170 C**

The same. 3rd ed. 1886. 12mo.   **10 E**

REED, Herbert.

The bills of sale act 1878. 3rd ed. 1880. 8vo.   **160 G**

. The bills of sale acts 1878, 1882. 7th ed. 1889. 8vo. **11 E**

REES, Abraham.

The Cyclopædia ; or, universal dictionary of arts, sciences, and
literature. 45 vols. 1819–20. 4to.   **147 C–F**

REEVES, John.

History of English law from the time of the Saxons to the
end of the reign of Philip and Mary. 2nd ed. 4 vols.
1787. 8vo.   **170 E**

The same. 3rd ed. brought down to the end of the reign of
Elizabeth. 5 vols. 1814–29. 8vo.   **170 E**

The same. New ed. by W. F. Finlason, with an introductory
dissertation on the nature and use of legal history, the rise
and progress of our laws and influence of the Roman law
in formation of our own. 3 vols. 1869. 8vo.   **170 E**

REFEREES, Court of.

Practice of the Court of Referees, on private bills in parliament, with reports of cases as to the Locus Standi of petitioners, 1867 to 1872. By F. Clifford and P. S. Stephens.
2 vols. 1870–73. 8vo.   **66 C**

Cases decided during the sessions 1873–1889 by the Court of
Referees on private bills in Parliament. By F. Clifford,
A. G. Rickards and M. J. Michael. 4 vols. 1876–91.
8vo.   **66 C**

Treatise on Court of Referees in Parliament, and reports of
cases decided in that court during last session. By J. H.
Fawcett. 1866. 8vo.   **66 A**

Practice of Referees' Courts in Parliament. By J. S. Will.
1866. 8vo.   **175 C**

See also Bills, Private and Public.

REFORM ACTS.

Analyse dè l'acte de Réforme du Parlement en Angleterre. Par C. H. Okey. Revue par N. M. Thevenin. Paris, 1832. 12mo. **166 D**

An Examination into certain errors and anomalies in the principles and detail of the registration clauses of the Reform Act 1832. By J. D. Chambers. 1833. [Pamphlets, vol. 4.] **144 A**

A History of the Reform bills of 1866 and 1867. By Homersham Cox. 1868. 8vo. **116 E**

A Letter on the Reform Act, with suggestions for its amendment. By A Revising Barrister. [D. C. Moylan.] 1839. [Pamphlets, vol. 4.] **144 A**

REFORMATION, THE.

Ecclesiastical memorials relating chiefly to religion under Henry VIII., Edward VI., and Mary I. By John Strype. 6 vols. Oxford, 1822. 8vo. **77 C**

The historie of the Reformation of the Church of Scotland; with some treatises conducing to the history. By John Knox. Edited by David Buchanan. 1644. folio. **113 F**

History of the Reformation of the Church of England. By Right Rev. Gilbert Burnet. New ed. 3 vols. in 6. Oxford, 1816. 4to. **115 H**

Narratives of the days of the reformation, chiefly from the manuscripts of John Foxe the Martyrologist. Edited by J. G. Nichols. [Camden Society, vol. 77.] 1859. 8vo. **85 B**

Original letters relative to the English reformation, written during the reigns of Henry VIII., Edward VI., and Mary, from the archives of Zurich. Translated and edited by Rev. H. Robinson. 2 vols. Cambridge, 1846–47. 8vo. **77 C**

The Zurich letters, comprising the correspondence of several English bishops and others with some of the Helvetian reformers during the reign of Queen Elizabeth. Translated and edited by Rev. H. Robinson. 2 vols. Cambridge, 1842–45. 8vo. **77 C**

See also HENRY VII. AND VIII., KINGS OF ENGLAND.

REGALITIES.

History of regalities and of the privilege of repledging. See Historical Law tracts, 2nd ed., 1761, pp. 187–205. **144 F**

REGISTER OFFICE.

A Plan of the universal register office established in the year 1749. By John Fielding. 6th ed. 1753. 8vo. **118 B**

REGISTRAR-GENERAL.

Inconsistencies of the English census of 1861, with the registrar-general's reports and deficiencies in local registry of births. By W. L. Sargant. 1865. [Pamphlets, vol. 26.] **144 B**

On certain results and defects of reports of registrar-general. By W. L. Sargant. 1864. [Pamphlets, vol. 26.] **144 B**

See also BIRTHS, DEATHS AND MARRIAGES.

REGISTRATION, PARLIAMENTARY AND MUNICIPAL.

A Digest of registration cases parliamentary and municipal. By J. J. H. Saint. 2nd ed. 1887. 8vo. **11 E**

Voters and their registration. By J. J. H. Saint. 1885. 8vo. **11 E**

Registration manual, parliamentary and municipal. By W. C. Glen. 4th ed. 1885. 12mo. **53 F**

Law of parliamentary and municipal registration. By A. J. Flaxman. 3rd ed. 1885. 8vo. **53 F**

REGRATING.

Inquiry into laws respecting Forestalling, Regrating, and Ingrossing. By Wm. Illingworth. 1800. 8vo. **168 E**

REGUERA VALDELOMAR, JUAN DE LA.

Guia para el estudio del derecho patrio, dividido en cinco tablas. Segunda edicion. Madrid, 1805. 8vo. **39 F**

REID, THOMAS.

Essays on the active powers of man. 1788. 4to. **78 G**

REILLY, FRANCIS SAVAGE.

Albert Arbitration. Lord Cairns's Decisions. 3 parts in 1 vol. 1872-5. 8vo. **146 D**

European Arbitration. Lord Westbury's Decisions. Part 1. [No more published.] 1873. 8vo. **146 D**

REIMES, PHILIPPE DE.

The romance of Blonde of Oxford and Jehan of Dammartin. Edited by M. Le Roux De Lincy. [Camden Society, vol. 72.] 1858. 8vo. **85 B**

RELEASES.

Dissertation on and precedents of Releases. See Bythewood and Jarman's Conveyancing, 4th ed., vol. 6, pp. 26-89. **13 D**

RELIGION.

De cultu exteriore secundum jus naturæ et jus publicum, Maximilianus Josephus Villers, Malmundariensis. Leodii, 1830. [Latin tracts on civil and canon law.] **118 E**

Dialogues concerning natural religion. See D. Hume's Treatise of human nature, vol. 2, 1886, pp. 375-468. **78 E**

What I believe. By Leon Tolstoi. Translated from the Russian by Constantine Popoff. 1885. 8vo. **77 A**

See also CLARKE, S. and NORDEN, J.

REMAINDERS.

An Essay on the learning of Contingent Remainders and Executory Devises. By Charles Fearne. 10th ed. by J. W. Smith. 2 vols. 1844. 8vo. **13 H**

Can Remainders be too remote? By W. D. Lewis. 1844. [Pamphlets, vol. 23.] **144 B**

RENFREWSHIRE.

Genealogical history of the royal family of the Stewarts ; with a general description of the Shire of Renfrew, and a deduction of noble families, proprietors there for upwards of 400 years. By G. Crawfurd. Edinburgh, 1710. folio. **113 F**

RENNELL, JAMES.

Description of roads in Bengal and Bahar. 1778. 12mo. **84 A**

RENTS AND RENT CHARGES.

Law of rents with special reference to the sale of land in consideration of a rent charge or chief rent. By W. A. Copinger and J. E. C. Munro. 1886. 8vo. **11 E**

Chief rents and other rent charges. By Wm. Harrison. 1884. 8vo. **11 E**

The art of valuing rents and tillages. By J. S. Bayldon. 9th ed. by J. C. Morton. 1876. 8vo. **11 E**

On the collection and recovery of rent charge. By C. J. Jones 2nd ed. 1849. 12mo. **53 F**

Law of annuities and rent charges. By W. G. Lumley. 1833 8vo. **52 A**

REPLEVIN.

The practice in the action of Replevin. By J. J. Wilkinson.
1825. 8vo.   175 C

Law and practice of Distresses and Replevins. By Lord chief
baron Gilbert. 4th ed. by W. J. Impey. 1823. 8vo. 165 G

Case of Buckworth and Thirkell in the King's Bench, Trinity
25 Geo. III. Special case reserved at the trial of a Replevin
at the last assizes for Cambridge. See Collectanea Juridica,
vol. 1, 1791, pp. 332–336.   144 G

See also DISTRESS.

REPORTERS, THE.

The reporters arranged and characterized, with incidental
remarks. By J. W. Wallace. 4th ed. by F. F. Heard.
Boston, 1882. 8vo.   82 C

REQUESTS, COURT OF.

Abstract of all the printed acts of parliament for the establishment of Courts of Requests in England and Wales. By
J. T. Pratt. 1824. 8vo.   175 C

The Court of Requests. By William Hutton, with a memoir
Edinburgh, 1840. [Law Tracts, vol. 7.]   144 E

RETTIE, MIDDLETON.

Cases decided in the Court of Session, Court of Justiciary
and House of Lords, 1873–1890. Reported by M. Rettie,
T. Crawford, G. F. Melville and others. Fourth series.
Vols. 1–17. 1874–90. 8vo.   14 G H

REVENUE AND TRADE.

Discourses on the publick revenues and on the trade of
England. [By C. Davenant.] Part 1. 1698. 12mo. 49 D

Great Britain's True system. By Malachy Postlethwayt.
1757. 8vo.   78 D

The great increase of the public expenditure, its cause and
how to check it. 1860. [Pamphlets, vol. 15.]   144 B

See also CUSTOMS, EXCISE, INCOME TAX, LEGACY DUTIES,
STAMPS and TAXES.

REVERSIONS.

Treatise on life assurance and reversions. By Arthur Scratchley. New ed. 1867. 8vo.   169 B

See also LANDLORD AND TENANT, LEASES and NEGLI-
GENCE.

REVISING BARRISTERS.

A Letter to the Lord Chancellor on subject of revising barristers. By C. R. Kennedy. [n.d.] [Pamphlets, vol. 4.] **144 A**

REVIVOR AND SUPPLEMENT.

The practice in equity by way of revivor and supplement.
By L. L. Pemberton. 1867. 8vo. **53 F**

Treatise on proceedings in equity by way of supplement and
revivor. By G. T. White. 1843. 8vo. **175 C**

REVOLUTIONS.

Revolutions in English history. By Rev. Robert Vaughan.
3 vols. 1859–63. 8vo. **115 G**

Revolutions which have taken place in different European
States, 1678 to 1794. See C. Mayo's European Chronology.
1795. folio. **115 I**

RHINE, THE.

The traveller's guide to the Rhine. Compiled from a work
by A. Schreiber. 4th ed. 1836. 12mo. **84 A**

RIBTON, THEODORE.

The law and practice in Bankruptcy. 1884. 8vo. **160 F**

RICART, ROBERT.

The Maire of Bristowe is kalendar. Edited by L. T. Smith.
[Camden Society, n.s. vol. 5.] 1872. 8vo. **85 C**

RICHARD I., KING OF ENGLAND.

Chronicles and Memorials of the reign of Richard I. Edited
by W. Stubbs. 2 vols. 1864–65. 8vo. **102 B**

Chronicles of the reigns of Stephen, Henry II. and Richard I.
Edited by R. Howlett. 4 vols. 1884–89. 8vo. **102 H**

Fines sive pedes finium in Curia domini regis, 1195–1199.
Edited by Rev. Joseph Hunter. 2 vols. 1835–44. 8vo. **98 A**

The great roll of the Pipe for the first year of the reign of
Richard I. Edited by Rev. J. Hunter. 1844. 8vo. **98 A**

The historical works of Gervase of Canterbury. Edited by
William Stubbs. 2 vols. 1879–80. 8vo. **102 G**

See also BENEDICT, LINGARD, REV. J., MARTYN, W. and
TURNER, S.

RICHARD II., King of England.
Alliterative poem on the death of Richard II. Ricardi May-
diston de concordia inter Ric. II. et civitatem London.
Edited by T. Wright. [Camden Society, vol. 3.] 1838.
8vo. **85 A**
An English chronicle of the reigns of Richard II., Henry IV.,
Henry V. and Henry VI.,written before 1471. Edited by Rev.
J. S. Davies. [Camden Society, vol. 64.] 1856. 8vo. **85 B**
See also LINGARD, REV. J., MARTYN, W. and TURNER, S.

RICHARD III., King of England.
Letters and papers illustrative of the reigns of Richard III.
and Henry VII. Edited by James Gairdner. 2 vols.
1861–63. 8vo. **101 E**
The reign of Richard III. See Polydore Vergil's English
history, edited by Sir H. Ellis, Camden Society, vol. 29,
1844, pp. 173–227. **85 A**
See also LINGARD, REV. J., MARTYN, W. and TURNER, S.

RICHARD, Canon of the Holy Trinity of London.
Itinerarium peregrinorum et gesta Regis Ricardi. Edited by
Rev. William Stubbs. 1864. 8vo. **102 B**

RICHARD OF CIRENCESTER.
The itinerary of Richard of Cirencester, with an account of
that author and his works. See W. Stukeley's Itinerarium
Curiosum, vol. 2, 1776, pp. 79–177. **85 I**
Speculum historiale de gestis regum Angliæ. Edited by
J. E. B. Mayor. 2 vols. 1863–69. 8vo. **101 I**

RICHARD OF DEVIZES.
The Chronicle of Richard of Devizes. See Chronicles of the
reigns of Stephen, &c. vol. 3, 1886, pp. 379–454. **102 H**

RICHARD OF MAIDSTONE.
De concordia inter Ric. II. et civitatem London. Edited by
T. Wright. [Camden Society, vol. 3.] 1838. 8vo. **85 A**

RICHARD, Prior of Hexham.
The Chronicle of Richard, Prior of Hexham. See Chronicles
of reigns of Stephen, &c. vol. 3, 1886, pp. 137–178. **102 H**

RICHARD, PRIOR OF HEXHAM—*continued.*
De statu et episcopis Hagustaldensis ecclesiæ, gestis regis
Stephani et bello Standardi. See Scriptores decem Hist.
Angl., vol. i, 1652, pp. 285–332. **114 H**

RICHARDS, EDWARD HARRINSON.
Table of offences in their relation to jurisdiction ·of district
commissioners of the colony of Lagos. 1889. 8vo. **37 D**

RICHARDS, OWEN.
A Book of Costs in common law, bankruptcy, and conveyancing.
1844. 12mo. **165 A**

RICHARDS, ROBERT SAMUEL.
Code Napoleon, being the French civil code literally translated. [1850.] 8vo. **55 C**

RICHARDS, WILLIAM.
The history of Lynn ; with the ancient and modern state of
Marshland, Wisbeach, and the Fens. 2 vols. Lynn, 1812.
8vo. **92 C**

RICHARDSON, CHARLES.
A New dictionary of the English language combining explanation with etymology. New ed. 2 vols. ·1858. 4to. **123 E**

RICHARDSON, ROBERT.
The attorney's practice in the court of Common Pleas. 5th
ed. 2 vols. 1778. 12mo. **163 A**
The attorney's practice in the court of King's Bench. By a
Gentleman of the Inner Temple. 1739. 12mo. **163 A**
The same. 3rd ed. 2 vols. 1750, and 5th ed. by R.
Richardson. 2 vols. 1769. 12mo. **163 A**
The same. 6th ed. 2 vols. 1776–79. 12mo. **163 A**
The law of Testaments and Wills. 2nd ed. 1769. 8vo. **178 B**

RICHARDSON, ROBERT HENRY.
A Practical treatise on solicitors' book-keeping by double
entry. 3rd ed. 1885. 8vo. **9 A**

RICHBOROUGH, KENT.
Antiquitates Rutupinæ. By Ven. John Battely. 2nd ed.
Oxoniæ, 1745. 8vo. **88 C**

RICHELIEU, Cardinal.
The prohibited comedy, Richelieu in love, or the youth of
Charles I. An historical comedy in five acts. By the
author of Whitefriars, &c. [Jane Robinson.] 1852.
[Pamphlets, vol. 23.] **144 B**

RICHEY, Alexander George.
Short history of the Irish people down to the date of the
plantation of Ulster. Edited by R. R. Kane. Dublin,
1887. 8vo. **115 C**

RICHINGS, Rev. Benjamin.
The Mancetter martyrs, the sufferings and martyrdoms of
Mr. Robert Glover and Mrs. Joice Lewis of Mancetter,
Warwickshire. 4th ed. 1860. 8vo. **79 B**

RICHMOND, Surrey.
Historical Richmond. By E. B. Chancellor. 1885. 8vo. **93 C**

RICHMOND AND RICHMONDSHIRE, Yorkshire.
The history of Richmond. [By Christopher Clarkson.]
Richmond, 1814. 12mo. **94 A**
History of Richmondshire. By T. D. Whitaker. 2 vols.
1823. folio. **95 H**
Registrum honoris de Richmond ; exhibens terrarum et villa-
rum quæ quondam fuerunt Edwini Comitis infra Rich-
mundshire, descriptionem, ex libro Domesday in thesauria
Domini Regis. [By Roger Gale.] 1722. folio. **95 H**

RICHMOND, Henry Fitzroy, 1 Duke of.
Inventories of the wardrobes, plate, chapel stuff &c. of H.
Fitzroy, Duke of Richmond. Edited with a memoir and
letters of the Duke of Richmond, by J. G. Nichols. [Cam-
den Society, vol. 61.] 1855. 8vo. **85 B**

RICKARDS, Arthur George and M. J. MICHAEL.
Cases decided during the sessions, 1885-6-7-8-9, by the
Court of Referees on Private Bills in Parliament. 1891.
8vo. **66 C**

RIDDELL, Henry.
Railway parliamentary practice ; with a treatise on the rights
of parties to oppose the preamble and clauses of a railway
bill. 1846. 12mo. **175 B**

[RIDDELL, JOHN.]
Reply to the misstatements of Dr. Hamilton of Bardowie in his
late ' Memoirs of the House of Hamilton corrected,' respecting the descent of his family.   1828.   8vo.   **80 C**

RIDGEWAY, WILLIAM.
Reports of cases in the high court of parliament in Ireland,
1784-1796.   3 vols.   Dublin, 1795-98.   8vo.   **15 F**
Reports of cases in the King's Bench and Chancery during the
time in which Lord Hardwicke presided in those courts.
1794.   8vo.   **5 H**

RIDGWAY, JAMES.
Ridgway's Peerage of the United Kingdom, 1834, 1835, 1837-
1841, 1843, 1844.   9 vols.   1834-44.   12mo.   **218 C D**
The speeches of Thomas Erskine when at the bar on subjects
connected with the liberty of the press and against constructive treasons.   4 vols.   1810.   8vo.   **83 G**
The speeches of Lord Erskine when at the bar on miscellaneous subjects.   1812.   8vo.   **83 G**

RIDLEY, NICHOLAS.
The works of Nicholas Ridley, D.D., sometime lord bishop of
London, martyr 1555.   Edited by Rev. H. Christmas.
Cambridge, 1841.   8vo.   **77 D**

RIGA, L. and G. W. YAPP.
Panorama de Paris.   Description des principaux monuments
et grands établissements, revue de l'industrie et du commerce
et guide de l'étranger.   Paris, 1857.   folio.   **84 H**

RIGGE, JOHN.
Observations on the statutes for registering deeds.   1798.
8vo.   **13 B**

RIGGE, WILLIAM.
Instructions for registring deeds, conveyances, wills and other
incumbrances affecting estates in the county of Middlesex.
1778.   12mo.   **172 F**

RIGHT TO BEGIN.
An Exposition of the practice relative to the Right to Begin
and Right to Reply in trials by jury and in appeals at
Quarter Sessions.   By W. M. Best.   1837.   8vo.   **167 D**

RIMMER, ALFRED.
Pleasant spots around Oxford. [1878.] 8vo.   **92 F**
Rambles round Eton and Harrow. 1882. 8vo.   **86 B**

RINGWOOD, RICHARD.
Outlines of the law of Torts. 1887. 8vo.   **64 F**
The principles of Bankruptcy. 1879. 8vo.   **160 F**
The same. 3rd ed. 1884. 8vo.   **160 F**
The same. 4th ed. 1887. 8vo.   **64 A**

RIOTS.
The law relating to riots. By S. Hastings. 1886. 8vo. **11 E**
A Summary of the law on Riots. By An Attorney. 1842.
-[Pamphlets, vol. 1.]   **144 A**

RIPLEY, GEORGE and CHARLES ANDERSON DANA.
The new American Cyclopædia, a popular dictionary of general
knowledge. 16 vols. New York, 1860–63. 8vo. **122 C D**

RIPLEY, WILLIAM RICHARD.
Court of Chancery. Trinity Term 1849. Salkeld, clerk, *v.*
Johnston and others. Report of the case with the Lord
Chancellor's Judgment and construction of 2 & 3 Wm. IV.
c. 100 (Lord Tenterden's Tithe act) 1849. Bound with
W. R. Ripley's Law of Tithes. 1846. 8vo.   **176 F**
The present state of the law of Tithes. 1846. 8vo. **176 F**
Three sermons. By A lay member of the Church of England
[W. R. Ripley]. 1873. [Pamphlets, vol. 40.]   **144 C**

RISDON, TRISTRAM.
The chorographical description or survey of the county of
Devon. 1811. 8vo.   **87 D**
A Review of part of Risdon's Survey of Devon, containing the
general description with corrections and additions. By
Wm. Chapple. Exeter, 1785. 8vo.   **87 B**

RISHANGER, WILLIAM.
Chronica et annales regnantibus Henrico Tertio et Edwardo
Primo. Edited by H. T. Riley. 1865. 8vo.   **101 G**
The chronicle of the Barons' wars. Edited by J. O. Halliwell.
[Camden Society, vol. 15.] 1840. 8vo.   **85 A**

RITSON, JOSEPH.

The office of Constable, an entirely new compendium of law concerning that ancient minister. 2nd ed. 1815. 8vo. **163 D**

Practical points ; or, Maxims in conveyancing. By A late eminent Conveyancer, with critical observations on the various and essential parts of a deed. 1804. 8vo. **163 G**

RITUAL, LEGAL.

The Bishop of Lincoln's Case. By E. S. Roscoe. 1891. 8vo. **53 F**

Legal Ritual. The judgments delivered by the Privy Council and Dean of Arches in recent cases of Martin *v.* Macko-nochie, and Elphinstone *v.* Purchas, and Herbert *v.* Purchas. A guide for incumbents, churchwardens and parishioners. By J. M. Dale. 1871. 12mo. **53 F**

RIVERS.

Opinions of counsel as to public rights in navigable rivers, on a case submitted on behalf of the corporation of Notting-ham. By P. E. Dove. 1887. [Pamphlets, vol. 40.] **144 C**

Rivers pollution prevention act, 1876. By A. Glen. 1876. 8vo. **11 E**

Law of navigable Rivers. By L. Houck. Boston, 1866. 8vo. **60 B**

The international law of navigable rivers. By John Castle. 1863. [Pamphlets, vol. 21.] **144 B**

See also CANALS, SEA and WATERS.

RIVIÈRE, HIPPOLYTE FÉRÉOL.

Codes Français et lois usuelles. 16me éd. 2 vols. Paris, 1888. 8vo. **55 C**

ROAD ACTS.

Public acts known as road acts, from 26 Geo. II. to 37 Geo. III. 47 vols. 1754–97. folio. **21 D-22 G**

ROADS.

Description of the direct and cross roads in England and Wales. By D. Paterson. 18th ed. 1829. 8vo. **86 A**

The traveller's pocket book ; or, Ogilby and Morgan's Book of the roads. 21st ed. 1782. 12mo. **86 A**

See RENNELL, J. and SPEED, J.

See also HIGHWAYS and TURNPIKES.

ROBBERS.
An Enquiry into the causes of the late increase of Robbers
&c. with some proposals for remedying this growing evil.
By Henry Fielding. 2nd ed. 1751. 12mo. **118 A**

ROBBINS, LEOPOLD GEORGE GORDON.
. Settled land statutes, with notes and precedents of settle-
ments &c. relating to settled land. 1882. 12mo. **53 G**
See also BYTHEWOOD, W. M.

ROBERT OF AVESBURY.
De gestis mirabilibus regis Edwardi Tertii. Edited by E. M.
Thompson. 1889. 8vo. **102 I**

ROBERT OF GLOUCESTER.
Metrical chronicle. Edited by W. A. Wright. 2 vols. 1887.
. 8vo. **102 I**

ROBERT OF TORIGNI.
The Chronicle of Robert of Torigni, abbot of the monastery
of St. Michael-in-Peril-of-the-Sea. See Chronicles of the ·
reigns of Stephen, &c. Vol. 4. 1889. **102 H**

ROBERTS, GEORGE.
History of Lyme Regis. Sherborne, 1823. 12mo. **87 C**

ROBERTS, THOMAS ARCHIBALD.
The principles of Equity as administered in the supreme
court of judicature. 3rd ed. 1877. 8vo. **167 D**

ROBERTS, WALWORTH HOWLAND and G. H. WALLACE.
Summary of the law on the liability of Employers for per-
sonal injuries. 2nd ed. 1882. 12mo. **166 E**
The same. 3rd ed. 1885. 8vo. **9 H**

ROBERTS, WILLIAM.
Construction of the statutes, 13 Eliz. c. 5 and 27 Eliz. c. 4,
relating to voluntary and fraudulent conveyances. 1800.
8vo. **164 E**
Treatise on the Statute of Frauds ; with a dissertation upon
the admissibility of parol and extrinsic evidence to explain
and controul written instruments. 1805. 12mo. **168 E**

ROBERTS, William—*continued.*
A Treatise upon Wills and Codicils. 1809. 8vo. **177 E**
The same. 2nd ed. 2 vols. 1815, and 3rd ed. 2 vols. 1826.
8vo. **177 E**

ROBERTS, W. H., H. LEEMING and J. E. WALLIS.
Reports of cases in superior courts on law and practice of new
County Courts, 1849–1851. 1 vol. 1851. 8vo. **68 A**

ROBERTSON, David.
Reports of cases on appeal from Scotland decided in the
House of Peers, 1707–1727. 1 vol. 1807. 8vo. **15 B**
A Tour through the Isle of Man ; with a review of the Manks
history. 1794. 8vo. **94 F**

ROBERTSON, John Elliot Pasley.
Reports of cases in the Ecclesiastical Courts at Doctors'
Commons, 1844–1853. 2 vols. 1850–53. 8vo. **8 H**

ROBERTSON, Rev. William.
Works. With an account of his life and writings. 9 vols.
1824. 8vo. **116 C**

ROBERTSON, William Henry.
Handbook to the Peak of Derbyshire and to the use of the
Buxton mineral waters. 1854. 8vo. **87 A**

ROBINSON, Benjamin Coulson.
Law of warrants of attorney, cognovits and consents to judges'
orders for judgment. 1844. 12mo. **177 D**

ROBINSON, Sir Christopher.
Reports of cases in the High Court of Admiralty, 1798–1802.
3 vols. 1799–1802. 8vo.
The same, 1798–1808. 6 vols. 1812–08. 8vo. **8 A**

ROBINSON, Conway.
The practice in courts of justice in England and the United
States. Vols. 5 and 6, as to the grounds and form of defence in personal actions. 2 vols. Richmond [U.S.], 1868–70.
8vo. **60 A**

ROBINSON, GEORGE.
Cases decided in House of Lords on appeal from courts of Scotland, 1840–1841. 2 vols. 1840–42. 8vo. **15 A**

ROBINSON, JAMES LUKIN.
Queen's Bench and Practice court reports, 1846–1862. 19 vols. Toronto, 1861–62. 8vo. **60 D**

[ROBINSON, JANE.]
The prohibited comedy, Richelieu in love, or the youth of Charles I. 1852. [Pamphlets, vol. 23.] **144 B**

ROBINSON, MARY.
Memoirs of the late Mrs. Robinson, written by herself. 1827. [Autobiography, vol. 1.] 1827. 12mo. **79 A**

ROBINSON, REV. THOMAS.
Essay towards a natural history of Westmoreland and Cumberland; with a vindication of the philosophical and theological paraphrase of the Mosaick system of the creation. 1709. 12mo. **93 F**

ROBINSON, SIR THOMAS.
Book of Special Entries of declarations, &c. and judicial process in such actions as are now in use. 1684. folio.

ROBINSON, THOMAS.
The common law of Kent, or the customs of Gavelkind; with an appendix concerning Borough-English. 1741, and 2nd ed. 1788. 12mo. **168 F**
The same. 3rd ed. by John Wilson. 1822. 12mo. **168 F**
The same. New ed. by J. D. Norwood. Ashford, 1858. 8vo. **10 B**

ROBINSON, WILLIAM, D.C.L.
Reports of cases in the high court of Admiralty, 1838–1850. 3 vols. 1844–52. 8vo. **8 A**

ROBINSON, WILLIAM, LL.D., F.S.A.
History and antiquities of Edmonton. 1819. 8vo. **89 D**
History and antiquities of Enfield. 1823. 8vo. **89 D**

ROBINSON, WILLIAM, LL.D., F.S.A.—*continued.*
History and antiquities of Hackney. 2 vols. 1842–43. 8vo. **89 D**
History and antiquities of Stoke Newington. 1820. 8vo.
89 D
History and antiquities of Tottenham High Cross ; with an
appendix containing the late Henry, Lord Coleraine's
History of Tottenham and The Rev. W. Bedwell's Brief
history of Tottenham. 1818. 8vo. **89 D**
The same. 2nd ed. 2 vols. 1840. 8vo. **89 D**
Magistrate's pocket-book ; or, an epitome of the duties and
practice of a justice of the peace. 2nd ed. by J. F. Archbold. 1837. 8vo. **172 B**

ROBINSON, WILLIAM GEORGE.
Concise view of law relating to the priority of incumbrances
and of other rights in property. 1873. 8vo. **11 C**

ROBSON, GEORGE YOUNG.
The law of Bankruptcy. 2nd ed. 1872. 8vo. **160 F**
The same. 4th ed. 1881. 8vo. **12 I**
The same. 6th ed. 1887. 8vo. **12 I**
The law of private arrangements with creditors, also prece-
dents of deeds of arrangement. 1888. 8vo. **12 I**

ROBSON, THOMAS.
The British herald ; or, cabinet of armorial bearings of the
nobility and gentry of Great Britain and Ireland. 3 vols.
Sunderland, 1830. 4to. **127 J**

ROBSON, WILLIAM.
Robson's British court and parliamentary guide 1832, 1834–
1838 and 1842. 7 vols. 1832–42. Bound with Robson's
Directory. 7 vols. 1832–42. 4to. **54 A B**
Robson's London commercial directory for 1824, 1828, 1830,
1832–1838 and 1842. 11 vols. 1824–42. 4to. **54 A B**
Robson's Royal court guide. 1839. 12mo. **218 H**

ROCCUS, FRANCISCUS.
De Navibus et Naulo, item de assecurationibus notabilia.
Amsterdam, 1708. 12mo. **49 A**

ROCHE, A. R.
Notes on the resources and capabilities of the Island of Anticosti. 1885. 8vo. **84 B**

ROCHE, Henry Philip and William HAZLITT.
Law and practice in Bankruptcy. 2nd ed. 1873. 8vo. **160 F**

ROCHEFOUCAULD, François, Duc de la.
Moral maxims and reflections. Now made English. 1694.
12mo. **83 A**

ROCHESTER, Kent.
Custumale Roffense ; with memorials of Rochester cathedral.
By John Thorpe. 1788. folio. **89 G**
The history and antiquities of Rochester and its environs.
[By Rev. Samuel Denne.] 2nd ed. enlarged by W. Wildash.
Rochester, 1817. 8vo. **88 C**
Poll for members of parliament to represent the city of
Rochester, taken on 5 July, 1802. Rochester, 1802. Bound
with Kent Poll book, 1803. 8vo. **107 K**
The same, taken 29 Oct. to 7 Nov. 1806. 1807. 8vo. **107 K**
Registrum Roffense ; or, a collection of ancient records
illustrating the ecclesiastical history and antiquities of the
diocese and cathedral church of Rochester. By John
Thorpe. 1769. folio. **89 G**
Repertory of endowments of vicarages in dioceses of Canter-
bury and Rochester. By A. C. Ducarel. 2nd ed. 1782.
8vo. **88 D**

ROCQUE, John.
Survey of the cities of London and Westminster and the
borough of Southwark. 1751. folio. **91 H**

ROE, Sir Thomas.
Letters from George Lord Carew to Sir T. Roe, 1615–1617.
Edited by John Maclean. [Camden Society, vol. 76.]
1860. 8vo. **85 B**
Letters relating to the mission of Sir Thomas Roe to Gus-
tavus Adolphus, 1629-30. Edited by S. R. Gardiner.
[Camden Society, n.s. vol. 14.] 1875. 8vo. **85 D**

ROGER OF WENDOVER.
The Flowers of history from the year of our Lord 1154.
Edited by H. G. Hewlett. 3 vols. 1886-89. 8vo. **102 H**

ROGERS, Arundel.
The law and practice of the supreme court of judicature.
1875. 8vo.   169 G
The law relating to Mines, Minerals, and Quarries in Great
Britain and Ireland ; with a summary of the laws of foreign
states. 1864. 8vo.   172 F
The same. 2nd ed. 1876. 8vo.   10 I

ROGERS, Rev. Charles.
The serpent's track, a narrative of twenty-two years' persecution. 1880. [Pamphlets, vol. 37.]   144 C

ROGERS, Francis Newman.
Law and practice of Elections. 2nd ed. 1830. 6th ed.
1841, and 12th ed. by F. S. P. Wolferstan. 1876. 12mo.
      166 D
The same. 14th ed. by J. C. Carter. 2 vols. 1885. 12mo. 52 F
Practical arrangement of ecclesiastical law. 1840. 8vo.
      166 A

ROGERS, Samuel.
The pleasures of memory. 6th ed. with some other poems.
1794. 12mo.   83 A

ROGERS, Thomas.
The catholic doctrine of the Church of England, an exposition
of the thirty-nine articles. Edited by Rev. J. J. S. Perowne.
Cambridge, 1854. 8vo.   77 E

ROGET, Peter Mark.
Animal and vegetable physiology considered with reference to
natural theology. 2nd ed. 2 vols. 1834. 8vo.   77 B

ROGRON, Joseph Adrien.
Les Codes Français expliqués par leurs motifs, par des
exemples et par la jurisprudence. 5me éd. Paris, 1863.
4to.   40 I

ROKEBY, Sir Thomas.
The diary of Mr. Justice Rokeby [1688-1697]. Printed from
a MS. in the possession of Sir Henry Peek, Bart. Privately
printed. [1888.] 4to.   80 F

ROLLE, Sir Henry.
Un abridgment des plusieurs cases et resolutions del common ley. 2 vols. 1688. folio.   38 G
Reports de divers cases en le Court del' Banke le Roy, 1614–1625. 2 vols. 1675–76. folio.   74 G

ROLLIN, Charles.
The ancient history of the Egyptians, Carthaginians, Assyrians, Babylonians, Medes and Persians, Grecians, and Macedonians. 18th ed. 6 vols. 1851. 8vo.   113 C

ROLT, Richard.
History of the Island of Man. 1773. 8vo.   94 F

ROMAN CATHOLICS.
A Guide to the laws of England affecting Roman Catholics. By T. C. Anstey. 1842. 8vo.   175 C

ROMAN LAW.
A Systematic and historical exposition of Roman law in the order of a code ; embodying the institutes of Gaius and the institutes of Justinian. By W. A. Hunter. Translated by J. A. Cross. 4th ed. 1887. 8vo.   63 E
The XII. Tables. By Frederick Goodwin. 1886. 8vo.   63 F
Historical introduction to the private law of Rome. By James Muirhead. Edinburgh, 1886. 8vo.   63 E
Roman law of damage to property. By Edwin Grueber. 1886. 8vo.   63 E
Introduction to Roman law. By W. A. Hunter. 3rd ed. 1885. 8vo.   63 E
The history and principles of the civil law of Rome. By Sheldon Amos. 1883. 8vo.   63 F
An Analysis and summary of the institutes of Roman law. By T. W. Greene. 3rd ed. 1875. 12mo.   63 E
A Treatise on the Roman law of Persons. By W. H. Rattigan. 1873. 8vo.   63 F
Early Roman law. The regal period. By E. C. Clark. 1872. 12mo.   63 E
An Epitome and analysis of Savigny's treatise on obligations in Roman law. By A. Brown. 1872. 8vo.   63 G
Bracton and his relation to Roman law. By Carl Gütterbock. Translated by B. Coxe. Philadelphia, 1866. 8vo.   63 F

ROMAN LAW—*continued.*

A Manual of Civil Law. By Patrick Cumin. 2nd ed. 1865. 8vo.   **63 G**

Studies in Roman Law, with comparative views of the laws of France, England, and Scotland. By Lord Mackenzie. 2nd ed. 1865. 8vo.   **63 E**

Private law among the Romans, from the Pandects. By J. G. Phillimore. 1863. 8vo.   **63 F**

Commentaries on the modern Civil law. By George Bowyer. 1848. 8vo.   **63 F**

Corpus juris civilis : ediderunt D. Albertus et D. Mauritius fratres Kriegelii. Editio stereotypa. 3 vols. Lipsiæ, 1833–44. 4to.   **48 G**

An Introduction to the study of the Civil law. By David Irving. 4th ed. 1837. 8vo.   **63 F**

An Analysis of the Civil Law. By Samuel Hallifax. New ed. with additions, by J. W. Geldart. Cambridge, 1836. 8vo.   **63 F**

A. J. Duymaer Van Twist, Commentatio continens responsum ad quæstionem : 'quæ fuit Peregrinorum, in imperio Romano, conditio, tum libera republica, tum sub Cæsaribus ?' 1831. [Latin Tracts on civil and canon law.]   **118 E**

Historical notices of the Roman law, and of the recent progress of its study in Germany. By John Reddie. Edinburgh, 1826. 8vo.   **63 E**

Petri De Ryckere, Oratio inauguralis de elegantiori juris Romani studio. 1817. [Latin Tracts on civil and canon law.]   **118 E**

De jure utilitatis innoxiæ, Sytso Fokkes Reiding. Groningæ, 1784. [Latin Tracts on civil and canon law.]   **118 E**

De jure Retentionis cum in veris tum in quasi contractibus, Pieter Rembt Sickinghe. Groningæ, 1768. [Latin Tracts on civil and canon law.]   **118 E**

De juris et facti Ignorantia, A. O. van Swinderen. Groningæ, 1759. [Latin Tracts on civil and canon law.]   **118 E**

De conjungendo studio juris civilis cum theologia . . . Abrah. Arnold van Toll. Harderovici, 1729. [Latin Tracts on civil and canon law.]   **118 E**

Corpus juris civilis. 2 vols. Amstelodami, 1681. 8vo. **48 F**

The same. 2 vols. in 1. Amstelodami, 1700. 8vo. **48 F**

Digestum vetus, Infortiatum, Digestum Novum ; seu, Pandectarum juris civilis ex pandectis Florentinis, quæ olim Pisanæ dicebantur, quoad eius fieri potuit, representatus. 3 vols. Parisiis, 1566. folio.

ROMAN LAW—*continued.*

Volumen Legum Paruum, quod vocant : in quo hæc insunt : tres posteriores libri Codicis Dn. Justiniani, eadem cura, qua priores nouem, emendati. Parisiis, 1566. folio.

See also ALBEŘICUS, AYLIFFE, J., AYRAULT, P., BEVER, T., BORCHOLTEN, J., BROWNE, A., BUTLER, C., BYNKERS-HOEK, C. V., COLQUHOUN, P. M. C. DE, CORVINUS, J. A., DOMAT, J., FULBECKE, W., GAIUS, GOUDSMIT, J. E., JUSTINIAN, LEUNCLAVIUS, J., MARTA, P., MASCARDUS, J., MOHEDANUS, J., ORTOLAN, J. L. E., OTTO, E., SALKOWSKI, C., SAVIGNY, F. C. V., SCHOLLAERT, F. J., SERRURIER, P., TAYLOR, J., TOMKINS, F., VINNIUS, A., VITRIARIUS, P. R., VOET, J., WENCK, C. F. C. and WOOD, T.

ROME, CHURCH OF AND POPES OF.

Cathedra Petri. A political history of the great Latin patriarchate. By T. Greenwood. 4 vols. 1861. 8vo. **77 C**

A Disputation on holy scriptures against the Papists. By Wm. Whitaker. Translated and edited by Rev. Wm. Fitzgerald. Cambridge, 1849. 8vo. **77 E**

The letters apostolic of Pope Pius IX. considered with reference to the law of England and the law of Europe. By Travers Twiss. 1851. 8vo. **77 B**

Pamphlets on the Vatican council of 1870. By David Urquhart. 1843–74. [Urquhart's Pamphlets, vol. 4.] **143 G**

Popery, the Inquisition and the Jesuits, historical facts exposing their profligate and dangerous tenets. [By E. R. Pickering.] 1851. 12mo. **77 A**

The Pope's brief of September 1850. Notes of some conclusions arrived at in conferences between certain Roman Catholic priests and a Queen's Counsel. Edited by C. P. Cooper. 2nd ed. 1851. [Pamphlets, vol. 8.] **144 A**

The Popes of Rome during the 16th and 17th centuries. By Leopold Ranke. Translated by Sarah Austin. 4th ed. 3 vols. 1866. 8vo. **113 C**

Popish Infallibility. By C. H. Collette. 1883. [Pamphlets, vol. 34.] **144 C**

Popish treaties not to be rely'd on : in a letter from a Gentleman at York to his friend in the Prince of Orange's camp. [n.d.] [Tracts, 1688–9.] **118 E**

The right of the returning officer at parliamentary elections to administer the oath of supremacy to Catholics. See H. Clifford's Southwark elections, 1797, pp. 401–413. **166 E**

ROME, Church of and Popes of—*continued.*

· Rise and fall of the Papacy. By Rev. R. Fleming. ·With an essay of Popery, by Rev. I. Cobbin. 1849. 8vo. **77 B**

The spirit of the Vatican, illustrated by historical and dramatic sketches during the reign of Henry II. By Joseph Turnley. 1845. 8vo. **83 H**

The ultra party amongst the English Roman Catholics. By C. P. Cooper. 4th ed. 1851. [Pamphlets, vol. 8.] **144 A**

See also COLLETTE, C. H., FULKE, W. and PRYNNE, W.

ROME, History and Antiquities of.

Chronological abridgment of Roman history from the foundation of the city to the extinction of the republic. By Philip Macquer. 1760. 8vo. **113 D**

Cl. Salmasii De Re Militari Romanorum Liber. Lugd. Bat. 1657. 4to. **47 G**

De Republica Romano-Germanica liber unus. Auctore Jacobo Lampadio, cum annotatis Hermanni Conringii. Helmestadt, 1671. 8vo. **113 C**

Dictionary of Greek and Roman antiquities. Edited by Wm. Smith. 2nd ed. 1873. 8vo. **84 C**

The history of the decline and fall of the Roman empire. By Edward Gibbon. New ed. 1831. 8vo. **113 D**

The history of the legal polity of the· Roman state and of the rise, progress, and extent of the Roman laws. By Thomas Bever. 1781. 4to. **113 G**

History of the Romans under the empire. By Charles Merivale. 7 vols. 1864–62. 8vo. **113 E**

Records of Roman history, as exhibited on the Roman coins. By Francis Hobler. 2 vols. 1860. 4to. **113 G**

The Romans of Britain. By H. C. Coote. 1878. 8vo. **113 C**

Romæ antiquæ notitia ; or, the antiquities of Rome. By Basil Kennett. 13th ed. 1763. 8vo. **113 D**

Topographical account of parish of Scampton in county of Lincoln and of Roman antiquities lately discovered there. By Rev. Cayley Illingworth. 1810. 4to. **118 F**

The works of Cornelius Tacitus. By Arthur Murphy. 4 vols. 1793. 4to. **113 E**

See also CLASSICS AND GREECE.

ROMILLY, Sir Samuel.

Memoirs of the life of Sir S. Romilly, written by himself. Edited by his sons. 3 vols. 1840. 8vo. **79 C**

ROMNEY MARSH.
The laws of Sewers ; or, the office and authority of commissioners of sewers ; with the laws relating to Rumney Marsh and other marshes and fens. 2nd ed. 1732. 12mo. **48 F**

ROOTS, GEORGE.
The charters of the town of Kingston upon Thames, translated into English ; with notes. 1797. 8vo. **93 C**

ROPER, ROPER SAMUEL DONNISON.
Law of Legacies. 3rd ed. by H. H. White. 2 vols. 1828. 8vo. **172 A**
The same. 4th ed. by H. H. White. 2 vols. 1847. 8vo. **10 F**
Law of property arising from relation between husband and wife. 2nd ed. by E. Jacob. 2 vols. 1826. 8vo. **168 G**

ROSCOE, EDWARD STANLEY.
Admiralty forms and precedents. 1884. 8vo. **12 D**
Admiralty jurisdiction and practice. 1878. 8vo. **160 A**
The same. 2nd ed. 1882. 8vo. **12 D**
The Bishop of Lincoln's Case. 1891. 8vo. **53 F**
Digest of cases relating to the construction of buildings. 2nd ed. 1883. 12mo. **9 B**
Digest of the law of Light. 1881. 12mo. **172 A**
The same. 2nd ed. 1886. 8vo. **10 G**

ROSCOE, HENRY.
Digest of the law of Evidence in criminal cases. 7th ed. by J. F. Stephen. 1868. 12mo. **167 E**
The same. 8th ed. by Horace Smith. 1874. 12mo. **167 E**
The same. 10th ed. by Horace Smith. 1884. 8vo. **52 E**
The same. 11th ed. by H. Smith and G. G. Kennedy. 1890. 8vo. **9 H**
Digest of the law of Evidence on the trial of actions at Nisi Prius. 4th ed. 1836. 12mo. **167 E**
The same. 6th ed. by E. Smirke. 1844. 12mo. **167 E**
The same. 10th ed. by E. Smirke. 1861. 12mo. **167 E**
The same. 12th ed. by J. C. Day and M. Powell. 1870. 12mo. **167 E**
The same. 15th ed. by M. Powell. 2 vols. 1884. 8vo. **9 H**

ROSCOE, HENRY—*continued*.
Law of actions relating to Real Property. 2 vols. 1825.
8vo. **174 F**
Lives of eminent British lawyers. [1833.] 8vo. **79 B**
Westminster Hall ; or, professional relics and anecdotes of
the bar, bench, and woolsack. [Compiled by Henry and
Thomas Roscoe.] 3 vols. 1825. 12mo. **79 A**

ROSCOMMON.
Statistical survey of the county of Roscommon. By Isaac
Weld. Dublin, 1832. 8vo. **95 F**

ROSE, GEORGE.
Cases in Bankruptcy, 1810–1816. 2nd ed. 2 vols. 1821.
8vo. **8 D**

ROSE, JAMES ANDERSON.
A Collection of engraved portraits, catalogued and exhibited
by J. A. Rose, at the opening of the new library and
museum of corporation of London. 1872. 8vo. **82 B**

ROSHER, GEORGE BRENCHLEY.
Treatise on the Principles of Rating. 1883. 8vo. **175 B**

ROSS, SIR JOHN.
Narrative of a second voyage in search of a north-west passage,
and of a residence in the Arctic regions during the years
1829–1833. 1835. 4to. **84 F**

ROSS, THOMAS.
Hastings and St. Leonards guide. 4th ed. [1846.] 12mo. **93 E**

ROUEN, SIEGE OF.
Journal of the siege of Rouen 1591. By Sir Thomas
Coningsby. Edited by J. G. Nichols. [Camden Society,
vol. 39.] 1847. 8vo. **85 B**
Poem on the siege of Rouen. By John Page. Edited by
J. Gairdner. [Camden Society, n.s. vol. 17.] 1876. 8vo. **85 D**

ROUMANIA.
Das Rumänische Handels-Gesetz-Buch vom Jahre 1887.
Durch Carl v. Boroschnay. Bukarest, 1887. 12mo. **55 C**

ROUS, John.

Diary of John Rous, incumbent of Santon Downham, Suffolk, from 1625 to 1642. Edited by M. A. E. Green. [Camden Society, vol. 66.] 1856. 8vo. **85 B**

ROUSE,. Rolla.

Building societies and borrowers, instructions and suggestions to borrowers and to building societies. 1874. 8vo. **161 A**

The Copyhold enfranchisement manual. 2nd ed. 1858. 12mo. **164 F**

The same. 3rd ed. 1866. 8vo. **13 B**

Practical conveyancer. 2nd ed. 2 vols. 1858. 12mo. **164 D**

The same. 3rd ed. 2 vols. 1867. 12mo. **13 G**

Precedents of mortgages, transfers of mortgages, and conveyances of mortgaged property. 1844. 12mo. **172 F**

Rouse's Practical Man. 8th ed. 1858. 12mo. **164 E**

The same. 12th ed. 1868. 12mo. **164 E**

The same. 15th ed. 2 vols. in 1. 1878. 12mo. **164 E**

The same. 16th ed. 1884. 12mo. **13 G**

The value of Advowsons. 1868. 8vo. **52 A**

ROUTIER, Charles.

Pratiques bénéficiales suivant l'usage général et celui de la province de Normandie. Rouen, 1757. 4to. **40 C**

Principes généraux du droit civil et coutumier de la province de Normandie. Rouen, 1742. 4to. **40 C**

The same. 2me éd. Rouen, 1748. 4to. **40 C**

ROUTLEDGE, Robert.

The education journal; or, magazine of general instruction. 1836. folio. **78 H**

ROWE, William Henry.

Practical observations on certain points of frequent occurrence in conveyancing. 1815. 8vo. **163 G**

Vindication of the Commentaries of Sir W. Blackstone, from some strictures contained in 'Remarks on the Commentaries of Sir W. Blackstone,' by J. Sedgwick. 1805. 8vo. **166 F**

ROWGHTON, Thomas.

Articuli ad officium Admiralitatis Angliæ spectantes e libro
nigro Admiralitatis summâ fide recogniti. See F. Clerke's
Admiralty Practice, 1743, pp. 107–178.   160 A

ROWLAND, Charles.

Abstract of the laws and regulations relating to shipping in
the port of London. 1842. 12mo.   92 A
The same. 2nd ed. 1843. 12mo.   92 A

ROWLAND, David.

A Manual of the English constitution ; with a review of its
rise, growth, and present state. 1859. 8vo.   116 B

ROWLANDS, Henry.

Mona antiqua restaurata ; an archæological discourse on the
antiquities of Isle of Anglesey. 2nd ed. 1766. 4to.   94 D

ROWZEE, Lodwich.

The Queens Wells, that is a treatise of the nature and vertues
of Tunbridge Water. 1671. 12mo.   118 A

ROXOLANA, the Podolian.

Roxolana, the Podolian, a tale of the sixteenth century. By
L. N. H. Musnicki. [1850.] [Pamphlets, vol. 23.]   144 B

ROYAL HOUSEHOLD.

Curialia ; or, an historical account of some branches of the
Royal Household. By S. Pegge. 1784. 4to.   83 J

ROYAL LITERARY FUND.

A Summary of facts drawn from records of the Society and
issued by the Committee. 1858. [Pamphlets, vol. 11.]   144 A

ROYAL SOCIETY OF LONDON.

The history of the Royal Society of London for the improving
of natural knowledge. By Thomas Sprat. 3rd ed. 1722.
8vo.   78 C

ROYAL SUPREMACY.

The royal supremacy in matters ecclesiastical in pre-reforma-
tion times. Bishop Gardiner's oration on true obedience.
Edited by B. A. Heywood. 1870. 12mo.   78 A

ROYALISTS.

Index nominum to the Royalist composition papers. Vol. I. A to F. Edited by W. P. W. Phillimore. [Index Library, vol. 3.] 1889. 8vo. **124 H**

ROYLE, WILLIAM.

The laws relating to English and foreign funds, shares, and securities. 1875. 8vo. **168 E**

RUBINSTEIN, JOSEPH SAMUEL.

The conveyancing and law of property act 1881, with intro-duction, notes, and precedents. 3rd ed. 1882. 8vo. **163 G**

The conveyancing acts 1881, 1882, and the Solicitors' remune-ration act 1881 ; with tables of costs and precedents. 4th ed. 1882. 8vo. **64 B**

Conveyancing costs under the Solicitors' remuneration act 1881. 2nd ed. 1882, and 3rd ed. 1883. 8vo. **165 A**

The same. 4th ed. 1888. 8vo. **9 F**

The Articled Clerk's handbook. By J. S. Rubinstein and S. Ward. 2nd ed. 1878. 12mo. **64 A**

RUDDER, SAMUEL.

The history and antiquities of Gloucester ; with a particular account of St. Peter's Abbey and other religious houses. Cirencester, 1781. 8vo. **87 F**

History of Gloucestershire. Cirencester, 1779. folio. **88 H**

RUDGE, EDWARD JOHN.

Short account of the history and antiquities of Evesham. Evesham, 1820. 8vo. **93 F**

RUFFHEAD, OWEN.

A Complete Index to the Statutes at Large, from Magna Charta to 10 George III. inclusive. 1772. 8vo. **31 D**

Statutes at large from Magna Charta to 41 George III. ; with preface by O. Ruffhead and an appendix [in vol. ix.] consisting of obsolete and curious acts. 18 vols. 1769–1800. 4to. **70 C D**

RUGBY SCHOOL.

Report of the proceedings respecting Rugby school before Lord Langdale, master of the Rolls ; with his lordship's judgment thereon. Rugby, 1839. 8vo. **93 F**

RUMSEY, Almaric.

A Chart of family inheritance according to orthodox Moohummudan law ; with an explanatory treatise. 1866, and
2nd ed. 1871. 8vo.   38 B

Moohummudan Law of Inheritance, and rights and relations
affecting it. 3rd ed. 1880. 8vo.   38 B

A Chart of Hindu family inheritance ; with an explanatory
treatise. 1868. 8vo.   38 B

The same. 2nd ed. 1877. 8vo.   38 B

County Court Jurisdiction before and after Jan. 1, 1868.
1867. 12mo.   165 C

RUNNINGTON, Charles.

The action of Ejectment. 1781. 12mo.   166 C

RURAL DEANS.

Horæ Decanicæ Rurales. An attempt to illustrate the name,
title, origin, appointment, and functions of Rural Deans.
By Wm. Dansey. 2nd ed. 2 vols. 1844. 8vo.   83 H

RUSHWORTH, John.

· Historical collections of private passages of state, weighty
matters in law and remarkable proceedings, 1618 to 1640.
2 vols. 1682–80. folio.   115 I

RUSSELL FAMILY.

An Account of the town of Woburn ; with a concise genealogy
of the house of Russell. By S. Dodd. Woburn, 1818.
8vo.   86 B

RUSSELL, Francis.

Treatise on the power and duty of an Arbitrator, and the law
of Submissions and Awards. 2nd ed. 1856. 8vo. 160 B

The same. 4th ed. 1870. 8vo.   160 B

The same. 5th ed. 1878. 8vo.   52 A

The same. 6th ed. by the author and H. Russell.   1882.
8vo.   9 A

RUSSELL, James.

Reports of cases in Court of Chancery during time of Lord
Chancellor Eldon, 1826–1829. 5 vols. 1827–29. 8vo. 3 D E

RUSSELL, James and James William MYLNE.
Reports of cases in the Court of Chancery, 1829–1832. 2 vols. 1832–37. 8vo. **3 E**

RUSSELL, John, Lord Chancellor.
Two speeches for opening parliament. See Camden Society, vol. 60, 1854, pp. xxxv–lxviii. **85 B**

RUSSELL, John Archibald.
A Treatise on Factors and Brokers. 1844. 12mo. **168 D**
A Treatise on Mercantile Agency. 2nd ed. 1873. 8vo. **10 I**

[RUSSELL, William.]
The history of modern Europe to the peace of Paris in 1763, in a series of letters from a nobleman to his son. New ed. with a continuation to 1825. 6 vols. 1827. 8vo. **113 C**

RUSSELL, William Oldnall.
A Treatise on Crimes and indictable misdemeanors. 2nd ed. 2 vols. 1826–28. 8vo. **165 E**
The same. 3rd ed. by C. S. Greaves. 2 vols. 1843, and 4th ed. by C. S. Greaves. 3 vols. 1865. 8vo. **165 E**
The same. 5th ed. by S. Prentice. 3 vols. 1877. 8vo. **9 G**

RUSSELL, William Oldnall and Edward RYAN.
Crown cases reserved for consideration and decided by the twelve judges of England, 1799 to 1824. 1 vol. 1825. 8vo. **1 H**

RUSSIA, History of.
The despots as revolutionists. To the German people. [By the Duke of Saxe-Coburg Gotha.] 1859. [Pamphlets, vol. 12.] **144 A**
Pamphlets on Russia and Turkey. By David Urquhart. 1839–67. [Urquhart's Pamphlets, vol. 3.] **143 G**
The rise, progress, and present state of the Northern governments. By John Williams. 2 vols. 1777. 4to. **113 F**

RUSSIA, Language of.
A New and complete Russian-English and English-Russian dictionary. By A. Alexandrow. 2 vols. 1884. 8vo. **123 B**

RUSSIA, LAW OF.

The Russian agrarian legislation of 1861. By Julius Faucher. See Systems of land tenure in various countries, 1881, pp. 313–350. **78 B**

Éléments de droit civil Russe. Par Ernest Lehr. Paris, 1877. 8vo. **55 C**

The grand instructions to the commissioners appointed to frame a new code of laws for the Russian Empire: composed by her Imperial Majesty Catherine II. Translated by M. Tatischeff. 1768. 8vo. **55 C**

RUTHERFORTH, THOMAS.

Institutes of natural law ; being the substance of a course of lectures on Grotius' de Jure belli ac pacis, read in S. John's college, Cambridge. 2 vols. Cambridge, 1754–56, and 2nd ed. 2 vols. Cambridge, 1779. 8vo. **48 E**

RUTLAND.

Calendar of wills relating to the counties of Northampton and Rutland, proved in the court of the archdeacon of Northampton, 1510 to 1652. Edited by W. P. W. Phillimore. [Index Library, vol. I.] 1888. 8vo. **124 H**

History and antiquities of the county of Rutland. By James Wright. 1684. folio. **93 H**

A Topographical and historical description of the county of Rutland. By F. C. Laird. 1818. 8vo. **92 F**

RUTTER, JOHN.

Delineations of Fonthill and its abbey. 1823. folio. **94 H**

Delineations of the north-western division of the county of Somerset. 1829. 8vo. **93 B**

RYAN, EDWARD and WILLIAM MOODY.

Reports of cases at Nisi Prius, 1823–1826. 1 vol. 1827. 8vo. **8 F**

RYDE, EDWARD and ARTHUR LYON RYDE.

Metropolitan rating. A summary of the appeals heard before the court of general assessment sessions, 1871–80. 3rd ed. 1881. 8vo. **175 B**

The same, 1871–85. 4th ed. by W. C. Ryde. 1885. 8vo. **11 D**

RYDE, Walter Cranley.
Reports of Rating Appeals heard during 1886–1890. 1890.
8vo.   11 D
Local government act, the County electors act 1888, the
Municipal corporations act 1882 ; with notes. By W. C.
Ryde and E. L. Thomas. 1888. 8vo.   10 G

RYE, Walter.
A History of Norfolk. 1885. 8vo.   92 C
Records and record searching, a guide to the genealogist and
topographer. 1888. 8vo.   124 G

RYLEY, William.
Pleadings in Parliament, with the judgements thereon, in the
reigns of Edward I. and Edward II. 1661. folio. 103 F
The visitation of Middlesex, began in the year 1663, by Wm.
Ryley and Henry Dethick. 1820. folio.   92 G

RYMER, Thomas and Robert SANDERSON.
Fœdera, conventiones, literæ, et cujuscunque generis acta
publica, inter reges Angliæ et alios quosvis imperatores,
reges, &c. 1101–1654. Editio tertia studio G. Holmes.
10 vols. Hagæ Comitis, 1745. folio.   116 H
Fœdera, &c. ab 1066 ad 1383. Denuo aucta et multis locis
emendata, accurantibus A. Clarke, F. Holbrooke et J. Caley.
4 vols. in 7. 1816–69. folio.   99 C
Syllabus (in English) of documents relating to England and
other kingdoms, contained in Rymer's Fœdera, 1066–1654.
By Sir T. D. Hardy. 3 vols. 1869–85. 8vo.   97 H

SACHEVERELL, Henry.
The tryal of H. Sacheverell before the House of Peers for
high crimes and misdemeanors. 1710. folio.   49 H
The same. Another copy. 1710. 8vo.   50 B

SACHEVERELL, William.
An Account of the Isle of Man. 1702. 12mo.   94 F

SACRAMENTS.
Pupilla oculi. De septem sacramentorum administratione, de
decem preceptis decalogi, ceterisque ecclesiasticorum officiis.
Joãnio de Burgo. Argentorati, 1514. 8vo.   118 B

SACRAMENTS—*continued.*
Writings and disputations of Thomas Cranmer, Archbishop of Canterbury, relative to the sacrament of the Lord's Supper. Edited by Rev. J. E. Cox. Cambridge, 1844. 8vo.   77 E

[SADE, JACQUES FRANÇOIS PAUL ALDONCE DE.]
Mémoires pour la vie de François Pétrarque, tirés de ses œuvres et des auteurs contemporains. 3 vols. Amsterdam, 1764–67. 4to.   81 F

SADLER, THOMAS.
Edwin Wilkins Field. A memorial sketch. 1872. 8vo. 79 B

SAFFERY, EDWIN.
Notes of the law and practice of the court of record for the town and borough of Southwark. 1868. 8vo.   12 A

SAINT, JOHN JAMES HEATH.
A Digest of parliamentary and municipal registration cases. 2nd ed. 1887. 8vo.   11 E
Voters and their registration. 1885. 8vo.   11 E

ST. ALBANS, HERTFORDSHIRE.
The Abbey church of St. Alban's. By J. W. C. Carr. 1877. 4to.   88 G
The charter and constitutions of the town of St. Albans. Translated by E. Farrinton. Edited by a member of the present corporation. St. Albans, 1813. 8vo.   88 C
Chronica Monasterii S. Albani. Edited by H. T. Riley. 7 vols. in 12. 1863–76. 8vo.   101 G H
The history of the Abbey of St. Alban. By Rev. Peter Newcome. 2 parts in 1 vol. 1795. 4to.   88 B

ST. ASAPH, FLINTSHIRE.
Willis's Survey of St. Asaph, considerably enlarged and brought down to the present time. By Edward Edwards. 2 vols. Wrexham, 1801. 8vo.   94 E

ST. BRIAVELS, GLOUCESTERSHIRE.
The laws of the Dean forest and hundred of Saint Briavels. By J. G. Wood. 1878. 8vo.   87 F

ST. CHRISTOPHER AND ST. CHRISTOPHER-NEVIS.

The statutes of the islands of Saint Christopher and Anguilla, 1711 to 1857. 1857. 8vo.   36 F

Acts of the Islands of Saint Christopher and St. Christopher-Nevis, 1857–1888. 3 vols. St. Christopher and Basseterre, 1857–88. folio.   36 F

See also NEVIS.

ST. CLEMENT DANES, PARISH OF.

Some account of the parish of Saint Clement Danes. By John Diprose. 2 vols. 1868–76. 8vo.   89 D

ST. DOMINGO.

Description de la partie Française de l'Isle Saint-Domingue. Par M. L. E. Moreau de Saint-Méry. 2 tomes. Philadelphie, 1797–98. 4to.   84 D

[SAINT-GERMAN, CHRISTOPHER.]

Doctor and Student. The dialogue in English betweene a Doctor of divinitie and a Student in the lawes of England. 3 vols. 1598. 12mo.   48 D

The same. 16th ed. 1761. 8vo.   48 D

An Abridgment of Doctor and Student. 1630. 12mo. 48 D

ST. GILES IN THE FIELDS, LONDON.

Bloomsbury and St. Giles's: past and present. By George Clinch. 1890. 4to.   89 F

Some account of the hospital and parish of St. Giles in the Fields. By John Parton. 1822. folio.   92 G

ST. HELENA.

Ordinances of St. Helena, 1857–1885. 2 vols. St. Helena, 1857–85. folio.   37·D

ST. KATHARINE'S HOSPITAL, LONDON.

Account of the royal hospital and collegiate church of Saint Katharine. By J. B. Nichols 1824. 4to.   89 F

The history of the royal hospital and collegiate church of St. Katharine. [By A. C. Ducarel.] 1782. 4to.   89 F

SAINT LOY.

The legend of St. Loy; with other poems. By J. A. Heraud. 1820. 8vo.   83 C

ST. LUCIA.
Code of civil procedure of Saint Lucia. 1881. 8vo.   **36 E**
Laws at present in force in St. Lucia. 1853. 8vo.   **36 E**
Laws of St. Lucia. New ed. Oxford, 1889. 8vo.   **36 E**
St. Lucia ordinances, 1853–1881, 1885–1888. 5 vols. St.
Lucia, 1853–88. folio.   **36 E**

ST. NEOTS, HUNTINGDON AND CORNWALL.
History of Eynesbury and St. Neot's, Hunts, and of St. Neot's,
Cornwall. By Rev. G. C. Gorham. 2 vols. 1824. 8vo.
   88 C

ST. PANCRAS, LONDON.
Acts for paving streets in parish of Saint Pancras, belonging to Ann, Dowager Baroness Southampton, 41st, 43rd,
52nd and 55th George III. [1800–15.] 12mo.   **92 A**
Marylebone and St. Pancras : their history, celebrities, buildings and institutions. By G. Clinch. 1890. 8vo.   **89 E**
Saint Pancras past and present. By F. Miller. 1874. 8vo.
   89 D
Sommers-Town, St. Pancras, Paving Acts. 29th Geo. III.
and 3rd Geo. IV. [1789–1822.] 12mo.   **92 A**

ST. PAUL'S CATHEDRAL, LONDON.
Annals of S. Paul's cathedral. By H. H. Milman. 2nd ed.
1869. 8vo.   **89 E**
Documents illustrating the history of S. Paul's cathedral.
Edited by W. S. Simpson. [Camden Society, n.s. vol. 26.]
1880. 8vo.   **85 D**
The Domesday of St. Paul's of the year M.CC.XXII. ; or, Regis-
trum de visitatione maneriorum. Per Robertum decanum ;
with an introduction and notes by W. H. Hale. [Camden
Society, vol. 69.] 1858. 8vo.   **85 B**
The history of St. Paul's cathedral. By Sir William Dug-
dale. Edited by Henry Ellis. 1818. folio.   **92 H**

ST. SAVIOUR'S, SOUTHWARK.
The history and antiquities of the parish of St. Saviour's,
Southwark. By Matthew Concanen junior and Aaron
Morgan. 1795. 8vo.   **93 C**

ST. VINCENT.
The colonial practice of Saint Vincent. By Charles Shephard.
1822. 8vo.   **55 D**

ST. VINCENT—*continued.*
Laws of St. Vincent, 1784–1884. 2 vols. 1884. 8vo. **36 D**
St. Vincent acts, 1857–1879. 6 vols. 1857–79. folio. **36 D**

SAINTE-PALAYE, JEAN BAPTISTE DE LA CURNE DE.
Memoirs of ancient chivalry. Translated by the translator of
the life of Petrarch [Mrs. S. Dobson]. 1784. 8vo. **125 C**

SALAMAN, JOSEPH SEYMOUR.
A Practical treatise on liquidation by arrangement and com-
position with creditors. 1871. 12mo. **165 G**
The same. Another ed. 1882. 8vo. **12 I**

SALE, GEORGE.
The Koran, commonly called the Alcoran of Mohammed,
translated from the original Arabic. New ed. 2 vols.
1825. 8vo. **77 B**

SALE, LAW OF.
Law of sale of personal property. By J. P. Benjamin. 4th
ed. by A. B. Pearson-Gee and H. F. Boyd. 1888. 8vo.
11 C
A Treatise on the effect of the contract of sale. By Colin
Blackburn. 2nd ed. by J. C. Graham. 1885. 8vo. **9 E**
The law relating to sales of land. By Aubrey St. John
Clerke and H. M. Humphrey. 1885. 8vo. **13 H**
Duties of solicitor to client as to sales, purchases, and mort-
gages of land. By E. F. Turner. 1883. 8vo. **11 G**
See CONDITIONS OF SALE and GOODS, SALE OF.
See also BAILLIE, N. B. E., DIGBY, R. E., HILLIARD, F. and
HUGHES, W.

SALISBURY, WILTSHIRE.
Antiquitates Sarisburienses; or, history and antiquities of Old
and New Sarum. New ed. Salisbury, 1777. 8vo. **93 F**
Brown's Shilling handbook and illustrated guide to Salisbury.
1866. 8vo. **93 F**
Guide to the cathedral church of Salisbury. By Wm. Dodsworth. 3rd ed. Salisbury, 1792. 12mo. **93 F**
Historical and descriptive account of Old Sarum. [n.d.]
12mo. **93 F**

SALISBURY, WILTSHIRE—*continued.*

Vetus registrum Sarisburiense alias dictum registrum S. Osmundi episcopi. The register of S. Osmund. Edited by W. H. R. Jones. 2 vols. 1883–84. 8vo.   102 H

SALKELD, WILLIAM.   ·

Reports of cases adjudged in the Court of King's Bench, with some special cases in the courts of Chancery, Common Pleas and Exchequer, 1689–1712. 3 vols. 1717–24. folio.

The same. 2nd ed. 2 vols. in 1. 1721–22. folio.

The same. 5th ed. by G. Wilson. 3 vols. 1773. folio.

The same. 6th ed. including the notes and references of Knightley D'Anvers and Mr. Serjeant Wilson, and additional notes by W. D. Evans. 3 vols. 1795. 8vo.   5 H

SALKOWSKI, CARL.

Institutes and history of Roman Private law ; with catena of texts. Translated by E. E. Whitfield. 1886. 8vo. 63 F

SALMASIUS, CLAUDIUS.

De re militari Romanorum Liber, opus posthumum. Lugd. Bat., 1657. 4to.   47 G

SALMON, NATHANIEL.

The history and antiquities of Essex. 1740. folio.   87 G

The history of Hertfordshire, describing the county and its ancient monuments. 1728. folio.   88 H

SALMON, THOMAS.

The Chronological historian; containing a regular account of all material transactions from the invasion of the Romans to the death of George I. 2nd ed. 1733. 12mo. 116 E

A New abridgement and critical review of the state trials, from the reign of Richard II. to the trial of Captain Porteous. 1738. folio.   48 I

The new universal geographical and historical grammar, being an improvement and continuation of Salmon's and Guthrie's grammars. 1777. 8vo.   84 A

Short view of the families of the present English nobility. 1751. 2nd ed. 1758, and 3rd ed. 1761. 12mo. 123 A

Short view of families of present Irish nobility. 1759. 12mo.   123 A

SALMON, THOMAS—*continued.*
Short view of families of Scottish nobility. 1759. 12mo. **123 A**
The universal gazetteer; or, short view of the several nations
of the world. 10th ed. 1777. 8vo. **84 A**

SALMON FISHERIES.
The Irish salmon question, socially, economically, and com-
mercially considered. By A Naturalist and an Epicure.
1863. [Pamphlets, vol. 19.] **144 B**
View of the present state of the Salmon fishery of Scotland.
By A Salmon fisher. [n.d.] 8vo. **78 C**
See also FISHERY LAWS.

SALOMONS, DAVID.
The case of David Salomons, Esq., being his address to the
court of aldermen on applying for admission as alderman of
the Ward of Portsoken, October 15, 1844. Revised by
himself. 1844. [Pamphlets, vol. 23.] **144 B**

SALT, WILLIAM.
Catalogue of the extensive and valuable library of Wm. Salt,
F.S.A. deceased, and important collection of manuscripts
and ancient deeds. 1868. 8vo. **82 B**
Index to the titles of the private acts of parliament passed
in the reigns of Queen Anne, George I. and George II.
Privately printed. 1863. folio. **31 E**

SALTOUN, ALEXANDER, 15 BARON.
Thoughts on the disqualification of the eldest sons of the peers
of Scotland to sit from that country in parliament. 2nd ed.
1789. 8vo. **124 F**

SALVAGE.
The law of Salvage. By H. Newson. 1886. 8vo. **11 E**
See also SHIPPING.

SAMS, WILLIAM.
Annual peerage of the British empire. Edited by Anne,
Eliza, and Maria Innes. 2 vols. 1827. 12mo. **124 F**

SAMSON, Abbot of St. Edmund's.
Chronica Jocelini De Brakelonda, de rebus gestis Samsonis
abbatis monasterii Sancti Edmundi. Curante J. G. Rokewode. [Camden Society, vol. 13.] 1840. 8vo. **85 A**

SAMSON, Charles Leopold.
The law and practice under the Bankruptcy act 1883 ; with
the rules and forms. 1884. 8vo. **12 I**

SAMUEL BROTHERS.
Wool and woollen manufactures of Great Britain. 1859.
8vo. **78 B**

SAMUEL, E.
An Historical account of the British army, and of the law
military. 1820. 8vo. **83 G**

SANCHEZ, Thomas.
De sancto matrimonii sacramento. 3 vols. in 1. Lugduni,
1739. folio. **48 H**

SANCTUARY, Rights of.
De Asylorum origine, usu et abusu apud præcipuas gentes
antiquas, Mordachæus Binger. 1828. [Latin Tracts on
civil and canon law.] **118 E**

SAND, George, i.e. A. L. A. DUDEVANT.
La Mare au Diable. Edited by J. F. Davis. 1890. 12mo.
83 C

SANDARS, Thomas Collett.
The Institutes of Justinian ; with English introduction. trans-
lation, and notes. 3rd ed. 1865. 8vo. **63 E**
The same. 5th ed. 1874, and 8th ed. 1888. 8vo. **63 E**

SANDERS, Francis Williams.
An Essay on the nature and laws of Uses and Trusts ; including a treatise on Conveyances at common law and
those deriving their effect from the Statute of Uses. 1791.
8vo. **176 G**
The same. 2nd ed. 2 vols. 1799, and 4th ed. 2 vols.
1824. 8vo. **176 G**

SANDERS, Francis Williams—*continued.*

The same. 5th ed. by G. W. Sanders and J. Warner. 2 vols.
1844. 8vo. **53 I**

Surrenders of copyhold property considered with reference to
future and springing uses. 1819. 12mo. **164 F**

SANDERS, George Williams.

Orders of the Court of Chancery from the earliest period to
the present time. 2 vols. 1845. 8vo. **161 B**

SANDERSON, Robert.

Seven lectures concerning the obligation of promissory oaths.
1655. 12mo. **48 B**

SANDERSON, William.

Compleat history of lives and reigns of Mary Queen of Scotland,
and of James VI., King of Scotland. 1656. 4to. **114 E**

SANDFORD, Francis.

The history of the Royal Family; or, a succinct account of
the marriages and issue of all the kings and queens of
England from the Conquest. 1741. 12mo. [An anonymous abridgment of F. Sandford's Genealogical history,
1707.] **115 D**

SANDYS, Charles.

A History of Gavelkind and other remarkable customs in the
county of Kent. 1851. 8vo. **10 B**

The Vindication, 'whereinne ye practices of a coontrie-atturney
bee notablie displaied and sette furth to ye contentacyon
and delite of ye gentille reader.' A romance of real life. 1847,
and A Letter to Messrs. Kingsford Son and Wightwick, solicitors, Canterbury. 1848. Bound with W. Gostling's
Canterbury. 1825. 8vo. **88 C**

SANDYS, Edwin.

Sermons and miscellaneous pieces. Edited by Rev. John Ayre.
Cambridge, 1841. 8vo. **77 D**

SANGER, George P.

Statutes at large, treaties and proclamations of the United
States of America, 1859–1869. 4 vols. Boston, 1863–69.
8vo. **32 B C**

SANGSTER, JOHN.

· The rights and duties of Property ; with a plan for paying off
the national debt. 1851. 12mo.   78 D

SAPPHO.

Sapphus, Poetriæ Lesbiæ, Fragmenta et elogia, cura et studio
Jo. Christiani Wolfii. Hamburgi, 1733. 4to.   47 F

SARDINIA.

Raccolta degli atti del governo di sua maestà il Re di Sardegna,
1828, 1829, 1830, 1859 and 1860. 11 vols. Torino, 1846-
60. 8vo.   56 C

SARGANT, CHARLES HENRY.

Ground-rents and building leases. 1886. 8vo.   11 E
Urban Rating, being an inquiry into ·the incidence of local
taxation in towns. 1890. 8vo.   11 E

SARGENT, RICHARD.

Burghersh ; or, the pleasures of a country life. [By R. Sargent]
1855. 8vo.   93 E
Principles of laws of England in various departments, and
also the practice of the superior courts in the form of question and answer. 2nd ed. 1843. 8vo.   ·   170 F

SARPI, PAOLO.

Discorso dell' origine, forma, leggi ed uso dell' officio dell' inquisitione, nella città e dominio di Venetia.   Del Paolo
dell' ordine de' Servi. 1639. 8vo.   118 A
· Histoire du concile de Trente, traduite en François, avec des
· notes par P. F. Le Courayer. 3 vols. Amsterdam, 1751.
4to.   120 F

SAUL : A DRAMATIC SKETCH.

Saul : a dramatic sketch.   Josephine to Napoleon ; with other
· poems and translations. 1844. 8vo.   83 D

SAUNDERS, SIR EDMUND.

Reports des divers Pleadings et Cases en le Court del Bank le
Roy, 1666-1673. 2 parts in 1 vol. 1686. folio.
· The same. 3rd ed. with notes and references by John Wil-
· liams. 2 vols. 1799-1802. 8vo.

SAUNDERS, Sir Edmund—*continued.*
· The same. 5th ed. by J. Patterson and E. V. Williams.
2 vols. in 3. 1824. 8vo.
The same. 6th ed. by E. V. Williams. 2 vols. in 3. 1845.
8vo. 5 H

SAUNDERS, Thomas William.
Law and practice of orders of Affiliation, and proceedings in
bastardy. 3rd ed. 1854, 4th ed. 1862, 5th ed. 1867,
6th ed. 1873, and 7th ed. 1878. 12mo. 160 A
The same. 8th ed. by T. W. Saunders and W. E. Saunders.
1884. 12mo. 52 A
The same. 9th ed. by T. W. Saunders and W. E. Saunders.
· 1888. 12mo. 9 A
The law applicable to Negligence. 1871. 12mo. 172 G
The law of Warranties and representations upon the sale of
personal chattels. 1874. 12mo. · 11 I
Municipal corporations act 1882. 1882. 8vo. 164 G
Practice of Magistrate's Courts. 3rd ed. 1867, and 4th ed.
1873. 12mo. 172 C
The same. 5th ed. by J. A. Foot. 1882. 12mo. 12 B
Public Health act 1875: with the Artizans' and labourers'
dwellings improvement act 1875. 1875. 12mo. 174 G
Criminal law consolidation acts. By T. W. Saunders and
E. W. Cox. 2nd ed. 1862. 12mo. 165 D
The same. 3rd ed. 1870. 12mo. 165 D
The law as applicable to the criminal offences of children
and young persons. By T. W. Saunders and W. E.
Saunders. 1887. 12mo. 52 E
Precedents of Indictments. By T. W. Saunders and W. E.
Saunders. 2nd ed. 1889. 12mo. 12 C

SAUNDERS, Thomas Wm. and Henry Thomas COLE.
Bail Court Reports, 1846–1848. 2 vols. 1847–49. 8vo. 4 B

SAUSSE, Matthew Richard and Vincent SCULLY.
Reports of cases in chancery in the Rolls court, 1837–1840.
Dublin, 1841. 8vo. 15 F

SAVAGE, James.
History of Taunton, originally written by the late Joshua
Toulmin. New ed. Taunton, 1822. 8vo. 93 B

SAVAGE, JAMES—*continued.*
History of the hundred of Carhampton in the county of Somerset. Bristol, 1830. 8vo. **93 B**

SAVARY DES BRUSLONS, JACQUES.
Dictionnaire universel de commerce. Nouvelle éd. par Philemon Louis Savary. 3 vols. Geneve, 1742. folio. **78 H**

SAVIGNY, FRIEDRICH CARL VON.
An Epitome and analysis of Savigny's Treatise on Obligations in Roman Law. By A. Brown. 1872. 8vo. **63 G**
Private international law. A treatise on the conflict of laws, translated by Wm. Guthrie. Edinburgh, 1869. 8vo. **55 A**
Treatise of Possession ; or, jus possessionis of the civil law. 6th ed. translated by Sir E. Perry. 1848. 8vo. **63 G**

SAVILE, HENRY.
Savile correspondence. Letters to and from Henry Savile, Esq., envoy at Paris and vice-chamberlain to Charles II. and James II. Edited by W. D. Cooper. [Camden Society, vol. 71.] 1858. 8vo. **85 B**

SAVILE, SIR JOHN.
Reports de divers special cases cybien en le Court de Common Bank come l'Exchequer, en le temps de Royne Elizabeth, 1580–1594. 1688. folio. **74 G**

SAVILE, THOMAS, 1 VISCOUNT.
Papers relating to the delinquency of Lord Savile, 1642–1646. Edited by J. J. Cartwright. [Camden Society, n.s. vol. 31.] 1883. 8vo. **85 D**

SAVINGS BANKS.
Law relating to trustee and post-office savings banks. By U. A. Forbes. 1878, and supplement 1884. 2 vols. 1878–84. 12mo. **11 E**
Instructions for the establishment of Savings Banks. 1837. 8vo. **144 F**
See also PRATT, J. T.

SAWTELL, GEORGE HENRY.
A Memoir of the life and death of Sir John King, written by his father in 1677 and now first printed with illustrative notes. 1855. 8vo. **79 B**

SAYER, JOSEPH.

Law of Costs. 1768, and 2nd ed. 1777. 12mo. **165 A**

Law of Damages. 1770. 8vo. **165 F**

Reports of cases adjudged in the court of King's Bench, 1751–1756. 1775. folio. **74 G**

SAYER, JOSEPH ROBERT and STANLEY SAVILL.

Labour disputes before magistrates. 1888. 8vo. **52 I**

SCAMPTON, LINCOLNSHIRE.

Topographical account of parish of Scampton and of Roman antiquities lately discovered there. By Rev. Cayley Illingworth. 1810. 4to. **118 G**

See also PECK, W.

SCAPULA, JOANNES.

Lexicon Græco-Latinum. Editio nova accurata. Lugduni, 1663. folio.

SCARBOROUGH, YORKSHIRE.

The history and antiquities of Scarborough. By Thomas Hinderwell. 3rd. ed. 1832. 8vo. **94 B**

The Scarborough guide. Scarborough, 1825. 12mo. **94 A**

SCARLETT, JOHN.

The stile of Exchanges, containing both their law and custom. 2nd ed. 1684. 12mo. **49 A**

SCHILLER, FRIEDRICH.

✎ English hexameter translations from Schiller, Göthe, Homer &c. 1847. 8vo. **83 A**

Maria Stuart. Ein Trauerspiel. Stuttgart, 1861. 12mo. **83 B**

Wallenstein. 1852. Wilhelm Tell. 1853. Die Braut von Messina. 1854. Die Jungfrau von Orleans. 1854. Maria Stuart. 1854. Stuttgart, 1852–54. 8vo. **83 B**

SCHOALES, JOHN and THOMAS LEFROY.

Reports of cases in the court of chancery in Ireland, 1802–1807. 2 vols. 1806–21. 8vo. **15 F**

SCHOLLAERT, Franciscus Jacobus.
Responsio ad quæstionem : Quid sit Possessio ? Quotuplex ?
Quomodo acquiratur, retineatur, et amittatur. Quænam
sint ejus commoda ? 1820. [Latin Tracts on civil and
canon law.] 118 E

SCHOMBERG, Isaac.
Naval chronology ; or, an historical summary of naval and
maritime events from the time of the Romans to the treaty of
peace 1802. 5 vols. in 3. 1802 8vo. 81 B

SCHOOLS.
Law of the building of churches, parsonages, and schools. By
C. F. Trower. 1874. 12mo. 9 A
Report of the meeting of head masters of schools, held at
Birmingham, on Dec. 27th and 28th, 1872. 1873. [Pam-
phlets, vol. 37.] 144 C
School Board guide and teacher's manual. By Thomas
Preston. 1871. 12mo. 166 C
See also CHARITY AND MORTMAIN, EDUCATION and
GRAMMAR SCHOOLS.

SCHREIBER, Aloysius Wilhelm.
Traveller's guide to the Rhine. 4th ed. 1836. 12mo. 84 A

SCHRODER, Herman.
Law of Bail in an action at common law. 1824. 12mo. 160 C

SCIENCE.
Alexandri Neckam De naturis rerum libri duo ; with the
poem, De laudibus divinæ sapientiæ. Edited by Thomas
Wright. 1863. 8vo. 102 A
De l'Origine des loix, des arts et des sciences, et de leur progrès chez les anciens peuples. [Par A. Y. Goguet.] 3 vols.
in 2. Paris, 1758. 4to. 78 H
A Dissertation exhibiting a general view of the progress
of mathematical and physical science, chiefly during the
eighteenth century. By Sir John Leslie. See Encyclopædia Britannica, 8th ed., vol. 1, pp. 691–793. 147 A
A Dissertation exhibiting a general view of the progress of
mathematical and physical science, since the revival of
letters in Europe. By John Playfair. See Encyclopædia
Britahnica, 8th ed., vol. 1, pp. 549–688. 147 A

SCIENCE—*continued.*

Elements of the logical and experimental sciences, considered in their relation to practice of law. 1835. 8vo.   78 C

Janua Scientiarum, or, a compendious introduction to geography, chronology, government, history, phylosophy. By Charles Blount. 1684. 12mo.   118 A

Leechdoms, wortcunning, and starcraft of early England. Edited by Rev. O. Cockayne. 3 vols. 1864–66. 8vo. 102 A

Of the advancement and proficience of learning; or, the partitions of sciences, ix bookes. By Francis Bacon, interpreted by G. Wats. Oxford, 1640. 4to.   78 G

The scientific and literary treasury. By Samuel Maunder. New ed. 1858. 12mo.   78 A

A Tribute to learning, fame, science and genius. By C. F. Cort. 1834. 4to.   83 I

SCILLY ISLANDS.

A Natural and historical account of the Islands of Scilly. By Robert Heath. 1750. 8vo.   87 A

Observations on ancient and present state of Islands of Scilly. By Wm. Borlase. Oxford, 1756. 4to.   86 F

A Survey of ancient and present state of Scilly Islands. By John Troutbeck. Sherborne, [1796.] 8vo.   87 A

SCIRE FACIAS.

A Treatise on the writ of Scire Facias. By T. C. Foster. 1851. 8vo.   175 D

SCOBELL, HENRY.

A Collection of Acts and ordinances of general use made in the Parliaments, 1640 to 1656. 1658. folio.   158 D

Remembrances of methods and proceedings used in the House of Lords; with The priviledges of the baronage of England, by John Selden. 1689. 12mo.   48 C

SCOTLAND, ANTIQUITIES AND TOPOGRAPHY OF.

The beauties of Scotland. By Robert Forsyth. 5 vols. Edinburgh, 1805–8. 8vo.   95 D

Border antiquities of England and Scotland. By Sir Walter Scott. 2 vols. 1814–17. 4to.   95 G

Leigh's New pocket road book of Scotland. 2nd ed. 1836. 12mo.   95 C

SCOTLAND, ANTIQUITIES AND TOPOGRAPHY OF—*continued.*

Observations on the present state of the Highlands of Scotland; with a view of the causes and probable consequences of emigration. By the Earl of Selkirk. 1805. 8vo. **95 C**

Reports upon the boundaries of the several cities, burghs, and towns in Scotland, in respect to the election of members to serve in parliament. 1832. folio. **153 A**

Sketches of the coast and islands of Scotland and the Isle of Man. By Lord Teignmouth. 2 vols. 1836. 12mo. **95 C**

The statistical account of Scotland. By Sir John Sinclair. 21 vols. Edinburgh, 1791–99. 8vo. **95 A B**

The new statistical account of Scotland. By the Ministers of the respective parishes. 15 vols. Edinburgh, 1845. 8vo. **95 B C**

SCOTLAND, HISTORY OF.

Facsimiles of the national manuscripts of Scotland. Photozincographed by Sir Henry James. Part I. Southampton, 1867. folio. **100 H**

Historical notes relating to Scotland, 1500–1603. By F. S. Thomas. 1856. 8vo. **99 A**

Historical papers and registers from the northern registers. Edited by James Raine. 1873. 8vo. **102 E**

The historie of the Reformation of the Church of Scotland; with some treatises conducing to the history. By John Knox. Edited by David Buchanan. 1644. folio. **113 F**

History of Scotland during the reigns of Queen Mary and of King James VI. till his accession to the crown of England; with a review of Scottish history previous to that period. By Wm. Robertson, D.D. [vols. 1 & 2 of his Works.] 2 vols. 1824. 8vo. **116 C**

The history of the Church of Scotland, from 203 to 1625. By John Spotswood. 3rd ed. 1668. folio. **113 F**

The history of the Union between England and Scotland. By Daniel De Foe. 1786. 4to. **113 F**

Inquiry into origins and limitations of feudal dignities of Scotland. By Wm. Borthwick. Edin., 1775. 12mo. **125 B**

Inquiry into rise and progress of parliament, chiefly in Scotland. By A. Wight. Edinburgh, 1784. 4to. **114 F**

The interest of Scotland considered with regard to its police, agriculture, trade, manufactures, and fisheries. [By Patrick Lindesay.] 1733. 8vo. **114 A**

Joannis de Fordun Scotichronicon, cum supplementis et continuatione Walteri Boweri, insulæ Sancti Columbæ abbatis. Curâ Walteri Goodall. 2 vols. Edinburghi, 1759. folio. **114 H**

SCOTLAND, HISTORY OF—*continued.*

The People and the Church of Scotland : a reply to Sir James Graham and the Government. By John White. 1843. [Pamphlets, vol. 23.] **144 B**

Proposals and reasons for constituting a council of trade in Scotland. By John Law. Glasgow, 1751. 12mo. **114 A**

Rotuli Scaccarii regum Scotorum. The exchequer rolls of Scotland, A.D. 1264–1436. Edited by George Burnett. 4 vols. Edinburgh, 1878–80. 8vo. **99 B**

Scotland's Soveraignty asserted, being a dispute concerning Homage. By Sir Thomas Craig. Translated from the Latin, by G. Ridpath. 1695. 8vo. **114 A**

See BÖETHIUS, H., JAMES I. and MARY, QUEEN OF SCOTS.

See also CHRONOLOGY, CONSTITUTIONAL HISTORY, ENGLAND HISTORY OF, RECORD COMMISSION, RECORDS and STATE PAPERS.

SCOTLAND, LANGUAGE OF.

Glossary of Scotch words. See Metrical Chronicle of Scotland, vol. 3, 1858, pp. 565–620. **101 B**

Jamieson's Dictionary of the Scottish language, abridged by John Johnston. New ed. by John Longmuir. Edinburgh, 1867. 8vo. **123 B**

SCOTLAND, LAW OF.

The law relating to the property of married persons. By David Murray. Glasgow, 1891. 8vo. **55 F**

Bell's Dictionary and digest of the law of Scotland. 7th ed. by George Watson. 1890. 8vo. **55 F**

Treatise on the law of leases in Scotland. By J. Rankine. 1887. 8vo. **55 F**

Principles of the law of Scotland. By John Erskine. 17th ed. by N[orman] M[acpherson]. 1886. 8vo. **55 F**

Rights and burdens incident to ownership of lands and other heritages in Scotland. By J. Rankine. 2nd ed. 1884. 8vo. **55 F**

Digest of the Scottish law of Evidence. By John Kirkpatrick. Edinburgh, 1882. 8vo. **55 F**

Principles of the law of Scotland. By G. J. Bell. 7th ed. by Wm. Guthrie. Edinburgh, 1876. 8vo. **55 F**

Brief summary of the law of intestate succession in Scotland. By P. H. Cameron. 1870. 8vo. **55 F**

SCOTLAND, LAW OF—*continued*.

Practical treatise on the law of Bankruptcy in Scotland. By J. B. Kinnear. 2nd ed. 1869. 8vo.   55 F

Digest of House of Lords cases decided on appeal from Scotland, 1709 to 1864; with glossary of Scottish law terms. By J. B. Kinnear. 1865. 8vo.   55 F

Lectures on the law of Scotland. By J. S. More. Edited by John McLaren. 2 vols. Edinburgh, 1864. 8vo.   55 F

A Compendium of English and Scotch law. By James Paterson. Edinburgh, 1860. 8vo.   55 F

Law and practice in appeals from Scotland to the House of Lords. By Thomas Paton. Edinburgh, 1858. 8vo. 55 G

A Complete system of Conveyancing adapted to the present practice of Scotland. By the Juridical Society of Edinburgh, 2 vols. Edinburgh, 1826–21. 4to.   157 A

Forms of writings used in the most common cases in Scotland. Edinburgh, 1784. 12mo.   55 G

See also ALEXANDER, W., ALISON, A., AMORY, S., BELL, R., BROWN, M. P., BURTON, J. H., DICKSON, W. G., FERGUSSON, J., FOUNTAINHALL, SIR J. L., HOPE, SIR T., INNES, J., MACKENZIE, SIR G., MACLAURIN, J., MARSHALL, J., MURRAY, D., MURRAY, SIR T., NICOLSON, W., NISBET, SIR J., PRATER, H., SKENE, SIR J., SPOTISWOOD, J. and STAIR, J. D.

SCOTT, BENJAMIN.

London's roll of fame : being complimentary votes and addresses from the City of London, on presentation of the honorary freedom of that city, 1757 to 1884. [By Benjamin Scott.] 1884. 4to.   89 F

A Statistical vindication of the City of London ; or, fallacies exploded and figures explained. 1867. 8vo.   91 C

SCOTT, CLEMENT.

Poppy-Land papers descriptive of scenery on the East coast. 1886. 12mo.   92 C

SCOTT, JOHN.

Cases in the Court of Common Pleas and Exchequer Chamber, 1834–1840. 8 vols. 1835–41. 8vo.   7 A

New reports in the Court of Common Pleas and Exchequer Chamber, 1840–1845. 8 vols. 1841–45. 8vo.   7 A B

SCOTT, JOHN—*continued.*

Costs in bankruptcy and liquidation under the Bankruptcy act 1869. [1873.] 12mo.   **165 A**

Costs in the superior courts of common law and probate and divorce and conveyancing. 2nd ed. 1860. 12mo. **165 A**

The same. 4th ed. 1880. 8vo.   **9 F**

Costs under the Judicature acts 1873 & 1875 ; with precedents of taxed bills. 1876. 12mo.   **165 A**

See also COMMON BENCH REPORTS.

SCOTT, ROBERT.

A Supplement to the third edition of Bridgman's Equity Digest, also, to Bridgman's practical digest in Equity. 2 parts in 1 vol. 1832. 8vo.   **63 B**

SCOTT, SIR WALTER.

Border antiquities of England and Scotland. 2 vols. 1814–17. 4to.   **95 G**

A Key to the Waverley novels, in chronological sequence. By Henry Grey. 1884. 8vo.   **83 A**

The Lady of the Lake. 8th ed. Edinburgh, 1810. 8vo. **83 E**

The Lay of the last minstrel. 13th ed. 1812. 8vo. **83 E**

Marmion, a tale of Flodden field. 7th ed. Edinburgh, 1811. 8vo.   **83 E**

The works of Jonathan Swift ; with notes and a life of the author. 2nd ed. 19 vols. Edinburgh, 1824. 8vo. **83 D**

SCOTT, WILLIAM JOHN STORROW.

The students' guide to the law and practice under the Bankruptcy act 1883. 1883. 12mo.   **64 A**

SCOTT, WILLIAM L. and MILTON P. JARNAGIN.

Law of Telegraphs. Boston, 1868. 8vo.   **60 B**

SCRATCHLEY, ARTHUR.

Decisions in life assurance law. 4th ed. 1878. 12mo. **169 B**

The same. Revised ed. 1887. 8vo.   **10 D**

Industrial investment and emigration : being a practical treatise on Benefit Building Societies and local enterprise encouragement companies. 4th ed. 1868. 8vo. **161 A**

Life assurance and reversions. New ed. 1867. 8vo. **169 B**

SCRATCHLEY, ARTHUR—*continued.*
The law of Building Societies. By A. Scratchley and E. W.
Brabrook. 1875. 12mo. **161 A**
The same. 2nd ed. 1882. 12mo. **9 B**

SCRIBNER, CHARLES H.
The law of Dower. 2 vols. Philadelphia, 1867. 8vo. **59 D**

SCRIVEN, JOHN.
Treatise on Copyholds, customary freeholds, ancient de-
mesne ; and the jurisdiction of courts baron and courts leet.
2nd ed. 2 vols. 1821. 8vo. **164 F**
The same. 3rd ed. 2 vols. 1833–34, and Supplement 1842.
8vo. **164 F**
The same. 4th ed. by H. Stalman. 2 vols. 1846. 8vo.
13 B
The same. 5th ed. by H. Stalman. 1867. 8vo. **52 C**
The same. 6th ed. by A. Brown. 1882. 8vo. **13 B**

SCRIVENERS.
The case of the free scriveners of London ; set forth in a report from a committee of the court of assistants of the
Company of Scriveners, London, to the master, wardens
and assistants of the company. 1749. 8vo. **89 E**
Report of the case of Adams *v.* Malkin ; being an issue out
of Chancery to try if a London attorney-at-law was liable
to the bankrupt laws as a money-scrivener ; with a copious
appendix relative to Scriveners. By Philip Hurd. 1814.
8vo. **50 B**
Symbolæographia ; which may be termed The art, description,
or image of instruments &c. or the Notarie or Scrivener.
By Wm. West. 1590. 12mo. **49 C**
See also ATTORNEYS and SOLICITORS.

SCROGGS, SIR WILLIAM.
Practice of Courts-Leet and Courts-Baron. 1701. 12mo. **165 C**
The same. 4th ed. 1728. 12mo. **165 C**

SCROPE, SIR RICHARD.
The controversy between Sir R. Scrope and Sir R. Grosvenor
in the Court of Chivalry, 1385–1390. By Sir N. H. Nicolas.
Privately printed. 2 vols. 1832. 4to. **118 F**

SCRUTTON, Thomas Edward.

The contract of affreightment as expressed in charterparties and bills of lading. 1886. 8vo.   **52 I**

The same. 2nd ed. 1890. 8vo.   **10 D**

Land in fetters; or, the history and policy of the laws restraining the alienation and settlement of land in England. 1886. 8vo.   **83 J**

The laws of Copyright. 1883. 8vo.   **52 D**

The same. 2nd ed. 1890. 8vo.   **9 E**

SCULCOATES, Yorkshire.

A Collection of statutes relating to the parish of Sculcoates. By Wm. Woolley. 1830. 8vo.   **94 B**

SCULPTURE.

Examples of ornamental Sculpture in Architecture, drawn by Lewis Vulliamy and engraved by H. Moses. 1818–22. folio.   **81 H**

A Guide to modelling in clay and wax; or, sculptural art made easy for beginners. By Morton Edwards. 1879. 12mo.   **78 A**

See also COPYRIGHT.

SEA AND SEASHORE.

History of the Foreshore and the law relating thereto, with an unpublished treatise by Lord Hale, Lord Hale's 'De jure maris' and Hall's Essay on the rights of the Crown in the sea-shore. By S. A. Moore. 1888. 8vo.   **11 E**

The Highway of the Seas in time of war. By H. W. Lord. 1862. 12mo.   **55 A**

Mare clausum : seu, de dominio maris libri duo. See J. Selden's Works, vol. 2, 1726, pp. 1179–1437.   **115 I**

A General treatise of the dominion of the sea, and a complete body of the sea-laws. [By Alexander Justice.] 3rd ed. [n.d.] 4to.   **78 C**

A Collection of all sea laws gathered for the use and benefit of all sea-faring men. See G. Malynes's Lex Mercatoria, 3rd ed., 1686. folio.   **118 G**

See BOROUGH, SIR J., MIEGE, G. and PYCROFT, J. W.

See also COLLISIONS, MARITIME LAW, MERCANTILE LAW and SHIPPING.

SEABORNE, Henry.

Concise manual of law relating to vendors and purchasers of real property. 1871, and 2nd ed. 1879. 12mo. **177 B**

The same. 3rd ed. 1884. 12mo. **64 F**

SEALS OF ENGLAND.

Jus Sigilli : or, the law touching His Majestie's four principal seales, viz. the Great Seale, the Privie Seale, the Exchequer Seale, and the Signet. By J. Brydall. 1673. 12mo. **49 A**

The Opening of the Great Seal of England. By Wm. Prynne. 1643. 8vo. **118 E**

SEARCHES.

On searches, containing a concise treatise on the law of judgments &c. as affecting land. By H. W. Elphinstone and J. W. Clark. 1887. With appendix, The land charges registration and searches act 1888. 1889. 8vo. **13 H**

SEBASTIAN, Lewis Boyd.

Digest of cases of trade mark, trade name, trade secret, goodwill, &c. 1879. 8vo. **11 H**

Law of Trade Marks and their registration, and matters connected therewith. 2nd ed. 1884. 8vo. **53 H**

The same. 3rd ed. 1890. 8vo. **11 H**

SECKFORD, Thomas.

The statutes and ordinances for the government of the almshouses in Woodbridge, founded by Thomas Seckford. Edited by Robert Loder. Woodbridge, 1792. 4to. **93 B**

SEDGWICK, James.

Remarks critical and miscellaneous on the Commentaries of Sir William Blackstone. 2nd ed. 1807. 4to. **156 B**

See also ROWE, W. H.

SEDGWICK, Theodore.

Treatise on the measure of Damages. 3rd ed. New York, 1858, and 4th ed. by H. D. Sedgwick. New York, 1868. 8vo. **59 D**

Treatise on the rules which govern the interpretation and application of statutory and constitutional law. New York, 1857. 8vo. **60 B**

SEEBOHM, FREDERIC.
The English village community, examined in its relations to the manorial and tribal systems, an essay in economic history. 2nd ed. 1883. 8vo. **83 H**

SEELEY, JOHN.
Stowe. A description of house and gardens of Duke of Buckingham and Chandos. Buckingham, 1827. 8vo. **86 C**

SEGAR, SIMON.
Honores Anglicani; or, Titles of honour the temporal nobility of the English nation. 1712. 12mo. **125 A**

SEGAR, SIR WILLIAM.
Honor, military and civill. 1602. folio. **126 I**

SEISIN.
The seisin of the freehold. By J. Williams. 1878. 8vo. **53 G**

SELBORNE, HAMPSHIRE.
The natural history and antiquities of Selborne. By Rev. Gilbert White. New ed. 1813. 4to. **88 B**

SELDEN, HENRY R.
Reports of cases in Court of Appeals of state of New York, 1851 to 1855. 6 vols. Albany, 1853–60. 8vo. **57 A B**

SELDEN, JOHN.
Fleta : seu, commentarius juris Anglicani ; subjungitur etiam Joannis Seldeni ad Fletam dissertatio historica. Editio secunda. 1685. 4to. **49 G**
An Historical and political discourse of the laws and government of England. Collected from some manuscript notes of J. Selden. By N. Bacon. 4th ed. 1739. folio. **78 H**
Opera omnia, tam edita quam inedita. Collegit ac recensuit, vitam auctoris, præfationes et indices adjecit David Wilkins. 3 vols. 1726. folio. **115 I**
The priviledges of the baronage of England. 1689. See H. Scobell's Remembrances, 1689. 12mo. **48 C**
Titles of Honor. 2nd ed. 1631. folio. **126 I**
The same. 3rd ed. 1672. folio. **126 I**

SELDEN, JOHN—*continued.*
Tracts, I. Jani Anglorum facies altera, II. England's
Epinomis, III. Of the original of ecclesiastical jurisdictions
of testaments, IV. Of the disposition or administration of
intestates goods. 1683. folio. **114 G**

SELDEN SOCIETY.
Publications of Selden Society. 3 vols. 1888–90. 8vo. **85 G**

> i. Select Pleas of the Crown. vol. I. A.D. 1200–1225. Edited by
> F. W. Maitland. 1888. 8vo.
> ii. Select Pleas in Manorial and other seignorial courts. vol. I.
> Reigns of Henry III. and Edward I. Edited by F. W. Mait-
> land. 1889. 8vo.
> iii. Select Civil Pleas. vol. I. A.D. 1200–1203. Edited by W. P.
> Baildon. 1890. 8vo.

SELECT CASES.
Select cases argued and adjudged in the high Court of
Chancery, before the late Lords Commissioners of the great
seal and the late Lord Chancellor King, 1724–1733. By
A Gentleman of the Temple. 1740. folio. **74 G**
The same. 2nd ed. by S. Macnaghten. 1850. 8vo. **3 E**

SELKIRK, THOMAS, 5 EARL OF.
Observations on the present state of the Highlands of Scotland ; with a view of the causes and probable consequences
of emigration. 1805. 8vo. **95 C**

SELLON, BAKER JOHN.
The practice of the courts of King's Bench and Common Pleas.
2 vols. 1792–96. 8vo. **162 F**

SELWYN, WILLIAM.
Abridgment of law of Nisi Prius. 2 vols. 1808. 8vo. **173 A**
The same. 8th ed. 2 vols. 1831, and 11th ed. 2 vols.
1845. 8vo. **173 A**
The same. 13th ed. by D. Keane and C. T. Smith. 2 vols.
1869. 8vo. **53 B**

SENECA, LUCIUS ANNÆUS.
Tragœdiæ, cum notis integris J. F. Gronovii et aliorum : recen-
suit, notas et animadversiones adjecit J. C. Schröderus.
Delphis, 1728. 4to. **47 G**

SENIOR, NASSAU WILLIAM.
Lecture on political economy. 3rd ed. 1831. 8vo. **78 D**
Legal provision for the Irish poor, commutation of tithes, and a provision for the Irish Roman Catholic clergy. 3rd ed. 1832. 8vo. **78 D**
Outline of science of Political Economy. 1836. 4to. **78 G**
Remarks on Emigration. 1831. 8vo. **78 D**
Three lectures on rate of wages. 2nd ed. 1831. 8vo. **78 D**
Three lectures on the cost of obtaining money and on some effects of private and government paper money. 1830. 8vo. **78 D**
Three lectures on the transmission of the precious metals from country to country, and the mercantile theory of wealth. 2nd ed. 1830. 8vo. **78 D**
Two lectures on Population ; with correspondence between the author and the Rev. T. R. Malthus. 1831. 8vo. **78 D**

SENIOR, WILLIAM.
Tutor and Pupils : talks about twelve law maxims. 1891. 8vo. **64 E**

SEPARATE USE.
Remarks on the separate use clause. By J. T. Cantrell. 1839. [Law Tracts, vol. 6.] **144 E**
A Critical examination of Mr. Cantrell's ' Remarks on the separate use clause.' By T. Swinburne. 1839. [Law Tracts, vol. 6.] **144 E**

SEPARATION DEEDS.
Dissertation on and precedents of Separation Deeds. See Bythewood and Jarman's Conveyancing, 4th ed., vol. 6, 1890, pp. 90–125. **13 D**
See also HUSBAND AND WIFE and MARRIAGE.

SERJEANTS-AT-LAW.
The order of the Coif. By A. Pulling. 1884. 8vo. **80 F**
Lives of eminent serjeants-at-law of the English bar. By H. W. Woolrych. 2 vols. 1869. 8vo. **80 F**
Inquiry into the justice and expediency of abolishing the

SERJEANTS-AT-LAW—*continued.*
rank of serjeant-at-law. By A Member of the Temple.
[1858.] [Pamphlets, vol. 12.] **144 A**
Observations touching the antiquity and dignity of the
degree of serjeant at law. By E. W. [Edward Wynne].
1765. 8vo. **80 F**
Origines juridiciales, or, historical memorials of the English
laws ; also A Chronologie of the serjeants at law. By Sir
Wm. Dugdale. 2nd ed. 1671. folio. **125 H**
See also DIGNITIES and HONOR.

SERMONS.
The Decades of Henry Bullinger. Edited by Rev. Thomas
Harding. 4 vols. Cambridge, 1849–52. 8vo. **77 E**
Sermon preach'd at the funeral of William Duke of Devon-
shire. By White Kennett. 1708. 8vo. **79 B**
Sermons, academical and occasional. By Rev. John Keble.
1847. 8vo. **77 B**
The sermons of Edwin Sandys, D.D. Edited by Rev. John
Ayre. Cambridge, 1841. 8vo. **77 C**
Three sermons. By a lay member of the Church of England
[W. R. Ripley]. 1873. [Pamphlets, vol. 40.] **144 C**
See also BRADFORD, J., HOOK, W. F. and LATIMER, H.

SERRELL, GEORGE.
The equitable doctrine of election. 1891. 12mo. **9 H**

SERRURIER, PHILIP.
Responsio ad quæstionem 'Quæritur expositio congruis ratio-
nibus adstructa totius theoriæ juris Romani et hodierni
circa obligationes dividuas et individuas.' 1823. [Latin
Tracts on civil and canon law.] **118 E**

SERVITUDES.
The American law of Easements and Servitudes. By Emory
Washburn. 2nd ed. Boston, 1867. 8vo. **59 D**
See also EASEMENTS.

SESSION, COURT OF, SCOTLAND.
Decisions of the Court of Session from its institution till 1764.
5 vols. 1774. 12mo.

SESSION, COURT OF, SCOTLAND—*continued.*

General synopsis of the decisions of the Court of Session from its institution until November 1827. By M. P. Brown. 4 vols. 1829. 4to.

Form of Process in Court of Session and Court of Teinds; with account of College of Justice. By J. Russell. Edinburgh, 1768. 12mo.

Scotch Acts of Sederunt of Lords of Council and Session, 1553–1790. 1790. folio.

See also MACLAURIN, J. and NISBET, SIR J.

SESSIONS LAW.

A Guide to the law and practice of Petty Sessions. By E. T. Ayers. 1884. 8vo.   12 B

The practice of the court of general assessment Sessions under the Valuation Metropolis act 1869, with forms. By E. W. Beal. 1883. 8vo.   11 E

Collection of several points of Sessions Law, alphabetically arranged. By Rev. S. Clapham. 1818. 8vo.   175 D

See also QUARTER SESSIONS.

SET-OFF.

Treatise on the law of Damages and the law of Set-off. By J. D. Mayne. 4th ed. 1884. 8vo.   9 G

The law of Set-off. By Basil Montagu. 1801. 8vo.   175 E

SETON, HENRY WILMOT.

Forms of decrees in equity and of orders connected with them. 1830. 8vo.   165 G

The same. 2nd ed. by W. H. Harrison and R. H. Leach, 1854, and 3rd ed. by W. H. Harrison and R. H. Leach. 2 vols. 1862. 8vo.   165 G

Forms of decrees, judgments, and orders in the high court of justice and courts of appeal having reference to the Chancery division. 4th ed. by R. H. Leach, F. G. A. Williams and H. W. May. 2 vols. in 3. 1877–79. 8vo.   12 G

SETTLED ESTATES.

Law and practice under the Settled land acts 1882 to 1890. By A. St. J. Clerke. 2nd ed. 1891. 8vo.   13 H

Statutes relating to Settled estates. By J. W. Middleton. 3rd ed. 1882. 8vo.   13 H

Settled land statutes, with notes and precedents of settlements &c. By L. G. G. Robbins. 1882. 12mo.   53 G

SETTLED ESTATES—*continued.*
The leases and sales of settled estates act [19 & 20 Vict. cap. 120]; with notes and a supplement containing the amending act 21 & 22 Vict. c. 77. By M. I. F. Brickdale. 1861. 12mo.   175 E
See also CONVEYANCING ACTS.

SETTLEMENTS.
Dissertation on and precedents of Settlements. See Bythewood and Jarman's Conveyancing, 4th ed., vol. 6, 1890, pp. 126–800.   13 D
A Treatise on the law of Settlements of property. By J. S. Vaizey. 2 vols. 1887. 8vo.   13 H
A Collection of precedents and forms; with references and additions to 'A Treatise on the law of Settlements.' By J. S. Vaizey. 1888. 8vo.   13 H
Settlement of real estates. By J. Williams. 1879. 8vo. 13 H
Tables of stamp duties on settlements, from 1815 to 1878. By W. A. Copinger. 1878. 8vo.   11 G
See ATHERLEY, E. G., CUTLER, J. and KEATINGE, T.
See also CONVEYANCES FRAUDULENT and MARRIAGE SETTLEMENTS.

SETTLEMENTS, PARISH.
The law of Settlement and removal of union poor. By John F. Symonds. 1887. 12mo.   11 E
Cases adjudged in the court of King's Bench concerning settlements and removals, 1710–1727. 2nd ed. 1729. 8vo.   74 F
See also PARISH LAW.

SÉVIGNÉ, MARIE DE RABUTIN CHANTAL, MARQUISE DE.
Letters to her daughter and her friends. 9 vols. 1811. 12mo.   83 A

SEWELL, RICHARD CLARKE.
Inquiry into constitution and practice of Chancellor's Court in University of Oxford. Oxford, 1839. 8vo.   92 E
A Treatise on the law of Sheriff. 1842. 8vo.   175 E

SEWELL, ROBERT.
The analytical history of India, from the earliest times to the abolition of East India Company. 1870. 12mo. 116 D

SEWERS.

The law of land drainage and sewers. By G. G. Kennedy
and J. S. Sandars. 1884. 8vo.   11 E
The law of sewers, including the drainage acts. By H. W.
Woolrych. 3rd ed. 1864. 8vo.   175 E
Commissions of sewers for Westminster and part of the county
of Middlesex. Statutes of sewers and laws ordinances,
and constitutions of the court. 1839. 8vo.   91 C
Reading upon the statute 23 Hen. VIII. cap. 5, of sewers. By
R. Callis. 4th ed. by W. J. Broderip. 1824. 8vo.   53 G
The laws of sewers, as far as they relate to the commissioner.
By C. M. 1762. 8vo.   175 E
See also LONDON SEWERS and ROMNEY MARSH.

SEYER, REV. SAMUEL.

Memoirs historical and topographical of Bristol and its neighbourhood. 2 vols. Bristol, 1821–23. 4to.   87 F

SHAEN, WILLIAM and EDEN KAYE GREVILLE.

A Book of chancery costs. 1857. 12mo.   165 A
The same. 2nd ed. by J. J. Bunning. 1870. 12mo.   165 A

SHAFTESBURY, DORSET.

History of the antient town of Shaftesbury, partly selected
from Hutchins. Shaftesbury, [1810.] 12mo.   87 C

SHAKESPEARE, WILLIAM.

An Argument on the assumed birthday of Shakespeare, reduced to shape A.D. 1864. By Bolton Corney. Privately
printed. 1864. [Pamphlets, vol. 26.]   144 B
The complete concordance to Shakespeare. By Mary Cowden Clarke. Revised ed. 1881. 8vo.   83 F
Historical account of the New Place, Stratford-upon-Avon,
the last residence of Shakespeare. By J. O. Halliwell.
1864. folio.   94 H
The plays of Wm. Shakespeare ; with the corrections and
illustrations of various commentators and notes by Sam.
Johnson. 8 vols. 1768. 8vo.   83 F
The tercentenary or the three hundredth birthday of William
Shakespeare. 1864. [Pamphlets, vol. 26.]   144 B
The works of Wm. Shakespeare. Edited by W. G. Clark
and John Glover. 9 vols. 1863–66. 8vo.   83 F
See also FARREN, G.

SHAREHOLDERS AND SHARES.
Shareholders' and Directors' Legal Companion. By F. B.
Palmer. 10th ed. 1890. 12mo.   **9 D**
Shareholder's handbook. By F. W. Pixley. 1884. 8vo. **9 D**
The sale and transfer of shares in companies. By K. E.
Digby. 1868. 12mo.   **169 D**
See also COMPANIES, LAW OF.

SHARKEY, PETER BURROWES.
Handbook of the practice of Election committees. 2nd ed.
1866. 12mo.   **166 D**

SHARP, SIR CUTHBERT.
A History of Hartlepool. Durham, 1816. 8vo.   **87 C**

SHARP, GRANVILLE.
Account of the ancient division of the English nation into
hundreds and tithings. 1784. 12mo.   **78 A**
Declaration of the people's natural right to a share in the
legislature. 2nd ed. 1775. 8vo.   **49 D**
. Remarks concerning the encroachments on the river Thames
near Durham Yard. 1771. 12mo.   **92 A**
Remarks on the opinions of some of the most celebrated
writers on crown law, respecting the due distinction between
manslaughter and murder. 1773. 12mo.   **118 B**

SHARP, THOMAS.
Illustrative papers on the history and antiquities of the city of
Coventry ; with corrections, additions, and a brief memoir of
the author. By W. G. Fretton. 1871. 4to.   **94 G**

SHARPE, HENRY.
A Concise history and description of Kenilworth Castle.
22nd ed. Warwick, 1835. 12mo.   **93 E**

SHARPE, REGINALD ROBINSON.
Calendar of letters from the mayor and corporation of the
City of London, circa 1350–1370. 1885. 8vo.   **91 F**
Calendar of wills proved and enrolled in the Court of Husting,
London, 1258–1688. 2 vols. 1889–90. 8vo.   **91 F**

SHAW, CHARLES.
The Inns of Court Calendar, a record of the members of the
English bar. 1877. 8vo. 80 F
The same. 2nd ed. 1878. 8vo. 80 F

SHAW, JOHN.
The predecessors of the high court of Madras. Madras, 1882.
8vo. 80 F

SHAW, JOSEPH.
Parish law; or, a guide to justices of the peace, church-
wardens, overseers, &c. 4th ed. by James Paterson. 1864.
12mo. 173 B
The same. 5th ed. by W. C. Glen. 1874. 12mo. 173 B
The same. 6th ed. by W. C. Glen. 1881. 12mo. 11 A

SHAW, PATRICK.
Cases decided in House of Lords on appeal from courts of
Scotland, 1821–1824. 2 vols. 1826–28. 8vo. 15 B
Digest of cases decided in the courts of sessions, teinds, and
justiciary, and in the House of Lords, 1821–1837. 2 vols.
Edinburgh, 1834–38. 8vo. 63 D

SHAW, PATRICK and CHARLES HOPE MACLEAN.
Cases decided in House of Lords on appeal from courts of
Scotland, 1835–1838. 3 vols. Edin., 1836–39. 8vo. 15 B

SHAW, PETER.
The philosophical works of Robert Boyle. 3 vols. 1725.
8vo. 78 E

SHAW, REV. STEBBING.
The history and antiquities of Staffordshire. 2 vols. 1798.
folio. 93 H

SHEAHAN, JAMES JOSEPH.
History of Buckinghamshire. 1862. 8vo. 86 C

SHEARWOOD, JOSEPH ALEXANDER.
Abridgment of law of personal property. 1882. 8vo. 64 E
Abridgment of law of real property. 3rd ed. 1885. 8vo. 64 F
Answers to digest of the questions set in bar and solicitors'
final examinations for last ten years. 1880. 8vo. 168 A

SHEARWOOD, JOSEPH ALEXANDER—*continued.*
Digest of questions set in the bar and solicitors' final examinations. 1879. 8vo. 168 A
The same. 2nd ed., with Answers. 1884. 8vo. 64 D
Introduction to Principles of Equity. 1885. 8vo. 64 D
Law Student's Annual, 1882 and 1884. 2 vols. 1882–84. 8vo. 64 D
An Outline of Contract. 1879. 8vo. 64 B
A Sketch of the law of Tort. 1886. 12mo. 64 F

[SHEBBEARE, JOHN.]
Authentic narrative of the oppressions of the islanders of Jersey; with a succinct history of that island. 2 vols. 1771. 8vo. 94 F

SHEE, JAMES.
Reports of cases decided in the Queen's Bench, Common Pleas and Exchequer in Ireland at the quarter sessions of the county and city of Kilkenny. Dublin, 1843. 8vo. 51 E

SHEFFIELD, YORKSHIRE.
History and topography of parish of Sheffield. By J. Hunter. New ed. by Rev. A. Gatty. [1869.] folio. 95 H

SHEFFIELD FAMILY.
A Character of John Sheffield, late Duke of Buckinghamshire; with an account of the pedigree of the Sheffield family. 1729. [Grimaldi's Tracts, vol. 3.] 118 B

SHELDON, FREDERICK.
History of Berwick-upon-Tweed; with notices of Tweedmouth, Spittal, Norham, Holy Island, Coldingham, &c. 1849. 8vo. 92 D

SHELFORD, LEONARD.
The act for the Commutation of Tithes in England and Wales with the Law of Tithes. 1837. 12mo. 176 F
The same. 3rd ed. 1848. 12mo. 11 H
The bankrupt law consolidation act 1849 and subsequent statutes. 2nd ed. 1854. 12mo. 160 F
The same. 3rd ed. 1862. 12mo. 52 A

SHELFORD, LEONARD—*continued.*

Law concerning lunatics, idiots, and persons of unsound mind. 2nd ed. 1847. 8vo. **53 A**

Law of Copyholds, in reference to the enfranchisement and commutation of manorial rights, and the Copyhold acts. 1853. 12mo. **13 B**

The law of Highways. 3rd ed. 1862. 12mo. **168 G**

The law of Joint Stock companies. 1863, and 2nd ed. by D. Pitcairn and F. L. Latham. 1870. 8vo. **169 D**

The law of marriage and divorce. 1841. 8vo. **172 D**

The law of mortmain and charitable uses and trusts. 1836. 8vo. **53 B**

The law of Railways. 2nd ed. 1846, and 4th ed. by W. C. Glen. 2 vols. 1869. 8vo. **175 A**

Law relating to probate, legacy and succession duties in England, Ireland and Scotland. 2nd ed. 1861. 12mo. **176 D**

Real Property statutes. 1833. 12mo. **174 F**

The same. 6th ed. 1856. 8vo. **174 F**

The same. 7th ed. 1863. 8vo. **53 F**

Statutes for relief of Insolvent Debtors. 1856. 12mo. **169 A**

SHELLEY'S CASE.

A Plea for Testators. Part I. The rule in Shelley's case : its mischief and a remedy suggested. By Wm. Wiley. Dublin, 1869. 8vo. **176 E**

A Letter to A. Amos, occasioned by a lecture lately delivered by him as professor of English law in University of London. By Wm. Hayes. 1830. [Jacob's Tracts, vol. 7.] **144 E**

Observations concerning the rule in Shelley's case, chiefly with a view to the application of the rule to last wills. See Hargrave's Law Tracts, 1787, pp. 549–578. **144 G**

See also WILLS.

[SHELTON, MAURICE.]

An Historical and critical essay on the true rise of Nobility. 1718. 8vo. **48 D**

SHEPHARD, CHARLES.

The colonial practice of Saint Vincent ; also, Observations on the common assurances in general use in the West Indies. 1822. 8vo. **55 E**

SHEPHARD, Horatio Hale.

Law of Limitation in India. Madras, 1883. 8vo. **38 D**
Commentaries on the transfer of property act 1882. By H.
H. Shephard and K. Brown. Madras, 1887. 8vo. **38 D**

SHEPPARD, William.

Actions upon the case for deeds. 2nd ed. 1675. 12mo.
49 B
The Court-Keeper's guide for the keeping of courts-leet and
courts-baron. 1649. 12mo. **49 B**
The same. 7th ed. by Wm. Browne. 1685. 12mo. **49 B**
Epitome of all the common and statute laws of this nation
now in force. 1656. folio. **48 G**
The justice of peace, his clark's cabinet ; or, a book of presidents or warrants. 1654. 12mo. **49 A**
The law of common assurances, touching deeds in general.
1669. folio. **48 G**
The practical counsellor in the law, touching fines, common
recoveries, judgements, statutes, recognizances, and bargain
and sale. 1671. folio. **48 G**
Sheppard's Precedent of precedents ; or, one general precedent
for common assurances by deeds. Modernized by T. W.
Williams. 1825. 8vo. **164 E**
A Survey of the county judicatures commonly called the
county court, hundred court and court baron. 1656.
12mo. **49 A**
Touchstone of common assurances. 7th ed. by Richard
Preston. 2 vols. 1820–21. 8vo. **164 B**
The same. 8th ed. by E. G. Atherley. 2 vols. in 1. 1826.
8vo. **13 A**

SHEPPY, Island of, Kent.

Rambles in the Island of Sheppy. By H. T. A. Turmine.
1843. 8vo. **88 D**

SHERBURN HOSPITAL, Durham.

Collections relating to Sherburn hospital in the county palatine of Durham. By George Allan. Privately printed.
1771. 4to. **118 F**

[SHERIDAN, Thomas.]

A Discourse on the rise and power of parliaments. 1685.
12mo. **49 A**

SHERIFF, ROBERT FFRENCH.
Consolidated laws of Gibraltar. 1890. 8vo.   **37 D**

SHERIFF AND UNDERSHERIFF.
Law of office and duties of sheriff. By C. Churchill. 2nd ed. 1882. 8vo.   **11 F**
A Treatise on the office of sheriff. By G. Atkinson. 6th ed. 1878. 8vo.   **11 F**
Lord lieutenant and high sheriff, correspondence upon the question of precedence. By J. M. Davenport. 1871. 8vo.   **92 E**
The attorney's office list of sheriffs, undersheriffs, and deputies, 1839–1843, and Laidman's List of sheriffs, undersheriffs, deputies, and agents, 1845–1847 and 1849–1860. [All bound in 1 vol.] 1839–60. folio.   **19 D**
Practice of the office of Sheriff and Under Sheriff. By John Impey. 3rd ed. 1812. 8vo.   **175 E**
Short treatise touching sheriffs accompts. By Sir Matthew Hale. 1716. 12mo.   **144 F**
The compleat sherriff, wherein is set forth his office and authority ; to which is added the office and duty of coroners. 1696. 12mo.   **49 C**
Ye offyce of Shyryffes, Baylyffes of lybertyes . . . 1552. 12mo.   **118 A**
See DALTON, M., GREENWOOD, W., SEWELL, R. C., SKIRROW, G. and WATSON, W. H.
See also EXECUTION and INTERPLEADER.

SHERIFFS' COURT.
Sheriffs' court of the City of London. By O. B. C. Harrison. 1860. 8vo.   **12 A**
On the constitution, jurisdiction, and practice of the Sheriffs' courts of London. By T. Lewis. 1833. 8vo.   **175 E**
The practice upon Writ of Trial for debts not exceeding 20l. before the sheriff. By G. B. Mansel. 1833. 12mo. **176 F**
The practice of Sheriffs' Court, London. 1657. 12mo. **48 A**

[SHERLOCK, WILLIAM.]
A Letter to a member of the Convention. [n.d.] 8vo. [Tracts, 1688–9.]   **118 E**

SHERWOOD, Thomas Moulden.
A Treatise on the proceedings to be adopted in conducting Private Bills through the House of Commons. 3rd ed. 1834. 8vo. **173 C**

SHILLIBEER, Henry Blatchford.
The ancient customs of the manor of Taunton Deane, collected from the records of the manor. 1821. 12mo. **93 A**

SHILLINGFORD, John.
Letters and papers of John Shillingford, mayor of Exeter, 1447–50. Edited by S. A. Moore. [Camden Society, n.s. vol. 2.] 1871. 8vo. **85 C**

SHIPBUILDING AND SHIPS.
Britain's glory ; or, ship-building unvail'd, being a general director for building and compleating the said machines. By Wm. Sutherland. 2nd ed. 1729. 4to. **78 G**
A Naval expositor shewing and explaining the words and terms of art belonging to ships. By T. R. Blanckley. 1750. 4to. **78 G**
The prices of the labour in ship-building adjusted, or the mystery of ship-building unveiled. By Wm. Sutherland. 1717. folio. **78 H**

SHIPLEY, Rev. Orby.
The Purgatory of prisoners ; or, an intermediate stage between the prison and the public. 1857. 8vo. **78 C**

SHIPMAN, Richard.
The law and practice relating to Landlords and Tenants, comprising the most approved modern precedents. 1839. 12mo. **170 C**
Shipman's attorney's new pocket-book, notary's manual, and conveyancer's assistant. By E. H. Cameron. 3rd ed. by G. S. Allnutt. 1849. 8vo. **13 G**

SHIP-MONEY.
An Humble Remonstrance against the Tax of Ship-Money lately imposed. By Wm. Prynne. 1643. 8vo. **118 E**
Notes of the judgment delivered by Sir George Croke in the case of ship-money. Edited by S. R. Gardiner. [Camden Society, n.s. vol. 14.] 1875. 8vo. **85 D**

SHIPPING, MERCHANT.
Admiralty procedure against Merchant ships and cargoes.
By R. G. M. Browne. 1887. 8vo. · 12 D
The law relative to Merchant ships and seamen. By C.
Abbott, Lord Tenterden. 12th ed. 1881. 8vo. 11 F
Compendium of law of Merchant shipping. By F. P. Maude
and C. E. Pollock. 4th ed. 2 vols. 1881. 8vo. 11 F
The law of Merchant shipping. By D. Maclachlan. 3rd ed.
1880. 8vo. 11 F
A Treatise on the law of Merchant shipping and freight. By
J. T. Foard. 1880. 8vo. 53 G
Consul's manual and shipowner's and shipmaster's guide in their
transactions abroad. By Lewis Joel. 1879. 8vo. 52 C
F. Rocci De Navibus et Naulo, item de assecurationibus
Notabilia. Amsterdam, 1708. 12mo. 49 A
See BOYD, A. C., HOLT, F. L., HOLT, W., KAY, J., LEES, J.,
NEWSON, H., OLIVER, W. A., PARKER, T., ROWLAND, C.,
SYMONDS, E. W. and WILKINSON, J. J.
See also MARITIME LAW and MERCANTILE LAW.

SHIPPING CASUALTIES.
Law of collisions at sea. By R. G. Marsden. 3rd ed. 1891.
8vo. 11 F
Wreck Inquiries. The law and practice relating to formal
investigations into shipping casualties. By W. Murton.
1884. 8vo. 53 I
A Digest of the judgments in Board of Trade inquiries into
shipping casualties, delivered by H. C. Rothery, 1876–1880.
By T. F. Squarey. 1882. 8vo. 53 I

SHIRLEY, EVELYN PHILIP.
History of the county of Monaghan. 1879. folio. 95 G

[SHIRLEY, JOHN.]
Life of the valiant and learned Sir Walter Raleigh, with his
Tryal at Winchester. 1677. 12mo. 79 A

SHIRLEY, WALTER SHIRLEY.
Elementary treatise on Magisterial law. 1881. 8vo. 64 E
John Wilkes, demagogue or patriot ? a sketch of the eighteenth
century. 1879. [Pamphlets, vol. 38.] 144 C
A Selection of leading cases in Common Law, with notes.
1880. 2nd ed. 1883, and 3rd ed. 1886. 8vo. 64 B

SHIRLEY, WALTER SHIRLEY—*continued.*
Selection of leading cases in Criminal law. 1888. 8vo.   **64 B**
A Sketch of thè Criminal Law.   1880.   8vo.   **64 B**
The same.   2nd ed. by C. S. Hunter.   1889.   8vo.   **64 B**

SHOREHAM, KENT.
Substance of the speech of M. Nolan before a committee of
the House of Commons, upon the Shoreham road bill.
1811.   [Jacob's Tracts, vol. 13.]   **144 F**

SHORT, FREDERICK HUGH.
The crown office rules and forms 1886; with notes.   1886.
8vo.   **52 E**
The taxation of costs in the crown office.   1879.   8vo.   **9 F**
Practice on the Crown Side of the Queen's Bench Division.
By F. H. Short and F. H. Mellor.   1890.   8vo.   **12 E**

SHORTHAND.
Institute of shorthand writers practising in the High court
of justice.   Amended constitution and bye-laws.   1882.
[Pamphlets, vol. 37.]   **144 C**
Shorthand notes and the practice relating to them.   By
M. Levy.   1886.   8vo.   **11 G**
Universal system of Shorthand (founded on system of Taylor).
By W. J. O. Michell.   1885.   [Pamphlets, vol. 40]   **144 C**

SHORTT, JOHN.
Informations, Mandamus and Prohibition.   1887.   8vo.   **10 C**
Law relating to works of literature and art.   1871.   8vo.   **52 D**
The same.   2nd ed.   1884.   8vo.   **9 E**

SHOWER, SIR BARTHOLOMEW.
Cases in Parliament resolved and adjudged, upon Petitions,
and Writs of Error.   1698.   folio.
The same.   3rd ed.   1740.   folio.   **74 G**
Reports of cases adjudged in the court of King's Bench in
the reigns of Charles II., James II. and Will. III.   2 vols.
1708–20.   folio.
The same.   2nd ed. with notes and references by Thomas
Leach.   2 vols.   1794.   8vo.   **5 H**

SHREWSBURY.
The history and antiquities of Shrewsbury ; with an appendix containing several particulars relative to castles, monasteries, &c. in Shropshire. By T. Phillips. Shrewsbury, 1779. 8vo. **93 B**
A History of Shrewsbury. By H. Owen and J. B. Blakeway. 2 vols. 1825. 4to. **92 F**

SHROPSHIRE. ·
Antiquities of Shropshire. By Rev. R. W. Eyton. 12 vols. 1854-60. 8vo. **93 A**
Antiquities of Shropshire. By T. F. Dukes. Shrewsbury, 1844. 4to. **93 G**
A Map of Shropshire. By R. Baugh. 1808. folio. **19 D**
A Selection of antiquities in the county of Salop ; with topographical and historical accounts to each view. [By W. Pearson.] 1824. 4to. **93 H**

SHUTE, W.
The generall historie of the magnificent state of Venice. By Thomas de Fougasses. Englished by W. Shute. 1612. folio. **113 G**

SICHEL, WALTER SYDNEY.
The practice relating to witnesses. 1887. 12mo. **11 I**
Law relating to interrogatories, production, inspection of documents and discovery. By W. S. Sichel and Wm. Chance. 1883. 8vo. **9 G**

SICILY, LAW OF.
Raccolta degli atti del governo della luogotenenza generale del re in Sicilia. Palermo, 1862. 8vo. **56 C**
Raccolta degli atti del governo dittatoriale e prodittatoriale in Sicilia (1860). Palermo, 1861. 8vo. **56 C**

SICKELMORE, RICHARD.
An Epitome of Brighton, topographical and descriptive. Brighton, [1815.] 12mo. **93 E**

SIDERFIN, THOMAS.
Reports des divers special Cases argue & adjudge en le court del Bank le Roy, et auxy en le Co. Ba. & l'Exchequer, en

SIDERFIN, THOMAS—*continued.*
les premier dix ans apres le Restauration de Charles II.
Part II., esteant plusieurs cases adjudge en le court del
Upper Banck, 1657–1659. 2 vols. 1683–84. folio.
The same. 2nd ed. corrigee par R. Dobyns, avec nouvelles
references par E. Chilton et R. Skinner. 2 parts in 1 vol.
1714. folio. **74 G**

SIELY, REV. THOMAS HURFORD.
A Letter to the lord bishop of London on the case of the
Rev. T. H. Siely, Ex-British chaplain at Lisbon. By An
officiating parish priest. 1846. [Pamphlets, vol. 5.] **144 A**

SIERRA LEONE.
Numerical and alphabetical index of the ordinances of Sierra
Leone. By F. F. Pinkett. 1887. folio. **37 D**
Sierra Leone ordinances, 1857–62 and 1885–90. 3 vols.
1857–90. folio. **37 D**

SIGNET BILLS.
An Index to bills of privy signet, commonly called Signet
Bills, 1584 to 1596 and 1603 to 1624 ; with a calendar of
writs of privy seal, 1601 to 1603. Edited by W. P. W.
Phillimore. [Index Library, vol. 4.] 1890. 8vo. **124 H**

SIGNIFICAVIT.
Case of Atwood *v.* Eyre in Chancery, on quashing a Significavit. See Collectanea Juridica, vol. 1, pp. 468–472. **144 G**

SIMEON, MONK OF DURHAM.
De Dunelmensi ecclesia. De gestis regum Anglorum cum
continuatione Joh. Prioris Hagustaldensis. See Scriptores
Decem Hist. Angl., vol. 1., 1652, pp. 1–282. **114 H**
Opera omnia. Edited by T. Arnold. 2 vols. 1882–85.
8vo. **102 G**
See also Monumenta Historica Britannica. 1848. folio. **99 B**

SIMMONS, THOMAS FREDERICK.
The constitution and practice of Courts Martial. 6th ed. by
his son T. F. Simmons. 1873. 8vo. **53 A**

SIMON, HENRY ANDREWS.
Law of Interpleader. 1842. 12mo. Bound with E. Lawes
on Bills of exchange. 1842.   160 G
                                                                   .

SIMONS, NICHOLAS.
Reports of cases in the Court of Chancery, 1826–1852.
17 vols. 1829–54. 8vo.   3 E F
Reports of cases in the Court of Chancery, new series, 1850–
1852. 2 vols. 1851–52. 8vo.   3 F

SIMONS, NICHOLAS and JOHN STUART.
Reports of cases decided in the court of Chancery, 1822–1826.
2 vols. 1824–27. 8vo.   3 F

SIMONY.
Law of Simony. By T. Cunningham. 1784. 8vo.   175 G
See also ECCLESIASTICAL LAW.

SIMPSON, ARCHIBALD HENRY.
Law and practice relating to Infants. 1875. 8vo.   . 52 I
The same. 2nd ed. by E. J. Elgood. 1890. 8vo.   . 10 C

SIMPSON, REV. HENRY TRAIL.
Archæologia Adelensis; or, a history of the parish of Adel
in the west riding of Yorkshire. 1879. 8vo.   94 B

SIMPSON, JOSEPH.
Reflections on the natural and acquired endowments requisite
for the study of the Law. 3rd ed. 1764. 12mo.   171 A
The same. 5th ed. by M. Dawes. [n.d.] 12mo.   171 A

SIMPSON, ROBERT.
A Collection of fragments illustrative of the history and antiquities of Derby. 2 vols. Derby, 1826. 8vo.   87 C

SIMPSON, REV. ROBERT.
The history and antiquities of the town of Lancaster. Lancaster, 1852. 8vo.   89 B

SIMS, RICHARD.
Handbook to library of British Museum ; with some account of the principal libraries in London. 1854. 8vo. **82 H**
An Index to the pedigrees and arms contained in the Heralds' visitations and other genealogical manuscripts in the British Museum. 1849. 8vo. **124 H** ·
A Manual for the genealogist, topographer, antiquary, and legal professor. 2nd ed. 1861. 8vo. **124 G**

SIMSON, ROBERT.
The elements of Euclid. Corrected by Samuel Maynard. 1839. 12mo. **255 H**
Sectionum Conicarum libri V. Edinburgi, 1735. 8vo. **255 H**

SINCLAIR, AUGUSTUS C. and LAWRENCE R. FYFE.
Handbook of Jamaica for 1882. Kingston, 1882. 8vo. **84 B**

SINCLAIR, SIR JOHN.
Observations on the Report of the bullion committee. 2nd ed. 1810. [Jacob's Tracts, vol. 13.] **144 F**
The statistical account of Scotland. 21 vols. Edinburgh, 1791–99. 8vo. **95 A B**

SIREY, JEAN BAPTISTE.
Les Codes annotés de Sirey, contenant toute la jurisprudence des arrêts et la doctrine des auteurs : édition entièrement refondue par P. Gilbert. 4me tirage. 3 vols. Paris, 1862–3. 8vo. **58 G**

SKEAT, REV. WALTER WILLIAM.
An Etymological dictionary of the English language. 2nd ed. Oxford, 1884. 4to. **123 E**

SKELTON, JOSEPH.
Oxonia antiqua restaurata, containing upwards of 190 engravings by Joseph Skelton and others, the literary portion by members of the university. 2nd ed. by E. J. Carlos. 1843. 4to. **92 G**

SKENE, SIR JOHN.
The exposition of termes and difficill wordes conteined in the foure buiks of Regiam Maiestatem. 1641. 8vo. **49 C**

SKENE, Sir John—*continued.*
The same. 1681. Reprinted at end of R. Bell's Dictionary of the law of Scotland, 3rd ed., vol. 2. 1826. 8vo.   **175 D**
Regiam Majestatem : the auld lawes and constitutions of Scotland.   Edinburgh, 1609.   folio.
See also D. Houard's Coutumes Anglo-Normandes, vol. 2, 1776, pp. 36–267.   **40 A**

SKERRIES, Anglesea.
The Skerries lighthouse compensation case.   The Rev. John Jones and others, Plaintiffs, and Corporation of Trinity-house, Defendants.   1841.   [Pamphlets, vol. 23.]   **144 B**

SKINNER, Robert.
Reports of cases in Court of King's Bench, 1681–1698 ; with some arguments in special cases.   1728.   folio.   **74 G**

SKINNER, Thomas.
The Stock Exchange year-book for 1888.   1888.   8vo.   **142 B**
The same for 1889.   1889.   8vo.   **142 B**
The same for 1890.   1890.   8vo.   **134 I**

SKINNER. Walter Robert.
The Mining Manual for 1888.   1888.   8vo.   **134 I**

SKIRBECK, Lincolnshire.
Collections for a topographical and historical account of Boston and the Hundred of Skirbeck.   By Pishey Thompson.   1820.   8vo.   **89 C**

SKIRROW, George.
The compleat practical Undersheriff, comprehending the duties of the office as exercised by the Sheriff in person or by his Undersheriff.   1811.   8vo.   **175 E**

SLADDEN, William.
The registry laws affecting lands in Upper Canada.   Toronto, 1857.   8vo.   **60 E**

SLANDER.
The law of Slander and Libel (founded on treatise of late Mr. Starkie).   5th ed. by H. C. Folkard.   1891.   8vo.   **11 F**

SLANDER—*continued.*
A Digest of the law of Libel and Slander. By Wm. Blake
Odgers. 2nd ed. 1887. 8vo. **11 F**
Actions for Slander. By John March. 1647. 12mo. **48 A**
See also LIBEL.

SLATER, JOHN HERBERT.
A Guide to the Legal Profession. 1884. 8vo. **64 E**
Law relating to copyright and trade marks, treated more
particularly with reference to infringement. 1884. 8vo. **9 E**

SLATER, JOSHUA.
Law of arbitration and awards. 2nd ed. 1886. 12mo. **52 A**
The principles of mercantile law. 1884. 12mo. **53 A**

SLAUGHTER, MIHILL.
Railway Intelligence. 2 vols. 1861–75. 8vo. **146 B**

SLAVERY.
De jure servorum tam veteri quam hodierno, H. J. Arnoldus
de Vries. Harderovici, 1764. [Latin tracts on civil and
canon law.] **118 E**
Digest of laws in the British colonies in America and the
West Indies; including laws for abolition of slave trade.
By Wm. Earnshaw. 1819. 8vo. **55 D**
Negroes and negro slavery. See J. D. B. De Bow's Industrial
resources of the southern and western states, vol. 2, pp. 196–
345. **84 D**
Opinions of Henry Brougham, Esq., on Negro slavery. 1830.
[Jacob's Tracts, vol. 13.] **144 F**
Slave law of Jamaica; with proceedings and documents relative
thereto. 1828. 8vo. **55 D**
Trial of P. De Zulueta junior, on a charge of slave trading;
with an address to the merchants of Great Britain. By
P. De Zulueta, junior. 1844. 8vo. **50 A**

SLEAFORD, LINCOLNSHIRE.
Sketches illustrative of the topography and history of New
and Old Sleaford. By James Creasey. Sleaford, 1825.
8vo. **89 C**

SLEIGH, WILLIAM ARTHUR WARNER.
An Annual digest of Criminal law, containing cases decided, and statutes passed relating to Criminal law, from Hilary, 1870, to Michaelmas, 1871. 1871. 12mo. **63 D**

SLEIGH, WILLIAM CAMPBELL.
A Handy book on criminal law applicable chiefly to commercial transactions. New ed. 1860. 12mo. **165 D**
Letter to the lord bishop of Exeter in reference to his speech in House of Lords against second reading of Earl St. Germans' bill for legalizing marriage with a deceased wife's sister. 2nd ed. 1851. [Pamphlets, vol. 24.] **144 B**
Personal wrongs and legal remedies. 1860. 12mo. **178 E**

SLIFORD, WILLIAM.
The court register and statesman's remembrancer, containing a series of all the great officers. 1741. 8vo. **124 G**
See also MUSGRAVE, SIR W.

SMALE, JOHN and JOHN WALTER DE L. GIFFARD.
Reports of cases adjudged in the court of Chancery, 1852–1857. 3 vols. 1855–58. 8vo. **3 G**

SMEE, JOHN.
A Complete collection of abstracts of acts of parliament and cases; with opinions of the judges upon Taxes. 2 vols. 1797. 8vo. **176 D**

SMETHURST, JAMES MELLOR.
Treatise on the Locus Standi of petitioners against private bills in Parliament. 1866, and 2nd ed. 1867. 12mo. **172 A**
The same. 3rd ed. 1876. 12mo. **53 A**

SMITH, ADAM.
Essays on philosophical subjects; with an account of the life and writings of the author, by Dugald Stewart. 1795. 4to. **78 G**
Inquiry into the nature and causes of the wealth of nations. Edited by J. E. T. Rogers. 2nd ed. 2 vols. Oxford, 1880. 8vo. **78 D**
Abridgment of Adam Smith's Inquiry into the nature and causes of the wealth of nations. By W. P. Emerton. Oxford, 1881. 8vo. **78 D**

SMITH, CHARLES. .
The ancient and present state of the county and city of Cork.
2nd ed. 2 vols. Dublin, 1774. 8vo.   95 E
The ancient and present state of the county and city of
Waterford. 2nd ed. Dublin, 1774. 8vo.   95 E
The ancient and present state of the county of Kerry. Dublin,
1774. 8vo.   95 E

SMITH, CHARLES MANLEY.
Treatise on the law of Master and Servant. 1852. 8vo. 172 D·
The same. 2nd ed. 1860. 8vo.   172 D
The same, including Masters and Workmen in every descrip-
tion of trade and occupation. 3rd ed. 1870. 8vo.   172 D
The same. 4th ed. 1885. 8vo.   10 H

SMITH, EDMUND.
Elementary view of practice of Conveyancing in solicitors'
offices. 1863. 12mo.   163 G

SMITH, EDWARD.
Manual for medical officers of health. 1872. 12mo.   172 E

SMITH, EDWARD ORFORD and CHARLES ALBERT CARTER.
The Birmingham corporation (consolidation) act 1883. 1883.
8vo.   93 E

SMITH, FRANCIS.
Ordinances of the settlement on the river Gambia, from
15th Sept. 1879 to 30th Dec. 1885. Vols. 2 and 3. 1886–7.
folio.   37 D

SMITH, FREDERICK JAMES.
A Vade Mecum of general practice in appellate and civil cases
at Quarter Sessions. 1882. 12mo.   12 B

SMITH, HENRY ARTHUR.
Practical exposition of principles of Equity. 1882. 8vo. 64 D
The same. 2nd ed. 1888. 8vo.   64 D

SMITH, HENRY STOOKS.
Register of contested elections. 1841. 12mo.   134 B

SMITH, HORACE.
Treatise on law of Negligence. 1880. 8vo.   **172 G**
The same. 2nd ed. 1884. 8vo.   **11 A**
A Manual of the law of Landlord and Tenant. By H. Smith
and T. S. Soden. Edited by L. W. Cave. 1871. 8vo. **170 D**
The same. 2nd ed., with forms. 1878. 8vo.   **170 D**

SMITH, JAMES WALTER.
Handy book on the law and practice of Public Meetings.
2nd ed. 1867. 12mo.   **175 A**
Handy book on the law of bills, cheques, notes, and I O U'S.
1887. 12mo.   **52 G**
Legal forms for common use. 6th ed. 1875. 12mo. **164 E**

SMITH, JOB ORTON.
The Lawyer and his profession. 1860. 8vo.   **170 F**

SMITH, JOHN GORDON.
An Analysis of Medical Evidence. 1825. 8vo.   **172 E**
Hints for examination of medical witnesses. 1829. 12mo. **118 A**

SMITH, JOHN PRINCE.
The law for surrender of effects and for personal liberation
of prisoners for debt. 1814. 8vo.   **169 A**
Reports of cases in the Court of King's Bench ; with some
cases in the Court of Chancery, 1803–1806. 3 vols. 1804-7.
8vo.   **5 H**

SMITH, JOHN SIDNEY.
Practice of the Court of Chancery. 2 vols. 1834-5. 8vo. **161 D**
The same. 5th ed. 1855. 8vo.   **161 D**
The same. 7th ed. by the author and Alfred Smith. 2 vols.
1862. 8vo.   **161 D**
A Treatise on the principles of Equity. 1856. 8vo. **167 C**

SMITH, JOHN THOMAS.
Antiquities of Westminster : the old palace, St. Stephen's
chapel (now the House of Commons), &c. &c. 1807. 4to.
    92 G

SMITH, JOHN WILLIAM.

Compendium of Mercantile law. 1834. 8vo.   **172 E**

The same. 3rd ed. 1843. 8vo.   **172 E**

The same. 8th ed. by G. M. Dowdeswell. 1871. 8vo.   **172 F**

The same. 10th ed. by J. Macdonell. 2 vols. 1890. 8vo.   **10 I**

Elementary view of the proceedings in an action at law. 3rd ed. by D. B. Ring. 1848. 12mo.   **160 A**

The same. 9th ed. by S. Prentice. 1866. 12mo.   **160 A**

The same. 12th ed. by W. D. I. Foulkes. 1876. 12mo.   **160 A**

The same. 14th ed. by W. D. I. Foulkes. 1884. 12mo.   **64 A**

Law of Contracts. 2nd ed. by J. G. Malcolm. 1855. 8vo. **163 E**

The same. 4th ed. by J. G. Malcolm. 1865. 8vo.   **163 E**

The same. 6th ed. by V. T. Thompson. 1874. 8vo.   **163 E**

The same. 8th ed. by V. T. Thompson. 1885. 8vo.   **9 E**

The law of Landlord and Tenant. Edited by F. P. Maude. 1855. 8vo.   **170 D**

The same. 2nd ed. by F. P. Maude. 1866. 8vo.   **170 D**

The same. 3rd ed. by V. T. Thompson. 1882. 8vo.   **10 E**

Selection of Leading Cases on various branches of the law; with notes. 2 vols. 1837–40. 8vo.   **171 C**

The same. 2nd ed. 2 vols. 1841–42. 8vo.   **171 C**

The same. 4th ed. by J. S. Willes and H. S. Keating. 2 vols. 1856. 8vo.   **171 C**

The same. 6th ed. by F. P. Maude and T. E. Chitty. 2 vols. 1867. 8vo.   **171 C**

The same. 8th ed. by R. H. Collins and R. G. Arbuthnot. 2 vols. 1879. 8vo.   **10 F**

The same. 9th ed. by R. H. Collins and R. G. Arbuthnot. 2 vols. 1887. 8vo.   **10 F**

SMITH, JOSHUA TOULMIN.

Centralization or Representation? A letter to the Metropolitan sanatory commissioners. 2nd ed. 1848. [Pamphlets, vol. 6.]   **144 A**

The Parish, its powers and obligations at law. 2nd ed. 1857. 8vo.   **53 B**

Practical proceedings for the removal of Nuisances to health and safety. 3rd ed. 1861. 12mo.   **173 B**

The same. 4th ed. 1867. 12mo.   **53 B**

SMITH, JOSIAH WILLIAM.

A Compendium of the law of Real and Personal Property connected with conveyancing. 1855. 8vo.   **174 F**

The same. 4th ed. 2 vols. 1870. 8vo.   **174 F**

The same. 5th ed. 2 vols. 1877. 8vo.   **174 F**

The same. 6th ed. by the author and J. Trustram. 2 vols. 1884. 8vo.   **11 C**

A Manual of Common law. 1862. 12mo.   **161 G**

The same. 4th ed. 1870, and 9th ed. 1880. 12mo. **161 G**

The same. 10th ed. by J. Trustram. 1887. 12mo.   **64 B**

A Manual of Equity jurisprudence as administered in England. 2nd ed. 1849. 12mo.   **167 C**

The same. 5th ed. 1856, and 9th ed. 1868. 12mo. **167 C**

The same. 13th ed. 1880. 12mo.   **64 C**

The same. 14th ed. by J. Trustram. 1889. 12mo. **64 C**

A Manual relating to bankruptcy and insolvency, and imprisonment for debt. 1873. 12mo.   **160 F**

A Succinct view of the operation of Fines and Recoveries. 1846. 12mo.   **168 D**

SMITH, SMALMAN.

Analytical index to the ordinances regulating the civil and criminal procedure of the Gold Coast Colony and of the colony of Lagos. 1888. 8vo.   **37 D**

SMITH, THOMAS.

A Topographical and historical account of the parish of St. Mary-Le-Bone. 1833. 8vo.   **89 E**

SMITH, THOMAS EUSTACE.

Summary of law and practice in Admiralty. 1880. 8vo. **160 A**

The same. 3rd ed. 1885. 8vo.   **64 A**

Summary of the law and practice in the Ecclesiastical Courts. 1880, and 2nd ed. 1883. 8vo.   **166 B**

The same. 3rd ed. 1888. 8vo.   **64 C**

Summary of the law of Companies. 1878. 8vo.   **169 D**

The same. 3rd ed. 1885, and 4th ed. 1890. 8vo. **64 B**

SMITH, WILLIAM, F.R.A.S.

A New history of the county of Warwick. 1829. 4to. **93 F**

SMITH, WILLIAM, LL.D., PH.D.
Dictionary of Greek and Roman antiquities. 2nd ed. *1873.* 8vo. **84 C**
Dictionary of Greek and Roman biography and mythology. 3 vols. 1864. 8vo. **81 G**
Dictionary of Greek and Roman geography. 2 vols. 1854–57. 8vo. **84 C**
Dictionary of the Bible. 3 vols. 1863. 8vo. **77 F**
A Latin-English dictionary, based upon the works of Forcellini and Freund. 1863. 8vo. **123 E**

SMITH, WILLIAM ROBERT.
The laws concerning Public Health. 1883. 8vo. **175 A**

SMITHERS, HENRY.
Liverpool, its commerce, statistics, and institutions; with a history of the cotton trade. Liverpool, 1825. 4to. **88 F**

SMOLLETT, TOBIAS GEORGE.
History of England from the Revolution to the death of George II., designed as a continuation of Mr. Hume's history. New ed. 4 vols. 1830. 8vo. **115 F**

SMYTH, CONSTANTINE JAMES.
Chronicle of the law officers of Ireland; containing lists of the judges, from the earliest period; also a chronological table of the law officers from the reign of Queen Elizabeth. 1839. 12mo. **80 F**

SMYTH, RICHARD.
The obituary of Richard Smyth; being a catalogue of all such persons as he knew in their life, extending from 1627 to 1674. Edited by Sir H. Ellis. [Camden Society, vol. 44.] 1849. 8vo. **85 B**

SMYTH, SIR THOMAS.
De Republica Anglorum. The maner of gouernement or policie of the realme of England. 1584. 8vo. **118 A**
The same. Another copy. **48 D**

SMYTH, William and Frederick LOWE

Narrative of a journey from Lima to Para, across the Andes and down the Amazon. 1836. 8vo. **84 E**

SMYTH, William Henry.

Ædes Hartwellianæ ; or, notices of the manor and mansion of Hartwell. Printed for private circulation. 1851. 4to. **86 G**

The cycle of celestial objects, continued at the Hartwell observatory to 1859 ; with a notice of recent discoveries. Printed for private circulation. 1860. 4to. **86 G**

Sidereal chromatics ; being a reprint with additions from the 'Bedford cycle of celestial objects' and its 'Hartwell continuation' on the colours of multiple stars. Privately printed. 1864. 8vo. **78 G**

SNAGG, William.

The laws of Grenada and the Grenadines, 1766–1852. Grenada, 1852. 8vo. **36 D**

SNELL, Edmund Henry Turner.

The Principles of Equity. 1868. 8vo. **167 C**

The same. 2nd ed. by J. R. Griffith. 1872. 8vo. **167 C**

The same. 4th ed. with An epitome of the equity practice, by A. Brown. 1878. 8vo. · **167 C**

The same. 8th ed. by A. Brown. [Practice in Equity omitted.] 1887. 8vo. **64 D**

The same. 9th ed. by A. Brown. 1889. 8vo. **64 D**

See also Blyth, E. E.

SNOW, Thomas and Herbert WINSTANLEY.

The Annual Chancery Practice. 1882. 8vo. **163 C**

The Lancaster chancery practice. 1885. 8vo. **12 H**

The principal statutes, orders, and rules of court of the court · of chancery of the county palatine of Lancaster. 1880. 8vo. **12 H**

SNOW, Thomas, H. WINSTANLEY and J. WALTON.

Annual Practice 1883–4 ; with copious notes, forms, &c. [1883.] 8vo. **163 C**

The same, 1884–5. New ed. [1884.] 8vo. **163 C**

The same, 1885–6. New ed. [1885.] 8vo. **163 C**

58

SNOW, THOMAS, H. WINSTANLEY and J. WALTON—
continued.
The same, 1886–7. New ed. [1886.] 8vo. **163 C**
The same, 1887–8. New ed. by the authors and F. A. Stringer.
[1887.] 8vo. **163 C**
The same, 1888–9. New ed. by the authors and F. A. Stringer,
with supplement. 2 vols. [1888.] 8vo. **163 C**
The same, 1889–90. New ed. by T. Snow, C. Burney and
F. A. Stringer, with Supplement. 2 vols. [1889.] 8vo. **12 F**
The same, 1890–1. New ed. by T. Snow, C. Burney and F. A.
Stringer, with Supplement. 2 vols. [1890.] 8vo. **12 F**

SNOWDEN, RALPH L.
Police officers' and constables' guide and magistrates' assistant.
6th ed. by W. C. Glen. 1866. 12mo. **172 C**
The same. 7th ed. by W. C. Glen. 1875. 12mo. **172 C**
The same. 8th ed. by T. H. Lees. 1885. 12mo. **12 C**

SOCIAL SCIENCE.
Journal of Social Science, Nov. 1865 to Oct. 1866. Edited
by Edwin Lankester. 1866. 8vo. **78 F**
Sessional papers of National Association for the promotion of
Social Science, 1865–6. 1866. 8vo. **78 F**
Transactions of National Association for the promotion of
Social Science, 1857–1884. 28 vols. 1858–85. 8vo. **78 F**
Conference on temperance legislation, London, 1886. 1886.
8vo. **78 F**
See also MILLER, REV. C.

SOCIALISM.
Fallacies of Socialism exposed ; being a reply to the manifesto
of the Democratic Federation. By Samuel Smith. 1884.
[Pamphlets, vol. 37.] **144 C**

SOCIETY.
Ancient law : its connection with the early history of society,
and its relation to modern ideas. By Sir H. S. Maine.
4th ed. 1870. 8vo. **83 I**
History of modern Europe ; with a view of the progress of
society from the rise of the modern kingdoms to the Peace
of Paris in 1763. [By Wm. Russell.] New ed. with a continuation to 1825. 6 vols. 1827. 8vo. **113 C**

SOCIETY—*continued.*

A View of society in Europe in its progress from rudeness to refinement. By G. Stuart. Edinburgh, 1778. 4to. **115 H**

SOLICITORS.

The Solicitor's clerk, a handy book upon the ordinary practical work of a solicitor's office. By C. Jones. 1891. 12mo. **11 G**

The law relating to solicitors. By A. Cordery. 2nd ed. 1888. 8vo. **11 G**

The organization of a solicitor's office. By E. F. Turner. 1886. 8vo. **11 G**

Duties of solicitor to client. By E. F. Turner. 2 vols. 1883-4. 8vo. **11 G**

The Solicitors' acts ; with notes and comments. By Charles Ford. 2nd ed. 1877. 8vo. **160 C**

An Essay in vindication of the Solicitors from the reflections cast upon them in a pamphlet entitled 'Considerations ; suggested by the Report made to His Majesty, under a commission authorizing the commissioners to make certain inquiries respecting the Court of Chancery.' 1826. [Jacob's Tracts, vol. 5.] **144 E**

The compleat solicitor, entring-clerk and attorney. 1683. 12mo. **48 B**

The Practick part of the law : shewing the office of an attorney, and a guide for solicitors. 1676. 12mo. **48 B**

The compleat sollicitor performing his duty. 1668, and 4th ed. 1672. 12mo. **48 B**

See also ADVOCACY, ATTORNEYS, LAW LISTS, LAWYERS and LEGAL EDUCATION.

SOLICITORS' JOURNAL.

The solicitors' journal and reporter, 1857–1890. 34 vols. 1857–90. 4to. **69 A-F**

SOLICITORS' REMUNERATION ACT.

The general order made under the solicitors' remuneration act 1881, and a digest. 1889. 8vo. **9 F**

See also CLERKE, A. ST. J., PRIDMORE, T. W., RUBENSTEIN, J. S. and WHITE, G. M.

SOLITUDE.

Solitude. Written originally by J. G. Zimmerman ; with the life of the author and notes historical and explanatory. 1798. [Vol. 1 only.] 8vo. **83 H**

SOMERS, JOHN, 1 BARON.

A Collection of scarce and valuable tracts on the most interesting and entertaining subjects, but chiefly such as relate to the history and constitution of these kingdoms, selected from public and private libraries, particularly that of Lord Somers. 2nd ed. by Walter Scott. 13 vols. 1809-15. 4to. **113 G**

The security of English-mens lives ; or, the trust, power, and duty of the Grand Jurys of England explained. [By Lord Somers.] 1682. 12mo. · **49 B**

The same. New ed. 1771. [Tracts on Libel, vol. 1.] **144 F**

SOMERSET.

Delineations of the north western division of the county of Somerset. By John Rutter. 1829. 8vo. **93 B**

Domesday studies, an analysis and digest of the Somerset survey and of the Somerset gheld inquest of A.D. 1084. By Rev. R. W. Eyton. 2 vols. 1880. 8vo. **93 B**

Ecclesiastical documents. A brief history of the bishoprick of Somerset from its foundation to the year 1174. By Rev. J. Hunter. [Camden Society, vol. 8.] 1840. 8vo. **85 A**

The history and antiquities of Somerset. By Rev. John Collinson. 3 vols. Bath, 1791. 4to. **93 G**

Topographical survey of Counties of Somerset, Gloucester, &c. By William Tunnicliff. Bath, 1789. 8vo. **93 B**

SOMERSET, HENRY FITZROY, 5 DUKE OF.

Inventories of the wardrobes, plate, chapel stuff, &c. of Henry Fitzroy, Duke of Somerset. Edited by J. G. Nichols. [Camden Society, vol. 61.] 1855. 8vo. **85 B**

SOMNER, WILLIAM.

The antiquities of Canterbury ; or, a survey of that ancient citie ; with the suburbs and cathedrall. 1640. 8vo. **88 C**

A Treatise of Gavelkind both name and thing ; with the life of the author, by White Kennett. 2nd ed. 1726. 8vo. **81 F**

Vocabularium Anglo-Saxonicum, Lexico magna parte auctius, opera Thomæ Benson. Oxoniæ, 1701. 8vo. **123 B**

SONNENSCHEIN, WILLIAM SWAN.
The best books. A reader's guide to the choice of the best available books (about 25,000) in every department of science, art and literature. 1887. 8vo. **82 E**

SORCERY.
A Contemporary narrative of the proceedings against Dame Alice Kyteler, prosecuted for sorcery in 1324, by Richard De Ledrede, bishop of Ossory. Edited by T. Wright. [Camden Society, vol. 24.] 1843. 8vo. **85 A**
See also WITCHCRAFT.

SORTAIN, REV. JOSEPH.
The life of Francis, Lord Bacon. [1851.] 8vo. **79 B**

SOULE, CHARLES C.
The lawyer's reference manual of law books and citations. Boston, 1883. 8vo. **82 D**

SOUTH AUSTRALIA.
Acts and ordinances of South Australia, 1837–1889. 16 vols. Adelaide, 1857–89. 4to. **35 A**
South Australia : a sketch of its history and resources. By J. F. Conigrave. 2nd ed. Adelaide, 1886. 8vo. **84 B**

SOUTH SEA BUBBLES.
Forty-eight pamphlets relating to the South Sea scheme, bound in 3 vols. endorsed South Sea Bubbles. 3 vols. 1712–35. 8vo. **118 B**

> An Appeal to Common Sense ; or some considerations offer'd to restore public credit. By E. Philips. 1720. [vol. 1.]
> The Battle of the Bubbles ; shewing their several constitutions, alliances, policies, and wars. By a Stander-By. 1720. [vol. 1.]
> Brittain's scheme to make a new coin of gold and silver to give in exchange for paper-money and South Sea Stock. By Charles Povey. 1720. [vol. 1.]
> Case of the borrowers on the South-Sea loans, stated. [n.d.] [vol. 1.]
> A Comparison between the proposals of the Bank and the South-Sea Company. 1720. [vol. 1.]
> Considerations recommending to the proprietors of South-Sea stock, the proposals for ingrafting part of that Company's funds into the stock of the Bank, and East-India Companies. 1722. [vol. 2.]
> A Detection of the whole management of the South-Sea Company. In a letter to John Ward of Hackney. 1721. [vol. 2.]

SOUTH SEA BUBBLES—*continued.*

A Dispassionate remonstrance of the nature and tendency of the laws now in force for the reduction of interest. 1751. [voL 3.]

An Essay on the practice of stock-jobbing, and some remarks on the right use, and regular improvement of Money. 1724. [voL 2.]

An Essay on the South-Sea Trade ; with an enquiry into the grounds and reasons of the present dislike and complaint against the settlement of a South-Sea Company. By the author of the Review. [Daniel Defoe.] 1712. [vol. 1.]

An Essay towards restoring of publick credit. By a faithful subject of the Best of Kings, and a well-wisher to the happiest constitution in the World. 1721. [vol. 1.]

Every one's interest in the South-Sea examined ; and by rules of . justice and equity settled, to their reciprocal advantage. 1721. [vol. 2.]

A Farther examination and explanation of the South-Sea Company's scheme. 1720. [voL 1.]

The Hardship of the South-Sea sufferers considered, and some proper remedies for their relief proposed. 1722. [voL 2.]

History of the rise and fall of South-Sea stock. [n.d.] [voL 1.]

An Impartial enquiry into the transactions of the late directors of the South-Sea Company ; with the Secret history of the South-Sea directors. 1735. [vol. 2.]

The Importance of the Ostend Company considered. 2nd ed. with a letter concerning his Majesty's Guaranteeship. 1721. [voL 3.]

A Letter from a merchant in Amsterdam to a friend in London, about the South Sea Trade. 1712. [vol. 1.]

A Letter of thanks from the author of the Comparison between the proposals of the Bank and the South-Sea &c. to the Author of the Argument. [n.d.] [vol. 1.]

A Letter to a conscientious man : concerning the use and the abuse of riches, and the right and wrong ways of acquiring them. 1720. [vol. 1.]

A Letter to a friend in the Country. By Eustace Budgell. 1721. [vol. 2.]

A Letter to a friend, in vindication of the directors of the South Sea Company. 1721. [voL 2.]

A Letter to a Member of Parliament, occasion'd by the South-Sea Company's scheme for reducing the public debts. 1720. [voL 1.]

A Letter to Mr. Law, upon his arrival in Great Britain. 4th ed. 1721. [vol. 3.]

A Second letter to Mr. Law. [n.d.] [voL 3.]

A Memorial of the contractants with Mr. Aislabie. In a letter to Licinius Stolo. 1721. [voL 2.]

Money and trade consider'd with a proposal for supplying the nation with money. By John Law. 1720. [voL 3.]

Mr. Law's Character vindicated, in the management of the stocks in France. By one who is disinterested, and was upon the place. 1721. [voL 3.]

A Nation a Family : being the sequel of the Crisis of property ; or, a plan for the improvement of the South-Sea Proposal. By Sir Richard Steele. 1720. [vol. 1.]

The Nation preserved ; or, the plot discovered. Addressed to Sir J—— B——. 1720. [vol. 1.]

SOUTH SEA BUBBLES—*continued.*

The Nature of contracts considered as they relate to the third and fourth subscriptions, taken in by the South Sea Company. By a tradesman of the City, whose name is not to be found in any of the subscriptions. 2nd ed. 1720. [vol. 1.]

Now or never ; or, a familiar discourse concerning the two schemes for restoring National Credit. By R. M. Esq. 1721. [vol. 2.]

Observations on the new system of the Finances of France. By Mr. Law. Translated by Sir J[ohn] E[yles]. 1720. [vol. 3.]

The Original plan, progress, and present state of the South-Sea-Company ; or, some occasional thoughts upon the state of the British Trade in the West Indies, more especially the South-Seas. By John Pullen. 1732. [vol. 2.]

The Pangs of credit : or, an argument to shew where it is most reasonable to bestow the two millions. By an Orphan Annuitant. 1722. [vol. 3.]

The Present state of the British credit consider'd. In a letter to W[illia]m S[ope]r, M.P. 1720. [vol. 2.]

Remarks on the celebrated calculations of the value of South-Sea stock, in the Flying-Post of the 9th of April, 1720. 1720. [vol. 1.]

Remarks on the occurrences of the years 1720 and 1721 ; relating to the South-Sea Scheme. 1732. [vol. 2.]

Remarks upon several pamphlets writ in opposition to the South-Sea scheme. 1720. [vol. 1.]

The Skreen removed ; in a list of all the names mention'd in the report of the committee of Secrecy. 1721. [vol. 2.]

Some considerations concerning the public funds, the public revenues, and the annual supplies, granted by parliament. [By Sir Robert Walpole.] 1735. [vol. 3.]

Some considerations upon the state of our publick debts in general, and of the civil list in particular. 1720. [vol. 3.]

Some general considerations concerning the alteration and improvement of public revenues. [By Sir Robert Walpole.] 1733. [vol. 3.]

Three letters concerning civil comprehension &c. the last of which is occasioned by the present distresses the directors of the South-Sea-Company have brought upon these kingdoms. 1721. [vol. 2.]

Three letters relating to the South Sea Company and the Bank. By James Milner. 1720. [vol. 1.]

A True account of the design, and advantages of the South-Sea Trade. 1711. [vol. 1.]

A True state of public credit ; or, a short view of the condition of the nation, with respect to our present calamities. 1721. [vol. 3.]

A True state of the contracts relating to the third money-subscription taken by the South-Sea Company. 1721. [vol. 2.]

Ways and means to make South-Sea stock more intrinsically worth than ready money. 1720. [vol. 1.]

SOUTH SEA COMPANY.

An Abstract of the several acts of parliament of the South Sea Company. 1718. 12mo.   **92 A**

SOUTH SEA COMPANY—*continued.*

A Letter to the proprietors of the South-Sea Company. By
Richard Coope. 1739. 8vo. **118 B**

List of the names of such proprietors of South-Sea capital,
stock, and the public funds transferable at the South-Sea
house as were entitled to dividends on or before 10 October
1822 and which remained unpaid 24 June 1823. 1823.
Bound with Bank of England Unclaimed Dividends. 1823.
8vo. **134 I**

The secret history of the late directors of the South-Sea-
Company. By D. Templeman. 1735. 8vo. **118 B**

A True state of the South-Sea-Scheme. 1732. 8vo. **118 B**

SOUTH WINFIELD, DERBYSHIRE.

History of the manor and manor-house of South Winfield.
By Thomas Blore. 1816. 4to. **87 B**

SOUTHAMPTON.

The charter of the town and county of Southampton, dated
the 27th of June 1641. Southampton, 1810. 12mo. **88 A**

History of Southampton. By Rev. J. S. Davies. 1883.
8vo. **88 B**

See also HAMPSHIRE.

SOUTHEY, ROBERT and JOSEPH COTTLE.

The works of Thomas Chatterton. 3 vols. 1803. 8vo. **83 E**

SOUTHWARK.

Etymology of Southwark. By Ralph Lindsay. 3rd ed.
1839. 12mo. **93 C**

A Report of the two cases of controverted elections of the
borough of Southwark in 1796. By Henry Clifford. 1797.
8vo. **166 E**

Survey of the cities of London and Westminster and the
borough of Southwark. By John Rocque. 1751. folio.
91 H

SOUTHWARK COURT OF RECORD.

Law and practice of the Southwark Court of Record. By
E. Saffery. 1868. 8vo. **12 A**

Analysis of the acts of parliament relating to the Southwark
Court of Requests, the general practice of the court and a
sketch of its origin and history. By F. W. Meymott. 1830.
8vo. **91 E**

SOUTHWARK COURT OF RECORD—*continued.*
An Address to the Commissioners of the Court of Requests
for the town and borough of Southwark &c. on some resolutions passed at a meeting held 6 May, 1819. By S. Lee.
1819. [City of London Tracts.]   91 C

SOUTHWELL, NOTTINGHAMSHIRE.
Visitations and Memorials of Southwell Minster. Edited
by A. F. Leach. [Camden Society, n.s. vol. 48.] 1891.
8vo.   85 E

SOUTHWOLD, SUFFOLK.
Historical account of Southwold. By T. Gardner. 1754.
4to.   93 B
Southwold and its vicinity, ancient and modern. By Robert
Wake. Yarmouth, 1839. 8vo.   93 C

SPAIN, HISTORY OF.
The British interests in Spain. By a Bondholder. 1860.
[Pamphlets, vol. 23.]   144 B
Calendar of letters, despatches, and state papers relating
to the negotiations between England and Spain, 1485–1542.
Edited by G. A. Bergenroth and P. de Gayangos. 6 vols.
in 11. 1862–90. 8vo.   97 F
Chronicles of England, France, Spain, and the adjoining
countries, 1326–1399. By Sir John Froissart. Translated
by Thomas Johnes. 2 vols. 1857. 8vo.   115 A
The Earl of Bristol's Defence of his negotiations in Spain.
Edited by S. R. Gardiner. [Camden Society, vol. 104.]
1871. 8vo.   85 C
History of the reign of Ferdinand and Isabella the Catholic
of Spain. By W. H. Prescott. 7th ed. revised. 2 vols.
1851. 8vo.   113 C
History of the war of the Succession in Spain. By Lord
Mahon. 1832. 8vo.   113 C
Sir Francis Drake's memorable service done against the
Spaniards in 1587. By Robert Leng. Now first edited
by C. Hopper. [Camden Society, vol. 87.] 1864. 8vo.
                                                    85 C

SPAIN, LANGUAGE OF.
Diccionario de la lengua Castellana compuesto por la real
academia Española, reducido á un tomo. Madrid, 1780,
and 3rd ed. Madrid, 1791. folio.   122 H

SPAIN, LANGUAGE OF—*continued.*

A Dictionary, Spanish and English, and English and Spanish. By J. Baretti. 2nd ed. 1778. folio. **123 H**

The same. New ed. 1807. 8vo. **123 B**

Glossary of Catalan words. See Black book of the Admiralty, vol. 4, 1876, pp. 201-238. **102 D**

Grammatik der Spanischen Sprache. Von Julius Wiggers. Leipzig, 1860. 8vo. **255 G**

Modelos de Literatura Española ; or, choice selections in prose, poetry, and the drama, from celebrated Spanish writers. By E. Del Mar. New ed. 1854. 12mo. **83 A**

A New and improved Spanish grammar. By Luis Josef Antonio McHenry. New ed. 1854. 12mo. **255 H**

A New dictionary, Spanish and English, and English and Spanish. By Captain John Stevens. 1726. 8vo. **123 C**

A Pocket dictionary of the Spanish and English languages. Compiled from the last improved edition of Neuman and Baretti. 1823. 12mo. **123 B**

A Pronouncing dictionary of the Spanish and English languages. By M. Velazquez de la Cadena. 2 vols. in 1. 1852. 8vo. **123 C**

See also MINSHEU, JOHN.

SPAIN, LAWS OF.

The Ley Hipotecaria of Spain ; or, law on the inscription of titles to immoveable property. Translated and edited by W. Grain. 1867. 8vo. **55 C**

Specimen of a catalogue of the books on foreign law, lately presented to Lincoln's Inn Library by C. P. Cooper. Laws of Spain. 1847. 8vo. **82 D**

Febrero Novísimo, ó Libreria de Jueces, Abogados y Escribanos, refundida; ordenada bajo nuevo método, y adicionada con un Tratado del Juicio Criminal, y algunos otros. Por Don E. de Tapia. 9 vols. Valencia, 1828-30. 8vo. **39 D**

Ley de Enjuiciamiento sobre los negocios y causas de Comercio decretada en 24 de Julio de 1830. Edicion oficial. [Madrid], 1830. 8vo. **39 E**

Novísima Recopilacion de las leyes de España dividida en XII libros. 5 vols. 1805. Tomo VI. Tres indices y el suplemento 1829. 6 vols. Madrid, 1805-29. 4to. **39 F**

Institutes of the civil law of Spain. By I. J de Asso y del Rio and M. de Manuel y Rodriguez. Translated with notes by Lewis F. C. Johnston. 1825. 8vo. **55 C**

SPAIN, Laws of—*continued.*
Las Siete Partidas del rey Don Alfonso el Sabio, cotejadas
con varios codices antiguos. Por la Real Academia de la
Historia. 3 vols. Madrid, 1807. 4to.   39 C
Guia para el estudio del Derecho Patrio dividido en cinco
tablas. Por Don Juan De La Reguera Valdelomar.
Segunda edicion. Madrid, 1805. folio.   39 F
See also LLORENTE, A. and MARINA, F. M.

SPARGO, Thomas.
The statistics of and observations upon the mines of Cornwall
and Devon. 1860. 8vo.   87 A

SPEAR, Samuel T.
The law of Extradition, international and inter-state. Albany,
1879. 8vo.   59 E

SPEARMAN, Rudolph Herries.
The common and statute law relating to Highways in England
and North Wales. 1881. 8vo.   168 G

SPECIFIC PERFORMANCE. See Contracts, Specific
Performance of.

SPECTATOR, The.
The Spectator. 1841–1847, and 1853–1890. 47 vols. 1841–
90. 4to.   Hall

SPEED, John.
The Theatre of the empire of Great Britaine. New ed. 1676.
folio.   85 I

SPELMAN, Sir Henry.
Codex legum veterum statutorum regni Angliæ, quæ ab in-
gressu Guilielmi I. usque ad annum nonum Henr. III.
edita sunt. See D. Wilkins's Leges Anglo-Saxonicæ, 1721,
pp. 284–387.   99 C
English works; and the life of the author, by Edmund
[Gibson], lord bishop of London. 2nd ed. 1727. folio.
     78 H

SPELMAN, Sir Henry—*continued.*

Glossarium archaiologicum, continens Latino-Barbara, pere-
grina, obsoleta, et novatæ significationis vocabula. Editio
tertia. 1687. folio. 123 H

Reliquiæ Spelmannianæ; the posthumous works of Sir H.
Spelman relating to the laws and antiquities of England;
with the life of the author. Oxford, 1698. 4to. 78 H

The same. 2nd ed. 1723. Bound with Spelman's English
Works, 2nd ed. 1727. folio. 78 H

Villare Anglicum; or, a view of the townes of England.
.1656. 8vo. 86 A

SPENCE, George.

The equitable jurisdiction of the Court of Chancery. 2 vols.
1846–49. 8vo. 52 G

An Essay on the origin of the English laws and institutions.
1812. 8vo. 170 F

An Inquiry into the origin of the laws and political institutions
of modern Europe, particularly of those of England. 1826.
8vo. 113 C

Reform of the Court of Chancery. 1830. [Pamphlets, vol.
17.] 144 B

The writs and abuses of the Court of Chancery and proposed
amendments. 1831. First address to the public on the
present unsatisfactory state of the Court of Chancery. 2nd
ed. 1839. Second address. 1839. Third address. 1840,
and Supplement to the three addresses. 1840. [Chancery
Pamphlets, vols. 1 and 2.] 144 A

SPENCE, Rev. Joseph.

Polymetis; or, an enquiry concerning the agreement between
the works of the Roman poets and the remains of the
antient artists. 1747. folio. 78 H

SPENCER, Herbert. See Guthrie, M.

SPENS, Walter Cook and Robert T. YOUNGER.

Employers and employed. Glasgow, 1887. 8vo. 9 H

SPIERS, Alexander.

General English and French, and French and English dictionary. New ed. 2 vols. [1865.] 8vo. 123 E

SPIKE, EDWARD.
The law of Master and Servant. 3rd ed. by C. H. Bromby.
1872. 12mo. **172 D**

SPILLER, BENJAMIN.
Index to the public general statutes of the United Kingdom,
1801–28. 1829. 4to. **31 E**

SPILSBURY, WILLIAM HOLDEN.
Catalogue of the printed books in the library of Lincoln's Inn.
1859. 8vo. **82 D**
Lincoln's Inn, its ancient and modern buildings; with an
account of the library. 1850. 12mo. **91 D**
The same. 2nd ed. 1873. 12mo. **91 D**

SPINKS, THOMAS.
Ecclesiastical and Admiralty Reports, 1853–1855. 2 vols.
1855. 8vo. **8 I**

SPINKS, WILLIAM.
The law and practice as to paving of private streets according
to The public health act, 1875. 1887. 8vo. **11 G**

SPIRITS.
An Enquiry as to the practicability and policy of reducing
the duties on Malt and Beer, and encreasing those on British
spirits. 1830. [Pamphlets, vol. 5.] **144 A**

SPOTISWOOD, JOHN.
Form of Process before the Lords of Council and Session;
with the present state of the College of Justice. Edinburgh,
1711. 12mo.
An Introduction to the knowledge of the Stile of Writs, simple
and compound, made use of in Scotland. 5th ed. Edinburgh,
1765. 12mo.

SPOTTISWOODE, JOHN.
History of the Church of Scotland, beginning A.D. 203 and
continued to the end of the reign of King James VI. 3rd
ed. 1668. folio. **113 F**

SPOUSALS.
A Treatise of spousals or matrimonial contracts. By Henry
Swinburne. 1686. 8vo. 49 E

SPRAGUE, PELEG.
Decisions in admiralty and maritime causes in the district
court of the United States for Massachusetts, 1841–1861.
Philadelphia, 1861. 8vo. . 59 B

SPRANGE, JASPER.
Tunbridge Wells guide. Tunbridge Wells, 1797. 8vo. 88 D
The same. Another ed. Tunbridge Wells, 1801. 8vo. 88 D

SPRAT, THOMAS.
The history of the Royal Society of London for the improving
of natural knowledge. 3rd ed. 1722. 8vo. 78 C
Observations on Monsieur de Sorbier's Voyage into England.
1665. 12mo. 118A

SPURZHEIM, JOHANN GASPAR.
Phrenology; or, the doctrine of the mind. 3rd ed. 1825.
8vo. 78 C
A Sketch of the natural laws of man. 1825. 12mo. 78 A
A View of the philosophical principles of Phrenology. 3rd
ed. [n.d.] 8vo. 78 C

SQUAREY, TUCKER FULTON.
Digest of the judgments in Board of Trade inquiries into
shipping casualties, delivered by H. C. Rothery, the wreck
commissioner, 1876–1880. 1882. 8vo. 53 I

SQUIBBS, ROBERT.
Auctioneers, their duties and liabilities. 2nd ed. 1891.
8vo. 9 A

STAËL-HOLSTEIN, A. L. G. NECKER, BARONNE DE.
Considérations sur les principaux événements de la révolution
Française. Le Directoire. Edited by Victor Oger. 2nd
ed. 1882. 8vo. 83 C

STAFFORD FAMILY.
The genealogical table of the royal house of Stafford, deduced down for nearly 2,000 years to 1818. 1818. 8vo. **127 I**

STAFFORDSHIRE.
Description of the country from thirty to forty miles round Manchester. By John Aikin. 1795. 4to. **88 F**

Domesday studies ; an analysis and digest of the Staffordshire survey. By Rev. R. W. Eyton. 1881. 4to. **93 B**

The history and antiquities of Staffordshire. By Rev. Stebbing Shaw. 2 vols. 1798–1801. folio. **93 H**

The natural history of Staffordshire. By Robert Plot. Oxford, 1686. folio. **93 G**

Staffordshire and Warwickshire, past and present. By J. A. Langford, C. S. Mackintosh and J. C. Tildesley. 2 vols. in 4. [1875–76.] 4to. **93 F**

A Survey of Staffordshire, containing the antiquities of that county. By Sampson Erdeswick, with additions by Rev. Thomas Harwood. 1820. 8vo. **93 B**

A Survey of the counties of Lancashire . . . and the Northern part of Staffordshire. 1797. 8vo. **89 B**

See also PENNANT, T. and TUNNICLIFF, W.

STAIR, JAMES, 1 VISCOUNT.
Institutions of the Law of Scotland, deduced from its originals and collated with Civil and Feudal Laws, and with the Customs of neighbouring nations. 4th ed. with commentaries and a supplement, by George Brodie. 2 vols. Edinburgh, 1826–31. folio.

STAMFORD, LINCOLNSHIRE.
Academia tertia Anglicana ; or, the antiquarian annals of Stanford. By Rev. Francis Peck. 1727. folio. **90 G**

An Essay of the ancient and present state of Stamford. By Francis Howgrave. 1726. 8vo. **89 C**

The Stamford Schism. By H. H. Henson. See Oxford Historical Society, vol. 5, 1885, pp. 1–56. **85 F**

STAMP, GEORGE.
Index to statute law of England. 2nd ed. 1853. 8vo. **31 D**

The same. 3rd ed. by J. E. Davis. 1862. 8vo. **31 D**

STAMP DUTIES.

A Digest of the law relating to Stamp duties. By E. N. Alpe. 1890. 12mo. **11 G**

Dissertation on Stamp Duties. See Bythewood and Jarman's Conveyancing, 4th ed., vol. 7, 1889, p. 1–303. **13 D**

A Digest of the stamp duties. By G. C. Griffith. 9th ed. 1886. 8vo. **11 G**

Tables of stamp duties from 1815 to the present time, on conveyances, mortgages, and settlements. By Walter Arthur Copinger. 1878. 8vo. **11 G**

A History and explanation of Stamp duties and laws. By Stephen Dowell. 1873. 8vo. **78 D**

A Treatise on the stamp laws. By H. Tilsley. 3rd ed. 1871. 8vo. **11 G**

A Practical treatise on the Stamp laws. By Joseph Chitty. 2nd ed. by J. W. Hulme. 1841. 12mo. **175 G**

Remarks upon the inequality of the stamp duties as now levied and Suggestions for their amendment. [By Charles Evans.] [n.d.] [Pamphlets, vol. 38.] **144 C**

Reply to the charge of fallacy brought against the exposition of the state of the stamp laws, contained in the Law and Commercial Remembrancer for 1833. 1833. [Pamphlets, vol. 21.] **144 B**

See also FISHER, R. A., HERAUD, J. A., HUGHES, W. and IMPEY, W. J.

STANDARD, BATTLE OF THE.

The ' Relatio de Standardo ' of St. Aelred, Abbot of Rievaulx. See Chronicles of the reigns of Stephen, Henry II. and Richard I., vol. 3, 1886, pp. 179–199. **102 H**

STANDING ORDERS.

History of the standing órders of Houses of Lords and Commons. See F. Clifford's History of private bill legislation, vol. 2, 1887, pp. 752–787. **83 I**

Standing orders of the Houses of Lords and Commons, relative to Private Bills, 1839, 1848, 1852, 1856, 1864–1890. 30 vols. 1839–89. 12mo. **173 B C**

The same for 1891. 1890. 12mo. **12 A**

STANHOPE, PHILIP HENRY, 5 EARL.
History of England ; comprising the reign of Queen Anne,
until the peace of Utrecht, 1701–1713. 4th ed. 2 vols.
1872. 8vo. 115 D
History of England, from peace of Utrecht to peace of Ver-
sailles, 1713–1783. 4th ed. 7 vols. 1853–54. 8vo. 115 G
History of war of Succession in Spain. 1832. 8vo. 113 C
The life of Louis, Prince of Condé, surnamed the Great. 1845.
8vo. 79 B
Life of William Pitt. 4 vols. 1861–62. 8vo. 79 B

STANLEY FAMILY.
History of the house of Stanley, from the conquest, to death
of Earl of Derby, in 1776. Preston, 1793. 8vo. 80 A
A Brief account of the travels of the celebrated Sir Wm.
Stanley. Liverpool, [n.d.] 8vo. 80 A

STANLEY, VERY REV. ARTHUR PENRHYN.
Historical memorials of Westminster Abbey. 2nd ed. 1868,
and Supplement. 1869. 2 vols. 1868–69. 8vo. 91 F
The life and correspondence of Thomas Arnold, D.D. 4th ed.
2 vols. 1845. 8vo. 80 B

STANNARIES, THE.
A Journal of the convocation, or parliament of tinners for the
Stannaries of Cornwall, held at Truro, 1710. See R. Carew's
Survey of Cornwall, 1811, pp. 397–432. 86 F
Laws of the Stannaries of Cornwall made at the convocation
or parliament of Tinners at Truro, Sept. 13, 1753, and the
laws made at Truro, 1703. [1753.] 8vo. 87 A
Laws of the Stannaries of Cornwall. 2nd ed. Truro, 1824.
8vo. 87 A
Laws of the Stannaries ; with The Stannaries' Courts Act
passed 20th of August, 1836. Truro, [1836.] 8vo. 87 A
A Letter to the Earl of Falmouth, on the present state of the
Stannary Courts of Cornwall. By F. Hill. Helston, 1835.
[Jacob's Tracts, vol. 12.] 144 F
Procedure in the court of the Vice warden of the Stannaries.
1856. 8vo. 12 A
Stannaries act 1869. By John Batten. 1873. 8vo. 12 A

STAPLE INN.
The Institute of Actuaries. Opening address by the President, Archibald Day. 'Staple Inn,' delivered 28 November, 1887. [1887.] 8vo.   **91 D**
The Society of Staple Inn; Inns of Court, &c. and Chancery and historical memoranda. By E. R. P[ickering]. [1859.] 8vo.   **91 D**
See also INNS OF COURT AND CHANCERY.

STAPLETON, AUGUSTUS GRANVILLE.
The political life of George Canning, from Sep. 1822 to Aug. 1827. 2nd ed. 3 vols. 1831. 8vo.   **79 B**
Suggestions for a conservative and popular reform in the Commons house of parliament. 1850. [Pamphlets, vol. 9, pt. 2.]   **144 A**

STAR CHAMBER.
Reports of cases in the courts of Star Chamber and High Commission. Edited by S. R. Gardiner. [Camden Society, n.s. vol. 39.] 1886. 8vo.   **85 D**
Speech of Sir Robert Heath in the cases of Alexander Leighton in the Star Chamber, June 4, 1630. Edited by S. R. Gardiner. [Camden Society, n.s. vol. 14.] 1875. 8vo. **85 D**
Star-chamber cases, collected for the most part out of Mr. Crompton his booke, entituled The jurisdiction of divers courts. 1641. [Law tracts and arguments, 1641.] **144 F**
Treatise on the Court of Star-Chamber. By Wm. Hudson. See Collectanea Juridica, vol. 2, 1792, pp. 1–240.   **144 G**

STARK, ADAM.
History and antiquities of Gainsburgh ; with an account of Stow. Gainsburgh, 1817. 8vo.   **89 C**

STARKIE, THOMAS.
Practical treatise of the law of Evidence and digest of proofs, in civil and criminal proceedings. 3rd ed. 3 vols. 1842. 8vo.   **167 G**
Reports of cases determined in the courts of King's Bench, at Nisi Prius, and on the circuit, 1814–1823. 3 vols. 1817–23. 8vo.   **8 F**
A Treatise on Criminal Pleading ; with precedents. 2 vols. 1814, and 2nd ed. 2 vols. 1822. 8vo.   **173 G**

STARKIE, THOMAS—*continued.*
Treatise on law of Slander and Libel, and incidentally of
malicious prosecutions. 2nd ed. 2 vols. 1830. 8vo. **175 G**
The same. 3rd ed. by H. C. Folkard. 1869. 8vo. **175 G**
The same. 4th ed. by H. C. Folkard. 1876. 8vo. **53 G**
The same. 5th ed. by H. C. Folkard. 1891. 8vo. **11 F**

STARLING, MATTHEW HENRY.
Indian criminal law and procedure. 1869. 8vo. **38 C**

STATE PAPERS.
British and foreign state papers, 1812–1881. Compiled by
Lewis Hertslet and Sir Edward Hertslet. 72 vols. 1841–
88. 8vo. **117 A–I**
Miscellanea Aulica ; or, a collection of State-Treatises, never
before publish'd. By T. Brown. 1702. 12mo. **145 B**
State papers during the reign of Henry VIII. 11 vols.
1830–52. 4to. **103 F**
See also CLARENDON, E. and RUSHWORTH, J.

STATE PAPERS, CALENDARS OF.
Calendarium genealogicum, Henry III. and Edward I. Edited
by Charles Roberts. 2 vols. 1865. 8vo. **96 B**
Calendar of state papers, domestic series, of the reigns of
Edward VI., Mary, Elizabeth, and James I., 1547–1625.
Edited by Robert Lemon and Mary Ann Everett Green.
12 vols. 1856–72. 8vo. **96 B C**
Calendar of state papers, domestic series, of the reign of
Charles I., 1625–1645. Edited by John Bruce and W. D.
Hamilton. 20 vols. 1858–90. 8vo. **96 C D**
Calendar of state papers, domestic series, during the Common-
wealth, 1649–1660. Edited by M. A. E. Green. 13 vols.
1875–85. 8vo. **96 D E**
Calendar of proceedings of the committee for the advance of
money, 1642–1656. Edited by M. A. E. Green. 3 parts.
1888. 8vo. **97 G**
Calendar of proceedings of the committee for compounding,
&c., 1643–1660. Edited by M. A. E. Green. Parts 1 & 2.
1889–90. 8vo. **97 H**
Calendar of state papers, domestic series, of the reign of
Charles II., 1660–1667. Edited by M. A. E. Green. 7 vols.
1860–66. 8vo. **96 F**

STATE PAPERS, CALENDARS OF—*continued.*

Calendar of Home Office papers, of the reign of George III., 1760–1772. Edited by Joseph Redington and R. A. Roberts. 3 vols. 1878–81. 8vo. **96 F**

Calendar of state papers relating to Scotland, 1509–1603. Edited by M. J. Thorpe. 2 vols. 1858. 8vo. **96 G**

Calendar of documents relating to Ireland, 1171–1307. Edited by H. S. Sweetman and G. F. Handcock. 5 vols. 1875–86. 8vo. **96 G**

Calendar of state papers relating to Ireland, of the reigns of Henry VIII., Edward VI., Mary, and Elizabeth, 1509–1596. Edited by H. C. Hamilton. 5 vols. 1860–90. 8vo. **96 G**

Calendar of state papers relating to Ireland, of the reign of James I., 1603–1625. Edited by Rev. C. W. Russell and J. P. Prendergast. 5 vols. 1872–80. 8vo. **96 G H**

Calendar of state papers, colonial series. Edited by W. Noel Sainsbury. 7 vols. 1860–89. 8vo. **96 I**

> Vols. i. v. vii. America and West Indies, 1574-1674.
> Vols. ii. iii. iv. vi. East Indies, China, and Japan, 1513-1629.

Calendars of letters and papers, foreign and domestic, of the reign of Henry VIII., 1509–1537. Edited by J. S. Brewer and James Gairdner. 12 vols. in 17. 1862–90. 8vo. **97 B C**

Calendar of state papers, foreign series, of the reigns of Edward VI. and Mary, 1547–1558. Edited by W. B. Turnbull. 2 vols. 1861. 8vo. **97 D**

Calendar of state papers, foreign series, of the reign of Elizabeth, 1558–1577. Edited by Rev. Joseph Stevenson and A. J. Crosby. 11 vols. 1863–80. 8vo. **97 D**

Calendar of treasury papers, 1557–1728. Edited by Joseph Redington. 6 vols. 1868–89. 8vo. **97 E**

Calendar of the Carew manuscripts in the archiepiscopal library at Lambeth, 1515–1624. Edited by Rev. J. S. Brewer and William Bullen. 6 vols. 1867–73. 8vo. **97 E**

Calendar of letters, despatches, and state papers, relating to the negotiations between England and Spain, 1485-1542. Edited by G. A. Bergenroth and Don Pascual de Gayangos. 6 vols. in 11. 1873–90. 8vo. **97 F**

Calendar of state papers relating to English affairs, existing in Venice and other libraries of Northern Italy, 1202-1580. Edited by Rawdon Brown and G. C. Bentinck. 7 vols. in 9. 1864–90. 8vo. **97 H**

STATE PAPERS, CALENDARS OF—*continued.* ✦

Syllabus (in English) of documents relating to England and other kingdoms, contained in Rymer's Fœdera, 1066–1654. By Sir T. D. Hardy. 3 vols. 1869–85. 8vo. **97 H**

Report to the Master of the Rolls upon the Carte and Carew papers in the Bodleian and Lambeth libraries. By T. D. Hardy and J. S. Brewer. 1864. 8vo. **97 H**

Report to the Master of the Rolls upon the documents in the archives and public libraries of Venice. By Thomas Duffus Hardy. 1866. 8vo. **97 H**

Acts of the Privy Council of England, new series, 1542–1550. Edited by J. R. Dasent. Vols. 1 & 2. 1890. 8vo. **99 A**

A Descriptive catalogue of Ancient Deeds in the Public Record Office. Edited by H. C. Maxwell Lyte. Vol. 1. 1890. 8vo. **97 H**

STATE TRIALS.

A Compleat collection of State-Tryals, and proceedings upon impeachments for High Treason, and other crimes and misdemeanours ; from Henry IV. to Queen Anne. 4 vols. 1719, and Supplement from Richard II. to George II. 2 vols. 1730. folio. **49 I**

The same. 3rd ed. 6 vols. 1742, and Supplement from Edward VI. to present time. 2 vols. 1735. folio. **49 I**

A Complete collection of State Trials and proceedings for high treason and other crimes and misdemeanors, from the earliest period to 1820. By T. B. Howell and T. J. Howell. 33 vols. 1816–26, and General index by David Jardine. 1 vol. 1828. 34 vols. 1816–28. 8vo. **50 I J**

Reports of State Trials, new series, 1820–1831. Edited by John Macdonell. Vols. 1 & 2. 1888–9. 8vo. **50 J**

A Select collection of remarkable trials (vols. 7 and 8 of an edition of State Trials). 2 vols. 1744. 8vo. **51 D**

State trials. Specimen of a new edition. By N. T. Moile. 1838. 8vo. **83 H**

See also SALMON, T. and WHARTON, F.

STATESMAN'S YEAR BOOK.

The statesman's year book : a statistical, genealogical, and historical account of the states and sovereigns of the civilised world. By F. Martin. 1864–1882, and by J. S. Keltie. 1883–1891. 28 vols. 1864–91. 12mo. **140 C D**

[ŞTATHAM, Nicholas.]
[An Abridgement of cases from Edward I. to Henry VI., in
Norman French. Rouen, 1495.] 4to. **158 D**

STATISTICAL SOCIETY.
Council and officers, list of fellows, rules, &c. of the Statistical
Society. 1874. 8vo. **146 E**

STATUTES, Collections and Indexes of.
Chitty's Collection of Statutes of practical utility. 4th ed.
containing the statutes and cases down to 1880, by J. M.
Lely. 6 vols. 1880. Annual continuations, 1881–1890,
by J. M. Lely. 2 vols. 8 vols. 1880–91. 8vo. **70 I**
Chronological table of and index to the statutes. 1870, 2nd
ed. 1873, 4th ed. 1878, 5th ed. 1879, 6th ed. 1880,
7th ed. 1881, 9th ed. 1884, and 10th ed. 1887. **158 A**
The same. 11th ed. 1890. 8vo. **71 C**
A Complete collection of practice statutes, orders, and rules.
By A. Emden. 2nd ed. 1886. 8vo. **71 I**
The Legal Prompter ; or, statute indicator, being a compila-
tion for immediate reference to Statutes most in use. By
H. W. Ibbotson. 1860. 12mo. **176 C**
An Index to the unrepealed Statutes connected with the
administration of the law in England and Wales, 1837–
1850. By T. G. Archer. 1851. 8vo. **176 C**
A Key to Statutes affected by enactments of Geo. IV. &
Wm. IV. By G. Farren, jun. 1837. 12mo. **176 C**
A Collection of Statutes connected with the general adminis-
tration of the law. By Sir W. D. Evans. 2nd ed. by
Anthony Hammond. 8 vols. 1823. 8vo. **176 B**
Abridgment of public statutes, Magna Charta to 1 Geo. III.
By J. Cay and H. B. Cay. 3 vols. 1739-66. folio. **158 C**
Public Statutes, 1707–1748. 21 vols. Edinburgh, 1718–54.
12mo. **21 F**
The statute law common-plac'd ; or, a general table to the
Statutes. By G. Jacob. 5th ed. 1748. 12mo. **176 C**
An Exact abridgment of all the Statutes in force and use,
from 9 Hen. III. to 9 Geo. II. 9 vols. 1730-37. 12mo. **176 C**
Readings upon the Statute Law, alphabetically digested.
By a Gentleman of the Middle Temple. 5 vols. 1723-25.
12mo. **176 C**
The Statutes at large in paragraphs and sections from Magna
Charta to 1680. By J. Keble. 1681. folio. **158 E**

STATUTES, COLLECTIONS AND INDEXES OF—*continued.*

· A Collection of the Statutes made in the reigns of Charles I. and Charles II. By Thomas Manby. 1667. folio. **158 D**

A Collection of all the Statutes at large, 1640–1667. 1667. folio. **158 D**

Abridgment of publick acts and ordinances of Parliament, 1640 to 1656. By Wm. Hughes. 1657. 4to. **158 D**

See PULTON, F., RAITHBY, J., RASTELL, W., RUFFHEAD, O. and WILLIAMS, T. W.

See also ACTS OF PARLIAMENT, ACTS OF PARLIAMENT, INDEXES OF and MAGNA CHARTA.

STATUTES, LAW AND INTERPRETATION OF.

The Student's Statute Law. By A. Gibson and A. Weldon. 1886, and 4 Supplements. 1888–91. 8vo. **64 F**

The Student's Statutes. By J. F. Haynes. 4th ed. 1889. 8vo. **64 F**

A Selection of Statutes for Students; with notes and cases. By J. C. Harrison. 1885. 8vo. **64 F**

On the interpretation of statutes. By Sir Peter Benson Maxwell. 2nd ed. 1883. 8vo. **11 G**

Statute Law: the principles which govern construction and operation of statutes. By E. Wilberforce. 1881. 8vo. **53 H**

Rules which govern the construction and effect of statutory law. By Henry Hardcastle. 1879. 8vo. **53 H**

The reform of the Statute book. See T. E. Holland's Essays upon the form of the law, 1870, pp. 101–181. **170 F**

Mr. Purton Cooper's memorandum respecting our statute book. London, 1858, reprinted Boulogne, 1860. [Pamphlets, vol. 15.] **144 B**

Confusion worse confounded; or, the statutes in 1852. By G. Willmore. 1852. [Pamphlets, vol. 9, part 2.] **144 A**

Rules for the construction of statutes, deeds, and wills. By Basil Montagu. 1837. 12mo. **176 C**

Observations on the more ancient statutes; with a proposal for new modelling the statutes. By Daines Barrington. 3rd ed. 1769. 4to. **158 A**

· The second part of the Institutes of the lawes of England, containing the Exposition of many ancient and other Statutes. By Sir E. Coke. 6th ed. 1681. folio. **155 C**

See also DWARRIS, SIR F., HENRY, JABEZ and SEDGWICK, T.

STATUTORY CHARGES AND DECLARATIONS.

On Searches : a concise treatise on the law of judgments . . . and statutory charges as affecting land. By H. W. Elphinstone and J. W. Clark. 1887-9. 8vo. **13 H**

Memorandum as to Oaths and statutory declarations, &c. By J. M. Davenport. Oxford, 1873. 8vo. **53 B**

STAUNDFORD, William.

An Exposition of the Kings Prerogatiue, collected out of the great abridgement of Justice Fitzherbert. 1607. Bound with Les Plees del' Corone, 1607. 8vo. **49 C**

Les Plees del' Corone, divisees in plusors titles et common lieux. 1607. 8vo. **49 C**

STAUNTON, Sir George Leonard.

An Authentic account of an embassy from the King of Great Britain to the emperor of China, taken chiefly from the papers of the Earl of Macartney. 2 vols. 1797. 4to.; with a volume of plates. 1797. folio. **84 F & H**

STAUNTON, Sir George Thomas.

Ta Tsing Leu Lee : being fundamental laws of penal code of China, translated from the Chinese. 1810. 4to. **83 J**

STEELE, Sir Richard.

The Crisis : or, a discourse representing, from the most authentick records, the just causes of the late happy Revolution ; with some seasonable remarks on the danger of a Popish Successor. 1714. 8vo. **49 F**

A Nation a Family : being the sequel of the Crisis of property : or, a plan for the improvement of the South-Sea Proposal. 1720. [South Sea Bubbles, vol. 1.] **118 B**

STEER, John.

Parish law : being a digest of the law relating to parishes, churches, ministers, &c. and the relief, settlement, and removal of the poor. 1830. 8vo. **173 B**

The same. 3rd ed. by H. J. Hodgson. 1857. 8vo. **173 B**

The same. 4th ed. by W. H. Macnamara. 1881. 8vo. **173 B**

The same. 5th ed. by W. H. Macnamara. 1887. 8vo. **11 A**

STEPHANUS, HENRICUS.
Thesaurus Græcæ linguæ, cum glossariis et appendice. 5 vols.
1573. folio.

STEPHANUS, ROBERTUS.
Thesaurus Linguæ Latinæ. 2 vols. Lugduni, 1573. folio.
The same. Editio nova, prioribus multo auctior et emendatior
[curis E. Law, J. Taylor, T. Johnson et S. Hutchinson].
4 vols. 1734–35. folio. 47 I

STEPHEN, KING OF ENGLAND.
Chronicles of the reign of Stephen, Henry II., and Richard I.
Edited by R. Howlett. 3 vols. 1884-86. 8vo. 102 H
Magnum rotulum Scaccarii ; vel, magnum rotulum Pipæ,
1135–1140. Edited by Rev. J. Hunter. 1833. 8vo. 98 A
See also LINGARD, REV. J., MARTYN, W. and TURNER, S.

STEPHEN, CARR.
The Indian registration act 1871. Calcutta, 1871. 8vo. 38 B
The same. 4th ed. Calcutta, 1877. 8vo. 38 B

STEPHEN, SIR GEORGE.
The juryman's guide. 1845. 12mo. 52 I

STEPHEN, HARRY LUSHINGTON.
The law of support and subsidence. 1890. 12mo. 9 B

STEPHEN, HENRY and REGINALD ARTHUR STEPHEN.
County Court acts, orders, and practice. 1889. 8vo. 12 H

STEPHEN, HENRY JOHN.
New commentaries on the laws of England (partly founded
on Blackstone). 4 vols. 1841–45. 8vo. 167 A
The same. 8th ed. by J. Stephen. 4 vols. 1880, and 9th ed.
by H. St. J. Stephen. 4 vols. 1883. 8vo. 167 A
The same. 10th ed. by A. Brown. 4 vols. 1886. 8vo. 64 C
The same. 11th ed. by A. Brown. 4 vols. 1890. 8vo. 10 E
The same. Another copy. 4 vols. 1890. 8vo. 64 C

STEPHEN, HENRY JOHN—*continued.*
Principles of Pleading in civil actions. 5th ed. 1843, and
6th ed. by James Stephen and F. F. Pinder. 1860. 8vo.
173 G
The same. 7th ed. by F. F. Pinder. 1866. 8vo. 173 G

STEPHEN, HERBERT.
The law relating to actions for malicious prosecution. 1888.
8vo. 12 C

STEPHEN, JAMES.
The Common law procedure act 1860 ; with notes and introduction. 1860. 12mo. 161 G
Questions for law students, on the Sixth edition of Mr. Serjeant Stephen's New commentaries on the laws of England.
1869. 8vo. 168 A

STEPHEN, SIR JAMES FITZJAMES.
A Digest of the criminal law. 1877. 8vo. 165 E
The same. 4th ed. 1887. 8vo. 52 E
A Digest of the law of Evidence. 1876. 12mo. 167 F
The same. 3rd ed. 1877. 12mo. 167 F
The same. 5th ed. 1887. 8vo. 9 H
General view of criminal law of England. 1863. 8vo. 165 E
The same. 2nd ed. 1890. 8vo. 52 E
A History of the Criminal law of England. 3 vols. 1883.
8vo. 52 E
A Digest of the law of criminal procedure in indictable offences.
By Sir J. F. Stephen and H. Stephen. 1883. 8vo. 52 E

STEPHENS, ARCHIBALD JOHN.
The law of Nisi Prius, evidence in civil actions, and arbitration
and awards. 3 vols. 1842. 8vo. 173 A
A Letter to Robert Monsey, Baron Cranworth, on the constitution of the ecclesiastical courts. 1853. 12mo. 166 A
A Letter to the Earl of Derby, upon a public speech, delivered in the House of Lords, by the Lord bishop of
Exeter on the Church discipline bill. 1856. [Pamphlets,
vol. 10.] 144 A
A Practical treatise of the laws relating to the clergy. 2 vols.
1848. 8vo. 9 C

STEPHENS, ARCHIBALD JOHN—*continued.*
Statutes relating to ecclesiastical and eleemosynary institutions of England, Wales, Ireland, India and the Colonies; with the decisions thereon. 2 vols. 1845. 8vo.   31 E
The substance of the argument of A. J. Stephens, delivered before the judicial committee of the Privy Council, in the case of T. B. Sheppard against W. J. E. Bennett, clerk; with an appendix containing their Lordships' judgment. 1872. 8vo.   51 F

STEPHENS, WILLIAM RICHARD WOOD.
A Memoir of Wm. Page Wood, Baron Hatherley; with selections from his correspondence. 2 vols. 1883. 8vo. 79 G

STERNE, LAURENCE.
Works. 8 vols. 1795. 12mo.   83 C

STERNHOLD, THOMAS.
The whole book of Psalms collected into English metre. . By Thomas Sternhold, John Hopkins and others, conferred with the Hebrew. 1724. Bound with Common Prayer, 1724. folio.   77 H

[STEUART, SIR HENRY.]
The genealogy of the Stewarts refuted, in a letter to Andrew Stuart, Esq. M.P. Edinburgh, 1799. 8vo.   113 F

STEVENS, JOHN.
A New Dictionary, Spanish and English, and English and Spanish. 1726. 8vo.   123 H

STEVENS, ROBERT.
An Essay on Average. 2nd ed. 1816. 8vo.   160 C

STEVENS, THOMAS MOFFITT.
The elements of Mercantile law. 1890. 12mo.   10 I

STEVENS, WILLIAM.
Report of the case of Spong and others *v.* Spong decided by the Lords April 13, 1829, relating to the distinction between real estates specifically devised to particular devisees and other real estate devised by a residuary clause in the same will. 1829. 8vo.   50 A

STEVENSON, WILLIAM, LAND SURVEYOR.

General view of the agriculture of the county of Surrey. 1809.
8vo.   93 C

STEVENSON, WILLIAM, F.S.A.

A Supplement to the first edition of Mr. Bentham's History
and antiquities of the cathedral and conventual church of
Ely ; with Addenda to the second edition and memoirs of
the late Rev. James Bentham. Norwich, 1817. 4to. 86 G

STEWART FAMILY.

A Genealogical history of the royal and illustrious family of
the Stewarts, from 1034 to 1710. By George Crawfurd.
Edinburgh, 1710. folio.   113 F

Genealogical history of the Stewarts from the earliest period
of their authentic history to the present times. By Andrew
Stuart. 1798, and Supplement, 1799. 2 vols. 1798-99.
.4to.   113 F

The genealogy of the Stewarts refuted, in a letter to Andrew
Stuart, Esq., M.P. [By Sir Henry Steuart.] Edinburgh,
1799. 8vo.   113 F

STEWART, DUGALD.

An Account of the life and writings of the late Adam Smith.
1795. 4to.   78 G

A Dissertation exhibiting a general view of the progress of
Metaphysical and Ethical Philosophy. See Encyclopædia
Britannica, 8th ed., vol. 1, pp. 1-289.   147 A

STEWART, DUNCAN.

The law and practice of the court of Bankruptcy. 1832.
12mo.   160 F

STEWART, JAMES.

The practice of Conveyancing. 3 vols. 1827-31. 8vo. 164 F

The principles of the law of Real Property. 1837. 8vo. 174 F

The principles of the law of Real and Personal Property.
1840. 8vo.   174 F

Suggestions as to reform in some branches of the law. 1842.
8vo.   170 F

[STEWART, Sir James.]
The life of a lawyer, written by himself. 1830. 8vo. **79 B**

STEWART, William.
The buik of the croniclis of Scotland ; or, a metrical version
of the history of Hector Boece. Edited by W. B. Turnbull.
3 vols. 1858. 8vo. **101 A B**

STILLINGFLEET, Edward, Bishop of Worcester.
Ecclesiastical cases relating to the duties and rights of the
parochial clergy, stated and resolved according to the prin-
ciples of conscience and law. 1698. 12mo. **49 E**
The same. 2nd ed. 1702. 12mo. **49 E**
The second part of Ecclesiastical cases. 1704. 12mo. **49 E**
The grand question, concerning the bishops' right to vote in
Parliament, in cases capital, stated and argued ; from the
Parliament-rolls and the history of former times. [By
Edward Stillingfleet.] 1680. 12mo. **48 C**
Miscellaneous discourses. 1735. 8vo. **77 B**
Works : with life and character. 6 vols. 1710. folio. **77 G**

STIMSON, Frederic J.
American statute law ; a digest of the constitutions and statutes
of all the states, relating to persons and property in force
January 1, 1886. Boston, 1886. 8vo. **32 C**

STIRLING.
The history of Stirling ; with a sketch of a tour to Callander
and the Trosachs. Stirling, 1812. 12mo. **95 C**

STIRLING, Earldom of.
The case of Alexander, Earl and Viscount of Stirling. Wor-
cester, [n.d.], and Summary of the case of Alexander Earl
of Stirling. Worcester, [n.d.] 8vo. **127 J**
The Stirling Peerage ; comprising an account of the resump-
tion of the titles by the present Earl of Stirling ; with An
epitome of the genealogy of the noble family of Alexander.
By T. C. Banks. 1826. 8vo. **127 J**
Trial of Alexander Humphrys or Alexander, styling himself
Earl of Stirling, before high court of justiciary for forgery.
Edited by W. Turnbull. Edinburgh, 1839. 8vo. **51 F**

STOCK EXCHANGE AND STOCKS.

Law and customs of the London Stock Exchange. By R. E. Melsheimer and Walter Laurence. 3rd ed. by R. E. Melsheimer and S. Gardner. 1891. 12mo.   11 G

List of members of the Stock Exchange. 1886. 8vo.   146 E

The United Kingdom stock and sharebrokers' directory for 1881–2. 1881. 8vo.   146 E

Financial Register and stock exchange manual 1873, 1876. 2 vols. 1873–76. 8vo.   146 E

Regulations adopted by the committee for general purposes of the Stock Exchange, to take effect from the 25th March, 1847. 1847. 12mo.   91 B

An Essay on the practice of stock-jobbing, and some remarks on the right use and regular improvement of money. 1724. [South Sea Bubbles, vol. 2.]   118 B

See also ASTON, J. J., BLEWERT, W., FUNDS, KEYSER, H., PATERSON, N. H., SKINNER, T. and TATE, W.

STOCKDALE, JOHN.

Parliamentary guide; or, member's and elector's complete companion. 1784. 8vo.   84 B

Present peerage of the United Kingdom, 1807, 1808, 1810–1814, by John Stockdale; 1815–1821, by Wm. Stockdale; 1831, 1832, 1834, 1835, 1837–1841, 1843 and 1844, by James Ridgway. 25 vols. 1807–44. Bound with the Imperial and Royal Calendars. 1807–44. 12mo.   217 & 218

Proceedings on the trial of an information exhibited ex officio by the king's attorney general against John Stockdale, for a libel on the House of Commons. 1790. 8vo.   50 B

STOCKDALE, WILLIAM.

Present baronetage of the United Kingdom, 1818–1821, by Wm. Stockdale; 1831, 1832, 1834, 1835, 1837–1841, 1843 and 1844, by James Ridgway. 15 vols. 1818–44. Bound with Imperial and Royal Calendars. 1818–44. 12mo.   217 & 218

STOCKTON ON TEES, DURHAM.

The parochial history and antiquities of Stockton. By Rev. John Brewster. Stockton, 1796. 4to.   87 D

STODDART, SIR JOHN.
A Letter to Lord Brougham on the opinions of the judges in
the Irish marriage cases, 1844 ; and Observations on the
opinion delivered by Lord Cottenham on the writ of error
in the case of The Queen *v.* Millis.   1844.   8vo.   **83 I**

STOKE NEWINGTON, MIDDLESEX.
The history and antiquities of the parish of Stoke Newington.
By William Robinson.   1820.   8vo.   **89 D**

STOKES, ANTHONY.
A View of the constitution of the British colonies in North
America and the West Indies, at the time the civil war
broke out on the continent of America.   1783.   8vo.   **55 D**

STOKES, CHARLES.
Observations and strictures upon the speech and reply of
D. W. Harvey, M.P., on the 14 June, 1832, in the House
of Commons, on moving for leave to bring in a bill to
empower the Court of King's Bench to regulate the admission of students and barristers.   1832.   8vo.   **78 B**

STOKES, WHITLEY.
The Anglo-Indian Codes. Vol. 1. Substantive law. 1887.
Vol. 2. Adjective law. 1888. 2 vols. 1887–8, and Sup-
plement. 1889. 8vo.   **38 D**
Precedents of powers of attorney. 1861. 8vo.   **53 D**
A Treatise on the liens of attornies, solicitors, and other legal
practitioners. 1860. 8vo.   **10 G**

. STONE, FREDERICK.
Procedure on elegit and equitable execution. 1882. 8vo.
                                                      12 F

STONE, JOHN.
Metropolitan Police manual. 2nd ed. 1841. 12mo. **172 C**
Practice of the Petty Sessions. 1836. 12mo.   **175 D**
The same. 7th ed. by T. Bell and L. W. Cave. 1861.
12mo.   **175 D**
Stone's practice for justices of the peace at petty and special
sessions. 9th ed. by W. H. Macnamara. 1882. 8vo. **12 B**

STONE, Samuel.
The Justices' Manual; or, guide to the ordinary duties of a justice of the peace. 9th ed. 1862. 12mo. 170 B
The same. 16th ed. 1873. 12mo. 170 B
The same. 22nd ed. by G. B. Kennett. 1884. 12mo. 170 B
The same. 25th ed. by G. B. Kennett. 1889. 12mo. 52 I
The same. 26th ed. by G. B. Kennett. 1891. 12mo. 12 C
The Town Councillors' manual; or, guide to the duties of Municipal Corporations. 1869. 12mo. 164 G

STONE, William.
A Practical treatise on Benefit Building Societies; also the principles and practice of Tontine building companies, Freehold land societies, &c. 1851. 12mo. 161 A

STONEHENGE.
The most notable antiquity of Great Britain, vulgarly called Stone-Heng on Salisbury Plain, restored by Inigo Jones; with The Chorea gigantum; or, Stone-Heng restored to the Danes, by Dr. Charleton; and Mr. Webb's Vindication of Stone-Heng restored. 1725. folio. 95 G
Stonehenge, a temple restored to the British Druids. By William Stukeley. 1740. folio. 95 G

STOPPAGE IN TRANSITU.
The law of Stoppage in Transitu. By J. Houston. 1866. 8vo. 11 G
The law of lien and stoppage in transitu. By John Cross. 1840. 8vo. 10 G
A Practical treatise on charter-parties &c. and stoppage in transitu. By E. Lawes. 1813. 8vo. 161 F

STOPS.
Stops; or, punctuation. See M. Montagu's Fifty more sonnets, 1861, pp. 31, 70–72. 83 D

STORR, John Stephens.
The City Solicitor's 'Painful Story;' being an epitome of Minutes of Evidence taken before special enquiry committee of Corporation of City of London. 1880. 8vo. 83 J

STORY, JOSEPH.

Commentaries on equity jurisprudence as administered in England and America. 3rd ed. 2 vols. 1843. 8vo.   **59 D**

The same.   7th ed. by E. H. Bennett. 2 vols. Boston, 1857, and 13th ed. by M. M. Bigelow. 2 vols. 1886. 8vo. **59 D**

The same.   1st English ed. by W. E. Grigsby.   1884.   8vo.
52 G

Commentaries on equity pleadings according to the practice of the Courts of Equity of England and America.   1838. 8vo.   **59 D**

The same.   6th ed. by E. H. Bennett. Boston, 1857, and 8th ed. by I. F. Redfield. Boston, 1870. 8vo.   **59 D**

Commentaries on the conflict of laws, foreign and domestic, in regard to contracts, rights, and remedies.   Edinburgh, 1835.   8vo.   **55 A**

The same.   5th ed. by E. H. Bennett. Boston, 1857, and 6th ed. by I. F. Redfield. Boston, 1865, and 8th ed. by M. M. Bigelow. Boston, 1883. 8vo.   **55 A**

Commentaries on the constitution of the United States. 3 vols. Boston, 1833.   8vo.   **59 A**

The same.   Abridged by the author for the use of colleges and high schools. Boston, 1833. 8vo.   **59 A**

Commentaries on the law of Agency. 5th ed. by E. H. Bennett. Boston, 1857. 8vo.   **59 B**

The same.   7th ed. by I. F. Redfield and W. A. Herrick. Boston, 1869. 8vo.   **11 C**

Commentaries on the law of Bailments, with illustrations from the civil and the foreign law. Edited by R. Charnock. 1839. 8vo.   **59 B**

The same.   7th ed. by E. H. Bennett. 1863. 8vo.   **59 B**

The same.   8th ed. by E. H. Bennett. 1870. 8vo.   **9 A**

Commentaries on the law of Bills of Exchange, foreign and inland, as administered in England and America. 4th ed. by E. H. Bennett. Boston, 1860. 8vo.   **59 E**

Commentaries on the law of Partnership. 5th ed. by E. H. Bennett. Boston, 1859, and 6th ed. by J. C. Gray, junior. Boston, 1868. 8vo.   **59 G**

The same.   7th ed. by W. F. Wharton. Boston, 1881. 8vo.
11 B

Commentaries on the law of promissory notes and checks on banks and bankers. 5th ed. Boston, 1859. 8vo.   **60 A**

STORY, JOSEPH—*continued.*
The same. 6th ed. Boston, 1868. 8vo. **60 A**
Life and letters of Joseph Story. Edited by his son W. W.
Story. 2 vols. 1851. 8vo. **80 D**

STORY, PHILIP.
Summary of military law and procedure. 1886. 8vo. **10 I**

STORY, WILLIAM WETMORE.
Law of Contracts. 4th ed. 2 vols. Boston, 1856. 8vo. **59 C**
Law of Sales of Personal Property, with illustrations from the
foreign law. 2nd ed. Boston, 1853. 8vo. **60 B**
Life and letters of Joseph Story. 2 vols. 1851. 8vo. **80 D**
Reports of cases in the Circuit court of the United States for
the first circuit, 1839 to 1845. 3 vols. Boston, 1851–55.
8vo. **57 A**

STOTHARD, ROBERT THOMAS.
The Propensitorial Zodiac ; or, psychoneurology of the mental
faculties. 1870. 8vo. **78 C**

STOURTON, WILTSHIRE.
The registers of Stourton, from 1570 to 1800. Edited by
Rev. John Henry Ellis. 1887. 8vo. **93 F**

STOW, LINCOLNSHIRE.
A Topographical and descriptive account of Stow, principally
in illustration of its claim to be considered as the Roman
Sidnacester. See Adam Stark's History of Gainsburgh,
1817, pp. 321–365. **89 C**

STOW, JOHN, ANTIQUARY.
Life of John Stow. See J. P. Malcolm's Lives of Topographers
and Antiquaries, 1815. 4to. **79 H**
The survey of London, containing the originall antiquitie, en-
crease, moderne estate, and description of that citie. 1603.
4to. **92 B**
The same. Another ed. by A[nthony] M[unday]. 1618
4to. **92 B**
The same. Another ed. by A[nthony] M[unday], H[enry]
D[yson], and others. 1633. folio. **92 G**

STOW, JOHN, ANTIQUARY—*continued*.

The same. 6th ed. by John Strype. 2 vols. 1754–55. folio. **92 H**

Three fifteenth-century chronicles ; with historical memoranda by John Stowe ; and contemporary notes of occurrences written by him in the reign of Queen Elizabeth. Edited by James Gairdner. [Camden Society, n.s. vol. 28.] 1880. 8vo. **85 D**

[STOW, JOHN,] OF CROOM'S HILL, GREENWICH.

A Biblical catechism, introductory to, or explanatory of the church catechism. By a lay member of the Church of England. 2nd ed. 1841. 12mo. **77 A**

Family prayers adapted from the Bible psalms ; with reflections and family and private prayers, principally from the Liturgy of the Church of England ; with additions. By a lay-member of that Church. 1840. 8vo. **77 C**

A Hermit's narrative of opinions of his solitary meditations, on divine revelation and christianity. 1861. 8vo. **77 A**

Reflections on the Epistles of St. Paul and on that to the Hebrews ; with scriptural illustrations. 1847. 8vo. **77 C**

Thoughts on the Book of Common Prayer used in the Church of England. By a lay-member of that church. 2 vols. 1850–56. 12mo. **77 A**

Thoughts on the Gospel of Jesus Christ. By a lay member of the Church of England. Greenwich, 1846. 8vo. **77 C**

A Version of the Psalms of David. By a lay member of the Church of England. 3rd ed. 1842. 12mo. **77 A**

STOWE, BUCKINGHAMSHIRE.

Catalogue of the collections of portraits and manuscripts, removed from Stowe house, Bucks., sold in London, March and June 1849. 1849. 8vo. **82 G**

Stowe. A description of the house and gardens of the Duke of Buckingham and Chandos. By J. Seeley. Buckingham, 1827. 8vo. **86 B**

[STRACHEY, MR.]

An Index to the Records, with directions to the several places where they are to be found ; and short explanations of the different kinds of Rolls, Writs, &c. 1739. 12mo. **97 I**

948

STRAFFORD AND TICKELL, Yorkshire.
The ancient state of the Wapentake of Strafford and Tickell.
By John Wainwright. Sheffield, 1829. 4to. **94 C**

STRAFFORD, Thomas, 1 Earl of.
Four letters of Lord Wentworth, afterwards Earl of Strafford ;
with a poem on his illness. Edited by S. R. Gardiner.
[Camden Society, n.s. vol. 31.] 1883. 8vo. **85 D**

STRAITS SETTLEMENTS.
Acts and ordinances of the Straits Settlements, 1867–1886.
By J. A. Harwood. 2 vols. 1886. 8vo. **37 F**
Straits Settlements acts and ordinances, 1867–1890. 13
vols. Singapore, 1867–91. folio and 8vo. **37 F G**
Indian acts passed during the period 1834 to 1867 and now
in force in the colony of the Straits Settlements. Singapore,
1890. 8vo. **37 G**
Orders and rules and regulations by the Governor in council
during 1890. Singapore, 1891. 8vo. **37 G**
Report on the working of ' The registration of deeds ordinance
1886,' during the six months ended 31st Dec. 1887, and
during the year 1888. By T. H. Kershaw. Singapore,
1888–89. folio. **37 F**

STRANGE, Sir John.
Reports of adjudged cases in the courts of Chancery, King's
Bench, Common Pleas and Exchequer, 1716–1749. Pub-
lished by his son, John Strange. 2 vols. 1755. folio.
The same. 2nd ed. 2 vols. 1782. 8vo.
The same. 3rd ed. with notes and additional references, by
Michael Nolan. 2 vols. 1795. 8vo. **5 I**

STRANGE, Sir Thomas.
Hindu law, principally with reference to such portions of it as
concern administration of justice in King's Courts in India.
3rd ed. by J. D. Mayne. Madras, 1859. 8vo. **38 B**

STRANGE, Thomas Lumisden.
A Manual of Hindoo law as prevailing in the presidency of
Madras. 2nd ed. Madras, 1863. 8vo. **38 B**

STRATFORD-UPON-AVON, Warwickshire.
A Guide to Stratford-upon-Avon. By R. B. Wheler. Stratford-upon-Avon, 1814. 12mo.   **93 E**

An Historical account of the New Place, Stratford-upon-Avon, the last residence of Shakespeare. By J. O. Halliwell. 1864. folio.   **94 H**

STRATHERN, Earldom of.
History of the Earldom of Strathern. By Sir N. H. Nicolas. 1842. 8vo.   **124 F**

STRAWBERRY HILL.
Catalogue of the classic contents of Strawberry Hill. Collected by Horace Walpole. 1842. 4to.   **118 F**

STREET, John Bamfield.
Law of public statutory undertakings. 1890. 8vo.   **11 G**

STREETS.
The law and practice as to paving of private streets according to The Public Health act, 1875. By Wm. Spinks. 1887. 8vo.   **11 G**

STRINGER, Francis Augustus.
Oaths and Affirmations in Great Britain and Ireland. 1890. 12mo.   **12 G**

STROUD, Frederick.
The Judicial Dictionary of words and phrases judicially interpreted. 1890. 8vo.   **123 F**

[STRUTT, Joseph.]
The history and description of Colchester. 2 vols. in 1. Colchester, 1803. 8vo.   **87 E**

STRYPE, John.
Ecclesiastical memorials relating chiefly to religion and the reformation of it, under Henry VIII., Edward VI., and Mary I. 6 vols. Oxford, 1822. 8vo.   **77 C**

Life of John Strype. See J. P. Malcolm's Lives of Topographers and Antiquaries. 1815. 4to.   **79 H**

STUART, Andrew.
Genealogical history of the Stewarts, from the earliest period
of their authentic history to the present times. 1798, and
Supplement 1799. 2 vols. 1798–99. 4to.   113 F
A Letter to the directors of the East India Company, re-
specting the conduct of brigadier general James Stuart at
Madras. 1778. 4to.   38 A

STUART, Gilbert.
History of Scotland, from establishment of the Reformation
till the death of Queen Mary. 2 vols. 1782. 4to.   113 F
Observations concerning the publick law and the constitutional
history of Scotland. Edinburgh, 1778. 8vo.   116 E
A View of society in Europe in its progress from rudeness
to refinement. Edinburgh, 1778. 4to.   115 H

STUART, James.
Historical memoirs of the City of Armagh, for a period of
1373 years. Newry, 1819. 8vo.   95 E

STUBBS, Thomas.
Chronica Pontificum Ecclesiæ Eboraci. See Scriptores Decem
Hist. Angl., 1652, pp. .1686–1734.   114 H

STUBBS, Rev. William.
The constitutional history of England in its origin and development. 3 vols. 1883–84. 12mo.   ·   116 D

STUBBS, W. and G. TALMASH.
The crown circuit companion, containing the practice of the
assizes on the crown side. 1738. 12mo.   165 D
The same. 7th ed. by Thomas Dogherty. 1799. 12mo. 165 D

STUDD, Edward Fairfax.
The law of Tithes and Tithe Rent-Charge. 1889. 12mo. 11 H

STUKELEY, William.
Abury, a temple of the British Druids; with some others
described. 1740. Bound with W. Stukeley's Stonehenge.
1740. folio.   95 G

STUKELEY, WILLIAM—*continued.*

Itinerarium Curiosum : or, an account of the antiquities and
remarkable curiosities in nature or art, observed in travels
through Great Britain. 2nd ed. 2 vols. in 1. 1776. folio.
85 I

Life of William Stukely. See Malcolm's Lives of Topographers and Antiquaries. 1815. 4to. 79 H

Stonehenge, a temple restored to the British Druids. 1740.
folio. 95 G

STURGES, DECIMUS. See FREND, H. T.

STUTFIELD, GEORGE HERBERT.

The law relating to betting, time-bargains, and gaming. 1884.
8vo. 10 B

STYLE, WILLIAM.

Narrationes modernæ ; or, modern reports in the Upper Bench
Court at Westminster, 1645–1656. 1658. folio. 74 G

Practical Register of rules, orders, and observations concerning
the practice of the Common law in the courts at Westminster. 4th ed. 1707. 12mo. 49 F

SUBPŒNA.

Two pieces concerning suits in Chancery by Subpœna. See
Hargrave's Law Tracts, 1787, pp. 321–355. 144 G

See also DISCOVERY, EVIDENCE and WITNESSES.

SUBSIDENCE.

The law of support and subsidence. By H. L. Stephen. 1890.
12mo. 9 B

SUCCESSION.

Principles of the law of Succession to deceased persons. By
T. R. Potts. 1888. 8vo. 11 G

The Succession laws of Christian countries. By Eyre Lloyd.
1877. 8vo. 11 G

The evidence of Succession to real and personal property and
peerages. By John Hubback. 1844. 8vo. 53 H

The Succession by a parent to a child. See R. Preston's
Tracts, 1797, pp. 78–83. 163 G

See DEMOLOMBE, J. C. F. and POTHIER, R. J.

See also LEGACY DUTIES.

SUCKLING, REV. ALFRED.

The history and antiquities of the county of Suffolk. 2 vols. 1846-48. 4to. **93 G**

SUDBURY, SUFFOLK.

Wills and inventories from the registers of the commissary of Bury St. Edmunds and the archdeacon of Sudbury. Edited by Samuel Tymms. [Camden Society, vol. 49.] 1850. 8vo. **85 B**

SUETONIUS TRANQUILLUS, CAIUS.

Opera omnia quæ extant, interpretatione et notis illustravit Augustinus Babelonius. Parisiis, 1684 4to. **47 G**

SUEZ CANAL.

L'Isthme de Suez. Son percement, examen au point de vue des intérêts commerciaux de la France et de l'Europe occidentale. Par A. De Simencourt. Paris, 1859. [Pamphlets, vol. 10.] **144 A**

SUFFOLK.

General view of the agriculture of the county of Suffolk; drawn up for the consideration of the board of agriculture. By the secretary to the board [Arthur Young]. 3rd ed. 1804. 8vo. **93 C**

The handbook to the rivers and broads of Norfolk and Suffolk. By G. C. Davies. 9th ed. 1887. 8vo. **92 C**

The history and antiquities of Suffolk. By Rev. Alfred Suckling. 2 vols. 1846-48. 4to. **93 G**

The history and antiquities of Suffolk. Thingoe hundred. By John Gage. 1838. folio. **93 H**

Holiday notes in East Anglia, being a selection of articles on the holiday resorts in Norfolk, Suffolk, and Essex. 1886. 12mo. **92 C**

The Suffolk traveller. By J. Kirby. 2nd ed. 1764. 8vo. **93 C**

The visitations of Suffolk 1561, 1577, and 1612. Edited by W. C. Metcalfe. Privately printed. Exeter, 1882. 4to. **93 B**

See also GARDNER, T., PARSONS, REV. P. and ROUS, J.

SUGDEN, Sir Edward Burtenshaw.

A Concise and practical view of the law of vendors and purchasers of estates. 1851. 8vo. **177 C**

The doctrine of presuming a surrender of terms assigned to
attend the inheritance. 4th ed. 1820. [Jacob's Tracts,
vol. 1.] **144 E**

Extracts from acts of parliament relating to the oaths to be
taken by members of Parliament. By E. B. S[ugden].
1829. [Jacob's Tracts, vol. 7.] **144 E**

Handy book on Property Law in a series of letters. 2nd ed.
1858, and 7th ed. 1863. 12mo. **174 D**

The law of property as administered by the House of Lords.
1849. 8vo. **53 E**

A Letter to James Humphreys, Esq., on his proposal to repeal
the laws of real property and substitute a new code. 1826.
[Jacob's Tracts, vol. 4.] **144 E**

A Letter to John Williams. Esq., M.P., in reply to his Observations upon the abuses of the Court of Chancery. 1825.
[Jacob's Tracts, vol. 1.] **144 E**

Lord St. Leonards' Act to further amend law of property and
to relieve trustees. By J. S. Vaizey. 1860. 12mo. **174 D**

Misrepresentations in Campbell's Lives of Lyndhurst and
Brougham, corrected by St. Leonards. 1869. 8vo. **79 G**

The new statutes relating to property. 1852. 8vo. **174 D**

The same. 2nd ed. 1862. 8vo. **53 F**

A Practical treatise of Powers. 4th ed. 1826. 8vo. **174 C**

The same. 6th ed. 2 vols. 1836. 8vo. **174 C**

The same. 8th ed. 1861. 8vo. **13 C**

A Practical treatise of the law of vendors and purchasers of
estates. 1805, and 2nd ed. 1806. 8vo. **177 B**

The same. 9th ed. 2 vols. 1834. 8vo. **177 B**

The same. 10th ed. 3 vols. 1839. 8vo. **177 C**

The same. 14th ed. 1862. 8vo. **13 I**

The present state of the appellate jurisdiction of the Court
of Chancery and House of Lords. 1835. [Chancery Pamphlets, vol. 1.] **144 A**

A Series of letters to a man of property, on the sale, purchase,
leasing, settlement, and devising of estates. 2nd ed. 1812,
and 5th ed. 1829. 8vo. **167 D**

Shall we register our deeds? Answered by Sir Edward Sugden. 1852. [Pamphlets, vol. 8.] **144 A**

SUGDEN, Sir Edward Burtenshaw—*continued*.
A Speech delivered in the House of Commons, 16th December
1830, upon the Court of Chancery. 1831. [Jacob's Tracts,
vol. 8.] **144 E**

SUGDEN, Henry.
An Essay on the law of Wills as altered by the 1 Victoria,
c. 26. 1837. 8vo. **178 C**

SUICIDE.
An Essay concerning self-murther. By John Adams. 1700.
12mo. **78 A**

SULLIVAN, Francis Stoughton.
An Historical treatise on the Feudal law and the constitution
and laws of England ; with a commentary on Magna Charta.
1772, and 2nd ed. by Gilbert Stuart. 1776. 4to. **157 B**

SULLY, Maximilian de Béthune, Duc de.
Memoirs of the Duke of Sully, prime minister of Henry the
Great ; with the trial of Francis Ravaillac for the murder
of Henry the Great. New ed. 5 vols. Edinburgh, 1819.
8vo. **80 A**

SUMMARY JURISDICTION.
The Summary Jurisdiction acts, 1848–1884, regulating the
duties of Justices of the Peace. By W. C. Glen. 6th ed.
by A. H. Bodkin and C. G. Douglas. 1887. 8vo. **12 C**
A Guide to the law and practice of Petty Sessions ; with the
Summary Jurisdiction act 1879. By E. T. Ayers. 1884.
8vo. **12 B**
See also Convictions, Judgments, Justices of the
Peace and Magisterial Law.

SUMMERHAYS, William Frank and T. TOOGOOD.
Precedents of bills of costs. 1877, 2nd ed. 1877, 3rd ed.
1879, and 4th ed. 1883. 8vo. **165 A**
The same. 5th ed. 1887. 8vo. **52 D**
The same. 6th ed. by Thornton Toogood. 1889. 8vo. **9 F**

SUMMONSES.
The law and practice appertaining to Originating Summons.
By G. N. Marcy and J. T. Dodd. 1889. 8vo. **12 F**

SUMMONSES—*continued.*

Forms of Summonses and Orders ; with notes for use at judges' chambers and in the district registries. By W. F. A. Archibald. 2nd ed. by W. F. A. Archibald and P. E. Vizard. 1886. 12mo. **12 G**

Forms of indorsements of writs of summons, pleadings, &c. By G. B. Allen and W. B. Allen. 1883. 8vo. **12 E**

SUMNER, CHARLES.

Reports of cases in the circuit court of the United States for the first circuit, 1829 to 1839. 2nd ed. 3 vols. Boston, 1848–51. 8vo. **57 A**

SUNDAY.

National conference of friends of Lord's-Day observance, held in Exeter hall, London, March 19 and 20, 1884. 1884. [Pamphlets, vol. 38.] **144 C**

The Sabbath. An essay. By a member of the English Bar [W. Griffith]. [1890.] 8vo. **77 A**

See also HILL, CHARLES.

SUPERSEDEAS.

An Argument of Lord Bacon on the writ De rege inconsulto in the case of the grant of the office of Supersedeas in the Common Pleas, 13 James I. See Collectanea Juridica, vol. 1, 1791, pp. 167–213. **144 G**

SUPPORT.

The law of support and subsidence. By H. L. Stephen. 1890. 12mo. **9 B**

SURREY.

Acts relative to the Roads in Surrey and Sussex, 1714–1770. 1772. 8vo. **93 C**

Domesday, translated with an introduction and notes ; comprehending the counties of Kent, Sussex, and Surrey. By Rev. S. Henshall and John Wilkinson. 1799. 4to. **88 E**

General view of the agriculture of Surrey. By William Stevenson. 1809. 8vo. **93 C**

Historical account of the part of Surrey within twelve miles of London. See Rev. D. Lysons's Environs of London, vol. 1, and vol. 4, pp. 577–617 and 661–663. **89 F**

SURREY—*continued.*

History and antiquities of the county of Surrey. By Rev. Owen Manning, continued to the present time by Wm. Bray. 3 vols. 1804–14. folio. **93 H**

A History of Surrey. By Thomas Allen. 2 vols. 1831. 4to. **93 D**

Plan shewing the extent of the Surrey and Sussex roads. 1850. 12mo. **93 E**

Report of some proceedings on the commission for the trial of the rebels in 1746 in the county of Surrey. By Sir M. Foster. 2nd ed. 1776. 8vo. **1 H**

The Rules of Customes pertaining unto West Sheen, Petersham, and Ham. See Collectanea Juridica, vol. 2, 1792, pp. 381–385. **144 G**

A Topographical history of Surrey. By E. W. Brayley, revised and edited by Edward Walford. 4 vols. [1878–81.] 4to. **93 G**

SURTEES, ROBERT.

The history and antiquities of the county palatine of Durham. 4 vols. 1816-40. folio. **87 H**

SURVIVORSHIP.

Arguments in the case of the representatives of General Stanwix and his daughter. See C. Fearne's Posthumous works, 1797, pp. 35–72. **175 C**

SUSSEX.

A Compendious history of Sussex, topographical, archæological, and anecdotical. By M. A. Lower. 2 vols. 1870. 8vo. **93 E**

East Sussex Election. List of the registered electors, with the votes of those who actually polled on the 4th and 5th August, 1837 ; for the election of knights of the shire to represent the eastern division of the county of Sussex in Parliament. Lewes, 1837. 8vo. **107 K**

The history, antiquities, and topography of Sussex. By T. W. Horsfield. Lewes, 1835. 4to. **94 G**

History of Chichester ; with notes on the county of Sussex. By A. Hay. Chichester, 1804. 8vo. **93 E**

History of the castles, mansions, and manors of Western Sussex. By D. G. C. Elwes. 3 parts in 1 vol. 1876–79. folio. **93 D**

SUSSEX—*continued.*

History of the western division of the county of Sussex. By James Dallaway, continued and completed by Rev. E. Cartwright. 2 vols. in 3. 1815–30. 4to.   **94 G**

Operations of the poor law amendment act in the county of Sussex. Reports of the auditor of the Uckfield union. By W. H. Newnham. 1836. 8vo.   **93 E**

Pedigrees of the families in the county of Sussex. By William Berry. 1830. folio.   **126 I**

Plan shewing the extent of the Surrey and Sussex roads. 1850. 12mo.   **93 E**

Proofs of age of Sussex families, temp. Edw. II. to Edw. IV. By W. D. Cooper. 1860. 8vo.   **93 E**

See also SURREY.

SUTHERLAND, DAVID.

The digest of Indian Law Reports. A compendium of the rulings of the high court of Calcutta from 1862, and of the Privy Council from 1831 to 1876. 1877. 8vo.   **38 F**

SUTHERLAND, WILLIAM.

Britain's glory; or, ship-building unvail'd, being a general director for building and compleating the said machines. 2nd ed. 1729. folio.   **78 H**

The prices of the labour in ship-building adjusted. 1717. folio. Bound with the preceding.   **78 H**

SUTTON, HENRY.

The Tramway acts of the United Kingdom. 1874. 8vo. **53 H**

The same. 2nd ed. 1883. 8vo.   **11 I**

SUTTON, THOMAS.

An Historical account of Thomas Sutton and of his foundation in Charter-House. By Rev. Philip Bearcroft. 1737. 8vo.   **91 C**

SWABEY, MAURICE CHARLES MERTTINS.

The act to amend the law relating to Divorce and Matrimonial Causes in England. 3rd ed. 1859. 8vo.   **166 A**

Reports of cases decided in the high court of Admiralty of England and on appeal to the Privy Council, 1855–1859. 1 vol. 1860. 8vo.   **8 B**

SWABEY, M. C. M. and THOMAS H. TRISTRAM.
Reports of cases decided in the court of Probate, and in the court for Divorce and Matrimonial Causes, 1858–1863. 4 vols. 1860–71. 8vo. **8 I**

SWAN, ROBERT.
The jurisdiction of the ecclesiastical courts, relating to probates and administrations. 1830. 8vo. **78 C**

SWANSTON, CLEMENT TUDWAY.
Observations on proposed changes in the law of Debtor and Creditor. 1868. [Pamphlets, vol. 32.] **144 C**
Reports of cases in the court of Chancery, during the time of Lord Chancellor Eldon, 1818–1819. 3 vols. 1821–27. 8vo. **3 G**

SWEDEN.
The rise, progress, and present state of the Northern governments. By John Williams. 2 vols. 1777. 4to. **113 F**
See also BANKS, SIR J.

SWEET, CHARLES.
A Dictionary of English law. 1882. 8vo. **123 G**

SWEET, GEORGE.
Concise precedents in conveyancing. 2nd ed. 1845. 8vo. **164 C**
The same. 3rd ed. by C. C. Tucker and G. Cave. 2 vols. 1884. 8vo. **53 D**
The same. 4th ed. by C. C. Tucker and G. Cave. 2 vols. 1886. 8vo. **13 F**
Impediments to the transfer of land. 1874. [Pamphlets, vol. 35.] **144 C**
Observations on the Land titles and transfer bills. 1874. [Pamphlets, vol. 35.] **144 C**

SWEET, JOSEPH.
The practice of the County Courts by Plaint and by original Writ of Justicies. 2nd ed. 1835. 8vo. **165 B**

SWEET, SAMUEL WHITE.
Memoir of the late Samuel White Sweet, Esq. 1841. [Law Tracts, vol. 7.] **144 E**

SWIFT, JONATHAN.
The memoirs of Captain John Creichton, from his own materials, drawn up and digested by Jonathan Swift. [Autobiography, vol. 20.] 1827. 12mo. **79 A**
Remarks on the life and writings of Jonathan Swift, in a series of letters from John Earl of Orrery to his son the hon. Hamilton Boyle. 3rd ed. 1752. 8vo. **83 C**
Works : with notes and a life of the author, by Sir Walter Scott. 2nd ed. 19 vols. Edinburgh, 1824. 8vo. **83 D**

SWIMMING.
A Few words on Swimming. With practical hints to beginners. By Ralph Harrington. [Ralph Thomas.] 1861. 12mo. **82 B**
Swimming. A bibliographical list of works on Swimming. By the author of The handbook of fictitious names. [Ralph Thomas.] 1868. 12mo. Bound with the preceding. **82 B**

SWINBURNE, HENRY.
Treatise of spousals or matrimonial contracts. 1686. 8vo. **49 E**
Treatise of testaments and last wills. 4th ed. 1677. 4to. **48 G**
The same, 5th ed. 1728, and 6th ed. 1743. folio. **48 H**

SWINDEN, HENRY.
The history and antiquities of the ancient burgh of Great Yarmouth. Norwich, 1772. 4to. **92 D**

SWINFIELD, RICHARD DE, BISHOP OF HEREFORD.
A Roll of the household expenses of R. de Swinfield, during part of the years 1289 and 1290. Edited by Rev. J. Webb. [Camden Society, vols. 59 and 62.] 1854-55. 8vo. **85 B**

SWITZERLAND.
Direct legislation by the people versus Representative government. Translated from the original Swiss pamphlets, by Eugene Oswald. 1869. [Pamphlets, vol. 35.] **144 C**

SWITZERLAND—*continued.*
A Handbook for travellers in Switzerland, and the Alps of
Savoy and Piedmont. New ed. 1842. 8vo. **84 A**

SYDENHAM, JOHN.
The history of the town and county of Poole ; with Appendix
illustrative of the botany of Poole and its neighbourhood,
by Thomas Bell Salter. Poole, 1839. 8vo. **87 D**

SYDENHAM, THOMAS.
Works, wherein not only the history and cures of acute diseases
are treated of, after a new and accurate method ; but also
the shortest and safest way of curing most chronical
diseases. 8th ed. by John Pechey. 1722. 12mo. **78 A**

SYKES, JOHN.
Local records ; or, historical register of remarkable events in
the counties of Durham and Northumberland, Newcastle
upon Tyne and Berwick upon Tweed. Newcastle, 1824.
8vo. **92 D**
The same. 2nd ed. 2 vols. Newcastle, 1833. 8vo. **92 D**

SYMONDS, JOHN FISH.
The law of settlement and removal of union poor. 2nd ed.
1887. 8vo. **11 E**

SYMONDS, RICHARD.
Diary of the marches of the royal army during the great civil
war. [Camden Society, vol. 74.] 1859. 8vo. **85 B**

SYMONS, EDWARD WILLIAM.
The law of Merchant Seamen. 2nd ed. 1839. 12mo. **175 G**

SYMS, FREDERICK RICHARD.
A Code of English law (principles and practice). 1870. 12mo.
170 F

SYON, MIDDLESEX.
The history and antiquities of Syon monastery. By George
James Aungier. 1840. 8vo. **89 D**

TABLES.
Popular tables giving information for ascertaining the value of lifehold, leasehold, and church property. By C. M. Willich. 10th ed. 1887. 8vo. **134 J**
Sinking fund tables, loan repayment and annuity tables and compound interest tables. By J. Fleming. 1886. 8vo. **11 H**
Tables for the purchasing of estates, renewing of leases and valuing reversionary estates. By W. Inwood. 22nd ed. 1884. 12mo. **134 J**
Tables for renewing and purchasing of leases, annuities, and reversions. By Sir I. Newton. 6th ed. 1808. 12mo. **176 D**
See also ANNUITY TABLES and INTEREST TABLES.

TACITUS, CAIUS CORNELIUS.
Opera interpretatione perpetua et notis illustravit Julianus Pichon. 4 vols. Paris, 1682–87. 4to. **47 F**
The works of Cornelius Tacitus. By Arthur Murphy; with an essay on the life and genius of Tacitus. 4 vols. 1793. 4to. **113 E**

TAGORE, PROSSONNO COOMAR.
Vivada Chintamani: a succinct commentary on the Hindoo law prevalent in Mithila. From the original Sanscrit of Vachaspati Misra. Calcutta, 1863. 8vo. **38 A**

TAIT'S EDINBURGH MAGAZINE.
Tait's Edinburgh Magazine, April 1832 to Jan. 1834. 4 vols. Edinburgh, 1832–34. 8vo. **251 E F**
The same. New Series. Feb. 1834 to Dec. 1860. 27 vols. Edinburgh, 1834–60. 8vo. **251 F G**

TALBOT, CHARLES, 1 BARON.
Cases in Equity during the time of lord chancellor Talbot, 1732–1736. [By Alexander Forrester.] 1741. folio.
The same. 2nd ed. 1753. folio. **74 C**
The same. 3rd ed. by J. G. Williams. 1792. 8vo. **3 G**

TALLACK, WILLIAM.
Defects in the criminal administration and penal legislation of Great Britain and Ireland ; with remedial suggestions. 1872, and The Cellular system of imprisonment as carried out at the prisons of Louvain, Amsterdam, &c. 1872. 8vo. **78 C**

TALLACK, WILLIAM—*continued.*
Humanity and humanitarianism ; with special reference to the prison systems of Great Britain and the United States. 1871. 8vo. **78 C**
Penological and preventive principles ; with special reference to Europe and America. 1889. 8vo. **78 C**

TAMLYN, JOHN.
Observations on the law of inheritance ; with the act for the amendment thereof 3 & 4 Wm. IV. c. 106. 1834. [Law Tracts, vol. 5.] **144 E**
Reports of cases decided in the court of Chancery by Sir John Leach, 1829–1831. 1 vol. 1831. 8vo. **3 G**
A Treatise on the disposition and conveyance of lands entailed. 1835. 8vo. **167 B**

TANJORE.
Copies of papers relative to the restoration of the King of Tanjore. 5 vols. 1777. 4to. **38 A**
The restoration of the King of Tanjore considered. 1777. 4to. **38 A**

TANNER, REV. THOMAS.
Notitia Monastica : or, an account of all the abbies, priories, and houses of friers, formerly in England and Wales, and of all the colleges and hospitals founded before 1540. Reprinted with many additions, by Rev. James Nasmith. Cambridge, 1787. folio. **85 I**

TAPESTRY.
Tapisseries du Roy ou sont representez les quatre elemens et les quatres saisons avec les devises qui les accompagnent et leur explication. 1687. folio. **118 G**

TAPIA, EUGENIO DE.
Febrero Novísimo, ó libreria de jueces, abogados y escribanos, refundida, ordenada bajo nuevo método, y adicionada con un tratado del juicio criminal. 9 vols. Valencia, 1828–30. 8vo. **39 D**

TAPP, WILLIAM JOHN.
An Inquiry into the present state of the law of Maintenance and Champerty. 1861. 12mo. **53 A**

TAPPING, Thomas.
The Derbyshire mining customs and mineral court act 1852.
1854. 12mo. **172 F**
Exposition of statutes passed for regulation of Ore-Mines,
Collieries, and Ironstone mines. 1861. 12mo. **172 F**
The High Peak mineral customs and mineral court act 1851 ;
with notes. 1851. 12mo. **172 F**
The law and practice of the high prerogative writ of Mandamus.
1848. 8vo. **53 A**
The Readwin prize essay on the Cost Book, its principles and
practice as applicable to Mining. 1853. 8vo. **164 G**
The same. 2nd ed. 1854. 8vo. **164 G**

TARBUCK, Edward Lance.
Handbook of House property. 1875. 12mo. **168 G**
The same. 2nd ed. 1880. 12mo. **168 G**
The same. 4th ed. 1887. 12mo. **10 B**

TARRING, Charles James.
British consular jurisdiction in the East ; with a collection of
statutes concerning consuls. 1887. 8vo. **55 D**
Chapters on the law relating to the colonies. 1882. 8vo. **55 D**

TARTARS, Western.
Histoire générale des Huns, des Turcs, des Mogols, et des
autres Tartares Occidentaux. Par Joseph de Guignes.
4 vols. in 5. Paris, 1756–58. 4to. **113 E**

TASMANIA.
The Acts of the parliament of Tasmania, 1857–1890. 10 vols.
Hobart, 1857–90. folio. **35 E**
Index to the statutes of Tasmania, 1826–1877. By H. M.
Hull. Hobart Town, 1877. folio. **35 E**
Report made to the third yearly general meeting of the Van
Diemen's Land Company ; 18th of March, 1828. 1828.
[Pamphlets, vol. 40.] **144 C**

TASWELL, William.
Autobiography and anecdotes, 1651–1682. Edited by G. P.
Elliott. [Camden Society, vol. 55.] 1853. 8vo. **85 B**

TATE, WILLIAM.
The calculations of life annuities and the public funds, simplified and explained. 1819. 8vo. **144 F**

TATISCHEV, MIKHAILO.
The grand instructions to the commissioners appointed to frame a new code of laws for the Russian empire : composed by Catherine II. Translated by Michael Tatischeff. 1768. 8vo. **55 C**

TATTERSHALL, LINCOLNSHIRE.
A Topographical account of Tattershall. [By G. Weir.] 2nd ed. Horncastle, 1813. Bound with W. Peck's Isle of Axholme. 1815. 4to. **90 G**

TAUNTON, SOMERSET.
The ancient customs of the manor of Taunton Deane, collected from the records of the manor. By H. B. Shillibeer. 1821. 12mo. **93 A**
The customs of the manor of Taunton and Taunton Deane. By Richard Locke. New ed. Taunton, 1816. 12mo. **93 A**
The history of Taunton, originally written by the late Joshua Toulmin. New ed. by James Savage. Taunton, 1822. 8vo. **93 B**

TAUNTON, WILLIAM PYLE.
Reports of cases in the Court of Common Pleas and other courts, 1807–1819. 8 vols. 1814–23. 8vo. **7 B C**

TAXATION AND TAXES.
A Complete collection of abstracts of acts of parliament and cases with opinions of the judges upon Taxes. By John Smee. 2 vols. 1797. 8vo. **176 D**
History of our customs, national debts and taxes. By Timothy Cunningham. 2nd ed. 1771. 8vo. **78 D**
History of taxation and taxes in England, from the earliest times to the year 1885. By S. Dowell. 2nd ed. 4 vols. 1888. 8vo. **78 D**
Local and imperial taxation. By J. G. Hubbard. 1875. [Pamphlets, vol. 38.] **144 C**
Reports of Tax cases under the act of 37 Vict. cap. 16 and under the Taxes management act, 1875–1890. 2 vols. 1884–91. 8vo. **68 B**

TAXATION AND TAXES—*continued.*

Sketch of the history of Taxes in England to the civil war 1642. By S. Dowell. 1876. 8vo. **78 D**

Tax tables 1808–12, 1820, 1822, 1825, 1826, 1829 and 1832. By G. Kearsley. 11 vols. 1808–32. 12mo. **176 D**

See also ASSESSED TAXES, HOUSE PROPERTY, INCOME TAX and LAND TAX.

TAYLER, GEORGE.

The Consolidation acts of 1845 and 1847 ; comprising the whole law of undertakings carried on by special act of parliament. 1857. 8vo. **163 D**

The laws of appeals to the superior courts of law by appeal case. 1865. 12mo. **160 B**

TAYLOR, ALFRED SWAINE.

Manual of Medical Jurisprudence. 6th ed. 1858. 12mo. **172 E**

The same. 11th ed. by T. Stevenson. 1886. 8vo. **10 H**

The principles and practice of Medical Jurisprudence. 1865. 8vo. **·172 E**

The same. 3rd ed. by T. Stevenson. 2 vols. 1883. 8vo. **10 H**

TAYLOR, ARTHUR.

The glory of regality, an historical treatise of the anointing and crowning of the kings and queens of England. 1820. 8vo. **116 B**

TAYLOR, EDGAR.

The book of rights ; or, constitutional acts and parliamentary proceedings affecting civil and religious liberty in England. 1833. 12mo. **118 E**

An Essay on religious offences indictable at common law. See L. M. Aspland's Law of blasphemy. 1884. [Pamphlets, vol. 30.] **144 B**

Memoir of Edgar Taylor, Esq., F.S.A. 1839. [Law Tracts, vol. 7.] **144 E**

TAYLOR, GEORGE.

Treatise on the act for the registration, regulation, and incorporation of joint stock companies. 1847. 8vo. **169 D**

TAYLOR, John, LL.D.
Elements of the civil law. 2nd ed. 1755. 4to. **48 G**

TAYLOR, John Pitt.
An Examination of Mr. Pitt Taylor's thesis ' On the ex-
pediency of passing an act to permit defendants in criminal
courts and their wives or husbands to testify on oath.' By
Francis Worsley. 1861. [Pamphlets, vol. 13.]   **144 A**
A Treatise on the law of Evidence as administered in England
and Ireland. 2 vols. 1848. 8vo.   **167 G**
The same. 5th ed. 2 vols. 1868. 8vo.   **167 G**
The same. 7th ed. 2 vols. 1878. 8vo.   **167 G**
The same. 8th ed. 2 vols. 1885. 8vo.   **9 I**

TAYLOR, John Robert.
Correspondence on the contemplated improvement of widening
the north end of Chancery Lane. 1850, and 2nd ed. 1850,
and Additional correspondence. 1850. [Pamphlets, vol. 7.]
144 A
Early closing on Saturdays. Correspondence compiled by
J. R. Taylor. 1855. [Pamphlets, vol. 13.]   **144 A**
The rise and progress of mechanics' institutes in England.
An address delivered at St. Pierres-Les-Calais, France ; to
the St. Pierre's Young men's mutual improvement society.
1861. [Pamphlets, vol. 21.]   **144 B**

TAYLOR, Joseph Smith.
A Manual on the winding up of companies by the Court of
Chancery. 1865. 12mo.   **169 D**

TAYLOR, Richard.
Index monasticus ; or, the monasteries, alien priories, friaries,
colleges and hospitals in the diocese of Norwich and the
ancient kingdom of East Anglia. 1821. folio.   **92 G**

TAYLOR, Silas, alias Domville.
The history and antiquities of Harwich and Dovercourt, first
collected by S. Taylor and now much enlarged by Samuel
Dale. 1730. 8vo.   **87 E**
The history of Gavel-kind ; with a short History of William
the Conquerour, written in Latin by an anonymous author
in the time of Henry I. 1663. 8vo.   **118 A**

TAYLOR, Thomas.
The philosophical and mathematical commentaries of Proclus, on the first book of Euclid's Elements ; and a translation of Proclus's Theological Elements. 2 vols. 1792. 4to.
78 G

TEIGNMOUTH, Charles John, 2 Baron.
. Sketches of the coasts and islands of Scotland and the Isle of Man. 2 vols. 1836. 12mo. 95 C

TELEGRAPHS.
Law of Telegraphs. By W. L. Scott and M. P. Jarnagin. Boston, 1868. 8vo. 60 B

TELEPHONES.
The Post Office and the Telephone Companies. 1884. 8vo.
53 H

TEMPERANCE.
Transactions of the National Association for the promotion of Social Science. Conference on temperance legislation. 1886. 8vo. 78 F

TEMPLE, Leofric and George MEW.
Reports of cases in the court of criminal appeal, 1848–1851. 1 vol. 1852. 8vo. 1 H

TEMPLE, Sir William.
Works : with his life. 2 vols. 1750. folio. 79 I

TEMPLE, The and TEMPLE BAR.
The history of the Knights Templars, the Temple church, and the Temple. By C. G. Addison. 1842. 8vo. 91 D
Memorials of Temple Bar ; with some account of Fleet street and the parishes of St. Dunstan and St. Bride. By T. C. Noble. 1869. 8vo. 89 D
The Temple church, an account of its restoration and repairs. By William Burge. 1843. 8vo. 91 D

TENANT-RIGHT.
Custom and tenant-right. By C. I. Elton. 1882. 12mo. 13 B
Can tenant-right owners be disturbed in possession ? The question argued and authorities adduced. By F. R. Jones. 1861. [Pamphlets, vol. 15.] 144 B

TENURES.

Systems of Land Tenure in various countries: a series of essays published under the sanction of the Cobden Club. By J. W. Probyn. New ed. 1881. 8vo. **78 B**

Tenures of land and customs of manors, originally collected by Thomas Blount. New ed. by W. C. Hazlitt. 1874. 8vo. **13 B**

The history of law of Tenures of land in England and Ireland. By W. F. Finlason. 1870. 8vo. **176 E**

The first part of the Institutes of the laws of England. By Sir E. Coke. 19th ed. by C. Butler. 2 vols. 1832. 8vo. **13 A**

Treatise of Tenures. By Sir Jeffray Gilbert. 4th ed. by Charles Watkins. 1796. 8vo. **176 D**

Introduction to the law of Tenures. By Sir Martin Wright. 3rd ed. 1768. 8vo. **176 D**

Baronia Anglica : an history of land-honors and baronies and of tenure in capite. By T. Madox. 1736. folio. **126 I**

Tenures in French and English. By T. Littleton. 1671. 12mo. **48 A**

See also ESTATES.

TERENTIUS AFER, PUBLIUS.

Comœdiæ. Birminghamiæ, 1772. 4to. **47 H**

TERM REPORTS.

Reports in the court of King's Bench, 1785–1800. By C. Durnford and E. H. East. 8 vols. 1794–1802. 8vo. **5 I**

Digested index to the Term Reports, containing all the points of law argued and determined in the court of King's Bench, 1785 to 1814, and in the court of Common Pleas, 1788 to 1815. By J. B. Moore. 2 vols. 1816. 8vo. **63 D**

TERMS.

The original of the four terms of the year, by Sir Henry Spelman. See Sir H. Spelman's English works, 1727, part 2, pp. 67–104. **78 H**

TERRA COTTA.

An Account of the history and manufacture of ancient and modern Terra Cotta. By J. M. Blashfield. 1855. [Pamphlets, vol. 40.] **144 C**

Examples of vases, tazzas, pateræ, &c. manufactured in Terra-Cotta. By J. M. Blashfield. 1853. 4to. **78 G**

TERRELL, THOMAS.
The law and practice relating to letters patent for inventions.
1884. 8vo. **173 E**
The same. 2nd ed. 1889. 8vo. **53 B**

TERRIEN, GUILLAUME.
Commentaires du Droit Civil tant public que privé, observé
au pays et duché de Normandie. Rouen, 1654. folio.
157 F

TERTULLIANUS, QUINTUS SEPTIMIUS FLORENS.
Opera quæ hactenus reperiri potuerunt omnia ; cum Jacobi
Pamelii argumentis et adnotationibus. Colon., 1617. folio.

TESTA DE NEVILL.
Testa de Nevill ; sive liber feodorum in Curia Scaccarii temp.
Hen. III. et Edw. I. 1807. folio. **98 E**

TESTATORS.
Practical advice to testators and executors. By Wm. Phippen.
7th ed. 1886. 12mo. **13 I**
See also SHELLEY'S CASE and WILLS.

TEWKESBURY, GLOUCESTERSHIRE.
The history of Tewkesbury. By James Bennett. Tewkesbury,
1830. 8vo. **87 F**

THAMES, THE.
History of the Thames Docks. See F. Clifford's History of
private bill legislation, vol. 2, 1887, pp. 625–675. **83 I**
The law of Pilotage on the river Thames. By W. H. Farn-
field. 1874. 12mo. **176 E**
Report from committee to whom the petition of proprietors
of stock of Governor and Company for raising the Thames
water in York Buildings is referred. 1733. Bound with
Lists of law officers, 1730–33. folio. **118 G**
Rules and bye-laws for the regulation of the watermen and
lightermen of the river Thames. 1828. [City of London
Tracts.] **91 C**
Rules, orders, and ordinances for the governing and regulating
all persons who shall fish or drudge on the river of Thames ;
and also in the waters of Medway. 1785. [City of London
Tracts.] **91 C**

THAMES, THE—*continued.*

Table of rates, prices, or fares to be taken by watermen on river Thames between New Windsor, Berks, and Yantlet Creek, Kent. 1828. [City of London Tracts.] **91 C**

The Thames conservancy. By E. H. Fishbourne. 1882. 12mo. **11 H**

Yantlett Creek. Rex *versus* J. Mountague, W. L. Newman, J. Nelson, and four others. Report of the trial on an indictment against the defendants in consequence of their having cut through an embankment at Grain Bridge for the purpose of restoring the junction of the waters of the rivers Thames and Medway in and through Yantlet Creek. 1824. [City of London Tracts.] **91 C**

See also BINNELL, R. and SHARP, G.

THANET, ISLE OF, KENT.

Delineations of the Isle of Thanet and the Cinque Ports. By E. W. Brayley. 2 vols. 1817–18. 8vo. **88 D**

The history and antiquities of the Isle of Tenet. By Rev. John Lewis. 2nd ed. 1736. 4to. **88 E**

A Tour through the Isle of Thanet ; and some other parts of East Kent. By Z. Cozens. 1793. 4to. **88 E**

THEATRES.

Law of theatres and music-halls. By W. N. M. Geary. 1885. 8vo. **11 H**

THEATRICAL TEARS.

Theatrical Tears, a poem occasioned by Familiar epistles to Frederick J[one]s, Esq. [By John Wilson Croker.] 1807. Bound with Attorney's Guide, 1807. 12mo. **118 A**

THELLUSSON ACT.

A Treatise on the Thellusson act 39 & 40 Geo. III. c. 98. By J. F. Hargrave. 1842. 8vo. **176 E**

Three arguments in two causes in Chancery, on the last will of Peter Thellusson. See Hargrave's Juridical Arguments, vol. 2, 1799, pp. 1–182, and Appendix, pp. i–xxiv. **144 G**

See also PERPETUITIES.

THELOALL, SIMON.

Le digest des briefes originals, et des choses concernants eux. 1687. See Registrum Brevium, 4th ed., 1687. folio. **157 C**

THEOBALD, HENRY STUDDY.
Concise treatise on construction of wills. 1876· 8vo. **178 A**
The same. 2nd ed. 1881. 8vo. **53 I**
The same. 3rd ed. 1885. 8vo. **13 I**

THEOBALD, WILLIAM.
Legislative acts of the governor general of India in council, 1834–1869. 7 vols. Calcutta, 1868–70. 8vo. **33 G**
A Practical treatise on the law of Principal and Surety. 1832. 8vo. . **174 C**
Summary of statements and arguments submitted to the president of the Board of Control [upon the law courts or India]. 1857. [Pamphlets, vol. 19.] **144 B**
What is special pleading ? A letter to Sir Thomas Denman in answer to this question ; with a proposal of emendations in the forms of actions. 1832. [Law Tracts, vol. 5.] **144 E**

THEOPHRASTUS.
The characters of Theophrastus ; with a translation into Latin. By R. Newton. Oxford, 1754. 8vo. **78 B**

THETFORD, NORFOLK.
The history of the ancient city and burgh of Thetford. By Rev. Francis Blomefield. Fersfield, 1739. 4to. **92 D**
The history of the town of Thetford. By Thomas Martin. Edited by Richard Gough. 1779. 4to. **92 D**

THICKNESSE, RALPH.
A Digest of the law of husband and wife, as it affects property. 1884. 8vo. **10 C**
The married women s property act 1882. 1882. 12mo. **53 A**

THINGOE HUNDRED, SUFFOLK.
The history and antiquities of Suffolk, Thingoe hundred. By John Gage. 1838. folio. **93 H**

THIRTY YEARS' WAR.
Letters and other documents illustrating the relations between England and Germany at the commencement of the thirty years' war. Edited by S. R. Gardiner. [Camden Society, vols. 90 and 98.] 1865–68. 8vo. **85 C**

THOMAS DE BURTON.
Chronica Monasterii de Melsa. Edited by E. A. Bond. 3 vols.
1866–68. 8vo. **102 C**

THOMAS OF ELMHAM.
Elmhami liber metricus de Henrico Quinto. See Memorials
of Henry the Fifth, 1858, pp. 79–165. **101 B**
Historia monasterii S. Augustini Cantuariensis. Edited by
C. Hardwick. 1858. 8vo. **101 B**

THOMAS, CHARLES.
Mining fields of the West : being a practical exposition of
the principal mines and mining districts in Cornwall and
Devon. 1867. [Pamphlets, vol. 36.] **144 C**

THOMAS, ERNEST CHESTER.
Leading cases in Constitutional law briefly stated. 1876.
8vo. **163 D**
The same. 2nd ed. 1885. 8vo. **64 B**
The Library Chronicle : a journal of librarianship and bibliography. Edited by E. C. Thomas. 5 vols. 1884–88. 8vo.
82 E

THOMAS, FRANCIS SHEPPARD.
Hand-book to the public records. 1853. 8vo. **98 A**
Historical Notes. 3 vols. 1856. 8vo. **99 A**
Notes of materials for the history of public departments. 1846.
folio. **99 E**

THOMAS, JOHN HENRY.
A Systematic arrangement of Lord Coke's First Institute of '
the laws of England, on the plan of Sir Matthew Hale's
analysis. 3 vols. 1818. 8vo. **176 E**

THOMAS, JOHN PENFORD.
A Treatise of universal jurisprudence. 1828, and 2nd ed.
1829. 8vo. **63 G**

[THOMAS, RALPH.]
A Bibliographical list of Lord Brougham's publications, arranged in chronological order. By the author of 'The
handbook of fictitious names.' Privately printed. 1873.
12mo. **82 B**

[THOMAS, RALPH]—*continued.*

A Bibliographical list of works on Swimming. By the author of The handbook of fictitious names. 1868. 12mo. **82 B**

A Few words on Swimming ; with practical hints to beginners. By Ralph Harrington. 1861. 12mo. **82 B**

Handbook for fictitious names : being a guide to authors, chiefly in the lighter literature of the xixth century, who have written under assumed names ; and to literary forgers, impostors, plagiarists and imitators. By Olphar Hamst, Esq. 1868. 8vo. **82 B**

How the parish of Debach borrowed £400 and refused to pay it all back. 1879. [Pamphlets, vol. 32.] **144 C**

A Martyr to Bibliography : a notice of the life and works of Joseph-Marie Quérard, bibliographer. By Olphar Hamst, Esq. Bibliophile, M. O. T. I. L. S. O. T. U. K., T. S. B. A., and A. O. A. F. W. O. S. 1867. 8vo. **82 B**

THOMAS, ST.

The skryvener's play. The incredulity of St. Thomas. Edited by J. P. Collier. [Camden Society, vol. 73.] 1859. 8vo. **85 B**

THOMPSON, J.

Historical sketches of Bridlington. Bridlington, 1821. 12mo. **94 A**

THOMPSON, PISHEY.

Collections for a topographical and historical account of Boston and the Hundred of Skirbeck. 1820. 8vo. **89 C**

The same. 1820. 4to. **90 G**

THOMPSON, RICHARD.

Letters to Henry Thompson of Escrick, co. York, 1684–93. Edited by J. J. Cartwright. [Camden Society, n.s. vol. 31.] 1883. 8vo. **85 D**

THOMPSON, SEYMOUR D.

The liability of stockholders in corporations. St. Louis, 1879. 8vo. **60 B**

THOMSON, HENRY BYERLEY.

Institutes of the laws of Ceylon. 2 vols. 1866. 8vo. **37 E**

The laws of War affecting commerce and shipping. 1854. [Pamphlets, vol. 9, pt. 2.] **144 A**

The same. 2nd ed. 1854. 8vo. **55 A**

THOMSON, JAMES.
Law Reports, containing decisions of bench of supreme court in Nova Scotia, 1834–1841. Halifax, 1853. 8vo. **55 E**

THOMSON, NINIAN HILL.
Act XIV. of 1859 regulating the limitation of civil suits in British India. 2nd ed. Calcutta, 1870. 8vo. **38 B**

THOMSON, RICHARD.
Chronicles of London Bridge. By An Antiquary. 1827. 8vo.
91 C
An Historical essay on the Magna Charta of King John. 1829. 8vo. **114 D**

THORESBY, RALPH.
Ducatus Leodiensis: or, the topography of the town and parish of Leeds, and parts adjacent. 2nd ed. by T. D. Whitaker. Leeds, 1816. folio. **95 H**
Life of Ralph Thoresby. See J. P. Malcolm's Lives of Topographers and Antiquaries. 1815. 4to. **79 H**

THORN, WILLIAM.
Chronica de rebus gestis abbatum S. Augustini Cantuariæ. See Scriptores Decem Hist. Angl. pp. 1758–2295. **114 H**

THORNBER, REV. WILLIAM.
Historical and descriptive account of Blackpool and its neighbourhood. Poulton, 1837. 12mo. **89 A**

THORNBURY, GEORGE WALTER and E. WALFORD.
Old and new London: a narrative of its history, its people, and its places. 6 vols. 1879–85. 8vo. **90 D**

THORNE, JAMES.
Handbook to the environs of London alphabetically arranged. 2 vols. 1876. 8vo. **89 C**

THORNTON, ABRAHAM.
Observations upon the case of Abraham Thornton, shewing the danger of pressing presumptive evidence too far. By E. Holroyd. 3rd ed. 1819. 8vo. **118 B**
See also BATTLE, TRIAL BY.

THORNTON, EDWARD.

A Gazetteer of the territories under the government of the East India company, and of the native states on the continent of India. 4 vols. 1854. 8vo.   84 G

THORNTON, JAMES B.

A Digest of the Conveyancing, testamentary, and registry laws of all the States of the Union. Philadelphia, 1847. 8vo.   •   59 C

THORNTON, ROBERT.

The Thornton romances. Early English metrical romances of Perceval, Isumbras, Eglamour and Degrevant. Edited by J. O. Halliwell. [Camden Society, vol. 30.] 1844. 8vo. 85 A

THORNTON, THOMAS.

Notes of cases in the Ecclesiastical and Maritime courts, 1841–1850. 7 vols. 1843–50. 8vo.   8 H

THOROTON, ROBERT.

The antiquities of Nottinghamshire. 1677. folio.   93 H
The same. 2nd ed. by John Throsby. 3 vols. 1797. 4to.
                                                                                       92 E

THORPE, JOHN.

Custumale Roffense, from the original manuscript in the archives of the dean and chapter of Rochester ; with memorials of that cathedral church. 1788. folio.   89 G
Registrum Roffense ; or, a collection of ancient records, illustrating the ecclesiastical history and antiquities of the diocese and cathedral church of Rochester. 1769. folio.   89 G

THRING, HENRY.

Law and practice of joint-stock companies. 2 vols. 1861–63, and 2nd ed. 2 vols. 1867. 12mo.   169 E
The same. 3rd ed. by G. Fitzgerald. 1875. 12mo. 169 E
The same. 4th ed. by G. Fitzgerald. 1880. 8vo.   52 C
The same. 5th ed. by J. M. Rendel. 1889. 8vo.   9 D
Simplification of the law. Practical Suggestions. 1875.
   [Pamphlets, vol. 35.]   144 C

THRING, THEODORE.
The criminal law of the navy. 1861. 12mo.   **172 G**
The same. 2nd ed. by T. Thring and C. E. Gifford. 1877.
12mo.   **172 G**
The Land Drainage act 1861. 1862. 12mo.   **170 C**

THROCKMORTON, SIR NICHOLAS.
Memoir and trial of Sir Nicholas Throckmorton. See Criminal
Trials, 1832, pp. 40–120.   **51 D**

THROOP, MONTGOMERY H.
Revised statutes of the state of New York. Edited by M. H.
Throop. 7th ed. 3 vols. New York, 1882. 8vo.   **32 D**
A Treatise on the validity of Verbal Agreements as affected
by the legislative enactments in England and the United
States, commonly called the Statute of Frauds. Vol. 1.
Albany, 1870. 8vo.   **59 B**

THROSBY, JOHN.
The history and antiquities of the ancient town of Leicester.
Leicester, 1791. 4to.   **90 G**
Select views in Leicestershire, containing seats of the nobility
and gentry, town views and ruins with descriptive and historical relations ; and a series of excursions to the villages
and places of note in the county. 2 vols. 1789–90. 4to.
                                                    89 C

THWAITES, CHARLES.
A Guide to Criminal Law at the Bar final. 1885. 8vo. **64 C**
The same. 2nd ed. 1888. 8vo.   **64 C**

TICHBORNE, SIR ROGER.
Charge of the lord chief justice of England, in the case of,
The Queen against Thomas Castro, otherwise Arthur
Orton, otherwise Sir Roger Tichborne. 2 vols. 1874–75.
8vo.   **118 E**
The Queen *v.* Castro, or Orton or Sir Roger C. D. Tichborne.
Summing up of the lord chief justice. [1874.] folio. **49 H**
The Tichborne case compared with previous impostures of
the same kind. By Joseph Brown. 1874. [Pamphlets,
vol. 38.]   **144 C**

TICHBORNE, Sir Roger—*continued*.
The Tichborne trial; the summing up by the lord chief justice of England; with the addresses of the judges, the
verdict and the sentence; and a history of the case. 1874.
8vo. **51 E**

TICKELL, Rev. John.
The history of the town and county of Kingston upon Hull.
Hull, 1798. 4to. **94 D**

TIDD, William.
Forms of practical proceedings chiefly intended as an appendix
to the practice of the court of King's Bench. 3rd ed. 1809,
7th ed. 1828, and 8th ed. 1840. 8vo. **163 B**
The practice of the courts of King's Bench and Common
Pleas in personal actions; with the law and practice of
Extents. 7th ed. 2 vols. 1821. 8vo. **163 B**
The same. 9th ed. 2 vols. 1828, and 2 Supplements
1830 & 1832. 4 vols. 1828–32. 8vo. **163 B**
The practice of the superior courts of law in personal actions
and ejectment, so far as it is altered or affected by the late
statutes. 1833, and New ed. 1837. 8vo. **163 B**

TIERNEY, Rev. Mark Aloysius.
The history and antiquities of the castle and town of Arundel;
including the biography of its earls. 2 vols. in 1. 1834.
8vo. **93 E**

TIGHE, Robert Richard and James Edward DAVIS.
Annals of Windsor; being a history of the castle and town;
with some account of Eton and places adjacent. 2 vols.
1858. 4to. **86 C**

TILSLEY, Hugh.
The new Stamp acts, with notes and explanatory observations.
6th ed. 1854. 8vo. **175 G**
A Digest of the Stamp acts. 8th ed. 1860. 8vo. **175 G**
The same. 9th ed. By E. H. Tilsley. 1865. 8vo. **175 G**
A Treatise on the Stamp laws in Great Britain and Ireland.
1847. 8vo. **53 H**
The same. 2nd ed. with supplement. 1850. 8vo. **53 H**
The same. 3rd ed. by E. H. Tilsley. 1871. 8vo. **11 G**

TIMBER.
An Essay on the nature and properties of timber. By
T. Tredgold. 2nd ed. 1828. 4to. 78 G

TIMBS, JOHN.
The Year-book of facts. 1868. 8vo. 146 C

TIME AND TIME TABLES.
A Chapter on Time. See W. T. Kime's Practical Hints,
1848, pp. 1–63. 162 G
The legal calculation and division of time. By Michael
Barry. 1842. [Lectures, &c. Ireland.] 144 G
Manual of times of procedure in chancery. By T. W. Braith-
waite. 1864. 8vo. 161 B
Time Tables for the high court of justice and the county
court. By J. W. Jeudwine. 2nd ed. 1884. 8vo. 169 G

TIMES, THE.
The Times, 1795–1804 and 1806–1891. 287 vols. 1795–
1891. folio. Hall
Index to The Times newspaper, 1842–1890. By Samuel
Palmer. 49 vols. 1891-76 & 1868–91. 8vo. 134 H I
Index to The Times and to the topics and events of years
1862–63. By J. Giddings. 2 vols. 1863-64. 8vo. 134 I
A Reprint from The Times. The annual summaries for a
quarter of a century, 1851–1875. 1876. 12mo. 146 F
The Times Law Reports, October 1884 to August 1891.
Edited by Stanley Boulter. 7 vols. 1885–91. 4to. 65 G
The Times parliamentary debates, 1886–1890. House of
Commons. 16 vols. 1886-90. 4to. 105 A
The Times parliamentary debates, 1886–1890. House of
Lords. 5 vols. 1886-90. 4to. 104 A
The Times register of events in 1885. 1886. 8vo. 146 F

TIMMINS, SAMUEL.
A History of Warwickshire. 1889. 8vo. 93 E

TINDAL, WILLIAM.
The history and antiquities of the abbey and borough of Evesham. Evesham, 1794. 4to. 93 F

TITE, WILLIAM.
Letters selected from the collection of autographs in the
possession of Wm. Tite, M.P.   [Camden Society, vol. 87.]
1864. 8vo.   85 C

TITHES.
The Tithe acts and the rules under the Tithe act 1891 with
notes and references and a short treatise on the recovery of
Tithe rent charge. By G. P. Leach. 1891. 12mo. 11 H
Tithe commutation tables. By C. M. Willich. 3rd ed. 1854,
and Annual Supplements 1838–1890. 2 vols. 1854–91.
8vo.   11 H
The law of Tithes and Tithe Rent-Charge. By E. F. Studd.
1889. 12mo.   11 H
The history of Tithes, from Abraham to Queen Victoria. By
H. W. Clarke. 1887. 8vo.   78 B
The Tithe acts. By T. H. Bolton. 1886. 12mo.   11 H
The acts for the commutation of Tithes. By L. Shelford.
3rd ed. 1848. 8vo.   11 H
The petition of Rev. C. Miller, respecting the Tithe Commu-
tation act, presented to the House of Lords by the bishop
of London, session 1840. 1841. [Pamphlets, vol. 5.] 144 A
Observations on the assessment of Tithes to the poor's rate.
By Wm. Blake. 1839. [Pamphlets, vol. 1.]   144 A
Observations on the due mode of rating Tithe and commuta-
tion of Tithe. By Thomas D'Oyly. 1839. [Pamphlets,
vol. 1.]   144 A
The Parson's Counsellor; with the law of tithes or tithing. By
Sir S. Degge. 7th ed. by C. Ellis. 1820. 8vo.   52 F
Laws concerning Tithes. By T. Cunningham. 3rd ed.
1748. 8vo.   176 E
Tythes. See Sir H. Spelman's English works, 2nd ed., 1727,
pp. 37–172.   78 H
See also ABBOTT, G., BEARBLOCK, REV. J., BOHUN, W.,
BOSANQUET, S. R., EAGLE, F. K., EAGLE, W., GWILLIM,
SIR H., HOWLETT, REV. J., LONDON TITHES, MIRE-
HOUSE, J., PEARSON, A., PLOWDEN, F., PRIDEAUX, H.,
RAYNER, J., RIPLEY, W. R., TOLLER, S., WHITE, F. M.,
WHITE, J. M. and WOOD, H.

TITHINGS.
Account of the ancient division of the English nation into
hundreds and tithings. By G. Sharp. 1784. 12mo. 78 A

TITLE AND TITLE DEEDS.

Hints as to advising on title, and practical suggestions for perusing and analysing abstracts. By W. H. Gover. 1889.
8vo. **13 H**

Rules for the interpretation of deeds. By H. W. Elphinstone, R. F. Norton and J. W. Clark. 1885. 8vo. **9 G**

See also ABSTRACTS OF TITLE and DEEDS.

TIVERTON, DEVONSHIRE.

Historical memoirs of the town and parish of Tiverton. By Martin Dunsford. Exeter, 1790. 4to. **87 D**

TIXALL, STAFFORDSHIRE.

A Topographical and historical description of the parish of Tixall. By Sir Thomas Clifford and Arthur Clifford. Paris, 1817. 4to. **93 B**

TOBAGO.

Acts and Ordinances of Tobago, 1857–1888. 7 vols. Tobago, 1857–88. folio. **36 E**

TODD, ALPHEUS.

Parliamentary government in the British colonies. 1880. 8vo. **116 C**

TODD, HENRY JOHN.

A Catalogue of the archiepiscopal manuscripts in the library at Lambeth Palace. 1812. folio. **81 H**

History of the College of Bonhommes, at Ashridge, in the county of Buckingham. 1823. folio. **91 H**

TOFTS, MARY.

Eleven tracts relating to Mary Tofts, the rabbit woman of Godalming. 1726–27. 8vo. **118 B**

TOLERATION.

Letters concerning Toleration. See J. Locke's Works, vol. 6, 1823. 8vo. **78 F**

TOLLER, SAMUEL.

The law of Executors and Administrators. 2nd ed. 1806, and 3rd ed. 1814. 8vo. **168 D**

The same. 7th ed. by F. Whitmarsh. 1838. 8vo. **168 D**

A Treatise of the law of Tithes. 1808. 8vo. **176 F**

The same. 2nd ed. 1816. 8vo. **176 F**

TOLLS.
The law of Tolls. By F. Gunning. 1833. 8vo. **176 F**

TOLSTOI, Leon.
What I believe. Translated from the Russian by Constantine
Popoff. 1885. 12mo. **77 A**

TOMKINS, Frederick.
The institutes of the Roman law. Part 1. 1867. 8vo. **63 E**
Commentaries of Gaius on the Roman law; with an English
translation and annotations. By F. Tomkins and W. G.
Lemon. 1869. 8vo. **63 E**

TOMLINS, Harold Nuttall.
Digested index to the Crown law; comprehending all the
points relating to criminal matters contained in Reports of
Blackstone, Burrow, Cowper, &c. 1816. 8vo. **63 D**

TOMLINS, Sir Thomas Edlyne.
A Digested Index to the Term Reports. 1799, 2nd ed. 1800,
and 4th ed. 1812. 8vo.
A Familiar, plain, and easy explanation of the laws of Wills
and Codicils. 4th ed. 1789. 8vo. **178 C**
The law dictionary, explaining the rise, progress, and present
state of the British law. 4th ed. by T. P. Granger. 2 vols.
1835. 4to. **123 G**
Repertorium Juridicum, index to all the cases and pleadings
in law and equity. By K. Freeman. New ed. by T. E.
Tomlins. 2 vols. Dublin, 1788. 8vo. **63 D**
The statutes of the United Kingdom of Great Britain and
Ireland, 1801–1869; with notes by T. E. Tomlins and
others. 29 vols. 1804–69. 4to. **70 D–G**

TONE, Theobald Wolfe.
The life of T. W. Tone, written by himself. Edited by his
son W. T. W. Tone. [Autobiography, vol. 16.] 1831.
12mo. **79 A**

TONG CASTLE, Shropshire.
Specifications of a freehold domain known as the Tong Castle
estate; comprising nearly the entire parish situate in the
county of Salop, which will be sold by auction by Messrs.
Driver on Tuesday, 11 Sep. 1855. 1855. folio. **93 H**

TONTINE,

A List of the existing nominees appointed by the contributors to the Tontine of 1789, 1809 and 1818. A List of the existing nominees appointed by the lords commissioners of His Majesty's treasury to hold shares on the part of the public in the Tontine of the years 1789, 1809 and 1818. 4 parts in 1 vol. 1809-18. 4to. **118 F**

See also STONE, W.

TOOKE, JOHN HORNE.

The Trial of John Horne Tooke, for high treason, at the sessions house in the Old Bailey, on 17th-22nd of November, 1794. Taken in short-hand by Joseph Gurney. 2 vols. in 1. 1795. 8vo. **50 B**

TOOKE, THOMAS.

Thoughts and details on the high and low prices of the last thirty years. 2 vols. 1823. 8vo. **78 D**

TOOKE, WILLIAM.

Lucian of Samosata, from the Greek ; with the comments and illustrations of Wieland and others. 2 vols. 1820. 4to. **83 J**

The monarchy of France, its rise, progress and fall. 1855. 8vo. **113 E**

Some account of the proceedings at the election for Truro, August 3-6, 1830, and Address on occasion of Mr. W. Tooke's visit to Truro, Sep.-Oct. 1833. 1830-33. 8vo. **86 E**

Verses. Edited by M. M. M. 2nd impression, and Supplement. For private distribution only. 1860-61. 8vo. **83 C**

TOONE, WILLIAM.

Magistrate's Manual ; or, a summary of duties and powers of a justice of the peace. 4th ed. 1828. 8vo. **172 B**

TOPOGRAPHY.

Catalogue of the Hoare library at Stourhead, co. Wilts. 1840. 8vo. **82 G**

Collectanea topographica et genealogica. [Edited by J. G. Nichols.] 8 vols. 1834-43. 8vo. **127 I**

An Essay on topographical literature, with accounts of the sources, objects, and uses of national and local records. By John Britton. [1843.] 4to. **85 I**

TOPOGRAPHY—*continued.*
Lives of topographers and antiquaries who have written concerning the antiquities of England ; with portraits of the authors. By J. P. Malcolm. 1815. 4to.   79 H
Manual for the genealogist, topographer, antiquary, and legal professor. By R. Sims. 2nd ed. 1861. 8vo.   124 G
Records and record searching, a guide to the genealogist and topographer. By Walter Rye. 1888. 8vo.   124 G

TORR, JOSEPH HOOLEY.
A Review of the ancient and modern position and duties, rights, and privileges of the judges of the Sheriffs' court of the City of London. 1869. [Pamphlets, vol. 37.]   144 C
A Review of the origin and present position of the Sheriffs' ·court of the City of London, and the right and privilege of the judge of the Sheriffs' court to sit as commissioner and assistant-judge of the Central Criminal court. 1868. [Pamphlets, vol. 37.]   144 C
The Sheriffs' (City of London) Court is a substantive court of original and special jurisdiction, and although statutably empowered to exercise the like jurisdictions as a county court, and subject to the like appeal, is not a county court. 1867. [Pamphlets, vol. 37.]   144 C

TORRINGTON, GEORGE, 1 VISCOUNT.
Memoirs relating to the Lord Torrington. Edited by J. K. Laughton. [Camden Society, n.s. vol. 46.] 1889. 4to. 85 E

TORTS.
Law of Torts. By J. F. Clerk and W. H. B. Lindsell. 1889. 8vo.   11 H
A Summary of the law of Torts. By Arthur Underhill. 5th ed. 1889. 12mo.   64 F
A Treatise on wrongs and their remedies. By C. G. Addison. 6th ed. 1887. 8vo.   11 H
Law of Torts. By F. Pollock. 1887. 8vo.   11 H
The law of Torts. By J. A. Shearwood. 1886. 12mo. 64 F
Principles of the law of Torts. By F. T. Piggott. 1885. 8vo.   11 H
A Treatise on Torts and the legal remedies for their redress. By S. Hastings. 1885. 8vo.   64 E

TORTS—*continued.*

Summary of the law on the liability of employers for personal injuries. By W. H. Roberts and G. H. Wallace. 3rd ed. 1885. 8vo. **9 H**

Leading cases on the law of Torts. By W. E. Ball. 1884. 8vo. **11 H**

Outlines of law, comprising injuries to persons and property. By R. Maugham. 1837. 12mo. **170 F**

See also BIGELOW, M. M., HILLIARD, F., RINGWOOD, F. and SLEIGH, W. C.

TORTURE.

A Reading on the use of Torture in the criminal law of England previously to the Commonwealth. By David Jardine. 1837. 8vo. ` **78 C**

TOSH, ANDREW.

A Statement of the law relating to securities over machinery. Edinburgh, 1887. 12mo. **55 F**

TOTHILL, WILLIAM.

The transactions of the high court of Chancery 1559–1646, collected by W. Tothill and since reviewed by Sir R. O. Holborne. 1820. 12mo. **161 E**

TOTNES, DEVONSHIRE.

Devonshire parishes, or the antiquities of twenty-eight parishes in the archdeaconry of Totnes. By C. Worthy. 2 vols. Exeter, 1887–89. 8vo. **87 D**

TOTTENHAM, MIDDLESEX.

The history and antiquities of the parish of Tottenham. By Wm. Robinson. 2nd ed. 2 vols. 1840. 8vo. **89 D**

TOTTILL, RICHARD.

Magna Charta cum statutis quæ antiqua vocantur, jam recens excusa, et summa fide emendata : quibus accesserunt nonnulla nunc primum typis edita. 1556. 12mo. **48 A**

The same. Another ed. partly in English. 1587. 12mo. **48 A**

TOULLIER, CHARLES BONAVENTURE MARIE.
Le Droit Civil Français, suivant l'ordre du Code . . . Continué
et complété par J. B. Duvergier. 6me éd. 7 vols. Paris,
[1846–48.] 8vo. **58 E F**

TOULMIN, JOSHUA.
The history of Taunton. New ed. by James Savage. Taunton,
1822. 8vo. **93 B**

TOULMIN, SAMUEL SIMPSON.
The statutes and orders relating to Practice and Pleading in
the high court of Chancery, from 1813 to Easter term 1847,
classified. 1847. 8vo. **173 G**

TOWAGE.
The law of salvage, towage and pilotage. By H. Newson.
1886. 8vo. **11 E**

TOWER OF LONDON.
The history and antiquities of the Tower of London, with
memoirs of royal and distinguished persons. By John
Bayley. 2nd ed. 1830. 8vo. **91 E**

TOWN COUNCILLORS.
The town councillors' and burgesses' manual. By Louis Gaches.
1875. 8vo. **176 F**
The town councillors' manual ; or, a guide to the duties of
municipal corporations. By S. Stone. 1869. 12mo. **164 G**

TOWNESEND, GEORGE.
A Preparative to Pleading. 3rd ed. 1713. 12mo. **173 G**
A Second book of Judgements in real, personal and mixt
actions and upon the statute. 1674. 12mo. **49 E**
Tables to most of the Presidents of Pleadings, Writs, and
Retorn of Writs, at the Common Law. 1667. folio.

TOWNS.
Index villaris, or an alphabetical table of all the cities, market
towns, parishes, villages and private seats in England and
Wales. By John Adams. 1680. folio. **85 I**
Villare Anglicum : or a view of the townes of England. Col-
lected by appointment of Sir H. Spelman. 1656. 8vo. **86 A**
See also COUNTY COURTS DIRECTORIES.

TOWNSEND, FRANCIS.
Calendar of Knights ; containing lists of knights bachelors,
British knights of foreign orders, also knights of the Garter,
Thistle, Bath, St. Patrick, and the Guelphic and Ionian
orders from 1760. 1828. 8vo. **125 E**

TOWNSEND, GEORGE HENRY.
The Hand-book of the year 1868. A register of facts, dates
and events. 1869. 8vo. **146 C**
The Manual of Dates. 1862. 8vo. **134 I**
Men of the time, a dictionary of contemporaries. 7th ed.
1868. 8vo. **81 D**

TOWNSHEND, HEYWOOD.
Historical collections, or an exact account of the proceedings
of the four last parliaments of Q. Elizabeth. 1680. folio.
115 H
TOWNSHEND, JOHN.
Code of procedure of the state of New York ; with revised
rules of the courts. New York, 1867. 12mo. **60 C**
Treatise on Slander and Libel. 2nd ed. New York, 1872.
8vo. and 3rd ed. New York, 1877. 8vo. **60 B**

TRADE.
A New discourse of Trade. By Sir Josiah Child. 4th ed.
[1698.] 12mo. **78 A**
Observations on the evils arising from the publication of
notices of warrants of attorney, cognovits, bills of sale, &c.
in the journals of Trade protection societies. By Wm.
Ford. 2nd ed. 1858. [Pamphlets, vol. 11.] **144 A**
Proposals and reasons for constituting a council of trade in
Scotland. By John Law. Glasgow, 1751. 12mo. **114 A**

TRADE MARKS.
The law of trade marks. By L. B. Sebastian. 3rd ed. 1890.
8vo. **11 H**
A Digest of cases of trade mark. By L. B. Sebastian. 1879.
8vo. **11 H**
A Treatise on the law of trade marks and trade names. By
H. Ludlow and H. Jenkyns. 1877. 8vo. **11 H**
The fraudulent imitation of trade marks. By A. Ryland.
Birmingham, 1860. [Pamphlets, vol. 23.] **144 B**
See COPYRIGHT and PATENTS.
See also ADAMS, F. M. and HARDINGHAM, G. G. M.

TRADE-UNIONS.

On the origin of trade-unions. By Lujo Brentano. 1870.
8vo.   78 B

The law relating to trade-unions. By Sir Wm. Erle. 1869.
8vo.   11 I

TRAIN, JOSEPH.

Historical and statistical account of the Isle of Man. 2 vols.
Douglas, 1845. 8vo.   94 F

TRAMWAYS.

History of tramways. See F. Clifford's History of private bill
legislation, vol. 1, 1885, pp. 184–194.   83 I

Tramway acts of the United Kingdom. By H. Sutton. 2nd
ed. 1883. 8vo.   11 I

TRAVELLING.

The Laws concerning Travelling. 1718. 12mo.   176 F

TREASON.

Cases of Treason. By Sir Francis Bacon. 1641. [Law
Tracts and Arguments, 1641.]   144 F

A Collection of trials of persons for high treason, murder &c.
[1603–1721.] folio.   118 G

Debate in the House of Commons upon Sir S. Romilly's bill
on the punishment for High Treason. By Basil Montagu.
1813. [Montagu's Law Tracts.]   144 F

A Discourse concerning Treason and bills of attainder. [By
R. West.] 2nd ed. 1717. [Law Tracts, vol. 1.]   144 E

Readings upon the Statute of Treasons. By Sir Robert Holbourne. 1681. 12mo.   49 B

Some considerations on the law of Forfeiture for high treason.
[By C. Yorke.] 4th ed. Edinburgh, 1778. 12mo. 168 E

The speeches of Thomas Erskine when at the bar against
constructive treasons. 4 vols. 1810. 8vo.   83 B

See also STATE TRIALS.

TREATIES.

A Collection of all the Treaties of peace, alliance, and commerce, between Great-Britain and other powers, 1688–1771.
2 vols. 1772. 8vo.   145 B

TREATIES—*continued.*
Extracts from the several treaties subsisting between Great-Britain and other kingdoms and states, of such articles and clauses as relate to the duty and conduct of the commanders of the king of Great-Britain's ships of war. [Collected by Henry Edmunds.] 1741. 4to. **158 C**
Lists of treaties, leagues, covenants, congresses &c. mentioned in history. See F. S. Thomas's Historical Notes, vol. 3, 1856, pp. 1329–1372. **99 A**
See also DUMONT, J., HERTSLET, L. and RYMER, T.

TREDGOLD, THOMAS.
Elementary principles of Carpentery ; with An essay on the nature and properties of timber. 2nd ed. 1828. 4to. **78 G**

TREDINNICK, RICHARD.
A Review of Cornish and Devon mining enterprise 1850 to 1856 inclusive. 1857. 8vo. **172 F**
A Review of Cornish copper mining enterprise. 2nd ed. 1858. 8vo. **172 F**

TREES AND WOODS.
Legal and equitable rights and liabilities as to trees and woods. By A. D. Craig. 1866. 8vo. **11 I**

TRELAWNY FAMILY.
Trelawny Papers. Edited by W. D. Cooper. [Camden Society, vol. 55.] 1853. 8vo. **85 B**

TREMAINE, SIR JOHN.
Placita coronæ, or pleas of the crown in matters criminal and civil, digested and revised by John Rice. 1723. folio. **49 H**

TRENT, COUNCIL OF.
Histoire du concile de Trente, écrite en Italien par Fra. |Paolo Sarpi, et traduite en François, avec des notes, par P. F. Le Courayer. 3 vols. Amsterdam, 1751. 4to. **120 F**

TRESPASS.
An Essay on waste, nuisance and trespass. By G. V. Yool. 1863. 8vo. **11 I**

TREVELYAN, Sir Charles.
Statement by Sir Charles Trevelyan of the circumstances connected with his recall from the government of Madras. 1860. [Pamphlets, vol. 14.] **144 A**

TREVELYAN FAMILY.
Trevelyan papers, part 1, prior to A.D. 1558. Edited by J. P. Collier. 1857 ; part 2, A.D. 1446 to 1643. Edited by J. P. Collier. 1863 ; part 3, with introduction to parts 1, 2, and 3. Edited by Sir W. C. Trevelyan and Sir C. E. Trevelyan. 1872. [Camden Society, vols. 67, 84 and 105.] 3 vols. 1857-72. 8vo. **85 B C**

TREVOR, Charles Cecil.
The taxes on Succession, a digest of the statutes and cases relating to the probate, legacy and succession duties. 1856. 8vo. **176 D**

The same. 3rd ed. by E. Freeth and R. J. Wallace. 1880. 8vo. **176 D**

The same. 4th ed. by E. Freeth and R. J. Wallace. 1881. 8vo. **53 H**

TRIAL BY JURY.
History of trial by jury. By Wm. Forsyth. 1852. 8vo. **83 I**

See also Juries.

TRIALS, Civil and Criminal.
Adams v. Malkin. See Scriveners.
Albert, Prince, v. Strange. See Art, Works of.
Allcard v. Skinner. Speech of the Solicitor-General (Sir Edward Clarke, Q.C., M.P.) for the defendant. 1887. 8vo. **51 G**
Annesley v. Anglesey. The trial in ejectment between C. Craig, lessee of J. Annesley, Esq. plaintiff, and Richard, Earl of Anglesey, defendant, in the Court of Exchequer in Ireland, Nov. 11-25, 1743. 1744. folio. **49 H**
Ashby v. White. See Parliamentary Reform.
Attorney General v. Shore. See Hewley, Lady Sarah.
Bagshaw v. Spencer. Case of Bagshaw and Spencer in Chancery, 22 Geo. II. See Collectanea Juridica, vol. 1, 1791, pp. 378-420. **144 G**
Bather v. Brayne. Report of the trial of the cause of, Doe, on the demise of H. F. Bather, plaintiff, and J. Brayne and J. Edwards, defendants, at the Shropshire Lent Assizes. 1848. Shrewsbury, 1848. 8vo. **51 E**

TRIALS, CIVIL AND CRIMINAL—*continued.*

Beal *v.* Liddell. See Moore, E. F.

Beaurain *v.* Scott. See Excommunication.

Bebb and others, Rex *v.* See Extents.

Beckwith *v.* Wood. Riots in London. The case of Beckwith
v. Wood and another tried before Lord Ellenborough and a
special jury of merchants of the City of London in the Court
of King's Bench. By Joseph Dowling. 1818. [City of London
Tracts.]   91 C

Bishops, The Seven. The proceedings and tryal in the case of
William, archbishop of Canterbury ; William, bishop of St.
Asaph ; Francis, bishop of Ely ; John, bishop of Chichester ;
Thomas, bishop of Bath and Wells ; Thomas, bishop of Peter-
borough ; and Jonathan, bishop of Bristol ; in the Court of King's
Bench, in Trinity Term, 1688. 1739. 12mo.   50 B

Brandon, James. The trial of James Brandon, for an assault and
false imprisonment, committed on the person of H. Clifford.
[n.d.] 12mo.   118 B

Brett *v.* Fisher. Report of the cause of Joseph Brett *v.* Thomas
Fisher and others, tried in the Court of King's Bench, December 1827, to determine legality of corporation of Cambridge
exacting certain tolls from the inhabitants. 1828. 8vo.   51 G

Brodie, William, and George Smith. An Account of the trial of
W. Brodie and G. Smith for breaking into and robbing the
general excise office of Scotland. By Wm. Creech, one of the
jury. 2nd ed. Edinburgh, 1788. 8vo.   118 B

Burke, T. F. and others. See Fenian Conspiracy.

Burrell *v.* Nicholson. Report of the trial in the Court of Queen's
Bench, in which Sir Charles Merrik Burrell, Bart., was plaintiff,
and Henry John Nicholson was defendant; respecting the
parochial rates claimed by the parish of St. Margaret, Westminster, from the inhabitants of Richmond Terrace, tried at
Westminster hall 9 Dec. 1833. 1834. 8vo.   51 G

Cadiere *v.* Girard. The accusation of Mary Catharine Cadiere,
against Father Girard and his defence. 1731. 12mo.   118 A

Canning, Elizabeth. The trial of Elizabeth Canning, for perjury.
See W. Robinson's History of Enfield, vol. 2, 1823, pp. 132–
151.   89 D

Cardigan, 7 Earl of. Trial of James Thomas, Earl of Cardigan,
before the House of Peers, in full Parliament for felony, 16
February 1841. 1841. 8vo.   50 A

Carew *v.* Burrell. Report of the trial of the cause Carew against
Burrell, Bart. and another, executors of the late Earl of Egre-
mont, at the Sussex Spring assizes March 18, 1840. 1840.
[Pamphlets, vol. 2.]   144 A

Carthew *v.* Brenton. See Halcomb, John.

Churcher's College, Case of. See Atcheson, N.

Clayton *v.* Duchy of Cornwall. See Cornwall.

Cochrane, Lord. Trial of C. R. De Berenger, Sir Thomas Cochrane,
commonly called Lord Cochrane and others, for a conspiracy,
in the Court of King's Bench. Taken in short hand by W. B.
Gurney. 1814. 8vo.   50 B

TRIALS, CIVIL AND CRIMINAL—*continued*.

Codrington, Sir Edward. Retrospect of the proceedings in the prosecution, Rex *v.* Woolcombe, at the suit of Vice admiral Sir E. Codrington, with remarks. Devonport, [n.d.] [Law Tracts, vol. 5.]   144 E

Crane *v.* Price. Remarks on the case of Crane *v.* Price and on the judgment in that action, establishing the validity of Mr. Crane's patent for the combined use of the hot air blast and anthracite or stone coal. By David Rowland. 1842. [Pamphlets, vol. 18.]   144 B

Dill *v.* Watson. An Authentic report of the Clough case, in the Court of Exchequer in Ireland, April 1836. By A. J. Macrory. Dublin, 1836. [Jacob's Tracts, vol. 13.]   144 F

Donaldson *v.* Becket. The cases of the appellants and respondents in the cause of Literary Property, before the House of Lords : wherein the decree of Lord Apsley was reversed. By A Gentleman of the Inner Temple. 1774. 4to.   157 B

Dunn, Elizabeth. Case of Elizabeth Dunn on a trial for Forgery. See Collectanea Juridica, vol. 1, 1791, pp. 481–485.   144 G

Elphinstone *v.* Purchas. See Dale, J. M.

Essex, Earl of. Memoir and trial of Robert, Earl of Essex. See Criminal Trials, vol. 1, 1832, pp. 277–388.   51 D

Exeter College, Oxford. The case of visitation of colleges, in the House of Lords, in Exeter College case. See E. Stillingfleet's Ecclesiastical Cases, part 2, 1704, pp. 411–436.   49 E

Exeter, Dean of, The Queen *v.* See Barnes, R.

Fabrigas *v.* Mostyn. The proceedings at large in a cause on an action brought by A. Fabrigas against John Mostyn, governor of the island of Minorca, for false imprisonment, tried before Mr. Justice Gould, in the Court of Common Pleas, in Guildhall, London. 1773. folio.   49 H

Fiennes, Nathaniel. A true and full relation of the prosecution, arraignment, tryall and condemnation of Nathaniel Fiennes, late colonel and governor of the city and castle of Bristoll. By W. Prynne and C. Walker. 1644. 8vo.   118 E

Flamank *v.* Simpson. See Phillimore, Sir R. J.

French Midwife. A Hellish Murder committed by a French midwife on the body of her husband Jan. 27, 168$\frac{7}{8}$, for which she was arraigned at the Old Baily and pleaded guilty and the day following received sentence to be burnt. 1688. [Tracts, 1688-9.]   118 E

Friend, Sir John. The tryal and condemnation of Sir John Friend, knight, for high treason. 1696. See Impeachment of Lords. 1701. folio.   118 G

Geddington, Rex *v.* See Amos, A.

Gesvres, Marquis de. The case of Impotency debated, in the late famous tryal at Paris, between the Marquis de Gesvres and Mademoiselle de Mascranny. 2 vols. 1714. 12mo.   118 A

Gibson *v.* Hargrave. Report of the trial (in Ejectment) Doe dem. Gibson and others, *v.* Hargrave and others, Lancaster Assizes, March 23, 1837. Preston, 1838. 8vo.   50 A

Gorham *v.* Bishop of Exeter. See Moore, E. F.

Grindall *v.* Grindall. Report of the trial of an action of Ejectment between Charles Edmund Grindall, as lessor of the plaintiff, and Captain Sturt Grindall, R.N. defendant. 1830. 8vo. 50 B

992

TRIALS, CIVIL AND CRIMINAL—*continued.*

Gurney and others, Regina *v.* Report of the case of the Queen *v.* Gurney and others in the Court of Queen's Bench. By W. F. Finlason. 1870. 8vo.   **51 G**

Halpin, William G. Report of the trial of W. G. Halpin, for treason felony, at the county of Dublin commission court, November 1867. Dublin, 1868. 8vo.   **50 A**

Hampden, Right Rev. R. D. See Jebb, R.

Hanson, Joseph. The trial of an indictment against Joseph Hanson, for a conspiracy to aid the weavers of Manchester in raising their wages. 1809. 8vo.   **51 E**

Harrison *v.* Alexander. See Attorneys.

Hebbert *v.* Purchas. See Dale, J. M.

Henry, W. C. and others *v.* Great Northern Railway Co. and others. A suit relating to the rights of preference shareholders in the Great Northern Railway Co. Report of the hearing before V.C. Sir W. P. Wood and his judgment and of the hearing before the full court of appeal in chancery and their lordships' judgments. 1857. 8vo.   **51 E**

Hiddingh *v.* South African Association. 'Wynberg Times' Law Reports Supplement. Hiddingh *versus* South African Association and others. 2nd ed. Wynberg, 1885. 12mo. **51 G**

Horner *v.* Liddiard. See Croke, A.

Hunt. The King *v.* John and Leigh Hunt. A report of the trial 'The King *v.* John and Leigh Hunt,' for a libel on the Prince Regent ; before Lord Ellenborough and a special jury. 1812. 12mo.   **118 B**

Jersey, States of the Island of, *v.* Nicolle. See Channel Islands.

Jones *v.* Corporation of Trinity-house. See Skerries.

Kelly, Robert. See Fenian Conspiracy.

Kinnear, John. The trial of John Kinnear, indicted with others for a conspiracy ; at Guildhall, London. 1819. 8vo. **51 F**

Lincoln, Bishop of. The Bishop of Lincoln's Case. By E. S. Roscoe. 1891. 8vo.   **53 F**

London, Bishop of. An exact account of the whole proceedings against Henry, lord bishop of London, before the lord chancellor and the other ecclesiastical commissioners. 1688. [Tracts, 1688–9.]   **118 E**

Long *v.* Bishop of Cape Town. The case of Long *v.* Bishop of Cape Town, embracing the opinions of the judges of the Colonial court, with the decision of the Privy Council. 1866. 8vo.   **51 G**

Luby, Thomas and others. See Fenian Conspiracy.

Mackreth, Robert. Argument for Mr. Mackreth's petition of rehearing, on a decree made at the Rolls and affirmed by the Lord Chancellor. See Hargrave's Juridical Arguments, vol. 1, 1797, pp. 453–470.   **144 G**

Maclean, Alexander. Cause in lunacy. Reduction of the will of the late Colonel Maclean. 1861. [Pamphlets, vol. 20.] **144 B**

Mander *v.* Pearson. Report of the Wolverhampton meeting house case, 'Attorney General and Mander *v.* Pearson,' before Lord Cottenham. 1836. [Law Tracts, vol. 4.]   **144 E**

Margarot, Maurice. The trial of Maurice Margarot, delegate from London to the British convention, before the high court of Justiciary at Edinburgh for sedition. 1794. 8vo. **50 B**

TRIALS, CIVIL AND CRIMINAL—*continued.*

Martin *v.* Mackonochie. See Dale, J. M. and Phillimore, Sir R. J.

Maybrick, Florence Elizabeth. The Maybrick case. By A. W. Macdougall. 1891. 8vo.   51 F

Millar *v.* Taylor. See Literature.

Milne and others, Rex *v.* Report of a trial (The King *v.* Milne and others) upon an indictment for conspiracy, against six defendants, in the Court of King's Bench, at Westminster, Feb. 21, 1818. The suppressed trial for conspiracy (Pitt *v.* Milne) in the Common Pleas at Westminster, Feb. 21, 1820. By Charles Pitt. 1820. [Jacob's Tracts, vol. 12.]   144 F

Morgan and Ridge *v.* London Dock Company. Report of the trial of Thomas Morgan the younger and Frederic Ridge *v.* The London Dock Company in the Court of Exchequer. 1860. 8vo.   50 B

Moss *v.* Smith. In the Common Pleas. Moss *v.* Smith. Tried before lord chief justice Wilde and a Special jury. [1850.] 8vo.   51 F

Mountague, J., W. L. Newman, J. Nelson, and four others, Rex *v.* See Thames, The.

Nelson and Brand, The Queen *v.* See Cockburn, Sir A. J. E.

Nightingale *v.* Stockdale. Report of the trial in an action for a libel contained in a review of the ' Portraiture of Methodism ' tried at Guildhall before Lord Ellenborough and a special jury, March 11, 1809. [n.d.] 8vo.   118 B

Norton *v.* Reilly. Decree of Lord Chancellor Northington in the remarkable case of Norton *v.* Reilly and others. See Collectanea Juridica, vol. 1, 1791, pp. 458–462.   144 G

Odwin *v.* Forbes. See Henry, J.

O'Keefe *v.* Cullen. Report of the action for Libel brought by Rev. Robert O'Keeffe against Cardinal Cullen. By H. C. Kirkpatrick. 1874. 8vo.   50 B

Onslow *v.* Horne. The whole proceedings in the cause on the action brought by George Onslow, Esq. against the Rev. Mr. Horne on April 6 at Kingston for a defamatory libel. 1770. [Tracts on Libel, vol. 3.]   144 F

Owen, William. The trial of Mr. Wm. Owen, bookseller, near Temple Bar, for publishing a libel : entitled ' The case of Alexander Murray, esq.' 1765. [Tracts on Libel, vol. 3.] 144 F

Paine, Thomas. Proceedings on the trial of Thomas Paine, for a libel upon the revolution and settlement of the crown and legal government as by law established ; tried in the court of King's Bench, 18 Dec. 1792. 1793. 8vo.   51 G

Panton *v.* Williams. Sir H. Jenner's Judgment in Panton *v.* Williams. 1840. [Pamphlets, vol. 1.]   144 A

Parry, William. Trial of Dr. William Parry. See Criminal Trials, 1832, pp. 246–276.   51 D

Paterson, Thomas. ' The Man Paterson.' God versus Paterson. The extraordinary Bow-Street Police Report [Trial of T. Paterson, editor of the ' Oracle of Reason,' charged with exhibiting to view a profane paper in a thoroughfare. Compiled by W. J. Birch. 1843] 8vo.   118 B

Perrin *v.* Blake. Case of Perrin and Blake in the King's Bench. See Collectanea Juridica, vol. 1, 1791, pp. 283–322.   144 G

TRIALS, CIVIL AND CRIMINAL—*continued.*

Preston, Thomas. Fairburn's edition of the proceedings on the arraignment and discharge of Thomas Preston. 1817. 8vo. **50 B**

Queens' College, Cambridge. The case of the President of Queens' College, Cambridge, determined in the Court of Chancery by Lord Eldon. Edited by C. Bowdler. 1821. [Jacob's Tracts, vol. 2.] **144 E**

Ravaillac, François. See Sully, Duc de.

Rayner, William. The tryal of William Rayner, for printing and publishing a libel intitled, Robin's Reign ; or, Seven's the Main. 1732. [Tracts on Libel, vol. 3.] **144 F**

Regicides, Twenty-nine. The indictment, arraignment, tryal and judgment at large of 29 Regicides, the murderers of King Charles the First. 1724. 8vo. **51 E**

Reynolds v. Buckley &c. A Report of the actions in the Queen's Bench of Reynolds v. Buckley and others, and Lyle v. Richards and others, and of the suit in Chancery, of Thomas v. Richards and others, to determine the boundary between the mines in Cornwall, known as West Basset and South Frances. By John Finch. 1872. 8vo. **51 G**

Rough, William. Report of Privy Council in the case of William Rough, sergeant at law, complainant, against John Murray, Esquire, respondent. 1825. 8vo. **51 F**

Rowe v. Grenfell and Rowe v. Brenton and another. See Halcomb, John.

St. Albans Raid. The St. Albans Raid : or Investigation into the charges against Lieut. Bennett H. Young and Command, for their acts at. St. Albans, Vt., on the 19 October 1864. By L. N. Benjamin. Montreal, 1865. 8vo. **51 E**

St. Asaph, Dean of. The speeches of the Dean of St. Asaph's counsel, in the Court of King's Bench, Westminster, in shewing cause why a new trial should be granted. 1785. [Tracts on libel, vol. 3.] **144 F**

See also LIBEL.

Salkeld v. Johnston and others. See Ripley, W. R.

Saunders v. Smith. See Crawford, G. M.

Sheppard v. Bennett. See Stephens, A. J.

Small v. Attwood. See Younge, E.

Smyth *versus* Smyth. A narrative of this extraordinary trial in the form of a speech by Sir Frederic Thesiger, Q.C., the defendant's counsel. 1869. [Pamphlets, vol. 38.] **144 C**

Statement relative to the ejectment, Smyth v. Smyth, tried at Gloucester August 10, 11, 12, 1853. 1854. By T. M. Cattlin. 1854. [Pamphlets, vol. 38.] **144 C**

Southampton, 4 Earl of. Memoir and trial of Robert Earl of Essex, and Henry Earl of Southampton. See Criminal Trials, vol. 1, 1832, pp. 277–388. **51 D**

Spong v. Spong. See Stevens, W.

Sullivan, A. M. and R. Pigott. See Fenian Conspiracy.

Tatham v. Wright. The great will cause, Tatham v. Wright, tried before Mr. Baron Gurney, and a special jury, at the Lancaster Lammas assizes. 1834. Lancaster, [n.d.] 12mo. **50 B**

TRIALS, CIVIL AND CRIMINAL—*continued.*

Teynham *v.* **Tyler.** Report of the proceedings on the trial of the cause, Doe, on the demise of Lord Teynham, against C. H. Tyler, in the Court of Common Pleas at Westminster. 1830. 8vo. **51 G**

Thornton, Abraham. See Battle, Trial by.

Throckmorton, Sir Nicholas. Memoir and trial of Sir N. Throckmorton. See Criminal Trials, 1832, pp. 40–120. **51 D**

Tooke, John Horne. Trial of J. H. Tooke for high treason, at the Old Bailey, November 1794. 2 vols. in 1. 1795. 8vo. **50 B**

Twycross *v.* **Grant.** Report of the case of Twycross *v.* Grant with notices of the previous cases on the liabilities of promoters of companies. By W. F. Finlason. 1877. 8vo. **51 E**

·Tyng, Rev. Stephen H., junior. Trial of the Rev. S. H. Tyng, jr., rector of the church of the Holy Trinity, New York, in the chapel of St. Peter's church, New York, February 1868. New York, 1868. 8vo. **60 B**

Walsh *v.* **Kebabi.** Constantinople consular law reports No. 1. Walsh *v.* Kebabi, before Sir Edmund Hornby. Constantinople, 1864. [Pamphlets, vol. 26.] **144 P**

Warren, John. Report of the trial of John Warren, for treason-felony, at the county Dublin commission, commencing the 30th October, 1867. Reported by W. G. Chamney. Dublin, 1867. 8vo. **50 A**

Watson, James, senior. Fairburn's Edition of the proceedings on the Trial of James Watson, senior, for high treason; with the arraignment and discharge of Arthur Thistlewood, Thomas Preston and John Hooper, tried in the court of King's Bench June 9, 1817, and following days. 1817. 8vo. **50 B**

West *v.* **Erissey.** Case of West *v.* Erissey in the Exchequer, Trinity 1726. See Collectanea Juridica, vol. 1, 1791, pp. 463–467. **144 G**

Westerton *v.* **Liddell.** See Moore, E. F.

Wilkes *v.* **Wood.** The case of general warrants, John Wilkes against Robert Wood. See C. Lofft's Reports of cases, 1776, pp. 1–19. **74 E**

Windham, William Frederick. An Inquiry into the state of mind of W. F. Windham of Fellbrigg hall, Norfolk, before Samuel Warren, Q.C. and a special jury. 1862. 8vo. **118 B**

Woodfall, Rex *v.* A Letter to the jurors of Great Britain, occasioned by an opinion of the Court of King's Bench, read by lord chief justice Mansfield, in the case of the King and Woodfall. By George Rous. 2nd ed. 1785. [Tracts on Libel, vol. 3.] **144 F**

Wooler, Thomas Jonathan. See Lincoln's Inn.

Zenger, John Peter. The trial of J. P. Zenger, of New-York, printer: who was charged with having printed and published a libel against the Government and acquitted. 1765. [Tracts on Libel, vol. 3.] **144 F**

See also ALEXANDRA, THE, ALMON, JOHN, TRIAL OF, AMEER KHAN, BANBURY PEERAGE, BANDA AND KIRWEE BOOTY, BARBER, W. H., BLOCKADE, BLUNDELL, B., CARR, SIR J., CAUSES CÉLÈBRES, COMMENDAMS, CRICKLADE CASE, D'ISRAELI, B., DOUGLAS, G., DYCE SOMBRE, D. O., FENIAN CONSPIRACY, GUNPOWDER PLOT, HABEAS CORPUS, HANOVER, HARVEY, D. W., HEWLEY, LADY S., HONE, W.,

TRIALS, CIVIL AND CRIMINAL—*continued.*
JOHNSON, A., JOHNSTON, G., QUO WARRANTO, RALEIGH, SIR W., RUGBY SCHOOL, SACHEVERELL, H., STIRLING, EARLDOM OF, STOCKDALE, J., TICHBORNE, SIR R., WELLESLEY, W. L. and ZULUETA, P. DE.

TRIALS, COLLECTIONS OF.
American criminal trials. By P. W. Chandler. 2 vols. Boston, 1841–44. 12mo. **59 D**
Central Criminal Court. Minutes of evidence from November 1834 to April 1891. 113 vols. 1835–91. 8vo. **50 C–H**
A Collection and abridgement of celebrated criminal trials in Scotland 1536 to 1784. By Hugo Arnot. Edinburgh, 1785. 4to. **49 H**
A Collection of trials chiefly for high treason. 1584–1685. folio. **118 G**
A Collection of trials for high treason, murder, rapes, &c. 1603–1721. folio. **118 G**
Criminal Trials. By David Jardine. 2 vols. 1832. 12mo. **51 D**
The history of the most remarkable tryals in Great Britain and Ireland in capital cases both by the methods of ordeal, combat and attainder and by the ecclesiastical, civil and common laws. 1715. 8vo. **51 D**
Reports of trials for murder by poisoning. By G. L. Browne and C. G. Stewart. 1883. 8vo. **50 B**
See also CHARLES II., NEWGATE CALENDAR and STATE TRIALS.

TRIGG MINOR DEANERY, CORNWALL.
Parochial and family history of deanery of Trigg Minor. By Sir John Maclean. 3 vols. 1873–79. 4to. **86 F**

TRINIDAD.
Chronological table of the royal orders in council and ordinances promulgated in Trinidad, 1831–1877. Port-of-Spain, 1877. 8vo. **36 C**
Laws of Trinidad, 1831 to 1848. 1852. 8vo. **36 C**
The same. 1832–1882. Revised ed. by G. L. Garcia. 5 vols. 1883–4. 8vo. **36 C**
Trinidad Ordinances, 1850–1888. 10 vols. Port-of-Spain, 1850–89. folio & 8vo. **36 C**

TRINITY HOUSE.

The royal charter of confirmation granted by King James II.
to the Trinity house of Deptford Strond. 1730. 8vo. **88 D**
The same. New ed. 1825. 8vo. **88 D**

TRIPIER, Louis.

Les Codes Français collationnés sur les textes officiels. 15me
éd. Paris, 1864. 8vo. **58 G**

TRISTRAM, Thomas Hutchinson.

The contentious practice of the high court of justice in respect
of grants of probates and administrations. 1881. 8vo. **53 E**
Coote's Common Form Practice and Tristram's Contentious
Practice. 10th ed. by T. H. Tristram. 1888. 8vo. **12 D**

TROKELOWE, John.

Johannis de Trokelowe et Henrici de Blaneforde, monachorum
S. Albani; Chronica et annales. Edited by H. T. Riley.
1866. 8vo. **101 G**

TROLLOPE, Rev. William.

History of royal foundation of Christ's hospital with memoirs
of eminent Blues. 1834. 4to. **89 F**

TROPLONG, Raymond Théodore.

De la contrainte par corps en matière civile et de commerce.
Paris, 1847. 8vo. **58 E**
De la prescription. 4me éd. 2 vols. Paris, 1857. 8vo. **58 E**
De la Vente. 5me éd. 2 vols. Paris, 1856. 8vo. **58 E**
De l'Echange et du Louage. 3me éd. 2 vols. Paris, 1859.
8vo. **58 D E**
Des donations entre-vifs et des testaments. 2me éd. 4 vols.
Paris, 1862. 8vo. **58 D**
Des priviléges et hypothèques, ou commentaire du titre XVIII
du livre III du Code Napoléon. 5me éd. et Commentaire
de la loi du 23 Mars 1855 sur la Transcription en matière
hypothécaire. 5 vols. Paris, 1854–56. 8vo. **58 E**
Du Cautionnement et des transactions. Paris, 1846. 8vo.
58 E
Du contrat de mariage et des droits respectifs des époux. Troisième édition. 4 vols. Paris, 1857. 8vo. **58 E**

TROPLONG, RAYMOND THÉODORE—*continuea*.
Du contrat de société civile et commerciale. 2 vols. Paris,
1843. 8vo. 58 E
Du dépôt et du séquestre, et des contrats aléatoires. Paris, 1845.
8vo. . 58 E
Du Mandat. Paris, 1846. 8vo. 58 E
Du Nantissement, du Gage et de l'Antichrèse. Paris, 1847.
8vo. 58 E
Du Prêt. Paris, 1845. 8vo. 58 E

TROTTER, JOHN GLASSE.
Appeals from the convictions and orders of justices. 1884.
8vo. 12 B

TROUTBECK, JOHN.
Survey of the ancient and present state of the Scilly Islands.
Sherborne, [1796.] 8vo. 87 A

TROVER.
A Treatise of Trover. 1696. 12mo. 49 C
See also NISI PRIUS and TORTS.

TROWBRIDGE.
A Concise history of Trowbridge. By James Bodman.
Bristol, 1814. 12mo. 93 F

TROWER, CHARLES FRANCIS.
The law of debtor and creditor. 1860. 8vo. 52 E
The law of building of churches, parsonages and schools ; and
of divisions of parishes and places. 1867. 8vo. 161 A
The same. 2nd ed. 1874. 8vo. 9 B

TRURO, CORNWALL.
Some account of the proceedings at the election for Truro,
August 3–6, 1830, as reported in the West Briton, Supplement containing petitions of the candidates and burgesses,
with a report of the proceedings before the select committee
of the House of Commons, Second supplement containing
a report of the proceedings at the election on the 3rd of May,
1831, Farther account of the election proceedings to their
successful termination on 15 December 1832, and Address
on occasion of Mr. W. Tooke's visit to Truro Sep.–Oct.
1833. 1830–33. 8vo. 87 A

TRUSTS AND TRUSTEES.

The law relating to Trusts and Trustees. By H. Godefroi.
2nd ed. 1891. 8vo.   11 I

The Trustee Acts, containing the trustee act 1850, the trustee
extension act 1852 and the trustee act 1888. By G. B.
Hamilton. 1889. 8vo.   11 I

The student's guide to Trusts and Partnerships. By John
Indermaur. 2nd ed. 1889. 8vo.   64 F

Manual of the law relating to Trusts and Trustees. By A.
Underhill. 3rd ed. 1888. 8vo.   64 F

Practical treatise on law of Trusts and Trustees. By T. Lewin.
8th ed. by F. A. Lewin. 1885. 8vo.   11 I

Lord St. Leonards' Act to further amend law of property and
to relieve trustees. By J. S. Vaizey. 1860. 12mo. 174 D

Relief of trustees desirous of relinquishing their trusts. By
G. R. Clarke. 1859. [Pamphlets, vol. 12.]   144 A

Law relating to Trustees. By James Hill. 1845. 8vo. 53 I

A Collection of cases on the question whether trustees take
the legal estate or not. See Law Journal Tracts, 1825–6,
pp. 275–328.   144 G

See COOKE, E., GRANT, H., HAMPSON, SIR G. F., LUCAS,
R. DE N. and WILLIS, J. W.

See also INVESTMENTS and USES.

TRUTH.

Search after truth. By Nicolas Malebranche. Translated by
R. Sault. 1694. 8vo.   78 A

Truth and its counterfeits. A lecture by Sir W. P. Wood,
delivered before the Young Men's Christian Association in
Exeter hall. 1856. [Pamphlets, vol. 23.]   144 B

TRYE, JOHN.

The Filacer's office in the Court of King's-Bench. 1684.
12mo.   49 B

TUCK, HENRY.

The railway shareholder's manual ; or, practical guide to all the
railways in the world. 6th ed. 1845. 12mo.   118 A

TUCKER, JOSIAH.

A Treatise concerning civil government, in three parts. 1781.
8vo.   49 E

TUDESCHIS, Nicolaus, Archiepiscopus Panormitanus.

Cum additionibus Z. Ferrerii, nuperrime in lucem editis et cum quibusdam aliis tractatibus alias non impressis'; prima [et secunda] pars. Abbatis Siculi Panor. super secundo Decretalium cum casuum Bernardi interpositione, &c. 2 vols in 1. Lugduni, 1513. folio.

Commentaria Juridica. 10 vols. in 4. Venetiis, 1617-18. folio.

Commentarium ; seu, Lectura Panormitani. 5 vols. in 3. Lugduni, 1524. folio.

TUDOR, Owen Davis.

Charitable trusts act 1853, and a selection of schemes preceded by a summary of the law of Charities. 1854, and 2nd ed. 1871. 12mo.   161 F

The law of Charities and Mortmain, being a third edition of Tudor's Charitable Trusts. By L. S. Bristowe and W. I. Cook. 1889. 8vo.   9 B

A Selection of leading cases on mercantile and maritime law. 1860, and 2nd ed. 1868. 8vo.   172 A

The same. 3rd ed. 1884. 8vo.   10 F

A Selection of leading cases on real property, conveyancing and the construction of wills and deeds. 1856. 8vo. 171 D

The same. 2nd ed. 1863. 8vo.   171 D

The same. 3rd ed. 1879. 8vo.   10 F

The statutes for the improvement of the jurisdiction of equity and other acts, all the new orders with notes. 1852. 12mo.   161 B

TUDORS, The.

A Chronicle of England during the reigns of the Tudors, 1485-1559. By Charles Wriothesley. Edited by W. D. Hamilton. [Camden Society, n.s. vols. 11 and 20.] 2 vols. 1875-77. 8vo.   85 D

TUFTON, Family of.

Memorials of the family of Tufton, Earls of Thanet, deduced from various sources of authentic information. Gravesend, 1800. 8vo.   79 C

TUKE, DANIEL HACK.
Rules and list of the present members of the Society for improving the condition of the Insane, and the Prize Essay entitled The progressive changes which have taken place since the time of Pinel in the moral management of the insane. 1854. 8vo. **172 B**

TUKE, JOHN.
General view of the agriculture of the north riding of Yorkshire. 1800. 8vo. **94 B**

TUNBRIDGE, KENT.
A Concise account of Tunbridge school and of its founder, governors and masters. 2nd ed. 1827. [Jacob's Tracts, vol. 5.] **144 E**
The Queens Wells, a treatise of the nature and vertues of Tunbridge Water. By L. Rowzee. 1671. 12mo. **118 A**
St. John Colbran's Guide to Tunbridge Wells and neighbourhood. 2nd ed. Tunbridge Wells, 1884. 8vo. **88 D**
Tunbridge Wells and its neighbourhood, illustrated by a series of etchings and historical descriptions. By Paul Amsinck. 1810. folio. **89 G**
The Tunbridge Wells guide. By Jasper Sprange. Tunbridge Wells, 1801. 8vo. **88 D**

TUNNICLIFF, WILLIAM.
A Topographical survey of the counties of Somerset, Gloucester, Worcester, Stafford, Chester and Lancaster. Bath, 1789. 8vo. **93 B**

TUPPER, CHARLES LEWIS.
Punjab customary law. 3 vols. Calcutta, 1881. 8vo. **38 C**

TURKS AND CAICOS ISLANDS.
Laws of the Turks and Caicos Islands, 1799–1860. By A. J. Duncombe. 1862. 8vo. **36 B**
Turks and Caicos islands ordinances, 1861–1889. 4 vols. 1861–89. folio. **36 B**

TURMINE, REV. HENRY T. A.
Rambles in the Island of Sheppy. 1843. 8vo. **88 D**

TURNER, EDWARD FRANCIS.
The duties of solicitor to client as to partnership agreements, leases, settlements and wills. 1884. 8vo. **11 G**
The duties of solicitor to client as to sales, purchases, and mortgages of land. 1883. 8vo. **11 G**
The organization of a solicitor's office. 1886. 8vo. **11 G**

TURNER, FRANCIS.
The Contract of Pawn. 1866. 12mo. **173 E**
The same. 2nd ed. 1883. 12mo. **11 B**
Pawnbrokers' Act 1872 with notes. 2nd ed. 1878. 12mo. **173 E**

TURNER, GEORGE and JAMES RUSSELL.
Reports of cases in the Court of Chancery during the time of Lord Chancellor Eldon, 1822–1824. 1 vol. 1832. 8vo. **3 G**

TURNER, SAMUEL.
Costs and present practice of the Court of Chancery. 2nd ed. 1795. 4to. **157 B**
The same. 3rd ed. by R. H. Venables. 2 vols. in 1. 1804. 8vo. **161 D**
The same. 4th ed. by Robert Venables. 2 vols. 1825. 8vo. **161 D**
An Epitome of the practice of the Court of Chancery. 2nd ed. 1809. 8vo. **163 B**
An Epitome of the practice on the equity side of the Court of Exchequer 1806. See Turner's Epitome 1809. 8vo. **163 B**

TURNER, SHARON.
History of England during the Middle Ages, comprising the reigns from William the Conqueror to the accession of Henry the Eighth. 2nd ed. 5 vols. 1825. 8vo. **115 E**
History of the Anglo-Saxons, from the earliest period to Norman Conquest. 5th ed. 3 vols. 1828. 8vo. **115 E**
History of the reign of Henry the Eighth. 2nd ed. 2 vols. 1827. 8vo. **115 E**
History of the reigns of Edward the Sixth, Mary and Elizabeth. 2nd ed. 2 vols. 1829. 8vo. **115 E**

TURNER, Thomas.

Counsel to inventors of improvements in the useful arts. 1850.
12mo.   78 A

The law of Patents and Registration of invention and design
in manufacture. 1851. 8vo.   173 E

Remarks on the amendment of the law of patents for inventions. 1851. [Pamphlets, vol. 8.]   144 A

TURNER, William Henry.

Selections from the records of the city of Oxford illustrating
the municipal history Henry VIII. to Elizabeth [1509–1583].
1880. 8vo.   .   92 E

TURNLEY, Joseph.

The spirit of the Vatican, illustrated by historical and
dramatic sketches during the reign of Henry the Second.
1845. 8vo.   83 H

TURNOR, Edmund.

Collections for the history of the town and soke of Grantham.
1806. 4to.   90 G

TURNOR, Lewis.

History of the ancient town and borough of Hertford. Hertford, 1830. 8vo.   88 C

TURNPIKES.

A Paper on Turnpike trusts and the abolition of tolls. By
H. Kinneir. Swindon, 1867. [Pamphlets, vol. 38.] 144 C

The laws of Turnpike roads by G. C. Oke. 2nd ed. 1860.
8vo.   .   176 G

A Collection of acts of parliament now in force for regulating the Turnpike Roads in England. 1828. 8vo. 176 G

On the mortgage of tolls under Turnpike road acts. See Law
Journal Tracts, 1825–6, pp. 97–114.   144 G

See also Bateman, J.

TUSCANY.

Edict of Grand Duke of Tuscany for reform of criminal
law in his dominions. Warrington, 1789. 8vo.   56 C

TUTBURY, STAFFORDSHIRE.

History of the castle, priory and town of Tutbury. By Sir
Oswald Mosley. 1832. 8vo. 93 C

TWISS, HORACE.

The public and private life of Lord Chancellor Eldon, with
selections from his correspondence. 2nd ed. 3 vols. 1844.
8vo. 79 G

TWISS, SIR TRAVERS.

The law of nations considered as independent political communities. On the rights and duties of nations in time of
peace. 1861, and 2nd ed. 1884. 8vo. 55 B

The law of nations considered as independent political communities. On the rights and duties of nations in time of
war. 2nd ed. 1875. 8vo. 55 B

The letters apostolic of Pope Pius IX., considered with reference to the law of England and the law of Europe. 1851.
8vo. 77 B

Monumenta Juridica. The black book of the Admiralty.
Edited by Sir T. Twiss. 4 vols. 1871–76. 8vo. 102 D

See also BRACTON, H. DE.

TWYSDEN, SIR ROGER.

Certaine considerations upon the government of England.
Edited by J. M. Kemble. [Camden Society, vol. 45.] 1849.
8vo. 85 B

Historiæ Anglicanæ Scriptores X. : Simeon Monachus Du-
nelmensis. Johannes Prior Hagustaldensis. Ricardus Prior
Hagustaldensis. Ailredus Abbas Rievallensis. Radulphus
de Diceto Londoniensis. Johannes Brompton Jorvallensis.
Gervasius Monachus Dorobornensis. Thomas Stubbs
Dominicanus. Gulielmus Thorn Cantuariensis. Henricus
Knighton Leicestrensis ; nunc primum in lucem editi.
1 vol. in 2. 1652. folio. 114 H

TYLER, RANSOM HUBERT.

American ecclesiastical law. Albany, 1866, 8vo. 59 D

Commentaries on the law of Infancy and the law of Coverture.
Albany, 1868. 8vo. 59 E

TYNDALE, WILLIAM.
An Answer to Sir Thomas More's Dialogue The supper of the Lord and Wm. Tracy's Testament expounded. Edited by Rev. Henry Walter. Cambridge, 1850. 8vo.   77 D
Doctrinal treatises and introductions to different portions of the holy scriptures. Edited by Rev. Henry Walter. Cambridge, 1848. 8vo.   77 D
Expositions and notes of sundry portions of the holy scriptures together with the practice of prelates. Edited by Rev. Henry Walter. Cambridge, 1849. 8vo.   77 C

TYRRELL, JOHN.
Suggestions sent to the commissioners appointed to inquire into the laws of real property. Privately printed. 1829. 8vo.   174 F

TYRWHITT, ROBERT PHILIP.
Reports of cases in the courts of Exchequer and Exchequer Chamber, 1830–1835. 5 vols. 1832–37. 8vo.   7 H I
A Digest of the public general statutes. By R. P. Tyrwhitt and T. W. Tyndale. 2 vols. 1822, and Supplement 1826. 3 vols. 1822–26. 4to.   31 E

TYRWHITT, ROBERT PHILIP and T. C. GRANGER.
Reports of cases in the courts of Exchequer and Exchequer Chamber, 1835–1836. 1 vol. 1837. 8vo.   7 I

TYSON, WILLIAM.
The Bristol Memorialist. Bristol, 1823. 8vo.   88 A

TYSSEN, AMHERST DANIEL.
The law of charitable bequests ; with an account of the Mortmain and Charitable uses act 1888. 1888. 8vo.   9 B

TYTLER, ALEXANDER FRASER.
An Essay on Military law and the practice of courts martial. 2nd ed. 1806. 8vo.   172 F

UCKFIELD, SUSSEX.
Operations of the poor law amendment act in the county of Sussex. Reports of the auditor of the Uckfield union. By W. H. Newnham. 1836. 8vo.   93 E

ULMAN, H. Charles.
Lawyers' record and official register of the United States; with a digest of the laws of the several states touching subjects of commercial law. New York, 1872. 8vo. 59 F

ULPIANUS, Domitius.
The Commentaries of Gaius and Rules of Ulpian : translated with notes. By J. T. Abdy and B. Walker. New ed. Cambridge, 1874. 8vo. 63 E
See also Cumin, P.

ULTRA VIRES.
A Treatise on the doctrine of Ultra Vires. By Seward Brice. 2nd ed. 1877. 8vo. 9 F

UMFREVILLE PEDIGREE.
The Umfrevilles, their ancestors and descendants. [1859.] 4to. 126 I

UNDERDOWN, Emanuel Maguire.
The law of art copyright. 1863. 12mo. 164 G

UNDERHILL, Arthur.
A Concise guide to Modern Equity. 1885. 12mo. 64 D
A Concise manual of the law relating to private Trusts and Trustees. 2nd ed. 1884. 12mo. 64 F
The same. 3rd ed. 1888. 12mo. 64 F
A Popular summary of the South Staffordshire Mines Drainage act, 1873. [1873.] 12mo. 172 F
The procedure of the Chancery division of the high court of justice. 1881. 8vo. 52 B
Settled land acts 1882 and 1884. 2nd ed. 1885. 12mo. 13 H
A Summary of the law of Torts. 1873. 12mo. 178 E
The same. 3rd ed. 1881. 12mo. 178 E
The same. 4th ed. 1884. 12mo. 64 F
The same. 5th ed. 1889. 12mo. 64 F

UNDERHILL, Edward.
Autobiographical anecdotes of E. Underhill, one of the band of Gentlemen Pensioners. See Camden Society, vol. 77, 1859, pp. 132–176. 85 B

UNION ASSESSMENT.

Fry's Union assessment committee acts. 7th ed. by R. C. Glen and A. D. Lawrie. 1887. 12mo.   11 I

The Union Assessment Committee act 1862. By W. G. Lumley. 7th ed. 1864. 12mo.   176 G

Practical remarks upon the Union Assessment Committee act 1862. By H. J. Castle. 1863. 8vo.   176 G

UNITED STATES.

The Bancroft library as material for Pacific States history. [1883.] [Pamphlets, vol. 30.]   144 B

Correspondence on the present relations between Great Britain and the United States of America. [Eleven letters between E. W. Field of London and C. G. Loring of Boston.] Boston, 1862. [Pamphlets, vol. 22.]   144 B

Manual of the Railroads of the United States for 1888 and Directory of railway officials. By H. V. Poor. 2 vols. 1888. 8vo.   129 J

Papers relating to foreign affairs, accompanying the annual message of the President to the second session, 38th congress. 2 vols. Washington, 1865. 8vo.   145 B

Public libraries in the United States of America, their history, condition and management. Special report. Department of the interior, bureau of education. Washington, 1876. 8vo.   82 C

Triumphant democracy; or, fifty years' march of the republic. By A. Carnegie. 1886. 12mo.   78 A

Zell's United States business directory for 1881. 3rd ed. Philadelphia, 1881. 8vo.   195 F

See also ALABAMA CLAIMS and AMERICA.

UNITED STATES, LAWS OF.

A Digest of the reports of the United States courts and of the acts of Congress, from the organization of the government to 1874. By B. V. Abbott. 6 vols. New York, 1867–74. 8vo.   32 D

A Digest of the decisions of the Federal courts from the organization of the government to the present time. By F. C. Brightly. Philadelphia, 1868. 8vo.   59 C

The first book of the Law. By J. P. Bishop. Boston, 1868. 8vo.   59 F

Commentaries on American law. By James Kent. 11th ed. by G. F. Comstock. 4 vols. Boston, 1866. 8vo.   59 A

UNITED STATES, LAWS OF—*continued.*

The organization, jurisdiction, and practice of the courts of the United States. By A. Conkling. 4th ed. Albany, 1864. 8vo.   60 A

A Law dictionary adapted to the constitution and laws of the United States of America. By J. Bouvier. 11th ed. 2 vols. Philadelphia, 1862. 8vo.   59 F

A Synoptical index to the laws and treaties of the United States of America, 1789 to 1851. Prepared under the direction of the Secretary of the Senate. Boston, 1856. 8vo.   32 C

Institutes of American law. By John Bouvier. 4 vols. Philadelphia, 1854. 8vo.   59 A

Commentaries on the constitution of the United States. By J. Story. 3 vols. Boston, 1833. 8vo.   59 A

Admiralty. Decisions in admiralty and maritime causes in the district court of the United States for Massachusetts, 1841-1861. By P. Sprague. Philadelphia, 1861. 8vo.
59 B

Admiralty. The Admiralty jurisdiction, law, and practice of the courts of the United States. By A. Conkling. 2nd ed. 2 vols. Albany, 1857. 8vo.   59 B

Agency. Commentaries on the law of Agency. By J. Story. 7th ed. by I. F. Redfield and W. A. Herrick. Boston, 1869. 8vo.   11 C

Agreements. A Treatise on the validity of verbal agreements as affected by the Statute of Frauds. By M. H. Throop. Vol. 1. Albany, 1870. 8vo.   59 B

Bailments. Commentaries on the law of Bailments. By J. Story. 8th ed. by E. H. Bennett. Boston, 1870. 8vo. 9 A

Banking. The banking system of the state of New York. By John Cleaveland. 2nd ed. by G. S. Hutchinson. New York, 1864. 8vo.   59 B

Bankruptcy. The Bankrupt law of the United States. By F. C. Brightly. Philadelphia, 1869. 8vo.   59 B

Bankruptcy. An Act to establish a uniform system of Bankruptcy throughout the United States. New York, 1842. 8vo.   59 A

Bills of Exchange. Commentaries on the law of Bills of Exchange as administered in England and America. By J. Story. 4th ed. by E. H. Bennett. Boston, 1860. 8vo.
59 E

1009

UNITED STATES, LAWS OF—*continued.*

Claims. History, jurisdiction, and practice of the court of claims of the United States. By Wm. Richardson. 2nd ed. Washington, 1885. [Pamphlets, vol. 39.]   **144 C**

Claims. Rules of the Court of Claims (United States) adopted June 1, 1885, and statutes applicable to the same. Washington, 1885. [Pamphlets, vol. 39.]   **144 C**

Consuls. United States consular regulations, a practical guide for consular officers. Washington, 1868. 8vo.   **59 B**

Contracts. The law of Contracts. By J. I. C. Hare. Boston, 1887. 8vo.   **59 C**

Contracts. Principles of the law of Contracts. By T. Metcalf. New York, 1868. 8vo.   **59 B**

Contracts. Law of Contracts. By T. Parsons. 4th ed. 2 vols. Boston, 1860. 8vo.   **59 B**

Contracts. Law of Contracts. By W. W. Story. 4th ed. 2 vols. Boston, 1856. 8vo.   **59 C**

Conveyancing. A Digest of the Conveyancing, testamentary, and registry laws of all the States of the Union. By J. B. Thornton. Philadelphia, 1847. 8vo.   **59 C**

Copyright. The law of property in intellectual productions. By E. S. Drone. Boston, 1879. 8vo.   **59 C**

Copyright. Patent and Copyright laws 1790 to 1868. By S. D. Law. 2nd ed. New York, 1867. 12mo.   **60 A**

Copyright. Law of Copyright. By G. T. Curtis. Boston, 1847. 8vo.   **59 C**

Corporations. Law of private corporations aggregate. By J. K. Angell and S. Ames. 8th ed. by J. Lathrop. Boston, 1866. 8vo.   **59 C**

Criminal law. Commentaries on the Criminal law. By J. P. Bishop. 3rd ed. 2 vols. Boston, 1865. 8vo.   **59 C**

Criminal Trials. American criminal trials. By P. W. Chandler. 2 vols. 1841–44. 8vo.   **59 D**

Damages. A Treatise on the measure of Damages. By T. Sedgwick. 4th ed. by H. D. Sedgwick. New York, 1868. 8vo.   **59 D**

Dower. The law of Dower. By C. H. Scribner. 2 vols. Philadelphia, 1867. 8vo.   **59 D**

Easements. The American law of Easements and Servitudes. By E. Washburn. 2nd ed. Boston, 1867. 8vo.   **59 D**

Ecclesiastical Law. American ecclesiastical law. By R. H. Tyler. Albany, 1866. 8vo.   **59 D**

UNITED STATES, LAWS OF—*continued.*

Equity. Commentaries on equity jurisprudence as administered in England and America. By J. Story. 13th ed. by M. M. Bigelow. 2 vols. 1886. 8vo.   **59 D**

Equity. Commentaries on equity pleadings according to the practice of the Courts of Equity of England and America. By J. Story. 8th ed. by I. F. Redfield. Boston, 1870. 8vo.   **59 D**

Evidence. The law of Evidence. By Simon Greenleaf. 3 vols. Boston, 1863–60. 8vo.   **59 E**

Extradition. The law of Extradition, international and interstate. By S. T. Spear. Albany, 1879. 8vo.   **59 E**

Highways. Law of Highways. By J. K. Angell and T. Durfee. 2nd ed. by G. F. Choate. 1868. 8vo.   **59 E**

Homicide. The law of Homicide in the United States. By F. Wharton. Philadelphia, 1855. 8vo.   **59 E**

Infancy. Commentaries on the law of Infancy. By R. H. Tyler. Albany, 1868. 8vo.   **59 E**

Insanity. Legislation on Insanity. A collection of all the lunacy laws of the states and territories of the United States, to the year 1883. By G. L. Harrison. Privately Printed. Philadelphia, 1884. 8vo.   **59 G**

Insanity. Medical jurisprudence of insanity. By Isaac Ray. Boston, 1860. 8vo.   **59 G**

Insurance. Digest of Fire Insurance decisions in the courts of Great Britain and North America. By H. A. Littleton and J. S. Blatchley. 2nd ed. New York, 1868. 8vo.   **59 F**

Insurance. The law of fire and life insurance. By J. K. Angell. 2nd ed. Boston, 1855. 8vo.   **59 E**

Insurance. The law and practice of Marine Insurance. By John Duer. 2 vols. New York, 1845–46. 8vo.   **59 E**

Land tenure. Farm land and land laws of the United States. By C. M. Fisher. See Systems of Land tenure, 1881, pp. 497–516.   **78 B**

Leading Cases. American leading cases, being select decisions of American courts in several departments of law. By J. I. C. Hare and H. B. Wallace. 4th ed. 2 vols. Philadelphia, 1857. 8vo.   **59 F**

Limitations of Actions. The limitation of actions at law and suits in equity and admiralty. By J. K. Angell. 5th ed. by J. W. May. Boston, 1869. 8vo.   **59 F**

Maritime Law. A Treatise of Maritime law. By T. Parsons. 2 vols. Boston, 1859. 8vo.   **59 G**

UNITED STATES, LAWS OF—*continued.*

Marriage and divorce. Commentaries on the law of marriage and divorce. By J. P. Bishop. 4th ed. 2 vols. Boston, 1864. 8vo.   **59 G**

Mortgages. A Treatise on the law of Mortgages of real property. By L. A. Jones. Boston, 1878. 8vo.   **59 G**

Mortgages. The law of Mortgages, being a general view of the English and American law upon that subject. By F. Hilliard. 2nd ed. 2 vols. Boston, 1856. 8vo.   **59 G**

Naval Courts-Martial. Law and practice of United States naval Courts-Martial. By A. A. Harwood. New York, 1867. 8vo.   **59 G**

Navigable Rivers. The law of navigable Rivers. By Louis Houck. Boston, 1868. 8vo.   **60 B**

Partnership. Exposition of principles of Partnership. By James Parsons. 1889. 8vo.   **59 G**

Partnership. Commentaries on the law of Partnership. By J. Story. 7th ed. by W. F. Wharton. Boston, 1881. 8vo.   **11 B**

Patents. Law of Patents for useful inventions in the United States of America. By G. T. Curtis. 3rd ed. Boston, 1867. 8vo.   **60 A**

Patents. Patent and Copyright laws 1790 to 1868. By S. D. Law. 2nd ed. New York, 1867. 12mo.   **60 A**

Personal actions. The practice in courts of justice in England and the United States. Vols. 5 and 6, as to the grounds and forms in personal actions. By C. Robinson. 2 vols. Richmond [U.S.], 1868–70. 8vo.   **60 A**

Promissory notes. Commentaries on the law of promissory notes and checks on banks and bankers. By Joseph Story. 6th ed. Boston, 1868. 8vo.   **60 A**

Railways. The law of Railways. By I. F. Redfield. 3rd ed. 2 vols. 1867. 8vo.   **60 A**

Real Property. A Treatise on the American law of Real Property. By E. Washburn. 3rd ed. 3 vols. Boston, 1868. 8vo.   **60 B**

Real property. American law of real property. By F. Hilliard. 3rd ed. 2 vols. New York, 1855. 8vo.   **60 B**

Sales. A Selection of cases on sales of personal property. By C. C. Langdell. Boston, 1872. 8vo.   **60 B**

Sales. The law of sales of personal property. By F. Hilliard. 2nd ed. Philadelphia, 1860. 8vo.   **60 B**

Sales. Law of sales of personal property. By W. W. Story. 2nd ed. Boston, 1853. 8vo.   **60 B**

UNITED STATES, LAWS OF—*continued.*

Slander and Libel. A Treatise on the wrongs called slander and libel. By John Townshend. 3rd ed. New York, 1877. 8vo. **60 B**

State Trials. State Trials during the administrations of Washington and Adams. By F. Wharton. Philadelphia, 1849. 8vo. **57 A**

Statutes. Analytical and compared digest of the constitutions and civil public statutes of all the states, relating to persons and property, in force January 1, 1886. By F. J. Stimson. Boston, 1886. 8vo. ˙ **32 C**

Statutes. Public statutes of United States of America, 1789–1845. By R. Peters. 8 vols. Boston, 1861–62. 8vo. **32 B**

The same, 1845–1855. By G. Minot. 2 vols. Boston, 1852–55. 8vo. **32 B**

The same, 1856–1859. By G. Minot and G. P. Sanger. Boston, 1859. 8vo. **32 B**

The same, 1859–1869. By G. P. Sanger. 4 vols. Boston, 1863–69. 8vo. **32 B C**

Stockholders. A Treatise on the liability of Stockholders in Corporations. By S. D. Thompson. St. Louis, 1879. 8vo. ˙ **60 B**

Tariff Laws. Tariff laws of the United States. By C. F. Williams. 1883. 8vo. **60 B**

Telegraphs. Treatise upon the law of telegraphs. By W. L. Scott and M. P. Jarnagin. Boston, 1868. 8vo. **60 B**

Tidal waters. The right of property in tide waters. By J. K. Angell. 2nd ed. Boston, 1847. 8vo. **60 B**

Torts. The law of remedies for Torts or private wrongs. By F. Hilliard. Boston, 1867. 8vo. **60 B**

Torts. The law of Torts. By F. Hilliard. 2 vols. Boston, 1859. 8vo. **60 B**

Wills. The law of Wills. By I. F. Redfield. 2nd ed. 2 vols. 1867. 8vo. **60 B**

See also AMERICAN LAW, INTERNATIONAL LAW, LAW LISTS and NEW YORK.

UNITED STATES REPORTS.

United States Reports, Supreme Court, 1790 to 1889. 162 vols. Boston, 1855–90. 8vo. **57 A–F**

UPCOTT, WILLIAM.

A Bibliographical account of the principal works relating to English topography. 3 vols. in 4. 1818. 4to. **82 I**

URLIN, RICHARD DENNY.
A Manual of the law relating to the office of trustee. 3rd ed.
1868. 12mo. 53 H

URQUHART, DAVID.
Pamphlets, 1840–1875. 5 vols. 1840–75. 8vo. 143 G
Vol. i. Constitutional and international.
Vol. ii., pt. i. England defenceless since the declaration of Paris ;
pt. ii. India.
Vol. iii. Russia and Turkey.
Vol. iv. The Vatican council of 1870.
Vol. v. Familiar words, effect of their misuse on the character of
men and the fate of nations.
Reflections on thoughts and things, moral, religious, and
political. 1844. 8vo. 78 C

URQUHART, GEORGE.
The experienced solicitor in proceedings under the appellant
jurisdiction of the House of Lords on appeals and writs of
error. 1773. folio. 156 D

URUGUAY.
Republic of Uruguay, International exhibition of mining and
metallurgy, Crystal Palace, London, 1890. Part I. Origin
of the auriferous region of Tacuarembo, by C. B. Posada.
Part II. Catalogue of Minerals and Mining code of the
Republic. 2 parts in 1 vol. 1890. 8vo. 84 D
The Republic of Uruguay. Prospects of 1889. A memorable
year. 1889. 12mo. 84 A
The Republic of Uruguay. Retrospect from 'La Razon.'
The country in 1888, statistical data. 1889. 12mo. 84 A
The Republic of Uruguay. The country in the Paris ex-
hibition. General description and statistical data. Liver-
pool, 1889. 4to. 84 D

USAGES.
The law of Usages and Customs. By J. H. B. Browne. 1875.
8vo. 11 I

USES AND TRUSTS.
A Digest of the law of Uses and Profits of Land. By S. M.
Leake. 1888. 8vo. 10 D
Law of Uses. By W. H. Jones. 1862. 8vo. 176 G

USES AND TRUSTS—*continued.*

An Essay on Uses and Trusts. By F. W. Sanders. 5th ed. 2 vols. 1844. 8vo. **53 I**

Law of Uses and Trusts. By Sir Jeffrey Gilbert. 3rd ed. by E. B. Sugden. 1811. 8vo. **53 I**

An Essay on Uses. By Wm. Cruise. 1795. 8vo. **176 G**

Reading on the law of Uses. By T. Carthew. See Collectanea Juridica, vol. 1, 1791, pp. 369–377. **144 G**

Case on the operation of the statute of Uses, with the opinions of Mr. Booth, and other learned counsel, thereon. See Collectanea Juridica, vol. 1, 1791, pp. 421–432. **144 G**

Reading on the statute of Uses. See Bacon's Law Tracts, 2nd ed., 1741. 8vo. **144 F**

USHER, JAMES, D.D.

The prophecy of Bishop Usher concerning a most dreadful persecution that would fall on the Protestant churches of Europe. 1688. [Tracts, 1688–9.] **118 E**

USURY LAWS.

Observations on the Usury laws. By J. B. Byles. 1845. 12mo. **53 I**

A Summary of the history and law of Usury. By J. B. Kelly. 1835. 8vo. **176 G**

Reasons against the repeal of the Usury laws. 1825. [Jacob's Tracts, vol. 3.] **144 E**

A Treatise on the principles of the Usury laws. By Robert Maugham. 1824. Bound with Laws of Literary Property. 1828. 8vo. **172 A**

A Small treatise against Usury. See Sir J. Child's Discourse of Trade, 4th ed., [1698], pp. 235–260. **78 A**

See also BENTHAM, J., PAWN and PLOWDEN, F.

UTTLEY, THOMAS FIELDEN.

Hints on Criminal law. 1888. 8vo. **64 C**

UXBRIDGE, MIDDLESEX.

The history of Uxbridge. By George Redford and T. H. Riches. Uxbridge, 1818. 8vo. **89 D**

VACCINATION.
Shaw's Manual of the Vaccination law. By A Barrister-at-law [John Lithiby]. 1887. 12mo.   11 I
The law relating to Vaccination. By D. P. Fry. 5th ed. 1872. 8vo.   176 G

VACHER, THOMAS BRITTAIN.
A Pocket digest of Stamp duties. 5th ed. 1862, and 6th ed. 1865. 12mo.   175 G
The same. 7th ed. by G. C. Griffith. 1874. 12mo. 175 G
The same. 8th ed. by G. C. Griffith. 1880. 12mo. 175 G
The same. 9th ed. by G. C. Griffith. 1886. 12mo. 11 G

VAIZEY, JOHN SAVILL.
Law relating to investment of trust money. 1890. 8vo. 11 I
Lord St. Leonards' Act to further amend the law of property, with notes. 1860. 12mo.   174 D
A Treatise on the law of Settlements of property. 2 vols. 1887. 8vo.   13 H
A Collection of precedents and forms; with references and additions to 'A Treatise on the law of Settlements.' 1888. 8vo.   13 H

VALDELOMAR, JUAN DE LA REGUERA.
Guia para el estudio del Derecho Patrio dividido en cinco tablas. Segunda edicion. Madrid, 1805. folio.   39 F

VALIN, RENÉ JOSUÉ.
Nouveau commentaire sur l'ordonnance de la Marine, du mois d'Août 1681. 2 vols. La Rochelle, 1760. 4to.   40 E

VALPY, ABRAHAM JOHN.
Scriptores Latini in usum Delphini, cum notis variorum, variis lectionibus, conspectu codicum et editionum et indicibus locupletissimis. 141 vols. 1819-30. 8vo.   46 A-J

VAN DER LINDEN, JOHANNES.
Institutes of the laws of Holland. Translated by Jabez Henry. 1828. 8vo.   55 D
Institutes of Holland; or, manual of law, practice, and mercantile law. Translated by Henry Juta. Cape Town, 1884. 8vo.   55 D

VAN DER LINDEN, JOHANNES—*continued*.
Judicial, practical, and mercantile guide. Translated from
the Dutch. George Town, 1814. 8vo.   **55 D**

VAN HEYTHUYSEN, F. M.
An Epitome of the Law Library; containing a second edition
of the Rudiments of English Law. Vol. I. The Constitution of the United Kingdom of Great Britain and Ireland.
1826. 12mo.   **116 D**
Equity Draftsman, a collection of precedents drawn by some
of the leading men at the equity bar. 1816. 8vo. **167 C**
The same. 2nd ed. by E. Hughes. 2 vols. 1828. 8vo. **167 C**

VAN LEEUWEN, SIMON.
Commentaries on Roman-Dutch law, revised by C. W. Decker.
Translated from the Dutch by J. G. Kotzé. 2 vols. 1881–
86. 8vo.   **55 D**

VAPEREAU, LOUIS GUSTAVE.
Dictionnaire universel des contemporains, contenant toutes
les personnes notables de la France et des pays étrangers.
3me éd. 1865. 8vo.   **81 E**

VARDON, THOMAS.
Index to the Local and Personal, and Private acts, 1798–1839.
1840. 8vo.   **31 E**

VATTEL, EMMERICH DE.
Law of Nations; or, principles of the law of Nature applied
to the conduct and affairs of Nations and Sovereigns.
2 vols. in I. 1759. 4to.   **155 B**
The same. New ed. 1797. 8vo.   **55 B**

VAUGHAN, SIR JOHN.
The reports and arguments of Sir John Vaughan, late chief
justice of the Court of Common Pleas, 1665–1674. Published by his son Edward Vaughan. 1677. folio. **74 G**

VAUGHAN, ROBERT.
British antiquities revived; or, a friendly contest touching the
soveraignty of the three princes of Wales in ancient times.
Bala, 1834. 4to.   **94 D**

VAUGHAN, REV. ROBERT.
Revolutions in English history. .3 vols. 1859–63. 8vo.
115 G

VAUX, JAMES HARDY.
Memoirs of J. H. Vaux, a swindler and thief, written by himself. [Autobiography, vol. 17.] 2nd ed. 1830. 12mo. 79 A

VEAL, JOHN.
The record and writ practice of the Court of Chancery. 2nd
ed. 1845. 12mo. 161 E

VELAZQUEZ DE LA CADENA, MARIANO.
A Pronouncing dictionary of the Spanish and English languages. 2 vols. in 1. 1852. 8vo. 123 C

VENDORS AND PURCHASERS.
Law and practice relating to vendors and purchasers of real
estate. By J. H. Dart. 6th ed. 2 vols. 1888. 8vo. 13 H
The law relating to vendors and purchasers of real property.
By H. Seaborne. 3rd ed. 1884. 12mo. 64 F
The law of vendors and purchasers of estates. By E. Sugden.
14th ed. 1862. 8vo. 13 I
A Practical treatise of the law of vendors and purchasers of
chattels personal. By T. C. Morton. 1836. 8vo. 177 B
See also CONVEYANCING ACTS, REAL PROPERTY STATUTES
and SALE, LAW OF.

VENEZUELA.
Correspondence between the Venezuelan government and
H.B.M.'s government about the question of the frontier.
Caracas, 1887. folio. 84 H
Emigrant's vade-mecum ; or, guide to the 'price grant' in
Venezuelan Guyana. By M. A. Pattison. 1868. 8vo. 84 A
Ministry of Fomento. Statistical annuary of the United
States of Venezuela. Caracas, 1887. folio. 84 H

VENICE.
Discorso dell' origine, forma, leggi ed uso dell' officio dell' inquisitione, nella città e dominio di Venetia. Del Paolo
dell' ordine de' Servi [father Paul Sarpi]. 1639. 8vo. 118 A
The generall historie of the magnificent state of Venice. By
Thomas de Fougasses. Englished by W. Shute. 1612.
folio. 113 G

VENICE—*continued.*
Report to the Master of .the Rolls upon the documents in the archives and public libraries of Venice. By T. D. Hardy. 1866. 8vo. **97 H**

VENTILATION.
The question of Ventilation considered, its importance and the consequences of its neglect. By R. A. Westbrook. 1861. [Pamphlets, vol. 15.] **144 B**
Ventilation, its vital importance and efficient application. [Pamphlets, vol. 27.] **144 B**

VENTRIS, SIR PEYTON.
Reports in two parts. Part I. Select cases adjudged in the King's Bench, 20–36 Car. II., 1668–1684. Part II. Choice cases adjudged in the Common Pleas, 21 Car. II. to 3 Will. and Mary, 1669–1691. With many remarkable and curious cases in the court of Chancery. 1696. folio.
The same. 3rd ed. by Serjeant Richardson. 2 vols. 1716. folio.
The same. 4th ed. 2 vols. in 1. 1726. folio. **74 G**

VERGIL, POLYDORE.
English history; vol. 1, containing the first eight books, comprising the period prior to the Norman conquest; vol. 2. Three books, comprising the reigns of Henry VI., Edward IV., and Richard III. Edited by Sir Henry Ellis. [Camden Society, vols. 36 and 29.] 2 vols. 1846–44. 8vo. **85 A**

VERNEY FAMILY.
Letters and papers of the Verney family down to the end of the year 1639. Edited by John Bruce. [Camden Society, vol. 56.] 1853. 8vo. **85 B**
Verney papers. Notes of proceedings in the Long Parliament, temp. Charles I., printed from original pencil memoranda taken in the House by Sir R. Verney. Edited by J. Bruce. [Camden Society, vol. 31.] 1845. 8vo. **85 A**

VERNON, CHRISTOPHER.
Considerations for regulating the Exchequer. 1642. 12mo. **48 B**

VERNON, GEORGE.
The life of Dr. Peter Heylyn, chaplain to Charles I. and Charles II. 1682. 12mo. **79 A**

VERNON, George William and J. B. SCRIVEN.
Irish reports ; or, reports of cases in the King's courts, Dublin ;
with select cases in the House of Lords of Ireland, 1786–
1788. Dublin, 1790. 8vo. **15 F**

VERNON, Thomas.
Cases argued and adjudged in the High Court of Chancery ;
published from his manuscripts by order of the Court.
2 vols. 1726–28. folio.
The same. 3rd ed. by John Raithby. 2 vols. 1828. 8vo. **3 G**

VESEY, Francis.
Reports of Cases argued and determined in the High Court
of Chancery, in the time of Lord Chancellor Hardwicke,
from 1746 to 1755. 2 vols. 1771. folio.
The same. 2nd ed. 2 vols. 1773. folio.
The same. 4th ed. by Robert Belt. 2 vols. 1818. 8vo. **3 G**
A Supplement to the Reports in Chancery. By Robert Belt.
2nd ed. 1825. 8vo. **3 G**

VESEY, Francis, Junior.
Reports of cases in the court of Chancery, 1789 to 1817.
2nd ed. 19 vols. 1827. 8vo. **3 H I**
A Digested index to the 19 vols. of reports by Francis Vesey.
By a Barrister. 1822. 8vo. **3 I**
A Supplement to the Reports of Francis Vesey. By J. E.
Hovenden. 2 vols. 1827. 8vo. **3 I**

VESEY, Francis and John BEAMES.
Reports of cases in the Court of Chancery in the time of Lord
Chancellor Eldon, 1812–1814. 2nd ed. 3 vols. 1818.
8vo. **3 I**

VESTRIUS, Octavianus.
Octaviani Vestrii jurisconsulti forocorneliensis in Romanæ
Aulæ actionem et judiciorum mores ad Jacobum Pellæum
ΕΙΣΑΓΩΓΗ. Venetiis, 1547. 12mo. **118 A**

VESTRY CLERKS.
A Manual for overseers . . . and vestry clerks. By H. Owen.
8th ed. 1887. 8vo. **11 A**

VICHY.
Vichy and its therapeutical resources. By Prosser James.
5th ed. 1883. 8vo. **84 A**

[VICTOR, BENJAMIN.]
The Widow of the Wood. 1755. 12mo. **118 A**

VICTORIA, AUSTRALIA.
Catalogue of the library of the Supreme Court of Victoria.
1861, and 2nd ed. 1873, and Catalogue of books recently
added to the library. 1864. 3 vols. Melbourne, 1861-73.
8vo. **82 C**
Illustrated handbook of Victoria. Edited by James Thomson.
Melbourne, 1886. 4to. **84 D**
Justice's manual, with the Justice's statute and notes thereon.
By J. J. Casey. Melbourne, 1872. 8vo. **55 D**
The Official Post Office Directory of Victoria, 1871-2, 1880,
1884-5. 3 vols. Melbourne, 1871-84. 8vo. **195 F**
Victorian Acts, 1855-1890. 21 vols. Melbourne, 1855-91.
4to. **35 B C**
Victorian Statutes, 1829-1865. 4 vols. Melbourne, 1866.
8vo. **35 B**
See also ADAMSON, T. and ARCHER, W. H.

VICTORIA, QUEEN OF ENGLAND.
A History of our own times, from the accession of Queen
Victoria to the general election of 1880. By Justin
McCarthy. 4 vols. 1881. 8vo. **116 G**
The Jubilee of Queen Victoria, an account of the procession
to Westminster Abbey, &c. By A. H. T[urnbull]. Edin-
burgh, 1887. 12mo. **78 A**

VIDIAN, ANDREW.
The Exact Pleader: a book of entries of choice, select, and
special pleadings in the court of King's Bench, in the reign
. of Charles II. 1684. folio.

VIEYRA, ANTONIO.
A Dictionary of the Portuguese and English languages, in
two parts. 2 vols. Transtagano, 1773. 4to. **123 G**

VILLAGE COMMUNITIES.
The English village community, an essay in economic history.
By Frederic Seebohm. 2nd ed. 1883. 8vo.   83 H
Village communities in the East and West. By H. S. Maine.
1871. 8vo.   83 I

VINCENT, CHARLES EDWARD HOWARD.
A Police code and manual of criminal law. 1881. 8vo. 12 B

VINER, CHARLES.
A General abridgment of law and equity ; with Index, by a
Gentleman of Lincoln's Inn. [Robert Kelham.] 24 vols.
in 23. Aldershot, 1742–58. folio.   38 G H
A Supplement to Viner's Abridgment. [Compiled by J. E.
Watson, S. Comyn, J. Sedgwick, and others.] 6 vols. 1799–
1806. 8vo.   14 A B

VINNIUS, ARNOLDUS.
Institutionum imperialium Commentarius. Editio ultima.
Lugd. Bat., 1709. 4to.   49 G

VIRGILIUS, PUBLIUS MARO.
Georgica in quinque linguas conversa. 1827. folio.   47 I
Hexametrical experiments ; or, a version of four of Virgil's
Pastorals, done in a structure of verse similar to that of the
original Latin. 1838. 4to.   83·J
See also Delphin Classics, vols. 1–8, 1819. 8vo.   46 A

VIRGIN ISLANDS.
Virgin Islands Ordinances, 1857–1870. 2 vols. 1857–70
folio.   36 F

VIRGINIA.
The acts of assembly now in force in the colony of Virginia.
Williamsburg, 1752. folio.   37 G
Acts of Assembly passed in the colony of Virginia, 1662 to
1715. 1727. folio.   37 G
The code of Virginia ; with the Declaration of independence
and Constitution of the United States and the Declaration
of rights and Constitution of Virginia. Richmond, 1849.
8vo.   60 C

1022

VIRGINIA—*continued.*
Emigration to Virginia (East) ' or the Old Dominion State.'
Report from J. Newton, of his second visit to this state.
3rd ed. [n.d.] [Pamphlets, vol. 38.]   **144 C**

VITRIARIUS, PHILIPPUS REINHARDUS.
Corpus juris publici ad ductum institutionum juris publici
P. R. Vitriarii, elaboratum a Johanne Friderico Pfeffingero.
4 vols. 1739–31. C. G. Riccii Repertorium in J. F. Pfeffin-
geri corpus juris publici i.e. Vitriarium illustratum universum.
1741. 5 vols. Gothæ, 1739–41. 4to.   **47 I**

VIVISECTION.
'The Woman' and The Age, a letter addressed to W. E.
Gladstone, M.P. by sundry members of the International
Association for the total suppression of vivisection. 1881.
[Pamphlets, vol. 38.]   **144 C**
See also ANIMALS.

VIZARD, JOHN.
A Compendium of principles in philosophy and divinity. 1836.
12mo.   **77 A**

VIZARD, PHILIP E.
A Concise manual of the practice of the Court in Banc. 1880.
8vo.   **52 A**

VIZARD, WILLIAM.
Letter to the speaker, on the subject of committees on Private
Bills. 1837. 8vo.   **173 B**
Remarks on the inconveniences resulting from the present
mode of proceeding in committees on Private Bills in Parlia-
ment. 1825. 8vo.   **173 B**

VOET, JOHANNES.
Commentarius ad Pandectas, in quo, præter Romani juris
principia ac controversias illustriores, jus etiam hodiernum,
et præcipuæ fori quæstiones excutiuntur. Editio sexta.
2 vols. Hagæ, 1734. folio.   **19 D**

VOLTAIRE, FRANÇOIS MARIE AROUET DE.
Memoirs of the life of Voltaire, written by himself. [Auto-
biography, vol. 4.] 1826. 12mo. **79 A**
Œuvres complètes de Voltaire. 70 vols. [Kehl], 1784–89.
8vo. **47 A–D**

VOLUNTEERS.
The Volunteer in the Field. By E. Palliser and W. C. Nangle.
1861. [Pamphlets, vol. 15.] **144 B**

VOTERS.
Voters and their registration. By J. J. H. Saint. 1885.
12mo. **11 E**
Law relating to the registration of Voters. By Charles Words-
worth. 2nd ed. 1843. 8vo. **166 E**
See also ELECTIONS and REGISTRATION.

VOWELL, JOHN, ALIAS HOKER.
The antique description and account of the city of Exeter :
in three parts. Part I. Containing the antient history, &c.
of the city. Part II. Containing a large and curious account
of the antiquity, foundation, and building of the Cathedral
Church of St. Peter. Part III. Contains the offices and
duties of those particular sworn officers, &c. of the city.
Edited by A. Brice. Exon, 1765. 8vo. **87 C**

VULLIAMY, LEWIS.
Examples of ornamental Sculpture, engraved by H. Moses.
1818–22. folio. **81 H**

WADDILOVE, ALFRED.
Digest of cases decided in court of Arches, Prerogative court
of Canterbury and Consistory court of London. 1849.
8vo. **63 D**

[WADE, JOHN.]
The Cabinet Lawyer, a popular digest of the laws of England.
22nd ed. 1867. 12mo. **171 B**
The same. 25th ed. with supplements. 1886. 12mo. **10 E**

WAGES.
Three lectures on the rate of wages. By N. W. Senior.
2nd ed. 1831. 8vo. **78 D**
See also POLITICAL ECONOMY.

WAGGETT, JOHN FRANCIS.
The law and practice relating to the prolongation of the term
of letters patent for inventions. 1887. 8vo.   53 B

WAINWRIGHT, JOHN.
Yorkshire. An historical and topographical introduction to
a knowledge of the ancient state of the Wapentake of
Strafford and Tickhill ; with ample accounts of Doncaster
and Conisbrough. Sheffield, 1829. 4to.   94 C

WAKE, ROBERT.
Southwold and its vicinity, ancient and modern. Yarmouth,
1839. 8vo.   93 C

WAKE, MOST REV. WILLIAM.
The genuine epistles of the Apostolical Fathers : S. Ignatius,
S. Clement, S. Polycarp, the Shepherd of Hermas, and the
Martyrdoms of St. Ignatius and St. Polycarp. Translated
with a large preliminary discourse. 1693. 12mo.   77 B

WAKEFIELD, EDWARD.
Account of Ireland, statistical and political. 2 vols. 1812.
4to.   95 F

WAKEFIELD, EDWARD GIBBON.
Facts relating to the punishment of death in the metropolis.
1831. 12mo.   78 A

WALCOTT, REV. MACKENZIE EDWARD CHARLES.
Westminster : memorials of the city, Saint Peter's college,
the parish, churches, palaces, streets and worthies. 1849.
8vo.   91 F

[WALDRON, GEORGE.]
History and description of Isle of Man. 1744. 12mo. 94 F

WALES, ANTIQUITIES AND TOPOGRAPHY OF.
Annals and antiquities of the counties and county families
of Wales. By Thomas Nicholas. 2 vols. 1872. 8vo. 94 E
British antiquities revived ; or, a friendly contest touching the
soveraignty of the three princes of Wales in ancient times.
By Robert Vaughan. Bala, 1834. 4to.   94 D

WALES, ANTIQUITIES AND TOPOGRAPHY OF—*continued.*

The Cambrian directory; or, cursory sketches of the Welsh territories. Salisbury, 1800. 12mo. 94 E

Giraldi Cambrensis Itinerarium Kambriæ et Descriptio Kambriæ. Edited by J. F. Dimock [vol. 6 of Giraldus Cambrensis]. 1868. 8vo. 101 E

Historical account of the ancient and modern state of the principality of Wales. By Sir John Doddridge. 2nd ed. 1714. 8vo. 94 E

The history of North Wales. By William Cathrall. 2 vols. Manchester, 1828. 4to. 94 E

The history of Wales. By John Jones. 1824. 8vo. 94 E

The itinerary of Archbishop Baldwin through Wales 1188. By Giraldus De Barri, translated into English by Sir R. C. Hoare. 2 vols. 1806. 4to. 94 D

A Run through South Wales, via the London and North Western railway. Shrewsbury, [1868]. 12mo. 94 E

A Second walk through Wales, in August and September 1798. By Rev. Richard Warner. Bath, 1799. 8vo. 94 E

A Topographical dictionary of the dominion of Wales. By Nicholas Carlisle. 1811. 4to. 94 D

A Tour through Monmouthshire and Wales. By H. P. Wyndham. 2nd ed. Salisbury, 1781. 4to. 95 G

The traveller's companion in a pedestrian excursion from Chester through North Wales. Chester, [n.d.] 12mo. 94 E

WALES, HISTORY OF.

Ancient laws and institutes of Wales. Edited by A. Owen. 1841. folio. 99 B

Annales Cambriæ. Edited by Rev. John Williams ab Ithel. 1860. 8vo. 101 D

Brut y Tywysogion ; or, the Chronicle of the Princes. Edited by Rev. John Williams ab Ithel. 1860. 8vo. 101 D

Cambria triumphans ; or, Brittain in its perfect lustre. By Percy Enderbie. 1661. folio. 95 H

Jurisdiction and practice of the court of great sessions of Wales upon the Chester circuit. [By Charles Abbot.] 1795. 8vo. 177 C

The Princes of Wales in their personal and political relations to the Crown and the Nation (from the Spectator, March 7, 1863). 1863. 4to. 114 H

WALES, Language of.

A Dictionary of the Welsh language explained in English. By Owen Williams. 2 vols. 1803. 4to. 123 C

A Dictionary of the Welsh language explained in English. By W. O. Pughe. 2 vols. in 1. Denbigh, 1832. 8vo. 123 C

Glossary of Welsh words. See Annales Cambriæ, 1860, pp. 111-127. 101 D

Glossary of Welsh words. See Brut y Tywysogion, 1860, pp. 377-418. 101 D

A Grammar of the Welsh language. By W. O. Pughe. 2nd ed. Denbigh, 1832. 8vo. 123 C

An Outline of the characteristics of the Welsh and its utility in connection with other ancient languages for developing the primitive speech of mankind. By W. O. Pughe. Denbigh, 1832. Bound with W. O. Pughe's Welsh grammar. 1832. 8vo. 123 C

See also MINSHEU, J.

WALFORD, Cornelius.

The Insurance Cyclopædia. 5 vols. [Aba-Han, all published.] 1871-78. 8vo. 122 A

Kings' Briefs ; their purposes and history. Printed for private circulation. 1882. 8vo. 78 B

WALFORD, Edward.

The county families of the United Kingdom. 3rd ed. 1865, 5th ed. 1869, and for the years 1872, 1875, 1876, and 1879 to 1890. 17 vols. 1865-90. 8vo. 126 F G

Greater London : a narrative of its history, its people, and its places. 2 vols. [1884.] 4to. 90 E

Speeches of Thomas Lord Erskine ; with memoir of his life. 2 vols. 1870. 8vo. 83 B

See also BRAYLEY, E. W. and THORNBURY, G. W.

WALFORD, Joseph Green.

The laws of the Customs. 1846. 8vo. 52 E

WALKER, Henry H.

The practice on signing judgement in the high court of justice. 1879. 8vo. 12 E

WALKER, JAMES DOUGLAS.
A Treatise on Banking law. 1877. 8vo.   160 C
The same. 2nd ed. 1885. 8vo.   78 D

WALKER, JOHN.
Critical pronouncing dictionary and expositor of the English
    language. 5th ed. 1810. 4to.   123 D
The same. New ed. by T. Young. Dublin, 1863. 8vo. 123 B

WALKER, WILLIAM GREGORY.
A Compendium of the law relating to executors and adminis-
    trators. 1880. 8vo.   52 G
The same. 2nd ed. by W. G. Walker and E. J. Elgood.
    1888. 8vo.   9 I
Partition acts 1868 and 1876: a manual of law of Partition
    and of sale in lieu of Partition. 2nd ed. 1882. 8vo. 13 B
The administration of the estates of deceased persons, by the
    Chancery division of the high court of justice. By W. G.
    Walker and E. J. Elgood. 1883. 8vo.   12 F

WALKLY, THOMAS.
A New catalogue of the peers of England, Scotland, and
    Ireland. 1658. 12mo.   125 A
The order and manner of the sitting of the Lords as Peeres
    of the Realme. 1628. 8vo.   49 D

WALLACE, GEORGE.
The nature and descent of ancient peerages connected with
    the state of Scotland. 2nd ed. Edinburgh, 1785. 8vo.
                                                           124 F
WALLACE, JOHN WILLIAM.
Cases argued and adjudged in the supreme court of the United
    States, December term 1863 to October term 1874. 23 vols.
    Washington, 1870–76. 8vo.   57 C D
The Reporters chronologically arranged ; with occasional
    remarks upon their respective merits. 4th ed. by F. F.
    Heard. Boston, 1882. 8vo. ,   82 D

WALLER, JOHN FRANCIS.
Report of the proceedings at a visitation holden in Trinity
    college, Dublin, to hear the appeals of G. F. Shaw and
    Robert Carmichael, fellows of the college. Dublin, 1858.
    8vo.   95 E

WALLER, William.
An Essay on the value of the mines late of Sir Carbery Price.
1698. 12mo. **94 E**

WALLIS, John.
The natural history and antiquities of Northumberland and
of so much of the county of Durham as lies between the
rivers Tyne and Tweed, commonly called North Bishoprick. 2 vols. 1769. 4to. **92 D**

WALMYSLEY, Thomas.
The expenses of the judges of assize, riding the Western and
Oxford circuits temp. Elizabeth 1596–1601. Edited from
the MS. account book of T. Walmysley, by W. D. Cooper.
[Camden Society, vol. 73.] 1859. 8vo. **85 B**

WALPOLE, Charles George.
A Rubric of the Common law, being a short digest of the
common law, illustrated by leading cases. 2nd ed. by
Sydney Hastings. 1891. 8vo. **64 B**

WALPOLE, Horace.
Catalogue of the classic contents of Strawberry Hill, collected
by Horace Walpole. 1842. 4to. **118 F**
A Catalogue of the royal and noble authors of England.
New ed. 1796. 8vo. **82 C**

WALPOLE, Sir Robert.
Genuine memoirs of the life and character of Sir Robert
Walpole, and of the family of the Walpoles. By Wm.
Musgrave. 1732. 8vo. **79 B**
Some considerations concerning the public funds, public re-
venues and annual supplies, granted by parliament. [By Sir
R. Walpole.] 1735. [South Sea Bubbles, vol. 3.] **118 B**
Some general considerations concerning the alteration and
improvement of public revenues. [By Sir R. Walpole.]
1733. [South Sea Bubbles, vol. 3.] **118 B**
Some reflections upon a pamphlet called The Old Whig.
[By Sir R. Walpole.] 1719. [Grimaldi's Tracts, vol. 2.]
118 B

WALSINGHAM, Sir Francis.
Journal of Sir F. Walsingham, from Dec. 1570 to April 1583.
Edited by C. T. Martin. [Camden Society, vol. 104.] 1871.
8vo **85 C**

WALSINGHAM, Thomas.
Gesta abbatum monasterii Sancti Albani regnante Ricardo
Secundo. Edited by H. T. Riley. 3 vols. 1867–69. 8vo.
101 G H
Historia Anglicana. Edited by H. T. Riley. 2 vols. 1863–
64. 8vo. 101 G
Ypodigma Neustriæ. Edited by H. T. Riley. 1876. 8vo.
101 H

WALTER OF COVENTRY.
Historical collections. Edited by W. Stubbs. 2 vols. 1872–
73. 8vo. 102 E

WALTER, James.
Manual of the statutes of Limitation. 3rd ed. 1879. 8vo.
172 A
The same. 4th ed. 1883. 8vo. 10 G

WALTHAM, Essex.
The history of the ancient town and once famous Abbey of
Waltham. By John Farmer. 1735. 8vo. 87 E
The history of the University of Cambridge and of Waltham
Abbey. By T. Fuller. New ed. by J. Nichols. 1840.
8vo. 86 C
Report on the present condition of the Abbey Church, Wal-
tham Holy Cross, Essex ; with a sketch of its history
and present state. By W. Burges. [1860.] Bound with
Gentleman's Magazine, vol. 8, n.s. 1860. 8vo. 128 F
See also Epping Forest.

WALTON, Joseph.
The practice and procedure of the Court of Common Pleas
at Lancaster. 1870. 12mo. 170 C

WANLEY, Humphrey.
Antiquæ literaturæ Septentrionalis liber alter, being vol. 2 of
Rev. George Hickes's Thesaurus. Oxoniæ, 1705. folio.
123 G

WANTING, Berkshire.
Parochial topography of the hundred of Wanting ; with other
miscellaneous records relating to the county of Berks. By
W. N. Clarke. Oxford, 1824. 4to. 86 B

WAR.

The art of War. See Machiavel's Works, 1680, pp. 432-523.
113 G

The Highway of the Seas in time of War. By H. W. Lord.
1862. 12mo. 55 A

The military engineer ; or, a treatise on the attack and defence of all kinds of fortified places. By G. Le Blond.
1759. 8vo. 78 B

New and extraordinary implements of war. Is England's safety or admiralty interest to be considered ? By F. P. Walesby. 3rd ed. 1841. [Pamphlets, vol. 5.] 144 A

On the effect of war. See T. Tooke's Thoughts and details, vol. 2, 1823, pp. 1–61. 78 D

A Treatise of captures in war. By Richard Lee. 2nd ed. 1803. 8vo. 55 A

What is contraband of war and what is not. By Joseph Moseley. 1861. 12mo. 55 A

See also INTERNATIONAL LAW.

WAR DEPARTMENT.

The statutory powers of Her Majesty's principal secretary of state for the war department. Ordnance branch. Selected and arranged by C. M. Clode. 1879. 8vo. 83 H

WARBLINGTON, HAMPSHIRE.

A Topographical account of the hundred of Bosmere, including the parish of Warblington. By C. J. Longcroft. 1857. 4to. 88 B

WARBURTON, JOHN, J. WHITELAW and R. WALSH.

History of the city of Dublin, from the earliest accounts to the present time. 2 vols. 1818. 4to. 95 F

WARBURTON, RIGHT REV. WILLIAM.

Tracts by Warburton and a Warburtonian [bishop Hurd]; not admitted into the collections of their respective works. [Edited by Dr. Samuel Parr.] 1789. 8vo. 78 B

The works of Alexander Pope; with the commentary and notes of his editor [Wm. Warburton.] 9 vols. 1770. 8vo. 83 E

WARD, DANIEL.

The practice at Parliamentary Elections. 1885. 12mo. 166 E

WARD, ROBERT.
Treatise of relative rights and duties of belligerent and neutral powers in maritime affairs. 1875. 8vo.   55 A

WARD, ROBERT ARTHUR.
A Treatise on Investments. 2nd ed. 1852. 8vo.   169 D

WARD, REV. WILLIAM PERCIVAL.
Isle of Mann and diocese of Sodor and Mann. Antient and authentic records relating to the history and constitution of that island. 1837. 8vo.   94 F

WARDE, DANIEL.
The practice of Interpleader by sheriffs and high bailiffs. 1887. 12mo.   12 E

WARDEN, ALEXANDER J.
Burgh laws of Dundee; with the history, statutes and proceedings of the guild of merchants and fraternities of crafts- • men. 1872. 8vo.   95 C

WARDS AND LIVERIES.
Reports of divers resolutions in law, arising upon cases in the Court of Wards and other courts at Westminster, 1608–1629. With a treatise of Wards and Liveries. By Sir James Ley. 1659. folio.   74 E

WARE, MARTIN.
The law reports. Digest of cases; with a digest of the important statutes, 1865–1885. 3 vols. 1882–86. 8vo.   73 F

WAREING, WILLIAM.
Practice of the Court of Common Pleas at Lancaster, in personal actions and ejectment. 1836. 12mo.   170 C

WARKWORTH, JOHN.
Chronicle of the first thirteen years of the reign of King Edward the Fourth. Edited by J. O. Halliwell. [Camden Society, vol. 10.] 1839. 8vo.   85 A

WARNEFORD LUNATIC ASYLUM, OXFORDSHIRE.
Brief history of the Warneford Lunatic Asylum. 1875. [Pamphlets, vol. 38.]   144 C

WARNER, REV. RICHARD.

Collections for the history of Hampshire and the bishopric of Winchester ; including the Isles of Wight, Jersey, Guernsey and Sarke, by D. Y. 5 vols. in 3. [1795.] 4to. **88 B**

Hampshire extracted from Domes-Day Book ; with an accurate English translation, a preface, and an introduction. 1789. 4to. **88 B**

The history of the Isle of Wight, military, ecclesiastical, civil, and natural. Southampton, 1795. 8vo. **88 A**

A Second walk through Wales, in August and September. 1798. Bath, 1799. 8vo. **94 E**

Topographical remarks relating to the South-Western parts of Hampshire; with a descriptive poem [Hengistbury Head]. 2 vols. in 1. 1793. 8vo. **88 A**

WARRANTIES.

Law of Warranties and representation upon the sale of personal chattels. By T. W. Saunders. 1874. 12mo. **11 I**

See also CONTRACTS and INSURANCE, LAW OF.

WARRANTS OF ATTORNEY.

The law of Warrants of Attorney, &c. By B. C. Robinson. 1844. 12mo. **177 D**

WARREN, SAMUEL.

A Manual of the parliamentary election law of the United Kingdom. 2 vols. 1852–53. 12mo. **166 E**

The moral, social, and professional duties of attornies and solicitors. 1848. 12mo. **160 C**

A Popular and practical introduction to Law studies. 1835, and 3rd ed. 2 vols. 1863. 12mo. **171 A**

Select extracts from Blackstone's Commentaries. 1837. 12mo. **166 F**

WARTON, REV. THOMAS.

The life of Sir Thomas Pope, founder of Trinity college, Oxford. 1772. 8vo. **79 B**

Specimen of a history of Oxfordshire [the history and antiquities of Kiddington]. 2nd ed. 1783. 4to. **92 E**

The same. 3rd ed. 1815. 4to. **92 E**

WARWICK.

An Account of Warwick and Leamington. By W. Field.
Warwick, 1815. 4to. **93 F**

History and succession of several Earls of Warwick since
Norman conquest and some account of Warwick Castle.
See J. Edmondson's Greville Family. 1766. 8vo. **80 C**

WARWICKSHIRE.

Antiquities of Warwickshire. By Sir William Dugdale. 2nd
ed. by W. Thomas. 2 vols. 1730. folio. **94 H**

Domesday book for the county of Warwick. Translated by
W. Reader. Coventry, 1835. 4to. **93 F**

History of Warwickshire. By S. Timmins. 1889. 8vo. **93 E**

New and complete history of the county of Warwick. By
William Smith. 1829. 4to. **93 F**

Staffordshire and Warwickshire past and present. By J. A.
Langford, C. S. Mackintosh and J. C. Tildesley. 2 vols. in 4.
[1875–76.] 4to. **93 F**

Warwickshire, being a concise topographical description of
the county of Warwick, from the elaborate work of Sir
Wm. Dugdale and other later authorities. By John Aston.
Coventry, 1817. 8vo. **93 E**

See also PENNANT, T.

WASHBURN, EMORY.

The American law of Easements and Servitudes. 2nd ed.
Boston, 1867. 8vo. **59 D**

The American law of Real Property. 3rd ed. 3 vols. Boston,
1868. 8vo. **60 A**

WASTE AND WASTE LANDS.

An Essay on Waste, Nuisance, and Trespass. By G. V. Yool.
1863. 8vo. **11 I**

Treatise on commons and waste lands. By C. I. Elton. 1868.
12mo. **52 B**

WATER SUPPLY AND WATERS.

Tabulated abstract of acts of parliament relating to Water
undertakings, 1879–1887. By E. K. Burstal. 1888. 12mo.
11 I

Payment of Water rates. By G. Wheeler. 1884. 8vo. **11 I**

The law relating to Gas and Water. By W. H. Michael and
J. S. Will. 3rd ed. by M. J. Michael. 1884. 8vo. **10 B**

WATER SUPPLY AND WATERS—*continued.*
The law relating to Waters. By H. J. W. Coulson and U. A. Forbes. 1880. 8vo.   11 I

Rights of Water. By J. B. Phear. 1859. 8vo.   11 I

The right of property in tide waters. By J. K. Angell. 2nd ed. Boston, 1847. 8vo.   60 B

See also CANALS, EASEMENTS, LONDON SEWERS AND WATER SUPPLY, RIVERS and SEA.

WATERFORD.
The ancient and present state of the county and city of Waterford. By Charles Smith. 2nd ed. Dublin, 1774. 8vo.   95 E

WATKINS, CHARLES.
An Essay towards the further elucidation of the law of Descents. 3rd ed. by R. S. Vidal. 1819. 8vo.   165 G

The same. 4th ed. by Joshua Williams. 1837. 12mo.   13 B

Principles of Conveyancing. 2nd ed. 1804. 4to. [an interleaved copy with many manuscript notes.]   118 E

The same. 3rd ed. by G. Morley and R. H. Coote. 1819. 8vo.   164 E

The same. 3rd ed. by R. Preston. 1819. 8vo.   164 E

The same. 4th ed. by R. Preston. 1823. 8vo.   164 F

The same. 5th ed. Part 1, by G. Morley and R. C. Coote. 1824. Part 2, by T. Coventry. 1827. 2 parts in 1 vol. 1824–27. 8vo.   164 F

The same. 8th ed. by J. Merrifield. 1833. 8vo.   164 F

The same. 8th ed. by H. H. White. 1838. 8vo.   52 D

A Treatise on Copyholds. 3rd ed. by R. S. Vidal. 2 vols. 1826. 8vo.   13 A

WATKINS, JOHN.
An Essay towards a history of Bideford in the county of Devon. Exeter, 1792. 8vo.   87 C

[WATSON, JAMES.]
Paramythia; or, mental pastimes, being original anecdotes. 1821. 12mo.   83 H

WATSON, Rev. John.
The history and antiquities of the parish of Halifax in Yorkshire. 1775. 4to. 94 C

WATSON, White.
A Delineation of the Strata of Derbyshire forming the surface
from Bolsover in the east to Buxton in the west, by a plate
designed from a tablet composed of the specimens of each
stratum within the above line. Sheffield, 1811. 8vo. 87 B

WATSON, Rev. William.
The Clergyman's law ; or, the complete incumbent. 3rd ed.
1725, and 4th ed. 1747. folio. 48 I

WATSON, William.
A Treatise of the law of Partnership. 1794. 8vo. 173 D
The same. 2nd ed. 1807. 8vo. 173 D

WATSON, William, F.A.S.
Historical account of Wisbech and of the circumjacent towns
and villages, the drainage of the great level of the Fens, the
origin of the royal franchise of the Isle of Ely. Wisbech,
1827. 8vo. 86 D

WATSON, William Henry.
The law of Arbitration and Awards. 1825. 8vo. 160 B
The same. 3rd ed. 1846. 8vo. 52 A
A Practical treatise on the law relating to the office and duty
of Sheriff. 1827. 8vo. 175 E

WATSON, William Webster.
A Practical compendium of Equity. 2 vols. 1873. 8vo. 167 D
The same. 2nd ed. by the author and B. P. Neuman. 2 vols.
1886. 8vo. 12 G

WATT, Robert.
Bibliotheca Britannica ; or, a general index to British and
foreign literature. 4 vols. Edinburgh, 1824. 4to. 82 F

WAUCH, Mansie.
The life of Mansie Wauch, tailor in Dalkeith, written by himself. [By D. M. Moir.] New ed. 1849. 12mo. 79 A

WAURIN, John de.
Recueil des Croniques et anchiennes istories de la Grant
Bretaigne. Edited by W. Hardy and E. L. C. P. Hardy.
5 vols. 1864–91. 8vo. **102 B**
A Collection of the Chronicles and Ancient Histories of
Great Britain, &c. Translated by W. Hardy and E. L. C. P.
Hardy. Vols. 1 & 2. 1864–87. 8vo. **102 B**

WAVERLEY ABBEY, Surrey.
Annales Monasterii de Waverleia A.D. 1–1291. See Annales
Monastici, vol. 2, 1865, pp. 127–414. **102 A**

WAYLEN, James.
Chronicles of the Devizes, being a history of the castle, parks,
and borough of that name. 1839. 8vo. **93 F**

WAYNFLETE, William.
The life of William Waynflete, bishop of Winchester. By
Richard Chandler. 1811. 8vo. **80 C**

WAYS.
A Treatise of the law of Ways. By H. W. Woolrych. 2nd ed.
1847. 8vo. **11 I**
See also Easements, Highways and Turnpikes.

WEALTH.
Three lectures on the transmission of the precious metals
from country to country, and the mercantile theory of
wealth. By N. W. Senior. 2nd ed. 1830. 8vo. **78 D**
See also Smith, A.

WEATHERLY, Edward.
A Practical guide in obtaining Probates, Administrations, &c.
in the Court of Probate. 2nd ed. 1858. 8vo. **174 D**

WEAVER, Charles.
A Collection of concise precedents of wills. 1882. 12mo. **13 I**

WEBB, John.
A Vindication of Stone-Heng restored, in which the orders
and rules of architecture observed by the ancient Romans
are discussed. 2nd ed. 1725. folio. **95 G**

WEBB, Locock.
The practice of the supreme court of judicature and of the House of Lords on appeals. 1877. 8vo. **12 A**

WEBSTER, Edward.
Parliamentary costs. 1859. 12mo. **165 B**
The same. 2nd ed. 1864, and 3rd ed. 1867. 12mo. **165 B**
The same. 4th ed. by C. Cavanagh. 1881. 12mo. **9 F**

WEBSTER, John.
Metallographia ; or, an history of metals. 1671. 12mo. **78 A**

WEBSTER, Noah.
A Dictionary of the English language. 2 vols. New York, 1828. Reprinted by E. H. Barker. 2 vols. 1832. 4to. **123 D**
The same. Revised and improved by C. A. Goodrich and Noah Porter. 2 vols. 1864. 4to. **123 D**

WEBSTER, Robert Grant.
The law relating to Canals : with the procedure and practice in private bill legislation and a map of the existing canals in England and Wales. 1885. 8vo. **9 B**

WEBSTER, Thomas.
The law and practice of Letters Patent for Inventions ; with supplement. 1841. 8vo. **173 E**
Reports and notes of cases on Letters Patent for Inventions, [1601–1855.] Vol. 1 and part 1 of vol. 2. [all published.] 1844–55. 8vo. **76 H**

WEBSTER, William Frederick.
The law relating to Particulars and Conditions of Sale on a sale of land. 1889. 8vo. **13 H**

WEDDERBURN, Alexander.
Statistical and practical observations relative to the province of New-Brunswick. Saint John, 1835. 4to. **84 E**

WEDGWOOD, William B. and I. S. HOMANS.
A Law manual for notaries public and bankers. New York, 1867. 8vo. **59 G**

WEEKLY NOTES.

The Weekly Notes ; being notes of cases heard and determined by House of Lords, superior courts of equity and common law, courts of probate and divorce, and admiralty court, 1866–1890. Vols. 1–25. 1866–90. 4to.   **69 G–I**

Another copy. Vols. 1–25. 1866–90. 4to.   **61 D E**

Digest of cases not reported in the Law Reports, 1866–1879. By G. M. White. 1880. 8vo.   **14 F**

Current index of all cases reported in The Law Reports and Weekly Notes, 1886–1890. By A. Pulling. 3 vols. 1888–90. 8vo.   **73 F**

WEEKLY REPORTER.

The Weekly Reporter, containing cases decided in the superior courts of equity and law, 1852–1890. Vols. 1–38. 1853–90. 4to.   **16 B–F**

Weekly Reporter Digest, 1853–1859. 2 vols. 1859. 4to. **16 B**

WEEVER, John.

Antient funeral monuments of Great Britain, Ireland, and the islands adjacent ; with the dissolved monasteries therein contained and a discourse on funeral monuments. 1767. 4to.   **81 F**

WEIGHTMAN, Hugh.

The law of Marriage and Legitimacy. 1871. 8vo.   **53 A**

The medical practitioners' legal guide. 1870. 8vo.   **172 E**

WEIGHTS AND MEASURES.

The law relating to weights and measures. By G. C. Whiteley. 1879. 8vo.   **11 I**

WEIR, Daniel.

History of the town of Greenock. Greenock, 1829. 8vo. **95 C**

[WEIR, George.]

A Topographical account of Tattershall. 2nd ed. Horncastle, 1813. Bound with W. Peck's Axholme. 1815. 4to. **90 G**

WELCH, Joseph.

A List of scholars of St. Peter's College, Westminster, from the foundation by Queen Elizabeth, MDLXI. to the present time. 1788. 4to.   **79 H**

WELD, ISAAC.
Statistical survey of the county of Roscommon. Dublin, 1832.
8vo.   95 F

WELFORD, RICHARD GRIFFITHS.
A Practical treatise on Equity Pleadings. 1842. 8vo. 173 G
New Practice Cases, 1844–1848. By R. G. Welford, A.
Bittleston, P. Parnell, &c. 3 vols. 1847–49. 8vo. 5 E

WELLBELOVED, REV. CHARLES.
Eburacum, or York under the Romans. York, 1842. 4to.
                                                            94 C

WELLESLEY, WILLIAM LONG.
Judgment of Earl Eldon, Lord Chancellor, on the petition
Wellesley v. The Duke of Beaufort, delivered at West-
minster Hall, on Feb. 1, 1827. 1827. [Jacob's Tracts,
vol. 6.]   144 B
A View of the Court of Chancery. 1830. 8vo.   118 C

WELLINGTON, ARTHUR, 1 DUKE OF.
The despatches of the Duke of Wellington, during his various
campaigns in India, Denmark, Portugal, Spain, The Low
Countries and France, from 1799 to 1818. By John Gur-
wood. New ed. 12 vols. 1837–38. 8vo.   114 A B
The general orders of the Duke of Wellington in Portugal,
Spain, and France, from 1809 to 1814, in the Low Countries
and France in 1815, and in France, army of occupation,
from 1816 to 1818. By John Gurwood. 1837. 8vo. 114 A
Supplementary despatches and memoranda. Edited by his
Son the Duke of Wellington. 10 vols. 1858–63. 8vo.
                                                          114 C D

WELLS, GEORGE.
The educational advantages of Bedford as a place of residence.
3rd ed. Bedford, 1886. 8vo.   86 B

WELLS, SAMUEL.
The history of the drainage of the great level of the Fens
called Bedford Level. 2 vols. 1820–28. 8vo.   86 B

WELSBY, W. N., E. T. HURLSTONE and J. GORDON.
Exchequer Reports, 1847–1854. 9 vols. 1849–54. 8vo. 7 D

WENCK, CARL FRIEDRICH CHRISTIAN.
Magister Vacarius, primus juris Romani in Anglia professor. Descriptio illustratus juris Romani in Bononiensis scholæ initiis fortunam illustrans emendationem interpretationem hodiernam juvans studiis C. F. C. Wenck. Lipsiæ, 1820. 8vo. **63 F**

WENDT, ERNST EMIL.
Papers on Maritime legislation ; with a translation of the German mercantile law relating to maritime commerce. 1868. 8vo. **172 E**
The same. 3rd ed. 1888. 8vo. **11 F**

WENEFREDE, SAINT.
The life and miracles of St. Wenefrede. [By William Fleetwood.] 2nd ed. 1713. 8vo. **79 B**

WENTWORTH, JOHN.
A Complete system of Pleading ; with an index of references to all the ancient and modern entries extant. 10 vols. Dublin, 1799. 8vo. **173 G**

WENTWORTH, THOMAS.
The office and duty of Executors. 4th ed. 1656. 12mo. **168 B**
The same. 1641. [Anon.] **49 D**
The same. Edited by Thomas Manley. 1676. 12mo. **168 B**
The same. 12th ed. by A Gentleman of the Inner Temple. 1763. 8vo. **168 B**
The same. 13th ed. by George Wilson. 1774. 8vo. **168 B**
The same. 14th ed. by H. Jeremy. 1829. 8vo. **52 G**

WERTHEIMER, JOHN.
The law relating to Clubs. 1885. 12mo. **52 B**
The same. 2nd ed. by A. W. Chaster. 1889. 8vo. **9 C**

WESKETT, JOHN.
Complete digest of the theory, laws, and practice of Insurance. 1781. 4to. **157 C**

WEST, EDWARD.
Law and practice of Extents in chief and in aid. 1817. 8vo. **168 D**

WEST, GILBERT.
Odes of Pindar ; with several other pieces in prose and verse,
translated from the Greek ; with a dissertation on the
Olympick Games. 1749. 4to. **83 J**

WEST INDIES.
The colonial practice of Saint Vincent ; also Observations on
the common assurances in general use in the West Indies.
By C. Shephard. 1822. 8vo. **55 E**
Digest of laws in the British colonies in America and the
West Indies. By Wm. Earnshaw. 1819. 8vo. **55 D**
The geographical and historical dictionary of America and
the West Indies. By A. De Alcedo. Translated from the
Spanish with large additions by G. A. Thompson. 5 vols.
1812-15. 4to. **84 E**
The original plan, progress, and present state of the South-
Sea-Company : or, some occasional thoughts upon the state
of the British Trade in the West Indies, more especially
the South-Seas. By John Pullen. 1732. [South Sea
Bubbles, vol. 2.] **118 B**
Six months in the West Indies in 1825. [By H. N. Coleridge.]
2nd ed. 1826. 8vo. **84 A**
A View of the constitution of the British colonies in North
America and the West Indies at the time the civil war
broke out on the continent of America. By Anthony
Stokes. 1783. 8vo. **55 D**
West Indian Incumbered estates acts. By R. J. Cust. 2nd
ed. with supplement. 2 vols. 1865-74. 12mo. **38 D**
See also BARBADOS, BERMUDA, CARRIBEE ISLANDS, &c.

WEST, MARTIN JOHN.
Cases heard and determined by the House of Lords, 1839-
1841. 1 vol. 1842. 8vo. **1 D**
A Letter to Viscount Melbourne on the present mode of
legislation in respect of public bills. 1836. 12mo. **173 B**
Reports of cases in the Court of Chancery, from 1736 to
July 1739, from the original manuscripts of Lord Chancellor
Hardwicke. 1827. 8vo. **3 I**

WEST, RAYMOND and JOHANN GEORG BÜHLER.
A Digest of Hindu law. Book 1. Inheritance. Bombay,
1867. 8vo. **38 B**

[WEST, RICHARD.]
A Discourse concerning treason and bills of attainder. 2nd
ed. 1717. [Law Tracts, vol. I.]   144 E
An Inquiry into the manner of creating peers. 2nd ed.
1719. 8vo.   49 C

WEST, THOMAS.
The antiquities of Furness ; or, an account of the royal abbey
of St. Mary, in the vale of Nightshade, belonging to
Lord George Cavendish. 1774. 4to.   88 F
The same. New ed. with additions by William Close.
Ulverston, 1813. 8vo.   89 B
A Guide to the lakes in Cumberland, Westmoreland, and
Lancashire. By the author of The Antiquities of Furness.
7th ed. 1799. 8vo.   87 A

WEST, WILLIAM.
Symbolæographia ; which may be termed The art of instruments or The Notarie or Scrivener. 1590. 12mo.   49 C

WESTBURY, RICHARD, I BARON.
European Assurance Arbitration: Lord Westbury's decisions,
reported by F. S. Reilly. Part I. 1873. 8vo.   145 D
The life of Richard, Lord Westbury. By Thomas Arthur
Nash. 2 vols. 1888. 8vo.   80 D

WESTERN AUSTRALIA.
Blue Book for the years 1887–1889. 3 vols. Perth, 1888–90.
folio.   35 F
Ordinances of Western Australia, 1858–1889. 7 vols. Perth,
1858–89. 4to.   35 F
Index to the ordinances of Western Australia, 1832–1862.
Perth, 1862. 4to.   35 F
The statutes of Western Australia. 2 vols. Melbourne, 1883.
8vo.   35 F
The supreme court act 1880 and rules of court. Perth, 1881.
4to.   37 G
Votes and proceedings of the Legislative Council, 1873–1875
and 1886–1888. 3 vols. Perth, 1873–88. folio.   35 F

WESTERN, Edward Young.
A History of the Bowes museum and park at Barnard Castle.
Barnard Castle, 1890. 8vo.   94 A

WESTERN, Thomas George.
Cases relating to the Tithes of the City of London, determined
in the several Courts of law and equity, and in Parliament.
1823. 8vo.   66 A
The juridical argument of T. G. Western against the decree
of Lord Brougham, upon case of late Sir William Clayton,
Bart. and the Duchy of Cornwall. 1835. 8vo.   87 A
Precedents in Conveyancing, illustrated with notes. 2 vols. in 1.
1839–40. 8vo. [these are vols. 3 and 4 of Bone's Precedents in Conveyancing.]   163 G

WESTLAKE, John.
A Treatise on private international law, with principal reference
to its practice in the English and other cognate systems of
jurisprudence. 1858. 8vo.   55 A
A Treatise on private international law. Being in lieu·of a
second edition of the above work. 1880. 8vo.   55 A

WESTMINSTER, Antiquities and History of.
Antiquities of Westminster : the old palace, St. Stephen's
chapel (now the House of Commons), &c. &c. By J. T.
Smith. 1807. 4to.   92 G
Historical memorials of Westminster Abbey. By A. P.
Stanley. 2nd ed. 1868, and Supplement. 1869. 2 vols.
1868–69. 8vo.   91 F
The history and antiquities of the abbey church of St. Peter,
Westminster. By E. W. Brayley, illustrated by J. P. Neale.
2 vols. 1818–23. folio.   91 H
History of abbey church of St. Peter's, Westminster, its an-
tiquities and monuments. [By Wm. Combe.] 2 vols. 1812.
4to.   92 G
History of the ancient palace and late Houses of Parliament
at Westminster. By E. W. Brayley and J. Britton. 1836.
8vo.   91 F
The new palace of Westminster. 1861. 8vo.   91 F
Report of the proceedings at a public meeting to promote
the admission of the public without charge to Westminster
Abbey and other public edifices. 1837. 8vo. [Pamphlets,
vol. 27.]   144 B

WESTMINSTER, ANTIQUITIES OF—*continued*.

Westminster, memorials of the city, Saint Peter's college, the parish, churches, palaces, streets, and worthies. By Rev. M. E. C. Walcott. 1849. 8vo. **91 F**

Westmonasterium; or, the history and antiquities of the abbey church of St. Peter's, Westminster; with Westminster Abbey, a poem. By Rev. J. Dart. 2 vols. 1742. folio. **91 H**

WESTMINSTER, COMMISSARY COURT OF.

A Calendar of grants of probate and administration of the Commissary Court of the Venerable the dean and chapter of Westminster. 1864. folio. **92 G**

WESTMINSTER, COURT OF BURGESSES FOR.

Instructions and directions given by the Court of Burgesses, for the city and liberty of Westminster to the Annoyance Jury. Westminster, 1801. 12mo. **91 B**

WESTMINSTER ELECTIONS.

Account of the Westminster election, Nov. 1806. Part I. [n.d.] 12mo. **118 B**

Copy of the poll, for electing two representatives in Parliament, for the city and liberty of Westminster, taken Oct. 11, 1774, and the fifteen following days. 1774. The same, taken 7–23 Sep. 1780. 1780, and The same, taken June 18–July 4, 1818. 1818. Bound in 2 vols. 1774–1818. 8vo. **107 K**

The rights of the people properly maintained in the choice of their representatives, addressed to the electors of Westminster. By An Elector. 1818. [Pamphlets, vol. 27.] **144 B**

WESTMINSTER REVIEW.

The Westminster Review, January, 1824 to December, 1890. 131 vols. 1824–90. 8vo. **253 A-G**

WESTMINSTER SCHOOL.

A List of scholars of St. Peter's college, Westminster, from the foundation by Queen Elizabeth MDLXI. to the present time. By Joseph Welch. 1788. 4to. **79 H**

WESTMORELAND.

An Essay towards a natural history of Westmoreland and Cumberland. By Thomas Robinson. 1709. 12mo. **93 F**

WESTMORELAND—*continued.*
The heraldic visitation of Westmoreland made in the year
1615, by Sir Richard St. George, Knt., Norroy king at arms.
1853. 12mo. **93 F**
The history and antiquities of the counties of Westmoreland
and Cumberland. By J. Nicholson and R. Burn. 2 vols.
1777. 4to. **94 G**
Translation of Domesday so far as relates to county of York,
parts of Lancashire, Westmoreland, &c. By Rev. Wm.
Bawdwen. Doncaster, 1809. 4to. **94 C**
See also LAKES, THE.

WHALE, GEORGE.
A Fragment on Political Education. 1882. [Pamphlets,
vol. 33.] **144 C**
Greater London and its government. 1888. 8vo. **10 G**

WHALLEY, LANCASHIRE.
An History of the parish of Whalley and honor of Clitheroe.
By Rev. T. D. Whitaker. 3rd ed. 1818. 4to. **88 F**

WHALLEY, GEORGE HAMMOND.
The whole of the Tithe acts, with a treatise on the recovery
of tithe rent-charge. 1879. 12mo. **176 E**
The same. 5th ed. by G. P. Leach. 1891. 8vo. **11 H**

WHALLEY, REV. PETER.
The history and antiquities of Northamptonshire, compiled
from the manuscript collections of J. Bridges. 2 vols.
Oxford, 1791. folio. **92 H**

WHARTON, CHARLES HENRY MARRIOTT.
The whole law relating to Innkeepers. 1876. 12mo. **10 D**

WHARTON, FRANCIS.
A Digest of the international law of the United States. 3 vols.
Washington, 1886. 8vo. **59 E**
The law of homicide in the United States. Philadelphia, 1855.
8vo. **59 E**
State Trials of the United States during the administrations
of Washington and Adams. 1849. 8vo. **57 A**
A Treatise on the conflict of laws, or private international
law. Philadelphia, 1872. 8vo. **55 B**

WHARTON, GEORGE.
Gesta Britannorum, or, a succinct chronologie of the actions and exploits, battails and other passages, which have happened from 1660 until 1661. 1661. 12mo. **118 A**

WHARTON, GEORGE FREDERICK.
Legal Maxims ; with observations and cases. 1865. 8vo. **64 E**

WHARTON, JOHN JANE SMITH.
The Law Lexicon ; or, dictionary of jurisprudence. 2nd ed. 1860, 3rd ed. 1864, and 4th ed. 1867. 8vo. **170 G**
The same. 5th ed. by J. S. Will. 1872. 8vo. **170 G**
The same. 6th ed. by J. S. Will. 1876. 8vo. **170 G**
The same. 7th ed. by J. M. Lely. 1883. 8vo. **52 I**
The same. 8th ed. by J. M. Lely. 1889. 8vo. **10 E**
A Manual for articled clerks. 8th ed. 1858. 12mo. **160 C**
The same. 9th ed. by C. H. Anderson. 1864. 12mo. **160 C**

WHARTON, THOMAS I.
A Digest of cases adjudged in the circuit court of the United States for the third circuit and in the courts of Pennsylvania. Philadelphia, 1822. 8vo. **57 A**

WHARTON, WILLIAM JAMES LLOYD.
A Short History of H.M.S. Victory. 1875. 12mo. **78 A**

WHATELY, REV. RICHARD.
A Dissertation exhibiting a general view of the rise, progress, and corruptions of Christianity. See Encyclopædia Britannica, 8th ed., vol. 1, 1860, pp. 447-545. **147 A**
Introductory lectures on political economy, delivered in Easter term, 1831. 2nd ed. 1832. 8vo. **78 D**
Logic. 2nd ed. 1869. 12mo. **78 A**

WHEATFIELD, SUFFOLK.
The history and antiquities of the ancient villa of Wheatfield. [By Rev John Clubbe.] 1758. Bound with Morant's Colchester, 1748. folio. **88 G**

WHEATLEY, HENRY BENJAMIN.
A List of English indexes. 1879. 8vo. **78 C**
London, past and present, its history, associations, and traditions. 3 vols. 1891. 8vo. **90 F**

WHEATLY, CHARLES.
A Rational illustration of the book of Common Prayer of the
Church of England.   Oxford, 1810.   8vo.   **77 B**

WHEATON, HENRY.
Elements of International law.   2nd ed.   By W. B. Lawrence.
1863, and Supplement, 1863.   8vo.   **55 B**
The same.   8th ed. by R. H. Dana.   1866.   8vo.   **55 B**
The same.   English ed. by A. C. Boyd.   1878.   8vo.   **55 B**
The same.   3rd ed. by A. C. Boyd.   1889.   8vo.   **55 B**
History of the law of nations in Europe and America.   New
York, 1845.   8vo.   **55 B**
Reports of decisions in the Supreme court of the United
States, 1816–1827.   12 vols.   See B. R. Curtis's Reports,
vols. 3-7.   Boston, 1855.   8vo.   **57 B**

WHEATSTONE, SIR CHARLES.
Authorship of the practical electric telegraph of Great Britain.
Edited by Rev. T. F. Cooke.   1868.   8vo.   **78 C**
The electric telegraph, was it invented by Professor Wheat-
stone?   By W. F. Cooke.   2 vols.   1857–56.   8vo.   **78 C**

WHEELER, GERALD.
Payment of water rates.   1884.   8vo.   **11 I**

WHEELER, JAMES.
Manchester, its political, social, and   commercial   history,
ancient and modern.   1836.   8vo.   **89 A**

WHELER, ROBERT BELL.
A   Guide   to   Stratford-upon-Avon.   Stratford-upon-Avon,
1814.   12mo.   **93 E**

WHEWELL, REV. WILLIAM.
Astronomy and general physics, considered with reference to
natural theology.   5th ed.   1836.   8vo.   **77 B**
An Elementary treatise on Mechanics.   5th ed.   Cambridge,
1836.   8vo.   **78 C**
The Elements of Morality, including polity.   2 vols.   1845.
8vo.   **77 B**

WHISHAW, Francis.
Analysis of railways, consisting of a series of reports on the twelve hundred miles of projected railways in England and Wales. 1837. 8vo.   77 B
New map of the whole manor and parish of Hendon. 1828. 4to.   89 E
Book of reference to the new map of the whole manor and parish of Hendon ; with an index of the names of owners of lands and tenements in Hendon. 1828. 4to.   89 E

WHISHAW, James.
A New Law Dictionary. 1829. 12mo.   171 A
A Synopsis of the members of the English bar, arranged in alphabetical and chronological order. 1835. 8vo.   80 F

WHISTON, William.
A New theory of the Earth. 4th ed. '1725. 12mo.   77 A
Sacred history of the old and new Testament, from the creation of the world till the days of Constantine the Great. Reduced into annals. 6 vols. 1745–46. 8vo.   77 A
The works of Flavius Josephus. Translated by Wm. Whiston. 1844. 8vo.   113 E

WHITAKER, Rev. John.
The history of Manchester. 2 vols. 1771–75. 4to.   88 F

WHITAKER, Richard.
A Treatise of the law relative to the rights of Lien and Stoppage in transitu. 1812. 8vo.   172 A

WHITAKER, Rev. Thomas Dunham.
History and antiquities of the deanery of Craven in the county of York. 2nd ed. 1812. folio.   95 H
History of Richmondshire in the north riding of the county of York. 2 vols. 1823. folio.   95 H
History of the original parish of Whalley and honor of Clitheroe, in counties of Lancaster and York ; with An account of the parish of Cartmell. 3rd ed. 1818. 4to.   88 F
Loidis and Elmete : or, an attempt to illustrate the districts described in those words by Bede, and supposed to embrace the lower portions of Aredale and Wharfdale, with the entire vale of Calder. Leeds, 1816. folio.   95 H
See also Thoresby, R.

WHITAKER, WILLIAM.
A Disputation on holy scripture against the Papists. Translated and edited by Rev. Wm. Fitzgerald. Cambridge, 1849. 8vo. **77 E**

WHITBY, YORKSHIRE.
A History of Whitby and Streoneshalh abbey. By Rev. George Young. 2 vols. Whitby, 1817. 8vo. **94 A**
The history of Whitby. By L. Charlton. 1779. 4to. **94 C**

WHITE, CHARLES.
A Compendium of the British peerage. 1825. 12mo. **125 A**

WHITE, FREDERICK MEADOWS.
A Report of the cases recently decided by the court of Queen's Bench on Rating of tithe commutation rent-charge; with an Appendix of observations. 1858. 8vo. **176 F**

WHITE, FREDERICK THOMAS and OWEN DAVIES TUDOR.
A Selection of leading cases in Equity, with notes. 2 vols. 1849-50, 2nd ed. 2 vols. 1858, 3rd ed. 2 vols. 1866, and 4th ed. 2 vols. 1872. 8vo. **171 E F**
The same. 5th ed. 2 vols. 1877. 8vo. **10 F**
The same. 6th ed. 2 vols. · 1886. 8vo. **10 F**

WHITE, GEORGE MERYON.
The Conveyancing acts 1881 and 1882 ; also the Solicitors' remuneration act 1881 ; with notes. 1883. 12mo. **64 B**
The weekly notes. Digest of cases not reported in the law reports, 1866-1879. 1880. 8vo. **14 F**

WHITE, GEORGE TOWRY.
A Treatise on proceedings in equity by way of Supplement and Revivor. 1843. 8vo. **175 C**

WHITE, REV. GILBERT.
The natural history and antiquities of Selborne in the county of Southampton ; with the naturalist's calendar, observations on various parts of nature and poems. New ed. 1813. 4to. **88 B**

WHITE HORSE IN BERKSHIRE.

A Letter to Dr. Mead, shewing that the White Horse is a monument of the West Saxons. By Rev. F. Wise. Oxford, 1738. 8vo. **86 B**

Further observations upon the White Horse; with An account of Whiteleaf-Cross in Bucks. By Rev. F. Wise. Oxford, • 1742. 8vo. **86 B**

WHITE, JOHN MEADOWS.

1 Vict. c. 69, Act to amend an act for the Commutation of Tithes in England and Wales; with notes. 1837. Bound with Bosanquet's Tithes. 1837. 12mo. **176 E**

WHITE, REV. JOSEPH BLANCO.

The law of anti-religious libel. Dublin, 1834. 8vo. **172 A**

WHITE, WILLIAM.

History, gazetteer, and directory of Hampshire and the Isle of Wight. Sheffield, 1859. 8vo. **88 A**

History, gazetteer, and directory of the east and north ridings of Yorkshire. Sheffield, 1840. 8vo. **94 A**

History, gazetteer, and directory of the west riding of Yorkshire; with the city of York and port of Hull. 2 vols. Sheffield, 1837–38. 8vo. **94 A**

WHITEFIELD, GEORGE.

Journal of a voyage from London to Savannah in Georgia. [Autobiography, vol. 19.] 1826. 12mo. **79 A**

WHITEFORD, FERDINAND MAUGER.

The law relating to Charities, especially charitable bequests and conveyances. 1878. 8vo. **52 B**

WHITEFORD, FLINTSHIRE.

The history of the parishes of Whiteford and Holywell. By Thomas Pennant. 1796. 4to. **95 G**

WHITELEY, GEORGE CRISPE.

The law relating to weights, measures, and weighing machines. 1879. 12mo. **11 I**

WHITELOCKE, SIR BULSTRODE.
Memorials of the English affairs, from the beginning of the reign of Charles I. to the Restoration. New ed. 4 vols. Oxford, 1853. 8vo. **115 C**
Notes upon the kings writt for choosing members of parliament XIII Car. II., being disquisitions on the government of England by king, lords, and commons. Published by Charles Morton. 2 vols. 1766. 4to. **114 F**

WHITELOCKE, SIR JAMES.
Liber famelicus . . . in the reigns of James I. and Charles I. Edited by John Bruce. [Camden Society, vol. 70.] 1858. 8vo. **85 B**

WHITEWAY, AUGUSTINE ROBERT.
Hints on practice ; or, practical notes on the Judicature acts ; with the rules of the Supreme court 1883. 2nd ed. 1883. 8vo. **52 I**

WHITGIFT, JOHN, ARCHBISHOP OF CANTERBURY.
A Sketch of the life of John Whitgift. See Rev. D. W. Garrow's History of Croydon, 1818, pp. 209–290. **93 C**
Works. Edited by Rev. John Ayre. 3 vols. Cambridge, 1851–53. 8vo. **77 E**

WHITMARSH, FRANCIS.
Treatise on Bankrupt laws. 2nd ed. 1817. 8vo. **160 D**

WHITMORE, WILLIAM WOLRYCHE.
Letter to the electors of Bridgenorth, upon the Corn laws. 1826. [Jacob's Tracts, vol. 7.] **144 E**

WHITTINGHAM, VERY REV. WILLIAM.
Life of W. Whittingham, dean of Durham. Edited by M. A. E. Green. [Camden Society, vol. 104.] 1871. 8vo. **85 C**

WHITTLE, P. A.
Bolton-le-Moors and the townships in the parish, an historical, statistical, civil, and moral account of the borough of Bolton, including a curious description of the parish of Deane. Bolton, 1855. 8vo. **89 B**

WHITWORTH, Charles.
A List of the English, Scots, and Irish nobility. 1765.
12mo. 125 A

WHYTE, Francis.
For the sacred law of the land. 1652. 12mo. 49 A

WICKSTEAD, John.
The attorney and agent's table of Costs in the courts of King's
Bench and Common Pleas. 1829. 8vo. 164 G

WICKSTEED, Gustavus W.
Index to statutes in force at end of session of 1856. Toronto,
1857. 8vo. 34 C
Table of the provincial statutes and ordinances of Lower
Canada. Toronto, 1857. 8vo. 34 C

WICLIFFE, John.
An Apology for Lollard doctrines, attributed to Wicliffe.
Edited by J. H. Todd. [Camden Society, vol. 20.] 1842.
8vo. 85 A
Fasciculi Zizaniorum cum Tritico. Edited by Rev. W. W.
Shirley. 1858. 8vo. 101 A

WIGAN.
The charters of the borough of Wigan in Latin and English.
Warrington, 1808. 4to. 88 F
The Mayor of Wigan, a tale. By Hillary Butler. 1760.
12mo. 118 C

WIGGERS, Julius.
Grammatik der Spanischen Sprache. Leipzig, 1860. 8vo.
255 G

WIGHT, Alexander.
Inquiry into the rise and progress of parliament, chiefly in
Scotland. Edinburgh, 1784. 4to. 114 F

WIGHT, Isle of.
A Companion to the Isle of Wight. By John Albin. 9th ed.
1823. 12mo. 88 A
Historical guide to the Isle of Wight. By John Bullar.
Southampton, 1806. 12mo. 88 A

WIGHT, ISLE OF—*continued.*

The history of the Isle of Wight. By Rev. Richard Warner. 1795. 8vo. **88 A**

A New history of the Isle of Wight. By J. Albin. 1795. 8vo. **88 A**

The pleasure-visitor's companion in surveying the Isle of Wight. By G. Brannon. Wootton, 1833. 12mo. **88 A**

See also WHITE, W., WOODWARD, B. B. and WORSLEY, R.

WIGHTWICK, JOHN.

Reports of cases in the court of Exchequer, 1810–1811. 1 vol. 1819. 8vo. **7 I**

WIGRAM, JAMES.

An Examination of the rules of law respecting the admission of extrinsic evidence in aid of the interpretation of wills, contained in observations on the case of Goblet *v.* Beechey and others. 1831. 8vo. **178 C**

The same. 4th ed. by W. K. Wigram. 1858. 8vo. **52 G**

Points in the law of Discovery. 1836. 8vo. **165 G**

WIGRAM, WILLIAM KNOX.

Justices' Note-Book. 1880, and 3rd ed. 1883. 12mo. **169 G**

The same. 5th ed. by W. S. Shirley. 1888. 12mo. **12 B**

WILBERFORCE, EDWARD.

Statute law : the principles which govern the construction and operation of statutes. 1881. 8vo. **53 H**

WILBERFORCE, REV. ROBERT ISAAC.

Church courts and church discipline. 1843. 8vo. **77 B**

WILDE, SAMUEL FRANCIS THOMAS.

A Lecture delivered at the Incorporated Law Society, introductory to a course on the principles and practice of conveyancing. 1833. [Pamphlets, vol. 3.] **144 A**

Supplement to Mr. Barton's Precedents in Conveyancing. 3rd ed. by C. Barton, jun. 3 vols. 1826. 8vo. **13 G**

WILEY, WILLIAM.

A Plea for Testators. Part 1. The rule in Shelley's case, its mischief and a remedy suggested. 1869. 8vo. **176 E**

WILKES, John.
John Wilkes, demagogue or patriot? a sketch of the eighteenth century. By W. S. Shirley. 1879. [Pamphlets, vol. 38.]
144 C

WILKINS, Cecil Ansdell.
General rules and circular orders of high court of judicature at Fort William in Bengal. Calcutta, 1881. 8vo. **38 B**

WILKINS, David.
Concilia Magnæ Britanniæ et Hiberniæ, a Synodo Verola-miensi, A.D. 446, ad Londinensem, A.D. 1717; accedunt constitutiones et alia ad historiam ecclesiæ Anglicanæ spectantia. 4 vols. 1737. folio. **113 H**
Leges Anglo-Saxonicæ, ecclesiasticæ et civiles; accedunt leges Edwardi Latinæ, Guilielmi Conquestoris Gallo-Nor-mannicæ, et Henrici I. Latinæ. 1721. folio. **99 C**

WILKINSON, James John.
The law of Shipping. 1843. 8vo. **175 G**
The law relating to the Public Funds. 1839. 12mo. **168 F**
The practice in the action of Replevin. 1825. 8vo. **175 C**
A Treatise on the Limitation of actions as affecting mercantile and other contracts. 1829. 8vo. **172 A**

WILKINSON, Rev. Joseph.
Select views in Cumberland, Westmoreland and Lancashire. 1821. folio. **91 H**

[WILKINSON, Martin.]
The practice of the court of Chancery of the county palatine of Durham. By A Solicitor of that court. Sunderland, 1807. 8vo. **166 A**

WILKINSON, Robert.
Londina illustrata : graphic and historic memorials of monas-teries, churches, chapels, schools, and modern and present theatres in the cities and suburbs of London and West-minster. 1819. folio. **92 H**

WILKINSON, Samuel.
The system of nature ; or, the laws of the moral and physical world, translated from the original French of M. De Mira-baud. 3 vols. 1820-21. 8vo. **83 B**

WILKINSON, THOMAS.
Every-day precedents in conveyancing. 3rd ed. 1881. 8vo.
13 F

WILKS, WASHINGTON.
The Half Century, its history, political and social. 1852.
12mo. 116 E

WILL, JOHN SHIRESS.
Changes in the jurisdiction and practice of the county courts
and superior courts effected by the County Courts act 1867.
1868. 8vo. 165 B
Practice of referees' courts in parliament. 1866. 8vo. 175 C

WILLCOCK, JOHN WILLIAM.
Laws of inns, hotels, and alehouses. 1829. 12mo. 169 A
Laws relating to the Medical profession. 1830. 8vo. 172 E
Laws relating to the ordering, relief, and settlement of the
Poor. 1829. 12mo. 174 B
The office of Constable, comprising the laws relating to con-
stables; with an account of their institution and appoint-
ment. 1827. 8vo. 163 D

WILLES, SIR JOHN.
Reports of adjudged cases in the Court of Common Pleas,
during the time Lord chief justice Willes presided in that
court, 1737–1758; with notes and references by C. Durnford. 1799. folio. 74 G

WILLIAM I. AND II., KINGS OF ENGLAND.
Guillaume le Conquérant; ou, l'Angleterre sous les Normands.
Par G. Guizot. Edited by A. J. Dubourg. 7th ed. 1878.
12mo. 83 C
History of Gavel-kind. By S. Taylor; with a short history
of William the Conquerour, written in Latin by an anony-
mous author in time of Henry I. 1663. 8vo. 118 A
The laws of William the Conqueror. See R. Kelham's Norman
Dictionary. 1779. 8vo. 123 B
Monumenta Historica Britannica. Vol. 1, extending to the
Norman Conquest. By H. Petrie and Rev. J. Sharpe;
completed by T. D. Hardy. 1848. folio. 99 B
See HOUARD, D., LINGARD, REV. J., MARTYN, W., TUR-
NER, S. and WILKINS, D.
See also NORMANDY, HISTORY OF.

WILLIAM III., KING OF ENGLAND.

An Account of the late proposals of the Archbishop of Canterbury with some other bishops to his Majesty, in a Letter to M. B. Esq. [n.d.] [Tracts, 1688-9.] **118 E**

Bishop Burnet's History of his own time from the restoration of Charles II. to the peace of Utrecht in the reign of Queen Anne. 4 vols. 1818. 8vo. **115 F**

The history of England from the accession of James II. By Lord Macaulay. 5 vols. 1860-61. 8vo. **115 G**

The history of the late conspiracy against the king and the nation; with a particular account of the Lancashire plot. 1696. 12mo. **115 D**

Memoirs of Great Britain and Ireland, 1681-1692. By Sir John Dalrymple. 2nd ed. 2 vols. 1771-73. 4to. **114 F**

A Prayer for the Prince and Princess of Orange, translated out of French. [n.d.] [Tracts, 1688-9.] **118 E**

The Declaration of William Henry, Prince of Orange, of the reasons inducing him to appear in arms, in the kingdom of England, for preserving of the Protestant religion, and for restoring the laws and liberties of England, Scotland and Ireland. 1688. [Tracts, 1688-9.] **118 E**

The Prince of Orange, his declaration shewing the reasons why he invades England; with a short preface and some modest remarks on it. [By Gilbert Burnet.] 1688. [Tracts, 1688-9.] **118 E**

WILLIAM OF CANTERBURY.

Materials for the history of Thomas Becket. Edited by J. C. Robertson and J. B. Sheppard. Vol. 1. William of Canterbury. 1875. 8vo. **102 F**

WILLIAM OF WORCESTER.

Liber Niger Scaccarii, nec non annales rerum Anglicarum; cum præfatione et appendice Thomæ Hearnii ad editionem primam Oxoniæ editam. Editio altera. 2 vols. 1771. 8vo. **97 I**

WILLIAM OF WYKEHAM.

Life of William of Wykeham, bishop of Winchester. By Robert Lowth. 3rd ed. Oxford, 1777. 8vo. **80 C**

WILLIAMS, CHARLES F.

Tariff laws of the United States. 1883. 8vo. **60 B**

[WILLIAMS, Charles Reynolds.]
Some professional recollections. By A former member of the
council of the Incorporated Law Society. 1883. 8vo.
86 G

WILLIAMS, David.
History of Monmouthshire. 1796. 4to.   92 C

WILLIAMS, Sir Edward Vaughan.
A Treatise on the law of Executors and Administrators.
2 vols. 1832, 2nd ed. 2 vols. 1838, 3rd ed. 2 vols.
1841, 4th ed. 2 vols. 1849, 5th ed. 2 vols. 1856, and
6th ed. 2 vols. 1867. 8vo.   168 C
The same. 7th ed. by Sir E. V. Williams and W. V. V.
Williams. 2 vols. 1873. 8vo.   52 G
The same. 8th ed. by R. L. V. Williams and W. V. V.
Williams. 2 vols. 1879. 8vo.   9 I

WILLIAMS, James.
Wills and intestate succession. 1891. 12mo.   13 I

WILLIAMS, John.
The rise, progress, and present state of the northern govern-
ments; viz. The United Provinces, Denmark, Sweden,
Russia and Poland. 2 vols. 1777. 4to.   113 F

WILLIAMS, John Griffith.
Cases in equity during the time of Lord Chancellor Talbot,
1730–1737. 3rd ed. 1792. 8vo.   3 G

WILLIAMS, Joshua.
An Essay on Real Assets. 1861. 8vo.   53 F
Letters to John Bull, Esq., on Lawyers and law reform.
1857. 12mo.   170 F
On the true remedies for the evils which affect the transfer of
land. 1862. [Pamphlets, vol. 19.]   144 B
Principles of law of Personal Property. 1848, 3rd ed. 1856,
9th ed. 1876, and 11th ed. 1881. 8vo.   174 E
The same. 12th ed. by T. C. Williams. 1884. 8vo.   64 F
The same. 13th ed. by T. C. Williams. 1887. 8vo.   64 F
Principles of law of Real Property. 1845, 4th ed. 1855, 8th ed.
1868, 11th ed. 1875, and 13th ed. 1880. 8vo.   174 E

WILLIAMS, JOSHUA—*continued.*
The same. 15th ed. by T. C. Williams. 1885. 8vo. **64 F**
The same. 16th ed. by T. C. Williams. 1887. 8vo. **64 F**
Rights of Common and other prescriptive rights; being twenty-four Lectures delivered in Gray's Inn Hall, in the year 1877. 1880. 8vo. **9 D**
The Seisin of the Freehold : being twelve Lectures delivered in Gray's Inn Hall in 1876. 1878. 8vo. **53 G**
The Settlement of real estates : being twenty-four Lectures delivered in Gray's Inn Hall in 1876. 1879. 8vo. **13 H**

WILLIAMS, OWEN.
A Dictionary of the Welsh language explained in English. 2 vols. 1803. 4to. **123 C**

WILLIAMS, ROBERT GRIFFITH and G. BRUCE.
The jurisdiction and practice of the high court of Admiralty. 1869. 8vo. **52 A**
The same. 2nd ed. by G. Bruce and C. F. Jemmett. 1886. 8vo. **12 D**

WILLIAMS, ROLAND VAUGHAN and W. V. WILLIAMS.
New law and practice in Bankruptcy. 1870. 8vo. **160 F**
The same. 2nd ed. 1876, and 3rd ed. 1884. 8vo. **160 F**
The same. 4th ed. 1886. 8vo. **52 A**
The same. 5th ed. by E. W. Hansell. 1891. 8vo. **12 I**

WILLIAMS, SAMUEL WELLS.
The Chinese commercial guide. 5th ed. Hongkong, 1863. 8vo. **78 A**

WILLIAMS, SYDNEY EDWARD.
The law and practice relating to Petitions in Chancery and Lunacy. 1880. 8vo. **11 C**

WILLIAMS, T.
Every man his own lawyer; or, a complete law library. 2nd ed. 1818. 8vo. **170 G**

WILLIAMS, THOMAS CYPRIAN.
Statutes affecting the practice of conveyancing, passed in the years 1874, 1881, 1882, 1884. 1884. 8vo. **13 G**

WILLIAMS, THOMAS WALTER.
Digest of the statute law, an abridgment of all public acts of
parliament now in force. 2 vols. 1791. 4to. **158 B**
The whole law relative to the duty and office of a Justice of
the Peace. 2nd ed. 4 vols. 1808. 8vo. **170 B**

WILLIAMS, WM. PEERE. See PEERE WILLIAMS, WM.

WILLIAMSON, REV. JOHN.
Glastonbury abbey, its history and ruins. Wells, 1865.
8vo. **93 A**

WILLIAMSON, SIR JOSEPH.
Letters addressed from London to Sir Joseph Williamson,
while plenipotentiary at the congress of Cologne 1673 and
1674. Edited by W. D. Christie. [Camden Society, n.s.
vols. 8 and 9.] 2 vols. 1873–74. 8vo. **85 D** .
See also W. Wynne's Life of Sir Leoline Jenkins, vol. 1. 1724,
pp. 1–346. **79 I**

WILLICH, CHARLES MADINGER.
Popular tables for ascertaining the value of lifehold, leasehold,
and church property. 3rd ed. 1853. 8vo. **134 J**
The same. 10th ed. 1887. 8vo. **134 J**
Tithe commutation tables. 3rd ed. 1854, and Annual
Supplements 1838–1891. 2 vols. 8vo. **11 H**

WILLIS, BROWNE.
The history and antiquities of the town, hundred, and deanery
of Buckingham. 1755. 4to. **86 C**
Notitia Parliamentaria; or, an history of the counties, cities,
and boroughs in England and Wales beginning with Bedford, Berks, Bucks, Cambridge, and Cheshire. 1715. 8vo.
84 B
A Survey of the cathedrals [of England and Wales]. 3 vols. in 2.
1742. 4to. **84 D**
Willis's Survey of St. Asaph considerably enlarged and brought
down to the present time. By Edward Edwards. 2 vols.
Wrexham, 1801. 8vo. **94 E**

WILLIS, EDWARD COOPER.
The law and practice in Bankruptcy. 1884. 8vo. **12 I**

WILLIS, JOHN WALPOLE.
A Digest of the rules and practice as to Interrogatories for the examination of witnesses. 1816. 8vo. 169 C
A Practical treatise on the duties and responsibilities of Trustees. 1827. 8vo. 176 F

WILLIS, ROBERT.
The architectural history of the University of Cambridge and of the colleges of Cambridge and Eton. Edited with large additions by J. W. Clark. [vol. 4; plans.] 4 vols. Cambridge, 1886. 4to. 86 D

WILLMORE, GRAHAM.
Confusion worse confounded ; or, the statutes at large in 1852. 1852. [Pamphlets, vol. 9, part 2.] 144 A
Mercantile and Maritime Guide. By Graham Willmore and Edwin Beedell. 1856. 8vo. 146 G

WILLMORE, G., F. L. WOLLASTON and H. DAVISON.
Reports of cases in the court of King's Bench, Exchequer Chamber and Bail Court 1837. 1 vol. 1839. 8vo. 5 I

WILLMORE, G., F. L. WOLLASTON and W. HODGES.
Reports of cases in the Court of Queen's Bench, Exchequer Chamber and Bail Court 1838. 1 vol. 1840. 8vo. 5 I

WILLOCK, JOHN.
Legal Facetiæ, satirical and humorous. 1887. 8vo. 78 B

WILLS.
Calendar of Wills proved and enrolled in the Court of Husting, London, A.D. 1258–A.D. 1688. Edited by R. R. Sharpe. 2 vols. 1889–90. 8vo. 91 D
Collection of all the wills, now known to be extant, of the kings and queens of England, princes and princesses of Wales, and every branch of the blood royal, from the reign of William the Conqueror to that of Henry VII. exclusive. By John Nichols. 1780. 4to. 114 D
A Selection from the wills of eminent persons proved in the Prerogative Court of Canterbury, 1495–1695. Edited by J. G. Nichols and John Bruce. [Camden Society, vol. 83.] 1863. 8vo. 85 C

WILLS—*continued.*

Testamenta Vetusta; being illustrations from wills, of manners, customs, &c. from Henry II. to accession of Queen Elizabeth. By Sir N. H. Nicolas. 2 vols. 1826. 8vo.   **114 D**

Wills and inventories from the registers of the Commissary of Bury St. Edmund's. Edited by Samuel Tymms. [Camden Society, vol. 49.] 1850. 8vo.   **85 B**

WILLS, LAW OF.

Dissertation on and precedents of Wills. See Bythewood and Jarman's Conveyancing, 4th ed., vol. 7, 1889, pp. 304–1055.   **13 D**

Practical advice to Testators and Executors. By Wm. Phippen. 7th ed. 1886. 12mo.   **13 I**

Law of Wills. By H. S. Theobald. 3rd ed. 1885. 8vo. **13 I**

The pitfalls of testators. A few hints about the making of wills. By J. C. H. Flood. 1884. 8vo.   **13 I**

Concise forms of Wills. By W. Hayes and T. Jarman. 9th ed. 1883. 8vo.   **13 I**

A Treatise on Wills. By T. Jarman. 4th ed. 2 vols. 1881. 8vo.   **13 I**

The law relating to Wills of personal property. By J. C. H. Flood. 1877. 8vo.   **13 I**

A Practical guide to making and proving Wills. By C. Hudson. 1876. 8vo.   **13 I**

The law of Wills. By I. F. Redfield. 2nd ed. 2 vols. 1867. 8vo.   **60 B**

Construction of Wills. By F. V. Hawkins. 1863. 8vo. **13 I**

Remarks on the Testamentary jurisdiction bill. By Thomas Falconer. 1854. [Pamphlets, vol. 12.]   **144 A**

How to make a will, a familiar exposition of the 1st Victoria cap. xxvi, commonly called the new law of wills; with an historical review. By The Editor of 'The Leigh Peerage.' 1837. 12mo.   **118 A**

Walpole case of mutual wills. See Hargrave's Juridical Arguments, vol. 2, 1799, pp. 272–315.   **144 G**

Opinions on a devise of real and personal estate. See Collectanea Juridica, vol. 2, 1792, pp. 255–257.   **144 G**

Opinions on a revocation of a will. See Collectanea Juridica, vol. 2, 1792, pp. 262–266.   **144 G**

Case on devise of real and personal estate, with Mr. Peere Williams's opinion. See Collectanea Juridica, vol. 1, 1791, pp. 473–475.   **144 G**

WILLS, LAW OF—*continued*.

A Treatise of testaments and last wills. By Henry Swinburne. 6th ed. 1743. folio. **48 I**

Of the original of ecclesiastical jurisdictions of testaments. By John Selden. See Selden's Tracts, 1683. folio. **114 G**

See ALLNUTT, G. S., DEANE, J. P., GODOLPHIN, J., INDERWICK, F. A., LOVELASS, P., POWELL, J. J., RAWLINSON, J., RICHARDSON, R., ROBERTS, W., SUGDEN, H., TOMLINS, SIR T. E., WEAVER, C., WIGRAM, J., WILLIAMS, J. and WORTHINGTON, G.

See also DEVISES and SHELLEY'S CASE.

WILLS, WILLIAM.

An Essay on the principles of circumstantial evidence. 4th ed. by Alfred Wills. 1862. 8vo. **52 G**

WILLSHIRE, WILLIAM.

The stranger's guide to Hampton Court palace and gardens. 1869. 12mo. **89 D**

WILMOT, SIR JOHN EARDLEY.

Memoirs of the life of Sir J. E. Wilmot, [by his son John Eardley Wilmot] and Notes of opinions and judgments delivered in different courts by Sir J. E. Wilmot. 1757–1770. 1802. 4to. **79 H**

Notes of opinions &c. Another copy. 1802. 4to. **74 G**

WILSON, ARTHUR.

The Supreme Court of Judicature acts. 1875, and 2nd ed. 1878. 12mo. **169 G**

The same. 3rd ed. by M. D. Chalmers. 1882. 12mo. **169 G**

The same. 4th ed. by M. D. Chalmers and M. M. Mackenzie. 1883. 12mo. **169 G**

The same. 5th ed. by M. M. Mackenzie and C. A. White. 1886. 12mo. **169 G**

The same. 6th ed. by C. Burney, M. M. Mackenzie and C. A. White. 1887. 8vo. **52 I**

The same. 7th ed. by C. Burney, M. M. Mackenzie and C. A. White. 1888. 8vo. **12 G**

1068

WILSON, Darcy Bruce.
The law and practice under the Bills of Sale acts 1854, 1866 and 1878 ; with notes on the law of fixtures and bankruptcy. 1879. 12mo.   160 G
The same. 2nd ed. 1881. 12mo.   160 G

WILSON, George.
The entries of Pleadings to the cases comprehended in Reports of cases in the Courts of King's Bench and Common Pleas by Robert, Lord Raymond. Dublin, 1792. 8vo.   5 H
Practical treatise of Fines and Recoveries. [By George Wilson.] 1753. 12mo.   168 E
The same. By George Wilson. 2nd ed. 1773. 12mo. 168 E
The same. 3rd ed. 1780, and 4th ed. 1793. 12mo. 168 E
Reports of cases argued and adjudged in the King's Courts at Westminster, 1743–1774. 2nd ed. 3 parts in 2 vols. 1779. folio.
The same. 3rd ed. 3 vols. 1799. 8vo.   7 C
The same. 4th ed. 3 vols. Dublin, 1792. 8vo.

WILSON, Rev. Harry Bristow.
Brief notices of the fabric and glebe of Saint Mary Aldermary in the City of London. 1840. [Pamphlets, vol. 1.]   144 A
History of Merchant-Taylors' school, from its foundation to the present time. 1814. 4to.   89 E
History of the parish of St. Lawrence Pountney, London ; including An account of Corpus Christi (or Pountney) college. 1831. 4to.   89 F
A Letter to the parishioners of Saint Thomas the Apostle. [1850.] [Pamphlets, vol. 7.]   144 A
Observations on the law and practice of sequestration of ecclesiastical benefices. 1836. [Pamphlets, vol. 1.]   144 A

WILSON, Horace Hayman.
The history of British India, from 1805 to 1835. 3 vols. 1848. 8vo.   116 B

WILSON, James and Patrick SHAW.
Cases decided in House of Lords, on Appeal from Courts of Scotland, 1825–1834. 7 vols. Edinburgh, 1829–39. 8vo.
                                                   15 B C

WILSON, JOHN.
A Discourse of Monarchy. 1684. 12mo. 49 B

WILSON, JOHN.
Reports of cases argued on the equity side of the court of Exchequer, 1805–1817. 1 vol. ' 1817. 8vo. 7 I
Reports of cases in Chancery, 1818–1819, vol. 1 and vol. 2, part 1. 1819. 8vo. 3 I

WILSON, JOSEPH.
Memorabilia Cantabrigiæ : or, an account of the different colleges in Cambridge. 1803. 8vo. 86 C

WILSON, JOSHUA.
A Biographical index to the present House of Commons. 1808. 12mo. 134 B

WILSON, ROBERT.
On the report of the Patent law commissioners. 1865. [Pamphlets, vol. 26.] 144 B
Outlines of a plan for adapting the machinery of the public funds to the transfer of real property. 1844. 8vo. 174 F
A Proposition to the Land Transfer commissioners. 1868. 8vo. 170 C
Registration of title to land ; what it is, why it is needed, and how it may be effected ; with maps and forms. 1863. 8vo. 170 C

WILSON, SIR ROLAND KNYVET.
History of modern English law. 1875. 12mo. 170 F

WILSON, REV. THOMAS.
Archæological dictionary ; or, classical antiquities of the Jews, Greeks, and Romans. 2nd ed. 1793. 8vo. 123 B

WILTES, EARLDOM OF.
A Dissertation on the history of hereditary dignities, with special reference to the case of the Earldom of Wiltes. By W. F. Finlason. 1869. 8vo. 124 F

WILTSHIRE.
The ancient history of North Wiltshire. By Sir R. C. Hoare. 1819. folio. 93 H

WILTSHIRE—*continued.*

The ancient history of South Wiltshire. By Sir R. C. Hoare.
1812. folio. 93 H

An Essay on topographical literature. By John Britton.
[Contains a list of MSS. and books relating to Wiltshire.]
1843. 4to. 85 I

The history of modern Wiltshire. By Sir R. C. Hoare and
11 others. 6 vols. in 4. 1822–44. folio. 94 H

Kaleidoscopiana Wiltoniensia ; or, a literary, political, and
moral view of the county of Wilts during the contested
election for its representation in June 1818, between Paul
Methuen, W. L. Wellesley and John Bennett. By An
Observer. 1818. 8vo. 93 F

The natural history of Wiltshire. By John Aubrey. Edited
by John Britton. 1847. 4to. 94 G

The Poll for the election of two knights for the county of
Wilts, to serve in Parliament. Taken on the 24th June to
the 3rd July, 1818. Salisbury, 1818. 8vo. 107 K

Wiltshire, extracted from Domesday book ; with a translation
of the original Latin into English. By H. P. Wyndham.
Salisbury, 1788. 8vo. 93 F

WIMBLEDON, SURREY.

Extracts from the court rolls of the manor of Wimbledon.
By P. H. Lawrence. 1866. 8vo. 93 C

Sketch of the law relating to public rights over Wastes and
Common Lands with some practical observations on the
Wimbledon Common question. By John Finlaison. 1867.
8vo. 163 C

WINCH, SIR HUMPHRY.

Le Beau-Pledeur. A book of entries, containing declarations,
informations, and other select and approved pleadings in the
courts at Westminster. 1680. folio.

Reports, containing many choice cases touching declarations,
&c., in points of law, 1621–1625. 1657. 4to. 74 G

WINCHESTER.

Historical and critical account of Winchester Cathedral, extracted from the Rev. Dr. Milner's History and antiquities
of Winchester ; with a Review of its modern monuments.
2nd ed. Winchester, 1807. 12mo. 88 A

WINCHESTER—*continued*.
History and antiquities of the cathedral church of Winchester.
Begun by Henry, late Earl of Clarendon, and continued by
Samuel Gale. 1715. 8vo. **88 A**
The history and antiquities of Winchester. 2 vols. Winton,
1773. 12mo. **88 A**
The history of Winchester. By Rev. John Milner. 2 vols.
Winchester, 1809. 4to. **88 B**
See also WARNER, REV. R. and WAYNFLETE, W.

WINDING UP COMPANIES.
Practice and forms in Winding up Companies. By Alfred
Emden. 4th ed. 1891. 8vo. **9 D**
See also COMPANIES, WINDING UP.

WINDSOR, BERKSHIRE.
Annals of Windsor. By R. R. Tighe and J. E. Davis. 2 vols.
1858. 4to. **86 B**
The history and antiquities of Windsor Castle. By Joseph
Pote. Eton, 1749–62. 4to. **86 B**
The history of Windsor and its neighbourhood. By James
Hakewill. 1813. 4to. **86 H**
A History of Windsor Forest, Sunninghill, and the Great
Park. By G. M. Hughes. 1890. 4to. **86 B**

WINGATE. EDMOND.
The body of the common law of England. By E[dmond]
W[ingate]. 1655. 12mo. **49 C**
Justice revived, being the whole office of a countrey justice of
the peace. By E. W. 1661. 12mo. **48 B**
Maximes of reason ; or, the reason of the common law of Eng-
land. 1658. folio. **49 G**

WINIWARTER, JOSEPH M. CHEVALIER DE.
General civil code for all the German hereditary provinces of
the Austrian monarchy. Vienna, 1866. 8vo. **55 C**

WINSLOW, LYTTLETON STEWART.
Manual of Lunacy, a handbook relating to the legal care and
treatment of the insane. 1874. 12mo. **172 B**

WINSLOW, Reginald.
Law of Artistic Copyright. 1889. 8vo.   9 E
Law of private arrangements between debtors and creditors.
1885. 8vo.   12 I
Law relating to Protestant Nonconformists. 1886. 12mo. 9 C

WINSTANLEY, James Winckworth.
The Chancery of the County Palatine of Lancaster, its practice
and modes of procedure. Liverpool, 1855. 8vo.   170 C

WIRKSWORTH, Derbyshire.
The rhymed chronicle of Edward Manlove, concerning the
liberties and customs of the lead mines within the Wapentake of Wirksworth. 2nd ed. by T. Tapping. 1851. 8vo.
    87 A

WISBEACH, Cambridgeshire.
The ancient and modern state of Wisbeach. See W. Richards's
History of Lynn. 2 vols. Lynn, 1812. 8vo.   92 C
Historical account of Wisbech. By W. Watson. Wisbech,
1827. 8vo.   86 D

WISBY, Sweden.
The ancient sea laws of Wisby, taken out of a French book,
intitled Les Us et Coutumes de la Mer. 1686. See G.
Malynes's Lex Mercatoria, 3rd ed. 1686. folio.   118 G

WISE, Bernhard Ringrose.
Outlines of Jurisprudence. Oxford, 1881. 12mo.   63 G

WISE, Edward.
A General index to the principal matters contained in Meeson
and Welsby's Reports. 1849. 8vo.   7 G

WISE, Rev. Francis.
A Letter to Dr. Mead concerning some antiquities in Berkshire, particularly shewing that the White Horse is a
monument of the West Saxons. Oxford, 1738. 8vo.   86 B
Further observations upon the White Horse and other antiquities in Berkshire ; with an account of Whiteleaf-Cross
in Buckinghamshire and of the Red Horse in Warwickshire.
Oxford, 1742. 8vo.   86 B

WISE, John R.
The New Forest, its history and its scenery. [3rd ed.] 1867.
8vo.   88 B

WISE, Thomas Alexander.
History of Paganism in Caledonia; with an examination into
the influence of Asiatic philosophy and the gradual development of Christianity in Pictavia. 1884. 4to.   85 I

WITCHCRAFT.
Potts's Discovery of witches in the county of Lancaster, re-
printed from the original edition of 1613; with an intro-
duction and notes by James Crossley. 1845. 8vo.   89 B
A Tryal of Witches at the assizes held at Bury St. Edmunds,
March 1664, before Sir Matthew Hale. 1716. 12mo. 144 F

WITHAM, Essex.
Witham in olden time. Two lectures. By Rev. John Bramston. Chelmsford, 1855. 12mo.   87 E

WITHY, Robert.
Practical treatise upon law of Annuities. 1800. 8vo. 160 B

WITNESSES.
The practice relating to Witnesses. By W. S. Sichel. 1887.
12mo.   11 I
See also Evidence.

WOBURN, Bedfordshire.
An Account of the town of Woburn; with a genealogy of the
house of Russell. By S. Dodd. Woburn, 1818. 12mo. 86 B

WOLFERSTAN, F. S. P. and S. B. BRISTOWE.
Reports of the decisions of election committees, 1859–1864.
1865. 8vo.   66 B

WOLFERSTAN, F. S. P. and E. L. DEWE.
Reports of the decisions of committees of the House of Commons in the trial of controverted elections, 1857–1858.
1859. 8vo.   66 B

WOLSEY, Thomas, Cardinal.
Correspondence between Henry VIII. and Cardinal Wolsey, 1518–1530. See State Papers, vol. 1, 1830, pp. 1–371.   98 F

WOLSTENHOLME, E. P. and R. O. TURNER.
The conveyancing and law of property act 1881, and the Vendor and purchaser act 1874, with forms adapted for use under the acts. 1882. 8vo.   52 D
The same. 2nd ed. 1882. 8vo.   52 D
The same. 3rd ed. 1883. 8vo.   52 D
The same. 4th ed. 1885. 8vo.   52 D
The conveyancing acts, 1881, 1882, the Vendor and purchaser act, 1874, the Land charges registration and searches act, 1888, the Trustee act, 1888, the Married women's property act, 1882, and the Settled land acts, 1882 to 1887.   5th ed. 1889. 8vo.   13 G
Forms and precedents adapted for use under the Conveyancing acts, and Settled Land acts 1881 to 1890. 5th ed. By E. P. Wolstenholme. 1891. 8vo.   13 G
The settled land act 1882. 1883. 8vo.   53 G
The same. 2nd ed. 1884. 8vo.   53 G

WOLVERHAMPTON, Staffordshire.
An Historical and descriptive account of the collegiate church of Wolverhampton. By Rev. George Oliver. Wolverhampton, 1836. 8vo.   93 C

WOMEN, Law relating to.
The position in law of Women. By Thomas Barrett-Lennard. 1883. 8vo.   172 D
The laws respecting Women, as they regard their natural rights or their connections and conduct. 1777. 8vo. 178 C
The Lawes resolutions of womens rights ; or the lawes provision for women. 1632. 12mo.   48 C
See also Husband and Wife, Marriage and Married Women's Property.

WOOD, Anthony À.
The antient and present state of the city of Oxford. With additions by the Rev. Sir J. Peshall. 1773. 4to.   92 F
Athenæ Oxonienses : an exact history of all the writers and bishops who have had their education in the University of

WOOD, ANTHONY Λ—*continued*.
Oxford ; with The Fasti or annals of the said University.
2 vols. in 1. 1691–92. folio. 79 H
The same. New ed. with additions and a continuation by
Philip Bliss. 4 vols. 1813–20. 4to. 79 H
The history and antiquities of the colleges and halls in the
University of Oxford. Edited by John Gutch. 2 vols.
1786–90. 4to. 92 F
The history and antiquities of the University of Oxford. Now
first published in English by John Gutch. 3 vols. Oxford,
1792. 4to. 92 F
Life of Anthony Wood. See Malcolm's Lives of Topographers
and Antiquaries. 1815. 4to. 79 H
'Survey of the Antiquities of the City of Oxford,' composed
in 1661–6. Edited by A. Clark. Vols. 1 & 2. [Oxford
Hist. Soc. vols. 15 & 17.] 2 vols. 1889–90. 8vo. 85 F

WOOD, REV. EDMUND GOUGH DE SALIS.
The regal power of the Church, or the fundamentals of the
Canon law, a dissertation. Cambridge, 1888. 8vo. 77 C

WOOD, EDWARD.
A Compleat body of Conveyancing in theory and practice.
4th ed. 3 vols. 1777. folio. 157 D
The same. 5th ed. by J. J. Powell. 3 vols. 1790–93. folio.
157 D

WOOD, FREDERICK.
The Legal Correspondent : (part 1). 1889. 8vo. 11 G
Solicitors' reports to residuary legatees as to the executors'
management of their testators' estates. 1887. 8vo. 9 I

WOOD, HUTTON.
A Collection of decrees by the Court of Exchequer in Tithe
causes, 1650–1798. 4 vols. 1798–99. 8vo. 66 A

WOOD, JAMES GEORGE.
The laws of the Dean Forest and Hundred of Saint Briavels
in the county of Gloucester. 1878. 8vo. 87 F

WOOD, JOHN.
An Essay towards a description of Bath. 2nd ed. 2 vols.
1749. 8vo. 93 A

WOOD, JOHN DENNISTOUN.
The interpretation of mercantile agreements. 1886. 8vo. **10 I**
The laws of Australasian colonies as to administration and
distribution of estate of deceased persons. 1884. 8vo. **55 D**

WOOD, THOMAS.
An Institute of the laws of England ; or, the laws of England
in their natural order according to common use. 2nd ed.
1722, and 6th ed. 1738. folio. **155 D**
The same. 7th ed. 1745. folio. **155 D**
The same. 10th ed. by a Sergeant at law. 1772. folio. **155 D**
A New institute of the Imperial or Civil law. 3rd ed. 1721.
12mo. **49 F**

WOODBRIDGE, SUFFOLK.
The statutes and ordinances for the government of the almshouses in Woodbridge, founded by Thomas Seckford, 1587 ;
with notes relating to Woodbridge priory. Edited by
Robert Loder. Woodbridge, 1792. 4to. **93 B**
The terrier of Woodbridge, exhibited at primary visitation
of Henry, Bishop of diocese of Norwich, held June 5th, 1806.
Edited by Robert Loder. 2nd ed. [Woodbridge.] 1811.
4to. Bound with the preceding. **93 B**

[WOODBURN, SAMUEL.]
Ecclesiastical topography. A collection of one hundred views
of churches in the environs of London, accompanied with
descriptions. 2 vols. in 1. 1807–10. folio. **91 G**

WOODDESON, RICHARD.
Elements of Jurisprudence treated of in the preliminary part
of a course of lectures on the laws of England. [By Richard
Wooddeson.] 1783. 4to. **63 F**
Lectures on the law of England. 2nd ed. by W. R. Williams.
3 vols. 1834. 12mo. **170 F**
A Systematical view of the laws of England. 3 vols. 1792–
93. 8vo. **170 G**

WOODFALL, WILLIAM.
The law of Landlord and Tenant. 2nd ed. 1804, and 5th
ed. 1819. 8vo. **170 D**
The same, entirely remodelled and greatly enlarged by S. B.
Harrison. 6th ed. by F. L. Wollaston. 1849. 8vo. **170 D**

WOODFALL, WILLIAM—*continued.*

The same.	7th ed. by H. Horn. 1856. 8vo.		170 D
The same.	9th ed. by W. R. Cole. 1867. 8vo.		170 D
The same.	11th ed. by J. M. Lely. 1877. 8vo.		170 D
The same.	13th ed. by J. M. Lely. 1886. 8vo.		52 I
The same.	14th ed. by J. M. Lely. 1889. 8vo.		10 E

[WOODHOUSE, JOHN CHAPPEL.]

A Short account of Lichfield cathedral. 4th ed. Lichfield, 1834. 8vo. 93 C

WOODMAN, JOSEPH VERE.

The Bengal Law Reports of decisions of the High Court at Fort William in its original and appellate jurisdictions, 1874–1875. Edited by J. V. Woodman. 4 vols. Calcutta, 1874–75. 8vo. 38 F

A Digest of Indian law cases ; containing high court reports and privy council reports of appeals from India, 1887–1889. Calcutta, 1890. 8vo. 38 F

WOODS, FORESTS AND LAND REVENUES.

Reports [1 to 26] of the Commissioners of woods, forests and land revenues. 6 vols. 1812–49. folio. 159 D

WOODS, GEORGE.

An Account of the past and present state of the Isle of Man. 1811. 8vo. 94 F

WOODWARD, B. B., T. C. WILKS and C. LOCKHART.

General history of Hampshire, or county of Southampton, including Isle of Wight. 3 vols. [1861–69.] folio. 88 G

WOOL AND WOOLLEN TRADE.

The request and suit of a true-hearted Englishman [concern-ing commerce of the Woollen manufacture] ; written by Wm. Cholmeley, 1553. Edited by W. J. Thoms. [Camden Society, vol. 55.] 1853. 8vo. 85 B

Wool and woollen manufactures of Great Britain : a historical sketch of rise, progress and present condition. By Samuel brothers. 1859. 8vo. 78 B

Yorkshire past and present. By T. Baines ; including an account of the woollen trade of Yorkshire, by Edward Baines. 2 vols. [1871–77.] 4to. 95 G

WOOLF, SIDNEY.
The law of Adulterations. 1874. 12mo. **160 A**
The law and practice of Compensation for taking or injuriously
affecting lands. By S. Woolf and J. W. Middleton.. 1884.
8vo. **9 D**

WOOLLEY, WILLIAM.
A Collection of statutes relating to the town of Kingston-upon-
Hull, the county of the same town ; and the parish of Scul-
coates in the county of York. 1830. 8vo. **94 B**

WOOLMAN, JOHN.
The journal of John Woolman ; with an introduction by J. G.
Whittier. Glasgow, 1882. 12mo. **79 A**

WOOLRYCH, EDMUND˙ HUMPHREY.
The Metropolis local management acts. 1863. 12mo. **172 F**
The same. 2nd ed. 1880. 8vo. **53 A**
The same. 3rd ed. by L. Goodrich. 1888. 8vo. **10 H**

WOOLRYCH, HUMPHRY WILLIAM.
The Criminal law as amended by the statutes of 1861 ; with
pleading, evidence, forms of indictment, cases and index.
1862. 8vo. **165 D**
The law of Party Walls and Fences. 1845. 8vo. **11 I**
The law of Waters and of Sewers. 1834. 8vo. **175 E**
The law of Sewers. 3rd ed. 1864. 8vo. **175 E**
The law of Ways. 2nd ed. 1847. 8vo. **11 I**
Lives of eminent serjeants-at-law of the English bar. 2 vols.
1869. 8vo. **80 F**
Metropolitan Building act, with notes. 1856. 12mo. **172 F**
The same. 2nd ed. by N. H. Paterson. 1877. 12mo. **172 F**
The same. 3rd ed. by W. H. Macnamara. 1882. 12mo. **10 I**
A Series of the lords chancellors . . . chief justices and
judges of the Courts of King's Bench, Common Pleas and
Exchequer, from the reign of Queen Elizabeth until the
present day. 1826. 12mo. **123 A**
A Treatise on Criminal statutes of 7 Will. IV. & 1 Vict.
cc. 84–91. 1837. 12mo. **165 C**
A Treatise on law of Rights of Common. 1824. 8vo. **163 C**
The same. 2nd ed. 1850. 8vo. **163 C**

68

WOOLSEY, ROBERT.
The doctrine and practice of Attachment in the Mayor's Court, London. 1816. 8vo. **172 D**

WOOLSEY, THEODORE DWIGHT.
Introduction to the study of international law. 3rd ed. New York, 1873. 8vo. **55 A**

WOOLTON, JOHN, BISHOP OF EXETER.
The Christian manual ; or, of the life and manners of true Christians. Cambridge, 1851. 12mo. **77 D**

WORCESTER.
Annales Prioratus de Wigornia. A.D. 1–1377. See Annales Monastici, vol. 4, 1869, pp. 355–567. **102 A**
History and antiquities of city and suburbs of Worcester. By Valentine Green. 2 vols. in 1. 1796. 4to. **95 G**
Registrum sive liber irrotularius et consuetudinarius Prioratus Beatæ Mariæ Wigorniensis. Edited by W. H. Hale. [Camden Society, vol. 91.] 1865. 8vo. **85 C**
A Survey of the city of Worcester. By Valentine Green. Worcester, 1764. 8vo. **93 F**

WORCESTERSHIRE.
Collections for the history of Worcestershire. By T. R. Nash. 2nd ed. 2 vols. 1799. folio. **94 H**
Topographical survey of counties of Somerset, Worcester, &c. By Wm. Tunnicliff. Bath, 1789. 8vo. **93 B**
The visitation of the county of Worcester, 1682–1683. Edited by W. C. Metcalfe. Privately printed. Exeter, 1883. 4to. **93 F**

WORDSWORTH, CHARLES FAVELL FORTH.
A Digest of all the Election reports, including the cases at Common Law. 1834. 8vo. **63 D**
The law and practice of Elections (for England and Wales) as altered by the Reform act. 1832. 8vo. **166 E**
The same. 2nd ed. 1835. 8vo. **166 E**
The law of Compensation by arbitration and by jury under the Lands and railways clauses acts. 1863. 8vo. **163 D**
The same. 2nd ed. 1867. 8vo. **163 D**

WORDSWORTH, CHARLES FAVELL FORTH—*continued.*
The law relating to railway, bank, insurance, mining and other Joint Stock companies. 2nd ed. 1837. 8vo. **169 E**
Law of Joint Stock companies. 4th ed. 1845. 8vo. **169 E**
The law of railway and other companies, requiring express authority of parliament. 6th ed. 1851. 8vo. **169 E**
The law of general Joint Stock companies, not requiring express authority of parliament. 6th ed. 1854. 8vo. **169 E**
The law of Joint Stock companies as altered by the act of 1862 ; with the whole law of winding-up. 10th ed. 1865. 8vo. **169 E**
Law relating to the Registration of Voters. 2nd ed. 1843. 8vo. **166 E**
The rules of Court, with notes and forms. 1834, and 2nd ed. 1835. 12mo. **163 B**

WORLD, THE.
A Dictionary of the various countries, places, and principal natural objects in the world. By J. R. M'Culloch. New ed. by F. Martin. 4 vols. in 2. 1866. ·8vo. **84 G**
The history of the World, in five books. By Sir Walter Ralegh. 1687. folio. **113 H**
See also ATLASES, COMENIUS, J. A., GAZETTEERS and GEOGRAPHY.

WORRALL, JOHN.
Bibliotheca legum : or a list of all the common and statute law books of this realm. 1732. 12mo. **82 A**
The same. Another ed. 1736. 12mo. **82 A**
The same. Part 1. New ed. 1788 ; with Supplement. 1800. Part 2. A general account of the laws and law writers of England to the reign of Edward III. By E. Brooke. 1788. 2 vols. 1788. 12mo. **82 A**

WORSLEY, RICHARD.
History of the Isle of Wight. 1781. 4to. **88 G**

WORTH, RICHARD NICHOLLS.
A History of Devonshire ; with sketches of its leading worthies. 1886. 8vo. **87 D**
History of Plymouth from the earliest period to the present time. 2nd ed. Plymouth, 1890. 8vo. **87 D**

WORTHINGTON, GEORGE.
A General precedent for Wills ; with practical notes. 3rd ed.
1830. 12mo.   178 C

WORTHY, CHARLES.
Devonshire parishes ; or, the antiquities, heraldry, and family
history of twenty-eight parishes in the Archdeaconry of
Totnes. 2 vols. Exeter, 1887–89. 8vo.   87 D

WOTTON, THOMAS.
The English baronets ; being a genealogical and historical
account of their families. 3 vols. 1727. 12mo.   124 B
The same. New ed. 4 vols. in 5. 1741. 8vo.   125 C
The same. New ed. by E. Kimber and R. Johnson. 3 vols.
1771. 8vo.   125 C

WRATISLAW, WILLIAM FERDINAND.
Memoir of the family of Wratislaw of Rugby, [n.d.] and
Wratislaw, a Bohemian ballad [translated from the German
by Albert Henry Wratislaw]. Rugby, 1845. 8vo. 80 C

WRAYSBURY, BUCKINGHAMSHIRE.
History of the parish of Wraysbury, Ankerwycke priory and
Magna Charta Island. By G. W. J. Gyll. 1862. 4to. 86 B

WRECK INQUIRIES.
The law and practice relating to formal investigations into
shipping casualties. By W. Murton. 1884. 8vo.   53 I

WRIGHT, ANDREW.
Court-hand restored ; or, the student's assistant in reading
old deeds, charters, &c. 3rd ed. 1786. 4to.   78 G
The same. 4th ed. 1815. 4to.   78 G

WRIGHT, REV. GEORGE NEWNHAM.
A Guide to the Giant's Causeway and the north-east coast of
the county of Antrim. 1823. 12mo.   95 E

[WRIGHT, I. H.]
The Horatii, a tragedy. 1846. [Pamphlets, vol. 23.] 144 B

WRIGHT, JAMES.
History and antiquities of Rutland. 1684. folio. **93 H**

WRIGHT, SIR MARTIN.
Introduction to the law of Tenures. 3rd ed. 1768. 8vo. **176 D**

WRIGHT, ROBERT SAMUEL.
Law of criminal conspiracies and agreements. 1873. 8vo. **52 E**
An Essay on Possession in the common law. By F. Pollock
and R. S. Wright. Oxford, 1888. 8vo. **53 C**

WRIGHT, THOMAS.
An Essay on the state of literature and learning under the
Anglo-Saxons. 1839. 8vo. **78 B**
The history and topography of the county of Essex. 2 vols.
in 3. 1836. 4to. **87 F**

WRIGHT, WILLIAM.
Advice on the study and practice of the Law. 3rd ed. 1824.
12mo. **171 A**
Observations on the judges of the Court of Chancery and
practice and delays complained of in that court. [By Wm.
Wright.] 1823. [Jacob's Tracts, vol. 1.] **144 E**

WRIOTHESLEY, CHARLES.
A Chronicle of England during the reign of the Tudors,
1485–1559. Edited by W. D. Hamilton. [Camden Society,
n.s. vols. 11 and 20.] 2 vols. 1875–77. 8vo. **85 D**

WRITING.
One hundred and fifty specimens of the manner of writing in
different ages, from the third to the fifteenth century. See
D. Casley's Catalogue of manuscripts. 1734. 4to. **118 F**
The origin and progress of writing as well hieroglyphic as
elementary. By Thomas Astle. 2nd ed. 1803. 4to. **78 G**

WRITS.
Kings' Briefs; their purposes and history. By Cornelius
Walford. Printed for private circulation. 1882. 8vo. **78 B**
The New Natura Brevium. By Anthony Fitzherbert; with
a Commentary containing curious notes and observations
on the most remarkable and useful writs, by Lord Chief
Justice Hale. 9th ed. 2 vols. 1794. 8vo. **178 D**

WRITS—*continued.*

History of Brieves. See Historical law tracts, 2nd ed., 1761, pp. 283–294. **144 F**

The New Retorna Brevium, collected from the many printed law books extant concerning the retorn of writs. By R[obert] G[ardiner]. 3rd ed. 1738. 12mo. **178 D**

Thesaurus Brevium ; or, a collection of approved forms of writs with their special directions to all cities and boroughs. Collected and published by J[ames] C[ornwall]. 2nd ed. 1687. folio. **157 C**

Registrum brevium tam originalium quam judicialium. Editio quarta unà cum libro Simonis Theloall cui titulus Le digest des briefs originals et des choses concernants eux. 1687. folio. **118 F**

Tables to most of the Presidents of Pleadings, Writs, and Retorn of Writs, at the Common Law. By G. Townesend. 1667. folio.

Brevia Selecta or choice writs. By R. Antrobus and J. Impey. 1663. 12mo. **48 C**

WURTZBURG, EDWARD ALBERT.

The Acts relating to Building Societies, with precedents of rules and assurances. 1886. 12mo. **9 B**

WYAT, SIR THOMAS.

The chronicle of Queen Jane and of two years of Queen Mary and especially of the rebellion of Sir T. Wyat. Written by a resident in the Tower of London. Edited by J. G. Nichols. [Camden Society, vol. 48.] 1850. 8vo. **85 B**

WYATT, JOHN.

The practical register in Chancery ; with the addition of the modern cases. 1800. 8vo. **161 D**

WYCOMBE, BUCKINGHAMSHIRE.

The history and antiquities of the deanery and borough town of Wycombe. By T. Langley. 1797. 4to. **86 B**

WYE, RIVER.

The excursion down the Wye from Ross to Monmouth. By Charles Heath. 1799. 8vo. **92 C**

WYKEHAM, William of.
The life of William of Wykeham, bishop of Winchester. By
Robert Lowth, D.D. 3rd ed. Oxford, 1777. 8vo. 80 C

WYNDHAM, Henry Penruddocke.
The diary of the late George Bubb Dodington, baron of Mel-
combe Regis, 1749–1761. Published from his Lordship's
original manuscripts. [Autobiography, vol. 3.] 1827.
12mo. 79 A
A Tour through Monmouthshire and Wales. 2nd ed. Salisbury, 1781. 4to. 95 G
Wiltshire, extracted from Domesday book : with a translation
of the Latin into English. Salisbury, 1788. 8vo. 93 F

WYNNE, Edward.
Eunomus ; or, dialogues concerning the law and constitution
of England. 2nd ed. 4 vols. 1785. 12mo. 170 F
Observations touching the antiquity and dignity of the degree
of sergeant at law. [By E. Wynne.] 1765. 8vo. 80 F
Strictures on the lives and characters of the most eminent
lawyers of present day. [By E. Wynne.] 1790. 8vo. 80 F

WYNNE, Sir John.
The history of the Gwedir family. 1770. 8vo. 79 B

WYNNE, William.
The life of Sir Leoline Jenkins, judge of the high court of
Admiralty. 2 vols. 1724. folio. 79 I

WYON, Frederick William.
The history of Great Britain during the reign of Queen Anne.
2 vols. 1876. 8vo. 115 G

XENOPHON.
A Discourse upon improving the revenue of the state of
Athens ; written originally in Greek by Xenophon, and
made English by W[alter] M[oyle]. 1697. See C.
Davenant, On Taxes. 1698. 12mo. 49 D
Xenophontis Anabasis. Nova editio. Lipsiæ, 1840. 12mo.
47 E

YACHT REGISTER.

Yacht Register, from 1st May, 1890, to 30th April, 1891; and Rules for 1890–91. 2 vols. 1890. 8vo. **146 F**
The same, from 1st May, 1891, to 30th April, 1892; and Rules for 1891–92. 2 vols. 1891. 8vo. **Hall**

YALE, GREGORY.

Legal titles to mining claims and water rights in California. San Francisco, 1867. 8vo. **60 B**

YARMOUTH, NORFOLK.

The history of Great Yarmouth. [By Rev. Charles Parkin.] Lynn, 1776. 8vo. **92 C**
The history of Great Yarmouth. By Henry Swinden. Norwich, 1772. 4to. **92 D**

YATES, REV. RICHARD.

An Illustration of the monastic history and antiquities of the town and abbey of St. Edmund's Bury. 1805. 4to. **93 G**

YATES, WILLIAM.

The county palatine of Lancaster surveyed. Engraved by Thomas Billinge. 1786. 4to. **88 F**

YEAR BOOKS.

Reports of law cases from the reign of Edward II. to the 27th Henry VIII.; with references to the Abridgments of Brooke, Fitzherbert, and Statham and indexes. 11 parts in 9 vols. 1678–79. folio. **99 E**
Year books of the reigns of Edward I. and III. Translated into English by A. J. Harwood and L. O. Pike. Vols. 1–10. 1863–89. 8vo. **101 I & 102 A**
Promptuaire; ou, Repertory generall de les annales et plusors auters livres del common ley Dengleterre. Per T. Ashe. 2 vols. 1614. 4to. **99 E**

YEATMAN, JOHN PYM.

The Mayor's Court of London procedure act. 1857; with notes and an outline of the practice thereof. 1870. 12mo. **172 D**
The same. 2nd ed. 1878. 12mo. **172 D**
Some observations upon the law of Ancient Demesne; with suggestions as to the origin of the families of Brewer, Brito, Hardwick, and Cavendish, the ancient Lords of the manor of Chesterfield. 1884. 8vo. **87 B**

YELVERTON, Sir Henry.
A Learned and necessary argument to prove that each subject hath a propriety in his goods. By a late learned judge of this kingdome [Sir H. Yelverton]. 1641. [Law Tracts and Arguments, 1641.] **144 F**
Reports de divers speciall cases en le court del Bank le Roy, 44 Eliz. to 10 Jac. I. Publie par Sir Wm. Wylde. 1661, and 2nd ed. 1674. folio.
The same. 3rd ed. translated into English. 1735. folio. **74 G**

YONGE, Walter.
Diary of Walter Yonge, written at Colyton and Axminster, co. Devon. Edited by George Roberts. [Camden Society, vol. 41.] 1848. 8vo. **85 B**

YOOL, George Valentine.
An Essay on waste, nuisance, and trespass. 1863. 8vo. **11 I**

YORK.
A Brief historical account of the cathedral of York, as also of the principal collegiate churches in the province of York. See Sir W. Dugdale's History of St. Paul's cathedral. 1818. folio. **92 H**
A Brief treatise of Bona Notabilia ; with an account of the archiepiscopal courts of probate within the province of York. By George Lawton. York, 1825. 8vo. **94 A**
Chronica Pontificum Ecclesiæ Eboraci. Autore T. Stubbs. See Scriptores Decem Hist. Angl., pp. 1686–1734. **114 H**
A Description of York. 9th ed. 1823. 12mo. **94 A**
Eboracum ; or, the history and antiquities of the city of York. By Francis Drake. 1736. folio. **94 H**
Eboracum ; or, the history and antiquities of the city of York. 2 vols. York, 1788. 8vo. **94 B**
Eburacum ; or, York under the Romans. By C. Wellbeloved. York, 1842. 4to. **94 C**
The historians of the church of York and its archbishops. Edited by Rev. James Raine. Vols. 1 & 2. 1879–86. 8vo. **102 G**
The Poll for members in Parliament for the city of York, begun 13th of May, 1741. York, 1741. 8vo. **107 K**
County of York. The Poll for knights of the shire, May 20th to June 5th, 1807. York, 1807. 8vo. **107 K**

1082

YORK, Frederick, 1 Duke of.
A Correct report of the speech delivered by Sir Francis Burdett in the House of Commons 13 March 1809, on the conduct of H.R.H. the Duke of York. 2nd ed. 1809. 8vo. 79 C

A Full report of the proceedings of the electors of Westminster at a meeting held in Westminster hall to express their sentiments on the inquiry into the conduct of the Duke of York, containing the speeches of Sir F. Burdett and Mr. Whitbread. 1809. 8vo. 79 C

[YORKE, Charles.]
Some considerations on the law of Forfeiture for High-Treason. 2nd ed. with an appendix concerning estates tail in Scotland. 1746. 12mo. 168 E
The same. 3rd ed. 1748. 12mo. 168 E
The same. 4th ed. Edinburgh, 1778. 12mo. 168 E

YORKSHIRE.
Description of the country from thirty to forty miles round Manchester. By John Aikin. 1795. 4to. 88 F
Description of Yorkshire. By W. Camden. [n.d.] 8vo. 94 B
History of Yorkshire. Wapentake of Gilling West. By G. H. De S. N. Plantagenet-Harrison. 1875. 8vo. 95 H
Map of Yorkshire. By Henry Teesdale. 1828. 4to. 95 G
Monasticon Eboracense ; or, the ecclesiastical history of Yorkshire. By John Burton. York, 1758. folio. 95 H
A New and complete history of the county of York. By Thomas Allen. 3 vols. 1829–31. 4to. 94 C
Sketch of a tour into Derbyshire and Yorkshire. By William Bray. 2nd ed. 1783. 8vo. 87 A
A Survey of the counties of Lancashire, West Riding of Yorkshire, &c. 1797. 8vo. 89 B
A Topographical and historical description of the county of York. By John Bigland. 1819. 8vo. 94 B
A Topographical dictionary of Yorkshire. By Thomas Langdale. Northallerton, 1809. 8vo. 94 B
Yorkshire gazetteer. By S. R. Clarke. 1828. 8vo. 94 B
Yorkshire past and present. By Thomas Baines. 2 vols. [1871–77.] 4to. 95 G
See also Parsons, E., Tuke, J., Whitaker, Rev. T. D. and White, W.

YORKSHIRE REGISTRY.
Dissertation on the Yorkshire registry and precedents of memorials, &c. See Bythewood and Jarman's Conveyancing, 4th ed., vol. 6, 1890, pp. 9–25.   13 D
A Manual on registration of deeds and other assurances in Yorkshire. By Henry Barker. 1885. 8vo.   · 13 B

YOUNG, ARCHIBALD.
An Historical sketch of the French bar from its origin to the present day. Edinburgh, 1869. 8vo.   79 B

[YOUNG, ARTHUR.] ·
General view of the agriculture of the county of Suffolk; drawn up for the consideration of the board of agriculture. By the secretary to the board. 3rd ed. 1804. 8vo. 93 C

[YOUNG, CHARLES GEORGE.]
A Table of precedency of men, with notes containing authorities upon which some parts are founded. [n.d.] 8vo. 125 C

YOUNG, REV. GEORGE.
A History of Whitby and Streoneshalh Abbey. Whitby, 2 vols. 1817. 8vo.   94 A

YOUNG, WALTER.
A Vade Mecum; or, table containing substance of such statutes wherein any one or more justices of the peace are inabled to act; with an Epitome of Mr. Stamford's Pleas of the Crown. 6th ed. 1660. 12mo.   48 A

YOUNGE, EDWARD.
A Report of the case of Small against Attwood in the Court of Exchequer. 1833. 8vo.   51 F
Reports of cases in the court of Exchequer in Equity, 1830–1832. 1 vol. 1833. 8vo.   7 I

YOUNGE, EDWARD and JOHN COLLYER.
Reports of cases decided in the Court of Chancery, by Sir J. L. Knight Bruce, 1841–1844. 2 vols. 1843–44. 8vo. 3 I
Reports of cases in the court of Exchequer in Equity, 1834–1842. 4 vols. 1836–46. 8vo.   7 I

YOUNGE, EDWARD and JOHN JERVIS.
Reports of cases in the courts of Exchequer and Exchequer
Chamber, 1826–1830. 3 vols. 1828–30. 8vo. 7 I

ZAEHNSDORF, JOSEPH WILLIAM.
The art of Bookbinding. 1880. 8vo. 82 B

ZAPPALÀ, BENEDETTO CRISAFULLI.
Autorità degl' Italiani su la scienza del diritto. Catania, 1862.
8vo. 56 C
Sullo studio giuridico, prelezione al corso della introduzione
generale per le scienze giuridiche e politico-amministrative:
storia del diritto. Catania, 1863. 8vo. Bound with the
preceding. · 56 C

ZIMMERMAN, JOHN GEORGE.
Solitude ; with the life of the author and notes historical and
explanatory. 1798. 8vo. [Vol. 1 only.] 83 H

ZOLA, ÉMILE.
L'Attaque du Moulin. Edited by F. Julien. 1888. 12mo.
83 C
ZOUCH, RICHARD.
Èlementa Jurisprudentiæ, definitionibus, regulis et sententiis
selectioribus juris civilis illustrata; accesserunt descriptiones
juris et judicii, sacri, militaris et maritimi. Amstelodami,
1652. 12mo. 48 A
The jurisdiction of the Admiralty of England asserted. 1686.
See G. Malynes's Lex Mercatoria. 1686. folio. 118 G

ZULUETA, PEDRO DE.
Trial of Pedro de Zulueta, jun., on a charge of slave-trading ;
with an address to the merchants of Great Britain. By
P. de Zulueta, junior. 1844. 8vo. 50 A

ZYPÆUS, FRANCISCUS. ·
Jus pontificum novum ; sive analytica postremi juris ecclesiastici enarratio. Coloniæ Agrippinæ, 1620. 8vo. 118 B

14

Lightning Source UK Ltd.
Milton Keynes UK
UKHW022149140119

335570UK00013B/833/P